edmunds.com SM

where smart car buyers start®

Used Cars & Trucks Buyer's Guide

2004

Where Smart Car Buyers Start®

Table of Contents

Edmunds.com Used Cars & Trucks Buyer's Guide

2004 Annual, Volume U3801 ISBN: 0-87759-685-9 ISSN: 1541-8510

Contents

Used Vehicle Information

Table of Contents

Cover Photos: Karl Brauer, American Honda Motor Company, Inc.

Publisher
Peter Steinlauf

President
Jeremy Anwyl

Executive Vice President, Sales
Mike Darrow

Vice President, Content
Matthew Kumin

Editor in Chief
Karl Brauer

Managing Editor
Donna DeRosa

Senior Road Test Editor
Ed Hellwig

Road Test Editors
John DiPietro, Brian Moody, Erin Riches

Road Test Coordinator
Kelly Stennick

Consumer Advice Editor
Phil Reed

Photo Editors
Scott Jacobs, Matt Landish

New Vehicle Reviews Editor
Jeffrey Bryan

Associate Editor
Warren Clarke

Copy Editor
Caroline Pardilla

Director, Creative Services
Guy Schackman

Book Designer and Master Layout
Jeff Zugale

Production Artists
Sara Flemming, Nadia Potiyenok

Vice President, EDS
Michael Kilander

Director, Automotive Research
Allyson Colgrove

Photographic Data Specialist
Matt Landish

Lead Programmer, Book Automation
John Song

Manager, Used Vehicle Data
Neil Lieberman

Director, Pricing and Market Analysis
Jesse Toprak

Director of Statistics
Ray Zhou

Senior Statistician
Sun Li

Printed in USA

Introduction

Welcome to the *Edmunds.com Used Cars & Trucks Buyer's Guide*

Ever since we produced our first automotive pricing guide in 1966, the name Edmunds has been associated with timely, accurate and unbiased vehicle information. For over 36 years, Edmunds.com has provided advice on getting the best deal when buying a vehicle; a complete breakdown of used car and truck pricing; straightforward, consumer-friendly explanations of terms like "trade-in" and "wholesale"; and other useful automotive consumer resources.

In 1994, Edmunds took a monumental step forward by offering all this valuable used vehicle content to Internet users…for free! As the first automotive resource to go on-line, we introduced used vehicle buyers and sellers to the concept of "information transparency," which essentially means giving consumers access to the same pricing information available to dealers and manufacturers. No one could match the quality of our on-line content offering in 1994, and 10 years later Edmunds.com continues to be the automotive information leader.

What You'll Find Inside This Book

Our used vehicle pricing and option information is presented in an easy to read format. We've grouped all years of each model together so you can more easily track values as the car ages. And, of course, we still present each vehicle's three True Market Value (TMV®) prices: the dealer trade-in price, the private party price and the dealer retail price. Keep in mind that the Edmunds.com True Market Value® prices are not the "asking" or "suggested" prices. TMV is our exclusive system for determining, and reporting to you, what others are paying and getting for similar used vehicles. Edmunds.com's True Market Value pricing system for new and used vehicles is the industry's best guide to market value pricing and the only pricing system designed with the consumer in mind.

Comprehensive Photography

We have provided at least one photograph for every "generation" of vehicle covered in this book (all non-exotic, U.S.-sold cars and trucks from 1994 to 2003). Most automakers substantially redesign their models about every four to seven years. While some changes are made to many models almost every year, it is during a redesign that a car or truck will often take on an entirely different look. By including over 700 images in this book we have provided you with an accurate visual representation of what each model looks like over the past 10 years.

In-Depth Buying and Selling Advice

You also get a comprehensive advice section with in-depth buying and selling articles, tips on how to use today's technology to research a vehicle's history, information on certified used vehicles and our picks for the "Best Bet" for a smart used car purchase. Specific advice articles include:

10 Steps to Buying and 10 Steps to Selling a Used Car (starts on page 7)

Buying this book is a smart first step on the path to buying or selling a used vehicle, but finding the car or truck that's right for you, and ensuring you get the vehicle at a fair price, can be a daunting process. Conversely, if you're trying to turn a car into cash, you'll want to understand how to properly prepare and accurately price the vehicle. To help you we've created our simple, straightforward "10 Steps" series. These tutorials, written by a former car salesman, will help guide you through the process to ensure you get a fair deal, regardless of whether you're buying or selling.

Vehicle History Reports (starts on page 17)

At one time there was no way to verify a used vehicle's history. But computer technology now allows car shoppers to use the Vehicle Identification Number (VIN) to reveal a car's (possibly) checkered past. As this article explains, vehicle history reports can be a valuable tool whether you are buying or selling a car.

Certified Used Vehicles (starts on page 612)

With so many manufacturers now offering a certified used vehicle program, it makes sense to consider such a vehicle when shopping for your next car or truck. We give you a basic description of each manufacturer's program, as well as some questions to consider when buying a certified used vehicle.

And Much More...

In addition to these features, you'll find a mileage chart (page 611) to further aid you in pricing a used vehicle. And as mentioned earlier, there's also a section devoted to our "Best Bet" used vehicles for 2004 (page 25). These are the cars and trucks we consider the best combination of reliability, safety and value in the used market. You'll also discover a glossary of used vehicle terms (page 22).

Don't Forget Our Web Site

There's no denying that the **Edmunds.com Used Cars & Trucks Buyer's Guide** is a powerful tool you can use in your quest to find the right used vehicle at the right price. As most car shoppers know, the Internet is another powerful tool for car-buying research. Consider this book a portable version of Edmunds.com. Use it to do basic vehicle research and as an easy reference guide (especially the pricing data and "10 Steps" section) when navigating the often treacherous waters that make up the used car buying process.

And don't forget that, despite our efforts to stuff everything you need to know about used cars into one book, you will always benefit from visiting our Web site at Edmunds.com. Once there you'll have access to a full array of new and used vehicle buying tools, including our True Market Value Used Vehicle Appraiser that calculates used vehicle values for specific models and styles based on color, options, mileage, condition and region. You'll also find used vehicle listings for your area, an on-line community of thousands of automotive consumers (some of them talking about the same car you're interested in buying), an on-line maintenance section listing recalls and technical service bulletins and hundreds of vehicle reviews dating back to 1996.

The technology available for researching a used vehicle purchase may have changed, but Edmunds.com's mission is still the same: To inform consumers, striving to give them the benefit of our knowledge, insight into the automotive industry, the experience of owning and driving vehicles and lessons we've learned about owning, buying and selling automobiles. We exist for the consumer, and write for that audience. Everything we publish is designed to make our readers better-educated car owners, buyers and sellers.

Karl Brauer
Editor in Chief
Edmunds.com

How To Use This Book

Our *Used Cars & Trucks Buyer's Guide* makes it easy for you to research used vehicle pricing. Here is a basic explanation of the information provided for each make, model and year.

Make:
Vehicle manufacturer

Model:
Vehicle model name

Body Styles:
This box lists the various body styles and trims available in a given year

TMV Pricing:
These figures represent the current True Market Value for a vehicle in terms of dealer trade-in, private party sale or dealer sale.

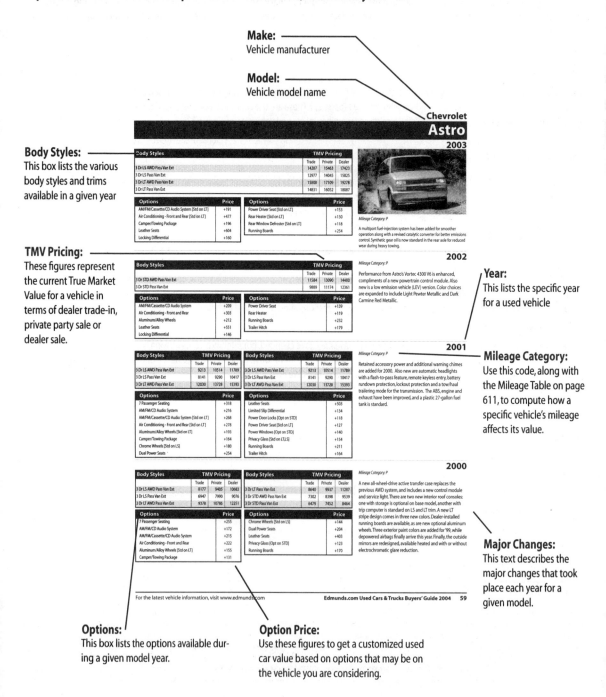

Year:
This lists the specific year for a used vehicle

Mileage Category:
Use this code, along with the Mileage Table on page 611, to compute how a specific vehicle's mileage affects its value.

Major Changes:
This text describes the major changes that took place each year for a given model.

Options:
This box lists the options available during a given model year.

Option Price:
Use these figures to get a customized used car value based on options that may be on the vehicle you are considering.

10 Steps to Buying a Used Car

The following steps will tell you how to locate, price and negotiate to buy the used car you want. Remember to consult our Glossary (page 22) if you find words here that you don't understand.

1. Starting Out

If you've decided to buy a used car, you've already made a smart decision. You can get a car that's almost as good as a brand-new one, without suffering the depreciation that wallops new car buyers as soon as they drive the car off the lot. Used cars — even those that are only one or two years old — are 20 to 30 percent cheaper than new cars.

But there are other good reasons to buy a used car:

- Buying a used car means you can buy a larger and/or more luxurious vehicle that you normally couldn't afford.
- You'll save money on insurance.
- The glut of cars coming off lease makes it easy to find one in good condition.
- Superior bargains are possible for the smart used car shopper.

Furthermore, the classic reasons to avoid used cars — lack of reliability and the expense of repairs — are less of an issue in modern times. Consider these related thoughts:

- Used cars are more reliable today than ever before.
- Some used cars are still covered by the factory warranty.
- Most new carmakers now sell certified used cars, which include warranties.
- The history of a used car can easily be traced using the VIN number.
- Finance rates for used cars have dropped in recent years.
- If you buy from a private party, the negotiation process is usually less stressful.

True, you can't be the first one on the block with the trendiest vehicle. But you'll have the satisfaction of knowing that you got a great deal and made a smart financial decision. So read on, as we guide you along the road to used car happiness.

2. How Much Can You Afford?

The smart shopper will consider how to finance the car at the beginning of the shopping process. This will avoid unpleasant surprises later in the game and help you make an unemotional decision that fits your budget. You will need to estimate three figures that will guide you as you go shopping:

- Monthly payment. If you are going to take out a loan, how much can you afford to pay each month?
- Down payment. How much cash can you put down to reduce your monthly payments?
- Purchase price of the car. Answering the first two questions will provide the answer to this final question.

Once you've determined how much you can spend for a down payment, a monthly payment and the purchase price of the car, print out these figures. Later, in the heat of the moment, when you are negotiating for a used car and need to stay within your budget, you might need to check your printout to keep yourself from overspending.

3. Locating the Right Used Car

It's possible that you need to expand your horizons when considering what to buy. You might want to think of other vehicles in the same class. For example, if you are considering a Toyota Camry, you should also look at the Honda Accord, Ford Taurus or Mitsubishi Galant. These cars were built for the same market, but they often have different features at lower prices.

10 Steps to Buying a Used Car

It's also important to remember the difference between your needs and your wants. You may want a luxury car or SUV for image purposes, but you really only need a midsize sedan to meet your passenger and cargo requirements. Obviously, you can buy whatever you want, but keep in mind that buying more car than you need is an unnecessary cost, at least in terms of covering your basic transportation goals.

4. Used Car Bargains

The cost of a used car is based on its condition, mileage, reliability, performance and popularity. Of course, you want a car that is reliable and performs well. But do you want the same used car everyone else wants? If so, you will pay a premium for it. In some cases, the only difference is the nameplate.

Some shoppers believe they can get a killer deal by going to police auctions or buying a car with a salvage title (one that has been declared a total loss by an insurance company). True, the initial cost is much lower, but you know little about what you are getting. It could have frame damage, a safety problem or a faulty transmission. For most people, it's better to stick to the more common used car sources: private parties and the used car department of the local dealership. You might even consider buying a certified used car that comes with a factory warranty. Then you get the best of both worlds: a break on the price and peace of mind.

5. Research Your Prospective Used Car

You will find all the information you need to make an informed decision about what to buy in the pages of this book. The major topics are covered, providing you with information on prices, standard features, specs, safety and warranties. If you can visit Edmunds.com, you can broaden your base of knowledge by reading the editorial reviews of the car and by checking out what current owners have to say in our Town Hall section. With over half a million registered users in Town Hall, you are almost guaranteed to find someone who has experience with the car (or cars) you are considering.

Another essential part of the used car buying process involves the Edmunds.com True Market Value (TMV®) pricing system, which serves as a guideline when car shopping. Again, by visiting Edmunds.com on-line you can get a "Customized Appraisal" that prices the car more accurately. The figures you can get are based upon thousands of similar sales across the country. We will go into more detail about how to use Edmunds.com's TMV later.

One last vital step to getting a great used car deal: you have to run a vehicle history report on any used car you are considering. Several companies sell these reports, which are based on the vehicle identification number (VIN), but Carfax (www.carfax.com) seems to be the most comprehensive. With these reports, you will find out the vital information about a used car, including whether it has a salvage title or its odometer has been rolled back.

6. Set Up Financing for Your Used Car

There are three ways to pay for your used car:

Cash. Need we say more? Money talks — you-know-what walks.

Financing through a bank, on-line lender or credit union. Assuming you can't pay in cash, we highly recommend this route because it will usually save money and give you the most control over the transaction.

Financing through the dealer. This can work for some people, depending on their credit scores and the current interest rates offered. Also, by prearranging financing through an independent source, the dealer may sometimes offer to beat the rate with a low-interest loan.

Financing through an independent source (on-line lender, bank or credit union) offers several advantages:

- Keeps negotiations simple in the dealership
- Allows you to shop competitive interest rates ahead of time

10 Steps to Buying a Used Car

- Removes dependency on dealership financing
- Encourages you to stick to your budgeted amount
- Low-interest loans can easily be arranged on-line through banks such as Capital One Auto Finance (http://www.capitaloneautofinance.com)

7. Used Car Markets

The three most common places to buy a used car are:

- Private parties
- New car dealerships
- Used car lots

Of these sources, private parties usually have the most reasonable prices. It is also a more relaxed transaction to buy a used car from a private party rather than face a salesman at a dealership.

Still, there are advantages to buying a used car from a new car dealership. Many used cars on these lots are trade-ins. Dealerships usually get these cars at rock-bottom prices. If you make a low offer — but one that gives them some profit — you just might get a great deal. Furthermore, many dealerships offer certified used cars that have been thoroughly inspected and are backed by attractive warranties. Search for your car by using Internet sites such as our Edmunds.com Used Vehicle Listings or in the classifieds of your local newspaper. When shopping on the Internet, you'll notice that some sites allow you to search according to specific criteria such as make, model, options and price range. In some cases, you can search the used car inventory of new car dealerships through their Web site.

While the Internet is an amazing resource, you should still try the conventional sources. Ask friends and relatives if they are selling a used car. Keep your eyes peeled for cars with "For Sale" signs in the window. Scan the bulletin boards at supermarkets or local schools and colleges. Finally, don't forget old faithful — the newspaper classifieds, particularly on Friday, Saturday and Sunday.

A lot of time can be saved by calling the selling party before you go see the vehicle. In this way, you can eliminate cars that have problems such as excessive mileage or a salvage title. Here are a few key questions to ask over the phone:

- What is the mileage? Why is it low? High? (12,000 to 15,000 miles a year is average)
- What color is the exterior? Interior? Does it have leather or cloth seats?
- How many doors?
- Is the engine a four-cylinder, V6 or V8?
- Is the transmission auto? Manual?
- Is the car still under warranty?
- Is there a salvage title?
- What options/add-ons does it have?
- What is the asking price?

If, after talking to the seller, the car still meets your needs, set up an appointment for a test-drive. If possible, make this appointment during the day so you can more accurately determine the car's condition. Also, ask for the VIN number so you can run a Carfax report. This will give you detailed information about the car's history.

8. Test-Driving a Used Car

Used car shopping will involve inspecting the vehicle to determine its condition. This process is simplified if you buy a certified used car that has passed a thorough inspection and is backed by a manufacturer's warranty. But while buying a certified used car removes a lot of the guesswork about the vehicle's mechanical condition, you pay for this service in the form of a higher purchase price.

10 Steps to Buying a Used Car

Most new cars are sold with a minimum three-year/36,000-mile basic warranty. Therefore, if you buy a car that is one to three years old, with less than 36,000 miles on the odometer, it will still be under the factory warranty. If anything goes wrong with the car you just bought, the problem will be fixed for free (provided it's not a wear item like brake pads). Warranties vary from one manufacturer to the next. Always read the restrictions of the warranty before buying the car.

If you are serious about buying a used car but have doubts about its condition, take it to a mechanic you trust. A private party will probably allow you to do this without much resistance. But at a dealership, it might be more difficult. If it is a factory-certified used car, you don't have to take it to a mechanic.

Once you get behind the wheel, your first impression will be the way the car feels when you sit in it. Is it a good fit? Does it offer enough head-room? Legroom? Are the gauges and controls conveniently positioned?

Try to arrange your test-drive so that you start the engine when it is completely cold. Some cars are harder to start after they have been sitting, and starting them up in this condition can reveal chronic problems. If you can have a friend stand behind the car to watch the tailpipe while you start it, even better. A condition to watch for is blue or white smoke emitted from the tailpipe for several seconds (or longer) after the engine starts. If you see steam or water vapor, don't worry about it. Turn off the radio before you start the vehicle — you want to hear the engine and concentrate on the driving experience.

On the test-drive, evaluate these additional points:

- Acceleration from a stop
- Visibility (Check for blind spots)
- Engine noise
- Passing acceleration (Does it downshift quickly and smoothly?)
- Hill-climbing power
- Braking
- Cornering (Do you feel in control when making turns?)
- Suspension (How does it ride?)
- Rattles and squeaks
- Cargo space
- Seat comfort/support
- Wear and tear (Are interior components mostly intact considering the car's age or does it feel like it's falling apart?)

On the test-drive, take your time and be sure to simulate the conditions of your normal driving patterns. If you do a lot of highway driving, be sure to merge and take the car up to 65 mph. If you go into the mountains, test the car on a steep slope. You don't want to find out — after you've bought the car — that it doesn't perform as needed.

After the test-drive, ask the owner if you can see the service records and if receipts are available. If so, note whether the car has had oil changes at regular intervals (at every 5,000 to 7,500 miles). Be cautious of buying a car that has had major repairs such as transmission rebuilds, valve jobs or engine overhauls.

9. Negotiating for a Used Car

Whether you are buying a used car from a dealer or a private party, let them know you have the cash in hand (or financing arranged) to make a deal on the spot. Preface your offer with a statement like, "I'm ready to make a deal now. I can give you cash (or a cashier's check) now. But we need to talk about the price."

At this point, you need to have a persuasive argument for why the price is too high. So let's talk about pricing. The foundation of successful negotiation is information. This is particularly true when buying a used car. Yet, the variable condition of used cars means prices will vary widely as well.

Edmunds.com has removed much of the guesswork in used car pricing by developing True Market Value pricing. After you have gathered information about a car you are considering, look it up in this book. If you can, visit www.edmunds.com and follow the link that gives you a "Customized Appraisal." When you're finished, print out the three TMV prices: Trade-In, Private Party and Dealer Retail.

Dealers have lots of negotiating experience. Most private party sellers do not. Therefore, buying a used car from a dealer or a private party will be two very different experiences. But there is one overriding similarity — they both want to sell the car. In fact, the incentive to sell the car might be greater to the dealer than to the private party owner.

You should, however, follow these guidelines when negotiating:

- Beware of negotiating with a salesperson (or private party seller) who makes you feel uncomfortable or intimidated.
- Make an opening offer that is low, but in the ballpark.
- Decide ahead of time how high you will go and leave when your limit is reached.
- Make it clear that you are prepared to walk away if a deal can't be made — this is your strongest negotiating tool.
- Be patient — plan to spend an hour or more negotiating at a dealership, much less with a private party.
- Leave the dealership if you get tired or hungry — in other words, don't sign the contract just to "get it over with."
- Don't be distracted by pitches for related items such as extended warranties or anti-theft devices.
- Try to keep the deal simple — negotiate the buying price and the trade-in price (if you have a trade-in) separately.
- Expect a closer (a second salesman) to come in during the final negotiations to try and improve the deal before you reach a final price.

Once you have a deal, you need to make sure the transaction is completed properly. The next section, the final step, will tell you what to expect and what you need to do.

10. Closing the Deal

If you are at a dealership, you still have to go through the finance and insurance (F&I) process. If you are buying a car from a private party, you have to make sure that payment is made and the title and registration are properly transferred.

In both cases, you also need to make sure you have insurance for the car you just bought before you drive it away. Also, at a dealership, the F&I person will probably try to sell you a number of additional items: an extended warranty, alarms or anti-theft services such as LoJack, prepaid service plans, fabric protection, rust proofing and emergency roadside kits. Some people swear by extended warranties, so this is something you might want to consider (unless your used car is certified or still under the manufacturer's warranty). However, the other items typically sold in the F&I room are expensive and hold little value for you.

The F&I person may seem like a financial advisor, but he or she is really an experienced salesperson. Some F&I people can become very persistent trying to sell these items. Be firm. Say, "I'm not interested in any aftermarket extras, thank you. I just want the car."

Once the contract is ready, review it thoroughly. In most states, it will contain the cost of the vehicle, a documentation fee, a smog fee, a small charge for a smog certificate, sales tax and license fees (also known as DMV fees). Make sure you understand the charges and question the appearance of any significant, sudden additions to the contract.

Finally, you should inspect the car before you take possession of it. If any repair work is required, and has been promised by the dealer, get it in writing in a "Due Bill." Make sure the temporary registration has been put in the proper place (usually on the lower part of the windshield) — and you're finally on your way.

When you buy a car from a private party, you will probably be asked to pay with a cashier's check or in cash. But before money changes hands, request the title (sometimes called the "pink slip") and have it signed over to you. Rules governing vehicle registration and licensing vary from state to state. Check with the DMV in your state (much of this information is now available on DMV Web sites).

Once all of the paperwork is complete, it is finally time to relax and begin enjoying your new purchase: a good used car.

10 Steps to Buying a Used Car

Checklist

1. Choose the right vehicle for you by making sure the car suits your needs.

2. Consider all cars in the class you have chosen (compact sedan, large SUV, midsize wagon, etc.)

3. Look up the car on Edmunds.com and check its reliability record, editorial reviews and consumer commentary.

4. Check the Edmunds.com TMV price in this book or visit **www.edmunds.com** to get the most accurate price on the car you want to buy (adjusted for mileage, options, color, condition and region).

5. Decide how much you have to spend: down payment, monthly payment and purchase price.

6. Decide how you are going to finance your car. If you are going through a bank, on-line lender or credit union, obtain loan approval before you start shopping.

7. Using the Internet, including Edmunds.com's Used Vehicle Listings, search for the used car you've decided to buy.

8. Call the seller and verify the pertinent information. Get the VIN. Run a Carfax report on the car.

9. Test-drive the car under your normal driving conditions. Take the car to a mechanic if it is not certified by the manufacturer or covered by a comprehensive warranty.

10. Negotiate your best deal.

11. Read the contract carefully before signing and always make sure you get a clean title.

12. Inspect the car for dents, dings and scratches before taking final delivery.

10 Steps to Selling a Used Car

Here are 10 simple steps to turn your used car into cash in the shortest amount of time.

1. Know the Market

Is your car going to be easy to sell? Is it a hot commodity? Or will you have to drop your price and search out additional avenues to sell it?

Here are a few general rules to answer these questions:

- Family sedans, while unexciting to many, are in constant demand by people needing basic, inexpensive transportation.
- SUVs are very popular right now and often move quickly, even older models.
- The sale of convertibles and sports cars is seasonal. Sunny weather brings out the buyers. Fall and winter months will be slow.
- Trucks and vans, used for work, are steady sellers and command competitive prices. Don't underestimate their value.
- Collector cars will take longer to sell and are often difficult to price. However, these cars can have unexpected value if you find the right buyer.

Your first step is to check classified ads in your local newspaper and on-line. See what is for sale and at what price. Edmunds.com and other Internet sites allow you to search with specific criteria. For example, select the year and trim level of your car and see how many similar cars are currently on the market. Take note of their condition, mileage, geographic location and selling price.

2. Price Your Car Competitively

The best way to price your car is to use the information in this book. If you want a more up-to-date price, visit Edmunds.com and look up the car you are selling. You will see a link under the "Used Car Prices, Reviews & Info" heading near the top of the page labeled "What is your car worth?" Click on this and follow the prompts. This will give you an Edmunds.com True Market Value® price that is adjusted for mileage, color, region, options and condition.

There are exceptions to the rules of pricing, so you should follow your intuition. And be sure to leave a little wiggle room in your asking price. You should always ask for more money than you are actually willing to accept. If you want to get $12,000 for the car, you should list the car at $12,500. That way, if you get $12,500 — great! But if you have to go lower, it won't be a terrible loss.

You may have noticed how creative used car dealers get in pricing cars. Their prices usually end in "995," as in $12,995. Are we not supposed to notice that the car basically costs $13,000? There is a lot of psychology in setting prices. A product that doesn't sell well at $20 might jump off the shelf at $19.95.

On the other hand, a private party doesn't want to look like a car dealer. Therefore, you might want to take a simple approach and set your price at a round figure such as $12,750 or $12,500.

3. Give Your Car "Curb Appeal"

When people come to look at your car, they will probably make up their minds to buy it or not within the first few seconds. This is based on their first look at the car. So you want this first look to be positive. You want your car to have "curb appeal."

Before you advertise your car for sale, make sure it looks as clean and attractive as is realistic. This goes beyond just taking it to the car wash. Here is a to-do list that will help you turn your heap into a cream puff:

- Make sure it is washed, waxed and detailed.
- Make sure your car is both mechanically sound and free from dents, dings and scrapes.
- Consider making low-cost repairs yourself rather than selling it "as is."
- Shovel out all the junk from the inside of the car. When prospects go for a test-drive, you don't want them to feel like they've walked into your messy bedroom. Let them visualize the car as theirs.
- Wipe the brake dust off the wheel covers and clean the tires with a product such as Armor All.

10 Steps to Selling a Used Car

* Thoroughly clean the windows (inside and out) and all the mirrored surfaces.
* Wipe down the dashboard and empty the ashtrays.
* Dig out all your maintenance records and have them ready to show buyers.
* If the car needs servicing or even a routine oil change, take care of that ahead of time.
* Have your mechanic check out your car and issue a report about its condition. You can use this to motivate a buyer who is on the fence.
* Order a Carfax report and show it to the buyer to prove the car's title is clean and the odometer reading is accurate.

4. Where to Advertise Your Car

Now that your car is looking great and running well, it's time to advertise it for sale. Traditionally, people advertise in newspaper classified ads. These ads can be expensive, but they get results. However, on-line ads are becoming more popular, particularly with hard-to-find or collector cars.

Here are the main markets for advertising used cars:

* On-line classified ads such as those on Edmunds.com
* Daily newspaper classified ads
* Weekly "shoppers" and giveaway newspapers
* Bulletin boards at your job, a local supermarket or on a college campus
* Word of mouth — tell your friends and family you have a car for sale
* Put a "For Sale" sign in the car window

Creativity is required when it comes to advertising. Think of unusual places to put ads (skywriting is probably too expensive), and you will get results.

One last word of advice about advertising: if you run an expensive classified ad, be sure you are available to take phone calls from possible buyers. Many people won't leave a message for a return call. So answer the phone — and be polite. This is the first hurdle to clear in getting buyers to come and see the car in person.

5. Create Ads That Sell

When creating "For Sale" signs or putting a classified ad in the paper, you have an opportunity to show how eager you are to sell the car. This can be done by inserting the following abbreviations and phrases:

Must Sell!: This often means the seller is leaving town and needs to dump the car at a fire sale price. This shows the seller is as eager as possible without giving the car away.

OBO: This stands for "Or Best Offer" and it indicates that you are willing to entertain offers below the stated price. This usually means you are eager to sell the car.

Asking price: This also communicates the feeling that you will negotiate, but it is one notch below OBO on the eagerness scale.

Firm: This word is used to rebuff attempts to negotiate. It indicates that you aren't in a hurry to sell the car — you are most interested in getting your price.

Think about what you are telling people by the way you phrase your ad. Little words convey a lot.

6. Showing Your Car

Keep in mind that when you sell your car, people will also be evaluating you. They will be thinking something like, "Here's the person who's owned this car for the past few years. Do I trust him/her?" Make the buyers feel comfortable. They will probably be uneasy about making a big decision and spending money. Put them at ease and answer their questions openly.

10 Steps to Selling a Used Car

Potential buyers will want to test-drive the car. Check to make sure they have a driver license. Ride along with them so you can answer any questions about the car's history and performance. Also, they may not know the area, so you might have to guide them.

There are many unexpected bumps in the road that can arise while selling a used car. These will be handled easily if you are dealing with a reasonable person. So, as you are contacted by prospective buyers, use your intuition to evaluate them. If they seem difficult, pushy or even shady, wait for another buyer. With the right person, selling a used car should be simple.

Some sellers feel uncomfortable about having buyers come to their house to see the car. However, you can generally screen buyers on the phone. If they sound suspicious, don't do business with them. If you don't want people knowing where you live, arrange to show the car at a park or shopping center located near your home. However, keep in mind that people will eventually see your address when you sign the title over to them.

Some buyers will want to take the car to a mechanic to have it inspected. If you have an inspection report from your mechanic, this might put their doubts to rest. However, if they still want to take the car to their mechanic, this is a reasonable request. By now, you should have a feeling for the person's trustworthiness. If you feel uncomfortable or have reason to think they will steal the car, decline the offer or go along with them.

Be ready for trick questions such as, "So, what's really wrong with the car?" If you get this, refer them to the mechanic's report or invite them to look over the car more carefully.

7. Negotiate for Your Best Price

If a person comes to look at the car and it passes their approval after a test-drive, you can expect them to make an offer. Most people are uncomfortable negotiating, so their opening offer might take several forms.

"I like the car, but..." This is the softest way to negotiate on the price. They may not even state that the price seems too high. However, if they say, "I like the car, but..." and then lapse into uncomfortable silence, you might consider an appropriate response. If you really want to move the car, you could say, "How much would you be willing to pay?"

"What's your best price?" This is a more direct way to probe the seller to find out how much he or she will come down. If you get this from a prospective buyer, don't seem too eager to reduce your price.

"Would you accept…?" Now we're getting somewhere. This buyer has thought it over and is making an offer. But the offer is being presented in a polite manner designed to allow for a counter offer.

"Take it or leave it." This buyer is making an offer that supposedly leaves no room for a counter offer. In reality, this buyer might be bluffing. Still, they are sending a message that they are close to their final price. The only way to know for sure whether it really is a "take it or leave it" offer is to leave it — and let them leave. They may return tomorrow ready to pay your price.

The above are just a few of the openers you might encounter. Think of your response ahead of time so you won't be caught unprepared. In general, it's a good idea to hold to your price when your car first goes up for sale. If you don't get any buyers right away, you'll know you have to be flexible about the price.

8. Handling Complications

In some cases, you might reach an agreement with a buyer that is contingent on performing repair work on the car. This can lead to misunderstandings down the line, so avoid this if you can. The best thing to do is have your car in good running order while being fully aware of any necessary repairs. If you state clearly in your ads that the car is being sold "as is," you can refer to this statement when it's time to close the deal.

Still, a trip to the prospective buyer's mechanic might turn up a new question about the car's condition. What to do?

This must be handled on a case-by-case basis. If the repair is needed, and you trust the mechanic's assessment, you could propose reducing the agreed-upon price by all, or part, of the amount for the repair. If the repair is questionable, but the buyer is insistent, split the difference, or have the car taken to your mechanic for further evaluation.

Remember, the older the car, the more problems a mechanic is likely to find. At some point, you have to draw the line. You may have to say to the buyer, "True, this work could be done. But the car drives well as it is. And the proposed repair isn't addressing a safety concern." After all, a used car — particularly an elderly one — isn't expected to be perfect.

10 Steps to Selling a Used Car

9. Finalize the Sale

Rules governing the sale of motor vehicles vary somewhat from state to state. Make sure you check with the department of motor vehicles (DMV) in your state, and keep in mind that much of the information is now available on DMV Web sites.

When selling your car, it's important to limit your liability. If someone drives away in the car you just sold, and they get into an accident, can you be held responsible? There are two ways to deal with this concern.

Once you have the money from the sale (it's customary to request either cash or a cashier's check) record the odometer reading and sign the car's title over to the buyer. In some states, the license plates go along with the car. A new title will be issued and mailed to the new owner.

But what if you still owe money on the car, and the bank is holding the title? One way to deal with this is to conclude the sale at the bank where the title is held. Call ahead and have the title ready. Then, once money has changed hands and the bank has been paid the balance of the loan, sign the title over to the buyer.

In some cases, however, an out-of-state bank might hold the title. In this instance, it is recommended that you go with the buyer to the DMV and get a temporary operating permit based on a bill of sale. Then, after you pay off the balance of the loan with the proceeds from the car sale, have the title mailed to the new owner. Sign it over to the new owner and the transaction is complete.

Finally, remember to contact your insurance agent to cancel your policy on the vehicle you have sold (or transfer the coverage to your new car).

Before your car drives away for the final time, take a last look through the glove compartment, the trunk and under the seats. You might find some long forgotten treasures you misplaced years ago.

10. After the Sale

In most states, the condition of a used car for sale is considered "as is" and no warranty is provided or implied. Therefore, if the car breaks down after you have sold it you are under no obligation to refund the buyer's money or pay to have it repaired. If you have sold a car to someone who took it for inspection at a garage and the mechanic found nothing wrong with it, you have done all you can to protect yourself and the buyer.

The best way to feel peace of mind after selling your used car is to make sure you did everything correctly. This means being open about the condition of the car before the sale and timely and complete in transferring DMV paperwork after the sale.

When done correctly, selling a used car can be a win-win situation. You have turned your used car into cash and provided reliable transportation for the next owner. Focus on the benefits to both parties and you are likely to have a smooth and successful experience.

Your Key to a Good Used Car

You're shopping for a used car when you think you've hit pay dirt. It's a '98 import with low miles. It drives great, and the price is right. When you question the owner about the car's history, he says he bought it from a used car lot only two years ago.

You're about to write a check when you have a troubling thought: This deal seems too good to be true. Maybe something's wrong with the car that the seller is keeping hidden. Who owned the car before? Is there any damage or problems you should know about?

At one time there was no way to verify a vehicle's history. Buyers could only examine the evidence in front of them, basing their decision on the mechanical condition of the car. But computer technology now allows car shoppers to use the Vehicle Identification Number (VIN) to reveal a car's possibly checkered past.

Vehicle history reports can be ordered from a number of Internet companies. The first company to offer this service is Carfax (www.carfax.com), which, as the name suggests, began faxing used car reports as early as 1986. Now, the Fairfax, Virginia-based company accesses 450 different information sources to compile reports that are e-mailed almost instantaneously to customers.

"We literally have every car on the road in our database back to 1981," said Carfax Vice President of Marketing Scott Fredericks. He notes that 1981 was when the U.S. government accepted the VIN as a standard tracking code for a vehicle's history. "Think of the Carfax as the DNA of the car — the Carfax report never forgets."

Vehicle History Reports — A Growing Field

While Carfax seems to be the leader in this new field, there are other companies vying for the consumer's business. Many of these companies draw on similar sources for their information and present the data in a compiled report at competitive prices. Carfax charges $19.99 for a single report and $24.99 for an unlimited number of reports for one month.

Consumer Guide (www.consumerguide.com) has taken the process one step further. Vehicle history information is drawn from the monster database of Experian (with 1.7 billion records) and coupled with Consumer Guide's repair information.

"What we do that is unique is marry the Consumer Guide data to [vehicle history reports] on the fly," said Grant Whitmore, general manager. "We also track trouble spots for the year, make and model of that vehicle." While the information doesn't pertain to that specific vehicle, it gives a buyer a general picture of the car's reliability and the replacement cost of parts, should something go wrong.

"If you are selling your car, you can buy the report and show it to the potential buyer," suggested Consumer Guide Product Manager Robin Kowalski. "This will show [consumers] there isn't some sort of wreck that they weren't aware of."

Consumer Guide launched its Vehicle History Reports in February 2001. Whitmore declined to give specifics about the number of reports that have been ordered but said, "It's been extremely popular."

Odometer Rollbacks

If you order a report from Carfax, your report is broken into categories: vehicle specifications, title check, odometer rollback check, problem check, registration check and vehicle history details. The different pieces of the report are summarized in a table that may flag problems. Details are listed later in the report.

Most importantly, Carfax provides an independent check of a vehicle's history. While the odometer of a used car might show that it has only 55,000 miles, the Carfax might indicate that the odometer readings at key events in the car's history — emissions tests or title changes — don't match up.

For example, the report might show that a certain vehicle was smog-checked in December 1999 at 55,000 miles. But then, when a change of title was issued two months later, the odometer reading was recorded as being 45,000 miles. Obviously, there was some kind of foul play here.

The number of miles a car is driven directly affects the price of the car. Therefore, a seller has a strong incentive to roll back the odometer. Each excess mile a car is driven — over the expected yearly average of between 12,000 to 15,000 — reduces its value. Therefore, turning back an odometer 10,000 miles can increase the sale price of the car by $600.

In another situation, a person might be ready to return a lease car and be faced with paying $2,000 in mileage penalties to the dealer. A quick trip

Vehicle History Reports

to a "spinner" — someone who turns back odometers — will save them lots of money. In this way, dealers are defrauded, and so is the next person who buys the car.

"Folks think because [the odometer] is digital, it is harder to roll back," Fredericks said. "But it's not. Anyone with a laptop [and the right software] can plug into the car's computer under the hood and do it." He added that some estimates have shown that 40 percent of lease cars have been involved in some type of scam.

Title Washing and Curb Stoning

Another scam detected by Carfax is called "title washing." This occurs when "state X might not recognize titles from state Y," Fredericks said. "People who are unscrupulous will take bad cars and move them into that state. This happens everyday."

But a Carfax report tracks the car as it crosses state lines. If a car has been "branded" in another state — with a salvage title, for example — this will be revealed on the report. Salvage titles are assigned to cars that have been considered a total loss by insurance companies. Of course, the car might still run and be drivable, but having a salvage title significantly reduces its value.

"Curb stoning" occurs when a dealer has an inferior or damaged car he can't sell on his lot. He gives the car to a salesperson to sell through the classifieds, as if it were a private party sale. However, a Carfax report will show that the title recently changed hands and may reveal that it is a lemon or an otherwise branded car. Fredericks recommends proceeding with extreme caution if the seller's name is different from the name on the title.

Edmunds Test-Drives Carfax

While we were writing this article, Carfax gave us an account to run a number of vehicle history reports. In many cases, reports were run on cars that were known to have salvage or lemon titles. Carfax reports caught those problems and flagged the pertinent information.

As a test case, we entered a VIN number for a '98 Corvette we knew had been branded as a lemon. Sure enough, the Carfax report clearly flagged the problem by stating: "LEMON LAW VEHICLE repurchased by manufacturer."

In other cases, we ran reports on cars we knew little about. In one instance, the report noted a "potential odometer rollback." Looking closely at the vehicle's file, however, it appeared the source of the rollback alert was probably a clerical error at a smog inspection station. Everything else about the car's history lined up.

"One of our fundamental tenets is 'Data authenticates data,'" Fredericks said. "This means that the more data sources we collect, the more verification we receive about the vehicle's history — including odometer rollbacks."

In another case, an Edmunds employee was considering buying a '95 Acura. He test-drove the car and felt it was in good mechanical condition. However, after running a Carfax report, it was discovered that the car was given a salvage title in 1996 and, several years later, a junk title (a junk vehicle is one that was reported to the DMV by an individual or a dismantler as having been dismantled). When the seller was confronted with this information, he said, "Oh yeah, I thought I told you about that."

In yet another case, an Edmunds editor ran the VIN number of a car she had owned several years ago. It was the only report that was returned listing an accident. It read, "Accident reported involving left side impact with another motor vehicle." Fredericks explained that Carfax is beginning to receive information from law enforcement sources reporting accidents. If a car is totaled in an accident, a salvage title is assigned. But prospective buyers will still want to know about minor accidents. In this way, they can find out if the damage was properly repaired.

Consumer Guide's Whitmore said their reports also list accident reports, usually if they were serious enough to cause damage to the car's frame.

What Does the Future Hold?

With the increased speed of data communications, the amount of information about vehicles will increase in the coming years. Both Carfax and Consumer Guide hope to tap into service and repair records in the near future. Then, a consumer can see if a car was maintained according to the manufacturer's requirements before purchasing it.

"We are working on [getting service records] now," Fredericks said. "That's our next big frontier."

Frequently Asked Questions

1. Why does it make good financial sense to buy a used car?

A new car depreciates between 20 and 30 percent as soon as you drive it off the lot. In the ensuing years of a car's life, it depreciates only about 5 to 10 percent. Therefore, if you buy a one-year-old car, someone else has paid for that steep depreciation. Furthermore, cars are more reliable now than ever before. Buying a yearling with about 12,000 miles on it means you are getting a car that will feel new at a significant savings.

2. What is the best way to check out the condition of a used car?

First, it is important to run a vehicle history report on the car you are considering. You can do this for a reasonable fee through a company such as Carfax (www.carfax.com). This will tell you who has owned the car and if it has a salvage title (that is, it has been declared a "total loss" by an insurance company due to an accident or flooding) or the odometer has been rolled back. If the vehicle history looks clear, consider taking it to your mechanic for an inspection. However, if you are buying a factory-certified used car, this will probably not be necessary. Also, check to see if the used car is still covered by the factory warranty (and make sure it is transferable). Should something go wrong with the car after you buy it, you can have it fixed at no cost if it's still under warranty.

3. I want to pay cash for my used car at the dealership. Do I have an advantage?

Not necessarily. You must remember that no matter how you pay for your car, it's all cash to the dealer. In the old days when dealers carried your note, you could save money by paying cash because there was no risk to the dealer. Today, dealerships finance through one of several lending institutions (banks, credit unions or the automaker's captive financing division) that pay them cash when the contract is presented. In fact, if dealerships do the financing on your behalf, they tend to make more money on your contract in the form of a reserve; anywhere from a one-half to a one-point spread on the interest. For example, if the published rate is 8.75 percent, the lender-to-dealer rate may be discounted to 8 percent. The remaining .75 percent is the reserve held by the dealer as additional profit. This may not sound like much, but it adds up to hundreds of thousands of dollars a year at larger dealerships. This is the reason you should always arrange financing before going to the dealership, and then ask the dealer if they can beat your preapproved rate.

Paying cash is an advantage if you suffer from poor credit or bankruptcy, because it allows you to avoid the higher interest rates charged on loans to people with past credit problems. The bottom line is that if you think you can invest your money at a higher return than the interest rate of the car loan, you could actually save money by not paying cash.

4. Why won't the dealer give me wholesale value for my trade-in?

When a dealership takes a car in on trade, it is responsible for the car. Before the trade-in can be resold, it must be inspected and often repaired. Sometimes, emissions work is necessary. All this inspection and repair work costs the dealership money. If the trade is in good condition and has low miles, the dealer will put the car on the used car lot for retail price. When the car sells, it is rarely for retail price, so the profit margin is shaved. The less a dealer pays for a trade-in, the more room he has to make a deal with a prospective buyer, and the more money the dealer will make due to increased profit margins.

If the car doesn't sell, has high miles or is in poor condition, the dealer will have to wholesale it. The dealer will likely sell the car for below wholesale value at the auction, and therefore expects to recoup some of the money spent reconditioning and inspecting the car on the front end. If the dealer offered you wholesale price when you traded in the car, it wouldn't make the money back in the event that the trade-in went to auction.

Regardless of the condition of your car, the dealer will anticipate taking the car to auction and will leave room to make money in that event. Your best bet is to sell your car on your own to a private party and forget about trading it in.

5. Should I buy an extended factory warranty for my used car?

Some people like the peace of mind an extended factory warranty provides. Other people like to save money and gamble. The decision is up to you. However, you should determine how much of the factory warranty is still in effect on the used car you are buying. The bumper-to-bumper warranty might have expired, but maybe the powertrain (which includes the major components that move the car, such as the engine and

Frequently Asked Questions

transmission) is still covered. Consider how long you expect to have the car. Will you keep it beyond the warranty that is in effect now? Also, keep in mind that extended warranties are negotiable; shop around for your best deal and you could save several hundred dollars.

6. When is the best time to purchase a car from a dealer?

There's as much advice about when to visit a dealer as there are days in a year. Some say that Mondays are good because business is slower on Monday than on the weekend. Some say holidays like Thanksgiving are good for the same reason: nobody else will be there, and the sales team will be hungry for a sale. Others advise to go when it's raining or snowing; after all, who wants to look at a car and get wet? Then there's the advice that the end of the month is the best time because the dealership needs to make its "quota" of car sales and will be more willing to cut a deal. Still others advise not to buy a car until the end of the model year, or in slow months like August or December when people are busy thinking about going back to school or shopping for Christmas gifts rather than buying a new car.

Our advice is don't buy a car until you're ready. That's usually the best time. By then you have had plenty of time to do your research for low-interest financing and you know what make and model best fits your needs.

7. When should a car be considered used?

Technically, a vehicle is considered used if it has been titled. However, some dealers can rack up hundreds or thousands of miles on a new car without titling it. In these cases, the ethical definition of a used car should include any car used for extensive demonstration or personal use by dealership staff members. The only miles a new car should have on the odometer when purchased are those put on during previous test-drives by prospective buyers (at dealerships where demonstrators are not used), and any miles driven during a dealer trade, within a reasonable limit. If the new car you're considering has more than 300 miles on the odometer, you should question how the car accumulated so many miles, and request a discount for the excessive mileage. We think a discount amounting to a dollar a mile up to 500 miles is reasonable. For higher mileage amounts, the cost deducted should be approximately 15 cents a mile for wear and tear inflicted by the dealership.

8. What's the difference between a demo car and a program car?

Both of these types of used cars might be sold at a discount by a new car dealership, so it's important to know what you are buying. A demo car is one used by the dealership for test-drives for potential buyers. Often, dealership personnel will use demo cars as personal transportation.

Program cars have been owned by the manufacturer and given to employees for a short time to use for company business. The idea is to have a Ford employee, for example, drive a late-model Ford to advertise the company's product. These cars are maintained by the factory and usually sent to auction before the odometer turns 10,000 miles. The cars are sold to Ford dealers at closed auctions and then put up for sale on the car lot and advertised as "program cars." Dealers like these cars because they can get them at low prices and then sell them at a good profit. Program cars have been well maintained, so in essence you are buying a nearly new car with no worries about mechanical problems.

9. Is it fair for a dealer to ask if my trade has ever been wrecked or damaged in any way?

Certainly. If you were buying a car from a used car dealer, you'd want to know the same thing, wouldn't you?

10. How do I determine a fair price for a used car?

Edmunds.com publishes True Market Value (TMV) prices for used cars back to 1980. If you can visit the site on-line, enter the information about the car you are considering into the Used Car Appraiser and you will find the average selling price in your region. Keep in mind that TMV is intended as a "transaction price" for the car — the price at which you actually close the deal — not an "asking price." When setting your price, it is also a good idea to look at used car prices in the local newspaper and through other on-line sources.

Frequently Asked Questions

11. How can I determine what a dealer paid for a used car at auction or in trade?

Unless the dealer discloses this amount, you can't determine the wholesale price. However, by making a low opening offer you will find the point at which the dealer firms up on price. When this happens, you've gotten about as low as you can go; any lower and the dealer figures it would be better to just hang onto the car.

12. Why does Edmunds.com's used car pricing differ from other price guides?

Each guide uses different sources to determine pricing. You must keep in mind that these publications, and Edmunds.com, are to be considered guides. The values contained within are not absolute; they are intended to give the user a range of values to consider when determining a fair price. Used car values depend on mileage, vehicle condition, geographic location, model popularity, seasonal demand and even color.

Also remember that the dealer will use whatever pricing guide works to its advantage in the deal. By providing pricing that favors the dealer, other guides make big bucks on subscriptions to industry personnel. Some even publish two different pricing guides — one for consumers and one for dealers. Rarely do dealers use values found at Edmunds.com. We believe that speaks volumes about the fairness of our published pricing to the consumer.

The most important thing to remember about buying, selling or trading a used car is this: a used car is only worth as much as somebody is willing to pay for it.

13. How often is Edmunds.com's used car pricing updated?

We update our used car pricing information on our Web site every six weeks. Our used car book comes out once a year.

14. Should I consider buying a car with a salvage title?

A salvage title means that the car has been damaged to a level that an insurance company has declared the car a "total loss." The car then is issued a salvage title to alert buyers to the car's history. However, the car may have been repaired, running well and capable of providing reliable transportation to someone. If the car has been thoroughly inspected by a mechanic, it might be a good deal for the right person. But keep in mind that when you try to resell the car, it will bring substantially less because the salvage title will scare away prospective buyers. In a nutshell, proceed with caution.

Glossary of Used Car Buying Terms

Add-ons: Extra items the dealership will try to sell you after you have made a deal on a vehicle. Examples are rust protection, extended warranties and insurance. These are high-profit sources for the dealer and are usually presented by the F&I person.

Advertising Fee: This is a fee that some dealers try to pass along to the buyer. You can try to remove this fee from the contract during negotiations. Or you can threaten to buy your car from a dealer who does not charge this fee.

Bait and Switch: Buyers are often lured into a dealership with the promise of a great deal on a specific car. This is the bait. When they ask to see that car, they are told that the car has already been sold but there is this other great car over here. The buyer has now been switched. This puts buyers at a disadvantage because they are now trying to negotiate a car they don't know much about (and it almost always costs more than the advertised car).

Certified Used Car: Certified used cars present a great option for used car shoppers. A certified car is one that has been thoroughly inspected — and where necessary, repaired — by factory-trained mechanics and is sold at a slightly higher price. The car comes with a limited time/mileage warranty and, in some cases, roadside assistance. The advantage for buyers is that they don't need to take the car to a mechanic for an inspection. They can buy the car with the knowledge that if it breaks down within the warranty period, the repairs will be covered.

Equity: Your car's equity is similar to the equity in your house. The car is worth a certain amount — and you probably owe a certain amount on it. Subtracting these figures will give you your car's equity. For example, if your car is worth $10,000 and you still owe $6,000, you have $4,000 of equity in the car. Unfortunately, it's easy to get "upside down" — the car is worth less than you owe on it — when buying a car. You might still owe $6,000 but the car could only be sold for $5,000. Even if you are upside down, keep in mind that you still have a car you can drive.

F&I Person: This stands for Finance and Insurance person. The F&I person will draw up a contract and present it to you once you have negotiated a deal with the salesperson. It is important to understand that the F&I person is really a "closer" — someone who makes sure you sign the contract. Therefore, the buyer needs to carefully read the contract to make sure it is the deal they reached with the salesman. This is also the person who will try to sell you "add-ons" at this stage of the purchase.

Market Value: This is a general term that defines how much you can get for your car if you sell it to a private party. In other words, if you advertise the car through the classifieds, or put a "For Sale" sign in the car window, the price you eventually sell the car for should theoretically be the market value. (See also "Trade-in Value.")

"No Haggle" or "No Dicker Sticker": When you shop for a TV or dishwasher, you check the price tag on the item assuming that it is not negotiable. Some dealers sell used cars the same way. This doesn't necessarily mean you are getting the best car for the fewest dollars. But it does reduce the time and trauma of haggling with aggressive salespeople over price.

Sticker Price: The sticker price of a new car (posted on the sticker displayed in the car's window) is also known as the MSRP or "Manufacturer's Suggested Retail Price." This translates to the dealer's "hoped for" price. The sticker price for new cars is set by the manufacturer and is as much as 10-percent above what the dealer bought the car for. The sticker price for a used car is set by the dealer. The buyer should, basically, ignore the sticker price. For a used car, begin your negotiations using the Edmunds.com TMV price.

Title: The title of your car is an official document that proves you own it. The title is given to you by your state's department of motor vehicles if you pay the full price for a car. If you buy a vehicle with a loan, a bank or other lending institution holds the title until the loan is paid in full. When you sell a car, you must sign the title over to the new owner.

Trade-in: When you use your old car as part of the purchase price for a new car at a dealership, it is called a "trade-in." You will never get the full market value of your car when you trade it in, because the dealer always leaves room to sell your old car at a profit (either to a private party or at a dealer auction). Despite the hassle of selling your old car on your own, you should consider doing this if you want to get maximum value for it.

Trade-in Value: This is the amount you should expect to get for your car when you use it as a trade-in toward the purchase of a new or newer car. (See also "Market Value.") This is not money in your pocket. It is the amount the dealer is willing to deduct from the purchase price of a new car.

"Turned Over" or T.O.: At some dealerships you are greeted by one salesman on the lot, then "turned over" to a more aggressive, experienced salesman who will actually negotiate the sale. You may then be "turned over" again to the F&I person. Many buyers find this process unpleasant. It is also designed to wear down your resistance and may cause you to take a deal just to get the whole thing over with. Never forget that you can simply walk away from the car lot if you are feeling unduly pressured or abused by these tactics.

Used Car Buying Quiz

Buying a used car should be pretty simple. Right? Well, actually, there are some pitfalls that could be costly. So just to make sure, take our used car buying quiz and see if you are ready.

Give yourself one point for each correct answer. If you score nine or above, you can expect to get a cream puff. If your score is six to eight, memorize your mechanic's home phone number. Scores of five and below, you'll probably be getting a visit from the repo man soon.

1. The best way to judge the mechanical condition of a used car is by pressing the preset radio station buttons on the car's sound system. That way, you can avoid buying a car from a heavy metal headbanger or someone else who would abuse the car. True or false?

2. When you go to inspect a used car, the only thing you need to do is ask for the service records. That tells the whole story of a used car. True or false?

3. A used car should be taken to a mechanic for inspection before you buy it. But there is one time when this isn't necessary. That is when:

    a)   The owner seems trustworthy.
    b)   The car comes with a certified pre-owned factory warranty.
    c)   The asking price is low and you don't want to blow the deal.

4. Name two places where the used cars on a new car dealer's lot come from:

    a)   _____
    b)   _____

5. The dealer makes more on used cars than on new cars. True or false?

6. Establishing the price for a used car is total guesswork. Look at the price, roll the dice and start haggling. True or false?

7. If your credit is weak, the place that will give you the best interest rate is:

    a)   The dealer
    b)   An on-line lender
    c)   A credit union

8. The best strategy in negotiating for a used car is to:

    a)   Try to intimidate the seller by using a lot of technical terms.
    b)   Ask the seller to throw in extras to get a good deal.
    c)   Make a low starting offer and gradually increase your price.

9. Leasing applies strictly to new cars. You can't lease a used car. True or false?

10. In comparison to new cars, interest rates for used cars are almost always higher. True or false?

Answers:

1. False. There are much better ways to find out about the potentially checkered past of a car's past life. See the next question.

2. False. Asking for service records is important. But the best thing to do is run a vehicle history report on the car you are interested in buying. Companies such as Carfax can reveal odometer rollbacks, salvage titles and, in some cases, accidents. Running a vehicle history report on a used car is essential.

3. B. The car comes with a certified pre-owned factory warranty. A certified used car means it has been thoroughly inspected by factory-trained mechanics. If something goes wrong after you buy it the repair will, for a limited time, be covered under the warranty.

Used Car Buying Quiz

4. Trade-ins and used car auctions, which sell one-year-old rentals and cars coming off lease. See the next answer for more on this subject.

5. True. Dealerships make more money selling used cars than new cars. (And, they make as much money servicing cars and selling parts as they do on both new and used cars combined.) The reason used cars are so lucrative is that there is a higher margin of profit. If you understand why, it might help you get a good deal on a used car.

The used cars on a new car dealership's lot come from trade-ins and auctions. The idea is to buy low and sell high. They buy as low as possible meaning that they will give the lowest possible price for a car that is offered as a trade-in. If they give an $8,000 credit for a car, they might try to sell it for as much as $14,000. This means they can comfortably bargain down to $9,500 or even $9,000 and still make money on the car. So, when you see a used car on a new car dealership, assume it has been marked up — way up. Moral of the story: Know beforehand how much a used car is worth by using Edmunds.com's TMV.

6. False. Several sources list current values for used cars. Edmunds.com has prices for used cars going back to 1980. Once you've looked up the car you want to buy or sell, make sure to click the "Customized Appraisal" bar and be realistic about the condition of the car.

7. B. An on-line lender. If your credit is weak, a dealer will likely mark up the interest rate and claim they are doing you a favor by letting you buy their car. In some cases, "nonprime" borrowers can pay as much as four interest points more than they should. It's a good idea to check your credit before you go to the dealership. Some on-line lenders have become very popular with consumers because they have tried to humanize the process by not humiliating "nonprime" borrowers. Try getting a loan through an on-line lender such as Capital One Auto Finance. For more information read Edmunds.com's "Tips for Subprime Borrowers."

8. C. Make a low starting offer and gradually increase your price. Even though there are pricing guides, such as Edmunds.com's True Market Value, you might be able to get an even lower price. It doesn't hurt to start low (but in the ballpark) and hear them say "no" several times. When they finally do say "yes" you'll know you are getting the lowest possible price. If you are negotiating in a car dealership, however, you might need to threaten to walk out before they will know it is your "take it or leave it" price.

9. False. Leasing is just another way of financing which can be applied to used cars as well as new cars. LeaseCompare.com is a good example of an on-line lender that has streamlined the leasing process.

10. True. Higher interest rates are one of the few bad things about buying a used car. The no-interest and super-low-interest rates offered by manufacturers usually pertain to new cars. However, the amount you save in depreciation when buying a used car will more than offset the higher interest rates.

2 0 0 4
Used Car
Best Bets

About Used Car Best Bets

Our editors are often asked what the best used car choices are, so we've decided to present the collective opinions of our editorial staff through our Edmunds.com Used Car Best Bets for 2004. In order to put together this list of our top choices in the used vehicle market, we emphasized the most important criteria that should be considered when researching and deciding on a vehicle: reliability, safety and availability. We also limited the eligible years from 1998 to 2002 for the following reasons: Older vehicles will probably have too many miles on them, and newer ones will suffer the large depreciation hit that typically makes a 2- or 3-year-old car (with low miles) the best value.

First, we looked at a number of sources that report on reliability and longevity, and applied our own experience and judgment to determine a vehicle's reliability. Second, we looked at how these vehicles rated in various crash tests conducted by the National Highway Traffic Safety Administration and the Insurance Institute for Highway Safety. And third, in most instances, we felt that the larger the spread of potential model years a buyer had to choose from the better. This is why one (more abundant) car may have beaten out another (less available one) if the two were otherwise closely matched.

Economy Car: 1998-2002 Honda Civic

For years, it's been the Civic and Toyota's Corolla fighting for the title of best economy car. Both are wise choices from a strictly utilitarian point of view; they're frugal with fuel, require minimal maintenance and are reliable. That said, the Civic gets our vote because it offers a few things that the Corolla line lacks: a sportier driving feel, a coupe body style in addition to a sedan and, in 1999, 2000 and 2002, an Si version that boasts a sizzling 160-horsepower inline four and a taut handling-biased suspension.

Midsize Car: 1998-2002 Toyota Camry

Fine build quality, legendary reliability and a hushed ride characterize the Camry. Though the arch rival Honda Accord may offer a more sporting drive, we picked the Camry based on its more serene cabin and compliant ride, qualities that are typically more appreciated in a family midsize car than apex-strafing proficiency. Furthermore, the Camry was redesigned in 1997 and this generation lasted through the 2001 model year, meaning all of these years are equally strong picks. An all-new Camry bowed for 2002, offering even more refinement and better driving dynamics.

Large Car: 1998-2002 Ford Crown Victoria/Mercury Grand Marquis

Ever wonder why police departments and taxi companies use these "old-tech" V8, rear-wheel-drive sedans? Because they're basically bullet-proof. Really, could a car have a tougher job than serving cab duty in New York City? Or cruiser duty in Los Angeles? Not only that, but these traditional American full-sizers are also very comfortable to ride in, have plenty of luggage capacity and are cheap to keep in light of their low maintenance requirements and commendable fuel efficiency (highway ratings are as high as 25 mpg). They also have very good crash test scores.

Luxury Car: 1998-2002 Lexus ES 300

As with the Camry, the Lexus ES 300 was revamped in 1997 and remained basically unchanged through 2001. Roomier than most entry-level luxury cars, silent and composed even when pushed, and boasting a level of fit and finish that holds up to the toughest scrutiny, the ES 300 doesn't ask for much more than the occasional oil change in return for thousands of miles of comfortable and stress-free motoring. An all-new ES 300 bowed for 2002, offering even more refinement and better driving dynamics.

Sporty Car: 1999-2002 Mazda Miata

Anyone who wonders how car enthusiasts can be so passionate about driving need only take a spin in a Miata. With ultraresponsive and communicative steering, an exuberant engine and a manual transmission with short, precise throws, even those who don't know a camshaft from a half shaft will be won over by Mazda's little two-seater. Yes, sports cars aren't the most practical things on four wheels, given their limited passenger and cargo capacities. But this is the Sporty Car category, and nothing within the average Joe's means represents affordable all-around automotive athleticism better than a Miata. Factor in great reliability, frugal fuel usage and plenty of aftermarket accessories and it's easy to see why so many Miata owners love their car as much as (maybe even more than) their significant other.

Mini-SUV: 1998-2002 Honda CR-V

It seems that everybody wants an SUV. The reasons for their overwhelming popularity include massive cargo capacity, the ability to traverse rugged and/or slippery terrain and a high seating position that affords a better view of the road ahead. Trouble is, most people who buy them will never come close to using a truck-based SUV's off-road capability, yet will have to endure the mediocre ride and handling and poor fuel mileage that accompany a "real" SUV. For those people who are more practical and less image-conscious, there is a better choice: the Honda CR-V. Combining the most practical attributes of an SUV (such as plenty of luggage capacity and all-wheel-drive traction for dealing with messy weather) with superior ride and handling characteristics, plenty of passenger room, excellent fuel economy and Honda's stout reliability history, the CR-V stands head and shoulders above most other SUVs, be they big or small. And in 2002, a roomier and more powerful CR-V debuted, cementing Honda's place in this segment.

SUV: 1999-2002 Nissan Pathfinder

With their dizzying array of driveline components, SUVs are rather complex beasts. Hence, they tend to be more maintenance-intensive than your everyday sedan. Unfortunately, that means more things that can go wrong. The Japanese SUVs have long enjoyed a big advantage over the American versions in the reliability area, and two of the best examples of this are the Toyota 4Runner and Nissan Pathfinder. We give the Pathfinder the nod because, in addition to matching the Toyota in build quality and dependability, the Pathfinder boasts a more comfortable ride and greater cargo capacity than its chief rival.

Minivan: 1999-2002 Honda Odyssey

Before 1999, the Odyssey couldn't compete with the more powerful V6-powered minivans from Dodge and Toyota. A four-cylinder engine, no matter how refined, isn't going to cut it when the van is loaded up with seven passengers and their belongings. That all changed when Honda brought out the completely revamped Odyssey in 1999. Boasting the most powerful V6 in the segment, along with a huge interior, hide-away third-row seat, top safety scores and Honda's solid reputation for quality and reliability, the Odyssey quickly jumped to the head of the class. You'll probably have to lay out a few more greenbacks for one of these vans, even in the used market, but consider it money well spent.

Small Pickup: 1998-2002 Ford Ranger/Mazda B-Series

With a wide range of trim levels and engines, including a big, torquey 4.0-liter V6, the Ranger and B-Series have something for everyone. In fact, these twins were the first compact pickups to offer four doors in an extended cab body style, a major benefit whether loading cargo or passengers. Factor in favorable reliability and these compact pickups are hard to beat.

Large Pickup: 1998-2002 Ford F-150

There must be a very good reason that the Ford F-150 has been the top-selling vehicle in America for the last two decades. We can think of many: a huge variety of cab styles and trim levels, a comfortable interior with sound ergonomics, a compliant ride, communicative and precise steering, smooth power plants and best-in-class brakes.

2001 Chevrolet Corvette

Trampled Under Foot

by Brent Romans

I recently traveled to a strange world, a twilight zone of sorts. Logic and practicality had little relevance, replaced by the holy worship of numbers and statistics. All of those who opposed my views thought that I should be smitten. The narrator's voice of this world was not Rod Sterling but someone who sounded a lot like the puberty-stricken 16-year-old teen working at the local car wash. For a week, I was on the bizzaro Planet of Bench Racing (PBR), transportation provided by a 2001 Chevrolet Corvette Z06.

During my time at Bench Racing, I saw very few females and no car with less than 250 horsepower. Conversations were centered on my Corvette. Comparisons were drawn. Questions were asked. How fast will it go? Can we go for a ride? Is it faster than a Ferrari? How much horsepower? What's it like? Can we go for a ride and do a big, smoky burnout? I did my best to answer these questions and speak the gospel of the Corvette, though responding got a bit tiresome after a while. (The food wasn't even that good on PBR, though I will note that it is better than what I've experienced at Planet Hollywood.)

During my stay at PBR, I picked up on some party tricks. Comparing weight-to-power ratios was always a crowd pleaser. Check out the following list:

Car	Mass	HP	Torque	Lbs./HP
2000 AM General Hummer	6,564	195	430	33.66
2001 Acura NSX	3,164	290	224	10.91
2000 Ford Mustang Cobra R	3,590	385	385	9.32
2000 Lotus Esprit V8	3,170	350	295	9.06
2001 BMW Z8	3,494	394	368	8.87
1995 Chevy Corvette ZR1	3,535	405	385	8.73
2001 Ferrari 360 Modena	3,241	395	275	8.21
2001 Porsche 911 Turbo	3,395	415	415	8.18
2001 Chevy Corvette Z06	3,133	385	385	8.13
2001 Dodge Viper ACR	3,447	460	500	7.49

Which one of these vehicles isn't like the others? That should be pretty obvious, but were you surprised by the Corvette's Z06's 8.13 pounds-per-horsepower ratio? We were. There is more beefy muscle on this list than a WWF SmackDown! event, and the Z06 manages to have the best power-to-weight ratio with the exception of the Viper. Need a kicker? The Z06 is the least-expensive vehicle on the list. For the same price as the Ferrari 360 Modena, you could get three Z06s! If your simple goal is to find a high-end factory sports car that delivers the mostest for the leastest, your quest has ended. Corvette Z06, all the way.

The Z06 arrives for the fifth year of production of the fifth-generation Corvette ("C5"). This isn't the first time a Z06 moniker has appeared on a Corvette, however. In 1962, GM was observing the Automobile Manufacturers Association's ban on all forms of competitive factory activity, a ban that had been in effect since 1957. Corvette granddaddy Zora Arkus-Duntov wasn't happy with the ban and came up with the Z06 factory option for the '63 Sting Ray.

Designed specifically for competition-minded Corvette owners, the Z06 package included upgraded brakes (finned drum brakes with sintered-metallic linings), thicker antiroll bars, stiffer springs, stronger shocks, a 36.5-gallon fiberglass fuel tank fitted to the luggage area and special cast-aluminum wheels. The 360-horsepower L84 V8 engine was the only engine offered. A total of 199 Z06 Vettes were ordered, but they didn't come cheap. The package added $1,818 to the Sting Ray's $4,257 base price, as well as requiring $661 of forced content in the form of fuel injection, a four-speed manual transmission and a Positraction rear axle. All together, the Z06 package resulted in an increase of about 58 percent of a Corvette's base price.

The resurrected '01 Z06 isn't so sharply focused on track duty as the '63, nor is it a replacement for the limited-production ZR1 model of '90 to '95. The Z06 takes over as the top-performance Corvette model, a position previously held by the short-lived '99-'00 hardtop model. Equipped with the Z51 suspension and mandatory six-speed manual transmission, the hardtop was otherwise just like every other Corvette and did little to justify its position as the best Corvette model. The Z06 makes an airtight case by starting with the hardtop's stiffer body and then one-upping it with a more powerful engine, tuned suspension components and 37 less pounds of curb weight.

About a dozen changes can be found on the Z06's engine when compared to the regular Corvette's power plant. Called the "LS6" (regular Corvette engines are labeled "LS1"), it looks very similar to the regular Vette V8 except for the red engine covers. Looks are deceiving though; this engine delivers almost 12 percent more power than the 2000 Corvette, totaling 385 horsepower at 6,000 rpm and 385 pound-feet of torque at 4,800 rpm. Both the horsepower and torque peaks are 400 rpm higher than the LS1's, but as the preceding chart shows, there is enough firepower here to take on any high-performance car and leave nearly all of them choking on the Vette's exhaust fumes.

Internally, the LS6 features a modified engine block, high-strength pistons, a revised camshaft, stronger valve springs, larger fuel injectors and new cylinder heads. The cylinder heads have altered intake and exhaust ports to improve flow, as well as smaller pent-roof combustion chambers that increase the compression ratio from 10.1:1 to 10.5:1. A new composite intake manifold is used to deliver larger amounts of air to the combustion chambers with less turbulence. The previous stainless steel exhaust manifolds have been replaced with new thin-wall cast-iron exhaust manifolds to improve durability in sustained high-speed situations. Those manifolds then dump gasses to a new exhaust system constructed out of titanium that weighs 50 percent less than a regular Corvette exhaust.

Hooked up to the LS6 engine is a unique manual transmission. It's still a rear-mounted six-speed Borg Warner transaxle with a 3.42:1 final drive, but the Z06's transmission has shorter gearing, allowing for more rapid acceleration and more usable torque at higher speeds. A temperature sensor has also been fitted and will warn the driver if thermal loads on the transmission become excessive.

Hopefully, we won't be activating that warning sensor on our watch. So, like, can we go for a ride and do a big, smoky burnout? Sure. Entry into the low-slung Z06 requires a familiar and ungraceful butt-first plop into the driver's seat. Once there, the view out the windshield shows off the pumped-up fenders and raised center cowling. It's certainly a pleasant landscape, and it encourages you to twist the ignition key. Doing so gives life to the V8. At first, it sounds just like the LS1, but listen more intently and you'll detect that the titanium exhaust adds a raspy edge to the exhaust note. As you let the engine warm up a bit and blip the throttle, you can feel the Vette shake subtly as the body structure is not substantial enough to control the motions of the idling engine. You understand that there is a big hairy monster under that shapely hood, and if you're not careful, it will eat you. And we wouldn't want it any other way.

Look around, and you'll see the Z06's interior follows typical Corvette design architecture, which means well thought-out ergonomics and build quality a cut above other GM products. It is not a model of refinement, however, as panel tolerances would be almost laughable if they were witnessed in a Honda or Toyota. It could also use more storage space, as there's only a glovebox, an anorexic center storage bin and a cupholder

2001 Chevrolet Corvette

designed exclusively for small Dixie cups. The Z06's hardtop format also drops cargo capacity from a generous 24.8 cubic feet found in the coupe to 13.3 cubic feet. Some optional equipment items aren't available on the Z06, such as the head-up display, the power tilt/telescope steering wheel, the power-adjustable passenger seat and the 12-disc CD changer.

To the car's credit, a fair amount of equipment is standard, such as keyless remote, dual-zone climate control with air conditioning, dual front airbags with a passenger-side shutoff switch and a decent-sounding audio system with a CD player. It also offers a few unique interior changes, including thicker side bolstering on the seats, drilled aluminum pedals, a stylized gauge cluster and a no-charge option package that adds red accents on the seats, the lower part of the instrument panel and the doors.

The Z06's mechanical modifications are instantly apparent as the car moves off into traffic. The shorter gearing offsets the LS6's higher power peaks and makes the transmission much more of a true six-speed rather than the coupe's tranny which often feels like a four-speed with two ridiculously tall overdrive gears. Some of our staff hoped the Z06 would go without the first-to-fourth gearshift fuel-saving feature, but alas, it's still quite alive. Chevrolet did remove the rubber bushings out of the Z06's shifter, improving shifter feel and accuracy. There doesn't seem to be any extra vibration coming through the stick, though the shifting effort is noticeably higher.

Around town, it's fun to drive the Z06 just like you would your average Chevy Cavalier, giving the car about two-fifths throttle as you pull away from a stoplight and then short shifting at around 4,000 in each gear. In the Cavalier, the result would be, well, normal acceleration. In the Z06, acceleration is thoroughly abnormal — and you're not even trying. Your fellow commuters back at the stoplight are now tiny dots in the Vette's rearview mirror, and the speedo shows that you are easily capable of getting a speeding ticket. Like a 12-year-old boy holding an M-80 firecracker, you can feel the power in your hands; you just need to find a devious way of exploiting it.

You quickly learn that stoplights and urban driving aren't the answer. As much fun as seeking out puny Mustang GTs might seem, the city is too confining of an environment, and the Z06's "FE4" suspension — consisting of thicker antiroll bars, a stiffer rear transverse leaf spring and stiffer dampers compared to all other Corvette suspensions — isn't really happy to be here, either. You feel every bump, crack and paint strip. Road construction baddies like sharp pavement elevation changes and large metal plates are to be avoided at all costs. There is compliance here, so we wouldn't go as far as saying the suspension is made out of concrete or anything. But it is obvious that the Z06 is meant for jobs outside the city.

Freeway entrance ramps seem to be the first thing more to the Z06's liking. Stomp on the throttle and you are the kid with the M-80. Blam! The Corvette snaps ferocious, hits warp nine, and slingshots up the ramp. The acceleration gives you tunnel vision, and it is all you can do to just point the wheels straight, let 'er rip and hope you don't run up into the back of a transit bus. Doing this for your first couple times numbs your brain like Novocain, and the only words that manage to tumble out of your mouth are monosyllable expressions like, "wow" or "whoa."

Once on the freeway and in top gear, the Z06 relaxes. The ride quality is more agreeable here, and visibility is decent thanks to minimally sized B-pillars, wide side mirrors and the low hood. This could be a great cross-country sports car like the coupe or convertible, but the increased road rumble, exhaust boom and smaller trunk conspire against it. The Z06 is fitted with 18-by-10.5-inch wheels with Goodyear Eagle F1 SC 295/35ZR-18 tires in back and 17-by-9.5-inch wheels with 265/40ZR-17 tires in front. This new combination is wider, grippier and gives better feedback, but it lacks the run-flat capabilities of the EMT tires. Since C5 Corvettes weren't designed to carry spare tires, the Z06 is fitted with a tire inflator kit.

The best place for the Z06, and the way that Zora Arkus-Duntov would have wanted it, is the racetrack, or at least sinuous and unpopulated roads. It is here that the car's modifications shine. If you can find the limits, that is. There is stupendous grip available, more than your average American consumer should have access to. Aim the car at a corner and it tracks through with zero drama. Hmm. Try harder on the next corner. Same thing. Am I getting old and driving like a grandma, or is the Vette just that good?

Mid- to high-speed corners are the Vette's favorite. Use the fade-free binders to haul the Z06 down from high speeds, let the car rail around the corner, and then nail the throttle to get a straight away shot toward the next bend. All the while, the LS6 V8 grunts and roars, feeding an endless supply of Herculean power to the rear wheels. Care must be taken with that power, however, as the stiffer rear leaf spring and shocks make the rear end feel greasy when midcorner bumps are encountered.

Tighter roads are also problematic. The Corvette's wide girth, which provided stability at high speeds, suddenly becomes a liability. The car is simply too big and cumbersome for this kind of work, and the steering does little to help matters. While the variable-rate steering rack is accurate enough, it feels heavy when quick transitions are asked for. The fun factor goes way down, and the Vette seems to know this. It grows bored, disenchanted, and seems to ask you, "Can't we go find some Porsche 911s to pick on?"

Once you are back at high speed and have enough confidence to get yourself in trouble, rest assured that all '01 Corvettes are equipped with a second-generation Active Handling system to help you out. Changes include a new pressure modulator and improved software. Chevy says the software allows Active Handling to take more precise control of rear braking. It has also gained sideslip angle rate control, a software algorithm that senses whether the driver has been too slow (or too fast) reacting to changing vehicle dynamics during evasive handling maneuvers. Unlike other stability control programs such as those found on high-end sedans, the Corvette's allows some mischievousness in the form of wheel spin or small degrees of oversteer. When the system does step in, it does so in a relatively unobtrusive manner. All of our editors thought highly of the new Active Handling system and left the system activated during hard driving.

Back from Corvette recess and parked in our garage, we pondered the level of success achieved by the Z06. Though we were unable to take our test car to a road course, we have no doubt the Z06 will make an excellent car for both autocrossing and road racing. As a daily driver, though, a coupe or convertible would make more sense because of their softer suspensions. Would the Z06 be a viable option to other cars like the Viper, M3 or 911? From a horsepower-per-dollar standpoint, sure. But there's more to vehicle ownership than just numbers, despite what the people from Planet Bench Racing think. The other cars still retain their own inherent advantages that make them equally appealing, from the Viper's unapologetic brashness to the M3's Teutonic smoothness and precision. To us, the Z06 is the Corvette for Corvette enthusiasts, the ones who are truly into performance and everything that the Corvette stands for. Love it or leave it, the Z06 is the true American sports car.

2002 Honda Odyssey

Trampling its Laurels

by Karl Brauer

If you read our 2001 Minivan Comparison Test, it's pretty obvious which minivan we preferred. The Honda Odyssey positively stomped the competition, beating its next closest rival, the Toyota Sienna, by 8 percentage points. We knew when the test posted there would be readers complaining that, when you figured in typical dealer gouging, the van was just too expensive to justify a purchase, no matter how good it was. For argument's sake, we ran all the final numbers with a $5,000 premium added to the Odyssey's price to see how things shook out. While the rankings got closer, the "big O" still won, proving that even with, ahem, "market price adjustments," as some dealers like to call them, Honda still offered the best people mover out there.

Despite this lofty position, there were some areas in which even the 2001 Odyssey fell short. It was one of the few vans in that test without a video entertainment system or a leather interior (with neither item available as a factory option). It also had rear drum brakes, no side airbags and one of the worst power point locations we'd ever seen. Many of these items, like side airbags and rear disc brakes, pertain more to sales brochures and advertisements than they do to everyday functionality. For instance, the Odyssey already had a five-star crash rating for side impacts; why add side airbags? So that when the young couple strolling through the Honda dealership asks, "Does this minivan have side airbags like the Dodge Grand Caravan?" the salesman can reply, "Yes, it does."

But a video entertainment system is something that minivan buyers use everyday. Like so many modern automotive features, you only miss them after they become available. Thankfully, when Honda finally decided to make the leap to in-car entertainment, the company didn't mess around. Opting for a DVD-based system that provides crystal-clear images on a 7-inch flip-down screen, along with wireless headphones, Honda has given Odyssey buyers one of the most valuable features they could hope for: rear-seat passenger pacification (we'll save the philosophical argument about kids staring at a video monitor instead of appreciating the world rolling by outside their windows for another story).

Another noticeable upgrade happens under the hood, where the 3.5-liter V6 jumps from 210 to 240 peak horsepower and the transmission goes from a four-speed to a five-speed unit. Like many of the previous van's components, the Odyssey's drivetrain was already among the best in class. During our last comparison test the Odyssey beat every other minivan in acceleration testing, including the slightly more powerful (215 horsepower) Chrysler Town & Country. But Chrysler had been threatening to bring out a more powerful V6, making 230 horsepower, by the end of 2001. Honda was likely responding to Chrysler's claims when it decided to put the 240-horse engine in the Odyssey for 2002. Even more interesting, Chrysler's engine never materialized, leaving the Odyssey with a healthy 25 (rather than just 10) horsepower advantage over the Pentastar offerings.

At the test track, this new drivetrain pushed the Odyssey to 60 mph in 7.9 seconds and through the quarter-mile in 16.2 seconds at 82 mph. Compare those numbers to the 2001 Odyssey's 9.1-second 0-to-60 figure and 16.9-second quarter-mile times, and it's clear that while last year's version was quick, the new one borders on sporty, despite its minivan status. Also worth mentioning is a drop of 7 feet, from 141 to 134, in stopping distance from 60 mph.

More subtle, but notable, upgrades include an honest-to-goodness tuning knob for the radio where previously there was a rocker switch, improved steering wheel controls for both audio and cruise control functions, heated seats, cupholders that deploy from the base of the second-row seats and quicker power-sliding doors.

In terms of ergonomics, Honda still has some finishing work to perform. For instance, the window switches and steering wheel controls aren't fully illuminated, making nighttime operation of these functions a "try and see" endeavor. Additionally, the shift lever partially blocks the temperature controls, and the power point is still located at the absolute bottom of the center stack just off the carpet (if you mount your radar detector on the sun visor, plan on getting an extension cord).

We'd also like to see Honda upgrade some of the interior materials used for the Odyssey. None of them are truly atrocious, but hard plastic on the top of the front door panels, where your arm is likely to rest on warm days, is something even the new Kia Sedona has addressed. The Sedona also offers a ratcheting armrest with multiple positions for the front seats, while the Odyssey's armrests are either up or down. And where is our outside temperature display and compass? Actually, you can get those on an Odyssey if you order the navigation system, but most other vans offer these useful bits of information as standard equipment.

If you get the sense that we're nitpicking, you're right. But that's all we're left to do after these latest upgrades to what was already the best minivan you could buy. Unless you're stuck on the SUV image (in which case, you'll be wanting the Odyssey-based Honda Pilot) or need to spend as little as possible (check out Kia's Sedona), this is simply the best vehicle you can buy for moving bodies around the planet.

Abbreviations

4A	4 speed automatic	GVWR	gross vehicle weight rating	PRNDL	Park, Reverse, Neutral, Drive, Low
5A	5 speed automatic	GPS	global positioning satellite	RBL	raised black-letter (tire)
6A	6 speed automatic	Hbk.	hatchback	Reg.	regular
2dr	2 door	HD	heavy duty	RH	right hand
4dr	4 door	Hp	horsepower	r/l	right and left
5M	5 speed manual	HUD	heads-up display	rpm	revolutions per minute
6M	6 speed manual	HVAC	heating, ventilation and air	RWD	rear-wheel drive
8V	8-valve		conditioning	SAE	Society of Automotive Engineers
12V	12-valve	I-4	inline four	SB	shortbed
16V	16-valve	I-5	inline five	SBR	steel-belted radial (tire)
24V	24-valve	I-6	inline six	Sdn	sedan
2WD	two-wheel drive	ISRV	inside rearview mirror	SFI	sequential fuel injection
4WD	four-wheel drive	KW	kilowatt	SLA	short/long arm
ABS	antilock braking system	L	liter	SMPI	sequential multi-port injection
A/C	air conditioning	LB	longbed	SOHC	single overhead cam
ALR	automatic locking retractor	lb(s).	pound(s)	SPI	sequential port injection
	(seatbelt)	lb-ft.	pound-feet	SRW	single rear wheels
Amp	ampere		(measurement of torque)	Std.	standard
A/S	all-season (tire)	LCD	liquid crystal display	SULEV	super ultra low emission vehicle
ASR	automatic slip regulation	LED	light emitting diode	SUV	sport utility vehicle
AT	automatic	LEV	low emission vehicle	SWB	short wheelbase
Auto	automatic	LH	left hand	TDI	turbocharged direct injection
AWD	all-wheel drive	LWB	long wheelbase	TMV®	Edmunds.com's True Market
BSW	black sidewall (tire)	mm	millimeter		Value®
Cass.	cassette	mpg	miles per gallon	TOD	torque on demand
CC	cubic centimeter	mph	miles per hour	ULEV	ultra low emission vehicle
CD	compact disc	MPI	multi-port injection	V6	V-type six
CFC	chloroflourocarbon	MSRP	manufacturer's suggested retail	V8	V-type eight
Conv.	convertible		price	V10	V-type ten
Cpe	coupe	N/A	not available OR not applicable	V12	V-type twelve
Cu. Ft.	cubic foot (feet)	NC	no charge	VR	v-rated
Cyl.	cylinder	NHTSA	National Highway and Traffic	VSC	vehicle skid control
DOHC	dual overhead cam		Safety Administration	VTEC	variable valve timing and
DRL	daytime running light(s)	NLEV	National Low Emission Vehicle		lift electronic control
DRW	dual rear wheels	Nm	Newton meters	VVT-i	variable valve timing, intelligence
DSC	dynamic stability control		(measurement of torque)	Wgn.	wagon
DVD	digital video disc	NVH	noise, vibration and harshness	WOL	white outline-letter (tire)
EDL	electronic differential lock	OD	overdrive	WS	work series (truck)
EFI	electronic fuel injection	OHC	overhead cam	WSW	white sidewall (tire)
EPA	Environmental Protection Agency	OHV	overhead valve	W/T	work truck
ETR	electronically-tuned radio	Opt.	option OR optional	X-Cab	extended cab
Ext.	extended	OSRV	outside rearview mirror		
FWD	front-wheel drive	OWL	outline white-letter (tire)		
Gal.	gallon(s)	Pass.	passenger		
GAWR	gross axle weight rating	PIO	Port Installed Option		
GVW	gross vehicle weight	Pkg.	package		

2003

Body Styles	TMV Pricing		
	Trade	Private	Dealer
2 Dr 3.2 Cpe	19419	20473	22230
2 Dr 3.2 Type-S Cpe	20344	21448	23289

Options	Price
Navigation System	+1651

Mileage Category: H

Acura has made a number of changes on its already highly competent luxury sport coupe. The biggest news is the availability of a six-speed manual transmission on the Type-S trim. If that doesn't interest you, there's certainly more. On the outside, the CL gains new wheels, updated headlights and taillights, a revised grille and new exhaust tips. Inside, Acura has added LATCH child safety seat attachments, a dual-stage and dual-threshold driver's front airbag and an auto-up driver's window. Cars with the optional navigation system also gain OnStar, the vehicle communications service.

2002

Body Styles	TMV Pricing		
	Trade	Private	Dealer
2 Dr 3.2 Cpe	16126	17143	18837
2 Dr 3.2 Type-S Cpe	17562	18669	20514

Options	Price
Navigation System	+1375

Mileage Category: H

Updated last year, the Acura CL is unchanged for 2002.

2001

Body Styles	TMV Pricing		
	Trade	Private	Dealer
2 Dr 3.2 Cpe	13865	15265	16558
2 Dr 3.2 Type-S Cpe	15037	16556	17958

Options	Price
Navigation System	+1176

Mileage Category: H

New from the ground up, the CL receives upgraded 3.2-liter V6 engines making up to 260 horsepower (in Type-S form), a five-speed automatic transmission with sequential SportShift and a full load of standard equipment for a bargain-basement price. A new sport-tuned Type-S is worth the extra money if you value performance over ride comfort.

1999

Body Styles	TMV Pricing		
	Trade	Private	Dealer
2 Dr 2.3 Cpe	8862	10145	11480
2 Dr 3.0 Cpe	9784	11200	12674

Options	Price
Automatic 4-Speed Transmission [Std on 3.0]	+326
Rear Spoiler	+183

Mileage Category: H

The previously optional Premium package, consisting of leather seats, is now standard.

1998

Body Styles	TMV Pricing		
	Trade	Private	Dealer
2 Dr 2.3 Cpe	6583	7632	8815
2 Dr 2.3 Premium Cpe	7032	8152	9415
2 Dr 3.0 Cpe	7711	8940	10325
2 Dr 3.0 Premium Cpe	7902	9161	10581

Options	Price
Automatic 4-Speed Transmission [Opt on 2.3, 2.3 Premium]	+330
Rear Spoiler	+186

Mileage Category: H

A new 2.3L engine replaces last year's 2.2L unit. All CL models get a revised grille and new alloy wheels.

1997

Mileage Category: H

Like many Acura products, the CL is based on a Honda platform, in this case the Honda Accord. The CL's sights are aimed squarely at BMW's 3 Series coupes.

Body Styles	TMV Pricing		
	Trade	Private	Dealer
2 Dr 2.2 Cpe	5579	6503	7633
2 Dr 2.2 Premium Cpe	6022	7020	8240
2 Dr 3.0 Cpe	6580	7670	9003
2 Dr 3.0 Premium Cpe	6917	8063	9463

Options	Price
Automatic 4-Speed Transmission [Opt on 2.2]	+243
Rear Spoiler	+137

Acura
Integra

2001

Body Styles	TMV Pricing			Body Styles	TMV Pricing		
	Trade	Private	Dealer		Trade	Private	Dealer
2 Dr GS Hbk	10043	11246	12357	4 Dr GS Sdn	10307	11542	12682
2 Dr GS-R Hbk	11063	12388	13612	4 Dr GS-R Sdn	11702	13104	14398
2 Dr LS Hbk	9407	10534	11574	4 Dr LS Sdn	9642	10797	11864
2 Dr Type R Hbk	12344	13823	15188				

Options	Price
Automatic 4-Speed Transmission	+470

Mileage Category: E

Carpeted floor mats are newly standard, and an emergency trunk release is added to the inside of the sedan's cargo area. Four new colors round out the changes for 2001, Integra's final year before an all-new model debuts for 2002.

2000

Mileage Category: E

The Type-R is back and it arrives with two more color choices. The four-speed automatic transmission has been enhanced for better shift quality, and all Integras now have a tune-up interval of 100,000 miles.

Body Styles	TMV Pricing			Body Styles	TMV Pricing		
	Trade	Private	Dealer		Trade	Private	Dealer
2 Dr GS Hbk	8904	10070	11213	4 Dr GS Sdn	9220	10427	11611
2 Dr GS-R Hbk	9997	11306	12589	4 Dr GS-R Sdn	10133	11460	12761
2 Dr LS Hbk	8472	9581	10669	4 Dr LS Sdn	8641	9772	10881
2 Dr Type R Hbk	10804	12219	13606				

Options	Price
Automatic 4-Speed Transmission	+478

1999

Mileage Category: E

In a small step upmarket, Acura has decided to kill the Integra's entry-level RS trim. The LS gets leather accents and 15-inch wheels, and the sporty GS-R now comes with leather seats. Type-R will return in limited numbers later in the year.

Body Styles	TMV Pricing			Body Styles	TMV Pricing		
	Trade	Private	Dealer		Trade	Private	Dealer
2 Dr GS Hbk	7782	8962	10190	4 Dr GS Sdn	8142	9377	10662
2 Dr GS-R Hbk	8867	10212	11611	4 Dr GS-R Sdn	8967	10327	11743
2 Dr LS Hbk	7314	8423	9578	4 Dr LS Sdn	7403	8526	9694

Options	Price
Alarm System	+137
Automatic 4-Speed Transmission	+326
Compact Disc Changer	+203

1998

Mileage Category: E

A revised front end, designed for a more aerodynamic approach, is added this year. LS, GS and GS-R models get a little more comfortable with a tilt- and height-adjustable driver seat and new alloy wheels appear on the LS and GS-R. The performance-edition Type-R is available again this year.

Body Styles	TMV Pricing			Body Styles	TMV Pricing		
	Trade	Private	Dealer		Trade	Private	Dealer
2 Dr GS Hbk	6762	7944	9277	2 Dr Type R Hbk	8278	9725	11357
2 Dr GS-R Hbk	7632	8966	10471	4 Dr GS Sdn	7107	8350	9751
2 Dr LS Hbk	6234	7324	8553	4 Dr GS-R Sdn	7489	8798	10275
2 Dr RS Hbk	5706	6704	7829	4 Dr LS Sdn	6490	7625	8904

Options	Price
Air Conditioning [Opt on RS,Type R]	+253
Alarm System	+117
Automatic 4-Speed Transmission	+279
Leather Seats [Std on GS]	+227

1997

Body Styles	TMV Pricing		
	Trade	Private	Dealer
2 Dr GS Hbk	6022	7206	8652
2 Dr GS-R Hbk	6367	7618	9147
2 Dr LS Hbk	5520	6605	7931
2 Dr RS Hbk	5098	6100	7324

Body Styles	TMV Pricing		
	Trade	Private	Dealer
2 Dr Type R Hbk	6436	7701	9246
4 Dr GS Sdn	6205	7424	8914
4 Dr GS-R Sdn	6505	7783	9345
4 Dr LS Sdn	5693	6812	8179

Mileage Category: E

Apart from the debut of the racy Type-R, no major changes.

Options	Price
AM/FM/Cassette/CD Audio System	+115
Automatic 4-Speed Transmission	+243
Leather Seats [Std on GS]	+198
Air Conditioning [Opt on RS,Type R]	+221

1996

Body Styles	TMV Pricing		
	Trade	Private	Dealer
2 Dr GS-R Hbk	5445	6586	8161
2 Dr LS Hbk	4779	5780	7163
2 Dr RS Hbk	4179	5055	6264
2 Dr Special Edition Hbk	5316	6430	7969

Body Styles	TMV Pricing		
	Trade	Private	Dealer
4 Dr GS-R Sdn	5520	6677	8274
4 Dr LS Sdn	5016	6067	7519
4 Dr RS Sdn	4372	5288	6553
4 Dr Special Edition Sdn	5456	6600	8179

Mileage Category: E

All Integras get new wheel cover and alloy wheel designs this year, as well as green-tinted glass. LS models receive body-colored moldings. Three new colors can be applied to the 1996 Integra: pearls in red, green or black.

Options	Price
Air Conditioning [Opt on RS]	+202
Automatic 4-Speed Transmission	+224
Compact Disc Changer	+140
Leather Seats [Opt on GS-R]	+182

1995

Body Styles	TMV Pricing		
	Trade	Private	Dealer
2 Dr GS-R Hbk	4474	5452	7081
2 Dr LS Hbk	3997	4870	6326
2 Dr RS Hbk	3420	4167	5413
2 Dr Special Edition Hbk	4375	5331	6924

Body Styles	TMV Pricing		
	Trade	Private	Dealer
4 Dr GS-R Sdn	4543	5536	7191
4 Dr LS Sdn	4169	5080	6598
4 Dr RS Sdn	3584	4367	5672
4 Dr Special Edition Sdn	4492	5474	7111

Mileage Category: E

A Special Edition model debuts, sporting leather interior, spoiler and larger tires. All LS models receive a sunroof.

Options	Price
Air Conditioning [Opt on RS]	+174
AM/FM/Cassette/CD Audio System	+91
AM/FM/CD Audio System	+78

Options	Price
Automatic 4-Speed Transmission	+192
Leather Seats [Opt on GS-R]	+156

1994

Body Styles	TMV Pricing		
	Trade	Private	Dealer
2 Dr GS-R Hbk	3716	4623	6134
2 Dr LS Hbk	3313	4122	5470
2 Dr RS Hbk	2822	3511	4659

Body Styles	TMV Pricing		
	Trade	Private	Dealer
4 Dr GS-R Sdn	4036	5021	6663
4 Dr LS Sdn	3276	4076	5408
4 Dr RS Sdn	2932	3648	4841

Mileage Category: E

Redesigned for 1994, the Integra sports a distinctive four-headlight front end. All models receive four-wheel disc brakes; LS and GS-R models get antilock brakes. GS-Rs get a 10-horsepower boost over last year to improve performance. Dual airbags replace the motorized seatbelts as the passive restraint system on the Integra.

Options	Price
Air Conditioning [Opt on RS]	+160
AM/FM/Cassette/CD Audio System	+83
Automatic 4-Speed Transmission	+177

Options	Price
Compact Disc Changer	+110
Leather Seats	+143

Acura
Legend/MDX

1995

Mileage Category: H

Body Styles	TMV Pricing		
	Trade	Private	Dealer
2 Dr L Cpe	5845	6900	8659
2 Dr LS Cpe	6906	8153	10230
4 Dr GS Sdn	6814	8044	10093

Body Styles	TMV Pricing		
	Trade	Private	Dealer
4 Dr L Sdn	5290	6245	7836
4 Dr LS Sdn	6289	7424	9316
4 Dr SE Sdn	6253	7382	9263

Options	Price
Automatic 4-Speed Transmission [Opt on GS,L,LS Cpe]	+192
Compact Disc Changer [Opt on L]	+144
Leather Seats [Opt on L Sdn]	+205

Last year for the Acura flagship, the 1996 replacement will bear Acura's new alphanumeric nomenclature. No changes for this year's model.

1994

Mileage Category: H

The base Legend is dropped from the lineup and a GS sedan is added. The new sedan offers the same 230-horsepower engine found in the coupe as well as traction control and a sport-tuned suspension. A new grille and bumpers find their way to all Legends and the LS coupe gets a new chin-spoiler. An automatically tilting steering wheel raises as soon as the key is removed from the ignition. Further improvements include a steering wheel position memory that is incorporated into the seat memory feature.

Body Styles	TMV Pricing		
	Trade	Private	Dealer
2 Dr L Cpe	5080	6201	8069
2 Dr LS Cpe	5914	7219	9394
4 Dr GS Sdn	5771	7045	9167

Body Styles	TMV Pricing		
	Trade	Private	Dealer
4 Dr L Sdn	4463	5448	7089
4 Dr LS Sdn	5168	6308	8209

Options	Price
Compact Disc Changer	+159
Leather Seats [Opt on L Sdn]	+368

Acura
MDX

2003

Body Styles	TMV Pricing		
	Trade	Private	Dealer
4 Dr STD 4WD SUV	30753	32249	34744
4 Dr Touring 4WD SUV	32877	34477	37142

Options	Price
Navigation System [Opt on Touring]	+1689
DVD Entertainment System [Opt on Touring]	+1152

Mileage Category: O

Further honing its already quite capable MDX, Acura has made a number of key improvements for 2003. First up is a 20-horsepower boost, giving the MDX a total of 260. To support the increased power, there's a revised five-speed automatic transmission, a new stability control system, a strengthened chassis, a retuned suspension and stronger brakes. Inside, the optional navigation system has gained voice recognition capability, enhanced graphics and expanded database coverage. There's also a tailgate-mounted rearview camera this year that transmits its view to the display screen when the vehicle is put in reverse. Lastly, Acura will be offering an optional DVD-based entertainment system as a factory option.

2002

Mileage Category: O

Introduced last year, Acura's capable SUV receives only minor changes for 2002. There are four new exterior colors, and enhancements have been made to reduce noise, vibration and harshness (NVH) for a quieter, more comfortable ride.

Body Styles	TMV Pricing		
	Trade	Private	Dealer
4 Dr STD 4WD SUV	28605	30004	32335
4 Dr Touring 4WD SUV	30016	31484	33931

Options	Price
Navigation System	+1375

2001

Body Styles	TMV Pricing		
	Trade	Private	Dealer
4 Dr STD 4WD SUV	25600	27721	29678
4 Dr Touring 4WD SUV	26813	29034	31085

Options	Price
Navigation System	+1176

Mileage Category: O

Acura brings a new sport-utility vehicle to the marketplace, combining great on-road performance, class-leading fuel economy and outstanding all-weather handling with seven-passenger seating and cavernous cargo capacity.

Acura
NSX

2003

Body Styles	TMV Pricing		
	Trade	Private	Dealer
2 Dr STD Cpe	71533	74088	78346

Mileage Category: R

There are no changes in store for Acura's supercar.

2002

Body Styles	TMV Pricing		
	Trade	Private	Dealer
2 Dr STD Cpe	66320	68856	73083

Mileage Category: R

For the first time since the car's introduction in 1991, Acura's midengined supercar receives a variety of styling enhancements. These include new fixed HID headlights, freshened front and rear bumpers and updated exhaust tips. Inside, six new color schemes are available. These schemes can be matched to the car's exterior color for a customized look. The center panel has also been updated with new chrome plating. Mechanically, the NSX remains unchanged, though the suspension has been retuned and larger wheels have been fitted.

2001

Body Styles	TMV Pricing		
	Trade	Private	Dealer
2 Dr STD Cpe	59438	63179	66632
2 Dr T Cpe	62241	66158	69774

Mileage Category: R

Acura's decade-old, aluminum-bodied, midengined supercar carries over for 2001 with no major changes.

2000

Body Styles	TMV Pricing		
	Trade	Private	Dealer
2 Dr STD Cpe	50398	54032	57594
2 Dr T Cpe	54096	57997	61821

Mileage Category: R

For 2000 the NSX gets improvements to its six-speed manual transmission, an upgraded perforated leather interior, and a cleaner engine that now qualifies it as a low emission vehicle.

1999

Body Styles	TMV Pricing		
	Trade	Private	Dealer
2 Dr STD Cpe	43764	47476	51340
2 Dr T Cpe	47971	52040	56276

Mileage Category: R

An Alex Zanardi Edition of the NSX is new this year, but only 50 will be made for sale in North America. The special-edition car features a fixed roof, lighter rear spoiler and manual steering in its quest to shed nearly 150 pounds. The Zanardi Edition adds BBS alloy wheels, a titanium shifter and softer red-stitched leather seats. And it wouldn't be a tribute to the CART champion without a stiffer suspension and lower height.

1998

Body Styles	TMV Pricing		
	Trade	Private	Dealer
2 Dr STD Cpe	40625	44411	48680
2 Dr T Cpe	42956	46959	51473

Mileage Category: R

No changes for 1998.

Acura
NSX/RL

1997

Mileage Category: R

The six-speed NSX comes to us this year with a larger 3.2-liter V6 engine that makes 290 ponies. Automatic NSXs continue with the 3.0-liter, 252-horse V6.

Body Styles	TMV Pricing		
	Trade	Private	Dealer
2 Dr STD Cpe	36395	39987	44378
2 Dr T Cpe	38567	42374	47026

1996

Mileage Category: R

The hardtop NSX is reintroduced to the Acura lineup.

Body Styles	TMV Pricing		
	Trade	Private	Dealer
2 Dr STD Cpe	31817	34991	39374
2 Dr T Cpe	34228	37643	42358

Options	Price
Automatic 4-Speed Transmission	+856

1995

Mileage Category: R

Acura offers an open-top version of the NSX, called the NSX-T. The "T" stands for targa (removable) top. Other than the pop-top, the NSX-T is identical to the standard NSX.

Body Styles	TMV Pricing		
	Trade	Private	Dealer
2 Dr T Cpe	29560	32372	37058

Options	Price
AM/FM/Cassette/CD Audio System	+107
Automatic 4-Speed Transmission	+701

1994

Mileage Category: R

No changes for the four-year-old NSX.

Body Styles	TMV Pricing		
	Trade	Private	Dealer
2 Dr STD Cpe	26727	29646	34512

Options	Price
Automatic 4-Speed Transmission	+644

Acura
RL

2003

Body Styles	TMV Pricing		
	Trade	Private	Dealer
4 Dr 3.5 Sdn	31953	33394	35796

Options	Price
Navigation System	+1536

Mileage Category: I

For 2003, Acura's RL receives only a few changes, including a new taillight design, restyled wheels and different interior trim colors.

2002

Mileage Category: I

The 3.5-liter RL now makes a generous 225 horsepower (up 15 from last year), and 231 pound-feet of torque, but a V8 engine still isn't available. The luxury sedan's double-wishbone suspension has been tuned for sportier handling characteristics this year, and wider, low-profile Michelins shoe the redesigned 16-inch alloy wheels. Noise and vibration should be quelled better by additional insulation material under the hood and dashboard, and the OnStar communications system makes its debut. Outside, the 2002 RL is freshened by new body-colored lower side sills, splash guards and roof strips.

Body Styles	TMV Pricing		
	Trade	Private	Dealer
4 Dr 3.5 Sdn	24057	25377	27578

Options	Price
Navigation System	+1375

2001

Body Styles	TMV Pricing		
	Trade	Private	Dealer
4 Dr 3.5 Sdn	21323	23107	24754

Options	Price
Navigation System	+1333

Mileage Category: I

Floor mats become standard, leaving the DVD-based navigation system alone on the factory option list. Also new is an emergency trunk release located on the inside of the cargo area.

2000

Body Styles	TMV Pricing		
	Trade	Private	Dealer
4 Dr 3.5 Sdn	17859	19727	21558

Options	Price
AM/FM/Cassette/CD Audio System	+192
Navigation System	+1025

Mileage Category: I

A new Vehicle Stability Assist system keeps the RL pointed straight, a new navigation system offers a larger screen and more information, and the 3.5-liter V6 now meets low-emission vehicle standards.

1999

Body Styles	TMV Pricing		
	Trade	Private	Dealer
4 Dr 3.5 Sdn	16443	18175	19979

Options	Price
AM/FM/Cassette/CD Audio System	+153
Navigation System	+650

Mileage Category: I

The suspension has been revised for better handling and a firmer ride, brake rotors have added mass, side airbags are standard, styling is more aggressive and the Premium features have been incorporated into one trim level.

1998

Body Styles	TMV Pricing		
	Trade	Private	Dealer
4 Dr 3.5 Premium Sdn	13384	14997	16817
4 Dr 3.5 Sdn	12614	14135	15850
4 Dr 3.5 Special Edition Sdn	12984	14550	16315

Options	Price
AM/FM/Cassette/CD Audio System	+131
Compact Disc Changer [Opt on STD]	+192
Navigation System	+558

Mileage Category: I

Slight suspension enhancements provide sportier handling without sacrificing ride.

1997

Body Styles	TMV Pricing		
	Trade	Private	Dealer
4 Dr 3.5 Premium Sdn	10008	11454	13222
4 Dr 3.5 Sdn	9543	10922	12607

Options	Price
AM/FM/Cassette/CD Audio System	+115
Compact Disc Changer [Opt on STD]	+168
Navigation System	+488

Mileage Category: I

No changes for the 1997 3.5RL.

1996

Body Styles	TMV Pricing		
	Trade	Private	Dealer
4 Dr 3.5 Premium Sdn	8583	9765	11397
4 Dr 3.5 Sdn	8123	9242	10786

Options	Price
Compact Disc Changer [Opt on 3.5]	+154
Navigation System	+447

Mileage Category: I

The replacement for the Legend arrives wearing Acura's new alphanumeric naming system: the 3.5 RL. The 3.5 refers to the Acura's engine size. The front wheels of the 3.5 RL are powered by a torquey V6 engine mated to an electronic four-speed automatic transmission. Other changes include 101 ways to isolate bumps, vibrations and road noise.

Acura

RSX/SLX

2003

Body Styles	TMV Pricing		
	Trade	Private	Dealer
2 Dr STD Hbk	15215	16296	18097
2 Dr Type-S Hbk	18023	19304	21438

Options	Price
Automatic 5-Speed Transmission [Opt on STD]	+691
Leather Seats [Std on Type-S]	+826

Mileage Category: O

Other than a new color, Redondo Red Pearl, there are no changes to the RSX in its sophomore year. Available from the dealer, however, is a new "Factory Performance" package that adds high-performance suspension components, better brakes, larger wheels and tires and a body kit.

2002

Mileage Category: E

The sporty RSX is an all-new replacement for the Acura Integra. Highlights include more powerful engines, higher levels of standard equipment and enhanced driving dynamics.

Body Styles	TMV Pricing		
	Trade	Private	Dealer
2 Dr STD Hbk	13953	14968	16660
2 Dr Type-S Hbk	16196	17374	19339

Options	Price
Automatic 5-Speed Transmission	+619
Leather Seats [Std on Type-S]	+687

Acura

SLX

1999

Body Styles	TMV Pricing		
	Trade	Private	Dealer
4 Dr STD 4WD SUV	9981	11505	13092

Mileage Category: O

The SLX is carried over unchanged from a year ago.

1998

Mileage Category: O

Acura's rebadged Isuzu Trooper gets more power and torque, a trick new 4WD system and revised styling for 1998.

Body Styles	TMV Pricing		
	Trade	Private	Dealer
4 Dr STD 4WD SUV	7852	9241	10808

1997

Mileage Category: O

No changes to Acura's upscale Isuzu Trooper twin.

Body Styles	TMV Pricing		
	Trade	Private	Dealer
4 Dr Premium 4WD SUV	6629	7934	9530
4 Dr STD 4WD SUV	6237	7466	8967

1996

Mileage Category: O

The SLX is one of the first luxury-badged sport-utes to be released in this country. Based on the successful Isuzu Trooper, the SLX is very similar to its twin.

Body Styles	TMV Pricing		
	Trade	Private	Dealer
4 Dr STD 4WD SUV	4600	5504	6752

Options	Price
Leather Seats	+277
Power Moonroof	+307

2003

Body Styles	TMV Pricing		
	Trade	Private	Dealer
4 Dr 3.2 Sdn	21264	22385	24254
4 Dr 3.2 Type-S Sdn	22029	23191	25127

Options	Price
Navigation System	+1651

Mileage Category: H

For 2003, all TL models equipped with the navigation system receive OnStar as standard equipment.

2002

Body Styles	TMV Pricing		
	Trade	Private	Dealer
4 Dr 3.2 Sdn	18541	19621	21421
4 Dr 3.2 Type-S Sdn	18978	20084	21926

Options	Price
Navigation System	+1375

Mileage Category: H

The TL Type-S makes its debut this year, sporting a 260-horsepower engine, sport-tuned suspension, Vehicle Stability Assist and 17-inch tires. 2002 also sees some styling revisions to the TL's front end and taillights. An in-dash six-disc changer, one-touch-up driver window and two-position memory system for driver seat and mirrors are standard on both the 3.2TL and the Type-S, and Acura has added insulation materials to the doors and reshaped the side mirrors to cut down on wind and road noise inside the cabin. Anthracite Metallic, Aegean Blue Pearl and Eternal Blue Pearl are the new exterior colors.

2001

Body Styles	TMV Pricing		
	Trade	Private	Dealer
4 Dr 3.2 Sdn	16427	17976	19405

Options	Price
Navigation System	+1176

Mileage Category: H

Standard equipment now includes floor mats and an emergency trunk release.

2000

Body Styles	TMV Pricing		
	Trade	Private	Dealer
4 Dr 3.2 Sdn	14093	15632	17141

Options	Price
Navigation System	+1025

Mileage Category: H

A new five-speed sequential SportShift automatic transmission and free-flowing intake manifold debut. A side-airbag system becomes standard as does a dual-stage inflator for the front-passenger airbag. The optional navigation system now features a DVD database.

1999

Body Styles	TMV Pricing		
	Trade	Private	Dealer
4 Dr 3.2 Sdn	12051	13599	15211

Options	Price
Chrome Wheels	+457
Compact Disc Changer	+264
Navigation System	+650
Rear Spoiler	+142

Mileage Category: H

The TL has been redesigned for 1999, with everything just getting better. The 2.5-liter engine is gone, making way for an all-new 3.2-liter V6. The transmission has been refined, the interior design makes better use of space, and the exterior is updated.

1998

Body Styles	TMV Pricing		
	Trade	Private	Dealer
4 Dr 2.5 Sdn	9681	11121	12744
4 Dr 3.2 Sdn	10082	11581	13272

Options	Price
Rear Spoiler	+122

Mileage Category: H

The premium level is gone, but the TL-Series gets more standard equipment.

1997

Body Styles	TMV Pricing		
	Trade	Private	Dealer
4 Dr 2.5 Premium Sdn	7707	9039	10666
4 Dr 2.5 Sdn	6952	8153	9621
4 Dr 3.2 Premium Sdn	9150	10730	12660
4 Dr 3.2 Sdn	7879	9239	10902

Mileage Category: H

The TL is unchanged for 1997.

1996

Mileage Category: H

Vigor replacement designed to do battle with new Infiniti I30 and the Lexus ES 300 in the near-luxury segment. Cleanly styled with room for four, the new TL-Series comes with either a 2.5-liter, inline five-cylinder or a smooth 3.2-liter V6.

Body Styles	TMV Pricing		
	Trade	Private	Dealer
4 Dr 2.5 Premium Sdn	5883	6999	8540
4 Dr 2.5 Sdn	5746	6836	8342
4 Dr 3.2 Premium Sdn	7294	8678	10590
4 Dr 3.2 Sdn	6140	7306	8915

Options	Price
Compact Disc Changer	+182

1995

Mileage Category: H

This "Touring/Luxury" replacement for the Vigor, aimed squarely at the Lexus ES 300, offers a choice of either inline-five-cylinder power (in the 2.5 TL) or more powerful V6 motivation (in the 3.2 TL). The five puts out 176 horsepower and the six makes 200 ponies. An automatic transmission is the sole gearbox and, as expected, the 3.2 TL has more standard features to go with its higher price tag.

Body Styles	TMV Pricing		
	Trade	Private	Dealer
4 Dr 2.5 Premium Sdn	4998	5971	7592
4 Dr 2.5 Sdn	4386	5240	6662

Options	Price
Rear Spoiler	+84

Acura
Vigor

1994

Body Styles	TMV Pricing		
	Trade	Private	Dealer
4 Dr GS Sdn	3977	4849	6302
4 Dr LS Sdn	3576	4360	5666

Options	Price
Automatic 4-Speed Transmission	+177
Keyless Entry System	+78

Mileage Category: H

Dual airbags are now standard on all Vigors. Burled walnut trim replaces the Zebrano wood trim and GS models get a standard CD player. This is the final year for the Vigor.

1994

Body Styles	TMV Pricing		
	Trade	Private	Dealer
4 Dr CS Sdn	3929	4918	6565
4 Dr CS quattro AWD Sdn	4083	5111	6823
4 Dr CS quattro AWD Wgn	4281	5358	7154

Body Styles	TMV Pricing		
	Trade	Private	Dealer
4 Dr S Sdn	3307	4139	5526
4 Dr S Wgn	3817	4777	6378

Options	Price
Automatic 4-Speed Transmission [Std on CS,Wgn]	+107
Bose Audio System [Opt on S Sdn]	+80
Compact Disc Changer	+80
Leather Seats	+117

Mileage Category: H

Base 100 sedan dropped. CS sedan gets standard automatic transmission. Rear ashtrays and cigarette lighters disappear from all models.

Audi
90

1995

Body Styles			TMV Pricing		
			Trade	Private	Dealer
4 Dr STD Sdn			3024	3685	4787
4 Dr Sport Sdn			3239	3947	5128
4 Dr quattro AWD Sdn			3613	4404	5721

Options	Price
Automatic 4-Speed Transmission	+184
Leather Seats	+253
Power Sunroof	+138

Mileage Category: H

Sport 90 model introduced, featuring lowered suspension.

1994

Body Styles			TMV Pricing		
			Trade	Private	Dealer
4 Dr CS Sdn			3027	3789	5058
4 Dr CS quattro AWD Sdn			3150	3943	5264
4 Dr S Sdn			2715	3398	4536

Options	Price
Automatic 4-Speed Transmission	+184
Leather Seats	+253
Power Sunroof	+138

Mileage Category: H

Passenger airbag newly standard. S model can be equipped with leather and a power sunroof.

Audi
A4

2003

Mileage Category: H

The big news is the arrival of the A4 Cabriolet, a fetching drop-top version of the A4. Initially, the company will offer only one drivetrain choice -- front-wheel drive with the 3.0-liter V6 engine and continuously variable transmission. Expect to see a 1.8T version midway through the model year and a 3.0 quattro Cab by October 2003. No word yet on the possibility of a manual transmission. The rest of the A4 lineup benefits from equipment upgrades. Leather is now optional on all 1.8T models, as are 12-way power front seats. All 3.0s will come swathed in leather, with more deluxe leather optional. Previous stand-alone options for the 3.0, including xenons and satellite steering wheel controls, have been swept up into the Premium Package. A new cold weather package includes seat heaters and a ski sack, and 17-inch all-season tires are a stand-alone extra.

2003 (cont'd)

Body Styles	TMV Pricing		
	Trade	Private	Dealer
2 Dr 1.8T Turbo Conv	28306	29621	31812
2 Dr 3.0 Conv	34580	36186	38863
4 Dr 1.8T Avant quattro Turbo AWD Wgn	21900	22917	24613
4 Dr 1.8T Turbo Sdn	19669	20582	22104

Body Styles	TMV Pricing		
	Trade	Private	Dealer
4 Dr 1.8T quattro Turbo AWD Sdn	21240	22227	23871
4 Dr 3.0 Avant quattro AWD Wgn	26148	27362	29386
4 Dr 3.0 Sdn	24545	25685	27585
4 Dr 3.0 quattro AWD Sdn	26101	27313	29333

Options	Price
Automatic 5-Speed Transmission [Opt on AWD]	+875
Bose Audio System	+494
Heated Front Seats	+247
Leather Seats	+723
Navigation System [Opt on 3.0]	+1027
Power Driver Seat [Opt on 1.8T]	+183
Power Moonroof [Opt on Sdn,Wgn]	+761
Power Passenger Seat [Opt on 3.0]	+183
Rear Side Airbag Restraints [Opt on Sdn,Wgn]	+266
Special Factory Paint	+342
Special Leather Seat Trim [Opt on 3.0]	+761

Options	Price
Sport Seats [Opt on Conv]	+1141
Sport Suspension	+228
OnStar Telematic System	+532
Power Rear Window Sunshade [Opt on 3.0 Sdn]	+285
Continuously Variable Transmission [Opt on FWD]	+875
16 Inch Wheels [Opt on 1.8T]	+342
17 Inch Wheels	+342
Automatic Dimming Sideview Mirror(s) [Opt on 3.0]	+152
Power Retractable Mirrors [Opt on 3.0]	+141
Power Driver Seat w/Memory [Opt on 3.0]	+228

2002

Mileage Category: H

Audi's entry-level sedan and wagon are all new for 2002. Along with a redesigned body structure and new sheet metal, the new A4 receives a variety of changes to make it sportier. It is motivated by either a 170-horsepower 1.8-liter turbocharged four or a completely new 3.0-liter 220-horsepower V6, which can be mated to a six-speed manual transmission. Making its debut this year for non-quattro models is a continuously variable transmission (CVT), also known as multitronic. An in-dash six-disc CD changer and a dual-zone auto climate control top the standard features list.

Body Styles	TMV Pricing		
	Trade	Private	Dealer
4 Dr 1.8T Avant quattro Turbo AWD Wgn	19462	20577	22434
4 Dr 1.8T Turbo Sdn	17479	18480	20149
4 Dr 1.8T quattro Turbo AWD Sdn	19199	20299	22131

Body Styles	TMV Pricing		
	Trade	Private	Dealer
4 Dr 3.0 Avant quattro AWD Wgn	23687	25044	27305
4 Dr 3.0 Sdn	21488	22719	24771
4 Dr 3.0 quattro AWD Sdn	22917	24230	26417

Options	Price
16 Inch Wheels [Opt on 1.8T]	+306
17 Inch Wheels	+306
Automatic 5-Speed Transmission	+714
Automatic Dimming Sideview Mirror(s)	+136
Bose Audio System	+442
Continuously Variable Transmission	+782
Heated Front and Rear Seats	+357
Leather Seats	+626
Metallic Paint	+306

Options	Price
Navigation System	+918
OnStar Telematic System	+577
Park Distance Control (Rear) [Opt on 3.0]	+238
Pearlescent Metallic Paint	+816
Power Driver Seat w/Memory [Opt on 3.0]	+204
Power Moonroof	+599
Power Rear Window Sunshade	+255
Rear Side Airbag Restraints	+238
Sport Suspension	+204

2001

Mileage Category: H

The entire Audi lineup receives a new 4-year/50,000-mile limited warranty and no-charge scheduled maintenance, a 12-year limited warranty against corrosion perforation, and 24-hour Roadside Assistance for four years. All A4s are now equipped with head protection airbags, have lengthier oil change intervals and an optional Electronic Stabilization Program (ESP). The 1.8T engine gets a horsepower boost from 150 to a racy 170 and meets ULEV standards.

Body Styles	TMV Pricing		
	Trade	Private	Dealer
4 Dr 1.8T Avant quattro Turbo AWD Wgn	15571	16995	18309
4 Dr 1.8T Turbo Sdn	13597	14840	15988
4 Dr 1.8T quattro Turbo AWD Sdn	15276	16673	17962

Body Styles	TMV Pricing		
	Trade	Private	Dealer
4 Dr 2.8 Avant quattro AWD Wgn	18172	19834	21368
4 Dr 2.8 Sdn	16761	18293	19708
4 Dr 2.8 quattro AWD Sdn	17479	19077	20553

Options	Price
17 Inch Wheels - Spoke	+261
Automatic 5-Speed Transmission [Std on 2.8 FWD]	+638
Automatic Dimming Sideview Mirror(s)	+116
Automatic Stability Control	+319
Bose Audio System	+377
Compact Disc Changer	+319
Heated Front Seats	+151

Options	Price
Leather Seats	+766
Metallic Paint	+261
Navigation System	+743
Pearlescent Metallic Paint	+261
Power Moonroof	+551
Sport Seats	+290
Sport Suspension	+232

2000

Body Styles	TMV Pricing		
	Trade	Private	Dealer
4 Dr 1.8T Avant quattro Turbo AWD Wgn	13444	14916	16359
4 Dr 1.8T Turbo Sdn	11416	12666	13891
4 Dr 1.8T quattro Turbo AWD Sdn	13103	14538	15944

Body Styles	TMV Pricing		
	Trade	Private	Dealer
4 Dr 2.8 Avant quattro AWD Wgn	15410	17097	18750
4 Dr 2.8 Sdn	13983	15514	17015
4 Dr 2.8 quattro AWD Sdn	14834	16458	18050

Options	Price
Automatic 5-Speed Transmission	+548
Bose Audio System	+315
Compact Disc Changer	+267
Front and Rear Head Airbag Restraints	+145
Heated Front Seats	+133
Leather Seats	+530

Options	Price
Navigation System	+620
Power Moonroof	+484
Special Factory Paint	+229
Spoke Wheels	+169
Sport Seats	+242
Sport Suspension	+218

Mileage Category: H

All A4 models receive minor updates to the interior, exterior and chassis. The front styling has been changed with new headlights, a new grille, new door handles and new mirror housings. Inside, you'll find a revised instrument cluster and center console, along with other minor interior changes. The rear seats have been modified to improve comfort. There are now optional head airbags and xenon headlights. The chassis has been reworked for improved ride comfort and responsiveness.

1999

Body Styles	TMV Pricing		
	Trade	Private	Dealer
4 Dr 1.8T Avant quattro Turbo AWD Wgn	10709	12338	14034
4 Dr 1.8T Turbo Sdn	9562	11017	12531
4 Dr 1.8T quattro Turbo AWD Sdn	10285	11850	13478

Body Styles	TMV Pricing		
	Trade	Private	Dealer
4 Dr 2.8 Avant quattro AWD Wgn	12628	14549	16549
4 Dr 2.8 Sdn	11477	13223	15040
4 Dr 2.8 quattro AWD Sdn	12220	14079	16014

Options	Price
Automatic 5-Speed Transmission	+467
Compact Disc Changer	+205
Leather Seats	+406
Power Moonroof	+371

Options	Price
Special Factory Paint	+195
Spoke Wheels	+130
Sport Seats	+185
Sport Suspension	+167

Mileage Category: H

Audi introduces the 1.8T Avant wagon to its lineup, while other A4 models gain standard equipment and new options.

1998

Body Styles	TMV Pricing		
	Trade	Private	Dealer
4 Dr 1.8T Turbo Sdn	7411	8729	10216
4 Dr 1.8T quattro Turbo AWD Sdn	7555	8899	10414
4 Dr 2.8 Avant Wgn	9003	10604	12409

Body Styles	TMV Pricing		
	Trade	Private	Dealer
4 Dr 2.8 Avant quattro AWD Wgn	9673	11393	13332
4 Dr 2.8 Sdn	8613	10145	11872
4 Dr 2.8 quattro AWD Sdn	8818	10386	12154

Options	Price
Automatic 5-Speed Transmission	+374
Bose Audio System	+196
Compact Disc Changer	+163
Leather Seats	+326
Metallic Paint	+137

Options	Price
Power Moonroof	+298
Special Factory Paint	+157
Sport Seats	+149
Sport Suspension	+134

Mileage Category: H

The 2.8 sedan gets a valve job resulting in 18 more horsepower and additional torque. Side-impact airbags are standard, as is traction control. Opt for the automatic and you'll get the same Tiptronic technology that allows Biff to manually shift Buffy's 911 Cabriolet. A new station wagon called Avant debuts, while the A4 1.8T gets new wheels, a sport package and an ambient temperature gauge. New colors and stereo improvements round out the changes for 1998.

1997

Body Styles	TMV Pricing		
	Trade	Private	Dealer
4 Dr 1.8T Turbo Sdn	6287	7504	8991
4 Dr 1.8T quattro Turbo AWD Sdn	6439	7686	9210
4 Dr 2.8 Sdn	6588	7863	9422
4 Dr 2.8 quattro AWD Sdn	6877	8209	9836

Options	Price
Automatic 5-Speed Transmission	+267
Bose Audio System	+162
Leather Seats	+269

Options	Price
Power Moonroof	+245
Special Factory Paint	+129
Sport Seats	+116

Mileage Category: H

A cheaper Audi A4 1.8T debuts, featuring a 150-horsepower, 20-valve, turbocharged inline four-cylinder engine and a base price in the low 20s. The 2.8 gains a revised deck lid and expanded central locking features. All models have new cloth upholstery, and the console and armrests are trimmed with the same fabric as the seats. Three new colors debut for 1997.

Audi

A4/A6

1996

Mileage Category: H

All new, the A4 replaces the compact 90. This car performs better than the lackluster 90, and features a full load of standard features. Plus, it's drop-dead gorgeous. For the first time, a five-speed automatic transmission is available with the optional Quattro all-wheel-drive system.

Body Styles	TMV Pricing		
	Trade	Private	Dealer
4 Dr 2.8 Sdn	5041	6149	7678
4 Dr 2.8 quattro AWD Sdn	5622	6858	8564

Options	Price
Automatic 5-Speed Transmission	+236
Bose Audio System	+146
Leather Seats	+250

Options	Price
Metallic Paint	+125
Power Moonroof	+226

Audi

A6

2003

Mileage Category: I

All 3.0 and 2.7T models get standard leather upholstery. In addition, the 2.7T now comes standard with a firmer sport-tuned suspension and 17-inch wheels and 235/45 high-performance tires (these items were previously available in the sport package). All models can be equipped with a cold weather package that includes front and rear seat heaters (front seats only in 3.0 models); a ski sack; and on the 4.2 sedan only, a heated steering wheel.

Body Styles	TMV Pricing		
	Trade	Private	Dealer
4 Dr 2.7T quattro Turbo AWD Sdn	31151	32593	34997
4 Dr 3.0 Avant quattro AWD Wgn	29409	30770	33039
4 Dr 3.0 Sdn	27035	28286	30372

Options	Price
Bose Audio System	+571
Heated Front Seats [Opt on 3.0]	+342
Heated Front and Rear Seats [Opt on 2.7T]	+437
Navigation System [Opt on 2.7T,4.2]	+1027
Power Moonroof	+669
Rear Side Airbag Restraints	+266
Special Leather Seat Trim [Opt on 2.7T]	+609
Sport Seats [Opt on 2.7T]	+380
Sport Suspension [Opt on 4.2]	+228

Body Styles	TMV Pricing		
	Trade	Private	Dealer
4 Dr 3.0 quattro AWD Sdn	28497	29816	32015
4 Dr 4.2 quattro AWD Sdn	36368	38052	40858

Options	Price
OnStar Telematic System	+532
Power Solar Sunroof [Opt on 4.2]	+418
Power Rear Window Sunshade [Opt on 2.7T]	+342
17 Inch Wheels	+342
Automatic Dimming Sideview Mirror(s)	+152
Power Retractable Mirrors	+141
Power Driver Seat w/Memory [Std on 4.2]	+228
Park Distance Control (Rear)	+266

2002

Mileage Category: I

The A6 gets a new 220-horsepower 3.0-liter V6 to replace last year's 2.8-liter. A continuously variable transmission (CVT) is available on front-wheel-drive models with this engine. Other mechanical changes this year include stronger brakes, an improved stability control system and BrakeAssist. OnStar telematics makes its way onto the options list, and you'll be pleased to find a standard six-disc changer in the dashboard. Styling in and around the car, such as the head and taillamps, is slightly modified and new interior and exterior colors expand your choices.

Body Styles	TMV Pricing		
	Trade	Private	Dealer
4 Dr 2.7T quattro Turbo AWD Sdn	27140	28566	30942
4 Dr 3.0 Avant quattro AWD Wgn	25293	26622	28837
4 Dr 3.0 Sdn	23092	24305	26326

Options	Price
17 Inch Wheels	+459
17 Inch Wheels - Spoke [Opt on 2.7T]	+459
Automatic Dimming Sideview Mirror(s) [Std on 4.2]	+136
Bose Audio System [Std on 4.2]	+510
Heated Front and Rear Seats	+170
Leather Seats [Std on 4.2]	+626
Navigation System	+918
OnStar Telematic System	+475
Park Distance Control (Rear)	+238
Pearlescent Metallic Paint	+816

Body Styles	TMV Pricing		
	Trade	Private	Dealer
4 Dr 3.0 quattro AWD Sdn	24505	25792	27938
4 Dr 4.2 quattro AWD Sdn	32181	33872	36689

Options	Price
Power Driver Seat w/Memory [Std on 4.2]	+204
Power Moonroof [Std on 4.2]	+599
Power Rear Window Sunshade	+238
Power Retractable Mirrors [Std on 4.2]	+126
Power Solar Sunroof	+442
Rear Side Airbag Restraints	+238
Sport Seats	+221
Sport Suspension	+289
Third Seat	+510

2001

Mileage Category: I

All 2001 Audis receive a new 4-year/50,000-mile limited warranty and no-charge scheduled maintenance, a 12-year limited warranty against corrosion perforation and 24-hour Roadside Assistance for four years. All A6s are now equipped with the high-tech Immobilizer III security system, side-curtain airbags, a 12-millimeter increase in the headrest height adjustment and an optional multifunction steering wheel.

Body Styles	TMV Pricing		
	Trade	Private	Dealer
4 Dr 2.7T quattro Turbo AWD Sdn	22292	24266	26088
4 Dr 2.8 Avant quattro AWD Wgn	20045	21820	23458
4 Dr 2.8 Sdn	18107	19710	21190

Body Styles	TMV Pricing		
	Trade	Private	Dealer
4 Dr 2.8 quattro AWD Sdn	19436	21157	22746
4 Dr 4.2 quattro AWD Sdn	25573	27837	29927

Options	Price
17 Inch Wheels [Opt on 2.7T,4.2]	+435
Automatic Dimming Sideview Mirror(s) [Std on 4.2]	+116
Automatic Stability Control [Opt on 2.8]	+319
Compact Disc Changer	+319
Forged Alloy Wheels	+580
Heated Front and Rear Seats	+193
Leather Seats [Std on 4.2]	+900
Navigation System	+743
Park Distance Control (Rear)	+203

Options	Price
Pearlescent Metallic Paint	+697
Power Driver Seat w/Memory [Opt on 2.7T]	+174
Power Moonroof [Std on 4.2]	+551
Power Rear Window Sunshade [Opt on 2.7T]	+261
Rear Side Airbag Restraints	+203
Sport Seats	+276
Sport Suspension	+248
Third Seat	+435

2000

Mileage Category: I

There are two new models joining the A6 2.8 and A6 2.8 Avant. The first is the A6 2.7T powered by a turbocharged V6 engine. The second model is the A6 4.2 powered by a virile V8.

Body Styles	TMV Pricing		
	Trade	Private	Dealer
4 Dr 2.7T quattro Turbo AWD Sdn	19244	21261	23239
4 Dr 2.8 Avant quattro AWD Wgn	17597	19442	21250
4 Dr 2.8 Sdn	15792	17448	19071

Body Styles	TMV Pricing		
	Trade	Private	Dealer
4 Dr 2.8 quattro AWD Sdn	17293	19106	20883
4 Dr 4.2 quattro AWD Sdn	22400	24749	27051

Options	Price
Third Seat	+339
Automatic Stability Control [Opt on 4.2]	+280
Bose Audio System [Std on 4.2]	+320
Compact Disc Changer	+278
Front and Rear Head Airbag Restraints [Opt on 2.7T,2.8]	+145
Heated Front and Rear Seats	+169
Leather Seats [Std on 4.2]	+605
Metallic Paint	+472
Navigation System	+620

Options	Price
Park Distance Control (Rear)	+178
Power Driver Seat w/Memory [Opt on 2.7T,2.8]	+153
Power Moonroof [Std on 4.2]	+484
Power Rear Window Sunshade	+229
Power Solar Sunroof	+433
Rear Side Airbag Restraints	+178
Spoke Wheels	+364
Sport Seats	+242
Sport Suspension	+218

1999

Mileage Category: I

The A6 continues basically unchanged after last year's redesign.

Body Styles		TMV Pricing		
		Trade	Private	Dealer
4 Dr 2.8 Avant quattro AWD Wgn		14656	16647	18719
4 Dr 2.8 Sdn		12408	14094	15848
4 Dr 2.8 quattro AWD Sdn		13532	15370	17283

Options	Price
Power Moonroof	+371
Power Rear Window Sunshade	+195
Power Solar Sunroof	+369
Rear Side Airbag Restraints	+152
Third Seat	+260
Heated Front and Rear Seats	+130

Options	Price
Leather Seats	+464
Metallic Paint	+212
Power Driver Seat w/Memory	+130
Bose Audio System	+245
Compact Disc Changer	+214

1998

Mileage Category: I

Stretch an A4 platform, add rounded styling with plenty of edges for character, toss in a sumptuously comfortable interior available in several "atmosphere" styles, blend it all with traditional Germanic handling and what do you get? The excellent new Audi A6 sedan. The wagon is carried over from 1997.

Body Styles		TMV Pricing		
		Trade	Private	Dealer
4 Dr 2.8 Avant Wgn		10009	11603	13401
4 Dr 2.8 Avant quattro AWD Wgn		10995	12746	14721
4 Dr 2.8 Sdn		9773	11329	13084
4 Dr 2.8 quattro AWD Sdn		10185	11807	13635

Options	Price
Bose Audio System	+196
Compact Disc Changer	+171
Leather Seats	+372
Metallic Paint	+169
Power Moonroof	+298

Options	Price
Power Passenger Seat [Opt on Wgn]	+163
Power Rear Window Sunshade [Opt on Sdn]	+157
Power Solar Sunroof [Opt on Sdn]	+296
Rear Side Airbag Restraints [Opt on Sdn]	+122

Audi
A6/A8

1997

Body Styles	TMV Pricing		
	Trade	Private	Dealer
4 Dr 2.8 Sdn	7123	8446	10064
4 Dr 2.8 Wgn	7771	9214	10978
4 Dr 2.8 quattro AWD Sdn	7588	8998	10721
4 Dr 2.8 quattro AWD Wgn	8650	10257	12220

Options	Price
Leather Seats	+307
Metallic Paint	+140
Power Moonroof	+245

Options	Price
Power Passenger Seat	+135
Bose Audio System	+162

Mileage Category: I

A new quattro Value Package is available with a power glass sunroof, larger alloy wheels, bigger tires and, of course, the quattro all-wheel-drive system. Selective unlocking capability expands to the remote keyless entry fob, and the alarm system now features interior monitoring. Jacquard cloth upholstery is new, and three new colors debut: Tornado Red, Volcano Black metallic and Byzantine metallic.

1996

Mileage Category: I

Traction control systems have been improved this year. Fans of the manual transmission will mourn the loss of it; all 1996 A6 models are saddled with an automatic shifter.

Body Styles	TMV Pricing		
	Trade	Private	Dealer
4 Dr 2.8 Sdn	5941	7114	8733
4 Dr 2.8 Wgn	6360	7616	9351
4 Dr 2.8 quattro AWD Sdn	6298	7542	9260
4 Dr 2.8 quattro AWD Wgn	7314	8758	10753

Options	Price
Bose Audio System	+146
Leather Seats	+285
Metallic Paint	+130

Options	Price
Power Moonroof	+224
Power Passenger Seat	+119

1995

Mileage Category: I

Subtle restyle of last year's 100 brings a new name. Sedan or wagon available in either front- or all-wheel drive. Wagon comes only with an automatic transmission.

Body Styles	TMV Pricing		
	Trade	Private	Dealer
4 Dr 2.8 Sdn	4050	4892	6296
4 Dr 2.8 Wgn	5027	6072	7814
4 Dr 2.8 quattro AWD Sdn	4979	6014	7739
4 Dr 2.8 quattro AWD Wgn	5178	6255	8049

Options	Price
Automatic 4-Speed Transmission [Std on Wgn]	+184
Bose Audio System	+127
Compact Disc Changer	+161

Options	Price
Leather Seats	+253
Power Moonroof	+180

Audi
A8

2003

Body Styles	TMV Pricing		
	Trade	Private	Dealer
4 Dr L quattro AWD Sdn	44385	46890	51065
4 Dr quattro AWD Sdn	44186	46680	50837

Mileage Category: I

A redesigned A8 is coming for the 2004 model year, so 2003 changes are minimal. Premium packages for both the A8 and A8 L now include the navigation system, parking assist system, tire pressure monitoring system and 17-inch wheels with 225/55R17 all-season tires. In addition, this year only the A8 L will be eligible for the optional 18-inch wheels and 245/45R18 performance tires.

Options	Price
Heated Front and Rear Seats [Opt on quattro]	+380
Navigation System	+1027
Pearlescent Metallic Paint	+913
OnStar Telematic System	+532
Power Solar Sunroof [Opt on L quattro]	+647

Options	Price
Power Rear Window Sunshade [Opt on quattro]	+342
17 Inch Wheels	+380
18 Inch Wheels [Opt on L quattro]	+685
Park Distance Control (Front and Rear) [Opt on L quattro]	+533

2002

Mileage Category: I

Audi will introduce the second generation of its flagship sedan next year, so 2002 sees only minor changes. Among them is a standard in-dash six-disc CD changer, OnStar telematics system as an option, an improved stability control system and updated navigation system software.

Body Styles	TMV Pricing		
	Trade	Private	Dealer
4 Dr L quattro AWD Sdn	39831	42359	46573
4 Dr quattro AWD Sdn	37529	39911	43881

Options	Price
17 Inch Wheels	+340
18 Inch Wheels - Spoke	+1020
Alcantra and Leather Package	+2041
Heated Front and Rear Seats [Std on L]	+340
Navigation System	+918

Options	Price
OnStar Telematic System	+475
Park Distance Control (Front and Rear)	+476
Pearlescent Metallic Paint	+816
Power Rear Window Sunshade [Std on L]	+306
Power Solar Sunroof	+578

2001

Mileage Category: I

The Electronic Stabilization Program (ESP) now comes standard, as does a multifunctional steering wheel with audio, telephone and Tiptronic controls. Audi adds an oil level sensor to the A8 and an Office Package consisting of an electrically folding desk and minibar/cold storage for the rear seat is added to the options list.

Body Styles	TMV Pricing		
	Trade	Private	Dealer
4 Dr L quattro AWD Sdn	33472	37098	40446
4 Dr quattro AWD Sdn	31419	34823	37965

Options	Price
17 Inch Wheels - Spoke [Opt on quattro]	+580
18 Inch Wheels [Opt on L quattro]	+871
Alcantra and Leather Package	+2032
Heated Front and Rear Seats [Opt on quattro]	+261
Navigation System [Std on L Quattro]	+743

Options	Price
Park Distance Control (Front and Rear)	+406
Pearlescent Metallic Paint	+697
Power Rear Window Sunshade [Opt on quattro]	+261
Power Solar Sunroof [Opt on L quattro]	+493
Power Sunroof [Std on L Quattro]	+493

2000

Mileage Category: I

Updated styling in the form of a revised grille, enlarged headlights, added chrome and aluminum trim and reshaped bumpers provides a subtle new look. Inside, new interior surfaces and standard Valcona leather intensify an already richly appointed cabin. Revised switchgear makes it easier to pilot the A8, and a new navigation system is available. A new 4.2-liter, 40-valve V8 resides under the hood, and aluminum suspension components reduce unsprung weight and enhance handling. A long wheelbase version (A8L) is now available for increased comfort of rear passengers, and comes standard with an electronic stability control system and navigation system.

Body Styles	TMV Pricing		
	Trade	Private	Dealer
4 Dr L quattro AWD Sdn	25634	28804	31911
4 Dr quattro AWD Sdn	25616	28784	31890

Options	Price
17 Inch Wheels - Spoke [Opt on L quattro]	+510
18 Inch Wheels [Opt on L quattro]	+765
Alcantra and Leather Package	+1611
Automatic Stability Control [Opt on quattro]	+280
Heated Front and Rear Seats [Opt on quattro]	+169

Options	Price
Navigation System	+620
Park Distance Control (Front and Rear)	+357
Power Rear Window Sunshade [Opt on quattro]	+229
Power Solar Sunroof	+433

1999

Mileage Category: I

The A8's warm weather package is modified to improve electronic accessory performance, while dual-pane laminated glass replaces insulated glass. Standard on the A8 is a larger right outside mirror, a first aid kit and a CD changer. A premium leather/Alcantra trim package and a new Volcano Black exterior paint color are optional. A8 prices will remain unchanged from 1998.

Body Styles	TMV Pricing		
	Trade	Private	Dealer
4 Dr STD Sdn	16436	18631	20916
4 Dr quattro AWD Sdn	19148	21705	24367

Options	Price
17 Inch Wheels	+434
Alcantra and Leather Package	+1235
Bose Audio System [Opt on STD]	+316
Heated Front and Rear Seats	+130

Options	Price
Metallic Paint	+212
Power Rear Window Sunshade	+195
Power Solar Sunroof	+369

Audi
A8/allroad quattro

1998

Mileage Category: I

Tiptronic automanual gear shifting is standard, as is a glass sunroof, dual-pane laminated window glass, an improved stereo and an upgraded antilock braking system.

Body Styles		TMV Pricing	
	Trade	Private	Dealer
4 Dr STD Sdn	13335	15374	17674
4 Dr quattro AWD Sdn	15494	17864	20536

Options	Price	Options	Price
17 Inch Wheels	+348	Metallic Paint	+169
Bose Audio System [Opt on STD]	+252	Power Rear Window Sunshade	+157
Compact Disc Changer	+160	Power Solar Sunroof	+296

1997

Mileage Category: I

Audi revolutionizes luxury sedan construction with the Audi Space Frame, which employs seven new aircraft-grade aluminum alloys to lighten weight and provide a tighter, more crashworthy structure. The new A8 is also the first passenger car equipped with six airbags. The usual accoutrements associated with a premium German sedan are all in place.

Body Styles		TMV Pricing	
	Trade	Private	Dealer
4 Dr STD Sdn	9348	10991	12999
4 Dr quattro AWD Sdn	12368	14542	17198

Options	Price	Options	Price
Power Solar Sunroof	+244	Power Solar Sunroof	+244
17 Inch Wheels	+287	17 Inch Wheels	+287
Bose Audio System [Opt on STD]	+196	Bose Audio System [Opt on STD]	+196

Audi
allroad quattro

2003

Body Styles		TMV Pricing	
	Trade	Private	Dealer
4 Dr Turbo AWD Wgn	29526	31270	34175

Options	Price	Options	Price
Automatic 5-Speed Transmission	+799	17 Inch Wheels - Spoke	+723
Bose Audio System	+571	OnStar Telematic System	+532
Heated Front and Rear Seats	+456	Automatic Dimming Sideview Mirror(s)	+152
Leather Seats	+669	Power Retractable Mirrors	+141
Navigation System	+1027	Power Driver Seat w/Memory	+228
Power Moonroof	+700	Park Distance Control (Rear)	+266
Rear Side Airbag Restraints	+266		

Mileage Category: I

Audi's rugged allroad quattro receives no changes, but the options list has been simplified. Rather than offering various "convenience," "preferred" and "warm weather" packages, a lengthy list of desirable features, including leather, xenons, sunroof and auto-dimming mirrors have been bundled into a handful of premium packages. A cold weather package includes front and rear seat heaters with a ski sack. The Parktronic parking assist system is now a stand-alone extra, and the rear-facing third-row seat has been deleted from the options list. Finally, for those who find the allroad's twin turbo V6 wanting, Audi is expected to introduce its 4.2-liter V8 sometime in the 2003 calendar year.

2002

Mileage Category: I

The height-adjustable allroad debuted last year to fill a slot left in Audi's lineup by the lack of an SUV. For 2002, a heated multifunctional steering wheel with Tiptronic is an option, as is an OnStar telematics system. Standard is an in-dash six-disc changer. Brushed aluminum-finish accents spruce up the interior.

Body Styles		TMV Pricing	
	Trade	Private	Dealer
4 Dr Turbo AWD Wgn	27507	29109	31778

Options	Price	Options	Price
17 Inch Wheels	+646	OnStar Telematic System	+475
Automatic 5-Speed Transmission	+714	Park Distance Control (Rear)	+238
Automatic Dimming Sideview Mirror(s)	+136	Power Moonroof	+626
Bose Audio System	+510	Power Retractable Mirrors	+126
Heated Front and Rear Seats	+374	Power Solar Sunroof	+1088
Leather Seats	+599	Rear Side Airbag Restraints	+238
Navigation System	+918	Third Seat	+510

2001

Body Styles	TMV Pricing		
	Trade	Private	Dealer
4 Dr Turbo AWD Wgn	25354	27626	29724

Options	Price	Options	Price
Automatic 5-Speed Transmission	+580	Power Driver Seat w/Memory	+174
Automatic Dimming Sideview Mirror(s)	+116	Power Moonroof	+580
Bose Audio System	+435	Power Passenger Seat w/Memory	+174
Compact Disc Changer	+319	Power Solar Sunroof	+987
Heated Front and Rear Seats	+261	Rear Side Airbag Restraints	+203
Navigation System	+743	Third Seat	+435
Park Distance Control (Rear)	+203		

Mileage Category: I

Based on the A6 platform, the height-adjustable allroad debuts this year to fill a slot left in Audi's lineup by the lack of an SUV. This luxury-station-wagon-turned-SUV is powered by the A6's 250-horsepower 2.7-liter V6 engine and features Audi's legendary quattro all-wheel-drive system. Audi blends these features in a distinctive vehicle that can handle a wide range of transportation needs.

Audi
Cabriolet

1998

Body Styles	TMV Pricing		
	Trade	Private	Dealer
2 Dr STD Conv	10381	12122	14085

Options	Price	Options	Price
Leather Seats	+382	Special Factory Paint	+137
Metallic Paint	+137	Sport Seats	+134
Power Convertible Top	+348		

Mileage Category: H

Based on the ancient 80/90 platform from the late '80s, the Cabriolet soldiers on with minimal change. A new steering wheel design is standard, and the Audi logo disappears from the side moldings.

1997

Body Styles	TMV Pricing		
	Trade	Private	Dealer
2 Dr STD Conv	8265	9804	11685

Options	Price
Bucket Seats	+292
Leather Seats	+316
Power Convertible Top	+287

Mileage Category: H

Base price drops a couple grand, but at the expense of the power top, burled walnut wood trim and leather seats. Opt for the Premium Equipment Package, and these items magically reappear. Casablanca White and Cactus Green join the list of paint colors, and three new top colors debut. Leather seats can be had in two new shades, too.

1996

Body Styles	TMV Pricing		
	Trade	Private	Dealer
2 Dr STD Conv	7089	8492	10430

Options	Price
Bucket Seats	+262

Mileage Category: H

Better acceleration, a new radio, a new color and revised alloy wheels are the only changes.

1995

Body Styles	TMV Pricing		
	Trade	Private	Dealer
2 Dr STD Conv	5823	7061	9123

Mileage Category: H

No changes.

1994

Body Styles	TMV Pricing		
	Trade	Private	Dealer
2 Dr STD Conv	4699	5805	7647

Mileage Category: H

Based on the 90 platform. Features dual airbags, ABS and 2.8-liter V6 engine. No manual transmission available. Rear window is plastic.

Audi
RS6/S4

Audi
RS6
2003

Body Styles		TMV Pricing	
	Trade	Private	Dealer
4 Dr quattro Turbo AWD Sdn	66570	68875	72718

Options	Price
Navigation System	+1027
Rear Side Airbag Restraints	+266
Power Solar Sunroof	+418
Power Rear Window Sunshade	+342

Mileage Category: F

The Audi RS 6 sedan is the product of a joint effort between Audi and its tuning division, quattro GmbH, and will be the fastest Audi to reach U.S. shores thus far. It will offer a considerably higher level of performance than the S6 Avant introduced last year, largely because two turbochargers will be affixed to its 4.2-liter V8, resulting in 450 horsepower and 415 pound-feet of torque, slotting it in between the BMW M5 and the 2003 Mercedes-Benz E55 -- just where Audi wants to be. Quattro GmbH also made a number of chassis upgrades to manage all this power -- highlights include the debut of Dynamic Ride Control, which uses hydraulics to adjust damping during cornering, an even stiffer suspension than the S6's, a quicker steering ratio and a new brake system. Indeed, it's a good time to be a wealthy enthusiast.

Audi
S4
2002

Body Styles		TMV Pricing	
	Trade	Private	Dealer
4 Dr Avant quattro Turbo AWD Wgn	28157	29809	32562
4 Dr quattro Turbo AWD Sdn	27726	29352	32063

Options	Price	Options	Price
Automatic Dimming Sideview Mirror(s)	+136	Nappa Leather Seat Trim	+136
Bose Audio System	+442	Navigation System	+918
Compact Disc Changer	+374	Pearlescent Metallic Paint	+816
Heated Front Seats	+306	Power Moonroof	+646

Mileage Category: F

Nothing new for 2002.

2001

Mileage Category: F

The Electronic Stabilization Program is made standard on the S4 sedan. The S4 Avant debuts for 2001, allowing for more cargo space and family-hauling capabilities. Casablanca White is made available as an exterior color, as are aluminum mirror housings in combination with the Pearl Napa/Alcantara sets and aluminum trim. A new four-year warranty concept is introduced this year.

Body Styles		TMV Pricing	
	Trade	Private	Dealer
4 Dr Avant quattro Turbo AWD Wgn	23634	26038	28257
4 Dr quattro Turbo AWD Sdn	23324	25696	27886

Options	Price	Options	Price
Alcantara and Leather Package	+261	Heated Front Seats	+145
Automatic Dimming Sideview Mirror(s)	+116	Navigation System	+743
Bose Audio System	+377	Pearlescent Metallic Paint	+697
Compact Disc Changer	+319	Power Moonroof	+551

2000

Mileage Category: F

The Audi S4 is a new sport sedan based off the excellent A4 platform introduced in 1996. Highlights include a turbocharged 250-horsepower engine, all-wheel drive and improved handling and braking.

Body Styles		TMV Pricing	
	Trade	Private	Dealer
4 Dr quattro Turbo AWD Sdn	19163	21535	23860

Options	Price	Options	Price
Bose Audio System	+315	Navigation System	+620
Compact Disc Changer	+267	Power Moonroof	+484
Heated Front Seats	+121		

1994

Body Styles	TMV Pricing		
	Trade	Private	Dealer
4 Dr quattro Turbo AWD Sdn	7233	8574	10810

Options	Price
Compact Disc Changer	+80

Mileage Category: F

No changes for the final year of the S4 based on the 90 platform.

Audi
S6

2003

Body Styles	TMV Pricing		
	Trade	Private	Dealer
4 Dr Avant quattro AWD Wgn	43347	45753	49762

Options	Price	Options	Price
Heated Front and Rear Seats	+190	OnStar Telematic System	+532
Navigation System	+1027	Power Solar Sunroof	+571
Rear Side Airbag Restraints	+266	Park Distance Control (Rear)	+266

Mileage Category: F

Audi makes no changes to the high-performance S6 in its second year on the U.S. market.

2002

Body Styles	TMV Pricing		
	Trade	Private	Dealer
4 Dr Avant quattro AWD Wgn	38404	40975	45260

Options	Price	Options	Price
Heated Front and Rear Seats	+170	Pearlescent Metallic Paint	+816
Navigation System	+918	Power Solar Sunroof	+510
OnStar Telematic System	+611	Rear Side Airbag Restraints	+238
Park Distance Control (Rear)	+238		

Mileage Category: F

Proving that even those burdened with the yoke of responsibility deserve a little fun, Audi releases a high-performance version of the A6 station wagon. Good for sub-7-second 0-to-60 acceleration runs, the S6 rides on a more muscular suspension structure to temper the 340-horsepower V8.

1995

Body Styles	TMV Pricing		
	Trade	Private	Dealer
4 Dr quattro Turbo AWD Sdn	9810	11370	13970

Options	Price
Compact Disc Changer	+120

Mileage Category: F

The former S4 is renamed the S6 to match Audi's new naming system. Last year for this model based on the 100 platform.

Audi
S8

2003

Body Styles	TMV Pricing		
	Trade	Private	Dealer
4 Dr quattro AWD Sdn	55248	57670	61706

Options	Price	Options	Price
Heated Front and Rear Seats	+190	Power Solar Sunroof	+647
Navigation System	+1027	Power Rear Window Sunshade	+342
OnStar Telematic System	+684	Park Distance Control (Front and Rear)	+533

Mileage Category: F

Changes to Audi's hot-rod version of the A8 flagship are minimal for 2003. Among them are a new set of 18-inch alloys; birch or sycamore wood interior trim; new black dash and door panel trim; and "Audi Exclusive" embossment for the headrests. Also, the premium package now includes the navigation, parking assist and tire pressure monitoring systems. Three limited-edition color combinations will be offered -- a silver exterior with a burgundy interior, a Ming Blue exterior with a platinum interior and a black exterior with a caramel interior -- but the Alcantara leather package has been discontinued.

Audi
S8/TT

2002
Mileage Category: I

The S8 is Audi's high-performance version of the flagship A8. For 2002, Audi has made an in-dash six-disc CD changer standard, and an OnStar telematics system and a tire-pressure monitor optional fare. It has also improved the stability control system and updated the navigation system software. New exterior and interior colors round out the changes.

Body Styles	TMV Pricing		
	Trade	Private	Dealer
4 Dr quattro AWD Sdn	51091	53393	57231

Options	Price	Options	Price
Alcantra and Leather Package	+2381	Park Distance Control (Front and Rear)	+476
Heated Front and Rear Seats	+170	Pearlescent Metallic Paint	+816
Navigation System	+918	Power Rear Window Sunshade	+306
OnStar Telematic System	+611	Power Sunroof	+578

2001
Mileage Category: I

The S8 is Audi's new high-performance version of the flagship A8. It's armed with more horsepower, a stiffer suspension and more powerful brakes. As with other 2001 A8s, the 2001 S8 has the Electronic Stabilization Program (ESP) and the new multifunctional steering wheel as standard equipment.

Body Styles	TMV Pricing		
	Trade	Private	Dealer
4 Dr quattro AWD Sdn	43319	46766	49947

Options	Price	Options	Price
Alcantra and Leather Package	+2032	Pearlescent Metallic Paint	+697
Navigation System	+743	Power Rear Window Sunshade	+261
Park Distance Control (Front and Rear)	+406	Power Sunroof	+493

Audi
TT

2003

Body Styles	TMV Pricing		
	Trade	Private	Dealer
2 Dr 225hp quattro Turbo AWD Conv	27417	29055	31784
2 Dr 225hp quattro Turbo AWD Cpe	26397	27974	30601
2 Dr Turbo Conv	25352	26866	29389
2 Dr Turbo Cpe	23660	25073	27428

Options	Price	Options	Price
Compact Disc Changer	+361	Special Leather Seat Trim	+761
Heated Front Seats	+342	Bose Mini Disc Player	+418
Navigation System	+1027	18 Inch Wheels [Opt on 225hp]	+590
Power Convertible Top [Opt on 180hp Conv]	+609		

Mileage Category: F

Never considered hard-edged performance cars in their respective segments, Audi's stylish 2003 TT coupe and roadster finally offer an automatic transmission -- and a six-speed unit at that. Unfortunately, it's available only on the front-drive, 180-horsepower coupe and roadster. In other news, the quattro version of the 180-hp coupe is no longer offered and the remaining cars get a new front grille and revised exterior badging. Cast-alloy wheel designs have been updated, and, this year, you'll be able to get optional 17-inch all-season tires on all TTs (you could only get summer performance tires in this size previously); 18-inch all-season rubber is available on 225-hp models. Finally, the optional Bose sound system gets AudioPilot technology, which uses volume and tonal adjustments to compensate for outside noise.

2002
Mileage Category: F

Two new colors join the TT palette, Brilliant White and Moro Blue. HomeLink is available as an option, and the navigation system gets an upgrade, as does the stereo. A blue top is available for the roadster, and the trunk gets an interior release. In the spring of 2002, Audi will appeal to collectors and offer the ALMS (American Le Mans Series) Commemorative Edition TT Coupe in a limited run of 1,000 cars. This special TT Coupe will come in two configurations -- a Misano Red exterior with a silver Silk napa leather interior or an Avus Silver exterior with a Brilliant Red interior. Although the ALMS is essentially a more exquisitely trimmed version of the 225-hp coupe, Audi will fit it with 18-inch wheels and Z-rated 225/40 high-performance tires.

Body Styles	TMV Pricing		
	Trade	Private	Dealer
2 Dr 225hp ALMS Edition quattro Turbo AWD Cpe	25250	26935	29743
2 Dr 225hp quattro Turbo AWD Conv	24449	26080	28798
2 Dr 225hp quattro Turbo AWD Cpe	22389	23882	26371

Body Styles	TMV Pricing		
	Trade	Private	Dealer
2 Dr Turbo Conv	20902	22297	24621
2 Dr Turbo Cpe	19512	20790	22919
2 Dr quattro Turbo AWD Cpe	20084	21424	23657

Options	Price	Options	Price
17 Inch Wheels [Std on 225hp ALMS]	+340	Heated Front Seats	+306
Bose Audio System	+420	Navigation System	+918
Compact Disc Changer	+356	Power Convertible Top [Std on 225hp]	+544

2001

Body Styles	TMV Pricing		
	Trade	Private	Dealer
2 Dr 225hp quattro Turbo AWD Conv	20755	23233	25520
2 Dr 225hp quattro Turbo AWD Cpe	19203	21489	23599
2 Dr Turbo Conv	17880	20014	21984

Options	Price
17 Inch Wheels - Spoke	+290
6-Speed Transmission	+522
Bose Audio System	+348
Compact Disc Changer	+304

Body Styles	TMV Pricing		
	Trade	Private	Dealer
2 Dr Turbo Cpe	16662	18652	20488
2 Dr quattro Turbo AWD Cpe	17151	19199	21089

Options	Price
Heated Front Seats	+138
Navigation System	+743
Power Convertible Top	+464

Mileage Category: F

For 2001 Audi introduces the TT Roadster, which retains the same interior and chassis as the coupe. Makes sense, as the coupe was designed with the roadster version in mind. There's also a 225-horsepower quattro version for both the coupe and convertible. The entire Audi lineup receives a new 4-year/50,000-mile limited warranty and no-charge scheduled maintenance, a 12-year limited warranty against corrosion perforation and 24-hour Roadside Assistance for four years.

2000

Body Styles			TMV Pricing
	Trade	Private	Dealer
2 Dr Turbo Cpe	13148	14978	16771
2 Dr quattro Turbo AWD Cpe	14555	16581	18566

Options	Price
Bose Audio System	+315
Compact Disc Changer	+267
Heated Front Seats	+121
Performance/Handling Package	+306

Mileage Category: F

Audi introduces the funky-looking TT Coupe for the 2000 model year. A turbocharged, 1.8-liter engine squeezes out 180 horsepower for this avant-garde sports car.

Audi
V8

1994

Body Styles			TMV Pricing
	Trade	Private	Dealer
4 Dr quattro AWD Sdn	5667	6763	8589

Mileage Category: I

Other than new foglights, no changes this year to the Audi V8.

3 Series

2003

Mileage Category: H

For 2003, BMW will finally offer a DVD-based navigation system -- meaning that you won't have to give up an in-dash CD player if you opt for the nav system. Other changes include a standard front armrest for all 325 models, as well as a rear center headrest for all sedans and wagons. Additionally, all wagons will come with a moonroof. In terms of options, the Premium Package for all 325s now includes automatic headlights and rain-sensing wipers, and the Sport Package for the 330xi includes double-spoke alloy wheels and run-flat tires.

Body Styles	TMV Pricing		
	Trade	Private	Dealer
2 Dr 325Ci Conv	29183	30760	33388
2 Dr 325Ci Cpe	22614	23836	25872
2 Dr 330Ci Conv	35373	37285	40470
2 Dr 330Ci Cpe	27156	28623	31069
4 Dr 325i Sdn	20281	21377	23204

Options	Price
Automatic 5-Speed Transmission	+1002
Hardtop Roof [Opt on Conv]	+1803
Harmon Kardon Audio System [Opt on 325]	+530
Heated Front Seats	+354
Leather Seats [Opt on 325]	+1139
Metallic Paint	+373
Navigation System	+1414
Power Convertible Top [Opt on 325Ci Conv]	+589

Body Styles	TMV Pricing		
	Trade	Private	Dealer
4 Dr 325i Wgn	22778	24009	26061
4 Dr 325xi AWD Sdn	21946	23132	25109
4 Dr 325xi AWD Wgn	23917	25209	27363
4 Dr 330i Sdn	25994	27399	29740
4 Dr 330xi AWD Sdn	27886	29393	31904

Options	Price
Power Moonroof	+825
Power Passenger Seat [Opt on 325]	+236
Rear Side Airbag Restraints	+303
Split Folding Rear Seat [Opt on Sdn]	+373
Sport Package	+471
18 Inch Wheels [Opt on 330]	+707
Power Driver Seat w/Memory [Opt on 325i,325Ci]	+369
Park Distance Control (Rear) [Opt on 330]	+275

2002

Mileage Category: H

BMW has seen fit to give the sedans and wagons a facelift for 2002. An in-dash CD player finally makes it onto the standard features list. The center stack has been altered to accommodate the new automatic climate controls. Steptronic automanual operation has been altered so that you move the transmission lever forward for downshifts and backward for upshifts. Bi-xenon headlamps are on the options list so that both low and high beams can glow a cold blue and can be set to automatic operation. Rear side airbags are available for coupes and convertibles. Two new colors, Electric Red and Gray Green (and a Natural Brown interior leather) join the color spectrum.

Body Styles	TMV Pricing		
	Trade	Private	Dealer
2 Dr 325Ci Conv	26844	28296	30715
2 Dr 325Ci Cpe	19910	20987	22783
2 Dr 330Ci Conv	31906	33631	36507
2 Dr 330Ci Cpe	24164	25471	27650
4 Dr 325i Sdn	18541	19543	21214

Options	Price
17 Inch Wheels	+216
18 Inch Wheels	+647
Automatic 5-Speed Transmission	+916
Hardtop Roof	+1649
Harmon Kardon Audio System [Std on 330]	+485
Heated Front Seats	+251
Leather Seats [Std on 330Ci Conv]	+1042
Metallic Paint	+341

Body Styles	TMV Pricing		
	Trade	Private	Dealer
4 Dr 325i Wgn	20220	21314	23136
4 Dr 325xi AWD Sdn	20011	21093	22897
4 Dr 325xi AWD Wgn	21887	23071	25044
4 Dr 330i Sdn	23307	24568	26669
4 Dr 330xi AWD Sdn	25326	26696	28980

Options	Price
Navigation System	+1293
Park Distance Control (Rear)	+251
Power Convertible Top [Std on 330Ci Conv]	+539
Power Driver Seat w/Memory [Std on 330]	+338
Power Moonroof	+754
Power Passenger Seat [Std on 330]	+338
Rear Side Airbag Restraints	+277
Sport Package	+431

2001

Mileage Category: H

A boost in engine displacement and technology, plus an available all-wheel-drive system, keeps BMW's venerable 3 Series at the top of its game in the competitive entry-level luxury market. Larger wheels and brakes are part of the engine upgrade. Addressing concerns that their cars are low on feature content, BMW adds automatic climate control, foglights, heated mirrors and cruise control as standard equipment for all 325 models. The 330s get power seats and a premium audio package at no extra cost.

Body Styles	TMV Pricing		
	Trade	Private	Dealer
2 Dr 325Ci Conv	24348	26482	28452
2 Dr 325Ci Cpe	18118	19705	21170
2 Dr 330Ci Conv	28495	30992	33297
2 Dr 330Ci Cpe	21805	23716	25480
4 Dr 325i Sdn	16785	18256	19614

Options	Price
AM/FM/CD Audio System	+126
Automatic 5-Speed Transmission	+802
Hardtop Roof	+1444
Harmon Kardon Audio System	+425
Heated Front Seats	+315
Leather Seats	+675
Metallic Paint	+299
Navigation System	+1133

Body Styles	TMV Pricing		
	Trade	Private	Dealer
4 Dr 325i Wgn	18358	19966	21451
4 Dr 325xi AWD Sdn	18392	20003	21491
4 Dr 325xi AWD Wgn	19898	21642	23251
4 Dr 330i Sdn	21153	23007	24719
4 Dr 330xi AWD Sdn	22465	24433	26249

Options	Price
Park Distance Control (Rear)	+220
Power Convertible Top [Opt on 325Ci Conv]	+472
Power Driver Seat w/Memory [Std on 330Ci,Conv]	+296
Power Moonroof	+661
Power Passenger Seat [Std on 330Ci,Conv]	+296
Rear Side Airbag Restraints	+242
Sport Package	+378

3 Series

2000

Mileage Category: H

Body Styles	TMV Pricing		
	Trade	Private	Dealer
2 Dr 323Ci Conv	19645	21639	23594
2 Dr 323Ci Cpe	16182	17825	19435
2 Dr 328Ci Cpe	18650	20543	22399

Body Styles	TMV Pricing		
	Trade	Private	Dealer
4 Dr 323i Sdn	14281	15731	17152
4 Dr 323iT Wgn	16524	18202	19846
4 Dr 328i Sdn	18075	19910	21708

For 2000 3 Series coupes, convertibles and wagons are all new; the hatchback has been discontinued. After last year's complete redesign, 2000 sedans see only minor improvements.

Options	Price
AM/FM/Cassette/CD Audio System	+267
AM/FM/CD Audio System	+116
Automatic 5-Speed Transmission	+500
Compact Disc Changer	+272
Cruise Control [Opt on 323i,323iT]	+129
Hardtop Roof	+961
Harman Kardon Audio System	+314
Heated Front Seats	+140
Leather Seats	+570
Metallic Paint	+221

Options	Price
Navigation System	+838
Park Distance Control (Rear) [Opt on 323iT,328]	+186
Power Driver Seat w/Memory [Opt on 323]	+252
Power Moonroof	+488
Power Passenger Seat [Opt on 323]	+252
Radio Navigation System	+559
Rear Side Airbag Restraints	+205
Split Folding Rear Seat [Opt on 323i,328i]	+221
Spoke Wheels	+232
Sport Suspension [Std on 323Ci,328Ci]	+174

1999

Body Styles	TMV Pricing		
	Trade	Private	Dealer
2 Dr 318ti Hbk	10846	12139	13485
2 Dr 318i Conv	16967	18990	21096
2 Dr 323is Cpe	14400	16117	17905
2 Dr 328i Conv	18600	20818	23127

Body Styles	TMV Pricing		
	Trade	Private	Dealer
2 Dr 328is Cpe	15637	17501	19441
4 Dr 323i Sdn	12583	14083	15645
4 Dr 328i Sdn	15714	17587	19537

Mileage Category: H

The 3 Series sedans, redesigned for 1999, offer 5 Series style along with more room for rear-seat passengers. Coupes and convertibles remain on old platform.

Options	Price
Alarm System [Opt on 323]	+123
Aluminum/Alloy Wheels [Opt on 323i]	+243
AM/FM/Cassette/CD Audio System	+217
Automatic 4-Speed Transmission	+368
Automatic 5-Speed Transmission [Opt on Sdn]	+454
Compact Disc Changer	+245
Hardtop Roof	+867
Harman Kardon Audio System	+324
Leather Seats	+463
Metallic Paint	+180
Navigation System	+544

Options	Price
Park Distance Control (Rear) [Opt on 328i]	+168
Power Convertible Top	+510
Power Driver Seat w/Memory [Opt on 323i]	+228
Power Moonroof	+397
Power Passenger Seat [Opt on 323i]	+228
Rear Side Airbag Restraints	+185
Rollover Protection System [Opt on Conv]	+696
Split Folding Rear Seat [Opt on Sdn]	+228
Sport Package	+265
Sport Suspension [Std on 318ti]	+142

1998

Mileage Category: H

Body Styles	TMV Pricing		
	Trade	Private	Dealer
2 Dr 318ti Hbk	8333	9468	10747
2 Dr 323i Conv	13674	15537	17637
2 Dr 323is Cpe	10876	12357	14026
2 Dr 328i Conv	16676	18947	21508

Body Styles	TMV Pricing		
	Trade	Private	Dealer
2 Dr 328is Cpe	12835	14582	16553
4 Dr 318i Sdn	9480	10771	12227
4 Dr 328i Sdn	12672	14397	16343

BMW adds a 2.5-liter inline-six engine to its entry-level coupe and convertible, making them the cheapest six-cylinder BMWs in years. Also new are standard side-impact airbags for front-seat passengers in all models except the 318ti, in which they're optional.

Options	Price
Sport Suspension	+124
Aluminum/Alloy Wheels [Opt on 318i,318ti]	+197
AM/FM/Cassette/CD Audio System	+190
Automatic 4-Speed Transmission	+321
Compact Disc Changer	+213
Front Side Airbag Restraints [Opt on 318ti]	+127
Hardtop Roof	+755
Harman Kardon Audio System	+222

Options	Price
Leather Seats	+403
Limited Slip Differential	+115
Metallic Paint	+157
Power Convertible Top	+444
Power Sunroof	+312
Rollover Protection System	+605
Sport Package	+230

3 Series

1997

Mileage Category: H

All-Season Traction is now standard on all models.

Body Styles	TMV Pricing		
	Trade	Private	Dealer
2 Dr 318i Conv	10300	12002	14083
2 Dr 318is Cpe	8655	10086	11835
2 Dr 318ti Hbk	6815	7942	9319
2 Dr 328i Conv	13227	15414	18087

Body Styles	TMV Pricing		
	Trade	Private	Dealer
2 Dr 328is Cpe	10198	11884	13945
4 Dr 318i Sdn	7785	9072	10645
4 Dr 328i Sdn	10123	11797	13842

Options	Price
Aluminum/Alloy Wheels [Opt on 318i,318ti]	+177
AM/FM/Cassette/CD Audio System	+170
Automatic 4-Speed Transmission	+289
Hardtop Roof	+680
Leather Seats [Std on 328i Conv]	+348

Options	Price
Metallic Paint	+141
Power Sunroof	+281
Premium Audio System [Opt on Cpe,Sdn]	+200
Rollover Protection System	+502
Sport Package	+311

1996

Mileage Category: H

BMW's highly acclaimed 3 Series receives new engines across the board. The 318 remains a 318 despite an increase in displacement to 1.9 liters. The six-cylinder model becomes the 328 with an improved engine that increases torque by a whopping 14 percent. Vented rear disc brakes aid the 328's stopping power by reducing brake fade. Automatic climate control is standard, except in the 318ti, and improved sound systems are optional on all models.

Body Styles	TMV Pricing		
	Trade	Private	Dealer
2 Dr 318i Conv	8328	9793	11815
2 Dr 318is Cpe	7316	8602	10378
2 Dr 318ti Hbk	5858	6888	8311
2 Dr 328i Conv	10618	12484	15062

Body Styles	TMV Pricing		
	Trade	Private	Dealer
2 Dr 328is Cpe	9140	10747	12966
4 Dr 318i Sdn	6760	7949	9590
4 Dr 328i Sdn	8840	10394	12539

Options	Price
Aluminum/Alloy Wheels [Opt on 318ti,318i]	+165
AM/FM/Cassette/CD Audio System	+158
Automatic 4-Speed Transmission	+298
Hardtop Roof	+631
Leather Seats [Std on 328i Conv]	+323

Options	Price
Metallic Paint	+131
Power Sunroof [Opt on 318ti]	+261
Premium Audio System [Opt on Cpe,Sdn]	+206
Rollover Protection System	+443
Sport Package	+198

1995

Mileage Category: H

The 318 series gains a convertible and a hatchback (318ti). Two new packages debut that allow a driver to choose between a sports or luxury orientation.

Body Styles	TMV Pricing		
	Trade	Private	Dealer
2 Dr 318i Conv	6015	7055	8789
2 Dr 318is Cpe	5442	6384	7953
2 Dr 318ti Hbk	4511	5292	6593
2 Dr 325i Conv	7757	9099	11336

Body Styles	TMV Pricing		
	Trade	Private	Dealer
2 Dr 325is Cpe	6744	7911	9855
4 Dr 318i Sdn	5076	5954	7418
4 Dr 325i Sdn	6505	7630	9506

Options	Price
Rollover Protection System [Opt on Conv]	+345
Premium Audio System [Opt on 318]	+145
Sport Package	+154
Sport Suspension	+81
Aluminum/Alloy Wheels [Opt on 318i Sdn]	+128
AM/FM/Cassette/CD Audio System	+123

Options	Price
Automatic 4-Speed Transmission	+209
Compact Disc Changer	+132
Leather Seats [Opt on 318i,318is,318ti]	+252
Limited Slip Differential	+75
Power Sunroof [Opt on 318ti]	+204

1994

Mileage Category: H

Dual airbags appear on all 3 Series models. A new six-cylinder convertible joins the stable, and traction control becomes optional for all cars.

Body Styles	TMV Pricing		
	Trade	Private	Dealer
2 Dr 318i Conv	4993	5949	7541
2 Dr 318is Cpe	4565	5439	6895
2 Dr 325i Conv	6851	8162	10348

Body Styles	TMV Pricing		
	Trade	Private	Dealer
2 Dr 325is Cpe	5921	7054	8942
4 Dr 318i Sdn	4304	5128	6501
4 Dr 325i Sdn	5616	6691	8483

Options	Price
Leather Seats [Opt on 318is,325i]	+217
Rollover Protection System [Opt on Conv]	+298
AM/FM/Cassette/CD Audio System	+107

Options	Price
Automatic 4-Speed Transmission	+180
Compact Disc Changer	+114

2003

Body Styles	TMV Pricing		
	Trade	Private	Dealer
4 Dr 525i Sdn	30096	31655	34254
4 Dr 525i Wgn	29065	30571	33081
4 Dr 530i Sdn	31334	32958	35664

Options	Price
6-Speed Transmission [Opt on 540]	+3143
Automatic 5-Speed Transmission [Opt on 525,530]	+1002
Automatic Load Leveling [Opt on Wgn]	+597
Comfort Seats [Opt on 540]	+943
Heated Front Seats	+354
Hi-Fi Audio System	+943
Leather Seats [Opt on 525,530]	+1061

Body Styles	TMV Pricing		
	Trade	Private	Dealer
4 Dr 540i Sdn	36624	38522	41684
4 Dr 540i Wgn	37441	39381	42614

Options	Price
Navigation System	+1414
Rear Side Airbag Restraints	+303
Split Folding Rear Seat [Opt on Sdn]	+373
Sport Package	+1572
Power Rear Window Sunshade [Opt on Wgn]	+452
Park Distance Control (Front and Rear)	+550

Mileage Category: I

This is your last chance to get a traditionally styled 5 Series -- next year, its styling becomes more closely aligned with the controversial 7 Series. For now, BMW will offer a DVD-based navigation system for the existing 5 Series -- but alas, you must still give up an in-dash CD player if you opt for the nav system. Besides that, rear head protection airbags (optional last year) are now standard across the line. Additionally, all six-cylinder models get a standard moonroof. Standard on the manual-shift 540i (and optional with the automatic) is a new sport package that includes 18-inch wheels, a revised sport suspension, front and rear spoilers, visible exhaust outlets, black side molding, a black headliner, titanium-ringed gauges and an M footrest for the driver. Finally, the 525i gets a new alloy wheel design, and its premium package now includes rain-sensing wipers.

2002

Mileage Category: I

Body Styles	TMV Pricing		
	Trade	Private	Dealer
4 Dr 525i Sdn	26752	28174	30544
4 Dr 525i Wgn	26933	28341	30687
4 Dr 530i Sdn	27947	29408	31842

Options	Price
17 Inch Wheels	+216
6-Speed Transmission	+1940
Automatic 5-Speed Transmission [Std on 540]	+916
Automatic Dimming Rearview Mirror [Std on 540]	+133
Automatic Load Leveling [Std on 540]	+546
Comfort Seats	+862
Digital Audio System	+862
Heated Front Seats	+287

Body Styles	TMV Pricing		
	Trade	Private	Dealer
4 Dr 540i Sdn	34553	36390	39451
4 Dr 540i Wgn	34848	36701	39788

Options	Price
Leather Seats [Std on 540]	+970
Navigation System	+1293
Park Distance Control (Front and Rear)	+503
Power Moonroof [Std on 540]	+754
Power Rear Window Sunshade	+395
Rear Head Airbag Restraints [Opt on Sdn]	+119
Rear Side Airbag Restraints	+277
Sport Package	+1078

This year a standard CD player, climate control and power seats. The 4.4-liter V8 of the 540 now makes 290 horsepower, up 8 from last year. Rear side-impact airbags are now a no-charge option, rather than standard.

2001

Mileage Category: I

Body Styles	TMV Pricing		
	Trade	Private	Dealer
4 Dr 525i Sdn	23519	25555	27434
4 Dr 525i Wgn	22739	24707	26524
4 Dr 530i Sdn	24682	26818	28790

Options	Price
6-Speed Transmission [Opt on 540i]	+1495
AM/FM/CD Audio System	+126
Automatic 5-Speed Transmission [Opt on 525,530i]	+802
Automatic Climate Control (2 Zone) - Driver and Passenger [Opt on 525]	+243
Automatic Dimming Rearview Mirror [Std on 540i]	+116
Automatic Load Leveling [Opt on 525i Wgn]	+478
Comfort Seats	+755
Heated Front Seats	+189

Body Styles	TMV Pricing		
	Trade	Private	Dealer
4 Dr 540i Sdn	30721	33380	35835
4 Dr 540i Wgn	31583	34317	36840

Options	Price
Leather Seats [Std on 540i]	+912
Navigation System	+1133
Park Distance Control (Front and Rear)	+441
Power Moonroof [Std on 540]	+661
Power Passenger Seat [Opt on 525,530i]	+252
Power Rear Window Sunshade [Opt on Sdn]	+362
Rear Side Airbag Restraints	+242
Sport Package	+944

The former base 2.8-liter engine gets bumped up to 3.0 liters, with an expected horsepower and torque increase to go along with the larger displacement. A new 2.5-liter engine premieres this year, as do rear-seat head airbags and a slightly freshened exterior. BMW also improved some of the optional equipment, including Park Distance Control for both the front and rear of the vehicle, a bigger LCD screen for the navigation system and an optional in-dash single-disc CD player.

5 Series

2000

Mileage Category: I

The 5 Series cars carry over from last year with small changes and no price increase.

Body Styles	TMV Pricing		
	Trade	Private	Dealer
4 Dr 528i Sdn	20169	22163	24118
4 Dr 528i Wgn	20454	22477	24459

Options	Price
6-Speed Transmission	+1261
Automatic 5-Speed Transmission [Opt on 528i]	+478
Automatic Load Leveling [Std on 540i Wgn]	+372
Comfort Seats	+588
Compact Disc Changer	+245
Heated Front Seats	+159
Hi-Fi Audio System	+588
Jump Seat(s)	+233
Leather Seats [Std on 540]	+721
Metallic Paint	+233
Navigation System	+882

Body Styles	TMV Pricing		
	Trade	Private	Dealer
4 Dr 540i Sdn	25635	28170	30655
4 Dr 540i Wgn	26702	29343	31931

Options	Price
Park Distance Control (Rear)	+186
Power Moonroof [Std on 540]	+514
Power Rear Window Sunshade [Opt on Sdn]	+306
Rear Side Airbag Restraints	+205
Rear Spoiler	+196
Split Folding Rear Seat [Opt on Sdn]	+282
Spoke Wheels	+387
Sport Package	+773
Sport Seats	+233
Sport Suspension	+367

1999

Mileage Category: I

New 528i and 540i sport wagons debut, all 5 Series models achieve low emission vehicle (LEV) status, and consumers will find extensive new standard and optional equipment on the cars.

Body Styles	TMV Pricing		
	Trade	Private	Dealer
4 Dr 528i Sdn	17241	19185	21209
4 Dr 528i Wgn	18080	20119	22241

Options	Price
17 Inch Wheels - Cross-Spoke [Opt on 528]	+349
6-Speed Transmission	+1025
Automatic 4-Speed Transmission	+388
Automatic Load Leveling [Opt on 528i Wgn]	+302
Automatic Stability Control [Opt on 528]	+240
Comfort Seats	+477
Compact Disc Changer	+199
Heated Front Seats	+130
Hi-Fi Audio System [Opt on 528]	+477
Leather Seats [Opt on 528]	+547
Metallic Paint	+190

Body Styles	TMV Pricing		
	Trade	Private	Dealer
4 Dr 540i Sdn	22709	25270	27935
4 Dr 540i Wgn	23574	26232	28999

Options	Price
Navigation System	+573
Park Distance Control (Rear)	+168
Power Moonroof [Opt on 528]	+418
Power Rear Window Sunshade [Opt on Sdn]	+276
Premium Audio System	+477
Rear Side Airbag Restraints	+185
Rear Spoiler	+159
Split Folding Rear Seat [Opt on Sdn]	+229
Sport Package	+911
Sport Seats	+190
Sport Suspension	+298

1998

Mileage Category: I

Side-impact airbags are now available for rear-seat passengers, as is break-resistant glass for the windows and moonroof.

Body Styles		Trade	Private	Dealer
4 Dr 528i Sdn		14519	16315	18340
4 Dr 540i Sdn		18194	20444	22982

Options	Price
17 Inch Wheels - Cross-Spoke	+304
6-Speed Transmission [Opt on 540i]	+892
Automatic 4-Speed Transmission	+338
Comfort Seats	+415
Leather Seats [Opt on 528i]	+567
Metallic Paint	+165
Navigation System	+692
Power Moonroof [Opt on 528i]	+364

Options	Price
Power Rear Window Sunshade	+240
Premium Audio System	+415
Rear Side Airbag Restraints	+161
Rear Spoiler	+138
Sport Package	+438
Sport Seats	+165
Sport Suspension	+203

1997

Body Styles	TMV Pricing		
	Trade	Private	Dealer
4 Dr 528i Sdn	12083	13644	15552
4 Dr 540i Sdn	14058	15874	18094

Options	Price
17 Inch Wheels - Cross-Spoke [Opt on 528i]	+277
6-Speed Transmission [Opt on 540i]	+726
AM/FM/Cassette/CD Audio System	+148
Automatic 4-Speed Transmission	+289
Comfort Seats	+355
Compact Disc Changer	+148
Leather Seats [Opt on 528i]	+408

Options	Price
Metallic Paint	+141
Navigation System	+663
Power Moonroof [Opt on 528i]	+299
Power Rear Window Sunshade	+199
Premium Audio System	+355
Rear Spoiler	+118
Sport Suspension	+222

Mileage Category: I

The 5 Series is redesigned and introduced midway through 1996 as a 1997 model. The Touring wagons are no longer available, and the 3.0-liter V8 is history. New 5 Series models can be had as a six-cylinder 528i or a V8 540i. Both models feature new engines, all-aluminum suspensions, improved brakes and available side-impact airbag protection.

1995

Body Styles	TMV Pricing		
	Trade	Private	Dealer
4 Dr 525i Sdn	6932	7935	9607
4 Dr 525i Wgn	7548	8640	10460
4 Dr 530i Sdn	7989	9144	11070

Body Styles	TMV Pricing		
	Trade	Private	Dealer
4 Dr 530i Wgn	8262	9458	11450
4 Dr 540i Sdn	8591	9834	11906

Options	Price
6-Speed Transmission	+525
AM/FM/CD Audio System	+75
Automatic 4-Speed Transmission [Std on Wgn]	+209
Compact Disc Changer	+107
Dual Power Sunroofs [Opt on 525i Wgn]	+315

Options	Price
Leather Seats [Opt on 525i]	+295
Metallic Paint	+102
Power Sunroof [Opt on 525i Wgn]	+190
Traction Control System	+107

Mileage Category: I

BMW improves its 540i by making a six-speed manual transmission available. That option includes 12-way power sport seats, a sport suspension and beefy antiroll bars. Unfortunately, all models lose their V-rated tires in favor of wimpy H-rated tires in an attempt to improve fuel economy.

1994

Body Styles	TMV Pricing		
	Trade	Private	Dealer
4 Dr 525i Sdn	5803	6768	8377
4 Dr 525i Wgn	6439	7510	9296
4 Dr 530i Sdn	6480	7558	9355

Body Styles	TMV Pricing		
	Trade	Private	Dealer
4 Dr 530i Wgn	6610	7710	9543
4 Dr 540i Sdn	6757	7881	9755

Options	Price
Automatic 4-Speed Transmission [Opt on 525i]	+185
Automatic 5-Speed Transmission [Opt on 530i]	+226
Dual Power Sunroofs [Opt on 525i Wgn]	+272
Traction Control System [Opt on 525i,540i]	+92

Options	Price
Automatic 4-Speed Transmission [Opt on 525i]	+185
Automatic 5-Speed Transmission [Opt on 530i]	+226
Dual Power Sunroofs [Opt on 525i Wgn]	+272
Traction Control System [Opt on 525i,540i]	+92

Mileage Category: I

A passenger airbag debuts on all models and two new V8s join the lineup. The 535i and M5 are dropped. BMW's traction control system becomes standard on the 530i Touring and optional on other models. Both 525i models gain a premium sound system.

2003

Body Styles	TMV Pricing		
	Trade	Private	Dealer
4 Dr 745Li Sdn	56695	58771	62232
4 Dr 745i Sdn	54419	56411	59732
4 Dr 760Li Sdn	92787	96185	101847

Mileage Category: I

The big news for 2003 is the late-fall arrival of the 760Li, which combines all the greatness of the 745 while adding a 6.0-liter V12. BMW has not released U.S. output ratings, but European specs have it at 408 horsepower and 442 pound-feet of torque. The more interesting aspect of the 760Li is that it's the first BMW with direct gasoline injection, which, in combination with the Valvetronic technology already used in the 745 models, allows for stellar performance, and according to BMW, "outstanding fuel economy." We'll wait and see on that one. In other news, all models get rear head-protection airbags, and Active Cruise Control finally makes it to the options list, along with run-flat tires. The Rear Comfort Seat package for the 745Li now includes rear-seat ventilation.

2003 (cont'd)

Options	Price
Automatic Load Leveling [Opt on 745]	+550
Comfort Seats [Opt on 745]	+707
Electronic Damping Suspension Control [Opt on 745]	+943
Heated Front and Rear Seats [Opt on 745]	+511
Power Rear Seat [Opt on 745]	+2750
Rear Side Airbag Restraints	+303
Sport Package	+2514
Ventilated Seats (Front) [Opt on 745i]	+707

Options	Price
Power Rear Window Sunshade [Opt on 745]	+589
Adaptive Cruise Control	+1729
AM/FM/CD Changer Audio System [Opt on 745]	+471
19 Inch Wheels [Opt on 745]	+1021
Power Trunk Closer	+589
Lexicon Audio System	+943
Power Passenger Seat w/Memory [Opt on 745i]	+393
Park Distance Control (Front and Rear) [Opt on 745]	+550

2002

Mileage Category: I

Completely and controversially redesigned, the 2002 BMW 7 Series arrives chock-full of innovative technology and luxury trimmings.

Body Styles	TMV Pricing		
	Trade	Private	Dealer
4 Dr 745Li Sdn	51370	54100	58651
4 Dr 745i Sdn	49536	52125	56439

Options	Price
19 Inch Wheels	+934
Automatic Load Leveling	+395
Comfort Seats	+1006
Compact Disc Changer	+431
Digital Audio System	+862
Electronic Damping Suspension Control	+575
Heated Front and Rear Seats	+467
Heated Front Seats	+323

Options	Price
Park Distance Control (Front and Rear)	+503
Power Passenger Seat w/Memory [Opt on 745i]	+359
Power Rear Seat	+2084
Power Rear Window Sunshade	+539
Power Trunk Closer	+719
Rear Side Airbag Restraints	+277
Ventilated Seats (Front)	+647

2001

Mileage Category: I

All 7 Series models receive an integrated Motorola StarTAC cell phone with BMW's Mayday function. Body-colored rocker panels and lower-bumper valances, as well as white turn signal lenses, enhance the 7 Series' exterior look. Sport Packages are now available on the 740iL and 750iL models.

Body Styles	TMV Pricing		
	Trade	Private	Dealer
4 Dr 740i Sdn	33996	36939	39655
4 Dr 740iL Protection Sdn	44347	48185	51728
4 Dr 740iL Sdn	35317	38374	41195

Body Styles	TMV Pricing		
	Trade	Private	Dealer
4 Dr 750iL Protection Sdn	56256	61125	65619
4 Dr 750iL Sdn	37517	40764	43761

Options	Price
Automatic Load Leveling [Opt on 740]	+472
Comfort Seats [Opt on 740]	+315
Electronic Damping Suspension Control [Opt on 740]	+724
Heated Front Seats [Opt on 740]	+315
Park Distance Control (Front and Rear) [Std on 750]	+566

Options	Price
Power Rear Window Sunshade [Opt on 740]	+362
Power Security Sunroof [Std on Protection]	+1636
Rear Side Airbag Restraints	+242
Sport Package	+1479

2000

Mileage Category: I

The Premium Package is standard on the 740i and 740iL and the Cold Weather Package now includes heated rear seats. Two new "Protection" trim levels are also available that provide light armor, bullet-resistant glass and run-flat tires.

Body Styles	TMV Pricing		
	Trade	Private	Dealer
4 Dr 740i Sdn	27475	30192	32856
4 Dr 740iL Protection Sdn	39026	42885	46668
4 Dr 740iL Sdn	28218	31009	33744

Body Styles	TMV Pricing		
	Trade	Private	Dealer
4 Dr 750iL Protection Sdn	49061	53913	58668
4 Dr 750iL Sdn	32920	36176	39367

Options	Price
Automatic Load Leveling [Opt on 740i,740iL]	+399
Comfort Seats [Opt on 740i]	+1010
Electronic Damping Suspension Control [Opt on 740i,740iL]	+611
Heated Front Seats [Opt on 740]	+245
Park Distance Control (Front and Rear) [Opt on 740]	+478

Options	Price
Power Rear Window Sunshade [Opt on 740]	+393
Power Sunroof	+722
Rear Side Airbag Restraints	+205
Spoke Wheels	+412
Sport Package	+1249

1999

Body Styles	TMV Pricing		
	Trade	Private	Dealer
4 Dr 740i Sdn	19605	22018	24530
4 Dr 740iL Sdn	21647	24311	27083

Body Styles	TMV Pricing		
	Trade	Private	Dealer
4 Dr 750iL Sdn	25174	28272	31497

Mileage Category: I

All 7 Series engines achieve low emission vehicle (LEV) status. Revised standard and optional equipment add to the cars' appeal.

Options	Price
Sport Package	+1128
Power Sunroof	+652
Rear Side Airbag Restraints	+185
Automatic Load Leveling [Opt on 740iL]	+319
Comfort Seats [Opt on 740i]	+576
Compact Disc Changer [Opt on 740]	+312
Electronic Damping Suspension Control [Opt on 740]	+756

Options	Price
Heated Front Seats [Opt on 740]	+199
Navigation System	+891
Park Distance Control (Front and Rear) [Opt on 740iL]	+432
Power Rear Window Sunshade [Opt on 740]	+355
Power Security Sunroof [Opt on 740iL]	+1034

1998

Body Styles	TMV Pricing		
	Trade	Private	Dealer
4 Dr 740i Sdn	16490	18530	20830
4 Dr 740iL Sdn	18285	20547	23097

Body Styles	TMV Pricing		
	Trade	Private	Dealer
4 Dr 750iL Sdn	21657	24336	27357

Mileage Category: I

BMW introduces Dynamic Stability Control (DSC). DSC is designed to automatically correct the yaw on all 7 Series cars, preventing plowing and fishtailing.

Options	Price
Automatic Load Leveling [Opt on 740iL]	+277
Comfort Seats [Opt on 740i]	+501
Compact Disc Changer	+271
Electronic Damping Suspension Control [Opt on 740i, 740iL]	+692
Heated Front Seats [Opt on 740i, 740iL]	+173

Options	Price
Navigation System	+776
Park Distance Control (Front and Rear) [Opt on 740iL]	+376
Power Security Sunroof [Opt on 740iL]	+900
Power Sunroof	+567
Rear Side Airbag Restraints	+161

1997

Body Styles	TMV Pricing		
	Trade	Private	Dealer
4 Dr 740i Sdn	14311	16160	18420
4 Dr 740iL Sdn	15779	17818	20310

Body Styles	TMV Pricing		
	Trade	Private	Dealer
4 Dr 750iL Sdn	18306	20671	23562

Mileage Category: I

BMW reintroduces the regular length 740i after the uproar caused over its cancellation for the 1996 model year. Like the rest of the 7 Series, the 740i has a standard equipment list that will leave the Sultan of Brunei drooling with desire.

Options	Price
Comfort Seats [Opt on 740i]	+416
Compact Disc Changer [Opt on 740i, 740iL]	+225
Electronic Damping Suspension Control [Opt on 740i, 740iL]	+563
Heated Front Seats [Opt on 740i, 740iL]	+148

Options	Price
Navigation System	+628
Automatic Load Leveling [Opt on 740iL]	+237
Park Distance Control (Front and Rear) [Opt on 740iL]	+286

1996

Body Styles	TMV Pricing		
	Trade	Private	Dealer
4 Dr 740iL Sdn	12578	14377	16861

Body Styles	TMV Pricing		
	Trade	Private	Dealer
4 Dr 750iL Sdn	15069	17224	20199

Mileage Category: I

BMW's flagship gets stretched; the only 7 Series models available for 1996 are long-wheelbase models. The 740iL receives a larger V8 that substantially increases torque. BMW's killer 440-watt sound system is now standard on the 750iL and optional on the 740iL. A sophisticated interior-motion theft-deterrent system is now available.

Options	Price
Automatic Load Leveling [Opt on 740iL]	+209
Comfort Seats [Opt on 740iL]	+330
Park Distance Control (Front and Rear) [Opt on 740iL]	+252

Options	Price
Power Rear Window Sunshade [Opt on 740iL]	+226
Premium Audio System [Opt on 740iL]	+443

1995

Mileage Category: I

The big Bimmer is totally redesigned for 1995. The flagship sedan now features sleek styling and a lengthened wheelbase. Three models are available for 1995, including a new 740i regular-wheelbase model. The V12 engine found in the 750iL gains 27 horsepower and 30 pound-feet of torque. New interior refinements include a residual heat system which will continue to heat the car after the power has been turned off, and 14-way power seats.

Body Styles	TMV Pricing		
	Trade	Private	Dealer
4 Dr 740i Sdn	7804	8933	10815
4 Dr 740iL Sdn	9361	10716	12973
4 Dr 750iL Sdn	11848	13562	16419

Options	Price	Options	Price
Comfort Seats [Opt on 740i,740iL]	+107	Park Distance Control (Front and Rear) [Opt on 740iL]	+196
Compact Disc Changer [Opt on 740i,740iL]	+155		
Heated Front Seats [Opt on 740i,740iL]	+81	Premium Audio System [Opt on 740i]	+171

1994

Body Styles	TMV Pricing		
	Trade	Private	Dealer
4 Dr 740i Sdn	6814	7948	9838
4 Dr 740iL Sdn	7253	8460	10472
4 Dr 750iL Sdn	9219	10754	13312

Options	Price
Compact Disc Changer [Opt on 740i,740iL]	+134
Electronic Damping Suspension Control	+259

Mileage Category: I

No changes for the 7 Series.

BMW
8 Series

1997

Body Styles	TMV Pricing		
	Trade	Private	Dealer
2 Dr 840Ci Cpe	21367	23363	25803
2 Dr 850Ci Cpe	24946	27277	30125

Options	Price
Forged Alloy Wheels	+277

Mileage Category: I

Engine displacement is bumped up, making the 1997 840Ci and 850Ci a bit stronger than last year's models. BMW's five-speed Steptronic is now standard on both models.

1996

Mileage Category: I

The high-performance 850CSi has been dropped. The remaining 850Ci and 840Ci models now feature the speed-sensitive variable assist steering system previously available only on the 850Ci. The 840Ci gets two upgrades previously exclusive to the V12 model: the Steptronic automatic transmission and Bird's Eye maple interior trim. A slightly larger displacement for the V8 engine results in more torque (310 lb-ft. vs. 295 lb-ft) at lower rpm but horsepower remains at 282. Both models receive a redesigned audio system and automatic-locking retractor seatbelts to better accommodate child seats.

Body Styles	TMV Pricing		
	Trade	Private	Dealer
2 Dr 840Ci Cpe	16788	18323	20442
2 Dr 850CSi Cpe	25878	28284	31606
2 Dr 850Ci Cpe	21349	23301	25996

Options	Price
Aluminum/Alloy Wheels	+343
Forged Alloy Wheels	+244

1995

Mileage Category: I

No changes for the 8 Series.

Body Styles	TMV Pricing		
	Trade	Private	Dealer
2 Dr 840Ci Cpe	12644	13888	15960
2 Dr 850CSi Cpe	23511	25858	29770
2 Dr 850Ci Cpe	16864	18523	21287

Options	Price
Aluminum/Alloy Wheels	+86
Electronic Damping Suspension Control	+300
Forged Alloy Wheels	+190

1994

Mileage Category: I

Body Styles	TMV Pricing		
	Trade	Private	Dealer
2 Dr 840Ci Cpe	10116	11384	13497
2 Dr 850CSi Cpe	18535	20908	24862
2 Dr 850Ci Cpe	14775	16627	19714

Options	Price
Electronic Damping Suspension Control	+308
Forged Alloy Wheels	+164

Two new models are introduced to the 8 Series: the 840Ci and the 850CSi. The 840Ci has the same V8 found in the 740 and 540. The 850CSi gets an increased displacement V12 that offers a whopping 372 horsepower. The CSi comes standard with a sports suspension and a six-speed manual transmission. Unfortunately, the introduction of the CSi takes away from the sportiness of the 850Ci, which is now saddled with a four-speed automatic as the only transmission choice.

2002

Body Styles	TMV Pricing		
	Trade	Private	Dealer
2 Dr STD Conv	29011	30732	33599
2 Dr STD Cpe	28386	30070	32876

Options	Price
Hardtop Roof	+1365
Power Moonroof	+216

Mileage Category: F

BMW makes a CD player part of the standard equipment list. No other changes are in store for the 2002 model year.

2001

Mileage Category: F

Body Styles	TMV Pricing		
	Trade	Private	Dealer
2 Dr STD Conv	23699	25849	27833
2 Dr STD Cpe	23432	25557	27519

Options	Price
AM/FM/CD Audio System	+126
Hardtop Roof [Opt on Conv]	+1196
Power Moonroof [Opt on Cpe]	+189

BMW's performance sport coupe and roadster are powered by a new inline six-cylinder engine capable of generating 315 horses. Complementing the increase in power is a more tautly sprung suspension. Standard equipment Dynamic Stability Control keeps overenthusiastic drivers in check, and a new tire-pressure monitoring system alerts you of underinflated rubber.

2000

Mileage Category: F

Body Styles	TMV Pricing		
	Trade	Private	Dealer
2 Dr STD Conv	20254	22200	24108
2 Dr STD Cpe	18031	19764	21463

Options	Price
Hardtop Roof [Opt on Conv]	+837
Power Moonroof [Opt on Cpe]	+485

The M cars carry over for 2000, save for two new exterior colors. Prices remain unchanged.

1999

Mileage Category: F

Body Styles	TMV Pricing		
	Trade	Private	Dealer
2 Dr STD Conv	18163	20073	22060
2 Dr STD Cpe	16036	17722	19476

These high-performance versions of the Z3 roadster and coupe make 240 M-power ponies.

1999 (cont'd)

Options	Price
Hardtop Roof [Opt on Conv]	+756
Power Moonroof [Opt on Cpe]	+438

1998

Mileage Category: F

The M Roadster, a 240-horsepower version of the Z3 convertible, arrives for 1998. An electric top also becomes available this year.

Body Styles	TMV Pricing		
	Trade	Private	Dealer
2 Dr STD Conv	16418	18259	20335

BMW
M3

2003

Mileage Category: F

For 2003, BMW will offer a DVD-based navigation system -- meaning that you won't have to give up an in-dash CD player if you opt for the nav system. Additionally, automatic headlights and rain-sensing wipers are now standard, while aluminum interior trim is a new stand-alone option. The power seat package has been excised from the coupe's option list, so you'll have to spring for the pricey premium package if you want power front seats (these come standard on the convertible).

Body Styles	TMV Pricing		
	Trade	Private	Dealer
2 Dr STD Conv	48312	50574	54343
2 Dr STD Cpe	42728	44728	48061

Options	Price	Options	Price
Hardtop Roof [Opt on Conv]	+1803	Rear Side Airbag Restraints	+303
Harman Kardon Audio System	+530	Nappa Leather Seat Trim [Opt on Cpe]	+864
Heated Front Seats	+354	6-Speed Sequential Semi-Manual Transmission	+1886
Metallic Paint	+373	19 Inch Wheels	+1375
Navigation System	+1414	Power Driver Seat w/Memory [Opt on Cpe]	+369
Power Moonroof [Opt on Cpe]	+825	Park Distance Control (Rear)	+275
Power Passenger Seat [Opt on Cpe]	+236		

2002

Mileage Category: F

An optional sequential manual gearbox makes its way into the M3s, which allows the driver to shift with almost instantaneous precision without a clutch. A CD player becomes standard, the automatic climate control has been revised and rear-seat side airbags are optional for both the coupe and convertible.

Body Styles	TMV Pricing		
	Trade	Private	Dealer
2 Dr STD Conv	43630	45840	49524
2 Dr STD Cpe	38406	40352	43596

Options	Price	Options	Price
6-Speed Sequential Semi-Manual Transmission	+1725	Navigation System	+1293
Hardtop Roof	+1649	Park Distance Control (Rear)	+251
Harman Kardon Audio System	+485	Power Driver Seat w/Memory [Opt on Cpe]	+338
Heated Front Seats	+251	Power Moonroof	+754
Metallic Paint	+341	Power Passenger Seat [Opt on Cpe]	+216
Nappa Leather Seat Trim	+790	Rear Side Airbag Restraints	+277

2001

Mileage Category: F

Powered by a 333-horsepower inline six, the athletic coupe and convertible possess the appeal, functionality and performance to back up their "M" badges.

Body Styles	TMV Pricing		
	Trade	Private	Dealer
2 Dr STD Conv	40385	43547	46466
2 Dr STD Cpe	35166	37919	40460

Options	Price	Options	Price
AM/FM/CD Audio System	+126	Park Distance Control (Rear)	+220
Hardtop Roof	+1444	Power Driver Seat w/Memory [Opt on Cpe]	+296
Harman Kardon Audio System	+425	Power Moonroof	+661
Heated Front Seats	+166	Power Passenger Seat [Opt on Cpe]	+296
Metallic Paint	+299	Rear Side Airbag Restraints	+242
Navigation System	+1133		

1999

Body Styles	TMV Pricing		
	Trade	Private	Dealer
2 Dr STD Conv	25745	28451	31267
2 Dr STD Cpe	21503	23763	26116

Options	Price	Options	Price
AM/FM/Cassette/CD Audio System	+269	Heated Front Seats	+199
Automatic 5-Speed Transmission	+477	Power Driver Seat	+228
Compact Disc Changer	+219	Power Moonroof	+378
Forged Alloy Wheels	+372	Power Passenger Seat	+228
Hardtop Roof	+913	Rear Spoiler	+140
Harman Kardon Audio System	+269		

Mileage Category: F

Production of M3 four-door sedans ends this year as BMW concentrates on selling the M3 coupe and recently introduced M3 convertible. These models go unchanged for 1999.

1998

Body Styles	TMV Pricing		
	Trade	Private	Dealer
2 Dr STD Conv	21167	23541	26217
2 Dr STD Cpe	17575	19546	21768
4 Dr STD Sdn	16303	18131	20192

Options	Price	Options	Price
Automatic 5-Speed Transmission [Opt on Conv,Sdn]	+395	Metallic Paint	+157
Compact Disc Changer	+213	Power Driver Seat	+177
Forged Alloy Wheels	+308	Power Passenger Seat	+177
Hardtop Roof [Opt on Conv]	+755	Power Sunroof [Opt on Cpe,Sdn]	+312
Harman Kardon Audio System [Opt on Cpe,Sdn]	+198	Rear Spoiler [Opt on Cpe,Sdn]	+115

Mileage Category: F

Newly standard side-impact airbags for front seat passengers.

1997

Body Styles	TMV Pricing		
	Trade	Private	Dealer
2 Dr STD Cpe	14698	16525	18759
4 Dr STD Sdn	13202	14843	16848

Options	Price	Options	Price
Automatic 5-Speed Transmission [Opt on Sdn]	+355	Metallic Paint	+141
Compact Disc Changer [Opt on Sdn]	+192	Power Sunroof	+281
Forged Alloy Wheels [Opt on Sdn]	+277	Premium Audio System [Opt on Cpe]	+200
Harman Kardon Audio System [Opt on Sdn]	+200		

Mileage Category: F

An M3 sedan is introduced. All-season traction control becomes standard on all models.

1996

Body Styles	TMV Pricing		
	Trade	Private	Dealer
2 Dr STD Cpe	12340	13953	16181

Options	Price
Power Sunroof	+261
Premium Audio System	+206

Mileage Category: F

No changes this year for the superb M3.

1995

Body Styles	TMV Pricing		
	Trade	Private	Dealer
2 Dr STD Cpe	10346	11580	13637

Options	Price	Options	Price
Automatic 5-Speed Transmission	+257	Power Passenger Seat	+77
Compact Disc Changer	+132	Power Sunroof	+204
Power Driver Seat	+77	Rear Spoiler	+75

Mileage Category: F

A new M3 coupe debuts with blistering performance and exceptional grace. Available only as a five-speed manual, the M3 has 240 horsepower, a limited-slip differential and 17-inch wheels.

BMW
M5

2003

Body Styles	TMV Pricing		
	Trade	Private	Dealer
4 Dr STD Sdn	59351	62584	67971

Options	Price
Split Folding Rear Seat	+373
Power Rear Window Sunshade	+452
Park Distance Control (Front and Rear)	+550

Mileage Category: F

For 2003, BMW will offer a DVD-based navigation system for the M5 -- but alas, you still can't get an in-dash CD player. Besides that, rear head protection airbags (optional last year) are now standard across the line. This is the last year for the current 5 Series -- the M5 being the higher-performance relative of the 540i -- as it will get a full redesign for the 2004 model year. If recent history holds, the M5 is likely to go on hiatus for a couple of years before returning to the welcoming arms and wallets of wealthy enthusiasts. And rumor has it that it will be coming back with a V10 under the hood.

2002
Mileage Category: F

BMW's top performance sedan gets some new exterior colors. Rear-side impact airbags are now a no-charge option, rather than standard.

Body Styles	TMV Pricing		
	Trade	Private	Dealer
4 Dr STD Sdn	53191	56289	61451

Options	Price	Options	Price
Digital Audio System	+647	Power Rear Window Sunshade	+413
Park Distance Control (Front and Rear)	+503	Split Folding Rear Seat	+341

2001
Mileage Category: F

BMW's top-performance sedan, the 394-horsepower M5, gets subtle exterior tweaks and a new head-protection airbag system for rear-seat passengers.

Body Styles	TMV Pricing		
	Trade	Private	Dealer
4 Dr STD Sdn	47234	51519	55474

Options	Price	Options	Price
Park Distance Control (Front and Rear)	+441	Split Folding Rear Seat	+299
Power Rear Window Sunshade	+362		

2000
Mileage Category: F

The M5 is a powerful (nearly 400 horsepower), all-new sport sedan based on the 540i.

Body Styles	TMV Pricing		
	Trade	Private	Dealer
4 Dr STD Sdn	40371	44251	48055

BMW
X5

2003

Body Styles	TMV Pricing		
	Trade	Private	Dealer
4 Dr 3.0i AWD SUV	31790	33339	35921
4 Dr 4.4i AWD SUV	39874	41817	45056
4 Dr 4.6is AWD SUV	52854	55430	59722

Mileage Category: F

This year, BMW will finally offer a DVD-based navigation system, though you must still give up the in-dash CD player if you opt for nav. Besides that, rear head protection airbags (optional last year) are now standard, as is an interesting new safety item called a brakeforce display -- during emergency braking situations, an extra set of rear brake lights will illuminate to warn motorists behind you. If you order the optional adjustable ride height suspension package, it no longer precludes the addition of the sport package. On the inside, new Dakota leather replaces the familiar Montana leather upholstery (it's optional on the 3.0i model and standard on the 4.4i). Individual model changes include a body-colored tailgate handle for any 3.0i equipped with the sport or premium package, and V-rated tires and an unlimited top speed for any sport package-equipped 4.4i.

Options	Price
Automatic 5-Speed Transmission [Opt on 3.0i]	+1002
Automatic Load Leveling [Std on 4.6is]	+550
Comfort Seats [Opt on 4.4i]	+943
Digital Audio System [Std on 4.6is]	+943
Electronic Suspension Control [Std on 4.6is]	+393
Heated Front Seats [Opt on 3.0i]	+354
Heated Front and Rear Seats [Opt on 4.4i]	+275
Leather Seats [Opt on 3.0i]	+1139
Navigation System	+1414
Power Moonroof [Std on 4.6is]	+825

Options	Price
Power Passenger Seat [Opt on 3.0i]	+236
Rear Side Airbag Restraints	+303
Sport Package [Std on 4.6is]	+1257
Sport Seats [Std on 4.6is]	+314
19 Inch Wheels [Opt on 4.4i]	+746
Automatic Climate Control (2 Zone) - Driver and Passenger [Opt on 3.0i]	+236
Automatic Dimming Sideview Mirror(s) [Std on 4.6is]	+138
Park Distance Control (Front and Rear) [Std on 4.6is]	+550

2002

Mileage Category: O

A sports car-quick X5 4.6is makes its debut, boasting a 340-hp 4.6-liter V8 making 350 pound-feet of torque. The 4.4-liter V8 has been upgraded to make 290 horsepower, up from last year's 282. The X5 now offers such goodies as enhanced Hill Descent Control, trailer stability control and a self-leveling suspension. A CD player finally makes its way onto the standard equipment list.

Body Styles	TMV Pricing		
	Trade	Private	Dealer
4 Dr 3.0i AWD SUV	28662	30165	32669
4 Dr 4.4i AWD SUV	35963	37878	41070
4 Dr 4.6is AWD SUV	47992	50548	54808

Options	Price
19 Inch Wheels [Opt on 4.4i]	+683
Automatic 5-Speed Transmission [Opt on 3.0]	+916
Automatic Climate Control [Opt on 3.0]	+216
Automatic Dimming Rearview Mirror [Std on 4.6is]	+180
Automatic Dimming Sideview Mirror(s) [Std on 4.6is]	+144
Automatic Load Leveling [Opt on 3.0]	+503
Digital Audio System [Std on 4.6is]	+862
Electronic Suspension Control [Std on 4.6is]	+359
Heated Front and Rear Seats [Std on 4.6is]	+467
Heated Front Seats [Std on 4.6is]	+216

Options	Price
Leather Seats [Opt on 3.0]	+1042
Navigation System	+1293
Park Distance Control (Front and Rear) [Std on 4.6is]	+503
Power Moonroof [Std on 4.6is]	+754
Power Passenger Seat [Opt on 3.0]	+216
Rear Head Airbag Restraints	+119
Rear Side Airbag Restraints	+277
Sport Package [Std on 4.6is]	+1150
Sport Seats [Opt on 3.0]	+287

2001

Mileage Category: O

A lower-priced X5, with a standard 3.0-liter inline six, is offered for 2001. Other newsworthy items include available sunshades for the back doors, as well as optional heated rear seats. The Sport package includes a sport steering wheel, and 16-way power front seats can be purchased. All X5s come with a self-leveling rear suspension as standard equipment.

Body Styles	TMV Pricing		
	Trade	Private	Dealer
4 Dr 3.0i AWD SUV	26121	28315	30341
4 Dr 4.4i AWD SUV	32481	35209	37728

Options	Price
AM/FM/CD Audio System	+126
Automatic 5-Speed Transmission [Opt on 3.0i]	+802
Automatic Climate Control [Opt on 3.0i]	+189
Automatic Dimming Rearview Mirror	+189
Automatic Dimming Sideview Mirror(s)	+126
Automatic Load Leveling	+478
Cast Alloy Wheels	+566
Comfort Seats	+755
Heated Front and Rear Seats [Opt on 4.4i]	+409

Options	Price
Heated Front Seats	+189
Leather Seats [Opt on 3.0i]	+912
Navigation System	+1252
Park Distance Control (Rear)	+220
Power Moonroof	+661
Power Passenger Seat [Opt on 3.0i]	+252
Rear Side Airbag Restraints	+242
Sport Seats	+299
Sport Suspension	+427

2000

Mileage Category: O

BMW joins the SUV craze with its all-new X5 SAV (sport activity vehicle), powered by the same superb V8 fitted to the 540i.

Body Styles	TMV Pricing		
	Trade	Private	Dealer
4 Dr 4.4i AWD SUV	29377	31885	34344

Options	Price
AM/FM/Cassette/CD Audio System	+282
Compact Disc Changer	+294
Heated Front and Rear Seats	+345
Heated Front Seats	+159
Navigation System	+974
Park Distance Control (Rear)	+186

Options	Price
Power Moonroof	+514
Premium Audio System	+438
Rear Side Airbag Restraints	+205
Sport Package	+490
Sport Seats	+258
Sport Suspension	+361

BMW
Z3

2002

Mileage Category: F

A CD player can be found on the standard features list. New hues color the sleek sportster, and aluminum-finish trim replaces maple wood inside the Z3 3.0i coupe.

Body Styles	TMV Pricing		
	Trade	Private	Dealer
2 Dr 2.5i Conv	20683	21887	23894
2 Dr 3.0i Conv	24530	25985	28409

Body Styles	TMV Pricing		
	Trade	Private	Dealer
2 Dr 3.0i Cpe	24099	25528	27910

Options	Price
Automatic 5-Speed Transmission	+916
Hardtop Roof	+1365
Harman Kardon Audio System [Opt on 2.5 Conv]	+485
Heated Front Seats	+287
Leather Seats [Opt on 2.5 Conv]	+539

Options	Price
Metallic Paint	+341
Power Convertible Top	+431
Power Moonroof	+216
Special Leather Seat Trim	+862
Sport Package	+431

2001

Mileage Category: F

Engine displacement in the 2.8 Roadster and Coupe is bumped from 2.8 liters to 3.0 liters. Horsepower and torque have been increased to 225 and 214 pound-feet, respectively. Bigger brakes and larger 17-inch wheels and tires accompany the new engine. The base 2.5-liter engine sees a 14-horsepower increase, and will appropriately be called the Z3 2.5i. An optional five-speed automatic with manual shifting capability replaces last year's four-speed automatic transmission.

Body Styles	TMV Pricing		
	Trade	Private	Dealer
2 Dr 2.5i Conv	18199	19850	21374
2 Dr 3.0i Conv	21988	23983	25824

Body Styles	TMV Pricing		
	Trade	Private	Dealer
2 Dr 3.0i Cpe	21582	23540	25347

Options	Price
17 Inch Wheels - Cross-Spoke [Opt on 3.0 Cpe]	+189
AM/FM/CD Audio System	+126
Automatic 5-Speed Transmission	+802
Hardtop Roof [Opt on Conv]	+1196
Harman Kardon Audio System [Opt on 2.5 Conv]	+425
Heated Front Seats	+205

Options	Price
Leather Seats [Opt on 2.5 Conv]	+572
Metallic Paint	+299
Power Convertible Top	+472
Power Moonroof	+189
Sport Package	+378
Sport Seats [Opt on Conv]	+252

2000

Mileage Category: F

Dynamic Stability Control is now standard on all Z3s. The cars also receive freshened exterior and interior styling and appointments.

Body Styles	TMV Pricing		
	Trade	Private	Dealer
2 Dr 2.3 Conv	16426	18005	19552
2 Dr 2.8 Conv	18536	20318	22064

Body Styles	TMV Pricing		
	Trade	Private	Dealer
2 Dr 2.8 Cpe	16866	18487	20076

Options	Price
17 Inch Wheels [Opt on 2.8]	+598
AM/FM/CD Audio System	+122
Automatic 4-Speed Transmission	+478
Chrome Wheels [Opt on 2.3 Conv]	+417
Cruise Control [Opt on 2.3 Conv]	+145
Hardtop Roof [Opt on Conv]	+931
Harman Kardon Audio System [Opt on 2.3 Conv]	+331
Heated Front Seats	+171

Options	Price
Leather Seats [Opt on 2.3 Conv]	+483
Metallic Paint	+233
Power Convertible Top [Opt on Conv]	+367
Power Moonroof [Opt on 2.8 Cpe]	+490
Special Factory Paint [Opt on Conv]	+233
Special Leather Seat Trim [Opt on 2.8]	+638
Spoke Wheels [Opt on 2.3 Conv]	+551
Sport Seats [Opt on Conv]	+196

1999

Mileage Category: F

The Z3 2.8 Coupe is new, side airbags are now standard on all models and a 2.5-liter inline six replaces the 1.9-liter four-cylinder engine on the entry-level roadster.

Body Styles	TMV Pricing		
	Trade	Private	Dealer
2 Dr 2.3 Conv	13852	15308	16824
2 Dr 2.8 Conv	16171	17871	19640

Body Styles	TMV Pricing		
	Trade	Private	Dealer
2 Dr 2.8 Cpe	14428	15945	17523

Options	Price
17 Inch Wheels - Spoke [Opt on 2.8 Cpe]	+540
Automatic 4-Speed Transmission	+388
Chrome Wheels	+338
Cruise Control [Opt on 2.3 Conv]	+118
Hardtop Roof	+756
Harman Kardon Audio System [Opt on 2.3 Conv]	+269
Heated Front Seats	+140
Leather Seats [Opt on 2.3 Conv]	+436

Options	Price
Metallic Paint	+190
Power Convertible Top	+298
Power Moonroof	+398
Special Factory Paint [Opt on Conv]	+190
Special Leather Seat Trim [Opt on 2.8]	+576
Spoke Wheels	+447
Sport Seats [Opt on Conv]	+159

1998

Body Styles		TMV Pricing		
		Trade	Private	Dealer
2 Dr 1.9 Conv		11552	12847	14308
2 Dr 2.8 Conv		14264	15863	17667

Options	Price	Options	Price
17 Inch Wheels - Spoke [Opt on 2.8]	+470	Metallic Paint	+165
Alarm System	+122	Power Convertible Top	+260
Automatic 4-Speed Transmission	+338	Special Factory Paint	+165
Harman Kardon Audio System [Opt on 1.9]	+282	Special Leather Seat Trim [Opt on 2.8]	+501
Heated Front Seats	+122	Sport Seats	+138
Leather Seats [Opt on 1.9]	+380		

Mileage Category: F

An electric top becomes available this year.

1997

Body Styles		TMV Pricing		
		Trade	Private	Dealer
2 Dr 1.9 Conv		9753	10966	12448
2 Dr 2.8 Conv		11898	13378	15186

Options	Price	Options	Price
17 Inch Wheels - Spoke [Opt on 2.8]	+390	Metallic Paint	+141
Automatic 4-Speed Transmission	+289	Special Factory Paint	+141
Compact Disc Changer	+163	Special Leather Seat Trim [Opt on 2.8]	+416
Leather Seats [Opt on 1.9]	+325	Traction Control System [Opt on 1.9]	+237

Mileage Category: F

BMW makes its 190-horsepower six-cylinder engine available in the Z3 2.8.

1996

Body Styles		TMV Pricing		
		Trade	Private	Dealer
2 Dr 1.9 Conv		8742	9885	11463

Options	Price	Options	Price
Automatic 4-Speed Transmission	+268	Special Factory Paint	+131
Leather Seats	+301	Traction Control System	+220
Metallic Paint	+131		

Mileage Category: F

BMW follows Mazda's lead and introduces a roadster. This dreamy two-seater made its debut in the James Bond movie, "GoldenEye", and has had enthusiasts across the country drooling over its smart styling and impressive refinement. Featured as the perfect Christmas gift in the 1995 Neiman Marcus Christmas catalog, BMW sold out of Z3s before the first one was released to the public.

2003

Body Styles		TMV Pricing		
		Trade	Private	Dealer
2 Dr 2.5i Conv		24958	26317	28582
2 Dr 3.0i Conv		28809	30378	32993

Options	Price	Options	Price
Automatic 5-Speed Transmission	+1002	Power Driver Seat	+236
Automatic Climate Control	+177	Power Passenger Seat	+236
Cruise Control [Opt on 2.5i]	+373	Special Leather Interior Trim [Opt on 3.0i]	+943
Heated Front and Rear Seats	+393	Sport Package	+943
Leather Seats [Opt on 3.0i]	+825	Premium Audio System [Opt on 2.5i]	+688
Metallic Paint	+373	6-Speed Sequential Semi-Manual Transmission	+1179
Navigation System	+1414	Automatic Dimming Sideview Mirror(s)	+161
Power Convertible Top	+471		

Mileage Category: F

The all-new Z4 roadster picks up where the Z3 left off. Well, sort of. There's no coupe version this time around. And the jury is still out on whether the Z4's "flame-surfaced" body is a welcome replacement for its predecessor's sexy corporate styling. In other respects, the newcomer offers much to like -- a more rigid chassis, a real glass rear window and, starting in the spring of 2003, a Sequential Manual Gearbox (SMG) like the one in the M3. All in all, the driving experience is exhilarating -- so if you can get past the styling and come up with the requisite cash, you know where this one belongs on your test drive list.

Buick
Century

2003

Body Styles	TMV Pricing		
	Trade	Private	Dealer
4 Dr Custom Sdn	9382	10322	11889

Options	Price	Options	Price
Aluminum/Alloy Wheels	+237	Power Driver Seat	+139
AM/FM/Cassette/CD Audio System	+156	Front Side Airbag Restraints	+195
Antilock Brakes	+390	Split Folding Rear Seat	+153
Leather Seats	+387	OnStar Telematic System	+387

Mileage Category: D

The deletion of the Century Limited trim level from the 2003 model lineup leaves us with a lone Century this year, and it offers only a short list of updates. Most important to note is that antilock brakes, OnStar and the driver side-impact airbag are now optional, instead of standard equipment. Other standard features that moved to the optional equipment list include the rear glass antenna, front bucket seats and accompanying center console, cassette player, sunroof, heated exterior mirrors and the 15-inch aluminum wheels. Other changes remain largely aesthetic; a new exterior appearance package adds revised fascias, updated door moldings and a graphite color grille. Inside, the Century benefits only from new wood switch plates. There's also a new starter for improved cold weather cranking and an impact-absorbing headliner that exceeds new federal requirements.

2002

Mileage Category: D

Buick's midsize Century remains relatively unchanged for 2002. LATCH child-seat attachment points are now standard, along with a revised cruise control system. Dark Bronze Mist is added to the color palette and Limited models get wood grain trim on the doors.

Body Styles	TMV Pricing		
	Trade	Private	Dealer
4 Dr Custom Sdn	8089	8974	10450
4 Dr Limited Sdn	9134	10134	11800

Options	Price	Options	Price
AM/FM/Cassette/CD Audio System	+135	Power Driver Seat [Opt on Custom]	+121
Chrome Wheels	+121	Power Passenger Seat	+121
OnStar Telematic System [Opt on Custom]	+218	Power Sunroof	+385

2001

Mileage Category: D

New rear-wheel house liners promise a quieter ride on wet roads, a special appearance package is offered and OnStar in-vehicle safety, security and information service is now standard on Limited models.

Body Styles	TMV Pricing		
	Trade	Private	Dealer
4 Dr Custom Sdn	6392	7538	8596
4 Dr Limited Sdn	7305	8614	9823

Options	Price	Options	Price
Aluminum/Alloy Wheels	+146	Power Passenger Seat	+125
OnStar Telematic System [Opt on Custom]	+185	Power Sunroof	+270
Power Driver Seat	+119		

2000

Mileage Category: D

Buick's midsize Century heads into the new millennium with a special-edition model commemorating the turn of the century and more horsepower in all three models from a revised 3.1-liter 3100 V6.

Body Styles	TMV Pricing		
	Trade	Private	Dealer
4 Dr Custom Sdn	5172	6239	7285
4 Dr Limited Sdn	5752	6939	8102

Options	Price
Aluminum/Alloy Wheels	+126
AM/FM/Cassette/CD Audio System	+141
OnStar Telematic System	+301
Power Moonroof	+233

1999

Mileage Category: D

The year 1999 brings a host of safety improvements, many of them standard. Additionally, the suspension has been retuned for less body roll, the sound systems have been upgraded and one new paint color, called Auburn Nightmist, has been added.

Body Styles	TMV Pricing		
	Trade	Private	Dealer
4 Dr Custom Sdn	3832	4710	5625
4 Dr Limited Sdn	4276	5256	6276

1999 (cont'd)

Options	Price
Leather Seats	+157
OnStar Telematic System	+250
Power Moonroof	+174

1998

Body Styles	TMV Pricing		
	Trade	Private	Dealer
4 Dr Custom Sdn	2969	3787	4710
4 Dr Limited Sdn	3321	4237	5270

Options	Price
Leather Seats [Opt on Limited]	+121
OnStar Telematic System	+220
Power Moonroof	+154

Mileage Category: D

The addition of second-generation airbags, three new exterior colors, one new interior color and the availability of OnStar mobile communications are this year's changes.

1997

Body Styles	TMV Pricing		
	Trade	Private	Dealer
4 Dr Custom Sdn	2193	2890	3743
4 Dr Limited Sdn	2824	3722	4820

Options	Price
Power Moonroof	+128

Mileage Category: D

Buick redesigns its bread-and-butter midsize sedan, dropping the wagon variant in the process. A 3.1-liter V6 engine, roomier interior, larger trunk and traditional Buick styling cues highlight the new Century.

1996

Body Styles	TMV Pricing		
	Trade	Private	Dealer
4 Dr STD Sdn	1695	2300	3135
4 Dr STD Wgn	1765	2395	3266

Mileage Category: D

Wagons get the V6 as standard equipment. Power windows, cassette player, rear window defogger and a remote trunk release make the standard equipment list as this ancient A-body rolls into its final year of production.

1995

Body Styles	TMV Pricing			Body Styles	TMV Pricing		
	Trade	Private	Dealer		Trade	Private	Dealer
4 Dr Custom Sdn	1205	1691	2502	4 Dr Special Sdn	1173	1647	2436
4 Dr Limited Sdn	1540	2162	3198	4 Dr Special Wgn	1180	1657	2452

Options	Price
3.1L V6 OHV 12V FI Engine [Opt on Special]	+89

Mileage Category: D

Instruments have new backlighting, and seats are revised.

1994

Body Styles	TMV Pricing		
	Trade	Private	Dealer
4 Dr Custom Sdn	913	1376	2148
4 Dr Special Sdn	831	1254	1958
4 Dr Special Wgn	870	1312	2049

Mileage Category: D

A driver airbag and ABS are standard on all models. This marks the first time ABS is offered on the Century. Coupe trimmed from lineup. The 2.2-liter engine gains 10 horsepower, and the optional 3.3-liter V6 is replaced by a 3.1-liter unit. When transmission is shifted into "Park," automatic door locks unlock themselves. Tilt steering is standard on Special. New gauges debut.

2003

Body Styles	TMV Pricing		
	Trade	Private	Dealer
4 Dr Custom Sdn	13145	14138	15793
4 Dr Limited Sdn	15330	16488	18418

Options	Price	Options	Price
Aluminum/Alloy Wheels [Opt on Custom]	+164	Front Side Airbag Restraints [Opt on Custom]	+195
Automatic Stability Control [Opt on Limited]	+276	Special Factory Paint [Opt on Limited]	+306
Heads-Up Display [Opt on Limited]	+167	OnStar Telematic System [Opt on Custom]	+387
Heated Front Seats [Opt on Custom]	+164	Satellite Radio System [Opt on Limited]	+181
Leather Seats [Opt on Custom]	+499	16 Inch Wheels - Chrome [Opt on Custom]	+220
Power Moonroof [Opt on Limited]	+554		

Mileage Category: G

To recognize the Buick LeSabre's successful 10-year sales record as the best-selling full-size car in America, and to celebrate Buick's centennial anniversary in 2003, Buick has added a new trim option for the LeSabre Limited model. Buick's product planners must have been feeling particularly creative when they named it; it's called the Celebration Edition. It features a new monochrome emblem, a blacked-out grille and license plate pocket and two new premium paints, Crimson Pearl and White Diamond. Additional Celebration exterior bits include body-color lower fascias and rocker moldings, turn-signal indicators in the side mirrors and new 16-inch chrome-plated aluminum wheels. Interior refinements are limited to two-tone leather seating and Black Cherry wood grain trim. It also includes a number of otherwise optional features, such as StabiliTrak. The rest of the LeSabre line is pretty much unchanged, with the exception of XM Satellite Radio, which is a new option on the Limited, and side-impact airbags, formerly standard on all LeSabres, are now optional on Custom models.

2002

Mileage Category: G

Buick's LeSabre receives only minor trim changes for 2002. Limited models get additional standard features and new 16-inch wheels, while all models get new radios, manual trunk release latches and the LATCH system for securing child safety seats.

Body Styles	TMV Pricing		
	Trade	Private	Dealer
4 Dr Custom Sdn	10730	11687	13281
4 Dr Limited Sdn	12486	13599	15455

Options	Price	Options	Price
16 Inch Wheels	+143	Heated Front Seats [Opt on Custom]	+143
Aluminum/Alloy Wheels [Opt on Custom]	+181	Leather Seats [Opt on Custom]	+433
AM/FM/Cassette/CD Audio System [Opt on Custom]	+133	OnStar Telematic System [Opt on Custom]	+230
Automatic Stability Control	+239	Power Passenger Seat [Opt on Custom]	+116
Chrome Wheels	+336	Power Sunroof	+435
Heads-Up Display	+145		

2001

Mileage Category: G

Changes include dual-stage airbags, standard (on the limited) OnStar in-vehicle safety, security and information service, and the engine oil change interval has been increased to 10,000 miles.

Body Styles	TMV Pricing		
	Trade	Private	Dealer
4 Dr Custom Sdn	8715	9957	11104
4 Dr Limited Sdn	10465	11957	13335

Options	Price	Options	Price
Aluminum/Alloy Wheels [Opt on Custom]	+126	Heated Front Seats [Opt on Limited]	+115
AM/FM/Cassette/CD Audio System	+136	Leather Seats	+304
Automatic Stability Control	+193	OnStar Telematic System [Opt on Custom]	+185
Compact Disc Changer	+232	Power Passenger Seat [Opt on Custom]	+128
Heads-Up Display [Opt on Limited]	+117	Power Sunroof	+350

2000

Mileage Category: G

Buick's LeSabre has been totally redesigned for the 2000 model year. Though it looks a lot like a '99, this car has undergone a remarkable transformation, riding on a new platform with mildly tweaked sheet metal and an entirely reworked cabin. Better ride, steering and seats, plus side airbags and integrated seatbelts, make it an even better value than before.

Body Styles	TMV Pricing		
	Trade	Private	Dealer
4 Dr Custom Sdn	7319	8521	9699
4 Dr Limited Sdn	8252	9607	10936

2000 (cont'd)

Options	Price	Options	Price
Automatic Stability Control	+166	OnStar Telematic System	+301
Compact Disc Changer	+200	Power Moonroof	+334
Leather Seats	+334		

1999

Body Styles	TMV Pricing		
	Trade	Private	Dealer
4 Dr Custom Sdn	5473	6540	7651
4 Dr Limited Sdn	6431	7685	8990

Options	Price
Leather Seats	+185
OnStar Telematic System	+250

Mileage Category: G

Buick has made some emissions system improvements for '99, and added two exterior metallic paint choices, Sterling Silver and Dark Bronze Mist.

1998

Body Styles	TMV Pricing		
	Trade	Private	Dealer
4 Dr Custom Sdn	4371	5403	6566
4 Dr Limited Sdn	5133	6345	7712

Options	Price
Leather Seats	+121
OnStar Telematic System	+220

Mileage Category: G

Cruise control is standard on base models, OnStar Mobile Communications is a dealer-installed option, Limited models get a couple of electrochromic mirrors and new colors are on tap inside and out. Second-generation airbags are made standard.

1997

Body Styles	TMV Pricing		
	Trade	Private	Dealer
4 Dr Custom Sdn	3548	4483	5626
4 Dr Limited Sdn	4127	5215	6544

Mileage Category: G

Buick freshens the LeSabre with new front and rear styling. Redesigned wheel selections, new seats on Custom models and walnut instrument panel appliques round out the visual changes. Structurally, the LeSabre now meets side-impact standards.

1996

Body Styles	TMV Pricing		
	Trade	Private	Dealer
4 Dr Custom Sdn	2559	3310	4347
4 Dr Limited Sdn	3170	4100	5385

Mileage Category: G

The Series II engine becomes standard on LeSabre. Order the Gran Touring suspension, and get the same magnetic variable effort steering found on the Park Avenue Ultra. Now standard on the Custom is an electric rear window defogger and storage armrest. Limited trim levels get Twilight Sentinel, dual automatic ComforTemp climate controls and a rear-seat center armrest.

1995

Body Styles	TMV Pricing		
	Trade	Private	Dealer
4 Dr Custom Sdn	1815	2399	3372
4 Dr Limited Sdn	2023	2674	3759

Mileage Category: G

New climate controls and radios are major changes.

1994

Body Styles	TMV Pricing		
	Trade	Private	Dealer
4 Dr Custom Sdn	1348	1860	2714
4 Dr Limited Sdn	1578	2177	3176

Mileage Category: G

Passenger airbag installed. Traction control system now cuts engine power to slipping wheels in addition to applying brake. Front-seat travel increased one inch.

Buick
Park Avenue

2003

Body Styles	TMV Pricing		
	Trade	Private	Dealer
4 Dr STD Sdn	17946	19131	21106
4 Dr Ultra S/C Sdn	23480	25030	27613

Options	Price
Automatic Stability Control [Std on Ultra]	+276
Chrome Wheels [Std on Ultra]	+423
Compact Disc Changer	+331
Heads-Up Display	+167
Power Moonroof	+610
Special Factory Paint	+306

Options	Price
Touring Suspension [Std on Ultra]	+159
Traction Control System [Std on Ultra]	+139
OnStar Telematic System [Std on Ultra]	+251
Premium Audio System [Std on Ultra]	+164
Park Distance Control (Rear)	+164

Mileage Category: H

A revamped Park Avenue Ultra, chock-full of aesthetic goodies, emerges for 2003. This Ultra model features a new grille, side mirror-mounted turn indicators, 17-inch chrome-plated aluminum wheels and retro-style fender portholes. The three holes on each front fender are meant to link the updated 2003 model to Buick's 40-plus years of design heritage. The Ultra also boasts an improved ride, largely due to the specially-tuned Gran Touring suspension and rear stabilizer bar, both of which are standard Ultra equipment. Inside, faux wood grain trim and a new gauge cluster graphics help define the Ultra's fresh look.

2002

Mileage Category: H

Buick's top-of-the-line luxury sedan remains virtually unchanged for 2002. Minor updates include wood grain trim on the doors and instrument panel and two new exterior colors.

Body Styles	TMV Pricing		
	Trade	Private	Dealer
4 Dr STD Sdn	15738	17002	19108
4 Dr Ultra S/C Sdn	18428	19908	22374

Options	Price
Automatic Stability Control [Opt on STD]	+239
Chrome Wheels	+368
Compact Disc Changer	+288
Heads-Up Display	+145
Heated Front and Rear Seats [Opt on STD]	+143

Options	Price
OnStar Telematic System [Opt on STD]	+206
Park Distance Control (Rear)	+143
Power Sunroof	+530
Premium Audio System [Opt on STD]	+143
Special Factory Paint	+218

2001

Mileage Category: H

Buick's full-size Park Avenue gets minor refinements in the areas of safety, convenience and colors for 2001. The biggest news is the addition of the Ultrasonic Rear Park Assist system, improving safety while backing up.

Body Styles	TMV Pricing		
	Trade	Private	Dealer
4 Dr STD Sdn	12150	13772	15269
4 Dr Ultra S/C Sdn	14128	16013	17753

Options	Price
Automatic Stability Control	+193
Chrome Wheels	+296
Compact Disc Changer	+232
Heads-Up Display	+117
Heated Front and Rear Seats [Opt on STD]	+115

Options	Price
Park Distance Control (Rear)	+115
Power Sunroof	+426
Premium Audio System [Opt on STD]	+115
Special Factory Paint	+175

2000

Mileage Category: H

The Park Avenue gets StabiliTrak, GM's advanced vehicle stability control system.

Body Styles	TMV Pricing		
	Trade	Private	Dealer
4 Dr STD Sdn	8975	10404	11805
4 Dr Ultra S/C Sdn	10696	12399	14069

Options	Price
Chrome Wheels	+233
Compact Disc Changer	+200
Leather Seats [Opt on STD]	+252

Options	Price
OnStar Telematic System	+301
Power Moonroof	+367
Special Factory Paint	+133

1999

Body Styles	TMV Pricing		
	Trade	Private	Dealer
4 Dr STD Sdn	6915	8223	9585
4 Dr Ultra S/C Sdn	8290	9858	11491

Options	Price	Options	Price
Chrome Wheels	+174	OnStar Telematic System	+250
Compact Disc Changer	+149	Power Moonroof	+275
Leather Seats [Opt on STD]	+188		

Mileage Category: H

The Park Avenue's taillamps are now similar to those found on the upscale Ultra model. Also new this year is an enhanced eight-speaker audio system dubbed Concert Sound III, a new hood-to-fender seal for improved appearance, an adjustable rubber bumper for the deck lid and four new exterior colors.

1998

Body Styles	TMV Pricing		
	Trade	Private	Dealer
4 Dr STD Sdn	5146	6319	7642
4 Dr Ultra S/C Sdn	7043	8649	10460

Options	Price	Options	Price
Chrome Wheels	+154	OnStar Telematic System	+220
Compact Disc Changer	+132	Power Moonroof	+220
Leather Seats [Opt on STD]	+133		

Mileage Category: H

Exterior mirrors can be folded away, a new optional feature tilts the exterior mirrors down for curb viewing during reversing, dealers can install an OnStar Communications system and new colors are available inside and out. Second-generation airbags are made standard.

1997

Body Styles	TMV Pricing		
	Trade	Private	Dealer
4 Dr STD Sdn	4033	5112	6431
4 Dr Ultra S/C Sdn	5063	6418	8073

Options	Price
Power Moonroof	+184
Chrome Wheels	+128

Mileage Category: H

Buick engineers substantially improve the Park Avenue for 1997 by strengthening the body structure, improving interior ergonomics, and introducing a sleek new look. Powertrains are carried over, and two models are available: base and Ultra.

1996

Body Styles	TMV Pricing		
	Trade	Private	Dealer
4 Dr STD Sdn	3081	3981	5224
4 Dr Ultra S/C Sdn	3802	4913	6447

Options	Price
Power Moonroof	+158

Mileage Category: H

Ultra gets new Series II supercharged engine as standard equipment, as well as magnetic variable effort steering gear. Colors and trim are revised, battery rundown protection is added, and long-life engine components keep the Park going longer between maintenance stops.

1995

Body Styles	TMV Pricing		
	Trade	Private	Dealer
4 Dr STD Sdn	2312	3101	4417
4 Dr Ultra S/C Sdn	2921	3918	5580

Options	Price
Leather Seats [Opt on STD]	+79
Power Moonroof	+131
Premium Audio System	+86

Mileage Category: H

Base engine upgraded to 3800 Series II status; makes 35 more horsepower than previous year. Base models get styling tweaks front and rear. New climate controls and radios are added.

1994

Mileage Category: H

Passenger airbag debuts, and Ultra model gets 20 more horsepower. Traction control system now cuts engine power to slipping wheels in addition to applying brake, and can be turned off if desired. Remote keyless entry, power trunk pull-down and auto-dimming rearview mirror added to Ultra standard equipment list. Front-seat travel increased one inch. Heated front seats are newly optional.

Body Styles	TMV Pricing		
	Trade	Private	Dealer
4 Dr STD Sdn	1606	2236	3287
4 Dr Ultra S/C Sdn	1990	2771	4073

Options	Price
Power Sunroof	+102

Buick
Regal

2003

Body Styles	TMV Pricing		
	Trade	Private	Dealer
4 Dr GS S/C Sdn	13444	14663	16694
4 Dr LS Sdn	11189	12203	13894

Options	Price
Aluminum/Alloy Wheels [Opt on LS]	+187
Antilock Brakes [Opt on LS]	+390
Chrome Wheels	+362
Heated Front Seats	+164
Leather Seats [Opt on LS]	+362
Monsoon Audio System	+220
Power Moonroof	+443

Options	Price
Power Passenger Seat	+195
Front Side Airbag Restraints	+195
Special Leather Seat Trim	+195
Split Folding Rear Seat [Opt on LS]	+153
OnStar Telematic System	+387
Automatic Climate Control (2 Zone) - Driver and Passenger [Opt on LS]	+139

Mileage Category: D

Many features that were on the standard equipment list for 2002 have been deemed optional, or deleted altogether, for the 2003 model. Deleted items are speed variable power-assisted steering, which is being downgraded to a nonspeed dependent system, and heated outside rearview mirrors. Side-impact airbags are now optional instead of standard (and continue to be available with leather seating surfaces only), as is a rear split-folding seat. Safety also comes with a separate price tag, as antilock brakes and traction control are now options on the lower Regal LS, but together with a tire inflation monitor, remain standard on the more upscale GS model. On the upside, all Regals receive an improved starter for cold weather cranking, and a new impact-absorbent headliner, plus two new packages to help Regal buyers group options for a better price. The new Luxury Package includes dual-zone climate control, illuminated visor mirrors, auto-dimming inside and outside rearview mirrors, AM/FM stereo with both cassette and CD player and steering wheel-mounted audio controls. The simpler Leather and Wheel Package includes leather seats, a split-folding rear seat and 15-inch aluminum wheels.

2002

Mileage Category: D

For 2002, the biggest news in the Regal lineup is the continuation of the upscale Joseph Abboud model along with a new Dark Bronze Mist exterior color. Additional wood grain trim will be added to all Regals later in the year and LATCH child seat attachment points are now standard.

Body Styles	TMV Pricing		
	Trade	Private	Dealer
4 Dr GS S/C Sdn	10617	11779	13716
4 Dr LS Sdn	9195	10201	11878

Options	Price
16 Inch Wheels [Opt on LS]	+145
Aluminum/Alloy Wheels [Opt on LS]	+162
Automatic Climate Control (2 Zone) - Driver and Passenger [Opt on LS]	+121
Chrome Wheels	+191
Heated Front and Rear Seats	+143
Leather Seats [Opt on LS]	+314

Options	Price
Monsoon Audio System	+143
OnStar Telematic System [Opt on LS]	+230
Power Moonroof	+336
Power Sunroof	+385
Touring Suspension	+121

2001

Body Styles	TMV Pricing		
	Trade	Private	Dealer
4 Dr GS S/C Sdn	8298	9786	11159
4 Dr LS Sdn	7069	8336	9506

2001 (cont'd)

Options	Price
Aluminum/Alloy Wheels [Opt on LS]	+130
Chrome Wheels	+154
Heated Front and Rear Seats	+115
Leather Seats [Opt on LS]	+214

Options	Price
Monsoon Audio System	+115
OnStar Telematic System [Opt on LS]	+185
Power Moonroof	+270
Power Passenger Seat	+128

Mileage Category: D

The "Car for the Supercharged Family" gets new rear-wheel house liners for a quieter ride, a standard trunk entrapment release and two new colors, Graphite Metallic and White. An Olympic appearance package is now available and OnStar in-vehicle safety, security and information service is standard on GS models.

2000

Mileage Category: D

Body Styles	TMV Pricing		
	Trade	Private	Dealer
4 Dr GS S/C Sdn	6841	8252	9635
4 Dr LS Sdn	5760	6947	8111
4 Dr LSE Sdn	6084	7338	8568

Options	Price
Chrome Wheels	+133
Compact Disc Changer	+184
Leather Seats [Opt on LS]	+218

Options	Price
OnStar Telematic System	+301
Power Moonroof	+233

New alloy wheels, a standard body-colored grille on the GS and two new colors, Gold Metallic and Sterling Silver debut. Inside, there's now a split-folding rear seat and an optional side airbag for the driver on leather-lined Regals.

1999

Mileage Category: D

Body Styles	TMV Pricing		
	Trade	Private	Dealer
4 Dr GS S/C Sdn	5249	6453	7706
4 Dr LS Sdn	4566	5614	6704

Options	Price
Compact Disc Changer	+138
Leather Seats [Opt on LS]	+163

Options	Price
OnStar Telematic System	+250
Power Moonroof	+174

Performance-oriented changes, such as more power, sporty tweaks to the steering and suspension, firmer motor mounts and the addition of a strut tower brace underhood, lead the news for the '99 Regal. Other changes include enhancements to the ABS and traction control systems, as well as the addition of a tire inflation monitor, perimeter lighting and the Concert Sound II audio system to Regal's already long list of standard equipment. New options include a self-dimming electrochromic outside rearview mirror, redesigned 15-inch alloy wheels and the eight-speaker, 220-watt Monsoon audio system. And that's all in addition to a new exterior paint color, Auburn Nightmist.

1998

Mileage Category: D

Body Styles	TMV Pricing		
	Trade	Private	Dealer
4 Dr 25th Anniv Sdn	4565	5823	7242
4 Dr GS S/C Sdn	4435	5657	7036
4 Dr LS Sdn	3782	4824	6000

Options	Price
Compact Disc Changer	+121
Leather Seats [Opt on LS]	+133

Options	Price
OnStar Telematic System	+220
Power Moonroof	+154

Regal LS gets a new standard four-speed automatic transmission, and three new exterior colors are available. Dealers will install an OnStar Mobile Communications system if the buyer desires, and second-generation airbags are added.

1997

Mileage Category: D

Body Styles	TMV Pricing		
	Trade	Private	Dealer
4 Dr GS S/C Sdn	3616	4765	6170
4 Dr LS Sdn	3167	4173	5403

Options	Price
Power Moonroof	+128

The complete redesign of the Regal means Buick finally has a viable entry in the midsize sedan marketplace. The standard equipment list is long, including ABS, traction control, dual-zone climate controls, heated exterior mirrors, retained accessory power and battery rundown protection.

1996

Body Styles	TMV Pricing		
	Trade	Private	Dealer
2 Dr Custom Cpe	2032	2757	3758
2 Dr Gran Sport Cpe	2393	3248	4428
4 Dr Custom Sdn	2069	2808	3828

Body Styles	TMV Pricing		
	Trade	Private	Dealer
4 Dr Gran Sport Sdn	2551	3461	4718
4 Dr Limited Sdn	2309	3133	4272
4 Dr Olympic Gold Sdn	2277	3091	4214

1996 (cont'd)

Mileage Category: D

The Series II 3.8-liter V6 is standard on Limited and Gran Sport, optional on base Custom models. Standard equipment now includes dual ComforTemp climate controls and a cassette player. Revised wheels, available in chrome, are standard on the Gran Sport. Base V6 is upgraded, and both engines feature long-life engine components.

1995

Mileage Category: D

New interior has dual airbags housed in revised instrument panel. Seats are new, too. Fake wood has been chopped from door panels. Exterior styling is updated.

Body Styles	TMV Pricing			Body Styles	TMV Pricing		
	Trade	Private	Dealer		Trade	Private	Dealer
2 Dr Custom Cpe	1597	2242	3317	4 Dr Custom Select Sdn	1523	2138	3163
2 Dr Gran Sport Cpe	1704	2393	3541	4 Dr Gran Sport Sdn	1695	2380	3521
4 Dr Custom Sdn	1622	2277	3369	4 Dr Limited Sdn	1647	2312	3421

Options	Price
Power Moonroof	+92

1994

Mileage Category: D

Driver airbag and ABS standard on all Regals. The 3.1-liter V6 gets 20 more horsepower. Power windows standard across the board, and automatic door locks unlock when car is shifted into "Park."

Body Styles	TMV Pricing			Body Styles	TMV Pricing		
	Trade	Private	Dealer		Trade	Private	Dealer
2 Dr Custom Cpe	1074	1620	2530	4 Dr Gran Sport Sdn	1142	1723	2690
2 Dr Gran Sport Cpe	1135	1712	2674	4 Dr Limited Sdn	1130	1703	2659
4 Dr Custom Sdn	1073	1619	2528				

Options	Price
Power Moonroof	+75
Power Sunroof	+102

Buick
Rendezvous

2003

Mileage Category: L

With just one year of production under its belt, Buick is already making some substantial content changes to its Rendezvous model line. Instead of offering standard all-wheel drive on its upscale CXL model, both the lower-level CX and the CXL will now come with front-wheel drive, with Versatrack all-wheel drive available on both models. Other formerly standard items that are now optional this year include: four-wheel disc brakes, ABS, side airbags, all-speed traction control and luggage rack crossbows. On the upside, both models get dual-zone climate control. The CXL also benefits from an optional DVD-based entertainment system and optional XM Satellite Radio for extra enjoyment.

Body Styles	TMV Pricing		
	Trade	Private	Dealer
4 Dr CX AWD SUV	16392	17558	19501
4 Dr CX SUV	14863	15920	17683
4 Dr CXL AWD SUV	19141	20503	22772
4 Dr CXL SUV	17313	18545	20597

Options	Price	Options	Price
AM/FM/Cassette/CD Audio System [Opt on CX]	+195	Front Side Airbag Restraints [Opt on CXL]	+195
Antilock Brakes [Opt on FWD]	+390	Third Seat	+259
Camper/Towing Package	+181	OnStar Telematic System [Opt on CXL]	+387
Captain Chairs (4)	+242	AM/FM/CD Changer Audio System [Opt on CXL]	+245
Heads-Up Display [Opt on CXL]	+153	Satellite Radio System [Opt on CXL]	+181
Heated Front Seats [Opt on CXL]	+125	Automatic Climate Control (2 Zone) - Driver and Passenger	+125
Leather Seats [Opt on CXL]	+276	DVD Entertainment System [Opt on CXL]	+613
Power Driver Seat [Opt on CX]	+150	16 Inch Wheels - Chrome	+164
Power Moonroof	+493	Park Distance Control (Rear) [Opt on CXL]	+164

2002

Body Styles	TMV Pricing		
	Trade	Private	Dealer
4 Dr CX AWD SUV	14136	15236	17068
4 Dr CX SUV	12775	13768	15424
4 Dr CXL AWD SUV	16435	17713	19843

Options	Price
16 Inch Wheels [Opt on CX]	+121
AM/FM/Cassette/CD Audio System [Opt on CX]	+169
AM/FM/CD Changer Audio System	+191
Captain Chairs (4)	+121
Heads-Up Display [Opt on CX]	+133
Leather Seats [Opt on CX]	+317
OnStar Telematic System [Opt on CX]	+206

Options	Price
Park Distance Control (Rear)	+143
Power Driver Seat [Opt on CX]	+145
Power Passenger Seat [Opt on CX]	+145
Power Sunroof	+336
Third Seat	+169
Traction Control System [Opt on CX]	+121

Mileage Category: L

The Rendezvous is one of a new breed of crossover vehicles that combines the look and utility of an SUV with the comfort of a touring car.

Buick
Riviera

1999

Body Styles	TMV Pricing		
	Trade	Private	Dealer
2 Dr S/C Cpe	7560	8989	10477

Options	Price
Chrome Wheels	+174
OnStar Telematic System	+250
Power Moonroof	+275

Mileage Category: H

Traction control is now standard on the Riviera and this year brings the choice of four new paint colors (Sterling Silver, Titanium Blue, Gold Firemist and Dark Bronze Mist). Buick decided to pull the plug on the big coupe so only approximately 2,000 Rivieras were built for the 1999 model year, along with a limited run of 200 special-edition models dubbed "Silver Arrow."

1998

Body Styles	TMV Pricing		
	Trade	Private	Dealer
2 Dr S/C Cpe	6062	7444	9002

Options	Price
Chrome Wheels	+154
OnStar Telematic System	+220
Power Moonroof	+220

Mileage Category: H

Supercharged power is now standard, OnStar satellite communications system is a new option and depowered airbags debut. Four exterior colors are new, suspension and steering have been massaged and a heated passenger seat with lumbar support has been added to the options list.

1997

Body Styles	TMV Pricing		
	Trade	Private	Dealer
2 Dr S/C Cpe	4696	5953	7489
2 Dr STD Cpe	4377	5548	6980

Options	Price
Chrome Wheels	+128
Leather Seats	+138
Power Moonroof	+202

Mileage Category: H

Upgraded transmissions, several new colors inside and out, additional standard equipment and new options summarize minimal changes to the Riviera.

Buick

Riviera/Roadmaster

1996

Mileage Category: H

Series II supercharged engine gives top-of-the-line Riv 240 horsepower. There are new colors inside and out, real wood on the dash and revised climate and radio controls. Chrome wheels are optional.

Body Styles	TMV Pricing		
	Trade	Private	Dealer
2 Dr S/C Cpe	3506	4530	5945
2 Dr STD Cpe	3398	4391	5763

Options	Price
Power Moonroof	+158

1995

Mileage Category: H

All-new debuts. Rivera dual airbags and ABS are standard. Base engine is 3800 Series II V6; optional is a supercharged 3.8-liter. Traction control is optional.

Body Styles	TMV Pricing		
	Trade	Private	Dealer
2 Dr S/C Cpe	2685	3602	5131
2 Dr STD Cpe	2535	3401	4843

Options	Price
Leather Seats	+92
Power Moonroof	+131

Buick

Roadmaster

1996

Body Styles	TMV Pricing		
	Trade	Private	Dealer
4 Dr Estate Wgn	4014	5191	6817
4 Dr Limited Sdn	3976	5142	6753
4 Dr STD Sdn	3469	4486	5891

Options	Price
Leather Seats	+123

Mileage Category: G

Last year for 260-horsepower land yacht. All models are designated Collector's Editions.

1995

Mileage Category: G

New radios and larger rearview mirrors are added. Cassette player is made standard. Wagon gets standard alloy wheels. New options are heated front seats and memory feature for power driver seat.

Body Styles	TMV Pricing		
	Trade	Private	Dealer
4 Dr Estate Wgn	2939	3883	5457
4 Dr Limited Sdn	2990	3951	5552
4 Dr STD Sdn	2746	3628	5099

Options	Price
Leather Seats	+102

1994

Mileage Category: G

Detuned Corvette engine transplanted into big Buick, giving Roadmaster 80 additional horsepower. Dual airbags housed in redesigned dashboard with new gauges.

Body Styles	TMV Pricing		
	Trade	Private	Dealer
4 Dr Estate Wgn	1989	2745	4004
4 Dr Limited Sdn	2223	3066	4472
4 Dr STD Sdn	1824	2516	3670

Options	Price
Leather Seats	+84

1998

Body Styles	TMV Pricing		
	Trade	Private	Dealer
4 Dr Custom Sdn	2368	3180	4095

Mileage Category: C

Skylark was sold strictly to fleets for 1998. If you're buying one used, chances are good that it was once a rental car.

1997

Body Styles	TMV Pricing		
	Trade	Private	Dealer
2 Dr Custom Cpe	1671	2395	3279
2 Dr Gran Sport Cpe	2095	3003	4112
4 Dr Custom Sdn	1701	2438	3339
4 Dr Gran Sport Sdn	2005	2874	3935

Mileage Category: C

Skylark gets minimal revisions this year. The standard equipment list is expanded.

1996

Body Styles	TMV Pricing		
	Trade	Private	Dealer
2 Dr Custom Cpe	1211	1822	2665
4 Dr Custom Sdn	1185	1782	2606
4 Dr Olympic Gold Sdn	1266	1904	2786

Mileage Category: C

Styling changes inside and out this year. Dual airbags are new, as are three-point seatbelts mounted to the B-pillar. A new twin-cam engine replaces the 2.3-liter Quad 4, and automatic transmissions include traction control. Air conditioning, a rear window defroster and a tilt wheel are now standard. Long-life engine components round out the long list of improvements.

1995

Body Styles	TMV Pricing		
	Trade	Private	Dealer
2 Dr Custom Cpe	925	1395	2179
2 Dr Gran Sport Cpe	1111	1675	2616
4 Dr Custom Sdn	928	1400	2186
4 Dr Gran Sport Sdn	1111	1675	2616

Options	Price
Power Moonroof	+78

Mileage Category: C

Rear suspension is revised. New base engine is 150-horsepower Quad 4. GS gets 3.1-liter V6 standard. Power sunroof is a new option.

1994

Body Styles	TMV Pricing		
	Trade	Private	Dealer
2 Dr Custom Cpe	783	1265	2067
2 Dr Gran Sport Cpe	930	1502	2456
4 Dr Custom Sdn	733	1184	1936

Body Styles	TMV Pricing		
	Trade	Private	Dealer
4 Dr Gran Sport Sdn	904	1461	2390
4 Dr Limited Sdn	831	1343	2195

Mileage Category: C

Driver airbag added to all models. New 3.1-liter V6 replaces 3.3-liter V6 from 1993. Automatic transmission gets overdrive gear. Gran Sport and Limited gain standard equipment including air conditioning, power windows, cruise control and tilt steering wheel. Automatic door locks unlock when car is put in "Park."

Cadillac
Catera

2001

Body Styles		TMV Pricing	
	Trade	Private	Dealer
4 Dr STD Sdn	10667	12134	13489

Options	Price	Options	Price
Bose Audio System	+436	Power Rear Window Sunshade	+132
Chrome Wheels	+356	Power Sunroof	+445
Heated Front Seats	+190		

Mileage Category: H

OnStar 2.6 in-vehicle safety, security and information service, vented rear disc brakes and the Solar Protect windshield are now standard on all models. The Catera Sport receives new seats, and projector beam headlamps are now standard on the base Catera.

2000
Mileage Category: H

Mildly successful front and rear styling enhancements and a revised interior update Catera for 2000. Side airbags are standard on all models, and an optional sport package finally arrives with 17-inch wheels, heated sport seats, a spoiler, rocker panel extensions, xenon HID headlights and brushed-aluminum interior trim. Electronic drive-by-wire throttle control and a revised torque converter improve oomph off the line. Revised suspension tuning better controls ride motions and body roll, while tightened steering improves road feel. Two new colors round out the changes.

Body Styles		TMV Pricing	
	Trade	Private	Dealer
4 Dr STD Sdn	9089	10566	12013
4 Dr Sport Sdn	9185	10677	12140

Options	Price	Options	Price
Power Rear Window Sunshade	+115	Heated Front and Rear Seats	+136
AM/FM/Cassette/CD Audio System	+136	Heated Front Seats [Opt on STD]	+165
Bose Audio System	+170	OnStar Telematic System	+348
Chrome Wheels	+309	Power Moonroof	+386
Compact Disc Changer	+175		

1999
Mileage Category: H

Catera's "black chrome" grille will be darkened this year, while new electronics and emissions systems make the '99 Catera the first Cadillac to meet the federal Low Emissions Vehicle (LEV) standards. There's also a redesigned fuel cap and tether with an instrument cluster light to indicate a loose fuel cap. Up to four remote entry key fobs can now be programmed for separate memory settings, all with enhanced automatic door lock/unlock functions. Cadillac is rumored to be working on a special Sport Edition planned for later in the model year.

Body Styles		TMV Pricing	
	Trade	Private	Dealer
4 Dr STD Sdn	6563	7885	9261

Options	Price	Options	Price
Chrome Wheels	+224	OnStar Telematic System	+279
Compact Disc Changer	+126	Power Moonroof	+279

1998
Mileage Category: H

New radios are available across the board, and a new option is a power rear sunshade. Second-generation airbags arrived during the middle of the model year.

Body Styles		TMV Pricing	
	Trade	Private	Dealer
4 Dr STD Sdn	4710	5892	7224

Options	Price	Options	Price
Chrome Wheels	+181	OnStar Telematic System	+226
Delco/Bose Audio System	+171	Power Moonroof	+226
Leather Seats	+341		

1997
Mileage Category: H

Cadillac leaps into the near luxury segment of the market with a stylish German-engineered sedan that features a 200-horsepower V6, an impressive load of standard equipment and proper rear-wheel drive.

Body Styles		TMV Pricing	
	Trade	Private	Dealer
4 Dr STD Sdn	3536	4505	5690

Options	Price
Chrome Wheels	+154
Leather Seats	+290
Power Moonroof	+193

Cadillac
CTS
2003

Body Styles	TMV Pricing		
	Trade	Private	Dealer
4 Dr STD Sdn	20033	21355	23559

Options	Price	Options	Price
Automatic Load Leveling	+165	Special Factory Paint	+494
Automatic Stability Control	+326	Split Folding Rear Seat	+297
Bose Audio System	+445	Sport Suspension	+132
Compact Disc Changer	+396	AM/FM/Cassette/CD Changer Audio System	+379
Heated Front Seats	+264	AM/FM/CD Changer Audio System	+396
Navigation System	+939	17 Inch Wheels	+363
Power Moonroof	+791	Power Driver Seat w/Memory	+148
Power Passenger Seat	+165		

Mileage Category: I

A replacement for the aging Catera sedan, the all-new CTS shares few parts with its German-built predecessor.

Cadillac
DeVille
2003

Body Styles	TMV Pricing		
	Trade	Private	Dealer
4 Dr DHS Sdn	28731	30140	32489
4 Dr DTS Sdn	29152	30582	32965
4 Dr STD Sdn	24702	25914	27933

Options	Price	Options	Price
Adaptive Seat Package [Opt on DHS,DTS]	+656	Special Factory Paint	+656
Automatic Stability Control [Opt on DHS,STD]	+231	17 Inch Wheels - Chrome [Opt on STD]	+524
Compact Disc Changer	+392	Night Vision [Opt on DHS,DTS]	+1483
Heated Front and Rear Seats [Opt on DTS]	+231	Satellite Radio System	+214
Navigation System	+1315	Power Tilt and Telescopic Steering Wheel [Opt on DTS]	+231
Power Moonroof	+1022		
Rear Side Airbag Restraints	+194	Park Distance Control (Rear) [Opt on DHS,STD]	+194

Mileage Category: I

In an effort to improve its DeVille, Cadillac has made a few changes for 2003. On all models, the side-view mirrors are now fully equipped with turn-signal indicators, and all models also have revised taillamps. A tire-pressure monitoring system is also new. On the inside, base DeVilles can now get the navigation system as an option, and all models can be had with the XM Satellite Radio feature.

2002

Mileage Category: I

Body Styles	TMV Pricing		
	Trade	Private	Dealer
4 Dr DHS Sdn	23625	25085	27519
4 Dr DTS Sdn	24334	25838	28344
4 Dr STD Sdn	21333	22651	24849

Options	Price	Options	Price
17 Inch Wheels - Chrome	+447	Park Distance Control (Rear)	+166
Adaptive Seat Package	+559	Power Driver Seat w/Memory [Opt on DTS]	+118
Automatic Stability Control [Opt on DHS]	+197	Power Sunroof	+871
Chrome Wheels [Opt on STD]	+447	Power Tilt and Telescopic Steering Wheel [Opt on DTS]	+197
Compact Disc Changer	+334	Rear Side Airbag Restraints	+166
Heated Front and Rear Seats [Opt on STD]	+197	Satellite Radio System	+166
Navigation System	+1121	Special Factory Paint	+365
Night Vision	+1264		

For 2002, the DeVille gets a host of minor refinements, many of which won't be available until later in the year. New shocks and strut valving have been added to shore up the ride quality, leather seating is standard on all models and an optional advanced navigation system with voice-recognition capabilities is offered. A Bose 4.0 sound system can now be ordered, while digital satellite radio provisions will be available later in the year. Dual-stage airbag inflators, an increased oil change interval and a new wreath and crest Cadillac badge round out the rest of this year's changes.

Cadillac
DeVille

2001

Mileage Category: I

After a complete redesign last year, changes for 2001 are minimal at best. A tire pressure monitoring system is available, Graphite replaces Parisian Blue and Polo Green paint schemes, Dark Gray is added as an interior color and all Devilles are now certified throughout the U.S. as low-emissions vehicles.

Body Styles	TMV Pricing		
	Trade	Private	Dealer
4 Dr DHS Sdn	20462	22529	24438
4 Dr DTS Sdn	20061	22088	23960
4 Dr STD Sdn	17808	19607	21268

Options	Price	Options	Price
17 Inch Wheels - Chrome [Opt on DTS]	+356	Navigation System	+893
Adaptive Seat Package [Opt on DHS,DTS]	+445	Night Vision	+1007
Automatic Stability Control [Std on DTS]	+222	Park Distance Control (Rear)	+132
Bose Audio System [Opt on DHS,DTS]	+546	Power Sunroof	+694
Chrome Wheels	+356	Power Tilt and Telescopic Steering Wheel [Opt on DTS]	+157
Compact Disc Changer	+266		
Heated Front and Rear Seats [Std on DHS]	+157	Rear Side Airbag Restraints	+132
Leather Seats [Opt on STD]	+351	Special Factory Paint	+291

2000

Mileage Category: I

The 2000 DeVille is all new inside and out and showcases new automotive technologies such as Night Vision, Ultrasonic Rear Parking Assist and the newest generation of GM's StabiliTrak traction-control system. It also boasts improvements to the Northstar V8 that not only improve fuel economy, but make this engine operate even smoother than before.

Body Styles	TMV Pricing		
	Trade	Private	Dealer
4 Dr DHS Sdn	16191	17988	19749
4 Dr DTS Sdn	16608	18452	20259
4 Dr STD Sdn	15093	16768	18410

Options	Price	Options	Price
Chrome Wheels [Opt on DHS,STD]	+309	Power Moonroof	+602
Compact Disc Changer	+214	Power Tilt and Telescopic Steering Wheel [Opt on DTS]	+136
Heated Front and Rear Seats [Opt on DHS,STD]	+136		
Leather Seats [Opt on STD]	+305	Rear Side Airbag Restraints	+115
Navigation System [Opt on DHS,DTS]	+775	Special Factory Paint	+252
Night Vision [Opt on DHS,DTS]	+775	Adaptive Seat Package [Opt on DHS,DTS]	+386
OnStar Telematic System	+348	AM/FM/Cassette/CD Audio System [Opt on STD]	+117
Park Distance Control (Rear)	+117	Automatic Stability Control [Opt on DHS,STD]	+186

1999

Body Styles	TMV Pricing		
	Trade	Private	Dealer
4 Dr Concours Sdn	10569	11896	13278
4 Dr D'elegance Sdn	10497	11815	13188
4 Dr STD Sdn	10432	11742	13106

Options	Price	Options	Price
Leather Seats [Opt on STD]	+220	Compact Disc Changer	+155
OnStar Telematic System	+279	AM/FM/Cassette/CD Audio System [Opt on STD]	+140
Power Moonroof	+436	Automatic Stability Control [Opt on Concours,D'elegance]	+155
Special Factory Paint	+183	Chrome Wheels [Std on D'elegance]	+224

Mileage Category: I

Comfort is big with Cadillac, so who else would offer massaging lumbar seats? Sure enough, this industry-first option is available on '99 d'Elegance and Concours models. All DeVilles get an electrochromic inside rearview mirror with compass added to the standard equipment list, in addition to an audible theft-deterrent system. There are three new exterior colors this year, and one different shade of leather inside. As if that weren't enough, side airbag deployment now communicates with the optional OnStar communications system, so the outside world will know when you've taken a broadside hit. Comforting, indeed. Look for a limited run of about 2,000 specially badged and optioned Golden Anniversary Edition DeVilles, painted White Diamond with gold trim, to celebrate the model's 50th anniversary.

DeVille

1998

Body Styles	TMV Pricing		
	Trade	Private	Dealer
4 Dr Concours Sdn	8070	9644	11418
4 Dr D'elegance Sdn	8001	9561	11320
4 Dr STD Sdn	7612	9096	10769

Options	Price
Chrome Wheels [Opt on Concours,STD]	+181
Compact Disc Changer	+125
Leather Seats [Opt on STD]	+178

Options	Price
OnStar Telematic System	+226
Power Moonroof	+352

Mileage Category: I

StabiliTrak, an integrated chassis control system that can prevent four-wheel lateral skids, is available on base and d'Elegance. New radio systems debut, and door lock programmability is enhanced. An idiot light is added to warn about loose fuel caps, and new colors are available inside and out. Heated seats are added to the d'Elegance and Concours while the Concours also gets a much needed alloy wheel redesign. Second-generation airbags debut as standard equipment.

1997

Body Styles	TMV Pricing		
	Trade	Private	Dealer
4 Dr Concours Sdn	6550	7927	9611
4 Dr D'elegance Sdn	6460	7819	9480
4 Dr STD Sdn	5904	7146	8664

Options	Price
Chrome Wheels	+154
Compact Disc Changer	+128
Leather Seats [Opt on STD]	+152

Options	Price
OnStar Telematic System	+192
Power Moonroof	+300

Mileage Category: I

DeVille undergoes a substantial revamp for 1997, including revised styling, the addition of standard side-impact airbags and a fresh interior that is actually functional. Concours receives stability enhancement and road texture detection as part of its Integrated Chassis Control System (ICCS), while a new d'Elegance model picks up where the defunct Fleetwood left off. Finally, the OnStar Services package provides DeVille owners with security and convenience features that will pinpoint the car's location at any given time or allow you to book a flight to Paris from the comfort of your driver seat.

1996

Body Styles	TMV Pricing		
	Trade	Private	Dealer
4 Dr Concours Sdn	5203	6376	7995
4 Dr STD Sdn	4450	5453	6838

Options	Price
Chrome Wheels	+130
Leather Seats [Opt on STD]	+128

Options	Price
OnStar Telematic System	+162
Power Moonroof	+253

Mileage Category: I

Northstar V8 is installed in base DeVille, along with a new transmission, Integrated Chassis Control System and Road Sensing Suspension. Concours gets 25 horsepower boost to 300, along with a higher final-drive ratio for quicker pickup and an improved continuously variable Road Sensing Suspension. Automatic windshield wipers and new variable-effort steering are standard on the Concours. Daytime running lights debut on both of these monsters.

1995

Body Styles	TMV Pricing		
	Trade	Private	Dealer
4 Dr Concours Sdn	3510	4367	5795
4 Dr STD Sdn	3116	3877	5145

Options	Price
Chrome Wheels	+101
Leather Seats [Opt on STD]	+100
Power Moonroof	+197

Mileage Category: I

Traction control (which can be shut off) is standard on base DeVille. Headlights come on automatically when windshield wipers are activated. Chrome wheels can be ordered on Concours. Garage door opener is optional on DeVille; standard on Concours.

1994

Body Styles	TMV Pricing		
	Trade	Private	Dealer
4 Dr Concours Sdn	2634	3398	4670
4 Dr STD Sdn	2135	2754	3786

Options	Price
Chrome Wheels	+84
Leather Seats [Opt on STD]	+83
Power Sunroof	+122

Mileage Category: I

Redesigned with dual airbags, height-adjustable seatbelts, and side-impact protection meeting 1997 standards. Base and Concours models available, with Concours replacing Touring Sedan. Concours comes with Northstar V8 and road-sensing suspension. Coupe DeVille and Sixty Special are retired. Base DeVille powered by 1993's 4.9-liter V8. Remote keyless entry is standard.

Cadillac
Eldorado

2002

Mileage Category: I

A special Collectors' Series package marks the final 1,600 coupes to come off the assembly line as the Eldorado heads for retirement.

Body Styles	TMV Pricing		
	Trade	Private	Dealer
2 Dr ESC Cpe	21716	22961	25037
2 Dr ETC Collectors Series Cpe	25489	26951	29388
2 Dr ETC Cpe	23090	24415	26622

Options	Price	Options	Price
AM/FM/Cassette/CD Audio System [Opt on ESC]	+225	Compact Disc Changer	+281
Automatic Stability Control [Opt on ESC]	+197	Power Driver Seat w/Memory [Opt on ESC]	+121
Bose Audio System [Opt on ESC]	+449	Power Sunroof	+871
Chrome Wheels	+447	Special Factory Paint	+365

2001

Mileage Category: I

Only three minor changes grace the Eldorado for 2001: Sequoia is added for an exterior color, Dark Gray is added for the interior and the Bose sound system with mini-disc player goes away.

Body Styles	TMV Pricing		
	Trade	Private	Dealer
2 Dr ESC Cpe	17246	18989	20598
2 Dr ETC Cpe	19392	21351	23160

Options	Price	Options	Price
Automatic Stability Control [Opt on ESC]	+222	Compact Disc Changer	+266
Bose Audio System [Opt on ESC]	+546	Power Sunroof	+694
Chrome Wheels	+356	Special Factory Paint	+291

2000

Mileage Category: I

The Northstar V8s have been improved, and the standard Eldorado gets a new logo, ESC (for Eldorado Sport Coupe). The racy Eldorado Touring Coupe (ETC) lands exterior enhancements such as body-color fascia moldings and side inserts (replacing chrome), new seven-spoke wheels with Cadillac logos in the center caps and a new ETC deck lid logo.

Body Styles	TMV Pricing		
	Trade	Private	Dealer
2 Dr ESC Cpe	14489	16097	17673
2 Dr ETC Cpe	15669	17408	19112

Options	Price	Options	Price
AM/FM/Cassette/CD Audio System [Opt on ESC]	+117	Compact Disc Changer	+214
Automatic Stability Control [Opt on ESC]	+192	OnStar Telematic System	+348
Bose Audio System [Opt on ESC]	+233	Power Moonroof	+602
Chrome Wheels	+309	Special Factory Paint	+194

1999

Mileage Category: I

Colors are big each year with Cadillac, and 1999 is no different. Cashmere, Parisian Blue and Sterling Silver replace Frost Beige, Baltic Blue Silver Mist and Shale on Eldorado's exterior color chart. Oatmeal leather replaces Cappuccino Cream as an interior color, while Pewter cloth has been deleted, leaving only Shale and Blue cloth available. In the hardware department, an electrochromic inside rearview mirror with compass and an audible theft-deterrent system are now standard equipment. The Eldorado Touring Coupe (ETC) also gets the Bose four-speaker AM/FM cassette/single-slot CD and Weather Band audio system standard, with the option of adding massaging lumbar seats that provide a gentle back rub as you drive.

Body Styles	TMV Pricing		
	Trade	Private	Dealer
2 Dr STD Cpe	11306	12831	14418
2 Dr Touring Cpe	12540	14231	15992

Options	Price	Options	Price
Automatic Stability Control [Opt on STD]	+155	Leather Seats [Opt on STD]	+220
Chrome Wheels	+224	OnStar Telematic System	+279
Compact Disc Changer	+155	Power Moonroof	+436
Delco/Bose Audio System [Opt on STD]	+342	Special Factory Paint	+140

1998

Mileage Category: I

New radios, a revised interior electrochromic mirror, enhanced programmable features, second-generation airbags and the addition of StabiliTrak to the base model's options list are the major improvements for 1998.

Body Styles	TMV Pricing		
	Trade	Private	Dealer
2 Dr STD Cpe	9356	10818	12466
2 Dr Touring Cpe	10656	12321	14198

Options	Price	Options	Price
Chrome Wheels	+181	Leather Seats [Opt on STD]	+178
Compact Disc Changer	+125	OnStar Telematic System	+226
Delco/Bose Audio System [Opt on STD]	+277	Power Moonroof	+352

1997

Body Styles	TMV Pricing		
	Trade	Private	Dealer
2 Dr STD Cpe	7612	8971	10631
2 Dr Touring Cpe	8390	9888	11718

Options	Price	Options	Price
Chrome Wheels	+154	OnStar Telematic System	+192
Delco/Bose Audio System	+236	Power Moonroof	+300
Leather Seats [Opt on STD]	+152		

Mileage Category: I

Structural, suspension and brake system enhancements are made across the board. Base models get MagnaSteer variable effort steering, while the Eldorado Touring Coupe (ETC) receives a new Integrated Chassis Control System (ICCS) that includes stability enhancement and road texture detection. All Eldos have slightly revised stereo and climate controls, and the OnStar services package is a slick new option that can notify emergency personnel where your disabled car is located or can allow you to book dinner reservations from the driver seat.

1996

Body Styles	TMV Pricing		
	Trade	Private	Dealer
2 Dr STD Cpe	5459	6772	8585
2 Dr Touring Cpe	5988	7429	9418

Options	Price	Options	Price
Chrome Wheels	+130	Leather Seats [Opt on STD]	+128
Compact Disc Changer	+126	OnStar Telematic System	+162
Delco/Bose Audio System	+131	Power Moonroof	+253

Mileage Category: I

Sea Mist Green is a new interior and exterior color, and daytime running lights are standard. Eldorado gets new seats and revised audio systems. Touring Coupe interior is revised, with a center-stack console, bigger gauges, and seamless passenger airbag. Rainsense, an automatic windshield wiper system, is standard on the ETC, as is an updated continuously variable Road Sensing Suspension.

1995

Body Styles	TMV Pricing		
	Trade	Private	Dealer
2 Dr STD Cpe	3851	4847	6508
2 Dr Touring Cpe	4189	5272	7078

Options	Price	Options	Price
Leather Seats [Opt on STD]	+100	Delco/Bose Audio System	+92
Power Moonroof	+197	Chrome Wheels	+101

Mileage Category: I

Northstar V8 power is increased. Electronic chassis controls now evaluate steering angle when deciding what to do with the Road Sensing Suspension, traction control and ABS. Styling is slightly revised front and rear. Headlights come on automatically when windshield wipers are activated.

1994

Body Styles	TMV Pricing		
	Trade	Private	Dealer
2 Dr STD Cpe	3076	4017	5584
2 Dr Touring Cpe	3313	4326	6014

Options	Price
Chrome Wheels	+84
Leather Seats [Opt on STD]	+83
Power Sunroof	+122

Mileage Category: I

Base model gets Northstar V8, Road Sensing Suspension and traction control. Remote keyless entry and automatic door locks are made standard.

2003

Body Styles	TMV Pricing		
	Trade	Private	Dealer
4 Dr STD AWD SUV	39545	41878	45765
4 Dr STD SUV	36777	38946	42561

Options	Price	Options	Price
Camper/Towing Package	+125	Special Factory Paint	+656
Chrome Wheels	+524	Satellite Radio System	+214
Navigation System	+1022	DVD Entertainment System	+854
Power Moonroof	+1022		

Cadillac
Escalade/Escalade ESV

2003 (cont'd)

Mileage Category: O

Despite brisk sales of the Escalade in 2002, there are numerous upgrades for 2003 to keep the luxury sport-ute at the top of its game. An improved StabiliTrak stability control system is now standard on both two- and all-wheel-drive models, while all Escalades get an improved braking system, High Intensity Discharge (HID) headlights, exterior mirrors with integrated turn signals and chrome wheels as an option. The interior has also been updated with new features like tri-zone climate control, satellite steering wheel controls and a redesigned instrument cluster and center console. The standard Bose audio system received some minor upgrades while new options include XM Satellite Radio, a DVD entertainment system and second-row captain's chairs. Added safety comes in the way of dual-stage airbags, adjustable pedals, a front-passenger seat sensor and three-point belts for all first- and second-row passengers.

2002

Mileage Category: O

No longer a mere Yukon Denali spin-off, the radiant new Escalade bursts onto the luxury SUV scene and attempts to maul its competitors with a monstrous 6.0-liter engine and enough technology to satisfy the target demographic.

Body Styles	TMV Pricing		
	Trade	Private	Dealer
4 Dr STD AWD SUV	34478	36779	40615
4 Dr STD SUV	31929	34060	37611

Options	Price
Power Moonroof	+871
Special Factory Paint	+559

2000

Body Styles	TMV Pricing		
	Trade	Private	Dealer
4 Dr STD 4WD SUV	19094	21451	23761

Mileage Category: O

The big change for 2000 is the availability of vertical-split rear cargo doors in addition to the standard split-tailgate rear-hatch design.

1999

Mileage Category: O

The new Cadillac Escalade is really more a 1999 GMC Yukon Denali than it is a Cadillac. (And GMC's Yukon Denali is really more Yukon than anything else -- except, perhaps, a Chevrolet Tahoe, but that's another story). Regardless of its origins, think of the Escalade as a big four-wheel-drive Cadillac limo for well-heeled outdoorsy types. Loaded with luxury touches and every possible convenience (even GM's OnStar mobile communications system), Escalade comes in four special colors and lacks only one thing: an options list. Why? It's got it all.

Body Styles	TMV Pricing		
	Trade	Private	Dealer
4 Dr STD 4WD SUV	16330	18438	20633

Options	Price
OnStar Telematic System	+279

Cadillac
Escalade ESV

2003

Body Styles	TMV Pricing		
	Trade	Private	Dealer
4 Dr STD AWD SUV	44026	46171	49747

Options	Price	Options	Price
Camper/Towing Package	+125	Special Factory Paint	+656
Chrome Wheels	+524	Satellite Radio System	+214
Navigation System	+1022	DVD Entertainment System	+854
Power Moonroof	+1022		

Mileage Category: O

The ESV is an all-new model in the Cadillac lineup. Essentially nothing more than a slightly stretched version of the standard Escalade, the ESV incorporates all of the improvements made to the standard Escalade for 2003.

Cadillac
Escalade EXT
2003

Body Styles	TMV Pricing		
	Trade	Private	Dealer
4 Dr STD AWD Crew Cab SB	37668	39851	43488

Options	Price	Options	Price
Camper/Towing Package	+125	Special Factory Paint	+656
Chrome Wheels	+524	Satellite Radio System	+214
Navigation System	+1022	DVD Entertainment System	+854
Power Moonroof	+1022		

Mileage Category: O

Despite strong sales in 2002, the EXT gets a host of new upgrades for 2003 to help maintain its momentum. An improved StabiliTrak stability control system is now standard along with an upgraded braking system, High Intensity Discharge (HID) headlights, exterior mirrors with integrated turn signals and chrome wheels as an option. The interior also has a number of improvements, including tri-zone climate control, satellite steering wheel controls and a redesigned instrument cluster and center console. The standard Bose audio system receives some minor upgrades while new options include XM Satellite Radio, a DVD entertainment system and bucket seats for the second row. Added safety comes in the way of dual-stage airbags, adjustable pedals, a front-passenger seat sensor and three-point belts for all first- and second-row passengers.

2002

Body Styles	TMV Pricing		
	Trade	Private	Dealer
4 Dr STD AWD Crew Cab SB	32305	34461	38055

Options	Price
Power Moonroof	+871
Special Factory Paint	+559

Mileage Category: O

In response to Lincoln's new Blackwood pickup, which is little more than a Ford F-150 Super Crew with a Navigator cabin grafted on, Cadillac trots out this Chevrolet Avalanche with an Escalade facelift.

Cadillac
Fleetwood
1996

Body Styles	TMV Pricing		
	Trade	Private	Dealer
4 Dr STD Sdn	5529	6679	8267

Options	Price
Chrome Wheels	+195
Leather Seats	+128
Power Moonroof	+253

Mileage Category: I

Final year for the longest production car sold in the U.S. Updates are limited to a new audio system, revised center storage armrest and prewiring for Cadillac's Dual Mode cellular phone.

1995

Mileage Category: I

Traction control gets on/off switch. Platinum-tipped spark plugs are added, allowing tune-ups to occur every 100,000 miles. Antilockout feature added. Remote keyless entry, central unlocking and fold-away outside mirrors are added. Garage door opener is new option.

Body Styles	TMV Pricing		
	Trade	Private	Dealer
4 Dr STD Sdn	3939	4901	6504

Options	Price	Options	Price
Power Moonroof	+197	Chrome Wheels	+152
Leather Seats	+100		

Cadillac
Fleetwood/Seville

1994
Mileage Category: I

Detuned Corvette 5.7-liter engine makes its way under Fleetwood's gargantuan hood. Performance is much improved. New transmission comes with new engine. Brougham package includes padded vinyl roof and alloy wheels. Flash-to-pass is a new feature, and a battery saver is installed.

Body Styles	TMV Pricing		
	Trade	Private	Dealer
4 Dr STD Sdn	2843	3667	5041

Options	Price
Chrome Wheels	+126
Leather Seats	+83

Options	Price
Power Sunroof	+122

Cadillac
Seville

2003

Mileage Category: I

The STS now sports standard 17-inch chrome wheels while all Sevilles can now couple XM Satellite Radio with the DVD navigation system. The SLS also gets a new body-colored grille and foglamps for a monochromatic look.

Body Styles	TMV Pricing		
	Trade	Private	Dealer
4 Dr SLS Sdn	23417	24870	27291
4 Dr STS Sdn	30501	32394	35548

Options	Price
Chrome Wheels [Opt on SLS]	+524
Compact Disc Changer	+363
Navigation System	+1187
Power Moonroof	+1022

Options	Price
Special Factory Paint	+656
Satellite Radio System	+214
Power Driver Seat w/Memory [Opt on SLS]	+142
Power Tilt and Telescopic Steering Wheel [Opt on SLS]	+231

2002
Mileage Category: I

An advanced navigation system with voice recognition and the Bose 4.0 sound system is new for 2002. Cadillac's restyled wreath and crest ornamentation is also added along with oil change intervals that have been increased from 10,000 to 12,500 miles. Later in the year, Seville gets two new colors, as well as provisions for Digital Satellite radio and a cellular integration package.

Body Styles	TMV Pricing		
	Trade	Private	Dealer
4 Dr SLS Sdn	20037	21605	24218
4 Dr STS Sdn	23273	25094	28128

Options	Price
17 Inch Wheels - Chrome	+449
AM/FM/Cassette/CD Changer Audio System	+225
Chrome Wheels	+447
Compact Disc Changer	+309
Navigation System	+1011

Options	Price
Power Driver Seat w/Memory [Opt on SLS]	+121
Power Sunroof	+871
Power Tilt and Telescopic Steering Wheel [Opt on SLS]	+197
Satellite Radio System	+166
Special Factory Paint	+365

2001
Mileage Category: I

Tire-pressure monitoring is now available on the STS, as well as an e-mail-capable Infotainment radio, a hands-free integrated cellular phone, 17-inch chrome wheels and high-intensity discharge headlamps. OnStar in-vehicle safety, security and information service is now standard fare on the STS and available on the SLS. Two new SLS and three STS packages round out the changes.

Body Styles	TMV Pricing		
	Trade	Private	Dealer
4 Dr SLS Sdn	17481	19690	21730
4 Dr STS Sdn	19486	21949	24223

Options	Price
Adaptive Seat Package	+445
Bose Audio System [Opt on SLS]	+425
Chrome Wheels	+356
Compact Disc Changer	+246
Park Distance Control (Rear)	+132

Options	Price
Power Sunroof	+694
Power Tilt and Telescopic Steering Wheel [Opt on SLS]	+157
Premium Audio System	+425
Special Factory Paint	+291

2000

Body Styles	TMV Pricing		
	Trade	Private	Dealer
4 Dr SLS Sdn	15267	17422	19534
4 Dr STS Sdn	16684	19038	21346

Options	Price
Adaptive Seat Package	+466
Bose Audio System [Opt on SLS]	+369
Bose Mini Disc Player [Opt on SLS]	+486
Chrome Wheels	+309
Compact Disc Changer	+214
Navigation System	+775

Options	Price
OnStar Telematic System	+348
Park Distance Control (Rear)	+115
Power Moonroof	+602
Power Tilt and Telescopic Steering Wheel [Opt on SLS]	+136
Special Factory Paint	+252

Mileage Category: l

The Northstar V8s have been improved, and all models get a new airbag suppression system and the revised version of GM's StabiliTrak. A new ultrasonic rear parking assist feature and an advanced navigation system are optional on both STS and SLS. There are also two new exterior colors, Midnight Blue and Bronzemist.

1999

Body Styles	TMV Pricing		
	Trade	Private	Dealer
4 Dr SLS Sdn	12555	14700	16932
4 Dr STS Sdn	13126	15369	17703

Options	Price
Adaptive Seat Package	+338
Chrome Wheels	+224
Compact Disc Changer	+155
Delco/Bose Audio System [Opt on SLS]	+232

Options	Price
OnStar Telematic System	+279
Power Moonroof	+436
Special Factory Paint	+183

Mileage Category: l

The Seville sees only minor changes after its successful redesign in 1998. Cadillac's new massaging lumbar seats are offered as an option on the STS. Heated seats become part of the adaptive seat package, which is now available on both SLS and STS trim levels. And the optional OnStar mobile communications system will automatically notify the OnStar customer assistance center in the case of any airbag deployment, front or side, so that the center can dispatch emergency services to the scene. Previously, notification occurred only with a front airbag deployment. There are also three new exterior colors, Cashmere, Parisian Blue and Sterling Silver, and one new interior shade called Oatmeal.

1998

Body Styles	TMV Pricing		
	Trade	Private	Dealer
4 Dr SLS Sdn	8261	9872	11689
4 Dr STS Sdn	9305	11119	13165

Options	Price
Adaptive Seat Package [Opt on STS]	+273
Chrome Wheels	+181
Compact Disc Changer	+125

Options	Price
Delco/Bose Audio System [Opt on SLS]	+187
OnStar Telematic System	+226
Power Moonroof	+352

Mileage Category: It

Cadillac redefines the American luxury car by debuting an all-new Seville that boasts the performance, style, refinement and technological innovation necessary to play ball on a global level.

1997

Body Styles	TMV Pricing		
	Trade	Private	Dealer
4 Dr SLS Sdn	6617	8010	9712
4 Dr STS Sdn	7614	9216	11175

Options	Price
Chrome Wheels	+154
Delco/Bose Audio System	+160
Leather Seats [Opt on SLS]	+152

Options	Price
OnStar Telematic System	+192
Power Moonroof	+300

Mileage Category: l

All Sevilles receive body structure, suspension, brake system and interior enhancements. STS models get a new stability enhancement feature designed to correct lateral skids, and road texture detection, which helps modulate the ABS more effectively on rough roads. Enhanced programmable memory systems are new to both models, as is a revised rear seat back and the availability of OnStar, a vehicle information and communications service. SLS models get MagnaSteer variable-effort steering.

Cadillac
Seville

1996

Mileage Category: I

All Sevilles get new seats and seat trim, redesigned sound systems, an (optional) integrated voice-activated cellular phone, daytime running lights and programmable door lock functions and seating positions. The STS also receives an updated instrument panel with big gauges and a new center console, the Cadillac-exclusive Rainsense Wiper System (which detects rainfall and turns the wipers on automatically) and a newly improved continuously variable road-sensing suspension. Magnasteer variable-assist steering replaces the old speed-sensitive gear on last year's STS.

Body Styles	TMV Pricing		
	Trade	Private	Dealer
4 Dr SLS Sdn	5481	6716	8422
4 Dr STS Sdn	5874	7198	9026

Options	Price	Options	Price
Chrome Wheels	+130	OnStar Telematic System	+162
Delco/Bose Audio System	+122	Power Moonroof	+253
Leather Seats	+128		

1995

Mileage Category: I

Northstar V8 power is increased. Electronic chassis controls now evaluate steering angle when deciding what to do with the road-sensing suspension, traction control and ABS. Headlights come on automatically when windshield wipers are activated. Chrome wheels are a new option.

Body Styles	TMV Pricing		
	Trade	Private	Dealer
4 Dr SLS Sdn	3882	4831	6412
4 Dr STS Sdn	4103	5105	6775

Options	Price	Options	Price
Chrome Wheels	+101	Power Moonroof	+197
Leather Seats [Opt on SLS]	+100		

1994

Mileage Category: I

Base model now called SLS. SLS gets Northstar V8, traction control and road-sensing suspension. Remote keyless entry is standard this year.

Body Styles	TMV Pricing		
	Trade	Private	Dealer
4 Dr STD Sdn	2838	3768	5317
4 Dr STS Sdn	2873	3815	5384

Options	Price	Options	Price
Chrome Wheels	+84	Leather Seats [Opt on STD]	+83
Delco/Bose Audio System	+79	Power Sunroof	+122

2003

Body Styles	TMV Pricing		
	Trade	Private	Dealer
3 Dr LS AWD Pass Van Ext	12757	13810	15564
3 Dr LS Pass Van Ext	11891	12872	14507
3 Dr LT AWD Pass Van Ext	14132	15298	17241

Body Styles	TMV Pricing		
	Trade	Private	Dealer
3 Dr LT Pass Van Ext	13276	14371	16197
3 Dr STD AWD Pass Van Ext	11967	12954	14600
3 Dr STD Pass Van Ext	11061	11974	13495

Options	Price
AM/FM/CD Audio System [Opt on LS]	+260
Camper/Towing Package	+197
Leather Seats [Opt on LT]	+606
Locking Differential	+161

Options	Price
Power Driver Seat [Opt on LS]	+153
Running Boards [Opt on LS]	+255
Air Conditioning - Front and Rear [Opt on LS]	+334

Mileage Category: P

All 2003 Astros have larger 16-inch aluminum wheels and an improved braking system.

2002

Mileage Category: P

A multiport fuel-injection system has been added for smoother operation along with a revised catalytic converter for better emissions control. Synthetic gear oil is now standard in the rear axle for reduced wear during heavy towing.

Body Styles	TMV Pricing		
	Trade	Private	Dealer
3 Dr LS AWD Pass Van Ext	10577	11501	13041
3 Dr LS Pass Van Ext	9608	10447	11846

Body Styles	TMV Pricing		
	Trade	Private	Dealer
3 Dr LT AWD Pass Van Ext	11704	12726	14430
3 Dr LT Pass Van Ext	10981	11940	13539

Options	Price
Air Conditioning - Front and Rear [Std on LT]	+430
AM/FM/Cassette/CD Audio System [Std on LT]	+172
Camper/Towing Package	+177
Leather Seats	+545

Options	Price
Locking Differential	+145
Power Driver Seat [Std on LT]	+138
Running Boards	+229

2001

Mileage Category: P

Performance from Astro's Vortec 4300 V6 is enhanced, compliments of a new powertrain control module. Also new is a low-emission-vehicle (LEV) version. Color choices are expanded to include Light Pewter Metallic and Dark Carmine Red Metallic.

Body Styles			TMV Pricing		
			Trade	Private	Dealer
3 Dr LS AWD Pass Van Ext			8886	10332	11666
3 Dr LS Pass Van Ext			7586	8820	9959

Options	Price
Air Conditioning - Front and Rear	+274
Aluminum/Alloy Wheels	+191
AM/FM/Cassette/CD Audio System	+189
Leather Seats	+498

Options	Price
Locking Differential	+132
Power Driver Seat	+125
Running Boards	+210

2000

Mileage Category: P

Retained accessory power and additional warning chimes are added for 2000. Also new are automatic headlights with a flash-to-pass feature, remote keyless entry, battery rundown protection, lockout protection and a tow/haul trailering mode for the transmission. The ABS, engine and exhaust have been improved, and a plastic 27-gallon fuel tank is standard.

Body Styles	TMV Pricing		
	Trade	Private	Dealer
3 Dr LS AWD Pass Van Ext	7108	8387	9641
3 Dr LS Pass Van Ext	6399	7550	8678
3 Dr LT AWD Pass Van Ext	8120	9581	11013

Body Styles	TMV Pricing		
	Trade	Private	Dealer
3 Dr LT Pass Van Ext	7179	8470	9736
3 Dr STD AWD Pass Van Ext	7027	8291	9530
3 Dr STD Pass Van Ext	5784	6824	7844

Options	Price
Running Boards	+187
7 Passenger Seating	+281
Air Conditioning - Front and Rear [Opt on LS]	+245
AM/FM/Cassette/CD Audio System [Opt on LS]	+237
AM/FM/CD Audio System	+190

Options	Price
Camper/Towing Package	+145
Chrome Wheels [Std on LS]	+159
Leather Seats	+444
Limited Slip Differential	+118
Power Windows [Opt on STD]	+123

1999

Body Styles	TMV Pricing		
	Trade	Private	Dealer
3 Dr LS AWD Pass Van Ext	5726	6871	8063
3 Dr LS Pass Van Ext	4866	5838	6850
3 Dr LT AWD Pass Van Ext	6569	7882	9249

Body Styles	TMV Pricing		
	Trade	Private	Dealer
3 Dr LT Pass Van Ext	5827	6992	8204
3 Dr STD AWD Pass Van Ext	5298	6357	7460
3 Dr STD Pass Van Ext	4702	5642	6620

1999 (cont'd)

Mileage Category: P

A new all-wheel-drive active transfer case replaces the previous AWD system, and includes a new control module and service light. There are two new interior roof consoles: one with storage is optional on base model, another with trip computer is standard on LS and LT trim. A new LT stripe design comes in three new colors. Dealer-installed running boards are available, as are new optional aluminum wheels. Three exterior paint colors are added for '99, while depowered airbags finally arrive this year. Finally, the outside mirrors are redesigned, available heated and with or without electrochromatic glare reduction.

Options	Price
Running Boards	+149
7 Passenger Seating	+224
Air Conditioning - Front and Rear	+195
Aluminum/Alloy Wheels [Std on LT]	+136
AM/FM/Cassette/CD Audio System	+189

Options	Price
AM/FM/CD Audio System	+151
Camper/Towing Package	+115
Chrome Wheels [Std on LS]	+127
Leather Seats	+355

1998

Mileage Category: P

New colors, improved clearcoating, a standard theft-deterrent system and the addition of composite headlights and an uplevel grille to base models are all that's different on this year's Astro. Full-power airbags continue for 1998.

Body Styles	TMV Pricing		
	Trade	Private	Dealer
3 Dr LS AWD Pass Van Ext	4685	5768	6990
3 Dr LS Pass Van Ext	4163	5126	6212
3 Dr LT AWD Pass Van Ext	4903	6037	7315

Body Styles	TMV Pricing		
	Trade	Private	Dealer
3 Dr LT Pass Van Ext	4502	5544	6718
3 Dr STD AWD Pass Van Ext	4130	5085	6162
3 Dr STD Pass Van Ext	3432	4225	5120

Options	Price
7 Passenger Seating	+189
8 Passenger Seating [Opt on STD]	+125
Air Conditioning - Front and Rear	+165

Options	Price
AM/FM/Cassette/CD Audio System	+160
AM/FM/CD Audio System	+128
Leather Seats	+299

1997

Mileage Category: P

Daytime running lights debut, and LT models can be equipped with leather upholstery. Also optional this year is a HomeLink three-channel transmitter. Delayed entry-exit lighting is now standard on all Astro passenger vans. Transmission refinements mean smoother shifts, and electronic variable orifice steering eases steering effort at low speeds.

Body Styles	TMV Pricing		
	Trade	Private	Dealer
3 Dr LS AWD Pass Van Ext	3707	4688	5886
3 Dr LS Pass Van Ext	3373	4265	5356
3 Dr LT AWD Pass Van Ext	4118	5207	6539

Body Styles	TMV Pricing		
	Trade	Private	Dealer
3 Dr LT Pass Van Ext	3851	4870	6115
3 Dr STD AWD Pass Van Ext	3448	4360	5474
3 Dr STD Pass Van Ext	2962	3745	4703

Options	Price
AM/FM/Cassette/CD Audio System	+144
AM/FM/CD Audio System	+116
Leather Seats	+270

Options	Price
7 Passenger Seating	+171
Air Conditioning - Front and Rear	+149

1996

Mileage Category: P

A new interior with dual airbags, new radio systems, an improved V6 and three new paint colors are the changes for this year.

Body Styles	TMV Pricing		
	Trade	Private	Dealer
3 Dr LS AWD Pass Van Ext	3010	3893	5113
3 Dr LS Pass Van Ext	2644	3420	4492
3 Dr LT AWD Pass Van Ext	3331	4309	5659

Body Styles	TMV Pricing		
	Trade	Private	Dealer
3 Dr LT Pass Van Ext	3242	4193	5507
3 Dr STD AWD Pass Van Ext	2945	3809	5003
3 Dr STD Pass Van Ext	2355	3046	4001

Options	Price
7 Passenger Seating	+135
Air Conditioning - Front and Rear	+135
AM/FM/Cassette/CD Audio System	+131

1995

Mileage Category: P

Front sheet metal is restyled. Regular-length versions are dropped from the lineup, leaving only the extended-length model. Multileaf steel springs replace single-leaf plastic springs. One engine is available, the 190-horsepower, 4.3-liter V6. Air conditioning is standard, and remote keyless entry is a new option.

Body Styles	TMV Pricing		
	Trade	Private	Dealer
3 Dr CL AWD Pass Van Ext	2491	3285	4607
3 Dr CL Pass Van Ext	2127	2805	3935
3 Dr CS AWD Pass Van Ext	2225	2935	4117
3 Dr CS Pass Van Ext	1926	2540	3564

Body Styles	TMV Pricing		
	Trade	Private	Dealer
3 Dr LT AWD Pass Van Ext	2669	3520	4937
3 Dr LT Pass Van Ext	2491	3285	4609
3 Dr STD AWD Pass Van Ext	2204	2907	4078
3 Dr STD Pass Van Ext	1909	2517	3531

Options	Price
Air Conditioning - Front and Rear	+121
AM/FM/CD Audio System	+91

Options	Price
7 Passenger Seating	+121
8 Passenger Seating [Std on CL,LT]	+80

1994

Body Styles	TMV Pricing		
	Trade	Private	Dealer
3 Dr CL AWD Pass Van	1656	2332	3458
3 Dr CL AWD Pass Van Ext	1715	2414	3580
3 Dr CL Pass Van	1390	1957	2901
3 Dr CL Pass Van Ext	1418	1997	2961
3 Dr LT AWD Pass Van	1835	2583	3829
3 Dr LT AWD Pass Van Ext	1863	2623	3889

Body Styles	TMV Pricing		
	Trade	Private	Dealer
3 Dr LT Pass Van	1579	2223	3295
3 Dr LT Pass Van Ext	1597	2248	3334
3 Dr STD AWD Pass Van	1555	2189	3246
3 Dr STD AWD Pass Van Ext	1568	2207	3273
3 Dr STD Pass Van	1301	1832	2716
3 Dr STD Pass Van Ext	1331	1874	2778

Options	Price
AM/FM/CD Audio System	+81
7 Passenger Seating	+96

Options	Price
Air Conditioning	+163
Air Conditioning - Front and Rear	+107

Mileage Category: P

Driver airbag is made standard. Side-door guard beams are stronger, and air conditioners use CFC-free refrigerant. A high-mount center brake light is added. Analog gauges get new graphics, and carpet is treated with Scotchgard.

Chevrolet
Avalanche

2003

Body Styles	TMV Pricing		
	Trade	Private	Dealer
4 Dr 1500 4WD Crew Cab SB	23802	25317	27841
4 Dr 1500 Crew Cab SB	21254	22607	24861
4 Dr 1500 North Face Edition 4WD Crew Cab SB	27234	28967	31855

Body Styles	TMV Pricing		
	Trade	Private	Dealer
4 Dr 2500 4WD Crew Cab SB	25199	26803	29475
4 Dr 2500 Crew Cab SB	22982	24444	26882

Mileage Category: K

Options	Price
Bose Audio System [Std on North Face]	+249
Bucket Seats [Std on North Face]	+128
Camper/Towing Package	+121
Heated Front Seats	+128
Leather Seats [Std on North Face]	+447
Locking Differential [Std on North Face]	+188
Power Moonroof	+699
Power Passenger Seat	+163
Front Side Airbag Restraints	+192
Side Steps	+373
OnStar Telematic System	+444

Options	Price
Power Adjustable Foot Pedals	+160
AM/FM/CD Changer Audio System	+255
Z71 Off-Road Suspension Package [Opt on 1500 4WD]	+667
Satellite Radio System	+207
Automatic Climate Control (2 Zone) - Driver and Passenger	+160
DVD Entertainment System	+827
Power Retractable Mirrors	+128
Z66 Suspension Package [Opt on 2WD]	+667

The Avalanche gets numerous interior upgrades for '03 in addition to the midyear introduction of a "decladded" version that does without the oft-derided extensive lower body trim. Dual-zone climate control is now standard equipment on all models along with multistage airbags and a passenger airbag sensor. A redesigned instrument panel houses a more comprehensive driver information display; and an optional multifunction steering wheel puts climate, radio and trip computer controls right in the palm of your hands. New entertainment options include a Bose stereo system, XM Satellite Radio and a rear passenger DVD video system. Other new options include the StabiliTrak stability control system on 2WD half-ton models, adjustable pedals, and a fully automatic multizone climate control system.

2002

Body Styles	TMV Pricing		
	Trade	Private	Dealer
4 Dr 1500 4WD Crew Cab SB	20666	22154	24635
4 Dr 1500 Crew Cab SB	18775	20127	22381
4 Dr 2500 4WD Crew Cab SB	21918	23496	26127
4 Dr 2500 Crew Cab SB	19948	21384	23779

Options	Price
Automatic Climate Control	+143
Bucket Seats	+172
Heated Front Seats	+115
Leather Seats	+401
Locking Differential [Opt on 2WD]	+163
Off-Road Suspension Package	+479

Options	Price
OnStar Telematic System	+244
Power Moonroof	+567
Power Passenger Seat	+115
Power Sunroof	+628
Side Steps	+335
Z71 Off-Road Suspension Package	+479

Mileage Category: K

The 2002 Chevrolet Avalanche is the newest addition to the Chevy truck lineup. Incorporating a unique convertible cab system, the Avalanche can transform itself from a five-passenger sport-utility with a 5-foot-3-inch bed into a standard cab pickup with a full 8-foot-1-inch utility bed. A 5300 Vortec V8 is standard along with a heavy-duty towing package.

Chevrolet
Beretta

1996

Mileage Category: C

Final year for Beretta. Only change is the addition of long-life coolant to the engine.

Body Styles	TMV Pricing		
	Trade	Private	Dealer
2 Dr STD Cpe	1314	1983	2906
2 Dr Z26 Cpe	1565	2362	3463

Options	Price
3.1L V6 OHV 12V FI Engine [Opt on STD]	+329
Automatic 3-Speed Transmission	+143
Automatic 4-Speed Transmission [Opt on STD]	+220
Sunroof	+129

1995

Mileage Category: C

Daytime running lights are newly standard. 170-horse Quad 4 engine is dropped, and 3.1-liter V6 loses five horsepower. Platinum-tipped spark plugs are standard on both engines.

Body Styles	TMV Pricing		
	Trade	Private	Dealer
2 Dr STD Cpe	935	1461	2338
2 Dr Z26 Cpe	1188	1857	2971

Options	Price
3.1L V6 OHV 12V FI Engine [Opt on STD]	+295
Automatic 3-Speed Transmission	+128
Automatic 4-Speed Transmission [Opt on STD]	+198
Sunroof	+116

1994

Mileage Category: C

GT and GTZ are dropped in favor of Z26 model, which offers a standard 170-horsepower Quad 4 engine. Base models get 10 more horsepower, and the 3.1-liter V6 makes an additional 20 horsepower, up to 160. Automatic transmission is unavailable with Quad 4; manual transmission is unavailable with V6. Door-mounted seat belts are added. Automatic door locks secure doors once Beretta is underway, and unlock when car is stopped. Disable this feature by yanking a fuse. Interior lights shut off after 10 minutes to save battery. Warning chime reminds driver that turn signal has been left on.

Body Styles	TMV Pricing		
	Trade	Private	Dealer
2 Dr STD Cpe	759	1277	2140
2 Dr Z26 Cpe	852	1433	2402

Options	Price
Automatic 4-Speed Transmission	+175
Sunroof	+102
Automatic 3-Speed Transmission	+114
3.1L V6 OHV 12V FI Engine	+108

Chevrolet
Blazer

2003

Mileage Category: M

The Blazer gets only a few minor changes for 2003. A new fuel-injection system helps smooth out the aging 4.3-liter V6 while the interior get refreshed with new seat fabrics. Two-door models are now available in a bright yellow exterior color while the Xtreme model gets new quarter-panel graphics.

Body Styles	TMV Pricing		
	Trade	Private	Dealer
2 Dr LS 4WD SUV	12599	13562	15166
2 Dr LS SUV	10830	11658	13037
2 Dr LS ZR2 4WD SUV	13826	14882	16643
2 Dr LS ZR2 SUV	12789	13766	15395

Options	Price
Automatic 4-Speed Transmission [Opt on 2 Dr]	+638
Camper/Towing Package [Opt on LS]	+134
Cruise Control	+115
Locking Differential	+172
Power Door Locks	+118

Body Styles	TMV Pricing		
	Trade	Private	Dealer
2 Dr Xtreme SUV	12111	13036	14578
4 Dr LS 4WD SUV	14493	15600	17446
4 Dr LS SUV	13295	14311	16003

Options	Price
Power Driver Seat	+153
Power Moonroof	+511
Power Windows	+144
AM/FM/CD Changer Audio System	+252

2002

Mileage Category: M

Body Styles	TMV Pricing		
	Trade	Private	Dealer
2 Dr LS 4WD SUV	10367	11290	12828
2 Dr LS SUV	8863	9652	10968
2 Dr Xtreme SUV	9963	10850	12329

Body Styles	TMV Pricing		
	Trade	Private	Dealer
4 Dr LS 4WD SUV	12025	13096	14882
4 Dr LS SUV	10996	11975	13607

Options	Price
AM/FM/CD Changer Audio System	+169
Automatic 4-Speed Transmission [Opt on 2 Dr]	+573
Bose Audio System	+284
Camper/Towing Package	+120
Compact Disc Changer	+227
Heated Front Seats	+143

Options	Price
Leather Seats	+430
Locking Differential	+155
Power Driver Seat	+138
Power Sunroof	+459
Power Windows	+129
Wide Stance Suspension Package	+1147

Most new additions for 2002 involve cosmetic enhancements such as new exterior colors and optional sport stripes on the Xtreme model. LS models get a monotone paint scheme along with newly styled wheels.

2001

Mileage Category: M

Body Styles	TMV Pricing		
	Trade	Private	Dealer
2 Dr LS 4WD SUV	8670	9894	11023
2 Dr LS SUV	7318	8351	9304
2 Dr Xtreme SUV	8387	9571	10663
4 Dr LS 4WD SUV	10876	12411	13827
4 Dr LS SUV	9874	11268	12554

Body Styles	TMV Pricing		
	Trade	Private	Dealer
4 Dr LT 4WD SUV	11978	13669	15229
4 Dr LT SUV	10928	12470	13893
4 Dr TrailBlazer 4WD SUV	12225	13950	15543
4 Dr TrailBlazer SUV	12103	13811	15387

Options	Price
Automatic 4-Speed Transmission [Opt on 2 Dr]	+525
Bose Audio System	+260
Compact Disc Changer	+207
Heated Front Seats	+131
Leather Seats [Opt on LT]	+446
Locking Differential	+174

Options	Price
Power Driver Seat [Std on LT]	+125
Power Passenger Seat [Std on Trailblazer]	+126
Power Sunroof	+420
Power Windows [Opt on LS]	+137
Wide Stance Suspension Package	+1049

Standard OnStar on premium models. Xtreme, a new trim level on the two-wheel-drive two-door that includes a low-riding sport suspension lowered by 2.5 inches, body cladding and special wheels, is now available.

2000

Mileage Category: M

Body Styles	TMV Pricing		
	Trade	Private	Dealer
2 Dr LS 4WD SUV	6719	7901	9060
2 Dr LS SUV	5133	6036	6921
4 Dr LS 4WD SUV	8120	9549	10949
4 Dr LS SUV	7527	8851	10149

Body Styles	TMV Pricing		
	Trade	Private	Dealer
4 Dr LT 4WD SUV	8348	9817	11257
4 Dr LT SUV	7896	9286	10648
4 Dr Trailblazer 4WD SUV	8813	10364	11884
4 Dr Trailblazer SUV	8608	10122	11607

Options	Price
AM/FM/CD Audio System [Opt on LS]	+154
Automatic 4-Speed Transmission [Opt on 2 Dr]	+468
Bose Audio System	+232
Compact Disc Changer	+187
Heated Front Seats	+117
Leather Seats [Opt on LT]	+398

Options	Price
Limited Slip Differential	+126
OnStar Telematic System	+325
Power Sunroof	+351
Power Windows [Opt on LS]	+122
ZR2 Highrider Suspension Package	+865

Base models are dropped. The engine, exhaust and ABS are refined for increased durability, and exterior trim on some models is modified. Two new colors are available.

1999

Mileage Category: M

Body Styles	TMV Pricing		
	Trade	Private	Dealer
2 Dr LS 4WD SUV	5991	7168	8393
2 Dr LS SUV	4587	5488	6426
2 Dr STD 4WD SUV	5462	6535	7652
2 Dr STD SUV	4466	5343	6256
4 Dr LS 4WD SUV	7136	8538	9997
4 Dr LS SUV	6503	7780	9110

Body Styles	TMV Pricing		
	Trade	Private	Dealer
4 Dr LT 4WD SUV	7642	9143	10706
4 Dr LT SUV	7178	8588	10056
4 Dr STD 4WD SUV	6371	7622	8925
4 Dr STD SUV	5549	6639	7773
4 Dr Trailblazer 4WD SUV	7648	9150	10714
4 Dr Trailblazer SUV	7309	8745	10239

Blazer gets automatic transmission improvements, new exterior colors and larger outside mirrors, while four-wheel-drive versions can be equipped with GM's AutoTrac active transfer case. Inside, there are new power-seating features, upgraded sound system options and available redundant radio controls in the steering wheel. On the safety side, the '99 Blazer now offers a vehicle content theft alarm, flash-to-pass headlamp feature and a liftgate ajar warning lamp. What's more, a new TrailBlazer trim package is available on four-door versions, featuring monochrome paint with gold accents, unique aluminum wheels, touring suspension and leather-lined interior.

1999 (cont'd)

Options	Price
AM/FM/CD Audio System [Std on 2 Dr]	+123
Automatic 4-Speed Transmission [Opt on 2 Dr]	+415
Compact Disc Changer	+149

Options	Price
Delco/Bose Audio System	+185
Power Sunroof [Opt on LS]	+280
ZR2 Highrider Suspension Package	+691

1998

Mileage Category: M

Blazer gets a front-end restyle and an interior redesign. New standard equipment includes a theft-deterrent system, automatic headlight control, four-wheel disc brakes and dual airbags incorporating second-generation technology to reduce the bags' inflation force. New radios, colors and a column-mounted automatic shift selector round out the major changes.

Body Styles	TMV Pricing		
	Trade	Private	Dealer
2 Dr LS 4WD SUV	5225	6330	7577
2 Dr LS SUV	4106	4975	5955
2 Dr STD 4WD SUV	4960	6009	7192
2 Dr STD SUV	3947	4782	5723
4 Dr LS 4WD SUV	5629	6820	8163

Body Styles	TMV Pricing		
	Trade	Private	Dealer
4 Dr LS SUV	5533	6703	8023
4 Dr LT 4WD SUV	6280	7608	9106
4 Dr LT SUV	5671	6870	8223
4 Dr STD 4WD SUV	5414	6559	7851
4 Dr STD SUV	4593	5564	6660

Options	Price
Power Sunroof	+218
Sport Suspension	+205
Wide Stance Suspension Package	+582
Automatic 4-Speed Transmission [Opt on 2 Dr]	+349

1997

Mileage Category: M

Those who prefer a liftgate over a tailgate have that option on 1997 four-door Blazers. A power sunroof is a new option for all Blazers, and models equipped with LT decor are equipped with a HomeLink transmitter that will open your garage, among other things. All-wheel-drive Blazers get four-wheel disc brakes, and automatic transmissions are revised for smoother shifting. Early-production 4WD two-door Blazers could be ordered with a ZR2 suspension package. Base Blazers get a chrome grille, while LT four-door models have body-color grilles in six exterior colors. Two new paint colors round out the changes.

Body Styles	TMV Pricing		
	Trade	Private	Dealer
2 Dr LS 4WD SUV	4237	5230	6444
2 Dr LS SUV	3674	4535	5587
2 Dr STD 4WD SUV	3968	4898	6034
2 Dr STD SUV	3215	3968	4889
4 Dr LS 4WD SUV	4572	5643	6953

Body Styles	TMV Pricing		
	Trade	Private	Dealer
4 Dr LS SUV	4472	5520	6801
4 Dr LT 4WD SUV	5016	6191	7628
4 Dr LT SUV	4667	5761	7097
4 Dr STD 4WD SUV	4360	5382	6630
4 Dr STD SUV	3651	4506	5552

Options	Price
Automatic 4-Speed Transmission [Opt on 2 Dr]	+316
Power Sunroof	+198
Wide Stance Suspension Package	+526

1996

Mileage Category: M

More power, available all-wheel drive and five new colors improve the 1996 Blazer. A five-speed manual transmission is optional on two-door models.

Body Styles	TMV Pricing		
	Trade	Private	Dealer
2 Dr LS 4WD SUV	3445	4369	5645
2 Dr LS SUV	3006	3812	4926
2 Dr STD 4WD SUV	2953	3745	4839
2 Dr STD SUV	2655	3367	4351
4 Dr LS 4WD SUV	3627	4600	5943

Body Styles	TMV Pricing		
	Trade	Private	Dealer
4 Dr LS SUV	3431	4351	5622
4 Dr LT 4WD SUV	3995	5066	6545
4 Dr LT SUV	3808	4830	6241
4 Dr STD 4WD SUV	3419	4336	5602
4 Dr STD SUV	2879	3651	4717

1995

Mileage Category: M

All-new SUV appears based on revamped S10. S10 nomenclature is dropped, and full-size Blazer becomes Tahoe. Four-wheel-drive models have electronic transfer case as standard equipment. Spare tire on four-door model is mounted beneath cargo bay instead of in it. Five different suspension packages are available. One engine, a 195-horsepower 4.3-liter V6, is available. All-wheel drive is optional. Driver airbag and air conditioning are standard equipment.

Body Styles	TMV Pricing		
	Trade	Private	Dealer
2 Dr LS 4WD SUV	2596	3330	4552
2 Dr LS SUV	2396	3073	4201
2 Dr STD 4WD SUV	2324	2982	4078
2 Dr STD SUV	2124	2725	3726
4 Dr LS 4WD SUV	2745	3521	4815

Body Styles	TMV Pricing		
	Trade	Private	Dealer
4 Dr LS SUV	2571	3293	4496
4 Dr LT 4WD SUV	3018	3871	5292
4 Dr LT SUV	2832	3633	4968
4 Dr STD 4WD SUV	2558	3281	4487
4 Dr STD SUV	2355	3022	4133

Options	Price
AM/FM/CD Audio System	+76

1994

Body Styles	TMV Pricing		
	Trade	Private	Dealer
2 Dr STD 4WD SUV	2502	3204	4375
2 Dr Silverado 4WD SUV	3436	4401	6009
2 Dr Sport 4WD SUV	3675	4707	6426

Options	Price
6.5L V8 Turbodiesel OHV 16V Engine	+641
Air Conditioning [Opt on STD]	+163
Automatic 4-Speed Transmission	+202

Mileage Category: N

Air conditioning receives CFC-free coolant. Side-door guard beams are added. A new grille appears, and models equipped with a decor package get composite headlamps. A turbocharged diesel is newly optional. Third brake light is added.

Chevrolet
C/K 1500 Series

1999

Body Styles	TMV Pricing		
	Trade	Private	Dealer
2 Dr C1500 LS Ext Cab SB	9926	11473	13083
2 Dr K1500 LS 4WD Ext Cab SB	11445	13229	15085

Options	Price
Leather Seats	+373
5.7L V8 OHV 16V FI Engine	+261
Aluminum/Alloy Wheels	+127

Mileage Category: K

A few new colors are added to Chevrolet's popular pickup in anticipation of the all-new Silverado.

1998

Mileage Category: K

This year's big news is a standard theft-deterrent system, revised color choices and fresh tailgate lettering. The Sport package has been dropped from the option list. Second-generation airbags are standard on models under 8,600 GVWR.

Body Styles	TMV Pricing		
	Trade	Private	Dealer
2 Dr C1500 Cheyenne Ext Cab LB	6826	8038	9405
2 Dr C1500 Cheyenne Ext Cab SB	6437	7580	8869
2 Dr C1500 Cheyenne Std Cab LB	5741	6760	7910
2 Dr C1500 Cheyenne Std Cab SB	5276	6213	7270
2 Dr C1500 Cheyenne Std Cab Step SB	5800	6830	7991
2 Dr C1500 Silverado Ext Cab LB	7722	9093	10640
2 Dr C1500 Silverado Ext Cab SB	7481	8810	10308
2 Dr C1500 Silverado Ext Cab Step SB	8467	9971	11666
2 Dr C1500 Silverado Std Cab LB	6479	7630	8927
2 Dr C1500 Silverado Std Cab SB	6265	7377	8632
2 Dr C1500 Silverado Std Cab Step SB	6555	7719	9031
2 Dr C1500 WT Std Cab LB	5104	6010	7032
2 Dr C1500 WT Std Cab SB	4989	5875	6874
2 Dr K1500 Cheyenne 4WD Ext Cab LB	8409	9902	11586
2 Dr K1500 Cheyenne 4WD Ext Cab SB	8003	9424	11027

Body Styles	TMV Pricing		
	Trade	Private	Dealer
2 Dr K1500 Cheyenne 4WD Std Cab LB	6904	8130	9512
2 Dr K1500 Cheyenne 4WD Std Cab SB	6862	8081	9455
2 Dr K1500 Cheyenne 4WD Std Cab Step SB	6961	8197	9591
2 Dr K1500 Silverado 4WD Ext Cab LB	8989	10585	12385
2 Dr K1500 Silverado 4WD Ext Cab SB	8817	10383	12148
2 Dr K1500 Silverado 4WD Ext Cab Step SB	10339	12175	14245
2 Dr K1500 Silverado 4WD Std Cab LB	8044	9472	11083
2 Dr K1500 Silverado 4WD Std Cab SB	7838	9230	10799
2 Dr K1500 Silverado 4WD Std Cab Step SB	8119	9561	11187
2 Dr K1500 WT 4WD Std Cab LB	6668	7852	9187
2 Dr K1500 WT 4WD Std Cab SB	6513	7669	8973

Options	Price
5.0L V8 OHV 16V FI Engine	+156
5.7L V8 OHV 16V FI Engine	+220
6.5L V8 Turbodiesel OHV 16V Engine	+1064
Air Conditioning [Std on Silverado]	+253

Options	Price
Automatic 4-Speed Transmission	+305
Bucket Seats	+121
Hinged Third Door	+132
Leather Seats	+314

1997

Mileage Category: K

On trucks under 8,600 pounds, the passenger airbag can be deactivated when a rear-facing child safety seat is installed. Low-speed steering effort is reduced this year, and a refined transmission fluid pump results in smoother shifts. An alternative fuel version of the Vortec 5700 is available, but only on a specific model. K1500's get a tighter turning radius, and three new colors debut. The third door option will be more widely available, because it is now a required option on all C/K 1500 short-bed extended cab trucks.

Body Styles	TMV Pricing		
	Trade	Private	Dealer
2 Dr C1500 Cheyenne Ext Cab LB	5675	6818	8214
2 Dr C1500 Cheyenne Ext Cab SB	5282	6345	7645
2 Dr C1500 Cheyenne Ext Cab Step SB	5564	6684	8053
2 Dr C1500 Cheyenne Std Cab LB	4664	5603	6751
2 Dr C1500 Cheyenne Std Cab SB	4484	5387	6490
2 Dr C1500 Cheyenne Std Cab Step SB	4776	5738	6913
2 Dr C1500 Silverado Ext Cab LB	6798	8167	9840
2 Dr C1500 Silverado Ext Cab SB	6181	7426	8947
2 Dr C1500 Silverado Ext Cab Step SB	6463	7764	9354
2 Dr C1500 Silverado Std Cab LB	5338	6413	7726
2 Dr C1500 Silverado Std Cab SB	5169	6210	7482
2 Dr C1500 Silverado Std Cab Step SB	5498	6605	7958
2 Dr C1500 WT Std Cab LB	4383	5265	6344
2 Dr C1500 WT Std Cab SB	4329	5200	6265
2 Dr K1500 Cheyenne 4WD Ext Cab LB	7177	8622	10388
2 Dr K1500 Cheyenne 4WD Ext Cab SB	6687	8033	9679

Body Styles	TMV Pricing		
	Trade	Private	Dealer
2 Dr K1500 Cheyenne 4WD Ext Cab Step SB	6967	8370	10084
2 Dr K1500 Cheyenne 4WD Std Cab LB	5844	7021	8459
2 Dr K1500 Cheyenne 4WD Std Cab SB	5618	6749	8132
2 Dr K1500 Cheyenne 4WD Std Cab Step SB	5943	7140	8602
2 Dr K1500 Silverado 4WD Ext Cab LB	7585	9112	10979
2 Dr K1500 Silverado 4WD Ext Cab SB	7319	8793	10594
2 Dr K1500 Silverado 4WD Ext Cab Step SB	7561	9083	10943
2 Dr K1500 Silverado 4WD Std Cab LB	6912	8304	10005
2 Dr K1500 Silverado 4WD Std Cab SB	6742	8100	9759
2 Dr K1500 Silverado 4WD Std Cab Step SB	7023	8437	10166
2 Dr K1500 WT 4WD Std Cab LB	5517	6628	7985
2 Dr K1500 WT 4WD Std Cab SB	5449	6546	7887

Options	Price
Hinged Third Door	+119
Leather Seats	+284
5.0L V8 OHV 16V FI Engine	+141
5.7L V8 OHV 16V FI Engine	+199

Options	Price
6.5L V8 Turbodiesel OHV 16V Engine	+961
Air Conditioning [Std on Silverado]	+229
Automatic 4-Speed Transmission	+276

1996

Mileage Category: K

A new series of engines is introduced, providing more power and torque than last year's offerings. Called Vortec, this family of engines includes a 4.3-liter V6 (the only six-cylinder of the bunch) capable of 200 hp at 4,400 rpm and 255 lb-ft of torque at 2,800 rpm; a 5.0-liter V8, producing 220 hp at 4,600 rpm and 285 lb-ft of torque at 2,800 rpm; and a 5.7-liter V8, rated at 250 hp at 4,600 rpm and 335 lb-ft of torque at 2,800 rpm. (There is also a 7.4-liter Vortec V8, but it's only available on the heavier-duty C/K 3500 trucks.) All of these figures represent increases in output when compared to their respective 1995 predecessors. An optional electronic shift transfer case for the K1500 (i.e. 4WD; C=2WD; K=4WD) rounds out the list of the most significant powertrain updates for the year.

Other noteworthy updates include the introduction of an optional passenger-side third door, called the "Easy-Access System," in GM vernacular. This feature is only available on the extended cab body styles.

Improved comfort and convenience comes in the way of such new features as illuminated entry, 12-volt power outlets, an electrochromic inside rearview mirror and height-adjustable D-rings for the shoulder section of the front three-point safety belts, among others. Daytime running lamps (DRLs) are part of the list of new exterior features.

A new level of sophistication in exhaust emissions monitoring is found with the addition of OBD II, the second generation of On-Board Diagnostics.

Body Styles	TMV Pricing		
	Trade	Private	Dealer
2 Dr C1500 Cheyenne Ext Cab LB	4820	5902	7397
2 Dr C1500 Cheyenne Ext Cab SB	4225	5174	6484
2 Dr C1500 Cheyenne Ext Cab Step SB	4448	5447	6826
2 Dr C1500 Cheyenne Std Cab LB	3805	4659	5839
2 Dr C1500 Cheyenne Std Cab SB	3881	4753	5956
2 Dr C1500 Cheyenne Std Cab Step SB	3795	4647	5824
2 Dr C1500 Silverado Ext Cab LB	5528	6769	8483
2 Dr C1500 Silverado Ext Cab SB	5031	6161	7721
2 Dr C1500 Silverado Ext Cab Step SB	5190	6356	7965
2 Dr C1500 Silverado Std Cab LB	4506	5518	6915
2 Dr C1500 Silverado Std Cab SB	4183	5122	6419
2 Dr C1500 Silverado Std Cab Step SB	4497	5507	6901
2 Dr C1500 WT Std Cab LB	3709	4541	5691
2 Dr C1500 WT Std Cab SB	3601	4410	5526
2 Dr K1500 Cheyenne 4WD Ext Cab LB	5773	7069	8859
2 Dr K1500 Cheyenne 4WD Ext Cab SB	5485	6716	8417

Body Styles	TMV Pricing		
	Trade	Private	Dealer
2 Dr K1500 Cheyenne 4WD Ext Cab Step SB	5553	6800	8521
2 Dr K1500 Cheyenne 4WD Std Cab LB	4874	5968	7479
2 Dr K1500 Cheyenne 4WD Std Cab SB	4766	5836	7314
2 Dr K1500 Cheyenne 4WD Std Cab Step SB	4926	6032	7560
2 Dr K1500 Silverado 4WD Ext Cab LB	6303	7718	9672
2 Dr K1500 Silverado 4WD Ext Cab SB	6355	7782	9752
2 Dr K1500 Silverado 4WD Ext Cab Step SB	6619	8105	10158
2 Dr K1500 Silverado 4WD Std Cab LB	5570	6821	8548
2 Dr K1500 Silverado 4WD Std Cab SB	5513	6751	8460
2 Dr K1500 Silverado 4WD Std Cab Step SB	5720	7004	8778
2 Dr K1500 WT 4WD Std Cab LB	4343	5318	6665
2 Dr K1500 WT 4WD Std Cab SB	4290	5253	6584

Options	Price
5.7L V8 OHV 16V FI Engine	+200
6.5L V8 Turbodiesel OHV 16V Engine	+1019
Air Conditioning [Std on Silverado]	+231

Options	Price
Automatic 4-Speed Transmission	+250
Leather Seats	+258
5.0L V8 OHV 16V FI Engine	+142

1995

Mileage Category: K

Body Styles	TMV Pricing		
	Trade	Private	Dealer
2 Dr C1500 Cheyenne Ext Cab LB	3915	4827	6346
2 Dr C1500 Cheyenne Ext Cab SB	3553	4380	5759
2 Dr C1500 Cheyenne Ext Cab Step SB	3860	4759	6257
2 Dr C1500 Cheyenne Std Cab LB	3187	3943	5204
2 Dr C1500 Cheyenne Std Cab SB	3061	3774	4962
2 Dr C1500 Cheyenne Std Cab Step SB	3239	3993	5250
2 Dr C1500 Silverado Ext Cab LB	4265	5258	6913
2 Dr C1500 Silverado Ext Cab SB	4010	4944	6500
2 Dr C1500 Silverado Ext Cab Step SB	4205	5184	6816
2 Dr C1500 Silverado Std Cab LB	3807	4694	6171
2 Dr C1500 Silverado Std Cab SB	3643	4491	5905
2 Dr C1500 Silverado Std Cab Step SB	3907	4817	6333
2 Dr C1500 WT Std Cab LB	3046	3755	4937
2 Dr C1500 WT Std Cab SB	2996	3694	4856
2 Dr K1500 Cheyenne 4WD Ext Cab LB	4316	5321	6995
2 Dr K1500 Cheyenne 4WD Ext Cab SB	4162	5131	6746

Body Styles	TMV Pricing		
	Trade	Private	Dealer
2 Dr K1500 Cheyenne 4WD Ext Cab Step SB	4260	5252	6904
2 Dr K1500 Cheyenne 4WD Std Cab LB	3904	4813	6327
2 Dr K1500 Cheyenne 4WD Std Cab SB	3858	4756	6253
2 Dr K1500 Cheyenne 4WD Std Cab Step SB	3959	4881	6417
2 Dr K1500 Silverado 4WD Ext Cab LB	5180	6386	8395
2 Dr K1500 Silverado 4WD Ext Cab SB	4924	6070	7981
2 Dr K1500 Silverado 4WD Ext Cab Step SB	5076	6258	8228
2 Dr K1500 Silverado 4WD Std Cab LB	4220	5203	6841
2 Dr K1500 Silverado 4WD Std Cab SB	4062	5007	6583
2 Dr K1500 Silverado 4WD Std Cab Step SB	4265	5258	6913
2 Dr K1500 WT 4WD Std Cab LB	3518	4352	5742
2 Dr K1500 WT 4WD Std Cab SB	3656	4507	5925

Options	Price
5.0L V8 OHV 16V FI Engine	+115
5.7L V8 OHV 16V FI Engine	+162
6.5L V8 Diesel OHV 16V Engine	+630
6.5L V8 Turbodiesel OHV 16V Engine	+782

Options	Price
7.4L V8 OHV 16V FI Engine	+195
Air Conditioning [Std on Silverado]	+186
Automatic 4-Speed Transmission	+224
Leather Seats	+231

A revised interior graces these full-size trucks this year. A new driver-side airbag and a shift interlock are added in the interest of safety. The latter requires the brake pedal to be depressed before the automatic transmission's gear selector can be shifted out of "Park," reducing the likelihood that the vehicle will move suddenly and unexpectedly. Power mirrors, revised climate controls and cupholders provide a more user-friendly interior environment.

Mechanical enhancements include the addition of standard four-wheel antilock brakes, improvements in the engines and modifications to the heavy-duty automatic gearbox. The four-wheel ABS replaces last year's rear-wheel-only antilock system. Various upgrades to the engines are intended to reduce noise improve durability and/or increase efficiency. The transmission is revised for quicker 1-2 upshifts during full-throttle applications.

1994

Mileage Category: K

Body Styles	TMV Pricing		
	Trade	Private	Dealer
2 Dr C1500 Cheyenne Ext Cab LB	3214	4117	5623
2 Dr C1500 Cheyenne Ext Cab SB	3075	3939	5379
2 Dr C1500 Cheyenne Ext Cab Step SB	3169	4060	5545
2 Dr C1500 Cheyenne Std Cab LB	2738	3508	4790
2 Dr C1500 Cheyenne Std Cab SB	2641	3384	4621
2 Dr C1500 Cheyenne Std Cab Step SB	2785	3568	4873
2 Dr C1500 Silverado Ext Cab LB	3367	4314	5891
2 Dr C1500 Silverado Ext Cab SB	3299	4226	5771
2 Dr C1500 Silverado Ext Cab Step SB	3359	4303	5876
2 Dr C1500 Silverado Std Cab LB	2878	3687	5036
2 Dr C1500 Silverado Std Cab SB	2827	3622	4947
2 Dr C1500 Silverado Std Cab Step SB	3121	3999	5461
2 Dr C1500 WT Std Cab LB	2262	2898	3958
2 Dr C1500 WT Std Cab SB	2065	2646	3613
2 Dr K1500 Cheyenne 4WD Ext Cab LB	3514	4502	6149
2 Dr K1500 Cheyenne 4WD Ext Cab SB	3418	4379	5980

Body Styles	TMV Pricing		
	Trade	Private	Dealer
2 Dr K1500 Cheyenne 4WD Ext Cab Step SB	3561	4562	6231
2 Dr K1500 Cheyenne 4WD Std Cab LB	3223	4129	5638
2 Dr K1500 Cheyenne 4WD Std Cab SB	2978	3815	5210
2 Dr K1500 Cheyenne 4WD Std Cab Step SB	3266	4184	5714
2 Dr K1500 Silverado 4WD Ext Cab LB	3987	5108	6975
2 Dr K1500 Silverado 4WD Ext Cab SB	3891	4985	6807
2 Dr K1500 Silverado 4WD Ext Cab Step SB	3948	5058	6908
2 Dr K1500 Silverado 4WD Std Cab LB	3375	4324	5905
2 Dr K1500 Silverado 4WD Std Cab SB	3365	4311	5887
2 Dr K1500 Silverado 4WD Std Cab Step SB	3265	4183	5713
2 Dr K1500 Sport 4WD Std Cab Step SB	3927	5031	6871
2 Dr K1500 WT 4WD Std Cab LB	2885	3696	5047
2 Dr K1500 WT 4WD Std Cab SB	2840	3638	4969

Options	Price
5.0L V8 OHV 16V FI Engine	+101
5.7L V8 OHV 16V FI Engine	+143
6.5L V8 Diesel OHV 16V Engine	+557
6.5L V8 Turbodiesel OHV 16V Engine	+691

Options	Price
Air Conditioning [Std on Silverado]	+165
Automatic 4-Speed Transmission	+198
Leather Seats	+204
LT Package [Opt on Silverado]	+346

Safety is enhanced with the side door guard beams designed to minimize intrusion into the passenger compartment during a side impact. A center high-mounted brake light is also added to enhance safety.

Chevy boasts it is the first automaker to offer a turbodiesel engine option in a vehicle with a gross vehicle weight rating less than 8,500 pounds.

Rust corrosion protection is improved while interior noise vibration and harshness is reduced. Rounding out the list of significant improvements are the addition of an "easy entry" feature to the front passenger seat on extended cab body styles to ease entry into the rear seating positions and the revision of the exterior front-end styling.

Chevrolet
C/K 2500 Series

2000

Mileage Category: K

One new paint color. Last year for "C/K" nomenclature.

Body Styles	TMV Pricing		
	Trade	Private	Dealer
2 Dr C2500 Ext Cab LB HD	10019	11337	12628
2 Dr C2500 LS Ext Cab LB HD	11948	13519	15059
2 Dr C2500 LS Std Cab LB HD	11024	12474	13895
2 Dr C2500 Std Cab LB HD	9413	10651	11864
2 Dr K2500 4WD Ext Cab LB HD	12684	14353	15988
2 Dr K2500 4WD Ext Cab SB HD	12555	14206	15825
2 Dr K2500 4WD Std Cab LB HD	11093	12551	13981

Body Styles	TMV Pricing		
	Trade	Private	Dealer
2 Dr K2500 LS 4WD Ext Cab LB HD	13445	15213	16945
2 Dr K2500 LS 4WD Ext Cab SB HD	13301	15050	16764
2 Dr K2500 LS 4WD Std Cab LB HD	12761	14439	16084
4 Dr C2500 Crew Cab SB HD	12164	13764	15332
4 Dr C2500 LS Crew Cab SB HD	13646	15441	17200
4 Dr K2500 4WD Crew Cab SB HD	13598	15386	17139

Options	Price
6.5L V8 Turbodiesel OHV 16V Engine	+1271
7.4L V8 OHV 16V FI Engine	+281
Air Conditioning	+377
AM/FM/Cassette/CD Audio System	+136

Options	Price
Automatic 4-Speed Transmission	+512
Bucket Seats	+126
Leather Seats	+468
Limited Slip Differential	+134

1999

Mileage Category: K

Model consolidation takes place in anticipation of the all-new Silverado. Trim levels have been changed from three to two (Base and LS) and two new Crew Cab Short Box models (C/K2500 and C/K3500 Series) are offered. Additionally, the C/K1500 will be available only as an LS Extended Cab Short Box with the third door. Mechanical upgrades include new internal components and seals for automatic transmissions, improved cooling system and starter motor durability and three new exterior paint colors.

Body Styles	TMV Pricing		
	Trade	Private	Dealer
2 Dr C2500 Ext Cab LB HD	8343	9643	10996
2 Dr C2500 LS Ext Cab LB HD	10230	11824	13483
2 Dr C2500 LS Std Cab LB HD	8851	10230	11665
2 Dr C2500 Std Cab LB HD	7904	9135	10417
2 Dr K2500 4WD Ext Cab LB HD	10649	12309	14036
2 Dr K2500 4WD Ext Cab SB HD	10436	12062	13754
2 Dr K2500 4WD Std Cab LB HD	9545	11033	12581

Body Styles	TMV Pricing		
	Trade	Private	Dealer
2 Dr K2500 LS 4WD Ext Cab LB HD	11488	13278	15141
2 Dr K2500 LS 4WD Ext Cab SB HD	11279	13037	14866
2 Dr K2500 LS 4WD Std Cab LB HD	10864	12557	14320
4 Dr C2500 Crew Cab SB HD	10295	11899	13569
4 Dr K2500 4WD Crew Cab SB HD	12074	13956	15914
4 Dr K2500 LS 4WD Crew Cab SB HD	13607	15728	17935

Options	Price
6.5L V8 Turbodiesel OHV 16V Engine	+1014
7.4L V8 OHV 16V FI Engine	+224
Air Conditioning	+300

Options	Price
Automatic 4-Speed Transmission	+372
Leather Seats	+438

1998

Mileage Category: K

This year's big news is a standard theft-deterrent system, revised color choices and fresh tailgate lettering. The Sport package has been dropped from the option list. Second-generation airbags are standard on models under 8,600 GVWR.

Body Styles	TMV Pricing		
	Trade	Private	Dealer
2 Dr C2500 Cheyenne Ext Cab LB HD	7478	8806	10304
2 Dr C2500 Cheyenne Ext Cab SB	7133	8401	9830
2 Dr C2500 Cheyenne Std Cab LB	5749	6770	7922
2 Dr C2500 Cheyenne Std Cab LB HD	6555	7720	9033
2 Dr C2500 Silverado Ext Cab LB HD	8854	10427	12201
2 Dr C2500 Silverado Ext Cab SB	8521	10035	11742
2 Dr C2500 Silverado Std Cab LB	6961	8198	9592
2 Dr C2500 Silverado Std Cab LB HD	7916	9323	10909

Body Styles	TMV Pricing		
	Trade	Private	Dealer
2 Dr K2500 Cheyenne 4WD Ext Cab LB HD	9063	10674	12490
2 Dr K2500 Cheyenne 4WD Ext Cab SB HD	9015	10617	12424
2 Dr K2500 Cheyenne 4WD Std Cab LB HD	7978	9396	10994
2 Dr K2500 Silverado 4WD Ext Cab LB HD	9928	11692	13681
2 Dr K2500 Silverado 4WD Ext Cab SB HD	9493	11180	13082
2 Dr K2500 Silverado 4WD Std Cab LB HD	9362	11026	12902

Options	Price
5.7L V8 OHV 16V FI Engine [Std on HD]	+220
6.5L V8 Turbodiesel OHV 16V Engine	+854
7.4L V8 OHV 16V FI Engine	+189
Air Conditioning [Std on Silverado]	+253

Options	Price
Automatic 4-Speed Transmission	+305
Bucket Seats	+121
Leather Seats	+314

1997

Body Styles	TMV Pricing		
	Trade	Private	Dealer
2 Dr C2500 Cheyenne Ext Cab LB HD	5911	7101	8555
2 Dr C2500 Cheyenne Ext Cab SB	6068	7290	8783
2 Dr C2500 Cheyenne Std Cab LB	4972	5973	7197
2 Dr C2500 Cheyenne Std Cab LB HD	5282	6345	7645
2 Dr C2500 Silverado Ext Cab LB HD	6685	8031	9676
2 Dr C2500 Silverado Ext Cab SB	6967	8370	10084
2 Dr C2500 Silverado Std Cab LB	5675	6818	8214
2 Dr C2500 Silverado Std Cab LB HD	6395	7683	9257

Body Styles	TMV Pricing		
	Trade	Private	Dealer
2 Dr K2500 Cheyenne 4WD Ext Cab LB HD	7315	8788	10589
2 Dr K2500 Cheyenne 4WD Ext Cab SB HD	7201	8651	10424
2 Dr K2500 Cheyenne 4WD Std Cab LB HD	6458	7759	9348
2 Dr K2500 Silverado 4WD Ext Cab LB HD	8066	9690	11675
2 Dr K2500 Silverado 4WD Ext Cab SB HD	8008	9621	11592

Options	Price
5.7L V8 OHV 16V FI Engine [Std on HD]	+199
6.5L V8 Turbodiesel OHV 16V Engine	+772
7.4L V8 OHV 16V FI Engine	+171

Options	Price
Air Conditioning [Std on Silverado]	+229
Automatic 4-Speed Transmission	+283
Leather Seats	+334

Mileage Category: K

On trucks under 8,600 pounds GVWR, the passenger airbag can be deactivated when a rear-facing child safety seat is installed. Low-speed steering effort is reduced this year, and a refined transmission fluid pump results in smoother shifts. An alternative fuel version of the Vortec 5700 is available, but only on a specific model. K1500's get a tighter turning radius, and three new colors debut. The third door option will be more widely available.

1996

Body Styles	TMV Pricing		
	Trade	Private	Dealer
2 Dr C2500 Cheyenne Ext Cab LB HD	5148	6248	7768
2 Dr C2500 Cheyenne Ext Cab SB	5014	6085	7565
2 Dr C2500 Cheyenne Std Cab LB	4177	5070	6302
2 Dr C2500 Silverado Ext Cab LB HD	5574	6766	8411
2 Dr C2500 Silverado Ext Cab SB	5430	6590	8193
2 Dr C2500 Silverado Std Cab LB	4616	5602	6964
2 Dr K2500 Cheyenne 4WD Ext Cab LB HD	6259	7597	9444

Body Styles	TMV Pricing		
	Trade	Private	Dealer
2 Dr K2500 Cheyenne 4WD Ext Cab SB HD	6179	7499	9322
2 Dr K2500 Cheyenne 4WD Std Cab LB HD	5272	6398	7954
2 Dr K2500 Silverado 4WD Ext Cab LB HD	7088	8603	10694
2 Dr K2500 Silverado 4WD Ext Cab SB HD	7025	8527	10600
2 Dr K2500 Silverado 4WD Std Cab LB HD	6482	7867	9780

Options	Price
Leather Seats	+258
5.7L V8 OHV 16V FI Engine [Std on HD]	+180
6.5L V8 Turbodiesel OHV 16V Engine	+700

Options	Price
7.4L V8 OHV 16V FI Engine	+155
Air Conditioning [Std on Silverado]	+207
Automatic 4-Speed Transmission	+278

Mileage Category: K

A new series of engines is introduced, providing more power and torque than last year's offerings. Called Vortec, this family of engines includes a 4.3-liter V6 (the only six-cylinder of the bunch) capable of 200 hp at 4,400 rpm and 255 lb-ft of torque at 2,800 rpm; a 5.0-liter V8, producing 220 hp at 4,600 rpm and 285 lb-ft of torque at 2,800 rpm; and a 5.7-liter V8, rated at 250 hp at 4,600 rpm and 335 lb-ft of torque at 2,800 rpm. (There is also a 7.4-liter Vortec V8, but it's only available on the heavier-duty C/K 3500 trucks.) All of these figures represent increases in output when compared to their respective 1995 predecessors. An optional electronic shift transfer case for the K1500 (i.e. 4WD; C=2WD; K=4WD) rounds out the list of the most significant powertrain updates for the year.

Other noteworthy updates include the introduction of an optional passenger-side third door, called the "Easy-Access System," in GM vernacular. This feature is only available on the extended cab body styles.

Improved comfort and convenience comes in the way of such new features as illuminated entry, 12-volt power outlets, an electrochromic inside rearview mirror and height-adjustable D-rings for the shoulder section of the front three-point safety belts, among others. Daytime running lamps (DRLs) are part of the list of new exterior features. A new level of sophistication in exhaust emissions monitoring is found with the addition of OBD II, the second generation of On-Board Diagnostics.

1995

Body Styles	TMV Pricing		
	Trade	Private	Dealer
2 Dr C2500 Cheyenne Ext Cab LB	4212	5193	6828
2 Dr C2500 Cheyenne Ext Cab SB	4162	5131	6746
2 Dr C2500 Cheyenne Std Cab LB	3493	4306	5662
2 Dr C2500 Silverado Ext Cab LB	4632	5703	7489
2 Dr C2500 Silverado Ext Cab SB	4589	5657	7437
2 Dr C2500 Silverado Std Cab LB	3619	4462	5866
2 Dr K2500 Cheyenne 4WD Ext Cab LB	5076	6258	8228

Body Styles	TMV Pricing		
	Trade	Private	Dealer
2 Dr K2500 Cheyenne 4WD Ext Cab SB	4568	5632	7405
2 Dr K2500 Cheyenne 4WD Std Cab LB	4113	5070	6666
2 Dr K2500 Silverado 4WD Ext Cab LB	5584	6884	9050
2 Dr K2500 Silverado 4WD Ext Cab SB	5432	6697	8804
2 Dr K2500 Silverado 4WD Std Cab LB	4517	5569	7321

Options	Price
5.0L V8 OHV 16V FI Engine	+162
5.7L V8 OHV 16V FI Engine	+162
6.5L V8 Diesel OHV 16V Engine	+630
6.5L V8 Turbodiesel OHV 16V Engine	+628
7.4L V8 OHV 16V FI Engine	+138

Options	Price
Air Conditioning [Std on Silverado]	+186
Automatic 4-Speed Transmission	+224
Driver Side Airbag Restraint [Opt on Std Cab]	+81
Leather Seats	+231

Mileage Category: K

A revised interior graces these full-size trucks this year. A new driver-side airbag and a shift interlock are added in the interest of safety. The latter requires the brake pedal to be depressed before the automatic transmission's gear selector can be shifted out of "Park," reducing the likelihood that the vehicle will move suddenly and unexpectedly. Power mirrors, revised climate controls and cupholders provide a more user-friendly interior environment.

Mechanical enhancements include the addition of standard four-wheel antilock brakes, improvements in the engines and modifications to the heavy-duty automatic gearbox. The four-wheel ABS replaces last year's rear-wheel-only antilock system. Various upgrades to the engines are intended to reduce noise improve durability and/or increase efficiency. The transmission is revised for quicker 1-2 upshifts during full-throttle applications.

Chevrolet

C/K 2500 Series/C/K 3500 Series

1994

Mileage Category: K

Safety is enhanced with the side door guard beams designed to minimize intrusion into the passenger compartment during a side impact. A center high-mounted brake light is also added to enhance safety.

Chevy boasts it is the first automaker to offer a turbodiesel engine option in a vehicle with a gross vehicle weight rating less than 8,500 pounds.

Rust corrosion protection is improved while interior noise vibration and harshness is reduced. Rounding out the list of significant improvements are the addition of an "easy entry" feature to the front passenger seat on extended cab body styles to ease entry into the rear seating positions and the revision of the exterior front-end styling.

Body Styles	TMV Pricing		
	Trade	Private	Dealer
2 Dr C2500 Cheyenne Ext Cab LB	3614	4630	6323
2 Dr C2500 Cheyenne Ext Cab SB	3553	4552	6216
2 Dr C2500 Cheyenne Std Cab LB	2881	3691	5041
2 Dr C2500 Silverado Ext Cab LB	3843	4923	6724
2 Dr C2500 Silverado Ext Cab SB	3775	4836	6604
2 Dr C2500 Silverado Std Cab LB	3025	3875	5292
2 Dr K2500 Cheyenne 4WD Ext Cab LB	4081	5229	7141

Body Styles	TMV Pricing		
	Trade	Private	Dealer
2 Dr K2500 Cheyenne 4WD Ext Cab SB	3793	4859	6636
2 Dr K2500 Cheyenne 4WD Std Cab LB	3330	4266	5827
2 Dr K2500 Silverado 4WD Ext Cab LB	4420	5662	7733
2 Dr K2500 Silverado 4WD Ext Cab LB	4035	5169	7059
2 Dr K2500 Silverado 4WD Std Cab LB	3717	4762	6504

Options	Price
5.0L V8 OHV 16V FI Engine	+143
5.7L V8 OHV 16V FI Engine	+143
6.5L V8 Diesel OHV 16V Engine	+557
6.5L V8 Turbodiesel OHV 16V Engine	+555

Options	Price
7.4L V8 OHV 16V FI Engine	+123
Air Conditioning [Std on Silverado]	+165
Automatic 4-Speed Transmission	+198

Chevrolet
C/K 3500 Series

2000

Mileage Category: K

One new paint color. Last year for "C/K" nomenclature.

Body Styles	TMV Pricing		
	Trade	Private	Dealer
2 Dr C3500 Ext Cab LB	11326	12815	14275
2 Dr C3500 LS Ext Cab LB	12265	13878	15459
2 Dr C3500 LS Std Cab LB	10691	12097	13475
2 Dr C3500 Std Cab LB	9510	10760	11986
2 Dr K3500 4WD Ext Cab LB	12283	13898	15482
2 Dr K3500 4WD Std Cab LB	10831	12255	13651
2 Dr K3500 LS 4WD Ext Cab LB	14308	16190	18034
2 Dr K3500 LS 4WD Std Cab LB	11548	13067	14555

Body Styles	TMV Pricing		
	Trade	Private	Dealer
4 Dr C3500 Crew Cab LB	10834	12259	13655
4 Dr C3500 Crew Cab SB	11358	12851	14315
4 Dr C3500 LS Crew Cab LB	13096	14818	16506
4 Dr C3500 LS Crew Cab SB	14295	16175	18017
4 Dr K3500 4WD Crew Cab LB	12321	13941	15529
4 Dr K3500 4WD Crew Cab SB	14178	16042	17870
4 Dr K3500 LS 4WD Crew Cab LB	14649	16575	18463
4 Dr K3500 LS 4WD Crew Cab SB	16098	18215	20290

Options	Price
6.5L V8 Turbodiesel OHV 16V Engine	+1271
7.4L V8 OHV 16V FI Engine	+281
Air Conditioning	+377
AM/FM/Cassette/CD Audio System	+136
Automatic 4-Speed Transmission	+465

Options	Price
Bucket Seats	+126
Dual Rear Wheels	+401
Leather Seats	+468
Limited Slip Differential	+134
Locking Differential	+134

1999

Mileage Category: K

Model consolidation takes place in anticipation of the all-new Silverado. Trim levels have been changed from three to two (Base and LS) and two new Crew Cab Short Box models (C/K2500 and C/K3500 Series) are offered. Additionally, the C/K1500 will be available only as an LS Extended Cab Short Box with the third door. Mechanical upgrades include new internal components and seals for automatic transmissions, improved cooling system and starter motor durability and three new exterior paint colors.

Body Styles	TMV Pricing		
	Trade	Private	Dealer
2 Dr C3500 Ext Cab LB	9299	10748	12256
2 Dr C3500 LS Ext Cab LB	10300	11905	13576
2 Dr C3500 LS Std Cab LB	8828	10203	11635
2 Dr C3500 Std Cab LB	7652	8845	10086
2 Dr K3500 4WD Ext Cab LB	10416	12039	13729
2 Dr K3500 4WD Std Cab LB	9064	10476	11946
2 Dr K3500 LS 4WD Ext Cab LB	12302	14219	16214
2 Dr K3500 LS 4WD Std Cab LB	10066	11634	13267

Body Styles	TMV Pricing		
	Trade	Private	Dealer
4 Dr C3500 Crew Cab LB	9240	10680	12179
4 Dr C3500 Crew Cab SB	9828	11360	12954
4 Dr C3500 LS Crew Cab LB	11499	13291	15156
4 Dr C3500 LS Crew Cab SB	12125	14014	15981
4 Dr K3500 4WD Crew Cab LB	10488	12123	13824
4 Dr K3500 4WD Crew Cab SB	11587	13393	15272
4 Dr K3500 LS 4WD Crew Cab LB	12360	14286	16291
4 Dr K3500 LS 4WD Crew Cab SB	12950	14968	17068

Options	Price
Dual Rear Wheels	+320
Leather Seats	+438
6.5L V8 Turbodiesel OHV 16V Engine	+1014

Options	Price
7.4L V8 OHV 16V FI Engine	+224
Air Conditioning	+300
Automatic 4-Speed Transmission	+372

1998

Body Styles	TMV Pricing		
	Trade	Private	Dealer
2 Dr C3500 Cheyenne Ext Cab LB	7693	9060	10601
2 Dr C3500 Cheyenne Std Cab LB	6401	7538	8821
2 Dr C3500 Silverado Ext Cab LB	8705	10251	11995
2 Dr C3500 Silverado Std Cab LB	7262	8552	10007
2 Dr K3500 Cheyenne 4WD Ext Cab LB	8711	10259	12004
2 Dr K3500 Cheyenne 4WD Std Cab LB	7476	8804	10302

Body Styles	TMV Pricing		
	Trade	Private	Dealer
2 Dr K3500 Silverado 4WD Ext Cab LB	9681	11401	13341
2 Dr K3500 Silverado 4WD Std Cab LB	8596	10124	11846
4 Dr Cheyenne Crew Cab LB	7530	8868	10377
4 Dr C3500 Silverado Crew Cab LB	9241	10883	12735
4 Dr K3500 Cheyenne 4WD Crew Cab LB	8738	10290	12041
4 Dr K3500 Silverado 4WD Crew Cab LB	10434	12288	14378

Options	Price
Automatic 4-Speed Transmission	+305
Bucket Seats	+121
Dual Rear Wheels	+269
Leather Seats	+314

Options	Price
6.5L V8 Turbodiesel OHV 16V Engine	+854
7.4L V8 OHV 16V FI Engine	+189
Air Conditioning [Std on Silverado]	+253

Mileage Category: K

The year 1998 brings subtle refinements to Chevy's one-ton truck. Passlock is added to aid in theft prevention. If someone starts the vehicle without the proper key, the engine will shut off immediately, not allowing the truck to move on its own power for 10 minutes.

The 4L60-E (light-duty) and 4L80-E (heavy-duty) electronically controlled four-speed automatic transmissions are updated to increase durability, improve gas mileage, reduce vibration (4L60-E only) and operate more smoothly overall.

Some exterior colors are replaced.

1997

Body Styles	TMV Pricing		
	Trade	Private	Dealer
2 Dr C3500 Cheyenne Ext Cab LB	6480	7785	9379
2 Dr C3500 Cheyenne Std Cab LB	5120	6151	7411
2 Dr C3500 Silverado Ext Cab LB	6721	8074	9728
2 Dr C3500 Silverado Std Cab LB	5978	7181	8652
2 Dr K3500 Cheyenne 4WD Ext Cab LB	7083	8509	10252
2 Dr K3500 Cheyenne 4WD Std Cab LB	6409	7699	9276

Body Styles	TMV Pricing		
	Trade	Private	Dealer
2 Dr K3500 Silverado 4WD Ext Cab LB	7595	9124	10993
2 Dr K3500 Silverado 4WD Std Cab LB	6613	7945	9572
4 Dr C3500 Cheyenne Crew Cab LB	6437	7733	9317
4 Dr C3500 Silverado Crew Cab LB	7556	9077	10937
4 Dr K3500 Cheyenne 4WD Crew Cab LB	7532	9048	10901
4 Dr K3500 Silverado 4WD Crew Cab LB	8532	10250	12350

Options	Price
6.5L V8 Turbodiesel OHV 16V Engine	+772
7.4L V8 OHV 16V FI Engine	+171
Air Conditioning [Std on Silverado]	+229

Options	Price
Automatic 4-Speed Transmission	+276
Dual Rear Wheels	+244
Leather Seats	+284

Mileage Category: K

On trucks under 8,600 pounds GVWR, the passenger airbag can be deactivated when a rear-facing child safety seat is installed. Low-speed steering effort is reduced this year, and a refined transmission fluid pump results in smoother shifts. An alternative fuel version of the Vortec 5700 is available, but only on a specific model. K1500s get a tighter turning radius, and three new colors debut. The third door option will be more widely available.

1996

Body Styles	TMV Pricing		
	Trade	Private	Dealer
2 Dr C3500 Cheyenne Ext Cab LB	5435	6655	8340
2 Dr C3500 Cheyenne Std Cab LB	4446	5444	6823
2 Dr C3500 Silverado Ext Cab LB	5784	7083	8876
2 Dr C3500 Silverado Std Cab LB	5039	6170	7732
2 Dr K3500 Cheyenne 4WD Ext Cab LB	6194	7585	9505
2 Dr K3500 Cheyenne 4WD Std Cab LB	5288	6475	8115

Body Styles	TMV Pricing		
	Trade	Private	Dealer
2 Dr K3500 Silverado 4WD Ext Cab LB	6391	7826	9807
2 Dr K3500 Silverado 4WD Std Cab LB	5733	7020	8797
4 Dr C3500 Cheyenne Crew Cab LB	5331	6528	8180
4 Dr C3500 Silverado Crew Cab LB	6324	7744	9705
4 Dr K3500 Cheyenne 4WD Crew Cab LB	6290	7702	9653
4 Dr K3500 Silverado 4WD Crew Cab LB	7264	8895	11147

Options	Price
6.5L V8 Turbodiesel OHV 16V Engine	+700
7.4L V8 OHV 16V FI Engine	+155
Air Conditioning [Std on Silverado]	+207

Options	Price
Automatic 4-Speed Transmission	+250
Dual Rear Wheels	+221
Leather Seats	+258

Mileage Category: K

A new series of engines is introduced, providing more power and torque than last year's offerings. Called Vortec, this family of engines includes a 4.3-liter V6 (the only six-cylinder of the bunch) capable of 200 hp at 4,400 rpm and 255 lb-ft of torque at 2,800 rpm; a 5.0-liter V8, producing 220 hp at 4,600 rpm and 285 lb-ft of torque at 2,800 rpm; and a 5.7-liter V8, rated at 250 hp at 4,600 rpm and 335 lb-ft of torque at 2,800 rpm. (There is also a 7.4-liter Vortec V8, but it's only available on the heavier-duty C/K 3500 trucks.) All of these figures represent increases in output when compared to their respective 1995 predecessors. An optional electronic shift transfer case for the K1500 (i.e. 4WD; C=2WD; K=4WD) rounds out the list of the most significant powertrain updates for the year.

Other noteworthy updates include the introduction of an optional passenger-side third door, called the "Easy-Access System," in GM vernacular. This feature is only available on the extended cab body styles.

Improved comfort and convenience comes in the way of such new features as illuminated entry, 12-volt power outlets, an electrochromic inside rearview mirror and height-adjustable D-rings for the shoulder section of the front three-point safety belts, among others. Daytime running lamps (DRLs) are part of the list of new exterior features.

A new level of sophistication in exhaust emissions monitoring is found with the addition of OBD II, the second generation of On-Board Diagnostics.

Chevrolet
C/K 3500 Series/Camaro

1995

Mileage Category: K

A revised interior graces these full-size trucks this year. A new driver-side airbag and a shift interlock are added in the interest of safety. The latter requires the brake pedal to be depressed before the automatic transmission's gear selector can be shifted out of "Park," reducing the likelihood that the vehicle will move suddenly and unexpectedly. Power mirrors, revised climate controls and cupholders provide a more user-friendly interior environment.

Mechanical enhancements include the addition of standard four-wheel antilock brakes, improvements in the engines and modifications to the heavy-duty automatic gearbox. The four-wheel ABS replaces last year's rear-wheel-only antilock system. Various upgrades to the engines are intended to reduce noise improve durability and/or increase efficiency. The transmission is revised for quicker 1-2 upshifts during full-throttle applications.

Body Styles	TMV Pricing		
	Trade	Private	Dealer
2 Dr C3500 Cheyenne Ext Cab LB	4344	5355	7041
2 Dr C3500 Cheyenne Std Cab LB	3832	4724	6210
2 Dr C3500 Silverado Ext Cab LB	5000	6164	8104
2 Dr C3500 Silverado Std Cab LB	4250	5239	6888
2 Dr K3500 Cheyenne 4WD Ext Cab LB	4905	6047	7950
2 Dr K3500 Cheyenne 4WD Std Cab LB	4289	5287	6951

Body Styles	TMV Pricing		
	Trade	Private	Dealer
2 Dr K3500 Silverado 4WD Ext Cab LB	5367	6617	8700
2 Dr K3500 Silverado 4WD Std Cab LB	4810	5930	7797
4 Dr C3500 Cheyenne Crew Cab LB	4306	5308	6979
4 Dr C3500 Silverado Crew Cab LB	5279	6508	8556
4 Dr K3500 Cheyenne 4WD Crew Cab LB	5045	6220	8177
4 Dr K3500 Silverado 4WD Crew Cab LB	6119	7544	9918

Options	Price
6.5L V8 Turbodiesel OHV 16V Engine	+628
7.4L V8 OHV 16V FI Engine	+138
Air Conditioning [Std on Silverado]	+186

Options	Price
Automatic 4-Speed Transmission	+224
Dual Rear Wheels	+185
Leather Seats	+231

1994

Mileage Category: K

Safety is enhanced with the side door guard beams designed to minimize intrusion into the passenger compartment during a side impact. A center high-mounted brake light is also added to enhance safety.

Chevy boasts it is the first automaker to offer a turbodiesel engine option in a vehicle with a gross vehicle weight rating less than 8,500 pounds.

Rust corrosion protection is improved while interior noise vibration and harshness is reduced. Rounding out the list of significant improvements are the addition of an "easy entry" feature to the front passenger seat on extended cab body styles to ease entry into the rear seating positions and the revision of the exterior front-end styling.

Body Styles	TMV Pricing		
	Trade	Private	Dealer
2 Dr C3500 Cheyenne Ext Cab LB	3671	4703	6423
2 Dr C3500 Cheyenne Std Cab LB	3230	4138	5651
2 Dr C3500 Silverado Ext Cab LB	4025	5157	7043
2 Dr C3500 Silverado Std Cab LB	3495	4477	6114
2 Dr K3500 Cheyenne 4WD Ext Cab LB	4070	5214	7121
2 Dr K3500 Cheyenne 4WD Std Cab LB	3558	4558	6225

Body Styles	TMV Pricing		
	Trade	Private	Dealer
2 Dr K3500 Silverado 4WD Ext Cab LB	4513	5781	7895
2 Dr K3500 Silverado 4WD Std Cab LB	3938	5045	6889
4 Dr C3500 Cheyenne Crew Cab LB	3425	4388	5993
4 Dr C3500 Silverado Crew Cab LB	3983	5102	6968
4 Dr K3500 4WD Crew Cab LB	4159	5328	7277
4 Dr K3500 Silverado 4WD Crew Cab LB	4732	6063	8280

Options	Price
Automatic 4-Speed Transmission	+198
Dual Rear Wheels	+163
Premium Audio System	+102

Options	Price
Air Conditioning [Std on Silverado]	+165
6.5L V8 Turbodiesel OHV 16V Engine	+555
7.4L V8 OHV 16V FI Engine	+123

Chevrolet
Camaro

2002

Mileage Category: E

Few changes are made to the Camaro in what is its final year of production. Minor additions include a special 35th anniversary package and Sebring Silver to the color palette.

Body Styles	TMV Pricing		
	Trade	Private	Dealer
2 Dr STD Conv	12364	13575	15592
2 Dr STD Hbk	8790	9651	11085

Body Styles	TMV Pricing		
	Trade	Private	Dealer
2 Dr Z28 Conv	14737	16180	18585
2 Dr Z28 Hbk	12202	13397	15389

Options	Price
17 Inch Wheels	+373
Automatic 4-Speed Transmission [Opt on STD]	+467
Chrome Wheels	+416
Compact Disc Changer	+341
Leather Seats	+287
Limited Slip Differential [Opt on STD]	+158

Options	Price
Monsoon Audio System [Opt on STD Hbk]	+201
Power Driver Seat [Std on Z28 Conv]	+138
Power Windows [Opt on Hbk]	+129
SS Package	+2079
Traction Control System	+143
T-Tops - Glass	+571

2001

Mileage Category: E

More horsepower is on tap for the Z28 and SS models, while styled chrome 16-inch wheels are a new option for base and Z28 models and Sunset Orange Metallic is added to the list of colors.

Body Styles	TMV Pricing		
	Trade	Private	Dealer
2 Dr STD Conv	10695	12356	13889
2 Dr STD Hbk	6857	7922	8906

Body Styles	TMV Pricing		
	Trade	Private	Dealer
2 Dr Z28 Conv	11754	13580	15266
2 Dr Z28 Hbk	10606	12253	13774

2001 (cont'd)

Options	Price
5.7L V8 OHV 16V FI w/Ram Air Engine	+2072
Aluminum/Alloy Wheels [Opt on STD]	+144
Automatic 4-Speed Transmission [Opt on STD]	+428
Chrome Wheels	+380
Compact Disc Changer	+312
Leather Seats	+262
Limited Slip Differential [Opt on STD]	+236

Options	Price
Monsoon Audio System	+184
Power Door Locks [Opt on STD,Cpe]	+115
Power Driver Seat [Opt on STD,Cpe]	+142
Power Windows [Opt on STD,Cpe]	+137
Traction Control System	+131
T-Tops - Glass	+522

2000

Mileage Category: E

New interior colors and fabrics, redundant steering-wheel audio controls, new alloy wheels, and a new exterior color debut. V6 and V8 engines meet California's low emission vehicle (LEV) standards.

Body Styles	TMV Pricing		
	Trade	Private	Dealer
2 Dr STD Conv	9546	11232	12885
2 Dr STD Hbk	5782	6803	7804
2 Dr Z28 Conv	9723	11441	13124

Body Styles	TMV Pricing		
	Trade	Private	Dealer
2 Dr Z28 Hbk	9163	10782	12368
2 Dr Z28 SS Conv	11167	13140	15073
2 Dr Z28 SS Hbk	9394	11053	12679

Options	Price
Aluminum/Alloy Wheels [Opt on STD]	+129
AM/FM/CD Audio System	+147
Automatic 4-Speed Transmission [Opt on STD]	+381
Compact Disc Changer	+278
Leather Seats	+210

Options	Price
Limited Slip Differential [Opt on STD]	+210
Monsoon Audio System	+164
Power Driver Seat [Opt on STD,Cpe]	+126
Power Windows [Opt on STD,Cpe]	+122
T-Tops - Glass	+465

1999

Mileage Category: E

Traction control (Acceleration Slip Regulation in Chevrolet parlance) is available on all models in 1999, and on the Z28 ASR allows for some tire slip before cutting the power to the rear wheels. Electronic throttle control is newly standard on V6 models, a new engine oil-life monitor tracks specific driving conditions to determine when the next change should occur and a Zexel Torsen differential is employed in the limited-slip rear axle.

Body Styles	TMV Pricing		
	Trade	Private	Dealer
2 Dr STD Conv	7564	9231	10967
2 Dr STD Hbk	4362	5323	6324
2 Dr Z28 Conv	7894	9634	11446

Body Styles	TMV Pricing		
	Trade	Private	Dealer
2 Dr Z28 Hbk	7430	9068	10773
2 Dr Z28 SS Conv	9208	11238	13351
2 Dr Z28 SS Hbk	7650	9336	11091

Options	Price
AM/FM/CD Audio System	+118
Automatic 4-Speed Transmission [Opt on STD]	+304
Chrome Wheels	+187
Compact Disc Changer	+222

Options	Price
Leather Seats	+205
Limited Slip Differential [Opt on STD]	+168
Performance/Handling Package	+448
T-Tops - Glass	+372

1998

Mileage Category: E

Chevrolet dumps a 305-horsepower version of the Corvette's V8 engine under a new front end, adds standard four-wheel disc brakes on all models, adds a couple of new colors, makes second-generation airbags standard and revises trim levels. The midyear SS package makes 320 horsepower.

Body Styles	TMV Pricing		
	Trade	Private	Dealer
2 Dr STD Conv	6225	7727	9421
2 Dr STD Hbk	3734	4635	5650
2 Dr Z28 Conv	6718	8339	10166

Body Styles	TMV Pricing		
	Trade	Private	Dealer
2 Dr Z28 Hbk	6152	7636	9309
2 Dr Z28 SS Conv	7992	9920	12094
2 Dr Z28 SS Hbk	6486	8051	9815

Options	Price
AM/FM/Cassette/CD Audio System [Opt on STD Cpe]	+141
Automatic 4-Speed Transmission [Opt on STD]	+256
Chrome Wheels	+157
Compact Disc Changer	+187

Options	Price
Leather Seats	+173
Limited Slip Differential [Opt on STD]	+141
Performance/Handling Package	+370
T-Tops - Glass	+313

1997

Mileage Category: E

Chevrolet celebrates the Camaro's 30th Anniversary with a special-edition Z28 that emulates the appearance of the 1969 SS Indy Pace Car with white paint, Hugger Orange stripes, and black-and-white houndstooth seat inserts. Interior revisions to seats, center console and dashboard freshen the look inside for 1997. Two new shades of gray are available for interiors, while exteriors get new green and purple hues. Tricolor taillamps debut, and new five-spoke alloy wheels are optional. On the safety front, daytime running lights are standard and side-impact regulations are met.

Body Styles	TMV Pricing		
	Trade	Private	Dealer
2 Dr RS Conv	4900	6255	7912
2 Dr RS Hbk	3961	5057	6396
2 Dr STD Conv	4833	6170	7804
2 Dr STD Hbk	3134	4001	5061

Body Styles	TMV Pricing		
	Trade	Private	Dealer
2 Dr Z28 Conv	5212	6653	8415
2 Dr Z28 Hbk	4744	6057	7661
2 Dr Z28 SS Conv	6635	8470	10713
2 Dr Z28 SS Hbk	5195	6632	8389

1997 (cont'd)

Options	Price
Automatic 4-Speed Transmission [Opt on STD]	+225
Chrome Wheels	+220
Compact Disc Changer	+169
Leather Seats	+156

Options	Price
Limited Slip Differential [Opt on RS,STD]	+128
Performance/Handling Package	+341
T-Tops - Glass [Opt on Hbk]	+283

1996

Mileage Category: E

A new 200-hp base V6 is available. Z28's 285-hp LT1 V8 (gets 10 more horsepower this year). SLP Engineering provides a 305-horse Z28 SS. The RS trim level returns, and chrome-aluminum wheels are optional.

Body Styles	TMV Pricing		
	Trade	Private	Dealer
2 Dr RS Conv	3893	5085	6730
2 Dr RS Hbk	3280	4283	5669
2 Dr STD Conv	3765	4917	6508
2 Dr STD Hbk	2499	3264	4320

Body Styles	TMV Pricing		
	Trade	Private	Dealer
2 Dr Z28 Conv	4381	5721	7572
2 Dr Z28 Hbk	3398	4438	5874
2 Dr Z28 SS Conv	5339	6973	9229
2 Dr Z28 SS Hbk	4098	5351	7082

Options	Price
Automatic 4-Speed Transmission	+204
Chrome Wheels	+129
Compact Disc Changer	+154
Delco/Bose Audio System	+156
Leather Seats	+142

Options	Price
Limited Slip Differential [Opt on RS,STD]	+116
Performance/Handling Package	+303
T-Tops - Glass	+250
Air Conditioning [Opt on STD,Cpe]	+231

1995

Mileage Category: E

Z28 gets optional traction control. Z28 can now be ordered with body-color roof and side mirrors (standard color is gloss black). Chrome-plated alloys are newly optional.

Body Styles	TMV Pricing		
	Trade	Private	Dealer
2 Dr STD Conv	2935	3849	5372
2 Dr STD Hbk	2148	2817	3932

Body Styles	TMV Pricing		
	Trade	Private	Dealer
2 Dr Z28 Conv	3733	4896	6834
2 Dr Z28 Hbk	2846	3733	5210

Options	Price
Air Conditioning	+207
Automatic 4-Speed Transmission	+162
Delco/Bose Audio System	+140

Options	Price
Leather Seats	+127
T-Tops - Glass	+224

1994

Mileage Category: E

Convertible returns in base and Z28 trim. First-to-fourth shift pattern added to six-speed manual transmission to meet fuel economy regulations. Z28 with manual transmission gets revised gearing for better acceleration.

Body Styles	TMV Pricing		
	Trade	Private	Dealer
2 Dr STD Conv	2500	3396	4888
2 Dr STD Hbk	1731	2351	3384

Body Styles	TMV Pricing		
	Trade	Private	Dealer
2 Dr Z28 Conv	3029	4113	5920
2 Dr Z28 Hbk	2084	2830	4073

Options	Price
Air Conditioning	+183
AM/FM/Cassette/CD Audio System	+108
Automatic 4-Speed Transmission	+123

Options	Price
Leather Seats	+112
T-Tops - Glass	+198

Chevrolet
Caprice

1996

Mileage Category: G

No changes as Caprice enters final year of production.

Body Styles	TMV Pricing		
	Trade	Private	Dealer
4 Dr STD Sdn	2934	3787	4965
4 Dr STD Wgn	3447	4449	5832

Options	Price
Sport Suspension	+131
5.7L V8 OHV 16V FI Engine [Opt on Sdn]	+157
Leather Seats	+222

1995

Body Styles	TMV Pricing		
	Trade	Private	Dealer
4 Dr STD Sdn	2420	3163	4401
4 Dr STD Wgn	2566	3354	4666

Options	Price
5.7L V8 OHV 16V FI Engine [Std on Wgn]	+141
AM/FM/CD Audio System	+91
Leather Seats	+180
Sport Suspension	+117

Mileage Category: G

Impala SS styling treatment for C-pillar is carried over to more mainstream sedan. New seats and radios debut. Outside mirrors can be folded in, and a new option is a radio with speed-compensated volume control.

1994

Body Styles	TMV Pricing		
	Trade	Private	Dealer
4 Dr LS Sdn	1893	2613	3813
4 Dr STD Sdn	1622	2239	3268
4 Dr STD Wgn	1858	2565	3744

Options	Price
AM/FM/CD Audio System	+81
Leather Seats	+158
Sport Suspension	+104

Mileage Category: G

Passenger airbag added. New base engine for sedan is a 200-horsepower, 4.3-liter V8. Optional on sedan and standard on wagon is a more powerful 260-horsepower, 5.7-liter V8. Automatic transmissions get electronic controls. Pass-Key II is a standard theft-deterrent system, and CFC-free refrigerant is added to air conditioning systems.

Chevrolet
Cavalier

2003

Body Styles	TMV Pricing		
	Trade	Private	Dealer
2 Dr LS Cpe	7895	8822	10366
2 Dr LS Sport Cpe	8620	9632	11319
2 Dr STD Cpe	6787	7584	8912

Body Styles	TMV Pricing		
	Trade	Private	Dealer
4 Dr LS Sdn	8056	9002	10578
4 Dr LS Sport Sdn	8688	9708	11408
4 Dr STD Sdn	6965	7783	9145

Options	Price
AM/FM/CD Audio System [Opt on STD]	+192
Antilock Brakes [Opt on STD]	+447
Automatic 4-Speed Transmission	+520
Cruise Control [Opt on STD]	+160
Keyless Entry System [Opt on STD]	+236

Options	Price
Power Moonroof [Opt on Cpe]	+415
Front Side Airbag Restraints	+223
OnStar Telematic System [Opt on LS,LS Sport]	+444
Satellite Radio System	+207

Mileage Category: B

The Cavalier gets a refresh this year that adds new front and rear fascias, revised headlights and taillights, redesigned ground effects, body-colored mirrors and door handles and a new hood. LS Sport models also get integrated foglights and new rocker moldings. The 2.2-liter Ecotec four-cylinder is now the only engine offered, as the Z24 model has been dropped from the lineup. Base model Cavs no longer come with standard ABS brakes, but it remains an available option. Inside, the Cavalier now features a center rear three-point seatbelt, a leather-wrapped steering wheel and shift lever, a rear 60/40-split bench seat, new child-seat anchors and optional side airbags. Finally, you can get XM Satellite Radio on all cars, and LS and LS Sport trims are available with the OnStar communications system.

2002

Body Styles	TMV Pricing		
	Trade	Private	Dealer
2 Dr LS Cpe	6146	7059	8581
2 Dr LS Sport Cpe	6752	7756	9428
2 Dr STD Cpe	5280	6065	7373
2 Dr Z24 Cpe	6448	7406	9003

Body Styles	TMV Pricing		
	Trade	Private	Dealer
4 Dr LS Sdn	6285	7219	8776
4 Dr LS Sport Sdn	6802	7813	9498
4 Dr STD Sdn	5345	6140	7464
4 Dr Z24 Sdn	6788	7797	9478

Options	Price
16 Inch Wheels [Opt on STD]	+330
2.4L I4 DOHC 16V FI Engine [Opt on LS]	+258
Aluminum/Alloy Wheels [Std on Z24]	+169
AM/FM/Cassette/CD Audio System [Opt on LS,STD]	+132

Options	Price
Automatic 4-Speed Transmission	+447
Cruise Control [Opt on STD]	+135
Keyless Entry System [Opt on STD]	+212
Power Sunroof [Opt on Cpe]	+341

Mileage Category: B

New LS Sport trim level for coupes and sedans that features an all-new 2.2-liter EcoTec engine. A Z24 sedan joins the Z24 coupe at the top end of the lineup, while both the LS and base model Cavalier gain additional standard equipment and an optional Sport appearance package. Both Z24 models get an upgraded stereo and an optional Sport appearance package will be available later in the year. Three new colors have also been added along with an upgraded cloth interior.

Chevrolet
Cavalier

2001

Mileage Category: B

Indigo Blue is added to the exterior palette. A CD player is made standard on the LS Sedan and Z24 Coupe. The Z24 Convertible has vanished from the lineup.

Body Styles	TMV Pricing				Body Styles	TMV Pricing		
	Trade	Private	Dealer			Trade	Private	Dealer
2 Dr STD Cpe	4278	5335	6311		4 Dr LS Sdn	5005	6241	7382
2 Dr Z24 Cpe	5462	6811	8057		4 Dr STD Sdn	4322	5390	6375

Options	Price		Options	Price
2.4L I4 DOHC 16V FI Engine [Opt on LS]	+236		Automatic 4-Speed Transmission [Std on LS]	+409
Aluminum/Alloy Wheels [Std on Z24]	+155		Power Sunroof	+312
AM/FM/CD Audio System	+168		Power Windows [Std on Z24]	+138
Automatic 3-Speed Transmission	+367			

2000

Mileage Category: B

Still available as a coupe, sedan or convertible, Chevy's best-selling car gets several subtle changes for 2000. Outside it has new body-colored front and rear facias, new headlamp/taillamp assemblies, new badging and restyled wheel covers/alloy wheels. Inside, the instrument panel now features an electronic odometer and tripmeter, a revamped center console with three front cupholders and an improved storage area. Functionally, it gets a better-shifting five-speed manual transaxle, smoother-operating ABS, Passlock II security system and standard air conditioning.

Body Styles	TMV Pricing				Body Styles	TMV Pricing		
	Trade	Private	Dealer			Trade	Private	Dealer
2 Dr STD Cpe	3462	4467	5453		4 Dr LS Sdn	3863	4985	6084
2 Dr Z24 Conv	5099	6580	8032		4 Dr STD Sdn	3504	4522	5519
2 Dr Z24 Cpe	4610	5949	7262					

Options	Price		Options	Price
2.4L I4 DOHC 16V FI Engine [Opt on LS]	+210		Automatic 4-Speed Transmission [Std on LS]	+365
Aluminum/Alloy Wheels [Std on Z24]	+138		Power Moonroof [Opt on Cpe]	+278
AM/FM/CD Audio System	+150		Power Windows [Std on Z24]	+123
Automatic 3-Speed Transmission	+281			

1999

Mileage Category: B

The 2.4 twin-cam engine benefits from reliability, emissions and fuel economy enhancements, and new front brake linings increase pad life. Minor interior and exterior revisions have been made, and new Fern Green Metallic and Sandrift Metallic replace Bright Aqua and Deep Purple on the paint chart.

Body Styles	TMV Pricing				Body Styles	TMV Pricing		
	Trade	Private	Dealer			Trade	Private	Dealer
2 Dr RS Cpe	2926	3878	4868		2 Dr Z24 Cpe	3837	5085	6383
2 Dr STD Cpe	2649	3510	4407		4 Dr LS Sdn	3242	4296	5394
2 Dr Z24 Conv	3855	5109	6415		4 Dr STD Sdn	2658	3523	4423

Options	Price		Options	Price
2.4L I4 DOHC 16V FI Engine [Opt on LS]	+168		Automatic 3-Speed Transmission	+224
Air Conditioning [Std on LS,Z24]	+297		Automatic 4-Speed Transmission [Std on LS]	+291
AM/FM/CD Audio System	+119		Power Sunroof	+222

1998

Mileage Category: B

A Z24 convertible is introduced, cruise control is standard on all but base models, power windows and remote keyless entry are no longer available on base cars, and buyers can no longer delete the AM/FM radio. Second-generation airbags debut on all models.

Body Styles	TMV Pricing				Body Styles	TMV Pricing		
	Trade	Private	Dealer			Trade	Private	Dealer
2 Dr RS Cpe	2242	3060	3982		2 Dr Z24 Cpe	2654	3622	4713
2 Dr STD Cpe	1971	2690	3500		4 Dr LS Sdn	2446	3338	4344
2 Dr Z24 Conv	3061	4178	5437		4 Dr STD Sdn	2005	2736	3561

Options	Price		Options	Price
2.4L I4 DOHC 16V FI Engine [Opt on LS]	+141		Automatic 4-Speed Transmission [Std on LS]	+245
Air Conditioning [Opt on RS,STD]	+250		Power Sunroof	+187
Automatic 3-Speed Transmission	+189			

1997

Mileage Category: B

The Rally Sport (RS) trim is available for 1997 on the coupe and slotted between base and Z24 editions of the Cavalier. RS trim nets buyers the rear spoiler from the Z24, 15-inch tires, AM/FM stereo, tachometer, interior and exterior trim upgrades and a 3D rear-quarter panel decal. Base coupes have new wheel covers and safety belt guide loops. All 1997 Cavaliers meet federal side-impact standards for the first time. One new interior color and three new exterior colors freshen the lineup.

Body Styles	TMV Pricing				Body Styles	TMV Pricing		
	Trade	Private	Dealer			Trade	Private	Dealer
2 Dr LS Conv	2572	3614	4888		2 Dr Z24 Cpe	2170	3050	4125
2 Dr RS Cpe	1865	2621	3544		4 Dr LS Sdn	2001	2812	3803
2 Dr STD Cpe	1594	2240	3029		4 Dr STD Sdn	1594	2240	3029

Options	Price
Air Conditioning [Opt on RS,STD]	+226
Automatic 3-Speed Transmission [Std on LS]	+156

Options	Price
Automatic 4-Speed Transmission	+226
Power Sunroof	+191

1996

Body Styles	TMV Pricing		
	Trade	Private	Dealer
2 Dr LS Conv	2045	2980	4270
2 Dr STD Cpe	1118	1629	2335
2 Dr Z24 Cpe	1587	2312	3314

Body Styles	TMV Pricing		
	Trade	Private	Dealer
4 Dr LS Sdn	1470	2142	3071
4 Dr STD Sdn	1182	1723	2469

Options	Price
Air Conditioning [Opt on STD]	+205
Automatic 3-Speed Transmission [Std on LS]	+142
Automatic 4-Speed Transmission	+205

Options	Price
Power Sunroof	+173
2.4L I4 DOHC 16V FI Engine [Opt on LS]	+121

Mileage Category: B

The 2.3-liter Quad 4 is replaced after just one year by a 2.4-liter twin-cam engine. Four-speed automatic transmission includes traction control. Daytime running lights debut, remote keyless entry is optional on LS and Z24 and base models get new interior fabrics and an Appearance Package.

1995

Body Styles	TMV Pricing		
	Trade	Private	Dealer
2 Dr LS Conv	1442	2213	3498
2 Dr STD Cpe	828	1271	2008
2 Dr Z24 Cpe	1163	1786	2823

Body Styles	TMV Pricing		
	Trade	Private	Dealer
4 Dr LS Sdn	999	1533	2422
4 Dr STD Sdn	836	1283	2028

Options	Price
2.3L I4 DOHC 16V FI Engine [Opt on LS Conv]	+150
Air Conditioning [Opt on STD]	+184
AM/FM/CD Audio System	+91

Options	Price
Automatic 3-Speed Transmission [Std on LS]	+127
Automatic 4-Speed Transmission	+81
Power Sunroof	+138

Mileage Category: B

First redesign since 1982 debut. Sedan, coupe and convertible are available. Wagon is dropped. Sedan comes in base and LS trim. Coupe comes in base and Z24 trim. Convertible is available as LS only. Dual airbags and ABS are standard. Base engine is a 2.2-liter, 120-horsepower four-cylinder engine. Optional on LS sedan and convertible is the Z24's standard power plant; a 2.3-liter, DOHC four-cylinder making 150 horsepower.

1994

Body Styles	TMV Pricing		
	Trade	Private	Dealer
2 Dr RS Conv	1060	1723	2827
2 Dr RS Cpe	780	1267	2079
2 Dr VL Cpe	724	1177	1931
2 Dr Z24 Conv	1152	1872	3073

Body Styles	TMV Pricing		
	Trade	Private	Dealer
2 Dr Z24 Cpe	855	1389	2279
4 Dr RS Sdn	791	1285	2108
4 Dr STD Wgn	800	1299	2131
4 Dr VL Sdn	738	1200	1969

Options	Price
3.1L V6 OHV 12V FI Engine [Std on Z24]	+140
Air Conditioning [Opt on VL]	+162
AM/FM/CD Audio System	+81

Options	Price
Automatic 3-Speed Transmission [Opt on RS Cpe,VL,Z24]	+112
Sunroof	+102

Mileage Category: B

Wagon is sold without trim designation. Base engine is up 10 horsepower to 120. Automatic door locks unlock when ignition is turned off.

1996

Body Styles	TMV Pricing		
	Trade	Private	Dealer
4 Dr STD Sdn	1176	1775	2602

Options	Price
3.1L V6 OHV 12V FI Engine	+172
Automatic 4-Speed Transmission	+180

Mileage Category: C

Long-life coolant is standard. Last year for Corsica.

Chevrolet
Corsica/Corvette

1995

Mileage Category: C

Daytime running lights debut. Rear suspension is revised, and larger tires are standard.

Body Styles	TMV Pricing		
	Trade	Private	Dealer
4 Dr STD Sdn	833	1301	2082

Options	Price	Options	Price
3.1L V6 OHV 12V FI Engine	+154	Automatic 4-Speed Transmission	+162
AM/FM/CD Audio System	+91	Power Windows	+79

1994

Mileage Category: C

Door-mounted seatbelts are added. Engines gain power; the 2.2-liter unit is up to 120 horsepower, and the optional 3.1-liter V6 now makes 160 horsepower. Sport Handling Package dropped from options list. Manual transmission dropped. Automatic door locks now unlock when car is shut off. Interior lights will shut off automatically after 10 minutes to save the battery. Warning chime sounds if turn signal is left on.

Body Styles	TMV Pricing		
	Trade	Private	Dealer
4 Dr STD Sdn	659	1108	1855

Options	Price	Options	Price
3.1L V6 OHV 12V FI Engine	+136	Automatic 4-Speed Transmission	+143
AM/FM/CD Audio System	+81		

Chevrolet
Corvette

2003

Body Styles	TMV Pricing		
	Trade	Private	Dealer
2 Dr STD Conv	37813	39770	43032
2 Dr STD Hbk	34536	36324	39303
2 Dr Z06 Cpe	39744	41801	45229

Options	Price	Options	Price
6-Speed Transmission [Opt on STD]	+584	Performance/Handling Package [Opt on STD]	+252
Compact Disc Changer [Opt on STD]	+383	Targa Top - Solid and Glass [Opt on Cpe]	+766
Electronic Damping Suspension Control [Opt on STD]	+1082	Special Factory Paint	+383
		Magnesium Wheels [Opt on STD]	+958
Targa Top - Glass [Opt on Cpe]	+479	Power Driver Seat w/Memory	+131
Heads-Up Display [Opt on STD]	+479	Power Tilt and Telescopic Steering Wheel	+192

Mileage Category: F

Most notable for 2003 is the 50th Anniversary package available on coupe and convertible models. The commemorative package includes Anniversary red exterior paint, a unique shale interior color, champagne-colored wheels and "50th Anniversary" exterior badging with matching embroidery on the headrests and floor mats. Also included in the Anniversary package (or as a stand-alone option on coupes and convertibles) is an all-new Magnetic Ride Control system that provides instantaneous shock adjustment for optimum ride quality and handling. All models also get additional standard equipment that includes sport seats, a power passenger seat, foglamps, dual-zone auto climate control and a parcel net and luggage shade on coupe models.

2002

Mileage Category: F

The track-ready Z06 model gains more power and performance. Electron Blue replaces Navy Blue metallic on the color palette, while Dark Bowling Green metallic gets dropped.

Body Styles	TMV Pricing		
	Trade	Private	Dealer
2 Dr STD Conv	33645	35623	38920
2 Dr STD Hbk	30166	31939	34894
2 Dr Z06 Cpe	34596	36630	40019

Options	Price	Options	Price
6-Speed Transmission [Std on Z06]	+525	Power Passenger Seat	+138
Automatic Climate Control (2 Zone) - Driver and Passenger [Std on Z06]	+330	Power Tilt and Telescopic Steering Wheel	+172
Compact Disc Changer	+344	Special Factory Paint	+344
Electronic Damping Suspension Control	+972	Sport Seats	+258
Metallic Paint	+344	Targa Top - Solid [Opt on Cpe]	+430
Performance/Handling Package [Std on Z06]	+227	Targa Top - Solid and Glass [Opt on Cpe]	+688
Power Driver Seat w/Memory	+118		

2001

Mileage Category: F

Body Styles	TMV Pricing		
	Trade	Private	Dealer
2 Dr STD Conv	29612	32404	34981
2 Dr STD Hbk	26210	28681	30962
2 Dr Z06 Cpe	29998	32827	35438

Options	Price	Options	Price
6-Speed Transmission	+428	Metallic Paint	+315
Automatic Climate Control (2 Zone) - Driver and Passenger	+302	Power Passenger Seat [Opt on STD]	+160
Compact Disc Changer	+315	Power Tilt and Telescopic Steering Wheel [Opt on STD]	+157
Electronic Damping Suspension Control	+889	Special Factory Paint	+315
Heads-Up Display	+197	Sport Seats	+236
Magnesium Wheels	+1049	Targa Top - Solid and Glass	+498

The entire Corvette lineup receives a dose of additional horsepower and torque. The Z06 model joins the lineup, and Active Handling is now standard on all Corvettes.

2000

Mileage Category: F

Body Styles	TMV Pricing		
	Trade	Private	Dealer
2 Dr STD Conv	26140	28941	31686
2 Dr STD Cpe	23045	25514	27935
2 Dr STD Hbk	23351	25854	28308

Options	Price	Options	Price
Automatic Climate Control (2 Zone) - Driver and Passenger	+171	Polished Aluminum/Alloy Wheels	+419
Automatic Stability Control	+234	Power Driver Seat [Opt on Cpe]	+143
Bose Audio System [Opt on Cpe]	+384	Power Passenger Seat	+143
Compact Disc Changer	+281	Power Tilt and Telescopic Steering Wheel	+164
Electronic Damping Suspension Control	+793	Special Factory Paint	+234
Heads-Up Display	+175	Sport Seats	+327
Magnesium Wheels	+936	Targa Top - Glass	+304
		Targa Top - Solid and Glass	+515

Minor refinements improve the Corvette for 2000. The Z51 performance-handling package has larger front and rear stabilizer bars for improved handling, while new thin-spoke alloy wheels with optional high-polish finish subtly change the outward appearance. Two new colors are available on coupe and convertible: extra-cost Millennium Yellow and no-cost Dark Bowling Green Metallic. A Torch Red interior can be ordered, the stupendous LS1 5.7-liter V8 engine meets LEV regulations in California, the remote keyless-entry system has been upgraded, and the passenger door-lock cylinder has been deleted.

1999

Mileage Category: F

Body Styles	TMV Pricing		
	Trade	Private	Dealer
2 Dr STD Conv	22509	25266	28136
2 Dr STD Cpe	20061	22518	25076
2 Dr STD Hbk	20363	22858	25454

Options	Price	Options	Price
Automatic Climate Control	+136	Power Passenger Seat [Opt on Conv,Hbk]	+127
Automatic Stability Control	+207	Sport Seats	+233
Compact Disc Changer	+224	Targa Top - Glass	+355
Delco/Bose Audio System [Opt on Cpe]	+306	Targa Top - Solid and Glass	+355
Electronic Damping Suspension Control	+633	Tilt and Telescopic Steering Wheel [Opt on Conv,Hbk]	+145
Magnesium Wheels	+1244		

A hardtop model aimed at enthusiasts is introduced, and its options list is short. Other Corvettes can be equipped with numerous options including a new heads-up display and a power tilt/telescope steering wheel.

1998

Mileage Category: F

Body Styles	TMV Pricing		
	Trade	Private	Dealer
2 Dr STD Conv	19553	22271	25335
2 Dr STD Hbk	17980	20479	23297

Options	Price	Options	Price
Automatic Climate Control	+115	Sport Seats	+196
Compact Disc Changer	+189	Targa Top - Glass	+205
Electronic Damping Suspension Control	+533	Targa Top - Solid and Glass	+299
Magnesium Wheels	+1048		

Two fresh colors are available, but the available convertible model is the big news. Equipped with a manual-folding top, a hard tonneau that extends along the rear wall of the passenger compartment and a trunk that holds golf bags. Lower-powered airbags are not available on the Corvette.

1997

Mileage Category: F

Fifth-generation Corvette debuts 44 years after the original, and is better than ever with world-class build quality and performance at a bargain price.

Body Styles	TMV Pricing		
	Trade	Private	Dealer
2 Dr STD Hbk	15368	17753	20669

Options	Price	Options	Price
Compact Disc Changer	+171	Targa Top - Glass	+185
Electronic Damping Suspension Control	+482	Targa Top - Solid and Glass	+270
Sport Seats	+178		

1996

Body Styles	TMV Pricing			Body Styles	TMV Pricing		
	Trade	Private	Dealer		Trade	Private	Dealer
2 Dr Grand Sport Conv	15189	17650	21048	2 Dr STD Conv	14085	16367	19518
2 Dr Grand Sport Hbk	13716	15939	19008	2 Dr STD Hbk	12153	14121	16839

Options	Price	Options	Price
Hardtop Roof	+514	Targa Top - Glass	+168
Sport Seats [Opt on STD]	+161	Targa Top - Solid and Glass	+168

Mileage Category: F

New 330-horsepower LT4 engine debuts on all manually shifted Corvettes. Two special editions are available, the Collector Edition and the Grand Sport. Next year, an all-new Corvette debuts. Other additions for 1996 include a Selective Real Time Damping system for the shock absorbers, and a stiffer Z51 suspension setup.

1995

Mileage Category: F

ZR-1's brakes trickle down to base models. Front fenders get revised gills. Only 448 ZR-1s produced in 1995.

Body Styles	TMV Pricing			Body Styles	TMV Pricing		
	Trade	Private	Dealer		Trade	Private	Dealer
2 Dr STD Conv	11855	13873	17235	2 Dr ZR1 Hbk	19982	23383	29050
2 Dr STD Hbk	10502	12289	15268				

Options	Price	Options	Price
AM/FM/Cassette/CD Audio System [Opt on STD]	+138	Performance/Handling Package	+393
Automatic Climate Control [Opt on STD]	+84	Sport Seats	+145
Delco/Bose Audio System [Opt on STD]	+91	Targa Top - Glass	+150
Electronic Suspension Control [Opt on STD]	+382	Targa Top - Solid and Glass	+150
Hardtop Roof	+461		

1994

Mileage Category: F

Passenger airbag is added. Traction control is standard. A new steering wheel and redesigned seats are added inside. Leather upholstery is standard. Automatic transmission gets electronic shift controls and brake/transmission shift interlock. Convertible gets glass rear window with defogger. ZR-1 has new five-spoke alloys. Power windows gain express-down feature for driver side. Selective Ride Control system has softer springs.

Body Styles	TMV Pricing			Body Styles	TMV Pricing		
	Trade	Private	Dealer		Trade	Private	Dealer
2 Dr STD Conv	9259	11302	14707	2 Dr ZR1 Hbk	16221	19800	25766
2 Dr STD Hbk	7980	9741	12675				

Options	Price	Options	Price
AM/FM/Cassette/CD Audio System	+123	Sport Seats	+128
Delco/Bose Audio System [Opt on STD]	+81	Targa Top - Glass	+133
Electronic Suspension Control	+337	Targa Top - Solid and Glass	+133
Hardtop Roof	+407		

Chevrolet
Express

2003

Mileage Category: Q

The Express van gains numerous improvements for the '03 model year. Under the hood, the Express now features GM's lineup of powerful Vortec engines, from the base 200-horsepower V6 all the way up to the hard-charging 300-hp 6.0-liter V8. All-wheel-drive models are also available for the first time, and all Express vans get four-wheel disc brakes with ABS. New driver-side 60/40 access doors have been added as an option along with revised front-end styling, larger stabilizer bars and a stronger frame. Inside, the Express gets redesigned seats, improved lighting and ventilation systems, more storage and dual-stage airbags on all light-duty versions.

2003 (cont'd)

Body Styles	TMV Pricing		
	Trade	Private	Dealer
3 Dr G1500 AWD Pass Van	15998	17334	19560
3 Dr G1500 LS AWD Pass Van	17155	18587	20974
3 Dr G1500 LS Pass Van	15286	16563	18690
3 Dr G1500 Pass Van	13393	14511	16375
3 Dr G2500 LS Pass Van	16410	17780	20064
3 Dr G2500 LS Pass Van Ext	16033	17372	19603

Body Styles	TMV Pricing		
	Trade	Private	Dealer
3 Dr G2500 Pass Van	15231	16503	18622
3 Dr G2500 Pass Van Ext	15771	17088	19282
3 Dr G3500 LS Pass Van	16678	18070	20391
3 Dr G3500 LS Pass Van Ext	16672	18064	20384
3 Dr G3500 Pass Van	15398	16684	18827
3 Dr G3500 Pass Van Ext	15981	17315	19539

Options	Price
15 Passenger Seating [Opt on G3500 Ext]	+239
Aluminum/Alloy Wheels	+255
AM/FM/CD Audio System	+131
AM/FM/Cassette/CD Audio System	+227
Chrome Wheels [Opt on G1500]	+160
Cruise Control [Std on LS] ·	+118
Locking Differential	+163
Power Door Locks [Std on LS]	+144

Options	Price
Power Driver Seat [Opt on LS]	+153
Power Passenger Seat [Opt on LS]	+153
Power Windows [Std on LS]	+169
OnStar Telematic System	+444
AM/FM/CD Changer Audio System	+354
Air Conditioning - Front and Rear [Std on LS]	+549
5.3L V8 OHV 16V FI Engine [Opt on G1500]	+954

2002

Mileage Category: Q

For 2002, Express gets only minor upgrades like the availability of rearview mirrors with an integrated compass and temperature reading, a more efficient starter, a stronger steering gear housing and low emission vehicle compliance for models equipped with either the 8100 V8 or 6.5-liter diesel and a GVWR of more than 8,600 pounds.

Body Styles	TMV Pricing		
	Trade	Private	Dealer
3 Dr G1500 LT Pass Van	16056	17659	20330
3 Dr G1500 Pass Van	11261	12385	14258
3 Dr G2500 Pass Van	12697	13965	16077

Body Styles	TMV Pricing		
	Trade	Private	Dealer
3 Dr G2500 Pass Van Ext	13170	14485	16676
3 Dr G3500 Pass Van	12830	14111	16245
3 Dr G3500 Pass Van Ext	13342	14674	16893

Options	Price
15 Passenger Seating	+213
5.0L V8 OHV 16V FI Engine [Opt on G1500]	+284
5.7L V8 OHV 16V FI Engine [Opt on G1500]	+685
6.5L V8 Turbodiesel OHV 16V Engine	+1755
8.1L V8 OHV 16V FI Engine	+487
Air Conditioning - Front and Rear [Std on Ext, G1500 LT]	+461
Aluminum/Alloy Wheels [Std on G1500 LT]	+143
AM/FM/Cassette/CD Audio System [Std on G1500 LT]	+368

Options	Price
AM/FM/CD Audio System	+311
AM/FM/CD Changer Audio System	+169
Camper/Towing Package	+178
Leather Seats	+746
Locking Differential [Std on G1500 LT]	+145
Power Door Locks [Std on G1500 LT]	+129
Power Driver Seat [Std on G1500 LT]	+138
Power Windows [Std on G1500 LT]	+152

2001

Mileage Category: Q

A new LT trim level with leather and an onboard entertainment system, and a more powerful V8 are the only major changes. Two new exterior colors and upgraded radios and alternators round out the updates for 2001.

Body Styles	TMV Pricing		
	Trade	Private	Dealer
3 Dr G1500 LT Pass Van	12865	14866	16714
3 Dr G1500 Pass Van	9112	10530	11838
3 Dr G2500 Pass Van	10561	12204	13721

Body Styles	TMV Pricing		
	Trade	Private	Dealer
3 Dr G2500 Pass Van Ext	10989	12699	14277
3 Dr G3500 Pass Van	10667	12327	13859
3 Dr G3500 Pass Van Ext	11150	12885	14486

Options	Price
15 Passenger Seating	+195
5.0L V8 OHV 16V FI Engine	+260
5.7L V8 OHV 16V FI Engine [Std on G3500]	+627
6.5L V8 Turbodiesel OHV 16V Engine	+1500
8.1L V8 OHV 16V FI Engine	+315
Air Conditioning - Front and Rear	+422
Aluminum/Alloy Wheels	+131
AM/FM/Cassette/CD Audio System [Std on LT]	+337

Options	Price
AM/FM/CD Audio System	+284
Compact Disc Changer	+155
Leather Seats [Std on LT]	+682
Locking Differential [Std on LT]	+132
Power Door Locks	+118
Power Driver Seat	+126
Power Passenger Seat [Std on LT]	+126
Power Windows	+126

Express

2000

Mileage Category: Q

Chevy updates the basic V6 for quieter operation, enhanced durability and reduced emissions. A new rear defogger (on models with fixed rear glass) improves visibility in inclement weather.

Body Styles	TMV Pricing		
	Trade	Private	Dealer
3 Dr G1500 LS Pass Van	7503	8779	10030
3 Dr G1500 Pass Van	7090	8296	9478
3 Dr G2500 LS Pass Van	8253	9657	11033
3 Dr G2500 LS Pass Van Ext	8530	9981	11403
3 Dr G2500 Pass Van	7707	9018	10303

Body Styles	TMV Pricing		
	Trade	Private	Dealer
3 Dr G2500 Pass Van Ext	8093	9470	10819
3 Dr G3500 LS Pass Van	8273	9680	11060
3 Dr G3500 LS Pass Van Ext	8684	10161	11609
3 Dr G3500 Pass Van	7759	9079	10373
3 Dr G3500 Pass Van Ext	8191	9584	10950

Options	Price
5.7L V8 OHV 16V FI Engine [Opt on G1500]	+559
6.5L V8 Turbodiesel OHV 16V Engine	+1338
7.4L V8 OHV 16V FI Engine	+281
Air Conditioning - Front and Rear [Opt on G1500]	+376
Aluminum/Alloy Wheels	+117
AM/FM/Cassette/CD Audio System	+301
AM/FM/CD Audio System	+254

Options	Price
Camper/Towing Package	+145
Chrome Wheels	+145
Limited Slip Differential	+118
Power Windows [Std on LS]	+123
15 Passenger Seating	+174
5.0L V8 OHV 16V FI Engine	+232

1999

Mileage Category: Q

The Chevy Express line of full-size vans now includes a variety of configurations, including the G1500 (1/2-ton), G2500 (3/4-ton) and G3500 (1-ton) series. Two wheelbases (135 inches and 155 inches) are available on 2500 and 3500 models. For '99, all Express vans get automatic transmission enhancements to increase durability and improve sealing, plus depowered dual front airbags. There are also two new exterior paint colors and one new interior shade for the 1999 model year.

Body Styles	TMV Pricing		
	Trade	Private	Dealer
3 Dr G1500 LS Pass Van	6440	7639	8886
3 Dr G1500 Pass Van	6115	7253	8438
3 Dr G2500 LS Pass Van	7314	8675	10092
3 Dr G2500 LS Pass Van Ext	7527	8928	10386
3 Dr G2500 Pass Van	6778	8039	9352

Body Styles	TMV Pricing		
	Trade	Private	Dealer
3 Dr G2500 Pass Van Ext	6971	8269	9619
3 Dr G3500 LS Pass Van	7343	8710	10132
3 Dr G3500 LS Pass Van Ext	7682	9111	10599
3 Dr G3500 Pass Van	6837	8110	9434
3 Dr G3500 Pass Van Ext	7129	8456	9837

Options	Price
15 Passenger Seating	+139
5.0L V8 OHV 16V FI Engine	+205
5.7L V8 OHV 16V FI Engine [Opt on G1500,G2500]	+496
6.5L V8 Turbodiesel OHV 16V Engine	+1186
7.4L V8 OHV 16V FI Engine	+249

Options	Price
Air Conditioning - Front and Rear	+321
AM/FM/Cassette/CD Audio System	+240
AM/FM/CD Audio System	+202
Camper/Towing Package	+116

1998

Mileage Category: Q

All vans equipped with airbags switch to mini-module bag designs for the driver, but they still deploy with more force than second-generation types. A theft-deterrent system is standard, and three new colors debut.

Body Styles	TMV Pricing		
	Trade	Private	Dealer
3 Dr G1500 LS Pass Van	5307	6372	7574
3 Dr G1500 Pass Van	4924	5912	7027
3 Dr G2500 LS Pass Van	5880	7061	8392
3 Dr G2500 LS Pass Van Ext	6024	7233	8597
3 Dr G2500 Pass Van	5354	6429	7642

Body Styles	TMV Pricing		
	Trade	Private	Dealer
3 Dr G2500 Pass Van Ext	5545	6658	7914
3 Dr G3500 LS Pass Van	5929	7119	8461
3 Dr G3500 LS Pass Van Ext	6074	7293	8668
3 Dr G3500 Pass Van	5402	6487	7710
3 Dr G3500 Pass Van Ext	5596	6719	7986

Options	Price
15 Passenger Seating	+117
5.0L V8 OHV 16V FI Engine [Opt on 1500]	+173
5.7L V8 OHV 16V FI Engine [Opt on 1500]	+337
6.5L V8 Turbodiesel OHV 16V Engine	+999

Options	Price
7.4L V8 OHV 16V FI Engine	+210
Air Conditioning - Front and Rear	+270
AM/FM/Cassette/CD Audio System	+202
AM/FM/CD Audio System	+171

1997

Mileage Category: Q

Dual airbags and DRLs appear on the G3500 model. Variable steering reduces effort at low speeds for easier parking, and automatic transmissions shift more smoothly.

Body Styles	TMV Pricing		
	Trade	Private	Dealer
3 Dr G1500 LS Pass Van	4148	5078	6214
3 Dr G1500 Pass Van	4013	4913	6013
3 Dr G2500 LS Pass Van	4644	5686	6959
3 Dr G2500 LS Pass Van Ext	4913	6015	7361
3 Dr G2500 Pass Van	4237	5187	6349

Body Styles	TMV Pricing		
	Trade	Private	Dealer
3 Dr G2500 Pass Van Ext	4464	5465	6688
3 Dr G3500 LS Pass Van	4809	5887	7204
3 Dr G3500 LS Pass Van Ext	5012	6136	7510
3 Dr G3500 Pass Van	4418	5408	6619
3 Dr G3500 Pass Van Ext	4508	5519	6755

Options	Price
5.0L V8 OHV 16V FI Engine [Opt on 1500]	+156
5.7L V8 OHV 16V FI Engine [Opt on 1500]	+305
6.5L V8 Turbodiesel OHV 16V Engine [Opt on 2500,3500]	+903
7.4L V8 OHV 16V FI Engine [Opt on 2500,3500]	+190

Options	Price
Air Conditioning - Front and Rear	+244
AM/FM/Cassette/CD Audio System	+183
AM/FM/CD Audio System	+154

1996

Body Styles	TMV Pricing		
	Trade	Private	Dealer
3 Dr G1500 Pass Van	3354	4183	5328
3 Dr G2500 Pass Van	3717	4636	5905
3 Dr G2500 Pass Van Ext	3836	4784	6094

Body Styles	TMV Pricing		
	Trade	Private	Dealer
3 Dr G3500 Pass Van	3762	4692	5976
3 Dr G3500 Pass Van Ext	3880	4839	6163

Options	Price
Air Conditioning - Front and Rear	+209
AM/FM/Cassette/CD Audio System	+166
AM/FM/CD Audio System	+139
7.4L V8 OHV 16V FI Engine	+172

Options	Price
5.0L V8 OHV 16V FI Engine [Opt on 1500]	+142
5.7L V8 OHV 16V FI Engine [Opt on 1500]	+276
6.5L V8 Turbodiesel OHV 16V Engine	+819

Mileage Category: Q

An all-new vehicle from the ground up, the Express is the successor to the Sportvan. The exterior looks totally different and offers improved functionality. The rear doors open wider and swing out away from the high-mounted taillights. Thus the taillights are still visible, even when the doors are open, as they could be at a loading dock.

Other functional improvements include longer wheelbases for the standard- and extended-length versions of this van (135 inches for the standard; 155 inches for the extended). The longer wheelbases ease entry/exit and improve ride quality and stability.

The spare tire no longer encroaches on cargo room; it's now banished to the underside of the van. Also, a 31-gallon gas tank offers a longer range between fill-ups. Dual front airbags are added to the standard safety equipment list of the vehicles with a gross vehicle weight rating (GVWR) of 8,600 pounds or lower. A new series of engines is introduced, providing more power and torque than last year's offerings.

Body Styles	TMV Pricing		
	Trade	Private	Dealer
4 Dr LS Sdn	13601	14750	16665
4 Dr STD Sdn	11480	12450	14066

Options	Price
Aluminum/Alloy Wheels [Opt on STD]	+223
AM/FM/CD Audio System	+156
Antilock Brakes [Opt on STD]	+447
Cruise Control [Opt on STD]	+118
Heated Front Seats	+176
Leather Seats	+383
Power Driver Seat [Opt on STD]	+153

Options	Price
Power Moonroof	+508
Power Passenger Seat	+153
Front Side Airbag Restraints [Opt on STD]	+223
OnStar Telematic System	+444
Satellite Radio System	+207
3.8L V6 OHV 12V FI Engine [Opt on STD]	+252

Mileage Category: G

There are only minor upgrades in store for the 2003 Impala. New options include a side airbag for the driver and XM Satellite Radio. Remote keyless entry is now standard and four new exterior colors are available. Both base and LS models get new wheel designs.

2002

Mileage Category: G

Now into its third year of production, the Impala soldiers on as Chevrolet's bread-and-butter family sedan. Minor upgrades this year include standard dual-zone air conditioning, an AM/FM stereo and LATCH child seat tether anchors. A leather-accented 60/40 split bench seat will be available later this year on LS models, and two new exterior colors have been added.

Body Styles	TMV Pricing		
	Trade	Private	Dealer
4 Dr LS Sdn	10878	11931	13687
4 Dr STD Sdn	9493	10412	11944

Options	Price
16 Inch Wheels	+172
3.8L V6 OHV 12V FI Engine [Std on LS]	+227
Aluminum/Alloy Wheels [Std on LS]	+201
AM/FM/Cassette/CD Audio System	+198
AM/FM/CD Audio System	+141
Antilock Brakes [Std on LS]	+401
Front Side Airbag Restraints [Std on LS]	+143

Options	Price
Heated Front Seats	+129
Leather Seats	+344
OnStar Telematic System [Std on LS]	+399
Power Driver Seat [Std on LS]	+138
Power Passenger Seat	+138
Power Sunroof	+456
Split Front Bench Seat [Std on STD]	+115

2001

Mileage Category: G

No changes this year.

Body Styles	TMV Pricing		
	Trade	Private	Dealer
4 Dr LS Sdn	9297	10711	12017
4 Dr STD Sdn	7608	8766	9834

Options	Price	Options	Price
3.8L V6 OHV 12V FI Engine [Std on LS]	+517	Heated Front Seats	+131
Aluminum/Alloy Wheels [Std on LS]	+157	Leather Seats	+328
AM/FM/Cassette/CD Audio System	+117	OnStar Telematic System [Std on LS]	+365
Antilock Brakes [Std on LS]	+357	Power Driver Seat	+160
Cruise Control [Std on LS]	+125	Power Passenger Seat	+160
Front Side Airbag Restraints [Std on LS]	+131	Power Sunroof	+417

2000

Mileage Category: G

GM has resurrected the Impala nameplate (a staple in Chevy's lineup from 1959 to the early '80s and then briefly from 1994 to '96) and put it on an all-new full-size sedan body that rides on the Lumina front-drive platform. Although the Lumina itself is back for the 2000 model year, Impala will eventually replace it as Chevy's large-car entry to battle the likes of Ford's Crown Victoria, Buick's LeSabre and Chrysler's LH cars.

Body Styles	TMV Pricing		
	Trade	Private	Dealer
4 Dr LS Sdn	7752	9118	10456
4 Dr STD Sdn	6126	7205	8263

Options	Price	Options	Price
3.8L V6 OHV 12V FI Engine [Std on LS]	+461	Front Side Airbag Restraints [Std on LS]	+117
Aluminum/Alloy Wheels [Std on LS]	+140	Heated Front Seats	+117
AM/FM/Cassette/CD Audio System	+236	Leather Seats	+292
AM/FM/CD Audio System	+189	OnStar Telematic System	+419
Antilock Brakes [Std on LS]	+318	Power Sunroof	+327

1996

Body Styles	TMV Pricing		
	Trade	Private	Dealer
4 Dr SS Sdn	7309	8552	10269

Mileage Category: G

A tachometer and floor shifter are available. Last year for this generation of Impala.

1995

Mileage Category: G

Dark Cherry and Green Gray paint colors join basic black. New seats and radios debut. Outside mirrors can be folded in, and a new option is a radio with speed-compensated volume control.

Body Styles	TMV Pricing		
	Trade	Private	Dealer
4 Dr SS Sdn	6400	7486	9297

Options	Price
Premium Audio System	+116

1994

Mileage Category: G

Caprice-based sedan powered by 260-horsepower, 5.7-liter V8 and sporting monochromatic black paint debuts. Has four-wheel disc brakes, dual airbags, ABS, five-spoke alloys and restyled C-pillars.

Body Styles	TMV Pricing		
	Trade	Private	Dealer
4 Dr SS Sdn	5532	6573	8309

2000

Body Styles	TMV Pricing		
	Trade	Private	Dealer
4 Dr STD Sdn	4688	5724	6739

Options	Price	Options	Price
Aluminum/Alloy Wheels	+140	Antilock Brakes	+318
AM/FM/CD Audio System	+152	Power Driver Seat	+143

Mileage Category: D

Base models receive additional standard equipment, while the standard 3.1-liter V6 gets more power and torque. The sporty LTZ and upscale LS models are dropped. This is the final year for the Lumina.

1999

Body Styles	TMV Pricing		
	Trade	Private	Dealer
4 Dr LS Sdn	3762	4741	5760
4 Dr LTZ Sdn	3902	4917	5974
4 Dr STD Sdn	3739	4712	5724

Options	Price	Options	Price
AM/FM/CD Audio System	+121	OnStar Telematic System	+371
Antilock Brakes [Opt on STD]	+282	Power Moonroof	+261
Leather Seats	+241		

Mileage Category: D

Chevrolet adds standard equipment to the LTZ and introduces Auburn Nightmist Medium Metallic to the base and LS models.

1998

Body Styles	TMV Pricing			Body Styles	TMV Pricing		
	Trade	Private	Dealer		Trade	Private	Dealer
4 Dr LS Sdn	3128	4056	5102	4 Dr STD Sdn	2926	3794	4773
4 Dr LTZ Sdn	3242	4204	5288				

Options	Price	Options	Price
3.8L V6 OHV 12V FI Engine [Opt on LTZ]	+141	OnStar Telematic System	+313
Antilock Brakes [Opt on STD]	+238	Power Moonroof	+220
Leather Seats	+202		

Mileage Category: D

Last year's aborted LTZ sport sedan comes on strong for 1998, with a 200-horsepower 3800 V6 engine and machine-faced aluminum wheels. Four new exterior colors and one new interior color are also available on all Lumina models. To help give Lumina a more upscale image than Malibu, an OnStar Mobile Communications system is a dealer-installed option. Second-generation airbags are standard equipment.

1997

Body Styles	TMV Pricing			Body Styles	TMV Pricing		
	Trade	Private	Dealer		Trade	Private	Dealer
4 Dr LS Sdn	2481	3318	4340	4 Dr STD Sdn	2455	3283	4294
4 Dr LTZ Sdn	2800	3744	4898				

Options	Price	Options	Price
3.4L V6 DOHC 24V FI Engine	+262	Leather Seats	+183
Antilock Brakes [Opt on STD]	+215	Power Moonroof	+199

Mileage Category: D

Performance-oriented Lumina LTZ debuts, with a spoiler, special front and rear styling, graphics and alloy wheels. Daytime running lamps are standard on all Luminas, and the power sunroof expected last year finally arrives. New colors and an oil life monitor round out changes to Lumina for 1997.

1996

Body Styles	TMV Pricing		
	Trade	Private	Dealer
4 Dr LS Sdn	2001	2750	3785
4 Dr STD Sdn	1857	2552	3512

Options	Price
Leather Seats	+166
Antilock Brakes [Std on LS]	+195
3.4L V6 DOHC 24V FI Engine	+238

Mileage Category: D

The ultimate family sedan is now available with an integrated child safety seat. Driver and passenger get their own climate controls. LS models offer available leather, and four-wheel disc brakes when equipped with the 3.4-liter V6.

Chevrolet
Lumina/Lumina Minivan

1995

Mileage Category: D

Midsize sedan is redesigned; features dual airbags. Base and LS trim levels are available. ABS is optional on base model; standard on LS. Standard power plant is a 160-horsepower, 3.1-liter V6. Optional on LS is a 210-horsepower, 3.4-liter V6. Air conditioning is standard.

Body Styles	TMV Pricing		
	Trade	Private	Dealer
4 Dr LS Sdn	1413	2051	3113
4 Dr STD Sdn	1244	1805	2740

Options	Price
3.4L V6 DOHC 24V FI Engine	+214
AM/FM/Cassette/CD Audio System	+117
AM/FM/CD Audio System	+75

Options	Price
Antilock Brakes [Std on LS]	+175
Premium Audio System	+116

1994

Body Styles	TMV Pricing		
	Trade	Private	Dealer
2 Dr Euro Cpe	953	1556	2562
2 Dr Z34 Cpe	1071	1750	2881

Options	Price
3.4L V6 DOHC 24V FI Engine [Std on Z34]	+189
Antilock Brakes [Opt on STD]	+154

Body Styles	TMV Pricing		
	Trade	Private	Dealer
4 Dr Euro Sdn	889	1452	2391
4 Dr STD Sdn	833	1361	2240

Options	Price
Bose Audio System	+77
Sport Suspension [Opt on Euro Sdn]	+77

Mileage Category: D

Base coupe is dropped from lineup. Manual transmission disappears.

Chevrolet
Lumina Minivan

1996

Body Styles	TMV Pricing		
	Trade	Private	Dealer
3 Dr STD Pass Van	2688	3477	4567

Options	Price
Air Conditioning - Front and Rear	+116

Mileage Category: P

Last year for this van. A 3.4-liter V6 good for 180 horsepower replaces standard and optional V6 engines from last year. Air conditioning, seven-passenger seating and an electronically controlled four-speed automatic transmission are standard.

1995

Mileage Category: P

Transmission gets brake/shift interlock.

Body Styles	TMV Pricing		
	Trade	Private	Dealer
3 Dr STD Pass Van	1965	2591	3634

Options	Price
Power Sliding Door	+81
Sunroof	+116
3.8L V6 OHV 12V FI Engine	+142
7 Passenger Seating	+127

Options	Price
Air Conditioning	+185
Air Conditioning - Front and Rear	+104
AM/FM/CD Audio System	+91
Automatic 4-Speed Transmission	+185

1994

Mileage Category: P

APV designation dropped in favor of more descriptive "minivan" nomenclature. Front styling is revised; overall length drops three inches. Driver airbag is standard. Integrated child seats and remote keyless entry are newly optional. Midyear, traction control becomes available on LS model.

Body Styles	TMV Pricing		
	Trade	Private	Dealer
3 Dr STD Pass Van	1324	1864	2763

Options	Price
3.8L V6 OHV 12V FI Engine	+126
7 Passenger Seating	+112
Air Conditioning	+163
Air Conditioning - Front and Rear	+92

Options	Price
AM/FM/CD Audio System	+81
Automatic 4-Speed Transmission	+163
Sunroof	+102

2003

Body Styles	TMV Pricing		
	Trade	Private	Dealer
4 Dr LS Sdn	8870	9790	11322
4 Dr STD Sdn	8359	9225	10669

Options	Price	Options	Price
Aluminum/Alloy Wheels [Opt on STD]	+239	Power Driver Seat [Opt on STD]	+153
Antilock Brakes [Opt on STD]	+447	Power Moonroof [Opt on LS]	+431
Cruise Control [Opt on STD]	+118	Power Windows [Opt on STD]	+156
Keyless Entry System [Opt on STD]	+121	Split Folding Rear Seat [Opt on STD]	+124
Leather Seats [Opt on LS]	+380		

Mileage Category: C

The Malibu gets little in the way of upgrades for 2003. There are two new colors to choose from -- Summit White and Medium Gray Metallic -- and a new seat fabric on LS models. ABS brakes are now optional on base models, but remain standard on the LS.

2002

Body Styles	TMV Pricing		
	Trade	Private	Dealer
4 Dr LS Sdn	7090	7966	9426
4 Dr STD Sdn	6464	7263	8594

Options	Price	Options	Price
Aluminum/Alloy Wheels [Opt on STD]	+215	Power Moonroof	+387
Cruise Control [Opt on STD]	+129	Power Windows [Opt on STD]	+152
Leather Seats [Opt on STD]	+341		

Mileage Category: C

Only minor changes are added to Chevrolet's midsize sedan. Floor mats and an AM/FM CD stereo are now standard on all models. Three new colors have been added along with newly styled 15-inch cast-aluminum wheels.

2001

Body Styles	TMV Pricing		
	Trade	Private	Dealer
4 Dr LS Sdn	5457	6600	7655
4 Dr STD Sdn	4869	5890	6832

Options	Price	Options	Price
Aluminum/Alloy Wheels [Opt on STD]	+163	Power Sunroof	+341
Cruise Control [Opt on STD]	+118	Power Windows [Opt on STD]	+137
Leather Seats	+312		

Mileage Category: C

Base models receive black rocker moldings, black molded-in-color outside rearview mirrors and a rear window defogger. LS models get front seat back map pockets. Both models receive auto headlamp on/off, new stereos and new cloth interiors.

2000

Body Styles	TMV Pricing		
	Trade	Private	Dealer
4 Dr LS Sdn	4417	5499	6559
4 Dr STD Sdn	3719	4631	5524

Options	Price	Options	Price
Aluminum/Alloy Wheels [Opt on STD]	+145	Power Driver Seat [Opt on STD]	+145
AM/FM/Cassette/CD Audio System [Opt on STD]	+197	Power Sunroof	+305
AM/FM/CD Audio System	+150	Power Windows [Opt on STD]	+122
Leather Seats	+278		

Mileage Category: C

Revised front styling ties Malibu to Impala, and the 1999's brushed-aluminum wheels have been redesigned. The 3.1-liter V6 engine is standard this year, and has been improved to offer more horsepower while meeting low emission vehicle (LEV) standards. A spoiler and a gold package are available.

1999

Body Styles	TMV Pricing			Body Styles	TMV Pricing		
	Trade	Private	Dealer		Trade	Private	Dealer
4 Dr LS Sdn	3507	4497	5528	4 Dr STD Sdn	3051	3913	4811

Options	Price	Options	Price
3.1L V6 OHV 12V FI Engine [Opt on STD]	+222	Power Driver Seat [Opt on STD]	+116
Aluminum/Alloy Wheels [Opt on STD]	+116	Power Sunroof	+243
Leather Seats	+222		

Mileage Category: C

The 1999 Malibu is identical to the 1998 model, except for the addition of Medium Bronzemist Metallic to the paint chart.

Chevrolet
Malibu/Metro

1998

Mileage Category: C

Leather trim is newly optional on LS models, aluminum wheels are revised, a sunroof can be ordered and Base models can be equipped with Medium Oak colored interior. Second-generation airbags debut.

Body Styles	TMV Pricing		
	Trade	Private	Dealer
4 Dr LS Sdn	2926	3884	4965

Options	Price
3.1L V6 OHV 12V FI Engine [Opt on STD]	+156
Leather Seats	+173

Body Styles	TMV Pricing		
	Trade	Private	Dealer
4 Dr STD Sdn	2492	3309	4231

Options	Price
Leather Seats	+173
Power Sunroof	+187

1997

Mileage Category: C

First year for new midsize sedan with classic name.

Body Styles	TMV Pricing		
	Trade	Private	Dealer
4 Dr LS Sdn	2264	3203	4350

Body Styles	TMV Pricing		
	Trade	Private	Dealer
4 Dr STD Sdn	1988	2812	3820

Chevrolet
Metro

2000

Mileage Category: A

Two new colors help buyers differentiate between 1999 and 2000 Metros.

Body Styles	TMV Pricing		
	Trade	Private	Dealer
2 Dr LSi Hbk	2364	3247	4112
2 Dr STD Hbk	2109	2897	3670
4 Dr LSi Sdn	2489	3419	4331

Options	Price
Air Conditioning	+367
AM/FM/Cassette Audio System	+257
AM/FM/CD Audio System	+210
Antilock Brakes	+318

Options	Price
Automatic 3-Speed Transmission	+278
Power Door Locks	+278
Power Steering	+136

1999

Mileage Category: A

After getting a makeover last year to mark its move from the old Geo nameplate to the Chevrolet model family, the Metro is a carryover product for 1999, save for the addition of two new exterior colors: Dark Green Metallic and Silver Metallic.

Body Styles	TMV Pricing		
	Trade	Private	Dealer
2 Dr LSi Hbk	1845	2678	3546
2 Dr STD Hbk	1654	2402	3181
4 Dr LSi Sdn	2032	2950	3906

Options	Price
Air Conditioning	+293
AM/FM/Cassette Audio System	+205
AM/FM/CD Audio System	+168

Options	Price
Antilock Brakes	+282
Automatic 3-Speed Transmission	+222

1998

Mileage Category: A

The Geo badge is replaced with a Chevy bowtie. Styling is updated front and rear. The LSi's four-cylinder engine gets four valves per cylinder for more power and better acceleration. Second-generation airbags are standard equipment. Wheel covers are revised, new radios, new interior fabrics and the addition of California Gold Metallic to the paint palette round out the changes.

Body Styles	TMV Pricing		
	Trade	Private	Dealer
2 Dr LSi Hbk	1325	1986	2732
2 Dr STD Hbk	1220	1829	2516
4 Dr LSi Sdn	1501	2250	3094

Options	Price
Air Conditioning	+247
AM/FM/Cassette Audio System	+173
AM/FM/CD Audio System	+141

Options	Price
Antilock Brakes	+238
Automatic 3-Speed Transmission	+187

2003

Body Styles	TMV Pricing		
	Trade	Private	Dealer
2 Dr LS Cpe	11432	12433	14101
2 Dr SS Cpe	13654	14849	16841

Options	Price	Options	Price
Aluminum/Alloy Wheels [Opt on LS]	+223	Power Passenger Seat	+153
AM/FM/CD Audio System	+220	Front Side Airbag Restraints	+223
Antilock Brakes [Opt on LS]	+447	Special Factory Paint [Opt on SS]	+255
Cruise Control [Opt on LS]	+153	OnStar Telematic System	+444
Leather Seats	+399	Satellite Radio System	+207
Power Driver Seat	+153	Jeff Gordon Signature Edition [Opt on SS]	+1979
Power Moonroof	+508	Pace Car Package [Opt on SS]	+1724

Mileage Category: D

The Monte Carlo receives only minor changes for the 2003 model year. The base LS model has been upgraded with standard four-wheel disc brakes, traction control and remote keyless entry. Both the LS and SS models sport newly styled wheels, four new exterior colors and the option of adding XM Satellite Radio.

2002

Mileage Category: D

Chevy's personal-luxury coupe receives only minor changes for 2002. LATCH child safety-seat anchors, dual-zone air conditioning and three-point seatbelts for rear passengers are now standard on all models. Bright Red and Medium Green Pearl replace Torch Red and Dark Jade Green as exterior color options.

Body Styles	TMV Pricing		
	Trade	Private	Dealer
2 Dr LS Cpe	9365	10325	11926
2 Dr SS Cpe	11184	12331	14243

Options	Price	Options	Price
16 Inch Wheels	+143	Leather Seats	+330
Aluminum/Alloy Wheels [Opt on LS]	+172	OnStar Telematic System [Opt on LS]	+244
AM/FM/Cassette/CD Audio System	+129	Power Driver Seat	+138
AM/FM/CD Audio System	+198	Power Moonroof	+456
Cruise Control [Opt on LS]	+137	Power Passenger Seat	+138
Front Side Airbag Restraints [Opt on LS]	+143	Special Factory Paint	+229

2001

Mileage Category: D

Chevy's personal-luxury coupe receives optional sport appearance packages, a standard driver-side-impact airbag and traction control and OnStar comes with the SS model.

Body Styles	TMV Pricing		
	Trade	Private	Dealer
2 Dr LS Cpe	7875	9219	10459
2 Dr SS Cpe	9143	10704	12144

Options	Price	Options	Price
Aluminum/Alloy Wheels [Opt on LS]	+157	OnStar Telematic System [Opt on LS]	+365
AM/FM/Cassette/CD Audio System	+117	Power Driver Seat	+160
Cruise Control [Opt on LS]	+125	Power Passenger Seat	+160
Front Side Airbag Restraints [Opt on LS]	+131	Power Sunroof	+417
Leather Seats	+328	Sport Package	+1102

2000

Mileage Category: D

Chevy's personal-luxury coupe is all new for 2000, based on the Impala platform and sporting distinctive, heritage styling cues.

Body Styles	TMV Pricing		
	Trade	Private	Dealer
2 Dr LS Cpe	6131	7485	8812

Body Styles	TMV Pricing		
	Trade	Private	Dealer
2 Dr SS Cpe	7250	8850	10419

Options	Price	Options	Price
Aluminum/Alloy Wheels [Opt on LS]	+140	OnStar Telematic System	+419
Leather Seats	+302	Power Moonroof	+327

1999

Mileage Category: D

Deep Purple paint is gone. First year for the optional OnStar communications system, a 24-hour roadside assistance network that is accessed through a dealer-installed cellular phone.

Body Styles	TMV Pricing		
	Trade	Private	Dealer
2 Dr LS Cpe	4504	5676	6895
2 Dr Z34 Cpe	4593	5788	7032

1999 (cont'd)

Options	Price
Leather Seats	+241
OnStar Telematic System	+371
Power Moonroof	+261

1998

Mileage Category: D

The Z34 model gets a different engine and fresh wheels. Second-generation airbags are added. New paint colors and one new interior hue round out the changes.

Body Styles	TMV Pricing		
	Trade	Private	Dealer
2 Dr LS Cpe	3410	4422	5563

Options	Price
Leather Seats	+202
OnStar Telematic System	+313

Body Styles	TMV Pricing		
	Trade	Private	Dealer
2 Dr Z34 Cpe	3834	4970	6252

Options	Price
Power Moonroof	+220

1997

Mileage Category: D

Z34 gets a new transmission, while all models have daytime running lights. A power sunroof is optional.

Body Styles	TMV Pricing		
	Trade	Private	Dealer
2 Dr LS Cpe	2718	3635	4755

Options	Price
Leather Seats	+183

Body Styles	TMV Pricing		
	Trade	Private	Dealer
2 Dr Z34 Cpe	3146	4207	5504

Options	Price
Power Sunroof	+199

1996

Mileage Category: D

Dual-zone climate controls reduce marital spats. The 3.4-liter V6 makes more power this year, and four-wheel disc brakes, standard on the Z34, are optional on the LS.

Body Styles	TMV Pricing		
	Trade	Private	Dealer
2 Dr LS Cpe	2201	3025	4162

Options	Price
Leather Seats	+166

Body Styles	TMV Pricing		
	Trade	Private	Dealer
2 Dr Z34 Cpe	2497	3432	4723

Options	Price
Power Sunroof	+180

1995

Mileage Category: D

Available in LS or Z34 trim levels. Dual airbags and ABS are standard. LS comes with 160-horsepower, 3.1-liter V6, while Z34 is powered by 3.4-liter, twin-cam V6 good for 210 horsepower. All Monte Carlos have automatic transmissions. Air conditioning is standard.

Body Styles	TMV Pricing		
	Trade	Private	Dealer
2 Dr LS Cpe	1513	2196	3334

Options	Price
Leather Seats	+149

Body Styles	TMV Pricing		
	Trade	Private	Dealer
2 Dr Z34 Cpe	1744	2531	3842

Options	Price
Premium Audio System	+116

Chevrolet
Prizm

2002

Body Styles	TMV Pricing		
	Trade	Private	Dealer
4 Dr LSi Sdn	6045	6944	8441

Options	Price
Aluminum/Alloy Wheels	+162
Antilock Brakes	+390
Automatic 3-Speed Transmission	+284
Automatic 4-Speed Transmission	+459

Body Styles	TMV Pricing		
	Trade	Private	Dealer
4 Dr STD Sdn	5303	6091	7404

Options	Price
Front Side Airbag Restraints	+169
Power Door Locks [Std on LSi]	+126
Power Sunroof	+387
Power Windows [Std on LSi]	+172

Mileage Category: B

The Prizm remains unchanged for 2002.

Prizm

2001

Body Styles	TMV Pricing		
	Trade	Private	Dealer
4 Dr LSi Sdn	4862	6064	7173
4 Dr STD Sdn	4337	5409	6398

Options	Price	Options	Price
Aluminum/Alloy Wheels	+148	Front Side Airbag Restraints	+155
AM/FM/Cassette Audio System [Std on LSi]	+291	Power Door Locks [Std on LSi]	+115
Antilock Brakes	+357	Power Sunroof	+344
Automatic 3-Speed Transmission	+260	Power Windows [Std on LSi]	+157
Automatic 4-Speed Transmission	+420		

Mileage Category: B

The Prizm remains relatively unchanged for 2001. An emergency trunk release becomes standard issue and Medium Red Metallic is added to the color palette.

2000

Body Styles	TMV Pricing		
	Trade	Private	Dealer
4 Dr LSi Sdn	3792	4894	5974
4 Dr STD Sdn	3425	4420	5396

Options	Price	Options	Price
Aluminum/Alloy Wheels	+157	Automatic 4-Speed Transmission	+374
AM/FM/Cassette Audio System [Opt on STD]	+260	Front Side Airbag Restraints	+138
AM/FM/CD Audio System	+306	Power Sunroof	+315
Antilock Brakes	+318	Power Windows [Opt on STD]	+140
Automatic 3-Speed Transmission	+232		

Mileage Category: B

New standard features improve the Prizm's value quotient, and variable valve timing boosts power and torque. The tweaked engine now meets low emission vehicle status in California, and three new colors freshen the exterior.

1999

Body Styles	TMV Pricing		
	Trade	Private	Dealer
4 Dr LSi Sdn	3060	4056	5093
4 Dr STD Sdn	2618	3470	4356

Options	Price	Options	Price
Air Conditioning [Opt on STD]	+293	Antilock Brakes	+282
Aluminum/Alloy Wheels	+125	Automatic 3-Speed Transmission	+185
AM/FM/Cassette Audio System [Opt on STD]	+207	Automatic 4-Speed Transmission	+298
AM/FM/CD Audio System	+244	Power Sunroof	+252

Mileage Category: B

After a thorough revision last year, the only changes for 1999 are four new paint colors.

1998

Body Styles	TMV Pricing		
	Trade	Private	Dealer
4 Dr LSi Sdn	2631	3590	4672
4 Dr STD Sdn	2212	3019	3928

Options	Price	Options	Price
Air Conditioning	+247	Automatic 3-Speed Transmission	+156
AM/FM/Cassette Audio System	+175	Automatic 4-Speed Transmission	+251
AM/FM/CD Audio System	+206	Power Sunroof	+212
Antilock Brakes	+238		

Mileage Category: B

Chevy replaces the Geo badge with its own on the completely redesigned Prizm. Among the improvements are a larger standard engine, optional side airbags, an optional handling package for LSi models and new colors inside and out. Front airbags are of the depowered variety.

Chevrolet
S-10

2003

Mileage Category: J

The S-10 gets few changes for what may be the final year of production of the current model. There's new cloth upholstery for the seats and door panels, a new fuel-injection system for the 4.3-liter V6 and a sport package for crew cab models.

Body Styles	TMV Pricing		
	Trade	Private	Dealer
2 Dr LS 4WD Ext Cab SB	13346	14642	16802
2 Dr LS Ext Cab SB	10510	11530	13231
2 Dr LS Std Cab LB	9480	10401	11935
2 Dr LS Std Cab SB	9233	10130	11624
2 Dr LS Xtreme Ext Cab SB	12268	13459	15444
2 Dr LS Xtreme Std Cab SB	10854	11908	13664

Body Styles	TMV Pricing		
	Trade	Private	Dealer
2 Dr LS ZR2 4WD Ext Cab SB	13764	15101	17328
2 Dr STD 4WD Ext Cab SB	12144	13323	15288
2 Dr STD Ext Cab SB	9340	10247	11758
2 Dr STD Std Cab LB	9260	10159	11658
2 Dr STD Std Cab SB	8324	9132	10479
4 Dr LS 4WD Crew Cab SB	14564	15978	18335

Options	Price
AM/FM/CD Audio System [Opt on STD]	+193
Automatic 4-Speed Transmission [Std on Crew, Std Cab LB]	+699
Bucket Seats	+218
Cruise Control [Opt on STD]	+118
Heated Front Seats [Opt on Crew]	+176
Keyless Entry System [Opt on LS,LS Xtreme,LS ZR2]	+118
Leather Seats [Opt on Crew]	+479
Locking Differential [Std on LS ZR2]	+172

Options	Price
Power Driver Seat [Opt on Crew]	+153
Power Moonroof	+444
Power Passenger Seat [Opt on Crew]	+153
Power Windows [Opt on LS,LS Xtreme,LS ZR2]	+153
Stepside Bed [Opt on LS,LS Xtreme]	+303
AM/FM/CD Changer Audio System	+252
ZQ8 Sport Suspension Package [Opt on LS 2WD]	+501
4.3L V6 OHV 12V FI Engine [Std on 4WD]	+638

2002

Mileage Category: J

Additional standard features are added to the S-10 for 2002 including a tachometer, air conditioning and a third door for extended-cab models. Vehicles sold in Northern states also get the Cold Weather package as standard equipment.

Body Styles	TMV Pricing		
	Trade	Private	Dealer
2 Dr LS 4WD Ext Cab SB	11650	12976	15187
2 Dr LS Ext Cab SB	8874	9884	11568
2 Dr LS Std Cab LB	8178	9096	10626
2 Dr LS Std Cab SB	7877	8774	10268
2 Dr STD 4WD Ext Cab SB	9807	10923	12784

Body Styles	TMV Pricing		
	Trade	Private	Dealer
2 Dr STD Ext Cab SB	7430	8276	9687
2 Dr STD Std Cab LB	7140	7953	9307
2 Dr STD Std Cab SB	6636	7391	8650
4 Dr LS 4WD Crew Cab SB	12139	13521	15823

Options	Price
4.3L V6 OHV 12V FI Engine [Std on 4WD]	+573
AM/FM/CD Audio System [Opt on STD]	+173
AM/FM/CD Changer Audio System [Opt on LS]	+227
Automatic 4-Speed Transmission [Std on LS]	+628
Heated Front Seats [Opt on LS Crew]	+146
Leather Seats [Opt on LS Crew]	+407
Locking Differential [Std on LS - Crew Cab,Ext 4WD]	+155
LS Xtreme Package [Opt on LS]	+1299

Options	Price
Power Door Locks [Std on LS Crew]	+129
Power Driver Seat [Opt on LS Crew]	+152
Power Passenger Seat [Opt on LS Crew]	+152
Power Windows [Std on LS Crew]	+146
Side Steps [Opt on LS Crew]	+172
ZQ8 Sport Suspension Package [Opt on LS]	+444
ZR2 Highrider Suspension Package	+1105

2001

Mileage Category: J

A new four-door crew cab 4WD version is offered with enough room for five passengers. Chevy's compact truck now offers a national low emission vehicle (NLEV) option.

Body Styles	TMV Pricing		
	Trade	Private	Dealer
2 Dr LS 4WD Ext Cab SB	9004	10574	12023
2 Dr LS Ext Cab SB	7006	8229	9357
2 Dr LS Std Cab LB	6052	7107	8081
2 Dr LS Std Cab SB	5909	6939	7890
2 Dr STD 4WD Ext Cab SB	8678	10191	11588

Body Styles	TMV Pricing		
	Trade	Private	Dealer
2 Dr STD Ext Cab SB	6767	7946	9035
2 Dr STD Std Cab LB	5820	6835	7771
2 Dr STD Std Cab SB	5706	6701	7620
4 Dr LS 4WD Crew Cab SB	11185	13135	14935

Options	Price
4.3L V6 OHV 12V FI Engine [Opt on 2WD]	+679
Air Conditioning [Opt on STD]	+422
Aluminum/Alloy Wheels [Opt on 2WD Reg Cab LB,LS,STD]	+147
AM/FM/Cassette/CD Audio System	+211
AM/FM/CD Audio System	+158
Automatic 4-Speed Transmission	+574
Bucket Seats	+179
Locking Differential	+122

Options	Price
LS Xtreme Package	+1149
Power Door Locks [Std on LS Wide Stance]	+118
Power Heated Mirrors [Std on LS Wide Stance]	+123
Power Windows [Std on LS Wide Stance]	+134
Sport Suspension [Std on LS]	+365
Stepside Bed	+249
Wide Stance Suspension Package	+2122

2000

Body Styles	TMV Pricing		
	Trade	Private	Dealer
2 Dr LS 4WD Ext Cab SB	7647	9072	10468
2 Dr LS 4WD Ext Cab Step SB	8375	9935	11464
2 Dr LS 4WD Std Cab SB	7364	8736	10081
2 Dr LS 4WD Std Cab Step SB	7475	8868	10233
2 Dr LS Ext Cab SB	5836	6923	7989
2 Dr LS Ext Cab Step SB	6351	7534	8694
2 Dr LS Std Cab LB	5237	6212	7168
2 Dr LS Std Cab SB	4947	5869	6772
2 Dr LS Std Cab Step SB	5259	6239	7199

Body Styles	TMV Pricing		
	Trade	Private	Dealer
2 Dr LS Wide Stance 4WD Ext Cab SB	10342	12269	14158
2 Dr LS Xtreme Ext Cab SB	7419	8801	10156
2 Dr LS Xtreme Ext Cab Step SB	7530	8933	10309
2 Dr LS Xtreme Std Cab SB	6072	7203	8311
2 Dr STD 4WD Ext Cab SB	7588	9001	10387
2 Dr STD 4WD Std Cab SB	6464	7668	8848
2 Dr STD Ext Cab SB	5734	6802	7849
2 Dr STD Std Cab LB	4722	5602	6464
2 Dr STD Std Cab SB	4664	5533	6385

Options	Price
4.3L V6 OHV 12V FI Engine [Std on 4WD]	+510
Air Conditioning [Opt on STD]	+377
Aluminum/Alloy Wheels [Opt on 2WD Reg Cab LB,LS,STD]	+131
AM/FM/Cassette/CD Audio System	+188
AM/FM/CD Audio System	+141
Automatic 4-Speed Transmission	+512

Options	Price
Bucket Seats	+136
Hinged Third Door [Std on LS Wide Stance]	+138
Limited Slip Differential [Std on LS Wide Stance]	+126
Locking Differential	+126
Power Windows [Std on LS Wide Stance]	+119
Sport Suspension [Std on LS Xtreme]	+326

Mileage Category: J

Performance and durability enhancements have been made to the engine, exhaust system, manual transmission and antilock braking system, but they don't result in more horsepower. Trucks equipped with the ZR2 package get a new axle ratio designed to improve acceleration. Extended cabs are available in Base trim this year, and LS models have revised exterior moldings.

1999

Body Styles	TMV Pricing		
	Trade	Private	Dealer
2 Dr LS 4WD Ext Cab SB	6642	7978	9368
2 Dr LS 4WD Ext Cab Step SB	7021	8432	9901
2 Dr LS 4WD Std Cab LB	6521	7832	9197
2 Dr LS 4WD Std Cab SB	6216	7466	8766
2 Dr LS 4WD Std Cab Step SB	6582	7905	9283
2 Dr LS Ext Cab SB	4715	5663	6650
2 Dr LS Ext Cab Step SB	5091	6115	7180
2 Dr LS Std Cab LB	4445	5339	6270
2 Dr LS Std Cab SB	4180	5020	5895
2 Dr LS Std Cab Step SB	4437	5329	6258

Body Styles	TMV Pricing		
	Trade	Private	Dealer
2 Dr LS Wide Stance 4WD Ext Cab SB	8681	10426	12243
2 Dr LS Wide Stance 4WD Std Cab SB	8055	9674	11360
2 Dr LS Xtreme Ext Cab SB	6144	7379	8665
2 Dr LS Xtreme Ext Cab Step SB	6268	7529	8841
2 Dr LS Xtreme Std Cab SB	5035	6047	7101
2 Dr STD 4WD Std Cab LB	6029	7242	8504
2 Dr STD 4WD Std Cab SB	5627	6758	7936
2 Dr STD Std Cab LB	4126	4956	5819
2 Dr STD Std Cab SB	4021	4829	5670

Options	Price
Automatic 4-Speed Transmission	+409
Sport Suspension	+259

Options	Price
Air Conditioning [Std on ZR2]	+300
AM/FM/Cassette/CD Audio System	+151

Mileage Category: J

An all-new sport package called the Xtreme debuts. All S-10s get automatic transmission enhancements to improve sealing and durability and larger outside mirrors with an optional power-heated mirror. Other changes for '99 include a content theft alarm, headlamp flash-to-pass feature, three new exterior paint choices and the availability of GM's AutoTrac electronic push-button transfer case on select four-wheel-drive models.

1998

Body Styles	TMV Pricing		
	Trade	Private	Dealer
2 Dr LS 4WD Ext Cab SB	5868	7128	8548
2 Dr LS 4WD Ext Cab Step SB	5920	7190	8623
2 Dr LS 4WD Std Cab LB	5395	6553	7858
2 Dr LS 4WD Std Cab SB	5185	6297	7552
2 Dr LS 4WD Std Cab Step SB	5406	6566	7874
2 Dr LS Ext Cab SB	4108	4989	5983
2 Dr LS Ext Cab Step SB	4277	5195	6230
2 Dr LS Std Cab LB	3810	4628	5550

Body Styles	TMV Pricing		
	Trade	Private	Dealer
2 Dr LS Std Cab SB	3731	4531	5434
2 Dr LS Std Cab Step SB	3867	4697	5633
2 Dr STD 4WD Std Cab LB	4846	5886	7059
2 Dr STD 4WD Std Cab SB	4477	5438	6521
2 Dr STD Std Cab LB	3598	4370	5241
2 Dr STD Std Cab SB	3495	4245	5090
2 Dr ZR2 4WD Ext Cab SB	7462	9063	10869
2 Dr ZR2 4WD Std Cab SB	7138	8670	10397

Options	Price
AM/FM/Cassette/CD Audio System	+126
Automatic 4-Speed Transmission [Std on ZR2]	+336
Sport Suspension	+218
Air Conditioning [Std on ZR2]	+253

Mileage Category: J

The S-10 gets a sheet metal makeover and a new interior with dual airbags that incorporate second-generation technology for reduced force deployments. The basic four-cylinder engine benefits from Vortec technology this year, while 4WD models now have four-wheel disc brakes and a more refined transfer case on trucks with an automatic transmission. New radios, automatic headlight control and a standard theft-deterrent system sum up the changes.

Chevrolet
S-10

1997

Mileage Category: J

Chevy strengthens the 2WD S-10 frame by using tougher components. Refinements to the automatic transmission result in improved efficiency and smoother shifts. Four-wheel-drive models have lighter-weight plug-in half shafts. Two new colors are available.

Body Styles	TMV Pricing		
	Trade	Private	Dealer
2 Dr LS 4WD Ext Cab SB	4969	6129	7546
2 Dr LS 4WD Ext Cab Step SB	5123	6318	7779
2 Dr LS 4WD Std Cab LB	4643	5727	7051
2 Dr LS 4WD Std Cab SB	4456	5496	6766
2 Dr LS 4WD Std Cab Step SB	4703	5800	7141
2 Dr LS Ext Cab SB	3361	4145	5104
2 Dr LS Ext Cab Step SB	3613	4456	5486

Options	Price
Air Conditioning	+229
Automatic 4-Speed Transmission	+304

Body Styles	TMV Pricing		
	Trade	Private	Dealer
2 Dr LS Std Cab LB	3206	3954	4869
2 Dr LS Std Cab SB	3150	3885	4784
2 Dr LS Std Cab Step SB	3219	3970	4888
2 Dr STD 4WD Std Cab LB	4054	5000	6156
2 Dr STD 4WD Std Cab LB	3899	4809	5922
2 Dr STD Std Cab LB	3126	3855	4747
2 Dr STD Std Cab SB	2871	3541	4359

Options	Price
Wide Stance Suspension Package	+496

1996

Mileage Category: J

Improved V6 engines make more power and torque this year. A new five-speed manual gives four-cylinder models better acceleration, and four-bangers also get four-wheel antilock brakes. Extended-cab models get third-door access panel on the driver side to make loading cargo and passengers easier. A new sport suspension turns the S-10 into a competent sports truck, and the new Sportside cargo box allows the S-Series to go head to head with the Ford Ranger Splash.

Body Styles	TMV Pricing		
	Trade	Private	Dealer
2 Dr LS 4WD Ext Cab SB	4065	5108	6549
2 Dr LS 4WD Ext Cab Step SB	4113	5169	6627
2 Dr LS 4WD Std Cab LB	4003	5030	6449
2 Dr LS 4WD Std Cab SB	3872	4866	6238
2 Dr LS 4WD Std Cab Step SB	3919	4925	6315
2 Dr LS Ext Cab SB	2903	3649	4678
2 Dr LS Ext Cab Step SB	3194	4014	5147

Options	Price
Wide Stance Suspension Package	+444
Air Conditioning	+207

Body Styles	TMV Pricing		
	Trade	Private	Dealer
2 Dr LS Std Cab LB	2564	3222	4131
2 Dr LS Std Cab SB	2515	3161	4052
2 Dr LS Std Cab Step SB	2662	3345	4288
2 Dr STD 4WD Std Cab LB	3375	4241	5437
2 Dr STD 4WD Std Cab SB	3211	4035	5174
2 Dr STD Std Cab LB	2323	2919	3743
2 Dr STD Std Cab SB	2275	2859	3666

Options	Price
Antilock Brakes [Opt on 2WD]	+195
Automatic 4-Speed Transmission	+276

1995

Mileage Category: J

Driver airbag is added, and daytime running lights are standard. ZR2 off-road package can be ordered on the extended cab. Power window and lock buttons are illuminated at night. Remote keyless entry is a new option. A single key operates both the door locks and the ignition. A manual transmission can now be ordered with the 191-horsepower, 4.3-liter V6.

Body Styles	TMV Pricing		
	Trade	Private	Dealer
2 Dr LS 4WD Ext Cab SB	3332	4258	5802
2 Dr LS 4WD Std Cab LB	3222	4118	5611
2 Dr LS 4WD Std Cab SB	3130	4000	5451
2 Dr LS Ext Cab SB	2312	2955	4027
2 Dr LS Std Cab LB	2170	2773	3778

Options	Price
Wide Stance Suspension Package	+399
4.3L V6 OHV 12V FI Engine [Opt on 2WD]	+229
4.3L V6 OHV 12V HO FI Engine	+129
Air Conditioning	+186
Aluminum/Alloy Wheels	+79

Body Styles	TMV Pricing		
	Trade	Private	Dealer
2 Dr LS Std Cab SB	1991	2545	3468
2 Dr STD 4WD Std Cab LB	2793	3570	4864
2 Dr STD 4WD Std Cab SB	2545	3253	4432
2 Dr STD Std Cab LB	1904	2433	3315
2 Dr STD Std Cab SB	1860	2377	3238

Options	Price
AM/FM/Cassette Audio System	+80
AM/FM/CD Audio System	+93
Antilock Brakes [Opt on 2WD]	+175
Automatic 4-Speed Transmission	+248

1994

Mileage Category: J

All-new truck debuts with more powerful engines and available four-wheel ABS. Side-door guard beams are standard. Rear ABS is standard on four-cylinder models; V6 trucks get the new four-wheel ABS system that works in both two- and four-wheel drive. ZR2 package is for serious off-roaders. Available only on regular-cab short-bed models, the ZR2 package includes four-inch-wider track, three-inch height increase, off-road suspension and tires, wheel flares and thick skid plates. Base engine is 118-horse, 2.2-liter four-cylinder. Standard on 4WD models is a 165-horsepower, 4.3-liter V6. Optional on all models is a 195-horsepower, high-output 4.3-liter V6. SS package available with high-output engine, sport suspension and alloy wheels.

Body Styles	TMV Pricing		
	Trade	Private	Dealer
2 Dr LS 4WD Ext Cab SB	2628	3516	4995
2 Dr LS 4WD Std Cab LB	2503	3348	4756
2 Dr LS 4WD Std Cab SB	2460	3290	4674
2 Dr LS Ext Cab SB	1822	2438	3464
2 Dr LS Std Cab LB	1739	2326	3305

Options	Price
Wide Stance Suspension Package	+194
4.3L V6 OHV 12V FI Engine [Opt on 2WD]	+202
4.3L V6 OHV 12V HO FI Engine	+114
Air Conditioning	+165

Body Styles	TMV Pricing		
	Trade	Private	Dealer
2 Dr LS Std Cab SB	1611	2155	3062
2 Dr STD 4WD Std Cab LB	1990	2662	3783
2 Dr STD 4WD Std Cab SB	1983	2653	3769
2 Dr STD Std Cab LB	1569	2099	2983
2 Dr STD Std Cab SB	1441	1928	2739

Options	Price
AM/FM/CD Audio System	+83
Antilock Brakes [Opt on 2WD]	+154
Automatic 4-Speed Transmission	+219

Chevrolet
S-10 Blazer

1994

Body Styles	TMV Pricing			Body Styles	TMV Pricing		
	Trade	Private	Dealer		Trade	Private	Dealer
2 Dr STD 4WD SUV	1856	2495	3560	4 Dr STD 4WD SUV	2054	2761	3939
2 Dr STD SUV	1737	2335	3332	4 Dr STD SUV	1798	2417	3448
2 Dr Tahoe 4WD SUV	2013	2706	3861	4 Dr Tahoe 4WD SUV	2051	2758	3935
2 Dr Tahoe LT 4WD SUV	2252	3027	4319	4 Dr Tahoe LT 4WD SUV	2402	3229	4606
2 Dr Tahoe LT SUV	1930	2595	3702	4 Dr Tahoe LT SUV	2144	2882	4111
2 Dr Tahoe SUV	1787	2402	3427	4 Dr Tahoe SUV	1795	2413	3443

Options	Price
4.3L V6 OHV 12V HO FI Engine	+82
Air Conditioning [Opt on STD,Tahoe]	+163
Automatic 4-Speed Transmission	+197

Mileage Category: M

Side-door guard beams and a high-mount center brake light are added. Front bench seat is now standard on four-door models.

Chevrolet
SSR

2003

Body Styles	TMV Pricing		
	Trade	Private	Dealer
2 Dr LS Conv Std Cab SB	37862	39689	42734

Options	Price	Options	Price
Bose Audio System	+192	Special Factory Paint	+223
Heated Front Seats	+271	AM/FM/CD Changer Audio System	+239

Mileage Category: K

Chevrolet brings to market a sport pickup with a retractable hardtop, retro styling and 300 horsepower.

Chevrolet
Silverado 1500

2003

Body Styles	TMV Pricing			Body Styles	TMV Pricing		
	Trade	Private	Dealer		Trade	Private	Dealer
2 Dr LS 4WD Std Cab LB	16881	17973	19793	4 Dr LS Ext Cab LB	18625	19830	21839
2 Dr LS 4WD Std Cab SB	16741	17824	19630	4 Dr LS Ext Cab SB	16979	18078	19909
2 Dr LS Std Cab LB	14963	15931	17545	4 Dr LT 4WD Ext Cab LB	23811	25352	27919
2 Dr LS Std Cab SB	14848	15808	17409	4 Dr LT 4WD Ext Cab SB	23200	24701	27203
2 Dr STD 4WD Std Cab LB	14779	15735	17329	4 Dr LT Ext Cab LB	21249	22624	24915
2 Dr STD 4WD Std Cab SB	14281	15205	16745	4 Dr LT Ext Cab SB	21039	22400	24669
2 Dr STD Std Cab LB	12196	12985	14301	4 Dr STD 4WD Ext Cab LB	19121	20358	22420
2 Dr STD Std Cab SB	12011	12788	14083	4 Dr STD 4WD Ext Cab SB	18293	19477	21450
2 Dr Work Truck 4WD Std Cab LB	14489	15427	16989	4 Dr STD Ext Cab LB	16710	17791	19593
2 Dr Work Truck Std Cab LB	12094	12877	14181	4 Dr STD Ext Cab SB	15291	16280	17929
4 Dr LS 4WD Ext Cab LB	20488	21814	24023	4 Dr Work Truck Ext Cab SB	15062	16037	17661
4 Dr LS 4WD Ext Cab SB	19804	21085	23221				

Mileage Category: K

The Silverado gets a makeover this year that includes a new front fascia and revised side moldings and taillights. Top-of-the-line models get power-folding heated mirrors with puddle lamps and turn signal indicators. On the inside, the Silverado is the first full-size pickup to offer a Bose stereo system and XM Satellite Radio. The instrument panel and center console have been redesigned, and Chevrolet has added new seats, a more comprehensive driver information center and a dual-zone climate control system. For increased safety, Silverados now feature a standard front-passenger-sensing system and dual-stage airbags. On the hardware side, all 4.3-liter V6-equipped Silverados and California-emission V8s are now ULEV-certified, while electronic throttle control is now standard on all V8 engines. The Autotrac four-wheel-drive system has been modified for less intrusiveness at low speeds, and the brake system received upgrades that provide better pedal feel and improved overall performance.

2003 (cont'd)

Options	Price
4 Wheel Steering [Opt on Ext Cab SB - LS,LT]	+2870
Aluminum/Alloy Wheels [Std on LT]	+128
AM/FM/CD Audio System [Opt on STD]	+163
Appearance Package	+322
Automatic 4-Speed Transmission [Std on Ext Cab LB,LT]	+699
Bose Audio System [Opt on LS]	+252
Bucket Seats [Opt on Ext Cab - LS,STD]	+271
Cruise Control [Opt on STD,Work]	+153
Electronic Suspension Control [Opt on LS,LT]	+207
Leather Seats [Opt on LS]	+511
Limited Slip Differential [Opt on Ext SB - LS,LT]	+188
Locking Differential	+188
Power Driver Seat [Std on LT]	+153

Options	Price
Power Mirrors [Opt on STD,Work]	+121
Power Windows [Opt on STD,Work]	+156
Traction Control System [Opt on 2WD]	+144
Two-Tone Paint [Opt on LS]	+160
OnStar Telematic System [Opt on LS]	+444
Stepside Bed [Opt on SB]	+508
AM/FM/CD Changer Audio System [Std on LT]	+255
Z71 Off-Road Suspension Package [Opt on LS 4WD]	+166
Satellite Radio System [Opt on LS,LT]	+207
Automatic Climate Control (2 Zone) - Driver and Passenger [Opt on LS]	+124
5.3L V8 OHV 16V FI Engine [Std on Ext Cab LB,LT]	+511
Power Retractable Mirrors [Opt on LS]	+117

2002

Mileage Category: K

Only minor changes are made to Chevrolet's bread-and-butter Silverado pickup for 2002. Some options packages have been revamped for easier ordering and all extended-cab models now come standard with a four-speed automatic transmission, with the manual no longer available.

Body Styles	TMV Pricing		
	Trade	Private	Dealer
2 Dr LS 4WD Std Cab LB	14163	15228	17002
2 Dr LS 4WD Std Cab SB	13935	14982	16728
2 Dr LS Std Cab LB	12668	13620	15207
2 Dr LS Std Cab SB	12584	13530	15106
2 Dr STD 4WD Std Cab LB	12632	13582	15164
2 Dr STD 4WD Std Cab SB	11902	12797	14288
2 Dr STD Std Cab LB	10094	10853	12117
2 Dr STD Std Cab SB	9977	10727	11977
2 Dr Work Truck 4WD Std Cab LB	12221	13139	14670
2 Dr Work Truck Std Cab LB	10052	10808	12067
4 Dr LS 4WD Ext Cab LB	17742	19076	21298

Body Styles	TMV Pricing		
	Trade	Private	Dealer
4 Dr LS 4WD Ext Cab SB	17286	18585	20751
4 Dr LS Ext Cab LB	16394	17626	19680
4 Dr LS Ext Cab SB	14581	15677	17504
4 Dr LT 4WD Ext Cab LB	19927	21425	23921
4 Dr LT 4WD Ext Cab SB	19730	21213	23684
4 Dr LT Ext Cab LB	18053	19410	21671
4 Dr LT Ext Cab SB	17875	19219	21458
4 Dr STD 4WD Ext Cab LB	16950	18224	20347
4 Dr STD 4WD Ext Cab SB	16160	17735	19399
4 Dr STD Ext Cab LB	14561	15656	17480
4 Dr STD Ext Cab SB	13184	14175	15826

Options	Price
4 Wheel Steering [Opt on Ext Cab - LS,LT]	+3028
5.3L V8 Flex Fuel OHV 16V FI Engine	+459
5.3L V8 OHV 16V FI Engine [Std on LS Ext LB,LT,STD Ext LB]	+459
Automatic 4-Speed Transmission [Std on Ext]	+628
Bucket Seats [Opt on LS]	+244
Chrome Wheels [Opt on STD]	+186
Cruise Control [Opt on STD,Work Truck]	+138

Options	Price
Electronic Suspension Control [Opt on LS,LT]	+186
Leather Seats [Std on LT]	+459
Locking Differential [Std on LT 4WD]	+163
Power Driver Seat [Opt on LS]	+138
Power Passenger Seat [Opt on LS]	+138
Traction Control System	+129
Two-Tone Paint [Opt on LS]	+143

2001

Mileage Category: K

A 1500HD crew cab makes its debut in 2001 featuring the 6.0-liter Vortec V8. An available PRO TEC composite truck box and optional traction control are also added to the Silverado this year along with new colors and the OnStar vehicle assistance system.

Body Styles	TMV Pricing		
	Trade	Private	Dealer
2 Dr LS 4WD Std Cab LB	12055	13530	14891
2 Dr LS 4WD Std Cab SB	11853	13303	14642
2 Dr LS Std Cab LB	10715	12026	13236
2 Dr LS Std Cab SB	10648	11951	13153
2 Dr STD 4WD Std Cab LB	10179	11424	12573
2 Dr STD 4WD Std Cab SB	9681	10865	11958
2 Dr STD Std Cab LB	8033	9015	9922
2 Dr STD Std Cab SB	8012	8992	9897
4 Dr LS 4WD Ext Cab LB	15360	17239	18973
4 Dr LS 4WD Ext Cab SB	15286	17156	18882

Body Styles	TMV Pricing		
	Trade	Private	Dealer
4 Dr LS Ext Cab LB	13728	15408	16958
4 Dr LS Ext Cab SB	12525	14057	15471
4 Dr LT 4WD Ext Cab LB	16542	18565	20433
4 Dr LT 4WD Ext Cab SB	16408	18415	20268
4 Dr LT Ext Cab LB	15463	17355	19101
4 Dr LT Ext Cab SB	15437	17325	19068
4 Dr STD 4WD Ext Cab LB	13864	15560	17125
4 Dr STD 4WD Ext Cab SB	13595	15258	16793
4 Dr STD Ext Cab LB	11765	13204	14533
4 Dr STD Ext Cab SB	10983	12327	13567

Options	Price
4.8L V8 OHV 16V FI Engine	+365
5.3L V8 OHV 16V FI Engine [Opt on LS,STD]	+420
Air Conditioning	+433
Automatic 4-Speed Transmission	+574
Cruise Control	+126
Electronic Suspension Control	+170
Leather Seats [Opt on LS]	+671

Options	Price
Locking Differential	+150
Off-Road Suspension Package	+207
Power Driver Seat [Opt on LS]	+126
Power Passenger Seat [Opt on LS]	+126
Stepside Bed [Opt on SB]	+417
Traction Control System	+118
Two-Tone Paint	+131

2000

Mileage Category: K

Body Styles	TMV Pricing		
	Trade	Private	Dealer
2 Dr LS 4WD Ext Cab LB	13252	14995	16703
2 Dr LS 4WD Ext Cab SB	13165	14896	16593
2 Dr LS 4WD Ext Cab Step SB	13417	15181	16911
2 Dr LS 4WD Std Cab LB	10701	12108	13487
2 Dr LS 4WD Std Cab SB	10544	11931	13290
2 Dr LS 4WD Std Cab Step SB	12247	13857	15436
2 Dr LS Ext Cab LB	11596	13121	14616
2 Dr LS Ext Cab SB	10495	11875	13228
2 Dr LS Ext Cab Step SB	11533	13050	14536
2 Dr LS Std Cab LB	9489	10737	11960
2 Dr LS Std Cab SB	9428	10668	11883
2 Dr LS Std Cab Step SB	10195	11536	12850
2 Dr LT 4WD Ext Cab LB	14647	16573	18461
2 Dr LT 4WD Ext Cab SB	14645	16571	18459
2 Dr LT 4WD Ext Cab Step SB	16459	18623	20745

Body Styles	TMV Pricing		
	Trade	Private	Dealer
2 Dr LT Ext Cab LB	13674	15472	17234
2 Dr LT Ext Cab SB	13481	15254	16992
2 Dr LT Ext Cab Step SB	14460	16362	18226
2 Dr STD 4WD Ext Cab LB	12268	13881	15463
2 Dr STD 4WD Ext Cab SB	11777	13325	14843
2 Dr STD 4WD Ext Cab Step SB	12773	14453	16099
2 Dr STD 4WD Std Cab LB	8892	10061	11207
2 Dr STD 4WD Std Cab SB	8633	9768	10881
2 Dr STD 4WD Std Cab Step SB	9370	10602	11810
2 Dr STD Ext Cab LB	10447	11821	13167
2 Dr STD Ext Cab SB	9387	10621	11831
2 Dr STD Ext Cab Step SB	10279	11631	12956
2 Dr STD Std Cab SB	7232	8183	9116
2 Dr STD Std Cab SB	7043	7969	8877
2 Dr STD Std Cab Step SB	7941	8985	10009

Options	Price
Camper/Towing Package	+134
Hinged Fourth Door	+155
Leather Seats [Opt on LS]	+537
Limited Slip Differential	+134
Off-Road Suspension Package [Opt on 4WD]	+185

Options	Price
Bucket Seats	+176
4.8L V8 OHV 16V FI Engine	+326
5.3L V8 OHV 16V FI Engine [Opt on LS,STD]	+374
Air Conditioning	+386
Automatic 4-Speed Transmission	+465

After a complete redesign last year, few changes make news for 2000. Most substantial is the addition of an optional fourth access door to extended cab models. The already potent Vortec 4800 and 5300 V8 engines make more power, and programmable door locks can be instructed to unlock automatically when the Silverado is shut off. A Sportside cargo box is available on 1500 LT models, and 1500 4WD trucks can be equipped with wheel flares this year. LS and LT trucks get a standard electrochromic self-dimming rearview mirror with compass and exterior temperature display, and a soft tonneau cover is available from the factory.

1999

Mileage Category: K

Body Styles	TMV Pricing		
	Trade	Private	Dealer
2 Dr LS 4WD Ext Cab LB	11590	13396	15276
2 Dr LS 4WD Ext Cab SB	11521	13316	15185
2 Dr LS 4WD Ext Cab Step SB	11908	13764	15695
2 Dr LS 4WD Std Cab LB	9623	11122	12683
2 Dr LS 4WD Std Cab SB	9371	10831	12351
2 Dr LS 4WD Std Cab Step SB	10241	11837	13498
2 Dr LS Ext Cab LB	9981	11536	13155
2 Dr LS Ext Cab SB	9223	10660	12156
2 Dr LS Ext Cab Step SB	9608	11105	12663
2 Dr LS Std Cab LB	8490	9813	11190
2 Dr LS Std Cab SB	8167	9440	10764
2 Dr LS Std Cab Step SB	8878	10262	11702
2 Dr LT 4WD Ext Cab LB	13178	15232	17369
2 Dr LT 4WD Ext Cab SB	13036	15067	17181

Body Styles	TMV Pricing		
	Trade	Private	Dealer
2 Dr LT Ext Cab LB	12040	13916	15869
2 Dr LT Ext Cab SB	11912	13768	15700
2 Dr STD 4WD Ext Cab LB	10468	12099	13797
2 Dr STD 4WD Ext Cab SB	10306	11912	13583
2 Dr STD 4WD Ext Cab Step SB	10825	12512	14267
2 Dr STD 4WD Std Cab LB	7778	8990	10251
2 Dr STD 4WD Std Cab SB	7712	8914	10165
2 Dr STD 4WD Std Cab Step SB	8103	9366	10680
2 Dr STD Ext Cab LB	9002	10405	11865
2 Dr STD Ext Cab SB	8296	9589	10934
2 Dr STD Ext Cab Step SB	8945	10339	11789
2 Dr STD Std Cab LB	6352	7342	8372
2 Dr STD Std Cab SB	6229	7200	8210
2 Dr STD Std Cab Step SB	6610	7640	8712

Options	Price
4.8L V8 OHV 16V FI Engine	+259
5.3L V8 OHV 16V FI Engine	+298
Air Conditioning [Opt on STD]	+308

Options	Price
Automatic 4-Speed Transmission	+372
Bucket Seats	+140
Leather Seats	+429

Chevrolet has redesigned the decade-old C/K pickup and given the truck a new name. Major structural, power, braking and interior enhancements characterize the new Silverado. Styling is evolutionary rather than revolutionary, inside and out.

Chevrolet
Silverado 1500 SS/Silverado 1500HD

Chevrolet
Silverado 1500 SS

2003

Body Styles	TMV Pricing		
	Trade	Private	Dealer
4 Dr STD AWD Ext Cab SB	29787	31224	33620

Options	Price	Options	Price
Camper/Towing Package	+137	Satellite Radio System	+207
OnStar Telematic System	+444	Automatic Climate Control (2 Zone) - Driver and Passenger	+124
AM/FM/CD Changer Audio System	+255		

Mileage Category: K

Introduced late in the model year, the SS version of the Silverado features a 6.0-liter V8 with 345 horsepower, all-wheel drive, 20-inch wheels and a more aggressive front end.

Chevrolet
Silverado 1500HD

2003

Body Styles	TMV Pricing			Body Styles	TMV Pricing		
	Trade	Private	Dealer		Trade	Private	Dealer
4 Dr LS 4WD Crew Cab SB HD	23242	24599	26861	4 Dr LT 4WD Crew Cab SB HD	25992	27510	30039
4 Dr LS Crew Cab SB HD	20652	21858	23867	4 Dr LT Crew Cab SB HD	23507	24880	27167

Options	Price	Options	Price
4 Wheel Steering	+2870	Power Driver Seat [Opt on LS]	+153
Aluminum/Alloy Wheels [Opt on LS]	+128	Traction Control System [Opt on 2WD]	+144
Bose Audio System [Opt on LS]	+252	OnStar Telematic System [Opt on LS]	+444
Bucket Seats [Opt on LS]	+271	AM/FM/CD Changer Audio System [Opt on LS]	+255
Electronic Suspension Control	+207	Satellite Radio System	+207
Leather Seats [Opt on LS]	+511	Automatic Climate Control (2 Zone) - Driver and Passenger [Opt on LS]	+124
Limited Slip Differential	+188	DVD Entertainment System	+827
Locking Differential	+188	Power Retractable Mirrors [Opt on LS]	+117

Mileage Category: K

The Silverado gets a makeover this year that includes a new front fascia and revised side moldings and taillights. Up-level LT models get power-folding heated mirrors with puddle lamps and turn signal indicators. On the inside, the Silverado offers new entertainment options, such as a Bose audio system with rear-seat controls, XM Satellite Radio and a DVD-based entertainment system. The instrument panel and center console have been redesigned, and Chevrolet has added new seats, a more comprehensive driver information center and a dual-zone climate control system. For increased safety, Silverados now feature a standard front-passenger-sensing system that deactivates the airbag for children. On the hardware side, the all-new Quadrasteer four-wheel steering system, which increases low-speed maneuverability and towing stability, is now optional. The standard 6.0-liter V8 gets electronic throttle control, as well as the ability to run exclusively on Compressed Natural Gas (CNG) or a mix of CNG and gasoline.

2002

Mileage Category: K

Debuting late last year as an all-new 2001 model, the 1500HD Crew Cab gets few changes for the 2002 model year. A high-capacity air cleaner is now standard, along with extended sunshades for both the driver and passenger.

Body Styles	TMV Pricing			Body Styles	TMV Pricing		
	Trade	Private	Dealer		Trade	Private	Dealer
4 Dr LS 4WD Crew Cab SB HD	20268	21623	23882	4 Dr LT 4WD Crew Cab SB HD	22283	23773	26256
4 Dr LS Crew Cab SB HD	18059	19267	21279	4 Dr LT Crew Cab SB HD	20117	21462	23704

Options	Price	Options	Price
Bucket Seats [Std on LT]	+244	Power Driver Seat [Opt on LS]	+138
Leather Seats [Std on LT]	+459	Power Passenger Seat [Opt on LS]	+138
Locking Differential [Opt on 2WD]	+169		

2001

Mileage Category: K

A 1500HD crew cab makes its debut in 2001 featuring the 6.0-liter Vortec V8. An available PRO TEC composite truck box and optional traction control are also added to the Silverado this year along with new colors and the OnStar vehicle assistance system.

Body Styles	TMV Pricing			Body Styles	TMV Pricing		
	Trade	Private	Dealer		Trade	Private	Dealer
4 Dr LS 4WD Crew Cab SB HD	17549	19409	21125	4 Dr LT 4WD Crew Cab SB HD	19302	21347	23235
4 Dr LS Crew Cab SB HD	15608	17262	18788	4 Dr LT Crew Cab SB HD	17403	19247	20950

Options	Price
Leather Seats [Opt on LS]	+708
Locking Differential [Std on LT]	+150

Options	Price
Power Driver Seat [Opt on LS]	+126
Power Passenger Seat [Opt on LS]	+126

2001 (cont'd)

Chevrolet
Silverado 2500

2003

Body Styles	TMV Pricing		
	Trade	Private	Dealer
2 Dr LS Std Cab LB	17548	18712	20651
2 Dr STD Std Cab LB	15663	16702	18433
2 Dr Work Truck Std Cab LB	15584	16618	18340

Body Styles	TMV Pricing		
	Trade	Private	Dealer
4 Dr LS 4WD Ext Cab SB	21757	23200	25605
4 Dr LT 4WD Ext Cab SB	24647	26281	29005
4 Dr STD 4WD Ext Cab SB	19866	21183	23379

Options	Price
Aluminum/Alloy Wheels [Opt on LS]	+128
AM/FM/CD Audio System [Opt on STD,Work]	+163
Appearance Package [Opt on LS]	+367
Automatic 4-Speed Transmission [Opt on Std Cab]	+699
Bose Audio System [Opt on LS Ext]	+252
Bucket Seats [Opt on LS Ext]	+271
Cruise Control [Opt on STD,Work]	+153
Leather Seats [Opt on LS Ext]	+511
Locking Differential	+188

Options	Price
Power Driver Seat [Opt on LS]	+153
Traction Control System [Opt on 2WD]	+144
Two-Tone Paint [Opt on LS Ext]	+160
OnStar Telematic System [Opt on LS Ext]	+444
AM/FM/CD Changer Audio System [Opt on LS]	+255
Satellite Radio System [Opt on LS,LT]	+207
Automatic Climate Control (2 Zone) - Driver and Passenger [Opt on LS Ext]	+124
Power Retractable Mirrors [Opt on LS]	+117

Mileage Category: K

The Silverado gets a makeover this year that includes a new front fascia and revised side moldings and taillights. Top-of-the-line models also get power-folding heated mirrors with puddle lamps and turn signal indicators. On the inside, the Silverado is the first full-size pickup to offer a Bose stereo system and XM Satellite Radio. The instrument panel and center console have been redesigned, and Chevrolet has added new seats, a more comprehensive driver information center and a dual-zone climate control system. For increased safety, Silverados now feature a standard front-passenger-sensing system and dual-stage airbags. On the hardware side, the standard 6.0-liter V8 gets electronic throttle control as well as the ability to run exclusively on Compressed Natural Gas (CNG) or a mix of CNG and gasoline.

2002

Body Styles	TMV Pricing		
	Trade	Private	Dealer
2 Dr LS Std Cab LB	15132	16222	18039
2 Dr STD Std Cab LB	13809	14804	16461
4 Dr LS 4WD Ext Cab SB	19303	20693	23010

Body Styles	TMV Pricing		
	Trade	Private	Dealer
4 Dr LT 4WD Ext Cab SB	21437	22981	25555
4 Dr STD 4WD Ext Cab SB	17610	18878	20992

Mileage Category: K

Three-quarter-ton Silverados get few changes for 2002. A high-capacity air cleaner and air conditioning are now standard on all models. All extended cabs get a four-speed automatic transmission standard.

Options	Price
Automatic 4-Speed Transmission [Std on Ext]	+628
Bucket Seats [Std on LT]	+244
Chrome Wheels [Opt on STD]	+186
Cruise Control [Std on LS,LT]	+138
Leather Seats [Std on LT]	+459

Options	Price
Locking Differential [Std on LT]	+169
Power Driver Seat [Opt on LS]	+138
Power Passenger Seat [Opt on LS]	+138
Traction Control System [Opt on LS]	+129
Two-Tone Paint [Opt on LS]	+143

2001

Body Styles	TMV Pricing		
	Trade	Private	Dealer
2 Dr LS Std Cab LB	13191	14705	16103
2 Dr STD Std Cab LB	11568	12896	14121
4 Dr LS 4WD Ext Cab SB	16135	17987	19696

Body Styles	TMV Pricing		
	Trade	Private	Dealer
4 Dr LT 4WD Ext Cab SB	18324	20427	22368
4 Dr STD 4WD Ext Cab SB	14370	16019	17542

Mileage Category: K

Both light- and heavy-duty 2500s sport new torsion bar front suspensions. Light-duty models get an 8,600-pound Gross Vehicle Weight Rating in addition to optional traction control and standard child safety-seat tether hooks. Heavy-duty models are completely redesigned for 2001 offering two new engines and transmissions, bigger interiors and numerous other improvements.

Options	Price
Air Conditioning	+433
Automatic 4-Speed Transmission	+574
Cruise Control	+126
Leather Seats [Opt on LS]	+671

Options	Price
Locking Differential	+150
Power Driver Seat [Opt on LS]	+126
Power Passenger Seat [Opt on LS]	+126
Two-Tone Paint	+131

Chevrolet
Silverado 2500/Silverado 2500HD

2000

Mileage Category: K

After a complete redesign last year, few changes make news for 2000. Most substantial is the addition of a fourth access door to extended cab models, but it's optional, unlike the standard quad-portal arrangement on the Ford F-150. The already potent Vortec 4800 and 5300 V8 engines make more power, and programmable door locks can be instructed to unlock automatically when the Silverado is shut off. LS and LT trucks get a standard electrochromic self-dimming rearview mirror with compass and exterior temperature display, and a soft tonneau cover is available from the factory.

Body Styles	TMV Pricing		
	Trade	Private	Dealer
2 Dr LS 4WD Ext Cab LB HD	15086	17083	19040
2 Dr LS 4WD Ext Cab SB HD	14851	16817	18744
2 Dr LS 4WD Std Cab LB HD	12031	13623	15184
2 Dr LS Ext Cab LB HD	12703	14384	16032
2 Dr LS Ext Cab SB	13049	14776	16469
2 Dr LS Std Cab LB	11688	13235	14751
2 Dr LS Std Cab LB HD	11240	12728	14186
2 Dr LT 4WD Ext Cab LB HD	17393	19695	21951
2 Dr LT 4WD Ext Cab SB HD	17142	19410	21634

Options	Price
6.0L V8 OHV 16V FI Engine	+166
Air Conditioning	+386
Automatic 4-Speed Transmission	+465
Bucket Seats	+176

Body Styles	TMV Pricing		
	Trade	Private	Dealer
2 Dr LT Ext Cab LB HD	15718	17798	19837
2 Dr LT Ext Cab SB	15017	17005	18953
2 Dr STD 4WD Ext Cab LB HD	13250	15004	16723
2 Dr STD 4WD Ext Cab SB HD	12962	14678	16360
2 Dr STD 4WD Std Cab LB HD	11681	13227	14742
2 Dr STD Ext Cab LB HD	11047	12509	13942
2 Dr STD Ext Cab SB	11115	12586	14028
2 Dr STD Std Cab LB	10148	11491	12808
2 Dr STD Std Cab LB HD	9682	10964	12220

Options	Price
Camper/Towing Package	+134
Hinged Fourth Door	+155
Leather Seats [Opt on LS]	+692
Limited Slip Differential	+134

1999

Mileage Category: K

Chevrolet has redesigned the decade-old C/K pickup and given the truck a new name. Major structural, power, braking and interior enhancements characterize the new Silverado. Styling is evolutionary rather than revolutionary, inside and out.

Body Styles	TMV Pricing		
	Trade	Private	Dealer
2 Dr LS 4WD Ext Cab LB HD	13281	15350	17504
2 Dr LS 4WD Ext Cab SB HD	12986	15009	17115
2 Dr LS 4WD Std Cab LB HD	10736	12408	14149
2 Dr LS Ext Cab LB HD	10692	12358	14092
2 Dr LS Ext Cab SB	10625	12281	14004
2 Dr LS Std Cab LB	9393	10857	12380
2 Dr LS Std Cab LB HD	9946	11496	13110
2 Dr LT 4WD Ext Cab LB HD	15356	17749	20239
2 Dr LT 4WD Ext Cab SB HD	15220	17592	20060

Options	Price
6.0L V8 OHV 16V FI Engine	+133
Air Conditioning [Opt on STD]	+308

Body Styles	TMV Pricing		
	Trade	Private	Dealer
2 Dr LT Ext Cab LB HD	14046	16235	18513
2 Dr LT Ext Cab SB	12622	14588	16635
2 Dr STD 4WD Ext Cab LB HD	11723	13550	15451
2 Dr STD 4WD Ext Cab SB HD	11409	13187	15038
2 Dr STD 4WD Std Cab LB HD	10442	12069	13762
2 Dr STD Ext Cab LB HD	10004	11563	13185
2 Dr STD Ext Cab SB	9389	10852	12375
2 Dr STD Std Cab LB	8556	9889	11277
2 Dr STD Std Cab LB HD	7558	8736	9962

Options	Price
Bucket Seats	+140
Leather Seats	+553

Chevrolet
Silverado 2500HD

2003

Mileage Category: K

The Silverado 2500HD now sports a new front fascia and revised side moldings and taillights. Top-of-the-line models also get power-folding heated mirrors with puddle lamps and turn signal indicators. On the inside, the Silverado offers numerous entertainment options including a Bose stereo system (with rear-seat controls on crew cab models), XM Satellite Radio and a rear-passenger DVD-based entertainment system (crew cab models only). The instrument panel and center console have been redesigned, and Chevrolet has added new seats, a more comprehensive driver information center and a dual-zone climate control system. On the hardware side, the standard 6.0-liter V8 gets electronic throttle control, as well as the ability to run exclusively on compressed natural gas (CNG) or a mix of CNG and gasoline.

Body Styles	TMV Pricing		
	Trade	Private	Dealer
2 Dr LS 4WD Std Cab LB HD	19954	21171	23200
2 Dr LS Std Cab LB HD	17498	18565	20344
2 Dr STD 4WD Std Cab LB HD	18204	19314	21165
2 Dr STD Std Cab LB HD	15939	16911	18531
2 Dr Work Truck 4WD Std Cab LB HD	18039	19139	20973
2 Dr Work Truck Std Cab LB HD	15741	16701	18302
4 Dr LS 4WD Crew Cab LB HD	23225	24642	27003
4 Dr LS 4WD Crew Cab SB HD	23084	24492	26839
4 Dr LS 4WD Ext Cab LB HD	21710	23034	25241
4 Dr LS 4WD Ext Cab SB HD	21647	22968	25169
4 Dr LS Crew Cab LB HD	21030	22313	24451
4 Dr LS Crew Cab SB HD	20818	22088	24204
4 Dr LS Ext Cab LB HD	19914	21129	23153
4 Dr LS Ext Cab SB HD	19626	20823	22818
4 Dr LT 4WD Crew Cab LB HD	27041	28690	31439

Body Styles	TMV Pricing		
	Trade	Private	Dealer
4 Dr LT 4WD Crew Cab SB HD	26851	28489	31219
4 Dr LT 4WD Ext Cab LB HD	25433	26984	29570
4 Dr LT 4WD Ext Cab SB HD	25195	26732	29293
4 Dr LT Crew Cab LB HD	24667	26172	28679
4 Dr LT Crew Cab SB HD	24454	25946	28432
4 Dr LT Ext Cab LB HD	23339	24763	27135
4 Dr LT Ext Cab SB HD	23249	24667	27031
4 Dr STD 4WD Crew Cab LB HD	21593	22910	25105
4 Dr STD 4WD Crew Cab SB HD	21415	22721	24898
4 Dr STD 4WD Ext Cab LB HD	20233	21467	23524
4 Dr STD 4WD Ext Cab SB HD	19896	21110	23132
4 Dr STD Crew Cab LB HD	19475	20663	22643
4 Dr STD Crew Cab SB HD	19261	20436	22394
4 Dr STD Ext Cab LB HD	18110	19215	21056
4 Dr STD Ext Cab SB HD	17704	18784	20584

2003 (cont'd)

Options	Price
AM/FM/CD Audio System [Opt on STD,Work]	+163
Appearance Package [Opt on STD]	+367
Automatic 4-Speed Transmission	+699
Automatic 5-Speed Transmission	+766
Bose Audio System [Opt on LS]	+252
Bucket Seats [Opt on LS]	+271
Cruise Control [Opt on STD,Work]	+153
Leather Seats [Opt on LS]	+511
Locking Differential	+188

Options	Price
Power Driver Seat [Opt on LS]	+153
OnStar Telematic System [Opt on LS]	+444
AM/FM/CD Changer Audio System [Opt on LS]	+255
Satellite Radio System [Opt on LS,LT]	+207
Automatic Climate Control (2 Zone) - Driver and Passenger [Opt on LS]	+124
DVD Entertainment System [Opt on Crew - LS,LT]	+827
8.1L V8 OHV 16V FI Engine	+543
6.6L V8 Turbodiesel OHV 32V Engine	+3198
Power Retractable Mirrors [Opt on LS]	+117

2002

Mileage Category: K

After undergoing a full redesign last year, Chevrolet's heavy-duty three-quarter-ton truck gets few changes for 2002. Air conditioning is now standard on all trim levels along with extendable sunshade visors and improved base model radios.

Body Styles	TMV Pricing		
	Trade	Private	Dealer
2 Dr LS 4WD Std Cab LB HD	17692	18966	21090
2 Dr LS Std Cab LB HD	15325	16429	18268
2 Dr STD 4WD Std Cab LB HD	16235	17405	19354
2 Dr STD Std Cab LB HD	13882	14882	16548
4 Dr LS 4WD Crew Cab LB HD	20412	21882	24332
4 Dr LS 4WD Crew Cab SB HD	20367	21834	24278
4 Dr LS 4WD Ext Cab LB HD	19375	20770	23096
4 Dr LS 4WD Ext Cab SB HD	19014	20384	22666
4 Dr LS Crew Cab LB HD	18531	19865	22089
4 Dr LS Crew Cab SB HD	18349	19671	21873
4 Dr LS Ext Cab LB HD	17689	18963	21086
4 Dr LS Ext Cab SB HD	17482	18741	20840
4 Dr LT 4WD Crew Cab LB HD	23384	25068	27875
4 Dr LT 4WD Crew Cab SB HD	23213	24885	27672

Body Styles	TMV Pricing		
	Trade	Private	Dealer
4 Dr LT 4WD Ext Cab LB HD	22038	23625	26271
4 Dr LT 4WD Ext Cab SB HD	21797	23367	25983
4 Dr LT Crew Cab LB HD	21251	22781	25332
4 Dr LT Crew Cab SB HD	21084	22602	25133
4 Dr LT Ext Cab LB HD	19921	21356	23747
4 Dr LT Ext Cab SB HD	19680	21098	23460
4 Dr STD 4WD Crew Cab LB HD	19135	20513	22810
4 Dr STD 4WD Crew Cab SB HD	18997	20365	22646
4 Dr STD 4WD Ext Cab LB HD	18237	19551	21740
4 Dr STD 4WD Ext Cab SB HD	17818	19101	21239
4 Dr STD Crew Cab LB HD	17410	18664	20753
4 Dr STD Crew Cab SB HD	17227	18468	20536
4 Dr STD Ext Cab LB HD	15868	17011	18916
4 Dr STD Ext Cab SB HD	15729	16862	18750

Options	Price
6.6L V8 Turbodiesel OHV 32V Engine	+2758
8.1L V8 OHV 16V FI Engine	+487
Automatic 4-Speed Transmission [Std on LT]	+628
Automatic 5-Speed Transmission	+688
Automatic Dimming Rearview Mirror [Std on LT]	+181
Bucket Seats [Std on LT]	+244

Options	Price
Cruise Control [Opt on STD]	+138
Leather Seats [Std on LT]	+459
Locking Differential	+169
Power Driver Seat [Opt on LS]	+138
Power Passenger Seat [Opt on LS]	+138

2001

Mileage Category: K

Both light- and heavy-duty 2500s sport new torsion bar front suspensions. Light-duty models get an 8,600-pound Gross Vehicle Weight Rating in addition to optional traction control and standard child safety-seat tether hooks. Heavy-duty models are completely redesigned for 2001 offering two new engines and transmissions, bigger interiors and numerous other improvements.

Body Styles	TMV Pricing		
	Trade	Private	Dealer
2 Dr LS 4WD Std Cab LB HD	15586	17382	19039
2 Dr LS Std Cab LB HD	13508	15064	16501
2 Dr STD 4WD Std Cab LB HD	14365	16020	17548
2 Dr STD Std Cab LB HD	11700	13048	14292
4 Dr LS 4WD Crew Cab LB HD	18300	20408	22354
4 Dr LS 4WD Crew Cab SB HD	17996	20069	21982
4 Dr LS 4WD Ext Cab LB HD	16931	18882	20682
4 Dr LS 4WD Ext Cab SB HD	16870	18813	20607
4 Dr LS Crew Cab LB HD	16147	18007	19723
4 Dr LS Crew Cab SB HD	15986	17828	19528
4 Dr LS Ext Cab LB HD	15439	17217	18859
4 Dr LS Ext Cab SB HD	14972	16697	18289
4 Dr LT 4WD Crew Cab LB HD	20422	22774	24946
4 Dr LT 4WD Crew Cab SB HD	20276	22611	24767

Body Styles	TMV Pricing		
	Trade	Private	Dealer
4 Dr LT 4WD Ext Cab LB HD	19585	21841	23923
4 Dr LT 4WD Ext Cab SB HD	19507	21754	23828
4 Dr LT Crew Cab LB HD	18531	20666	22637
4 Dr LT Crew Cab SB HD	18389	20507	22462
4 Dr LT Ext Cab LB HD	17992	20065	21978
4 Dr LT Ext Cab SB HD	17857	19914	21813
4 Dr STD 4WD Crew Cab LB HD	16207	18074	19797
4 Dr STD 4WD Crew Cab SB HD	16001	17844	19546
4 Dr STD 4WD Ext Cab LB HD	15653	17456	19121
4 Dr STD 4WD Ext Cab SB HD	15270	17029	18652
4 Dr STD Crew Cab LB HD	14691	16383	17945
4 Dr STD Crew Cab SB HD	14535	16209	17755
4 Dr STD Ext Cab LB HD	13526	15084	16522
4 Dr STD Ext Cab SB HD	13406	14950	16375

Options	Price
6.6L V8 Turbodiesel OHV 32V Engine	+2523
8.1L V8 OHV 16V FI Engine	+446
Air Conditioning [Opt on STD]	+433
Automatic 4-Speed Transmission [Std on LT]	+574
Automatic 5-Speed Transmission	+630

Options	Price
Cruise Control [Opt on STD]	+126
Leather Seats [Std on LT]	+671
Locking Differential [Std on LT]	+150
Power Driver Seat [Opt on LS]	+126
Power Passenger Seat [Opt on LS]	+126

Chevrolet
Silverado 3500

2003

Mileage Category: K

The Silverado 3500 now sports the same look as its light-duty siblings, including a new front fascia and revised side moldings and taillights. Top-of-the-line models also get power-folding heated mirrors with puddle lamps and turn signal indicators. On the inside, the 2003 Silverado offers numerous entertainment options, including a Bose stereo system (with rear-seat controls on crew cab models), XM Satellite Radio and a DVD-based entertainment system (crew cab models only). The instrument panel and center console have been redesigned, and Chevrolet has added new seats, a more comprehensive driver information center and a dual-zone climate control system. On the hardware side, the standard 6.0-liter V8 gets electronic throttle control as well as the ability to run exclusively on compressed natural gas (CNG) or a mix of CNG and gasoline.

Body Styles	TMV Pricing		
	Trade	Private	Dealer
2 Dr LS 4WD Std Cab LB DRW	20551	21751	23751
2 Dr STD 4WD Std Cab LB DRW	19083	20197	22054
4 Dr LS 4WD Crew Cab LB DRW	23877	25271	27595
4 Dr LS 4WD Ext Cab LB DRW	22464	23775	25961
4 Dr LS Crew Cab LB DRW	21579	22839	24939
4 Dr LS Ext Cab LB DRW	20235	21416	23385
4 Dr LT 4WD Crew Cab LB DRW	26885	28455	31071

Options	Price
AM/FM/CD Audio System [Opt on STD]	+163
Automatic 4-Speed Transmission	+699
Automatic 5-Speed Transmission	+766
Bose Audio System [Opt on LS]	+252
Bucket Seats [Opt on LS]	+271
Cruise Control [Opt on STD]	+153
Leather Seats [Opt on LS]	+511
Locking Differential	+188
Power Driver Seat [Opt on LS]	+153

Body Styles	TMV Pricing		
	Trade	Private	Dealer
4 Dr LT 4WD Ext Cab LB DRW	25514	27004	29487
4 Dr LT Crew Cab LB DRW	24830	26280	28696
4 Dr LT Ext Cab LB DRW	23540	24914	27205
4 Dr STD 4WD Crew Cab LB DRW	22304	23606	25777
4 Dr STD 4WD Ext Cab LB DRW	21069	22299	24349
4 Dr STD Crew Cab LB DRW	19983	21150	23094
4 Dr STD Ext Cab LB DRW	18572	19657	21464

Options	Price
OnStar Telematic System [Opt on LS]	+444
AM/FM/CD Changer Audio System [Opt on LS]	+255
Satellite Radio System [Opt on LS,LT]	+207
Automatic Climate Control (2 Zone) - Driver and Passenger [Opt on LS]	+124
DVD Entertainment System [Opt on Crew - LS,LT]	+827
8.1L V8 OHV 16V FI Engine	+543
6.6L V8 Turbodiesel OHV 32V Engine	+3198
Power Retractable Mirrors [Opt on LS]	+152

2002

Mileage Category: K

After undergoing a full redesign last year, Chevrolet's heavy-duty one-ton truck gets few changes for 2002. Air conditioning is now standard on all trim levels along with extendable sunshade visors and improved base model radios.

Body Styles	TMV Pricing		
	Trade	Private	Dealer
2 Dr LS 4WD Std Cab LB	17860	19054	21044
2 Dr STD 4WD Std Cab LB	16697	17813	19674
4 Dr LS 4WD Crew Cab LB	20844	22238	24560
4 Dr LS 4WD Ext Cab LB	19480	20782	22953
4 Dr LS Crew Cab LB	18737	19990	22078
4 Dr LS Ext Cab LB	17596	18772	20733
4 Dr LT 4WD Crew Cab LB	22416	23915	26413

Options	Price
6.6L V8 Turbodiesel OHV 32V Engine	+2758
8.1L V8 OHV 16V FI Engine	+487
Automatic 4-Speed Transmission [Std on LT]	+628
Automatic 5-Speed Transmission	+688
Bucket Seats [Std on LT]	+244
Camper/Towing Package	+123

Body Styles	TMV Pricing		
	Trade	Private	Dealer
4 Dr LT 4WD Ext Cab LB	21384	22814	25197
4 Dr LT Crew Cab LB	20985	22388	24726
4 Dr LT Ext Cab LB	20165	21513	23760
4 Dr STD 4WD Crew Cab LB	19347	20641	22797
4 Dr STD 4WD Ext Cab LB	18537	19776	21842
4 Dr STD Crew Cab LB	17267	18422	20346
4 Dr STD Ext Cab LB	16117	17195	18991

Options	Price
Cruise Control [Opt on STD]	+138
Leather Seats [Std on LT]	+459
Locking Differential	+169
Power Driver Seat [Opt on LS]	+138
Power Passenger Seat [Opt on LS]	+138

2001

Mileage Category: K

Chevrolet's heavy-duty pickups get a complete redesign for 2001 including two new engines and transmissions, new exterior styling, and numerous other improvements.

Body Styles	TMV Pricing		
	Trade	Private	Dealer
2 Dr LS 4WD Std Cab LB	15450	17149	18717
2 Dr STD 4WD Std Cab LB	14084	15633	17062
4 Dr LS 4WD Crew Cab LB	18037	20021	21852
4 Dr LS 4WD Ext Cab LB	16849	18702	20412
4 Dr LS Crew Cab LB	16177	17956	19598
4 Dr LS Ext Cab LB	15201	16873	18416
4 Dr LT 4WD Crew Cab LB	19313	21437	23397

Options	Price
6.6L V8 Turbodiesel OHV 32V Engine	+2523
8.1L V8 OHV 16V FI Engine	+446
Air Conditioning [Opt on STD]	+433
Automatic 4-Speed Transmission [Std on LT]	+574
Automatic 5-Speed Transmission	+630

Body Styles	TMV Pricing		
	Trade	Private	Dealer
4 Dr LT 4WD Ext Cab LB	18442	20470	22342
4 Dr LT Crew Cab LB	18105	20096	21934
4 Dr LT Ext Cab LB	17435	19352	21122
4 Dr STD 4WD Crew Cab LB	16242	18028	19677
4 Dr STD 4WD Ext Cab LB	15759	17492	19092
4 Dr STD Crew Cab LB	14417	16002	17466
4 Dr STD Ext Cab LB	13612	15109	16491

Options	Price
Cruise Control [Opt on STD]	+126
Leather Seats [Std on LT]	+671
Locking Differential	+150
Power Driver Seat [Opt on LS]	+126
Power Passenger Seat [Opt on LS]	+126

Sportvan/Suburban

Chevrolet
Sportvan

1996

Body Styles	TMV Pricing		
	Trade	Private	Dealer
3 Dr G30 Beauville Pass Van	4351	5426	6910
3 Dr G30 Beauville Pass Van Ext	4431	5526	7039

Options	Price
6.5L V8 Diesel OHV 16V Engine	+822
7.4L V8 OHV 16V FI Engine	+173

Mileage Category: Q

Body Styles	TMV Pricing		
	Trade	Private	Dealer
3 Dr G30 Pass Van	4236	5283	6729
3 Dr G30 Pass Van Ext	4282	5340	6802

Options	Price
Air Conditioning [Std on Beauville]	+252
Air Conditioning - Front and Rear	+406

No changes to final year of Sportvan, replaced by Express.

1995

Body Styles	TMV Pricing		
	Trade	Private	Dealer
3 Dr G20 Beauville Pass Van Ext	3278	4146	5592
3 Dr G20 Pass Van	2820	3567	4811
3 Dr G30 Beauville Pass Van	3411	4314	5820

Options	Price
16 Passenger Seating	+92
5.0L V8 OHV 16V FI Engine [Opt on G20]	+148
5.7L V8 OHV 16V FI Engine [Opt on G20]	+217
6.5L V8 Diesel OHV 16V Engine	+737

Body Styles	TMV Pricing		
	Trade	Private	Dealer
3 Dr G30 Beauville Pass Van Ext	3458	4373	5899
3 Dr G30 Pass Van	3189	4033	5440
3 Dr G30 Pass Van Ext	3322	4202	5668

Options	Price
7.4L V8 OHV 16V FI Engine	+155
Air Conditioning [Std on Beauville]	+225
Air Conditioning - Front and Rear	+364
Bucket Seats	+93

Mileage Category: Q

No significant changes as Chevrolet readies a replacement set to debut next year.

1994

Body Styles	TMV Pricing		
	Trade	Private	Dealer
3 Dr G20 Beauville Pass Van Ext	2563	3409	4818
3 Dr G20 Pass Van	2275	3025	4275
3 Dr G30 Beauville Pass Van	2729	3629	5128

Options	Price
15 Passenger Seating	+76
5.0L V8 OHV 16V FI Engine [Opt on G20]	+131
5.7L V8 OHV 16V FI Engine [Opt on G20]	+192
6.5L V8 Diesel OHV 16V Engine	+651

Body Styles	TMV Pricing		
	Trade	Private	Dealer
3 Dr G30 Beauville Pass Van Ext	2812	3739	5284
3 Dr G30 Pass Van	2522	3354	4740
3 Dr G30 Pass Van Ext	2688	3575	5052

Options	Price
7.4L V8 OHV 16V FI Engine	+137
Air Conditioning [Std on Beauville]	+199
Air Conditioning - Front and Rear	+321
Premium Audio System	+102

Mileage Category: Q

Safety is enhanced with side door guard beams and the addition of a driver-side airbag (on the G20s). Also a center high-mounted brake light is added.

The gasoline engines receive refinements to improve durability and reduce noise. Last year's diesel engine offerings are replaced with more sophisticated units. The new 6.5-liter diesel V8 offered in the lighter-duty G20 provides 15 more horsepower (for a total of 155) and 20 lb-ft more torque (totaling 275) when compared to the 6.2-liter diesel engine it replaces. Additionally, that 6.5-liter has a more sophisticated fuel injection system that improves fuel economy, reduces diesel exhaust smoke, improves cold starting and offers better idle quality.

The optional 4L80-E heavy-duty four-speed automatic transmission (offered on the heavy-duty G30) is revised to provide smoother shifts.

Chevrolet
Suburban
2003

Body Styles	TMV Pricing		
	Trade	Private	Dealer
4 Dr 1500 LS 4WD SUV	26658	28238	30870
4 Dr 1500 LS SUV	23380	24765	27074
4 Dr 1500 LT 4WD SUV	28922	30636	33492
4 Dr 1500 LT SUV	27129	28737	31416

Body Styles	TMV Pricing		
	Trade	Private	Dealer
4 Dr 2500 LS 4WD SUV	27878	29530	32283
4 Dr 2500 LS SUV	25837	27368	29920
4 Dr 2500 LT 4WD SUV	29847	31616	34563
4 Dr 2500 LT SUV	28119	29785	32562

Mileage Category: N

The Suburban gets numerous functional enhancements for 2003. The Quadrasteer four-wheel steering system is now available on 3/4-ton models for increased maneuverability and better stability when towing, while 1/2-ton versions now offer the StabiliTrak stability control system. New power heated mirrors feature puddle lamps, in-glass turn signal indicators and a memory function, and extendable power camper mirrors are optional. The interior gets numerous upgrades that include tri-zone climate control, an enhanced driver-information center, a redesigned center console and options such as second-row captain's chairs and adjustable pedals. A revised lineup of entertainment options includes a Bose audio system as well as XM Satellite Radio and a DVD-based entertainment system. For increased safety, the Suburban now features a standard front-passenger-sensing system and dual-stage airbags.

Suburban

2003 (cont'd)

Options	Price
4 Wheel Steering [Opt on 2500]	+2870
Automatic Stability Control [Opt on 1500]	+479
Bose Audio System [Opt on LS]	+223
Captain Chairs (4)	+313
Heated Front Seats	+223
Leather Seats [Opt on LS]	+575
Limited Slip Differential [Opt on 2500]	+188
Locking Differential	+188
Power Moonroof	+631
Power Passenger Seat [Opt on LS]	+153
Front Side Airbag Restraints	+223

Options	Price
Traction Control System [Opt on 2500 2WD]	+144
Autoride Suspension Package	+715
OnStar Telematic System [Opt on LS]	+524
AM/FM/Cassette/CD Changer Audio System [Opt on LS]	+252
Power Adjustable Foot Pedals	+176
Z71 Off-Road Suspension Package [Opt on 1500 LS 4WD]	+3299
Satellite Radio System	+207
DVD Entertainment System	+827
8.1L V8 OHV 16V FI Engine [Opt on 2500]	+447
Power Retractable Mirrors [Opt on LS]	+227

2002

Mileage Category: N

The base trim level has been dropped. New for this year on LS are standard six-way power driver and front passenger seats, heated outside mirrors, exterior side steps that make getting in and out easier and the HomeLink system that can be programmed to control automatic garage doors or community gates all from one keypad. 5300 V8s can now burn gasoline/ethanol mixed fuels.

Body Styles	TMV Pricing		
	Trade	Private	Dealer
4 Dr 1500 LS 4WD SUV	23427	25048	27750
4 Dr 1500 LS SUV	20185	21582	23910
4 Dr 1500 LT 4WD SUV	25301	27052	29970
4 Dr 1500 LT SUV	23736	25379	28116

Body Styles	TMV Pricing		
	Trade	Private	Dealer
4 Dr 2500 LS 4WD SUV	24522	26219	29047
4 Dr 2500 LS SUV	22700	24271	26889
4 Dr 2500 LT 4WD SUV	26074	27879	30886
4 Dr 2500 LT SUV	24593	26295	29131

Options	Price
8.1L V8 OHV 16V FI Engine	+401
Autoride Suspension Package	+502
Captain Chairs (4)	+281
Leather Seats [Std on LT]	+510
Locking Differential [Opt on 2WD]	+145

Options	Price
OnStar Telematic System [Std on LT]	+399
Power Sunroof	+538
Traction Control System [Opt on 2WD]	+172
Z71 Off-Road Suspension Package [Opt on K1500 LS]	+1302

2001

Mileage Category: N

Though completely redesigned last year, 2001 still sees improvements to the powertrain. Chevy has upped the horsepower rating of the Vortec 6000 to 320, and 360 pound-feet of torque is now made at 4,000 revs. A new 8.1-liter engine cranks out 340 horsepower at 4,200 rpm and 455 lb-ft of torque at 3,200 rpm. The recommended oil change interval goes from 7,500 miles to 10,000 miles.

Body Styles	TMV Pricing		
	Trade	Private	Dealer
4 Dr 1500 4WD SUV	15979	17736	19357
4 Dr 1500 LS 4WD SUV	19980	22176	24204
4 Dr 1500 LS SUV	17230	19124	20872
4 Dr 1500 LT 4WD SUV	22570	25051	27341
4 Dr 1500 LT SUV	21383	23734	25904
4 Dr 1500 SUV	14097	15647	17077

Body Styles	TMV Pricing		
	Trade	Private	Dealer
4 Dr 2500 4WD SUV	17028	18900	20628
4 Dr 2500 LS 4WD SUV	20963	23267	25394
4 Dr 2500 LS SUV	19210	21322	23271
4 Dr 2500 LT 4WD SUV	22859	25372	27691
4 Dr 2500 LT SUV	21670	24052	26251
4 Dr 2500 SUV	15408	17102	18665

Options	Price
8.1L V8 OHV 16V FI Engine	+367
Air Conditioning [Opt on STD]	+424
Autoride Suspension Package	+367
Leather Seats	+498
Locking Differential [Opt on STD]	+132
Off-Road Suspension Package	+1781
OnStar Telematic System [Std on LT]	+365

Options	Price
Power Driver Seat [Opt on LS]	+126
Power Moonroof	+495
Power Passenger Seat [Opt on LS]	+126
Running Boards [Opt on LS]	+207
Split Front Bench Seat [Opt on STD]	+330
Third Seat	+645
Traction Control System	+242

2000

Mileage Category: N

The 2000 Chevrolet Suburban is completely redesigned. It's roomier, safer, more comfortable and a more powerful ride.

Body Styles	TMV Pricing		
	Trade	Private	Dealer
4 Dr 1500 4WD SUV	13378	15054	16696
4 Dr 1500 LS 4WD SUV	16775	18876	20936
4 Dr 1500 LS SUV	14943	16815	18649
4 Dr 1500 LT 4WD SUV	18557	20882	23160
4 Dr 1500 LT SUV	17406	19587	21724
4 Dr 1500 SUV	11604	13058	14483

Body Styles	TMV Pricing		
	Trade	Private	Dealer
4 Dr 2500 4WD SUV	14259	16045	17796
4 Dr 2500 LS 4WD SUV	17658	19870	22038
4 Dr 2500 LS SUV	16746	18844	20900
4 Dr 2500 LT 4WD SUV	19931	22428	24875
4 Dr 2500 LT SUV	18391	20695	22953
4 Dr 2500 SUV	12931	14551	16139

2000 (cont'd)

Options	Price
Leather Seats	+444
OnStar Telematic System [Opt on LS]	+325
Power Moonroof	+442
Side Steps	+145
Traction Control System	+216
Air Conditioning - Front and Rear	+620

Options	Price
AM/FM/Cassette/CD Audio System	+179
AM/FM/CD Audio System	+134
Autoride Suspension Package [Opt on 4WD]	+327
Bucket Seats	+120
Center and Rear Bench Seat [Std on LS,LT]	+486

1999

Body Styles	TMV Pricing		
	Trade	Private	Dealer
4 Dr C1500 SUV	9875	11359	12903
4 Dr C2500 SUV	10954	12600	14313

Body Styles	TMV Pricing		
	Trade	Private	Dealer
4 Dr K1500 4WD SUV	11211	12896	14649
4 Dr K2500 4WD SUV	11584	13324	15136

Mileage Category: N

Options	Price
Running Boards	+115
6.5L V8 Turbodiesel OHV 16V Engine	+1186
7.4L V8 OHV 16V FI Engine	+249
Air Conditioning	+299
Air Conditioning - Front and Rear	+495
AM/FM/Cassette/CD Audio System	+143

Options	Price
Center and Rear Bench Seat	+389
Heated Front Seats	+124
Leather Seats	+394
LS Package	+1088
LT Package	+1646
OnStar Telematic System	+288

A couple of new colors are the only modifications to the Suburban as Chevrolet prepares a redesigned model for 2000.

1998

Mileage Category: N

New colors, a standard theft-deterrent system, optional heated seats, second-generation airbags and an automatic 4WD system improve the 1998 Suburban.

Body Styles	TMV Pricing		
	Trade	Private	Dealer
4 Dr C1500 SUV	8573	10018	11647
4 Dr C2500 SUV	9569	11182	13000

Body Styles	TMV Pricing		
	Trade	Private	Dealer
4 Dr K1500 4WD SUV	9713	11350	13196
4 Dr K2500 4WD SUV	9977	11658	13554

Options	Price
6.5L V8 Turbodiesel OHV 16V Engine [Opt on 2500]	+999
7.4L V8 OHV 16V FI Engine [Opt on 2500]	+210
Air Conditioning	+253
Air Conditioning - Front and Rear	+417
Center and Rear Bench Seat	+328

Options	Price
Leather Seats	+332
LS Package	+1146
LT Package	+1387
OnStar Telematic System	+243

1997

Mileage Category: N

Dual airbags debut, and a cargo area power lock switch makes locking up the vehicle after unloading cargo more convenient. Variable power steering lightens low-speed steering effort, and automatic transmissions are improved. Two new exterior colors are added to the paint roster.

Body Styles	TMV Pricing		
	Trade	Private	Dealer
4 Dr C1500 SUV	7185	8547	10212
4 Dr C2500 SUV	7774	9248	11049

Body Styles	TMV Pricing		
	Trade	Private	Dealer
4 Dr K1500 4WD SUV	8156	9702	11592
4 Dr K2500 4WD SUV	8369	9956	11895

Options	Price
Leather Seats	+300
LS Package	+1035
LT Package	+1254
Third Seat	+373

Options	Price
6.5L V8 Turbodiesel OHV 16V Engine	+772
7.4L V8 OHV 16V FI Engine	+190
Air Conditioning	+228
Air Conditioning - Front and Rear	+350

1996

Mileage Category: N

Improved engines generate more horsepower and torque. Four-wheel-drive models get an optional electronic shift transfer case. Daytime running lights, rear-seat heating ducts and two new paint colors summarize the changes.

Body Styles	TMV Pricing		
	Trade	Private	Dealer
4 Dr C1500 SUV	6116	7381	9129
4 Dr C2500 SUV	6487	7829	9683

Body Styles	TMV Pricing		
	Trade	Private	Dealer
4 Dr K1500 4WD SUV	6858	8277	10236
4 Dr K2500 4WD SUV	6966	8407	10398

Options	Price
6.5L V8 Turbodiesel OHV 16V Engine	+809
7.4L V8 OHV 16V FI Engine	+172
Air Conditioning	+207
Air Conditioning - Front and Rear	+317

Options	Price
Leather Seats	+245
LS Package	+869
LT Package	+1067
Third Seat	+338

Chevrolet
Suburban/Tahoe

1995

Mileage Category: N

New interior with driver airbag debuts. New dashboard features modular design with controls that are much easier to read and use. The 1500 models can now be ordered with turbodiesel engine. Brake/transmission shift interlock is added to automatic transmission. Seats and door panels are revised. New console on models with bucket seats features pivoting writing surface, along with rear cupholders and storage drawer. Uplevel radios come with automatic volume controls that raise or lower the volume depending on vehicle speed.

Body Styles	TMV Pricing		
	Trade	Private	Dealer
4 Dr C1500 SUV	4409	5402	7057
4 Dr C2500 SUV	4845	5937	7756

Options	Price
6.5L V8 Turbodiesel OHV 16V Engine	+726
7.4L V8 OHV 16V FI Engine	+154
Air Conditioning	+185
Air Conditioning - Front and Rear	+285

Body Styles	TMV Pricing		
	Trade	Private	Dealer
4 Dr K1500 4WD SUV	5049	6187	8083
4 Dr K2500 4WD SUV	5203	6375	8329

Options	Price
Leather Seats	+219
LS Package	+779
LT Package	+957

1994

Mileage Category: N

Side-door guard beams are added, as well as a high-mounted center brake light. A turbocharged diesel is newly optional on 2500 models. A new grille appears.

Body Styles	TMV Pricing		
	Trade	Private	Dealer
4 Dr C1500 SUV	3224	4130	5639
4 Dr C2500 SUV	3370	4316	5893

Options	Price
6.5L V8 Turbodiesel OHV 16V Engine	+641
7.4L V8 OHV 16V FI Engine	+137
Air Conditioning	+164
Air Conditioning - Front and Rear	+251

Body Styles	TMV Pricing		
	Trade	Private	Dealer
4 Dr K1500 4WD SUV	3433	4397	6003
4 Dr K2500 4WD SUV	3575	4578	6250

Options	Price
Center and Rear Bench Seat	+212
Leather Seats	+183
Premium Audio System	+97

Chevrolet
Tahoe

2003

Body Styles	TMV Pricing		
	Trade	Private	Dealer
4 Dr LS 4WD SUV	24268	25706	28102
4 Dr LS SUV	22278	23598	25798

Options	Price
Automatic Stability Control	+479
Bose Audio System [Opt on LS]	+223
Camper/Towing Package	+182
Captain Chairs (4)	+313
Leather Seats [Opt on LS]	+479
Locking Differential	+188
Power Moonroof	+631
Power Passenger Seat [Opt on LS]	+153
Front Side Airbag Restraints	+223

Body Styles	TMV Pricing		
	Trade	Private	Dealer
4 Dr LT 4WD SUV	26888	28481	31136
4 Dr LT SUV	24776	26244	28691

Options	Price
Third Seat	+319
Autoride Suspension Package [Opt on LT]	+715
OnStar Telematic System [Opt on LS]	+524
AM/FM/Cassette/CD Changer Audio System [Opt on LS]	+252
Power Adjustable Foot Pedals	+176
Z71 Off-Road Suspension Package [Opt on LS 4WD]	+3299
Satellite Radio System	+207
DVD Entertainment System	+827

Mileage Category: N

The Tahoe gets a host of upgrades for 2003. On the inside, you'll find tri-zone climate controls, an enhanced driver-information center and a redesigned center console and instrument panel. Second-row bucket seats are now available when leather buckets are specified in front. A revised lineup of entertainment options offers buyers Bose sound, as well as XM Satellite Radio and a DVD-based entertainment system. For increased safety, there are dual-stage airbags, a standard front-passenger-sensing system and three-point belts for all second-row passengers. Like many Ford products, the Tahoe now has adjustable gas and brake pedals. The braking system has also been upgraded for what Chevrolet says is better pedal feel and performance. Two- and four-wheel-drive trucks with the 5.3-liter engine can be ordered with an optional stability control system. Trucks sold in California now earn ULEV certification. No longer standard are third-row floormats, an underhood light, a 7-to-4 pin trailer brake adapter, an auxiliary door lock switch in the cargo area and a lock for the center console.

2002

Mileage Category: N

All models get the previously optional Premium Ride suspension. LS Tahoes get six-way power driver and front passenger seats, along with foglights, heated outside mirrors, side-mounted assist steps and a programmable HomeLink transmitter for opening garage doors or automatic gates. The 5300 V8 is now capable of running gasoline/ethanol fuel blends.

Body Styles	TMV Pricing		
	Trade	Private	Dealer
4 Dr LS 4WD SUV	21119	22581	25017
4 Dr LS SUV	19449	20795	23038
4 Dr LT 4WD SUV	23389	25008	27705
4 Dr LT SUV	21483	22970	25447

2002 (cont'd)

Options	Price
5.3L V8 Flex Fuel OHV 16V FI Engine [Opt on 1500]	+401
Autoride Suspension Package	+502
Camper/Towing Package	+149
Leather Seats [Opt on LS]	+660
Locking Differential [Opt on 2WD]	+145

Options	Price
OnStar Telematic System [Std on LT]	+399
Power Sunroof	+538
Third Seat	+287
Traction Control System [Opt on 2WD]	+172
Z71 Off-Road Suspension Package [Opt on LS 4WD]	+1793

2001

Mileage Category: N

Two new exterior colors and OnStar availability are the only changes for 2001.

Body Styles	TMV Pricing		
	Trade	Private	Dealer
4 Dr LS 4WD SUV	18183	20182	22027
4 Dr LS SUV	16616	18443	20129
4 Dr LT 4WD SUV	20694	22969	25069

Body Styles	TMV Pricing		
	Trade	Private	Dealer
4 Dr LT SUV	19104	21204	23143
4 Dr STD 4WD SUV	15489	17191	18763
4 Dr STD SUV	13910	15439	16850

Options	Price
Air Conditioning [Opt on STD]	+424
Autoride Suspension Package	+367
Camper/Towing Package	+142
Leather Seats [Opt on LS]	+656
Locking Differential	+132
Off-Road Suspension Package	+1781
OnStar Telematic System [Opt on LS]	+365

Options	Price
Power Driver Seat [Opt on LS]	+126
Power Moonroof	+498
Power Passenger Seat [Opt on LS,LT]	+126
Running Boards [Opt on LS]	+207
Third Seat	+374
Traction Control System	+125

2000

Mileage Category: N

The engineers at Chevy redesigned the Tahoe from top to bottom, making it safer, more powerful and a more pleasurable vehicle to drive.

Body Styles	TMV Pricing		
	Trade	Private	Dealer
4 Dr LS 4WD SUV	16619	18701	20742
4 Dr LS SUV	15163	17062	18924
4 Dr LT 4WD SUV	18039	20299	22514

Body Styles	TMV Pricing		
	Trade	Private	Dealer
4 Dr LT SUV	16787	18890	20951
4 Dr STD 4WD SUV	14082	15846	17575
4 Dr STD SUV	12547	14119	15660

Options	Price
Automatic Load Leveling	+163
Bucket Seats [Opt on LS]	+167
Camper/Towing Package	+127
Leather Seats [Opt on LS]	+400
OnStar Telematic System [Opt on LS]	+325

Options	Price
Power Moonroof	+391
Running Boards [Opt on LS]	+145
Third Seat	+333
5.3L V8 OHV 16V FI Engine [Opt on STD]	+311
Air Conditioning [Opt on STD]	+378

1999

Body Styles	TMV Pricing		
	Trade	Private	Dealer
2 Dr LS 4WD SUV	11361	13068	14845
2 Dr LS SUV	11005	12658	14379
2 Dr LT 4WD SUV	11532	13264	15067
2 Dr LT SUV	11253	12944	14703
2 Dr STD 4WD SUV	10132	11654	13239

Body Styles	TMV Pricing		
	Trade	Private	Dealer
2 Dr STD SUV	8729	10041	11406
4 Dr LS 4WD SUV	11713	13473	15305
4 Dr LS SUV	11313	13013	14782
4 Dr LT 4WD SUV	12078	13893	15782
4 Dr LT SUV	11449	13169	14960

Mileage Category: N

The standard cargo net is deleted, and new colors are added as Tahoe enters final model year on this platform.

Options	Price
6.5L V8 Turbodiesel OHV 16V Engine	+1172
Air Conditioning [Opt on STD]	+299
Air Conditioning - Front and Rear	+195

Options	Price
Heated Front Seats	+115
OnStar Telematic System [Opt on LS,LT]	+288
Running Boards	+115

1998

Mileage Category: N

Autotrac is a new optional automatic four-wheel-drive system that switches from 2WD to 4WD automatically as conditions warrant. A new option package includes heated seats and heated exterior mirrors. Second-generation airbags deploy with less force than last year. A theft-deterrent system is standard, and color selections are modified.

Body Styles	TMV Pricing		
	Trade	Private	Dealer
2 Dr LS 4WD SUV	8802	10286	11960
2 Dr LS SUV	8465	9892	11502
2 Dr LT 4WD SUV	9825	11482	13350
2 Dr LT SUV	8530	9968	11590
2 Dr STD 4WD SUV	7779	9091	10570

Body Styles	TMV Pricing		
	Trade	Private	Dealer
2 Dr STD SUV	6520	7619	8859
4 Dr LS 4WD SUV	9903	11573	13456
4 Dr LS SUV	8658	10118	11764
4 Dr LT 4WD SUV	9955	11633	13526
4 Dr LT SUV	8949	10458	12159

1998 (cont'd)

Options	Price
6.5L V8 Turbodiesel OHV 16V Engine [Opt on 2 Dr]	+987
Air Conditioning [Opt on STD]	+253
Air Conditioning - Front and Rear	+164

Options	Price
Camper/Towing Package	+132
OnStar Telematic System [Opt on LS,LT]	+243

1997

Mileage Category: N

A passenger-side airbag is added, and the automatic transmission is improved. Variable steering debuts, and cargo areas have a power door lock switch. A new center console comes with high-back bucket seats, and two new paint colors are available.

Body Styles	TMV Pricing		
	Trade	Private	Dealer
2 Dr LS 4WD SUV	7409	8813	10530
2 Dr LS SUV	6717	7991	9547
2 Dr LT 4WD SUV	8327	9906	11835
2 Dr LT SUV	6933	8247	9853
2 Dr STD 4WD SUV	6187	7360	8793

Body Styles	TMV Pricing		
	Trade	Private	Dealer
2 Dr STD SUV	5653	6724	8034
4 Dr LS 4WD SUV	7619	9063	10828
4 Dr LS SUV	6728	8004	9563
4 Dr LT 4WD SUV	8387	9976	11919
4 Dr LT SUV	7490	8910	10645

Options	Price
6.5L V8 Turbodiesel OHV 16V Engine	+892
Air Conditioning [Opt on STD]	+228

Options	Price
Air Conditioning - Front and Rear	+148

1996

Mileage Category: N

For 1996, Tahoe gets 50 additional horsepower and more torque out of a new 5700 V8. Other improvements include rear-seat heating ducts, quieter-riding P-metric tires, improved automatic transmissions and extended interval service schedules. Daytime running lights are new for 1996.

Body Styles	TMV Pricing		
	Trade	Private	Dealer
2 Dr LS 4WD SUV	5912	7135	8824
2 Dr LS SUV	5486	6621	8188
2 Dr LT 4WD SUV	6436	7767	9606
2 Dr LT SUV	5545	6692	8276
2 Dr STD 4WD SUV	5407	6526	8071

Body Styles	TMV Pricing		
	Trade	Private	Dealer
2 Dr STD SUV	4169	5032	6223
4 Dr LS 4WD SUV	6452	7787	9631
4 Dr LS SUV	5584	6739	8335
4 Dr LT 4WD SUV	7007	8457	10459
4 Dr LT SUV	5774	6969	8619

Options	Price
6.5L V8 Turbodiesel OHV 16V Engine	+809

Options	Price
Air Conditioning [Opt on STD]	+207

1995

Mileage Category: N

Full-size SUV gets a new name as S10-based model takes Blazer moniker. New interior with driver airbag debuts. New dashboard features modular design with controls that are much easier to read and use. New five-door model is added midyear, sized between Blazer and Suburban. New model is offered only in LS or LT trim with a 5.7-liter V8 and an automatic transmission in either 2WD or 4WD. Brake/transmission shift interlock is added to automatic transmission. New console on models with bucket seats features pivoting writing surface, along with rear cupholders and storage drawer.

Body Styles	TMV Pricing		
	Trade	Private	Dealer
2 Dr LS 4WD SUV	4757	5828	7614
2 Dr LT 4WD SUV	5153	6313	8247
2 Dr STD 4WD SUV	4271	5233	6836
4 Dr LS 4WD SUV	4928	6038	7888

Body Styles	TMV Pricing		
	Trade	Private	Dealer
4 Dr LS SUV	4555	5581	7291
4 Dr LT 4WD SUV	5083	6228	8136
4 Dr LT SUV	4925	6034	7883

Options	Price
Automatic 4-Speed Transmission [Std on 4 Dr]	+229
6.5L V8 Turbodiesel OHV 16V Engine	+726

Options	Price
Air Conditioning [Opt on STD]	+185

Chevrolet

Tahoe Limited/Z71

2000

Body Styles	TMV Pricing		
	Trade	Private	Dealer
4 Dr Limited SUV	15437	17371	19266
4 Dr Z71 4WD SUV	17233	19391	21507

Options	Price
Camper/Towing Package	+127
Heated Front Seats	+140

Mileage Category: N

All old-style Tahoes are dropped, except these two four-door special editions. The 4WD Z71 is for off-road use, while the 2WD Limited appeals to on-road customers.

Tracker

2003

Body Styles	TMV Pricing		
	Trade	Private	Dealer
2 Dr STD 4WD Conv	8655	9476	10845
2 Dr STD Conv	8061	8826	10101
2 Dr ZR2 4WD Conv	9870	10807	12368
4 Dr LT 4WD SUV	11402	12484	14287

Options	Price
Aluminum/Alloy Wheels [Opt on STD]	+128
Antilock Brakes	+447
Automatic 4-Speed Transmission [Opt on 2 Dr - STD,ZR2]	+699

Body Styles	TMV Pricing		
	Trade	Private	Dealer
4 Dr LT SUV	10666	11678	13365
4 Dr STD 4WD SUV	9047	9905	11336
4 Dr STD SUV	8460	9263	10601
4 Dr ZR2 4WD SUV	11156	12215	13979

Options	Price
Leather Seats [Opt on LT,ZR2]	+380
Power Door Locks [Opt on STD]	+134
Power Windows [Opt on STD]	+153
2.5L V6 DOHC 24V FI Engine [Opt on 4 Dr STD]	+469

Mileage Category: L

The aging Tracker gets only minimal changes for 2003. Yellow has been added to the color palette while LT models get monochromatic paint. Tinted windows are now available and base models get a chrome grille.

2002

Body Styles	TMV Pricing		
	Trade	Private	Dealer
2 Dr STD 4WD Conv	7065	7848	9152
2 Dr STD Conv	6410	7120	8303
2 Dr ZR2 4WD Conv	7958	8839	10308
4 Dr LT 4WD SUV	9212	10232	11933

Options	Price
Aluminum/Alloy Wheels [Opt on STD]	+209
Antilock Brakes	+401
Automatic 4-Speed Transmission [Std on LT,ZR2 4 Dr]	+573

Body Styles	TMV Pricing		
	Trade	Private	Dealer
4 Dr LT SUV	8571	9520	11102
4 Dr STD 4WD SUV	7230	8031	9365
4 Dr STD SUV	6744	7491	8736
4 Dr ZR2 4WD SUV	9003	10000	11662

Options	Price
Leather Seats	+341
Power Door Locks [Opt on STD]	+120
Power Windows [Opt on STD]	+137

Mileage Category: L

The Tracker gets only minor changes for 2002. An AM/FM/CD stereo is now standard equipment on all models, while both LT and ZR2 models get new alloy wheel designs. Four new colors have been added to the color palette: Medium Green Pearl Metallic, Medium Red Metallic, Light Bronzemist Metallic and Indigo Blue Metallic.

2001

Body Styles	TMV Pricing		
	Trade	Private	Dealer
2 Dr STD 4WD Conv	5840	6890	7859
2 Dr STD Conv	5303	6256	7136
2 Dr ZR2 4WD Conv	6641	7835	8938
4 Dr LT 4WD SUV	7767	9164	10453

Options	Price
Aluminum/Alloy Wheels	+191
Antilock Brakes	+357
Automatic 4-Speed Transmission	+525

Body Styles	TMV Pricing		
	Trade	Private	Dealer
4 Dr LT SUV	7209	8505	9701
4 Dr STD 4WD SUV	6038	7124	8126
4 Dr STD SUV	5566	6566	7490
4 Dr ZR2 4WD SUV	7501	8849	10094

Options	Price
Leather Seats	+312
Power Windows	+125

Mileage Category: L

The Tracker gets two new trim packages (LT and ZR2) and a new V6 on four-door models. Air conditioning, AM/FM cassette stereo and child-seat tether anchors are now standard on all models. The base 1.6-liter engine has been dropped in favor of the more powerful 127-horsepower 2.0-liter that is now standard on all two-door and base four-door models.

2000

Body Styles	TMV Pricing		
	Trade	Private	Dealer
2 Dr STD 4WD Conv	4422	5337	6233
2 Dr STD Conv	3995	4821	5631

Options	Price
2.0L I4 DOHC 16V FI Engine [Std on Wgn]	+187
Air Conditioning	+437
Aluminum/Alloy Wheels	+171

Body Styles	TMV Pricing		
	Trade	Private	Dealer
4 Dr STD 4WD SUV	4823	5820	6798
4 Dr STD SUV	4450	5371	6273

Options	Price
AM/FM/CD Audio System	+150
Antilock Brakes	+318
Automatic 4-Speed Transmission	+468

Mileage Category: L

After a complete redesign in 1999, new colors sum up the changes for 2000.

1999

Body Styles	TMV Pricing		
	Trade	Private	Dealer
2 Dr STD 4WD Conv	3721	4620	5555
2 Dr STD Conv	3209	3984	4791

Body Styles	TMV Pricing		
	Trade	Private	Dealer
4 Dr STD 4WD SUV	3996	4961	5966
4 Dr STD SUV	3859	4791	5761

Mileage Category: L

The redesigned-for-1999 Tracker, available in either two-door convertible or four-door hardtop versions and in two- or four-wheel drive, features sporty new looks, more power, improved ride and handling and a roomier, more comfortable interior.

Chevrolet
Tracker/TrailBlazer

1999 (cont'd)

Options	Price
2.0L I4 DOHC 16V FI Engine [Std on Wgn]	+149
Air Conditioning	+349
Aluminum/Alloy Wheels	+136

Options	Price
AM/FM/CD Audio System	+119
Antilock Brakes	+282
Automatic 4-Speed Transmission	+373

1998

Body Styles	TMV Pricing		
	Trade	Private	Dealer
2 Dr STD 4WD Conv	3253	4060	4971
2 Dr STD Conv	2888	3604	4412

Body Styles	TMV Pricing		
	Trade	Private	Dealer
4 Dr STD 4WD SUV	3490	4356	5332
4 Dr STD SUV	3318	4141	5070

Options	Price
Air Conditioning	+294
Aluminum/Alloy Wheels	+115
AM/FM/Cassette Audio System	+165
AM/FM/CD Audio System	+165

Options	Price
Antilock Brakes	+238
Automatic 3-Speed Transmission	+196
Automatic 4-Speed Transmission	+314

Mileage Category: L

Geo is gone, so all Trackers are now badged as Chevrolets. The LSi models are dropped, though an LSi equipment package is available on Base models. Two new colors are available. Second-generation airbags are standard.

Chevrolet
TrailBlazer

2003

Mileage Category: M

For 2003, a new trim package, named The North Face Edition, comes with items that Chevy hopes will attract people who like to venture off the beaten path. Starting with a TrailBlazer LTZ or TrailBlazer EXT with the Leather Plus Package, Chevy adds body-color cladding, unique seats, mesh map pockets, rain-sensing wipers, liftgate lighting, an underfloor storage cargo liner, heavy-duty cargo mats, an adjustable cargo shelf (EXT model only) and The North Face duffel bags and blanket. Not for you? Perhaps a V8 will suit your fancy. Chevy's 5.3-liter V8 is available on the TrailBlazer EXT only. Other changes for 2003 include a larger 22-gallon fuel tank (late fall availability) and additional child-seat anchors on EXT models. Chevy has also made some previously standard equipment optional, such as the side airbags, rear cargo shade, interior lighting and auto-dimming driver-side mirror.

Body Styles	TMV Pricing		
	Trade	Private	Dealer
4 Dr EXT LS 4WD SUV	20471	22035	24641
4 Dr EXT LS SUV	19070	20527	22955
4 Dr EXT LT 4WD SUV	21629	23281	26035
4 Dr EXT LT SUV	20155	21695	24261
4 Dr LS 4WD SUV	18296	19694	22024

Body Styles	TMV Pricing		
	Trade	Private	Dealer
4 Dr LS SUV	16169	17404	19463
4 Dr LT 4WD SUV	20316	21868	24455
4 Dr LT SUV	18863	20304	22706
4 Dr LTZ 4WD SUV	22450	24165	27024
4 Dr LTZ SUV	20970	22572	25242

Options	Price
Bose Audio System [Opt on LT,LTZ]	+316
Cruise Control [Opt on LS]	+118
Heated Front Seats [Opt on EXT LT,LTZ]	+160
Leather Seats [Opt on LT]	+511
Locking Differential	+172
Power Moonroof	+351
Power Passenger Seat [Opt on LT]	+144
Running Boards	+239

Options	Price
Front Side Airbag Restraints	+223
Traction Control System [Opt on 2WD]	+124
OnStar Telematic System [Opt on LS,LT]	+444
AM/FM/CD Changer Audio System [Opt on LT,LTZ]	+188
DVD Entertainment System [Opt on LT,LTZ]	+638
5.3L V8 OHV 16V FI Engine [Opt on EXT]	+958
The Northface Edition [Opt on EXT LT,LTZ]	+974
Power Driver Seat w/Memory [Opt on EXT LT]	+131

2002
Mileage Category: M

This fully redesigned TrailBlazer now sports a longer, wider and noticeably stiffer chassis, along with an all-new 4.2-liter inline six-cylinder engine and a more refined suspension compared to its predecessor, the Blazer. Unique sheet metal now differentiates the TrailBlazer from its GM cousins, the GMC Envoy and Oldsmobile Bravada, while a restyled interior makes better use of the additional passenger room. An extended wheelbase EXT model offers true seven-passenger seating and class-leading cargo capacity.

Body Styles	TMV Pricing		
	Trade	Private	Dealer
4 Dr EXT LT 4WD SUV	18916	20541	23249
4 Dr EXT LT SUV	17616	19129	21651
4 Dr LS 4WD SUV	15898	17264	19540
4 Dr LS SUV	14631	15888	17982

Body Styles	TMV Pricing		
	Trade	Private	Dealer
4 Dr LT 4WD SUV	17749	19274	21815
4 Dr LT SUV	16478	17893	20252
4 Dr LTZ 4WD SUV	19557	21237	24037
4 Dr LTZ SUV	18249	19817	22429

Options	Price
AM/FM/CD Changer Audio System	+169
Bose Audio System	+284
DVD Entertainment System [Opt on LS,LTZ]	+571
Heated Front Seats	+143
Leather Seats [Opt on LT]	+459
Locking Differential [Opt on 2WD]	+155

Options	Price
OnStar Telematic System [Opt on LS]	+399
Power Driver Seat w/Memory [Opt on LT]	+118
Power Moonroof	+459
Power Passenger Seat [Opt on LT]	+129
Running Boards	+215

Venture

2003

Body Styles	TMV Pricing		
	Trade	Private	Dealer
4 Dr LS AWD Pass Van Ext	14788	16147	18411
4 Dr LS Pass Van	12584	13740	15666
4 Dr LS Pass Van Ext	12863	14045	16014
4 Dr LT AWD Pass Van Ext	17068	18636	21249
4 Dr LT Entertainer Pass Van Ext	15020	16400	18699
4 Dr LT Pass Van Ext	14627	15971	18210

Options	Price
8 Passenger Seating [Opt on LS]	+185
Aluminum/Alloy Wheels [Opt on LS,STD]	+188
AM/FM/CD Audio System [Opt on STD]	+236
Antilock Brakes [Opt on STD,Value]	+606
Automatic Load Leveling [Opt on LS,Warner]	+230
Heated Front Seats [Opt on LT,LT Entertainer]	+124
Leather Seats [Opt on LT,LT Entertainer]	+399
Power Driver Seat [Opt on LS]	+166

Body Styles	TMV Pricing		
	Trade	Private	Dealer
4 Dr STD Pass Van	12143	13258	15117
4 Dr STD Pass Van Ext	12481	13627	15538
4 Dr Value Pass Van	10463	11424	13026
4 Dr Warner Brothers AWD Pass Van Ext	17647	19268	21970
4 Dr Warner Brothers Pass Van Ext	16811	18355	20929

Options	Price
Power Dual Sliding Doors [Opt on LS,LT,Warner]	+246
Power Sliding Door [Opt on LS]	+370
Rear Window Defroster [Opt on STD,Value]	+115
Traction Control System [Opt on LS,Warner]	+124
OnStar Telematic System [Opt on LS,LT]	+271
AM/FM/CD Changer Audio System	+252
Air Conditioning - Front and Rear [Opt on Ext - LS,STD]	+303
Park Distance Control (Rear) [Opt on LS,LT,Warner]	+140

Mileage Category: P

The Venture remains relatively unchanged for 2003. Base vans now have additional color options but many previously standard features are now optional to keep prices down.

2002

Body Styles	TMV Pricing		
	Trade	Private	Dealer
4 Dr LS AWD Pass Van Ext	12049	13278	15326
4 Dr LS Pass Van	10286	11322	13049
4 Dr LS Pass Van Ext	10654	11741	13553
4 Dr LT AWD Pass Van Ext	14484	15962	18424
4 Dr LT Pass Van Ext	12219	13466	15543
4 Dr Plus Pass Van	10205	11246	12980

Options	Price
Air Conditioning - Front and Rear [Std on LT,Warner Brothers]	+272
Aluminum/Alloy Wheels [Opt on Plus,Value]	+169
Automatic Load Leveling [Opt on LS]	+206
Captain Chairs (4) [Opt on LS]	+166
Compact Disc Changer	+169

Body Styles	TMV Pricing		
	Trade	Private	Dealer
4 Dr Plus Pass Van Ext	10340	11395	13153
4 Dr STD Pass Van	9533	10505	12125
4 Dr Value Pass Van	8564	9437	10893
4 Dr Warner Brothers AWD Pass Van Ext	14928	16451	18988
4 Dr Warner Brothers Pass Van Ext	12741	14024	16163

Options	Price
Leather Seats [Opt on LT]	+358
Park Distance Control (Rear) [Opt on LS Ext]	+126
Power Driver Seat [Std on LT,Warner Brothers]	+155
Power Dual Sliding Doors	+201
Power Sliding Door [Opt on Plus]	+201

Mileage Category: P

The Venture becomes the first minivan to offer a factory-installed DVD video player; it comes standard on the popular Warner Bros. Edition. The WB and LT models get an all-new AWD option package. Two new colors and LATCH child safety-seat anchors sum up the changes for 2002.

2001

Body Styles	TMV Pricing		
	Trade	Private	Dealer
4 Dr LS Pass Van	8615	10016	11309
4 Dr LS Pass Van Ext	9062	10535	11895
4 Dr LT Pass Van Ext	9948	11565	13058
4 Dr Plus Pass Van	8359	9718	10973

Options	Price
8 Passenger Seating	+152
Air Conditioning - Front and Rear [Opt on LS,Plus]	+249
Aluminum/Alloy Wheels [Opt on Plus]	+155
Automatic Load Leveling [Std on LT]	+212
Compact Disc Changer	+207

Body Styles	TMV Pricing		
	Trade	Private	Dealer
4 Dr Plus Pass Van Ext	8639	10044	11340
4 Dr Value Pass Van	7051	8197	9255
4 Dr Warner Brothers Pass Van Ext	10228	11891	13426

Options	Price
Leather Seats [Opt on LT]	+328
Park Distance Control (Rear) [Std on LT,Warner Bros]	+115
Power Sliding Door [Opt on LS,Plus]	+378
Rear Window Defroster [Opt on Value]	+160

Mileage Category: P

A new grille and front fascia give the 2001 Venture an updated look, while a rear parking aid system helps keep extended wheelbase drivers from inadvertently updating the tail. OnStar is now standard on all models except the Value Van; a six-disc CD changer and fold-flat captain's chairs are available options on passenger models.

2000

Body Styles	TMV Pricing		
	Trade	Private	Dealer
4 Dr LS Pass Van	7065	8336	9581
4 Dr LS Pass Van Ext	7546	8904	10235
4 Dr LT Pass Van Ext	8075	9527	10951
4 Dr Plus Pass Van	6890	8129	9344

Body Styles	TMV Pricing		
	Trade	Private	Dealer
4 Dr Plus Pass Van	7065	8336	9581
4 Dr STD Pass Van	6452	7612	8750
4 Dr Value Pass Van	5792	6834	7856
4 Dr Warner Brothers Pass Van Ext	8470	9994	11488

Mileage Category: P

Chevy adds two new models on either end of the price spectrum for 2000. On the low end, a new Value Van includes basic equipment for a low price, while on the high end, a Warner Bros. Edition provides leather and a video entertainment system. New radios include radio data system (RDS) on uplevel versions. Three-door models die this year, while remaining models get new interior fabric patterns and a redesigned gauge cluster with a scratch-resistant lens. Smokey Carmel is a new paint color.

Chevrolet
Venture

2000 (cont'd)

Options	Price
8 Passenger Seating	+131
Air Conditioning - Front and Rear [Opt on LS,Plus]	+222
Aluminum/Alloy Wheels [Opt on Plus]	+138
AM/FM/Cassette/CD Audio System [Opt on LS,Plus,STD]	+219
AM/FM/CD Audio System	+173

Options	Price
Captain Chairs (4) [Std on LT]	+131
Leather Seats [Opt on LT]	+419
OnStar Telematic System	+419
Power Driver Seat	+126
Power Sliding Door [Opt on LS,Plus]	+210
Rear Window Defroster [Opt on Value]	+143

1999

Mileage Category: P

Venture gets some performance and safety enhancements. Other changes include additional seating choices, four new exterior and two new interior colors, as well as wider standard tires. There's a new LT model that packages an upgraded audio system with a touring suspension, traction control and captain's seats with available leather.

Body Styles	TMV Pricing		
	Trade	Private	Dealer
3 Dr STD Pass Van	5120	6145	7211
4 Dr LS Pass Van	5931	7117	8352
4 Dr LS Pass Van Ext	6225	7470	8766

Body Styles	TMV Pricing		
	Trade	Private	Dealer
4 Dr LT Pass Van Ext	6802	8163	9579
4 Dr STD Pass Van	5478	6574	7714
4 Dr STD Pass Van Ext	5755	6906	8104

Options	Price
Air Conditioning - Front and Rear [Std on LT]	+178
AM/FM/Cassette/CD Audio System [Std on LT]	+175
AM/FM/CD Audio System	+139

Options	Price
Leather Seats	+334
OnStar Telematic System [Opt on LS,LT]	+371
Power Sliding Door [Std on LT]	+168

1998

Mileage Category: P

Venture is the first minivan to get side-impact airbags. Other changes include the availability of a cargo van edition, a wider variety of dual door models, and an optional power sliding door on regular wheelbase vans. Power rear window vents are also added for 1998. Front airbags deploy with less force thanks to second-generation technology.

Body Styles		TMV Pricing	
	Trade	Private	Dealer
3 Dr LS Pass Van	4387	5402	6547
3 Dr LS Pass Van Ext	4612	5678	6880
3 Dr STD Pass Van	4002	4927	5971
3 Dr STD Pass Van Ext	4349	5355	6489

Options	Price
Air Conditioning - Front and Rear	+141
AM/FM/Cassette/CD Audio System	+148
AM/FM/CD Audio System	+116
Bucket Seats	+141

Options	Price
OnStar Telematic System [Opt on LS]	+313
Power Sliding Door	+137
Sliding Driver Side Door	+121

1997

Mileage Category: P

Complete redesign of Chevy's minivan results in a new name, a left-side sliding door, optional traction control, a powerful standard engine and a fun-to-drive demeanor.

Body Styles		TMV Pricing	
	Trade	Private	Dealer
3 Dr LS Pass Van	3591	4542	5704
3 Dr LS Pass Van Ext	3717	4701	5903
3 Dr STD Pass Van	3350	4236	5319
3 Dr STD Pass Van Ext	3571	4516	5671

Options	Price
Air Conditioning - Front and Rear	+128
AM/FM/Cassette/CD Audio System	+133
Bucket Seats [Opt on LS]	+128
Power Sliding Door	+128

2003

Body Styles	TMV Pricing		
	Trade	Private	Dealer
4 Dr STD Sdn	17781	19004	21043
4 Dr Special Sdn	19123	20439	22633

Options	Price	Options	Price
Power Moonroof	+534	17 Inch Wheels - Chrome [Opt on STD]	+447
Front Side Airbag Restraints	+233	AM/FM/Cassette/CD Changer Audio System [Opt on STD]	+262
Sport Suspension [Opt on Special]	+334		

Mileage Category: H

For 2003, Chrysler introduces the option of a factory-installed Sirius Satellite Radio, a first for Chrysler vehicles. Other changes include an updated audio system that features a six-disc CD changer in place of the old four-disc unit.

2002

Body Styles	TMV Pricing		
	Trade	Private	Dealer
4 Dr STD Sdn	14421	15667	17743
4 Dr Special Sdn	15464	16800	19026

Options	Price	Options	Price
17 Inch Wheels - Chrome	+390	Power Moonroof	+466
Front Side Airbag Restraints	+203	Sport Suspension	+291

Mileage Category: H

A special 300M debuts this year, called the Special. Designed to appeal to performance enthusiasts, the Special comes with 18-inch wheels wearing 245/45ZR18 Michelin Pilot Sport tires, a firmer suspension, increased-effort steering and an upgraded brake system. All models get a revised grille.

2001

Body Styles	TMV Pricing		
	Trade	Private	Dealer
4 Dr STD Sdn	12404	14130	15723

Options	Price	Options	Price
Chrome Wheels	+336	Power Moonroof	+401
Compact Disc Changer	+231	Sport Package	+251
Front Side Airbag Restraints	+175		

Mileage Category: H

DaimlerChrysler ups the feature content for the 300M by including standard steering wheel controls for the stereo, offering the option of side airbags and adding a luxury group package that includes real wood trim and an overhead console-mounted vehicle information center. The rear end gets a makeover in the form of clear-lens taillamps and chrome dual-exhaust outlets while new 17-inch wheels and anodized aluminum window trim dresses up the 300M's profile. There's now a three-point shoulder/lap belt for the central rear-seat passenger and an internal emergency trunk release. Additional luxury package features include an auto-dimming rearview mirror and exterior mirrors that tilt down automatically when the vehicle is placed in reverse. Two new exterior colors (Black and Deep Sapphire Blue) plus three new interior colors (Sandstone, Dark Slate Grey and Taupe) round out the changes for 2001.

2000

Body Styles	TMV Pricing		
	Trade	Private	Dealer
4 Dr STD Sdn	10281	12053	13790

Options	Price
Chrome Wheels	+254
Compact Disc Changer	+187
Power Moonroof	+289

Mileage Category: H

There are five new colors, interior upgrades such as rear-seat cupholders and color-keyed switches and a four-disc in-dash CD player. The rear suspension has been improved for less noise, vibration and harshness. The 2000 has the brake-shift interlock safety feature, which won't allow the driver to shift out of "Park" unless his foot is on the brake.

1999

Body Styles	TMV Pricing		
	Trade	Private	Dealer
4 Dr STD Sdn	8065	9734	11471

Options	Price
Chrome Wheels	+202
Power Moonroof	+230

Mileage Category: H

This all-new car from Chrysler will try to win some international recognition for the marque.

2000

Body Styles	TMV Pricing		
	Trade	Private	Dealer
4 Dr LX Sdn	4888	5980	7051
4 Dr LXi Sdn	5432	6646	7835

Options	Price	Options	Price
Chrome Wheels	+127	Automatic 4-Speed Transmission [Opt on LX]	+381
Compact Disc Changer	+138	AM/FM/CD Audio System	+123
Power Driver Seat [Opt on LX]	+118	Antilock Brakes [Opt on LX]	+247
Premium Audio System [Opt on LX]	+205		

Mileage Category: C

With a redesigned Cirrus successor modeled after the exceptionally attractive Concorde due in showrooms for 2001, the 2000 model is essentially a carryover model. Child-seat tethers have been added behind the backseat, and four new colors debut.

1999

Mileage Category: C

A slightly revised suspension gives the Cirrus a softer ride, and the interior improvements include a new instrument cluster and lower NVH levels. Outside, 15-inch chrome wheel covers are standard, and a winged Chrysler badge now decorates the front grille.

Body Styles	TMV Pricing		
	Trade	Private	Dealer
4 Dr LXi Sdn	4193	5273	6397

Options	Price
Compact Disc Changer	+159
Leather Seats	+289
Power Moonroof	+168

1998

Mileage Category: C

LX model is dropped. A powered driver seat, a 2.5-liter V6 engine, a tilt wheel and power windows, locks, and mirrors are now standard equipment. The LXi also comes in five new colors and as with all other Chrysler products, depowered airbags are standard.

Body Styles	TMV Pricing		
	Trade	Private	Dealer
4 Dr LXi Sdn	3340	4366	5522

Options	Price
Compact Disc Changer	+136
Leather Seats	+247
Power Moonroof	+143

1997

Mileage Category: C

The LXi trim level gets chrome wheels and the LX gets optional aluminum wheels. The Gold Package is also available on the LX. An in-dash CD changer is now available on LX and LXi models, as is a trip computer.

Body Styles	TMV Pricing		
	Trade	Private	Dealer
4 Dr LX Sdn	2350	3160	4151
4 Dr LXi Sdn	2708	3642	4784

Options	Price
2.5L V6 SOHC 24V FI Engine	+165

1996

Mileage Category: C

Base LX model gets a four-cylinder engine. Uplevel LXi gets a revised torque converter for better V6 response. A power sunroof, chrome-plated aluminum wheels and new colors are available for 1996.

Body Styles	TMV Pricing		
	Trade	Private	Dealer
4 Dr LX Sdn	1798	2526	3532
4 Dr LXi Sdn	2149	3020	4223

Options	Price
2.5L V6 SOHC 24V FI Engine [Opt on LX]	+142

1995

Mileage Category: C

The Cirrus is replacing the LeBaron sedan. A cab-forward design, a 164-horsepower V6 coupled with an automatic transmission, dual airbags, antilock brakes, air conditioning, power door locks and power windows are just a few of the improvements this car has over the LeBaron.

Body Styles	TMV Pricing		
	Trade	Private	Dealer
4 Dr LX Sdn	1466	2137	3256
4 Dr LXi Sdn	1600	2332	3553

2003

Body Styles	TMV Pricing		
	Trade	Private	Dealer
4 Dr LX Sdn	11495	12397	13901
4 Dr LXi Sdn	12811	13816	15492
4 Dr Limited Sdn	15597	16821	18861

Options	Price	Options	Price
Aluminum/Alloy Wheels [Opt on LX]	+209	Special Factory Paint	+119
AM/FM/CD Audio System [Opt on LX]	+119	Traction Control System [Opt on LXi]	+149
Antilock Brakes [Std on Limited]	+406	17 Inch Wheels - Chrome [Opt on LXi]	+388
Power Moonroof	+534	AM/FM/Cassette/CD Changer Audio System	+253
Front Side Airbag Restraints	+233		

Mileage Category: G

Three new colors -- Deep Lava Red, Brilliant Black Crystal and Deep Graphite -- burst onto the palette. Instead of a four-disc in-dash CD changer, you now get to insert six discs.

2002

Mileage Category: G

The Concorde goes uptown by adopting the LHS' (which is dropped this year) front and rear styling. More power is on tap for the LXi. And a new trim level debuts -- the Limited, which essentially replaces the LHS.

Body Styles	TMV Pricing		
	Trade	Private	Dealer
4 Dr LX Sdn	9129	9979	11397
4 Dr LXi Sdn	10399	11367	12981
4 Dr Limited Sdn	12948	14154	16165

Options	Price	Options	Price
16 Inch Wheels [Opt on LX]	+182	Antilock Brakes [Std on Limited]	+354
17 Inch Wheels - Chrome [Opt on LXi]	+338	Front Side Airbag Restraints	+203
AM/FM/Cassette/CD Changer Audio System	+195	Power Sunroof	+487
AM/FM/CD Changer Audio System [Opt on Limited]	+130	Traction Control System [Opt on LXi]	+130

2001

Mileage Category: G

Supplemental side airbags are a new option for the year, and an internal trunk release and center shoulder belt for the rear seat are standard. A center console power outlet exists for those models equipped with bucket seats, and all models get steering wheel-mounted audio controls. Two new exterior colors and three new interior colors are available this year, and both engines now meet LEV standards for all 50 states.

Body Styles	TMV Pricing		
	Trade	Private	Dealer
4 Dr LX Sdn	7575	8728	9792
4 Dr LXi Sdn	8679	9999	11217

Options	Price	Options	Price
Aluminum/Alloy Wheels [Opt on LX]	+164	Leather Seats [Opt on LX]	+336
AM/FM/Cassette/CD Changer Audio System [Opt on LXi]	+258	Power Passenger Seat [Opt on LX]	+170
Antilock Brakes [Opt on LX]	+305	Power Sunroof	+425
Chrome Wheels	+269	Premium Audio System [Opt on LX]	+258
Front Side Airbag Restraints	+175		

2000

Mileage Category: G

All models are given a more refined touring suspension, and variable-assist, speed-proportional steering is standard on LXi. Five new colors come aboard, and the instrument panel has been freshened.

Body Styles	TMV Pricing		
	Trade	Private	Dealer
4 Dr LX Sdn	6337	7441	8523
4 Dr LXi Sdn	6861	8056	9228

Options	Price	Options	Price
Aluminum/Alloy Wheels [Opt on LX]	+132	Infinity Audio System	+134
AM/FM/Cassette/CD Audio System [Opt on LX]	+134	Leather Seats [Opt on LX]	+361
Antilock Brakes [Opt on LX]	+247	Power Moonroof	+289
Chrome Wheels	+218	Power Passenger Seat [Opt on LX]	+138
Compact Disc Changer	+127		

Chrysler
Concorde

1999

Mileage Category: G

Bigger sway bar links and tubular rear trailing arms will be phased in during the model year, two changes that Chrysler promises will provide more road isolation for a more luxurious ride. Premium carpeting is added to the interior, and the LXi leather is improved.

Body Styles	TMV Pricing		
	Trade	Private	Dealer
4 Dr LX Sdn	5284	6349	7457
4 Dr LXi Sdn	5439	6535	7677

Options	Price	Options	Price
Antilock Brakes [Opt on LX]	+218	Power Moonroof	+230
Leather Seats [Opt on LX]	+287	Power Passenger Seat [Opt on LX]	+122

1998

Mileage Category: G

The Concorde is all new for 1998. The only thing they didn't change is the name.

Body Styles	TMV Pricing		
	Trade	Private	Dealer
4 Dr LX Sdn	4348	5403	6593
4 Dr LXi Sdn	4445	5524	6741

Options	Price
Antilock Brakes [Opt on LX]	+186
Leather Seats	+245
Power Moonroof	+196

1997

Mileage Category: G

The 3.5-liter engine is now standard on the LX trim level. An upgraded stereo debuts along with hood-mounted windshield-washer nozzles. The automatic transmission receives refinements.

Body Styles	TMV Pricing		
	Trade	Private	Dealer
4 Dr LX Sdn	3119	3975	5022
4 Dr LXi Sdn	3723	4744	5993

Options	Price
AM/FM/Cassette/CD Audio System	+124
Antilock Brakes [Std on LXi]	+156
Leather Seats [Opt on LX]	+206
Power Moonroof	+149

1996

Mileage Category: G

Improved headlight illumination, a revised exterior appearance, a quieter interior and new colors bow on all Concorde models. Base cars get standard 16-inch wheels. LXi models get gold-accented wheels and trim.

Body Styles	TMV Pricing		
	Trade	Private	Dealer
4 Dr LX Sdn	2235	2930	3890
4 Dr LXi Sdn	2633	3453	4585

Options	Price
3.5L V6 SOHC 24V FI Engine	+128
Leather Seats [Opt on LX]	+177
Power Moonroof	+128

1995

Mileage Category: G

No significant changes for the 1995 Concorde.

Body Styles	TMV Pricing		
	Trade	Private	Dealer
4 Dr STD Sdn	1918	2558	3624

Options	Price
3.5L V6 SOHC 24V FI Engine	+106
Leather Seats	+146
Power Moonroof	+106

1994

Body Styles	TMV Pricing		
	Trade	Private	Dealer
4 Dr STD Sdn	1323	1822	2653

Options	Price
Leather Seats	+101

Mileage Category: G

The base 3.3-liter engine is upped to 161 horsepower. A flexible-fuel version of the Concorde is available that will allow the car to run on alternative fuels such as methanol. Variable-assist power steering and a touring suspension are also added to the standard equipment list.

Chrysler
Grand Voyager

2000

Body Styles	TMV Pricing		
	Trade	Private	Dealer
4 Dr SE Pass Van Ext	7336	8538	9716
4 Dr STD Pass Van Ext	6819	7937	9032

Options	Price	Options	Price
Air Conditioning - Front and Rear [Opt on SE]	+218	Camper/Towing Package	+158
Aluminum/Alloy Wheels [Opt on SE]	+151	Captain Chairs (4) [Opt on SE]	+252
Antilock Brakes [Opt on STD]	+247	Infinity Audio System [Opt on SE]	+152

Mileage Category: P

With Plymouth's impending death, the Grand Voyager turns into a Chrysler this year, but it is otherwise unchanged. Four new colors and a new Value-Plus option package that includes a V6 and power features are new this year.

Chrysler
LHS

2001

Body Styles	TMV Pricing		
	Trade	Private	Dealer
4 Dr STD Sdn	11140	12690	14120

Options	Price
Compact Disc Changer	+231
Front Side Airbag Restraints	+175
Power Sunroof	+401

Mileage Category: H

An optional luxury package includes automatic adjusting side mirrors, electrochromic driver-side mirror, walnut wood trim and an overhead console-mounted vehicle information display. There's an additional electrical power outlet in the center console, an overhead console with a driver information display, standard steering wheel-mounted stereo controls and three new interior colors. The LHS' 17-inch wheels now come in a Sparkle Silver finish while aluminum replaces the chrome window molding trim and two new exterior colors, Black and Deep Sapphire Blue Pearl Coat, further dress up this upscale sedan. For safety's sake, an internal trunk release and a center shoulder belt for the rear seat come standard while side airbags are now optional for front passengers.

2000

Body Styles	TMV Pricing		
	Trade	Private	Dealer
4 Dr STD Sdn	9117	10789	12428

Options	Price
Chrome Wheels	+254
Compact Disc Changer	+187
Power Moonroof	+289

Mileage Category: H

Nothing dramatically changes for 2000. There are interior upgrades, including an in-dash four-disc CD changer, and a modified rear suspension for less noise, vibration and harshness. An automatic transaxle brake-shift interlock is now standard, and there are four more color choices.

1999

Mileage Category: H

The luxury-tuned LHS has been completely redesigned for 1999.

Body Styles	TMV Pricing		
	Trade	Private	Dealer
4 Dr STD Sdn	6780	8328	9940

Options	Price
Chrome Wheels	+202
Power Moonroof	+230

1997

Mileage Category: H

The automatic transmission receives some fine-tuning.

Body Styles	TMV Pricing		
	Trade	Private	Dealer
4 Dr STD Sdn	4392	5703	7305

Options	Price
Power Moonroof	+165

1996

Mileage Category: H

A quieter interior and new colors entice buyers for 1996. Revised sound systems and a HomeLink Universal transmitter that opens your garage door for you when you pull in the driveway debut.

Body Styles	TMV Pricing		
	Trade	Private	Dealer
4 Dr STD Sdn	2941	3983	5421

Options	Price
Power Moonroof	+141

1995

Mileage Category: H

No changes this year.

Body Styles	TMV Pricing		
	Trade	Private	Dealer
4 Dr STD Sdn	2198	3061	4499

Options	Price
Power Moonroof	+117

1994

Mileage Category: H

The dechromed LHS model is the sporty edition of the New Yorker.

Body Styles	TMV Pricing		
	Trade	Private	Dealer
4 Dr STD Sdn	1544	2274	3491

Options	Price
Power Moonroof	+81

Chrysler
Le Baron

1995

Body Styles	TMV Pricing		
	Trade	Private	Dealer
2 Dr GTC Conv	1452	2117	3224

Options	Price
Antilock Brakes	+111
Leather Seats	+110

Mileage Category: C

The last of the K-Cars, the LeBaron convertible rides into the sunset in GTC trim.

1994

Body Styles	TMV Pricing		
	Trade	Private	Dealer
2 Dr GTC Conv	874	1362	2174
4 Dr LE Sdn	742	1156	1846
4 Dr Landau Sdn	1006	1567	2503

Options	Price
Air Conditioning [Opt on LE]	+81
Antilock Brakes	+77
Automatic 4-Speed Transmission [Opt on LE]	+81
Leather Seats	+76

Mileage Category: C

The two-door coupe is cancelled, leaving the convertible and sedan in place. The 100-horsepower four-cylinder engine is dropped, leaving the 141-horsepower V6 as the sole power plant.

Chrysler
New Yorker

1996

Body Styles	TMV Pricing		
	Trade	Private	Dealer
4 Dr STD Sdn	2750	3724	5068

Options	Price
Leather Seats	+192
Power Moonroof	+141

Mileage Category: H

After a short 1996 production run, the New Yorker is cut from the lineup in favor of the more popular LHS.

1995

Body Styles	TMV Pricing		
	Trade	Private	Dealer
4 Dr STD Sdn	1859	2590	3807

Options	Price
Infinity Audio System	+96
Leather Seats	+159
Power Moonroof	+117

Mileage Category: H

No changes to the New Yorker this year.

1994

Body Styles	TMV Pricing		
	Trade	Private	Dealer
4 Dr STD Sdn	1217	1793	2753

Options	Price
Leather Seats	+109
Power Moonroof	+81

Mileage Category: H

An all-new New Yorker debuts. Improved handling, styling and luxury mark a significant improvement for this nameplate.

Chrysler
PT Cruiser

2003

Body Styles	TMV Pricing		
	Trade	Private	Dealer
4 Dr Dream Cruiser Series 2 Turbo Wgn	14184	15443	17540
4 Dr GT Turbo Wgn	12755	13887	15773
4 Dr Limited Wgn	11729	12770	14504

Body Styles	TMV Pricing		
	Trade	Private	Dealer
4 Dr STD Wgn	10206	11112	12621
4 Dr Touring Wgn	10748	11702	13291

PT Cruiser

2003 (cont'd)

Mileage Category: L

The PT Turbo debuts with a 215-horsepower engine that gives the unique and versatile Cruiser a much needed boost in performance.

Options	Price
Antilock Brakes [Opt on Limited,STD,Touring]	+447
Automatic 4-Speed Transmission	+262
Chrome Wheels [Opt on Touring]	+358
Cruise Control [Opt on STD]	+140
Heated Front Seats [Opt on GT,Limited]	+149
Keyless Entry System [Opt on STD]	+119

Options	Price
Power Door Locks [Opt on STD]	+134
Power Moonroof [Opt on GT,Touring]	+415
Front Side Airbag Restraints [Opt on GT,STD,Touring]	+233
Special Factory Paint	+119
17 Inch Wheels - Chrome [Opt on GT]	+358

2002

Mileage Category: L

Taking a cue from custom cars of the past, Chrysler offers a flame-accented paint job on its popular retro-styled PT Cruiser. The optional flames, which are actually a decal. Also, two new trim levels debut this year: the Touring Edition (which was previously an option package) and the Dream Cruiser. A Woodie appearance option is also available.

Body Styles	TMV Pricing		
	Trade	Private	Dealer
4 Dr Dream Cruiser Series I Wgn	11675	12862	14839
4 Dr Limited Edition Wgn	10452	11514	13284

Body Styles	TMV Pricing		
	Trade	Private	Dealer
4 Dr STD Wgn	8627	9493	10936
4 Dr Touring Edition Wgn	8978	9890	11411

Options	Price
Antilock Brakes [Std on Dream Cruiser]	+390
Automatic 4-Speed Transmission	+429
Chrome Wheels [Opt on Touring]	+312
Cruise Control [Std on Dream Cruiser,Limited]	+122

Options	Price
Front Side Airbag Restraints [Std on Dream Cruiser,Limited]	+182
Heated Front Seats [Std on Dream Cruiser]	+130
Power Door Locks [Opt on STD]	+117
Power Moonroof [Opt on STD]	+310

2001

Mileage Category: L

Classic styling and modern utility were the guiding forces behind Chrysler's all-new PT Cruiser. Based loosely on the Neon platform, this small van offers a flexible interior, head-turning looks and, sadly, only 150 horsepower. But feature content is high and a more powerful engine is reportedly in the works for 2002.

Body Styles	TMV Pricing		
	Trade	Private	Dealer
4 Dr Limited Edition Wgn	9157	10548	11832
4 Dr STD Wgn	7290	8398	9421

Options	Price
Aluminum/Alloy Wheels	+135
Antilock Brakes	+336
Automatic 4-Speed Transmission	+370

Options	Price
Chrome Wheels [Opt on STD]	+179
Front Side Airbag Restraints [Opt on STD]	+157
Power Moonroof [Opt on STD]	+269

Chrysler
Prowler

2002

Body Styles	TMV Pricing		
	Trade	Private	Dealer
2 Dr STD Conv	30982	32803	35838

Options	Price
Special Factory Paint	+234

Mileage Category: F

One new color, Inca Gold, is added.

2001

Mileage Category: F

In January, the Plymouth brand was dropped from the Prowler name, and it became a Chrysler. To mark the change, a new "Mulholland Edition" was introduced in a dark blue coupe with white pinstriping. Also new this year, Chrysler is offering two new paint schemes for its Prowler. A two-tone version (the top of the car will be black and the sides will be silver), called the "Black Tie Edition," will appear. It also includes a silver instrument cluster bezel and silver floor mats. And, later in 2001, a new color, Prowler Orange, will also be available. Silver will still be offered, but red, yellow, black and purple are discontinued.

Body Styles	TMV Pricing		
	Trade	Private	Dealer
2 Dr STD Conv	27897	30261	32443

Options	Price
Special Factory Paint	+897

2003

Body Styles	TMV Pricing		
	Trade	Private	Dealer
2 Dr GTC Conv	14201	15316	17173
2 Dr LX Conv	13045	14069	15775
2 Dr LX Cpe	10952	11810	13241
2 Dr LXi Conv	14273	15393	17260

Body Styles	TMV Pricing		
	Trade	Private	Dealer
2 Dr LXi Cpe	12131	13082	14667
2 Dr Limited Conv	16941	18270	20486
4 Dr LX Sdn	9055	9766	10950
4 Dr LXi Sdn	11096	11966	13417

Options	Price
Aluminum/Alloy Wheels [Opt on LX]	+233
Antilock Brakes [Std on GTC,Limited]	+429
Compact Disc Changer [Opt on LX Cvt]	+253
Cruise Control [Opt on LX Cvt]	+140
Heated Front Seats [Opt on Limited Cnv,LXi Cnv,LXi Sdn]	+149
Infinity Audio System [Opt on GTC Cnv,LXi Cnv]	+283
Leather Seats [Opt on LXi Cpe,LXi Sdn]	+304
Power Driver Seat [Std on Limited Cnv,LXi Cnv,LXi Sdn]	+122
Power Moonroof [Opt on LX Cpe,LXi Cpe,LXi Sdn]	+415

Options	Price
Front Side Airbag Restraints [Opt on LX Cpe,LXi Cpe]	+233
Special Factory Paint	+119
Sport Suspension [Opt on LXi Sdn]	+116
17 Inch Wheels - Chrome [Opt on LXi Cpe]	+447
Premium Audio System [Opt on LXi Sdn]	+149
AM/FM/Cassette/CD Changer Audio System [Opt on GTC,Limited,LXi]	+179
Front and Rear Head Airbag Restraints [Opt on LX Sdn,LXi Sdn]	+268
16 Inch Wheels - Chrome [Opt on LXi Sdn]	+447

Mileage Category: D

For 2003, a six-disc in-dash CD changer replaces last year's four-disc in-dash model in the Sebring convertible. The Sebring LX sedan has been dressed with new 15-inch painted 10-spoke wheel covers. And the Sebring coupe gets a complete makeover this year. Its exterior has been freshened with a new hood, front and rear fascias, side sill moldings, deck lid, grille, headlamps, taillamps and foglamps. Within its cabin, the Sebring coupe gets a new instrument panel, gauge cluster, center console, center stack, door trim style and bezel surface appearance.

2002

Body Styles	TMV Pricing		
	Trade	Private	Dealer
2 Dr GTC Conv	11586	12669	14473
2 Dr LX Conv	10586	11575	13223
2 Dr LX Cpe	8565	9335	10619
2 Dr LXi Conv	12413	13573	15507
2 Dr LXi Cpe	9865	10753	12232

Body Styles	TMV Pricing		
	Trade	Private	Dealer
2 Dr Limited Conv	13687	14966	17098
4 Dr LX Plus Sdn	7494	8194	9361
4 Dr LX Sdn	7378	8041	9145
4 Dr LXi Sdn	8693	9505	10859

Options	Price
17 Inch Wheels - Chrome [Opt on LXi Cpe]	+390
2.7L V6 DOHC 24V FI Engine [Opt on LX,LX Plus]	+442
3.0L V6 SOHC 24V FI Engine [Opt on LX Cpe]	+460
Aluminum/Alloy Wheels [Opt on LX,LX Plus]	+169
AM/FM/CD Changer Audio System [Opt on LX Cpe]	+174
Antilock Brakes [Std on GTC,Limited]	+375
Chrome Wheels [Opt on LXi Sdn]	+312
Compact Disc Changer	+130

Options	Price
Cruise Control [Opt on LX Conv,LX Sdn]	+122
Front and Rear Head Airbag Restraints [Opt on Sdn]	+203
Heated Front Seats [Opt on Conv - Limited,LXi]	+130
Infinity Audio System [Opt on Conv - GTC,LX]	+247
Leather Seats [Opt on LXi]	+338
Power Sunroof	+362
Premium Audio System [Opt on LXi,LX Plus Sdn]	+130
Sport Suspension [Opt on LXi Sdn]	+130

Mileage Category: D

Even though it was revamped last year, the Sebring line receives a number of changes. An Enthusiast package for the sedan debuts, as will a sporty GTC convertible later in the model year. And to put the Sebring ragtop in reach of more buyers, a lower-priced LX version with the 2.4-liter inline four becomes available.

2001

Body Styles	TMV Pricing		
	Trade	Private	Dealer
2 Dr LX Conv	10032	11527	12907
2 Dr LX Cpe	7386	8492	9513
2 Dr LXi Conv	10128	11637	13030
2 Dr LXi Cpe	8098	9311	10431

Body Styles	TMV Pricing		
	Trade	Private	Dealer
2 Dr Limited Conv	11186	12853	14392
4 Dr LX Sdn	6248	7179	8038
4 Dr LXi Sdn	7702	8850	9909

Options	Price
17 Inch Wheels - Chrome	+336
2.7L V6 DOHC 24V FI Engine [Opt on LXi Sdn]	+359
3.0L V6 SOHC 24V FI Engine [Opt on LX Cpe]	+426
Aluminum/Alloy Wheels [Opt on LX]	+146
Antilock Brakes [Std on Limited]	+305
Automatic 4-Speed Transmission [Opt on LXi Cpe]	+370

Options	Price
Chrome Wheels [Opt on LXi Sdn]	+247
Compact Disc Changer	+168
Front and Rear Head Airbag Restraints [Opt on Sdn]	+175
Infinity Audio System [Opt on LX Conv]	+213
Leather Seats [Opt on LXi Cpe]	+381
Power Sunroof	+307

Mileage Category: D

The Sebring sedan debuts for 2001 along with redesigned versions of the coupe and convertible. A new, more powerful V6 joins the enlarged four-cylinder, with a manual five-speed available in the coupe. The Autostick automanual is still an option for those who can't decide where they stand on the shift issue, but only on upscale LXi models with the V6. An Infinity premium sound system with an in-dash CD changer is also new this year.

2000

Mileage Category: D

For 2000, the standard-equipment list has increased. Also, Ice Silver is the newest color, and the LX trim fabric has been updated.

Body Styles	TMV Pricing		
	Trade	Private	Dealer
2 Dr JX Conv	6758	8021	9259
2 Dr JXi Conv	7665	9098	10502
2 Dr JXi Limited Conv	8753	10389	11992

Options	Price
Antilock Brakes [Opt on Cpe]	+247
Chrome Wheels [Opt on JXi]	+127
Compact Disc Changer [Opt on Conv]	+181

Body Styles	TMV Pricing		
	Trade	Private	Dealer
2 Dr LX Cpe	5956	7068	8158
2 Dr LXi Cpe	6734	7991	9224

Options	Price
Infinity Audio System [Opt on Cpe]	+118
Power Sunroof [Opt on Cpe]	+249
Traction Control System [Opt on JXi]	+145

1999

Mileage Category: D

Body-colored mirrors lend the Sebring LXi a more elegant style.

Body Styles	TMV Pricing		
	Trade	Private	Dealer
2 Dr JX Conv	5859	7152	8498
2 Dr JXi Conv	6015	7342	8723

Options	Price
Power Sunroof	+185
Traction Control System [Opt on JXi]	+115
2.5L V6 SOHC 24V FI Engine [Opt on JX,LX]	+221
Antilock Brakes [Opt on Cpe]	+218

Body Styles	TMV Pricing		
	Trade	Private	Dealer
2 Dr LX Cpe	4445	5433	6462
2 Dr LXi Cpe	5690	6955	8272

Options	Price
Automatic 4-Speed Transmission [Opt on LX]	+201
Compact Disc Changer [Opt on Conv]	+144
Leather Seats [Opt on LXi]	+217

1998

Mileage Category: D

Evolutionary, mostly aesthetic changes enhance the Sebrings this year. The Sebring Coupe LX and LXi now offer a black and gray interior, and a new exterior color, Caffe Latte.

Body Styles	TMV Pricing		
	Trade	Private	Dealer
2 Dr JX Conv	3974	5001	6159
2 Dr JXi Conv	4827	6074	7480

Options	Price
2.5L V6 SOHC 24V FI Engine [Opt on JX,LX]	+188
Aluminum/Alloy Wheels [Opt on JX,LX]	+121
Antilock Brakes [Opt on JX,LX]	+186
Automatic 4-Speed Transmission [Opt on LX]	+171

Body Styles	TMV Pricing		
	Trade	Private	Dealer
2 Dr LX Cpe	3749	4719	5812
2 Dr LXi Cpe	4642	5842	7196

Options	Price
Compact Disc Changer	+123
Leather Seats [Opt on LXi]	+185
Power Sunroof	+158

1997

Mileage Category: D

After just one year in production, the Sebring Convertible receives several changes. The most significant are a quieter intake manifold for the 2.4-liter engine and the availability of Chrysler's AutoStick transmission. Other changes include the addition of new colors, auto-dimming mirror, trip computer, enhanced vehicle theft system and damage-resistant power antenna to the options list.

Body Styles	TMV Pricing		
	Trade	Private	Dealer
2 Dr JX Conv	3315	4285	5471
2 Dr JXi Conv	4070	5261	6717

Options	Price
2.5L V6 SOHC 24V FI Engine [Opt on JX,LX]	+158
Antilock Brakes [Opt on JX,LX]	+156
Automatic 4-Speed Transmission [Opt on LX]	+144

Body Styles	TMV Pricing		
	Trade	Private	Dealer
2 Dr LX Cpe	2838	3678	4705
2 Dr LXi Cpe	3932	5095	6517

Options	Price
Leather Seats [Opt on LXi]	+155
Power Sunroof	+133

1996

Mileage Category: D

Remote keyless-entry system gets a panic feature, and a HomeLink Universal Transmitter debuts on this suave sport coupe. Three new paint colors are also available. Chrysler dumps its final K-Car variant this year in favor of the Sebring Convertible. Based on the Cirrus platform and drivetrains, this drop top shares only the name of the Sebring Coupe.

Body Styles	TMV Pricing		
	Trade	Private	Dealer
2 Dr JX Conv	2741	3624	4844
2 Dr JXi Conv	3511	4643	6206

Options	Price
Leather Seats [Opt on LXi]	+133
2.5L V6 SOHC 24V FI Engine [Opt on JX,LX]	+136

Body Styles	TMV Pricing		
	Trade	Private	Dealer
2 Dr LX Cpe	2393	3169	4241
2 Dr LXi Cpe	3177	4208	5632

Options	Price
Antilock Brakes [Opt on JX]	+134
Automatic 4-Speed Transmission [Opt on LX]	+124

1995

Body Styles	TMV Pricing		
	Trade	Private	Dealer
2 Dr LX Cpe	1937	2644	3823
2 Dr LXi Cpe	2344	3200	4626

Options	Price
2.5L V6 SOHC 24V FI Engine [Opt on LX]	+112
Automatic 4-Speed Transmission [Opt on LX]	+102
Leather Seats	+110

Options	Price
Power Sunroof	+94
Premium Audio System	+124

Mileage Category: E

Chrysler's replacement for the LeBaron coupe is the Sebring. Based on the Dodge Avenger, the Sebring offers more luxury than its corporate cousin. The Sebring is available as a four-cylinder LX or an upscale 2.5-liter V6 LXi; both come standard with an automatic transmission.

Chrysler

Town & Country

2003

Body Styles	TMV Pricing		
	Trade	Private	Dealer
4 Dr EX Pass Van Ext	17071	18326	20418
4 Dr LX Pass Van Ext	16002	17179	19140
4 Dr LXi AWD Pass Van Ext	20824	22355	24907
4 Dr LXi Pass Van Ext	19019	20418	22749

Body Styles	TMV Pricing		
	Trade	Private	Dealer
4 Dr Limited AWD Pass Van Ext	24161	25938	28899
4 Dr Limited Pass Van Ext	23025	24719	27541
4 Dr STD Pass Van Ext	16052	17233	19200
4 Dr eL Pass Van Ext	15166	16282	18141

Options	Price
Alarm System [Opt on LXi]	+116
Automatic Load Leveling	+173
Camper/Towing Package [Opt on Limited,LXi]	+212
Captain Chairs (4) [Opt on LX]	+444
Compact Disc Changer [Opt on LXi]	+119
Heated Front Seats [Opt on LXi]	+149
Power Driver Seat [Opt on LX]	+143
Power Moonroof [Opt on Limited,LXi]	+534
Power Sliding Door [Opt on LX]	+239

Options	Price
Front Side Airbag Restraints [Std on Limited]	+233
Special Factory Paint	+119
Power Rear Liftgate [Opt on LX]	+239
16 Inch Wheels [Opt on LX]	+161
Air Conditioning - Front and Rear [Opt on STD]	+119
Automatic Climate Control (3 Zone) [Opt on STD]	+164
DVD Entertainment System [Opt on Limited,LXi]	+537
3.8L V6 OHV 12V FI Engine [Opt on eL,LX]	+200

Mileage Category: P

Two new options debut -- a one-touch power sunroof (that Chrysler boasts is one of the largest available in a minivan) and a factory-, not dealer-, installed DVD entertainment system that comes with wireless headphones. Audiophiles will appreciate the new six-CD changer, an upgrade over the previous four-disc unit. Note that the LX AWD model has been discontinued, thus requiring buyers who want all-wheel drive to step up to the more expensive LXi and Limited models to get it.

2002

Body Styles	TMV Pricing		
	Trade	Private	Dealer
4 Dr EX Pass Van Ext	13900	15145	17221
4 Dr LX AWD Pass Van Ext	15874	17296	19666
4 Dr LX Pass Van Ext	12947	14107	16040
4 Dr LXi AWD Pass Van Ext	16799	18304	20812

Body Styles	TMV Pricing		
	Trade	Private	Dealer
4 Dr LXi Pass Van Ext	14641	15952	18138
4 Dr Limited AWD Pass Van Ext	19816	21591	24550
4 Dr Limited Pass Van Ext	18899	20592	23413
4 Dr eL Pass Van Ext	12275	13375	15207

Options	Price
16 Inch Wheels [Opt on EX]	+195
3.8L V6 OHV 12V FI Engine [Opt on LXi 2WD]	+174
Air Conditioning - Front and Rear [Opt on LX 2WD]	+258
Aluminum/Alloy Wheels [Opt on LX,LXi FWD]	+232
AM/FM/Cassette/CD Audio System [Opt on LX 2WD,LXi]	+117
Automatic Load Leveling [Opt on FWD - LX,LXi]	+151
Captain Chairs (4) [Opt on LX 2WD]	+388
DVD Entertainment System	+468

Options	Price
Front Side Airbag Restraints [Std on Limited]	+203
Heated Front Seats	+130
Infinity Audio System [Opt on LX]	+258
Leather Seats [Opt on LXi]	+463
Power Driver Seat [Opt on LX 2WD]	+192
Power Dual Sliding Doors [Opt on EX]	+208
Power Passenger Seat [Opt on LXi]	+192
Power Rear Liftgate [Std on EX,Limited]	+208
Power Sliding Door [Opt on eL,LX FWD]	+208

Mileage Category: P

Chrysler makes this already opulent minivan more luxurious with the availability of power-adjustable pedals, rear-seat audio with wireless headsets and a DVD video system for the rear seat that also includes wireless headsets. A value-leader eL model is introduced that lists for around $24,000.

2001

Body Styles	TMV Pricing		
	Trade	Private	Dealer
4 Dr EX Pass Van Ext	11324	13021	14588
4 Dr LX AWD Pass Van Ext	12432	14295	16015
4 Dr LX Pass Van Ext	10304	11848	13273
4 Dr LXi AWD Pass Van Ext	13054	15011	16817

Body Styles	TMV Pricing		
	Trade	Private	Dealer
4 Dr LXi Pass Van Ext	11355	13057	14628
4 Dr Limited AWD Pass Van Ext	15675	18024	20193
4 Dr Limited Pass Van Ext	14327	16475	18457

Mileage Category: P

Chrysler's top-of-the-line minivans are all new for the 2001 model year, with new gewgaws such as a power liftgate and a removable center console with three power outlets.

2001 (cont'd)

Options	Price
3.8L V6 OHV 12V FI Engine [Opt on LXi 2WD]	+206
Air Conditioning - Front and Rear [Opt on LX 2WD]	+247
Aluminum/Alloy Wheels	+186
Automatic Climate Control (3 Zone) [Opt on LX]	+146
Automatic Load Leveling [Std on Limited,AWD]	+130
Front Side Airbag Restraints	+175

Options	Price
Infinity Audio System [Opt on LX]	+222
Leather Seats [Opt on LXi]	+399
Power Driver Seat [Opt on LX 2WD]	+166
Power Rear Liftgate [Opt on LX,LXi]	+179
Power Sliding Door [Opt on LX 2WD]	+173

2000

Mileage Category: P

The model lineup changes this year, and telling the difference between the LX and LXi will be easier to the untrained eye, thanks to distinctive exterior and interior modifications. New colors for 2000 are Shale Green, Bright White, Patriot Blue, Bright Silver and Inferno Red.

Body Styles	TMV Pricing		
	Trade	Private	Dealer
4 Dr LX AWD Pass Van Ext	9819	11428	13005
4 Dr LX Pass Van Ext	8595	10003	11383
4 Dr LXi AWD Pass Van Ext	10949	12743	14501

Body Styles	TMV Pricing		
	Trade	Private	Dealer
4 Dr LXi Pass Van Ext	9780	11383	12954
4 Dr Limited AWD Pass Van Ext	12011	13979	15908
4 Dr Limited Pass Van Ext	11671	13583	15458

Options	Price
3.8L V6 OHV 12V FI Engine [Opt on LXi FWD]	+167
Air Conditioning - Front and Rear [Opt on LX,LXi]	+172
Aluminum/Alloy Wheels	+151
AM/FM/Cassette/CD Audio System [Opt on LX,LXi]	+143

Options	Price
Compact Disc Changer	+199
Infinity Audio System [Opt on LX]	+127
Leather Seats [Opt on LXi]	+323
Power Passenger Seat [Opt on LXi]	+167

1999

Mileage Category: P

The top-of-the-line trim level is now called "Limited," and it offers more standard equipment (hence less options) than any other Chrysler minivan. Leather upgrades, steering wheel-mounted stereo controls and a center armrest in the rear bench are new this year, and the exterior features such details as 16-inch 15-spoke chrome wheels and chrome door handles.

Body Styles	TMV Pricing		
	Trade	Private	Dealer
4 Dr LX AWD Pass Van Ext	8527	10077	11691
4 Dr LX Pass Van Ext	7375	8716	10112
4 Dr LXi AWD Pass Van Ext	9538	11272	13077
4 Dr LXi Pass Van Ext	8601	10165	11792

Body Styles	TMV Pricing		
	Trade	Private	Dealer
4 Dr Limited AWD Pass Van Ext	9928	11733	13611
4 Dr Limited Pass Van Ext	9413	11125	12906
4 Dr SX Pass Van	8184	9672	11221

Options	Price
3.8L V6 OHV 12V FI Engine [Opt on SX,LX FWD]	+132
Air Conditioning - Front and Rear [Opt on LX]	+144
Aluminum/Alloy Wheels [Opt on LX]	+120

Options	Price
Compact Disc Changer	+159
Leather Seats [Opt on LX,SX]	+257

1998

Mileage Category: P

Chrysler's luxury minivans get a few improvements this year, with the addition of a new Chrysler-signature grille, more powerful 3.8-liter V6, high-performance headlights and three fancy new colors.

Body Styles	TMV Pricing		
	Trade	Private	Dealer
4 Dr LX AWD Pass Van Ext	6526	7943	9541
4 Dr LX Pass Van Ext	6047	7360	8841
4 Dr LXi AWD Pass Van Ext	7478	9102	10933

Body Styles	TMV Pricing		
	Trade	Private	Dealer
4 Dr LXi Pass Van Ext	6888	8384	10071
4 Dr SX Pass Van	5701	6939	8336

Options	Price
Compact Disc Changer	+136
Leather Seats [Std on LXi]	+219

1997

Mileage Category: P

Chrysler's luxury minivans get a few improvements this year, as AWD extended length models are added to the lineup. Also new this year is a sporty SX model, which replaces last year's LX as the regular length Town & Country. Families with kids will love the standard left-side sliding door on this vehicle.

Body Styles	TMV Pricing		
	Trade	Private	Dealer
4 Dr LX AWD Pass Van Ext	4842	6099	7635
4 Dr LX Pass Van Ext	4604	5799	7259
4 Dr LXi AWD Pass Van Ext	5653	7120	8912

Body Styles	TMV Pricing		
	Trade	Private	Dealer
4 Dr LXi Pass Van Ext	5439	6850	8575
4 Dr SX Pass Van	4531	5706	7143

Options	Price
Leather Seats [Std on LXi]	+184

Town & Country/Voyager

1996

Body Styles	TMV Pricing		
	Trade	Private	Dealer
3 Dr LX Pass Van	3337	4318	5673
3 Dr LX Pass Van Ext	3423	4430	5820
4 Dr LXi Pass Van Ext	4036	5223	6863

Options	Price
Leather Seats [Std on LXi]	+158

Mileage Category: P

Totally redesigned for 1996, the T&C raises the bar for luxury minivans. In a departure from last year, the T&C is offered in a short wheelbase version, and is available in two trim levels: LX and LXi. New innovations include a driver-side passenger door, dual-zone temperature controls and a one-hand latch system on the integrated child safety seats.

1995

Mileage Category: P

There are no changes for the 1995 Town & Country.

Body Styles	TMV Pricing		
	Trade	Private	Dealer
3 Dr STD AWD Pass Van Ext	2814	3692	5154
3 Dr STD Pass Van Ext	2525	3313	4625

1994

Mileage Category: P

A passenger airbag joins the standard equipment list of the Chrysler Town & Country, once again pushing the envelope of the growing minivan segment. A larger engine is also available in the 1994 Town & Country.

Body Styles	TMV Pricing		
	Trade	Private	Dealer
3 Dr STD AWD Pass Van Ext	2026	2784	4047
3 Dr STD Pass Van Ext	1960	2694	3916

Chrysler
Voyager

2003

Body Styles	TMV Pricing		
	Trade	Private	Dealer
4 Dr LX Pass Van	11986	12868	14337

Options	Price	Options	Price
Child Seat (1)	+134	Front Side Airbag Restraints	+233
Power Door Locks	+140	3.3L V6 Flex Fuel OHV 12V FI Engine	+579
Power Driver Seat	+221	3.3L V6 OHV 12V FI Engine	+579
Power Windows	+158		

Mileage Category: P

Chrysler has reorganized the lineup, eliminating all "base" models as well as the four-cylinder-only "eC" model (extra-cheap?). Now there's only one trim level, LX. If you stick with the base Value Package, you'll get the 2.4-liter four-cylinder engine. If you opt for the Popular Equipment Package, you'll get the 3.3-liter V6. Mercifully, Chrysler has done away with the archaic three-speed automatic formerly available on four-cylinder models. New exterior colors include Satin Jade and Butane Blue.

2002

Mileage Category: P

Chrysler brings out the Voyager eC, a value leader that lists for just $17,000. Power-adjustable pedals debut as well.

Body Styles	TMV Pricing		
	Trade	Private	Dealer
4 Dr LX Pass Van	10284	11194	12710
4 Dr STD Pass Van	8287	9030	10267
4 Dr eC Pass Van	7011	7639	8686

Options	Price	Options	Price
3.3L V6 OHV 12V FI Engine [Opt on STD]	+505	Front Side Airbag Restraints	+203
AM/FM/Cassette/CD Audio System [Opt on LX]	+117	Infinity Audio System [Opt on LX]	+258
Antilock Brakes	+375	Power Door Locks [Std on LX]	+117
Automatic 4-Speed Transmission [Opt on STD]	+156	Power Driver Seat [Opt on LX]	+192

Voyager

2002 (cont'd)

Options	Price
Captain Chairs (4) [Opt on LX]	+336
Center and Rear Bench Seat	+117
Child Seat (1)	+117
Compact Disc Changer [Opt on LX]	+195

Options	Price
Power Sliding Door [Opt on LX]	+208
Power Windows [Std on LX]	+137
Temperature Controls - Driver and Passenger [Opt on LX]	+117

2001

Mileage Category: P

Chrysler's low-end minivan receives an available 3.3-liter V6 engine that's been massaged to put forth more power; an improved suspension and drivetrain to increase ride comfort and reduce vibrations; upgraded brakes; standard dual sliding doors; and available side airbags, all under new, sleek sheet metal.

Body Styles	TMV Pricing		
	Trade	Private	Dealer
4 Dr LX Pass Van	8201	9431	10566
4 Dr STD Pass Van	6183	7110	7965

Options	Price
3.3L V6 OHV 12V FI Engine [Opt on STD]	+435
Antilock Brakes [Opt on STD]	+305
Automatic Load Leveling	+130
Compact Disc Changer	+312
Front Side Airbag Restraints	+175

Options	Price
Infinity Audio System	+222
Power Driver Seat	+166
Power Sliding Door	+173
Power Windows [Opt on STD]	+118
Temperature Controls - Driver and Passenger [Opt on LX]	+123

2000

Mileage Category: P

With Plymouth's impending death, the Voyager turns into a Chrysler this year, but it is otherwise unchanged. Four new colors and a new Value-Plus option package that includes a V6 and power features are new this year.

Body Styles	TMV Pricing		
	Trade	Private	Dealer
3 Dr STD Pass Van	4719	5492	6250
4 Dr SE Pass Van	6633	7720	8786

Options	Price
Camper/Towing Package	+158
Captain Chairs (4)	+252
Infinity Audio System	+152
Sliding Driver Side Door [Opt on STD]	+216
3.0L V6 SOHC 12V FI Engine [Opt on STD]	+291

Options	Price
3.3L V6 Flex Fuel OHV 12V FI Engine [Opt on STD]	+352
7 Passenger Seating [Opt on STD]	+136
Air Conditioning [Opt on STD]	+313
Aluminum/Alloy Wheels	+151
Antilock Brakes [Opt on STD]	+247

Daewoo
Lanos/Leganza

2002

Body Styles	TMV Pricing		
	Trade	Private	Dealer
2 Dr S Hbk	2143	2965	4336
2 Dr Sport Hbk	3110	4304	6293

Body Styles	TMV Pricing		
	Trade	Private	Dealer
4 Dr S Sdn	2521	3489	5101

Options	Price
Air Conditioning [Opt on S]	+311
AM/FM/Cassette/CD Audio System [Opt on S]	+207
Automatic 4-Speed Transmission	+332

Mileage Category: A

A new Comfort Package for the S Hatchback and S Sedan includes air conditioning and power steering, while the Convenience Package adds power windows, power locks and a power passenger-side exterior mirror.

2001

Body Styles	TMV Pricing		
	Trade	Private	Dealer
2 Dr S Hbk	1729	2715	3625
2 Dr Sport Hbk	2450	3848	5138

Body Styles	TMV Pricing		
	Trade	Private	Dealer
4 Dr S Sdn	2056	3229	4312

Options	Price
Air Conditioning [Opt on S]	+250
Aluminum/Alloy Wheels [Opt on S]	+134
Automatic 4-Speed Transmission	+267

Mileage Category: A

Daewoo adds the new Sport Hatchback model to the Lanos lineup for 2001, but discontinues the SE Hatchback and SX Sedan. Pacific Blue Mica and Red Rock Mica are added to the palette for the sedan and hatchback, while Super Red and Granada Black Mica are available exclusively on the Sport. The new premium package available on the S models includes power windows, door locks and passenger rearview mirror; tilt steering wheel; AM/cassette/CD stereo; digital clock; and variable intermittent wipers.

2000

Body Styles	TMV Pricing		
	Trade	Private	Dealer
2 Dr S Hbk	1371	2272	3156
2 Dr SE Hbk	1572	2607	3622

Body Styles	TMV Pricing		
	Trade	Private	Dealer
4 Dr S Sdn	1551	2571	3571
4 Dr SX Sdn	1722	2855	3966

Options	Price
Air Conditioning [Opt on S,SE]	+212
Antilock Brakes	+205

Options	Price
Automatic 4-Speed Transmission	+242
Power Moonroof	+151

Mileage Category: A

The three-door SX disappears, as does the SE Sedan. Daewoo picks up the tab for all scheduled maintenance during the warranty period and has added ownership peace of mind with 24-hour roadside assistance for three years or 36,000 miles.

1999

Body Styles	TMV Pricing		
	Trade	Private	Dealer
2 Dr S Hbk	1013	1700	2416
2 Dr SE Hbk	1139	1912	2716
2 Dr SX Hbk	1282	2152	3058

Body Styles	TMV Pricing		
	Trade	Private	Dealer
4 Dr S Sdn	1093	1834	2605
4 Dr SE Sdn	1162	1949	2769
4 Dr SX Sdn	1380	2316	3290

Options	Price
Air Conditioning [Opt on S,SE]	+148
Antilock Brakes	+160

Options	Price
Automatic 4-Speed Transmission	+169

Mileage Category: A

This entry into the subcompact class is Daewoo's attack on the Honda Civic.

Daewoo
Leganza

2002

Body Styles	TMV Pricing		
	Trade	Private	Dealer
4 Dr CDX Sdn	4890	6326	8718

Body Styles	TMV Pricing		
	Trade	Private	Dealer
4 Dr SE Sdn	3713	4803	6619

Options	Price
AM/FM/Cassette/CD Audio System [Opt on SE]	+116
Antilock Brakes [Opt on CDX]	+282
Automatic 4-Speed Transmission [Opt on SE]	+415

Options	Price
Leather Seats [Opt on CDX]	+270
Power Moonroof [Opt on CDX]	+290
Traction Control System [Opt on CDX]	+124

Mileage Category: C

The Leganza is a carryover. The midlevel SX trim has been eliminated, leaving the base SE and the upscale CDX. To help bridge the gap, the CDX has been decontented and its price lowered.

Daewoo
Leganza/Nubira

2001

Mileage Category: C

Scarlet Mica and Harbor Mist Mica are the new exterior colors. Outside rearview mirrors get a blue tint and a new audio head unit is added for improved sound quality. A new option package for the SE includes front and rear power windows, power door locks, AM/FM/cassette/CD stereo with six speakers, dual body-color heated power rearview mirrors, anti-theft alarm with remote keyless entry, tilt steering wheel and front foglamps.

Body Styles	TMV Pricing		
	Trade	Private	Dealer
4 Dr CDX Sdn	3609	5665	7562
4 Dr SE Sdn	2638	4141	5528
4 Dr SX Sdn	2658	4173	5571

Options	Price
Aluminum/Alloy Wheels [Opt on SX]	+167
Automatic 4-Speed Transmission [Opt on SE]	+267

Options	Price
Compact Disc Changer	+150
Power Moonroof [Opt on SX]	+217

2000

Mileage Category: C

Content is pulled from the base SE model, but all Leganzas have new grilles and larger stereo knobs. New seat fabric on SE models, revised alloy wheels and a more convenient remote keyless-entry design debut, and buyers now get 24-hour roadside assistance and free scheduled maintenance for the duration of the basic warranty period. New colors round out the changes.

Body Styles	TMV Pricing		
	Trade	Private	Dealer
4 Dr CDX Sdn	2818	4652	6450
4 Dr SE Sdn	2006	3312	4593
4 Dr SX Sdn	2080	3434	4761

Options	Price
Automatic 4-Speed Transmission [Opt on SE]	+242
Compact Disc Changer	+157
Power Moonroof [Opt on SX]	+257

1999

Mileage Category: C

The whole car is new to the United States, as is the motor company that makes it.

Body Styles	TMV Pricing		
	Trade	Private	Dealer
4 Dr CDX Sdn	2375	3973	5637
4 Dr SE Sdn	1521	2544	3609
4 Dr SX Sdn	1569	2625	3724

Options	Price
Automatic 4-Speed Transmission [Opt on SE]	+169
Power Moonroof [Opt on SX]	+179

Daewoo
Nubira

2002

Mileage Category: B

Daewoo trims the Nubira ranks for 2002 -- you can now purchase either an SE sedan or a CDX wagon.

Body Styles	TMV Pricing		
	Trade	Private	Dealer
4 Dr CDX Wgn	3621	4795	6751
4 Dr SE Sdn	3072	4068	5728

Options	Price
Air Conditioning [Opt on SE]	+332
AM/FM/Cassette/CD Audio System	+118
Automatic 4-Speed Transmission	+332

Nubira

2001

Body Styles	TMV Pricing		
	Trade	Private	Dealer
4 Dr CDX Sdn	2408	3659	4813
4 Dr CDX Wgn	3076	4673	6147
4 Dr SE Sdn	2366	3594	4728

Options	Price
Air Conditioning [Opt on SE]	+284
Automatic 4-Speed Transmission	+267
Leather Seats	+217
Power Moonroof	+167

Mileage Category: B

You can pick up a Daewoo Nubira with Diamond Blue Metallic paint. The sedan gets a new 14-inch standard wheel cover and the wagon has a fresh rear taillamp design.

2000

Body Styles	TMV Pricing		
	Trade	Private	Dealer
4 Dr CDX Sdn	1974	3101	4205
4 Dr CDX Wgn	2508	3939	5341
4 Dr SE Sdn	1838	2887	3915

Options	Price
Air Conditioning [Opt on SE]	+212
Automatic 4-Speed Transmission	+242
Leather Seats	+151
Power Moonroof	+151

Mileage Category: B

Nubira, already the most appealing choice from the Daewoo buffet, is restyled inside and out and becomes even more attractive to cash-strapped buyers. Firmer springs and a new rear stabilizer bar tighten handling, and the new SE trim level replaces last year's SX model. The five-door hatchback is dropped, but four new colors debut. Scheduled maintenance for the duration of the basic warranty, and three-year/36,000-mile 24-hour roadside assistance is standard.

1999

Body Styles	TMV Pricing			Body Styles	TMV Pricing		
	Trade	Private	Dealer		Trade	Private	Dealer
4 Dr CDX Hbk	1605	2536	3504	4 Dr SX Hbk	1456	2301	3180
4 Dr CDX Sdn	1581	2498	3453	4 Dr SX Sdn	1387	2191	3027
4 Dr CDX Wgn	2221	3509	4850	4 Dr SX Wgn	1498	2366	3270

Options	Price
Antilock Brakes [Opt on SX]	+160
Automatic 4-Speed Transmission	+169

Mileage Category: B

In an attempt to lure consumers away from the likes of Honda and Toyota, the new Korean upstart fields its loaded-with-features Nubira. Air conditioning, power windows, keyless entry, four-wheel disc brakes, 129 horsepower and a funny name all come as standard equipment.

Dodge
Avenger

2000

Body Styles		TMV Pricing	
	Trade	Private	Dealer
2 Dr ES Cpe	6503	7820	9110
2 Dr STD Cpe	5460	6564	7647

Options	Price	Options	Price
Alarm System [Opt on STD]	+138	Infinity Audio System	+147
AM/FM/Cassette/CD Audio System [Opt on STD]	+197	Power Moonroof	+289
Antilock Brakes	+307		

Mileage Category: E

Base Avengers get new standard equipment, including the 2.5-liter V6 and automatic transmission from the uplevel ES, new cloth fabric on the seats and standard 16-inch wheels with luxury wheelcovers. A sport package is optional. A power leather-trimmed driver's seat is included with ES trim for 2000. Two key fobs come with the remote keyless-entry system this year, and two new colors are available. The Avenger will be completely redesigned and take the Stratus nameplate for 2001.

1999

Mileage Category: E

One new color for the exterior: Shark Blue (replaces Silver Mist).

Body Styles		TMV Pricing	
	Trade	Private	Dealer
2 Dr ES Cpe	4957	6171	7434
2 Dr STD Cpe	4328	5387	6490

Options	Price	Options	Price
Power Moonroof	+236	Antilock Brakes	+278
2.5L V6 SOHC 24V FI Engine	+225	Automatic 4-Speed Transmission	+255
Air Conditioning [Opt on STD]	+291	Infinity Audio System [Opt on STD]	+120
Aluminum/Alloy Wheels [Opt on STD]	+181	Leather Seats	+203
AM/FM/Cassette/CD Audio System	+120		

1998

Mileage Category: E

Interior fabrics are new, as is a black and gray color scheme. The ES model gets a new Sport package that affects appearance, not performance. Also available for the ES are new 16-inch aluminum wheels and a rear sway bar that improves handling.

Body Styles		TMV Pricing	
	Trade	Private	Dealer
2 Dr ES Cpe	4652	5751	6990
2 Dr STD Cpe	3776	4668	5674

Options	Price	Options	Price
2.5L V6 SOHC 24V FI Engine	+199	Automatic 4-Speed Transmission	+227
Air Conditioning [Opt on STD]	+257	Leather Seats	+179
Aluminum/Alloy Wheels [Opt on STD]	+160	Power Sunroof	+209
Antilock Brakes	+246		

1997

Mileage Category: E

Front and rear styling is updated, while ES models lose the standard V6 engine. The V6 is available on base and ES models, and includes 17-inch wheels and tires on the ES. New colors inside and out and two additional speakers with cassette stereos further broaden the appeal of this roomy coupe.

Body Styles		TMV Pricing	
	Trade	Private	Dealer
2 Dr ES Cpe	4012	5094	6416
2 Dr STD Cpe	3187	4046	5095

Options	Price	Options	Price
2.5L V6 SOHC 24V FI Engine	+175	Antilock Brakes [Opt on STD]	+217
Air Conditioning [Opt on STD]	+226	Automatic 4-Speed Transmission	+196
Aluminum/Alloy Wheels [Opt on STD]	+140	Compact Disc Changer	+129
AM/FM/Cassette/CD Audio System	+125	Leather Seats	+158
AM/FM/CD Audio System [Opt on STD]	+125	Power Sunroof	+183

1996

Mileage Category: E

Dodge's sporty coupe gets a panic mode for the remote keyless entry system and a HomeLink transmitter that will open your garage door. ES models get new seat fabric, and three new colors are on the roster.

Body Styles		TMV Pricing	
	Trade	Private	Dealer
2 Dr ES Cpe	3343	4371	5790
2 Dr STD Cpe	2669	3489	4622

1996 (cont'd)

Options	Price
AM/FM/Cassette/CD Audio System	+220
Antilock Brakes [Opt on STD]	+197
Automatic 4-Speed Transmission [Opt on STD]	+178
Leather Seats	+144

Options	Price
Power Sunroof	+167
Premium Audio System	+143
Air Conditioning [Opt on STD]	+206
Aluminum/Alloy Wheels	+121

1995

Body Styles	TMV Pricing		
	Trade	Private	Dealer
2 Dr ES Cpe	2439	3201	4470

Options	Price
Air Conditioning [Opt on STD]	+181
AM/FM/CD Audio System	+100
Antilock Brakes [Opt on STD]	+172
Automatic 4-Speed Transmission [Opt on STD]	+156

Body Styles	TMV Pricing		
	Trade	Private	Dealer
2 Dr Highline Cpe	2054	2695	3764

Options	Price
Leather Seats	+126
Power Sunroof	+146
Premium Audio System	+125

Mileage Category: E

New coupe is late replacement for Daytona. Based on a Mitsubishi Galant platform, the Avenger is about the size of a Camry coupe. Base and ES models are available. Base cars have a 2.0-liter, 140-horsepower four-cylinder engine underhood. ES gets a Mitsubishi-built 2.5-liter V6 making 155 horsepower. An automatic is the only transmission available on the ES. ABS is optional on base models; standard on ES. All Avengers have dual airbags, height-adjustable driver's seat, split-folding rear seat, rear defroster, and tilt steering wheel.

Dodge
Caravan

2003

Body Styles	TMV Pricing		
	Trade	Private	Dealer
4 Dr SE Pass Van	11317	12251	13807

Options	Price
AM/FM/Cassette/CD Audio System [Opt on Sport]	+142
Antilock Brakes [Opt on SE]	+430
Captain Chairs (4) [Opt on Sport]	+471
Child Seats (2)	+142
Cruise Control [Opt on CV,SE]	+117
Power Heated Mirrors [Opt on CV,SE]	+123
Infinity Audio System [Opt on Sport]	+313
Power Door Locks [Opt on CV,SE]	+148
Power Driver Seat	+234
Power Sliding Door [Opt on Sport]	+253

Body Styles	TMV Pricing		
	Trade	Private	Dealer
4 Dr Sport Pass Van	12654	13698	15439

Options	Price
Power Windows [Opt on CV,SE]	+167
Front Side Airbag Restraints	+246
Special Factory Paint	+126
Split Folding Rear Seat [Opt on Sport]	+126
Power Adjustable Foot Pedals	+117
AM/FM/CD Changer Audio System [Opt on Sport]	+126
16 Inch Wheels [Opt on Sport]	+237
3.3L V6 Flex Fuel OHV 12V FI Engine [Opt on SE]	+613
3.3L V6 OHV 12V FI Engine [Opt on SE]	+613

Mileage Category: P

A new trim level dubbed "CV" has been added. The bargain-basement, four-cylinder-only "eC" model (extra-cheap?) has been dropped, but we doubt its passing will be mourned.

2002

Body Styles	TMV Pricing		
	Trade	Private	Dealer
4 Dr SE Pass Van	8938	9835	11330
4 Dr Sport Pass Van	10308	11343	13068

Options	Price
3.3L V6 OHV 12V FI Engine [Opt on SE]	+527
7 Passenger Seating [Opt on eC]	+245
AM/FM/Cassette/CD Audio System [Opt on Sport]	+122
Antilock Brakes [Opt on SE,Sport]	+370
Automatic 4-Speed Transmission [Opt on SE]	+163
Captain Chairs (4) [Opt on Sport]	+408
Center and Rear Bench Seat [Opt on Sport]	+122
Child Seat (1) [Opt on Sport]	+122
Child Seats (2) [Opt on SE]	+122

Body Styles	TMV Pricing		
	Trade	Private	Dealer
4 Dr eC Pass Van	7436	8183	9427

Options	Price
Compact Disc Changer [Opt on Sport]	+204
Front Side Airbag Restraints	+212
Infinity Audio System [Opt on Sport]	+269
Power Door Locks [Std on Sport]	+128
Power Driver Seat [Opt on SE,Sport]	+201
Power Sliding Door [Opt on Sport]	+217
Power Windows [Opt on SE]	+144
Temperature Controls - Driver and Passenger [Opt on Sport]	+163

Mileage Category: P

Dodge brings out the Caravan eC, a value leader that lists for just $17,000. Power adjustable pedals debut as well.

2001

Body Styles	TMV Pricing		
	Trade	Private	Dealer
4 Dr SE Pass Van	7539	8697	9766

Body Styles	TMV Pricing		
	Trade	Private	Dealer
4 Dr Sport Pass Van	8275	9546	10719

Mileage Category: P

America's best-selling minivan has been revised for 2001 and boasts new sheet metal, boosted horsepower, a refined suspension, upgraded brakes, improved safety features and plenty of additional gadgets. Third-row seats are now easier to remove and install, but still don't fold flat.

Dodge
Caravan

2001 (cont'd)

Options	Price
Aluminum/Alloy Wheels	+339
Antilock Brakes [Opt on SE]	+339
Automatic Load Leveling	+145
Captain Chairs (4) [Opt on Sport]	+372
Compact Disc Changer	+347
Front Side Airbag Restraints	+195
Infinity Audio System	+247

Options	Price
Power Door Locks [Opt on SE]	+157
Power Driver Seat	+185
Power Sliding Door [Opt on Sport]	+200
Power Windows [Opt on SE]	+130
Rear Window Defroster [Opt on SE]	+115
Temperature Controls - Driver and Passenger [Opt on Sport]	+187

2000

Mileage Category: P

New colors and more standard equipment keep Chrysler's best-selling minivans up to date until the redesigned 2001 model arrives.

Body Styles	TMV Pricing		
	Trade	Private	Dealer
3 Dr STD Pass Van	5134	6040	6929

Body Styles	TMV Pricing		
	Trade	Private	Dealer
4 Dr SE Pass Van	6460	7601	8719

Options	Price
3.0L V6 SOHC 12V FI Engine [Opt on SE,STD]	+361
3.3L V6 Flex Fuel OHV 12V FI Engine	+438
3.3L V6 OHV 12V FI Engine	+438
Air Conditioning [Opt on STD]	+389
Aluminum/Alloy Wheels	+119
AM/FM/Cassette/CD Audio System	+140

Options	Price
Antilock Brakes [Opt on STD]	+307
Automatic Load Leveling	+131
Camper/Towing Package	+136
Captain Chairs (4)	+314
Compact Disc Changer	+181
Infinity Audio System	+204

1999

Mileage Category: P

A revised front fascia is common to all models.

Body Styles	TMV Pricing		
	Trade	Private	Dealer
3 Dr STD Pass Van	4093	4916	5772
4 Dr LE Pass Van	5861	7039	8266

Body Styles	TMV Pricing		
	Trade	Private	Dealer
4 Dr SE Pass Van	4975	5976	7017

Options	Price
3.0L V6 SOHC 12V FI Engine	+295
3.3L V6 OHV 12V FI Engine	+357
3.8L V6 OHV 12V FI Engine	+138
7 Passenger Seating	+138
Air Conditioning	+317
AM/FM/Cassette/CD Audio System	+146
AM/FM/CD Audio System [Opt on STD]	+120

Options	Price
Antilock Brakes	+278
Automatic Load Leveling	+119
Captain Chairs (4)	+219
Infinity Audio System [Opt on SE]	+265
Leather Seats [Opt on LE]	+293
Power Door Locks [Std on LE]	+123
Sliding Driver Side Door [Opt on STD]	+219

1998

Mileage Category: P

Available this year is a 3.8-liter V6 that puts out 180 horsepower and 240 foot-pounds of torque. And for convenience, Caravans come with rear-seat mounted grocery bag hooks, and driver's-side easy-entry Quad seating. All Chrysler products are equipped with "Next Generation" depowered airbags.

Body Styles	TMV Pricing		
	Trade	Private	Dealer
3 Dr STD Pass Van	3475	4286	5200
4 Dr LE Pass Van	4969	6129	7437

Body Styles	TMV Pricing		
	Trade	Private	Dealer
4 Dr SE Pass Van	4214	5198	6307

Options	Price
Sliding Driver Side Door [Opt on STD]	+194
3.0L V6 SOHC 12V FI Engine [Opt on STD]	+251
3.3L V6 OHV 12V FI Engine [Opt on SE,STD]	+316
3.8L V6 OHV 12V FI Engine [Opt on LE,SE]	+122
Air Conditioning [Std on LE]	+281

Options	Price
AM/FM/Cassette/CD Audio System	+129
Antilock Brakes [Opt on STD]	+246
Captain Chairs (4)	+218
Leather Seats	+259

1997

Mileage Category: P

Traction control is a new option, so long as you get LE or ES trim, and an enhanced accident response system will automatically unlock the doors and illuminate the interior when an airbag deploys. Appearance and equipment refinements complete the modest changes to this best-in-class minivan.

Body Styles	TMV Pricing		
	Trade	Private	Dealer
3 Dr SE Pass Van	3493	4434	5584
3 Dr STD Pass Van	2876	3650	4597

Body Styles	TMV Pricing		
	Trade	Private	Dealer
4 Dr ES Pass Van	4562	5791	7292
4 Dr LE Pass Van	4173	5297	6670

Options	Price
Air Conditioning [Opt on SE,STD]	+247
Antilock Brakes [Opt on STD]	+217
Captain Chairs (4)	+171

Options	Price
Leather Seats	+228
Sliding Driver Side Door [Opt on STD]	+171

1996

Body Styles	TMV Pricing		
	Trade	Private	Dealer
3 Dr ES Pass Van	3457	4489	5913
3 Dr LE Pass Van	3414	4433	5839

Options	Price
3.0L V6 SOHC 12V FI Engine	+201
3.3L V6 Flex Fuel OHV 12V FI Engine	+229
3.3L V6 OHV 12V FI Engine [Opt on SE]	+232
Air Conditioning [Opt on SE,STD]	+225
Air Conditioning - Front and Rear	+232

Body Styles	TMV Pricing		
	Trade	Private	Dealer
3 Dr SE Pass Van	2871	3727	4909
3 Dr STD Pass Van	2266	2942	3876

Options	Price
Antilock Brakes [Opt on SE,STD]	+197
Captain Chairs (4)	+163
Leather Seats	+208
Sliding Driver Side Door	+156

Mileage Category: P

A complete redesign yields a cavernous interior, best-in-class driveability, and new innovations such as the optional driver's side passenger door. And although the all-wheel drive version is discontinued for now, Caravan dethrones the Ford Windstar and once again reigns as king of the minivans.

1995

Body Styles	TMV Pricing		
	Trade	Private	Dealer
3 Dr ES Pass Van	2462	3293	4679
3 Dr LE Pass Van	2343	3134	4453

Options	Price
3.3L V6 Flex Fuel OHV 12V FI Engine	+200
7 Passenger Seating [Opt on STD]	+80
Air Conditioning [Opt on SE,STD]	+196

Mileage Category: P

Body Styles	TMV Pricing		
	Trade	Private	Dealer
3 Dr SE Pass Van	2122	2839	4033
3 Dr STD Pass Van	1709	2286	3247

Options	Price
Antilock Brakes	+172
Captain Chairs (4)	+136
Infinity Audio System [Opt on ES,SE]	+77

Newly optional is a 3.3-liter V6 engine designed to operate on compressed natural gas. Sport and SE decor packages are available this year. The five-speed manual transmission, available only with the four-cylinder engine, has been canceled.

1994

Body Styles	TMV Pricing		
	Trade	Private	Dealer
3 Dr ES Pass Van	1718	2426	3605
3 Dr LE Pass Van	1645	2322	3451

Options	Price
Air Conditioning [Opt on SE,STD]	+165
Antilock Brakes	+145

Body Styles	TMV Pricing		
	Trade	Private	Dealer
3 Dr SE Pass Van	1581	2232	3317
3 Dr STD Pass Van	1329	1876	2788

Options	Price
Captain Chairs (4)	+114
Leather Seats	+153

Mileage Category: P

A passenger airbag is added to a redesigned dashboard, and new side-door guard beams meet 1997 passenger car safety standards. All-wheel drive is no longer available on regular-length models. Bumpers are restyled, and seats with integrated child seats can be reclined for the first time.

Dodge
Colt

1994

Body Styles	TMV Pricing		
	Trade	Private	Dealer
2 Dr ES Cpe	483	846	1450
2 Dr STD Cpe	459	804	1379

Options	Price
Air Conditioning	+134
Antilock Brakes	+145

Body Styles	TMV Pricing		
	Trade	Private	Dealer
4 Dr ES Sdn	528	925	1587
4 Dr STD Sdn	505	885	1518

Options	Price
Automatic 3-Speed Transmission	+105
Automatic 4-Speed Transmission	+149

Mileage Category: B

A driver airbag debuts. ES trim replaces GL nomenclature. Order ABS on an ES sedan and you'll get rear discs instead of drums. The optional 1.8-liter engine is available on the coupe this year, but only with ES trim. Sedans gain standard power steering. Air conditioners use CFC-free refrigerant.

Dodge
Dakota

2003

Mileage Category: J

Finally realizing that a 120-horsepower engine has no business being in a 3,500-pound (or more) pickup, Dodge drops the 2.5-liter inline four from the Dakota's powertrain roster. An optional five-speed automatic transmission for the 4.7-liter V8 debuts, as does a Stampede package that provides the show but not the go of the R/T model. Speaking of the R/T, that model receives four-wheel disc brakes this year.

Body Styles	TMV Pricing		
	Trade	Private	Dealer
2 Dr R/T Ext Cab	16433	17731	19895
2 Dr R/T Std Cab SB	14409	15548	17445
2 Dr SLT 4WD Ext Cab SB	13917	15017	16849
2 Dr SLT 4WD Std Cab SB	12623	13621	15283
2 Dr SLT Ext Cab SB	11760	12689	14238
2 Dr SLT Plus 4WD Ext Cab SB	15069	16260	18244
2 Dr SLT Plus 4WD Std Cab SB	13573	14646	16433
2 Dr SLT Plus Ext Cab SB	12721	13726	15401
2 Dr SLT Plus Std Cab SB	11246	12135	13616
2 Dr SLT Std Cab SB	10273	11085	12438
2 Dr STD 4WD Ext Cab SB	13904	15002	16833
2 Dr STD 4WD Std Cab SB	11904	12845	14413
2 Dr STD Ext Cab SB	11713	12639	14181
2 Dr STD Std Cab SB	10160	10963	12301
2 Dr SXT 4WD Ext Cab SB	14312	15443	17327
2 Dr SXT 4WD Std Cab SB	13182	14223	15959
2 Dr SXT Ext Cab SB	12291	13262	14880
2 Dr SXT Std Cab SB	10447	11272	12648

Body Styles	TMV Pricing		
	Trade	Private	Dealer
2 Dr Sport 4WD Ext Cab SB	13918	15018	16850
2 Dr Sport 4WD Std Cab SB	12599	13595	15254
2 Dr Sport Ext Cab SB	11721	12647	14191
2 Dr Sport Plus 4WD Ext Cab SB	15082	16274	18260
2 Dr Sport Plus 4WD Std Cab SB	13643	14721	16517
2 Dr Sport Plus Ext Cab SB	12712	13716	15390
2 Dr Sport Plus Std Cab SB	11398	12298	13799
2 Dr Sport Std Cab SB	10652	11494	12896
4 Dr SLT 4WD Crew Cab SB	14924	16103	18068
4 Dr SLT Crew Cab SB	13117	14154	15881
4 Dr SLT Plus 4WD Crew Cab SB	16405	17701	19861
4 Dr SLT Plus Crew Cab SB	14280	15408	17289
4 Dr SXT 4WD Crew Cab SB	15133	16329	18322
4 Dr SXT Crew Cab SB	13516	14584	16364
4 Dr Sport 4WD Crew Cab SB	15044	16233	18214
4 Dr Sport Crew Cab SB	13174	14215	15950
4 Dr Sport Plus 4WD Crew Cab SB	16286	17573	19717
4 Dr Sport Plus Crew Cab SB	14286	15415	17296

Options	Price
Alarm System	+142
Antilock Brakes	+430
Automatic 4-Speed Transmission	+332
Automatic 5-Speed Transmission	+692
Camper/Towing Package	+174
Cruise Control [Opt on SLT,Sport]	+117
Infinity Audio System	+300
Leather Seats [Opt on R/T,Sport Plus,SLT Plus]	+303

Options	Price
Limited Slip Differential	+180
Power Door Locks [Opt on R/T,SLT,Sport]	+145
Power Driver Seat [Opt on SLT Plus,Sport Plus]	+202
Power Windows [Opt on R/T,SLT,Sport]	+180
Rear Window Defroster [Opt on Crew Cab,EXT Cab]	+145
Two-Tone Paint [Opt on SLT]	+123
AM/FM/CD Changer Audio System	+126
5.9L V8 OHV 16V FI Engine [Opt on Sport,SLT]	+404

2002

Mileage Category: J

A new value-priced Dakota SXT debuts and includes 16-inch alloys, automatic tranny, air conditioning, bucket seats and CD player. An appearance group consisting of graphite-colored bumpers, grille and fender flares is also fitted to the SXT.

Body Styles	TMV Pricing		
	Trade	Private	Dealer
2 Dr SLT 4WD Ext Cab SB	11232	12318	14128
2 Dr SLT 4WD Std Cab SB	10140	11120	12754
2 Dr SLT Ext Cab SB	9184	10072	11552
2 Dr SLT Plus 4WD Ext Cab SB	11806	12948	14850
2 Dr SLT Plus 4WD Std Cab SB	10697	11731	13454
2 Dr SLT Plus Ext Cab SB	10138	11118	12752
2 Dr SLT Plus Std Cab SB	8689	9529	10929
2 Dr SLT Std Cab SB	8089	8871	10174
2 Dr STD 4WD Ext Cab SB	11242	12329	14140
2 Dr STD 4WD Std Cab SB	9216	10107	11592
2 Dr STD Ext Cab SB	8637	9472	10863
2 Dr STD Std Cab SB	7044	7725	8860
2 Dr SXT 4WD Ext Cab SB	10996	12059	13831
2 Dr SXT 4WD Std Cab SB	9665	10599	12156
2 Dr SXT Ext Cab SB	9070	9947	11408
2 Dr SXT Std Cab SB	7798	8552	9808

Body Styles	TMV Pricing		
	Trade	Private	Dealer
2 Dr Sport 4WD Ext Cab SB	11165	12244	14043
2 Dr Sport 4WD Std Cab SB	10102	11079	12706
2 Dr Sport Ext Cab SB	8765	9613	11025
2 Dr Sport Plus 4WD Ext Cab SB	11726	12860	14749
2 Dr Sport Plus 4WD Std Cab SB	10825	11872	13616
2 Dr Sport Plus Ext Cab SB	9766	10710	12283
2 Dr Sport Plus Std Cab SB	8974	9842	11288
2 Dr Sport Std Cab SB	7795	8549	9805
4 Dr SLT 4WD Crew Cab SB	11922	13075	14996
4 Dr SLT Crew Cab SB	10520	11537	13232
4 Dr SLT Plus 4WD Crew Cab SB	13348	14638	16789
4 Dr SLT Plus Crew Cab SB	11290	12381	14200
4 Dr Sport 4WD Crew Cab SB	12136	13309	15265
4 Dr Sport Crew Cab SB	10647	11676	13392
4 Dr Sport Plus 4WD Crew Cab SB	13129	14398	16513
4 Dr Sport Plus Crew Cab SB	11313	12407	14230

Options	Price
16 Inch Wheels [Opt on SLT,SLT Plus]	+253
17 Inch Wheels [Opt on Sport Plus]	+381
3.9L V6 OHV 12V FI Engine [Opt on 2WD - Sport,STD]	+275
4.7L V8 SOHC 16V FI Engine	+321
5.9L V8 OHV 16V FI Engine	+612
Alarm System [Opt on SLT Plus,Sport Plus]	+122

Options	Price
Antilock Brakes	+370
Automatic 4-Speed Transmission	+530
Automatic 5-Speed Transmission	+530
Camper/Towing Package	+149
Infinity Audio System	+258
Leather Seats [Opt on Crew - SLT Plus,Sport Plus]	+315

Options	Price
Limited Slip Differential	+155
Power Door Locks [Opt on Crew - SLT,Sport]	+125
Power Driver Seat [Opt on SLT Plus,Sport Plus]	+174

Options	Price
Power Windows [Opt on Crew - SLT,Sport]	+141
Rear Window Defroster	+125
Sport Suspension [Opt on Sport Plus 2WD]	+163

2001

Body Styles	TMV Pricing		
	Trade	Private	Dealer
2 Dr SLT 4WD Ext Cab SB	9894	11354	12702
2 Dr SLT 4WD Std Cab SB	9147	10496	11742
2 Dr SLT Ext Cab SB	8192	9400	10516
2 Dr SLT Std Cab SB	7298	8375	9369
2 Dr STD 4WD Ext Cab SB	9697	11128	12448
2 Dr STD 4WD Std Cab SB	8020	9203	10295
2 Dr STD Ext Cab SB	7554	8668	9697
2 Dr STD Std Cab SB	6077	6973	7801

Body Styles	TMV Pricing		
	Trade	Private	Dealer
2 Dr Sport 4WD Ext Cab SB	9683	11112	12431
2 Dr Sport 4WD Std Cab SB	8731	10020	11209
2 Dr Sport Ext Cab SB	7960	9134	10218
2 Dr Sport Std Cab SB	6806	7810	8737
4 Dr SLT 4WD Crew Cab SB	11003	12626	14125
4 Dr SLT Crew Cab SB	9610	11028	12336
4 Dr Sport 4WD Crew Cab SB	10716	12297	13757
4 Dr Sport Crew Cab SB	9058	10394	11628

Mileage Category: J

The Dakota gets a redesigned interior with upgraded audio components, optional steering wheel controls, larger exterior mirrors and a redesigned front fascia on the Sport models. Four-wheel-drive models get a dash-mounted, electronically controlled transfer case. New 15x7-inch cast aluminum wheels are standard on Sport and SLT models, and a leather interior is now available in Quad Cab models. Quad Cabs also benefit from front seatbelt pre-tensioners, Club Cabs have added rear window defrost as an option, and Sentry Key Engine Immobilizer technology is now part of the optional security alarm system. Finally, the 3.9-liter V6, 4.7-liter V8 and 5.9-liter V8 engines meet low-emission-vehicle standards for 2001.

Options	Price
4.7L V8 SOHC 16V FI Engine	+294
5.9L V8 OHV 16V FI Engine	+561
Air Conditioning	+399
AM/FM/Cassette/CD Audio System	+329
AM/FM/CD Audio System	+239
Antilock Brakes	+339
Automatic 4-Speed Transmission	+486

Options	Price
Camper/Towing Package	+137
Leather Seats [Opt on Crew Cab]	+289
Limited Slip Differential	+142
Power Driver Seat	+160
Rear Window Defroster [Opt on SLT,Sport]	+115
Sport Suspension [Opt on SLT,Sport]	+175

2000

Body Styles	TMV Pricing		
	Trade	Private	Dealer
2 Dr R/T Sport Ext Cab SB	9946	11555	13133
2 Dr R/T Sport Std Cab SB	8280	9620	10933
2 Dr SLT 4WD Ext Cab SB	8750	10166	11554
2 Dr SLT 4WD Std Cab SB	8341	9691	11014
2 Dr SLT Ext Cab SB	7053	8194	9313
2 Dr SLT Plus 4WD Ext Cab SB	10066	11695	13292
2 Dr SLT Plus 4WD Std Cab SB	8684	10089	11467
2 Dr SLT Plus Ext Cab SB	8308	9652	10970
2 Dr SLT Plus Std Cab SB	6914	8033	9130
2 Dr SLT Std Cab SB	6201	7204	8188
2 Dr STD 4WD Ext Cab SB	8450	9818	11158
2 Dr STD 4WD Std Cab SB	6904	8021	9116
2 Dr STD Ext Cab SB	6630	7703	8755
2 Dr STD Std Cab SB	5299	6156	6997

Body Styles	TMV Pricing		
	Trade	Private	Dealer
2 Dr Sport 4WD Ext Cab SB	8857	10291	11696
2 Dr Sport 4WD Std Cab SB	7820	9086	10327
2 Dr Sport Ext Cab SB	7071	8215	9337
2 Dr Sport Plus 4WD Ext Cab SB	9435	10962	12459
2 Dr Sport Plus 4WD Std Cab SB	8337	9686	11009
2 Dr Sport Plus Ext Cab SB	7756	9011	10242
2 Dr Sport Plus Std Cab SB	6076	7059	8023
2 Dr Sport Std Cab SB	5842	6787	7714
4 Dr SLT 4WD Crew Cab SB	10172	11819	13433
4 Dr SLT Crew Cab SB	8549	9932	11288
4 Dr SLT Plus 4WD Crew Cab SB	11093	12888	14648
4 Dr SLT Plus Crew Cab SB	8785	10207	11600
4 Dr Sport 4WD Crew Cab SB	10125	11763	13369
4 Dr Sport Plus Crew Cab SB	8587	9977	11339

Mileage Category: J

The biggest change this year is design oriented -- the Dakota is now available with four full-size doors, and with that comes a family name: Quad Cab. A 4.7-liter V8 has been added, but the 8-foot bed is gone. You can select from five more colors as well.

Options	Price
AM/FM/CD Audio System	+127
Antilock Brakes	+307
Automatic 4-Speed Transmission [Std on R/T Sport - Ext Cab,Std Cab]	+441
Compact Disc Changer	+181
Limited Slip Differential [Std on R/T Sport - Ext Cab,Std Cab]	+129
Power Driver Seat	+145

Options	Price
AM/FM/Cassette/CD Audio System	+163
3.9L V6 OHV 12V FI Engine [Opt on Std Cab]	+253
4.7L V8 SOHC 16V FI Engine	+239
5.9L V8 OHV 16V FI Engine [Std on R/T Sport]	+508
Air Conditioning	+361

1999

Body Styles	TMV Pricing		
	Trade	Private	Dealer
2 Dr R/T Sport Ext Cab SB	8162	9622	11141
2 Dr R/T Sport Std Cab SB	6930	8170	9460

Body Styles	TMV Pricing		
	Trade	Private	Dealer
2 Dr SLT 4WD Ext Cab SB	7363	8680	10051
2 Dr SLT 4WD Std Cab SB	6965	8211	9507

Mileage Category: J

Solar Yellow paint is now available. Other un-pickuplike refinements include an express down feature for the driver window, extra storage space for cassettes or CDs, and remote radio controls on the steering wheel.

Dodge
Dakota

1999 (cont'd)

Mileage Category: J

Solar Yellow paint is now available. Other un-pickuplike refinements include an express down feature for the driver window, extra storage space for cassettes or CDs, and remote radio controls on the steering wheel.

Body Styles	TMV Pricing		
	Trade	Private	Dealer
2 Dr SLT Ext Cab SB	6019	7096	8216
2 Dr SLT Std Cab LB	5717	6739	7803
2 Dr SLT Std Cab SB	5562	6557	7593
2 Dr STD 4WD Ext Cab SB	7070	8334	9650
2 Dr STD 4WD Std Cab SB	5972	7040	8152
2 Dr STD Ext Cab SB	5876	6927	8021
2 Dr STD Std Cab LB	5256	6196	7174

Body Styles	TMV Pricing		
	Trade	Private	Dealer
2 Dr STD Std Cab SB	4520	5329	6170
2 Dr Sport 4WD Ext Cab SB	7061	8324	9638
2 Dr Sport 4WD Std Cab SB	6301	7428	8601
2 Dr Sport Ext Cab SB	5833	6876	7962
2 Dr Sport Std Cab LB	5534	6524	7554
2 Dr Sport Std Cab SB	5292	6238	7223

Options	Price
5.2L V8 OHV 16V FI Engine	+217
Air Conditioning [Std on SLT]	+295
AM/FM/Cassette/CD Audio System	+243
AM/FM/CD Audio System	+177

Options	Price
Antilock Brakes	+278
Automatic 4-Speed Transmission [Std on R/T Sport]	+399
Compact Disc Changer	+276
Power Driver Seat	+118

1998

Mileage Category: J

The Dakota R/T, featuring a 250-horsepower V8, is available for those seeking a performance pickup. The passenger airbag can now be deactivated in all Dakotas, so a rear-facing child seat can be used. The Dakota is also available in three new colors.

Body Styles	TMV Pricing		
	Trade	Private	Dealer
2 Dr R/T Sport Ext Cab SB	6119	7422	8891
2 Dr R/T Sport Std Cab SB	5113	6202	7430
2 Dr SLT 4WD Ext Cab SB	6220	7544	9038
2 Dr SLT 4WD Std Cab SB	5583	6772	8113
2 Dr SLT Ext Cab SB	5258	6378	7641
2 Dr SLT Std Cab LB	4660	5653	6772
2 Dr SLT Std Cab SB	4505	5465	6547
2 Dr STD 4WD Ext Cab SB	5968	7239	8673
2 Dr STD 4WD Std Cab SB	5249	6367	7628

Body Styles	TMV Pricing		
	Trade	Private	Dealer
2 Dr STD Ext Cab SB	4768	5784	6929
2 Dr STD Std Cab LB	4193	5086	6093
2 Dr STD Std Cab SB	3786	4593	5502
2 Dr Sport 4WD Ext Cab SB	6307	7650	9165
2 Dr Sport 4WD Std Cab SB	5413	6566	7866
2 Dr Sport Ext Cab SB	4922	5970	7153
2 Dr Sport Std Cab LB	4453	5401	6470
2 Dr Sport Std Cab SB	4272	5181	6207

Options	Price
3.9L V6 OHV 12V FI Engine [Opt on Std Cab RWD - SLT,Sport,STD]	+181
5.2L V8 OHV 16V FI Engine	+214
Air Conditioning [Std on SLT]	+261
AM/FM/Cassette/CD Audio System	+215

Options	Price
AM/FM/CD Audio System	+156
Antilock Brakes	+246
Automatic 4-Speed Transmission [Std on R/T Sport]	+344

1997

Mileage Category: J

Powertrains are carried over, but everything else is new. Distinctions? Tightest turning circle in class, roomiest cabs and dual airbags are standard. Faux pas? No third door option, and the passenger airbag cannot be deactivated, so a rear-facing child seat is out of the question unless you cram it into the rear of the Club Cab.

Body Styles	TMV Pricing		
	Trade	Private	Dealer
2 Dr SLT 4WD Ext Cab SB	5625	6962	8596
2 Dr SLT 4WD Std Cab SB	4981	6165	7612
2 Dr SLT Ext Cab SB	4456	5515	6810
2 Dr SLT Std Cab LB	4018	4973	6140
2 Dr SLT Std Cab SB	3619	4479	5530
2 Dr STD 4WD Ext Cab SB	5249	6497	8022
2 Dr STD 4WD Std Cab SB	4402	5448	6727
2 Dr STD Ext Cab SB	4251	5262	6497

Body Styles	TMV Pricing		
	Trade	Private	Dealer
2 Dr STD Std Cab LB	3481	4309	5320
2 Dr STD Std Cab SB	3308	4095	5056
2 Dr Sport 4WD Ext Cab SB	5331	6598	8147
2 Dr Sport 4WD Std Cab SB	4811	5954	7352
2 Dr Sport Ext Cab SB	4069	5036	6218
2 Dr Sport Std Cab LB	3532	4372	5398
2 Dr Sport Std Cab SB	3505	4338	5356

Options	Price
3.9L V6 OHV 12V FI Engine	+223
5.2L V8 OHV 16V FI Engine	+187
Air Conditioning [Std on SLT]	+229
AM/FM/Cassette/CD Audio System	+189

Options	Price
AM/FM/CD Audio System	+138
Antilock Brakes	+217
Automatic 4-Speed Transmission	+279

1996

Mileage Category: J

America's first midsized pickup gets a more powerful standard four-cylinder engine, revised sound system, and three new colors.

Body Styles	TMV Pricing		
	Trade	Private	Dealer
2 Dr SLT 4WD Ext Cab SB	4398	5519	7066
2 Dr SLT 4WD Std Cab LB	4212	5285	6767

Body Styles	TMV Pricing		
	Trade	Private	Dealer
2 Dr SLT 4WD Std Cab SB	4034	5062	6481
2 Dr SLT Ext Cab SB	3387	4250	5442

1996 (cont'd)

Body Styles	TMV Pricing		
	Trade	Private	Dealer
2 Dr SLT Std Cab LB	3247	4074	5216
2 Dr SLT Std Cab SB	3068	3850	4929
2 Dr STD 4WD Ext Cab SB	4247	5329	6822
2 Dr STD 4WD Std Cab LB	3842	4820	6171
2 Dr STD 4WD Std Cab SB	3756	4713	6034
2 Dr STD Ext Cab SB	3316	4160	5326
2 Dr STD Std Cab LB	2562	3214	4115
2 Dr STD Std Cab SB	2760	3463	4434

Body Styles	TMV Pricing		
	Trade	Private	Dealer
2 Dr Sport 4WD Ext Cab SB	4134	5187	6641
2 Dr Sport 4WD Std Cab SB	3711	4656	5962
2 Dr Sport Ext Cab SB	3294	4133	5292
2 Dr Sport Std Cab SB	2620	3287	4209
2 Dr WS 4WD Std Cab LB	3453	4332	5547
2 Dr WS 4WD Std Cab SB	3312	4156	5321
2 Dr WS Std Cab LB	2373	2977	3812
2 Dr WS Std Cab SB	2293	2877	3683

Options	Price
3.9L V6 OHV 12V FI Engine	+203
5.2L V8 OHV 16V FI Engine	+170
Air Conditioning [Std on SLT]	+208

Options	Price
AM/FM/CD Audio System	+125
Antilock Brakes	+197
Automatic 4-Speed Transmission	+269

1995

Body Styles	TMV Pricing		
	Trade	Private	Dealer
2 Dr SLT 4WD Ext Cab SB	3294	4241	5819
2 Dr SLT 4WD Std Cab LB	3069	3951	5421
2 Dr SLT 4WD Std Cab SB	3005	3869	5308
2 Dr SLT Ext Cab SB	2616	3368	4622
2 Dr SLT Std Cab LB	2482	3195	4384
2 Dr SLT Std Cab SB	2192	2822	3872
2 Dr STD 4WD Ext Cab SB	3213	4137	5677
2 Dr STD 4WD Std Cab LB	2998	3860	5297
2 Dr STD 4WD Std Cab SB	2932	3775	5180
2 Dr STD Ext Cab SB	2573	3313	4546

Body Styles	TMV Pricing		
	Trade	Private	Dealer
2 Dr STD Std Cab LB	2067	2661	3651
2 Dr STD Std Cab SB	2112	2719	3731
2 Dr Sport 4WD Ext Cab SB	3049	3926	5387
2 Dr Sport 4WD Std Cab SB	2889	3720	5105
2 Dr Sport Ext Cab SB	2437	3138	4306
2 Dr Sport Std Cab SB	1888	2431	3335
2 Dr WS 4WD Std Cab LB	2900	3733	5122
2 Dr WS 4WD Std Cab SB	2573	3313	4545
2 Dr WS Std Cab LB	2014	2593	3558
2 Dr WS Std Cab SB	1851	2383	3270

Options	Price
3.9L V6 OHV 12V FI Engine	+127
5.2L V8 OHV 16V FI Engine	+149
Air Conditioning [Std on SLT]	+182

Options	Price
AM/FM/CD Audio System	+110
Antilock Brakes	+172
Automatic 4-Speed Transmission	+235

Mileage Category: J

A 2WD Club Cab Sport is added to the model mix.

1994

Body Styles	TMV Pricing		
	Trade	Private	Dealer
2 Dr SLT 4WD Ext Cab SB	2383	3247	4686
2 Dr SLT 4WD Std Cab LB	2177	2966	4281
2 Dr SLT 4WD Std Cab SB	2143	2919	4213
2 Dr SLT Ext Cab SB	1937	2639	3809
2 Dr SLT Std Cab LB	1663	2266	3270
2 Dr SLT Std Cab SB	1537	2094	3022
2 Dr STD 4WD Ext Cab SB	2263	3083	4450
2 Dr STD 4WD Std Cab LB	2092	2850	4114
2 Dr STD 4WD Std Cab SB	2005	2732	3943
2 Dr STD Ext Cab SB	1816	2474	3570

Body Styles	TMV Pricing		
	Trade	Private	Dealer
2 Dr STD Std Cab LB	1550	2112	3048
2 Dr STD Std Cab SB	1454	1981	2859
2 Dr Sport 4WD Ext Cab SB	2193	2988	4313
2 Dr Sport 4WD Std Cab SB	1984	2704	3903
2 Dr Sport Ext Cab SB	1782	2428	3505
2 Dr Sport Std Cab SB	1366	1861	2686
2 Dr WS 4WD Std Cab LB	1920	2616	3775
2 Dr WS 4WD Std Cab SB	1890	2575	3717
2 Dr WS Std Cab LB	1474	2009	2900
2 Dr WS Std Cab SB	1210	1648	2379

Options	Price
3.9L V6 OHV 12V FI Engine [Std on 4WD,LB]	+113
5.2L V8 OHV 16V FI Engine	+110
Air Conditioning [Opt on Sport,STD,WS]	+153

Options	Price
Antilock Brakes	+145
Automatic 4-Speed Transmission	+191
Driver Side Airbag Restraint	+77

Mileage Category: J

Driver airbag is added, along with side-door guard beams. LE trim level now called SLT. A strengthened roof now meets passenger car crush standards. The 5.2-liter V8 loses horsepower but gains torque.

Dodge
Durango

2003

Mileage Category: M

Entry-level Sport model gets bigger wheels (16s versus last year's 15s) and all Durangos now have four-wheel disc brakes. Inside, you'll find a six-disc CD changer as a new option. A redesign is due for 2004.

Body Styles	TMV Pricing		
	Trade	Private	Dealer
4 Dr R/T 4WD SUV	21126	22596	25047
4 Dr SLT 4WD SUV	18020	19274	21365
4 Dr SLT Plus 4WD SUV	19816	21196	23495
4 Dr SLT Plus SUV	18728	20032	22204
4 Dr SLT SUV	16118	17240	19110

Body Styles	TMV Pricing		
	Trade	Private	Dealer
4 Dr SXT 4WD SUV	15970	17081	18934
4 Dr SXT SUV	14937	15977	17710
4 Dr Sport 4WD SUV	15498	16577	18375
4 Dr Sport SUV	14624	15642	17338

Options	Price
Antilock Brakes	+430
Camper/Towing Package	+373
Infinity Audio System [Opt on SLT]	+338
Leather Seats [Opt on SLT]	+502
Limited Slip Differential [Std on R/T]	+180

Options	Price
Running Boards [Opt on SLT]	+250
Third Seat [Opt on SXT]	+423
Air Conditioning - Front and Rear [Opt on SXT]	+385
Front Head Airbag Restraints	+313

2002

Mileage Category: M

Like its sibling, the Dakota, the Durango gets a new trim level dubbed SXT that serves as the entry-level Durango. Other improvements this year include side-curtain airbags, a five-speed automatic gearbox and an optional DVD video entertainment system.

Body Styles	TMV Pricing		
	Trade	Private	Dealer
4 Dr R/T 4WD SUV	17382	18777	21103
4 Dr SLT 4WD SUV	14791	15978	17957
4 Dr SLT Plus 4WD SUV	16343	17655	19841
4 Dr SLT Plus SUV	15484	16727	18799
4 Dr SLT SUV	13780	14886	16731

Body Styles	TMV Pricing		
	Trade	Private	Dealer
4 Dr SXT 4WD SUV	13502	14587	16394
4 Dr SXT SUV	12378	13372	15028
4 Dr Sport 4WD SUV	13048	14096	15842
4 Dr Sport SUV	12112	13079	14690

Options	Price
5.9L V8 OHV 16V FI Engine [Opt on SLT,SLT Plus]	+323
Antilock Brakes	+370
Camper/Towing Package	+253
Front and Rear Head Airbag Restraints	+269

Options	Price
Infinity Audio System [Opt on SLT]	+291
Leather Seats [Opt on SLT]	+432
Limited Slip Differential	+155
Running Boards [Opt on SXT,SLT]	+215

2001

Mileage Category: M

Dodge's brute of a midsize 'ute receives numerous improvements for 2001. An electronic transfer case for its four-wheel drive system is now standard on 4WD models. A new instrument panel, center console with cupholders, interior trim and upgraded stereo has been added, and a tilt steering column is now standard on all Durangos. The 5.2-liter V8 engine is dropped, leaving the more efficient 4.7-liter V8 as standard equipment in both 4x2 and 4x4 Durangos. A variable-delay intermittent rear wiper is offered, and auto-dimming, heated outside power mirrors can be had on in SLT trim. A new appearance option group for the SLT includes 16-inch aluminum wheels, along with special body side moldings, running boards and lower panels. New 15-inch Sparkle Silver aluminum wheels are standard across the Durango lineup.

Body Styles	TMV Pricing		
	Trade	Private	Dealer
4 Dr SLT 4WD SUV	13001	14675	16221
4 Dr SLT SUV	11591	13084	14462

Body Styles	TMV Pricing		
	Trade	Private	Dealer
4 Dr Sport 4WD SUV	11819	13342	14748
4 Dr Sport SUV	10884	12286	13580

Options	Price
5.9L V8 OHV 16V FI Engine [Opt on SLT]	+296
Air Conditioning - Front and Rear	+399
AM/FM/Cassette/CD Audio System	+150
Antilock Brakes	+339
Camper/Towing Package	+137

Options	Price
Heated Front Seats [Opt on SLT]	+137
Leather Seats	+299
Limited Slip Differential	+142
Power Passenger Seat [Opt on SLT]	+224
Third Seat	+249

2000

Mileage Category: M

The next-generation 4.7-liter V8 is now available on four-wheel-drive models and is linked to an all-new automatic transmission. Rack-and-pinion steering becomes standard for both two- and four-wheel-drives. A performance-oriented R/T model has been added to the lineup that already includes the SLT and the decked-out SLT Plus.

Body Styles	TMV Pricing		
	Trade	Private	Dealer
4 Dr R/T 4WD SUV	13721	15516	17276
4 Dr SLT 4WD SUV	11080	12530	13951
4 Dr SLT Plus 4WD SUV	13388	15139	16855
4 Dr SLT Plus SUV	11332	12815	14268

Body Styles	TMV Pricing		
	Trade	Private	Dealer
4 Dr SLT SUV	9744	11019	12269
4 Dr Sport 4WD SUV	10234	11573	12886
4 Dr Sport SUV	9695	10963	12206

Options	Price
5.9L V8 OHV 16V FI Engine [Std on R/T 4WD Wgn]	+268
Air Conditioning - Front and Rear	+194
AM/FM/Cassette/CD Audio System [Std on R/T 4WD Wgn]	+136
Antilock Brakes	+307
Camper/Towing Package	+124

Options	Price
Infinity Audio System [Std on R/T 4WD Wgn]	+149
Limited Slip Differential	+129
Running Boards [Opt on SLT]	+178
Third Seat	+249

1999

Body Styles	TMV Pricing		
	Trade	Private	Dealer
4 Dr SLT 4WD SUV	9266	10745	12284
4 Dr SLT SUV	8455	9804	11208

Options	Price
5.9L V8 OHV 16V FI Engine	+219
Air Conditioning - Front and Rear	+176
Antilock Brakes	+278
Infinity Audio System	+122

Options	Price
Leather Seats	+247
Power Driver Seat	+118
Third Seat	+203

Mileage Category: M

Two-wheel drive models finally show up for true flatlander use, and all Durangos gain a rear power outlet. Also available are steering wheel-mounted radio controls, heated mirrors, and two new colors: Bright Platinum Metallic and Patriot Blue.

1998

Body Styles	TMV Pricing		
	Trade	Private	Dealer
4 Dr SLT 4WD SUV	8603	9935	11437
4 Dr STD 4WD SUV	8579	9908	11406

Options	Price
5.9L V8 OHV 16V FI Engine	+129
Air Conditioning - Front and Rear	+140
Antilock Brakes	+246

Options	Price
Leather Seats	+218
Third Seat	+180

Mileage Category: M

As the most recent addition to the Dodge truck lineup, the Durango makes quite an entry. Offering the most cargo space in its class, along with eight-passenger seating and three-and-a-half tons of towing capacity, the Durango is the most versatile sport-utility on the market.

Dodge
Grand Caravan

2003

Body Styles	TMV Pricing		
	Trade	Private	Dealer
4 Dr ES AWD Pass Van Ext	18490	19960	22409
4 Dr ES Pass Van Ext	18271	19723	22144
4 Dr SE Pass Van Ext	12364	13347	14984
4 Dr Sport AWD Pass Van Ext	16672	17997	20206

Body Styles	TMV Pricing		
	Trade	Private	Dealer
4 Dr Sport Pass Van Ext	14851	16032	17999
4 Dr eL Pass Van Ext	13165	14211	15955
4 Dr eX Pass Van Ext	14478	15629	17546

Options	Price
Alarm System [Opt on CV,ES]	+123
AM/FM/Cassette/CD Audio System [Opt on SE,Sport]	+142
Automatic Load Leveling [Opt on ES,SE,Sport]	+190
Camper/Towing Package [Opt on ES,Sport]	+224
Compact Disc Changer [Opt on ES,Sport]	+126
Cruise Control [Opt on CV,SE]	+117
Heated Front Seats [Opt on ES]	+158
Leather Seats [Opt on ES,EX]	+521
Power Door Locks [Opt on CV,SE]	+142
Power Driver Seat [Opt on SE,Sport]	+234
Power Dual Sliding Doors [Opt on eX]	+253

Options	Price
Power Moonroof [Opt on ES]	+565
Power Sliding Door [Opt on eL,Sport]	+253
Power Windows [Opt on CV,SE]	+164
Front Side Airbag Restraints	+246
Special Factory Paint	+126
Power Rear Liftgate [Opt on eL,Sport]	+253
Power Adjustable Foot Pedals	+117
Air Conditioning - Front and Rear [Opt on SE]	+174
Automatic Climate Control (3 Zone) [Opt on SE]	+237
DVD Entertainment System [Opt on ES,eX,Sport]	+569
3.8L V6 OHV 12V FI Engine [Opt on eL,Sport]	+212

Mileage Category: P

Two new options debut, a power sunroof (that Dodge boasts as one of the largest available in a minivan) and a factory-, not dealer-, installed DVD entertainment system that comes with wireless headphones. Audiophiles will appreciate the CD changer being upgraded from four-disc capacity to six.

2002

Body Styles	TMV Pricing		
	Trade	Private	Dealer
4 Dr ES AWD Pass Van Ext	15420	16866	19276
4 Dr ES Pass Van Ext	13697	14981	17122
4 Dr SE Pass Van Ext	10167	11121	12710
4 Dr Sport AWD Pass Van Ext	13852	15151	17316

Body Styles	TMV Pricing		
	Trade	Private	Dealer
4 Dr Sport Pass Van Ext	11358	12423	14199
4 Dr eL Pass Van Ext	10903	11926	13630
4 Dr eX Pass Van Ext	12064	13195	15081

Options	Price
16 Inch Wheels [Opt on Sport 2WD]	+149
17 Inch Wheels - Chrome [Opt on ES FWD]	+299
Air Conditioning - Front and Rear [Opt on SE,Sport FWD]	+353

Options	Price
AM/FM/Cassette/CD Audio System [Opt on Sport]	+122
AM/FM/CD Audio System [Opt on SE]	+122
Automatic Load Leveling [Opt on FWD - ES,Sport]	+163

Mileage Category: P

Dodge brings out the Caravan eL, a value leader that lists for around $24,000. The luxury factor on higher-line trims is boosted with the availability of power adjustable pedals, rear-seat audio with wireless headsets and the coupe de grace: a DVD video system for the rear seat, which also includes wireless headsets.

Grand Caravan

2002 (cont'd)

Options	Price
Captain Chairs (4) [Opt on Sport]	+405
Center and Rear Bench Seat [Opt on Sport 2WD]	+122
Child Seats (2) [Opt on SE,Sport FWD]	+122
Front Side Airbag Restraints	+212
Heated Front Seats [Opt on ES]	+136
Infinity Audio System [Opt on Sport]	+269
Leather Seats [Opt on ES,eX]	+448
Power Door Locks [Opt on SE]	+122

Options	Price
Power Driver Seat [Opt on Sport]	+130
Power Dual Sliding Doors [Opt on eX]	+217
Power Rear Liftgate [Opt on ES,Sport]	+217
Power Sliding Door [Opt on eL,Sport FWD]	+217
Power Windows [Opt on SE]	+141
Temperature Controls - Driver and Passenger [Opt on SE,Sport FWD]	+177

2001

Mileage Category: P

America's best-selling minivan is all new for 2001, with many industry-first features including a power rear tailgate, a power sliding door obstacle detection system, a removable and powered center console and a pop-up rear cargo organizer, all residing under new sheet metal.

Body Styles	TMV Pricing		
	Trade	Private	Dealer
4 Dr ES AWD Pass Van Ext	12518	14412	16160
4 Dr ES Pass Van Ext	11183	12875	14436
4 Dr EX Pass Van Ext	10378	11948	13397

Body Styles	TMV Pricing		
	Trade	Private	Dealer
4 Dr SE Pass Van Ext	8518	9807	10996
4 Dr Sport AWD Pass Van Ext	12135	13970	15664
4 Dr Sport Pass Van Ext	9484	10918	12242

Options	Price
17 Inch Wheels - Chrome [Opt on ES]	+339
3.8L V6 OHV 12V FI Engine [Std on AWD]	+167
Air Conditioning - Front and Rear [Opt on Sport]	+274
Aluminum/Alloy Wheels	+339
Automatic Climate Control (3 Zone) [Opt on Sport]	+200
Automatic Load Leveling	+145
Camper/Towing Package [Opt on ES,Sport]	+304
Front Side Airbag Restraints	+195
Heated Front Seats [Opt on ES]	+125

Options	Price
Infinity Audio System [Opt on Sport]	+247
Leather Seats [Opt on ES]	+623
Power Driver Seat [Opt on Sport]	+185
Power Heated Mirrors [Opt on SE]	+125
Power Rear Liftgate [Opt on ES,Sport]	+200
Power Sliding Door [Opt on Sport]	+192
Power Windows [Opt on SE]	+130
Rear Window Defroster [Opt on SE]	+115

2000

Mileage Category: P

New colors, more standard equipment, and an AWD Sport model keep Chrysler's best-selling minivans up to date until the redesigned 2001 model arrive

Body Styles	TMV Pricing		
	Trade	Private	Dealer
4 Dr ES AWD Pass Van Ext	9642	11344	13013
4 Dr ES Pass Van Ext	8737	10280	11792
4 Dr LE AWD Pass Van Ext	9079	10682	12253
4 Dr LE Pass Van Ext	8504	10005	11477

Body Styles	TMV Pricing		
	Trade	Private	Dealer
4 Dr SE Pass Van Ext	6672	7850	9005
4 Dr STD Pass Van Ext	6291	7401	8490
4 Dr Sport AWD Pass Van Ext	8585	10101	11586

Options	Price
3.3L V6 OHV 12V FI Engine [Opt on FWD - LE,SE,STD]	+438
3.8L V6 OHV 12V FI Engine [Opt on LE FWD]	+230
Air Conditioning - Front and Rear [Opt on ES,SE,Sport]	+271
Aluminum/Alloy Wheels [Opt on LE,SE,Sport]	+119
AM/FM/Cassette/CD Audio System	+140
Antilock Brakes [Opt on STD]	+310
Automatic Load Leveling [Opt on FWD]	+131

Options	Price
Captain Chairs (4)	+270
Infinity Audio System [Opt on SE,Sport]	+326
Leather Seats [Opt on LE,ES]	+359
Power Door Locks [Opt on STD]	+152
Power Driver Seat [Opt on SE,Sport]	+126
Power Passenger Seat [Opt on ES]	+172
Power Windows [Opt on STD]	+117

1999

Mileage Category: P

A revised front fascia is common to all models. The Grand Caravan ES gets an AutoStick transmission, 17-inch wheels and tires, and steering wheel-mounted radio controls.

Body Styles	TMV Pricing		
	Trade	Private	Dealer
4 Dr ES AWD Pass Van Ext	7938	9535	11198
4 Dr ES Pass Van Ext	7245	8703	10220
4 Dr LE AWD Pass Van Ext	7747	9306	10929
4 Dr LE Pass Van Ext	6883	8268	9710

Body Styles	TMV Pricing		
	Trade	Private	Dealer
4 Dr SE AWD Pass Van Ext	6788	8154	9576
4 Dr SE Pass Van Ext	5492	6597	7748
4 Dr STD Pass Van Ext	5198	6244	7332

Options	Price
Air Conditioning	+184
Air Conditioning - Front and Rear	+255
3.8L V6 OHV 12V FI Engine	+170
Aluminum/Alloy Wheels	+153

Options	Price
AM/FM/Cassette/CD Audio System	+120
AM/FM/CD Audio System [Opt on STD]	+120
Antilock Brakes	+281
Automatic Load Leveling [Opt on STD AWD]	+119

1999 (cont'd)

Options	Price
Camper/Towing Package	+155
Captain Chairs (4)	+247
Compact Disc Changer	+166
Infinity Audio System [Opt on SE]	+265

Options	Price
Leather Seats	+328
Power Passenger Seat [Opt on ES]	+131
3.0L V6 SOHC 12V FI Engine	+295
3.3L V6 OHV 12V FI Engine	+357

1998

Body Styles	TMV Pricing		
	Trade	Private	Dealer
4 Dr ES AWD Pass Van Ext	6463	7972	9674
4 Dr ES Pass Van Ext	5806	7161	8690
4 Dr LE AWD Pass Van Ext	6452	7959	9658
4 Dr LE Pass Van Ext	5795	7148	8674

Body Styles	TMV Pricing		
	Trade	Private	Dealer
4 Dr SE AWD Pass Van Ext	5777	7126	8648
4 Dr SE Pass Van Ext	4418	5450	6613
4 Dr STD Pass Van Ext	4178	5154	6254

Options	Price
3.8L V6 OHV 12V FI Engine [Opt on FWD]	+122
Air Conditioning [Opt on STD,SE]	+281
Air Conditioning - Front and Rear	+290
AM/FM/Cassette/CD Audio System	+129

Options	Price
Antilock Brakes [Opt on STD]	+248
Captain Chairs (4) [Opt on ES,LE,SE]	+218
Infinity Audio System [Opt on SE]	+129
Leather Seats [Opt on ES,LE]	+259

Mileage Category: P

Available this year is a 3.8-liter V6 that puts out 180 horsepower and 240 pound-feet of torque. Caravans come with rear-seat mounted grocery bag hooks, and driver-side easy-entry Quad seating. All Chrysler products are equipped with "Next Generation" depowered airbags.

1997

Body Styles	TMV Pricing		
	Trade	Private	Dealer
3 Dr SE AWD Pass Van Ext	4430	5623	7081
3 Dr SE Pass Van Ext	3533	4485	5648
3 Dr STD Pass Van Ext	3266	4146	5221
4 Dr ES AWD Pass Van Ext	5150	6537	8232

Body Styles	TMV Pricing		
	Trade	Private	Dealer
4 Dr ES Pass Van Ext	4586	5821	7331
4 Dr LE AWD Pass Van Ext	5134	6517	8208
4 Dr LE Pass Van Ext	4571	5802	7307

Options	Price
Air Conditioning [Opt on SE,STD]	+247
Air Conditioning - Front and Rear [Opt on ES,LE,SE]	+255
Antilock Brakes [Opt on STD]	+219
Captain Chairs (4) [Opt on ES,LE,SE]	+171

Options	Price
Compact Disc Changer [Opt on ES]	+158
Leather Seats [Opt on ES,LE]	+228
Sliding Driver Side Door [Opt on SE,STD]	+171
Sport Package [Opt on SE]	+355

Mileage Category: P

After a one year hiatus, all-wheel drive returns to the lineup, available on SE and LE models. Traction control is newly available, and an enhanced accident response system will automatically unlock the doors and illuminate the interior when an airbag deployment is detected. A Sport decor group is newly available on Grand Caravan SE.

1996

Body Styles	TMV Pricing		
	Trade	Private	Dealer
3 Dr ES Pass Van Ext	3557	4618	6082
3 Dr LE Pass Van Ext	3442	4468	5885

Body Styles	TMV Pricing		
	Trade	Private	Dealer
3 Dr SE Pass Van Ext	3004	3899	5136
3 Dr STD Pass Van Ext	2703	3509	4623

Options	Price
3.0L V6 SOHC 12V FI Engine [Opt on STD]	+201
3.3L V6 OHV 12V FI Engine [Opt on SE]	+232
Air Conditioning [Opt on SE,STD]	+225
Air Conditioning - Front and Rear [Opt on ES,LE,SE]	+232

Options	Price
Antilock Brakes [Opt on STD]	+199
Captain Chairs (4) [Opt on ES,LE,SE]	+163
Leather Seats [Opt on ES,LE]	+208
Sliding Driver Side Door	+156

Mileage Category: P

A complete redesign yields a cavernous interior, best-in-class driveability and new innovations such as the optional driver-side passenger door. And although the all-wheel-drive version is discontinued for now, Caravan dethrones the Ford Windstar and once again reigns as king of the minivans.

1995

Body Styles	TMV Pricing		
	Trade	Private	Dealer
3 Dr ES AWD Pass Van Ext	2572	3441	4889
3 Dr ES Pass Van Ext	2477	3313	4707
3 Dr LE AWD Pass Van Ext	2549	3410	4845
3 Dr LE Pass Van Ext	2358	3154	4481

Body Styles	TMV Pricing		
	Trade	Private	Dealer
3 Dr SE AWD Pass Van Ext	2288	3061	4348
3 Dr SE Pass Van Ext	2166	2898	4117
3 Dr STD Pass Van Ext	1949	2607	3703

Options	Price
3.8L V6 OHV 12V FI Engine [Opt on ES,LE]	+85
Air Conditioning [Opt on SE,STD]	+196
Air Conditioning - Front and Rear	+159
Antilock Brakes [Opt on SE,STD]	+174

Options	Price
Captain Chairs (4) [Opt on ES,LE,SE]	+136
Infinity Audio System [Opt on ES,SE]	+77
Leather Seats [Opt on ES,LE]	+182

Mileage Category: P

Newly optional is a 3.3-liter V6 engine designed to operate on compressed natural gas, and new Sport and SE decor packages are available this year.

Dodge
Grand Caravan/Intrepid

1994

Mileage Category: P

A passenger airbag is added to a redesigned dashboard, and new side-door guard beams meet 1997 passenger car safety standards. Bumpers are restyled, and seats with integrated child seats can be reclined for the first time.

Body Styles	TMV Pricing		
	Trade	Private	Dealer
3 Dr ES AWD Pass Van Ext	1866	2635	3916
3 Dr ES Pass Van Ext	1773	2503	3720
3 Dr LE AWD Pass Van Ext	1777	2509	3729
3 Dr LE Pass Van Ext	1756	2480	3686

Body Styles	TMV Pricing		
	Trade	Private	Dealer
3 Dr SE AWD Pass Van Ext	1676	2367	3518
3 Dr SE Pass Van Ext	1620	2287	3399
3 Dr STD Pass Van Ext	1583	2235	3322

Options	Price
Air Conditioning [Opt on SE,STD]	+165
Air Conditioning - Front and Rear	+133
AM/FM/Cassette/CD Audio System [Opt on STD]	+76

Options	Price
Antilock Brakes	+146
Captain Chairs (4) [Opt on ES,LE,SE]	+114
Leather Seats [Opt on ES,LE]	+153

Dodge
Intrepid

2003

Mileage Category: G

The high-performance R/T model is dropped, although the new SXT offers virtually all of the go-fast goodies, including the 244-horsepower V6 and firmer suspension tuning. Music buffs will appreciate the new six-disc CD changer that replaces the former four-disc unit.

Body Styles	TMV Pricing		
	Trade	Private	Dealer
4 Dr ES Sdn	12637	13903	16014
4 Dr SE Sdn	9864	10853	12501

Body Styles	TMV Pricing		
	Trade	Private	Dealer
4 Dr SXT Sdn	12480	13731	15816

Options	Price
Aluminum/Alloy Wheels [Opt on ES,SE]	+186
Antilock Brakes	+490
Compact Disc Changer	+268
Cruise Control [Opt on SE]	+117
Power Driver Seat [Opt on SE]	+152

Options	Price
Power Moonroof	+565
Front Side Airbag Restraints	+246
Special Factory Paint	+126
Split Folding Rear Seat [Opt on SE]	+133

2002

Mileage Category: G

A few functional upgrades take place. The 3.2-liter V6 is dropped as the 3.5-liter engine becomes an option on the ES model, a new SXT model debuts, sporting the R/T's higher-output engine, and the antilock brakes now have Electronic Brakeforce Distribution.

Body Styles	TMV Pricing		
	Trade	Private	Dealer
4 Dr ES Sdn	9764	10799	12525
4 Dr R/T Sdn	11488	12706	14735

Body Styles	TMV Pricing		
	Trade	Private	Dealer
4 Dr SE Sdn	8052	8906	10328
4 Dr SXT Sdn	10432	11538	13382

Options	Price
16 Inch Wheels [Opt on SE]	+160
AM/FM/Cassette/CD Changer Audio System	+204
Antilock Brakes [Std on R/T]	+421
Chrome Wheels [Opt on ES]	+326

Options	Price
Front Side Airbag Restraints	+212
Leather Seats	+326
Power Driver Seat [Opt on SE]	+130
Power Moonroof	+487

2001

Mileage Category: G

Changes to this family sedan for the 2001 model year include optional side airbags, a shoulder belt for the central rear passenger, an internal trunk release, three new interior colors, two additional exterior colors and an additional power outlet in the center console if you get a model with bucket seats. For those cars equipped with the Infinity sound system, you'll receive steering wheel-mounted controls and a four-disc in-dash CD player. SE is now the base Intrepid designation (previously it was the mid-level model), and it includes higher grade fabric this year. All engine choices meet LEV standards, and all models receive thicker side glass and upgraded windshield moldings for a quieter ride.

Body Styles	TMV Pricing		
	Trade	Private	Dealer
4 Dr ES Sdn	7546	8923	10194
4 Dr R/T Sdn	8296	9810	11208
4 Dr SE Sdn	6595	7798	8909

Options	Price
3.2L V6 SOHC 24V FI Engine	+249
Aluminum/Alloy Wheels [Opt on STD]	+195
AM/FM/Cassette/CD Audio System [Std on R/T]	+287
Antilock Brakes [Std on R/T]	+387
Compact Disc Changer	+175

Options	Price
Front Side Airbag Restraints	+195
Leather Seats	+436
Power Driver Seat [Std on ES]	+190
Power Passenger Seat [Opt on R/T]	+190
Power Moonroof	+446

2000

Body Styles	TMV Pricing		
	Trade	Private	Dealer
4 Dr ES Sdn	6008	7208	8384
4 Dr R/T Sdn	6712	8052	9365

Options	Price
3.2L V6 SOHC 24V FI Engine	+226
AM/FM/Cassette/CD Audio System [Opt on ES,STD]	+260
AM/FM/CD Audio System	+147
Antilock Brakes [Opt on ES,STD]	+350
Compact Disc Changer	+159

Body Styles	TMV Pricing		
	Trade	Private	Dealer
4 Dr STD Sdn	5572	6685	7775

Options	Price
Infinity Audio System	+260
Leather Seats	+395
Power Passenger Seat [Opt on ES]	+172
Power Moonroof	+359

Mileage Category: G

A performance R/T model is onboard for 2000. Intrepids get five new colors, new seat fabric in Base models, and added horsepower and torque to ES models powered by the 2.7-liter V6. AutoStick is available with that engine, and ES buyers can order an in-dash CD changer. Tether-ready child-seat anchors have been added behind the rear seat, and cars sold in California meet LEV standards.

1999

Body Styles	TMV Pricing		
	Trade	Private	Dealer
4 Dr ES Sdn	5275	6443	7659

Options	Price
AM/FM/Cassette/CD Audio System	+182
AM/FM/CD Audio System	+120
Antilock Brakes [Opt on STD]	+317
Compact Disc Changer	+129

Body Styles	TMV Pricing		
	Trade	Private	Dealer
4 Dr STD Sdn	4611	5632	6694

Options	Price
Leather Seats	+323
Power Passenger Seat [Opt on ES]	+156
Power Moonroof	+293

Mileage Category: G

Minor appearance tweaks such as chrome badging and improved floor carpeting debut for 1999. A new engine immobilizer is available on the ES.

1998

Body Styles	TMV Pricing		
	Trade	Private	Dealer
4 Dr ES Sdn	4027	5108	6326

Options	Price
AM/FM/Cassette/CD Audio System	+162
Antilock Brakes [Opt on STD]	+281
Leather Seats	+285

Body Styles	TMV Pricing		
	Trade	Private	Dealer
4 Dr STD Sdn	3421	4339	5374

Options	Price
Power Moonroof	+259
Power Passenger Seat [Opt on ES]	+138

Mileage Category: G

Completely redesigned for 1998, the Intrepid is a sedan that has the graceful styling of a coupe, thanks to a continuation of Chrysler's cab-forward design. Dodge's trademark cross hair grille dominates the front end along with two large, sparkling headlights. And the new Intrepid is powered by your choice of two new V6 engines.

1997

Body Styles	TMV Pricing		
	Trade	Private	Dealer
4 Dr ES Sdn	2937	3854	4974

Options	Price
Leather Seats	+251
Power Moonroof	+228
Power Passenger Seat [Opt on ES]	+121
Premium Audio System	+201

Body Styles	TMV Pricing		
	Trade	Private	Dealer
4 Dr STD Sdn	2578	3383	4366

Options	Price
3.5L V6 SOHC 24V FI Engine [Std on ES]	+208
AM/FM/Cassette/CD Audio System	+142
Antilock Brakes [Std on ES]	+247

Mileage Category: G

Few changes as first-generation Intrepid enters final year of production. A Sport Group including the 3.5-liter V6 engine is optional on base models, which also get an upgraded cassette stereo standard. Bolt-on wheel covers debut, and a new exterior color is introduced. Automatic transmissions get new software.

1996

Body Styles	TMV Pricing		
	Trade	Private	Dealer
4 Dr ES Sdn	2329	3148	4278

Options	Price
Power Moonroof	+208
Antilock Brakes [Std on Sport]	+225
Leather Seats	+229

Body Styles	TMV Pricing		
	Trade	Private	Dealer
4 Dr STD Sdn	2057	2780	3778

Mileage Category: G

ES carries over, but the base model gets several improvements to remain competitive with the new Ford Taurus. ES styling cues and 16-inch wheels come standard on the base Intrepid. New colors and seat fabrics update this full-size sedan, and all Intrepids get noise, vibration and harshness improvements.

Dodge
Intrepid/Neon

1995

Mileage Category: G

ABS is standard on ES. Traction control is a new ES option.

Body Styles	TMV Pricing		
	Trade	Private	Dealer
4 Dr ES Sdn	1675	2299	3338
4 Dr STD Sdn	1612	2212	3213

Options	Price
3.5L V6 SOHC 24V FI Engine	+165
Antilock Brakes [Opt on STD]	+197
Infinity Audio System	+137

Options	Price
Leather Seats	+200
Power Moonroof	+182

1994

Mileage Category: G

Base engine is upgraded with eight more horsepower. A flexible-fuel model is introduced to all states except California. Standard equipment includes air conditioning and a touring suspension. ES models gain variable-assist power steering, which is optional on base models with the Wheel and Handling Group. New options include a power sunroof, security alarm and power passenger seat.

Body Styles	TMV Pricing		
	Trade	Private	Dealer
4 Dr ES Sdn	1320	1884	2823

Body Styles	TMV Pricing		
	Trade	Private	Dealer
4 Dr STD Sdn	1171	1671	2504

Options	Price
AM/FM/Cassette/CD Audio System	+95
Antilock Brakes	+165
Infinity Audio System	+115

Options	Price
Leather Seats	+167
Power Moonroof	+153
3.5L V6 SOHC 24V FI Engine	+139

Dodge
Neon

2003

Mileage Category: B

All Neons receive a facelift in the form of new front and rear ends as well as interior changes that include a new steering wheel.

Body Styles	TMV Pricing		
	Trade	Private	Dealer
4 Dr R/T Sdn	8147	9103	10697
4 Dr SE Sdn	6340	7084	8325
4 Dr SXT Sdn	6563	7333	8617

Options	Price
Air Conditioning [Opt on SE]	+632
Antilock Brakes [Opt on SE,SXT]	+430
Automatic 4-Speed Transmission [Opt on SE,SXT]	+521
Chrome Wheels [Opt on SXT]	+190
Cruise Control [Opt on SE,SXT]	+158

Options	Price
Leather Seats [Opt on R/T]	+452
Power Moonroof [Opt on R/T,SXT]	+439
Front Side Airbag Restraints [Opt on R/T,SE,SXT]	+246
AM/FM/Cassette/CD Changer Audio System [Opt on SXT]	+190

2002

Mileage Category: B

A four-speed automatic gearbox replaces the archaic three-speed unit, a new base model is introduced, as is a value-packed SXT. Both SE and ES trims are relegated to fleet-only sales, and all Neons get a new "Dodge-signature" (crosshair-style) front end.

Body Styles	TMV Pricing		
	Trade	Private	Dealer
4 Dr ACR Sdn	5285	6079	7401
4 Dr ES Sdn	5367	6173	7517
4 Dr R/T Sdn	6275	7217	8788

Body Styles	TMV Pricing		
	Trade	Private	Dealer
4 Dr SE Sdn	5128	5898	7182
4 Dr STD Sdn	4372	5028	6122
4 Dr SXT Sdn	4883	5616	6838

Options	Price
Air Conditioning	+353
Aluminum/Alloy Wheels [Opt on SE]	+193
AM/FM/Cassette/CD Changer Audio System	+166
Antilock Brakes [Std on ACR,R/T]	+370
Automatic 4-Speed Transmission	+448

Options	Price
Chrome Wheels [Opt on SE,SXT]	+326
Front Side Airbag Restraints	+160
Leather Seats	+302
Power Sunroof	+321

2001

Body Styles	TMV Pricing		
	Trade	Private	Dealer
4 Dr Highline ACR Sdn	4477	5584	6605
4 Dr Highline ES Sdn	4255	5306	6277

Options	Price
Air Conditioning [Opt on ES]	+349
Alarm System [Opt on ACR]	+125
Aluminum/Alloy Wheels	+204
AM/FM/CD Audio System	+197
Antilock Brakes	+339
Automatic 3-Speed Transmission	+299

Body Styles	TMV Pricing		
	Trade	Private	Dealer
4 Dr Highline R/T Sdn	5052	6300	7452
4 Dr Highline SE Sdn	3731	4653	5504

Options	Price
Compact Disc Changer	+187
Cruise Control [Std on ES]	+117
Front Side Airbag Restraints	+175
Leather Seats	+329
Power Sunroof	+296
Power Windows [Std on ES]	+127

Mileage Category: B

The Neon R/T and Neon ACR, both models sporting a 2.0-liter 150-horsepower engine, make their much-anticipated return this year. Side-impact airbags and leather seats are available, as is a new interior color and four new exterior colors. An internal trunk release keeps young and old from being trapped in the Neon's cargo hold, and four new option packages, one of which includes a four-disc in-dash CD player, further widen its appeal to buyers seeking an American-made economy car.

2000

Body Styles	TMV Pricing		
	Trade	Private	Dealer
4 Dr ES Sdn	3188	4114	5021
4 Dr Highline Sdn	3115	4020	4907

Options	Price
Air Conditioning [Opt on ES]	+452
Aluminum/Alloy Wheels	+160
AM/FM/CD Audio System	+178
Antilock Brakes	+307

Options	Price
Automatic 3-Speed Transmission	+271
Compact Disc Changer	+226
Power Moonroof	+268
Power Windows [Std on ES Sdn]	+115

Mileage Category: B

Everything's new inside and out, as the second-generation Neon grows up, not old. A totally redesigned suspension and steering system, low-speed traction control, and a complete exterior redesign head up the notable changes.

1999

Body Styles	TMV Pricing		
	Trade	Private	Dealer
2 Dr Competition Cpe	2424	3235	4079
2 Dr Highline Cpe	2502	3339	4211
2 Dr R/T Cpe	2896	3865	4874
2 Dr Sport Cpe	2859	3816	4813

Options	Price
Air Conditioning [Std on R/T,Sport]	+368
Aluminum/Alloy Wheels [Std on R/T]	+131
AM/FM/CD Audio System	+146
Antilock Brakes	+278

Body Styles	TMV Pricing		
	Trade	Private	Dealer
4 Dr Competition Sdn	2483	3315	4180
4 Dr Highline Sdn	2519	3362	4240
4 Dr R/T Sdn	2938	3921	4945
4 Dr Sport Sdn	2823	3768	4751

Options	Price
Automatic 3-Speed Transmission	+246
Compact Disc Changer	+184
Competition Package	+759
Power Moonroof	+219

Mileage Category: B

One new color is available for the Neon Style Package: Inferno Red.

1998

Body Styles	TMV Pricing		
	Trade	Private	Dealer
2 Dr Competition Cpe	1883	2642	3498
2 Dr Highline Cpe	1949	2734	3619
2 Dr R/T Cpe	2079	2917	3861
2 Dr Sport Cpe	2014	2826	3742

Options	Price
AM/FM/CD Audio System	+121
Antilock Brakes	+246
Automatic 3-Speed Transmission	+196
Compact Disc Changer	+163

Body Styles	TMV Pricing		
	Trade	Private	Dealer
4 Dr Competition Sdn	1930	2708	3585
4 Dr Highline Sdn	1981	2779	3679
4 Dr R/T Sdn	2119	2973	3936
4 Dr Sport Sdn	2050	2876	3808

Options	Price
Competition Package	+671
Power Moonroof	+194
Air Conditioning [Opt on Competition,Highline]	+326
Aluminum/Alloy Wheels [Opt on Competition,Highline]	+116

Mileage Category: B

An R/T appearance package debuts. Improved option packages, LEV emissions and next-generation airbags round out the changes.

1997

Mileage Category: B

Sport trim level disappears in favor of Sport Package for Highline models. Twin-cam engine is optional on Highline models. Federal side-impact standards are met for the first time. More work has been done to quiet the Neon's boisterous demeanor.

1997 (cont'd)

Body Styles	TMV Pricing			Body Styles	TMV Pricing		
	Trade	Private	Dealer		Trade	Private	Dealer
2 Dr Highline Cpe	1522	2241	3119	4 Dr Highline Sdn	1539	2266	3155
2 Dr STD Cpe	1447	2131	2967	4 Dr STD Sdn	1487	2189	3047
2 Dr Sport Cpe	1540	2268	3157	4 Dr Sport Sdn	1611	2372	3302

Options	Price	Options	Price
Air Conditioning [Opt on STD]	+287	Compact Disc Changer	+143
Antilock Brakes	+217	Competition Package	+591
Automatic 3-Speed Transmission	+172	Power Moonroof	+171

1996

Mileage Category: B

A raft of improvements make the sprightly Neon even more attractive to compact buyers. Base models get more equipment, and the gray bumpers are discontinued. A base coupe is newly available. Interior noise levels are supposedly subdued this year. ABS is available across the board this year.

Body Styles	TMV Pricing			Body Styles	TMV Pricing		
	Trade	Private	Dealer		Trade	Private	Dealer
2 Dr Highline Cpe	1123	1729	2566	4 Dr Highline Sdn	1129	1739	2581
2 Dr STD Cpe	1096	1688	2505	4 Dr STD Sdn	1109	1708	2536
2 Dr Sport Cpe	1293	1991	2954	4 Dr Sport Sdn	1265	1948	2890

Options	Price	Options	Price
Air Conditioning	+261	Compact Disc Changer	+131
AM/FM/CD Audio System	+125	Competition Package [Opt on STD]	+473
Antilock Brakes	+197	Power Moonroof	+156
Automatic 3-Speed Transmission	+174		

1995

Mileage Category: B

Neon is the new Shadow replacement. Base, Highline and Sport models are available. Coupe and sedan body styles are offered. All except Sport Coupe have a 132-horsepower, 2.0-liter four-cylinder engine. Sport Coupe gets a 150-horsepower twin-cam edition of the base motor. Dual airbags are standard on all models; ABS is standard on Sport and optional on others. Integrated child seats are optional.

Body Styles	TMV Pricing			Body Styles	TMV Pricing		
	Trade	Private	Dealer		Trade	Private	Dealer
2 Dr Highline Cpe	903	1447	2353	4 Dr STD Sdn	773	1239	2016
2 Dr Sport Cpe	1005	1610	2619	4 Dr Sport Sdn	955	1531	2491
4 Dr Highline Sdn	876	1404	2284				

Options	Price	Options	Price
Premium Audio System	+114	Antilock Brakes	+172
Air Conditioning	+228	Automatic 3-Speed Transmission	+152
Aluminum/Alloy Wheels	+77	Leather Seats [Opt on Sport]	+126
AM/FM/CD Audio System	+96		

Dodge
Neon SRT-4

2003

Body Styles	TMV Pricing		
	Trade	Private	Dealer
4 Dr Turbo Sdn	11758	13133	15425

Mileage Category: E

The fire-breathing Neon SRT-4 debuts, sporting a 215-horsepower turbocharged engine, a tweaked suspension and Viper-inspired sport seats. Zero to 60 takes only about 6 seconds.

Dodge
Ram Pickup 1500

2003

Mileage Category: K

Two new packages debut, "Off-Road" and "Work Special," and the old Laramie trim level returns to replace the SLT Plus. For better performance, a five-speed automatic transmission is now optional on the 3.7-liter V6 and 4.7-liter V8 engines.

Body Styles	TMV Pricing		
	Trade	Private	Dealer
2 Dr Laramie 4WD Std Cab LB	20032	21415	23719
2 Dr Laramie 4WD Std Cab SB	19787	21153	23429
2 Dr Laramie Std Cab LB	17492	18700	20712
2 Dr Laramie Std Cab SB	17296	18490	20480
2 Dr SLT 4WD Std Cab LB	16122	17235	19089
2 Dr SLT 4WD Std Cab SB	15880	16976	18803
2 Dr SLT Std Cab LB	13863	14820	16414
2 Dr SLT Std Cab SB	13353	14275	15811
2 Dr ST 4WD Std Cab LB	14598	15606	17285
2 Dr ST 4WD Std Cab SB	14192	15172	16804
2 Dr ST Std Cab LB	11400	12187	13498
2 Dr ST Std Cab SB	11196	11969	13257

Body Styles	TMV Pricing		
	Trade	Private	Dealer
4 Dr Laramie 4WD Crew Cab LB	22890	24470	27103
4 Dr Laramie 4WD Crew Cab SB	22686	24252	26862
4 Dr Laramie Crew Cab LB	20406	21815	24162
4 Dr Laramie Crew Cab SB	20232	21629	23956
4 Dr SLT 4WD Crew Cab LB	18454	19728	21851
4 Dr SLT 4WD Crew Cab SB	18231	19489	21586
4 Dr SLT Crew Cab LB	16293	17418	19292
4 Dr SLT Crew Cab SB	16075	17185	19034
4 Dr ST 4WD Crew Cab LB	17205	18393	20372
4 Dr ST 4WD Crew Cab SB	16978	18150	20103
4 Dr ST Crew Cab LB	14933	15964	17681

Options	Price
Alarm System [Opt on SLT]	+120
Aluminum/Alloy Wheels [Opt on SLT]	+190
Antilock Brakes [Std on Laramie]	+430
Automatic 5-Speed Transmission [Opt on SLT,ST]	+739
Camper/Towing Package	+212
Cruise Control [Opt on ST]	+117
Infinity Audio System [Opt on SLT]	+190
Limited Slip Differential	+180
Off-Road Suspension Package [Opt on Laramie,SLT]	+550

Options	Price
Two-Tone Paint	+142
Velour/Cloth Seats [Opt on ST]	+174
AM/FM/CD Changer Audio System [Opt on SLT]	+600
20 Inch Wheels [Opt on Laramie,SLT]	+483
Front Head Airbag Restraints [Opt on STD Cab]	+246
Front and Rear Head Airbag Restraints [Opt on Crew Cab]	+310
4.7L V8 SOHC 16V FI Engine [Opt on ST]	+373
5.7L V8 OHV 16V FI Engine	+565

Mileage Category: K

Just about everything on the truck has undergone a complete redesign with improvements in safety, passenger comfort and handling.

Body Styles	TMV Pricing		
	Trade	Private	Dealer
2 Dr SLT 4WD Std Cab LB	13196	14242	15985
2 Dr SLT 4WD Std Cab SB	12983	14012	15727
2 Dr SLT Plus 4WD Std Cab LB	16492	17799	19978
2 Dr SLT Plus 4WD Std Cab SB	16268	17557	19706
2 Dr SLT Plus Std Cab LB	14338	15474	17368
2 Dr SLT Plus Std Cab SB	14157	15279	17149
2 Dr SLT Std Cab LB	11093	11972	13438
2 Dr SLT Std Cab SB	10679	11525	12936
2 Dr ST 4WD Std Cab LB	11749	12680	14232
2 Dr ST 4WD Std Cab SB	11555	12471	13997
2 Dr ST Std Cab LB	9165	9891	11102
2 Dr ST Std Cab SB	8986	9698	10885

Body Styles	TMV Pricing		
	Trade	Private	Dealer
4 Dr SLT 4WD Crew Cab LB	15204	16409	18418
4 Dr SLT 4WD Crew Cab SB	14987	16175	18155
4 Dr SLT Crew Cab LB	13335	14392	16154
4 Dr SLT Crew Cab SB	13143	14185	15921
4 Dr SLT Plus 4WD Crew Cab LB	19097	20611	23133
4 Dr SLT Plus 4WD Crew Cab SB	18916	20415	22914
4 Dr SLT Plus Crew Cab LB	16958	18302	20542
4 Dr SLT Plus Crew Cab LB	16805	18137	20357
4 Dr ST 4WD Crew Cab LB	14150	15272	17141
4 Dr ST 4WD Crew Cab SB	13958	15064	16908
4 Dr ST Crew Cab LB	12190	13156	14766
4 Dr ST Crew Cab SB	12058	13014	14607

Options	Price
17 Inch Wheels - Chrome [Opt on SLT Plus,ST]	+163
20 Inch Wheels [Opt on SLT,SLT Plus]	+367
4.7L V8 SOHC 16V FI Engine [Opt on ST Std Cab 2WD]	+321
5.9L V8 OHV 16V FI Engine [Std on SLT Plus]	+323
Antilock Brakes [Opt on SLT,ST]	+370
Automatic 4-Speed Transmission [Std on SLT Plus]	+530
Camper/Towing Package	+182

Options	Price
Front and Rear Head Airbag Restraints [Opt on Crew Cab]	+266
Front Head Airbag Restraints [Opt on Std Cab]	+212
Infinity Audio System [Opt on SLT]	+353
Leather Seats [Opt on SLT Crew]	+476
Limited Slip Differential	+155
Power Driver Seat [Std on SLT Plus]	+196
Two-Tone Paint	+122

Body Styles	TMV Pricing		
	Trade	Private	Dealer
2 Dr SLT 4WD Ext Cab SB	11877	13436	14875
2 Dr SLT 4WD Std Cab LB	11233	12707	14068
2 Dr SLT 4WD Std Cab SB	11065	12517	13858

Body Styles	TMV Pricing		
	Trade	Private	Dealer
2 Dr SLT Ext Cab SB	10436	11806	13070
2 Dr SLT Std Cab LB	9324	10548	11678
2 Dr SLT Std Cab SB	9058	10247	11345

2001

Mileage Category: K

Electronic cruise control is offered for the Cummings turbodiesel models with a manual transmission, two new exterior colors debut and child-seat anchors are mounted on the rear of the cab. A high-output Cummings turbodiesel model, with a six-speed transmission, 245 horsepower and 505 foot-pounds of torque, is offered in addition to a slightly improved 235-horsepower/460-ft-lbs version, available with a manual or automatic tranny.

Body Styles	TMV Pricing		
	Trade	Private	Dealer
2 Dr ST 4WD Ext Cab SB	10877	12305	13623
2 Dr ST 4WD Std Cab LB	10010	11324	12537
2 Dr ST 4WD Std Cab SB	9841	11133	12326
2 Dr ST Ext Cab SB	8773	9925	10988
2 Dr ST Std Cab LB	8009	9060	10031
2 Dr ST Std Cab SB	7725	8739	9675
2 Dr WS Std Cab LB	7490	8473	9381
2 Dr WS Std Cab SB	7367	8334	9227
4 Dr SLT 4WD Ext Cab LB	12742	14414	15958
4 Dr SLT 4WD Ext Cab SB	12554	14202	15723

Body Styles	TMV Pricing		
	Trade	Private	Dealer
4 Dr SLT Ext Cab LB	11126	12587	13935
4 Dr SLT Ext Cab SB	10959	12398	13726
4 Dr SLT Plus 4WD Ext Cab LB	14692	16621	18401
4 Dr SLT Plus 4WD Ext Cab SB	14535	16443	18204
4 Dr SLT Plus Ext Cab LB	13050	14763	16344
4 Dr SLT Plus Ext Cab SB	12920	14616	16181
4 Dr ST 4WD Ext Cab LB	11617	13142	14549
4 Dr ST 4WD Ext Cab SB	11452	12955	14343
4 Dr ST Ext Cab LB	9926	11229	12432

Options	Price
5.2L V8 OHV 16V FI Engine [Opt on ST Std Cab 2WD]	+294
5.9L V8 OHV 16V FI Engine [Std on SLT Plus]	+297
Air Conditioning [Std on SLT Plus]	+402
AM/FM/Cassette/CD Audio System	+344
AM/FM/CD Audio System [Std on SLT Plus]	+254
Antilock Brakes	+339
Automatic 4-Speed Transmission [Std on SLT Plus]	+486

Options	Price
Camper/Towing Package	+137
Infinity Audio System	+254
Leather Seats [Std on SLT Plus]	+324
Limited Slip Differential	+142
Power Driver Seat [Std on SLT Plus]	+180
Side Steps [Opt on ST]	+150

2000

Mileage Category: K

The Ram 1500 Pickup Club Cab models with the 8-foot bed have been discontinued; also eliminated for 2000 are the 2500 Club Cabs. All Ram Pickups receive a new front suspension and steering system to improve ride quality and steering precision, and 2500s and 3500s have a revised rear suspension for a better ride when loaded. An off-road package is now available for the short-wheelbase four-wheel-drive 1500.

Body Styles	TMV Pricing		
	Trade	Private	Dealer
2 Dr SLT 4WD Ext Cab SB	10340	11821	13273
2 Dr SLT 4WD Std Cab LB	9828	11236	12616
2 Dr SLT 4WD Std Cab SB	9646	11027	12381
2 Dr SLT Ext Cab SB	9279	10608	11911
2 Dr SLT Std Cab LB	7806	8924	10020
2 Dr SLT Std Cab SB	7750	8860	9949
2 Dr ST 4WD Ext Cab SB	9646	11027	12381
2 Dr ST 4WD Std Cab LB	8612	9846	11055
2 Dr ST 4WD Std Cab SB	8590	9820	11026
2 Dr ST Ext Cab SB	7892	9022	10130
2 Dr ST Std Cab LB	7036	8043	9031

Body Styles	TMV Pricing		
	Trade	Private	Dealer
2 Dr ST Std Cab SB	6731	7695	8640
2 Dr WS Std Cab LB	6362	7274	8167
2 Dr WS Std Cab SB	6334	7241	8130
4 Dr SLT 4WD Ext Cab LB	11161	12759	14326
4 Dr SLT 4WD Ext Cab SB	11001	12577	14121
4 Dr SLT Ext Cab LB	9733	11127	12493
4 Dr SLT Ext Cab SB	9535	10901	12239
4 Dr ST 4WD Ext Cab LB	10216	11679	13113
4 Dr ST 4WD Ext Cab SB	10000	11432	12836
4 Dr ST Ext Cab LB	8601	9833	11041
4 Dr ST Ext Cab SB	8221	9399	10553

Options	Price
5.2L V8 OHV 16V FI Engine	+267
5.9L V8 OHV 16V FI Engine	+268
Air Conditioning	+364
AM/FM/Cassette/CD Audio System	+312
AM/FM/CD Audio System	+192
Antilock Brakes	+307
Automatic 4-Speed Transmission	+441

Options	Price
Camper/Towing Package	+124
Infinity Audio System [Opt on SLT]	+206
Leather Seats	+565
Limited Slip Differential	+129
Off-Road Suspension Package	+395
Power Driver Seat	+145

1999

Mileage Category: K

The Sport model gets a new front bumper, fascia, grille, headlamps, graphics and Solar Yellow exterior color just to make sure it won't go unnoticed in traffic. All Ram Pickups get an express-down feature for the power windows, a new headlamp switch and four-wheel ABS are standard on vehicles over 10,000 pounds.

Body Styles	TMV Pricing		
	Trade	Private	Dealer
2 Dr Laramie SLT 4WD Ext Cab LB	9399	10886	12433
2 Dr Laramie SLT 4WD Ext Cab SB	9064	10498	11991
2 Dr Laramie SLT 4WD Std Cab LB	8785	10175	11622
2 Dr Laramie SLT 4WD Std Cab SB	8607	9969	11386
2 Dr Laramie SLT Ext Cab LB	8211	9510	10862
2 Dr Laramie SLT Ext Cab SB	8093	9373	10706
2 Dr Laramie SLT Std Cab LB	6943	8042	9185

Body Styles	TMV Pricing		
	Trade	Private	Dealer
2 Dr Laramie SLT Std Cab SB	6694	7753	8856
2 Dr ST 4WD Ext Cab LB	8649	10018	11442
2 Dr ST 4WD Ext Cab SB	8625	9990	11410
2 Dr ST 4WD Std Cab LB	7638	8846	10104
2 Dr ST 4WD Std Cab SB	7453	8632	9860
2 Dr ST Ext Cab LB	7192	8330	9514

Body Styles	TMV Pricing		
	Trade	Private	Dealer
2 Dr ST Ext Cab SB	7061	8178	9341
2 Dr ST Std Cab LB	6309	7307	8346
2 Dr ST Std Cab SB	6142	7114	8125
2 Dr WS Std Cab LB	5698	6600	7538
2 Dr WS Std Cab SB	5654	6549	7480
4 Dr Laramie SLT 4WD Ext Cab LB	10125	11727	13394
4 Dr Laramie SLT 4WD Ext Cab SB	9798	11348	12961

Body Styles	TMV Pricing		
	Trade	Private	Dealer
4 Dr Laramie SLT Ext Cab LB	8648	10016	11440
4 Dr Laramie SLT Ext Cab SB	8520	9868	11270
4 Dr ST 4WD Ext Cab LB	8944	10359	11831
4 Dr ST 4WD Ext Cab SB	8925	10337	11806
4 Dr ST Ext Cab LB	7487	8672	9905
4 Dr ST Ext Cab SB	7268	8418	9615

Options	Price
Leather Seats	+460
Power Driver Seat	+118
Infinity Audio System [Opt on Laramie SLT]	+168
5.2L V8 OHV 16V FI Engine [Opt on Std Cab - Laramie SLT,ST]	+217
5.9L V8 OHV 16V FI Engine	+146

Options	Price
Air Conditioning [Opt on ST,WS]	+297
AM/FM/Cassette/CD Audio System	+203
AM/FM/CD Audio System	+156
Antilock Brakes	+278
Automatic 4-Speed Transmission	+359

1998

Body Styles	TMV Pricing		
	Trade	Private	Dealer
2 Dr Laramie SLT 4WD Ext Cab LB	8230	9683	11321
2 Dr Laramie SLT 4WD Ext Cab SB	7846	9231	10793
2 Dr Laramie SLT 4WD Std Cab LB	7621	8967	10484
2 Dr Laramie SLT 4WD Std Cab SB	7448	8763	10246
2 Dr Laramie SLT Ext Cab LB	7125	8383	9802
2 Dr Laramie SLT Ext Cab SB	7086	8337	9747
2 Dr Laramie SLT Std Cab LB	5993	7051	8244
2 Dr Laramie SLT Std Cab SB	5863	6898	8065
2 Dr SS/T Std Cab SB	6740	7930	9271
2 Dr ST 4WD Ext Cab LB	7555	8888	10392
2 Dr ST 4WD Ext Cab SB	7413	8721	10197
2 Dr ST 4WD Std Cab SB	6392	7520	8793
2 Dr ST 4WD Std Cab SB	6230	7330	8570
2 Dr ST Ext Cab LB	6103	7180	8395

Body Styles	TMV Pricing		
	Trade	Private	Dealer
2 Dr ST Ext Cab SB	6016	7078	8276
2 Dr ST Std Cab LB	5363	6310	7377
2 Dr ST Std Cab SB	5044	5934	6938
2 Dr WS Std Cab LB	4691	5519	6452
2 Dr WS Std Cab SB	4621	5436	6356
4 Dr Laramie SLT 4WD Ext Cab LB	8456	9949	11632
4 Dr Laramie SLT 4WD Ext Cab SB	8327	9797	11455
4 Dr Laramie SLT Ext Cab LB	7518	8845	10342
4 Dr Laramie SLT Ext Cab SB	7284	8570	10020
4 Dr ST 4WD Ext Cab LB	7721	9084	10621
4 Dr ST 4WD Ext Cab SB	7690	9047	10578
4 Dr ST Ext Cab LB	6306	7419	8675
4 Dr ST Ext Cab SB	6195	7289	8522

Options	Price
5.2L V8 OHV 16V FI Engine [Opt on Std Cab - Laramie SLT,ST]	+192
Air Conditioning [Opt on ST,WS]	+262
AM/FM/Cassette/CD Audio System	+180
AM/FM/CD Audio System	+138

Options	Price
Antilock Brakes	+246
Automatic 4-Speed Transmission [Std on SS/T]	+310
Leather Seats	+407

Mileage Category: K

The Ram Quad Cab, as in four doors, becomes the first pickup on the market with two rear access doors. And for convenience, the front seatbelts are now integrated into the front seats, making for obstruction-free rear access. All Ram Pickups get a totally redesigned interior, standard passenger-side airbag with cutoff switch, and all airbags are "depowered" for safety.

1997

Body Styles	TMV Pricing		
	Trade	Private	Dealer
2 Dr LT 4WD Std Cab LB	5649	6767	8133
2 Dr LT 4WD Std Cab SB	5537	6632	7971
2 Dr LT Std Cab LB	4745	5684	6831
2 Dr LT Std Cab SB	4577	5482	6589
2 Dr Laramie SLT 4WD Ext Cab LB	7297	8741	10505
2 Dr Laramie SLT 4WD Ext Cab SB	6963	8341	10025
2 Dr Laramie SLT 4WD Std Cab LB	6454	7731	9292
2 Dr Laramie SLT 4WD Std Cab SB	5939	7114	8549
2 Dr Laramie SLT Ext Cab LB	5818	6969	8376
2 Dr Laramie SLT Ext Cab SB	5743	6879	8268

Body Styles	TMV Pricing		
	Trade	Private	Dealer
2 Dr Laramie SLT Std Cab LB	5117	6129	7366
2 Dr Laramie SLT Std Cab SB	4759	5701	6852
2 Dr SS/T Std Cab SB	5677	6800	8173
2 Dr ST 4WD Ext Cab LB	6857	8214	9872
2 Dr ST 4WD Ext Cab SB	6338	7592	9124
2 Dr ST Ext Cab LB	5386	6452	7754
2 Dr ST Ext Cab SB	5156	6176	7423
2 Dr WS Std Cab LB	4041	4841	5818
2 Dr WS Std Cab SB	3891	4661	5602

Options	Price
Leather Seats	+358
5.2L V8 OHV 16V FI Engine [Opt on Std Cab - Laramie SLT,LT]	+169

Options	Price
Air Conditioning [Opt on LT,ST,WS]	+231
AM/FM/Cassette/CD Audio System	+158

Mileage Category: K

No major changes to this popular truck for 1997. Refinements include available leather seating and woodgrain trim on SLT models, optional remote keyless entry, and standard deep-tinted quarter glass on Club Cab models. Also available is a combination CD/cassette stereo. Items from the 1996 Indy 500 Special Edition are available in a new Sport Package upgrade. Fresh interior and exterior colors sum up the changes this year.

1997 (cont'd)

Options	Price
AM/FM/CD Audio System	+122
Antilock Brakes	+217
Automatic 4-Speed Transmission	+272

1996

Mileage Category: K

The Ram Pickup gets some mild mechanical changes, including electronically governed automatic transmissions and a torque increase for the optional 5.9L turbodiesel V8 to 440 lb-ft. CD controls are added to cassette audio systems and cast alloy wheels are standard with SLT and Sport trims. New color offerings are Light Kiwi Pearl and Spruce Pearl.

Body Styles	TMV Pricing		
	Trade	Private	Dealer
2 Dr LT 4WD Std Cab LB	4726	5753	7172
2 Dr LT 4WD Std Cab SB	4520	5503	6860
2 Dr LT Std Cab LB	3802	4629	5770
2 Dr LT Std Cab SB	3750	4565	5691
2 Dr Laramie SLT 4WD Ext Cab LB	5845	7116	8871
2 Dr Laramie SLT 4WD Ext Cab SB	5268	6413	7995
2 Dr Laramie SLT 4WD Std Cab LB	5206	6338	7901
2 Dr Laramie SLT 4WD Std Cab SB	5158	6279	7828
2 Dr Laramie SLT Ext Cab LB	5053	6152	7669

Body Styles	TMV Pricing		
	Trade	Private	Dealer
2 Dr Laramie SLT Ext Cab SB	4829	5879	7328
2 Dr Laramie SLT Std Cab LB	4262	5189	6468
2 Dr Laramie SLT Std Cab SB	4035	4912	6124
2 Dr ST 4WD Ext Cab LB	5011	6100	7605
2 Dr ST 4WD Ext Cab SB	4977	6059	7553
2 Dr ST Ext Cab LB	4452	5420	6757
2 Dr ST Ext Cab SB	4118	5013	6250
2 Dr WS Std Cab LB	3444	4193	5227
2 Dr WS Std Cab SB	3121	3799	4736

Options	Price
Leather Seats	+366
5.2L V8 OHV 16V FI Engine [Opt on Std Cab - Laramie SLT,LT]	+153
Air Conditioning [Std on Laramie SLT]	+208

Options	Price
Antilock Brakes	+197
Automatic 4-Speed Transmission	+242
Compact Disc Changer	+143

1995

Mileage Category: K

After a complete redesign in 1994, the Ram Pickup offers a club cab body on a 134.7-inch wheelbase. Torque increases to 430 pound-feet with the Cummins 5.9L diesel with manual transmission. Optional equipment includes a natural gas 5.2L V8 and Infinity CD audio system. Foglights are bundled with the Sport Package.

Body Styles	TMV Pricing		
	Trade	Private	Dealer
2 Dr LT 4WD Std Cab LB	3931	4845	6368
2 Dr LT 4WD Std Cab SB	3861	4758	6254
2 Dr LT Std Cab LB	3164	3899	5125
2 Dr LT Std Cab SB	3133	3862	5076
2 Dr Laramie SLT 4WD Ext Cab LB	4832	5956	7828
2 Dr Laramie SLT 4WD Ext Cab SB	4640	5719	7516
2 Dr Laramie SLT 4WD Std Cab LB	4472	5512	7245
2 Dr Laramie SLT 4WD Std Cab SB	4431	5461	7178
2 Dr Laramie SLT Ext Cab LB	4125	5084	6683

Body Styles	TMV Pricing		
	Trade	Private	Dealer
2 Dr Laramie SLT Ext Cab SB	4011	4943	6497
2 Dr Laramie SLT Std Cab LB	3354	4134	5434
2 Dr Laramie SLT Std Cab SB	3304	4072	5353
2 Dr ST 4WD Ext Cab LB	4441	5473	7194
2 Dr ST 4WD Ext Cab SB	4314	5317	6988
2 Dr ST Ext Cab LB	3684	4541	5968
2 Dr ST Ext Cab SB	3372	4156	5463
2 Dr WS Std Cab LB	2597	3201	4208
2 Dr WS Std Cab SB	2592	3195	4199

Options	Price
Infinity Audio System	+76
Power Driver Seat	+75
5.2L V8 OHV 16V FI Engine [Opt on Std Cab - Laramie SLT,LT]	+134

Options	Price
Air Conditioning [Std on Laramie SLT]	+182
AM/FM/CD Audio System	+97
Antilock Brakes	+172
Automatic 4-Speed Transmission	+212

1994

Body Styles	TMV Pricing		
	Trade	Private	Dealer
2 Dr LT 4WD Std Cab LB	3233	4173	5739
2 Dr LT 4WD Std Cab SB	3204	4136	5689
2 Dr LT Std Cab LB	2508	3237	4452
2 Dr LT Std Cab SB	2285	2949	4056
2 Dr Laramie SLT 4WD Std Cab LB	3533	4560	6272
2 Dr Laramie SLT 4WD Std Cab SB	3488	4502	6192
2 Dr Laramie SLT Std Cab LB	2733	3528	4852

Body Styles	TMV Pricing		
	Trade	Private	Dealer
2 Dr Laramie SLT Std Cab SB	2667	3443	4735
2 Dr ST 4WD Std Cab LB	3331	4300	5915
2 Dr ST 4WD Std Cab SB	3219	4155	5715
2 Dr ST Std Cab LB	2611	3371	4637
2 Dr ST Std Cab SB	2407	3107	4273
2 Dr WS Std Cab LB	2036	2628	3615
2 Dr WS Std Cab SB	2013	2598	3573

Options	Price
5.2L V8 OHV 16V FI Engine [Opt on 2WD Std Cab]	+113
Air Conditioning [Std on Laramie SLT]	+153
AM/FM/Cassette/CD Audio System	+105

Options	Price
Antilock Brakes	+145
Automatic 4-Speed Transmission	+177

Mileage Category: K

Sharing the limelight with its 1500 Series younger brother, Dodge's 3/4-ton hauler also gets a complete makeover. Sporting curved, muscular sheet metal and a brash Kenworth semi truck-styled grill and headlight assembly, Dodge's light- and heavy-duty truck boasts an impressive array of upgrades inside and out. Offered in 118.7-inch and 134.7-inch wheelbases (6.5-foot and 8-foot boxes respectively), the Magnum engine line equips 2- and 4WD drivelines with new 2500 series nomenclature. A standard 5.2L V8 producing 220 horsepower/300 pound-feet can be swapped for the optional 5.9L gas V8 (230 hp/330 lb-ft), a brawny 5.9L straight six Cummins turbo diesel (175 hp/420 lb-ft) or the newly introduced version of the Viper motor, a behemoth 8.0L V10 cranking out 300 hp and 450 lb-ft of torque. A standard five-speed manual transmission can be upgraded to a four-speed automatic and three axle ratios (3.55, 3.90, 4.10) are available. Only offered as a regular cab body, a myriad of power and convenience packages are configurable, or choose the SLT trim with a 40/20/40 cloth bench, power windows and door locks, AC, cruise control, a fold-down center armrest (capable of housing a cell phone, laptop and music media) and leather-wrapped steering wheel. Choose Claret Red, Flame Red, Light Driftwood, Emerald Green, Dark or Brilliant Blue, Black, Sabre Gray, Silver or Bright White exterior paint with Medium Quartz, Slate Blue, Crimson Red or Medium Driftwood interior colors.

Dodge
Ram Pickup 2500

2003

Body Styles	TMV Pricing			Body Styles	TMV Pricing		
	Trade	Private	Dealer		Trade	Private	Dealer
2 Dr Laramie 4WD Std Cab LB	20583	21893	24076	4 Dr Laramie Crew Cab SB	22874	24330	26756
2 Dr Laramie Std Cab LB	18200	19358	21289	4 Dr SLT 4WD Crew Cab LB	19749	21006	23100
2 Dr SLT 4WD Std Cab LB	18066	19216	21132	4 Dr SLT 4WD Crew Cab SB	19627	20876	22958
2 Dr SLT Std Cab LB	15768	16772	18444	4 Dr SLT Crew Cab LB	17557	18675	20537
2 Dr ST 4WD Std Cab LB	16696	17758	19529	4 Dr SLT Crew Cab SB	17421	18530	20377
2 Dr ST Std Cab LB	14409	15326	16854	4 Dr ST 4WD Crew Cab LB	18315	19481	21423
4 Dr Laramie 4WD Crew Cab LB	22743	24191	26603	4 Dr ST 4WD Crew Cab SB	18229	19389	21322
4 Dr Laramie 4WD Crew Cab SB	20235	21523	23669	4 Dr ST Crew Cab LB	16236	17269	18991
4 Dr Laramie Crew Cab LB	20393	21691	23854	4 Dr ST Crew Cab SB	15976	16993	18687

Options	Price	Options	Price
6-Speed Transmission	+253	Two-Tone Paint	+142
Alarm System [Opt on SLT]	+120	AM/FM/CD Changer Audio System [Opt on SLT]	+600
Aluminum/Alloy Wheels [Opt on SLT]	+190	Front Head Airbag Restraints [Opt on STD Cab]	+246
Automatic 4-Speed Transmission	+692	Front and Rear Head Airbag Restraints [Opt on Crew Cab]	+310
Automatic 5-Speed Transmission	+739	5.9L I6 Turbodiesel OHV 24V Engine	+2922
Camper/Towing Package	+174	8.0L V10 OHV 20V FI Engine	+379
Cruise Control [Opt on ST]	+117	5.9L I6 Turbodiesel OHV 24V HO Engine	+3301
Limited Slip Differential	+180		

Mileage Category: K

Dodge redid its Ram 1500 full-size truck for 2002. For 2003, the heavies -- the 2500 and 3500 -- get their day in the sun. Along with the new Ram styling, these trucks receive more powerful engines, increased towing capacities, improved handling characteristics and additional safety equipment.

2002

Body Styles	TMV Pricing			Body Styles	TMV Pricing		
	Trade	Private	Dealer		Trade	Private	Dealer
2 Dr SLT 4WD Std Cab LB	14655	15817	17753	4 Dr SLT Plus 4WD Ext Cab LB	18075	19508	21896
2 Dr SLT Std Cab LB	12714	13722	15401	4 Dr SLT Plus 4WD Ext Cab SB	17949	19371	21742
2 Dr ST 4WD Std Cab LB	13261	14312	16064	4 Dr SLT Plus Ext Cab LB	16199	17483	19623
2 Dr ST Std Cab LB	11344	12243	13741	4 Dr SLT Plus Ext Cab SB	16052	17324	19445
4 Dr SLT 4WD Ext Cab LB	15905	17166	19267	4 Dr SLT 4WD Ext Cab LB	14521	15672	17590
4 Dr SLT 4WD Ext Cab SB	15811	17064	19153	4 Dr SLT 4WD Ext Cab SB	14389	15529	17430
4 Dr SLT Ext Cab LB	14059	15173	17030	4 Dr ST Ext Cab LB	12653	13656	15327
4 Dr SLT Ext Cab SB	13927	15031	16870	4 Dr ST Ext Cab SB	12517	13509	15163

Options	Price	Options	Price
5.9L I6 Turbodiesel OHV 24V Engine	+2514	Appearance Package [Opt on SLT, SLT Plus]	+179
5.9L I6 Turbodiesel OHV 24V HO Engine	+2840	Automatic 4-Speed Transmission	+530
6-Speed Transmission	+544	Camper/Towing Package	+149
8.0L V10 OHV 20V FI Engine	+326	Leather Seats [Opt on SLT]	+299
Air Conditioning	+381	Limited Slip Differential	+155
AM/FM/Cassette/CD Audio System [Opt on SLT]	+375	Power Driver Seat [Opt on SLT]	+174
AM/FM/CD Audio System [Opt on SLT]	+277	Two-Tone Paint	+122

Mileage Category: K

Three new colors: Atlantic Blue and Light Almond Pearls and Graphite metallic are added for 2002. Although the Ram 1500 was completely revamped this year, the heavier-duty 2500 Ram pickup must wait one more year for its update.

Dodge
Ram Pickup 2500

2001

Mileage Category: K

Electronic cruise control is now offered for the Cummings turbodiesel models with a manual transmission, improved braking systems with standard ABS come on all 2500 and 3500 Rams, two new exterior colors debut and child-seat anchors are mounted on the rear of the cab. A high-output Cummings turbodiesel model, with a six-speed transmission, 245 horsepower and 505 pound-feet of torque, is offered in addition to a slightly improved 235-horsepower/460-lb-ft version, available with a manual or automatic tranny.

Body Styles	TMV Pricing		
	Trade	Private	Dealer
2 Dr SLT 4WD Std Cab LB	12635	14293	15824
2 Dr SLT Std Cab LB	10947	12384	13711
2 Dr ST 4WD Std Cab LB	11518	13030	14425
2 Dr ST Std Cab LB	9762	11043	12226
4 Dr SLT 4WD Ext Cab LB	13716	15517	17179
4 Dr SLT 4WD Ext Cab SB	13636	15426	17078
4 Dr SLT Ext Cab LB	12118	13709	15177
4 Dr SLT Ext Cab SB	12001	13577	15031

Body Styles	TMV Pricing		
	Trade	Private	Dealer
4 Dr SLT Plus 4WD Ext Cab LB	14811	16755	18550
4 Dr SLT Plus 4WD Ext Cab SB	14700	16630	18411
4 Dr SLT Plus Ext Cab LB	13193	14925	16523
4 Dr SLT Plus Ext Cab SB	13065	14780	16363
4 Dr ST 4WD Ext Cab LB	12589	14242	15767
4 Dr ST 4WD Ext Cab SB	12552	14199	15720
4 Dr ST Ext Cab LB	10896	12327	13647
4 Dr ST Ext Cab SB	10780	12195	13501

Options	Price
5.9L I6 Turbodiesel OHV 24V Engine	+2307
5.9L I6 Turbodiesel OHV 24V HO Engine	+2606
6-Speed Transmission	+200
8.0L V10 OHV 20V FI Engine	+234
Air Conditioning [Opt on ST]	+402
AM/FM/Cassette/CD Audio System [Opt on SLT]	+344
AM/FM/CD Audio System [Opt on SLT]	+254

Options	Price
Automatic 4-Speed Transmission	+486
Camper/Towing Package	+137
Infinity Audio System [Opt on SLT]	+254
Leather Seats [Opt on SLT]	+624
Limited Slip Differential	+142
Power Driver Seat [Opt on SLT]	+160

2000

Mileage Category: K

The Ram Pickup 1500 Club Cab models with the 8-foot bed box have been discontinued; also eliminated for 2000 are the 2500 Club Cabs. All Ram Pickups receive a new front suspension and steering system to improve ride quality and steering precision, and 2500s and 3500s have a revised rear suspension for a better ride when loaded. An off-road package is now available for the short-wheelbase four-wheel-drive 1500.

Body Styles	TMV Pricing		
	Trade	Private	Dealer
2 Dr SLT 4WD Std Cab LB	11137	12770	14371
2 Dr SLT Std Cab LB	9648	11063	12449
2 Dr ST 4WD Std Cab LB	10211	11708	13176
2 Dr ST Std Cab LB	8494	9739	10960
4 Dr SLT 4WD Ext Cab LB	11952	13704	15422
4 Dr SLT 4WD Ext Cab SB	11908	13654	15366

Body Styles	TMV Pricing		
	Trade	Private	Dealer
4 Dr SLT Ext Cab LB	10577	12128	13648
4 Dr SLT Ext Cab SB	10483	12020	13527
4 Dr ST 4WD Ext Cab LB	11071	12694	14285
4 Dr ST 4WD Ext Cab SB	11034	12652	14238
4 Dr ST Ext Cab LB	9445	10830	12188
4 Dr ST Ext Cab SB	9310	10675	12013

Options	Price
Power Driver Seat	+145
5.9L I6 Turbodiesel OHV 24V Engine	+2090
8.0L V10 OHV 20V FI Engine	+212
Air Conditioning	+364
AM/FM/Cassette/CD Audio System	+312
AM/FM/CD Audio System	+192

Options	Price
Antilock Brakes	+307
Automatic 4-Speed Transmission	+441
Camper/Towing Package	+124
Chrome Wheels	+147
Leather Seats	+565
Limited Slip Differential	+129

1999

Mileage Category: K

The Sport model gets a new front bumper, fascia, grille, headlamps, graphics and Solar Yellow exterior color just to make sure it won't go unnoticed in traffic. All Ram Pickups get an express-down feature for the power windows, a new headlamp switch and four-wheel ABS are standard on vehicles over 10,000 pounds.

Body Styles	TMV Pricing		
	Trade	Private	Dealer
2 Dr Laramie SLT 4WD Ext Cab LB	11123	12883	14715
2 Dr Laramie SLT 4WD Ext Cab SB	11042	12789	14608
2 Dr Laramie SLT 4WD Std Cab LB	9786	11334	12945
2 Dr Laramie SLT Ext Cab LB	9702	11237	12834
2 Dr Laramie SLT Ext Cab SB	9510	11014	12580
2 Dr Laramie SLT Std Cab LB	8502	9847	11247
2 Dr ST 4WD Ext Cab LB	9716	11253	12853
2 Dr ST 4WD Ext Cab SB	10143	11747	13417
2 Dr ST 4WD Std Cab LB	9114	10556	12057
2 Dr ST Ext Cab LB	8428	9761	11149

Body Styles	TMV Pricing		
	Trade	Private	Dealer
2 Dr ST Ext Cab SB	8315	9631	11000
2 Dr ST Std Cab LB	7593	8794	10044
4 Dr Laramie SLT 4WD Ext Cab LB	10770	12475	14249
4 Dr Laramie SLT 4WD Ext Cab SB	10699	12392	14153
4 Dr Laramie SLT Ext Cab LB	9628	11151	12737
4 Dr Laramie SLT Ext Cab SB	9713	11249	12848
4 Dr ST 4WD Ext Cab LB	10133	11736	13405
4 Dr ST 4WD Ext Cab SB	10087	11683	13344
4 Dr ST Ext Cab LB	8521	9869	11272
4 Dr ST Ext Cab SB	8460	9798	11191

Options	Price
5.9L I6 Turbodiesel OHV 24V Engine	+1894
8.0L V10 OHV 20V FI Engine	+173
Air Conditioning [Opt on ST]	+297
AM/FM/Cassette/CD Audio System	+255
AM/FM/CD Audio System	+156

Options	Price
Antilock Brakes	+278
Automatic 4-Speed Transmission	+359
Chrome Wheels [Opt on ST]	+120
Leather Seats	+460
Power Driver Seat	+118

1998

Body Styles	TMV Pricing		
	Trade	Private	Dealer
2 Dr Laramie SLT 4WD Ext Cab LB	9043	10639	12439
2 Dr Laramie SLT 4WD Ext Cab SB	8872	10439	12205
2 Dr Laramie SLT 4WD Std Cab LB	8670	10200	11926
2 Dr Laramie SLT Ext Cab LB	8518	10022	11717
2 Dr Laramie SLT Ext Cab SB	8420	9907	11583
2 Dr Laramie SLT Std Cab LB	7367	8667	10134
2 Dr ST 4WD Ext Cab LB	8666	10196	11921
2 Dr ST 4WD Ext Cab SB	8600	10118	11830
2 Dr ST 4WD Std Cab LB	8145	9583	11204
2 Dr ST Ext Cab LB	7322	8615	10072

Body Styles	TMV Pricing		
	Trade	Private	Dealer
2 Dr ST Ext Cab SB	7296	8584	10036
2 Dr ST Std Cab LB	6531	7684	8984
4 Dr Laramie SLT 4WD Ext Cab LB	9309	10952	12805
4 Dr Laramie SLT 4WD Ext Cab SB	9275	10912	12758
4 Dr Laramie SLT Ext Cab LB	8659	10187	11911
4 Dr Laramie SLT Ext Cab SB	8557	10068	11771
4 Dr ST 4WD Ext Cab LB	8774	10323	12069
4 Dr ST 4WD Ext Cab SB	8694	10229	11960
4 Dr ST Ext Cab LB	7668	9022	10548
4 Dr ST Ext Cab SB	7606	8949	10463

Options	Price
AM/FM/Cassette/CD Audio System	+225
AM/FM/CD Audio System	+138
Antilock Brakes	+246
Automatic 4-Speed Transmission	+310
Leather Seats	+407

Options	Price
5.9L I6 Turbodiesel OHV 12V Engine	+1376
5.9L I6 Turbodiesel OHV 24V Engine	+1675
8.0L V10 OHV 20V FI Engine	+318
Air Conditioning [Opt on ST]	+262

Mileage Category: K

Available as a sedan! The Ram Quad Cab, as in four doors, becomes the first pickup on the market with two rear access doors. And for convenience, the front seatbelts are now integrated into the front seats, making for obstruction-free rear access. All Ram Pickups get a totally redesigned interior, standard passenger-side airbag with cutoff switch, and all airbags are "depowered" for safety.

1997

Body Styles	TMV Pricing		
	Trade	Private	Dealer
2 Dr LT 4WD Std Cab LB	6498	7784	9355
2 Dr LT Std Cab LB	5310	6361	7645
2 Dr Laramie SLT 4WD Ext Cab LB	7739	9270	11142
2 Dr Laramie SLT 4WD Ext Cab SB	7682	9202	11060
2 Dr Laramie SLT 4WD Std Cab LB	6778	8119	9758
2 Dr Laramie SLT Ext Cab LB	6674	7995	9609
2 Dr Laramie SLT Ext Cab SB	6667	7986	9598

Body Styles	TMV Pricing		
	Trade	Private	Dealer
2 Dr Laramie SLT Std Cab LB	6039	7233	8693
2 Dr ST 4WD Ext Cab LB	6741	8074	9704
2 Dr ST 4WD Ext Cab SB	6692	8016	9634
2 Dr ST 4WD Std Cab LB	6584	7886	9478
2 Dr ST Ext Cab LB	5989	7174	8622
2 Dr ST Ext Cab SB	5934	7108	8542
2 Dr ST Std Cab LB	5381	6445	7746

Options	Price
5.9L I6 Turbodiesel OHV 12V Engine	+1416
8.0L V10 OHV 20V FI Engine	+279
Air Conditioning [Opt on LT,ST]	+231
AM/FM/Cassette/CD Audio System	+198
AM/FM/CD Audio System	+122

Options	Price
Antilock Brakes	+217
Automatic 4-Speed Transmission	+279
Leather Seats	+358
Premium Audio System	+122

Mileage Category: K

No major changes for 1997. Refinements include available leather seating and woodgrain trim on SLT models, optional remote keyless entry, and standard deep-tinted quarter glass on Club Cab models. Also available is a combination CD/cassette stereo. Fresh interior and exterior colors sum up the changes this year.

1996

Body Styles	TMV Pricing		
	Trade	Private	Dealer
2 Dr LT 4WD Std Cab LB	5054	6153	7670
2 Dr LT Std Cab LB	4285	5217	6503
2 Dr Laramie SLT 4WD Ext Cab LB	6748	8215	10241
2 Dr Laramie SLT 4WD Ext Cab SB	6802	8281	10323
2 Dr Laramie SLT 4WD Std Cab LB	5733	6980	8701
2 Dr Laramie SLT Ext Cab LB	5891	7172	8940
2 Dr Laramie SLT Ext Cab SB	5785	7042	8779

Body Styles	TMV Pricing		
	Trade	Private	Dealer
2 Dr Laramie SLT Std Cab LB	4839	5891	7344
2 Dr Laramie SLT 4WD Ext Cab LB	6058	7375	9193
2 Dr ST 4WD Ext Cab SB	5968	7265	9056
2 Dr ST 4WD Std Cab LB	5118	6231	7767
2 Dr ST Ext Cab LB	5242	6381	7955
2 Dr ST Ext Cab SB	5208	6340	7904
2 Dr ST Std Cab LB	4394	5350	6669

Options	Price
Compact Disc Changer	+176
Infinity Audio System	+133
5.9L I6 Turbodiesel OHV 12V Engine	+1202
8.0L V10 OHV 20V FI Engine	+122

Options	Price
Air Conditioning [Opt on LT,ST]	+208
Antilock Brakes	+197
Automatic 4-Speed Transmission	+242

Mileage Category: K

The Ram Pickup gets some mild mechanical changes, including electronically governed automatic transmissions and a torque increase for the optional 5.9L turbodiesel V8 to 440 pound-feet. CD controls are added to cassette audio systems and cast alloy wheels are standard with SLT and Sport trims. New color offerings are Light Kiwi Pearl and Spruce Pearl.

Dodge
Ram Pickup 2500/Ram Pickup 3500

1995

Mileage Category: K

After a complete redesign in 1994, the Ram Pickup offers a club cab on a 134.7-inch wheelbase. Torque increases to 430 pound-feet with the Cummins 5.9L diesel with manual transmission and an illuminated overdrive lockout switch is standard. An Infinity CD audio system is optional and foglights are included with the Sport Package.

Body Styles	TMV Pricing		
	Trade	Private	Dealer
2 Dr LT 4WD Std Cab LB	4099	5053	6642
2 Dr LT Std Cab LB	3454	4257	5596
2 Dr Laramie SLT 4WD Ext Cab LB	5586	6885	9051
2 Dr Laramie SLT 4WD Ext Cab SB	5536	6823	8969
2 Dr Laramie SLT 4WD Std Cab LB	4755	5861	7705
2 Dr Laramie SLT Ext Cab LB	4860	5990	7874
2 Dr Laramie SLT Std Cab LB	4150	5115	6724
2 Dr ST 4WD Ext Cab LB	5078	6259	8228

Body Styles	TMV Pricing		
	Trade	Private	Dealer
2 Dr ST 4WD Ext Cab SB	4977	6135	8065
2 Dr ST 4WD Std Cab LB	4217	5198	6832
2 Dr ST Ext Cab LB	4268	5261	6916
2 Dr ST Ext Cab SB	4247	5235	6881
2 Dr ST Std Cab LB	3500	4314	5670
2 Dr Sport 4WD Ext Cab SB	5182	6387	8395
2 Dr Sport Ext Cab SB	4688	5779	7596

Options	Price
5.9L I6 Turbodiesel OHV 12V Engine	+964
8.0L V10 OHV 20V FI Engine	+107
Air Conditioning [Opt on LT,Sport,ST]	+182
AM/FM/CD Audio System	+97

Options	Price
Antilock Brakes	+172
Automatic 4-Speed Transmission	+212
Infinity Audio System	+117

1994

Mileage Category: K

All new this year, Dodge's pickup sports a more user-friendly cabin and aggressive styling highlighted by a big rig facade.

Body Styles	TMV Pricing		
	Trade	Private	Dealer
2 Dr LT 4WD Std Cab LB	3410	4402	6055
2 Dr LT Std Cab LB	2727	3521	4843
2 Dr Laramie SLT 4WD Std Cab LB	3659	4724	6498

Body Styles	TMV Pricing		
	Trade	Private	Dealer
2 Dr Laramie SLT Std Cab LB	2886	3726	5125
2 Dr ST 4WD Std Cab LB	3450	4454	6127
2 Dr ST Std Cab LB	2781	3590	4937

Options	Price
5.9L I6 Turbodiesel OHV 12V Engine	+809
8.0L V10 OHV 20V FI Engine	+90
Air Conditioning [Std on Laramie SLT]	+153

Options	Price
Antilock Brakes	+145
Automatic 4-Speed Transmission	+177

Dodge
Ram Pickup 3500

2003

Mileage Category: K

Dodge redid its Ram 1500 full-size truck for 2002. For 2003, the heavies -- the 2500 and 3500 -- get their day in the sun. Along with the new Ram styling, these trucks receive more powerful engines, increased towing capacities, improved handling characteristics and additional safety equipment.

Body Styles	TMV Pricing		
	Trade	Private	Dealer
2 Dr Laramie 4WD Std Cab LB DRW	21391	22696	24870
2 Dr Laramie Std Cab LB DRW	19213	20385	22338
2 Dr SLT 4WD Std Cab LB DRW	18975	20132	22061
2 Dr SLT Std Cab LB DRW	16779	17802	19508
2 Dr ST 4WD Std Cab LB DRW	18022	19121	20953
2 Dr ST Std Cab LB DRW	15836	16802	18412
4 Dr Laramie 4WD Crew Cab LB DRW	24319	25803	28275
4 Dr Laramie 4WD Crew Cab SB	25903	27483	30116
4 Dr Laramie Crew Cab LB DRW	21870	23204	25427

Body Styles	TMV Pricing		
	Trade	Private	Dealer
4 Dr Laramie Crew Cab SB	23128	24539	26890
4 Dr SLT 4WD Crew Cab LB DRW	21222	22517	24674
4 Dr SLT 4WD Crew Cab SB	22833	24226	26547
4 Dr SLT Crew Cab LB DRW	19031	20192	22127
4 Dr SLT Crew Cab SB	21264	22561	24723
4 Dr ST 4WD Crew Cab LB DRW	20241	21476	23533
4 Dr ST 4WD Crew Cab SB	22087	23434	25680
4 Dr ST Crew Cab LB DRW	18096	19200	21040
4 Dr ST Crew Cab SB	20291	21529	23592

Options	Price
6-Speed Transmission	+253
Alarm System [Opt on SLT]	+120
Automatic 4-Speed Transmission	+692
Automatic 5-Speed Transmission	+739
Camper/Towing Package	+174
Cruise Control [Opt on ST]	+117
Two-Tone Paint	+142

Options	Price
AM/FM/CD Changer Audio System [Opt on SLT]	+600
Front Head Airbag Restraints [Opt on STD Cab]	+246
Front and Rear Head Airbag Restraints [Opt on Crew Cab]	+310
5.9L I6 Turbodiesel OHV 24V Engine [Std on HD]	+2922
8.0L V10 OHV 20V FI Engine	+379
5.9L I6 Turbodiesel OHV 24V HO Engine	+379

2002

Body Styles	TMV Pricing		
	Trade	Private	Dealer
2 Dr SLT 4WD Std Cab LB	15325	16540	18564
2 Dr SLT Std Cab LB	13473	14541	16321
2 Dr ST 4WD Std Cab LB	14294	15427	17315
2 Dr ST Std Cab LB	12442	13428	15072
4 Dr SLT 4WD Ext Cab LB	17027	18377	20626

Body Styles	TMV Pricing		
	Trade	Private	Dealer
4 Dr SLT Ext Cab LB	15201	16406	18414
4 Dr SLT Plus 4WD Ext Cab LB	19158	20676	23207
4 Dr SLT Plus Ext Cab LB	17327	18700	20989
4 Dr ST 4WD Ext Cab LB	16042	17314	19433
4 Dr ST Ext Cab LB	14157	15279	17149

Options	Price
5.9L I6 Turbodiesel OHV 24V Engine	+2514
5.9L I6 Turbodiesel OHV 24V HO Engine	+2840
6-Speed Transmission	+544
8.0L V10 OHV 20V FI Engine	+326
Air Conditioning	+381
AM/FM/Cassette/CD Audio System [Opt on SLT]	+375
AM/FM/CD Audio System [Opt on SLT]	+277

Options	Price
Appearance Package [Opt on SLT,SLT Plus]	+179
Automatic 4-Speed Transmission	+530
Camper/Towing Package	+149
Leather Seats [Opt on SLT]	+788
Limited Slip Differential	+155
Power Driver Seat [Opt on SLT]	+174

Mileage Category: K

Three new colors: Atlantic Blue and Light Almond Pearls and Graphite metallic are available for 2002. Although the Ram 1500 was completely revamped this year, the heavy-duty 3500 Ram pickups must wait one more year for their update.

2001

Mileage Category: K

Body Styles	TMV Pricing		
	Trade	Private	Dealer
2 Dr SLT 4WD Std Cab LB	13183	14885	16456
2 Dr SLT Std Cab LB	11610	13109	14493
2 Dr ST 4WD Std Cab LB	12321	13912	15380
2 Dr ST Std Cab LB	10714	12098	13375
4 Dr SLT 4WD Ext Cab LB	14693	16590	18341

Body Styles	TMV Pricing		
	Trade	Private	Dealer
4 Dr SLT Ext Cab LB	13080	14769	16328
4 Dr SLT Plus 4WD Ext Cab LB	15746	17779	19656
4 Dr SLT Plus Ext Cab LB	14166	15995	17684
4 Dr ST 4WD Ext Cab LB	13790	15570	17214
4 Dr ST Ext Cab LB	12202	13778	15232

Options	Price
5.9L I6 Turbodiesel OHV 24V Engine	+2307
5.9L I6 Turbodiesel OHV 24V HO Engine	+2606
6-Speed Transmission	+200
8.0L V10 OHV 20V FI Engine	+234
Air Conditioning [Opt on ST]	+402
AM/FM/Cassette/CD Audio System [Opt on SLT]	+344

Options	Price
AM/FM/CD Audio System [Opt on SLT]	+254
Automatic 4-Speed Transmission	+486
Camper/Towing Package	+137
Leather Seats [Opt on SLT]	+624
Limited Slip Differential	+142
Power Driver Seat [Opt on SLT]	+160

Electronic cruise control is offered for the Cummings turbodiesel models with a manual transmission, improved braking systems with standard ABS come on all 2500 and 3500 Rams, two new exterior colors debut and child-seat anchors are mounted on the rear of the cab. A high-output Cummings turbodiesel model, with a six-speed transmission, 245 horsepower and 505 foot-pounds of torque, is offered in addition to a slightly improved 235-horsepower/460-ft-lbs version, available with a manual or automatic tranny.

2000

Body Styles	TMV Pricing		
	Trade	Private	Dealer
2 Dr SLT 4WD Std Cab LB	11115	12707	14267
2 Dr SLT Std Cab LB	9994	11425	12828
2 Dr ST 4WD Std Cab LB	10755	12295	13805
2 Dr ST Std Cab LB	9063	10361	11633

Body Styles	TMV Pricing		
	Trade	Private	Dealer
4 Dr SLT 4WD Ext Cab LB	13064	14936	16770
4 Dr SLT Ext Cab LB	10775	12318	13831
4 Dr ST 4WD Ext Cab LB	11733	13414	15061
4 Dr ST Ext Cab LB	10600	12118	13606

Options	Price
5.9L I6 Turbodiesel OHV 24V Engine	+2090
6-Speed Transmission	+181
8.0L V10 OHV 20V FI Engine	+212
Air Conditioning	+364
AM/FM/Cassette/CD Audio System	+312
AM/FM/CD Audio System	+230

Options	Price
Automatic 4-Speed Transmission	+441
Camper/Towing Package	+124
Leather Seats	+565
Limited Slip Differential	+129
Power Driver Seat	+145

Mileage Category: K

The 1500 Club Cab models with the 8-foot bed box have been discontinued; also eliminated for 2000 are the 2500 Club Cabs. All Ram Pickups receive a new front suspension and steering system to improve ride quality and steering precision, and 2500s and 3500s have a revised rear suspension for a better ride when loaded. An off-road package is now available for the short-wheelbase four-wheel-drive 1500.

1999

Body Styles	TMV Pricing		
	Trade	Private	Dealer
2 Dr Laramie SLT 4WD Std Cab LB	10030	11617	13268
2 Dr Laramie SLT Std Cab LB	8789	10180	11627
2 Dr ST 4WD Std Cab LB	9674	11204	12797
2 Dr ST Std Cab LB	8100	9381	10714

Body Styles	TMV Pricing		
	Trade	Private	Dealer
4 Dr Laramie SLT 4WD Ext Cab LB	11777	13640	15579
4 Dr Laramie SLT Ext Cab LB	9870	11432	13057
4 Dr ST 4WD Ext Cab LB	10602	12279	14025
4 Dr ST Ext Cab LB	9571	11085	12661

Mileage Category: K

The Sport model gets a new front bumper, fascia, grille, headlamps, graphics and Solar Yellow exterior color just to make sure it won't go unnoticed in traffic. All Ram Pickups get an express-down feature for the power windows, a new headlamp switch, and four-wheel ABS is standard on vehicles over 10,000 pounds.

1999 (cont'd)

Options	Price
5.9L I6 Turbodiesel OHV 24V Engine	+1894
8.0L V10 OHV 20V FI Engine	+173
Air Conditioning [Opt on ST]	+297
AM/FM/Cassette/CD Audio System	+255

Options	Price
AM/FM/CD Audio System	+188
Automatic 4-Speed Transmission	+359
Leather Seats	+460
Power Driver Seat	+118

1998

Mileage Category: K

All Ram Pickups get a totally redesigned interior, standard passenger-side airbag with cutoff switch, and all airbags are "depowered" for safety.

Body Styles	TMV Pricing		
	Trade	Private	Dealer
2 Dr Laramie SLT 4WD Std Cab LB	8721	10261	11998
2 Dr Laramie SLT Std Cab LB	7518	8846	10343
2 Dr ST 4WD Std Cab LB	8024	9441	11039
2 Dr ST Std Cab LB	7117	8374	9791

Body Styles	TMV Pricing		
	Trade	Private	Dealer
4 Dr Laramie SLT 4WD Ext Cab LB	10298	12117	14168
4 Dr Laramie SLT Ext Cab LB	8736	10279	12019
4 Dr ST 4WD Ext Cab LB	9236	10867	12707
4 Dr ST Ext Cab LB	8100	9531	11144

Options	Price
5.9L I6 Turbodiesel OHV 12V Engine	+1376
5.9L I6 Turbodiesel OHV 24V Engine	+1675
8.0L V10 OHV 20V FI Engine	+318
Air Conditioning [Opt on ST]	+262
AM/FM/Cassette/CD Audio System	+225

Options	Price
AM/FM/CD Audio System	+166
Antilock Brakes	+246
Automatic 4-Speed Transmission	+310
Leather Seats	+407

1997

Mileage Category: K

No major changes for 1997. Refinements include available leather seating and woodgrain trim on SLT models, optional remote keyless entry, and standard deep-tinted quarter glass on Club Cab models. Also available is a combination CD/cassette stereo. Fresh interior and exterior colors sum up the changes this year.

Body Styles	TMV Pricing		
	Trade	Private	Dealer
2 Dr LT 4WD Std Cab LB	6802	8175	9852
2 Dr LT Std Cab LB	6153	7395	8912
2 Dr Laramie SLT 4WD Ext Cab LB	8398	10092	12163
2 Dr Laramie SLT 4WD Std Cab LB	7708	9263	11163
2 Dr Laramie SLT Ext Cab LB	7080	8508	10254

Body Styles	TMV Pricing		
	Trade	Private	Dealer
2 Dr Laramie SLT Std Cab LB	6622	7958	9590
2 Dr ST 4WD Ext Cab LB	7615	9151	11029
2 Dr ST 4WD Std Cab LB	6962	8367	10084
2 Dr ST Ext Cab LB	6329	7606	9167
2 Dr ST Std Cab LB	6290	7559	9109

Options	Price
8.0L V10 OHV 20V FI Engine	+279
Air Conditioning [Opt on LT,ST]	+231
AM/FM/Cassette/CD Audio System	+198
AM/FM/CD Audio System	+146

Options	Price
Antilock Brakes	+217
Automatic 4-Speed Transmission	+279
Leather Seats	+358
5.9L I6 Turbodiesel OHV 12V Engine	+1416

1996

Mileage Category: K

The Ram Pickup gets some mild mechanical changes, including electronically governed automatic transmissions and a torque increase for the optional 5.9L turbodiesel V8 to 440 pound-feet. CD controls are added to cassette audio systems and cast alloy wheels are standard with SLT and Sport trims. New color offerings are Light Kiwi Pearl and Spruce Pearl.

Body Styles	TMV Pricing		
	Trade	Private	Dealer
2 Dr LT 4WD Std Cab LB	6070	7390	9212
2 Dr LT Std Cab LB	5196	6325	7885
2 Dr Laramie SLT 4WD Ext Cab LB	7039	8569	10683
2 Dr Laramie SLT 4WD Std Cab LB	6786	8261	10299
2 Dr Laramie SLT Ext Cab LB	6303	7673	9565

Body Styles	TMV Pricing		
	Trade	Private	Dealer
2 Dr Laramie SLT Std Cab LB	5859	7133	8892
2 Dr ST 4WD Ext Cab LB	6758	8227	10256
2 Dr ST 4WD Std Cab LB	6188	7533	9391
2 Dr ST Ext Cab LB	5599	6816	8497
2 Dr ST Std Cab LB	5222	6357	7925

Options	Price
5.9L I6 Turbodiesel OHV 12V Engine	+1202
8.0L V10 OHV 20V FI Engine	+122
Air Conditioning [Opt on LT,ST]	+208

Options	Price
AM/FM/CD Audio System	+133
Antilock Brakes	+197
Automatic 4-Speed Transmission	+242

1995

Mileage Category: K

After a complete redesign in 1994, the Ram Pickup offers a club cab on a 134.7-inch wheelbase. Torque increases to 430 pound-feet with the Cummins 5.9L diesel with manual transmission, and an illuminated overdrive lockout switch is standard. An Infinity CD audio system, foglights and four-wheel ABS are optional.

Body Styles	TMV Pricing		
	Trade	Private	Dealer
2 Dr LT 4WD Std Cab LB	5078	6259	8226
2 Dr LT Std Cab LB	4139	5101	6704
2 Dr Laramie SLT 4WD Ext Cab LB	5902	7274	9561
2 Dr Laramie SLT 4WD Std Cab LB	5669	6987	9184
2 Dr Laramie SLT Ext Cab LB	5259	6481	8519

Body Styles	TMV Pricing		
	Trade	Private	Dealer
2 Dr Laramie SLT Std Cab LB	4916	6059	7964
2 Dr ST 4WD Ext Cab LB	5609	6913	9087
2 Dr ST Ext Cab LB	4589	5656	7434
2 Dr ST Std Cab LB	4376	5393	7088

Options	Price
Infinity Audio System	+76
5.9L I6 Turbodiesel OHV 12V Engine	+964
8.0L V10 OHV 20V FI Engine	+107
Air Conditioning [Opt on LT,ST]	+182

Options	Price
AM/FM/CD Audio System	+117
Antilock Brakes	+172
Automatic 4-Speed Transmission	+212

1994

Body Styles	TMV Pricing		
	Trade	Private	Dealer
2 Dr LT 4WD Std Cab LB	4162	5373	7391
2 Dr LT Std Cab LB	3089	3988	5486
2 Dr Laramie SLT 4WD Std Cab LB	4567	5896	8110

Body Styles	TMV Pricing		
	Trade	Private	Dealer
2 Dr Laramie SLT Std Cab LB	4111	5307	7300
2 Dr ST 4WD Std Cab LB	4514	5827	8015
2 Dr ST Std Cab LB	3659	4724	6498

Options	Price
5.9L I6 Turbodiesel OHV 12V Engine	+809
8.0L V10 OHV 20V FI Engine	+90
Air Conditioning [Std on Laramie SLT]	+153
Automatic 4-Speed Transmission	+177

Mileage Category: K

Mirroring changes to its 3/4-ton sibling, Dodge's one-ton patriarch is all-new in both single and dual rear wheel models. Sporting curved, muscular sheet metal and a brash Kenworth semi truck-styled grill and headlight assembly, the newly badged 3500 boasts an impressive array of upgrades inside and out. Offered in 118.7-inch and 134.7-inch wheelbases (6.5-foot and 8-foot boxes, respectively), the Magnum engine line equips 2- and 4WD drivelines. A standard 5.9L gas V8 producing 230 horsepower and 330 pound-feet of torque can be upgraded to a brawny 5.9L straight six Cummins turbo diesel(175 horsepower/420 pound-feet of torque) or the newly introduced truck version of the Viper motor, a behemoth 8.0L gas V10 cranking out 300 hp and 450 lb-ft of torque. A standard 5-speed manual transmission can be upgraded to a four-speed automatic and three axle ratios (3.55, 3.90, 4.10) are available. Only offered as a regular cab body, a myriad of power and convenience packages are configurable, or choose the SLT trim with a 40/20/40 cloth bench, power windows and door locks, A/C, cruise control, a fold-down center armrest (capable of housing a cell phone, laptop and music media) and leather-wrapped steering wheel. Choose Claret Red, Flame Red, Light Driftwood, Emerald Green, Dark or Brilliant Blue, Black, Sabre Gray, Silver or Bright White exterior paint with Medium Quartz, Slate Blue, Crimson Red or Medium Driftwood interior colors.

Dodge
Ram Wagon

2002

Body Styles	TMV Pricing		
	Trade	Private	Dealer
3 Dr 1500 Pass Van	10778	11926	13838
3 Dr 2500 Pass Van Ext	11450	12670	14702

Body Styles	TMV Pricing		
	Trade	Private	Dealer
3 Dr 3500 Maxi Pass Van Ext	13007	14392	16700

Options	Price
5.2L V8 Flex Fuel OHV 16V FI Engine [Opt on 2500,3500]	+2346
5.2L V8 OHV 16V FI Engine [Opt on 1500]	+321
5.9L V8 OHV 16V FI Engine [Opt on 2500,3500]	+323
Air Conditioning - Front and Rear [Opt on 2500,3500]	+149
AM/FM/Cassette/CD Audio System	+122
Antilock Brakes	+370

Options	Price
Automatic 4-Speed Transmission [Opt on 1500]	+163
Infinity Audio System	+247
Limited Slip Differential	+155
Power Driver Seat	+163
Power Windows	+147

Mileage Category: Q

No changes for 2002.

2001

Body Styles	TMV Pricing		
	Trade	Private	Dealer
3 Dr 1500 Pass Van	9094	10596	11983
3 Dr 2500 Pass Van Ext	9660	11256	12730
3 Dr 3500 Maxi Pass Van Ext	11024	12846	14527

Options	Price
5.2L V8 Flex Fuel OHV 16V FI Engine	+2152
5.2L V8 OHV 16V FI Engine [Opt on 1500]	+294
5.9L V8 OHV 16V FI Engine	+294
Air Conditioning - Front and Rear	+387
Antilock Brakes	+339
Automatic 4-Speed Transmission [Opt on 1500]	+150

Options	Price
Cruise Control	+127
Infinity Audio System	+227
Limited Slip Differential	+142
Power Driver Seat	+150
Power Windows	+132

Mileage Category: Q

A new trailer tow package and a Class IV receiver hitch. The tilt steering wheel comes with three new positions.

Dodge
Ram Wagon

2000

Mileage Category: Q

Minor changes come with the 2000 model year, including hood-mounted windshield-washer nozzles and chrome-clad wheels. Sealing has been improved to reduce noise and keep out the weather, and Ram Wagons get a six-speaker audio system as standard equipment.

Body Styles	TMV Pricing		
	Trade	Private	Dealer
3 Dr 1500 Pass Van	7025	8290	9530
3 Dr 2500 Pass Van Ext	7678	9060	10415

Options	Price
Air Conditioning - Front and Rear	+382
Antilock Brakes	+307
Automatic 4-Speed Transmission [Opt on 1500]	+136
5.9L V8 OHV 16V FI Engine	+267
Cruise Control	+115
Infinity Audio System	+206

Body Styles	TMV Pricing		
	Trade	Private	Dealer
3 Dr 3500 Maxi Pass Van Ext	8768	10347	11894

Options	Price
Limited Slip Differential	+129
Power Driver Seat	+136
Power Windows	+119
12 Passenger Seating	+129
5.2L V8 OHV 16V FI Engine [Opt on 1500]	+267

1999

Mileage Category: Q

Seat track travel has increased substantially, and the remote keyless entry has been improved. For fleet customers, Ram Vans and Wagons have an available 5.2-liter Compressed Natural Gas V8 engine.

Body Styles	TMV Pricing		
	Trade	Private	Dealer
3 Dr 1500 Pass Van	5977	7230	8534
3 Dr 2500 Pass Van Ext	6634	8025	9473

Options	Price
5.2L V8 OHV 16V FI Engine [Opt on 1500]	+217
Air Conditioning - Front and Rear	+311
AM/FM/Cassette/CD Audio System	+245

Body Styles	TMV Pricing		
	Trade	Private	Dealer
3 Dr 3500 Maxi Pass Van Ext	7142	8639	10198

Options	Price
AM/FM/CD Audio System	+179
Antilock Brakes	+278

1998

Mileage Category: Q

A minor redesign this year includes better build quality. Of note are the appearance of dual airbags in the revised dash and upgrades to the brakes, front doors and sound system. The V8 engines have also been relocated forward to reduce the size of the central "hump" in the cabin.

Body Styles	TMV Pricing		
	Trade	Private	Dealer
3 Dr 1500 Pass Van	4720	5847	7118
3 Dr 1500 SLT Pass Van	4866	6027	7337
3 Dr 2500 Pass Van Ext	5156	6387	7775

Options	Price
Premium Audio System	+180
5.2L V8 OHV 16V FI Engine [Opt on 1500]	+192
5.9L V8 OHV 16V FI Engine	+129
Air Conditioning - Front and Rear	+287

Body Styles	TMV Pricing		
	Trade	Private	Dealer
3 Dr 2500 SLT Pass Van Ext	5346	6623	8062
3 Dr 3500 Maxi Pass Van Ext	5684	7041	8572
3 Dr 3500 SLT Maxi Pass Van Ext	5781	7161	8718

Options	Price
AM/FM/Cassette/CD Audio System	+217
AM/FM/CD Audio System	+158
Antilock Brakes	+246

1997

Mileage Category: Q

New this year are wider cargo doors, upgraded stereo systems, and an improved ignition switch with anti-theft protection. Front quarter vent windows disappear for 1997, and underhood service points feature colored identification.

Body Styles	TMV Pricing		
	Trade	Private	Dealer
3 Dr 1500 Pass Van	3854	4871	6113
3 Dr 1500 SLT Pass Van	4170	5270	6615
3 Dr 2500 Pass Van Ext	4081	5157	6473
3 Dr 2500 SLT Pass Van Ext	4352	5500	6904

Options	Price
5.2L V8 OHV 16V FI Engine [Opt on 1500,2500]	+188
Air Conditioning - Front and Rear [Opt on 1500]	+252
AM/FM/CD Audio System	+139

Body Styles	TMV Pricing		
	Trade	Private	Dealer
3 Dr 3500 Maxi Pass Van Ext	4398	5559	6977
3 Dr 3500 Pass Van Ext	4214	5326	6685
3 Dr 3500 SLT Maxi Pass Van Ext	5077	6417	8054
3 Dr 3500 SLT Pass Van Ext	4443	5615	7048

Options	Price
Antilock Brakes	+217
Premium Audio System	+158

1996

Mileage Category: Q

Base GVWR raised to 6,010 pounds and automatics are electronically governed. CD controls are added to cassette audio systems and an "on" indicator now accompanies cruise control readout. New color offerings include Medium Red, Dark and Light Spruce with Blue Spruce and Camel offered on conversion interior trims only.

Body Styles	TMV Pricing		
	Trade	Private	Dealer
3 Dr 1500 Pass Van	3221	4126	5375
3 Dr 1500 SLT Pass Van	3613	4628	6030
3 Dr 2500 Pass Van Ext	3533	4525	5896
3 Dr 2500 SLT Pass Van Ext	3749	4802	6257

Body Styles	TMV Pricing		
	Trade	Private	Dealer
3 Dr 3500 Maxi Pass Van Ext	3786	4849	6318
3 Dr 3500 Pass Van Ext	3666	4696	6118
3 Dr 3500 SLT Maxi Pass Van Ext	4258	5454	7106
3 Dr 3500 SLT Pass Van Ext	3819	4892	6374

For the latest vehicle information, visit www.edmunds.com

Options	Price
Air Conditioning - Front and Rear	+282
Antilock Brakes	+197

Options	Price
5.2L V8 OHV 16V FI Engine [Opt on 1500,2500]	+170

1995

Body Styles	TMV Pricing		
	Trade	Private	Dealer
3 Dr 1500 Pass Van	2553	3262	4444
3 Dr 1500 SLT Pass Van	2816	3598	4902
3 Dr 2500 Maxi Pass Van Ext	3035	3879	5285
3 Dr 2500 Pass Van Ext	2948	3767	5132
3 Dr 2500 SLT Maxi Pass Van Ext	3343	4272	5821

Body Styles	TMV Pricing		
	Trade	Private	Dealer
3 Dr 2500 SLT Pass Van Ext	3210	4102	5589
3 Dr 3500 Maxi Pass Van Ext	3133	4003	5454
3 Dr 3500 Pass Van Ext	3016	3855	5252
3 Dr 3500 SLT Maxi Pass Van Ext	3607	4610	6281
3 Dr 3500 SLT Pass Van Ext	3403	4349	5925

Mileage Category: Q

Model/engine designations follow Ram truck suit with the 1500, 2500 and 3500 nameplates. Upgrades include chrome-styled wheels, driver airbag with knee bolsters and under-seat storage. "SLT" replaces Luxury Interior Decor Group. Infinity CD sound systems, power driver seats and reading lamps are optional. Hunter Green color available.

Options	Price
12 Passenger Seating	+143
15 Passenger Seating	+194
5.2L V8 OHV 16V FI Engine [Opt on 1500,2500]	+149

Options	Price
8 Passenger Seating	+137
Air Conditioning	+152
Air Conditioning - Front and Rear	+152

1994

Body Styles	TMV Pricing		
	Trade	Private	Dealer
3 Dr B150 LE Pass Van	2111	2843	4063
3 Dr B150 Pass Van	1697	2285	3265
3 Dr B250 LE Pass Van Ext	2436	3281	4688
3 Dr B250 Maxi Pass Van Ext	2341	3153	4506
3 Dr B250 Pass Van Ext	2122	2858	4085

Body Styles	TMV Pricing		
	Trade	Private	Dealer
3 Dr B350 LE Maxi Pass Van Ext	2514	3357	4762
3 Dr B350 LE Maxi Pass Van Ext	2817	3794	5421
3 Dr B350 LE Pass Van Ext	2906	3914	5594
3 Dr B350 Maxi Pass Van Ext	2524	3400	4859
3 Dr B350 Pass Van Ext	2462	3316	4739

Mileage Category: Q

The smoother, more aerodynamic lines and signature crosshair grille step in line with its truck brethren while benefiting from the same Magnum engines. Increased torque for the 3.9L V6 and 5.2L V8 raise the numbers to 225 and 295, respectively. A choice of 107- and 127-inch wheelbases, a three- or four-speed automatic transmission and available 5.9L V8 with 330 lb-ft of torque promise capability for hauling cargo and up to 16 people. Among the many upgrades are ABS, remote keyless entry, Infinity sound system and aluminum road wheels. The manual transmission is no longer offered, and color choices expand to include Light or Medium Turquoise and Dark or Light Gray.

Options	Price
Antilock Brakes	+145
12 Passenger Seating	+120
15 Passenger Seating	+163
5.2L V8 OHV 16V FI Engine [Opt on 1500,2500]	+125

Options	Price
8 Passenger Seating	+115
Air Conditioning	+128
Air Conditioning - Front and Rear	+128

Dodge
Shadow

1994

Body Styles	TMV Pricing		
	Trade	Private	Dealer
2 Dr ES Hbk	596	1044	1790
2 Dr STD Hbk	566	993	1704

Body Styles	TMV Pricing		
	Trade	Private	Dealer
4 Dr ES Hbk	711	1246	2138
4 Dr STD Hbk	580	1017	1744

Options	Price
Antilock Brakes	+145
Automatic 3-Speed Transmission	+105
Automatic 4-Speed Transmission	+144

Options	Price
2.5L I4 SOHC 8V FI Engine [Std on ES]	+86
3.0L V6 SOHC 12V FI Engine	+133
Air Conditioning	+144

Mileage Category: B

Four-door hatchback production stops midyear. Front passengers are now restrained by motorized seatbelt to comply with federal regulations. Air conditioning runs on CFC-free coolant this year.

Dodge
Spirit

1995

Body Styles	TMV Pricing		
	Trade	Private	Dealer
4 Dr STD Sdn	988	1483	2309

Dodge
Spirit/Sprinter/Stealth

1995 (cont'd)

Options	Price
3.0L V6 SOHC 12V FI Engine	+158

Mileage Category: C

Flexible fuel model and optional four-speed automatic transmission are dropped. A three-speed automatic continues as standard equipment.

1994

Mileage Category: C

Motorized seatbelt is introduced for front passengers. Highline and ES trim designations are retired. All 1994 Spirits come equipped one way, with various option packages available.

Body Styles	TMV Pricing		
	Trade	Private	Dealer
4 Dr STD Sdn	684	1120	1846

Options	Price
2.5L I4 Flex Fuel SOHC 8V FI Engine	+106
3.0L V6 SOHC 12V FI Engine	+133

Options	Price
Antilock Brakes	+156
Automatic 4-Speed Transmission	+144

Dodge
Sprinter

2003

Mileage Category: Q

Dodge takes a major leap of faith by replacing the aging Ram Van with a European-styled commercial design engineered by Mercedes-Benz.

Body Styles	TMV Pricing		
	Trade	Private	Dealer
3 Dr 2500 High Roof 140 WB Pass Van Ext	22982	24253	26372
3 Dr 2500 High Roof 158 WB Pass Van Ext	24263	25605	27842
3 Dr 2500 High Roof Pass Van	21416	22601	24575

Body Styles	TMV Pricing		
	Trade	Private	Dealer
3 Dr 2500 Pass Van	20222	21341	23205
3 Dr 2500 Pass Van Ext	21788	22993	25002

Options	Price
Alarm System	+221
AM/FM/CD Audio System	+205
Camper/Towing Package	+164
Cruise Control	+117
Heated Front Seats	+253

Options	Price
Keyless Entry System	+126
Power Door Locks	+136
Power Windows	+167
Special Factory Paint	+221
Air Conditioning - Front and Rear	+616

Dodge
Stealth

1996

Body Styles	TMV Pricing		
	Trade	Private	Dealer
2 Dr R/T Hbk	6079	7350	9104
2 Dr R/T Turbo AWD Hbk	7775	9400	11645

Body Styles	TMV Pricing		
	Trade	Private	Dealer
2 Dr STD Hbk	4252	5179	6460

Options	Price
18 Inch Wheels [Opt on R/T AWD]	+265
Antilock Brakes	+208
Automatic 4-Speed Transmission	+230

Options	Price
Compact Disc Changer	+157
Leather Seats	+220
Power Moonroof	+184

Mileage Category: F

Final year for Japanese-built sports car. A new rear spoiler and body-color roof mark the 1996 model. A chrome 18-inch wheel package is available with Pirelli P-Zero tires and base models get an optional Infinity sound system.

1995

Mileage Category: F

Chromed 18-inch aluminum wheels are available on R/T Turbo.

1995 (cont'd)

Body Styles	TMV Pricing				Body Styles	TMV Pricing		
	Trade	Private	Dealer			Trade	Private	Dealer
2 Dr R/T Hbk	4374	5487	7343		2 Dr STD Hbk	3287	4157	5607
2 Dr R/T Turbo AWD Hbk	5833	7318	9792					

Options	Price		Options	Price
Antilock Brakes [Opt on R/T,STD]	+182		Leather Seats	+192
Automatic 4-Speed Transmission	+224		Moonroof	+92
Compact Disc Changer	+137		18 Inch Wheels [Opt on R/T AWD]	+231
Infinity Audio System [Opt on R/T,R/T AWD]	+89			

1994

Body Styles	TMV Pricing				Body Styles	TMV Pricing		
	Trade	Private	Dealer			Trade	Private	Dealer
2 Dr R/T Hbk	2866	3799	5355		2 Dr R/T Turbo AWD Hbk	4314	5720	8062
2 Dr R/T Luxury Hbk	3374	4473	6305		2 Dr STD Hbk	2193	2937	4176

Options	Price		Options	Price
18 Inch Wheels [Opt on R/T AWD]	+194		Compact Disc Changer	+104
Air Conditioning [Opt on R/T,STD]	+134		Leather Seats	+162
Antilock Brakes [Opt on R/T,STD]	+149		Moonroof	+77
Automatic 4-Speed Transmission	+169		Premium Audio System [Opt on R/T,STD]	+96

Mileage Category: F

Passenger airbag is added. R/T Turbo gains 20 horsepower and a six-speed transmission. ES trim level is dropped. Styling is slightly revised front and rear, revealing the addition of projector-beam headlamps in place of the hidden lights used previously. CFC-free refrigerant is used in the air conditioning system, and R/T models can be painted a bright shade of yellow.

Dodge

Stratus

2003

Body Styles	TMV Pricing				Body Styles	TMV Pricing		
	Trade	Private	Dealer			Trade	Private	Dealer
2 Dr R/T Cpe	11511	12701	14684		4 Dr R/T Sdn	11284	12453	14402
2 Dr SXT Cpe	9081	10020	11585		4 Dr SE Sdn	8954	9882	11428
4 Dr ES Sdn	10544	11637	13458		4 Dr SXT Sdn	8872	9792	11324

Options	Price		Options	Price
Aluminum/Alloy Wheels [Opt on SE]	+268		Front Side Airbag Restraints [Opt on Cpe]	+246
Antilock Brakes	+430		Special Factory Paint	+126
Automatic 4-Speed Transmission [Opt on R/T,SXT Cpe]	+521		17 Inch Wheels - Chrome [Opt on R/T Cpe]	+474
Leather Seats [Opt on ES,R/T]	+379		Premium Audio System [Opt on ES]	+221
Power Door Locks [Opt on SE]	+126		AM/FM/Cassette/CD Changer Audio System [Opt on ES,R/T Sdn]	+190
Power Driver Seat	+130		Front and Rear Head Airbag Restraints [Opt on Sdn]	+246
Power Moonroof	+439			

Mileage Category: C

The 2003 Stratus coupe gains revisions to its front and rear styling and an updated instrument panel and center console. The SE coupe is dropped in a sense; it will only be available to fleet buyers, such as rental car agencies. Sedans continue as before except the SE Plus is subtracted and the V6 engine (with the automatic transmission) is now flexible fuel-rated, meaning it can run on ethanol as well as gasoline.

2002

Body Styles	TMV Pricing				Body Styles	TMV Pricing		
	Trade	Private	Dealer			Trade	Private	Dealer
2 Dr R/T Cpe	8927	10032	11874		4 Dr R/T Sdn	8985	10108	11979
2 Dr SE Cpe	7160	8047	9524		4 Dr SE Plus Sdn	7714	8678	10284
2 Dr SXT Cpe	7389	8304	9830		4 Dr SE Sdn	7117	8007	9490
4 Dr ES Sdn	8487	9505	11201		4 Dr SXT Sdn	7093	7945	9364

Options	Price		Options	Price
17 Inch Wheels [Opt on R/T]	+204		Chrome Wheels [Opt on ES Sdn]	+326
2.7L V6 DOHC 24V FI Engine [Opt on Sdn - SE,SE Plus]	+462		Cruise Control [Opt on SE Plus Sdn]	+128
3.0L V6 SOHC 24V FI Engine [Opt on SE Cpe]	+481		Front and Rear Head Airbag Restraints [Opt on Sdn]	+212
Aluminum/Alloy Wheels [Opt on SE Cpe]	+198		Leather Seats [Opt on ES,R/T]	+326
AM/FM/Cassette/CD Changer Audio System [Std on R/T Sdn,SXT]	+136		Power Driver Seat [Opt on R/T]	+144
Antilock Brakes [Std on R/T Sdn]	+370		Power Sunroof [Opt on Cpe,Sdn]	+378

Mileage Category: C

A new R/T sedan joins the lineup, complete with a healthy V6 and manual gearbox. Other additions to the family include the SE Plus and SXT sedans and an SXT coupe. All Strati gain a "battery saver" device and new audio features. For coupes, a stereo with a four-CD in-dash changer is available in the Touring Package and is standard on the R/T model. For sedans the new option of a stereo with both CD and cassette players debuts. New color choices include Steel Blue, Onyx Green and Light Almond Pearl now available for sedans, and Dark Titanium and Caffe Latte added to the coupes' color palette.

Dodge
Stratus

2001
Mileage Category: C

The Avenger nameplate has been dropped from the Dodge lineup, replaced by the all-new Stratus Coupe. The Stratus Sedan continues with a full redesign but retains much of its predecessor's look and feel. A new engine debuts along with additional safety features that make the Stratus a family sedan in the truest sense.

Body Styles	TMV Pricing		
	Trade	Private	Dealer
2 Dr R/T Cpe	7749	9259	10652
2 Dr SE Cpe	6141	7336	8440

Options	Price
3.0L V6 SOHC 24V FI Engine [Opt on SE Cpe]	+424
Aluminum/Alloy Wheels	+175
AM/FM/Cassette/CD Audio System	+125
AM/FM/Cassette/CD Changer Audio System [Opt on ES,SE]	+125
Antilock Brakes	+339
Automatic 4-Speed Transmission [Opt on Cpe]	+411

Body Styles	TMV Pricing		
	Trade	Private	Dealer
4 Dr ES Sdn	6462	7722	8886
4 Dr SE Sdn	6263	7484	8612

Options	Price
Chrome Wheels [Opt on SE Sdn]	+299
Front and Rear Head Airbag Restraints [Opt on Sdn]	+195
Leather Seats	+289
Power Driver Seat	+189
Power Sunroof	+342
Premium Audio System	+175

2000

Body Styles	TMV Pricing		
	Trade	Private	Dealer
4 Dr ES Sdn	4697	5827	6934

Options	Price
AM/FM/Cassette/CD Audio System	+154
Antilock Brakes [Opt on SE]	+307
Automatic 4-Speed Transmission [Opt on SE]	+475
Compact Disc Changer	+249

Mileage Category: C

Body Styles	TMV Pricing		
	Trade	Private	Dealer
4 Dr SE Sdn	4032	5002	5952

Options	Price
Power Driver Seat	+171
Power Sunroof	+314
Power Windows [Opt on SE]	+117
2.4L I4 DOHC 16V FI Engine [Opt on SE]	+204

A new entry-level SE replaces last year's Base model and comes with so much standard equipment. The upper-level ES steps up to a 2.5-liter V6, and new colors also debut.

1999
Mileage Category: C

The instrument panel gauges are now white-faced, wheels are better looking, and some work has been done to reduce the interior noise levels.

Body Styles	TMV Pricing		
	Trade	Private	Dealer
4 Dr ES Sdn	3580	4591	5644

Options	Price
2.4L I4 DOHC 16V FI Engine	+166
AM/FM/Cassette/CD Audio System	+203
Antilock Brakes [Opt on STD]	+278
Automatic 4-Speed Transmission [Opt on STD]	+387

Body Styles	TMV Pricing		
	Trade	Private	Dealer
4 Dr STD Sdn	3196	4100	5040

Options	Price
Compact Disc Changer	+203
Leather Seats	+230
Power Driver Seat	+140
Power Sunroof	+214

1998
Mileage Category: C

The 2.4-liter engine with automatic transmission is now standard on the ES. New colors are available this year and numerous refinements are made to reduce noise and vibration.

Body Styles	TMV Pricing		
	Trade	Private	Dealer
4 Dr ES Sdn	2722	3639	4674

Options	Price
Power Sunroof	+189
2.4L I4 DOHC 16V FI Engine [Opt on STD]	+146
2.5L V6 SOHC 24V FI Engine	+310
AM/FM/Cassette/CD Audio System	+180
Antilock Brakes	+246

Body Styles	TMV Pricing		
	Trade	Private	Dealer
4 Dr STD Sdn	2345	3136	4029

Options	Price
Automatic 4-Speed Transmission [Opt on STD]	+342
Compact Disc Changer	+180
Leather Seats	+203
Power Driver Seat	+124

1997
Mileage Category: C

Subtle styling revisions are the most obvious change to the Stratus for 1997. Sound systems have been improved, rear seat heat ducts benefit from improved flow, and the optional 2.4-liter engine runs quieter. New colors and a revised console round out changes.

Body Styles	TMV Pricing		
	Trade	Private	Dealer
4 Dr ES Sdn	2040	2810	3751

Options	Price
2.4L I4 DOHC 16V FI Engine	+129
2.5L V6 SOHC 24V FI Engine	+272
AM/FM/Cassette/CD Audio System	+158
Antilock Brakes [Std on ES]	+217

Body Styles	TMV Pricing		
	Trade	Private	Dealer
4 Dr STD Sdn	1852	2551	3406

Options	Price
Automatic 4-Speed Transmission	+236
Compact Disc Changer	+158
Leather Seats	+179

1996

Body Styles	TMV Pricing		
	Trade	Private	Dealer
4 Dr ES Sdn	1515	2174	3083

Options	Price
Power Sunroof	+151
2.4L I4 DOHC 16V FI Engine	+117
2.5L V6 SOHC 24V FI Engine	+248
AM/FM/CD Audio System	+129

Body Styles	TMV Pricing		
	Trade	Private	Dealer
4 Dr STD Sdn	1457	2090	2964

Options	Price
Antilock Brakes [Std on ES]	+197
Automatic 4-Speed Transmission	+215
Leather Seats	+163

Mileage Category: C

Excellent midsized sedan gets a more responsive torque converter when equipped with the 2.5-liter V6. New colors and a power sunroof are also new for 1996.

1995

Body Styles	TMV Pricing		
	Trade	Private	Dealer
4 Dr ES Sdn	1237	1858	2894

Options	Price
2.4L I4 DOHC 16V FI Engine	+102
Antilock Brakes [Opt on STD]	+172
Automatic 4-Speed Transmission [Opt on STD]	+188

Body Styles	TMV Pricing		
	Trade	Private	Dealer
4 Dr STD Sdn	1104	1658	2580

Options	Price
Leather Seats	+143
Power Driver Seat	+80
Premium Audio System	+84

Mileage Category: C

Spirit replacement features cutting-edge styling and class-leading accommodations. Dual airbags and ABS are standard. Base and ES models are available. Base model has 2.0-liter, four-cylinder engine making 132 horsepower and a five-speed manual transmission. ES is powered by 155-horsepower, Mitsubishi 2.5-liter V6. A credit option on the ES is the Neon's 2.0-liter four hooked to a five-speed manual transmission.

Dodge
Viper

2003

Body Styles	TMV Pricing		
	Trade	Private	Dealer
2 Dr SRT-10 Conv	66200	68879	73343

Mileage Category: R

Dodge hatches a new snake with a real roadster body, scary output figures (how's 500 horsepower sound?) and improved build quality.

2002

Body Styles	TMV Pricing		
	Trade	Private	Dealer
2 Dr ACR Competition Cpe	62966	65864	70694
2 Dr GTS Cpe	55292	57837	62078

Options	Price
Alpine Audio System [Opt on ACR]	+217
AM/FM/CD Audio System [Opt on ACR]	+245

Body Styles	TMV Pricing		
	Trade	Private	Dealer
2 Dr RT/10 Conv	54609	57122	61311

Options	Price
Special Factory Paint	+1631
Special Leather Seat Trim	+408

Mileage Category: R

Nothing's new except for an available color scheme on the GTS: Graphite metallic with silver stripes.

2001

Body Styles	TMV Pricing		
	Trade	Private	Dealer
2 Dr ACR Competition Cpe	58629	62780	66612
2 Dr GTS Cpe	50204	53758	57039

Options	Price
AM/FM/CD Audio System [Std on GTS,R/T 10]	+275
Hardtop Roof	+1247

Body Styles	TMV Pricing		
	Trade	Private	Dealer
2 Dr RT/10 Conv	49951	53488	56753

Options	Price
Special Factory Paint [Opt on ACR,GTS]	+1496

Mileage Category: R

Slightly refining the snake's venomous bite are standard four-wheel disc ABS, an ACR option group with air conditioning and a CD player, and an internal trunk. New Race Yellow or Deep Sapphire Blue exterior hues are offered.

Dodge
Viper

2000

Mileage Category: R

The 2000 Viper is available in a new Steel Gray color and the new ACR version offers additional performance.

Body Styles	TMV Pricing		
	Trade	Private	Dealer
2 Dr ACR Competition Cpe	54332	58507	62600
2 Dr GTS Cpe	44315	47720	51058

Body Styles	TMV Pricing		
	Trade	Private	Dealer
2 Dr RT/10 Conv	43907	47281	50588

Options	Price
AM/FM/CD Audio System [Opt on ACR]	+249
Hardtop Roof	+1130

Options	Price
Special Factory Paint [Opt on GTS]	+1130

1999

Mileage Category: R

Goodies for the '99 Viper include power mirrors, Connolly leather for various interior surfaces, a new shift knob, aluminum interior accents, and a remote release for the glass hatch on the GTS. Black is again an exterior color choice, available with or without silver stripes. New 18-inch aluminum wheels with the Viper logo on the caps round out the changes.

Body Styles	TMV Pricing		
	Trade	Private	Dealer
2 Dr GTS Cpe	40030	43694	47508

Body Styles	TMV Pricing		
	Trade	Private	Dealer
2 Dr RT/10 Conv	39815	43459	47252

Options	Price
Hardtop Roof	+921

Options	Price
Special Factory Paint [Opt on GTS]	+737

1998

Mileage Category: R

Tubular, stainless steel exhaust manifolds help reduce emissions and weight. Silver Metallic paint is a new option and the powerful Dodge gets a passenger airbag cutoff switch and second-generation depowered airbags.

Body Styles	TMV Pricing		
	Trade	Private	Dealer
2 Dr GTS Cpe	34794	38153	41941

Body Styles	TMV Pricing		
	Trade	Private	Dealer
2 Dr RT/10 Conv	34248	37555	41284

Options	Price
Hardtop Roof	+815

Options	Price
Special Factory Paint [Opt on GTS]	+489

1997

Mileage Category: R

One new color, flame red, with or without white stripes, is available for 1997. Silver, sparkle gold or yellow gold wheels come with red Vipers. The original blue with white stripes paint scheme is available as an option, as are last year's standard polished aluminum wheels. The RT/10 roadster is set to return later this year, with dual airbags, power windows and door locks, and the 450-horsepower V10 from the GTS. Also set to debut on the revamped drop top are the four-wheel independent suspension and adjustable pedals from the GTS.

Body Styles	TMV Pricing		
	Trade	Private	Dealer
2 Dr GTS Cpe	32182	35489	39531

Body Styles	TMV Pricing		
	Trade	Private	Dealer
2 Dr RT/10 Conv	30537	33675	37511

Options	Price
Hardtop Roof	+717

Options	Price
Special Factory Paint [Opt on GTS]	+344

1996

Mileage Category: R

Final year for Viper in current form. More power is offered from the V10 engine via a low-restriction rear outlet exhaust system, and an optional hardtop with sliding side curtains is available. Five-spoke aluminum wheels and three exterior styling themes replace the trim on the 1995 Viper. GTS coupe begins production when convertibles have completed their run. The GTS arrives with dual airbags and air conditioning.

Body Styles	TMV Pricing		
	Trade	Private	Dealer
2 Dr GTS Cpe	29789	32948	37311

Body Styles	TMV Pricing		
	Trade	Private	Dealer
2 Dr RT/10 Conv	27318	30215	34216

Options	Price
Air Conditioning [Opt on RT/10]	+348

Options	Price
Hardtop Roof	+653

1995

Mileage Category: R

No changes.

Body Styles		TMV Pricing		
		Trade	Private	Dealer
2 Dr RT/10 Conv		25317	27951	32342

Options	Price
Air Conditioning	+304

Options	Price
AM/FM/CD Audio System	+125

1994

Mileage Category: R

Air conditioning with CFC-free refrigerant can be installed at the factory when the appropriate option box is checked. Green and yellow are added to the color chart. Green cars get a new black-and-tan interior.

Body Styles		TMV Pricing		
		Trade	Private	Dealer
2 Dr RT/10 Conv		22689	25272	29576

Options	Price
Air Conditioning	+255

1996

Body Styles	TMV Pricing		
	Trade	Private	Dealer
2 Dr DL Cpe	1031	1459	2050
2 Dr ESi Cpe	1139	1612	2264
4 Dr DL Wgn	1459	2064	2900
4 Dr ESi Sdn	1391	1967	2763

Body Styles	TMV Pricing		
	Trade	Private	Dealer
4 Dr LX Sdn	1316	1862	2617
4 Dr LX Wgn	1602	2267	3185
4 Dr STD AWD Wgn	1688	2389	3356

Options	Price
Air Conditioning	+147
Antilock Brakes	+131
Automatic 4-Speed Transmission	+129

Mileage Category: B

Nothing changes for the Mitsubishi-built Summit except a new choice of paint colors. The Summit wagon, cross between a sedan and a minivan, gets new colors and seat fabrics.

1995

Mileage Category: B

Dual airbags for the slow-selling Eagle Summit are the only change for 1995.

Body Styles	TMV Pricing		
	Trade	Private	Dealer
2 Dr DL Cpe	791	1132	1699
2 Dr ESi Cpe	921	1318	1980
4 Dr DL Wgn	1053	1507	2263
4 Dr ESi Sdn	1019	1459	2191

Body Styles	TMV Pricing		
	Trade	Private	Dealer
4 Dr LX Sdn	987	1413	2122
4 Dr LX Wgn	1151	1647	2474
4 Dr STD AWD Wgn	1184	1694	2544

Options	Price
Air Conditioning	+123
Antilock Brakes	+109

Options	Price
Automatic 3-Speed Transmission	+76
Automatic 4-Speed Transmission	+108

1994

Mileage Category: B

A driver airbag is added to the standard equipment list of the Eagle Summit. CFC-free air conditioning is now standard on all models equipped with air conditioning. Power steering is standard on all sedan models.

Body Styles	TMV Pricing		
	Trade	Private	Dealer
2 Dr DL Cpe	494	742	1156
2 Dr ES Cpe	586	880	1370
2 Dr ESi Cpe	650	975	1517
4 Dr DL Wgn	772	1159	1803
4 Dr ES Sdn	741	1113	1732

Body Styles	TMV Pricing		
	Trade	Private	Dealer
4 Dr ESi Sdn	835	1253	1949
4 Dr LX Sdn	680	1021	1588
4 Dr LX Wgn	916	1375	2140
4 Dr STD AWD Wgn	937	1406	2188

Options	Price
Air Conditioning	+106
Antilock Brakes	+94
Automatic 4-Speed Transmission	+92

1998

Body Styles	TMV Pricing		
	Trade	Private	Dealer
2 Dr ESi Hbk	4179	4973	5868
2 Dr STD Hbk	4058	4829	5698

Body Styles	TMV Pricing		
	Trade	Private	Dealer
2 Dr TSi Turbo AWD Hbk	5513	6560	7740
2 Dr TSi Turbo Hbk	5089	6055	7145

Options	Price
Air Conditioning	+260
Aluminum/Alloy Wheels [Opt on ESi]	+154
AM/FM/Cassette/CD Audio System	+122
AM/FM/CD Audio System	+122
Antilock Brakes	+238

Options	Price
Automatic 4-Speed Transmission	+225
Infinity Audio System	+240
Leather Seats	+166
Power Sunroof	+220

Mileage Category: E

New silver exterior badging and a new black and gray interior mark the Eagle in its final year of production. A new four-speaker CD/cassette player is now optional on the ESi, and all Talons benefit from Chrysler's next-generation depowered airbags.

Eagle
Talon/Vision

1997

Mileage Category: E

New front and rear fascias, bodyside cladding, bright new paint colors and "sparkle" wheels and wheel covers are guaranteed to attract attention to this overshadowed model.

Body Styles	TMV Pricing		
	Trade	Private	Dealer
2 Dr ESi Hbk	3432	4174	5080
2 Dr STD Hbk	3258	3962	4823

Options	Price
Air Conditioning	+199
Aluminum/Alloy Wheels [Opt on ESi]	+117
AM/FM/Cassette Audio System [Opt on ESi,STD]	+116
Antilock Brakes	+182

Body Styles	TMV Pricing		
	Trade	Private	Dealer
2 Dr TSi Turbo AWD Hbk	4573	5562	6771
2 Dr TSi Turbo Hbk	4231	5145	6263

Options	Price
Automatic 4-Speed Transmission	+208
Leather Seats	+127
Power Sunroof	+169
Premium Audio System	+171

1996

Mileage Category: E

Based on Mitsubishi mechanicals, Talon receives minor upgrades for 1996, including revised sound systems, a panic alarm, a HomeLink transmitter and two new colors. ESi trim level gets standard 16-inch wheels.

Body Styles	TMV Pricing		
	Trade	Private	Dealer
2 Dr ESi Hbk	2545	3233	4183
2 Dr STD Hbk	2442	3102	4014

Options	Price
Power Sunroof	+127
Air Conditioning	+149
AM/FM/Cassette/CD Audio System	+137

Body Styles	TMV Pricing		
	Trade	Private	Dealer
2 Dr TSi Turbo AWD Hbk	3168	4024	5207
2 Dr TSi Turbo Hbk	2909	3695	4781

Options	Price
Antilock Brakes	+137
Automatic 4-Speed Transmission	+155

1995

Mileage Category: Et

The Talon is redesigned for 1995. The new model features a new body and more power. Base engine creeps up to 140 horsepower, the turbo to 210 horsepower. Dual airbags replace the antiquated motorized seatbelts on the previous edition, and the Talon now meets 1997 federal side-impact standards.

Body Styles	TMV Pricing		
	Trade	Private	Dealer
2 Dr ESi Hbk	1876	2504	3550
2 Dr TSi Turbo AWD Hbk	2381	3177	4504
2 Dr TSi Turbo Hbk	2106	2811	3985

Options	Price
Air Conditioning	+124
Antilock Brakes	+114
Automatic 4-Speed Transmission	+108

Options	Price
Leather Seats	+80
Power Sunroof	+106

1994

Mileage Category: E

No changes for the Talon.

Body Styles	TMV Pricing		
	Trade	Private	Dealer
2 Dr DL Hbk	1158	1659	2494
2 Dr ES Hbk	1329	1904	2863

Options	Price
Air Conditioning	+107
Antilock Brakes	+98
Automatic 4-Speed Transmission	+92

Body Styles	TMV Pricing		
	Trade	Private	Dealer
2 Dr TSi Turbo AWD Hbk	1714	2456	3692
2 Dr TSi Turbo Hbk	1458	2090	3142

Options	Price
Premium Audio System	+92
Sunroof	+81

Eagle
Vision

1997

Body Styles	TMV Pricing		
	Trade	Private	Dealer
4 Dr ESi Sdn	2481	3222	4127
4 Dr TSi Sdn	2878	3738	4788

Options	Price
AM/FM/Cassette/CD Audio System	+139
Antilock Brakes [Opt on ESi]	+182
Compact Disc Changer [Opt on ESi]	+161

Options	Price
Infinity Audio System	+131
Leather Seats	+143
Power Moonroof	+166

Mileage Category: G

1997 (cont'd)

The 3.5-liter engine, formerly exclusive to the TSi, is now available on the ESi. Automatic transmission refinements are intended to improve shifting. Eagle Vision ESi gets an improved stereo. A new color, Deep Amethyst Pearl, is now available.

1996

Mileage Category: G

An automanual transmission called AutoStick gives the 1996 Vision a feature to distinguish it as Chrysler's premier sport sedan. Interiors have been quieted down, and the ESi gets standard 16-inch wheels. Headlight illumination has been improved, new colors and seat fabrics are on board, and improved sound systems debut.

Body Styles	TMV Pricing		
	Trade	Private	Dealer
4 Dr ESi Sdn	2071	2706	3584
4 Dr TSi Sdn	2424	3168	4196

Options	Price
Antilock Brakes [Opt on ESi]	+137
Power Moonroof	+125

1995

Mileage Category: G

No changes to the Vision.

Body Styles	TMV Pricing		
	Trade	Private	Dealer
4 Dr ESi Sdn	1694	2246	3165
4 Dr TSi Sdn	2032	2693	3795

Options	Price	Options	Price
Power Moonroof	+104	Antilock Brakes [Opt on ESi]	+114
AM/FM/CD Audio System	+76	Leather Seats	+90

1994

Mileage Category: G

ESi models restyled to resemble their TSi stablemates by adding body cladding and a similar front fascia. The ESi's engine gains an increase in horsepower for 1994 as well. A flexible fuel version of the Vision is released in all states but California.

Body Styles	TMV Pricing		
	Trade	Private	Dealer
4 Dr ESi Sdn	1509	2063	2985
4 Dr TSi Sdn	1758	2403	3477

Options	Price
Antilock Brakes [Opt on ESi]	+98
Leather Seats	+77
Power Moonroof	+90

Ford
Aerostar/Aspire

1997

Body Styles	TMV Pricing		
	Trade	Private	Dealer
3 Dr XLT AWD Pass Van Ext	2987	3842	4888
3 Dr XLT Pass Van	2305	2965	3771

Options	Price
Air Conditioning - Front and Rear	+255
AM/FM/Cassette Audio System	+119

Mileage Category: P

Body Styles	TMV Pricing		
	Trade	Private	Dealer
3 Dr XLT Pass Van Ext	2700	3473	4418

Options	Price
Captain Chairs (4)	+197

Ford's aging minivan gets a five-speed automatic transmission this year. The sound systems are upgraded and the seats are restyled as well.

1996

Mileage Category: P

Smoother shifting transmission debuts, along with revised air conditioning controls and a new radio with visible controls. Solar-tinted glass is standard.

Body Styles	TMV Pricing		
	Trade	Private	Dealer
3 Dr XLT AWD Pass Van Ext	2309	3026	4016
3 Dr XLT Pass Van	1827	2394	3177

Options	Price
Captain Chairs (2)	+122
Captain Chairs (4)	+174

Body Styles	TMV Pricing		
	Trade	Private	Dealer
3 Dr XLT Pass Van Ext	2172	2846	3777

Options	Price
Air Conditioning - Front and Rear	+227

1995

Mileage Category: P

The XL and Eddie Bauer trim levels are dropped; only the XLT remains. The AWD system is available only in extended-length versions. Antilock brakes become standard for the Aerostar.

Body Styles	TMV Pricing		
	Trade	Private	Dealer
3 Dr XLT AWD Pass Van Ext	1618	2204	3180
3 Dr XLT Pass Van	1337	1822	2629

Options	Price
Air Conditioning - Front and Rear	+196
Aluminum/Alloy Wheels	+82

Body Styles	TMV Pricing		
	Trade	Private	Dealer
3 Dr XLT Pass Van Ext	1493	2033	2934

Options	Price
Captain Chairs (4)	+151

1994

Mileage Category: P

A high-mounted rear brake light is standard. No other changes to Ford's venerable minivan.

Body Styles	TMV Pricing		
	Trade	Private	Dealer
3 Dr Eddie Bauer AWD Pass Van	1335	1951	2977
3 Dr Eddie Bauer AWD Pass Van Ext	1420	2075	3167
3 Dr Eddie Bauer Pass Van	1233	1802	2751
3 Dr Eddie Bauer Pass Van Ext	1278	1868	2851
3 Dr XL AWD Pass Van	1081	1580	2412
3 Dr XL AWD Pass Van Ext	1115	1629	2486
3 Dr XL Pass Van	850	1243	1897
3 Dr XL Pass Van Ext	947	1384	2113

Options	Price
Air Conditioning [Std on XLT]	+165
Air Conditioning - Front and Rear [Std on Eddie Bauer]	+165
Automatic 4-Speed Transmission [Std on Eddie Bauer, XLT, 4WD]	+124

Body Styles	TMV Pricing		
	Trade	Private	Dealer
3 Dr XL Plus AWD Pass Van	1131	1653	2523
3 Dr XL Plus AWD Pass Van Ext	1164	1701	2596
3 Dr XL Plus Pass Van	964	1409	2151
3 Dr XL Plus Pass Van Ext	1022	1493	2279
3 Dr XLT AWD Pass Van	1199	1753	2675
3 Dr XLT AWD Pass Van Ext	1228	1794	2738
3 Dr XLT Pass Van	1068	1561	2383
3 Dr XLT Pass Van Ext	1165	1703	2599

Options	Price
Captain Chairs (4)	+128
Leather Seats	+133

Ford
Aspire

1997

Mileage Category: A

This Kia-built entry-level Ford gets a higher final drive ratio on models equipped with an automatic transmission. New wheel covers, paint choices and interior trim are the only other changes.

Body Styles	TMV Pricing		
	Trade	Private	Dealer
2 Dr STD Hbk	967	1478	2103
4 Dr STD Hbk	1022	1562	2223

Options	Price
Air Conditioning	+242
AM/FM/Cassette Audio System	+151
Antilock Brakes	+222
Automatic 3-Speed Transmission	+193

1996

Body Styles	TMV Pricing		
	Trade	Private	Dealer
2 Dr STD Hbk	684	1080	1628

Options	Price
Air Conditioning	+215
AM/FM/Cassette Audio System	+121

Body Styles	TMV Pricing		
	Trade	Private	Dealer
4 Dr STD Hbk	735	1162	1752

Options	Price
Antilock Brakes	+197
Automatic 3-Speed Transmission	+172

Mileage Category: A

The Aspire loses the SE trim level and several items of standard and optional equipment. Four new colors debut.

1995

Body Styles	TMV Pricing		
	Trade	Private	Dealer
2 Dr SE Hbk	576	925	1506
2 Dr STD Hbk	542	871	1418

Options	Price
Air Conditioning	+186
AM/FM/Cassette Audio System	+105
AM/FM/CD Audio System	+79

Body Styles	TMV Pricing		
	Trade	Private	Dealer
4 Dr STD Hbk	561	901	1468

Options	Price
Antilock Brakes	+170
Automatic 3-Speed Transmission	+149

Mileage Category: A

Available as a two- or four-door hatchback, the Aspire comes with dual airbags and available antilock brakes.

1994

Body Styles	TMV Pricing		
	Trade	Private	Dealer
2 Dr SE Hbk	424	727	1231
2 Dr STD Hbk	378	648	1099

Options	Price
Air Conditioning	+157
AM/FM/Cassette Audio System	+89

Body Styles	TMV Pricing		
	Trade	Private	Dealer
4 Dr STD Hbk	423	725	1229

Options	Price
Antilock Brakes	+144
Automatic 3-Speed Transmission	+126

Mileage Category: A

Ford introduces the Korean-built Aspire as a replacement for the aging Festiva. This little econobox has a 1.3-liter inline-four that produces 63 horsepower. The Aspire is available with a five-speed manual or a three-speed automatic transmission.

Ford
Bronco

1996

Body Styles	TMV Pricing		
	Trade	Private	Dealer
2 Dr Eddie Bauer 4WD SUV	6375	7640	9387
2 Dr XL 4WD SUV	5098	6109	7506
2 Dr XLT 4WD SUV	5680	6807	8363

Options	Price
Leather Seats	+181
Air Conditioning [Opt on XL,XLT]	+205
Automatic 4-Speed Transmission [Opt on XL,XLT]	+268

Mileage Category: N

Trick new turn signal system is embedded in sideview mirrors. Otherwise, minor trim changes mark the passing of the last Bronco.

Ford
Bronco/Contour

1995

Mileage Category: N

An available Sport Package and new exterior styling for the Eddie Bauer model are the sole changes for 1995.

Body Styles	TMV Pricing		
	Trade	Private	Dealer
2 Dr Eddie Bauer 4WD SUV	5027	6157	8039
2 Dr XL 4WD SUV	4044	4953	6467

Body Styles	TMV Pricing		
	Trade	Private	Dealer
2 Dr XLT 4WD SUV	4412	5404	7056

Options	Price
Air Conditioning [Opt on XL,XLT]	+177
AM/FM/CD Audio System	+98
Automatic 4-Speed Transmission [Opt on XL,XLT]	+232

Options	Price
Camper/Towing Package	+81
Chrome Wheels	+90
Leather Seats	+157

1994

Mileage Category: N

The 1994 Bronco receives a driver airbag and door guard beams. ABS now works in two-wheel drive and four-wheel drive.

Body Styles	TMV Pricing		
	Trade	Private	Dealer
2 Dr Eddie Bauer 4WD SUV	3954	5076	6946
2 Dr XL 4WD SUV	3328	4272	5846

Body Styles	TMV Pricing		
	Trade	Private	Dealer
2 Dr XLT 4WD SUV	3524	4523	6189

Options	Price
Air Conditioning [Opt on XL,XLT]	+150
AM/FM/CD Audio System	+83
Automatic 4-Speed Transmission [Opt on XL,XLT]	+196

Options	Price
Chrome Wheels	+76
Leather Seats	+133

Ford
Contour

2000

Mileage Category: C

The Contour LX is dropped, leaving either the Contour SE Sport or SVT Contour to pick from. New colors are offered and an emergency trunk-release handle is standard.

Body Styles		TMV Pricing		
		Trade	Private	Dealer
4 Dr SE Sdn		3743	4574	5389
4 Dr SE Sport Sdn		3753	4587	5404

Options	Price
Power Driver Seat	+165
Power Moonroof	+280
2.5L V6 DOHC 24V FI Engine [Opt on SE]	+233
Aluminum/Alloy Wheels [Opt on SE]	+200

Options	Price
AM/FM/Cassette/CD Audio System	+130
AM/FM/CD Audio System	+130
Antilock Brakes	+320
Automatic 4-Speed Transmission	+384

1999

Mileage Category: C

Base and GL models are both dropped and the LX and SE receive minor suspension tweaks.

Body Styles		TMV Pricing		
		Trade	Private	Dealer
4 Dr LX Sdn		2913	3675	4468
4 Dr SE Sdn		2969	3746	4554

Options	Price
2.5L V6 DOHC 24V FI Engine [Std on SE]	+193
Aluminum/Alloy Wheels	+165
Antilock Brakes	+293
Automatic 4-Speed Transmission	+317

Options	Price
Leather Seats [Opt on SE]	+348
Power Driver Seat	+136
Power Moonroof	+231
Power Windows [Opt on LX]	+138

1998

Mileage Category: C

A redesigned face gives this Ford more character, but the new taillight treatment is almost identical to the Contour's sibling, the Mercury Mystique. New alloy wheels and a slightly more commodious rear seat debut. Midyear changes included a model consolidation, the addition of depowered airbags, as well as improved handling and new wheels for the SVT.

Body Styles		TMV Pricing		
		Trade	Private	Dealer
4 Dr GL Sdn		2144	2883	3717
4 Dr LX Sdn		2239	3011	3882
4 Dr SE Sdn		2367	3183	4103
4 Dr STD Sdn		1983	2667	3438

1998 (cont'd)

Options	Price
2.5L V6 DOHC 24V FI Engine	+157
Air Conditioning	+255
Aluminum/Alloy Wheels	+135
Antilock Brakes	+240

Options	Price
Automatic 4-Speed Transmission	+259
Compact Disc Changer	+143
Leather Seats	+284
Power Moonroof	+188

1997

Body Styles	TMV Pricing		
	Trade	Private	Dealer
4 Dr GL Sdn	1475	2178	3038
4 Dr LX Sdn	1528	2257	3148

Body Styles	TMV Pricing		
	Trade	Private	Dealer
4 Dr SE Sdn	1721	2542	3545

Mileage Category: C

The addition of a Sport Package for the GL and LX models and the inclusion of a standard trunk light are the only changes for the 1997 Contour.

Options	Price
2.5L V6 DOHC 24V FI Engine [Std on SE]	+317
Air Conditioning	+233
Aluminum/Alloy Wheels [Std on SE]	+124
Antilock Brakes	+222

Options	Price
Automatic 4-Speed Transmission	+239
Leather Seats	+262
Power Moonroof	+174

1996

Body Styles	TMV Pricing		
	Trade	Private	Dealer
4 Dr GL Sdn	1021	1575	2339
4 Dr LX Sdn	1071	1651	2453

Body Styles	TMV Pricing		
	Trade	Private	Dealer
4 Dr SE Sdn	1219	1880	2793

Mileage Category: C

Designers sculpt and adjust interior seating to make more leg- and headroom in the backseat. Five new colors are available and improvements to shift effort on manual transmission models make the 1996 Contour more competitive.

Options	Price
2.5L V6 DOHC 24V FI Engine [Opt on GL,LX]	+282
Air Conditioning	+204
Antilock Brakes	+197

Options	Price
Automatic 4-Speed Transmission	+213
Leather Seats	+168
Power Moonroof	+155

1995

Body Styles	TMV Pricing		
	Trade	Private	Dealer
4 Dr GL Sdn	862	1331	2112
4 Dr LX Sdn	887	1368	2170

Body Styles	TMV Pricing		
	Trade	Private	Dealer
4 Dr SE Sdn	1002	1547	2454

Mileage Category: C

The Contour replaces the Tempo to compete with European and Japanese compacts. Based on the European Mondeo, the Contour has front-wheel drive and dual airbags. Traction control and antilock brakes are available on all models, as is a V6 engine that produces an impressive 170 horsepower.

Options	Price
AM/FM/CD Audio System	+79
Antilock Brakes	+170
Automatic 4-Speed Transmission	+184
Leather Seats	+146
Power Moonroof	+134

Options	Price
Power Windows	+77
2.5L V6 DOHC 24V FI Engine [Opt on GL,LX]	+112
Air Conditioning	+176
Aluminum/Alloy Wheels	+96

Ford
Contour SVT

2000

Body Styles	TMV Pricing		
	Trade	Private	Dealer
4 Dr STD Sdn	7533	9209	10852

Options	Price
AM/FM/CD Audio System	+130
Power Moonroof	+280

Mileage Category: E

The 2000 Contour is unchanged from 1999.

Contour SVT/Crown Victoria

1999

Mileage Category: E

After being introduced, and receiving midyear tweaks for 1998, Ford's bargain sport sedan stands pat for its sophomore year.

Body Styles	TMV Pricing		
	Trade	Private	Dealer
4 Dr STD Sdn	6510	8220	10000

Options	Price
Power Moonroof	+231

1998

Mileage Category: E

Ford's SVT gurus turn their attention to the Contour, and the end result is this thoroughly enjoyable, near 200-horsepower sport sedan. As with all Contour models for this year, the SVT has the new face that gives this Ford more character (though the new taillight treatment is almost identical to the Contour's cousin, the Mercury Mystique). Halfway through the model year, the SVT got new wheels and tires, a slightly revised suspension and depowered airbags.

Body Styles	TMV Pricing		
	Trade	Private	Dealer
4 Dr STD Sdn	5376	7220	9300

Options	Price
Power Moonroof	+188

Ford

Crown Victoria

2003

Body Styles	TMV Pricing		
	Trade	Private	Dealer
4 Dr LX Sdn	13781	14863	16665
4 Dr STD Sdn	11743	12665	14201

Options	Price	Options	Price
AM/FM/Cassette/CD Audio System [Opt on STD]	+119	Leather Seats [Opt on LX]	+319
Automatic Load Leveling [Opt on LX]	+161	Front Side Airbag Restraints [Opt on LX]	+164
Bucket Seats [Opt on LX]	+171	Sport Suspension [Opt on LX]	+129
Digital Instrument Panel [Opt on LX]	+152	17 Inch Wheels [Opt on LX]	+274
Keyless Entry System [Opt on STD]	+155	4.6L V8 CNG SOHC 16V FI Engine [Opt on STD]	+4486

Mileage Category: G

Ford's big sedan receives a number of updates for 2003. A new full-perimeter frame uses strong, lightweight hydroformed steel sections for the front rails to improve frontal and offset crash performance. Redesigned frame crossmembers and new optional side impact airbags improve side impact crash performance. Additionally, the new frame -- combined with a redesigned independent front suspension and new monotube shock absorbers -- contributes to a smoother, more controlled ride and improved handling. Other changes include a new variable ratio rack and pinion steering system with variable power assist and a new dual-rate brake booster that automatically supplies full braking power in a panic stop. Inside, revised seats offer improved comfort and appearance; the cupholders are new; and a three-point seatbelt has been added for the rear center passenger.

2002

Mileage Category: G

A new Crown Vic LX Sport model with 235 horsepower, boosted torque, a performance-oriented axle ratio and five-spoke 17-inch wheels debuts. The Sport also comes with leather front bucket seats and a nifty center console. Standard Crown Vics get new included equipment like an auto-dimming rearview mirror, front seat back pockets and wheel covers. Newly optional on Standard models is luxury cloth seating and power-adjustable pedals. Those pedals, floor mats, heated side mirrors, antilock brakes, 12-spoke alloy wheels and steering wheel controls for the stereo and climate controls are now standard on LX models. Electronic gauges have been thoughtfully moved to the LX options list. LX and LX Sport get an optional trunk storage system. All Vics benefit from upgraded cupholders.

Body Styles	TMV Pricing		
	Trade	Private	Dealer
4 Dr LX Sdn	10813	11868	13627
4 Dr STD Sdn	9362	10276	11799

Options	Price	Options	Price
16 Inch Wheels [Opt on LX]	+206	Digital Instrument Panel [Opt on LX]	+138
4.6L V8 CNG SOHC 16V FI Engine [Opt on STD]	+3971	Keyless Entry System [Opt on STD]	+141
Antilock Brakes [Opt on STD]	+400	Leather Seats [Opt on LX]	+291
Automatic Load Leveling [Opt on LX]	+147	Sport Suspension [Opt on LX]	+118
Compact Disc Changer [Opt on LX]	+206		

2001

Mileage Category: G

Power from the V8 engine is increased. The interior gets minor improvements and an optional adjustable pedal assembly. Safety has been improved via a crash severity sensor, safety belt pre-tensioners, dual-stage airbags and seat-position sensors.

Body Styles	TMV Pricing		
	Trade	Private	Dealer
4 Dr LX Sdn	8228	9520	10712
4 Dr STD Sdn	7533	8716	9808

Crown Victoria

Options	Price	Options	Price
4.6L V8 Flex Fuel SOHC 16V FI Engine	+3248	Keyless Entry System [Opt on STD]	+126
Aluminum/Alloy Wheels	+224	Leather Seats	+387
Antilock Brakes	+358	Power Driver Seat	+190
Automatic Load Leveling	+142	Power Passenger Seat	+184
Compact Disc Changer	+184	Traction Control System	+132

2000

Body Styles	TMV Pricing		
	Trade	Private	Dealer
4 Dr LX Sdn	6952	8178	9379
4 Dr STD Sdn	6363	7485	8584

Options	Price	Options	Price
Aluminum/Alloy Wheels	+200	Leather Seats	+346
Automatic Load Leveling	+127	Power Driver Seat [Opt on STD]	+170
Compact Disc Changer	+165	Power Passenger Seat [Opt on LX]	+170

Mileage Category: G

New safety items have been added, including an emergency trunk release, child seat-anchor brackets and the Belt Minder system. The rear-axle ratio for Crown Victorias with the handling package changes from 3.27 to 3.55, for quicker acceleration. Two new shades of green are offered -- Tropical Green and Dark Green Satin.

1999

Body Styles	TMV Pricing		
	Trade	Private	Dealer
4 Dr LX Sdn	5723	6900	8126
4 Dr STD Sdn	5260	6343	7470

Options	Price	Options	Price
Aluminum/Alloy Wheels	+165	Leather Seats	+286
Automatic Load Leveling	+117	Power Driver Seat [Opt on STD]	+140
Compact Disc Changer	+136	Power Passenger Seat [Opt on LX]	+155

Mileage Category: G

Antilock brakes are now standard on Base and LX models. A stereo with cassette player is also newly standard on the Base model. Deep Wedgewood Blue, Light Blue and Harvest Gold are new exterior colors. Medium Wedgewood Blue, Light Denim Blue and Light Prairie Tan are no longer available.

1998

Body Styles	TMV Pricing		
	Trade	Private	Dealer
4 Dr LX Sdn	4340	5388	6570
4 Dr STD Sdn	3875	4811	5867

Options	Price	Options	Price
Aluminum/Alloy Wheels	+135	Leather Seats	+233
Antilock Brakes	+240	Power Passenger Seat [Opt on LX]	+127

Mileage Category: G

A formal roofline graces this favorite of police officers and taxi drivers. To further add to the Crown Victoria's driving excitement, the power steering and suspension have been improved.

1997

Body Styles	TMV Pricing		
	Trade	Private	Dealer
4 Dr LX Sdn	3381	4278	5375
4 Dr STD Sdn	3082	3901	4901

Options	Price	Options	Price
Power Passenger Seat [Opt on LX]	+117	Aluminum/Alloy Wheels	+124
Leather Seats	+216	Antilock Brakes	+222

Mileage Category: G

After a mild facelift last year, the Crown Vic soldiers on with a few color changes, improved power steering and the addition of rear air suspension to the handling package.

1996

Body Styles	TMV Pricing		
	Trade	Private	Dealer
4 Dr LX Sdn	2544	3324	4402
4 Dr STD Sdn	2325	3039	4024

Options	Price
Antilock Brakes	+197
Leather Seats	+168
Performance/Handling Package	+177

Mileage Category: G

A new steering wheel and gas cap are standard, and some equipment has been dropped from the roster, including the JBL sound system and trailer towing package.

1995

Mileage Category: G

New grille, trunk lid, wheels and bumpers freshen the Crown Victoria's styling. Rear window defroster and heated outside mirrors move from the options list to the standard equipment roster. A new interior includes a revised stereo, backlit door switches, restyled instrument panel and a fresh climate control system.

Body Styles	TMV Pricing		
	Trade	Private	Dealer
4 Dr LX Sdn	1789	2402	3424
4 Dr STD Sdn	1631	2191	3123

Options	Price	Options	Price
Aluminum/Alloy Wheels	+96	Performance/Handling Package	+153
Antilock Brakes	+170	Power Driver Seat [Opt on STD]	+81
JBL Audio System	+124	Power Passenger Seat [Opt on LX]	+90
Leather Seats	+146		

1994

Mileage Category: G

A passenger airbag is now standard. Air conditioning gets CFC-free refrigerant.

Body Styles	TMV Pricing		
	Trade	Private	Dealer
4 Dr LX Sdn	1313	1837	2709
4 Dr S Sdn	1252	1752	2584
4 Dr STD Sdn	1254	1754	2588

Options	Price	Options	Price
Aluminum/Alloy Wheels	+81	JBL Audio System	+105
Antilock Brakes	+144	Leather Seats	+123

Ford
E-150

1998

Body Styles	TMV Pricing			Body Styles	TMV Pricing		
	Trade	Private	Dealer		Trade	Private	Dealer
3 Dr Chateau Club Wgn Pass Van	5825	7084	8503	3 Dr XLT Club Wgn Pass Van	5596	6805	8169
3 Dr XL Club Wgn Pass Van	5501	6690	8031				

Options	Price	Options	Price
4.6L V8 SOHC 16V FI Engine	+254	Air Conditioning - Front and Rear	+291
5.4L V8 SOHC 16V FI Engine	+458		

Mileage Category: Q

Ford's full-size vans greet 1998 relatively unchanged. The XL trim level previously available is replaced by interior and exterior appearance packages, yet is still applicable to Club Wagon models. Optional audio units receive minor styling changes while instrument panel lighting goes from blue-green to green. Models equipped with power door locks get a rear door lock switch and the previously standard engine block heater for diesel models becomes optional. Colorwise, Colonial White is dropped, Denim Blue replaces Crystal Blue, and Deep Forest Green, Carribean Green and Light Blue Metallic are introduced.

1997

Mileage Category: Q

Ford's full-size vans receive minior enhancements. The new 4.2L V6 replaces the 4.9L as standard, and optional power plants now include the new Triton 4.6L and 5.4L V8s. A new front bumper and grille refresh the outside while a revised dash and front console, redesigned seats, an extra power point and seatbelt pre-tensioners round out the inside changes. A 3.31 limited-slip rear axle is offered and the three-speed automatic transmission is deleted.

Body Styles	TMV Pricing			Body Styles	TMV Pricing		
	Trade	Private	Dealer		Trade	Private	Dealer
3 Dr Chateau Club Wgn Pass Van	5116	6318	7786	3 Dr XLT Club Wgn Pass Van	4887	6035	7437
3 Dr XL Club Wgn Pass Van	4297	5306	6539				

Options	Price	Options	Price
4.6L V8 SOHC 16V FI Engine	+235	Air Conditioning [Opt on STD,XL]	+318
5.4L V8 SOHC 16V FI Engine	+424	Air Conditioning - Front and Rear	+269

1996

Mileage Category: Q

Ford's full-size vans receive modest changes, including the replacement of last year's swing-out rear door windows with fixed glass on all styles except Club Wagon and RV models. The under-hood light is dropped from the Light and Convenience Group option, and anti-theft is deleted from the remote keyless-entry system. Standard on all models are 15-inch wheel covers and new color choices of Deep Violet, Toreador Red, Light Saddle and Medium Wedgewood Blue.

Body Styles	TMV Pricing			Body Styles	TMV Pricing		
	Trade	Private	Dealer		Trade	Private	Dealer
3 Dr Chateau Club Wgn Pass Van	4568	5722	7315	3 Dr XLT Club Wgn Pass Van	4141	5187	6632
3 Dr XL Club Wgn Pass Van	3556	4454	5695				

Options	Price	Options	Price
5.0L V8 OHV 16V FI Engine	+207	Air Conditioning [Opt on STD,XL]	+282
5.8L V8 OHV 16V FI Engine	+272	Air Conditioning - Front and Rear [Std on Chateau]	+204
7 Passenger Seating [Opt on XLT]	+174		

E-150/E-350

1995

Body Styles	TMV Pricing		
	Trade	Private	Dealer
3 Dr Chateau Club Wgn Pass Van	3902	4949	6695
3 Dr XL Club Wgn Pass Van	3002	3808	5150

Options	Price
5.0L V8 OHV 16V FI Engine	+179
5.8L V8 OHV 16V FI Engine	+235
Air Conditioning [Opt on STD,XL]	+186

Body Styles	TMV Pricing		
	Trade	Private	Dealer
3 Dr XLT Club Wgn Pass Van	3516	4460	6033

Options	Price
Air Conditioning - Front and Rear	+186
Captain Chairs (4) [Opt on XLT]	+122
Power Driver Seat	+81

Mileage Category: Q

Miniscule changes this year for Ford's biggest people-hauler, among them optional 16-inch aluminum wheels (on Super XLT trims) and an XL Plus PEP Package is offered on the Chateau and Club Wagons.

1994

Body Styles	TMV Pricing		
	Trade	Private	Dealer
3 Dr Chateau Club Wgn Pass Van	3036	4088	5841
3 Dr XL Club Wgn Pass Van	2336	3145	4494

Options	Price
5.0L V8 OHV 16V FI Engine	+152
5.8L V8 OHV 16V FI Engine	+199
Air Conditioning [Opt on STD,XL]	+157

Body Styles	TMV Pricing		
	Trade	Private	Dealer
3 Dr XLT Club Wgn Pass Van	2762	3719	5314

Options	Price
Air Conditioning - Front and Rear [Std on Chateau]	+157
Captain Chairs (4) [Opt on XLT]	+103

Mileage Category: Q

Among the minor changes, nomenclature for Custom styles is replaced with XL for all base models. All Club Wagons and RV series receive four-wheel ABS, and a brake/shift interlock system and side door beams are standard. A CFC-free air conditioning is offered to all models and an electronic four-speed wide-ratio transmission with overdrive is standard with the 5.0L engine.

Ford

E-350

1998

Body Styles	TMV Pricing		
	Trade	Private	Dealer
3 Dr Chateau Club Wgn Pass Van	6454	7849	9422
3 Dr XL Club Wgn Pass Van	5810	7065	8481
3 Dr XL Club Wgn Pass Van Ext	5985	7278	8736

Options	Price
Power Driver Seat	+124
5.4L V8 CNG SOHC 16V FI Engine	+2200
6.8L V10 SOHC 20V FI Engine	+196

Body Styles	TMV Pricing		
	Trade	Private	Dealer
3 Dr XLT Club Wgn Pass Van	6168	7501	9005
3 Dr XLT Club Wgn Pass Van Ext	6361	7736	9286

Options	Price
7.3L V8 Turbodiesel OHV 16V Engine	+1649
Air Conditioning - Front and Rear	+291

Mileage Category: Q

Ford's full-size vans greet 1998 relatively unchanged. The XL trim level previously available is replaced by a gaggle of interior and exterior appearance packages, yet is still applicable to Club Wagon models. Optional audio units receive minor styling changes while instrument panel lighting goes from blue-green to green. Models equipped with power door locks get a rear door lock switch and the previously standard engine block heater for diesel models becomes optional. Colorwise, Colonial White is dropped, Denim Blue replaces Crystal Blue and Deep Forest Green, Carribean Green and Light Blue Metallic are introduced.

1997

Body Styles	TMV Pricing		
	Trade	Private	Dealer
3 Dr Chateau Club Wgn Pass Van	5758	7110	8762
3 Dr XL Club Wgn Pass Van	5098	6295	7758
lub Wgn Pass Van Ext	5239	6469	7972

Options	Price
5.4L V8 CNG SOHC 16V FI Engine	+1060
6.8L V10 SOHC 20V FI Engine	+135
7.3L V8 Turbodiesel OHV 16V Engine	+1435

Body Styles	TMV Pricing		
	Trade	Private	Dealer
3 Dr XLT Club Wgn Pass Van	5429	6703	8261
3 Dr XLT Club Wgn Pass Van Ext	5655	6983	8606

Options	Price
Air Conditioning [Opt on STD,XL]	+318
Air Conditioning - Front and Rear	+269

Mileage Category: Q

While its cousins, the F-150 and F-250, receive ground-up redesigns, Ford's full-size vans receive minor enhancements. The new 4.2L V6 replaces the 4.9L as standard, and optional power plants now include the new Triton 4.6L and 5.4L V8s. A new front bumper and grille refresh the outside while a revised dash and front console, redesigned seats, an extra power point and seatbelt pre-tensioners round out the inside changes. A 3.31 limited-slip rear axle is offered and the three-speed automatic transmission is deleted.

1996

Mileage Category: Q

Ford's full-size vans receive modest changes, including the replacement of last year's swing-out rear door windows with fixed glass on all styles except Club Wagon and RV models. The under-hood light is dropped from the Light and Convenience Group option, and anti-theft is deleted from the remote keyless-entry system. Standard on all models are 15-inch wheel covers, and new color choices of Deep Violet, Toreador Red, Light Saddle and Medium Wedgewood Blue.

Body Styles	TMV Pricing		
	Trade	Private	Dealer
3 Dr Chateau Club Wgn Pass Van	5059	6337	8103
3 Dr XL Club Wgn Pass Van	4194	5254	6718
3 Dr XL Club Wgn Pass Van Ext	4422	5539	7082

Options	Price
Air Conditioning [Opt on XL,XLT]	+282
Air Conditioning - Front and Rear [Std on Chateau]	+161
7.5L V8 OHV 16V FI Engine	+412

Body Styles	TMV Pricing		
	Trade	Private	Dealer
3 Dr XLT Club Wgn Pass Van	4501	5638	7209
3 Dr XLT Club Wgn Pass Van Ext	4727	5921	7571

Options	Price
5.8L V8 OHV 16V FI Engine	+272
7 Passenger Seating [Opt on XLT]	+221
7.3L V8 Turbodiesel OHV 16V Engine	+1275

1995

Mileage Category: Q

Miniscule changes this year for Ford's biggest people-hauler, among them optional 16-inch aluminum wheels (on Super XLT trims) and an XL Plus PEP Package are offered on the Chateau and Club Wagons.

Body Styles	TMV Pricing		
	Trade	Private	Dealer
3 Dr Chateau Club Wgn Pass Van	4159	5275	7135
3 Dr XL Club Wgn Pass Van	3348	4246	5743
3 Dr XL Club Wgn Pass Van Ext	3516	4460	6032

Options	Price
5.8L V8 OHV 16V FI Engine	+235
7.3L V8 Turbodiesel OHV 16V Engine	+1102
7.5L V8 OHV 16V FI Engine	+356
Air Conditioning [Std on Chateau]	+219

Body Styles	TMV Pricing		
	Trade	Private	Dealer
3 Dr XLT Club Wgn Pass Van	3645	4623	6253
3 Dr XLT Club Wgn Pass Van Ext	3773	4785	6472

Options	Price
Air Conditioning - Front and Rear	+186
Automatic 4-Speed Transmission	+75
Power Driver Seat	+87

1994

Mileage Category: Q

Among the minor changes, nomenclature for Custom styles is replaced with XL for all base models. All Club Wagons and RV series receive four-wheel ABS, and a brake/shift interlock system and side door beams are standard. A CFC-free air conditioning is offered to all models and an electronic four-speed wide-ratio transmission with overdrive is standard with the 5.0L engine.

Body Styles	TMV Pricing		
	Trade	Private	Dealer
3 Dr Chateau Club Wgn Pass Van	3268	4401	6289
3 Dr XL Club Wgn Pass Van	2591	3488	4984
3 Dr XL Club Wgn Pass Van Ext	2841	3825	5466

Options	Price
5.8L V8 OHV 16V FI Engine	+199
7.3L V8 Diesel OHV 16V Engine	+792
7.5L V8 OHV 16V FI Engine	+301

Body Styles	TMV Pricing		
	Trade	Private	Dealer
3 Dr XLT Club Wgn Pass Van	2957	3982	5690
3 Dr XLT Club Wgn Pass Van Ext	2957	3982	5690

Options	Price
Air Conditioning [Opt on STD,XL]	+186
Air Conditioning - Front and Rear [Std on Chateau]	+157

Ford
Econoline Wagon

2003

Body Styles	TMV Pricing		
	Trade	Private	Dealer
3 Dr E-150 XL Pass Van	12999	14084	15893
3 Dr E-150 XLT Pass Van	14758	15990	18044
3 Dr E-350 Super Duty XL Pass Van	14960	16209	18291
3 Dr E-350 Super Duty XL Pass Van Ext	15611	16915	19087

Body Styles	TMV Pricing		
	Trade	Private	Dealer
3 Dr E-350 Super Duty XLT Pass Van	16360	17726	20002
3 Dr E-350 Super Duty XLT Pass Van Ext	16620	18008	20320

Mileage Category: Q

Ford has deleted the family-friendly Traveler Package from the options list for the E-150 XLT, but two-tone exterior paint, running boards and a rear cargo organizer have been added to the Chateau Package. You can pick up the rest of the Traveler features -- including leather upholstery, rear entertainment system and trailer preparation -- as stand-alone options. Additionally, all models get a standard set of power exterior mirrors. If that's not enough, there's an upgraded set with convex blind-spot mirrors and puddle lamps newly optional across the line. Inside, XLT models are now equipped with dual-illuminated vanity mirrors. Finally, the Ford emblem is moved from the hood to the grille.

2003 (cont'd)

Options	Price
Aluminum/Alloy Wheels	+200
AM/FM/Cassette/CD Audio System [Opt on XLT]	+177
Camper/Towing Package	+168
Cruise Control [Opt on XL]	+155
Keyless Entry System	+129
Leather Seats [Opt on XLT]	+551
Limited Slip Differential	+174
Power Door Locks [Opt on XL]	+161
Power Driver Seat [Opt on XLT]	+252
Power Windows [Opt on XL]	+184

Options	Price
Running Boards	+206
Velour/Cloth Seats [Opt on XL]	+155
VCR Entertainment System	+800
AM/FM/CD Changer Audio System [Opt on XLT]	+258
Air Conditioning - Front and Rear [Opt on XL]	+532
4.6L V8 SOHC 16V FI Engine [Opt on E-150]	+516
5.4L V8 SOHC 16V FI Engine [Opt on E-150]	+1000
6.8L V10 SOHC 20V FI Engine [Opt on E-350]	+451
7.3L V8 Turbodiesel OHV 16V Engine [Opt on E-350]	+3412
5.4L V8 CNG SOHC 16V FI Engine [Opt on E-350]	+4802

2002

Mileage Category: Q

All Econolines get A-pillar grab handles, tilt steering, backlit cruise control switches, an illuminated rear auxiliary climate control switch, low-fuel and cruise-control-on indicators in the gauge cluster. Newly optional on the XL is an overhead console. XLT has standard dual illuminated sun visors and front floor mats. E-350 Super Duty models can now be equipped with the luxury Traveler package, while E-350 Super Duty Extended vans get an upgraded transmission. Optional on XLT is an in-dash six-CD changer, and models equipped with the Chateau package get a dual-media cassette/CD stereo, privacy glass and an overhead console.

Body Styles	TMV Pricing		
	Trade	Private	Dealer
3 Dr E-150 XL Pass Van	10988	12085	13912
3 Dr E-150 XLT Pass Van	12267	13491	15532
3 Dr E-350 Super Duty XL Pass Van	12451	13694	15766

Body Styles	TMV Pricing		
	Trade	Private	Dealer
3 Dr E-350 Super Duty XL Pass Van Ext	12998	14296	16458
3 Dr E-350 Super Duty XLT Pass Van	13638	14999	17268
3 Dr E-350 Super Duty XLT Pass Van Ext	13864	15248	17554

Options	Price
4.6L V8 SOHC 16V FI Engine [Opt on E-350]	+442
5.4L V8 CNG SOHC 16V FI Engine [Opt on E-350]	+4133
5.4L V8 SOHC 16V FI Engine [Opt on E-150]	+912
6.8L V10 SOHC 20V FI Engine [Opt on E-350]	+412
7.3L V8 Turbodiesel OHV 16V Engine [Opt on E-350]	+2525
Air Conditioning - Front and Rear [Opt on XL]	+486
AM/FM/Cassette/CD Audio System [Opt on XLT]	+147
AM/FM/CD Changer Audio System [Opt on XLT]	+235
Camper/Towing Package	+153
Captain Chairs (4) [Opt on XLT]	+177

Options	Price
Cruise Control [Opt on XL]	+141
Keyless Entry System	+118
Leather Seats [Opt on E-150 XLT]	+633
Limited Slip Differential	+159
Power Door Locks [Opt on XL]	+147
Power Driver Seat [Opt on XLT]	+221
Power Windows [Opt on XL]	+168
Running Boards	+188
VCR Entertainment System	+559

2001

Mileage Category: Q

2001 Econoline Wagons are virtually the same as last year, with a deluxe engine cover console, dual illuminated sun visors and a heavy-duty battery now standard on all models. One interesting new option is the Traveling Package for the E-150 XLT. This package features seven-passenger leather seating, a video cassette player with two 6-inch headliner mounted LCD screens, a electronic AM/FM/clock/cassette/CD sound system, a leather-wrapped steering wheel and a unique two-tone paint combination.

Body Styles	TMV Pricing		
	Trade	Private	Dealer
3 Dr E-150 XL Pass Van	9236	10673	12000
3 Dr E-150 XLT Pass Van	10384	11999	13490
3 Dr E-350 Super Duty XL Pass Van	10407	12026	13521

Body Styles	TMV Pricing		
	Trade	Private	Dealer
3 Dr E-350 Super Duty XL Pass Van Ext	10931	12631	14201
3 Dr E-350 Super Duty XLT Pass Van	11487	13274	14924
3 Dr E-350 Super Duty XLT Pass Van Ext	11691	13509	15188

Options	Price
4.6L V8 SOHC 16V FI Engine	+395
5.4L V8 CNG SOHC 16V FI Engine	+3372
5.4L V8 SOHC 16V FI Engine [Std on E350]	+817
6.8L V10 SOHC 20V FI Engine	+369
7 Passenger Seating	+171
7.3L V8 Turbodiesel OHV 16V Engine	+2629
Air Conditioning - Front and Rear [Opt on XL]	+435
Aluminum/Alloy Wheels [Opt on XLT]	+163
AM/FM/Cassette/CD Audio System	+145

Options	Price
Camper/Towing Package	+137
Captain Chairs (4) [Opt on XL,XLT]	+132
Leather Seats	+659
Limited Slip Differential	+142
Power Door Locks [Opt on XL]	+119
Power Driver Seat	+205
Power Windows [Std on XLT]	+132
Running Boards	+169
VCR Entertainment System [Opt on E-150 XLT]	+682

2000

Mileage Category: Q

The 5.4-liter V8 and the 6.8-liter V10 gas engines generate more horsepower and torque. Four-wheel antilock brakes are now standard on all models. The Light Convenience Group (including courtesy lights, a rear cargo light, a chime warning module, a "headlamps on" alert and illuminated courtesy door lights) is now standard on all models. The handling package has been made standard on all Econolines. The towing package is standard on all wagons. The instrument panel has been simplified. Remote keyless entry and power sail-mount mirrors are standard on recreational vans.

Body Styles	TMV Pricing		
	Trade	Private	Dealer
3 Dr E-150 Chateau Pass Van	9020	10555	12059
3 Dr E-150 XL Pass Van	7792	9118	10417
3 Dr E-150 XLT Pass Van	9098	10646	12163
3 Dr E-350 Super Duty Chateau Pass Van	9903	11587	13238

Body Styles	TMV Pricing		
	Trade	Private	Dealer
3 Dr E-350 Super Duty XL Pass Van	8703	10183	11634
3 Dr E-350 Super Duty XL Pass Van Ext	9206	10773	12308
3 Dr E-350 Super Duty XLT Pass Van	9968	11664	13326
3 Dr E-350 Super Duty XLT Pass Van Ext	10134	11858	13548

2000 (cont'd)

Options	Price
4.6L V8 SOHC 16V FI Engine	+353
5.4L V8 CNG SOHC 16V FI Engine	+3016
5.4L V8 SOHC 16V FI Engine [Std on E350]	+731
6.8L V10 SOHC 20V FI Engine	+330
7.3L V8 Turbodiesel OHV 16V Engine	+2352
Air Conditioning - Front and Rear [Opt on XL - E150,E350 SD]	+389
Aluminum/Alloy Wheels [Opt on XLT]	+147

Options	Price
AM/FM/Cassette/CD Audio System	+130
Camper/Towing Package	+123
Captain Chairs (2)	+127
Limited Slip Differential	+127
Power Door Locks [Opt on XL]	+118
Power Driver Seat	+184
Power Windows [Std on Chateau,XLT]	+154

1999

Mileage Category: Q

An all-new alphanumeric vehicle badging system is being applied to all Econoline Van and Club Wagon models. This will replace the past Club Wagon and Econoline badges. Four-wheel disc brakes with ABS are now standard on all E-350 Super Duty vans. The 4R70W electronic four-speed automatic is now standard on all E-150/250 models. Improved "fail-safe" cooling is now a feature on all Econoline gasoline engines.

Body Styles	TMV Pricing		
	Trade	Private	Dealer
3 Dr E-150 Chateau Pass Van	7744	9235	10786
3 Dr E-150 XL Pass Van	6526	7782	9089
3 Dr E-150 XLT Pass Van	7124	8495	9922
3 Dr E-350 Super Duty Chateau Pass Van	8434	10057	11746

Body Styles	TMV Pricing		
	Trade	Private	Dealer
3 Dr E-350 Super Duty XL Pass Van	7521	8969	10476
3 Dr E-350 Super Duty XL Pass Van Ext	7963	9495	11090
3 Dr E-350 Super Duty XLT Pass Van	7978	9514	11112
3 Dr E-350 Super Duty XLT Pass Van Ext	8471	10101	11798

Options	Price
4.6L V8 SOHC 16V FI Engine [Opt on E-150]	+367
5.4L V8 Flex Fuel SOHC 16V FI Engine	+2738
5.4L V8 SOHC 16V FI Engine [Opt on E-150]	+669
6.8L V10 SOHC 20V FI Engine [Opt on E-350]	+302
7.3L V8 Turbodiesel OHV 16V Engine [Opt on E-350]	+2138

Options	Price
Air Conditioning - Front and Rear	+356
Aluminum/Alloy Wheels [Opt on E-150]	+120
Power Driver Seat	+151
Power Windows [Opt on E-150 XL,E-350]	+126

Ford
Escape

2003

Body Styles	TMV Pricing		
	Trade	Private	Dealer
4 Dr Limited 4WD SUV	17195	18418	20457
4 Dr Limited SUV	16186	17337	19256
4 Dr XLS 4WD SUV	13989	14984	16643

Body Styles	TMV Pricing		
	Trade	Private	Dealer
4 Dr XLS SUV	11969	12821	14240
4 Dr XLT 4WD SUV	15312	16401	18217
4 Dr XLT SUV	14156	15163	16841

Options	Price
Aluminum/Alloy Wheels [Opt on XLS]	+242
Antilock Brakes [Opt on XLS]	+439
Automatic 4-Speed Transmission [Opt on XLS 2WD]	+451
Camper/Towing Package	+226
Cruise Control [Opt on XLS]	+116
Leather Seats [Opt on XLT]	+319

Options	Price
Power Moonroof [Opt on Limited,XLT]	+377
Running Boards [Opt on XLS,XLT]	+177
Front Side Airbag Restraints [Opt on XLS,XLT]	+223
AM/FM/CD/MP3 Audio System [Opt on XLS]	+145
MACH Audio System [Opt on XLT]	+326
3.0L V6 DOHC 24V FI Engine [Opt on XLS 2WD]	+451

Mileage Category: L

Need more luxury when you Escape? For 2003, Ford will offer a new Limited edition that includes body-color trim, polished aluminum wheels, a reverse sensing system, a Mach audio system with six-disc CD changer, heated front seats and sideview mirrors, premium leather seats, front side airbags and an autodimming rearview mirror. The XLT can also be upgraded this year with an appearance package that includes special wheels, side step bars and body-color exterior trim. For all Escapes, there are upgraded interior materials and fabrics, an available two-tone cabin color scheme, illuminated power window and lock switches and three new colors. Finally, the XLS 4WD with a four-cylinder engine and a manual transmission is dropped for 2003.

2002

Mileage Category: L

Additional standard equipment makes Escape an even better value for 2002. XLS models get a dual-media cassette/CD stereo, while XLT adds a V6 engine, privacy glass, power driver seat and an in-dash six-CD changer. New Sport packages also debut. The XLS Sport includes 15-inch alloy wheels with larger tires, side-step bars, Sport-embroidered floor mats and dark tinted privacy glass. The XLT Sport, new for 2002, provides, in addition to XLS Sport equipment, a special No Boundaries roof rack system and unique 16-inch alloy wheels with meatier rubber. Four new colors are also available.

Body Styles	TMV Pricing		
	Trade	Private	Dealer
4 Dr XLS 4WD SUV	11703	12683	14316
4 Dr XLS SUV	10265	11124	12556
4 Dr XLT 4WD SUV	13144	14245	16079
4 Dr XLT SUV	12281	13309	15023

2002 (cont'd)

Options	Price
3.0L V6 DOHC 24V FI Engine [Opt on XLS]	+412
Aluminum/Alloy Wheels [Opt on XLS]	+147
AM/FM/Cassette/CD/MP3 Audio System [Opt on XLS]	+174
AM/FM/CD/MP3 Audio System [Opt on XLT]	+174
Antilock Brakes [Opt on XLS]	+400
Automatic 4-Speed Transmission [Opt on XLS]	+506

Options	Price
Compact Disc Changer [Opt on XLT]	+206
Front Side Airbag Restraints	+147
Leather Seats [Opt on XLT]	+291
Locking Differential [Opt on XLT 4WD]	+118
MACH Audio System [Opt on XLT]	+132
Power Moonroof [Opt on XLT]	+344

2001

Body Styles	TMV Pricing		
	Trade	Private	Dealer
4 Dr XLS 4WD SUV	10737	12079	13317
4 Dr XLS SUV	9327	10492	11568

Body Styles	TMV Pricing		
	Trade	Private	Dealer
4 Dr XLT 4WD SUV	11525	12965	14294
4 Dr XLT SUV	10290	11575	12762

Options	Price
3.0L V6 DOHC 24V FI Engine	+369
Aluminum/Alloy Wheels [Std on XLT]	+198
Antilock Brakes [Std on XLT]	+358
Automatic 4-Speed Transmission	+369
Compact Disc Changer	+308
Cruise Control [Std on XLT]	+119

Options	Price
Front Side Airbag Restraints	+182
Leather Seats	+342
Power Driver Seat	+126
Power Moonroof	+308
Running Boards	+145

Mileage Category: L

The Escape is Ford's new SUV. Smaller in size than the Explorer (and dwarfed by an Excursion), the Escape competes in the same class as the Honda CR-V and Toyota RAV4. Its main calling cards are an optional V6 engine and a large interior.

Ford
Escort

2003

Body Styles	TMV Pricing		
	Trade	Private	Dealer
2 Dr ZX2 Cpe	6484	7291	8636

Options	Price
Air Conditioning	+448
Antilock Brakes	+439
Automatic 4-Speed Transmission	+526
Cruise Control	+119

Options	Price
Keyless Entry System	+116
Power Door Locks	+132
Power Windows	+158

Mileage Category: B

The aged Escort ZX2 receives a few changes this year. On the outside, there are stylistic changes to its front and rear fascias, including standard foglamps. Inside, new cloth spruces up the seats, and the standard model receives a cassette player. Fifteen-inch wheels are standard on all models, and two new colors make their debut. For 2003, Ford has renamed the options packages "deluxe" and "premium." The deluxe package gets you a CD player, a leather-wrapped steering wheel that tilts, cruise control and map lights as standard equipment. Premium models also get power windows, locks and remote keyless entry. Finally, the in-dash six-disc CD changer is no longer available.

2002

Body Styles	TMV Pricing		
	Trade	Private	Dealer
2 Dr ZX2 Cpe	5172	5889	7085

Options	Price
Air Conditioning	+353
Antilock Brakes	+400
Automatic 4-Speed Transmission	+480

Mileage Category: B

Other than a couple of new exterior colors, the Escort ZX2 is unchanged for 2002. The Comfort and Power Groups have been replaced by the Deluxe and Premium Groups, which include new items of standard equipment.

2001

Body Styles	TMV Pricing		
	Trade	Private	Dealer
2 Dr ZX2 Cpe	4340	5274	6137

Mileage Category: B

Other than a couple of new exterior colors, the Escort ZX2 is unchanged for 2001. The high-performance S/R Package is no longer available.

2001 (cont'd)

Options	Price
Air Conditioning	+419
AM/FM/Cassette/CD Changer Audio System	+155
Antilock Brakes	+358
Automatic 4-Speed Transmission	+429

Options	Price
Chrome Wheels	+313
Leather Seats	+261
Power Moonroof	+313
Power Windows	+121

2000

Mileage Category: B

The 2000 Escort line has been simplified. The station wagon is discontinued, and there is now only one trim level for the sedan and coupe models.

Body Styles	TMV Pricing		
	Trade	Private	Dealer
2 Dr ZX2 Cpe	3276	4203	5112
4 Dr STD Sdn	3279	4208	5118

Options	Price
Air Conditioning	+375
Aluminum/Alloy Wheels [Std on ZX2]	+125
AM/FM/Cassette/CD Audio System	+139
Antilock Brakes	+320
Automatic 4-Speed Transmission	+384

Options	Price
Chrome Wheels	+280
Compact Disc Changer	+139
Leather Seats	+233
Power Moonroof	+280

1999

Mileage Category: B

Ford's entry-level car gets new colors, new interior fabrics and revised options. An AM/FM stereo with cassette is now standard on the Escort SE. An interior trunk release is now standard on all models. The sedans and wagon get all-door remote keyless entry added to their standard equipment lists. An integrated child seat is no longer available.

Body Styles	TMV Pricing		
	Trade	Private	Dealer
2 Dr ZX2 Cool Cpe	2504	3407	4347
2 Dr ZX2 Hot Cpe	2868	3902	4979
4 Dr LX Sdn	2484	3380	4312

Body Styles	TMV Pricing		
	Trade	Private	Dealer
4 Dr SE Sdn	2799	3809	4860
4 Dr SE Wgn	2991	4069	5192

Options	Price
Air Conditioning [Std on SE,ZX2 Hot]	+309
Antilock Brakes	+293
Automatic 4-Speed Transmission	+317

Options	Price
Compact Disc Changer	+115
Power Moonroof	+231

1998

Mileage Category: B

Packages are reshuffled on Ford's entry-level cars. Available this year as sedans, wagons or stylish coupes, the Ford Escort now qualifies as a low emissions vehicle, thanks to the car's split-port induction 2.0-liter four-cylinder engine.

Body Styles	TMV Pricing		
	Trade	Private	Dealer
2 Dr ZX2 Cool Cpe	2001	2835	3775
2 Dr ZX2 Hot Cpe	2210	3131	4170
4 Dr LX Sdn	1902	2695	3590

Body Styles	TMV Pricing		
	Trade	Private	Dealer
4 Dr SE Sdn	2117	3000	3995
4 Dr SE Wgn	2331	3303	4400

Options	Price
Air Conditioning	+252
AM/FM/Cassette/CD Audio System [Opt on ZX2]	+163
AM/FM/CD Audio System [Opt on SE Sdn]	+163

Options	Price
Antilock Brakes	+240
Automatic 4-Speed Transmission	+259
Power Moonroof	+188

1997

Mileage Category: B

The Ford Escort is totally redesigned this year with improvements across the board. The most noticeable improvements are in the powertrain and ride quality. New sheet metal gives the Escort a rounder, more aerodynamic appearance as well. The GT hatchback version is dropped.

Body Styles	TMV Pricing		
	Trade	Private	Dealer
4 Dr LX Sdn	1514	2270	3193
4 Dr LX Wgn	1600	2399	3375

Body Styles	TMV Pricing		
	Trade	Private	Dealer
4 Dr STD Sdn	1448	2171	3054

Options	Price
Air Conditioning	+233
Antilock Brakes	+222

Options	Price
Automatic 4-Speed Transmission	+239

1996

Body Styles	TMV Pricing		
	Trade	Private	Dealer
2 Dr GT Hbk	1271	1981	2962
2 Dr LX Hbk	1095	1707	2553
2 Dr STD Hbk	1024	1596	2386

Body Styles	TMV Pricing		
	Trade	Private	Dealer
4 Dr LX Hbk	1115	1738	2599
4 Dr LX Sdn	1146	1787	2671
4 Dr LX Wgn	1210	1887	2821

1996 (cont'd)

Options	Price
Air Conditioning	+205
AM/FM/Cassette Audio System [Std on LX]	+121
Antilock Brakes	+197
Automatic 4-Speed Transmission	+213

Mileage Category: B

Last year for the second-generation Escort. The 1.9-liter engine gets 100,000-mile tune-up interval. Automatic transmissions have lower final drive ratio when coupled with 1.9-liter engine to improve acceleration. Sport/Appearance Group available on four-door models. Ultra Violet decor no longer offered on GT. Integrated child safety seat, added during 1995 model year, continues for 1996 on sedan and wagon.

1995

Body Styles	TMV Pricing		
	Trade	Private	Dealer
2 Dr GT Hbk	933	1482	2397
2 Dr LX Hbk	802	1274	2060
2 Dr STD Hbk	736	1170	1893

Body Styles	TMV Pricing		
	Trade	Private	Dealer
4 Dr LX Hbk	818	1300	2102
4 Dr LX Sdn	848	1346	2177
4 Dr LX Wgn	884	1404	2271

Options	Price
Air Conditioning	+177
Antilock Brakes	+170

Options	Price
Automatic 4-Speed Transmission	+184
Power Moonroof	+96

Mileage Category: B

A passenger airbag is now available. A more powerful, optional air conditioner appears in the revised instrument panel. An integrated child seat is available on sedans and wagons.

1994

Body Styles	TMV Pricing		
	Trade	Private	Dealer
2 Dr GT Hbk	758	1291	2178
2 Dr LX Hbk	650	1106	1866
2 Dr STD Hbk	587	1000	1688

Body Styles	TMV Pricing		
	Trade	Private	Dealer
4 Dr LX Hbk	663	1128	1904
4 Dr LX Sdn	678	1154	1947
4 Dr LX Wgn	700	1192	2013

Options	Price
Air Conditioning	+150
Antilock Brakes	+144

Options	Price
Automatic 4-Speed Transmission	+156
Power Moonroof	+81

Mileage Category: B

A driver airbag debuts on all models. Antilock brakes are now available on the GT. The LX-E sedan is dropped from the lineup.

2003

Body Styles	TMV Pricing		
	Trade	Private	Dealer
4 Dr Eddie Bauer 4WD SUV	24545	26131	28773
4 Dr Eddie Bauer SUV	23293	24798	27305
4 Dr Limited 4WD SUV	24826	26430	29103

Body Styles	TMV Pricing		
	Trade	Private	Dealer
4 Dr Limited SUV	23587	25111	27650
4 Dr XLT 4WD SUV	22973	24457	26930
4 Dr XLT SUV	20323	21636	23824

Options	Price
Captain Chairs (2) [Opt on XLT]	+164
Captain Chairs (4) [Opt on Eddie Bauer, Limited]	+513
Compact Disc Changer	+164
Limited Slip Differential [Opt on Eddie Bauer, Limited]	+161
Power Driver Seat [Opt on XLT]	+155
Power Passenger Seat [Opt on XLT]	+155

Options	Price
AM/FM/CD Changer Audio System [Opt on Eddie Bauer, XLT]	+164
DVD Entertainment System	+835
7.3L V8 Turbodiesel OHV 16V Engine	+2667
6.0L V8 Turbodiesel OHV 32V Engine	+871
Park Distance Control (Rear) [Opt on XLT]	+158

Mileage Category: N

A new Eddie Bauer trim level debuts. It's equipped similarly to last year's Limited trim and also includes Arizona Beige exterior trim, two-tone leather seating and available second-row captain's chairs. Limited models get as standard equipment a six-disc in-dash CD changer, new aluminum wheels, cherrywood interior trim and a reversible cargo mat. In terms of mechanical changes, a new 6.0-liter turbodiesel engine arrives mid-year with more power and efficiency, connected to an all new five-speed TorqShift automatic transmission. Why anyone would use this mammoth rig to go trail busting we have no idea, but Ford will be offering an off-road package shortly after the first of the year. Finally, all Excursions get revised front suspensions for improved ride and handling.

Ford
Excursion/Expedition

2002

Mileage Category: N

Excursions get crystalline headlamp lenses for 2002, as well as "smart" intermittent front and rear wipers. XLTs gain a new auto-lock feature as well as standard third-row child seat tethers with a BeltMinder system. Excursion Limited receives a chrome side strip, automatic climate control and power-adjustable pedals. New options on XLT include power-adjustable pedals and a power front passenger seat. Limited models can be equipped with memory seats and pedals, second-row captain's chairs and redundant controls for climate and audio on the steering wheel. Both XLT and Limited will get a DVD-based entertainment system for rear-seat passengers later this year. Skid plates are no longer optional.

Body Styles	TMV Pricing		
	Trade	Private	Dealer
4 Dr Limited 4WD SUV	20894	22466	25086
4 Dr Limited SUV	19885	21381	23874

Options	Price
7.3L V8 Turbodiesel OHV 16V Engine	+2155
Captain Chairs (2) [Opt on XLT]	+235
Captain Chairs (4) [Opt on Limited]	+468
Compact Disc Changer	+150
Heated Front and Rear Seats [Opt on Limited]	+171

Body Styles	TMV Pricing		
	Trade	Private	Dealer
4 Dr XLT 4WD SUV	19491	20957	23401
4 Dr XLT SUV	17051	18334	20472

Options	Price
Limited Slip Differential	+147
Park Distance Control (Rear) [Opt on XLT]	+144
Power Driver Seat [Opt on XLT]	+153
Power Passenger Seat [Opt on XLT]	+153

2001

Mileage Category: N

Performance is beefed up to 250 horsepower on the 7.3-liter Power Stroke turbodiesel V8 and all engines are now LEV compliant. An in-dash six-disc CD player is made available. The Excursion XLT gets platinum cladding and standard chrome steel wheels, and the Limited offers standard power signal aero mirrors, foglamps and an optional rear-seat entertainment system.

Body Styles	TMV Pricing		
	Trade	Private	Dealer
4 Dr Limited 4WD SUV	18005	20087	22009
4 Dr Limited SUV	16685	18615	20396

Options	Price
6.8L V10 SOHC 20V FI Engine [Std on 4WD]	+313
7.3L V8 Turbodiesel OHV 16V Engine	+2142
Aluminum/Alloy Wheels [Opt on XLT]	+163
Compact Disc Changer	+134
Heated Front Seats [Opt on Limited]	+153

Body Styles	TMV Pricing		
	Trade	Private	Dealer
4 Dr XLT 4WD SUV	15303	17073	18706
4 Dr XLT SUV	14967	16698	18296

Options	Price
Leather Seats [Opt on XLT]	+558
Limited Slip Differential	+132
Park Distance Control (Rear) [Opt on XLT]	+129
Power Driver Seat [Opt on XLT]	+126
VCR Entertainment System [Opt on Limited]	+803

2000

Mileage Category: N

The Excursion is an entirely new SUV based on Ford's F-250 Super Duty truck platform. It is the largest vehicle of its type, outgunning even the Chevy Suburban in terms of overall size and interior space.

Body Styles	TMV Pricing		
	Trade	Private	Dealer
4 Dr Limited 4WD SUV	15560	17624	19648
4 Dr Limited SUV	14413	16325	18199

Options	Price
6.8L V10 SOHC 20V FI Engine [Std on 4WD]	+280
7.3L V8 Turbodiesel OHV 16V Engine	+2060
Chrome Wheels	+147
Compact Disc Changer	+233

Body Styles	TMV Pricing		
	Trade	Private	Dealer
4 Dr XLT 4WD SUV	13501	15293	17049
4 Dr XLT SUV	12663	14344	15991

Options	Price
Heated Front Seats	+137
Leather Seats [Opt on XLT]	+518
Limited Slip Differential	+118
Park Distance Control (Rear) [Opt on XLT]	+115

Ford
Expedition

2003

Body Styles	TMV Pricing		
	Trade	Private	Dealer
4 Dr Eddie Bauer 4WD SUV	26137	27825	30639
4 Dr Eddie Bauer SUV	22553	24010	26438

Options	Price
Aluminum/Alloy Wheels [Opt on XLT]	+161
Automatic Load Leveling	+316
Automatic Stability Control [Opt on Eddie Bauer]	+319
Captain Chairs (2) [Opt on XLT]	+248
Captain Chairs (4) [Opt on Eddie Bauer]	+513
Leather Seats [Opt on XLT]	+580
Limited Slip Differential [Opt on XLT]	+164
Navigation System [Opt on Eddie Bauer]	+1287
Power Driver Seat [Opt on XLT]	+155
Power Moonroof [Opt on Eddie Bauer]	+555
Running Boards [Opt on XLT]	+210

Body Styles	TMV Pricing		
	Trade	Private	Dealer
4 Dr XLT 4WD SUV	20569	21898	24112
4 Dr XLT SUV	18685	19892	21904

Options	Price
Traction Control System [Opt on Eddie Bauer]	+193
Ventilated Seats (Front) [Opt on Eddie Bauer]	+484
AM/FM/CD Changer Audio System [Opt on Eddie Bauer, XLT]	+164
Air Conditioning - Front and Rear [Opt on XLT]	+387
DVD Entertainment System	+967
Front and Rear Head Airbag Restraints	+419
5.4L V8 SOHC 16V FI Engine [Opt on XLT, Eddie Bauer 2WD]	+332
Power Third Seat [Opt on Eddie Bauer]	+319
FX4 Off-Road Suspension Package [Opt on XLT 4WD]	+2432
Park Distance Control (Rear) [Opt on XLT]	+164

Expedition

Mileage Category: N

Ford's full-size SUV sports changes inside and out. Outside, the Expedition looks bigger and bolder. Some of its new styling cues, such as the egg-crate grille and raised hood, are from its little brother, the Explorer. Inside you'll find fold-flat second- and third-row seats, with a power-folding option for the third row. The second row is split-40/20/40 enabling the middle section to slide forward. The Eddie Bauer package has an in-dash six-disc changer (optional on the XLT) and steering wheel-mounted stereo and climate controls, as well as an optional DVD player, navigation system and heated-cooled seats.

But the big changes are the ones you can't readily see. Underneath the skin a double-wishbone independent rear suspension system and a rack and pinion steering configuration improve road handling. AdvanceTrac stability control, along with ControlTrac four-wheel-drive system and an increased width of 1.7 inches should help keep the rubber down and the shiny side up.

Body Styles	TMV Pricing		
	Trade	Private	Dealer
4 Dr Eddie Bauer 4WD SUV	21288	22890	25559
4 Dr Eddie Bauer SUV	19299	20751	23171

Options	Price
17 inch Wheels	+235
5.4L V8 SOHC 16V FI Engine [Opt on 2WD,XLT 4WD]	+409
Air Conditioning - Front and Rear [Std on Eddie Bauer]	+353
Automatic Load Leveling	+288
Camper/Towing Package	+230
Captain Chairs (2) [Opt on XLT]	+227
Captain Chairs (4) [Opt on Eddie Bauer]	+265
Compact Disc Changer [Opt on XLT]	+291

Body Styles	TMV Pricing		
	Trade	Private	Dealer
4 Dr XLT 4WD SUV	17604	18929	21136
4 Dr XLT SUV	15901	17098	19092

Options	Price
DVD Entertainment System	+792
Front Side Airbag Restraints	+233
Heated Front Seats [Opt on Eddie Bauer]	+174
Leather Seats [Opt on XLT]	+530
Limited Slip Differential	+150
Park Distance Control (Rear)	+118
Power Driver Seat [Opt on XLT]	+141
Power Moonroof	+471
Running Boards [Opt on XLT]	+191

Mileage Category: N

2002

For 2002, the Expedition gets Ford's BeltMinder audible warning system to remind buyers to buckle up. The XLT can be equipped with a rear video entertainment system for the first time. Eddie Bauer models can be done up in Premier Group packaging, which includes monochromatic exterior paint, second-row captain's chairs, moonroof, 17-inch alloy wheels, foglights and illuminated running boards.

Body Styles	TMV Pricing		
	Trade	Private	Dealer
4 Dr Eddie Bauer 4WD SUV	18303	20420	22374
4 Dr Eddie Bauer SUV	16815	18760	20555

Options	Price
5.4L V8 SOHC 16V FI Engine [Opt on XLT,2WD]	+366
Air Conditioning - Front and Rear [Opt on XLT]	+398
Automatic Load Leveling	+258
Camper/Towing Package	+205
Front Side Airbag Restraints	+208
Heated Front Seats	+155
Leather Seats [Opt on XLT]	+558

Body Styles	TMV Pricing		
	Trade	Private	Dealer
4 Dr XLT 4WD SUV	15281	17048	18680
4 Dr XLT SUV	13758	15350	16819

Options	Price
Limited Slip Differential	+134
Power Driver Seat [Opt on XLT]	+126
Power Moonroof	+421
Premium Audio System [Opt on XLT]	+261
Running Boards [Opt on XLT]	+229
VCR Entertainment System [Opt on Eddie Bauer]	+709

Mileage Category: N

2001

Ford's second-largest SUV changes little for 2001. XLT models get privacy glass as standard equipment, while the upscale Eddie Bauer trim level now comes with HomeLink and a class IV trailer towing package (4x4 models only). Eddie Bauers also get second-row leather captain's chairs and a rear-seat entertainment system as optional equipment. A new "No Boundaries" option package includes a monochromatic black exterior, side body cladding, 17-inch wheels, illuminated running boards and special front seats.

Mileage Category: N

2000

The Expedition receives power-adjustable foot pedals, a rear sonar system for when the vehicle is backing up, optional side airbags, a revised center console and restyled wheels.

Body Styles	TMV Pricing		
	Trade	Private	Dealer
4 Dr Eddie Bauer 4WD SUV	14509	16434	18321
4 Dr Eddie Bauer SUV	13652	15463	17239
4 Dr XLT 4WD SUV	12488	14145	15769
4 Dr XLT SUV	11080	12551	13992

Options	Price
Compact Disc Changer [Opt on XLT]	+224
Front Side Airbag Restraints	+186
Heated Front Seats	+137
Leather Seats [Opt on XLT]	+471
Limited Slip Differential	+120
Park Distance Control (Rear)	+115
Power Moonroof	+377
Running Boards [Opt on XLT]	+205

Options	Price
5.4L V8 SOHC 16V FI Engine [Opt on XLT,2WD]	+328
Air Conditioning - Front and Rear [Opt on XLT]	+332
Aluminum/Alloy Wheels	+147
AM/FM/Cassette/CD Audio System	+167
Automatic Load Leveling	+231
Camper/Towing Package	+414
Captain Chairs (2) [Opt on XLT]	+132
Captain Chairs (4)	+375

1999

Mileage Category: N

Power output is improved for both Triton V8 engines on Ford's full-size sport-ute. Package content is added for both XLT and Eddie Bauer trim levels. Power-adjustable accelerator and brake pedals have been added. An updated Command Trac four-wheel-drive system allows automatic four-wheel-drive operation when required. Spruce Green, Harvest Gold, Tropic Green and Deep Wedgewood Blue replace Light Prairie Tan, Vermont Green, Light Denim Blue and Pacific Green on the color chart.

Body Styles	TMV Pricing		
	Trade	Private	Dealer
4 Dr Eddie Bauer 4WD SUV	12056	14007	16037
4 Dr Eddie Bauer SUV	10678	12406	14205

Options	Price
5.4L V8 SOHC 16V FI Engine [Opt on XLT,2WD]	+258
Air Conditioning - Front and Rear [Opt on XLT]	+274
AM/FM/Cassette/CD Audio System	+138
Automatic Load Leveling	+352
Camper/Towing Package	+151

Body Styles	TMV Pricing		
	Trade	Private	Dealer
4 Dr XLT 4WD SUV	10220	11874	13595
4 Dr XLT SUV	8537	9918	11356

Options	Price
Compact Disc Changer	+185
Leather Seats [Opt on XLT]	+388
Power Moonroof	+311
Running Boards [Opt on XLT]	+169
Third Seat [Opt on XLT]	+249

1998

Mileage Category: N

No changes.

Body Styles	TMV Pricing		
	Trade	Private	Dealer
4 Dr Eddie Bauer 4WD SUV	9026	10675	12534
4 Dr Eddie Bauer SUV	8313	9832	11544

Options	Price
Compact Disc Changer	+151
Leather Seats [Opt on XLT]	+317
Power Moonroof	+254
Running Boards	+138
Third Seat	+190

Body Styles	TMV Pricing		
	Trade	Private	Dealer
4 Dr XLT 4WD SUV	8254	9762	11462
4 Dr XLT SUV	7583	8969	10531

Options	Price
5.4L V8 SOHC 16V FI Engine	+211
Air Conditioning - Front and Rear	+224
Automatic Load Leveling	+173
Camper/Towing Package	+159

1997

Mileage Category: N

Ford's replacement for the aging Bronco is the all-new Expedition. Based on the 1997 F-150 platform, this full-size sport-utility vehicle is poised to do battle with the Chevrolet Tahoe and GMC Yukon.

Body Styles	TMV Pricing		
	Trade	Private	Dealer
4 Dr Eddie Bauer 4WD SUV	7587	9187	11143
4 Dr Eddie Bauer SUV	7249	8779	10649

Options	Price
5.4L V8 SOHC 16V FI Engine	+166
Air Conditioning - Front and Rear	+207
Automatic Load Leveling	+160
Camper/Towing Package	+161
Compact Disc Changer	+139

Body Styles	TMV Pricing		
	Trade	Private	Dealer
4 Dr XLT 4WD SUV	7108	8608	10441
4 Dr XLT SUV	6435	7792	9451

Options	Price
Leather Seats [Opt on XLT]	+293
Power Moonroof	+228
Running Boards	+128
Third Seat	+176

Ford
Explorer

2003

Body Styles	TMV Pricing		
	Trade	Private	Dealer
4 Dr Eddie Bauer 4WD SUV	21163	22660	25154
4 Dr Eddie Bauer AWD SUV	20313	21750	24144
4 Dr Eddie Bauer SUV	19610	20997	23308
4 Dr Limited 4WD SUV	21376	22888	25407
4 Dr Limited AWD SUV	20807	22279	24731
4 Dr Limited SUV	19913	21321	23668
4 Dr NBX 4WD SUV	18676	19997	22198

Body Styles	TMV Pricing		
	Trade	Private	Dealer
4 Dr NBX SUV	17419	18651	20704
4 Dr XLS 4WD SUV	16028	17162	19051
4 Dr XLS AWD SUV	16465	17629	19570
4 Dr XLS SUV	13956	14943	16588
4 Dr XLT 4WD SUV	17652	18900	20981
4 Dr XLT AWD SUV	18011	19285	21408
4 Dr XLT SUV	17018	18221	20227

Mileage Category: M

Sport versions of the XLS and XLT debut, along with a new trim level called NBX (No Boundaries Experience). The NBX includes special exterior trim, unique 17-inch alloy wheels, all-terrain tires, a Yakima roof rack, rubber floormats and a cargo area liner. All-wheel drive is newly available on all but the NBX model. XLS models come standard with an automatic transmission and a CD player for 2003, while XLT models get a chrome grille and metallic interior accents. Eddie Bauer models have satin-finish 17-inch wheels this year. Limited models get upgrades such as chromed exterior trim, chrome wheels, a leather-upholstered center console cover and new woodgrain interior trim. A tire-pressure monitoring system is available on Limited models. An Off-Road Package including underbody skid plates, suspension upgrades, front tow hooks and unique wheels debuts. Finally, a rear seat DVD-based entertainment system will be available later in the year.

2003 (cont'd)

Options	Price
Aluminum/Alloy Wheels [Opt on XLS]	+290
Camper/Towing Package	+255
Leather Seats [Opt on XLT]	+422
Limited Slip Differential [Opt on XLS]	+187
Power Moonroof [Opt on Eddie Bauer,Limited,XLT]	+516
Running Boards [Opt on XLT]	+255
Side Steps [Opt on XLS,XLT]	+177
Special Factory Paint [Opt on Limited]	+129
Special Leather Seat Trim [Opt on Limited]	+577

Options	Price
Third Seat	+432
AM/FM/CD Changer Audio System [Opt on NBX,XLT]	+329
17 Inch Wheels [Opt on XLT]	+319
Air Conditioning - Front and Rear	+393
DVD Entertainment System	+835
Front and Rear Head Airbag Restraints	+361
4.6L V8 SOHC 16V FI Engine	+516
Park Distance Control (Rear) [Opt on Eddie Bauer,Limited,XLT]	+164

2002

Body Styles	TMV Pricing		
	Trade	Private	Dealer
4 Dr Eddie Bauer 4WD SUV	18038	19535	22031
4 Dr Eddie Bauer SUV	16655	18038	20342
4 Dr Limited 4WD SUV	18155	19662	22174
4 Dr Limited SUV	16868	18268	20602

Body Styles	TMV Pricing		
	Trade	Private	Dealer
4 Dr XLS 4WD SUV	14103	15274	17226
4 Dr XLS SUV	11462	12413	13999
4 Dr XLT 4WD SUV	14724	15947	17984
4 Dr XLT SUV	14397	15592	17584

Mileage Category: M

Ford has overhauled its Explorer for model-year 2002 in an attempt to make it more carlike than ever before. Among the improvements are a 2.5-inch-wider stance and 2-inch-longer wheelbase for improved handling and roominess, a new independent rear suspension that improves ride and handling, while at the same time accommodating an optional third row of seats, larger door openings with a lower step-in height, an optional side curtain airbag system and an optional Reverse Sensing System.

Options	Price
17 Inch Wheels [Opt on XLT]	+294
4.6L V8 SOHC 16V FI Engine	+471
Air Conditioning - Front and Rear	+359
Aluminum/Alloy Wheels [Opt on XLS]	+162
AM/FM/CD Changer Audio System [Opt on XLT]	+171
Automatic 5-Speed Transmission [Opt on XLS]	+645
Camper/Towing Package	+233
Chrome Wheels	+144
Front and Rear Head Airbag Restraints	+147

Options	Price
Leather Seats [Opt on XLT]	+309
Park Distance Control (Rear)	+150
Pearlescent Metallic Paint [Opt on Limited]	+118
Power Moonroof	+471
Power Passenger Seat [Opt on XLT]	+191
Rollover Protection System	+147
Running Boards [Opt on XLT]	+233
Sport Seats [Opt on XLT]	+159
Third Seat	+394

2001

Body Styles	TMV Pricing		
	Trade	Private	Dealer
4 Dr Eddie Bauer 4WD SUV	14367	16268	18022
4 Dr Eddie Bauer AWD SUV	14845	16809	18621
4 Dr Eddie Bauer SUV	13231	14981	16597
4 Dr Limited 4WD SUV	14458	16370	18135
4 Dr Limited AWD SUV	14856	16821	18635
4 Dr Limited SUV	13618	15419	17081

Body Styles	TMV Pricing		
	Trade	Private	Dealer
4 Dr XLS 4WD SUV	11485	13004	14406
4 Dr XLS SUV	10276	11635	12890
4 Dr XLT 4WD SUV	11962	13544	15004
4 Dr XLT AWD SUV	11973	13556	15018
4 Dr XLT SUV	11616	13153	14571

Mileage Category: M

A complete redesign is planned for 2002, so the Explorer changes little in 2001. The SOHC V6 is standard on all models, and the 4.0-liter OHV V6 and manual transmission are no longer available. Additional child safety-seat tether anchors have been added to the second-row seats.

Options	Price
5.0L V8 OHV 16V FI Engine	+222
Automatic Load Leveling	+184
Camper/Towing Package	+187
Compact Disc Changer	+208
Front Side Airbag Restraints	+208
Heated Front Seats [Opt on Eddie Bauer]	+134

Options	Price
Leather Seats [Opt on Sport,XLT]	+500
Park Distance Control (Rear) [Opt on Eddie Bauer,Limited,XLT]	+134
Power Moonroof	+421
Power Passenger Seat [Opt on XLT]	+171
Running Boards [Opt on XLS,XLT]	+208
Sport Seats	+148

2000

Body Styles	TMV Pricing		
	Trade	Private	Dealer
2 Dr Sport 4WD SUV	7822	9073	10300
2 Dr Sport SUV	6763	7845	8905
4 Dr Eddie Bauer 4WD SUV	10773	12497	14186
4 Dr Eddie Bauer AWD SUV	10946	12697	14414
4 Dr Eddie Bauer SUV	10144	11768	13359
4 Dr Limited 4WD SUV	10887	12629	14337
4 Dr Limited AWD SUV	11017	12780	14508
4 Dr Limited SUV	10252	11893	13501

Body Styles	TMV Pricing		
	Trade	Private	Dealer
4 Dr XL 4WD SUV	8243	9562	10855
4 Dr XL SUV	7028	8152	9254
4 Dr XLS 4WD SUV	8454	9807	11133
4 Dr XLS SUV	7925	9194	10437
4 Dr XLT 4WD SUV	9301	10789	12247
4 Dr XLT AWD SUV	9449	10961	12443
4 Dr XLT SUV	8772	10176	11552

Mileage Category: M

A color-keyed, two-spoke leather-wrapped steering wheel (with auxiliary audio, climate and speed control) is now standard on Eddie Bauer models. XLT Sport/Eddie Bauer/Limited models with 5.0-liter V8s receive a trailer-towing package as standard equipment. The XL is available only for fleet sales, and the XLS replaces the XL Appearance as the base retail model.

2000 (cont'd)

Options	Price
4.0L V6 SOHC 12V FI Engine [Opt on Sport,XL,XLS,XLT]	+254
5.0L V8 OHV 16V FI Engine	+198
Automatic 5-Speed Transmission [Opt on Sport,XL,XLS]	+516
Automatic Load Leveling	+165
Bucket Seats [Opt on XLT]	+132
Camper/Towing Package	+167
Captain Chairs (2) [Opt on XL]	+132
Compact Disc Changer	+175
Front Side Airbag Restraints	+184

Options	Price
Heated Front Seats [Opt on Eddie Bauer]	+115
Leather Seats [Opt on Sport,XLT]	+448
Limited Slip Differential	+147
Park Distance Control (Rear)	+120
Power Driver Seat [Opt on Sport]	+123
Power Moonroof	+377
Power Passenger Seat [Opt on Sport,XLT]	+123
Running Boards [Opt on XL,XLS,XLT]	+186
Side Steps	+139
Split Front Bench Seat [Opt on XL,XLS]	+137

1999

Mileage Category: M

The Explorer gets exterior revisions including new foglamps, rocker panel moldings, wheel moldings, running boards and wheels. Harvest Gold, Chestnut, Deep Wedgewood, Spruce Green and Tropic Green replace Light Prairie Tan, Desert Violet, Light Denim Blue, Pacific Green and Evergreen Frost on the color chart. New options include a reverse sensing system and rear load leveling. Side-impact airbags are also newly available.

Body Styles	TMV Pricing		
	Trade	Private	Dealer
2 Dr Sport 4WD SUV	6071	7209	8393
2 Dr Sport SUV	5268	6255	7283
4 Dr Eddie Bauer 4WD SUV	8213	9752	11354
4 Dr Eddie Bauer AWD SUV	8285	9838	11455
4 Dr Eddie Bauer SUV	7765	9221	10736
4 Dr Limited 4WD SUV	8410	9986	11626
4 Dr Limited AWD SUV	8461	10047	11698
4 Dr Limited SUV	8170	9701	11295

Body Styles	TMV Pricing		
	Trade	Private	Dealer
4 Dr XL 4WD SUV	6294	7473	8701
4 Dr XL SUV	5446	6467	7529
4 Dr XLS 4WD SUV	6473	7686	8949
4 Dr XLS SUV	6437	7644	8900
4 Dr XLT 4WD SUV	7141	8480	9873
4 Dr XLT AWD SUV	7189	8536	9938
4 Dr XLT SUV	6562	7791	9071

Options	Price
4.0L V6 SOHC 12V FI Engine [Opt on Sport,XL,XLS,XLT]	+210
5.0L V8 OHV 16V FI Engine	+167
AM/FM/Cassette/CD Audio System [Opt on Sport,XL,XLS,XLT]	+124
Automatic 4-Speed Transmission	+367
Automatic 5-Speed Transmission [Opt on Sport,XL,XLS]	+413
Automatic Load Leveling	+151
Camper/Towing Package	+138

Options	Price
Compact Disc Changer	+144
Front Side Airbag Restraints	+168
Leather Seats [Std on Eddie Bauer,Limited]	+369
Limited Slip Differential	+120
Power Moonroof	+311
Power Passenger Seat [Opt on Sport,XLT]	+119
Running Boards [Std on Eddie Bauer,Limited]	+154
Side Steps [Opt on Sport]	+115

1998

Mileage Category: M

The Ford Explorer gets a restyled tailgate for 1998.

Body Styles	TMV Pricing		
	Trade	Private	Dealer
2 Dr Sport 4WD SUV	4895	5920	7076
2 Dr Sport SUV	4558	5513	6590
4 Dr Eddie Bauer 4WD SUV	6636	8027	9595
4 Dr Eddie Bauer AWD SUV	6299	7618	9106
4 Dr Eddie Bauer SUV	6169	7462	8920
4 Dr Limited 4WD SUV	7233	8749	10458
4 Dr Limited AWD SUV	6978	8440	10088

Body Styles	TMV Pricing		
	Trade	Private	Dealer
4 Dr Limited SUV	6764	8182	9780
4 Dr XL 4WD SUV	5190	6278	7505
4 Dr XL SUV	4765	5763	6889
4 Dr XLT 4WD SUV	5701	6896	8243
4 Dr XLT AWD SUV	5487	6637	7934
4 Dr XLT SUV	5232	6329	7565

Options	Price
Power Moonroof	+254
Running Boards [Opt on Eddie Bauer,XL,XLT]	+125
4.0L V6 SOHC 12V FI Engine [Opt on Sport,XLT]	+190
5.0L V8 OHV 16V FI Engine	+152

Options	Price
Automatic 4-Speed Transmission	+299
Automatic 5-Speed Transmission [Opt on Sport,XL,XLT]	+338
Compact Disc Changer	+117
Leather Seats [Opt on Eddie Bauer,Sport,XLT]	+208

Explorer

Body Styles	TMV Pricing		
	Trade	Private	Dealer
2 Dr Sport 4WD SUV	4348	5356	6587
2 Dr Sport SUV	3954	4870	5990
2 Dr XL 4WD SUV	4192	5163	6350
2 Dr XL SUV	3798	4678	5753
4 Dr Eddie Bauer 4WD SUV	5841	7195	8849
4 Dr Eddie Bauer AWD SUV	5545	6829	8399
4 Dr Eddie Bauer SUV	5413	6667	8200
4 Dr Limited 4WD SUV	6224	7666	9429

Body Styles	TMV Pricing		
	Trade	Private	Dealer
4 Dr Limited AWD SUV	6180	7612	9363
4 Dr Limited SUV	6120	7538	9270
4 Dr XL 4WD SUV	4391	5409	6653
4 Dr XL SUV	3975	4896	6022
4 Dr XLT 4WD SUV	4902	6038	7426
4 Dr XLT AWD SUV	4782	5889	7243
4 Dr XLT SUV	4476	5513	6781

Options	Price
Automatic 4-Speed Transmission	+277
Automatic 5-Speed Transmission [Opt on Sport,XL,XLT]	+312
JBL Audio System [Std on Limited]	+161
Leather Seats [Std on Limited]	+192

Options	Price
Power Moonroof	+235
Running Boards [Std on Limited]	+116
4.0L V6 SOHC 12V FI Engine [Opt on Sport,XL,XLT]	+124
5.0L V8 OHV 16V FI Engine	+232

Mileage Category: M

Ford's best-selling Explorer receives a few appreciated improvements this year. A new SOHC V6 engine is now available, providing nearly as much power as the 5.0-liter V8. Also new is a five-speed automatic transmission, the first ever offered by an American auto manufacturer, which is standard on V6 models equipped with automatic.

Body Styles	TMV Pricing		
	Trade	Private	Dealer
2 Dr Sport 4WD SUV	3519	4423	5671
2 Dr Sport SUV	3267	4107	5266
2 Dr XL 4WD SUV	3349	4209	5397
2 Dr XL SUV	3095	3890	4988
4 Dr Eddie Bauer 4WD SUV	4734	5950	7630
4 Dr Eddie Bauer AWD SUV	4827	6067	7779
4 Dr Eddie Bauer SUV	4399	5529	7089
4 Dr Limited 4WD SUV	5050	6347	8137

Body Styles	TMV Pricing		
	Trade	Private	Dealer
4 Dr Limited AWD SUV	4949	6220	7975
4 Dr Limited SUV	4915	6177	7920
4 Dr XL 4WD SUV	3603	4529	5807
4 Dr XL SUV	3288	4133	5300
4 Dr XLT 4WD SUV	4023	5057	6484
4 Dr XLT AWD SUV	4101	5154	6608
4 Dr XLT SUV	3704	4656	5970

Options	Price
Power Moonroof	+209
5.0L V8 OHV 16V FI Engine	+251
Automatic 4-Speed Transmission [Opt on Sport,XL,XLT]	+246

Options	Price
JBL Audio System [Std on Limited]	+144
Leather Seats [Std on Limited]	+163

Mileage Category: M

The long-awaited V8 AWD Explorers are available in XLT, Eddie Bauer or Limited Edition flavors. An integrated child safety seat is optional, and the Expedition model has been replaced by a Premium trim package for the Sport.

Body Styles	TMV Pricing		
	Trade	Private	Dealer
2 Dr Expedition 4WD SUV	3352	4300	5880
2 Dr Sport 4WD SUV	2766	3549	4853
2 Dr Sport SUV	2527	3242	4433
2 Dr XL 4WD SUV	2727	3499	4785
2 Dr XL SUV	2221	2850	3897
4 Dr Eddie Bauer 4WD SUV	3820	4900	6701
4 Dr Eddie Bauer SUV	3546	4549	6221

Body Styles	TMV Pricing		
	Trade	Private	Dealer
4 Dr Limited 4WD SUV	4038	5180	7083
4 Dr Limited SUV	3889	4989	6822
4 Dr XL 4WD SUV	2884	3700	5060
4 Dr XL SUV	2539	3258	4455
4 Dr XLT 4WD SUV	3236	4151	5677
4 Dr XLT SUV	2923	3750	5128

Options	Price
Automatic 4-Speed Transmission [Opt on Sport,XL,XLT]	+213
Camper/Towing Package	+77
Compact Disc Changer	+83
JBL Audio System [Std on Limited]	+124

Options	Price
Leather Seats [Std on Limited]	+141
Power Moonroof	+180
Running Boards [Std on Limited]	+89

Mileage Category: M

Dual airbags top the changes for the redesigned Explorer. Integrated child safety seats are optional on four-door models. Exterior changes include new sheet metal, headlights, grille, taillights and side moldings. The Control-Trac four-wheel-drive system automatically sends power to front wheels if it senses rear-wheel slippage. This feature can be locked in for full-time four-wheeling.

Ford
Explorer/Explorer Sport

1994

Mileage Category: M

New wheels and a power equipment group for the Eddie Bauer model are the only changes to this year's Explorer.

Body Styles	TMV Pricing		
	Trade	Private	Dealer
2 Dr Eddie Bauer 4WD SUV	2308	3129	4496
2 Dr Eddie Bauer SUV	2168	2939	4223
2 Dr Sport 4WD SUV	2063	2796	4017
2 Dr Sport SUV	1857	2517	3616
2 Dr XL 4WD SUV	1922	2605	3744
2 Dr XL SUV	1573	2132	3064
4 Dr Eddie Bauer 4WD SUV	2551	3458	4970

Body Styles	TMV Pricing		
	Trade	Private	Dealer
4 Dr Eddie Bauer SUV	2375	3220	4628
4 Dr Limited 4WD SUV	2916	3953	5680
4 Dr Limited SUV	2551	3458	4970
4 Dr XL 4WD SUV	2028	2749	3950
4 Dr XL SUV	1849	2506	3601
4 Dr XLT 4WD SUV	2272	3080	4426
4 Dr XLT SUV	2131	2889	4151

Options	Price
Running Boards	+76
Air Conditioning [Std on Limited]	+143
Automatic 4-Speed Transmission [Std on Limited]	+180

Options	Price
JBL Audio System	+105
Leather Seats [Std on Limited]	+119

Ford
Explorer Sport

2003

Body Styles	TMV Pricing		
	Trade	Private	Dealer
2 Dr XLS 4WD SUV	13616	14736	16602
2 Dr XLS SUV	11655	12613	14210

Body Styles	TMV Pricing		
	Trade	Private	Dealer
2 Dr XLT 4WD SUV	14711	15921	17937
2 Dr XLT SUV	13067	14141	15932

Options	Price
Limited Slip Differential	+229
Power Driver Seat [Opt on XLT]	+168
Side Steps [Opt on XLT]	+135

Options	Price
AM/FM/CD Changer Audio System [Opt on XLT]	+193
Pioneer Audio System [Opt on XLT]	+135

Mileage Category: M

Very few changes are in store for this two-door SUV. Trim levels equipped with the Comfort Group now includes power lumbar support. This, along with heated seats, will also be included if you opt for the leather trim. Two coat hooks and a power point make an appearance in the cargo area, and Red Fire Clearcoat Metallic replaces Toreador Red Clearcoat Metallic.

2002

Mileage Category: M

Sixteen-inch aluminum wheels are made standard, along with an AM/FM/CD/cassette stereo. You now have a choice between an automatic or manual transmission with the base model.

Body Styles					TMV Pricing		
					Trade	Private	Dealer
2 Dr STD 4WD SUV					11357	12439	14242
2 Dr STD SUV					10035	10991	12585

Options	Price
AM/FM/CD Changer Audio System	+177
Automatic 5-Speed Transmission	+615
Front Side Airbag Restraints	+233
Leather Seats	+386
Limited Slip Differential	+209

Options	Price
Pioneer Audio System	+124
Power Driver Seat	+153
Power Moonroof	+471
Running Boards	+118

2001

Mileage Category: M

The 2001 Ford Explorer Sport receives a few styling changes as well as minor mechanical and interior improvements.

Body Styles					TMV Pricing		
					Trade	Private	Dealer
2 Dr STD 4WD SUV					10087	11511	12825
2 Dr STD SUV					8658	9880	11008

Options	Price
AM/FM/CD Changer Audio System	+163
Automatic 5-Speed Transmission	+577
Bucket Seats	+148
Front Side Airbag Restraints	+205
Leather Seats	+500

Options	Price
Limited Slip Differential	+187
Power Driver Seat	+137
Power Moonroof	+421
Running Boards	+208

2003

Body Styles	TMV Pricing		
	Trade	Private	Dealer
4 Dr XLS 4WD Crew Cab SB	15931	17236	19412
4 Dr XLS Crew Cab SB	14091	15246	17170

Options	Price
Limited Slip Differential	+229
Power Driver Seat [Opt on XLT]	+168
Side Steps [Opt on XLT]	+135

Body Styles	TMV Pricing		
	Trade	Private	Dealer
4 Dr XLT 4WD Crew Cab SB	17093	18493	20827
4 Dr XLT Crew Cab SB	15368	16627	18725

Options	Price
AM/FM/CD Changer Audio System [Opt on XLT]	+193
Pioneer Audio System [Opt on XLT]	+135
Front and Rear Head Airbag Restraints	+361

Mileage Category: J

Ford updates the Sport Trac's interior with new low-back bucket seats, revised door trim and updated colors. When leather upholstery is ordered, the front seats are six-way power adjustable and can be heated and equipped with power lumbar support. To improve safety, Ford's Safety Canopy side airbag system with rollover sensors is newly available, as are standard rear disc brakes. Lastly, an Adrenaline Edition debuts mid-year with a 485-watt Pioneer sound system and new colors.

2002

Body Styles	TMV Pricing		
	Trade	Private	Dealer
4 Dr STD 4WD Crew Cab SB	14415	15787	18074
4 Dr STD Crew Cab SB	12820	14040	16074

Options	Price	Options	Price
AM/FM/CD Changer Audio System	+182	Pioneer Audio System	+118
Automatic 5-Speed Transmission	+615	Power Driver Seat	+153
Leather Seats	+386	Power Moonroof	+471
Limited Slip Differential	+209	Side Steps	+127

Mileage Category: J

The Explorer Sport Trac enters 2002 with slightly more power and torque from its 4.0-liter V6 engine, some new exterior colors and a simplified options list. You can now also get an automatic transmission with the value package.

2001

Body Styles	TMV Pricing		
	Trade	Private	Dealer
4 Dr STD 4WD Crew Cab SB	12810	14666	16380
4 Dr STD Crew Cab SB	11410	13064	14590

Options	Price	Options	Price
AM/FM/CD Changer Audio System	+163	Power Driver Seat	+137
Automatic 5-Speed Transmission	+577	Power Moonroof	+421
Leather Seats	+500	Running Boards	+208
Limited Slip Differential	+187		

Mileage Category: J

The Sport Trac is a combination of a pickup and an SUV. Basically, Ford has grafted a small cargo bed to the back of an updated Ford Explorer.

Ford
F-150
2003

Mileage Category: K

Arriving in 2003 for the XLT supercab styleside configuration is the Heritage Edition, which includes 17-inch wheels, a chrome cab step and various stylistic flairs such as a black bedliner, a lower valance, paint striping and a paint scheme with a raised cut-line. Also new is an STX edition for the XL- and XLT-trimmed regular and supercabs that includes an MP3 player combined with a monochromatic color scheme and clear lights, among others. Upgrades for the fancy King Ranch flavor consist of fake wood for the interior, lighted step bars and an in-dash six-disc CD changer. For the Lariat, expect a standard rear window defroster and a Pioneer CD and cassette system (the latter is also newly available on the XL and XLT). Harley-Davidson models have the option of getting a two-tone black-and-silver paint. Finally, a new LATCH system helps you tie down the kiddie seats properly.

Body Styles	TMV Pricing		
	Trade	Private	Dealer
2 Dr XL 4WD Std Cab LB	14792	15773	17408
2 Dr XL 4WD Std Cab SB	14592	15560	17172
2 Dr XL 4WD Std Cab Step SB	15225	16235	17917
2 Dr XL Std Cab LB	12468	13295	14673
2 Dr XL Std Cab SB	12264	13077	14433
2 Dr XL Std Cab Step SB	12919	13776	15204
2 Dr XLT 4WD Std Cab LB	16604	17705	19541

Body Styles	TMV Pricing		
	Trade	Private	Dealer
2 Dr XLT 4WD Std Cab SB	16348	17432	19239
2 Dr XLT 4WD Std Cab Step SB	16987	18114	19991
2 Dr XLT Std Cab LB	14343	15294	16880
2 Dr XLT Std Cab SB	14109	15045	16605
2 Dr XLT Std Cab Step SB	14769	15749	17381
4 Dr Harley-Davidson S/C Crew Cab SB	27932	29785	32872

2003 (cont'd)

Body Styles	TMV Pricing		
	Trade	Private	Dealer
4 Dr King Ranch 4WD Crew Cab SB	25077	26740	29512
4 Dr King Ranch 4WD Ext Cab Step SB	23602	25167	27775
4 Dr King Ranch Crew Cab SB	22504	23997	26484
4 Dr King Ranch Ext Cab Step SB	21443	22865	25235
4 Dr Lariat 4WD Crew Cab SB	23522	25082	27681
4 Dr Lariat 4WD Ext Cab LB	20904	22290	24600
4 Dr Lariat 4WD Ext Cab SB	20671	22042	24326
4 Dr Lariat 4WD Ext Cab Step SB	21342	22757	25116
4 Dr Lariat Crew Cab SB	20001	21327	23538
4 Dr Lariat Ext Cab LB	18713	19954	22022
4 Dr Lariat Ext Cab SB	18373	19591	21622
4 Dr Lariat Ext Cab Step SB	19019	20280	22382
4 Dr XL 4WD Ext Cab LB	16982	18108	19985

Body Styles	TMV Pricing		
	Trade	Private	Dealer
4 Dr XL 4WD Ext Cab SB	16794	17908	19764
4 Dr XL 4WD Ext Cab Step SB	17419	18574	20500
4 Dr XL Ext Cab LB	14323	15273	16856
4 Dr XL Ext Cab SB	14094	15029	16587
4 Dr XL Ext Cab Step SB	14751	15729	17360
4 Dr XLT 4WD Crew Cab SB	20852	22235	24539
4 Dr XLT 4WD Ext Cab LB	18802	20049	22127
4 Dr XLT 4WD Ext Cab SB	18596	19829	21884
4 Dr XLT 4WD Ext Cab Step SB	19223	20498	22622
4 Dr XLT Crew Cab SB	18625	19860	21919
4 Dr XLT Ext Cab LB	16140	17210	18994
4 Dr XLT Ext Cab SB	15960	17018	18782
4 Dr XLT Ext Cab Step SB	16593	17693	19527

Options	Price
Aluminum/Alloy Wheels [Opt on XL]	+161
AM/FM/CD Audio System [Opt on XL]	+123
Automatic 4-Speed Transmission [Opt on XL,XLT]	+706
Camper/Towing Package	+226
Captain Chairs (2) [Opt on Lariat,XLT]	+316
Compact Disc Changer [Opt on Lariat,XLT]	+145
Cruise Control [Opt on XL]	+116
Heated Front and Rear Seats	+158
Limited Slip Differential	+184
Polished Aluminum/Alloy Wheels [Opt on XL]	+129
Power Driver Seat [Opt on XLT]	+187
Power Moonroof	+522
Power Rear Window	+158

Options	Price
Running Boards	+158
Split Front Bench Seat [Opt on XL]	+126
Two-Tone Paint [Opt on Lariat,XLT]	+145
VCR Entertainment System	+835
17 Inch Wheels [Opt on XLT]	+322
4.6L V8 SOHC 16V FI Engine [Opt on XL,XLT]	+484
5.4L V8 SOHC 16V FI Engine	+516
FX4 Off-Road Suspension Package [Opt on Lariat,XLT]	+555
STX Edition [Opt on XL,XLT]	+642
Heritage Edition [Opt on XLT]	+774
5.4L V8 CNG SOHC 16V FI Engine [Opt on XL,XLT]	+5054
5.4L V8 Propane SOHC 16V FI Engine [Opt on XL,XLT]	+5054

2002

Mileage Category: K

A new King Ranch SuperCab arrives for 2002, joining the SuperCrew version near the top of the F-150 food chain. All King Ranch trucks get lighted visor mirrors with a HomeLink universal transmitter and a Travel Note recording device, while KR SuperCrews have automatic climate control and an available second-row bench seat that replaces the standard rear captain's chairs. Get the Harley-Davidson edition for a supercharged 5.4-liter Triton V-8 engine that adds 80 horsepower and new styling cues in the form of flame pin striping and chrome accessories, a new upper chrome billet grille, clear-lens headlamps and clear-lens parking lamps embossed with the label and rivets surrounding the center cap of the 20-inch wheels. The lower-line F-150 XL gets standard air conditioning, and its 4.2-liter V6 receives a ULEV rating. An FX4 off-road equipment package can be added to XLT or Lariat 4WD models and includes upgrades like Rancho shocks, skid plates, special wheels and unique trim. Carryover improvements from late 2001 include seat-mounted seatbelts on SuperCabs, child seat-tether anchors and rear head restraints on SuperCrew models. Also added late in 2001 were optional heated front seats (XLT and Lariat), a power sunroof (XLT and Lariat SuperCab and Crew) and a rear-seat entertainment system (XLT and Lariat SuperCrew).

Body Styles	TMV Pricing		
	Trade	Private	Dealer
2 Dr XL 4WD Std Cab LB	13050	14043	15697
2 Dr XL 4WD Std Cab SB	12855	13833	15462
2 Dr XL 4WD Std Cab Step SB	13492	14518	16229
2 Dr XL Std Cab LB	11049	11889	13290
2 Dr XL Std Cab SB	10883	11711	13090
2 Dr XL Std Cab Step SB	11510	12386	13845
2 Dr XLT 4WD Std Cab LB	14373	15466	17288
2 Dr XLT 4WD Std Cab SB	14216	15298	17100
2 Dr XLT 4WD Std Cab Step SB	14805	15931	17808
2 Dr XLT Std Cab LB	12364	13305	14872
2 Dr XLT Std Cab SB	12163	13088	14630
2 Dr XLT Std Cab Step SB	12791	13764	15386
4 Dr Harley-Davidson S/C Crew Cab SB	24628	26502	29624
4 Dr King Ranch 4WD Crew Cab SB	23052	24806	27728
4 Dr King Ranch 4WD Ext Cab SB	21589	23231	25968
4 Dr King Ranch Crew Cab SB	20963	22558	25215
4 Dr King Ranch Ext Cab SB	17495	18826	21044
4 Dr Lariat 4WD Crew Cab SB	20985	22581	25241
4 Dr Lariat 4WD Ext Cab LB	17996	19365	21646

Body Styles	TMV Pricing		
	Trade	Private	Dealer
4 Dr Lariat 4WD Ext Cab SB	17760	19111	21363
4 Dr Lariat 4WD Ext Cab Step SB	18433	19835	22172
4 Dr Lariat Crew Cab SB	17171	18477	20654
4 Dr Lariat Ext Cab LB	15985	17201	19227
4 Dr XLT 4WD Crew Cab SB	18075	19450	21741
4 Dr XLT 4WD Ext Cab LB	16301	17541	19608
4 Dr XLT 4WD Ext Cab SB	16112	17338	19380
4 Dr XLT 4WD Ext Cab Step SB	16706	17977	20095
4 Dr XLT Crew Cab SB	16148	17377	19424
4 Dr XLT Ext Cab LB	14038	15106	16886
4 Dr XLT Ext Cab SB	13861	14916	16673
4 Dr XLT Ext Cab Step SB	14490	15592	17429
4 Dr Lariat Ext Cab SB	15802	17004	19007
4 Dr Lariat Ext Cab Step SB	16401	17649	19728
4 Dr XL 4WD Ext Cab LB	14904	16038	17927
4 Dr XL 4WD Ext Cab SB	14756	15878	17749
4 Dr XL 4WD Ext Cab Step SB	15349	16517	18463
4 Dr XL Ext Cab LB	12639	13601	15203
4 Dr XL Ext Cab SB	12448	13395	14973
4 Dr XL Ext Cab Step SB	13062	14056	15712

Options	Price
17 Inch Wheels [Opt on XLT]	+294
4.6L V8 SOHC 16V FI Engine [Std on Crew,Lariat,Ext LB]	+442
5.4L V8 CNG SOHC 16V FI Engine	+4612
5.4L V8 Flex Fuel SOHC 16V FI Engine	+921
5.4L V8 Propane SOHC 16V FI Engine	+4630

Options	Price
5.4L V8 SOHC 16V FI Engine	+471
AM/FM/Cassette/CD Changer Audio System [Std on King Ranch]	+174
Automatic 4-Speed Transmission [Std on Crew,Lariat]	+645
Camper/Towing Package	+206

Options	Price
Captain Chairs (2) [Opt on Lariat,XLT]	+288
Compact Disc Changer [Opt on Harley]	+174
Heated Front Seats	+144
Limited Slip Differential	+168
Power Driver Seat [Std on Harley,King Ranch,Lariat]	+165
Power Moonroof	+477

Options	Price
Power Rear Window	+144
Running Boards [Std on Harley,King Ranch]	+144
Side Steps	+235
Split Front Bench Seat [Opt on XL]	+235
Two-Tone Paint	+132
VCR Entertainment System	+762

2001

Body Styles	TMV Pricing		
	Trade	Private	Dealer
2 Dr XL 4WD Std Cab LB	10928	12302	13570
2 Dr XL 4WD Std Cab SB	10762	12115	13363
2 Dr XL 4WD Std Cab Step SB	11312	12734	14047
2 Dr XL Std Cab LB	9194	10349	11416
2 Dr XL Std Cab SB	9051	10189	11239
2 Dr XL Std Cab Step SB	9596	10802	11916
2 Dr XLT 4WD Std Cab LB	12485	14054	15503
2 Dr XLT 4WD Std Cab SB	12350	13903	15336
2 Dr XLT 4WD Std Cab Step SB	12860	14476	15968
2 Dr XLT Std Cab LB	10747	12098	13345
2 Dr XLT Std Cab SB	10582	11912	13140
2 Dr XLT Std Cab Step SB	11117	12514	13804
4 Dr Harley-Davidson Crew Cab SB	19623	22090	24367
4 Dr King Ranch 4WD Crew Cab SB	20635	23229	25623
4 Dr King Ranch Crew Cab SB	15846	17838	19677
4 Dr Lariat 4WD Crew Cab SB	16566	18649	20571
4 Dr Lariat 4WD Ext Cab LB	15766	17748	19577
4 Dr Lariat 4WD Ext Cab SB	15622	17586	19398
4 Dr Lariat 4WD Ext Cab Step SB	16137	18166	20038

Body Styles	TMV Pricing		
	Trade	Private	Dealer
4 Dr Lariat Crew Cab SB	14790	16649	18365
4 Dr Lariat Ext Cab LB	14082	15852	17486
4 Dr Lariat Ext Cab SB	13921	15671	17286
4 Dr Lariat Ext Cab Step SB	14442	16257	17933
4 Dr XL 4WD Ext Cab LB	12537	14113	15567
4 Dr XL 4WD Ext Cab SB	12408	13967	15407
4 Dr XL 4WD Ext Cab Step SB	12920	14544	16043
4 Dr XL Ext Cab LB	10573	11902	13129
4 Dr XL Ext Cab SB	10409	11717	12925
4 Dr XL Ext Cab Step SB	10943	12318	13588
4 Dr XLT 4WD Crew Cab SB	15663	17632	19450
4 Dr XLT 4WD Ext Cab LB	14158	15937	17580
4 Dr XLT 4WD Ext Cab SB	14033	15797	17425
4 Dr XLT 4WD Ext Cab Step SB	14509	16333	18016
4 Dr XLT Crew Cab SB	13994	15753	17377
4 Dr XLT Ext Cab LB	12193	13725	15140
4 Dr XLT Ext Cab SB	12044	13558	14955
4 Dr XLT Ext Cab Step SB	12586	14168	15629

Mileage Category: K

Besides the introduction of the four-door SuperCrew and limited-edition Harley-Davidson and King Ranch models, America's most popular truck receives only minor changes in 2001. Power-adjustable accelerator and brake pedals are now standard on all F-150 Lariat models and optional on XL and XLT trucks. The Work Series model is no longer available, but there is a new Work Truck option group that deletes certain equipment from the XL model. Child safety-seat anchors and four-wheel ABS are now standard equipment on all trucks. XL and XLT trucks have upgraded standard-equipment radios.

Options	Price
4.6L V8 SOHC 16V FI Engine	+395
5.4L V8 CNG SOHC 16V FI Engine	+3485
5.4L V8 Propane SOHC 16V FI Engine	+3561
5.4L V8 SOHC 16V FI Engine	+421
Air Conditioning	+424
AM/FM/Cassette/CD Changer Audio System [Opt on Harley,Lariat,XLT]	+155
Automatic 4-Speed Transmission	+577
Camper/Towing Package	+156
Captain Chairs (2)	+258

Options	Price
Heated Front Seats [Opt on Harley,Lariat,XLT]	+129
Limited Slip Differential	+150
Off-Road Suspension Package	+237
Power Driver Seat [Opt on XLT]	+190
Power Moonroof	+427
Running Boards	+132
Split Front Bench Seat [Opt on XL]	+211
Two-Tone Paint [Opt on Lariat,XLT]	+119
VCR Entertainment System [Opt on Crew]	+682

2000

Body Styles	TMV Pricing		
	Trade	Private	Dealer
2 Dr Work 4WD Std Cab LB	8884	10170	11430
2 Dr Work 4WD Std Cab SB	8833	10112	11365
2 Dr Work Std Cab LB	7504	8590	9655
2 Dr Work Std Cab SB	7374	8442	9488
2 Dr XL 4WD Std Cab LB	9395	10755	12088
2 Dr XL 4WD Std Cab SB	9253	10592	11905
2 Dr XL 4WD Std Cab Step SB	9747	11158	12541
2 Dr XL Std Cab LB	7831	8965	10076
2 Dr XL Std Cab SB	7795	8924	10030
2 Dr XL Std Cab Step SB	8159	9340	10497
2 Dr XLT 4WD Std Cab LB	10808	12372	13906
2 Dr XLT 4WD Std Cab SB	10590	12123	13626
2 Dr XLT 4WD Std Cab Step SB	11146	12759	14341
2 Dr XLT Std Cab LB	9222	10557	11865
2 Dr XLT Std Cab SB	9029	10336	11617
2 Dr XLT Std Cab Step SB	9437	10803	12142

Body Styles	TMV Pricing		
	Trade	Private	Dealer
4 Dr Harley-Davidson Ext Cab Step SB	15994	18309	20579
4 Dr Lariat 4WD Ext Cab LB	13480	15431	17343
4 Dr Lariat 4WD Ext Cab SB	13410	15351	17254
4 Dr Lariat 4WD Ext Cab Step SB	13613	15584	17515
4 Dr Lariat Ext Cab LB	12203	13969	15701
4 Dr Lariat Ext Cab SB	11914	13639	15329
4 Dr Lariat Ext Cab Step SB	12557	14374	16156
4 Dr Work 4WD Ext Cab LB	10478	11995	13481
4 Dr Work 4WD Ext Cab SB	10465	11980	13465
4 Dr Work Ext Cab LB	8755	10023	11265
4 Dr Work Ext Cab SB	8621	9869	11093
4 Dr XL 4WD Ext Cab LB	10809	12373	13907
4 Dr XL 4WD Ext Cab SB	10763	12321	13848
4 Dr XL 4WD Ext Cab Step SB	11162	12777	14361
4 Dr XL Ext Cab LB	9089	10405	11694

Mileage Category: K

The F-150 SuperCrew, a crew-cab truck with full-size doors and a larger rear-passenger compartment, will bow in the first quarter of 2000 as a 2001 model. A limited-edition Harley-Davidson F-150 is available for 2000. The under-8,500-pound GVW F-250 has been discontinued and replaced by the F-150 7700 Payload Group. A new overhead console and left- and right-side visor vanity mirrors are optional on XL models and standard on XLT and Lariat F-150 pickups. A driver-side keypad entry system is available on Lariat models. Chromed steel wheels and 17-inch tires are now available on 4x2 models. A comfort-enhancing flip-up 40/60 rear seat has been added to the F-150 SuperCab.

2000 (cont'd)

Body Styles	TMV Pricing		
	Trade	Private	Dealer
4 Dr XL Ext Cab SB	8943	10237	11506
4 Dr XL Ext Cab Step SB	9400	10760	12094
4 Dr XLT 4WD Ext Cab LB	12217	13986	15719
4 Dr XLT 4WD Ext Cab SB	12004	13742	15445

Options	Price
4.6L V8 SOHC 16V FI Engine	+353
5.4L V8 CNG SOHC 16V FI Engine	+3479
5.4L V8 Propane SOHC 16V FI Engine	+3186
5.4L V8 SOHC 16V FI Engine	+377
Air Conditioning	+379
Aluminum/Alloy Wheels	+151
AM/FM/CD Audio System [Opt on XL,XLT]	+151
Antilock Brakes	+320
Automatic 4-Speed Transmission	+516
Camper/Towing Package	+140

Body Styles	TMV Pricing		
	Trade	Private	Dealer
4 Dr XLT 4WD Ext Cab Step SB	12578	14399	16183
4 Dr XLT Ext Cab LB	10492	12011	13499
4 Dr XLT Ext Cab SB	10550	12077	13574
4 Dr XLT Ext Cab Step SB	10808	12372	13906

Options	Price
Captain Chairs (2)	+231
Compact Disc Changer	+189
Limited Slip Differential	+127
Off-Road Suspension Package	+292
Power Driver Seat [Opt on XLT]	+170
Running Boards	+118
Side Steps	+139
Split Front Bench Seat [Opt on XL]	+123
Velour/Cloth Seats [Opt on Work]	+118

1999

Mileage Category: K

The "Standard" trim level is replaced by the "Work" trim level. XLT and Lariat models get standard four-wheel antilock brakes, and the XLT gets standard air conditioning. All SuperCab models get a fourth door and horsepower is improved for engines across the board. Option content is shuffled and simplified as Ford reduces the number of optional features.

Body Styles	TMV Pricing		
	Trade	Private	Dealer
2 Dr Lariat 4WD Std Cab LB	10345	12101	13929
2 Dr Lariat 4WD Std Cab SB	10119	11837	13625
2 Dr Lariat 4WD Std Cab Step SB	10776	12605	14509
2 Dr Lariat Std Cab LB	8816	10312	11870
2 Dr Lariat Std Cab SB	8743	10227	11772
2 Dr Lariat Std Cab Step SB	9025	10557	12152
2 Dr Work 4WD Std Cab LB	7323	8566	9860
2 Dr Work 4WD Std Cab SB	7313	8555	9847
2 Dr Work Std Cab LB	5992	7009	8068
2 Dr Work Std Cab SB	5877	6875	7913
2 Dr XL 4WD Std Cab LB	7671	8973	10329
2 Dr XL 4WD Std Cab SB	7542	8823	10156
2 Dr XL 4WD Std Cab Step SB	7798	9122	10500
2 Dr XL Std Cab LB	6229	7286	8387
2 Dr XL Std Cab SB	6101	7137	8215
2 Dr XL Std Cab Step SB	6518	7625	8777
2 Dr XLT 4WD Std Cab LB	8854	10357	11921
2 Dr XLT 4WD Std Cab SB	8790	10283	11836
2 Dr XLT 4WD Std Cab Step SB	9249	10819	12454
2 Dr XLT Std Cab LB	7505	8779	10105
2 Dr XLT Std Cab SB	7344	8591	9888
2 Dr XLT Std Cab Step SB	7767	9086	10458

Body Styles	TMV Pricing		
	Trade	Private	Dealer
4 Dr Lariat 4WD Ext Cab LB	11022	12893	14841
4 Dr Lariat 4WD Ext Cab SB	10970	12832	14771
4 Dr Lariat 4WD Ext Cab Step SB	11118	13005	14970
4 Dr Lariat Ext Cab LB	9602	11232	12929
4 Dr Lariat Ext Cab SB	9506	11120	12800
4 Dr Lariat Ext Cab Step SB	10255	11996	13808
4 Dr Work 4WD Ext Cab LB	8576	10032	11547
4 Dr Work 4WD Ext Cab SB	8354	9772	11248
4 Dr Work Ext Cab LB	7029	8223	9465
4 Dr Work Ext Cab SB	6915	8089	9311
4 Dr XL 4WD Ext Cab LB	8938	10456	12035
4 Dr XL 4WD Ext Cab SB	8844	10346	11909
4 Dr XL 4WD Ext Cab Step SB	9314	10895	12541
4 Dr XL Ext Cab LB	7453	8718	10035
4 Dr XL Ext Cab SB	7328	8572	9867
4 Dr XL Ext Cab Step SB	7708	9017	10379
4 Dr XLT 4WD Ext Cab LB	10185	11914	13714
4 Dr XLT 4WD Ext Cab SB	9795	11458	13189
4 Dr XLT 4WD Ext Cab Step SB	10399	12164	14002
4 Dr XLT Ext Cab LB	8644	10112	11639
4 Dr XLT Ext Cab SB	8360	9779	11256
4 Dr XLT Ext Cab Step SB	8857	10360	11925

Options	Price
4.6L V8 SOHC 16V FI Engine [Std on Lariat]	+291
5.4L V8 Flex Fuel SOHC 16V FI Engine	+352
5.4L V8 Propane SOHC 16V FI Engine	+2488
5.4L V8 SOHC 16V FI Engine	+287
Air Conditioning [Opt on XL,Work]	+312
Aluminum/Alloy Wheels [Opt on XL]	+124
AM/FM/CD Audio System [Opt on XL,XLT]	+124

Options	Price
Antilock Brakes [Opt on XL,Work]	+293
Automatic 4-Speed Transmission [Std on Lariat]	+387
Camper/Towing Package	+115
Captain Chairs (2) [Opt on XLT]	+190
Compact Disc Changer	+155
Power Driver Seat [Opt on XLT]	+140
Side Steps	+115

1998

Mileage Category: K

The 1998 F-150 gets a 50th Anniversary decal affixed to the lower left corner of the windshield. Other changes include making the locking tailgate standard on XLT and Lariat trims, optional on XL and Standard models. Foglights become optional this year on all four-wheel-drive models except for the Lariat, which gets them standard. An STX package featuring 17-inch tires, aluminum wheels and color-keyed grille debuts as an option for the XLT 2WD. The Lariat receives a color-keyed steering column, leather-wrapped steering wheel and outside power signal mirrors. Silver Metallic paint replaces Silver Frost paint, and Light Denim Blue replaces Portofino Blue.

Body Styles	Trade	Private	Dealer
2 Dr Lariat 4WD Ext Cab LB	9106	10802	12714
2 Dr Lariat 4WD Ext Cab SB	9033	10715	12612
2 Dr Lariat 4WD Ext Cab Step SB	9169	10877	12802
2 Dr Lariat 4WD Std Cab LB	8417	9984	11752
2 Dr Lariat 4WD Std Cab SB	8331	9882	11632
2 Dr Lariat 4WD Std Cab Step SB	8514	10099	11887
2 Dr Lariat Ext Cab LB	8142	9658	11368
2 Dr Lariat Ext Cab SB	8063	9564	11257
2 Dr Lariat Ext Cab Step SB	8444	10017	11790
2 Dr Lariat Std Cab LB	7246	8595	10117
2 Dr Lariat Std Cab SB	7147	8478	9979
2 Dr Lariat Std Cab Step SB	7482	8875	10446
2 Dr STD 4WD Ext Cab LB	7196	8536	10047
2 Dr STD 4WD Ext Cab SB	7100	8422	9913
2 Dr STD 4WD Std Cab LB	6058	7186	8459
2 Dr STD 4WD Std Cab SB	6005	7123	8384
2 Dr STD Ext Cab LB	5899	6998	8237
2 Dr STD Ext Cab SB	5665	6720	7909
2 Dr STD Std Cab LB	5129	6084	7161
2 Dr STD Std Cab SB	4736	5618	6613
2 Dr XL 4WD Ext Cab LB	7782	9231	10865
2 Dr XL 4WD Ext Cab SB	7554	8961	10547

Body Styles	Trade	Private	Dealer
2 Dr XL 4WD Ext Cab Step SB	7999	9488	11168
2 Dr XL 4WD Std Cab LB	6596	7825	9210
2 Dr XL 4WD Std Cab SB	6413	7607	8954
2 Dr XL 4WD Std Cab Step SB	6658	7898	9296
2 Dr XL Ext Cab LB	6244	7407	8718
2 Dr XL Ext Cab SB	6134	7276	8564
2 Dr XL Ext Cab Step SB	6399	7591	8935
2 Dr XL Std Cab LB	5330	6323	7442
2 Dr XL Std Cab SB	5220	6192	7288
2 Dr XL Std Cab Step SB	5564	6600	7768
2 Dr XLT 4WD Ext Cab LB	8695	10314	12140
2 Dr XLT 4WD Ext Cab SB	8573	10170	11970
2 Dr XLT 4WD Ext Cab Step SB	8873	10526	12389
2 Dr XLT 4WD Std Cab LB	7491	8886	10459
2 Dr XLT 4WD Std Cab SB	7392	8769	10321
2 Dr XLT 4WD Std Cab Step SB	7702	9136	10753
2 Dr XLT Ext Cab LB	7352	8721	10265
2 Dr XLT Ext Cab SB	7252	8603	10126
2 Dr XLT Ext Cab Step SB	7505	8903	10479
2 Dr XLT Std Cab LB	6251	7415	8727
2 Dr XLT Std Cab SB	6144	7288	8578
2 Dr XLT Std Cab Step SB	6538	7756	9129

Options	Price
4.6L V8 SOHC 16V FI Engine	+202
5.4L V8 SOHC 16V FI Engine	+211
Air Conditioning	+255
Antilock Brakes	+240

Options	Price
Automatic 4-Speed Transmission	+308
Captain Chairs (2) [Opt on XLT]	+155
Compact Disc Changer	+127

1997

Mileage Category: K

New engines, new sheet metal and a new suspension compliment dual airbags and class-leading side-impact protection in this user-friendly heavy hauler. All SuperCab models get a third door for easy access to the rear compartment. Grille styling is slightly different depending on what drive system is selected.

Body Styles	Trade	Private	Dealer
2 Dr Lariat 4WD Ext Cab LB	7513	9065	10962
2 Dr Lariat 4WD Ext Cab SB	7435	8971	10848
2 Dr Lariat 4WD Ext Cab Step SB	7584	9151	11066
2 Dr Lariat 4WD Std Cab LB	6963	8402	10160
2 Dr Lariat 4WD Std Cab SB	6938	8371	10123
2 Dr Lariat 4WD Std Cab Step SB	7036	8490	10266
2 Dr Lariat Ext Cab LB	6892	8316	10056
2 Dr Lariat Ext Cab SB	6840	8253	9980
2 Dr Lariat Ext Cab Step SB	6981	8423	10186
2 Dr Lariat Std Cab LB	6226	7512	9084
2 Dr Lariat Std Cab SB	6150	7421	8974
2 Dr Lariat Std Cab Step SB	6573	7931	9591
2 Dr STD 4WD Ext Cab LB	6187	7465	9028
2 Dr STD 4WD Ext Cab SB	6073	7328	8862
2 Dr STD 4WD Std Cab LB	5446	6571	7946
2 Dr STD 4WD Std Cab SB	5309	6406	7746
2 Dr STD Ext Cab LB	5019	6056	7324
2 Dr STD Ext Cab SB	4960	5985	7238
2 Dr STD Std Cab LB	4354	5254	6353
2 Dr STD Std Cab SB	3875	4676	5654
2 Dr XL 4WD Ext Cab LB	6683	8064	9752
2 Dr XL 4WD Ext Cab SB	6661	8038	9720

Body Styles	Trade	Private	Dealer
2 Dr XL 4WD Ext Cab Step SB	6821	8230	9953
2 Dr XL 4WD Std Cab LB	5707	6886	8327
2 Dr XL 4WD Std Cab SB	5668	6839	8270
2 Dr XL 4WD Std Cab Step SB	5859	7069	8548
2 Dr XL Ext Cab LB	5374	6484	7841
2 Dr XL Ext Cab SB	5294	6388	7724
2 Dr XL Ext Cab Step SB	5497	6633	8021
2 Dr XL Std Cab LB	4476	5401	6532
2 Dr XL Std Cab SB	4413	5325	6439
2 Dr XL Std Cab Step SB	4731	5708	6903
2 Dr XLT 4WD Ext Cab LB	7262	8762	10596
2 Dr XLT 4WD Ext Cab SB	7115	8585	10382
2 Dr XLT 4WD Ext Cab Step SB	7390	8917	10783
2 Dr XLT 4WD Std Cab LB	6481	7820	9457
2 Dr XLT 4WD Std Cab SB	6389	7709	9322
2 Dr XLT 4WD Std Cab Step SB	6596	7959	9625
2 Dr XLT Ext Cab LB	6237	7525	9100
2 Dr XLT Ext Cab SB	6195	7475	9040
2 Dr XLT Ext Cab Step SB	6528	7877	9526
2 Dr XLT Std Cab LB	5453	6580	7957
2 Dr XLT Std Cab SB	5333	6435	7782
2 Dr XLT Std Cab Step SB	5786	6981	8442

Options	Price
4.6L V8 SOHC 16V FI Engine	+187
5.4L V8 SOHC 16V FI Engine	+166
Air Conditioning	+236
Antilock Brakes	+222

Options	Price
Automatic 4-Speed Transmission	+285
Captain Chairs (2)	+144
Compact Disc Changer	+118
Off-Road Suspension Package	+202

F-150

1996

Mileage Category: K

Flareside styles and the Lightning model are dropped in 1996, and the silver instrument panel trim is replaced by a new black finish for all but Eddie Bauer styles which instead get wood grain trim on instrument and door panels. Improvements are made to the hub-locking systems and transfer case on 4WD styles, and XLT exteriors receive the slotted style front bumper. Interior upgrades include a new seat design with integrated headrest and Automatic Locking Restraint/Emergency Locking Restraint safety belts for all outboard seating positions.

Body Styles	TMV Pricing		
	Trade	Private	Dealer
2 Dr Eddie Bauer 4WD Ext Cab LB	6359	7820	9838
2 Dr Eddie Bauer 4WD Ext Cab SB	6561	8069	10151
2 Dr Eddie Bauer 4WD Ext Cab Step SB	6622	8143	10244
2 Dr Eddie Bauer 4WD Std Cab LB	5788	7118	8954
2 Dr Eddie Bauer 4WD Std Cab SB	5644	6941	8731
2 Dr Eddie Bauer 4WD Std Cab Step SB	6105	7508	9445
2 Dr Eddie Bauer Ext Cab LB	5686	6993	8797
2 Dr Eddie Bauer Ext Cab SB	5498	6761	8506
2 Dr Eddie Bauer Ext Cab Step SB	5820	7157	9004
2 Dr Eddie Bauer Std Cab LB	4840	5952	7488
2 Dr Eddie Bauer Std Cab SB	4737	5825	7328
2 Dr Eddie Bauer Std Cab Step SB	5080	6247	7858
2 Dr Special 4WD Std Cab LB	4529	5570	7007
2 Dr Special 4WD Std Cab SB	4487	5518	6942
2 Dr Special Ext Cab LB	4135	5085	6397
2 Dr Special Ext Cab SB	4052	4983	6268
2 Dr Special Std Cab LB	3633	4468	5621
2 Dr Special Std Cab SB	3602	4429	5572
2 Dr XL 4WD Ext Cab LB	5214	6412	8067
2 Dr XL 4WD Ext Cab SB	5194	6387	8035
2 Dr XL 4WD Ext Cab Step SB	5417	6662	8381

Body Styles	TMV Pricing		
	Trade	Private	Dealer
2 Dr XL 4WD Std Cab LB	4622	5684	7151
2 Dr XL 4WD Std Cab SB	4536	5578	7017
2 Dr XL 4WD Std Cab Step SB	4750	5841	7348
2 Dr XL Ext Cab LB	4506	5541	6971
2 Dr XL Ext Cab SB	4384	5391	6782
2 Dr XL Ext Cab Step SB	4562	5610	7058
2 Dr XL Std Cab LB	3795	4667	5871
2 Dr XL Std Cab SB	3776	4644	5842
2 Dr XL Std Cab Step SB	4158	5114	6433
2 Dr XLT 4WD Ext Cab LB	6132	7541	9486
2 Dr XLT 4WD Ext Cab SB	5795	7127	8966
2 Dr XLT 4WD Ext Cab Step SB	6143	7555	9504
2 Dr XLT 4WD Std Cab LB	5040	6198	7797
2 Dr XLT 4WD Std Cab SB	5472	6729	8466
2 Dr XLT 4WD Std Cab Step SB	5145	6327	7960
2 Dr XLT Ext Cab LB	5118	6294	7917
2 Dr XLT Ext Cab SB	5047	6207	7808
2 Dr XLT Ext Cab Step SB	5325	6548	8238
2 Dr XLT Std Cab LB	4498	5532	6959
2 Dr XLT Std Cab SB	4362	5365	6749
2 Dr XLT Std Cab Step SB	4664	5735	7215

Options	Price
5.0L V8 OHV 16V FI Engine	+166
5.8L V8 OHV 16V FI Engine	+286
Air Conditioning [Opt on Special, XL]	+210

Options	Price
Automatic 4-Speed Transmission	+253
Captain Chairs (2)	+127

1995

Mileage Category: K

Ford introduces the premium Eddie Bauer model. Adorned with two-toned paint, air conditioning, a full array of power features, deep-dish aluminum wheels and signature badging, it's fair to say that this truck paves the way for the ultraluxury truck segment to come. Other changes include optional privacy glass for side and rear windows (including manual-sliding rear window, when equipped) and cab steps for regular and SuperCab Styleside trims.

Body Styles	TMV Pricing		
	Trade	Private	Dealer
2 Dr Eddie Bauer 4WD Ext Cab LB	4766	5915	7829
2 Dr Eddie Bauer 4WD Ext Cab SB	4737	5878	7781
2 Dr Eddie Bauer 4WD Ext Cab Step SB	4884	6061	8023
2 Dr Eddie Bauer 4WD Std Cab LB	4319	5360	7095
2 Dr Eddie Bauer 4WD Std Cab SB	4244	5267	6972
2 Dr Eddie Bauer 4WD Std Cab Step SB	4421	5487	7263
2 Dr Eddie Bauer Ext Cab LB	4306	5343	7073
2 Dr Eddie Bauer Ext Cab SB	4255	5280	6990
2 Dr Eddie Bauer Ext Cab Step SB	4402	5464	7232
2 Dr Eddie Bauer Std Cab LB	3789	4702	6224
2 Dr Eddie Bauer Std Cab SB	3742	4644	6147
2 Dr Eddie Bauer Std Cab Step SB	3926	4872	6449
2 Dr Special 4WD Std Cab LB	3576	4437	5874
2 Dr Special 4WD Std Cab SB	3507	4352	5761
2 Dr Special Ext Cab LB	3311	4109	5439
2 Dr Special Ext Cab SB	3262	4048	5358
2 Dr Special Std Cab LB	2964	3678	4868
2 Dr Special Std Cab SB	2907	3608	4775
2 Dr XL 4WD Ext Cab LB	4045	5020	6645
2 Dr XL 4WD Ext Cab SB	4016	4983	6597
2 Dr XL 4WD Ext Cab Step SB	4163	5166	6839

Body Styles	TMV Pricing		
	Trade	Private	Dealer
2 Dr XL 4WD Std Cab LB	3699	4591	6077
2 Dr XL 4WD Std Cab SB	3638	4515	5976
2 Dr XL 4WD Std Cab Step SB	3815	4734	6267
2 Dr XL Ext Cab LB	3585	4449	5889
2 Dr XL Ext Cab SB	3499	4343	5748
2 Dr XL Ext Cab Step SB	3683	4571	6050
2 Dr XL Std Cab LB	3153	3913	5180
2 Dr XL Std Cab SB	3106	3855	5103
2 Dr XL Std Cab Step SB	3290	4083	5405
2 Dr XLT 4WD Ext Cab LB	4416	5480	7254
2 Dr XLT 4WD Ext Cab SB	4386	5444	7206
2 Dr XLT 4WD Ext Cab Step SB	4534	5626	7448
2 Dr XLT 4WD Std Cab LB	4097	5084	6730
2 Dr XLT 4WD Std Cab SB	4064	5044	6677
2 Dr XLT 4WD Std Cab Step SB	4241	5263	6967
2 Dr XLT Ext Cab LB	3993	4955	6559
2 Dr XLT Ext Cab SB	3942	4892	6476
2 Dr XLT Ext Cab Step SB	4126	5120	6777
2 Dr XLT Std Cab LB	3500	4344	5750
2 Dr XLT Std Cab SB	3504	4349	5756
2 Dr XLT Std Cab Step SB	3688	4577	6058

Options	Price
5.0L V8 OHV 16V FI Engine	+144
5.8L V8 OHV 16V FI Engine	+247
Air Conditioning [Opt on Special, XL]	+182

Options	Price
Automatic 4-Speed Transmission	+219
Captain Chairs (2)	+110

1994

Body Styles	TMV Pricing		
	Trade	Private	Dealer
2 Dr S 4WD Std Cab LB	2839	3708	5155
2 Dr S 4WD Std Cab SB	2789	3642	5064
2 Dr S Ext Cab LB	2548	3328	4627
2 Dr S Ext Cab SB	2511	3279	4560
2 Dr S Std Cab LB	2214	2892	4021
2 Dr S Std Cab SB	2132	2784	3871
2 Dr XL 4WD Ext Cab LB	3134	4093	5691
2 Dr XL 4WD Ext Cab SB	3108	4059	5644
2 Dr XL 4WD Ext Cab Step SB	3224	4210	5853
2 Dr XL 4WD Std Cab LB	2941	3841	5341
2 Dr XL 4WD Std Cab SB	2855	3728	5184
2 Dr XL 4WD Std Cab Step SB	3031	3958	5504
2 Dr XL Ext Cab LB	2750	3592	4994
2 Dr XL Ext Cab SB	2696	3520	4894
2 Dr XL Ext Cab Step SB	2811	3671	5104

Body Styles	TMV Pricing		
	Trade	Private	Dealer
2 Dr XL Std Cab LB	2458	3210	4464
2 Dr XL Std Cab SB	2373	3099	4309
2 Dr XL Std Cab Step SB	2549	3329	4629
2 Dr XLT 4WD Ext Cab LB	3536	4618	6420
2 Dr XLT 4WD Ext Cab SB	3500	4571	6355
2 Dr XLT 4WD Ext Cab Step SB	3645	4760	6618
2 Dr XLT 4WD Std Cab LB	3507	4580	6369
2 Dr XLT 4WD Std Cab SB	3188	4163	5788
2 Dr XLT 4WD Std Cab Step SB	3356	4382	6093
2 Dr XLT Ext Cab LB	3108	4059	5643
2 Dr XLT Ext Cab SB	3065	4002	5564
2 Dr XLT Ext Cab Step SB	3185	4160	5784
2 Dr XLT Std Cab LB	2824	3688	5127
2 Dr XLT Std Cab SB	2766	3613	5024
2 Dr XLT Std Cab Step SB	2981	3893	5412

Options	Price
5.0L V8 OHV 16V FI Engine	+121
5.8L V8 OHV 16V FI Engine	+210
Air Conditioning [Opt on S,XL]	+153

Options	Price
Automatic 4-Speed Transmission	+185
Captain Chairs (2)	+93

Mileage Category: K

Ford's bread-and-butter truck receives minor changes that include the implementation of a CFC-free air conditioning system, the addition of side door beams, a center high-mounted stop lamp, a driver-side airbag (for under-8,500-pound GVWR models) and a brake shift interlock system for all automatics. A premium 40/20/40 bench seat option is added to XLT Crew- and SuperCab styles and a wide-ratio four-speed automatic transmission with overdrive accompanies the 5.0L engine.

Ford
F-150 SVT Lightning

2003

Body Styles	TMV Pricing		
	Trade	Private	Dealer
2 Dr S/C Std Cab Step SB	24418	25694	27820

Mileage Category: K

In the face of new competition from Dodge and General Motors, Ford updates the SVT F-150 Lightning to remain competitive in the sport-truck class. The steering is upgraded and retuned for better on-center feel, while suspension tweaks raise payload capacity from 800 to 1,400 pounds. The standard 18-inch alloy wheels are redesigned, and the interior gets door handles finished in a brushed aluminum appearance and upgraded carpet. A six-disc in-dash CD changer is standard this year, and new colors include Dark Shadow Gray and Sonic Blue.

2002

Body Styles	TMV Pricing		
	Trade	Private	Dealer
2 Dr S/C Std Cab Step SB	22590	23803	25824

Mileage Category: K

Ford's bad-boy pickup receives minimal changes in 2002. True Blue Clearcoat Metallic is a new color option and locking lug nuts and keyless entry keypad are added as standard equipment.

2001

Body Styles	TMV Pricing		
	Trade	Private	Dealer
2 Dr S/C Std Cab Step SB	19319	21214	22963

Mileage Category: K

Ford's bad-boy pickup receives a few changes in 2001. Acceleration times should be even faster thanks to an increase in power and a shorter final drive ratio. The front turn signals and taillights have unique clear lenses. Styling of the 18-by-9.5-inch wheels is new. A six-disc CD changer is now standard.

2000

Body Styles	TMV Pricing		
	Trade	Private	Dealer
2 Dr S/C Std Cab Step SB	16519	18377	20198

Mileage Category: K

Completely new in 1999, the 2000 Lightning is the same, except for a new Silver Clearcoat exterior color.

1999

Body Styles	TMV Pricing		
	Trade	Private	Dealer
2 Dr S/C Std Cab Step SB	14637	16406	18247

Mileage Category: K

Ford has revived its F-150-based performance truck with all-new features like an Eaton supercharger, performance suspension and Z-rated Goodyear tires.

1999 (cont'd)

Options	Price
Side Steps	+115

1995

Mileage Category: K

The somewhat rare and aptly named Lightning, with its tire-smoking 240 horsepower, 5.8-liter V8, continues unchanged for this year.

Body Styles	TMV Pricing		
	Trade	Private	Dealer
2 Dr STD Std Cab SB	4809	5969	7901

Options	Price
Premium Audio System	+124

1994

Mileage Category: K

After joining the lineup last year, the aptly named Lightning, with its tire-smoking 240 horsepower, 5.8-liter V8, continues unchanged for this year.

Body Styles	TMV Pricing		
	Trade	Private	Dealer
2 Dr STD Std Cab SB	3844	5020	6980

Options	Price
Premium Audio System	+105

Ford
F-250

1999

Mileage Category: K

The "Standard" trim level is replaced by the "Work" trim level. XLT and Lariat models get standard four-wheel antilock brakes, and the XLT gets standard air conditioning. All SuperCab models get a fourth door and horsepower is improved for engines across the board. Option content is shuffled and simplified as Ford reduces the number of optional features to a mere 78.

Body Styles	TMV Pricing		
	Trade	Private	Dealer
2 Dr Lariat 4WD Std Cab LB	11033	12906	14856
2 Dr Lariat Std Cab LB	9700	11346	13060
2 Dr Work 4WD Std Cab LB	8292	9700	11165
2 Dr Work Std Cab LB	7234	8462	9740
2 Dr XL 4WD Std Cab LB	8616	10079	11601
2 Dr XL Std Cab LB	7246	8476	9757
2 Dr XLT 4WD Std Cab LB	9852	11524	13265
2 Dr XLT Std Cab LB	8551	10003	11514

Body Styles	TMV Pricing		
	Trade	Private	Dealer
4 Dr Lariat 4WD Ext Cab SB	11821	13828	15917
4 Dr Lariat Ext Cab SB	10556	12348	14213
4 Dr Work 4WD Ext Cab SB	9699	11345	13059
4 Dr Work Ext Cab SB	8275	9680	11142
4 Dr XL 4WD Ext Cab SB	9832	11501	13238
4 Dr XL Ext Cab SB	8506	9950	11453
4 Dr XLT 4WD Ext Cab SB	11146	13038	15008
4 Dr XLT Ext Cab SB	9776	11436	13163

Options	Price
5.4L V8 SOHC 16V FI Engine	+258
Air Conditioning [Opt on XL,Work]	+312
AM/FM/CD Audio System [Opt on XL]	+117
Antilock Brakes [Opt on XL,Work]	+293
Automatic 4-Speed Transmission [Opt on XL,XLT,Work]	+387

Options	Price
Automatic Load Leveling	+190
Camper/Towing Package	+115
Captain Chairs (2) [Opt on XLT]	+190
Power Driver Seat [Opt on XLT]	+140
Side Steps	+115

1998

Mileage Category: K

The 1998 F-150 gets a 50th Anniversary decal affixed to the lower left corner of the windshield. Other changes include making the locking tailgate standard on XLT and Lariat trims, optional on XL and Standard models. Foglights become optional this year on all four-wheel-drive models except for the Lariat, which gets them standard. An STX package featuring 17-inch tires, aluminum wheels and color-keyed grille debuts as an option for the XLT 2WD. The Lariat receives a color-keyed steering column, leather-wrapped steering wheel and outside power signal mirrors. Silver Metallic paint replaces Silver Frost paint, and Light Denim Blue replaces Portofino Blue.

Body Styles	TMV Pricing		
	Trade	Private	Dealer
2 Dr Lariat 4WD Ext Cab SB	9480	11245	13236
2 Dr Lariat 4WD Std Cab LB	9166	10873	12798
2 Dr Lariat Ext Cab SB	8460	10035	11812
2 Dr Lariat Std Cab LB	7529	8931	10512
2 Dr STD 4WD Ext Cab SB	7510	8908	10485
2 Dr STD 4WD Std Cab LB	6887	8170	9616
2 Dr STD Ext Cab SB	6871	8150	9593
2 Dr STD Std Cab LB	5875	6969	8203

Body Styles	TMV Pricing		
	Trade	Private	Dealer
2 Dr XL 4WD Ext Cab SB	8228	9760	11488
2 Dr XL 4WD Std Cab LB	7356	8726	10271
2 Dr XL Ext Cab SB	7043	8355	9834
2 Dr XL Std Cab LB	5980	7093	8349
2 Dr XLT 4WD Ext Cab SB	9276	11003	12951
2 Dr XLT 4WD Std Cab LB	8292	9836	11578
2 Dr XLT Ext Cab SB	7952	9432	11102
2 Dr XLT Std Cab LB	7243	8592	10113

Options	Price
5.4L V8 SOHC 16V FI Engine	+211
Air Conditioning	+255
Antilock Brakes	+240
Automatic 4-Speed Transmission	+308

Options	Price
Automatic Load Leveling	+155
Camper/Towing Package	+143
Captain Chairs (2)	+155
Compact Disc Changer	+127

1997

Mileage Category: K

Ford's F-250 joins the F-150 this year in a dramatic redesign. The new model has swoopy styling, a greatly improved interior, a much more rigid chassis, and carlike handling.

Body Styles	TMV Pricing			Body Styles	TMV Pricing		
	Trade	Private	Dealer		Trade	Private	Dealer
2 Dr Lariat 4WD Ext Cab SB	8087	9758	11800	2 Dr XL Std Cab LB	5092	6144	7430
2 Dr Lariat 4WD Std Cab LB	7953	9596	11604	2 Dr XL Std Cab LB HD	5718	6899	8343
2 Dr Lariat Ext Cab SB	7422	8956	10830	2 Dr XLT 4WD Ext Cab LB HD	7965	9611	11622
2 Dr Lariat Std Cab LB	6929	8361	10111	2 Dr XLT 4WD Ext Cab SB	8079	9748	11788
2 Dr STD 4WD Ext Cab SB	6838	8251	9978	2 Dr XLT 4WD Ext Cab SB HD	8028	9687	11714
2 Dr STD 4WD Std Cab LB	6100	7360	8901	2 Dr XLT 4WD Std Cab LB	7321	8833	10682
2 Dr STD Ext Cab SB	5823	7026	8497	2 Dr XLT 4WD Std Cab LB HD	7393	8921	10788
2 Dr STD Std Cab LB	4946	5968	7217	2 Dr XLT Ext Cab LB HD	7024	8476	10250
2 Dr XL 4WD Ext Cab LB HD	7239	8735	10563	2 Dr XLT Ext Cab SB	6916	8344	10089
2 Dr XL 4WD Ext Cab SB	7326	8839	10689	2 Dr XLT Ext Cab SB HD	7081	8544	10332
2 Dr XL 4WD Ext Cab SB HD	7295	8802	10644	2 Dr XLT Std Cab LB	6424	7751	9373
2 Dr XL 4WD Std Cab LB	6646	8019	9698	2 Dr XLT Std Cab LB HD	6475	7813	9448
2 Dr XL 4WD Std Cab LB HD	6633	8003	9678	4 Dr XL 4WD Crew Cab SB HD	7576	9141	11054
2 Dr XL Ext Cab LB HD	5987	7224	8736	4 Dr XL Crew Cab SB HD	6863	8281	10014
2 Dr XL Ext Cab SB	6002	7242	8758	4 Dr XLT 4WD Crew Cab SB HD	8114	9790	11839
2 Dr XL Ext Cab SB HD	6373	7690	9299	4 Dr XLT Crew Cab SB HD	7485	9031	10921

Options	Price	Options	Price
Captain Chairs (2) [Opt on XLT]	+182	Air Conditioning	+262
Compact Disc Changer	+118	Antilock Brakes [Std on Lariat]	+222
5.4L V8 SOHC 16V FI Engine [Std on HD]	+166	Automatic 4-Speed Transmission	+285
7.3L V8 Turbodiesel OHV 16V Engine	+1115	Automatic Load Leveling	+144

1996

Mileage Category: K

Short wheelbase Crew Cab and Superab styles are now offered with a 6.75-foot box in 2- and 4WD configurations, and an improved hub-locking system and transfer case equip all 4WD models. The 7.5L V8 receives a standard integral oil cooler, and a throttle-control module for power takeoffs with the 7.3L diesel is now optional. Interior improvements include black finish on instrument panels, a revised seat design with integrated headrest and Automatic Locking Restraint/Emergency Locking Restraint safety belts for all outboard seating positions. A standard slotted style front bumper and trailer tow wiring harness (except chassis cab) complete the changes.

Body Styles	TMV Pricing			Body Styles	TMV Pricing		
	Trade	Private	Dealer		Trade	Private	Dealer
2 Dr XL 4WD Ext Cab LB HD	6095	7495	9429	2 Dr XLT 4WD Std Cab LB HD	6355	7815	9831
2 Dr XL 4WD Ext Cab SB HD	6204	7629	9598	2 Dr XLT Ext Cab LB HD	5495	6758	8502
2 Dr XL 4WD Std Cab LB HD	5443	6693	8420	2 Dr XLT Ext Cab SB HD	5607	6895	8674
2 Dr XL Ext Cab LB HD	4926	6058	7621	2 Dr XLT Std Cab LB	4817	5924	7452
2 Dr XL Ext Cab SB HD	4960	6099	7673	2 Dr XLT Std Cab LB HD	5371	6605	8309
2 Dr XL Std Cab LB	4001	4920	6190	4 Dr XL 4WD Crew Cab LB HD	6769	8324	10472
2 Dr XL Std Cab LB HD	4227	5198	6539	4 Dr XL Crew Cab LB HD	5486	6746	8487
2 Dr XLT 4WD Ext Cab LB HD	6813	8378	10540	4 Dr XLT 4WD Crew Cab LB HD	7365	9057	11394
2 Dr XLT 4WD Ext Cab SB HD	6956	8554	10761	4 Dr XLT Crew Cab LB HD	6684	8220	10341

Options	Price	Options	Price
Split Front Bench Seat [Opt on XLT]	+137	Air Conditioning [Opt on XL]	+210
5.0L V8 OHV 16V FI Engine [Opt on 2WD Std Cab - XL,XLT]	+166	Automatic 3-Speed Transmission	+194
5.8L V8 OHV 16V FI Engine [Opt on 2WD Std Cab - XL,XLT]	+286	Automatic 4-Speed Transmission	+258
7.3L V8 Turbodiesel OHV 16V Engine	+884	Captain Chairs (2)	+127

1995

Mileage Category: K

The F-Super Duty's Stripped Commercial Chassis is deleted, optional privacy glass now includes manual-sliding rear windows (when equipped), forged aluminum wheels are offered and cab steps on regular and SuperCab Styleside trims are available.

Body Styles	TMV Pricing			Body Styles	TMV Pricing		
	Trade	Private	Dealer		Trade	Private	Dealer
2 Dr Special Ext Cab LB	4109	5098	6746	2 Dr XLT 4WD Ext Cab LB	5419	6723	8896
2 Dr XL 4WD Ext Cab LB	5022	6231	8245	2 Dr XLT 4WD Std Cab LB	5271	6540	8655
2 Dr XL 4WD Std Cab LB	4553	5649	7475	2 Dr XLT Ext Cab LB	4642	5760	7622
2 Dr XL Ext Cab LB	4276	5305	7021	2 Dr XLT Std Cab LB	4173	5178	6852
2 Dr XL Std Cab LB	3452	4283	5668				

Options	Price	Options	Price
5.0L V8 OHV 16V FI Engine [Opt on 2WD Std Cab - XL,XLT]	+144	Aluminum/Alloy Wheels [Opt on XL]	+86
5.8L V8 OHV 16V FI Engine [Opt on 2WD Std Cab - XL,XLT]	+247	Automatic 3-Speed Transmission	+167
7.3L V8 Turbodiesel OHV 16V Engine	+856	Automatic 4-Speed Transmission [Opt on XL,XLT]	+219
7.5L V8 OHV 16V FI Engine	+87	Captain Chairs (2)	+110
Air Conditioning [Opt on Special,XL]	+182		

Ford
F-250/F-250 Super Duty

1994

Mileage Category: K

Ford's 3/4-ton hauler receives only slight mechanical and chassis refinements. Two versions of the 7.3L turbodiesel, direct injection and indirect injection, are offered on models above 8,500 pounds GVWR. Environmentally friendly CFC-free air conditioning is offered, and standard equipment grows with the addition of side door beams, a center high-mounted stop lamp, a driver-side airbag (for under-8,500 GVWR models) and a brake shift interlock system for all automatics. A premium 40/20/40 bench seat option is added to XLT Crew- and SuperCab styles and a wide-ratio four-speed automatic transmission with overdrive accompanies the 5.0L engine.

Body Styles	TMV Pricing		
	Trade	Private	Dealer
2 Dr S Ext Cab LB	3370	4401	6119
2 Dr XL 4WD Ext Cab LB	3915	5113	7109
2 Dr XL 4WD Std Cab LB	3584	4680	6507
2 Dr XL Ext Cab LB	3375	4407	6128
2 Dr XL Std Cab LB	2785	3637	5057

Options	Price
5.0L V8 OHV 16V FI Engine [Opt on 2WD Std Cab - XL,XLT]	+121
5.8L V8 OHV 16V FI Engine [Opt on 2WD Std Cab - XL,XLT]	+210
7.3L V8 Diesel OHV 16V Engine	+526
7.3L V8 Turbodiesel OHV 16V Engine	+725

Body Styles	TMV Pricing		
	Trade	Private	Dealer
2 Dr XLT 4WD Ext Cab LB	4085	5335	7417
2 Dr XLT 4WD Std Cab LB	4064	5307	7378
2 Dr XLT Ext Cab LB	3695	4826	6710
2 Dr XLT Std Cab LB	3305	4316	6002

Options	Price
Air Conditioning [Opt on S,XL]	+153
Automatic 3-Speed Transmission	+142
Automatic 4-Speed Transmission	+185
Captain Chairs (2)	+94

Ford
F-250 Super Duty

2003

Mileage Category: K

The 2003 model year sees a new FX4 Off-Road Package with skid plates, Rancho front and rear shocks, a steering damper and decals. The regular off-road package is no longer available, but a skid plate package can still be had on all 4WD trucks. All XLs can be had with a vinyl 40/20/40 reclining split bench that has a fold down armrest with a console and cupholders. Ford has also upgraded seat material quality, and installed a tailgate lock on this trim level. If you order a SuperCab or Crew Cab in XLT trim with the Sport Package, you can also order a reverse sensing system and a power driver seat. Late-availability additions include an optional power moonroof for Crew Cabs and optional heated telescoping trailer tow mirrors with integrated turn signals. A King Ranch version of the Crew Cab will also appear later in the year. Finally, the torque rating for the 7.3-liter turbodiesel V8 has been boosted to 525 pound feet. By mid-year, expect an even more-powerful 6.0-liter diesel to appear.

Body Styles	TMV Pricing		
	Trade	Private	Dealer
2 Dr XL 4WD Std Cab LB	16573	17699	19575
2 Dr XL Std Cab LB	14200	15165	16773
2 Dr XLT 4WD Std Cab LB	18540	19800	21899
2 Dr XLT Std Cab LB	16604	17732	19612
4 Dr Lariat 4WD Crew Cab LB	23595	25198	27869
4 Dr Lariat 4WD Crew Cab SB	23443	25036	27690
4 Dr Lariat 4WD Ext Cab LB	22050	23548	26045
4 Dr Lariat 4WD Ext Cab SB	21839	23323	25795
4 Dr Lariat Crew Cab LB	21432	22888	25315
4 Dr Lariat Crew Cab SB	21305	22753	25165
4 Dr Lariat Ext Cab LB	19925	21279	23535
4 Dr Lariat Ext Cab SB	19784	21128	23368
4 Dr XL 4WD Crew Cab LB	18982	20272	22421
4 Dr XL 4WD Crew Cab SB	18861	20142	22278

Options	Price
Air Conditioning [Opt on XL]	+519
Aluminum/Alloy Wheels [Opt on XLT]	+119
Automatic 4-Speed Transmission	+706
Automatic 5-Speed Transmission	+955
Captain Chairs (4) [Opt on Lariat]	+400
Cruise Control [Opt on XL]	+119
Heated Front and Rear Seats [Opt on Lariat]	+142
Limited Slip Differential	+193
Power Driver Seat [Opt on XLT]	+187
Power Moonroof [Opt on Lariat,XLT]	+522
Power Passenger Seat [Opt on XLT]	+187
Side Steps [Opt on XLT]	+177

Body Styles	TMV Pricing		
	Trade	Private	Dealer
4 Dr XL 4WD Ext Cab LB	17992	19215	21252
4 Dr XL 4WD Ext Cab SB	17855	19068	21089
4 Dr XL Crew Cab LB	16833	17977	19883
4 Dr XL Crew Cab SB	16701	17836	19727
4 Dr XL Ext Cab LB	15855	16932	18727
4 Dr XL Ext Cab SB	15738	16807	18589
4 Dr XLT 4WD Crew Cab LB	21935	23425	25909
4 Dr XLT 4WD Crew Cab SB	21805	23286	25755
4 Dr XLT 4WD Ext Cab LB	20636	22038	24374
4 Dr XLT 4WD Ext Cab SB	20492	21884	24204
4 Dr XLT Crew Cab LB	19744	21085	23321
4 Dr XLT Crew Cab SB	19604	20936	23156
4 Dr XLT Ext Cab LB	18445	19698	21787
4 Dr XLT Ext Cab SB	18310	19554	21627

Options	Price
Special Leather Seat Trim [Opt on Lariat]	+242
Split Front Bench Seat [Opt on XL]	+258
Tilt Steering Wheel [Opt on XL]	+116
Two-Tone Paint [Opt on Lariat,XLT]	+145
AM/FM/CD Changer Audio System [Opt on Lariat,XLT]	+135
6.8L V10 SOHC 20V FI Engine	+387
7.3L V8 Turbodiesel OHV 16V Engine	+3122
Power Retractable Mirrors [Opt on Lariat,XLT]	+142
6.0L V8 Turbodiesel OHV 32V Engine	+3280
FX4 Off-Road Suspension Package	+145
King Ranch Package [Opt on Lariat]	+1932
Park Distance Control (Rear) [Opt on Lariat,XLT]	+158

2002

Mileage Category: K

A six-speed manual transmission is now standard with the 5.4- and 6.8-liter V8 gas engines, and the 6.8-liter has been enhanced to provide better performance. If you order an automatic transmission, a gauge that measures transmission oil temperature replaces the battery gauge, and you can opt to add adjustable pedals to your Super Duty XLT or Lariat truck. Trucks with the Power Stroke diesel get an air filter service indicator. All F-250s get roof ride handles standard for 2002, and the available telescoping trailer mirrors can now be folded forward. SuperCabs have new rear door panel map pockets with molded-in cupholders. XL gets upgraded visors, while XLT and Lariat get new seats with increased width, bolstering and lumbar support; jewellike headlamp lenses and an available Advanced Security Group that includes remote keyless entry, automatic door locks and automatic headlamps. Optional on the XLT Crew Cab and standard on the Lariat Crew Cab is a power front passenger seat. The Lariat also gets a larger standard overhead console with improved storage.

Body Styles	TMV Pricing			Body Styles	TMV Pricing		
	Trade	Private	Dealer		Trade	Private	Dealer
2 Dr XL 4WD Std Cab LB	14766	15881	17740	4 Dr XL 4WD Ext Cab LB	15902	17112	19128
2 Dr XL Std Cab LB	12648	13610	15214	4 Dr XL 4WD Ext Cab SB	15788	16989	18991
2 Dr XLT 4WD Std Cab LB	16253	17489	19550	4 Dr XL Crew Cab LB	15060	16206	18116
2 Dr XLT Std Cab LB	14344	15435	17253	4 Dr XL Crew Cab SB	14975	16114	18012
4 Dr Lariat 4WD Crew Cab LB	20462	22019	24613	4 Dr XL Ext Cab LB	14087	15158	16944
4 Dr Lariat 4WD Crew Cab SB	20344	21892	24471	4 Dr XL Ext Cab SB	13964	15026	16797
4 Dr Lariat 4WD Ext Cab LB	19190	20650	23082	4 Dr XLT 4WD Crew Cab LB	19046	20495	22910
4 Dr Lariat 4WD Ext Cab SB	19076	20527	22946	4 Dr XLT 4WD Crew Cab SB	18934	20374	22775
4 Dr Lariat Crew Cab LB	18632	20050	22412	4 Dr XLT 4WD Ext Cab LB	17966	19333	21610
4 Dr Lariat Crew Cab SB	18520	19929	22277	4 Dr XLT 4WD Ext Cab SB	17847	19205	21467
4 Dr Lariat Ext Cab LB	17361	18682	20883	4 Dr XLT Crew Cab LB	17174	18481	20658
4 Dr Lariat Ext Cab SB	17229	18540	20724	4 Dr XLT Crew Cab SB	17031	18327	20486
4 Dr XL 4WD Crew Cab LB	16758	18033	20157	4 Dr XLT Ext Cab LB	16093	17317	19357
4 Dr XL 4WD Crew Cab SB	16651	17918	20029	4 Dr XLT Ext Cab SB	15952	17166	19188

Options	Price	Options	Price
6.8L V10 SOHC 20V FI Engine	+353	Leather Seats [Opt on XLT]	+291
7.3L V8 Turbodiesel OHV 16V Engine	+2849	Limited Slip Differential	+168
Air Conditioning [Opt on XL]	+474	Park Distance Control (Rear) [Opt on Lariat,XLT]	+144
AM/FM/CD Changer Audio System	+124	Power Driver Seat [Std on Lariat]	+171
Automatic 4-Speed Transmission	+645	Power Passenger Seat [Std on Lariat]	+341
Bucket Seats [Opt on XL]	+118	Two-Tone Paint	+132
Heated Front and Rear Seats [Opt on Lariat]	+130		

2001

Mileage Category: K

A trailer tow package is standard on all models, as is four-wheel ABS. XLT and Lariat models can be equipped with an ultrasonic reverse vehicle-aid sensor, an in-dash six-disc CD changer and chrome tubular cab steps. Heated seats are available on Lariat models. Rounding out the 2001 changes are minor interior updates and a horsepower upgrade for the 7.3-liter Power Stroke turbodiesel engine.

Body Styles	TMV Pricing			Body Styles	TMV Pricing		
	Trade	Private	Dealer		Trade	Private	Dealer
2 Dr XL 4WD Std Cab LB	12786	14393	15877	4 Dr XL 4WD Ext Cab LB	14016	15778	17404
2 Dr XL Std Cab LB	11211	12620	13921	4 Dr XL 4WD Ext Cab SB	13930	15681	17297
2 Dr XLT 4WD Std Cab LB	14313	16112	17773	4 Dr XL Crew Cab LB	13101	14748	16268
2 Dr XLT Std Cab LB	12652	14243	15711	4 Dr XL Crew Cab SB	13004	14639	16148
4 Dr Lariat 4WD Crew Cab LB	17458	19652	21678	4 Dr XL Ext Cab LB	12447	14012	15456
4 Dr Lariat 4WD Crew Cab SB	17104	19254	21238	4 Dr XL Ext Cab SB	12343	13895	15327
4 Dr Lariat 4WD Ext Cab LB	16556	18637	20558	4 Dr XLT 4WD Crew Cab LB	16430	18495	20402
4 Dr Lariat 4WD Ext Cab SB	16455	18524	20433	4 Dr XLT 4WD Crew Cab SB	16333	18386	20281
4 Dr Lariat Crew Cab LB	15874	17870	19712	4 Dr XLT 4WD Ext Cab LB	15544	17498	19301
4 Dr Lariat Crew Cab SB	15779	17763	19594	4 Dr XLT 4WD Ext Cab SB	15442	17383	19175
4 Dr Lariat Ext Cab LB	14972	16854	18591	4 Dr XLT Crew Cab LB	14803	16664	18382
4 Dr Lariat Ext Cab SB	14858	16726	18450	4 Dr XLT Crew Cab SB	14679	16524	18227
4 Dr XL 4WD Crew Cab LB	14710	16559	18266	4 Dr XLT Ext Cab LB	13921	15671	17286
4 Dr XL 4WD Crew Cab SB	14618	16456	18152	4 Dr XLT Ext Cab SB	13799	15534	17135

Options	Price	Options	Price
6.8L V10 SOHC 20V FI Engine	+316	Limited Slip Differential	+150
7.3L V8 Turbodiesel OHV 16V Engine	+2487	Park Distance Control (Rear) [Opt on Lariat,XLT]	+129
Air Conditioning [Opt on XL]	+424	Power Driver Seat [Opt on XLT]	+153
Automatic 4-Speed Transmission	+577	Two-Tone Paint	+119
Heated Front Seats [Opt on Lariat]	+116		

2000

Mileage Category: K

Four-wheel antilock brakes are now standard on F-250 and F-350 trucks with Lariat trim levels. XL trim level trucks now have optional bucket seats. Clean fuel (LEV) gasoline engines are standard on all Super Duty trucks. Power windows and locks are now standard on XLT trim levels. The trailer/tow mirrors now telescope manually. Rear bumpers are standard on all F-250 and F-350 pickups. All Super Duty trucks get new interior and exterior colors.

F-250 Super Duty

2000 (cont'd)

Body Styles	TMV Pricing			Body Styles	TMV Pricing		
	Trade	Private	Dealer		Trade	Private	Dealer
2 Dr Lariat 4WD Std Cab LB	13470	15385	17262	4 Dr XL 4WD Crew Cab SB	12615	14408	16166
2 Dr Lariat Std Cab LB	11464	13094	14692	4 Dr XL 4WD Ext Cab LB	11992	13697	15368
2 Dr XL 4WD Std Cab LB	10867	12412	13926	4 Dr XL 4WD Ext Cab SB	11944	13642	15306
2 Dr XL Std Cab LB	9448	10791	12108	4 Dr XL Crew Cab LB	11156	12742	14297
2 Dr XLT 4WD Std Cab LB	12141	13867	15559	4 Dr XL Crew Cab SB	11057	12629	14170
2 Dr XLT Std Cab LB	10678	12196	13684	4 Dr XL Ext Cab LB	10572	12075	13548
4 Dr Lariat 4WD Crew Cab LB	15211	17373	19493	4 Dr XL Ext Cab SB	10470	11958	13417
4 Dr Lariat 4WD Crew Cab SB	15000	17133	19223	4 Dr XLT 4WD Crew Cab LB	14312	16347	18341
4 Dr Lariat 4WD Ext Cab LB	14234	16258	18241	4 Dr XLT 4WD Crew Cab SB	14176	16191	18167
4 Dr Lariat 4WD Ext Cab SB	13947	15930	17873	4 Dr XLT 4WD Ext Cab LB	13582	15513	17405
4 Dr Lariat Crew Cab LB	13852	15821	17751	4 Dr XLT 4WD Ext Cab SB	13498	15417	17298
4 Dr Lariat Crew Cab SB	13743	15697	17612	4 Dr XLT Crew Cab LB	12563	14349	16099
4 Dr Lariat Ext Cab LB	12526	14307	16052	4 Dr XLT Crew Cab SB	12473	14246	15984
4 Dr Lariat Ext Cab SB	12392	14153	15880	4 Dr XLT Ext Cab LB	11609	13259	14877
4 Dr XL 4WD Crew Cab LB	12673	14474	16240	4 Dr XLT Ext Cab SB	11556	13199	14809

Options	Price	Options	Price
Antilock Brakes	+320	Side Steps [Opt on XL,XLT]	+139
Automatic 4-Speed Transmission	+516	6.8L V10 SOHC 20V FI Engine	+283
Camper/Towing Package	+189	7.3L V8 Turbodiesel OHV 16V Engine	+2060
Captain Chairs (2)	+231	Air Conditioning	+379
Limited Slip Differential	+134	Aluminum/Alloy Wheels	+179
Power Driver Seat [Opt on XLT]	+170		

1999

Mileage Category: K

The all-new Super Duty F-Series is a full-size truck developed and built on a separate platform from the under-8,500lb GVWR F150 and F250. For '99 the Super Duty is available in Regular Cab, four-door Super Cab or Crew Cab models, as well as in a class A Motor Home Chassis model.

Body Styles	TMV Pricing			Body Styles	TMV Pricing		
	Trade	Private	Dealer		Trade	Private	Dealer
2 Dr Lariat 4WD Std Cab LB	11182	13021	14936	4 Dr XL 4WD Crew Cab SB	11199	13041	14959
2 Dr Lariat Std Cab LB	9839	11457	13142	4 Dr XL 4WD Ext Cab LB	10538	12272	14076
2 Dr XL 4WD Std Cab LB	9691	11285	12945	4 Dr XL 4WD Ext Cab SB	10735	12501	14340
2 Dr XL Std Cab LB	8347	9720	11150	4 Dr XL Crew Cab LB	9942	11578	13280
2 Dr XLT 4WD Std Cab LB	10289	11981	13743	4 Dr XL Crew Cab SB	9855	11476	13164
2 Dr XLT Std Cab LB	8945	10416	11948	4 Dr XL Ext Cab LB	9194	10707	12281
4 Dr Lariat 4WD Crew Cab LB	12777	14879	17066	4 Dr XL Ext Cab SB	9109	10607	12166
4 Dr Lariat 4WD Crew Cab SB	12691	14778	16951	4 Dr XLT 4WD Crew Cab LB	11885	13840	15874
4 Dr Lariat 4WD Ext Cab LB	11937	13901	15945	4 Dr XLT 4WD Crew Cab SB	11797	13738	15758
4 Dr Lariat 4WD Ext Cab SB	11942	13907	15952	4 Dr XLT 4WD Ext Cab LB	11136	12968	14875
4 Dr Lariat Crew Cab LB	11433	13314	15271	4 Dr XLT 4WD Ext Cab SB	11051	12868	14760
4 Dr Lariat Crew Cab SB	11347	13213	15156	4 Dr XLT Crew Cab LB	10541	12275	14079
4 Dr Lariat Ext Cab LB	10595	12337	14151	4 Dr XLT Crew Cab SB	10455	12174	13963
4 Dr Lariat Ext Cab SB	10508	12236	14035	4 Dr XLT Ext Cab LB	9793	11404	13081
4 Dr XL 4WD Crew Cab LB	11285	13142	15074	4 Dr XLT Ext Cab SB	9706	11303	12965

Options	Price	Options	Price
6.8L V10 SOHC 20V FI Engine	+136	Automatic 4-Speed Transmission	+387
7.3L V8 Turbodiesel OHV 16V Engine	+1679	Camper/Towing Package	+115
Air Conditioning	+312	Leather Seats	+214
Aluminum/Alloy Wheels	+124	Limited Slip Differential	+124
AM/FM/Cassette/CD Audio System	+126	Side Steps [Opt on XL,XLT]	+115
Antilock Brakes	+293		

1997

Body Styles	TMV Pricing			Body Styles	TMV Pricing		
	Trade	Private	Dealer		Trade	Private	Dealer
2 Dr XL 4WD Std Cab LB	7010	8457	10226	2 Dr XLT Std Cab LB	6744	8137	9840
2 Dr XL Ext Cab LB	6967	8406	10164	4 Dr XL 4WD Crew Cab LB	8079	9747	11786
2 Dr XL Std Cab LB	5878	7092	8575	4 Dr XL Crew Cab LB	7165	8645	10453
2 Dr XLT 4WD Std Cab LB	7653	9233	11165	4 Dr XLT 4WD Crew Cab LB	9021	10884	13162
2 Dr XLT Ext Cab LB	7401	8930	10798	4 Dr XLT Crew Cab LB	7853	9475	11457

Options	Price
Automatic 4-Speed Transmission	+285
Dual Rear Wheels	+230
7.3L V8 Turbodiesel OHV 16V Engine	+1115
Air Conditioning [Opt on XL]	+236

Mileage Category: K

While its younger siblings receive complete redesigns, the elder 350 remains virtually unchanged. The 7.3L diesel receives minor improvements and the three-speed automatic transmission is eliminated.

1996

Body Styles	TMV Pricing			Body Styles	TMV Pricing		
	Trade	Private	Dealer		Trade	Private	Dealer
2 Dr XL 4WD Std Cab LB	5860	7206	9065	2 Dr XLT Std Cab LB	5594	6879	8654
2 Dr XL Ext Cab LB	5882	7234	9100	4 Dr XL 4WD Crew Cab LB	6817	8384	10547
2 Dr XL Std Cab LB	5052	6212	7815	4 Dr XL Crew Cab LB	6005	7385	9290
2 Dr XLT 4WD Std Cab LB	6529	8029	10101	4 Dr XLT 4WD Crew Cab LB	7516	9243	11628
2 Dr XLT Ext Cab LB	6309	7758	9760	4 Dr XLT Crew Cab LB	6621	8142	10243

Options	Price	Options	Price
7.3L V8 Turbodiesel OHV 16V Engine	+1025	Automatic 4-Speed Transmission	+260
Air Conditioning [Opt on XL]	+210	Dual Rear Wheels	+151
Automatic 3-Speed Transmission	+194	Split Front Bench Seat [Opt on XLT]	+137

Mileage Category: K

Minimal changes include an improved hub-locking system and transfer case for all 4WD models. The 7.5L V8 receives a standard integral oil cooler, and a throttle-control module for power takeoffs with the 7.3L diesel is now optional. Interior improvements include black finish on instrument panels, a revised seat design with integrated headrest and Automatic Locking Restraint/Emergency Locking Restraint safety belts for all outboard seating positions. A standard slotted-style front bumper and trailer tow wiring harness (except chassis cab) complete the changes.

1995

Body Styles	TMV Pricing			Body Styles	TMV Pricing		
	Trade	Private	Dealer		Trade	Private	Dealer
2 Dr XL 4WD Std Cab LB	4796	5951	7875	2 Dr XLT Std Cab LB	4828	5991	7928
2 Dr XL Ext Cab LB	4941	6131	8114	4 Dr XL 4WD Crew Cab LB	5598	6946	9193
2 Dr XL Std Cab LB	4321	5362	7097	4 Dr XL Crew Cab LB	4875	6049	8005
2 Dr XLT 4WD Std Cab LB	5398	6698	8865	4 Dr XLT 4WD Crew Cab LB	6230	7730	10231
2 Dr XLT Ext Cab LB	5235	6496	8598	4 Dr XLT Crew Cab LB	5411	6714	8886

Options	Price	Options	Price
Dual Rear Wheels	+131	Air Conditioning [Opt on XL]	+180
Power Sunroof	+180	Automatic 3-Speed Transmission	+167
7.3L V8 Turbodiesel OHV 16V Engine	+856	Automatic 4-Speed Transmission	+219
7.5L V8 OHV 16V FI Engine	+87		

Mileage Category: K

Mirroring that of its smaller F-250 sibling, the F-Super Duty's Stripped Commercial Chassis is deleted, optional privacy glass now includes manual-sliding rear windows (when equipped), forged aluminum wheels are offered and cab steps on regular and SuperCab Styleside trims are available.

1994

Body Styles	TMV Pricing			Body Styles	TMV Pricing		
	Trade	Private	Dealer		Trade	Private	Dealer
2 Dr XL 4WD Std Cab LB	3863	5045	7015	2 Dr XLT Std Cab LB	3982	5200	7231
2 Dr XL Ext Cab LB	3955	5165	7182	4 Dr XL 4WD Crew Cab LB	4439	5797	8060
2 Dr XL Std Cab LB	3510	4584	6374	4 Dr XL Crew Cab LB	3855	5034	7000
2 Dr XLT 4WD Std Cab LB	4263	5567	7740	4 Dr XLT 4WD Crew Cab LB	4904	6404	8905
2 Dr XLT Ext Cab LB	4366	5701	7927	4 Dr XLT Crew Cab LB	4278	5586	7767

Options	Price	Options	Price
Air Conditioning [Opt on XL]	+153	Dual Rear Wheels	+111
Automatic 3-Speed Transmission	+142	7.3L V8 Diesel OHV 16V Engine	+542
Automatic 4-Speed Transmission	+185	7.3L V8 Turbodiesel OHV 16V Engine	+725

Mileage Category: K

Ford's one-ton hauler receives only slight mechanical and chassis refinements. Two versions of the 7.3L turbodiesel, direct injection and indirect injection, are offered on models above 8,500 pounds GVWR. Environmentally friendly CFC-free air conditioning is offered, and standard equipment grows with the addition of side door beams, a center high-mounted stop lamp, a driver-side airbag (for under-8,500-pound GVWR models) and a brake shift interlock system for all automatics. A premium 40/20/40 bench seat option is added to XLT Crew- and SuperCab styles and a wide-ratio four-speed automatic transmission with overdrive accompanies the 5.0L engine.

2003

Mileage Category: K

The 2003 model year sees a new FX4 Off-Road Package with skid plates, Rancho front and rear shocks, a steering damper and decals. The regular off-road package is no longer available, but a skid plate package can still be had on all 4WD trucks. All XLs can be had with a vinyl 40/20/40 reclining split bench that has a fold-down armrest with a console and cupholders. Ford has also upgraded seat material quality and installed a tailgate lock on this trim level. If you order a SuperCab or Crew Cab in XLT trim with the Sport Package, you can also order a reverse sensing system and a power driver seat. Late-availability additions include an optional power moonroof for Crew Cabs and optional heated telescoping trailer tow mirrors with integrated turn signals. A King Ranch version of the Crew Cab will also appear later in the year. Finally, the torque rating for the 7.3-liter turbodiesel V8 has been boosted to 525 pound-feet. By mid-year, expect an even more powerful 6.0-liter diesel to appear.

Body Styles	TMV Pricing		
	Trade	Private	Dealer
2 Dr XL 4WD Std Cab LB	16668	17801	19688
2 Dr XL Std Cab LB	14523	15510	17154
2 Dr XLT 4WD Std Cab LB	19124	20423	22588
2 Dr XLT Std Cab LB	16917	18066	19982
4 Dr Lariat 4WD Crew Cab LB	24109	25747	28477
4 Dr Lariat 4WD Crew Cab SB	23959	25587	28300
4 Dr Lariat 4WD Ext Cab LB	22775	24322	26901
4 Dr Lariat 4WD Ext Cab SB	22639	24177	26740
4 Dr Lariat Crew Cab LB	22173	23680	26191
4 Dr Lariat Crew Cab SB	22067	23566	26065
4 Dr Lariat Ext Cab LB	20639	22041	24378
4 Dr Lariat Ext Cab SB	20510	21904	24226
4 Dr XL 4WD Crew Cab LB	19444	20765	22966
4 Dr XL 4WD Crew Cab SB	19339	20653	22842

Body Styles	TMV Pricing		
	Trade	Private	Dealer
4 Dr XL 4WD Ext Cab LB	18568	19830	21932
4 Dr XL 4WD Ext Cab SB	18415	19666	21751
4 Dr XL Crew Cab LB	17319	18495	20456
4 Dr XL Crew Cab SB	17099	18261	20197
4 Dr XL Ext Cab LB	16396	17510	19367
4 Dr XL Ext Cab SB	16258	17362	19203
4 Dr XLT 4WD Crew Cab LB	22513	24042	26591
4 Dr XLT 4WD Crew Cab SB	22377	23897	26431
4 Dr XLT 4WD Ext Cab LB	21446	22903	25331
4 Dr XLT 4WD Ext Cab SB	21310	22758	25171
4 Dr XLT Crew Cab LB	20524	21919	24243
4 Dr XLT Crew Cab SB	20354	21737	24041
4 Dr XLT Ext Cab LB	19372	20688	22881
4 Dr XLT Ext Cab SB	19131	20431	22597

Options	Price
Air Conditioning [Opt on XL]	+519
Aluminum/Alloy Wheels [Opt on XLT]	+119
Automatic 4-Speed Transmission	+706
Automatic 5-Speed Transmission	+955
Captain Chairs (4) [Opt on Lariat]	+226
Cruise Control [Opt on XL]	+119
Dual Rear Wheels	+648
Heated Drivers Seat [Opt on Lariat]	+142
Leather Seats [Opt on XLT]	+319
Limited Slip Differential	+193
Power Driver Seat [Opt on XLT]	+187
Power Moonroof [Opt on Lariat,XLT]	+522

Options	Price
Power Passenger Seat [Opt on XLT]	+187
Running Boards [Opt on XL,XLT]	+126
Special Leather Seat Trim [Opt on Lariat]	+577
Tilt Steering Wheel [Opt on XL]	+116
Two-Tone Paint [Opt on Lariat,XLT]	+145
AM/FM/CD Changer Audio System [Opt on Lariat,XLT]	+135
7.3L V8 Turbodiesel OHV 16V Engine	+3122
Power Retractable Mirrors [Opt on Lariat,XLT]	+142
6.0L V8 Turbodiesel OHV 32V Engine	+3280
FX4 Off-Road Suspension Package	+145
King Ranch Package [Opt on Lariat]	+1932
Park Distance Control (Rear) [Opt on Lariat,XLT]	+158

2002

Mileage Category: K

A six-speed manual transmission is now standard with the 5.4- and 6.8-liter V8 gas engines, and the 6.8-liter has been enhanced to provide better performance and shift feel than before. If you order an automatic transmission, a gauge that measures transmission oil temperature replaces the battery gauge, and you can opt to add adjustable pedals to your Super Duty XLT or Lariat truck. Trucks with the Power Stroke diesel get an air filter service indicator. All F-350s get roof ride handles standard for 2002, and the available telescoping trailer mirrors can now be folded forward. SuperCabs have new rear door panel map pockets with molded-in cupholders. XL gets upgraded visors, while XLT and Lariat get new seats with increased width, bolstering and lumbar support; jewellike headlamp lenses and an available Advanced Security Group that includes remote keyless entry, automatic door locks and automatic headlamps. Optional on the XLT Crew Cab and standard on the Lariat Crew Cab is a power front passenger seat. The Lariat also gets a larger standard overhead console with improved storage.

Body Styles	TMV Pricing		
	Trade	Private	Dealer
2 Dr XL 4WD Std Cab LB	14759	15882	17753
2 Dr XL Std Cab LB	12909	13891	15528
2 Dr XLT 4WD Std Cab LB	16735	18008	20129
2 Dr XLT Std Cab LB	14832	15960	17841
4 Dr Lariat 4WD Crew Cab LB	20996	22593	25255
4 Dr Lariat 4WD Crew Cab SB	20872	22459	25105
4 Dr Lariat 4WD Ext Cab LB	19792	21298	23807
4 Dr Lariat 4WD Ext Cab SB	19679	21176	23671
4 Dr Lariat Crew Cab LB	19210	20671	23107
4 Dr Lariat Crew Cab SB	19101	20554	22976
4 Dr Lariat Ext Cab LB	17973	19340	21619
4 Dr Lariat Ext Cab SB	17858	19216	21480
4 Dr XL 4WD Crew Cab LB	17141	18445	20618
4 Dr XL 4WD Crew Cab SB	17080	18379	20545

Body Styles	TMV Pricing		
	Trade	Private	Dealer
4 Dr XL 4WD Ext Cab LB	16417	17666	19747
4 Dr XL 4WD Ext Cab SB	16261	17498	19560
4 Dr XL Crew Cab LB	15314	16479	18420
4 Dr XL Crew Cab SB	15182	16337	18262
4 Dr XL Ext Cab LB	14520	15624	17465
4 Dr XL Ext Cab SB	14408	15504	17331
4 Dr XLT 4WD Crew Cab LB	19545	21032	23510
4 Dr XLT 4WD Crew Cab SB	19421	20898	23360
4 Dr XLT 4WD Ext Cab LB	18643	20061	22425
4 Dr XLT 4WD Ext Cab SB	18541	19951	22302
4 Dr XLT Crew Cab LB	17777	19129	21383
4 Dr XLT Crew Cab SB	17710	19057	21303
4 Dr XLT Ext Cab LB	16787	18064	20192
4 Dr XLT Ext Cab SB	16675	17943	20057

Options	Price
6.8L V10 SOHC 20V FI Engine	+353
7.3L V8 Turbodiesel OHV 16V Engine	+2849
Air Conditioning [Opt on XL]	+474
AM/FM/CD Changer Audio System [Opt on Lariat]	+206
Automatic 4-Speed Transmission	+645
Bucket Seats [Opt on XL]	+118
Dual Rear Wheels	+353
Heated Front Seats [Opt on Lariat]	+130

Options	Price
Leather Seats [Opt on XLT]	+291
Limited Slip Differential	+168
Park Distance Control (Rear) [Opt on Lariat,XLT]	+144
Power Driver Seat [Std on Lariat]	+171
Power Passenger Seat [Std on Lariat]	+341
Premium Audio System	+124
Side Steps [Opt on XLT]	+118
Two-Tone Paint	+132

2001

Mileage Category: K

Body Styles	TMV Pricing		
	Trade	Private	Dealer
2 Dr XL 4WD Std Cab LB	13037	14676	16189
2 Dr XL Std Cab LB	11433	12870	14196
2 Dr XLT 4WD Std Cab LB	14730	16582	18291
2 Dr XLT Std Cab LB	13084	14729	16247
4 Dr Lariat 4WD Crew Cab LB	17802	20040	22105
4 Dr Lariat 4WD Crew Cab SB	17695	19920	21973
4 Dr Lariat 4WD Ext Cab LB	17079	19226	21207
4 Dr Lariat 4WD Ext Cab SB	16979	19114	21084
4 Dr Lariat Crew Cab LB	16301	18350	20242
4 Dr Lariat Crew Cab SB	16204	18241	20121
4 Dr Lariat Ext Cab LB	15486	17432	19229
4 Dr Lariat Ext Cab SB	15383	17317	19102
4 Dr XL 4WD Crew Cab LB	15042	16933	18678
4 Dr XL 4WD Crew Cab SB	14956	16836	18571

Body Styles	TMV Pricing		
	Trade	Private	Dealer
4 Dr XL 4WD Ext Cab LB	14442	16257	17933
4 Dr XL 4WD Ext Cab SB	14331	16132	17795
4 Dr XL Crew Cab LB	13453	15144	16705
4 Dr XL Crew Cab SB	13339	15015	16563
4 Dr XL Ext Cab LB	12822	14433	15921
4 Dr XL Ext Cab SB	12722	14322	15798
4 Dr XLT 4WD Crew Cab LB	16827	18942	20895
4 Dr XLT 4WD Crew Cab SB	16739	18843	20786
4 Dr XLT 4WD Ext Cab LB	16133	18161	20033
4 Dr XLT 4WD Ext Cab SB	16045	18062	19924
4 Dr XLT Crew Cab LB	15329	17256	19035
4 Dr XLT Crew Cab SB	15225	17139	18906
4 Dr XLT Ext Cab LB	14521	16347	18032
4 Dr XLT Ext Cab SB	14428	16242	17916

Options	Price
6.8L V10 SOHC 20V FI Engine	+316
7.3L V8 Turbodiesel OHV 16V Engine	+2302
Air Conditioning [Opt on XL]	+424
Automatic 4-Speed Transmission	+577
Dual Rear Wheels	+448

Options	Price
Heated Front Seats [Opt on Lariat]	+116
Limited Slip Differential	+150
Park Distance Control (Rear) [Opt on Lariat,XLT]	+129
Power Driver Seat [Opt on XLT]	+153
Two-Tone Paint	+119

The Trailer Tow package is standard on all models, as is four-wheel ABS. XLT and Lariat models can be equipped with an ultrasonic reverse vehicle-aid sensor, an in-dash six-disc CD changer and chrome tubular cab steps. Heated seats are available on Lariat models. Rounding out the 2001 changes are minor interior updates and a horsepower upgrade to the 7.3-liter diesel engine.

2000

Mileage Category: K

Body Styles	TMV Pricing		
	Trade	Private	Dealer
2 Dr Lariat 4WD Std Cab LB	13477	15380	17246
2 Dr Lariat Std Cab LB	12219	13946	15638
2 Dr XL 4WD Std Cab LB	11170	12748	14295
2 Dr XL Std Cab LB	9707	11078	12422
2 Dr XLT 4WD Std Cab LB	12643	14429	16180
2 Dr XLT Std Cab LB	11084	12650	14185
4 Dr Lariat 4WD Crew Cab LB	15733	17956	20135
4 Dr Lariat 4WD Crew Cab SB	14977	17093	19167
4 Dr Lariat 4WD Ext Cab LB	14631	16698	18724
4 Dr Lariat 4WD Ext Cab SB	14475	16520	18524
4 Dr Lariat Crew Cab LB	13860	15818	17737
4 Dr Lariat Crew Cab SB	13732	15672	17574
4 Dr Lariat Ext Cab LB	13097	14947	16761
4 Dr Lariat Ext Cab SB	13027	14867	16671
4 Dr XL 4WD Crew Cab LB	13023	14863	16666

Body Styles	TMV Pricing		
	Trade	Private	Dealer
4 Dr XL 4WD Crew Cab SB	12856	14672	16452
4 Dr XL 4WD Ext Cab LB	12543	14315	16052
4 Dr XL 4WD Ext Cab SB	12485	14248	15977
4 Dr XL Crew Cab LB	11498	13122	14714
4 Dr XL Crew Cab SB	11388	12996	14573
4 Dr XL Ext Cab LB	10941	12487	14002
4 Dr XL Ext Cab SB	10842	12374	13875
4 Dr XLT 4WD Crew Cab LB	14302	16323	18303
4 Dr XLT 4WD Crew Cab SB	14234	16245	18216
4 Dr XLT 4WD Ext Cab LB	13650	15578	17468
4 Dr XLT 4WD Ext Cab SB	13560	15476	17354
4 Dr XLT Crew Cab LB	13040	14882	16688
4 Dr XLT Crew Cab SB	12897	14719	16505
4 Dr XLT Ext Cab LB	12321	14062	15768
4 Dr XLT Ext Cab SB	12277	14011	15711

Options	Price
Camper/Towing Package	+162
Dual Rear Wheels	+274
Limited Slip Differential	+134
Power Driver Seat	+137
Side Steps [Opt on XL,XLT]	+139

Options	Price
6.8L V10 SOHC 20V FI Engine	+283
7.3L V8 Turbodiesel OHV 16V Engine	+2060
Air Conditioning	+379
Antilock Brakes	+320
Automatic 4-Speed Transmission	+516

Four-wheel antilock brakes are now standard on F-250 and F-350 trucks with Lariat trim levels. XL trim level trucks now have optional bucket seats. Clean fuel (LEV) gasoline engines are standard on all Super Duty trucks. Power windows and locks are now standard on XLT trim levels. The trailer/tow mirrors now telescope manually. Rear bumpers are standard on all F-250 and F-350 pickups. All Super Duty trucks get new interior and exterior colors.

1999

Mileage Category: K

Body Styles	TMV Pricing		
	Trade	Private	Dealer
2 Dr Lariat 4WD Std Cab LB	10961	12822	14759
2 Dr Lariat Std Cab LB	9545	11165	12852
2 Dr XL 4WD Std Cab LB	9409	11006	12669
2 Dr XL Std Cab LB	7840	9171	10556
2 Dr XLT 4WD Std Cab LB	9894	11574	13323
2 Dr XLT Std Cab LB	8834	10333	11894
4 Dr Lariat 4WD Crew Cab LB	12861	15044	17317
4 Dr Lariat 4WD Crew Cab SB	12327	14420	16598

Body Styles	TMV Pricing		
	Trade	Private	Dealer
2 Dr Lariat 4WD Std Cab LB	10961	12822	14759
2 Dr Lariat Std Cab LB	9545	11165	12852
2 Dr XL 4WD Std Cab LB	9409	11006	12669
2 Dr XL Std Cab LB	7840	9171	10556
2 Dr XLT 4WD Std Cab LB	9894	11574	13323
2 Dr XLT Std Cab LB	8834	10333	11894
4 Dr Lariat 4WD Crew Cab LB	12861	15044	17317

The all-new Super Duty F-Series is a full-size truck developed and built on a separate platform from the under-8,500-pound GVWR F150 and F250. For '99 the Super Duty is available in Regular Cab, four-door SuperCab or Crew Cab models.

1999 (cont'd)

Body Styles	TMV Pricing		
	Trade	Private	Dealer
4 Dr XL 4WD Crew Cab SB	10945	12803	14737
4 Dr XL 4WD Ext Cab LB	10209	11942	13746
4 Dr XL 4WD Ext Cab SB	10115	11832	13620
4 Dr XL Crew Cab LB	9729	11380	13099
4 Dr XL Crew Cab SB	9645	11282	12986
4 Dr XL Ext Cab LB	8975	10499	12085
4 Dr XL Ext Cab SB	8956	10476	12059
4 Dr XLT 4WD Crew Cab LB	11491	13442	15472

Body Styles	TMV Pricing		
	Trade	Private	Dealer
4 Dr XLT 4WD Crew Cab SB	11426	13366	15385
4 Dr XLT 4WD Ext Cab LB	11041	12916	14867
4 Dr XLT 4WD Ext Cab SB	10972	12834	14773
4 Dr XLT Crew Cab LB	10313	12064	13886
4 Dr XLT Crew Cab SB	10277	12022	13838
4 Dr XLT Ext Cab LB	9794	11457	13188
4 Dr XLT Ext Cab SB	9686	11330	13042

Options	Price
Side Steps	+115
6.8L V10 SOHC 20V FI Engine	+136
7.3L V8 Turbodiesel OHV 16V Engine	+1679
Air Conditioning	+312
AM/FM/Cassette/CD Audio System	+126

Options	Price
Antilock Brakes	+293
Automatic 4-Speed Transmission	+387
Camper/Towing Package	+115
Dual Rear Wheels	+225
Leather Seats	+214

Ford
Focus

2003

Mileage Category: B

Minor changes are in store for the Focus. Two new trim levels increase the breadth of prices for Ford's economy car; a base trim for the three door hatchback renders air conditioning optional and only comes with a manual transmission. For the five door hatchback, a tilt and telescoping steering wheel, cruise control, front reading lights and a center console are available when you step up to the comfort trim level from the base level. Heated front seats are a new option, as is a traction control and ABS package. New colors for the exterior brighten up the color palette, and the interior is freshened with two new fabric trims. Finally, a CD/MP3 player is now standard on the ZX3 and ZX5.

Body Styles	TMV Pricing		
	Trade	Private	Dealer
2 Dr ZX3 Hbk	6611	7364	8619
4 Dr LX Sdn	6737	7504	8783
4 Dr SE Sdn	7425	8271	9681
4 Dr SE Wgn	8803	9806	11477

Body Styles	TMV Pricing		
	Trade	Private	Dealer
4 Dr ZTS Sdn	8484	9450	11061
4 Dr ZTW Wgn	9901	11029	12908
4 Dr ZX5 Hbk	8413	9372	10969

Options	Price
Air Conditioning [Opt on LX,ZX3]	+513
Antilock Brakes	+439
Automatic 4-Speed Transmission [Opt on SE,ZTS,ZX5]	+526
Automatic Stability Control [Opt on ZTS,ZTW]	+371
Cruise Control	+119
Heated Front Seats [Opt on ZTS,ZTW]	+177
Leather Seats [Opt on ZTS,ZTW,ZX5]	+448

Options	Price
Power Moonroof [Opt on ZTS,ZTW,ZX5]	+371
Power Windows [Opt on LX,ZX3]	+142
Front Side Airbag Restraints	+226
Special Leather Seat Trim [Opt on ZTS]	+513
Tilt and Telescopic Steering Wheel [Std on ZTS,ZTW]	+129
AM/FM/CD Changer Audio System	+181
2.0L I4 DOHC 16V FI Engine [Opt on SE]	+164

2002

Mileage Category: B

Four new Focus models debut for 2002: the ZX5 five-door hatchback, the well-equipped ZTW wagon, the sport-tuned SVT hatchback and the Mach Audio ZTS. No matter what Focus you pick in 2002, a power moonroof can now be ordered. The high-end ZTS Sedan loses its standard ABS and crummy fake wood dash trim while gaining a rear spoiler. An in-dash six-disc CD changer is standard on ZX5, ZTS and ZTW but optional on all other Foci except the LX Sedan.

Body Styles	TMV Pricing		
	Trade	Private	Dealer
2 Dr ZX3 Hbk	5296	6007	7192
4 Dr LX Sdn	5333	6073	7306
4 Dr SE Sdn	5806	6612	7954
4 Dr SE Wgn	6974	7942	9554

Body Styles	TMV Pricing		
	Trade	Private	Dealer
4 Dr ZTS Sdn	6388	7274	8751
4 Dr ZTW Wgn	7933	8998	10774
4 Dr ZX5 Hbk	6956	7891	9448

Options	Price
2.0L I4 DOHC 16V FI Engine [Opt on SE Sdn]	+165
Air Conditioning [Opt on LX,ZX3]	+468
AM/FM/CD Changer Audio System [Opt on ZTS,ZX3]	+165
Antilock Brakes	+400
Automatic 4-Speed Transmission [Std on Wgn]	+480
Automatic Stability Control	+338

Options	Price
Front Side Airbag Restraints	+206
Leather Seats [Opt on ZTS,ZX5]	+409
MACH Audio System [Opt on ZTS]	+306
Power Moonroof	+350
Power Windows [Opt on ZX3]	+130
Traction Control System	+147

2001

Body Styles	TMV Pricing		
	Trade	Private	Dealer
2 Dr ZX3 Hbk	4262	5180	6027
4 Dr LX Sdn	4437	5393	6275
4 Dr SE Sdn	5084	6178	7188
4 Dr SE Wgn	5986	7275	8465

Options	Price
2.0L I4 DOHC 16V FI Engine [Opt on SE]	+148
Air Conditioning [Opt on LX,SE]	+419
Antilock Brakes [Std on ZTS]	+358
Automatic 4-Speed Transmission [Std on Wgn]	+429
Automatic Stability Control [Opt on Street,ZTS,ZX3]	+303
Compact Disc Changer	+184

Body Styles	TMV Pricing		
	Trade	Private	Dealer
4 Dr Street Sdn	4887	5939	6911
4 Dr Street Wgn	6290	7645	8895
4 Dr ZTS Sdn	5669	6889	8016

Options	Price
Front Side Airbag Restraints	+184
Leather Seats	+366
Moonroof	+261
Power Windows [Std on ZTS]	+118
Traction Control System	+132

Mileage Category: B

Raising the bar for compact vehicles, Ford is offering its stability system -- called AdvanceTrac -- on ZTS Sedans and ZX3 Hatchbacks. Ford has also made previously optional features standard equipment. Highlights include a driver armrest on every model except LX and power windows on SE Sedans and Wagons. SE Wagons also get the Zetec engine as standard and can be ordered with a manual transmission. A new manual moonroof is offered on the ZX3 and new 16-inch wheels are standard on ZTS Sedans and optional on ZX3 Coupes.

2000

Body Styles	TMV Pricing		
	Trade	Private	Dealer
2 Dr ZX3 Hbk	3389	4349	5290
4 Dr LX Sdn	3549	4554	5540
4 Dr SE Sdn	4100	5262	6400

Options	Price
2.0L I4 DOHC 16V FI Engine [Opt on SE]	+132
Air Conditioning [Opt on LX,SE]	+375
Aluminum/Alloy Wheels [Opt on LX]	+170
Antilock Brakes [Std on ZTS]	+320

Body Styles	TMV Pricing		
	Trade	Private	Dealer
4 Dr SE Wgn	4936	6334	7704
4 Dr Sony Limited Sdn	4576	5872	7142
4 Dr ZTS Sdn	4630	5941	7226

Options	Price
Automatic 4-Speed Transmission [Std on Wgn]	+384
Front Side Airbag Restraints	+165
Kona Mountain Bike Package	+705
Leather Seats	+328

Mileage Category: B

This is Ford's all-new "world car" that will be sold initially concurrently with the Escort. Everything from interior room to performance has been addressed to make this European-engineered compact a winner in the small-car segment.

2003

Body Styles	TMV Pricing		
	Trade	Private	Dealer
2 Dr STD Hbk	11186	12460	14584
4 Dr STD Hbk	11346	12638	14792

Options	Price
AM/FM/CD Changer Audio System	+181
Heated Front Seats	+129
Leather Seats	+448

Options	Price
Power Moonroof	+384
Premium Audio System	+129
Traction Control System	+126

Mileage Category: B

A four-door version of the hot-rod Focus hatchback debuts later in the year, making for a more practical choice for those with family obligations.

2002

Mileage Category: B

Ford's in-house tuning team, known as SVT, works its magic on the Focus ZX3 hatchback. The result is a well-balanced, 170-horsepower canyon carver.

Body Styles	TMV Pricing		
	Trade	Private	Dealer
2 Dr STD Hbk	9014	10265	12349

Options	Price
AM/FM/CD Changer Audio System	+280
Heated Front Seats	+118
Power Moonroof	+350

Options	Price
Premium Audio System	+306
Traction Control System	+115

Ford
Mustang

2003

Body Styles	TMV Pricing		
	Trade	Private	Dealer
2 Dr GT Conv	18206	19322	21182
2 Dr GT Cpe	14753	15657	17164
2 Dr Mach 1 Cpe	19391	20579	22560

Body Styles	TMV Pricing		
	Trade	Private	Dealer
2 Dr STD Conv	14896	15809	17331
2 Dr STD Cpe	10974	11647	12768

Options	Price
Antilock Brakes [Opt on STD]	+439
Automatic 4-Speed Transmission [Opt on GT,STD,MACH 1]	+526
Cruise Control [Opt on STD]	+119
Leather Seats [Opt on GT,STD]	+384
Power Driver Seat [Opt on STD]	+158

Options	Price
Rear Spoiler [Opt on STD]	+139
Traction Control System [Opt on STD]	+135
AM/FM/CD Changer Audio System [Opt on GT,STD]	+210
MACH Audio System [Opt on GT,STD]	+190

Mileage Category: E

Heavily updated is the 2003 SVT Mustang Cobra, which makes 390 horsepower and 390 pound-feet of torque thanks to the addition of an Eaton supercharger. A new six-speed manual transmission drives the rear wheels through a 3.55 rear axle ratio. Larger wheels and tires come standard, along with stiffer springs and a tubular cross brace. Cobra convertibles have a cloth top, while both cars get new seats with upgraded leather and suede upholstery. A limited-production Mach 1 model arrives later in the year with a massaged 4.6-liter V8 engine making at least 300 horsepower and 300 pound-feet of torque, a functional shaker hood with ram-air scoop, black striping, unique leather seating and retro-design Magnum 500 alloy wheels, and, of course, a Mach 460 audio system. Mach 1 can be ordered in a variety of colors with either a manual or automatic transmission. Like the Mustang Bullitt before it, the Mach 1 comes with a lowered, retuned suspension and additional frame rail connectors for a stiffer body. Large 13-inch Brembo front rotors and upgraded calipers are standard.

Standard V6 and V8 GT models change little for 2003. A V6 Pony Package includes 16-inch polished alloy wheels and the GT's scooped hood. All V6 models get a new hood design, and four new colors debut.

2002

Mileage Category: E

Lower-line V6 models get standard 16-inch alloy wheels and a new hood while losing the fake side scoops. Premium models can be equipped with a Mach 1000 audio system. Both this system and the Mach 460 get speed-sensitive volume. Later this year, an MP3 player will be available. Performance Red paint is replaced with Torch Red.

Body Styles	TMV Pricing		
	Trade	Private	Dealer
2 Dr GT Conv	15101	16427	18638
2 Dr GT Cpe	12458	13552	15375

Body Styles	TMV Pricing		
	Trade	Private	Dealer
2 Dr STD Conv	12310	13391	15193
2 Dr STD Cpe	9194	10001	11347

Options	Price
16 Inch Wheels [Opt on STD]	+191
AM/FM/CD Changer Audio System	+191
Antilock Brakes [Opt on STD]	+400
Automatic 4-Speed Transmission	+383

Options	Price
Leather Seats	+309
MACH Audio System	+174
Power Driver Seat [Opt on STD Cpe]	+147
Traction Control System [Opt on STD]	+135

2001

Mileage Category: E

GT models get unique hood and side scoops. They also receive standard 17-inch wheels, and V6 Convertibles get 16-inch wheels as standard. All cars have a revised center console and blacked-out headlights and spoilers. The Mach 460 stereo system comes with an in-dash six-disc CD changer. A new "premium" trim line is created for both V6 and V8 models.

Body Styles	TMV Pricing		
	Trade	Private	Dealer
2 Dr GT Bullitt Cpe	13034	14792	16414
2 Dr GT Conv	13122	14892	16525
2 Dr GT Cpe	11039	12528	13902

Body Styles	TMV Pricing		
	Trade	Private	Dealer
2 Dr STD Conv	11013	12498	13869
2 Dr STD Cpe	8023	9105	10103

Options	Price
AM/FM/Cassette/CD Changer Audio System	+184
Antilock Brakes [Opt on STD]	+358
Automatic 4-Speed Transmission	+429

Options	Price
Leather Seats	+248
Sport Seats [Opt on STD Conv]	+132
Traction Control System	+132

2000

Mileage Category: E

The Mustang has three updated colors: Performance Red, Amazon Green and Sunburst Gold. A child safety-seat anchoring system is standard on both the coupe and convertible. New 16-inch wheels and tires are offered as an option on appearance package-equipped V6 Mustangs. The 2000 Mustang also features a tri-color bar emblem on the sides of the front fenders.

Body Styles	TMV Pricing		
	Trade	Private	Dealer
2 Dr GT Conv	10879	12550	14187
2 Dr GT Cpe	9088	10484	11852

Body Styles	TMV Pricing		
	Trade	Private	Dealer
2 Dr STD Conv	9273	10697	12092
2 Dr STD Cpe	6711	7741	8751

Options	Price
Antilock Brakes [Opt on STD]	+320
Automatic 4-Speed Transmission	+384

Options	Price
Leather Seats	+236
MACH Audio System	+186

1999

Body Styles	TMV Pricing		
	Trade	Private	Dealer
2 Dr GT Conv	8767	10382	12062
2 Dr GT Cpe	7557	8949	10397

Options	Price
AM/FM/Cassette Audio System	+154
Antilock Brakes [Opt on STD]	+293
Automatic 4-Speed Transmission	+317
Bucket Seats	+194

Body Styles	TMV Pricing		
	Trade	Private	Dealer
2 Dr STD Conv	7618	9021	10481
2 Dr STD Cpe	5813	6884	7998

Options	Price
Compact Disc Changer [Opt on STD]	+174
Leather Seats	+214
Spoke Wheels	+194

Mileage Category: E

Ford gives its sports car fresh styling and more motor. The 3.8-liter V6 engine makes 190 horsepower and 220 pound-feet of torque. The SOHC V8 found in GT models gets an 16-percent increase in horsepower. Improvements to the V6 and GT suspension and steering gear, as well as a styling update.

1998

Body Styles	TMV Pricing		
	Trade	Private	Dealer
2 Dr GT Conv	6986	8491	10189
2 Dr GT Cpe	5663	6884	8260

Options	Price
AM/FM/Cassette Audio System	+125
Antilock Brakes	+240

Body Styles	TMV Pricing		
	Trade	Private	Dealer
2 Dr STD Conv	5762	7003	8403
2 Dr STD Cpe	4683	5692	6830

Options	Price
Automatic 4-Speed Transmission	+259
Leather Seats	+159

Mileage Category: E

The Mustang gains standard equipment, such as power windows and door locks, air conditioning, and premium sound. Options are shuffled as well, making it easier to choose the car you want. GT models get a slight boost in power.

1997

Body Styles	TMV Pricing		
	Trade	Private	Dealer
2 Dr GT Conv	6008	7389	9077
2 Dr GT Cpe	4313	5304	6516

Options	Price
Air Conditioning	+262
AM/FM/Cassette/CD Audio System	+116
Antilock Brakes	+222
Automatic 4-Speed Transmission	+239

Body Styles	TMV Pricing		
	Trade	Private	Dealer
2 Dr STD Conv	5158	6344	7793
2 Dr STD Cpe	3990	4907	6028

Options	Price
Bucket Seats	+147
Leather Seats	+147
Premium Audio System [Opt on Conv]	+116

Mileage Category: E

GT models and base convertibles get new interior color options, and cars equipped with an automatic transmission get a thicker shift lever. New 17-inch aluminum wheels are optional on the GT. The Passive Anti-Theft System has been introduced to all Mustangs.

1996

Body Styles	TMV Pricing		
	Trade	Private	Dealer
2 Dr GT Conv	5136	6402	8150
2 Dr GT Cpe	3834	4779	6083

Options	Price
Antilock Brakes	+197
Automatic 4-Speed Transmission	+213
Leather Seats	+130

Body Styles	TMV Pricing		
	Trade	Private	Dealer
2 Dr STD Conv	4284	5340	6798
2 Dr STD Cpe	3129	3900	4965

Options	Price
17 Inch Wheels [Opt on GT]	+116
Air Conditioning	+234

Mileage Category: E

Ford plugs a 4.6-liter modular V8 into its pony car. Base cars also get engine improvements, and all Mustangs get minor styling revisions. The GTS model, a midyear 1995 V8 base Mustang, has been dropped.

1995

Body Styles	TMV Pricing		
	Trade	Private	Dealer
2 Dr GT Conv	4230	5299	7081
2 Dr GT Cpe	3292	4124	5510
2 Dr GTS Cpe	2847	3567	4766

Options	Price
Air Conditioning	+202
AM/FM/Cassette/CD Audio System	+89
Antilock Brakes	+170

Body Styles	TMV Pricing		
	Trade	Private	Dealer
2 Dr STD Conv	3511	4399	5878
2 Dr STD Cpe	2466	3089	4128

Options	Price
Automatic 4-Speed Transmission	+184
Compact Disc Changer	+101
Leather Seats [Opt on GT]	+135

Mileage Category: E

A power driver seat moves from the standard equipment list to the options list. A powerful new stereo with a CD changer also debuts on the options list.

1994

Mileage Category: E

New sheet metal for the venerable pony. The LX model and hatchback are dropped. The base Mustang gets a 3.8-liter V6, and GT models receive a boost in horsepower. Four-wheel disc brakes are standard on both Mustangs and ABS becomes an available option. A passenger airbag, power driver seat, and tilt steering wheel become standard in 1994. Convertibles are available with a removable hardtop.

Body Styles	TMV Pricing		
	Trade	Private	Dealer
2 Dr GT Conv	2984	4019	5743
2 Dr GT Cpe	2561	3449	4929

Options	Price
Air Conditioning	+171
AM/FM/Cassette/CD Audio System	+76
Antilock Brakes	+144

Body Styles	TMV Pricing		
	Trade	Private	Dealer
2 Dr STD Conv	2770	3731	5332
2 Dr STD Cpe	1789	2410	3444

Options	Price
Automatic 4-Speed Transmission	+156
Compact Disc Changer	+86
Leather Seats	+115

Ford
Mustang SVT Cobra

2003

Heavily updated is the 2003 SVT Mustang Cobra, which makes 390 horsepower and 390 pound-feet of torque thanks to the addition of an Eaton supercharger. A new six-speed manual transmission drives the rear wheels through a 3.55 rear axle ratio. Larger wheels and tires come standard, along with stiffer springs and a tubular strut tower brace. Cobra convertibles have a cloth top, while both cars get new seats with upgraded leather and suede upholstery.

Body Styles	TMV Pricing		
	Trade	Private	Dealer
2 Dr 10th Anniv S/C Conv	27611	29303	32123
2 Dr 10th Anniv S/C Cpe	24604	26112	28625

Options	Price
17 Inch Wheels - Chrome	+448

Mileage Category: E

Body Styles	TMV Pricing		
	Trade	Private	Dealer
2 Dr S/C Conv	26616	28247	30966
2 Dr S/C Cpe	23554	24997	27403

2001

Mileage Category: E

After a one-year hiatus, the Ford SVT Mustang Cobra returns to the Mustang stable.

Body Styles	TMV Pricing		
	Trade	Private	Dealer
2 Dr STD Conv	16808	19075	21167

Body Styles	TMV Pricing		
	Trade	Private	Dealer
2 Dr STD Cpe	14785	16779	18619

1999

Mileage Category: E

A new SVT Cobra debuts, boasting 320 ponies, an independent rear suspension and the fresh but controversial styling that all Mustangs received this year.

Body Styles		TMV Pricing		
		Trade	Private	Dealer
2 Dr STD Conv		11617	13756	15983
2 Dr STD Cpe		9988	11827	13741

Options	Price
Leather Seats	+220

1998

Body Styles		TMV Pricing		
		Trade	Private	Dealer
2 Dr STD Conv		9016	10959	13149
2 Dr STD Cpe		7818	9502	11402

Options	Price
AM/FM/Cassette Audio System	+125
Leather Seats	+180

Mileage Category: E

The Cobra sees virtually no changes as a heavily revamped version is due next year.

1997

Body Styles	TMV Pricing		
	Trade	Private	Dealer
2 Dr STD Conv	7847	9651	11856

Options	Price
AM/FM/Cassette/CD Audio System	+116

Body Styles	TMV Pricing		
	Trade	Private	Dealer
2 Dr STD Cpe	6740	8289	10183

Options	Price
Leather Seats	+147

Mileage Category: E

After last year's significant underhood upgrade, the SVT folks saw no reason to make changes to the Cobra for this year.

1996

Body Styles	TMV Pricing		
	Trade	Private	Dealer
2 Dr STD Conv	6573	8193	10429

Options	Price
Leather Seats	+148

Body Styles	TMV Pricing		
	Trade	Private	Dealer
2 Dr STD Cpe	5918	7376	9390

Options	Price
Special Factory Paint	+420

Mileage Category: E

Ford's most potent pony gets a 32-valve, 305-horsepower version of the Mustang's new 4.6-liter V8. The Cobra also receives the subtle styling tweaks, such as the vertically themed taillights, that its stablemates received this year.

1995

Body Styles	TMV Pricing		
	Trade	Private	Dealer
2 Dr R Cpe	6540	8193	10948
2 Dr STD Conv	5412	6780	9060

Options	Price
Air Conditioning	+202
AM/FM/Cassette/CD Audio System	+89

Body Styles	TMV Pricing		
	Trade	Private	Dealer
2 Dr STD Cpe	4575	5731	7658

Options	Price
Automatic 4-Speed Transmission	+184
Leather Seats	+135

Mileage Category: E

No changes for this year.

1994

Body Styles	TMV Pricing		
	Trade	Private	Dealer
2 Dr STD Conv	4091	5510	7875

Options	Price
Air Conditioning	+171
AM/FM/Cassette/CD Audio System	+76

Body Styles	TMV Pricing		
	Trade	Private	Dealer
2 Dr STD Cpe	3502	4716	6739

Options	Price
Leather Seats	+115

Mileage Category: E

Like the other Mustangs, the Cobra was redesigned this year and sports 235 horsepower, the most in the Mustang stable.

Ford
Probe

1997

Body Styles	TMV Pricing		
	Trade	Private	Dealer
2 Dr GT Hbk	2963	3789	4798

Options	Price
Air Conditioning	+262
Aluminum/Alloy Wheels [Opt on STD]	+138
AM/FM/CD Audio System	+126
Antilock Brakes	+222

Body Styles	TMV Pricing		
	Trade	Private	Dealer
2 Dr STD Hbk	2496	3192	4042

Options	Price
Automatic 4-Speed Transmission	+262
Leather Seats	+147
Power Sunroof	+181

Mileage Category: E

Ford adds a GTS Sport Appearance Package to the GT's option sheet. The package includes a rear spoiler, racing stripes and 16-inch chrome wheels.

1996

Body Styles	TMV Pricing		
	Trade	Private	Dealer
2 Dr GT Hbk	2238	2856	3710
2 Dr SE Hbk	1935	2470	3208
2 Dr STD Hbk	1820	2323	3017

Mileage Category: E

Ford concentrates on the SE and GT trim levels this year, revising and simplifying options lists and making minor cosmetic and trim revisions.

1996 (cont'd)

Options	Price
Leather Seats	+130
Power Sunroof	+161
Air Conditioning	+234

Options	Price
Aluminum/Alloy Wheels	+139
Antilock Brakes	+197
Automatic 4-Speed Transmission	+213

1995

Mileage Category: E

Base and GT models receive new taillights. GTs receive 16-inch directional wheels. The rear-window wiper washer, four-way seat-height adjuster and graphic equalizer have been deleted from the options list.

Body Styles	TMV Pricing		
	Trade	Private	Dealer
2 Dr GT Hbk	1705	2216	3068
2 Dr SE Hbk	1499	1949	2698

Body Styles	TMV Pricing		
	Trade	Private	Dealer
2 Dr STD Hbk	1434	1863	2579

Options	Price
Leather Seats	+113
Power Sunroof	+139
Air Conditioning [Std on SE]	+202
Aluminum/Alloy Wheels	+106
AM/FM/Cassette/CD Audio System	+124

Options	Price
AM/FM/CD Audio System	+97
Antilock Brakes	+170
Automatic 4-Speed Transmission	+184
Chrome Wheels	+88

1994

Mileage Category: E

Dual airbags are now standard on all Probes. A Sport Appearance Package is available for base models.

Body Styles	TMV Pricing		
	Trade	Private	Dealer
2 Dr GT Hbk	1283	1845	2781
2 Dr SE Hbk	1053	1514	2282

Body Styles	TMV Pricing		
	Trade	Private	Dealer
2 Dr STD Hbk	994	1429	2154

Options	Price
Air Conditioning	+171
Aluminum/Alloy Wheels	+90
AM/FM/CD Audio System	+82
Antilock Brakes	+144

Options	Price
Automatic 4-Speed Transmission	+156
Leather Seats	+95
Power Sunroof	+118

Ford

Ranger

2003

Mileage Category: J

Ford's popular compact pickup receives a number of minor changes for 2003. The 2002 Tremor package, with its ear-splitting 485-watt sound system, returns for 2003 as a trim level, joining XL, Edge and XLT in the lineup. A chrome appearance package for select XLT models is available, and last year's FX4 package for four-wheel-drive Rangers is offered in two guises: Off Road and Level II. New Sonic Blue paint is unique to FX4 Level II Rangers. Other changes include covered visor vanity mirrors for XLT models, standard step bars on XLT 4WD SuperCab and Edge 4WD models and minor interior trim and fabric revisions on some models. Finally, crew cab rear seats get LATCH anchors, and some new colors are available.

Body Styles	TMV Pricing		
	Trade	Private	Dealer
2 Dr Edge Ext Cab SB	10278	11276	12940
2 Dr Edge Plus 4WD Std Cab SB	11486	12601	14460
2 Dr Edge Std Cab SB	8815	9671	11097
2 Dr Tremor Ext Cab SB	11190	12276	14087
2 Dr XL 4WD Ext Cab SB	11779	12920	14822
2 Dr XL 4WD Std Cab LB	11677	12810	14699
2 Dr XL Ext Cab SB	9950	10916	12527
2 Dr XL Std Cab LB	8398	9213	10572
2 Dr XL Std Cab SB	7848	8610	9880
2 Dr XLT 4WD Ext Cab SB	12114	13290	15250
2 Dr XLT Ext Cab SB	10097	11078	12712

Body Styles	TMV Pricing		
	Trade	Private	Dealer
2 Dr XLT Std Cab LB	10018	10991	12612
2 Dr XLT Std Cab SB	8515	9342	10720
4 Dr Edge 4WD Ext Cab SB	12553	13772	15803
4 Dr Edge Plus Ext Cab SB	11850	13001	14918
4 Dr Tremor Plus Ext Cab SB	12303	13498	15489
4 Dr XL 4WD Ext Cab SB	12801	14044	16115
4 Dr XL Ext Cab SB	10662	11697	13422
4 Dr XLT 4WD Ext Cab SB	13030	14295	16404
4 Dr XLT Ext Cab	11832	12981	14896
4 Dr XLT FX4 4WD Ext Cab SB	14623	16043	18409

Options	Price
Air Conditioning	+419
Aluminum/Alloy Wheels [Opt on EDGE]	+145
AM/FM/CD Audio System [Opt on XL]	+177
Automatic 5-Speed Transmission [Std on Tremor]	+645
Bucket Seats [Opt on XLT FX4]	+161
Chrome Wheels [Opt on XLT]	+148
Compact Disc Changer [Opt on XLT]	+190
Cruise Control	+119
Limited Slip Differential	+190

Options	Price
Power Windows	+139
Side Steps	+190
Sport Seats [Opt on EDGE,XLT]	+129
Stepside Bed	+319
AM/FM/CD Changer Audio System [Opt on EDGE]	+210
3.0L V6 Flex Fuel OHV 12V FI Engine [Opt on XLT]	+252
3.0L V6 OHV 12V FI Engine [Opt on XL,XLT]	+252
4.0L V6 SOHC 12V FI Engine [Opt on EDGE,XL,XLT]	+116

2002

Mileage Category: J

A new FX4 model debuts, designed to appeal to Ranger XLT Extended Cab buyers who need to do some serious off-roading. Among the hardware goodies are a limited-slip differential, 31-inch BFGoodrich all-terrain tires, special 15-inch alloy wheels, tow hooks, skid plates, Bilstein shocks, special exterior trim and sport seats. All Rangers get a SecuriLock antitheft system, while XLT and Edge 4WD models have a new 16-inch wheel design. An MP3 player is newly optional, and models equipped with a 3.0-liter V6 get improved fuel economy.

Body Styles	TMV Pricing		
	Trade	Private	Dealer
2 Dr Edge Ext Cab SB	8642	9568	11110
2 Dr Edge Plus 4WD Std Cab SB	9634	10666	12386
2 Dr Edge Std Cab SB	7450	8248	9579
2 Dr Tremor Ext Cab SB	9442	10454	12140
2 Dr XL 4WD Ext Cab SB	9781	10829	12576
2 Dr XL 4WD Std Cab LB	9613	10643	12360
2 Dr XL Ext Cab SB	8142	9014	10468
2 Dr XL Std Cab LB	7173	7941	9222
2 Dr XL Std Cab SB	6592	7299	8477

Body Styles	TMV Pricing		
	Trade	Private	Dealer
2 Dr XLT 4WD Ext Cab SB	10326	11433	13277
2 Dr XLT Ext Cab SB	8431	9335	10841
2 Dr XLT Std Cab LB	8516	9416	10916
2 Dr XLT Std Cab SB	7287	8068	9369
4 Dr Edge 4WD Ext Cab SB	10588	11722	13612
4 Dr Edge Plus 4WD Ext Cab SB	11881	13154	15275
4 Dr Edge Plus Ext Cab SB	9857	10913	12673
4 Dr XLT FX4 4WD Ext Cab SB	12610	13962	16214

Options	Price
3.0L V6 OHV 12V FI Engine [Opt on 2WD - XL,XLT]	+230
Air Conditioning	+383
Aluminum/Alloy Wheels [Opt on Edge 2WD]	+132
AM/FM/CD Audio System [Opt on XL]	+162
AM/FM/CD Changer Audio System [Opt on Edge,XLT]	+174
Appearance Package [Opt on XLT Ext Cab]	+356
Automatic 5-Speed Transmission [Opt on Edge,Edge Plus,XL,XLT]	+589
Chrome Wheels [Opt on XLT]	+191

Options	Price
Hinged Fourth Door [Opt on 2 Dr Ext Cab]	+391
Limited Slip Differential [Std on FX4]	+174
Off-Road Suspension Package [Opt on XLT]	+983
Power Windows [Std on Edge,Edge Plus,Tremor,XLT]	+115
Running Boards	+174
Sport Seats [Opt on Edge,Edge Plus,XLT Ext Cab]	+118
Stepside Bed	+291

2001

Mileage Category: J

Most notable for the '01 Ranger is the availability of the Explorer's 207-horsepower, 4.0-liter SOHC V6. In other engine news, the flexible-fuel feature on the 3.0-liter V6 has been dropped and there is a new base 2.3-liter four-cylinder. ABS is now standard on all models. A new Edge trim level has a monochromatic appearance, which includes color-keyed bumpers and wheel lip moldings. Exterior changes are numerous. All models get a new grille, bumpers and headlamps, while the XLT 4x4 and Edge get a new hood and wheel lip moldings. Four colors are new as well as an optional in-dash six-disc CD changer.

Body Styles	TMV Pricing		
	Trade	Private	Dealer
2 Dr Edge Ext Cab SB	7171	8416	9566
2 Dr Edge Plus 4WD Std Cab SB	8287	9726	11054
2 Dr Edge Plus 4WD Std Cab Step SB	8590	10082	11459
2 Dr Edge Plus Ext Cab SB	7899	9271	10538
2 Dr Edge Plus Ext Cab Step SB	8092	9497	10794
2 Dr Edge Plus Std Cab Step SB	6713	7878	8954
2 Dr Edge Std Cab SB	6191	7267	8260
2 Dr XL Ext Cab SB	6811	7994	9086
2 Dr XL Std Cab LB	5485	6438	7317
2 Dr XL Std Cab SB	5090	5975	6791

Body Styles	TMV Pricing		
	Trade	Private	Dealer
2 Dr XLT Ext Cab SB	6980	8192	9311
2 Dr XLT Ext Cab Step SB	8703	10215	11610
2 Dr XLT Std Cab LB	6861	8053	9154
2 Dr XLT Std Cab SB	5878	6899	7842
2 Dr XLT Std Cab Step SB	6074	7129	8103
4 Dr Edge 4WD Ext Cab SB	8572	10061	11435
4 Dr Edge Plus 4WD Ext Cab SB	9821	11527	13101
4 Dr Edge Plus 4WD Ext Cab Step SB	9997	11733	13335
4 Dr XLT 4WD Ext Cab SB	9076	10652	12107
4 Dr XLT 4WD Ext Cab Step SB	9361	10987	12487

Options	Price
4.0L V6 SOHC 12V FI Engine	+290
Air Conditioning	+342
AM/FM/CD Audio System [Opt on XL]	+126
Appearance Package [Opt on XLT]	+171
Automatic 4-Speed Transmission	+527
Automatic 5-Speed Transmission	+527

Options	Price
Hinged Fourth Door	+350
Limited Slip Differential	+155
Off-Road Suspension Package [Opt on XLT]	+387
Power Door Locks	+126
Power Windows	+145
Running Boards [Opt on Edge,Edge Plus]	+155

2000

Mileage Category: J

For 2000, the 2WD can be had with a "Trailhead" off-road style suspension package complete with larger tires and wheels, giving it the tough look of its 4WD cousin. All Ranger models have new wheel designs, and the XLT 4WD Off-Road Group receives a stainless-steel front-suspension skid plate.

Body Styles	TMV Pricing		
	Trade	Private	Dealer
2 Dr XL 4WD Ext Cab SB	6079	7302	8501
2 Dr XL 4WD Std Cab LB	5699	6846	7970
2 Dr XL 4WD Std Cab SB	5559	6677	7773
2 Dr XL Ext Cab SB	5226	6278	7310
2 Dr XL Ext Cab Step SB	5224	6275	7305
2 Dr XL Std Cab LB	4179	5020	5845
2 Dr XL Std Cab SB	4036	4849	5645
2 Dr XL Std Cab Step SB	4140	4973	5789
2 Dr XLT 4WD Ext Cab SB	6887	8273	9631

Body Styles	TMV Pricing		
	Trade	Private	Dealer
2 Dr XLT 4WD Ext Cab Step SB	6839	8215	9564
2 Dr XLT 4WD Std Cab LB	6469	7770	9046
2 Dr XLT 4WD Std Cab SB	6318	7589	8835
2 Dr XLT 4WD Std Cab Step SB	6450	7748	9021
2 Dr XLT Ext Cab SB	5517	6627	7716
2 Dr XLT Ext Cab Step SB	5509	6617	7704
2 Dr XLT Std Cab LB	4941	5935	6910
2 Dr XLT Std Cab SB	4751	5706	6643
2 Dr XLT Std Cab Step SB	4892	5876	6841

Ford
Ranger

2000 (cont'd)

Options	Price
Power Windows	+130
Split Front Bench Seat [Opt on XL]	+137
3.0L V6 Flex Fuel OHV 12V FI Engine [Opt on XL,XLT]	+186
4.0L V6 OHV 12V FI Engine	+328
Air Conditioning	+379
Aluminum/Alloy Wheels	+118
AM/FM/Cassette/CD Audio System	+137

Options	Price
Antilock Brakes	+320
Automatic 4-Speed Transmission	+516
Automatic 5-Speed Transmission	+540
Bucket Seats	+170
Compact Disc Changer	+236
Hinged Fourth Door	+271
Limited Slip Differential	+162

1999

Mileage Category: J

This year's changes include standard 15-inch silver styled wheels, a class III frame-mounted hitch receiver for V6 applications, and a spare tire access lock. All models get dual front cupholders and Dark Graphite has been added to the interior colors options list while Willow Green and Denim Blue have been removed as interior choices. The "Splash" model has been discontinued. A 3.0-liter V6 flexible fuel engine is available that is designed specifically for ethanol/gasoline fuel blends.

Body Styles	TMV Pricing		
	Trade	Private	Dealer
2 Dr XL 4WD Ext Cab SB	5312	6476	7688
2 Dr XL 4WD Ext Cab Step SB	5447	6642	7885
2 Dr XL 4WD Std Cab LB	4864	5930	7040
2 Dr XL 4WD Std Cab SB	4676	5701	6768
2 Dr XL 4WD Std Cab Step SB	4807	5861	6958
2 Dr XL Ext Cab SB	4553	5551	6589
2 Dr XL Ext Cab Step SB	4692	5721	6791
2 Dr XL Std Cab LB	3649	4449	5281
2 Dr XL Std Cab SB	3475	4236	5029
2 Dr XL Std Cab Step SB	3644	4443	5275

Body Styles	TMV Pricing		
	Trade	Private	Dealer
2 Dr XLT 4WD Ext Cab SB	5938	7240	8596
2 Dr XLT 4WD Ext Cab Step SB	6077	7410	8797
2 Dr XLT 4WD Std Cab LB	5604	6832	8110
2 Dr XLT 4WD Std Cab SB	5431	6622	7861
2 Dr XLT 4WD Std Cab Step SB	5566	6787	8058
2 Dr XLT Ext Cab SB	4760	5804	6891
2 Dr XLT Ext Cab Step SB	4947	6031	7160
2 Dr XLT Std Cab LB	4313	5258	6242
2 Dr XLT Std Cab SB	4154	5065	6013
2 Dr XLT Std Cab Step SB	4323	5271	6258

Options	Price
3.0L V6 OHV 12V FI Engine [Std on 4WD]	+202
4.0L V6 OHV 12V FI Engine	+262
Air Conditioning	+312
Antilock Brakes [Std on XLT 4WD]	+293
Automatic 4-Speed Transmission	+426

Options	Price
Automatic 5-Speed Transmission	+439
Bucket Seats	+140
Compact Disc Changer	+194
Hinged Fourth Door [Opt on XLT]	+300

1998

Mileage Category: J

The Ranger gets new sheet metal, a new grille and revised headlamps. The wheelbase on regular cab models has been stretched to provide more cabin room and the displacement of the base engine has been increased. A short- and long-arm (SLA) suspension replaces the Twin-I-Beam suspension found on last year's models. A four-door Ranger join the lineup midyear.

Body Styles	TMV Pricing		
	Trade	Private	Dealer
2 Dr Splash 4WD Ext Cab Step SB	5465	6785	8274
2 Dr Splash 4WD Std Cab Step SB	5046	6265	7639
2 Dr Splash Ext Cab Step SB	4635	5754	7016
2 Dr Splash Std Cab Step SB	4099	5089	6206
2 Dr XL 4WD Ext Cab SB	4815	5977	7288
2 Dr XL 4WD Ext Cab Step SB	4936	6128	7472
2 Dr XL 4WD Std Cab LB	4365	5418	6606
2 Dr XL 4WD Std Cab SB	4233	5256	6409
2 Dr XL 4WD Std Cab Step SB	4354	5406	6592
2 Dr XL Ext Cab SB	4024	4995	6091
2 Dr XL Ext Cab Step SB	4109	5101	6220
2 Dr XL Std Cab LB	3218	3995	4872

Body Styles	TMV Pricing		
	Trade	Private	Dealer
2 Dr XL Std Cab SB	2867	3559	4340
2 Dr XL Std Cab Step SB	3205	3979	4852
2 Dr XLT 4WD Ext Cab SB	5057	6278	7655
2 Dr XLT 4WD Ext Cab Step SB	5200	6456	7873
2 Dr XLT 4WD Std Cab LB	4987	6192	7550
2 Dr XLT 4WD Std Cab SB	4837	6005	7322
2 Dr XLT 4WD Std Cab Step SB	4958	6155	7505
2 Dr XLT Ext Cab SB	4131	5129	6254
2 Dr XLT Ext Cab Step SB	4298	5335	6505
2 Dr XLT Std Cab LB	3698	4591	5598
2 Dr XLT Std Cab SB	3523	4374	5333
2 Dr XLT Std Cab Step SB	3673	4560	5560

Options	Price
3.0L V6 OHV 12V FI Engine [Std on 4WD,Splash 2WD Ext Cab]	+143
4.0L V6 OHV 12V FI Engine	+214
Air Conditioning	+255
Antilock Brakes	+240

Options	Price
Automatic 4-Speed Transmission	+347
Automatic 5-Speed Transmission	+351
Compact Disc Changer	+159

Ranger

Body Styles	TMV Pricing		
	Trade	Private	Dealer
2 Dr STX 4WD Ext Cab SB	4552	5733	7176
2 Dr STX 4WD Std Cab LB	4421	5569	6971
2 Dr STX 4WD Std Cab SB	4285	5397	6755
2 Dr Splash 4WD Ext Cab Step SB	4787	6029	7547
2 Dr Splash 4WD Std Cab Step SB	4568	5753	7201
2 Dr Splash Ext Cab Step SB	3898	4910	6146
2 Dr Splash Std Cab Step SB	3476	4378	5481
2 Dr XL 4WD Ext Cab SB	4245	5347	6693
2 Dr XL 4WD Ext Cab Step SB	4354	5484	6864
2 Dr XL 4WD Std Cab LB	3981	5014	6277
2 Dr XL 4WD Std Cab SB	3822	4814	6027
2 Dr XL 4WD Std Cab Step SB	3981	5014	6277
2 Dr XL Ext Cab SB	3356	4227	5291
2 Dr XL Ext Cab Step SB	3492	4397	5504

Body Styles	TMV Pricing		
	Trade	Private	Dealer
2 Dr XL Std Cab LB	2646	3333	4173
2 Dr XL Std Cab SB	2392	3013	3771
2 Dr XL Std Cab Step SB	2695	3394	4248
2 Dr XLT 4WD Ext Cab SB	4572	5758	7207
2 Dr XLT 4WD Ext Cab Step SB	4676	5889	7372
2 Dr XLT 4WD Std Cab LB	4365	5497	6881
2 Dr XLT 4WD Std Cab SB	4228	5325	6666
2 Dr XLT 4WD Std Cab Step SB	4334	5458	6832
2 Dr XLT Ext Cab SB	3493	4399	5506
2 Dr XLT Ext Cab Step SB	3597	4530	5670
2 Dr XLT Std Cab LB	3077	3875	4851
2 Dr XLT Std Cab SB	2958	3726	4664
2 Dr XLT Std Cab Step SB	3061	3855	4825

Options	Price
Dual Front Airbag Restraints	+118
3.0L V6 OHV 12V FI Engine	+197
Air Conditioning	+236
Antilock Brakes	+222

Options	Price
Automatic 4-Speed Transmission	+314
Automatic 5-Speed Transmission	+345
Compact Disc Changer	+132

Mileage Category: J

Ford introduces its brand-new five-speed automatic transmission to the Ranger lineup. Available with the V6 engines, the five-speed automatic is designed to improve the Ranger's acceleration, towing and hill-climbing ability.

Body Styles	TMV Pricing		
	Trade	Private	Dealer
2 Dr STX 4WD Ext Cab SB	3843	4888	6332
2 Dr STX 4WD Std Cab LB	3721	4734	6132
2 Dr STX 4WD Std Cab SB	3605	4586	5941
2 Dr Splash 4WD Ext Cab Step SB	4049	5150	6671
2 Dr Splash 4WD Std Cab Step SB	3848	4895	6341
2 Dr Splash Ext Cab Step SB	3128	3979	5154
2 Dr Splash Std Cab Step SB	2808	3572	4626
2 Dr XL 4WD Ext Cab SB	3583	4557	5903
2 Dr XL 4WD Ext Cab Step SB	3675	4674	6054
2 Dr XL 4WD Std Cab LB	3303	4202	5444
2 Dr XL 4WD Std Cab SB	3165	4026	5216
2 Dr XL 4WD Std Cab Step SB	3300	4197	5436
2 Dr XL Ext Cab SB	2715	3453	4473
2 Dr XL Ext Cab Step SB	2829	3599	4662

Body Styles	TMV Pricing		
	Trade	Private	Dealer
2 Dr XL Std Cab LB	2122	2700	3498
2 Dr XL Std Cab SB	2009	2555	3310
2 Dr XL Std Cab Step SB	2183	2777	3597
2 Dr XLT 4WD Ext Cab SB	3874	4928	6383
2 Dr XLT 4WD Ext Cab Step SB	3943	5016	6497
2 Dr XLT 4WD Std Cab LB	3629	4616	5979
2 Dr XLT 4WD Std Cab SB	3514	4469	5788
2 Dr XLT 4WD Std Cab Step SB	3594	4571	5920
2 Dr XLT Ext Cab SB	2809	3573	4628
2 Dr XLT Ext Cab Step SB	2897	3685	4772
2 Dr XLT Std Cab LB	2486	3162	4095
2 Dr XLT Std Cab SB	2364	3007	3896
2 Dr XLT Std Cab Step SB	2445	3110	4029

Options	Price
3.0L V6 OHV 12V FI Engine	+174
Air Conditioning	+210
Antilock Brakes [Opt on 2WD]	+197

Options	Price
Automatic 4-Speed Transmission	+272
Compact Disc Changer	+117

Mileage Category: J

An optional passenger-side airbag is available, and it comes with a switch that will disable the system if a child seat is installed in the truck. Super Cab models get standard privacy glass, Splash models lose that putrid green tape stripe, and the Flareside box from the Splash is now available on two-wheel-drive, four-cylinder XL and XLT models.

Body Styles	TMV Pricing		
	Trade	Private	Dealer
2 Dr STX 4WD Ext Cab SB	3203	4120	5647
2 Dr STX 4WD Std Cab LB	3165	4071	5580
2 Dr STX 4WD Std Cab SB	3046	3918	5371
2 Dr Splash 4WD Ext Cab Step SB	3399	4371	5992
2 Dr Splash 4WD Std Cab Step SB	3240	4167	5711
2 Dr Splash Ext Cab Step SB	2579	3317	4546
2 Dr Splash Std Cab Step SB	2270	2919	4001
2 Dr XL 4WD Ext Cab SB	2983	3837	5259
2 Dr XL 4WD Std Cab LB	2773	3567	4889
2 Dr XL 4WD Std Cab SB	2617	3366	4614

Body Styles	TMV Pricing		
	Trade	Private	Dealer
2 Dr XL Ext Cab SB	2149	2764	3788
2 Dr XL Std Cab LB	1826	2349	3220
2 Dr XL Std Cab SB	1737	2234	3063
2 Dr XLT 4WD Ext Cab SB	3243	4171	5718
2 Dr XLT 4WD Std Cab LB	3085	3968	5439
2 Dr XLT 4WD Std Cab SB	2954	3799	5208
2 Dr XLT Ext Cab SB	2263	2910	3989
2 Dr XLT Std Cab LB	2109	2712	3718
2 Dr XLT Std Cab SB	1994	2564	3514
2 Dr XLT Std Cab Step SB	2070	2663	3650

Mileage Category: J

A driver airbag and optional four-wheel antilock brakes are two of the features added to the safety equipment roster of the capable Ford Ranger. SuperCab models can now be had with a power driver seat.

1995 (cont'd)

Options	Price		Options	Price
3.0L V6 OHV 12V FI Engine	+101		Bucket Seats	+81
Air Conditioning	+182		Compact Disc Changer	+101
Antilock Brakes [Opt on XL,XLT]	+170		Sport Seats	+81
Automatic 4-Speed Transmission	+236			

1994

Mileage Category: J

Side-impact door beams are installed on the Ranger to protect occupants. The Splash model is now available as a SuperCab.

Body Styles	TMV Pricing			Body Styles	TMV Pricing		
	Trade	Private	Dealer		Trade	Private	Dealer
2 Dr STX 4WD Ext Cab SB	2566	3493	5039	2 Dr XL 4WD Std Cab LB	2159	2939	4240
2 Dr STX 4WD Std Cab LB	2632	3583	5168	2 Dr XL 4WD Std Cab SB	2019	2748	3964
2 Dr STX 4WD Std Cab SB	2489	3388	4887	2 Dr XL Ext Cab SB	1722	2344	3381
2 Dr STX Ext Cab SB	2023	2754	3971	2 Dr XL Std Cab LB	1495	2035	2935
2 Dr STX Std Cab LB	1905	2594	3741	2 Dr XL Std Cab SB	1417	1929	2782
2 Dr STX Std Cab SB	1804	2456	3543	2 Dr XLT 4WD Ext Cab SB	2562	3488	5030
2 Dr Splash 4WD Ext Cab Step SB	2813	3830	5524	2 Dr XLT 4WD Std Cab LB	2453	3340	4817
2 Dr Splash 4WD Std Cab Step SB	2662	3624	5227	2 Dr XLT 4WD Std Cab SB	2346	3193	4605
2 Dr Splash Cab Step SB	2102	2861	4127	2 Dr XLT Ext Cab SB	1840	2505	3613
2 Dr Splash Std Cab Step SB	1823	2482	3580	2 Dr XLT Std Cab LB	1731	2357	3400
2 Dr XL 4WD Ext Cab SB	2344	3191	4602	2 Dr XLT Std Cab SB	1615	2199	3171

Options	Price		Options	Price
Split Front Bench Seat	+128		Air Conditioning	+153
3.0L V6 OHV 12V FI Engine	+86		Automatic 4-Speed Transmission	+199

Ford
Taurus

2003

Mileage Category: D

New for 2003, the SEL trim level offers a unique instrument cluster with a satin-finish background, as well as Imola leather trimmed seats and dark wood trim. You can now get a real wood- and leather-trimmed steering wheel, and you'll want to note that power windows and locks, as well as tilt steering and floor mats, are standard on all models.

Body Styles	TMV Pricing			Body Styles	TMV Pricing		
	Trade	Private	Dealer		Trade	Private	Dealer
4 Dr LX Sdn	8477	9355	10817	4 Dr SEL Sdn	11281	12449	14395
4 Dr SE Sdn	8758	9665	11176	4 Dr SEL Wgn	11811	13034	15071
4 Dr SE Wgn	9602	10596	12252	4 Dr SES Sdn	9507	10491	12131

Options	Price		Options	Price
AM/FM/Cassette Audio System [Opt on LX]	+119		Rear Spoiler [Opt on SE,SEL,SES]	+148
Antilock Brakes [Opt on LX,SE]	+439		Front Side Airbag Restraints [Opt on SE,SEL,SES]	+252
Compact Disc Changer [Opt on SEL,SES]	+119		Special Leather Seat Trim [Opt on SEL]	+610
Cruise Control [Opt on LX]	+119		Premium Audio System [Opt on SES,SEL]	+223
Leather Seats [Opt on SES,SEL]	+577		AM/FM/CD Changer Audio System [Opt on SE]	+168
Power Driver Seat [Opt on LX,SE]	+155		MACH Audio System [Opt on SES,SEL]	+171
Power Moonroof [Opt on SES,SEL]	+577		3.0L V6 DOHC 24V FI Engine [Opt on SE,SEL,SES]	+306

2002

Mileage Category: D

Floor mats become standard on all Taurus models, and the base V6 benefits from improved fuel economy. All but the base LX get security approach lamps, while LX and SE come standard with six-passenger seating. A slew of no-charge options are available on various Taurus models for 2002: SE gets a free power driver seat and CD player; SES comes with free leather or a moonroof (regionally available); SEL adds leather or moonroof, or both (regionally available). SEL also has standard adjustable pedals for 2002. A new SEL Wagon debuts. A new SEL premium package includes a Mach audio system, side airbags and traction control. Optional on SES and SEL is a new Luxury and Convenience group, which provides an auto-dimming rearview mirror with compass and heated side mirrors. Four new colors round out the list of changes.

Body Styles	TMV Pricing			Body Styles	TMV Pricing		
	Trade	Private	Dealer		Trade	Private	Dealer
4 Dr LX Sdn	6527	7317	8633	4 Dr SEL Sdn	9583	10743	12675
4 Dr SE Sdn	7008	7856	9270	4 Dr SEL Wgn	9689	10862	12817
4 Dr SE Wgn	7490	8396	9907	4 Dr SES Sdn	7321	8171	9587

Options	Price		Options	Price
3.0L V6 DOHC 24V FI Engine [Opt on SE Wgn,SES]	+409		MACH Audio System [Opt on SEL Wgn]	+188
Antilock Brakes [Opt on LX,SE Sdn]	+400		Power Driver Seat [Opt on SE Sdn]	+141
Compact Disc Changer [Opt on SEL Wgn]	+124		Power Moonroof [Opt on Sdn - SE,SEL]	+412
Front Side Airbag Restraints	+147		Power Passenger Seat [Opt on SEL Sdn]	+141
Leather Seats [Std on SEL Wgn]	+265			

Taurus

Body Styles	TMV Pricing		
	Trade	Private	Dealer
4 Dr LX Sdn	5485	6595	7620
4 Dr SE Sdn	5532	6653	7688
4 Dr SE Wgn	6055	7281	8413

Options	Price
Antilock Brakes [Opt on LX,SE]	+358
Front Side Airbag Restraints	+205
Leather Seats [Opt on LX]	+472
Power Driver Seat [Opt on LX,SE]	+184

Body Styles	TMV Pricing		
	Trade	Private	Dealer
4 Dr SEL Sdn	6418	7719	8919
4 Dr SES Sdn	6012	7230	8354

Options	Price
Power Moonroof	+469
Power Passenger Seat	+184
Premium Audio System	+169
Rear Spoiler	+121

Mileage Category: D

After the 2000 redesign, updates are minor. A Lower Anchor and Tether for Children (LATCH) is now standard on all models. LATCH is an anchoring system for child safety seats. Also new is Spruce Green Clearcoat Metallic, an increase in fuel tank capacity to 18 gallons, a six-disc CD changer is standard on SES models, power locks are standard on LX and an optional rear spoiler can give your Taurus that extra bit of attitude.

Body Styles	TMV Pricing		
	Trade	Private	Dealer
4 Dr LX Sdn	4408	5384	6340
4 Dr SE Sdn	4720	5765	6789
4 Dr SE Wgn	5033	6147	7239

Options	Price
3.0L V6 DOHC 24V FI Engine	+328
3.0L V6 Flex Fuel OHV 12V FI Engine	+549
Aluminum/Alloy Wheels [Opt on LX]	+148
Antilock Brakes [Opt on LX,SE]	+320
Compact Disc Changer	+165
Front Side Airbag Restraints	+184

Body Styles	TMV Pricing		
	Trade	Private	Dealer
4 Dr SEL Sdn	5263	6429	7571
4 Dr SES Sdn	4954	6051	7126

Options	Price
Leather Seats [Opt on LX]	+422
Power Door Locks [Opt on LX]	+125
Power Driver Seat [Opt on LX,SE]	+165
Power Moonroof	+349
Power Passenger Seat [Opt on SEL]	+165
Rear Spoiler	+118

Mileage Category: D

Many changes are in store for the 2000 Taurus. Styling is the most obvious, with a new look for both the front and rear. Improved safety comes from a new airbag-deployment system, adjustable pedals, seatbelt pre-tensioners and child safety-seat anchors. The ride has been made more comfortable and the powertrain has been updated for more power and less noise. The V8-powered SHO has been dropped from the lineup.

Body Styles	TMV Pricing		
	Trade	Private	Dealer
4 Dr LX Sdn	3527	4400	5308
4 Dr SE Sdn	3570	4453	5372

Options	Price
3.0L V6 DOHC 24V FI Engine	+193
3.0L V6 Flex Fuel OHV 12V FI Engine	+452
Aluminum/Alloy Wheels	+123
Antilock Brakes [Opt on LX,SE]	+293
Chrome Wheels [Opt on SE]	+193
Compact Disc Changer [Opt on SE]	+136

Body Styles	TMV Pricing		
	Trade	Private	Dealer
4 Dr SE Wgn	3691	4604	5554
4 Dr SHO Sdn	5946	7416	8947

Options	Price
Leather Seats [Opt on SE]	+348
Power Driver Seat	+170
Power Moonroof [Opt on SE]	+288
Power Passenger Seat [Opt on SE]	+170
Spoke Wheels	+225

Mileage Category: D

The light group and speed control are now optional on LX level cars. Chrome wheels on the SE models have been replaced with five-spoke aluminum wheels.

Body Styles	TMV Pricing		
	Trade	Private	Dealer
4 Dr LX Sdn	2751	3552	4455
4 Dr SE Sdn	2784	3594	4507

Options	Price
3.0L V6 DOHC 24V FI Engine [Opt on LX,SE]	+157
3.0L V6 Flex Fuel OHV 12V FI Engine	+369
Antilock Brakes [Std on SHO]	+240
Chrome Wheels [Opt on SE]	+157
Leather Seats	+180

Body Styles	TMV Pricing		
	Trade	Private	Dealer
4 Dr SE Wgn	3063	3955	4960
4 Dr SHO Sdn	4644	5996	7521

Options	Price
Power Driver Seat	+123
Power Moonroof [Opt on SE]	+235
Power Passenger Seat [Opt on SE]	+123
Premium Audio System [Opt on SE]	+127

Mileage Category: D

A mild facelift, revised trim levels and fewer options are the only changes to Ford's midsize sedan.

1997

Mileage Category: D

A few new exterior color choices are added and there are minor changes to a couple of optional equipment packages.

Body Styles	TMV Pricing		
	Trade	Private	Dealer
4 Dr G Sdn	1916	2550	3325
4 Dr GL Sdn	2040	2715	3541
4 Dr GL Wgn	2200	2928	3818

Options	Price
Leather Seats	+291
Power Moonroof	+217
3.0L V6 Flex Fuel OHV 12V FI Engine	+342

Body Styles	TMV Pricing		
	Trade	Private	Dealer
4 Dr LX Sdn	2233	2972	3875
4 Dr LX Wgn	2452	3263	4255
4 Dr SHO Sdn	3644	4850	6324

Options	Price
Antilock Brakes	+222
Chrome Wheels	+145
Compact Disc Changer	+174

1996

Mileage Category: D

All-new Taurus debuts in sedan and wagon format, available in GL, LX and SHO trim levels. New or substantially revised engines and suspensions improve the performance of the Taurus, while several functional innovations make the car easier and more enjoyable to drive.

Body Styles	TMV Pricing		
	Trade	Private	Dealer
4 Dr GL Sdn	1605	2207	3038
4 Dr GL Wgn	1728	2376	3271
4 Dr LX Sdn	1816	2497	3438

Options	Price
Chrome Wheels	+129
Compact Disc Changer	+155
JBL Audio System	+130
Leather Seats [Opt on LX]	+258

Body Styles	TMV Pricing		
	Trade	Private	Dealer
4 Dr LX Wgn	1945	2675	3682
4 Dr SHO Sdn	2992	4115	5666

Options	Price
Antilock Brakes [Std on SHO]	+197
Power Moonroof	+193
3.0L V6 Flex Fuel OHV 12V FI Engine	+304

1995

Mileage Category: D

Sport-edition model is introduced as an SE. The SE includes aluminum wheels, sport bucket seats, air conditioning and a rear defroster. The base engine has been revised to decrease engine noise.

Body Styles	TMV Pricing		
	Trade	Private	Dealer
4 Dr GL Sdn	1001	1474	2263
4 Dr GL Wgn	1047	1542	2367
4 Dr LX Sdn	1061	1563	2400

Options	Price
3.0L V6 Flex Fuel OHV 12V FI Engine	+256
3.8L V6 OHV 12V FI Engine	+125
AM/FM/Cassette/CD Audio System	+94
Antilock Brakes [Std on SHO]	+170
Automatic 4-Speed Transmission [Opt on SHO]	+198

Body Styles	TMV Pricing		
	Trade	Private	Dealer
4 Dr LX Wgn	1154	1700	2610
4 Dr SE Sdn	1041	1533	2354
4 Dr SHO Sdn	1461	2153	3305

Options	Price
JBL Audio System	+113
Leather Seats	+124
Power Driver Seat [Opt on GL]	+77
Power Moonroof	+167

1994

Mileage Category: D

The passenger airbag is finally a standard equipment item. GL models receive 15-inch wheels and all Tauruses get a new steering wheel. Cellular phones are a new option.

Body Styles	TMV Pricing		
	Trade	Private	Dealer
4 Dr GL Sdn	659	1084	1792
4 Dr GL Wgn	724	1191	1969
4 Dr LX Sdn	791	1300	2148

Options	Price
3.0L V6 Flex Fuel OHV 12V FI Engine [Opt on GL]	+153
3.8L V6 OHV 12V FI Engine [Opt on GL,LX]	+106
Air Conditioning [Std on LX,SHO]	+143
AM/FM/Cassette/CD Audio System	+105
Antilock Brakes [Std on SHO]	+144

Body Styles	TMV Pricing		
	Trade	Private	Dealer
4 Dr LX Wgn	812	1336	2208
4 Dr SHO Sdn	966	1589	2626

Options	Price
Automatic 4-Speed Transmission [Opt on SHO]	+124
JBL Audio System	+95
Leather Seats [Std on SHO]	+115
Power Moonroof	+142

Ford
Tempo
1994

Body Styles	TMV Pricing		
	Trade	Private	Dealer
2 Dr GL Cpe	520	885	1493
4 Dr GL Sdn	520	885	1493

Options	Price
3.0L V6 OHV 12V FI Engine	+131
Air Conditioning	+133

Body Styles	TMV Pricing		
	Trade	Private	Dealer
4 Dr LX Sdn	565	962	1623

Options	Price
Automatic 3-Speed Transmission	+105
Driver Side Airbag Restraint	+76

Mileage Category: B

CFC-free air conditioning refrigerant and redesigned seatbelts are the only changes this year. The Tempo is retired after this model year in favor of the new Contour.

Ford
Thunderbird
2003

Body Styles			TMV Pricing		
			Trade	Private	Dealer
2 Dr STD Conv			25834	27328	29819

Options	Price
Hardtop Roof	+1609
Heated Front Seats	+223

Options	Price
17 Inch Wheels - Chrome	+451

Mileage Category: H

Now in its second year, the Thunderbird gains 28 more horsepower and 25 more pound-feet of torque, bringing the totals to 280 and 286, respectively. The bump in power is due to new electronic throttle control and variable cam timing. All-speed traction control comes standard, and heated seats are now available as options. The instrument cluster has been revised, and new exterior and colors brighten up the palette. Finally, a new saddle interior package makes its debut with full saddle-style leather for the seats, steering wheel and shift knob.

2002

Body Styles	TMV Pricing		
	Trade	Private	Dealer
2 Dr Neiman Marcus Edition Conv	31510	33031	35566

Options	Price
17 Inch Wheels - Chrome [Opt on STD]	+412
Hardtop Roof [Opt on STD]	+1472

Body Styles	TMV Pricing		
	Trade	Private	Dealer
2 Dr STD Conv	23230	24351	26220

Options	Price
Traction Control System [Opt on STD]	+177

Mileage Category: H

Following a four-year absence, the Thunderbird nameplate returns on an all-new two-seat roadster platform designed to recall the first-generation '55-'57 T-Birds.

1997

Body Styles			TMV Pricing		
			Trade	Private	Dealer
2 Dr LX Cpe			2443	3252	4241

Options	Price
4.6L V8 SOHC 16V FI Engine	+332
Antilock Brakes	+222
Chrome Wheels	+170

Options	Price
Leather Seats	+161
Power Moonroof	+217
Premium Audio System	+126

Mileage Category: D

The Thunderbird receives few updates this year. A revised center console, a few new colors, and standard four-wheel disc brakes are the big news for 1997.

Ford
Thunderbird/Windstar

1996

Mileage Category: D

Revised styling greatly improves the look of the Thunderbird for 1996. The Super Coupe is deleted, replaced by a Sport Package for the V8 model. Base V6 engines have been upgraded, and go 100,000 miles between tune-ups. Equipment rosters have been shuffled.

Body Styles	TMV Pricing		
	Trade	Private	Dealer
2 Dr LX Cpe	1803	2480	3414

Options	Price	Options	Price
4.6L V8 SOHC 16V FI Engine	+327	Leather Seats	+143
Antilock Brakes	+197	Power Moonroof	+193
Chrome Wheels	+151		

1995

Mileage Category: D

The trunk-mounted CD changer is deleted in favor of an in-dash CD-player. Variable-assist power steering is lost from the standard equipment list.

Body Styles	TMV Pricing		
	Trade	Private	Dealer
2 Dr LX Cpe	1338	1808	2590
2 Dr SC S/C Cpe	2947	3970	5675

Options	Price	Options	Price
4.6L V8 SOHC 16V FI Engine	+255	Leather Seats [Opt on LX]	+124
AM/FM/CD Audio System	+97	Power Moonroof	+167
Antilock Brakes [Opt on LX]	+170	Premium Audio System	+97
Automatic 4-Speed Transmission [Opt on SC]	+147		

1994

Mileage Category: D

Dual airbags make their first appearance on the Thunderbird. An optional 4.6-liter V8 replaces last year's 5.0-liter V8. Dual cupholders complement the center console and the airbags are housed in a restyled dashboard.

Body Styles	TMV Pricing			Body Styles	TMV Pricing		
	Trade	Private	Dealer		Trade	Private	Dealer
2 Dr LX Cpe	877	1316	2048	2 Dr SC S/C Cpe	2143	3197	4953

Options	Price	Options	Price
4.6L V8 SOHC 16V FI Engine	+216	JBL Audio System	+105
Antilock Brakes [Opt on LX]	+144	Leather Seats	+105
Automatic 4-Speed Transmission [Opt on SC]	+124	Power Moonroof	+142
Compact Disc Changer	+115	Premium Audio System	+82

Ford
Windstar

2003

Mileage Category: P

AdvanceTrac stability control system was supposed to be available for 2002, but it was postponed. It makes its appearance for the 2003 model year. The LX base trim level is rechristened to Windstar.

Body Styles	TMV Pricing			Body Styles	TMV Pricing		
	Trade	Private	Dealer		Trade	Private	Dealer
4 Dr LX Pass Van	12336	13598	15700	4 Dr SEL Pass Van	16077	17721	20460
4 Dr Limited Pass Van	18213	20075	23178	4 Dr STD Pass Van	11727	12926	14925
4 Dr SE Pass Van	13662	15059	17387				

Options	Price	Options	Price
Alarm System [Opt on SE,SEL]	+161	Traction Control System [Opt on SE,SEL]	+226
Camper/Towing Package [Opt on SEL]	+287	VCR Entertainment System	+642
Captain Chairs (4) [Opt on LX]	+481	Power Adjustable Foot Pedals [Opt on LX]	+161
Power Driver Seat [Opt on LX]	+171	16 Inch Wheels [Opt on LX]	+190
Power Dual Sliding Doors [Opt on SE]	+580	Air Conditioning - Front and Rear [Opt on STD]	+306
Front Side Airbag Restraints [Std on Limited]	+252	Park Distance Control (Rear) [Opt on SE,SEL]	+193

2002

Mileage Category: P

The biggest news is the availability of the AdvanceTrac stability control system. All Windstars have sliding doors on both sides for 2002. Entry-level LX models get upgraded appearance items, and buyers of this trim can opt for the Autovision entertainment system and 16-inch alloy wheels for the first time. The short-lived SE Sport model is dropped, and SE buyers can no longer have leather seats. Four new colors freshen the outside of the Windstar.

Body Styles	TMV Pricing		
	Trade	Private	Dealer
4 Dr LX Pass Van	10349	11431	13234
4 Dr Limited Pass Van	15210	16781	19399
4 Dr SE Pass Van	12517	13809	15963
4 Dr SEL Pass Van	13781	15222	17624

For the latest vehicle information, visit www.edmunds.com

Options	Price
Air Conditioning - Front and Rear [Opt on LX]	+471
Aluminum/Alloy Wheels [Opt on LX]	+206
Camper/Towing Package [Opt on SEL]	+262
Front Side Airbag Restraints [Std on Limited]	+230
Park Distance Control (Rear) [Opt on SE,SEL]	+177

Options	Price
Power Dual Sliding Doors [Opt on SE]	+530
Tilt Steering Wheel [Opt on LX]	+118
Traction Control System [Std on Limited]	+206
VCR Entertainment System	+586

2001

Body Styles	TMV Pricing		
	Trade	Private	Dealer
3 Dr LX Pass Van	8407	9835	11153
4 Dr LX Pass Van	9362	10953	12421
4 Dr Limited Pass Van	12026	14069	15955

Body Styles	TMV Pricing		
	Trade	Private	Dealer
4 Dr SE Pass Van	10525	12313	13963
4 Dr SE Sport Pass Van	9842	11514	13058
4 Dr SEL Pass Van	10755	12583	14270

Mileage Category: P

There are several model/series changes for Windstar this year, as well as updates to the exterior, interior and powertrain. Ford says a new transmission has improved shift quality and the 3.8-liter V6 is standard on all Windstars. The base model is now called the Windstar LX three-door. The SE Sport is a new trim level and it includes driving lights, painted bumpers and body-side molding, a rear liftgate spoiler, second-row bucket/console seats, a roof rack with brushed aluminum crossbars, black rocker cladding and different wheels and tires.

Options	Price
Air Conditioning - Front and Rear	+263
Aluminum/Alloy Wheels [Opt on LX]	+219
AM/FM/Cassette/CD Audio System [Opt on LX,SE]	+132
Camper/Towing Package [Std on Limited]	+234
Front Side Airbag Restraints [Std on Limited]	+205
Leather Seats [Opt on SE]	+456

Options	Price
Power Driver Seat [Opt on LX]	+171
Power Dual Sliding Doors [Opt on SE]	+474
Power Sliding Door [Opt on LX,SE]	+474
Traction Control System [Std on Limited]	+208
VCR Entertainment System	+524

2000

Body Styles	TMV Pricing		
	Trade	Private	Dealer
3 Dr LX Pass Van	6558	7813	9043
3 Dr STD Pass Van	6146	7322	8474
4 Dr Limited Pass Van	9373	11165	12921

Body Styles	TMV Pricing		
	Trade	Private	Dealer
4 Dr SE Pass Van	7247	8633	9991
4 Dr SEL Pass Van	8560	10198	11803

Mileage Category: P

The Windstar now has standard power-adjustable pedals and an optional rear-seat video entertainment center. There's also a new trim level called the Limited. Available midyear 2000, it will contain more standard features than the previously top-line SEL.

Options	Price
Power Driver Seat [Opt on LX]	+153
Power Dual Sliding Doors [Opt on SE]	+424
Power Sliding Door [Opt on LX,SE]	+236
Sliding Driver Side Door [Opt on LX,STD]	+165
Traction Control System [Opt on LX,SE,SEL]	+186
VCR Entertainment System [Opt on LX,SE,SEL]	+611
3.8L V6 OHV 12V FI Engine [Opt on STD]	+323
Air Conditioning - Front and Rear [Opt on LX]	+224

Options	Price
Aluminum/Alloy Wheels [Opt on LX]	+196
AM/FM/Cassette/CD Audio System [Opt on LX,SE]	+141
Camper/Towing Package [Opt on LX,SE,SEL]	+205
Captain Chairs (4) [Opt on Limited,LX]	+337
Compact Disc Changer [Opt on LX]	+189
Front Side Airbag Restraints [Std on Limited]	+184
Leather Seats [Opt on SE]	+408

1999

Body Styles	TMV Pricing		
	Trade	Private	Dealer
3 Dr LX Pass Van	5557	6776	8045
3 Dr STD Pass Van	4919	5997	7120
4 Dr SE Pass Van	6187	7545	8958
4 Dr SEL Pass Van	6781	8270	9819

Mileage Category: P

This year the Windstar has been totally redesigned. The biggest news for '99, in addition to the completely new exterior and interior styling, is a left-hand sliding door. The second- and third-row seats are now on rollers for easier removal/interchangeability and the instrument panel has been redesigned for improved ergonomics. There's also a more powerful and cleaner-burning 3.8-liter V6 plus upgraded suspension, transmission, brakes and air conditioning components. New options include side airbags and a trick reverse sensing system.

Options	Price
Air Conditioning [Opt on STD]	+332
Air Conditioning - Front and Rear [Opt on LX]	+185
Aluminum/Alloy Wheels [Opt on LX]	+161
AM/FM/Cassette/CD Audio System [Std on SEL]	+117
Bucket Seats	+190
Camper/Towing Package	+169
Captain Chairs (4) [Opt on LX]	+278
Compact Disc Changer	+155

Options	Price
Front Side Airbag Restraints	+151
Leather Seats [Opt on SE]	+336
Power Driver Seat [Opt on LX,SE]	+126
Power Dual Sliding Doors [Opt on SE]	+311
Power Sliding Door	+194
Sliding Driver Side Door [Opt on LX,STD]	+136
Traction Control System	+154

Ford
Windstar

1998

Mileage Category: P

Ford widens the driver door as a stop-gap measure until the 1999 Windstar arrives with a fourth door. Subtle styling revisions and a new Limited model round out the changes for 1998.

Body Styles	TMV Pricing		
	Trade	Private	Dealer
3 Dr GL Pass Van	3806	4781	5880
3 Dr LX Pass Van	3971	4988	6135
3 Dr Limited Pass Van	4820	6055	7447
3 Dr STD Pass Van	3329	4181	5142

Options	Price
Traction Control System	+125
3.8L V6 OHV 12V FI Engine [Opt on GL]	+217
Air Conditioning [Std on LX]	+272
Air Conditioning - Front and Rear [Opt on GL,LX]	+151
Aluminum/Alloy Wheels [Opt on GL]	+132

Options	Price
Camper/Towing Package	+130
Captain Chairs (4) [Opt on GL]	+227
JBL Audio System	+162
Leather Seats [Opt on LX]	+274

1997

Mileage Category: P

Nothing is new for the 1997 Ford Windsar.

Body Styles	TMV Pricing		
	Trade	Private	Dealer
3 Dr GL Pass Van	2943	3787	4818
3 Dr LX Pass Van	3160	4066	5173

Options	Price
3.8L V6 OHV 12V FI Engine [Opt on GL]	+201
Air Conditioning	+251
Air Conditioning - Front and Rear	+139
Aluminum/Alloy Wheels	+122

Options	Price
Captain Chairs (4)	+204
JBL Audio System	+149
Leather Seats	+254

1996

Mileage Category: P

Ford boosted output on the 3.8-liter V6 from 155 to 200 horsepower. Trim and equipment have been revised, and four-wheel disc brakes come with traction control or the tow package. A new integrated child safety seat has been added to the options list. Tune-ups happen every 100,000 miles. Traction control is now optional.

Body Styles	TMV Pricing		
	Trade	Private	Dealer
3 Dr GL Pass Van	2227	2918	3873
3 Dr LX Pass Van	2652	3476	4613

Options	Price
Air Conditioning [Std on LX]	+223
Air Conditioning - Front and Rear	+124
Captain Chairs (4)	+156

Options	Price
JBL Audio System	+133
Leather Seats [Opt on LX]	+225
3.8L V6 OHV 12V FI Engine [Std on LX]	+178

1995

Mileage Category: P

This year, Ford introduces its version of the front-wheel drive minivan. Designed to replace the Aerostar, the Windstar offers an extensive standard equipment list. Dual airbags, antilock brakes, a four-speed automatic transmission and V6 power are just a few of the things Windstar owners will find included on their vehicle. The Windstar has seating for seven that includes a unique integrated child seat.

Body Styles	TMV Pricing		
	Trade	Private	Dealer
3 Dr GL Pass Van	1760	2398	3460
3 Dr GL Pass Van (1995.5)	1855	2527	3647
3 Dr LX Pass Van	2013	2742	3957
3 Dr LX Pass Van (1995.5)	2202	3000	4329

Options	Price
Air Conditioning [Std on LX]	+193
Air Conditioning - Front and Rear	+107
Aluminum/Alloy Wheels [Opt on GL]	+94
Bucket Seats [Opt on LX]	+110
Camper/Towing Package [Std on LX]	+79

Options	Price
Captain Chairs (4)	+135
Compact Disc Changer	+90
JBL Audio System	+115
Leather Seats	+195
Premium Audio System	+124

1997

Body Styles	TMV Pricing		
	Trade	Private	Dealer
2 Dr LSi Hbk	876	1390	2019
2 Dr STD Hbk	816	1296	1883
4 Dr LSi Sdn	933	1481	2151

Options	Price
Air Conditioning	+149
Antilock Brakes	+144

Mileage Category: A

Geo drops the base sedan variant of the Metro for 1997. A new convenience package is available on LSi models, and the LSi hatchback comes with the larger 1.3-liter engine standard. Two new colors debut.

1996

Mileage Category: A

A zoned rear window defroster clears the center of the Metro's tiny rear backlight first, base coupes get dual exterior mirrors and LSi coupes get hubcaps and body-color bumpers.

Body Styles	TMV Pricing		
	Trade	Private	Dealer
2 Dr LSi Hbk	626	1034	1597
2 Dr STD Hbk	611	1010	1560

Body Styles	TMV Pricing		
	Trade	Private	Dealer
4 Dr LSi Sdn	726	1199	1853
4 Dr STD Sdn	673	1111	1717

Options	Price
Antilock Brakes	+124

1995

Mileage Category: A

All-new car is larger than previous model, and comes as a two-door hatchback or four-door sedan in base or LSi trim. Dual airbags are standard. ABS is optional on all models. Hatchbacks get the carryover 1.0-liter three-cylinder motor. Optional on LSi hatchback and standard on sedans is a 70-horsepower, 1.3-liter four-cylinder engine. Daytime running lights are standard.

Body Styles	TMV Pricing		
	Trade	Private	Dealer
2 Dr LSi Hbk	479	805	1347
2 Dr STD Hbk	453	761	1273

Body Styles	TMV Pricing		
	Trade	Private	Dealer
4 Dr LSi Sdn	538	903	1512
4 Dr STD Sdn	497	836	1400

Options	Price
AM/FM/Cassette/CD Audio System	+81
Antilock Brakes	+107

Options	Price
Air Conditioning	+85

1994

Mileage Category: A

Convertible is dropped as is LSi trim level. CFC-free refrigerant is added to air conditioning systems.

Body Styles	TMV Pricing		
	Trade	Private	Dealer
2 Dr STD Hbk	296	535	934
2 Dr XFi Hbk	291	526	918
4 Dr STD Hbk	302	547	955

Options	Price
Air Conditioning	+76

Geo
Prizm
1997

Body Styles	TMV Pricing		
	Trade	Private	Dealer
4 Dr LSi Sdn	1743	2585	3614
4 Dr STD Sdn	1648	2444	3417

Options	Price	Options	Price
Air Conditioning	+152	Automatic 4-Speed Transmission	+152
Antilock Brakes	+144	Power Sunroof	+129

Mileage Category: B

The Prizm is essentially carried over for 1997, sporting new door trim panels, standard power steering, new exterior colors, and strengthened side-impact protection.

Geo
Prizm/Tracker

1996
Mileage Category: B

An integrated child safety seat is optional on the LSi, and daytime running lights debut. Three new exterior colors and added equipment to the base model round out the changes to this excellent compact.

Body Styles	TMV Pricing		
	Trade	Private	Dealer
4 Dr LSi Sdn	1286	2018	3029
4 Dr STD Sdn	1200	1883	2827

Options	Price
Air Conditioning	+130
Antilock Brakes	+124
Automatic 4-Speed Transmission	+131

1995
Mileage Category: B

Base 1.6-liter engine loses horsepower. All models get new wheel covers, and leather is newly optional on LSi.

Body Styles	TMV Pricing		
	Trade	Private	Dealer
4 Dr LSi Sdn	862	1422	2356
4 Dr STD Sdn	788	1300	2154

Options	Price	Options	Price
Antilock Brakes	+107	Power Sunroof	+95
Automatic 4-Speed Transmission	+113	Air Conditioning	+112
Leather Seats	+84		

1994
Mileage Category: B

Passenger airbag is added. Air conditioners get CFC-free coolant.

Body Styles	TMV Pricing		
	Trade	Private	Dealer
4 Dr LSi Sdn	642	1175	2064
4 Dr STD Sdn	577	1057	1857

Options	Price	Options	Price
Air Conditioning	+100	Leather Seats	+75
Antilock Brakes	+95	Power Sunroof	+85
Automatic 4-Speed Transmission	+101		

Geo
Tracker
1997

Body Styles	TMV Pricing			Body Styles	TMV Pricing		
	Trade	Private	Dealer		Trade	Private	Dealer
2 Dr STD 4WD Conv	1974	2658	3493	4 Dr LSi SUV	2085	2807	3689
2 Dr STD Conv	1837	2472	3249	4 Dr STD 4WD SUV	2088	2811	3694
4 Dr LSi 4WD SUV	2191	2950	3877	4 Dr STD SUV	2025	2726	3583

Options	Price	Options	Price
Air Conditioning	+159	Automatic 3-Speed Transmission	+119
Antilock Brakes	+144	Automatic 4-Speed Transmission	+181

Mileage Category: L

After a heavy makeover for 1996, changes for 1997 are limited. Convertibles get a standard fold-and-stow rear bench seat along with an enhanced evaporative emissions system. All Trackers can be painted Sunset Red Metallic or Azurite Blue Metallic for the first time.

1996

Mileage Category: L

Body Styles	TMV Pricing		
	Trade	Private	Dealer
2 Dr LSi 4WD Conv	1748	2366	3219
2 Dr LSi Conv	1580	2139	2910
2 Dr STD 4WD Conv	1638	2217	3016
2 Dr STD Conv	1451	1963	2671

Body Styles	TMV Pricing		
	Trade	Private	Dealer
4 Dr LSi 4WD SUV	1883	2549	3468
4 Dr LSi SUV	1762	2384	3244
4 Dr STD 4WD SUV	1788	2420	3292
4 Dr STD SUV	1688	2285	3109

Options	Price
Air Conditioning	+122
Antilock Brakes	+124
Automatic 4-Speed Transmission	+131

A new four-door model joins the lineup, and dual airbags are standard on all Trackers. Four-wheel antilock brakes are optional. Revised styling freshens the new exterior, and daytime running lights make the Tracker more conspicuous to motorists. Cruise control is a new convenience option.

1995

Mileage Category: L

Body Styles	TMV Pricing		
	Trade	Private	Dealer
2 Dr LSi 4WD Conv	1439	1951	2805
2 Dr LSi 4WD SUV	1493	2024	2909
2 Dr STD 4WD Conv	1309	1775	2551

Body Styles	TMV Pricing		
	Trade	Private	Dealer
2 Dr STD 4WD SUV	1275	1729	2486
2 Dr STD Conv	1122	1521	2186

Options	Price
AM/FM/Cassette/CD Audio System	+81
Automatic 3-Speed Transmission	+84

Options	Price
Hardtop Roof	+106
Air Conditioning	+105

All 4WD models and Massachusetts-bound Trackers get 95-horsepower engine. Convertible top has been redesigned for easier operation. Expressions Packages offer color-coordinated tops and wheels.

1994

Mileage Category: L

Body Styles	TMV Pricing		
	Trade	Private	Dealer
2 Dr LSi 4WD Conv	1181	1651	2434
2 Dr LSi 4WD SUV	1192	1667	2458
2 Dr STD 4WD Conv	1027	1436	2117

Body Styles	TMV Pricing		
	Trade	Private	Dealer
2 Dr STD 4WD SUV	1057	1478	2180
2 Dr STD Conv	880	1230	1814

Options	Price
Air Conditioning	+94
Automatic 3-Speed Transmission	+75

Trackers sold in California and New York get 95-horsepower version of 1.6-liter engine to clear emissions hurdles. Four-wheel-drive models trade on-/off-road tires for better riding all-season type rubber. Alloy wheels have been restyled. Center console gets cupholders. Interior fabrics are new. Optional is a CD/cassette player.

GMC
Envoy

2003

Mileage Category: O

For 2003, Envoy buyers are able to order certain options individually, rather than as part of an equipment package, adding potential savings and increased flexibility. The sport-ute's already powerful Vortec 4.2-liter inline six also gets a slight bump in horsepower, up from 270 to 275, and Envoys now boast a new four-position headlamp switch that permits drivers to turn off the vehicle's daytime running lamps and automatic headlamps when necessary. Additionally, the Envoy gets a larger fuel tank that holds 22 gallons. Previously standard side airbags are now optional, while autodimming side mirrors and the rear seat overhead compartment have been deleted.

Body Styles	TMV Pricing		
	Trade	Private	Dealer
4 Dr SLE 4WD SUV	20384	21598	23620
4 Dr SLE SUV	19259	20405	22316

Options	Price
Automatic Load Leveling	+241
Bose Audio System [Opt on SLT]	+319
Heated Front Seats [Opt on SLT]	+161
Locking Differential	+174
Power Driver Seat [Opt on SLE]	+177
Power Moonroof	+515

Body Styles	TMV Pricing		
	Trade	Private	Dealer
4 Dr SLT 4WD SUV	24164	25603	28000
4 Dr SLT SUV	22660	24009	26257

Options	Price
Power Passenger Seat [Opt on SLE]	+177
Running Boards	+241
Front Side Airbag Restraints	+225
OnStar Telematic System [Opt on SLE]	+447
AM/FM/CD Changer Audio System	+158
DVD Entertainment System	+644

2002

Mileage Category: O

Long overdue for a redesign, GMC's all-new Envoy finally gets the goods to compete in the highly competitive midsize SUV segment. An all-aluminum inline six-cylinder engine replaces the aging 4.3-liter V6, and a revised suspension dramatically improves the ride. Unlike the 2000 Envoy that was virtually indistinguishable from its Chevrolet and Oldsmobile siblings, the 2002 model now sports a new look that is unique to the GMC brand.

Body Styles	TMV Pricing		
	Trade	Private	Dealer
4 Dr SLE 4WD SUV	17765	18955	20938
4 Dr SLE SUV	16502	17607	19449

Options	Price
17 Inch Wheels	+237
AM/FM/CD Changer Audio System	+147
Automatic Load Leveling	+150
Bose Audio System [Opt on SLT]	+180
Compact Disc Changer [Opt on SLE]	+299
DVD Entertainment System	+539

Body Styles	TMV Pricing		
	Trade	Private	Dealer
4 Dr SLT 4WD SUV	19288	20580	22734
4 Dr SLT SUV	17996	19201	21209

Options	Price
Heated Front Seats [Opt on SLT]	+150
Locking Differential [Opt on 2WD]	+162
Power Moonroof	+479
Power Passenger Seat [Opt on SLE]	+135
Running Boards	+195

2000

Body Styles	TMV Pricing		
	Trade	Private	Dealer
4 Dr STD 4WD SUV	11164	12730	14264

Options	Price
Limited Slip Differential	+134
OnStar Telematic System	+445

Options	Price
Power Moonroof	+373

Mileage Category: O

Upgraded seats and V6 engine improvements headline changes to GM's high-end compact SUV. There's also a new metallic paint color, and a heavy-duty battery is now standard.

1999

Mileage Category: O

After its debut as General Motors' high-end compact SUV last year, the GMC Envoy gets equipment upgrades for '99. A new mini-module for the driver airbag allows for steering wheel radio controls, and the turn signal stalk now incorporates a flash-to-pass headlamp feature. Heated, eight-way power front seating is improved, thanks to available two-position memory for the driver and power recliners. A liftgate ajar telltale resides in the instrument cluster, and the outside rearview mirrors have been redesigned, featuring electrochromic dimming and power-folding capability. GM's advanced AutoTrac active transfer case is now standard, while a new shift lever-mounted button selects a tow/haul mode to optimize transmission shift points. There are three new metallic exterior paint colors: Topaz Gold, Meadow Green and Indigo Blue.

Body Styles	TMV Pricing		
	Trade	Private	Dealer
4 Dr STD 4WD SUV	9497	10992	12548

Options	Price
OnStar Telematic System	+401
Power Moonroof	+302

1998

Mileage Category: O

GMC introduces its finest luxury compact SUV to date: the Envoy.

Body Styles	TMV Pricing		
	Trade	Private	Dealer
4 Dr STD 4WD SUV	8282	9682	11261

Options	Price
Power Moonroof	+260

For the latest vehicle information, visit www.edmunds.com

Envoy XL/Jimmy

GMC
Envoy XL
2003

Body Styles	TMV Pricing		
	Trade	Private	Dealer
4 Dr SLE 4WD SUV	20412	22012	24678
4 Dr SLE SUV	19222	20728	23239

Options	Price
Automatic Load Leveling	+241
Bose Audio System [Opt on SLT]	+319
Heated Front Seats [Opt on SLT]	+161
Locking Differential	+174
Power Driver Seat [Opt on SLE]	+177
Power Moonroof	+515
Power Passenger Seat [Opt on SLE]	+177

Body Styles	TMV Pricing		
	Trade	Private	Dealer
4 Dr SLT 4WD SUV	22484	24246	27182
4 Dr SLT SUV	21110	22764	25521

Options	Price
Running Boards	+241
Front Side Airbag Restraints	+225
OnStar Telematic System [Opt on SLE]	+447
AM/FM/CD Changer Audio System	+158
DVD Entertainment System	+644
5.3L V8 OHV 16V FI Engine	+966

Mileage Category: M

For 2003, Envoy XL buyers are able to order options individually, rather than as part of an equipment package, adding potential savings and increased flexibility. The sport-ute's already powerful 4.2-liter inline six engine also gets a slight bump in horsepower, up from 270 to 275; XL buyers seeking increased low-end torque, greater cargo-hauling and trailering capability and speedier acceleration may step up to the newly offered 5.3-liter V8, which spews 290 horsepower and 325 pound-feet of torque. Additionally, Envoy XLs now boast a new four-position headlamp switch that permits drivers to turn off the vehicle's daytime running lamps and automatic headlamps as necessary.

2002

Body Styles	TMV Pricing		
	Trade	Private	Dealer
4 Dr SLE 4WD SUV	18111	19656	22231
4 Dr SLE SUV	16863	18301	20698

Options	Price
17 Inch Wheels	+269
AM/FM/CD Changer Audio System	+147
Automatic Load Leveling	+150
Bose Audio System [Opt on SLT]	+150
DVD Entertainment System	+539

Body Styles	TMV Pricing		
	Trade	Private	Dealer
4 Dr SLT 4WD SUV	19646	21322	24114
4 Dr SLT SUV	18386	19954	22568

Options	Price
Heated Front Seats [Opt on SLT]	+150
Locking Differential [Opt on 2WD]	+135
Power Passenger Seat [Opt on SLE]	+135
Power Sunroof	+479

Mileage Category: M

Debuting as a midyear addition to the Envoy lineup, the Envoy XL is an extended-wheelbase seven-passenger version of the standard Envoy.

GMC
Jimmy
2001

Body Styles	TMV Pricing		
	Trade	Private	Dealer
2 Dr SLS 4WD SUV	8139	9385	10535
2 Dr SLS Convenience 4WD SUV	9206	10616	11917
2 Dr SLS Convenience SUV	8083	9321	10463
2 Dr SLS SUV	6960	8026	9010
4 Dr Diamond Edition 4WD SUV	12181	14046	15767
4 Dr Diamond Edition SUV	11395	13140	14750

Options	Price
Automatic 4-Speed Transmission [Opt on SLS]	+546
Bose Audio System	+270
Camper/Towing Package	+115
Compact Disc Changer	+216
Heated Front Seats	+137
Locking Differential	+147
OnStar Telematic System	+380

Body Styles	TMV Pricing		
	Trade	Private	Dealer
4 Dr Diamond Edition Special 4WD SUV	13695	15792	17728
4 Dr SLE 4WD SUV	10719	12361	13876
4 Dr SLE SUV	9877	11390	12786
4 Dr SLT 4WD SUV	11449	13202	14820
4 Dr SLT SUV	10272	11845	13297

Options	Price
Power Door Locks [Opt on SLS]	+123
Power Driver Seat	+131
Power Passenger Seat	+131
Power Sunroof	+437
Power Windows [Opt on SLS]	+131
Two-Tone Paint	+123

Mileage Category: M

The Vortec 4300 V6 enjoys another round of improvements, plus the Jimmy adds programmable door locks and a new cargo management system to its long list of features for 2001. A floor-shift option is now available on two-door models with automatic transmission, and the four-wheel-drive SLE version touts restyled alloy wheels. The tarted-up Envoy has been redesigned for 2002, but the glitzy Diamond Edition, introduced last year to mark the 30th anniversary of the Jimmy nameplate, is back -- packing more pizzazz.

GMC
Jimmy

2000
Mileage Category: M

For 2000, GMC is celebrating the 30th anniversary of its Jimmy nameplate with a Diamond Edition model. Other changes center on new equipment and suspension packaging. A heavy-duty battery is now standard, and Jimmy's V6 has been upgraded with a roller timing chain, sprocket and rocker arms for improved durability and reduced noise. There are also two new exterior colors, while the SLE gets a revised cloth interior.

Body Styles	TMV Pricing		
	Trade	Private	Dealer
2 Dr SLS 4WD SUV	6787	8018	9224
2 Dr SLS Convenience 4WD SUV	7597	8975	10325
2 Dr SLS Convenience SUV	6533	7718	8879
2 Dr SLS SUV	5705	6740	7754
4 Dr Diamond Edition 4WD SUV	9306	10994	12648

Options	Price
AM/FM/Cassette/CD Audio System	+170
Automatic 4-Speed Transmission [Opt on SLS]	+497
Automatic Load Leveling	+125
Compact Disc Changer	+197
Delco/Bose Audio System	+246
Heated Front Seats	+125

Body Styles	TMV Pricing		
	Trade	Private	Dealer
4 Dr Diamond Edition SUV	8635	10201	11736
4 Dr SLE 4WD SUV	8510	10053	11566
4 Dr SLE SUV	7656	9044	10405
4 Dr SLT 4WD SUV	8685	10260	11804
4 Dr SLT SUV	8350	9864	11349

Options	Price
Limited Slip Differential [Std on SLS,STD 2WD 2 Dr]	+134
Power Driver Seat [Opt on SLE,SLS,SLS Convenience]	+119
Power Moonroof	+373
Power Passenger Seat	+119
Power Windows [Opt on SLS]	+125

1999
Mileage Category: M

There are three new colors and revised outside mirrors, but most changes to the '99 Jimmy are inside. You'll find new power-seating features, redundant radio controls and a mini-module depowered airbag in the steering wheel, as well as a new Bose premium sound system and six-disc CD changer. A vehicle content theft alarm, flash-to-pass headlamp feature and liftgate ajar warning lamp have also been added. Four-wheel-drive versions get the new AutoTrac active transfer case and four-door models gain a tow/haul mode for the transmission. Finally, the optional Z85 Euro-Ride suspension has been retuned.

Body Styles	TMV Pricing		
	Trade	Private	Dealer
2 Dr SL 4WD SUV	5852	7014	8224
2 Dr SL SUV	4876	5844	6852
2 Dr SLS Sport 4WD SUV	5982	7170	8407
2 Dr SLS Sport SUV	4977	5966	6995
4 Dr SL 4WD SUV	6468	7753	9091

Options	Price
AM/FM/Cassette/CD Audio System	+137
Automatic 4-Speed Transmission [Std on SLE,SLS Sport,SLT,Wgn]	+403
Compact Disc Changer	+159

Body Styles	TMV Pricing		
	Trade	Private	Dealer
4 Dr SL SUV	5936	7115	8343
4 Dr SL 4WD SUV	7765	9308	10913
4 Dr SLE SUV	6503	7795	9139
4 Dr SLT 4WD SUV	7899	9468	11101
4 Dr SLT SUV	7413	8885	10418

Options	Price
Delco/Bose Audio System	+200
Power Moonroof	+302

1998
Mileage Category: M

A revised interior contains dual second-generation airbags, improved climate controls and available premium sound systems. Outside, the front bumper, grille and headlights are new. Side cladding is restyled and SLT models have new alloy wheels. Fresh colors inside and out sum up the changes.

Body Styles	TMV Pricing		
	Trade	Private	Dealer
2 Dr SL 4WD SUV	4991	6056	7257
2 Dr SL SUV	4206	5104	6116
2 Dr SLS Sport 4WD SUV	5326	6463	7745
2 Dr SLS Sport SUV	4472	5427	6503
4 Dr SL 4WD SUV	5374	6521	7814
4 Dr SL SUV	5039	6114	7327

Options	Price
Power Moonroof	+260
AM/FM/Cassette/CD Audio System	+118

Body Styles	TMV Pricing		
	Trade	Private	Dealer
4 Dr SLE 4WD SUV	6028	7314	8764
4 Dr SLE SUV	5451	6614	7926
4 Dr SLS Sport 4WD SUV	5791	7027	8421
4 Dr SLS Sport SUV	5226	6341	7599
4 Dr SLT 4WD SUV	6404	7770	9311
4 Dr SLT SUV	5839	7085	8490

Options	Price
Compact Disc Changer	+137

1997
Mileage Category: M

Highrider off-road package deleted as GMC realigns Jimmy as luxury sport-ute. Instead, buyers can opt for a Gold Edition in one of four colors. New options include a power sunroof and HomeLink universal transmitter. Radar Purple and Bright Teal paint colors are replaced by Fairway Green and Smoky Caramel.

Body Styles	TMV Pricing		
	Trade	Private	Dealer
2 Dr SLS 4WD SUV	3947	4861	5979
2 Dr SL SUV	3584	4414	5428
2 Dr SLS Sport 4WD SUV	4007	4935	6070
2 Dr SLS Sport SUV	4001	4928	6061
4 Dr SL 4WD SUV	4057	4997	6145
4 Dr SL SUV	3636	4478	5508

Options	Price
Power Moonroof	+218

Body Styles	TMV Pricing		
	Trade	Private	Dealer
4 Dr SLE 4WD SUV	4802	5914	7274
4 Dr SLE SUV	4242	5225	6426
4 Dr SLS Sport 4WD SUV	4475	5512	6779
4 Dr SLS Sport SUV	4101	5051	6213
4 Dr SLT 4WD SUV	4942	6087	7486
4 Dr SLT SUV	4522	5569	6849

1996

Body Styles	TMV Pricing		
	Trade	Private	Dealer
2 Dr SL 4WD SUV	3364	4211	5380
2 Dr SL SUV	3179	3979	5084
2 Dr SLS 4WD SUV	3594	4498	5747
2 Dr SLS SUV	3270	4093	5230
2 Dr STD 4WD SUV	3195	3999	5109
2 Dr STD SUV	2796	3500	4471
4 Dr SL 4WD SUV	3640	4556	5820
4 Dr SL SUV	3307	4139	5289

Body Styles	TMV Pricing		
	Trade	Private	Dealer
4 Dr SLE 4WD SUV	3949	4943	6315
4 Dr SLE SUV	3638	4553	5817
4 Dr SLS 4WD SUV	3859	4830	6171
4 Dr SLS SUV	3548	4441	5674
4 Dr SLT 4WD SUV	4256	5327	6807
4 Dr SLT SUV	3902	4884	6241
4 Dr STD 4WD SUV	3462	4333	5536
4 Dr STD SUV	3106	3888	4967

Mileage Category: M

GMC's popular compact sport-utility gets an optional off-road package called Highrider, as well as an available five-speed transmission. Either of these are available on two-door models only. All Jimmys receive glow-in-the-day headlights and long-life engine coolant. Spark plugs last 100,000 miles. All-wheel drive, which became optional in mid-1995, continues. Conspicuously absent is a passenger airbag.

1995

Body Styles	TMV Pricing		
	Trade	Private	Dealer
2 Dr SL 4WD SUV	2461	3150	4297
2 Dr SL SUV	2187	2799	3819
2 Dr SLS 4WD SUV	2867	3670	5007
2 Dr SLS SUV	2426	3105	4237
2 Dr STD 4WD SUV	2408	3082	4205
2 Dr STD SUV	2154	2757	3761
4 Dr SLE 4WD SUV	2985	3821	5213

Body Styles	TMV Pricing		
	Trade	Private	Dealer
4 Dr SLE SUV	2855	3654	4986
4 Dr SLS 4WD SUV	3192	4086	5575
4 Dr SLS SUV	2901	3713	5066
4 Dr SLT 4WD SUV	3440	4403	6008
4 Dr SLT SUV	3192	4086	5575
4 Dr STD 4WD SUV	2820	3609	4925
4 Dr STD SUV	2387	3055	4169

Options	Price
AM/FM/Cassette/CD Audio System [Opt on SLS]	+88

Options	Price
AM/FM/CD Audio System	+85

Mileage Category: M

All-new SUV appears based on revamped Sonoma. Four-wheel-drive models have electronic transfer case as standard equipment. Spare tire on four-door model is mounted beneath cargo bay instead of in it. Five different suspension packages are available. One engine, a 195-horsepower 4.3-liter V6, is available. All-wheel drive is optional. Driver airbag and air conditioning are standard equipment.

1994

Body Styles	TMV Pricing		
	Trade	Private	Dealer
2 Dr SLE 4WD SUV	1945	2566	3600
2 Dr SLE SUV	1507	1988	2790
2 Dr SLS 4WD SUV	1984	2618	3674
2 Dr SLS SUV	1627	2146	3012
2 Dr SLT 4WD SUV	2341	3088	4334
2 Dr SLT SUV	2143	2827	3967
2 Dr STD 4WD SUV	1825	2408	3379
2 Dr STD SUV	1442	1903	2670

Body Styles	TMV Pricing		
	Trade	Private	Dealer
4 Dr SLE 4WD SUV	2380	3140	4407
4 Dr SLE SUV	2235	2949	4138
4 Dr SLS 4WD SUV	2184	2882	4044
4 Dr SLS SUV	1588	2095	2939
4 Dr SLT 4WD SUV	2422	3195	4483
4 Dr SLT SUV	2181	2877	4038
4 Dr STD 4WD SUV	2221	2930	4112
4 Dr STD SUV	1706	2251	3158

Options	Price
Air Conditioning [Opt on SLS,STD]	+162
AM/FM/CD Audio System	+81
Automatic 4-Speed Transmission	+230

Options	Price
Premium Audio System	+75
4.3L V6 OHV 12V HO FI Engine	+105

Mileage Category: M

Side-door guard beams and a high-mounted center brake light are added. Front bench seat is now standard on four-door models.

Body Styles	TMV Pricing		
	Trade	Private	Dealer
3 Dr G35 Pass Van	4612	5618	7007
3 Dr G35 Pass Van Ext	4764	5803	7238
3 Dr G35 STX Pass Van	4866	5928	7394
3 Dr G35 STX Pass Van Ext	5072	6178	7706

Options	Price
6.5L V8 Diesel OHV 16V Engine	+885
7.4L V8 OHV 16V FI Engine	+187
Air Conditioning [Std on STX]	+271
Air Conditioning - Front and Rear	+347

Mileage Category: Q

All-new Savana replaces this aged warhorse later in this model year.

GMC
Rally Wagon/Safari

1995
Mileage Category: Q

No significant changes as GMC readies a replacement set to debut next year.

Body Styles	TMV Pricing		
	Trade	Private	Dealer
3 Dr G25 Pass Van	3485	4268	5573
3 Dr G25 STX Pass Van	4151	5084	6639
3 Dr G35 Pass Van	3796	4649	6071

Options	Price
15 Passenger Seating	+96
5.0L V8 OHV 16V FI Engine [Opt on G25]	+165
5.7L V8 OHV 16V FI Engine [Opt on G25]	+242
6.5L V8 Diesel OHV 16V Engine	+822
7.4L V8 OHV 16V FI Engine	+173

Body Styles	TMV Pricing		
	Trade	Private	Dealer
3 Dr G35 Pass Van Ext	4178	5117	6682
3 Dr G35 STX Pass Van	4232	5183	6768
3 Dr G35 STX Pass Van Ext	4281	5243	6847

Options	Price
Air Conditioning [Std on STX]	+251
Air Conditioning - Front and Rear	+251
AM/FM/CD Audio System [Opt on STX]	+102
Bucket Seats [Opt on G35]	+104
Camper/Towing Package	+80

1994
Mileage Category: Q

Safety is increased via new side door guard beams and a driver airbag. Longevity is increased via improved rust proofing. Engines and transmissions are tweaked for quieter, more efficient performance.

Body Styles	TMV Pricing		
	Trade	Private	Dealer
3 Dr G25 Pass Van	2936	3719	5024
3 Dr G25 STX Pass Van	3002	3803	5137

Options	Price
15 Passenger Seating [Opt on G35]	+86
5.7L V8 OHV 16V FI Engine [Opt on G25]	+218
6.5L V8 Diesel OHV 16V Engine	+741
7.4L V8 OHV 16V FI Engine	+156

Body Styles	TMV Pricing		
	Trade	Private	Dealer
3 Dr G35 Pass Van	2988	3785	5112
3 Dr G35 Pass Van Ext	3350	4243	5732

Options	Price
Air Conditioning [Std on STX]	+227
Air Conditioning - Front and Rear	+227
AM/FM/CD Audio System	+92
Premium Audio System	+128

GMC
Safari

2003

Mileage Category: P

All 2003 Safaris have larger 16-inch aluminum wheels and an improved braking system.

Body Styles	TMV Pricing		
	Trade	Private	Dealer
3 Dr SLE AWD Pass Van Ext	14623	15902	18033
3 Dr SLE Pass Van Ext	13972	15194	17230
3 Dr SLT AWD Pass Van Ext	17551	19086	21644

Options	Price
AM/FM/CD Audio System [Opt on STD]	+262
Camper/Towing Package	+199
Leather Seats [Opt on SLT]	+612
Locking Differential	+162

Body Styles	TMV Pricing		
	Trade	Private	Dealer
3 Dr SLT Pass Van Ext	16480	17922	20324
3 Dr STD AWD Pass Van Ext	14366	15622	17716
3 Dr STD Pass Van Ext	13278	14439	16374

Options	Price
Power Driver Seat [Opt on SLE]	+155
Rear Window Defroster [Opt on SLE]	+119
Running Boards [Opt on SLE,SLT]	+258
Air Conditioning - Front and Rear [Std on SLT]	+337

2002
Mileage Category: P

The standard Vortec V6 gets multipoint fuel injection for better overall drivability, while the rear axle now receives a standard dose of synthetic gear oil for reduced heat buildup and longer bearing life.

Body Styles	TMV Pricing		
	Trade	Private	Dealer
3 Dr SLE AWD Pass Van Ext	12042	13156	15012
3 Dr SLE Pass Van Ext	11233	12272	14003

Options	Price
Air Conditioning - Front and Rear [Opt on SLE]	+389
AM/FM/Cassette/CD Audio System [Opt on SLE]	+269
Camper/Towing Package	+185
Leather Seats [Opt on SLT]	+569

Body Styles	TMV Pricing		
	Trade	Private	Dealer
3 Dr SLT AWD Pass Van Ext	14986	16372	18682
3 Dr SLT Pass Van Ext	14014	15310	17470

Options	Price
Locking Differential	+151
Power Driver Seat [Opt on SLE]	+144
Running Boards	+240

2001

Body Styles	TMV Pricing		
	Trade	Private	Dealer
3 Dr SLE AWD Pass Van Ext	9529	11083	12517
3 Dr SLE Pass Van Ext	8907	10360	11701

2001 (cont'd)

Options	Price
Air Conditioning - Front and Rear	+286
AM/FM/Cassette/CD Audio System	+276
Leather Seats	+519

Options	Price
Locking Differential	+138
Power Driver Seat	+131
Running Boards	+218

Mileage Category: P

Safari gets still more engineering enhancements for its 4.3-liter V6, and higher-output alternators. Door locks have been improved for increased security and remote keyless entry has been made standard on passenger van models. To reduce build complexity, preferred equipment groups have been revised and trim levels cut from three to two.

2000

Body Styles	TMV Pricing		
	Trade	Private	Dealer
3 Dr SL AWD Pass Van Ext	7217	8528	9813
3 Dr SL Pass Van Ext	6698	7914	9106
3 Dr SLE AWD Pass Van Ext	7547	8918	10262

Body Styles	TMV Pricing		
	Trade	Private	Dealer
3 Dr SLE Pass Van Ext	6886	8137	9363
3 Dr SLT AWD Pass Van Ext	8929	10551	12140
3 Dr SLT Pass Van Ext	8310	9820	11300

Options	Price
AM/FM/Cassette/CD Audio System [Opt on SLE]	+252
AM/FM/CD Audio System	+203
Camper/Towing Package	+174
Chrome Wheels [Opt on SL]	+170
Leather Seats	+473
Limited Slip Differential	+125
Power Driver Seat [Opt on SLE]	+119

Options	Price
Power Passenger Seat [Opt on SLE]	+119
Power Windows [Opt on SL]	+236
Running Boards	+199
7 Passenger Seating	+197
Air Conditioning - Front and Rear [Opt on SLE]	+261
Aluminum/Alloy Wheels [Opt on SLE]	+152

Mileage Category: P

The 2000 Safari gets engineering enhancements for its 4.3-liter V6 and ABS components, a tow/haul mode for its four-speed automatic transmission, revised lighting and power-locking functions, a larger (27-gallon) composite fuel tank and a third-row seat as standard equipment.

1999

Body Styles	TMV Pricing		
	Trade	Private	Dealer
3 Dr SL AWD Pass Van Ext	6493	7767	9092
3 Dr SL Pass Van Ext	5814	6954	8141
3 Dr SLE AWD Pass Van Ext	6638	7939	9294

Body Styles	TMV Pricing		
	Trade	Private	Dealer
3 Dr SLE Pass Van Ext	6113	7312	8559
3 Dr SLT AWD Pass Van Ext	7702	9213	10785
3 Dr SLT Pass Van Ext	7121	8518	9972

Options	Price
7 Passenger Seating	+159
Air Conditioning - Front and Rear	+211
Aluminum/Alloy Wheels [Std on SLT]	+122
AM/FM/Cassette/CD Audio System	+205

Options	Price
AM/FM/CD Audio System [Std on SLT]	+164
Camper/Towing Package	+124
Leather Seats [Opt on SLT]	+383

Mileage Category: P

There are two new exterior paint and body-cladding colors, restyled wheels and outside mirrors, an overhead console and new optional integrated running boards. Additionally, all-wheel-drive Safari models get the new AutoTrac transfer case, and GM's OnStar communications system is now available.

1998

Body Styles	TMV Pricing		
	Trade	Private	Dealer
3 Dr SLE AWD Pass Van Ext	5753	7008	8424
3 Dr SLE Pass Van Ext	5130	6250	7512
3 Dr SLT AWD Pass Van Ext	6332	7715	9274

Body Styles	TMV Pricing		
	Trade	Private	Dealer
3 Dr SLT Pass Van Ext	5798	7064	8491
3 Dr SLX AWD Pass Van Ext	5083	6192	7443
3 Dr SLX Pass Van Ext	4549	5542	6662

Options	Price
7 Passenger Seating	+257
8 Passenger Seating [Opt on SLX]	+137
Air Conditioning - Front and Rear	+182

Options	Price
AM/FM/Cassette/CD Audio System	+176
AM/FM/CD Audio System [Std on SLT]	+141
Leather Seats	+330

Mileage Category: P

New colors, a theft-deterrent system and automatic transmission refinements are the changes to the Safari. This van is one of the few GM models that retains full-power airbags for 1998.

1997

Body Styles	TMV Pricing		
	Trade	Private	Dealer
3 Dr SLE AWD Pass Van Ext	4578	5653	6967
3 Dr SLE Pass Van Ext	4106	5071	6250
3 Dr SLT AWD Pass Van Ext	5090	6286	7747

Body Styles	TMV Pricing		
	Trade	Private	Dealer
3 Dr SLT Pass Van Ext	4621	5706	7033
3 Dr SLX AWD Pass Van Ext	4192	5177	6380
3 Dr SLX Pass Van Ext	3722	4596	5664

Options	Price
7 Passenger Seating	+233
8 Passenger Seating [Opt on SLX ,SLE Pass Van Ext]	+124
Air Conditioning - Front and Rear	+164

Options	Price
AM/FM/Cassette/CD Audio System	+159
AM/FM/CD Audio System	+128
Leather Seats	+298

Mileage Category: P

Illuminated entry and daytime running lights debut this year, along with a couple of new colors and automatic transmission improvements. SLT models can be equipped with leather seating, and a HomeLink three-channel transmitter is optional. Speed-sensitive power steering makes parking easier.

GMC
Safari/Savana

1996

Mileage Category: P

An all-new interior debuts with dual airbags, more leg- and foot room, and a host of other features. Important among them are the availability of dual-integrated child seats and a child-proof lock on the right-side sliding door. Under-seat heat ducts help warm the rear passengers, and new audio systems include a radio that can be tuned independently by rear-seat passengers without disturbing the listening pleasure, or program, that the front occupants are enjoying.

Body Styles	TMV Pricing		
	Trade	Private	Dealer
3 Dr SLE AWD Pass Van Ext	3589	4528	5824
3 Dr SLE Pass Van Ext	3216	4057	5218
3 Dr SLT AWD Pass Van Ext	3967	5004	6436
3 Dr SLT Pass Van Ext	3631	4581	5893

Options	Price
7 Passenger Seating	+205

Body Styles	TMV Pricing		
	Trade	Private	Dealer
3 Dr SLX AWD Pass Van Ext	3466	4372	5624
3 Dr SLX Pass Van Ext	3131	3950	5080
3 Dr STD AWD Pass Van Ext	3372	4254	5471
3 Dr STD Pass Van Ext	2991	3773	4854

Options	Price
Air Conditioning - Front and Rear	+145

1995

Mileage Category: P

Front sheet metal is restyled. Regular-length versions are dropped from the lineup, leaving only the extended model. Multileaf steel springs replace single-leaf plastic springs. One engine is available, the 190-horsepower, 4.3-liter V6. Air conditioning is newly standard, and remote keyless entry is a new option.

Body Styles	TMV Pricing		
	Trade	Private	Dealer
3 Dr SLE AWD Pass Van Ext	2874	3675	5011
3 Dr SLE Pass Van Ext	2479	3171	4323
3 Dr SLT AWD Pass Van Ext	3069	3926	5353
3 Dr SLT Pass Van Ext	2914	3727	5081

Options	Price
7 Passenger Seating	+191
8 Passenger Seating [Opt on SLX,STD]	+102
Air Conditioning - Front and Rear	+135

Body Styles	TMV Pricing		
	Trade	Private	Dealer
3 Dr SLX AWD Pass Van Ext	2636	3371	4597
3 Dr SLX Pass Van Ext	2361	3020	4117
3 Dr STD AWD Pass Van Ext	2597	3322	4529
3 Dr STD Pass Van Ext	2282	2919	3980

Options	Price
AM/FM/CD Audio System	+105
Camper/Towing Package	+80
Captain Chairs (4)	+116

1994

Mileage Category: P

Driver airbag is made standard. Side-door guard beams are stronger, and air conditioners use CFC-free refrigerant. A high-mount center brake light is added. Analog gauges get new graphics, and carpet is treated with Scotchgard.

Body Styles	TMV Pricing		
	Trade	Private	Dealer
3 Dr SLE AWD Pass Van Ext	2298	3051	4306
3 Dr SLE Pass Van	1846	2451	3459
3 Dr SLE Pass Van Ext	1893	2514	3548
3 Dr SLT AWD Pass Van Ext	2372	3149	4445
3 Dr SLT Pass Van	2336	3101	4377
3 Dr SLT Pass Van Ext	2186	2902	4095
3 Dr SLX AWD Pass Van Ext	2261	3002	4236

Options	Price
4.3L V6 OHV 12V HO FI Engine [Std on 4WD]	+129
7 Passenger Seating	+172
8 Passenger Seating	+92

Body Styles	TMV Pricing		
	Trade	Private	Dealer
3 Dr SLX Pass Van	1736	2305	3254
3 Dr SLX Pass Van Ext	1808	2401	3388
3 Dr STD AWD Pass Van	1936	2571	3628
3 Dr STD AWD Pass Van Ext	1957	2599	3669
3 Dr STD Pass Van	1694	2250	3176
3 Dr STD Pass Van Ext	1728	2295	3239

Options	Price
Air Conditioning	+162
Air Conditioning - Front and Rear	+121
AM/FM/CD Audio System	+94

GMC
Savana

2003

Body Styles	TMV Pricing		
	Trade	Private	Dealer
3 Dr G1500 AWD Pass Van	16853	18043	20025
3 Dr G1500 Pass Van	13507	14460	16048
3 Dr G1500 SLE AWD Pass Van	18041	19314	21435
3 Dr G1500 SLE Pass Van	15862	16981	18847
3 Dr G2500 Pass Van	15645	16749	18589
3 Dr G2500 Pass Van Ext	16223	17368	19275

Body Styles	TMV Pricing		
	Trade	Private	Dealer
3 Dr G2500 SLE Pass Van	17259	18477	20506
3 Dr G2500 SLE Pass Van Ext	17253	18470	20499
3 Dr G3500 Pass Van	15960	17086	18963
3 Dr G3500 Pass Van Ext	16825	18012	19991
3 Dr G3500 SLE Pass Van	17761	19014	21102
3 Dr G3500 SLE Pass Van Ext	17750	19003	21090

Mileage Category: Q

The Savana gains numerous improvements for the '03 model year. Under the hood, GMC's cargo hauler now features GM's lineup of powerful Vortec engines, from the base 200-horsepower V6 all the way up to the hard-charging 300-hp 6.0-liter V8. All-wheel-drive models are also available for the first time, and all Savanas get four-wheel disc brakes with ABS. Driver-side 60/40 access doors and swing-up access panels have also been added as an option along with revised front-end styling, larger stabilizer bars and a stronger frame. Inside, the Savana gets redesigned seats, improved lighting and ventilation systems and dual-stage airbags on all light-duty versions.

2003 (cont'd)

Options	Price
15 Passenger Seating [Opt on G3500]	+241
Aluminum/Alloy Wheels	+258
AM/FM/CD Audio System	+132
AM/FM/Cassette/CD Audio System	+229
Chrome Wheels [Opt on G1500]	+161
Cruise Control [Std on SLE]	+119
Locking Differential	+164
Power Door Locks [Std on SLE]	+132

Options	Price
Power Driver Seat [Opt on SLE]	+155
Power Passenger Seat [Opt on SLE]	+155
Power Windows [Std on SLE]	+171
OnStar Telematic System	+447
AM/FM/CD Changer Audio System	+357
Air Conditioning - Front and Rear [Std on SLE]	+554
5.3L V8 OHV 16V FI Engine [Opt on G1500]	+963

2002

Body Styles	TMV Pricing		
	Trade	Private	Dealer
3 Dr G1500 Pass Van	11528	12560	14280
3 Dr G1500 SLT Pass Van	16940	18457	20984
3 Dr G2500 Pass Van	12679	13814	15705

Body Styles	TMV Pricing		
	Trade	Private	Dealer
3 Dr G2500 Pass Van Ext	13223	14407	16379
3 Dr G3500 Pass Van	12966	14127	16061
3 Dr G3500 Pass Van Ext	13848	15087	17153

Mileage Category: Q

GMC's full-size van gets only minor improvements, such as a more efficient starter and a stronger steering gear housing. Models with an 8,600-pound or above GVWR and either the 8100 V8 or 6.5-liter diesel engine are newly certified as low emissions vehicles in California.

Options	Price
15 Passenger Seating [Opt on G3500 Ext]	+222
5.0L V8 OHV 16V FI Engine [Opt on G1500]	+296
5.7L V8 OHV 16V FI Engine [Opt on G1500]	+716
6.5L V8 Turbodiesel OHV 16V Engine [Opt on G2500,G3500]	+1832
8.1L V8 OHV 16V FI Engine [Opt on G3500]	+509
Air Conditioning - Front and Rear [Std on Ext,G1500 SLT]	+389
Aluminum/Alloy Wheels [Std on G1500 SLT]	+150
AM/FM/Cassette/CD Audio System [Std on G1500 SLT]	+384

Options	Price
AM/FM/CD Audio System	+325
AM/FM/CD Changer Audio System	+177
Camper/Towing Package	+186
Leather Seats [Opt on G1500 SLT]	+778
Locking Differential [Std on G1500 SLT]	+151
Power Driver Seat [Std on G1500 SLT]	+144
Power Windows [Std on G1500 SLT]	+159

2001

Body Styles	TMV Pricing		
	Trade	Private	Dealer
3 Dr G1500 Pass Van	9236	10591	11842
3 Dr G1500 SLT Pass Van	14095	16163	18072
3 Dr G2500 Pass Van	10153	11643	13018

Body Styles	TMV Pricing		
	Trade	Private	Dealer
3 Dr G2500 Pass Van Ext	10750	12327	13783
3 Dr G3500 Pass Van	10586	12139	13573
3 Dr G3500 Pass Van Ext	11073	12698	14198

Mileage Category: Q

GMC's full-size van gets a bigger, more powerful Big Block V8 engine, the Vortec 8100. There are also more advanced powertrain control modules for the other gas engines in the Savana line, and an improved torque converter for the 4L80-E four-speed automatic transmission. Other changes for 2001 include more robust door and ignition locks, upgraded audio systems, quieter alternators and longer-lasting brake pads. A luxury-lined SLT, complete with leather upholstery and on-board entertainment system, debuted midway through the model year.

Options	Price
15 Passenger Seating	+203
5.0L V8 OHV 16V FI Engine [Opt on 1500]	+270
5.7L V8 OHV 16V FI Engine [Opt on 1500]	+653
6.5L V8 Turbodiesel OHV 16V Engine	+1562
8.1L V8 OHV 16V FI Engine	+328
Air Conditioning - Front and Rear [Std on SLT]	+439
Aluminum/Alloy Wheels	+137
AM/FM/Cassette/CD Audio System [Std on SLT]	+351

Options	Price
AM/FM/CD Audio System	+296
Compact Disc Changer	+161
Leather Seats [Opt on SLT]	+710
Locking Differential [Std on SLT]	+138
Power Door Locks [Std on SLT]	+120
Power Driver Seat [Std on SLT]	+131
Power Passenger Seat [Std on SLT]	+131
Power Windows [Std on SLT]	+137

2000

Body Styles	TMV Pricing		
	Trade	Private	Dealer
3 Dr G1500 Pass Van	7621	8899	10151
3 Dr G1500 SLE Pass Van	8139	9504	10842
3 Dr G2500 Pass Van	8398	9806	11186
3 Dr G2500 Pass Van Ext	9019	10531	12013
3 Dr G2500 SLE Pass Van	9174	10713	12221

Body Styles	TMV Pricing		
	Trade	Private	Dealer
3 Dr G2500 SLE Pass Van Ext	10057	11743	13396
3 Dr G3500 Pass Van	8916	10411	11876
3 Dr G3500 Pass Van Ext	9070	10591	12082
3 Dr G3500 SLE Pass Van	9470	11058	12615
3 Dr G3500 SLE Pass Van Ext	10107	11802	13464

Mileage Category: Q

Improved powertrains, increased trailer ratings, seat-mounted tether anchors for installing child safety seats and an optional rear-window defogger mark the improvements for 2000.

Options	Price
15 Passenger Seating	+185
5.0L V8 OHV 16V FI Engine [Opt on 1500]	+246
5.7L V8 OHV 16V FI Engine [Opt on 1500]	+595
6.5L V8 Turbodiesel OHV 16V Engine	+1352
7.4L V8 OHV 16V FI Engine	+299

Options	Price
Air Conditioning - Front and Rear	+428
Aluminum/Alloy Wheels	+125
AM/FM/Cassette Audio System	+220
AM/FM/Cassette/CD Audio System	+320
AM/FM/CD Audio System	+270

2000 (cont'd)

Options	Price
Camper/Towing Package	+154
Chrome Wheels	+125
Limited Slip Differential	+125

Options	Price
Power Driver Seat	+119
Power Passenger Seat [Opt on SLE]	+119
Power Windows [Std on SLE]	+126

1999

Mileage Category: Q

Two new exterior colors, one new interior color and automatic transmission enhancements.

Body Styles	TMV Pricing		
	Trade	Private	Dealer
3 Dr G1500 Pass Van	6259	7473	8736
3 Dr G1500 SLE Pass Van	6539	7807	9127
3 Dr G2500 Pass Van	6638	7925	9265
3 Dr G2500 Pass Van Ext	6972	8324	9731
3 Dr G2500 SLE Pass Van	7080	8453	9882

Body Styles	TMV Pricing		
	Trade	Private	Dealer
3 Dr G2500 SLE Pass Van Ext	7375	8805	10294
3 Dr G3500 Pass Van	6917	8258	9654
3 Dr G3500 Pass Van Ext	7026	8389	9807
3 Dr G3500 SLE Pass Van	7293	8707	10179
3 Dr G3500 SLE Pass Van Ext	7422	8861	10359

Options	Price
15 Passenger Seating	+150
5.0L V8 OHV 16V FI Engine	+200
5.7L V8 OHV 16V FI Engine [Std on G2500, G3500]	+482
6.5L V8 Turbodiesel OHV 16V Engine	+1094
7.4L V8 OHV 16V FI Engine	+242

Options	Price
Air Conditioning - Front and Rear	+346
AM/FM/Cassette Audio System	+178
AM/FM/Cassette/CD Audio System	+259
AM/FM/CD Audio System	+218
Camper/Towing Package	+125

1998

Mileage Category: Q

New colors, transmission enhancements, more power for the diesel engine, revised uplevel stereos and the addition of a PassLock theft-deterrent system mark the changes for 1998. A mini-module driver airbag is new, but it and the passenger airbag still deploy at full-force levels.

Body Styles	TMV Pricing		
	Trade	Private	Dealer
3 Dr G1500 Pass Van	5511	6593	7813
3 Dr G1500 SLE Pass Van	5804	6944	8229
3 Dr G2500 Pass Van	5952	7121	8440
3 Dr G2500 Pass Van Ext	6199	7416	8789
3 Dr G2500 SLE Pass Van	6284	7518	8910

Body Styles	TMV Pricing		
	Trade	Private	Dealer
3 Dr G2500 SLE Pass Van Ext	6592	7887	9347
3 Dr G3500 Pass Van	6052	7240	8580
3 Dr G3500 Pass Van Ext	6247	7474	8857
3 Dr G3500 SLE Pass Van	6445	7711	9138
3 Dr G3500 SLE Pass Van Ext	6642	7946	9417

Options	Price
15 Passenger Seating	+129
5.0L V8 OHV 16V FI Engine	+172
5.7L V8 OHV 16V FI Engine [Std on G2500]	+335
6.5L V8 Turbodiesel OHV 16V Engine	+942
7.4L V8 OHV 16V FI Engine	+208

Options	Price
Air Conditioning - Front and Rear	+298
AM/FM/Cassette Audio System	+154
AM/FM/Cassette/CD Audio System	+223
AM/FM/CD Audio System	+188

1997

Mileage Category: Q

G3500 models get dual airbags, while daytime running lights are a new standard feature. Speed-sensitive steering reduces effort at low speeds. Chrome-plated wheels are a new option. Remote keyless entry key fobs are redesigned, and automatic transmissions provide better fuel economy and smoother shifts.

Body Styles	TMV Pricing		
	Trade	Private	Dealer
2 Dr G2500 SLE Pass Van	5514	6663	8067
2 Dr G2500 SLE Pass Van Ext	5700	6886	8336
3 Dr G1500 Pass Van	4710	5692	6893
3 Dr G1500 SLE Pass Van	4968	6005	7272
3 Dr G2500 Pass Van	5188	6271	7594

Body Styles	TMV Pricing		
	Trade	Private	Dealer
3 Dr G2500 Pass Van Ext	5382	6505	7878
3 Dr G3500 Pass Van	5237	6330	7665
3 Dr G3500 Pass Van Ext	5429	6562	7947
3 Dr G3500 SLE Pass Van	5525	6678	8087
3 Dr G3500 SLE Pass Van Ext	5718	6911	8369

Options	Price
15 Passenger Seating	+117
5.0L V8 OHV 16V FI Engine	+156
5.7L V8 OHV 16V FI Engine [Std on G3500]	+303
6.5L V8 Turbodiesel OHV 16V Engine	+853

Options	Price
7.4L V8 OHV 16V FI Engine	+188
Air Conditioning - Front and Rear [Opt on G1500]	+270
AM/FM/Cassette/CD Audio System	+201
AM/FM/CD Audio System	+170

1996

Mileage Category: Q

The Savana is a fully redesigned version of GMC's former Rally Wagon. It features a new line of more powerful engines, a larger overall size and numerous functional improvements that give it an edge over its aging competitors.

Body Styles	TMV Pricing		
	Trade	Private	Dealer
3 Dr G1500 Pass Van	3927	4809	6026
3 Dr G2500 Pass Van	4449	5448	6828
3 Dr G2500 Pass Van Ext	4750	5816	7289

Body Styles	TMV Pricing		
	Trade	Private	Dealer
3 Dr G3500 Pass Van	4470	5474	6860
3 Dr G3500 Pass Van Ext	4795	5871	7358

Options	Price
5.0L V8 OHV 16V FI Engine	+138
5.7L V8 OHV 16V FI Engine [Std on G2500,G3500]	+267
6.5L V8 Turbodiesel OHV 16V Engine	+755
7.4L V8 OHV 16V FI Engine	+166

Options	Price
Air Conditioning - Front and Rear	+223
AM/FM/Cassette/CD Audio System	+178
AM/FM/CD Audio System	+151

GMC
Sierra 1500
2003

Body Styles	TMV Pricing		
	Trade	Private	Dealer
2 Dr SLE 4WD Std Cab LB	17162	18305	20211
2 Dr SLE 4WD Std Cab SB	16985	18117	20003
2 Dr SLE Std Cab LB	14606	15579	17200
2 Dr SLE Std Cab SB	14405	15365	16964
2 Dr STD 4WD Std Cab LB	14907	15900	17555
2 Dr STD 4WD Std Cab SB	14730	15711	17347
2 Dr STD Std Cab LB	12034	12835	14171
2 Dr STD Std Cab SB	11857	12647	13963
2 Dr Work Truck 4WD Std Cab LB	14488	15453	17062
2 Dr Work Truck Std Cab LB	11614	12388	13677
4 Dr Denali AWD Ext Cab SB	27294	29112	32143
4 Dr SLE 4WD Ext Cab LB	19137	20412	22537

Body Styles	TMV Pricing		
	Trade	Private	Dealer
4 Dr SLE 4WD Ext Cab SB	18490	19722	21776
4 Dr SLE Ext Cab LB	17312	18466	20388
4 Dr SLE Ext Cab SB	16666	17776	19627
4 Dr SLT 4WD Ext Cab LB	20219	21566	23811
4 Dr SLT 4WD Ext Cab SB	19572	20876	23050
4 Dr SLT Ext Cab LB	18394	19620	21662
4 Dr SLT Ext Cab SB	17748	18930	20901
4 Dr STD 4WD Ext Cab LB	17524	18691	20637
4 Dr STD 4WD Ext Cab SB	16878	18002	19876
4 Dr STD Ext Cab LB	15759	16809	18558
4 Dr STD Ext Cab SB	15113	16120	17797
4 Dr Work Truck Ext Cab SB	13935	14864	16411

Options	Price
4 Wheel Steering [Opt on SLE,SLT]	+2894
Aluminum/Alloy Wheels [Opt on SLE,SLT]	+129
AM/FM/CD Audio System [Std on SLE,SLT]	+164
Automatic 4-Speed Transmission [Opt on STD,Work]	+705
Bose Audio System [Opt on SLE,SLT]	+129
Bucket Seats [Opt on SLE,SLT]	+274
Chrome Wheels [Opt on STD,Work]	+200
Cruise Control [Opt on STD,Work]	+155
Electronic Suspension Control [Opt on SLE,SLT]	+209
Limited Slip Differential	+190
Locking Differential	+190
Power Driver Seat [Opt on SLE]	+155
Power Passenger Seat [Opt on SLT]	+158

Options	Price
Power Windows [Opt on STD,Work]	+171
Traction Control System [Opt on STD,SLE,SLT]	+145
Two-Tone Paint [Opt on SLE,SLT]	+161
OnStar Telematic System [Opt on SLE]	+447
Stepside Bed [Opt on STD,SLE,SLT]	+512
AM/FM/CD Changer Audio System [Opt on SLE,SLT]	+383
Z71 Off-Road Suspension Package [Opt on SLE,SLT]	+177
Satellite Radio System [Opt on Denali,SLE,SLT]	+209
Automatic Climate Control (2 Zone) - Driver and Passenger [Opt on SLE]	+126
5.3L V8 Flex Fuel OHV 16V FI Engine	+515
5.3L V8 OHV 16V FI Engine	+515
Power Retractable Mirrors [Opt on SLE,SLT]	+118

Mileage Category: K

The Sierra gets a revised look this year that includes a new front fascia, revised side moldings and an additional wheel design. Top-of-the-line models get power-folding heated mirrors with puddle lamps and turn signal indicators. Inside, the Sierra now offers a Bose stereo system and XM Satellite Radio. The instrument panel and center console have been redesigned, and GMC has added new seats, a more comprehensive driver information center, optional satellite steering wheel controls and a dual-zone climate control system. For increased safety, Sierras now feature a standard front-passenger-sensing system and dual-stage airbags. All 4.3-liter V6-equipped Sierras and California-emission V8s are now ULEV certified, while electronic throttle control is now standard on all V8 engines. Finally, the Autotrac four-wheel-drive system has been modified for less intrusiveness at low speeds, and the brake system received upgrades that provide better pedal feel and improved overall performance.

2002

Body Styles	TMV Pricing		
	Trade	Private	Dealer
2 Dr HT 4WD Std Cab SB	14760	15846	17655
2 Dr HT Std Cab SB	12800	13742	15311
2 Dr SL 4WD Std Cab LB	13959	14986	16697
2 Dr SL 4WD Std Cab SB	13895	14917	16620
2 Dr SL Std Cab LB	11044	11857	13211
2 Dr SL Std Cab SB	10885	11686	13020
2 Dr SLE 4WD Std Cab LB	15251	16373	18243
2 Dr SLE 4WD Std Cab SB	15079	16189	18038
2 Dr SLE Std Cab LB	13442	14431	16079
2 Dr SLE Std Cab SB	13294	14272	15902
2 Dr STD 4WD Std Cab LB	12898	13847	15428
2 Dr STD 4WD Std Cab SB	12789	13730	15298
2 Dr STD Std Cab LB	10220	10972	12226
2 Dr STD Std Cab SB	10127	10872	12114
2 Dr Work Truck 4WD Std Cab LB	12776	13716	15282
2 Dr Work Truck Std Cab LB	9746	10451	11626
4 Dr Denali AWD Ext Cab SB	24453	26252	29250

Body Styles	TMV Pricing		
	Trade	Private	Dealer
4 Dr SL 4WD Ext Cab LB	15931	17103	19057
4 Dr SL 4WD Ext Cab SB	15770	16930	18864
4 Dr SL Ext Cab LB	14281	15331	17082
4 Dr SL Ext Cab SB	14106	15144	16874
4 Dr SLE 4WD Ext Cab LB	16826	18064	20127
4 Dr SLE 4WD Ext Cab SB	16645	17869	19910
4 Dr SLE Ext Cab LB	15104	16215	18066
4 Dr SLE Ext Cab SB	14903	15999	17826
4 Dr SLT 4WD Ext Cab LB	17822	19133	21319
4 Dr SLT 4WD Ext Cab SB	17650	18948	21112
4 Dr SLT Ext Cab LB	16065	17247	19217
4 Dr SLT Ext Cab SB	15879	17047	18994
4 Dr STD 4WD Ext Cab LB	15332	16460	18340
4 Dr STD 4WD Ext Cab SB	15171	16287	18147
4 Dr STD Ext Cab LB	13996	15026	16742
4 Dr STD Ext Cab SB	13935	14960	16669

Mileage Category: K

The Sierra C3 gets a name change to Sierra Denali in addition to a trick new four-wheel steering system. On standard Sierras, the previously optional Z85 firm-ride suspension is now standard on all 1500 models for improved handling and towing capacity. Base SL models now include air conditioning while uplevel SLE and SLT models add deep-tinted glass to the standard feature list.

GMC
Sierra 1500

2002 (cont'd)

Options	Price
4 Wheel Steering [Opt on Ext Cab - SLE,SLT]	+3105
4.8L V8 OHV 16V FI Engine [Opt on Std Cab 2WD - SL,STD,Work]	+416
5.3L V8 OHV 16V FI Engine	+479
Air Conditioning [Opt on Std Cab - STD,Work]	+494
AM/FM/CD Audio System [Opt on Ext Cab - SLE,SLT]	+117
Automatic 4-Speed Transmission [Opt on Std Cab 2WD - SL,STD,Work]	+656
Bucket Seats [Opt on SLE,SLT]	+153
Cruise Control [Std on SLE,SLT]	+144

Options	Price
Electronic Suspension Control [Opt on SLE,SLT]	+195
Locking Differential [Std on Denali,SLT 4WD]	+171
Off-Road Suspension Package [Opt on 4WD - SLE,SLT]	+180
Power Driver Seat [Opt on SLE]	+147
Power Passenger Seat [Opt on SLE]	+147
Running Boards [Opt on Ext Cab SB - Denali,SLE,SLT]	+150
Traction Control System [Opt on 2WD]	+135
Two-Tone Paint [Opt on Ext Cab SB - SLE,SLT]	+150

2001
Mileage Category: K

Reliability improvements for all Vortec V6 and V8 engines top the list of changes this year. Consequently, oil-change intervals have been extended to 7,500 miles. A traction assist feature is now available on two-wheel-drive V8 automatics, thanks to a new electronic throttle control system. Factory-installed OnStar, GM's mobile communications and security system, has been made standard with the SLT trim level. New this year is a 325-horse, all-wheel-drive performance version called the C3.

Body Styles	TMV Pricing		
	Trade	Private	Dealer
2 Dr SL 4WD Std Cab LB	12061	13430	14694
2 Dr SL 4WD Std Cab SB	12000	13362	14619
2 Dr SL Std Cab LB	8915	9926	10860
2 Dr SL Std Cab SB	8782	9779	10699
2 Dr SLE 4WD Std Cab LB	13820	15388	16836
2 Dr SLE 4WD Std Cab SB	13659	15209	16640
2 Dr SLE Std Cab LB	12157	13537	14810
2 Dr SLE Std Cab SB	12117	13492	14761
4 Dr SL 4WD Ext Cab LB	14155	15761	17244
4 Dr SL 4WD Ext Cab SB	14006	15596	17063

Body Styles	TMV Pricing		
	Trade	Private	Dealer
4 Dr SL Ext Cab LB	12515	13936	15247
4 Dr SL Ext Cab SB	12349	13750	15044
4 Dr SLE 4WD Ext Cab LB	15453	17207	18826
4 Dr SLE 4WD Ext Cab SB	15281	17015	18616
4 Dr SLE Ext Cab LB	13854	15426	16878
4 Dr SLE Ext Cab SB	13674	15226	16658
4 Dr SLT 4WD Ext Cab LB	16572	18453	20189
4 Dr SLT 4WD Ext Cab SB	16495	18368	20096
4 Dr SLT Ext Cab LB	14994	16695	18266
4 Dr SLT Ext Cab SB	14659	16323	17859

Options	Price
4.8L V8 OHV 16V FI Engine [Opt on SL Std Cab 2WD]	+380
5.3L V8 OHV 16V FI Engine	+437
Air Conditioning [Opt on SL]	+440
Automatic 4-Speed Transmission [Opt on SL]	+598
Bucket Seats	+137
Chrome Wheels [Opt on SL]	+169
Electronic Suspension Control	+177
Heated Front Seats	+137

Options	Price
Locking Differential	+156
Off-Road Suspension Package	+216
Power Driver Seat [Opt on SLE]	+131
Power Passenger Seat [Opt on SLE]	+131
Stepside Bed [Opt on SB]	+434
Traction Control System [Opt on 2WD]	+123
Two-Tone Paint	+137

2000
Mileage Category: K

After a complete redesign last year, GMC's Silverado-based pickup finally gets a fourth door on the extended cab. There's also more power on tap from the 4.8- and 5.3-liter engines, increased trailer ratings and standard programmable automatic door locks. New factory appearance items, such as wheel-lip flares and a soft tonneau cover, are now available on some models.

Body Styles	TMV Pricing		
	Trade	Private	Dealer
2 Dr SL 4WD Ext Cab LB	11852	13343	14805
2 Dr SL 4WD Ext Cab SB	11716	13191	14636
2 Dr SL 4WD Ext Cab Step SB	12120	13645	15140
2 Dr SL 4WD Std Cab LB	9171	10325	11457
2 Dr SL 4WD Std Cab SB	9037	10174	11289
2 Dr SL 4WD Std Cab Step SB	9441	10629	11793
2 Dr SL Ext Cab LB	10472	11790	13081
2 Dr SL Ext Cab SB	10335	11636	12911
2 Dr SL Ext Cab Step SB	10739	12090	13415
2 Dr SL Std Cab LB	7784	8764	9724
2 Dr SL Std Cab SB	7648	8611	9554
2 Dr SL Std Cab Step SB	8052	9066	10059
2 Dr SLE 4WD Ext Cab LB	12931	14558	16152
2 Dr SLE 4WD Ext Cab SB	12795	14404	15982
2 Dr SLE 4WD Ext Cab Step SB	13153	14808	16430

Body Styles	TMV Pricing		
	Trade	Private	Dealer
2 Dr SLE 4WD Std Cab LB	10839	12204	13541
2 Dr SLE 4WD Std Cab SB	10705	12052	13372
2 Dr SLE 4WD Std Cab Step SB	11062	12454	13819
2 Dr SLE Ext Cab LB	11549	13002	14426
2 Dr SLE Ext Cab SB	11414	12850	14258
2 Dr SLE Ext Cab Step SB	11771	13253	14705
2 Dr SLE Std Cab LB	9458	10649	11816
2 Dr SLE Std Cab SB	9323	10497	11648
2 Dr SLE Std Cab Step SB	9682	10901	12095
2 Dr SLT 4WD Ext Cab LB	13887	15635	17348
2 Dr SLT 4WD Ext Cab SB	13751	15482	17179
2 Dr SLT 4WD Ext Cab Step SB	14111	15887	17627
2 Dr SLT Ext Cab LB	12338	13890	15412
2 Dr SLT Ext Cab SB	12203	13738	15243
2 Dr SLT Ext Cab Step SB	12561	14142	15692

Options	Price
4.8L V8 OHV 16V FI Engine [Opt on SL,SLE]	+346
5.3L V8 OHV 16V FI Engine [Opt on SLE,SLT]	+399
Air Conditioning [Opt on SL]	+401
Aluminum/Alloy Wheels	+154
AM/FM/Cassette/CD Audio System	+144
Automatic 4-Speed Transmission [Opt on SL,SLE]	+545
Bucket Seats	+125

Options	Price
Chrome Wheels [Opt on SLE]	+154
Heated Front Seats	+125
Hinged Fourth Door	+164
Limited Slip Differential	+134
Power Driver Seat [Opt on SLE]	+119
Power Passenger Seat [Opt on SLE]	+119

1999

Mileage Category: K

Finally, the decade-old, full-size GMC pickup based on the C/K gets a complete redesign from the ground-up. Major structural, power, braking and interior enhancements characterize the all-new Sierra. Styling is evolutionary rather than revolutionary, both inside and out.

Body Styles	Trade	Private	Dealer
2 Dr SL 4WD Ext Cab LB	10116	11548	13039
2 Dr SL 4WD Ext Cab SB	9998	11414	12888
2 Dr SL 4WD Ext Cab Step SB	10561	12056	13612
2 Dr SL 4WD Std Cab LB	7794	8897	10046
2 Dr SL 4WD Std Cab SB	7677	8764	9895
2 Dr SL 4WD Std Cab Step SB	7948	9073	10244
2 Dr SL Ext Cab LB	8922	10185	11499
2 Dr SL Ext Cab SB	8804	10051	11348
2 Dr SL Ext Cab Step SB	9075	10360	11697
2 Dr SL Std Cab LB	6594	7527	8498
2 Dr SL Std Cab SB	6475	7392	8347
2 Dr SL Std Cab Step SB	6747	7703	8697
2 Dr SLE 4WD Ext Cab LB	11305	12905	14571
2 Dr SLE 4WD Ext Cab SB	11184	12767	14415
2 Dr SLE 4WD Ext Cab Step SB	11416	13032	14713

Body Styles	Trade	Private	Dealer
2 Dr SLE 4WD Std Cab LB	9254	10564	11928
2 Dr SLE 4WD Std Cab SB	9138	10432	11778
2 Dr SLE 4WD Std Cab Step SB	9370	10696	12077
2 Dr SLE Ext Cab LB	9789	11176	12619
2 Dr SLE Ext Cab SB	9673	11043	12468
2 Dr SLE Ext Cab Step SB	9905	11307	12767
2 Dr SLE Std Cab LB	8060	9201	10389
2 Dr SLE Std Cab SB	7943	9068	10238
2 Dr SLE Std Cab Step SB	8175	9332	10537
2 Dr SLT 4WD Ext Cab LB	12173	13896	15690
2 Dr SLT 4WD Ext Cab SB	12053	13759	15535
2 Dr SLT 4WD Ext Cab Step SB	12405	14161	15988
2 Dr SLT Ext Cab LB	10793	12321	13912
2 Dr SLT Ext Cab SB	10674	12185	13758
2 Dr SLT Ext Cab Step SB	10911	12456	14064

Options	Price
4.8L V8 OHV 16V FI Engine [Std on SLT]	+239
5.3L V8 OHV 16V FI Engine	+282
Air Conditioning [Opt on SL]	+324
Aluminum/Alloy Wheels [Std on SLT]	+125

Options	Price
AM/FM/Cassette/CD Audio System	+117
Automatic 4-Speed Transmission [Std on SLT]	+401
Chrome Wheels [Opt on SL]	+125

1998

Mileage Category: K

With an all-new Sierra just one year away, changes are minimal. Diesel engines make more power and torque, extended cab models get rear heater ducts, a PassLock theft-deterrent system is standard, 1500-Series trucks get reduced rolling resistance tires and three new colors debut. Second-generation airbags are standard.

Body Styles	Trade	Private	Dealer
2 Dr C1500 SL Ext Cab LB	6777	7892	9149
2 Dr C1500 SL Ext Cab SB	6506	7577	8784
2 Dr C1500 SL Std Cab LB	5929	6904	8004
2 Dr C1500 SL Std Cab SB	5826	6785	7866
2 Dr C1500 SL Std Cab Step SB	6021	7012	8130
2 Dr C1500 SLE Ext Cab LB	7383	8598	9968
2 Dr C1500 SLE Ext Cab SB	7111	8282	9602
2 Dr C1500 SLE Ext Cab Step SB	8117	9453	10959
2 Dr C1500 SLE Std Cab LB	6535	7610	8823
2 Dr C1500 SLE Std Cab SB	6432	7491	8685
2 Dr C1500 SLE Std Cab Step SB	6628	7719	8949
2 Dr C1500 SLT Ext Cab LB	8170	9514	11030
2 Dr C1500 SLT Ext Cab SB	7898	9199	10666
2 Dr C1500 SLT Ext Cab Step SB	8735	10173	11795
2 Dr C1500 SLT Std Cab LB	7300	8501	9856
2 Dr C1500 SLT Std Cab SB	7199	8383	9719
2 Dr C1500 SLT Std Cab Step SB	7393	8610	9982
2 Dr C1500 Special Std Cab LB	5450	6347	7359
2 Dr C1500 Special Std Cab SB	5341	6220	7212
2 Dr K1500 SL 4WD Ext Cab LB	7795	9078	10524
2 Dr K1500 SL 4WD Ext Cab SB	7524	8762	10159

Body Styles	Trade	Private	Dealer
2 Dr K1500 SL 4WD Std Cab LB	6947	8091	9380
2 Dr K1500 SL 4WD Std Cab SB	6844	7971	9242
2 Dr K1500 SL 4WD Std Cab Step SB	7040	8199	9506
2 Dr K1500 SLE 4WD Ext Cab LB	8400	9783	11343
2 Dr K1500 SLE 4WD Ext Cab SB	8130	9469	10978
2 Dr K1500 SLE 4WD Ext Cab Step SB	9136	10640	12335
2 Dr K1500 SLE 4WD Std Cab LB	7554	8797	10199
2 Dr K1500 SLE 4WD Std Cab SB	7451	8678	10061
2 Dr K1500 SLE 4WD Std Cab Step SB	7646	8905	10325
2 Dr K1500 SLT 4WD Ext Cab LB	9190	10702	12407
2 Dr K1500 SLT 4WD Ext Cab SB	8918	10386	12041
2 Dr K1500 SLT 4WD Ext Cab Step SB	9755	11360	13170
2 Dr K1500 SLT 4WD Std Cab LB	8318	9688	11232
2 Dr K1500 SLT 4WD Std Cab SB	8217	9570	11095
2 Dr K1500 SLT 4WD Std Cab Step SB	8412	9797	11358
2 Dr K1500 Special 4WD Std Cab LB	6708	7812	9057
2 Dr K1500 Special 4WD Std Cab SB	6598	7684	8909

Options	Price
Hinged Third Door	+146
5.0L V8 OHV 16V FI Engine	+172
5.7L V8 OHV 16V FI Engine	+243
6.5L V8 Turbodiesel OHV 16V Engine	+1173

Options	Price
Air Conditioning [Opt on SL,Special]	+279
Aluminum/Alloy Wheels	+118
Automatic 4-Speed Transmission	+337

1997

Mileage Category: K

A passenger airbag is added to models with a GVWR under 8,600 pounds, and all models get speed-sensitive steering that reduces low-speed effort. K1500 models have a tighter turning radius for better maneuverability. Automatic transmissions are refined to provide smoother shifts and improved efficiency. Three new paint colors debut.

Body Styles	Trade	Private	Dealer
2 Dr C1500 GT Std Cab SB	5768	6787	8033
2 Dr C1500 SL Ext Cab LB	5929	6976	8255
2 Dr C1500 SL Ext Cab SB	5629	6623	7838
2 Dr C1500 SL Ext Cab Step SB	5802	6827	8079

Body Styles	Trade	Private	Dealer
2 Dr C1500 SL Std Cab LB	5094	5994	7093
2 Dr C1500 SL Std Cab SB	5002	5886	6967
2 Dr C1500 SL Std Cab Step SB	5176	6090	7208
2 Dr C1500 SLE Ext Cab LB	6504	7653	9057

1997 (cont'd)

Body Styles	TMV Pricing		
	Trade	Private	Dealer
2 Dr C1500 SLE Ext Cab SB	6206	7302	8641
2 Dr C1500 SLE Ext Cab Step SB	6529	7682	9091
2 Dr C1500 SLE Std Cab LB	5670	6671	7895
2 Dr C1500 SLE Std Cab SB	5579	6565	7769
2 Dr C1500 SLE Std Cab Step SB	5753	6769	8010
2 Dr C1500 SLT Ext Cab LB	7022	8262	9777
2 Dr C1500 SLT Ext Cab SB	6722	7909	9360
2 Dr C1500 SLT Ext Cab Step SB	7045	8290	9811
2 Dr C1500 SLT Std Cab LB	6166	7255	8587
2 Dr C1500 SLT Std Cab SB	6076	7149	8461
2 Dr C1500 SLT Std Cab Step SB	6249	7353	8702
2 Dr C1500 Special Std Cab LB	4706	5537	6553
2 Dr C1500 Special Std Cab SB	4580	5389	6378
2 Dr K1500 SL 4WD Ext Cab LB	6770	7966	9427
2 Dr K1500 SL 4WD Ext Cab SB	6473	7616	9013
2 Dr K1500 SL 4WD Ext Cab Step SB	6645	7819	9254
2 Dr K1500 SL 4WD Std Cab LB	5995	7054	8349
2 Dr K1500 SL 4WD Std Cab SB	5905	6948	8223

Body Styles	TMV Pricing		
	Trade	Private	Dealer
2 Dr K1500 SL 4WD Std Cab Step SB	6078	7152	8464
2 Dr K1500 SLE 4WD Ext Cab LB	7345	8643	10229
2 Dr K1500 SLE 4WD Ext Cab SB	7049	8294	9815
2 Dr K1500 SLE 4WD Ext Cab Step SB	7371	8673	10264
2 Dr K1500 SLE 4WD Std Cab LB	6571	7732	9151
2 Dr K1500 SLE 4WD Std Cab SB	6481	7626	9025
2 Dr K1500 SLE 4WD Std Cab Step SB	6654	7829	9266
2 Dr K1500 SLT 4WD Ext Cab LB	7780	9155	10835
2 Dr K1500 SLT 4WD Ext Cab SB	7565	8902	10535
2 Dr K1500 SLT 4WD Ext Cab Step SB	7739	9106	10776
2 Dr K1500 SLT 4WD Std Cab LB	7070	8318	9844
2 Dr K1500 SLT 4WD Std Cab SB	6978	8211	9718
2 Dr K1500 SLT 4WD Std Cab Step SB	7152	8415	9959
2 Dr K1500 Special 4WD Std Cab LB	5788	6810	8060
2 Dr K1500 Special 4WD Std Cab SB	5693	6698	7927

Options	Price
5.0L V8 OHV 16V FI Engine	+156
5.7L V8 OHV 16V FI Engine	+220
6.5L V8 Turbodiesel OHV 16V Engine	+1062

Options	Price
Air Conditioning [Opt on SL,Special]	+253
Automatic 4-Speed Transmission	+305
Hinged Third Door	+132

1996

Mileage Category: K

A new series of engines is introduced, providing more power and torque than last year's offerings. Called Vortec, this family of engines includes a 4.3-liter V6 (the only six-cylinder of the bunch) capable of 200 hp @ 4,400 rpm and 255 lb-ft of torque @ 2,800 rpm; a 5.0-liter V8, producing 220 hp @ 4,600 rpm and 285 lb-ft of torque @ 2,800 rpm; and a 5.7-liter V8, rated at 250 hp @ 4,600 rpm and 335 lb-ft of torque @ 2,800 rpm. (There is also a 7.4-liter Vortec V8, but it's only available on the heavier duty C/K 3500 trucks.) All of these figures represent increases in output when compared to their respective 1995 predecessors. An optional electronic shift transfer case for the K1500 (i.e. 4WD; C= 2WD; K= 4WD) rounds out the list of the most significant powertrain updates for this year.

Other noteworthy updates include the introduction of an optional passenger-side third door, called the "Easy-Access System," in GM vernacular. This feature is only available on the extended cab body styles.

Improved comfort and convenience comes in the way of such new features as illuminated entry, 12-volt power outlets, an electrochromic inside rearview mirror and height-adjustable D-rings for the shoulder section of the front three-point safety belts, among others. Daytime Running Lamps (DRLs) are part the list of new exterior features.

A new level of sophistication in exhaust emissions monitoring is found with the addition of OBD II, the second generation of On-Board Diagnostics.

Body Styles	TMV Pricing		
	Trade	Private	Dealer
2 Dr C1500 SL Ext Cab LB	4982	5911	7193
2 Dr C1500 SL Ext Cab SB	4737	5620	6839
2 Dr C1500 SL Ext Cab Step SB	4844	5747	6993
2 Dr C1500 SL Std Cab LB	4273	5069	6168
2 Dr C1500 SL Std Cab SB	4278	5075	6175
2 Dr C1500 SL Std Cab Step SB	4200	4982	6063
2 Dr C1500 SLE Ext Cab LB	5613	6658	8102
2 Dr C1500 SLE Ext Cab SB	5366	6366	7747
2 Dr C1500 SLE Ext Cab Step SB	5500	6525	7940
2 Dr C1500 SLE Std Cab LB	4903	5816	7077
2 Dr C1500 SLE Std Cab SB	4829	5729	6971
2 Dr C1500 SLE Std Cab Step SB	5041	5980	7277
2 Dr C1500 SLT Ext Cab LB	6057	7186	8744
2 Dr C1500 SLT Ext Cab SB	5812	6894	8389
2 Dr C1500 SLT Ext Cab Step SB	5944	7052	8581
2 Dr C1500 SLT Std Cab LB	5329	6322	7693
2 Dr C1500 SLT Std Cab SB	5257	6236	7589
2 Dr C1500 SLT Std Cab Step SB	5468	6487	7894
2 Dr C1500 Special Std Cab LB	3936	4670	5683
2 Dr C1500 Special Std Cab SB	3832	4546	5532
2 Dr K1500 SL 4WD Ext Cab LB	5651	6704	8158
2 Dr K1500 SL 4WD Ext Cab SB	5449	6464	7866

Body Styles	TMV Pricing		
	Trade	Private	Dealer
2 Dr K1500 SL 4WD Ext Cab Step SB	5556	6592	8022
2 Dr K1500 SL 4WD Std Cab LB	5035	5973	7268
2 Dr K1500 SL 4WD Std Cab SB	4958	5881	7156
2 Dr K1500 SL 4WD Std Cab Step SB	5103	6054	7367
2 Dr K1500 SLE 4WD Ext Cab LB	6280	7451	9067
2 Dr K1500 SLE 4WD Ext Cab SB	6079	7212	8776
2 Dr K1500 SLE 4WD Ext Cab Step SB	6212	7370	8968
2 Dr K1500 SLE 4WD Std Cab LB	5664	6719	8177
2 Dr K1500 SLE 4WD Std Cab SB	5587	6628	8065
2 Dr K1500 SLE 4WD Std Cab Step SB	5734	6802	8277
2 Dr K1500 SLT 4WD Ext Cab LB	6725	7978	9709
2 Dr K1500 SLT 4WD Ext Cab SB	6523	7738	9417
2 Dr K1500 SLT 4WD Ext Cab Step SB	6631	7867	9573
2 Dr K1500 SLT 4WD Std Cab LB	6090	7225	8793
2 Dr K1500 SLT 4WD Std Cab SB	6013	7134	8681
2 Dr K1500 SLT 4WD Std Cab Step SB	6160	7308	8893
2 Dr K1500 Special 4WD Std Cab LB	4825	5724	6965
2 Dr K1500 Special 4WD Std Cab SB	4772	5661	6889

Options	Price
5.0L V8 OHV 16V FI Engine	+138
5.7L V8 OHV 16V FI Engine	+194
6.5L V8 Turbodiesel OHV 16V Engine	+939

Options	Price
Air Conditioning [Opt on SL,Special]	+223
Automatic 4-Speed Transmission	+269
Hinged Third Door	+116

Mileage Category: K

Body Styles	TMV Pricing		
	Trade	Private	Dealer
2 Dr C1500 SL Ext Cab LB	4328	5145	6506
2 Dr C1500 SL Ext Cab SB	4133	4913	6212
2 Dr C1500 SL Ext Cab Step SB	4253	5056	6393
2 Dr C1500 SL Std Cab LB	3703	4402	5566
2 Dr C1500 SL Std Cab SB	3636	4322	5466
2 Dr C1500 SL Std Cab Step SB	3827	4549	5753
2 Dr C1500 SLE Ext Cab LB	4816	5725	7239
2 Dr C1500 SLE Ext Cab SB	4594	5461	6905
2 Dr C1500 SLE Ext Cab Step SB	4714	5604	7086
2 Dr C1500 SLE Std Cab LB	4141	4922	6224
2 Dr C1500 SLE Std Cab SB	4075	4844	6125
2 Dr C1500 SLE Std Cab Step SB	4265	5070	6412
2 Dr C1500 SLT Ext Cab LB	5268	6262	7919
2 Dr C1500 SLT Ext Cab SB	5046	5999	7586
2 Dr C1500 SLT Ext Cab Step SB	5167	6142	7767
2 Dr C1500 Special Std Cab LB	3400	4041	5110
2 Dr C1500 Special Std Cab SB	3305	3929	4969
2 Dr K1500 SL 4WD Ext Cab LB	4859	5776	7303
2 Dr K1500 SL 4WD Ext Cab SB	4703	5590	7068
2 Dr K1500 SL 4WD Ext Cab Step SB	4799	5705	7214

Body Styles	TMV Pricing		
	Trade	Private	Dealer
2 Dr K1500 SL 4WD Std Cab LB	4316	5131	6488
2 Dr K1500 SL 4WD Std Cab SB	4245	5046	6382
2 Dr K1500 SL 4WD Std Cab Step SB	4436	5273	6669
2 Dr K1500 SLE 4WD Ext Cab LB	5416	6438	8141
2 Dr K1500 SLE 4WD Ext Cab SB	5163	6138	7762
2 Dr K1500 SLE 4WD Ext Cab Step SB	5260	6253	7908
2 Dr K1500 SLE 4WD Std Cab LB	4753	5650	7146
2 Dr K1500 SLE 4WD Std Cab SB	4683	5567	7040
2 Dr K1500 SLE 4WD Std Cab Step SB	4875	5795	7328
2 Dr K1500 SLS 4WD Ext Cab SB	4702	5589	7068
2 Dr K1500 SLS 4WD Ext Cab Step SB	4799	5705	7214
2 Dr K1500 SLT 4WD Ext Cab LB	5797	6891	8715
2 Dr K1500 SLT 4WD Ext Cab SB	5617	6677	8443
2 Dr K1500 SLT 4WD Ext Cab Step SB	5713	6791	8588
2 Dr K1500 Special 4WD Std Cab LB	4138	4919	6220
2 Dr K1500 Special 4WD Std Cab SB	4089	4861	6148

Options	Price
Automatic 4-Speed Transmission	+250
Compact Disc Changer	+142
5.0L V8 OHV 16V FI Engine	+128
5.7L V8 OHV 16V FI Engine	+180

Options	Price
6.5L V8 Turbodiesel OHV 16V Engine	+873
Air Conditioning [Opt on SL,SLS,Special]	+207
AM/FM/Cassette/CD Audio System	+75

A revised interior graces these full-size trucks this year. A new driver-side airbag and a shift interlock are added in the interest of safety. The latter requires the brake pedal to be depressed before the automatic transmission's gear selector can be shifted out of "park." This reduces the likelihood that the vehicle will move suddenly and unexpectedly when the transmission is taken out of "park." Power mirrors, revised climate controls and cupholders provide a more user-friendly interior environment.

Mechanical enhancements include the addition of standard 4-wheel antilock brakes, improvements in the engines and modifications to the heavy-duty 4L80-E. The four-wheel ABS replaces last year's rear-wheel-only antilock system. Various upgrades to the engines are intended to reduce noise, improve durability and/or increase efficiency. The transmission is revised for quicker 1-2 upshifts during full-throttle applications.

1994

Mileage Category: K

Body Styles	TMV Pricing		
	Trade	Private	Dealer
2 Dr C1500 SL Ext Cab LB	3563	4398	5789
2 Dr C1500 SL Ext Cab SB	3289	4060	5344
2 Dr C1500 SL Ext Cab Step SB	3458	4268	5617
2 Dr C1500 SL Std Cab LB	3080	3802	5004
2 Dr C1500 SL Std Cab SB	2981	3679	4842
2 Dr C1500 SL Std Cab Step SB	3078	3799	5001
2 Dr C1500 SLE Ext Cab LB	3619	4467	5880
2 Dr C1500 SLE Ext Cab SB	3528	4354	5731
2 Dr C1500 SLE Ext Cab Step SB	3755	4634	6099
2 Dr C1500 SLE Std Cab LB	3067	3785	4982
2 Dr C1500 SLE Std Cab SB	3096	3821	5030
2 Dr C1500 SLE Std Cab Step SB	3279	4047	5327
2 Dr C1500 SLT Ext Cab LB	2259	3014	4273
2 Dr C1500 SLT Ext Cab SB	4116	5080	6686
2 Dr C1500 SLT Ext Cab Step SB	4371	5395	7102
2 Dr C1500 Special Std Cab LB	2633	3250	4278
2 Dr C1500 Special Std Cab SB	2583	3188	4197
2 Dr K1500 SL 4WD Ext Cab LB	4074	5028	6618

Body Styles	TMV Pricing		
	Trade	Private	Dealer
2 Dr K1500 SL 4WD Ext Cab SB	3678	4539	5974
2 Dr K1500 SL 4WD Ext Cab Step SB	3975	4906	6457
2 Dr K1500 SL 4WD Std Cab LB	3576	4414	5810
2 Dr K1500 SL 4WD Std Cab SB	3428	4231	5568
2 Dr K1500 SL 4WD Std Cab Step SB	3498	4317	5683
2 Dr K1500 SLE 4WD Ext Cab LB	4072	5026	6616
2 Dr K1500 SLE 4WD Ext Cab SB	4122	5088	6697
2 Dr K1500 SLE 4WD Ext Cab Step SB	4173	5151	6780
2 Dr K1500 SLE 4WD Std Cab LB	3716	4586	6037
2 Dr K1500 SLE 4WD Std Cab SB	3821	4716	6207
2 Dr K1500 SLE 4WD Std Cab Step SB	3912	4829	6356
2 Dr K1500 SLT 4WD Ext Cab LB	4504	5556	7310
2 Dr K1500 SLT 4WD Ext Cab SB	4650	5739	7554
2 Dr K1500 SLT 4WD Ext Cab Step SB	4679	5775	7602
2 Dr K1500 Special 4WD Std Cab LB	3329	4109	5409

Options	Price
Automatic 4-Speed Transmission	+225
6.5L V8 Diesel OHV 16V Engine	+592
6.5L V8 Turbodiesel OHV 16V Engine	+786
Air Conditioning	+187

Safety is enhanced with the side door guard beams designed to minimize intrusion into the passenger compartment during a side impact. A center high-mounted brake light is also added to enhance safety.

An optional 6.5-liter turbodiesel is offered as an option; the 5.0- and 5.7-liter engines receive some new hardware, intended to improve reliability and durability.

Rust corrosion protection is improved while interior noise vibration and harshness is reduced. Rounding out the list of significant improvements are the addition of an "easy entry" feature to the front passenger seat on extended cab body styles to ease entry into the rear seating positions and the revision of the exterior front end styling.

GMC
Sierra 1500HD
2003

Body Styles	TMV Pricing		
	Trade	Private	Dealer
4 Dr SLE 4WD Crew Cab SB HD	21620	22888	25002
4 Dr SLE Crew Cab SB HD	19553	20700	22611

Options	Price
4 Wheel Steering	+2894
Aluminum/Alloy Wheels	+129
Bose Audio System	+129
Bucket Seats	+274
Electronic Suspension Control	+209
Limited Slip Differential	+190
Locking Differential	+190
Power Driver Seat [Opt on SLE]	+155

Body Styles	TMV Pricing		
	Trade	Private	Dealer
4 Dr SLT 4WD Crew Cab SB HD	22950	24296	26540
4 Dr SLT Crew Cab SB HD	20789	22009	24041

Options	Price
Power Passenger Seat [Opt on SLT]	+158
Traction Control System	+145
OnStar Telematic System [Opt on SLE]	+447
AM/FM/CD Changer Audio System	+383
Satellite Radio System	+209
Automatic Climate Control (2 Zone) - Driver and Passenger [Opt on SLE]	+126
DVD Entertainment System	+834
Power Retractable Mirrors	+118

Mileage Category: K

The Sierra gets a new look this year that includes a new front fascia and revised side moldings. On the inside, the Sierra offers new entertainment options, such as a Bose audio system with rear seat controls, XM Satellite Radio and a rear-passenger DVD entertainment system. The instrument panel and center console have been redesigned, and GMC has added new seats, a more comprehensive driver information center and a dual-zone climate control system. For increased safety, Sierras now feature a standard front-passenger-sensing system that deactivates the airbag for children. On the hardware side, the all-new Quadrasteer four-wheel steering system, which increases low-speed maneuverability and towing stability, is now optional. The standard 6.0-liter V8 gets electronic throttle control, as well as the ability to run exclusively on Compressed Natural Gas (CNG) or a mix of CNG and gasoline.

2002

Body Styles	TMV Pricing		
	Trade	Private	Dealer
4 Dr SLE 4WD Crew Cab SB HD	20043	21383	23616
4 Dr SLE Crew Cab SB HD	17972	19193	21229

Options	Price
Bucket Seats	+254

Body Styles	TMV Pricing		
	Trade	Private	Dealer
4 Dr SLT 4WD Crew Cab SB HD	21143	22580	24974
4 Dr SLT Crew Cab SB HD	19021	20314	22468

Options	Price
Locking Differential [Opt on 2WD]	+177

Mileage Category: K

Debuting late last year as an all-new 2001 model, the 1500HD Crew Cab gets few changes for the 2002 model year. Deep-tinted glass is now standard, and a Cold Weather option package with heated exterior mirrors and a rear window defogger have been added.

2001
Mileage Category: K

A crew cab version debuts, called Sierra 1500HD. Oil-change intervals have been extended to 10,000 miles. A traction control system is now available on two-wheel-drive V8 automatics, thanks to a new electronic throttle control system. OnStar, GM's mobile communications and security system, has been made standard with the SLT trim level.

Body Styles	TMV Pricing		
	Trade	Private	Dealer
4 Dr SLE 4WD Crew Cab SB HD	17510	19357	21061
4 Dr SLE Crew Cab SB HD	15656	17307	18831

Options	Price
Bucket Seats [Opt on SLE]	+137
Heated Front Seats	+137
Leather Seats [Opt on SLE]	+699

Body Styles	TMV Pricing		
	Trade	Private	Dealer
4 Dr SLT 4WD Crew Cab SB HD	18498	20449	22250
4 Dr SLT Crew Cab SB HD	16601	18352	19968

Options	Price
Locking Differential	+156
Power Driver Seat [Opt on SLE]	+131
Power Passenger Seat [Opt on SLE]	+131

GMC
Sierra 2500
2003

Body Styles	TMV Pricing		
	Trade	Private	Dealer
2 Dr SLE Std Cab LB	17124	18219	20044
2 Dr STD Std Cab LB	15130	16097	17709
2 Dr Work Truck Std Cab LB	14546	15476	17025

Body Styles	TMV Pricing		
	Trade	Private	Dealer
4 Dr SLE 4WD Ext Cab SB	21480	22853	25142
4 Dr SLT 4WD Ext Cab SB	22643	24091	26504
4 Dr STD 4WD Ext Cab SB	19646	20902	22996

2003 (cont'd)

Options	Price
AM/FM/CD Audio System [Opt on STD,Work]	+164
Automatic 4-Speed Transmission [Opt on SLE,STD,Work]	+705
Bose Audio System [Opt on SLE,SLT]	+129
Bucket Seats [Opt on SLE,SLT]	+274
Chrome Wheels [Opt on STD]	+200
Cruise Control [Opt on STD,Work]	+155
Locking Differential	+190
Power Driver Seat [Opt on SLE]	+155

Options	Price
Power Passenger Seat [Opt on SLT]	+158
Traction Control System [Opt on SLE,STD]	+145
Two-Tone Paint [Opt on SLE,SLT]	+161
OnStar Telematic System [Opt on SLE]	+447
AM/FM/CD Changer Audio System [Opt on SLE,SLT]	+383
Satellite Radio System [Opt on SLE,SLT]	+209
Automatic Climate Control (2 Zone) - Driver and Passenger [Opt on SLE]	+126
Power Retractable Mirrors [Opt on SLE,SLT]	+118

Mileage Category: K

The Sierra gets a revised look this year that includes a new front fascia, revised side moldings and an additional wheel design. Top-of-the-line models get power-folding heated mirrors with puddle lamps and turn signal indicators. On the inside, the Sierra now offers a Bose stereo system and XM Satellite Radio. The instrument panel and center console have been redesigned, and GMC has added new seats, a more comprehensive driver information center, optional satellite steering wheel controls and a dual-zone climate control system. For increased safety, Sierras now feature a standard front-passenger-sensing system and dual-stage airbags. On the hardware side, the standard 6.0-liter V8 gets electronic throttle control, as well as the ability to run exclusively on compressed natural gas (CNG) or a mix of CNG and gasoline. The Autotrac four-wheel-drive system has been modified for less intrusiveness at low speeds, and the brake system received upgrades that provide better pedal feel and improved overall performance.

2002

Body Styles	Trade	Private	Dealer
2 Dr SL Std Cab LB	14392	15420	17133
2 Dr SLE Std Cab LB	15034	16108	17897
2 Dr STD Std Cab LB	13114	14050	15611
4 Dr SL 4WD Ext Cab SB	18221	19522	21691

Body Styles	Trade	Private	Dealer
4 Dr SLE 4WD Ext Cab SB	19366	20749	23054
4 Dr SLT 4WD Ext Cab SB	20418	21876	24306
4 Dr STD 4WD Ext Cab SB	17394	18636	20707

Options	Price
Air Conditioning [Opt on STD Std Cab]	+494
AM/FM/CD Audio System [Opt on STD]	+117
Automatic 4-Speed Transmission [Opt on Std Cab]	+656
Bucket Seats [Opt on SLE,SLT]	+254
Cruise Control [Opt on SL,STD]	+144

Options	Price
Locking Differential [Opt on 2WD]	+177
Power Driver Seat [Opt on SLE]	+147
Power Passenger Seat [Opt on SLE]	+147
Traction Control System [Opt on 2WD]	+135
Two-Tone Paint [Opt on Ext Cab SB - SLE,SLT]	+150

Mileage Category: K

GMC's light-duty 2500s get only minor changes for 2002. Base model SLs now come standard with air conditioning, while uplevel SLE and SLT models get standard deep-tinted glass. All Sierras get redesigned badging and extendable sun visors.

2001

Body Styles	Trade	Private	Dealer
2 Dr SL Std Cab LB	11920	13235	14448
2 Dr SLE Std Cab LB	13211	14668	16012
4 Dr SL 4WD Ext Cab SB	15394	17092	18659

Body Styles	Trade	Private	Dealer
4 Dr SLE 4WD Ext Cab SB	16729	18573	20276
4 Dr SLT 4WD Ext Cab SB	17932	19909	21734

Options	Price
Air Conditioning [Opt on SL]	+440
Automatic 4-Speed Transmission [Opt on SL,SLE]	+598
Bucket Seats	+137
Heated Front Seats	+137
Locking Differential	+156

Options	Price
Power Driver Seat [Opt on SLE]	+131
Power Passenger Seat [Opt on SLE]	+131
Traction Control System [Opt on Std Cab]	+123
Two-Tone Paint	+137

Mileage Category: K

Both light- and heavy-duty 2500s sport new torsion bar front suspensions. Light-duty models now offer optional traction control and standard child safety-seat tethers. Heavy-duty Sierras are completely redesigned for 2001 offering two new engines and transmissions, bigger interiors and numerous other improvements aimed at buyers looking for a "professional grade" truck from GM.

2000

Body Styles	Trade	Private	Dealer
2 Dr SL 4WD Ext Cab LB HD	13704	15417	17096
2 Dr SL 4WD Ext Cab SB HD	13569	15265	16928
2 Dr SL 4WD Std Cab LB HD	11924	13414	14875
2 Dr SL Ext Cab LB HD	12199	13724	15218
2 Dr SL Ext Cab SB	11379	12801	14195
2 Dr SL Std Cab LB	10597	11922	13220
2 Dr SL Std Cab LB HD	10347	11640	12908
2 Dr SLE 4WD Ext Cab LB HD	14870	16728	18550
2 Dr SLE 4WD Ext Cab SB HD	14735	16577	18382

Body Styles	Trade	Private	Dealer
2 Dr SLE 4WD Std Cab LB HD	13090	14726	16330
2 Dr SLE Ext Cab LB HD	13207	14858	16476
2 Dr SLE Ext Cab SB	12884	14494	16073
2 Dr SLE Std Cab LB	11723	13189	14625
2 Dr SLE Std Cab LB HD	11259	12666	14045
2 Dr SLT 4WD Ext Cab LB HD	16438	18492	20506
2 Dr SLT 4WD Ext Cab SB HD	16293	18330	20326
2 Dr SLT Ext Cab LB HD	13908	15646	17350
2 Dr SLT Ext Cab SB	13764	15485	17171

Options	Price
6.0L V8 OHV 16V FI Engine	+177
Air Conditioning [Opt on SL]	+401
AM/FM/Cassette/CD Audio System	+144

Options	Price
Automatic 4-Speed Transmission [Opt on SL,SLE]	+545
Bucket Seats	+125
Heated Front Seats	+125

Mileage Category: K

After a complete redesign last year, GMC's Silverado-based pickup finally gets a fourth door on the extended cab. There's also more power on tap in the 4.8- and 5.3-liter engines, increased trailer ratings and standard programmable automatic door locks. New factory appearance items, such as wheel-lip flares and a soft tonneau cover, are now available on some models.

2000 (cont'd)

Options	Price
Hinged Fourth Door	+164
Limited Slip Differential	+134

Options	Price
Power Driver Seat [Opt on SLE]	+119
Power Passenger Seat [Opt on SLE]	+119

1999

Mileage Category: K

Finally, the decade-old, full-size GMC pickup based on the C/K gets a complete redesign from the ground up. Major structural, power, braking and interior enhancements characterize the all-new Sierra. Styling is evolutionary rather than revolutionary, both inside and out.

Body Styles	TMV Pricing		
	Trade	Private	Dealer
2 Dr SL 4WD Ext Cab LB HD	12095	13808	15590
2 Dr SL 4WD Ext Cab SB HD	11968	13662	15426
2 Dr SL 4WD Std Cab LB HD	10416	11891	13426
2 Dr SL Ext Cab LB HD	10427	11903	13439
2 Dr SL Ext Cab SB	9979	11392	12862
2 Dr SL Std Cab LB	9265	10577	11942
2 Dr SL Std Cab LB HD	8656	9881	11157
2 Dr SLE 4WD Ext Cab LB HD	13024	14868	16787
2 Dr SLE 4WD Ext Cab SB HD	13006	14847	16764

Body Styles	TMV Pricing		
	Trade	Private	Dealer
2 Dr SLE 4WD Std Cab LB HD	11328	12932	14601
2 Dr SLE Ext Cab LB HD	11535	13168	14867
2 Dr SLE Ext Cab SB	11103	12675	14311
2 Dr SLE Std Cab LB	9942	11350	12815
2 Dr SLE Std Cab LB HD	9803	11191	12635
2 Dr SLT 4WD Ext Cab LB HD	14604	16672	18824
2 Dr SLT 4WD Ext Cab SB HD	14404	16443	18566
2 Dr SLT Ext Cab LB HD	12292	14032	15844
2 Dr SLT Ext Cab SB	12059	13766	15543

Options	Price
6.0L V8 OHV 16V FI Engine [Std on SLT]	+201
Air Conditioning [Opt on SL]	+324

Options	Price
AM/FM/Cassette/CD Audio System	+117
Automatic 4-Speed Transmission [Std on SLT]	+401

1998

Mileage Category: K

With an all-new Sierra just one year away, changes are minimal. Diesel engines make more power and torque, extended cab models get rear heater ducts, a PassLock theft-deterrent system is standard, 1500-Series trucks get reduced rolling resistance tires and three new colors debut. Second-generation airbags are standard.

Body Styles	TMV Pricing		
	Trade	Private	Dealer
2 Dr C2500 SL Ext Cab LB HD	7871	9166	10627
2 Dr C2500 SL Ext Cab SB	7812	9098	10548
2 Dr C2500 SL Std Cab LB	6789	7907	9167
2 Dr C2500 SL Std Cab LB HD	7221	8410	9750
2 Dr C2500 SLE Ext Cab LB HD	8759	10201	11827
2 Dr C2500 SLE Ext Cab SB	8713	10147	11764
2 Dr C2500 SLE Std Cab LB	7693	8959	10387
2 Dr C2500 SLE Std Cab LB HD	7939	9246	10719
2 Dr C2500 SLT Ext Cab LB HD	9300	10831	12557
2 Dr C2500 SLT Ext Cab SB	9291	10820	12545
2 Dr C2500 SLT Std Cab LB	8227	9581	11108

Body Styles	TMV Pricing		
	Trade	Private	Dealer
2 Dr C2500 SLT Std Cab LB HD	8686	10116	11728
2 Dr K2500 SL 4WD Ext Cab LB HD	8833	10287	11926
2 Dr K2500 SL 4WD Ext Cab SB HD	8819	10270	11907
2 Dr K2500 SL 4WD Std Cab LB HD	8252	9611	11143
2 Dr K2500 SLE 4WD Ext Cab LB HD	9937	11573	13417
2 Dr K2500 SLE 4WD Ext Cab SB HD	9864	11487	13318
2 Dr K2500 SLE 4WD Std Cab LB HD	9106	10605	12295
2 Dr K2500 SLT 4WD Ext Cab LB HD	10154	11825	13710
2 Dr K2500 SLT 4WD Ext Cab SB HD	10099	11761	13636
2 Dr K2500 SLT 4WD Std Cab LB HD	9826	11443	13267

Options	Price
5.7L V8 OHV 16V FI Engine [Std on HD]	+243
6.5L V8 Turbodiesel OHV 16V Engine	+942
7.4L V8 OHV 16V FI Engine	+208

Options	Price
Air Conditioning [Opt on SL]	+279
Automatic 4-Speed Transmission	+337
Hinged Third Door	+146

1997

Mileage Category: K

A passenger airbag is added to models with a GVWR under 8,600 pounds, and all models get speed-sensitive steering that reduces low-speed effort. K1500 models have a tighter turning radius for better maneuverability. Automatic transmissions are refined to provide smoother shifts and improved efficiency. Three new paint colors debut.

Body Styles	TMV Pricing		
	Trade	Private	Dealer
2 Dr C2500 SL Ext Cab LB HD	6711	7897	9346
2 Dr C2500 SL Ext Cab SB	6745	7937	9393
2 Dr C2500 SL Std Cab LB	5828	6858	8116
2 Dr C2500 SL Std Cab LB HD	6134	7218	8542
2 Dr C2500 SLE Ext Cab LB HD	7522	8851	10475
2 Dr C2500 SLE Ext Cab SB	7549	8883	10513
2 Dr C2500 SLE Std Cab LB	6654	7829	9266
2 Dr C2500 SLE Std Cab LB HD	6813	8017	9488
2 Dr C2500 SLT Ext Cab LB HD	7963	9369	11088
2 Dr C2500 SLT Ext Cab SB	8100	9531	11279
2 Dr C2500 SLT Std Cab LB	7175	8442	9991

Body Styles	TMV Pricing		
	Trade	Private	Dealer
2 Dr C2500 SLT Std Cab LB HD	7463	8782	10393
2 Dr K2500 SL 4WD Ext Cab LB HD	7577	8915	10551
2 Dr K2500 SL 4WD Ext Cab SB HD	7556	8891	10522
2 Dr K2500 SL 4WD Std Cab LB HD	6974	8206	9712
2 Dr K2500 SLE 4WD Ext Cab LB HD	8415	9901	11718
2 Dr K2500 SLE 4WD Ext Cab SB HD	8415	9901	11718
2 Dr K2500 SLE 4WD Std Cab LB HD	7875	9266	10966
2 Dr K2500 SLT 4WD Ext Cab LB HD	8612	10133	11993
2 Dr K2500 SLT 4WD Ext Cab SB HD	8426	9915	11734
2 Dr K2500 SLT 4WD Std Cab LB HD	8297	9762	11553

Options	Price
5.7L V8 OHV 16V FI Engine [Std on HD]	+220
6.5L V8 Turbodiesel OHV 16V Engine	+1062
7.4L V8 OHV 16V FI Engine	+188

Options	Price
Air Conditioning [Opt on SL]	+253
Automatic 4-Speed Transmission	+305
Hinged Third Door	+132

1996

Body Styles	TMV Pricing		
	Trade	Private	Dealer
2 Dr C2500 SL Ext Cab LB HD	5605	6649	8090
2 Dr C2500 SL Ext Cab SB	5562	6598	8028
2 Dr C2500 SL Std Cab LB	4855	5759	7008
2 Dr C2500 SLE Ext Cab LB HD	6680	7924	9642
2 Dr C2500 SLE Ext Cab SB	6284	7454	9070
2 Dr C2500 SLE Std Cab LB	5533	6563	7986
2 Dr C2500 SLT Ext Cab SB	6852	8128	9890
2 Dr C2500 SLT Std Cab LB	5945	7052	8581

Body Styles	TMV Pricing		
	Trade	Private	Dealer
2 Dr K2500 SL 4WD Ext Cab LB HD	6624	7858	9562
2 Dr K2500 SL 4WD Ext Cab SB HD	6624	7858	9562
2 Dr K2500 SL 4WD Std Cab LB HD	6057	7185	8743
2 Dr K2500 SLE 4WD Ext Cab LB HD	7359	8729	10622
2 Dr K2500 SLE 4WD Ext Cab SB HD	7303	8663	10541
2 Dr K2500 SLE 4WD Std Cab LB HD	6737	7992	9725
2 Dr K2500 SLT 4WD Ext Cab LB HD	7852	9314	11334
2 Dr K2500 SLT 4WD Std Cab LB HD	7190	8529	10379

Options	Price
5.7L V8 OHV 16V FI Engine [Std on HD]	+194
6.5L V8 Turbodiesel OHV 16V Engine	+755
7.4L V8 OHV 16V FI Engine	+166

Options	Price
Air Conditioning [Opt on SL]	+223
Automatic 4-Speed Transmission	+269
Hinged Third Door	+116

Mileage Category: K

Vortec, a new family of engines, is introduced, providing more power and torque than last year's offerings. The Vortec engines available on the C/K 2500 pickups include a 5.0-liter V8, producing 220 hp @ 4,600 rpm and 285 lb-ft of torque @ 2,800 rpm and a 5.7-liter V8, rated at 250 hp @ 4,600 rpm and 335 lb-ft of torque @ 2,800 rpm. All of these figures represent increases in output when compared to their respective 1995 predecessors.

Noteworthy comfort and convenience additions include illuminated entry, additional 12-volt power outlets, an electrochromic inside rearview mirror and height-adjustable front safety belts.

Daytime Running Lamps (DRLs) are added this year as well.

1995

Body Styles	TMV Pricing		
	Trade	Private	Dealer
2 Dr C2500 SL Ext Cab LB HD	4839	5752	7274
2 Dr C2500 SL Ext Cab SB	4715	5605	7088
2 Dr C2500 SL Std Cab LB	4052	4817	6091
2 Dr C2500 SLE Ext Cab LB HD	5653	6720	8498
2 Dr C2500 SLE Ext Cab SB	5477	6511	8234
2 Dr C2500 SLE Std Cab LB	4570	5433	6870
2 Dr C2500 SLT Ext Cab LB HD	5880	6990	8839
2 Dr C2500 SLT Ext Cab SB	5819	6917	8748

Body Styles	TMV Pricing		
	Trade	Private	Dealer
2 Dr K2500 SL 4WD Ext Cab LB HD	5705	6782	8576
2 Dr K2500 SL 4WD Ext Cab SB	5471	6504	8225
2 Dr K2500 SL 4WD Std Cab LB	4675	5557	7028
2 Dr K2500 SLE 4WD Ext Cab LB HD	6291	7478	9456
2 Dr K2500 SLE 4WD Ext Cab SB	6143	7302	9234
2 Dr K2500 SLE 4WD Std Cab LB	5438	6464	8174
2 Dr K2500 SLT 4WD Ext Cab LB HD	6854	8148	10304
2 Dr K2500 SLT 4WD Ext Cab SB	6546	7781	9840

Options	Price
7.4L V8 OHV 16V FI Engine	+154
6.5L V8 Turbodiesel OHV 16V Engine	+701
Air Conditioning [Opt on SL]	+207
AM/FM/Cassette/CD Audio System	+75

Options	Price
Automatic 4-Speed Transmission	+250
5.0L V8 OHV 16V FI Engine [Opt on Std Cab - SL,SLE 2WD/4WD]	+148
5.7L V8 OHV 16V FI Engine	+180

Mileage Category: K

A revised interior graces these full-size trucks this year. A new driver-side airbag and a shift interlock are added in the interest of safety. The latter requires the brake pedal to be depressed before the automatic transmission's gear selector can be shifted out of "park." This reduces the likelihood that the vehicle will move suddenly and unexpectedly when the transmission is taken out of "park." Power mirrors, revised climate controls and cupholders provide a more user-friendly interior environment.

Mechanical enhancements include the addition of standard 4-wheel antilock brakes, improvements in the engines and modifications to the heavy-duty 4L80-E. The four-wheel ABS replaces last year's rear-wheel-only antilock system. Various upgrades to the engines are intended to reduce noise, improve durability and/or increase efficiency. The transmission is revised for quicker 1-2 upshifts during full-throttle applications.

1994

Body Styles	TMV Pricing		
	Trade	Private	Dealer
2 Dr C2500 Ext Cab LB HD	4169	5142	6763
2 Dr C2500 Ext Cab SB	3969	4903	6460
2 Dr C2500 SL Ext Cab LB HD	4060	5011	6597
2 Dr C2500 SL Ext Cab SB	3896	4809	6330
2 Dr C2500 SL Std Cab LB	3508	4330	5700
2 Dr C2500 SLE Ext Cab LB HD	4583	5657	7446
2 Dr C2500 SLE Ext Cab SB	4480	5530	7279
2 Dr C2500 SLE Std Cab LB	3631	4482	5899
2 Dr C2500 Std Cab LB	3477	4288	5639

Body Styles	TMV Pricing		
	Trade	Private	Dealer
2 Dr K2500 4WD Ext Cab LB HD	4788	5910	7780
2 Dr K2500 4WD Ext Cab SB	4414	5445	7162
2 Dr K2500 4WD Std Cab LB	3909	4824	6350
2 Dr K2500 SL 4WD Ext Cab LB HD	4614	5700	7510
2 Dr K2500 SL 4WD Ext Cab SB	4532	5594	7363
2 Dr K2500 SL 4WD Std Cab LB	3655	4511	5938
2 Dr K2500 SLE 4WD Ext Cab LB HD	5006	6179	8133
2 Dr K2500 SLE 4WD Ext Cab SB	4946	6105	8036
2 Dr K2500 SLE 4WD Std Cab LB	4427	5465	7194

Options	Price
5.7L V8 OHV 16V FI Engine	+163
6.5L V8 Diesel OHV 16V Engine	+629
6.5L V8 Turbodiesel OHV 16V Engine	+631
7.4L V8 OHV 16V FI Engine	+139

Options	Price
Air Conditioning [Opt on SL,STD]	+187
Automatic 4-Speed Transmission	+225
Premium Audio System	+128

Mileage Category: K

Safety is enhanced with the side door guard beams designed to minimize intrusion into the passenger compartment during a side impact. A center high-mounted brake light is also added to enhance safety.

An optional 6.5-liter turbodiesel V8 engine is available even on vehicles with a gross vehicle weight rating less than 8,500 pounds. The 5.0-, 5.7- and 7.4-liter engines all receive some enhancements.

Rust corrosion protection is improved while interior noise vibration and harshness is reduced. Rounding out the list of significant improvements are the addition of an "easy entry" feature to the front passenger seat on extended cab body styles to ease entry into the rear seating positions and the revision of the exterior front end styling.

GMC
Sierra 2500HD

2003

Mileage Category: K

The Sierra gets a revised look this year that includes a new front fascia, revised side moldings and optional multifunction, fold-away mirrors. On the inside, GMC has added new seats, a more comprehensive driver information center, a redesigned instrument panel and optional dual-zone climate control and satellite steering wheel controls. On the hardware side, the standard 6.0-liter V8 gets electronic throttle control as well as the ability to run exclusively on Compressed Natural Gas (CNG) or a mix of CNG and gasoline. Other upgrades include an improved Insta-Trac part-time four-wheel drive system for reduced service costs, a more efficient starter for the 8.1-liter V8 and a revised headlight switch that allows drivers to turn off the daytime running lamps.

Body Styles	TMV Pricing		
	Trade	Private	Dealer
2 Dr SLE 4WD Std Cab LB HD	19318	20502	22474
2 Dr SLE Std Cab LB HD	17387	18452	20228
2 Dr STD 4WD Std Cab LB HD	17830	18922	20743
2 Dr STD Std Cab LB HD	16041	17024	18662
2 Dr Work Truck 4WD Std Cab LB HD	17250	18307	20069
2 Dr Work Truck Std Cab LB HD	15436	-16382	17959
4 Dr SLE 4WD Crew Cab LB HD	23283	24710	27088
4 Dr SLE 4WD Crew Cab SB HD	23092	24507	26865
4 Dr SLE 4WD Ext Cab LB HD	21782	23117	25342
4 Dr SLE 4WD Ext Cab SB HD	21592	22915	25121
4 Dr SLE Crew Cab LB HD	21217	22517	24684
4 Dr SLE Crew Cab SB HD	21027	22316	24463
4 Dr SLE Ext Cab LB HD	19994	21219	23261
4 Dr SLE Ext Cab SB HD	19803	21017	23039
4 Dr SLT 4WD Crew Cab LB HD	24462	25961	28459

Body Styles	TMV Pricing		
	Trade	Private	Dealer
4 Dr SLT 4WD Crew Cab SB HD	24269	25756	28235
4 Dr SLT 4WD Ext Cab LB HD	23103	24519	26878
4 Dr SLT 4WD Ext Cab SB HD	22911	24315	26654
4 Dr SLT Crew Cab LB HD	22534	23915	26216
4 Dr SLT Crew Cab SB HD	22342	23711	25992
4 Dr SLT Ext Cab LB HD	21166	22463	24624
4 Dr SLT Ext Cab SB HD	20974	22259	24401
4 Dr STD 4WD Crew Cab LB HD	21608	22932	25139
4 Dr STD 4WD Crew Cab SB HD	21418	22731	24918
4 Dr STD 4WD Ext Cab LB HD	20177	21413	23474
4 Dr STD 4WD Ext Cab SB HD	19986	21211	23252
4 Dr STD Crew Cab LB HD	19692	20899	22910
4 Dr STD Crew Cab SB HD	19500	20695	22687
4 Dr STD Ext Cab LB HD	18420	19548	21429
4 Dr STD Ext Cab SB HD	18229	19346	21207

Options	Price
AM/FM/CD Audio System [Opt on STD,Work]	+164
Automatic 4-Speed Transmission	+705
Automatic 5-Speed Transmission	+773
Bose Audio System [Opt on SLE,SLT]	+254
Bucket Seats [Opt on SLE,SLT]	+274
Chrome Wheels [Opt on STD]	+200
Cruise Control [Opt on STD,Work]	+155
Locking Differential	+190
Power Driver Seat [Opt on SLE]	+155

Options	Price
Power Passenger Seat [Opt on SLT]	+158
OnStar Telematic System [Opt on SLE]	+447
AM/FM/CD Changer Audio System [Opt on SLE,SLT]	+258
Satellite Radio System [Opt on SLE,SLT]	+209
Automatic Climate Control (2 Zone) - Driver and Passenger [Opt on SLE,SLT]	+126
DVD Entertainment System	+834
8.1L V8 OHV 16V FI Engine	+547
6.6L V8 Turbodiesel OHV 32V Engine	+3226
Power Retractable Mirrors [Opt on SLE,SLT]	+118

2002

Mileage Category: K

Fully redesigned last year, the Sierra 2500HD gets only minor updates for 2002. Air conditioning is now standard on all trim levels along with extendable sunshade visors and redesigned exterior badging.

Body Styles	TMV Pricing		
	Trade	Private	Dealer
2 Dr SL 4WD Std Cab LB HD	16252	17413	19347
2 Dr SL Std Cab LB HD	14513	15550	17277
2 Dr SLE 4WD Std Cab LB HD	17048	18266	20295
2 Dr SLE Std Cab LB HD	15193	16278	18087
2 Dr STD 4WD Std Cab LB HD	15377	16475	18306
2 Dr STD Std Cab LB HD	13336	14289	15876
4 Dr SL 4WD Crew Cab LB HD	19834	21250	23611
4 Dr SL 4WD Crew Cab SB HD	19652	21056	23395
4 Dr SL 4WD Ext Cab LB HD	18602	19931	22145
4 Dr SL 4WD Ext Cab SB HD	18429	19745	21939
4 Dr SL Crew Cab LB HD	17991	19276	21417
4 Dr SL Crew Cab SB HD	17694	18958	21064
4 Dr SL Ext Cab LB HD	16868	18073	20081
4 Dr SL Ext Cab SB HD	16651	17840	19822
4 Dr SLE 4WD Crew Cab LB HD	20699	22177	24641
4 Dr SLE 4WD Crew Cab SB HD	20528	21994	24437
4 Dr SLE 4WD Ext Cab LB HD	19523	20917	23241
4 Dr SLE 4WD Ext Cab SB HD	19500	20892	23213
4 Dr SLE Crew Cab LB HD	18827	20171	22412

Body Styles	TMV Pricing		
	Trade	Private	Dealer
4 Dr SLE Crew Cab SB HD	18674	20008	22231
4 Dr SLE Ext Cab LB HD	17625	18884	20982
4 Dr SLE Ext Cab SB HD	17613	18871	20967
4 Dr SLT 4WD Crew Cab LB HD	21786	23342	25935
4 Dr SLT 4WD Crew Cab SB HD	21574	23115	25683
4 Dr SLT 4WD Ext Cab LB HD	20584	22054	24504
4 Dr SLT 4WD Ext Cab SB HD	20375	21830	24255
4 Dr SLT Crew Cab LB HD	19911	21333	23703
4 Dr SLT Crew Cab SB HD	19714	21122	23468
4 Dr SLT Ext Cab LB HD	18866	20213	22459
4 Dr SLT Ext Cab SB HD	18790	20132	22368
4 Dr STD 4WD Crew Cab LB HD	18871	20219	22465
4 Dr STD 4WD Crew Cab SB HD	18739	20078	22309
4 Dr STD 4WD Ext Cab LB HD	18022	19309	21454
4 Dr STD 4WD Ext Cab SB HD	17883	19160	21289
4 Dr STD Crew Cab LB HD	16951	18162	20180
4 Dr STD Crew Cab SB HD	16672	17863	19847
4 Dr STD Ext Cab LB HD	16316	17481	19423
4 Dr STD Ext Cab SB HD	16019	17163	19070

Options	Price
6.6L V8 Turbodiesel OHV 32V Engine	+2880
8.1L V8 OHV 16V FI Engine	+509
Air Conditioning [Opt on STD]	+494
AM/FM/CD Audio System [Opt on STD]	+117
Automatic 4-Speed Transmission [Opt on Std Cab]	+656
Automatic 5-Speed Transmission	+719

Options	Price
Bucket Seats [Opt on SLE,SLT]	+153
Cruise Control [Opt on STD]	+144
Locking Differential	+177
Power Driver Seat [Opt on SLE]	+147
Power Passenger Seat [Opt on SLE]	+147
Running Boards [Opt on Ext Cab SB - SLE,SLT]	+150

Mileage Category: K

Both light- and heavy-duty 2500s sport new torsion bar front suspensions. Light-duty models now offer optional traction control and standard child safety-seat tethers. Heavy-duty Sierras are completely redesigned for 2001 offering two new engines and transmissions, bigger interiors and numerous other improvements aimed at buyers looking for a "professional grade" truck from GM.

Body Styles	TMV Pricing			Body Styles	TMV Pricing		
	Trade	Private	Dealer		Trade	Private	Dealer
2 Dr SL 4WD Std Cab LB HD	13708	15220	16615	4 Dr SLE 4WD Ext Cab LB HD	17120	19008	20750
2 Dr SL Std Cab LB HD	12151	13491	14728	4 Dr SLE 4WD Ext Cab SB HD	16945	18813	20538
2 Dr SLE 4WD Std Cab LB HD	14947	16595	18117	4 Dr SLE Crew Cab LB HD	16425	18236	19908
2 Dr SLE Std Cab LB HD	13404	14882	16246	4 Dr SLE Crew Cab SB HD	16133	17912	19555
4 Dr SL 4WD Crew Cab LB HD	16750	18597	20302	4 Dr SLE Ext Cab LB HD	15569	17286	18870
4 Dr SL 4WD Crew Cab SB HD	16599	18429	20119	4 Dr SLE Ext Cab SB HD	15395	17092	18659
4 Dr SL 4WD Ext Cab LB HD	16117	17894	19534	4 Dr SLT 4WD Crew Cab LB HD	19568	21725	23717
4 Dr SL 4WD Ext Cab SB HD	15862	17611	19225	4 Dr SLT 4WD Crew Cab SB HD	19517	21669	23656
4 Dr SL Crew Cab LB HD	15103	16768	18305	4 Dr SLT 4WD Ext Cab LB HD	18181	20186	22037
4 Dr SL Crew Cab SB HD	14607	16218	17705	4 Dr SLT 4WD Ext Cab SB HD	17993	19977	21809
4 Dr SL Ext Cab LB HD	14307	15885	17341	4 Dr SLT Crew Cab LB HD	17406	19325	21097
4 Dr SL Ext Cab SB HD	14100	15655	17090	4 Dr SLT Crew Cab SB HD	17303	19211	20972
4 Dr SLE 4WD Crew Cab LB HD	18103	20099	21942	4 Dr SLT Ext Cab LB HD	16547	18372	20056
4 Dr SLE 4WD Crew Cab SB HD	17499	19429	21210	4 Dr SLT Ext Cab SB HD	16380	18186	19853

Options	Price	Options	Price
6.6L V8 Turbodiesel OHV 32V Engine	+2627	Cruise Control [Opt on SL]	+131
8.1L V8 OHV 16V FI Engine	+464	Heated Front Seats	+137
Air Conditioning [Opt on SL]	+451	Locking Differential	+156
Automatic 5-Speed Transmission	+655	Power Driver Seat [Opt on SLE]	+131
Bucket Seats [Opt on SLE]	+137	Power Passenger Seat [Opt on SLE]	+131
Chrome Wheels [Opt on SL]	+169		

Body Styles	TMV Pricing			Body Styles	TMV Pricing		
	Trade	Private	Dealer		Trade	Private	Dealer
2 Dr SLE 4WD Std Cab LB	19931	21152	23187	4 Dr SLT 4WD Ext Cab LB	24133	25612	28077
2 Dr STD 4WD Std Cab LB	18167	19280	21136	4 Dr SLT Crew Cab LB	23258	24683	27059
4 Dr SLE 4WD Crew Cab LB	24175	25656	28125	4 Dr SLT Ext Cab LB	22080	23433	25688
4 Dr SLE 4WD Ext Cab LB	22939	24345	26687	4 Dr STD 4WD Crew Cab LB	22343	23712	25994
4 Dr SLE Crew Cab LB	22168	23526	25790	4 Dr STD 4WD Ext Cab LB	21380	22690	24873
4 Dr SLE Ext Cab LB	20814	22089	24215	4 Dr STD Crew Cab LB	20192	21429	23491
4 Dr SLT 4WD Crew Cab LB	25411	26968	29563				

Options	Price	Options	Price
AM/FM/CD Audio System [Opt on STD]	+164	OnStar Telematic System [Opt on SLE]	+447
Automatic 4-Speed Transmission	+705	AM/FM/CD Changer Audio System [Opt on SLE,SLT]	+258
Automatic 5-Speed Transmission	+773	Satellite Radio System [Opt on SLE]	+209
Bose Audio System [Opt on SLE,SLT]	+254	Automatic Climate Control (2 Zone) - Driver and Passenger [Opt on SLE]	+126
Bucket Seats [Opt on SLE,SLT]	+274	DVD Entertainment System	+834
Cruise Control [Opt on STD,Work]	+155	8.1L V8 OHV 16V FI Engine	+547
Locking Differential	+190	6.6L V8 Turbodiesel OHV 32V Engine	+3226
Power Driver Seat [Opt on SLE]	+155	Power Retractable Mirrors [Opt on SLE,SLT]	+153
Power Passenger Seat [Opt on SLT]	+158		

Mileage Category: K

The Sierra gets a revised look this year that includes a new front fascia, revised side moldings and optional multifunction, fold-away mirrors. On the inside, GMC has added new seats, a more comprehensive driver information center, a redesigned instrument panel and optional dual-zone climate control and satellite steering wheel controls. On the hardware side, the standard 6.0-liter V8 gets electronic throttle control as well as the ability to run exclusively on compressed natural gas (CNG) or a mix of CNG and gasoline. Other upgrades include an improved Insta-Trac part-time four-wheel-drive system for reduced service costs, a more efficient starter for the 8.1-liter V8 and a revised headlight switch that allows drivers to turn off the daytime running lamps.

Body Styles	TMV Pricing			Body Styles	TMV Pricing		
	Trade	Private	Dealer		Trade	Private	Dealer
2 Dr SL 4WD Std Cab LB	16968	18168	20169	4 Dr SLE 4WD Crew Cab LB	21321	22829	25343
2 Dr SLE 4WD Std Cab LB	17771	19007	21068	4 Dr SLE 4WD Ext Cab LB	20247	21680	24067
2 Dr STD 4WD Std Cab LB	15968	17098	18980	4 Dr SLE Crew Cab LB	19454	20830	23124
4 Dr SL 4WD Crew Cab LB	20484	21933	24348	4 Dr SLE Ext Cab LB	18387	19688	21856
4 Dr SL 4WD Ext Cab LB	19355	20724	23006	4 Dr SLT 4WD Crew Cab LB	22399	23984	26625
4 Dr SL Crew Cab LB	18607	19923	22117	4 Dr SLT 4WD Ext Cab LB	21325	22834	25349
4 Dr SL Ext Cab LB	17506	18745	20809	4 Dr SLT Crew Cab LB	20509	21960	24378

Mileage Category: K

After undergoing a full redesign last year, the Sierra 3500 gets only minor changes for 2002. Air conditioning is now standard on all trim levels, and a Cold Weather package is now available that includes heated exterior mirrors and a rear window defogger.

2002 (cont'd)

Body Styles	TMV Pricing		
	Trade	Private	Dealer
4 Dr SLT Ext Cab LB	19499	20878	23177
4 Dr STD 4WD Crew Cab LB	19657	21048	23365
4 Dr STD 4WD Ext Cab LB	18812	20143	22361

Body Styles	TMV Pricing		
	Trade	Private	Dealer
4 Dr STD Crew Cab LB	17887	19152	21261
4 Dr STD Ext Cab LB	16971	18171	20172

Options	Price
6.6L V8 Turbodiesel OHV 32V Engine	+2880
8.1L V8 OHV 16V FI Engine	+509
Air Conditioning [Opt on STD]	+494
AM/FM/CD Audio System [Opt on STD]	+117
Automatic 4-Speed Transmission [Opt on Std Cab]	+656
Automatic 5-Speed Transmission	+719

Options	Price
Bucket Seats [Opt on SLE,SLT]	+254
Cruise Control [Opt on STD]	+144
Locking Differential	+177
Power Driver Seat [Opt on SLE]	+147
Power Passenger Seat [Opt on SLE]	+147

2001

Mileage Category: K

The General's brand-new HD truck lineup debuts with stronger frames; beefed-up suspensions, axles, brakes and cooling systems; new sheet metal; bigger interiors; and a trio of powerful new V8s -- a 6.6-liter Duramax turbodiesel and two gas engines, a hefty 8.1-liter and an improved 6.0-liter. One of the four transmissions, a new Allison five-speed automatic, is designed especially for towing and hauling with GM's helpful tow/haul mode and a new "grade-braking" feature.

Body Styles	TMV Pricing		
	Trade	Private	Dealer
2 Dr SL 4WD Std Cab LB	14901	16472	17923
2 Dr SL Ext Cab LB	15050	16638	18103
2 Dr SL Std Cab LB	13830	15289	16635
2 Dr SLE 4WD Std Cab LB	15537	17176	18688
2 Dr SLE Std Cab LB	14060	15543	16912
4 Dr SL 4WD Crew Cab LB	18063	19968	21727
4 Dr SL 4WD Ext Cab LB	16704	18466	20092
4 Dr SL Crew Cab LB	16013	17702	19262

Body Styles	TMV Pricing		
	Trade	Private	Dealer
4 Dr SLE 4WD Crew Cab LB	18660	20628	22445
4 Dr SLE 4WD Ext Cab LB	18223	20145	21919
4 Dr SLE Crew Cab LB	16990	18782	20436
4 Dr SLE Ext Cab LB	16102	17800	19368
4 Dr SLT 4WD Crew Cab LB	19740	21822	23744
4 Dr SLT 4WD Ext Cab LB	18809	20793	22624
4 Dr SLT Crew Cab LB	18246	20171	21947
4 Dr SLT Ext Cab LB	17328	19156	20843

Options	Price
6.6L V8 Turbodiesel OHV 32V Engine	+2627
8.1L V8 OHV 16V FI Engine	+464
Air Conditioning [Opt on SL]	+451
Automatic 4-Speed Transmission	+598
Automatic 5-Speed Transmission	+655
Bucket Seats [Opt on SLE]	+137

Options	Price
Chrome Wheels [Opt on SL]	+169
Cruise Control [Opt on SL]	+131
Heated Front Seats	+137
Locking Differential	+156
Power Driver Seat [Opt on SLE]	+131
Power Passenger Seat [Opt on SLE]	+131

1998

Mileage Category: K

Diesel engines make more power and torque, extended cab models get rear heater ducts, a PassLock theft-deterrent system is standard and three new colors debut. Second-generation airbags are standard.

Body Styles	TMV Pricing		
	Trade	Private	Dealer
2 Dr C3500 SL Ext Cab LB	9107	10525	12125
2 Dr C3500 SL Std Cab LB	7728	8932	10289
2 Dr C3500 SLE Ext Cab LB	9928	11474	13218
2 Dr C3500 SLE Std Cab LB	8711	10067	11597
2 Dr C3500 SLT Ext Cab LB	10922	12623	14541
2 Dr C3500 SLT Std Cab LB	9321	10773	12410
2 Dr K3500 SL 4WD Ext Cab LB	10070	11638	13407
2 Dr K3500 SL 4WD Std Cab LB	8825	10200	11750
2 Dr K3500 SLE 4WD Ext Cab LB	11026	12743	14679

Body Styles	TMV Pricing		
	Trade	Private	Dealer
2 Dr K3500 SLE 4WD Std Cab LB	9871	11408	13141
2 Dr K3500 SLT 4WD Ext Cab LB	11433	13213	15221
2 Dr K3500 SLT 4WD Std Cab LB	10611	12264	14127
4 Dr C3500 SL Crew Cab LB	8997	10398	11978
4 Dr C3500 SLE Crew Cab LB	10884	12579	14491
4 Dr C3500 SLT Crew Cab LB	11009	12723	14656
4 Dr K3500 SL 4WD Crew Cab LB	10486	12119	13960
4 Dr K3500 SLE 4WD Crew Cab LB	11215	12962	14932
4 Dr K3500 SLT 4WD Crew Cab LB	12144	14035	16168

Options	Price
6.5L V8 Turbodiesel OHV 16V Engine	+942
7.4L V8 OHV 16V FI Engine	+208
Air Conditioning [Opt on SL]	+279

Options	Price
Automatic 4-Speed Transmission	+337
Dual Rear Wheels	+297

1997

Mileage Category: K

A passenger airbag is added to models with a GVWR under 8,600 pounds, and all models get speed-sensitive steering that reduces low-speed effort. Automatic transmissions are refined to provide smoother shifts and improved efficiency. Three new paint colors debut.

Body Styles	TMV Pricing		
	Trade	Private	Dealer
2 Dr C3500 SL Ext Cab LB	7999	9342	10983
2 Dr C3500 SL Std Cab LB	6778	7916	9306
2 Dr C3500 SLE Ext Cab LB	8441	9858	11589
2 Dr C3500 SLE Std Cab LB	7436	8684	10210
2 Dr C3500 SLT Ext Cab LB	9462	11051	12992

Body Styles	TMV Pricing		
	Trade	Private	Dealer
2 Dr C3500 SLT Std Cab LB	8275	9664	11362
2 Dr K3500 SL 4WD Ext Cab LB	8976	10483	12324
2 Dr K3500 SL 4WD Std Cab LB	7748	9049	10638
2 Dr K3500 SLE 4WD Ext Cab LB	9598	11209	13178
2 Dr K3500 SLE 4WD Std Cab LB	8414	9826	11552

1997 (cont'd)

Body Styles	TMV Pricing		
	Trade	Private	Dealer
2 Dr K3500 SLT 4WD Ext Cab LB	9851	11504	13525
2 Dr K3500 SLT 4WD Std Cab LB	9415	10995	12926
4 Dr C3500 SL Crew Cab LB	7958	9294	10926
4 Dr C3500 SLE Crew Cab LB	9426	11008	12942

Body Styles	TMV Pricing		
	Trade	Private	Dealer
4 Dr C3500 SLT Crew Cab LB	9562	11167	13128
4 Dr K3500 SL 4WD Crew Cab LB	9046	10564	12420
4 Dr K3500 SLE 4WD Crew Cab LB	9794	11438	13447
4 Dr K3500 SLT 4WD Crew Cab LB	10442	12195	14337

Options	Price
6.5L V8 Turbodiesel OHV 16V Engine	+853
7.4L V8 OHV 16V FI Engine	+188
Air Conditioning [Opt on SL]	+253

Options	Price
Automatic 4-Speed Transmission	+305
Dual Rear Wheels	+269

1996

Body Styles	TMV Pricing		
	Trade	Private	Dealer
2 Dr C3500 SL Ext Cab LB	6760	7960	9618
2 Dr C3500 SL Std Cab LB	5809	6841	8265
2 Dr C3500 SLE Ext Cab LB	7128	8393	10141
2 Dr C3500 SLT Ext Cab LB	8009	9431	11394
2 Dr C3500 SLT Std Cab LB	6984	8224	9936
2 Dr K3500 SL 4WD Ext Cab LB	7594	8942	10804
2 Dr K3500 SL 4WD Std Cab LB	6604	7777	9396
2 Dr K3500 SLE 4WD Ext Cab LB	8039	9466	11437
2 Dr K3500 SLE 4WD Std Cab LB	7794	9178	11089

Body Styles	TMV Pricing		
	Trade	Private	Dealer
2 Dr K3500 SLT 4WD Ext Cab LB	8445	9944	12015
2 Dr K3500 SLT 4WD Std Cab LB	7794	9178	11089
4 Dr C3500 SL Crew Cab LB	6667	7851	9485
4 Dr C3500 SLE Crew Cab LB	7990	9408	11367
4 Dr C3500 SLT Crew Cab LB	8044	9472	11445
4 Dr K3500 SL 4WD Crew Cab LB	7661	9021	10899
4 Dr K3500 SLE 4WD Crew Cab LB	8350	9833	11880
4 Dr K3500 SLT 4WD Crew Cab LB	8924	10508	12696

Options	Price
6.5L V8 Turbodiesel OHV 16V Engine	+755
7.4L V8 OHV 16V FI Engine	+166
Air Conditioning [Opt on SL]	+223

Options	Price
Automatic 4-Speed Transmission	+269
Dual Rear Wheels	+238

Mileage Category: K

Vortec, a new family of engines, is introduced, providing more power and torque than last year's offerings. The Vortec engines available on the Sierra 3500 pickups include a 5.7-liter V8, rated at 250 hp at 4,600 rpm and 355 lb-ft of torque at 2,800 rpm and a 7.4-liter V8, capable of 290 hp at 4,200 rpm and 410 lb-ft of torque at 3,200 rpm.

Noteworthy comfort and convenience additions include illuminated entry, additional 12-volt power outlets, an electrochromic inside rearview mirror and height-adjustable front safety belts. Also the crew cab body styles get rear-seat heating ducts.

Daytime Running Lamps (DRLs) are added this year as well.

1995

Body Styles	TMV Pricing		
	Trade	Private	Dealer
2 Dr C3500 SL Ext Cab LB	5652	6719	8496
2 Dr C3500 SL Std Cab LB	4726	5618	7104
2 Dr C3500 SLE Ext Cab LB	5921	7039	8901
2 Dr C3500 SLE Std Cab LB	5346	6355	8036
2 Dr C3500 SLT Ext Cab LB	6583	7825	9896
2 Dr K3500 SL 4WD Ext Cab LB	6249	7428	9394
2 Dr K3500 SL 4WD Std Cab LB	5398	6417	8114

Body Styles	TMV Pricing		
	Trade	Private	Dealer
2 Dr K3500 SLE 4WD Ext Cab LB	6726	7995	10110
2 Dr K3500 SLE 4WD Std Cab LB	5853	6957	8798
2 Dr K3500 SLT 4WD Ext Cab LB	7083	8420	10648
4 Dr C3500 SL Crew Cab LB	5482	6517	8241
4 Dr C3500 SLE Crew Cab LB	6474	7695	9731
4 Dr K3500 SL 4WD Crew Cab LB	6313	7504	9489
4 Dr K3500 SLE 4WD Crew Cab LB	6934	8242	10423

Options	Price
6.5L V8 Turbodiesel OHV 16V Engine	+701
7.4L V8 OHV 16V FI Engine	+154
Air Conditioning [Opt on SL]	+207

Options	Price
AM/FM/Cassette/CD Audio System	+75
Automatic 4-Speed Transmission	+250
Dual Rear Wheels	+221

Mileage Category: K

A revised interior graces these full-size trucks this year. A shift interlock is added, requiring the brake pedal to be depressed before the automatic transmission's gear selector can be shifted out of "park." This reduces the likelihood that the vehicle will move suddenly and unexpectedly when the transmission is taken out of "park." Power mirrors, revised climate controls and cupholders provide a more user-friendly interior environment.

Mechanical enhancements include the addition of standard 4-wheel antilock brakes, improvements in the engines and modifications to the heavy-duty 4L80-E. The four-wheel ABS replaces last year's rear-wheel-only antilock system. Various upgrade to the engines are intended to reduce noise, improve durability and/or increase efficiency. The transmission is revised for quicker 1-2 upshifts during full-power applications.

1994

Body Styles	TMV Pricing		
	Trade	Private	Dealer
2 Dr C3500 SL Ext Cab LB	4669	5763	7586
2 Dr C3500 SL Std Cab LB	4050	4999	6580
2 Dr C3500 SLE Ext Cab LB	4926	6080	8002
2 Dr C3500 SLE Std Cab LB	4264	5263	6927
2 Dr K3500 SL 4WD Ext Cab LB	5383	6644	8745
2 Dr K3500 SL 4WD Std Cab LB	4657	5748	7565

Body Styles	TMV Pricing		
	Trade	Private	Dealer
2 Dr K3500 SLE 4WD Ext Cab LB	5527	6822	8979
2 Dr K3500 SLE 4WD Std Cab LB	4809	5935	7812
4 Dr C3500 SL Crew Cab LB	4638	5724	7534
4 Dr C3500 SLE Crew Cab LB	5196	6413	8441
4 Dr K3500 SL 4WD Crew Cab LB	5703	7039	9265
4 Dr K3500 SLE 4WD Crew Cab LB	5803	7162	9428

Options	Price
6.5L V8 Turbodiesel OHV 16V Engine	+631
7.4L V8 OHV 16V FI Engine	+139
Air Conditioning	+187

Options	Price
Automatic 4-Speed Transmission	+225
Dual Rear Wheels	+199
Premium Audio System	+128

Mileage Category: K

Safety is enhanced with the side door guard beams designed to minimize intrusion into the passenger compartment during a side impact. A center high-mounted brake light is also added to enhance safety.

An optional 6.5-liter turbodiesel V8 engine is available even on vehicles with a gross vehicle weight rating less than 8,500 pounds. The 5.0-, 5.7- and 7.4-liter engines all receive some enhancements.

Rust corrosion protection is improved while interior noise vibration and harshness is reduced. Rounding out the list of significant improvements are the addition of an "easy entry" feature to the front passenger seat on extended cab body styles to ease entry into the rear seating positions and the revision of the exterior front end styling.

Sierra C3/Sierra Classic 1500/Sierra Classic 2500

GMC
Sierra C3
2001

Body Styles	TMV Pricing		
	Trade	Private	Dealer
4 Dr STD AWD Ext Cab SB	19735	21662	23440

Mileage Category: K

The extended-cab C3 is a new truck based on the Sierra 1500 half-ton full-size pickup. It's powered by a specially tuned version of the 6.0-liter Vortec V8. It also gets full-time all-wheel drive, 3/4-ton brakes and a standard heavy-duty suspension. With styling cues and feature content similar to GMC's SUVs, think of the C3 as the Denali version of the Sierra.

GMC
Sierra Classic 1500
1999

Body Styles	TMV Pricing		
	Trade	Private	Dealer
2 Dr C1500 SLE Ext Cab SB	11012	12590	14233
2 Dr C1500 SLT Ext Cab SB	11343	13084	14896

Options	Price
5.7L V8 OHV 16V FI Engine	+282
Aluminum/Alloy Wheels	+125
AM/FM/Cassette/CD Audio System	+117

Mileage Category: K

Body Styles	TMV Pricing		
	Trade	Private	Dealer
2 Dr K1500 SLE 4WD Ext Cab SB	12502	14293	16158
2 Dr K1500 SLT 4WD Ext Cab SB	12487	14376	16342

Options	Price
Bucket Seats	+121
Chrome Wheels	+125

With an all-new Sierra 1500 just months away, changes are limited to a few new colors.

GMC
Sierra Classic 2500
2000

Mileage Category: K

GM has refined the Sierra Classic lineup, dropping all 1500 Series (half-ton) trucks in favor of workhorse 2500 (three-quarter-ton) and 3500 (one-ton) Series models. The only other news is the addition of a new paint color, as this old truck platform (based on the previous-generation C/K pickup) soldiers on for a final year.

Body Styles	TMV Pricing		
	Trade	Private	Dealer
2 Dr C2500 SL Ext Cab LB HD	10919	12304	13662
2 Dr C2500 SL Std Cab LB HD	9767	11006	12220
2 Dr C2500 SLE Ext Cab LB HD	12321	13884	15416
2 Dr C2500 SLE Std Cab LB HD	11001	12396	13764
2 Dr C2500 SLT Ext Cab LB HD	13532	15248	16931
2 Dr C2500 SLT Std Cab LB HD	11727	13215	14673
2 Dr K2500 SL 4WD Ext Cab LB HD	12934	14574	16182
2 Dr K2500 SL 4WD Ext Cab SB HD	12855	14486	16084
2 Dr K2500 SL 4WD Std Cab LB HD	11232	12657	14053
2 Dr K2500 SLE 4WD Ext Cab LB HD	13799	15549	17264
2 Dr K2500 SLE 4WD Ext Cab SB HD	13770	15516	17228

Options	Price
Limited Slip Differential	+142
Power Driver Seat [Std on SLT]	+119
6.5L V8 Turbodiesel OHV 16V Engine	+1352
7.4L V8 OHV 16V FI Engine	+299

Body Styles	TMV Pricing		
	Trade	Private	Dealer
2 Dr K2500 SLE 4WD Std Cab LB HD	13016	14667	16285
2 Dr K2500 SLT 4WD Ext Cab LB HD	15224	17155	19048
2 Dr K2500 SLT 4WD Ext Cab SB HD	15085	16998	18874
2 Dr K2500 SLT 4WD Std Cab LB HD	13707	15445	17149
4 Dr C2500 SL Crew Cab SB	12814	14439	16032
4 Dr C2500 SLE Crew Cab SB	14327	16144	17926
4 Dr C2500 SLT Crew Cab SB	15226	17157	19050
4 Dr K2500 SL 4WD Crew Cab SB	13914	15679	17409
4 Dr K2500 SLE 4WD Crew Cab SB	15498	17463	19390
4 Dr K2500 SLT 4WD Crew Cab SB	16886	19028	21127

Options	Price
Air Conditioning [Opt on SL]	+401
AM/FM/Cassette/CD Audio System	+144
Automatic 4-Speed Transmission	+545
Bucket Seats	+187

Sierra Classic 2500/Sierra Classic 3500

Body Styles	TMV Pricing		
	Trade	Private	Dealer
2 Dr C2500 SL Ext Cab LB HD	9208	10599	12046
2 Dr C2500 SL Std Cab LB HD	8132	9360	10638
2 Dr C2500 SLE Ext Cab LB HD	10554	12147	13806
2 Dr C2500 SLE Std Cab LB HD	9582	11029	12535
2 Dr C2500 SLT Ext Cab LB HD	11603	13355	15178
2 Dr C2500 SLT Std Cab LB HD	10461	12041	13685
2 Dr K2500 SL 4WD Ext Cab LB HD	10806	12438	14137
2 Dr K2500 SL 4WD Ext Cab SB HD	10714	12331	14015
2 Dr K2500 SL 4WD Std Cab LB HD	9744	11215	12747
2 Dr K2500 SLE 4WD Ext Cab LB HD	11954	13759	15638
2 Dr K2500 SLE 4WD Ext Cab SB HD	11895	13691	15561
2 Dr K2500 SLE 4WD Std Cab LB HD	11151	12835	14588

Body Styles	TMV Pricing		
	Trade	Private	Dealer
2 Dr K2500 SLT 4WD Ext Cab LB HD	12904	14853	16881
2 Dr K2500 SLT 4WD Ext Cab SB HD	12687	14602	16596
2 Dr K2500 SLT 4WD Std Cab LB HD	11677	13441	15276
4 Dr C2500 SL Crew Cab SB HD	10641	12248	13921
4 Dr C2500 SLE Crew Cab SB HD	11531	13272	15084
4 Dr C2500 SLT Crew Cab SB HD	12653	14564	16553
4 Dr K2500 SL 4WD Crew Cab SB HD	12050	13869	15763
4 Dr K2500 SLE 4WD Crew Cab SB HD	12781	14711	16720
4 Dr K2500 SLT 4WD Crew Cab SB HD	14069	16193	18404

Options	Price
6.5L V8 Turbodiesel OHV 16V Engine	+1094
7.4L V8 OHV 16V FI Engine	+242
Air Conditioning [Opt on SL]	+324
AM/FM/Cassette/CD Audio System [Opt on SLE,SLT]	+117

Options	Price
Automatic 4-Speed Transmission	+401
Bucket Seats	+121
Locking Differential	+115

Mileage Category: K

Mechanical upgrades include new internal components and seals for automatic transmissions, improved cooling system and starter motor durability, and three new exterior paint colors. With an all-new Sierra 2500 just months away, changes are limited to a few new colors.

Sierra Classic 3500

Body Styles	TMV Pricing		
	Trade	Private	Dealer
2 Dr C3500 SL Ext Cab LB	11928	13418	14878
2 Dr C3500 SL Std Cab LB	10642	11971	13274
2 Dr C3500 SLE Ext Cab LB	13395	15068	16708
2 Dr C3500 SLE Std Cab LB	11399	12823	14219
2 Dr C3500 SLT Ext Cab LB	14196	15969	17707
2 Dr C3500 SLT Std Cab LB	12479	14038	15566
2 Dr K3500 SL 4WD Ext Cab LB	13643	15347	17018
2 Dr K3500 SL 4WD Std Cab LB	11775	13246	14688
2 Dr K3500 SLE 4WD Ext Cab LB	14917	16780	18606
2 Dr K3500 SLE 4WD Std Cab LB	13310	14972	16602
2 Dr K3500 SLT 4WD Ext Cab LB	15473	17406	19300
2 Dr K3500 SLT 4WD Std Cab LB	13801	15525	17215

Body Styles	TMV Pricing		
	Trade	Private	Dealer
4 Dr C3500 SL Crew Cab LB	11855	13336	14787
4 Dr C3500 SL Crew Cab SB	12936	14552	16136
4 Dr C3500 SLE Crew Cab LB	14024	15776	17493
4 Dr C3500 SLE Crew Cab SB	14747	16589	18394
4 Dr C3500 SLT Crew Cab LB	15069	16951	18796
4 Dr C3500 SLT Crew Cab SB	15790	17763	19696
4 Dr K3500 SL 4WD Crew Cab LB	13727	15441	17122
4 Dr K3500 SL 4WD Crew Cab SB	14601	16425	18212
4 Dr K3500 SLE 4WD Crew Cab LB	15945	17937	19889
4 Dr K3500 SLE 4WD Crew Cab SB	18182	20453	22679
4 Dr K3500 SLT 4WD Crew Cab LB	15996	17994	19953
4 Dr K3500 SLT 4WD Crew Cab SB	17328	19492	21614

Mileage Category: K

GM has refined the Sierra Classic's lineup, dropping all 1500 Series (half-ton) trucks in favor of workhorse 2500 (three-quarter-ton) and 3500 (one-ton) Series models. The only other news is the addition of a new paint color, as this old truck platform (based on the previous-generation C/K pickup) soldiers on into its second decade.

Options	Price
6.5L V8 Turbodiesel OHV 16V Engine	+1352
7.4L V8 OHV 16V FI Engine [Std on Crew Cab]	+299
Air Conditioning [Opt on SL]	+401
AM/FM/Cassette/CD Audio System	+144
Automatic 4-Speed Transmission	+545

Options	Price
Bucket Seats	+134
Dual Rear Wheels [Std on SLE,SLT]	+495
Limited Slip Differential	+125
Power Driver Seat [Opt on SLE]	+119

Sierra Classic 3500/Sonoma

1999

Mileage Category: K

Mechanical upgrades include new internal components and seals for automatic transmissions, improved cooling system and starter motor durability, and three new exterior paint colors. With an all-new Sierra just months away, changes are limited to a few new colors.

Body Styles	TMV Pricing		
	Trade	Private	Dealer
2 Dr C3500 SL Ext Cab LB	10327	11789	13310
2 Dr C3500 SL Std Cab LB	9178	10477	11829
2 Dr C3500 SLE Ext Cab LB	11649	13298	15014
2 Dr C3500 SLE Std Cab LB	9966	11377	12845
2 Dr C3500 SLT Ext Cab LB	12866	14687	16583
2 Dr C3500 SLT Std Cab LB	11045	12609	14236
2 Dr K3500 SL 4WD Ext Cab LB	11821	13494	15236
2 Dr K3500 SL 4WD Std Cab LB	10097	11526	13014
2 Dr K3500 SLE 4WD Ext Cab LB	13381	15275	17247
2 Dr K3500 SLE 4WD Std Cab LB	11566	13204	14908
2 Dr K3500 SLT 4WD Ext Cab LB	13667	15602	17616
2 Dr K3500 SLT 4WD Std Cab LB	12469	14234	16071

Body Styles	TMV Pricing		
	Trade	Private	Dealer
4 Dr C3500 SL Crew Cab LB	10253	11704	13215
4 Dr C3500 SL Crew Cab SB	11137	12714	14355
4 Dr C3500 SLE Crew Cab LB	12687	14483	16352
4 Dr C3500 SLE Crew Cab SB	13177	15042	16984
4 Dr C3500 SLT Crew Cab LB	13347	15236	17203
4 Dr C3500 SLT Crew Cab SB	13617	15545	17551
4 Dr K3500 SL 4WD Crew Cab LB	12026	13728	15500
4 Dr K3500 SL 4WD Crew Cab SB	13034	14879	16800
4 Dr K3500 SLE 4WD Crew Cab LB	13663	15597	17610
4 Dr K3500 SLE 4WD Crew Cab SB	14170	16176	18263
4 Dr K3500 SLT 4WD Crew Cab LB	14276	16297	18401
4 Dr K3500 SLT 4WD Crew Cab SB	15141	17285	19516

Options	Price
6.5L V8 Turbodiesel OHV 16V Engine	+1094
7.4L V8 OHV 16V FI Engine	+242
Air Conditioning [Opt on SL]	+324

Options	Price
AM/FM/Cassette/CD Audio System	+117
Automatic 4-Speed Transmission	+401
Dual Rear Wheels	+345

GMC
Sonoma
2003

Mileage Category: J

The Sonoma gets a few changes for what will be the final year of production of the current model. There's a new split-folding bench seat on all two-wheel-drive models, new seat materials, an optional six-disc CD changer and a sport package for crew-cab models.

Body Styles	TMV Pricing		
	Trade	Private	Dealer
2 Dr SL 4WD Ext Cab SB	11964	13139	15096
2 Dr SL Ext Cab SB	9261	10170	11685
2 Dr SL Std Cab LB	8207	9013	10355
2 Dr SL Std Cab SB	7382	8107	9315
2 Dr SLS 4WD Ext Cab SB	13830	15188	17451

Body Styles	TMV Pricing		
	Trade	Private	Dealer
2 Dr SLS Ext Cab SB	10814	11876	13645
2 Dr SLS Std Cab LB	10626	11669	13408
2 Dr SLS Std Cab SB	9121	10017	11509
2 Dr SLS ZR2 4WD Ext Cab SB	14153	15542	17858
4 Dr SLS 4WD Crew Cab SB	14505	15929	18302

Options	Price
AM/FM/CD Audio System [Opt on SL]	+194
Automatic 4-Speed Transmission	+705
Bucket Seats	+220
Cruise Control [Opt on SL]	+119
Heated Front Seats [Opt on SLS]	+177
Keyless Entry System [Opt on SLS]	+119
Leather Seats [Opt on SLS]	+483
Locking Differential	+174
Power Door Locks [Opt on SLS]	+138

Options	Price
Power Driver Seat [Opt on SLS]	+155
Power Moonroof [Opt on SLS]	+447
Power Passenger Seat [Opt on SLS]	+155
Power Windows [Opt on SLS]	+158
Side Steps	+161
Stepside Bed [Opt on SLS]	+306
AM/FM/CD Changer Audio System [Opt on SLS]	+254
ZQ8 Sport Suspension Package [Opt on SLS]	+505
4.3L V6 OHV 12V FI Engine [Std on 4WD]	+644

2002

Mileage Category: J

In what is likely the last year of production before a full redesign, the Sonoma gets a host of minor equipment upgrades. All extended cabs get a standard third door, while all models get a bed extender and upgraded stereos. The top-of-the-line SLE trim level has been discontinued along with the regular cab, long-bed model. Graphite leather trim is now available on crew cab models and Sandalwood has been added to the color palette.

Body Styles	TMV Pricing		
	Trade	Private	Dealer
2 Dr SL 4WD Ext Cab SB	10392	11532	13433
2 Dr SL Ext Cab SB	7798	8653	10079
2 Dr SL Std Cab LB	6675	7407	8627
2 Dr SL Std Cab SB	6408	7111	8283
2 Dr SLS 4WD Ext Cab SB	12408	13770	16039

Body Styles	TMV Pricing		
	Trade	Private	Dealer
2 Dr SLS Ext Cab SB	9533	10579	12321
2 Dr SLS Std Cab LB	9528	10573	12315
2 Dr SLS Std Cab SB	7957	8830	10286
4 Dr SLS 4WD Crew Cab SB	12846	14256	16605

Options	Price
4.3L V6 OHV 12V FI Engine [Opt on 2WD]	+599
AM/FM/CD Audio System [Opt on SL]	+181
AM/FM/CD Changer Audio System [Opt on SLS]	+177
Automatic 4-Speed Transmission [Opt on SL SB]	+656

Options	Price
Bucket Seats [Opt on SLS]	+159
Cruise Control [Opt on SL]	+117
Leather Seats [Opt on Crew Cab]	+928
Locking Differential	+162

Options	Price
Power Door Locks [Opt on SLS]	+129
Power Driver Seat [Opt on Crew Cab]	+144
Power Passenger Seat [Opt on Crew Cab]	+144
Power Windows [Opt on SLS]	+147
Side Steps [Opt on Crew Cab]	+150

Options	Price
Tilt Steering Wheel [Opt on SL]	+117
ZQ8 Sport Suspension Package [Opt on SLS 2WD]	+464
ZR2 Highrider Suspension Package [Opt on SLS 4WD Ext Cab]	+1154

2001

Mileage Category: J

An all-new model has been added to the Sonoma lineup for 2001, a four-door Crew Cab, complete with Vortec 4300 V6, automatic transmission, InstaTrac four-wheel-drive system and SLS trim. Powertrain improvements incorporate an advanced control module for the V6 and flex-fuel capability for the four-cylinder. There are also new aluminum wheels with the sport suspension, and programmable automatic power door locks.

Body Styles	TMV Pricing		
	Trade	Private	Dealer
2 Dr SL 4WD Ext Cab SB	8680	10229	11658
2 Dr SL Ext Cab SB	7016	8268	9423
2 Dr SL Std Cab LB	5757	6784	7732
2 Dr SL Std Cab SB	5436	6406	7301
2 Dr SLS Sport 4WD Ext Cab SB	9593	11304	12884

Body Styles	TMV Pricing		
	Trade	Private	Dealer
2 Dr SLS Sport Ext Cab SB	7316	8621	9825
2 Dr SLS Sport Std Cab LB	6656	7843	8939
2 Dr SLS Sport Std Cab SB	6232	7344	8370
4 Dr SLS 4WD Crew Cab SB	11272	13283	15139

Options	Price
4.3L V6 OHV 12V FI Engine [Std on 4WD]	+707
Air Conditioning	+440
Aluminum/Alloy Wheels	+153
AM/FM/CD Audio System	+165
Automatic 4-Speed Transmission	+598

Options	Price
Locking Differential	+147
Power Windows	+131
Sport Suspension	+402
ZR2 Highrider Suspension Package	+1035

2000

Mileage Category: J

Four-wheel-drive Sonomas get a higher-output V6 and a handling/trailering suspension standard. GMC drops the 4WD long-bed and High-Rider regular-cab models and adds a new, lower-priced base-trim extended-cab model. All versions get a boost in trailer ratings and a new paint color.

Body Styles	TMV Pricing		
	Trade	Private	Dealer
2 Dr SL 4WD Ext Cab SB	7008	8379	9723
2 Dr SL 4WD Std Cab SB	6687	7995	9277
2 Dr SL Ext Cab SB	5669	6778	7866
2 Dr SL Std Cab LB	4763	5695	6608
2 Dr SL Std Cab SB	4521	5406	6273
2 Dr SLE 4WD Ext Cab SB	7919	9468	10987
2 Dr SLE 4WD Std Cab SB	7063	8444	9798
2 Dr SLE Ext Cab SB	6635	7933	9205
2 Dr SLE Std Cab SB	5242	6268	7273
2 Dr SLS Sport 4WD Ext Cab SB	7489	8954	10390

Body Styles	TMV Pricing		
	Trade	Private	Dealer
2 Dr SLS Sport 4WD Ext Cab Step SB	7704	9211	10688
2 Dr SLS Sport 4WD Std Cab SB	6902	8252	9576
2 Dr SLS Sport 4WD Std Cab Step SB	6954	8314	9648
2 Dr SLS Sport Ext Cab SB	5938	7100	8239
2 Dr SLS Sport Ext Cab Step SB	6152	7355	8535
2 Dr SLS Sport Std Cab LB	5179	6192	7185
2 Dr SLS Sport Std Cab SB	5135	6139	7124
2 Dr SLS Sport Std Cab Step SB	5201	6219	7216

Options	Price
4.3L V6 OHV 12V FI Engine	+645
Air Conditioning	+401
Aluminum/Alloy Wheels	+139
AM/FM/Cassette/CD Audio System	+200
AM/FM/CD Audio System	+150
Automatic 4-Speed Transmission	+545

Options	Price
Bucket Seats	+145
Hinged Third Door	+147
Limited Slip Differential	+134
Power Windows	+119
Sport Suspension	+366
ZR2 Highrider Suspension Package	+893

1999

Mileage Category: J

The '99 Sonoma touts four new exterior colors, a new steering wheel with mini-module depowered airbag and larger, more robust outside rearview mirrors, with the uplevel power mirror gaining a heated feature. AutoTrac, GM's electronic push-button two-speed transfer case, is now standard on four-wheel-drive models, and all Sonomas get a content theft alarm with remote keyless entry as well as a flash-to-pass headlamp feature for the smart stalk. Serious four-wheelers can now order composite skid plates.

Body Styles	TMV Pricing		
	Trade	Private	Dealer
2 Dr SL 4WD Std Cab LB	5661	6852	8092
2 Dr SL 4WD Std Cab SB	5498	6655	7860
2 Dr SL Std Cab LB	4185	5066	5983
2 Dr SL Std Cab SB	3981	4819	5692
2 Dr SLE 4WD Ext Cab SB	6973	8441	9969
2 Dr SLE 4WD Std Cab SB	6333	7666	9053
2 Dr SLE Ext Cab SB	5428	6570	7759
2 Dr SLE Std Cab SB	4696	5685	6714
2 Dr SLS Sport 4WD Ext Cab SB	6639	8036	9491

Body Styles	TMV Pricing		
	Trade	Private	Dealer
2 Dr SLS Sport 4WD Ext Cab Step SB	6938	8398	9918
2 Dr SLS Sport 4WD Std Cab LB	6183	7485	8840
2 Dr SLS Sport 4WD Std Cab SB	5820	7045	8320
2 Dr SLS Sport 4WD Std Cab Step SB	6281	7603	8979
2 Dr SLS Sport Ext Cab SB	5002	6055	7151
2 Dr SLS Sport Ext Cab Step SB	5360	6488	7663
2 Dr SLS Sport Std Cab LB	4442	5376	6349
2 Dr SLS Sport Std Cab SB	4388	5312	6274
2 Dr SLS Sport Std Cab Step SB	4645	5623	6641

Sonoma

1999 (cont'd)

Options	Price
Air Conditioning	+324
AM/FM/Cassette/CD Audio System	+162
AM/FM/CD Audio System	+122
Automatic 4-Speed Transmission	+431

Options	Price
Bucket Seats	+117
Hinged Third Door	+119
Sport Suspension	+296
ZR2 Highrider Suspension Package	+723

1998

Mileage Category: J

Styling is retuned inside and out, resulting in a sleeker look and better interior ergonomics. Dual second-generation airbags are standard, and seats are upgraded for improved comfort and appearance. Four-wheel disc brakes are standard on 4WD models and uplevel stereos are new for 1998. New colors inside and out round out the changes.

Body Styles	TMV Pricing		
	Trade	Private	Dealer
2 Dr SL 4WD Std Cab LB	4814	5891	7105
2 Dr SL 4WD Std Cab SB	4673	5718	6897
2 Dr SL Std Cab LB	3554	4349	5246
2 Dr SL Std Cab SB	3515	4301	5188
2 Dr SLE 4WD Ext Cab SB	5984	7322	8831
2 Dr SLE 4WD Std Cab SB	5595	6847	8258
2 Dr SLE Ext Cab SB	4577	5601	6755
2 Dr SLE Std Cab SB	4089	5004	6036
2 Dr SLS Sport 4WD Ext Cab SB	5796	7093	8555

Body Styles	TMV Pricing		
	Trade	Private	Dealer
2 Dr SLS Sport 4WD Ext Cab Step SB	6160	7538	9092
2 Dr SLS Sport 4WD Std Cab LB	5393	6599	7959
2 Dr SLS Sport 4WD Std Cab SB	5230	6400	7719
2 Dr SLS Sport 4WD Std Cab Step SB	5539	6778	8175
2 Dr SLS Sport Ext Cab SB	4430	5421	6539
2 Dr SLS Sport Ext Cab Step SB	4527	5540	6682
2 Dr SLS Sport Std Cab LB	3812	4665	5626
2 Dr SLS Sport Std Cab SB	3681	4504	5433
2 Dr SLS Sport Std Cab Step SB	4040	4944	5963

Options	Price
Air Conditioning	+279
AM/FM/Cassette/CD Audio System	+118
Automatic 4-Speed Transmission	+371

Options	Price
Hinged Third Door	+130
Sport Suspension	+158
ZR2 Highrider Suspension Package	+623

1997

Mileage Category: J

Changes are limited to new colors, availability of the Sport Suspension on extended cab models, engine and transmission improvements, lighter-weight plug-in half shafts for 4WD Sonomas and console-mounted shifter for trucks equipped with a center console and bucket seats.

Body Styles	TMV Pricing		
	Trade	Private	Dealer
2 Dr SL 4WD Std Cab LB	4374	5399	6651
2 Dr SL 4WD Std Cab SB	4123	5090	6271
2 Dr SL Std Cab LB	3061	3778	4655
2 Dr SL Std Cab SB	3019	3726	4591
2 Dr SLE 4WD Ext Cab SB	5441	6716	8275
2 Dr SLE 4WD Ext Cab Step SB	5953	7348	9052
2 Dr SLE 4WD Std Cab SB	4939	6096	7510
2 Dr SLE 4WD Std Cab Step SB	5103	6299	7760
2 Dr SLE Ext Cab SB	4098	5058	6231
2 Dr SLE Ext Cab Step SB	4115	5079	6258
2 Dr SLE Std Cab SB	3603	4447	5479

Body Styles	TMV Pricing		
	Trade	Private	Dealer
2 Dr SLE Std Cab Step SB	3750	4629	5703
2 Dr SLS Sport 4WD Ext Cab SB	5233	6460	7959
2 Dr SLS Sport 4WD Ext Cab Step SB	5339	6590	8119
2 Dr SLS Sport 4WD Std Cab LB	4803	5928	7304
2 Dr SLS Sport 4WD Std Cab SB	4683	5780	7121
2 Dr SLS Sport 4WD Std Cab Step SB	4852	5989	7378
2 Dr SLS Sport Ext Cab SB	3901	4815	5933
2 Dr SLS Sport Ext Cab Step SB	4049	4998	6158
2 Dr SLS Sport Std Cab LB	3403	4200	5175
2 Dr SLS Sport Std Cab SB	3087	3810	4694
2 Dr SLS Sport Std Cab Step SB	3555	4388	5406

Options	Price
ZR2 Highrider Suspension Package	+419
Air Conditioning	+253
AM/FM/CD Audio System	+127

Options	Price
Automatic 4-Speed Transmission	+336
Hinged Third Door	+118
Sport Suspension	+221

1996

Mileage Category: J

Extended-cab models get an optional driver-side rear access panel. All Sonomas are now equipped with four-wheel ABS. A new sport suspension provides sporty handling, and a snazzy Sportside box ends Ford's reign as lord of compact stepsides. A new five-speed transmission improves shifter location and operation when equipped with the base four-cylinder. Still missing is the availability of a passenger airbag.

Body Styles	TMV Pricing		
	Trade	Private	Dealer
2 Dr SL 4WD Std Cab LB	3732	4632	5876
2 Dr SL 4WD Std Cab SB	3614	4486	5690
2 Dr SL Std Cab LB	2571	3191	4047
2 Dr SL Std Cab SB	2489	3090	3919
2 Dr SLE 4WD Ext Cab SB	4788	5943	7538
2 Dr SLE 4WD Ext Cab Step SB	4914	6099	7736
2 Dr SLE 4WD Std Cab SB	3802	4720	5987
2 Dr SLE Ext Cab SB	3544	4399	5579
2 Dr SLE Ext Cab Step SB	3590	4456	5653
2 Dr SLE Std Cab SB	2768	3436	4358

Body Styles	TMV Pricing		
	Trade	Private	Dealer
2 Dr SLS Sport 4WD Ext Cab SB	4318	5360	6798
2 Dr SLS Sport 4WD Ext Cab Step SB	4410	5475	6945
2 Dr SLS Sport 4WD Std Cab LB	4016	4985	6323
2 Dr SLS Sport 4WD Std Cab SB	3896	4836	6135
2 Dr SLS Sport 4WD Std Cab Step SB	3942	4893	6206
2 Dr SLS Sport Ext Cab SB	3165	3929	4983
2 Dr SLS Sport Ext Cab Step SB	3497	4340	5505
2 Dr SLS Sport Std Cab LB	3004	3729	4729
2 Dr SLS Sport Std Cab SB	2783	3455	4382
2 Dr SLS Sport Std Cab Step SB	3051	3787	4804

1996 (cont'd)

Options	Price
ZR2 Highrider Suspension Package	+479
Air Conditioning	+223
Automatic 4-Speed Transmission	+297

1995

Body Styles	TMV Pricing		
	Trade	Private	Dealer
2 Dr SL 4WD Std Cab LB	2947	3655	4834
2 Dr SL 4WD Std Cab SB	2853	3539	4681
2 Dr SL Std Cab LB	2027	2513	3324
2 Dr SL Std Cab SB	1980	2456	3248
2 Dr SLE 4WD Ext Cab SB	4124	5114	6764
2 Dr SLE 4WD Std Cab SB	3132	3884	5137
2 Dr SLE Ext Cab SB	2764	3428	4534

Options	Price
4.3L V6 OHV 12V FI Engine	+255
4.3L V6 OHV 12V HO FI Engine	+144
Air Conditioning	+207
Antilock Brakes [Opt on 2WD]	+195

Body Styles	TMV Pricing		
	Trade	Private	Dealer
2 Dr SLE Std Cab SB	2395	2970	3928
2 Dr SLS 4WD Ext Cab SB	3766	4670	6177
2 Dr SLS 4WD Std Cab LB	3223	3997	5286
2 Dr SLS 4WD Std Cab SB	3132	3884	5137
2 Dr SLS Ext Cab SB	2718	3371	4458
2 Dr SLS Std Cab LB	2534	3142	4156
2 Dr SLS Std Cab SB	2256	2798	3701

Options	Price
Automatic 4-Speed Transmission	+276
Sport Suspension	+117
ZR2 Highrider Suspension Package	+400

Mileage Category: J

Driver airbag is added, and daytime running lights are standard. Highrider off-road package can be ordered on the Club Coupe. Power window and lock buttons are illuminated at night. Remote keyless entry is a new option. A single key operates both the door locks and the ignition. A manual transmission can now be ordered with the 191-horsepower, 4.3-liter V6.

1994

Body Styles	TMV Pricing		
	Trade	Private	Dealer
2 Dr SL 4WD Std Cab LB	2399	3053	4143
2 Dr SL 4WD Std Cab SB	2355	2997	4068
2 Dr SL Std Cab LB	1621	2063	2800
2 Dr SL Std Cab SB	1615	2055	2789
2 Dr SLE 4WD Ext Cab SB	3382	4305	5842
2 Dr SLE 4WD Std Cab LB	2825	3595	4879
2 Dr SLE Ext Cab SB	2268	2887	3918

Options	Price
4.3L V6 OHV 12V FI Engine	+230
4.3L V6 OHV 12V HO FI Engine	+130
Air Conditioning	+187

Body Styles	TMV Pricing		
	Trade	Private	Dealer
2 Dr SLE Std Cab LB	1969	2506	3401
2 Dr SLE Std Cab SB	1841	2343	3179
2 Dr SLS 4WD Ext Cab SB	3212	4088	5547
2 Dr SLS 4WD Std Cab SB	2571	3272	4440
2 Dr SLS Ext Cab SB	2227	2834	3846
2 Dr SLS Std Cab SB	1713	2180	2959

Options	Price
AM/FM/CD Audio System	+94
Automatic 4-Speed Transmission	+249

Mileage Category: J

All-new truck debuts with more powerful engines and available four-wheel ABS. Side-door guard beams are standard. Rear ABS is standard on four-cylinder models; V6 trucks get the new four-wheel ABS system that works in both two- and four-wheel drive. Highrider package is for serious off-roaders. Available only on regular-cab shortbed models, the Highrider includes four-inch wider track, three-inch height increase, off-road suspension and tires, wheel flares and thick skid plates. Base engine is 118-horse, 2.2-liter four cylinder. Standard on 4WD models is a 165-horsepower, 4.3-liter V6. Optional on all models is a 195-horsepower, high-output 4.3-liter V6.

GMC
Suburban

1999

Body Styles	TMV Pricing		
	Trade	Private	Dealer
4 Dr C1500 SUV	10038	11484	12988
4 Dr C2500 SUV	10553	12073	13655

Options	Price
Aluminum/Alloy Wheels	+119
Air Conditioning - Front and Rear	+534
Center and Rear Bench Seat	+419
Heated Front Seats	+134
Leather Seats	+478
OnStar Telematic System	+311

Body Styles	TMV Pricing		
	Trade	Private	Dealer
4 Dr K1500 4WD SUV	11066	12659	14318
4 Dr K2500 4WD SUV	11768	13463	15227

Options	Price
Running Boards	+124
SLE Package	+1467
SLT Package	+1777
6.5L V8 Turbodiesel OHV 16V Engine [Opt on 2500]	+1094
7.4L V8 OHV 16V FI Engine [Opt on 2500]	+230
Air Conditioning	+323

Mileage Category: N

A couple of new colors are the only modifications to the Suburban.

GMC
Suburban

1998
Mileage Category: N

Depowered second-generation airbags protect front-seat occupants for 1998. Carpeted floor mats become standard. Standard equipment also includes PassLock theft-deterrent system, electrochromic rearview mirror and automatic four-wheel drive on K-series models.

Body Styles	TMV Pricing		
	Trade	Private	Dealer
4 Dr C1500 SUV	8825	10222	11798
4 Dr C2500 SUV	9341	10820	12488

Options	Price
6.5L V8 Turbodiesel OHV 16V Engine [Opt on 2500]	+942
7.4L V8 OHV 16V FI Engine [Opt on 2500]	+198
Air Conditioning	+279
Air Conditioning - Front and Rear	+460
Center and Rear Bench Seat	+361

Body Styles	TMV Pricing		
	Trade	Private	Dealer
4 Dr K1500 4WD SUV	9720	11259	12995
4 Dr K2500 4WD SUV	10219	11837	13661

Options	Price
Heated Front Seats	+115
Leather Seats	+412
OnStar Telematic System	+268
SLE Package	+1264
SLT Package	+1530

1997
Mileage Category: N

GMC has added a passenger-side airbag and a power lock switch in the cargo compartment. SLE and SLT trim now includes rear heat and air conditioning, as well as remote keyless entry. Uplevel SLT trim also includes a combination CD and cassette player stereo system. All Suburbans receive speed-sensitive power steering, and 4WD models have a tighter turning circle. Two new colors freshen the dated exterior design this year.

Body Styles	TMV Pricing		
	Trade	Private	Dealer
4 Dr C1500 SUV	7386	8666	10231
4 Dr C2500 SUV	7840	9199	10861

Options	Price
Leather Seats	+335
SLE Package	+1144
SLT Package	+1385
Third Seat	+412

Body Styles	TMV Pricing		
	Trade	Private	Dealer
4 Dr K1500 4WD SUV	8217	9641	11382
4 Dr K2500 4WD SUV	8634	10131	11960

Options	Price
6.5L V8 Turbodiesel OHV 16V Engine	+853
7.4L V8 OHV 16V FI Engine	+179
Air Conditioning	+252
Air Conditioning - Front and Rear	+416

1996
Mileage Category: N

Giant SUV gets daytime running lights to make it more visible to other drivers. New V8s, quieter tires and long-life spark plugs and coolant make the Suburban less costly to maintain. Rear passengers get warmer faster, thanks to new rear-seat heat ducting. Illuminated entry is newly standard, and electronic 4WD controls are a new option.

Body Styles	TMV Pricing		
	Trade	Private	Dealer
4 Dr C1500 SUV	6393	7526	9091
4 Dr C2500 SUV	6775	7976	9634

Options	Price
SLE Package	+936
SLT Package	+1149
Third Seat	+365
6.5L V8 Turbodiesel OHV 16V Engine	+755
7.4L V8 OHV 16V FI Engine	+158

Body Styles	TMV Pricing		
	Trade	Private	Dealer
4 Dr K1500 4WD SUV	7044	8292	10016
4 Dr K2500 4WD SUV	7397	8708	10518

Options	Price
Air Conditioning	+223
Air Conditioning - Front and Rear	+342
Compact Disc Changer	+158
Leather Seats	+296

1995
Mileage Category: N

New interior with driver airbag debuts. New dashboard features modular design with controls that are much easier to read and use. The 1500 models can now be ordered with turbodiesel engine. Brake/transmission shift interlock is added to automatic transmission. Seats and door panels are revised. New console on models with bucket seats features pivoting writing surface, along with rear cupholders and storage drawer. Uplevel radios come with automatic volume controls that raise or lower the volume depending on vehicle speed.

Body Styles	TMV Pricing		
	Trade	Private	Dealer
4 Dr C1500 SUV	4945	5823	7285
4 Dr C2500 SUV	5355	6305	7888

Options	Price
SLE Package	+869
SLT Package	+1068
6.5L V8 Turbodiesel OHV 16V Engine	+701
7.4L V8 OHV 16V FI Engine	+147

Body Styles	TMV Pricing		
	Trade	Private	Dealer
4 Dr K1500 4WD SUV	5522	6502	8135
4 Dr K2500 4WD SUV	5911	6960	8707

Options	Price
Air Conditioning	+207
Air Conditioning - Front and Rear	+318
Compact Disc Changer	+147
Leather Seats	+275

1994
Mileage Category: N

Side-door guard beams are added, as well as a high-mounted center brake light. A turbocharged diesel is optional on 2500 models. A new grille appears.

Body Styles	TMV Pricing		
	Trade	Private	Dealer
4 Dr C1500 SUV	4139	4991	6412
4 Dr C2500 SUV	4229	5100	6551

Options	Price
6.5L V8 Turbodiesel OHV 16V Engine	+631
7.4L V8 OHV 16V FI Engine	+132
Air Conditioning	+186
Air Conditioning - Front and Rear	+286

Body Styles	TMV Pricing		
	Trade	Private	Dealer
4 Dr K1500 4WD SUV	4540	5475	7033
4 Dr K2500 4WD SUV	4706	5675	7290

Options	Price
Center and Rear Bench Seat	+242
Leather Seats	+248
Premium Audio System	+122
SLE Package	+573

For the latest vehicle information, visit www.edmunds.com

2003

Body Styles	TMV Pricing		
	Trade	Private	Dealer
4 Dr Denali AWD SUV	33040	35095	38520
4 Dr SLE 4WD SUV	24764	26294	28843
4 Dr SLE SUV	22989	24409	26775

Body Styles	TMV Pricing		
	Trade	Private	Dealer
4 Dr SLT 4WD SUV	26202	27821	30519
4 Dr SLT SUV	24402	25909	28421

Options	Price
Automatic Stability Control [Opt on SLE,SLT]	+195
Bose Audio System [Opt on SLE]	+254
Bucket Seats [Opt on SLE]	+274
Camper/Towing Package	+200
Captain Chairs (4)	+315
Navigation System [Opt on Denali]	+1285
Off-Road Suspension Package [Opt on SLT]	+411
Power Moonroof	+644
Power Passenger Seat [Opt on SLE,SLT]	+155

Options	Price
Running Boards [Opt on SLE]	+254
Front Side Airbag Restraints [Opt on SLE,SLT]	+161
Third Seat [Opt on SLE,SLT]	+232
Autoride Suspension Package [Opt on SLT]	+721
OnStar Telematic System [Opt on SLE,SLT]	+447
AM/FM/Cassette/CD Changer Audio System [Opt on SLE,SLT]	+161
Satellite Radio System [Opt on SLE,SLT]	+225
DVD Entertainment System	+834
Power Driver Seat w/Memory [Opt on SLT]	+132

Mileage Category: N

Despite numerous 2003 upgrades, there's not much different on the outside other than optional multifunction mirrors and new machined aluminum wheels for SLT models. Inside, you'll find tri-zone climate controls, an enhanced driver-information center and a redesigned center console and instrument panel. Satellite steering wheel controls are now optional (standard on Denali models) as are second-row captain's chairs. New entertainment options include a Bose audio system, as well as XM Satellite Radio and a DVD-based entertainment system. For increased safety, there are a standard front-passenger sensing system, three-point belts for all second-row passengers, adjustable pedals and an available StabiliTrak stability control system. GMC also upgraded the braking system for better pedal feel and performance and retuned the Autotrac four-wheel-drive system for better efficiency and less binding at low speeds. Finally, Yukons sold in California are fitted with a new catalytic converter that earns the truck ULEV certification.

2002

Body Styles	TMV Pricing		
	Trade	Private	Dealer
4 Dr Denali AWD SUV	28813	30751	33980
4 Dr SLE 4WD SUV	22202	23692	26175
4 Dr SLE SUV	20529	21907	24203

Body Styles	TMV Pricing		
	Trade	Private	Dealer
4 Dr SLT 4WD SUV	23473	25048	27673
4 Dr SLT SUV	21787	23249	25685

Options	Price
5.3L V8 Flex Fuel OHV 16V FI Engine	+419
5.3L V8 OHV 16V FI Engine	+419
Autoride Suspension Package	+509
Bucket Seats [Opt on SLE]	+225
Cast Alloy Wheels [Opt on SLT]	+120
Off-Road Suspension Package [Opt on 4WD]	+371

Options	Price
OnStar Telematic System [Opt on SLT]	+416
Power Driver Seat w/Memory [Opt on SLT]	+123
Power Moonroof	+562
Running Boards	+237
Third Seat	+216

Mileage Category: N

GMC's strong-selling Yukon heads into 2002 with few changes. The 5300 V8 is now ultralow emission certified (ULEV) for California. For states with less restrictive emission requirements, the Yukon offers flexible fuel capability with the use of cleaner burning gasoline blends. A more efficient starter, more durable steering gear housing and LATCH child seat attachments anchors round out the Yukon's upgrades for 2002.

2001

Body Styles	TMV Pricing		
	Trade	Private	Dealer
4 Dr Denali AWD SUV	24095	26695	29095
4 Dr SLE 4WD SUV	19562	21683	23641
4 Dr SLE SUV	17949	19895	21691

Body Styles	TMV Pricing		
	Trade	Private	Dealer
4 Dr SLT 4WD SUV	20356	22563	24600
4 Dr SLT SUV	18743	20775	22650

Options	Price
5.3L V8 OHV 16V FI Engine	+382
Autoride Suspension Package	+382
Bucket Seats	+205
Camper/Towing Package	+116
Locking Differential [Opt on 2WD]	+138

Options	Price
OnStar Telematic System	+380
Power Sunroof	+512
Running Boards	+216
Third Seat	+355

Mileage Category: N

The recently redesigned Yukon is virtually unchanged from last year. The high-level Yukon Denali is now based on the revamped Yukon. The Denali gets a 6.0-liter V8 engine along with standard all-wheel drive and a host of other new features designed to elevate the top-of-the-line GMC above and beyond its more basic Yukon cousin.

2000

Body Styles	TMV Pricing		
	Trade	Private	Dealer
4 Dr SLE 4WD SUV	16711	18808	20864
4 Dr SLE SUV	15844	17833	19782

Body Styles	TMV Pricing		
	Trade	Private	Dealer
4 Dr SLT 4WD SUV	17806	20041	22232
4 Dr SLT SUV	16490	18560	20589

Mileage Category: N

Completely redesigned, Yukon is based on the new Sierra pickup platform with zippy V8 engines and a stouter chassis for a better, more isolated ride.

2000 (cont'd)

Options	Price
5.3L V8 OHV 16V FI Engine	+348
Bucket Seats	+118
Compact Disc Changer	+274
Heated Front Seats	+174
Limited Slip Differential	+125

Options	Price
OnStar Telematic System [Opt on SLT]	+346
Power Moonroof	+372
Running Boards	+162
Third Seat	+475

1999

Body Styles	TMV Pricing		
	Trade	Private	Dealer
4 Dr Denali 4WD SUV	14527	16666	18893
4 Dr SLE 4WD SUV	11084	12742	14468
4 Dr SLE SUV	10283	11822	13423

Body Styles	TMV Pricing		
	Trade	Private	Dealer
4 Dr SLT 4WD SUV	11545	13272	15070
4 Dr SLT SUV	10657	12251	13911

Options	Price
Air Conditioning - Front and Rear	+222
Compact Disc Changer	+222
Heated Front Seats	+141

Options	Price
OnStar Telematic System [Opt on SLE,SLT]	+311
Running Boards	+131

Mileage Category: N

An upscale version of the Yukon dubbed the Yukon Denali joins the lineup featuring distinct exterior colors, chrome wheels and a fully optioned interior.

1998

Mileage Category: N

The two-door model gets the ax this year. Rear-seat passengers are cooled by a newly optional rear air conditioning system. A host of new standard features has been added, including carpeted floor mats. Three new colors spruce up the outside a bit, and second-generation airbags are standard inside.

Body Styles	TMV Pricing		
	Trade	Private	Dealer
4 Dr SLE 4WD SUV	9796	11346	13094
4 Dr SLE SUV	8962	10381	11982

Body Styles	TMV Pricing		
	Trade	Private	Dealer
4 Dr SLT 4WD SUV	10325	11959	13802
4 Dr SLT SUV	9552	11065	12771

Options	Price
Air Conditioning - Front and Rear [Opt on SLE]	+190
Bucket Seats	+135
Compact Disc Changer	+190

Options	Price
Heated Front Seats	+121
OnStar Telematic System	+268

1997

Mileage Category: N

Dual airbags, speed-sensitive steering and a tighter turning circle for 4WD models. A power lock switch is added to the cargo compartment, and SLT models have a standard CD/cassette combo stereo. Remote keyless entry is standard on four-door models, and on SLE and SLT two-door models. Optional on four-door models is a rear air conditioning unit.

Body Styles	TMV Pricing		
	Trade	Private	Dealer
2 Dr SL 4WD SUV	6621	7769	9171
2 Dr SL SUV	6012	7055	8329
2 Dr SLE 4WD SUV	7337	8609	10163
2 Dr SLE SUV	7062	8286	9783
2 Dr SLT 4WD SUV	7557	8867	10469

Body Styles	TMV Pricing		
	Trade	Private	Dealer
2 Dr SLT SUV	7216	8467	9996
4 Dr SLE 4WD SUV	7378	8657	10220
4 Dr SLE SUV	7121	8356	9865
4 Dr SLT 4WD SUV	7661	8989	10612
4 Dr SLT SUV	7345	8618	10174

Options	Price
6.5L V8 Turbodiesel OHV 16V Engine	+986
Air Conditioning [Opt on SL]	+265

Options	Price
Air Conditioning - Front and Rear	+265

1996

Mileage Category: N

A two-wheel-drive two-door Yukon becomes available. A new 5700 Vortec V8 gets long-life coolant and spark plugs, as well as a hefty bump in power and torque. Passenger car tires on less stout Yukons result in a softer, quieter ride. Rear heat ducts, illuminated entry, and height-adjustable seatbelts debut. Four-wheel-drive models get an optional electronic shift mechanism.

Body Styles	TMV Pricing		
	Trade	Private	Dealer
2 Dr SL 4WD SUV	5555	6578	7991
2 Dr SL SUV	5073	6007	7297
2 Dr SLE 4WD SUV	6124	7252	8809
2 Dr SLE SUV	5988	7091	8613
2 Dr SLT 4WD SUV	6412	7593	9224

Body Styles	TMV Pricing		
	Trade	Private	Dealer
2 Dr SLT SUV	6116	7242	8798
4 Dr SLE 4WD SUV	6223	7369	8952
4 Dr SLE SUV	6028	7138	8671
4 Dr SLT 4WD SUV	6511	7710	9366
4 Dr SLT SUV	6152	7285	8849

Options	Price
6.5L V8 Turbodiesel OHV 16V Engine	+871
Air Conditioning [Opt on SL]	+234

1995

Body Styles	TMV Pricing		
	Trade	Private	Dealer
2 Dr SLE 4WD SUV	4917	5790	7245
2 Dr SLT 4WD SUV	5194	6116	7652
2 Dr STD 4WD SUV	4653	5479	6856
4 Dr SLE 4WD SUV	5324	6269	7845

Options	Price
6.5L V8 Turbodiesel OHV 16V Engine	+810
Air Conditioning [Opt on STD]	+217

Body Styles	TMV Pricing		
	Trade	Private	Dealer
4 Dr SLE SUV	5061	5959	7456
4 Dr SLT 4WD SUV	5613	6609	8270
4 Dr SLT SUV	5252	6184	7738

Options	Price
Aluminum/Alloy Wheels	+80
Automatic 4-Speed Transmission [Std on Wgn]	+255

Mileage Category: N

New interior with driver airbag debuts. New dashboard features modular design with controls that are much easier to read and use. New four-door model is added midyear, nicely sized between Jimmy and Suburban. New model is offered only in SLE or SLT trim with a 5.7-liter V8 and an automatic transmission in either 2WD or 4WD. Brake/transmission shift interlock is added to automatic transmission. New console on models with bucket seats features pivoting writing surface, along with rear cupholders and storage drawer.

1994

Body Styles	TMV Pricing		
	Trade	Private	Dealer
2 Dr SLE 4WD SUV	4253	5128	6587
2 Dr STD 4WD SUV	3970	4787	6149

Options	Price
6.5L V8 Turbodiesel OHV 16V Engine	+729
Air Conditioning [Std on Sport]	+196

Body Styles	TMV Pricing		
	Trade	Private	Dealer
2 Dr Sport 4WD SUV	4086	4927	6328

Options	Price
Automatic 4-Speed Transmission	+230
Premium Audio System	+128

Mileage Category: N

Air conditioning receives CFC-free coolant. Side-door guard beams are added. A new grille appears, and models equipped with a decor package get composite headlamps. A turbocharged diesel is newly optional. Third brake light is added.

GMC
Yukon Denali

2000

Body Styles	TMV Pricing		
	Trade	Private	Dealer
4 Dr Denali 4WD SUV	20035	22730	25372

Mileage Category: O

For the 2000 model year, GMC's Yukon Denali gets a new exterior color and adds GM's OnStar communications system.

GMC
Yukon XL

2003

Body Styles	TMV Pricing		
	Trade	Private	Dealer
4 Dr 1500 SLE 4WD SUV	27126	28801	31594
4 Dr 1500 SLE SUV	24864	26400	28959
4 Dr 1500 SLT 4WD SUV	28304	30052	32966
4 Dr 1500 SLT SUV	27367	29057	31874
4 Dr 2500 SLE 4WD SUV	27938	29664	32540

Body Styles	TMV Pricing		
	Trade	Private	Dealer
4 Dr 2500 SLE SUV	26095	27707	30393
4 Dr 2500 SLT 4WD SUV	29535	31359	34400
4 Dr 2500 SLT SUV	28050	29783	32670
4 Dr Denali AWD SUV	33543	35629	39105

Options	Price
4 Wheel Steering [Opt on SLE,SLT]	+2894
Automatic Stability Control [Opt on SLE,SLT]	+195
Bucket Seats [Opt on SLE]	+274
Camper/Towing Package	+138
Captain Chairs (4)	+315
Limited Slip Differential [Opt on SLE,SLT]	+190
Navigation System [Opt on Denali]	+1285
Power Moonroof	+644
Power Passenger Seat [Opt on SLE,SLT]	+155

Options	Price
Running Boards [Opt on SLE]	+254
Front Side Airbag Restraints [Opt on SLE,SLT]	+161
Autoride Suspension Package [Opt on SLT]	+721
OnStar Telematic System [Opt on SLE,SLT]	+447
AM/FM/Cassette/CD Changer Audio System [Opt on SLT]	+161
Satellite Radio System [Opt on SLE,SLT]	+225
DVD Entertainment System	+834
8.1L V8 OHV 16V FI Engine [Opt on SLE,SLT]	+451

Mileage Category: N

The Yukon XL gains numerous functional enhancements for 2003. The Quadrasteer four-wheel steering system is now available on 3/4-ton models for increased maneuverability and better stability when towing, while 1/2-ton versions now offer the Stabilitrak stability control system. Also this year, buyers get a choice of two new optional exterior mirrors: a multifunction power fold-away version with puddle lamps and integrated turn signal lights or extended camper mirrors that are also power foldable. The interior gets numerous upgrades that include tri-zone climate control, an enhanced driver-information center and a redesigned center console and instrument panel. Steering wheel-mounted audio controls are now optional, as are second-row captain's chairs and power adjustable pedals. A revised lineup of entertainment options offers buyers a Bose audio system as well as XM Satellite Radio and a DVD-based entertainment system. Finally, for increased safety, the Yukon XL now features a standard front-passenger-sensing system, dual-stage airbags and three point seatbelts for all positions in the first and second rows.

Yukon XL

2002

Mileage Category: N

Three-quarter-ton models equipped with the 8100 V8 get the new 4L85 heavy-duty transmission, while the previous 4L80 version also gets upgraded with more durable internal parts. A more efficient starter and a stronger steering gear housing have also been added to all gas engines along with flexible fuel capability for the 5300 V8.

Body Styles	TMV Pricing		
	Trade	Private	Dealer
4 Dr 1500 SLE 4WD SUV	24504	26148	28889
4 Dr 1500 SLE SUV	22269	23763	26254
4 Dr 1500 SLT 4WD SUV	25364	27066	29902
4 Dr 1500 SLT SUV	24142	25762	28462
4 Dr 2500 SLE 4WD SUV	25216	26908	29728

Body Styles	TMV Pricing		
	Trade	Private	Dealer
4 Dr 2500 SLE SUV	23479	25055	27680
4 Dr 2500 SLT 4WD SUV	26575	28358	31330
4 Dr 2500 SLT SUV	24959	26634	29425
4 Dr Denali AWD SUV	29004	30932	34145

Options	Price
8.1L V8 OHV 16V FI Engine [Opt on 2500]	+841
Autoride Suspension Package	+509
Bucket Seats [Opt on SLE]	+225
Captain Chairs (4) [Opt on Denali,SLT]	+293

Options	Price
Cast Alloy Wheels [Opt on SLT]	+120
OnStar Telematic System [Opt on SLT]	+416
Power Sunroof	+562
Running Boards [Opt on SLE,SLT]	+237

2001

Mileage Category: N

The Yukon XL gets a new top-of-the-line engine in addition to more horsepower for the 6.0-liter V8. Debuting this year is the Yukon Denali XL featuring standard all-wheel drive and a host of other new features designed to elevate the top-of-the-line GMC above and beyond its more basic Yukon XL stablemate.

Body Styles	TMV Pricing		
	Trade	Private	Dealer
4 Dr 1500 SLE 4WD SUV	21214	23488	25588
4 Dr 1500 SLE SUV	19442	21526	23450
4 Dr 1500 SLT 4WD SUV	22550	24968	27200
4 Dr 1500 SLT SUV	21015	23268	25348
4 Dr 2500 SLE 4WD SUV	22063	24429	26613

Body Styles	TMV Pricing		
	Trade	Private	Dealer
4 Dr 2500 SLE SUV	20573	22778	24814
4 Dr 2500 SLT 4WD SUV	23316	25816	28123
4 Dr 2500 SLT SUV	21748	24080	26232
4 Dr Denali AWD SUV	26217	29015	31598

Options	Price
8.1L V8 OHV 16V FI Engine	+631
Autoride Suspension Package	+329
Bucket Seats	+205
Heated Front Seats	+137

Options	Price
OnStar Telematic System	+380
Power Sunroof	+546
Running Boards	+216

2000

Mileage Category: N

The 2000 GMC Yukon XL is a complete redesign of last year's Suburban model, adding mechanical and comfort upgrades.

Body Styles	TMV Pricing		
	Trade	Private	Dealer
4 Dr C1500 SLE SUV	16709	18806	20861
4 Dr C1500 SLT SUV	18176	20457	22693
4 Dr C2500 SLE SUV	17932	20183	22389
4 Dr C2500 SLT SUV	18911	21284	23611

Body Styles	TMV Pricing		
	Trade	Private	Dealer
4 Dr K1500 SLE 4WD SUV	18290	20585	22835
4 Dr K1500 SLT 4WD SUV	19788	22272	24706
4 Dr K2500 SLE 4WD SUV	19520	21970	24372
4 Dr K2500 SLT 4WD SUV	21276	23946	26564

Options	Price
Limited Slip Differential	+125
OnStar Telematic System [Opt on SLT]	+346
Power Moonroof	+495
Running Boards	+162

Options	Price
Autoride Suspension Package	+300
Bucket Seats	+187
Camper/Towing Package	+129
Heated Front Seats	+125

2003

Body Styles	TMV Pricing			Body Styles	TMV Pricing		
	Trade	Private	Dealer		Trade	Private	Dealer
2 Dr EX Cpe	15786	16984	18980	4 Dr EX Sdn	15538	16717	18681
2 Dr EX V6 Cpe	18800	20226	22603	4 Dr EX V6 Sdn	17915	19274	21538
2 Dr LX Cpe	14377	15468	17286	4 Dr LX Sdn	14058	15125	16903
2 Dr LX V6 Cpe	16547	17802	19895	4 Dr LX V6 Sdn	16450	17698	19778
4 Dr DX Sdn	12306	13239	14795				

Options	Price
Leather Seats [Opt on EX]	+1014
Navigation System [Opt on EX]	+1560
Front Side Airbag Restraints [Opt on LX]	+195

Mileage Category: D

The Honda Accord -- one of America's favorite vehicles -- has been substantially changed for 2003. Continuing as a sedan and a coupe, the '03 Accord features more powerful and fuel-efficient engines, increased safety and higher levels of interior comfort. A voice-activated GPS navigation system is optional, and a sporty EX coupe debuts in early 2003.

2002

Body Styles	TMV Pricing			Body Styles	TMV Pricing		
	Trade	Private	Dealer		Trade	Private	Dealer
2 Dr EX Cpe	13482	14685	16691	4 Dr EX Sdn	13211	14391	16357
2 Dr EX V6 Cpe	15440	16818	19115	4 Dr EX V6 Sdn	15275	16639	18912
2 Dr LX Cpe	12244	13337	15159	4 Dr LX Sdn	12162	13248	15059
2 Dr LX V6 Cpe	13910	15152	17221	4 Dr LX V6 Sdn	14040	15294	17383
2 Dr SE Cpe	13203	14382	16347	4 Dr SE Sdn	13172	14348	16309
4 Dr DX Sdn	10414	11344	12893	4 Dr Value Sdn	11274	12281	13958

Options	Price	Options	Price
Antilock Brakes [Opt on LX]	+671	Front Side Airbag Restraints [Std on EX,EX V6]	+168
Automatic 4-Speed Transmission [Std on V6]	+537	Leather Seats [Std on EX V6]	+772

Mileage Category: D

Honda has added a new trim level for 2002, the SE. The Accord SE is based on the LX four-cylinder coupe or sedan trim level with an automatic transmission. Features setting the SE apart from LX models include an upgraded audio system, a driver seat power height adjustment, interior wood grain trim, antilock brakes, remote keyless entry and 15-inch alloy wheels.

2001

Body Styles	TMV Pricing			Body Styles	TMV Pricing		
	Trade	Private	Dealer		Trade	Private	Dealer
2 Dr EX Cpe	11470	13063	14534	4 Dr EX Sdn	11361	12939	14397
2 Dr EX V6 Cpe	13201	15035	16729	4 Dr EX V6 Sdn	13141	14966	16651
2 Dr LX Cpe	10502	11960	13307	4 Dr LX Sdn	10444	11895	13234
2 Dr LX V6 Cpe	11754	13387	14894	4 Dr LX V6 Sdn	11718	13346	14848
4 Dr DX Sdn	8640	9840	10949	4 Dr Value Sdn	9379	10681	11884

Options	Price	Options	Price
Antilock Brakes [Opt on LX]	+408	Leather Seats [Opt on EX]	+570
Automatic 4-Speed Transmission [Opt on DX,EX,LX]	+480	Power Driver Seat [Opt on EX]	+132
Front Side Airbag Restraints [Opt on EX]	+150		

Mileage Category: D

Freshened exterior styling debuts for 2001, with a more aggressive-looking front fascia and hood and a new taillight design. Honda also ups the safety features list, making dual-stage, dual-threshold front airbags standard and side airbags available on all models. All Accords now either meet or exceed California's low-emission vehicle (LEV) standards (some Accords meet ULEV standards, and one model sold in California is rated SULEV). Improvements aimed at reducing road and wind noise have been made, while EX models get a standard in-dash six-disc CD changer, and all V6 models come with traction control. Midyear, a DX four-banger equipped with a special value package debuted, adding an automatic transmission, air conditioning, a CD player, floor mats, fake wood interior accents and special exterior trim.

2000

Body Styles	TMV Pricing			Body Styles	TMV Pricing		
	Trade	Private	Dealer		Trade	Private	Dealer
2 Dr EX Cpe	9832	11325	12788	4 Dr EX Sdn	9885	11385	12856
2 Dr EX V6 Cpe	11324	13043	14727	4 Dr EX V6 Sdn	11364	13089	14780
2 Dr LX Cpe	8939	10297	11627	4 Dr LX Sdn	9040	10412	11757
2 Dr LX V6 Cpe	9954	11465	12946	4 Dr LX V6 Ldn	10004	11522	13011
4 Dr DX Sdn	7404	8528	9630	4 Dr SE Sdn	9658	11124	12562

Mileage Category: D

The four-cylinder engines now have a 100,000-mile no-tune-up service life. Side airbags are standard for all V6 models and EX four-cylinders with the leather interior. The feature-laden Accord SE Sedan makes its debut this year. In the paint department, Nighthawk Black replaces Starlight Black, and Naples Gold Metallic replaces Heather Mist Metallic; Raisin and Currant have been dropped.

Honda
Accord

2000 (cont'd)

Options	Price
Air Conditioning [Opt on DX]	+276
AM/FM/Cassette/CD Audio System	+152
Antilock Brakes [Opt on LX]	+375
Automatic 4-Speed Transmission [Std on V6]	+442
Compact Disc Changer	+249

Options	Price
Front Side Airbag Restraints [Opt on EX]	+138
Leather Seats [Opt on EX]	+510
Power Driver Seat [Opt on EX]	+121
Rear Spoiler	+193

1999

Mileage Category: D

The coupes remain unchanged after their recent overhaul, but the sedans receive new seat fabric, and the LX and EX sedans now feature fold-away side mirrors.

Body Styles	TMV Pricing		
	Trade	Private	Dealer
2 Dr EX Cpe	8349	9768	11245
2 Dr EX V6 Cpe	9687	11333	13046
2 Dr LX Cpe	7645	8944	10296
2 Dr LX V6 Cpe	8588	10047	11566
4 Dr DX Sdn	6153	7199	8287

Body Styles	TMV Pricing		
	Trade	Private	Dealer
4 Dr EX Sdn	8396	9823	11309
4 Dr EX V6 Sdn	9719	11371	13090
4 Dr LX Sdn	7700	9008	10370
4 Dr LX V6 Sdn	8337	9754	11228

Options	Price
Air Conditioning [Opt on DX]	+319
Aluminum/Alloy Wheels [Opt on LX,LX V6]	+123
AM/FM/Cassette/CD Audio System	+147

Options	Price
Antilock Brakes [Opt on LX]	+333
Automatic 4-Speed Transmission [Std on V6]	+392
Leather Seats [Std on EX V6]	+417

1998

Mileage Category: D

Honda redesigns its best-seller for 1998. A 3.0-liter V6 engine makes its debut in LX V6 and EX V6 models, marking the first six-cylinder VTEC in the Honda lineup. The standard 2.3-liter four-cylinder is also re-engineered, as is the chassis. The new Accord is also larger, and the interior boasts more room inside.

Body Styles	TMV Pricing		
	Trade	Private	Dealer
2 Dr EX Cpe	7130	8488	10019
2 Dr EX V6 Cpe	8406	10007	11813
2 Dr LX Cpe	6329	7535	8895
2 Dr LX V6 Cpe	7418	8831	10424
4 Dr DX Sdn	5003	5956	7031

Body Styles	TMV Pricing		
	Trade	Private	Dealer
4 Dr EX Sdn	7081	8429	9949
4 Dr EX V6 Sdn	8353	9944	11738
4 Dr LX Sdn	6353	7563	8927
4 Dr LX V6 Sdn	7187	8555	10098

Options	Price
Antilock Brakes [Std on EX,V6]	+285
Automatic 4-Speed Transmission [Std on EX V6,LX V6]	+302
Leather Seats [Std on EX V6]	+349

Options	Price
Rear Spoiler [Opt on Sdn]	+132
Air Conditioning [Opt on DX]	+189

1997

Mileage Category: D

Changes to the ever-popular Accord include the deletion of antilock brakes on the LX five-speed models and the discontinuation of the EX Coupes with leather. No other changes for the 1997 Accord.

Body Styles	TMV Pricing		
	Trade	Private	Dealer
2 Dr EX Cpe	5916	7129	8613
2 Dr LX Cpe	5194	6259	7561
2 Dr Special Edition Cpe	5857	7058	8527
4 Dr DX Sdn	3834	4620	5581
4 Dr EX Sdn	5982	7209	8708
4 Dr EX V6 Sdn	7113	8572	10356

Body Styles	TMV Pricing		
	Trade	Private	Dealer
4 Dr EX Wgn	7043	8488	10253
4 Dr LX Sdn	5194	6260	7562
4 Dr LX V6 Sdn	6448	7770	9387
4 Dr LX Wgn	5822	7016	8476
4 Dr Special Edition Sdn	5883	7090	8564
4 Dr Value Sdn	4762	5738	6932

Options	Price
Air Conditioning [Opt on DX]	+168
Antilock Brakes [Opt on LX]	+285
Automatic 4-Speed Transmission [Opt on DX,EX,LX]	+269

Options	Price
Compact Disc Changer	+152
Leather Seats [Opt on EX]	+311
Rear Spoiler	+117

1996

Mileage Category: D

All Accords get revised styling, featuring new taillights and bumper covers. Wagons have a new roof rack, while sedans boast a new pass-through ski sack.

Body Styles	TMV Pricing		
	Trade	Private	Dealer
2 Dr EX Cpe	5093	6199	7726
2 Dr LX Cpe	4684	5701	7105
4 Dr 25th Anniv Sdn	4591	5587	6964
4 Dr DX Sdn	3414	4155	5178
4 Dr EX Sdn	5281	6428	8012

Body Styles	TMV Pricing		
	Trade	Private	Dealer
4 Dr EX V6 Sdn	6394	7783	9700
4 Dr EX Wgn	5986	7286	9081
4 Dr LX Sdn	4691	5710	7117
4 Dr LX V6 Sdn	5545	6749	8412
4 Dr LX Wgn	5068	6168	7688

Options	Price
Antilock Brakes [Opt on LX]	+288
Automatic 4-Speed Transmission [Opt on DX,EX,LX]	+243
Compact Disc Changer	+137

Options	Price
Leather Seats [Opt on EX]	+280
Air Conditioning [Opt on DX]	+151

1995

Body Styles	TMV Pricing		
	Trade	Private	Dealer
2 Dr EX Cpe	4462	5481	7179
2 Dr LX Cpe	3715	4563	5977
4 Dr DX Sdn	2934	3604	4720
4 Dr EX Sdn	4538	5574	7301
4 Dr EX V6 Sdn	5465	6713	8793

Body Styles	TMV Pricing		
	Trade	Private	Dealer
4 Dr EX Wgn	4869	5980	7833
4 Dr LX Sdn	3753	4610	6039
4 Dr LX V6 Sdn	4714	5790	7584
4 Dr LX Wgn	4448	5464	7157

Mileage Category: D

A V6 is offered in this midsize Honda. Unfortunately, it fails to improve performance figures because of the mandatory automatic transmission. V6 Accords gain different front styling as a result of the increased size of the engine bay. All V6 Accords come with standard antilock brakes.

Options	Price
Air Conditioning [Opt on DX]	+134
Antilock Brakes [Opt on LX]	+203
Automatic 4-Speed Transmission [Opt on DX,EX,LX]	+215

Options	Price
Compact Disc Changer	+120
Leather Seats [Std on EX V6]	+248

1994

Body Styles	TMV Pricing		
	Trade	Private	Dealer
2 Dr DX Cpe	2851	3597	4840
2 Dr EX Cpe	3640	4592	6179
2 Dr LX Cpe	3159	3985	5362
4 Dr DX Sdn	2631	3319	4466

Body Styles	TMV Pricing		
	Trade	Private	Dealer
4 Dr EX Sdn	3674	4635	6237
4 Dr EX Wgn	4196	5294	7123
4 Dr LX Sdn	3190	4024	5415
4 Dr LX Wgn	3586	4524	6089

Mileage Category: D

Once again, Honda's best-selling model is redesigned. Changes for 1994 make the vehicle more competitive with its midsize rival, the Ford Taurus. Shorter and wider than the previous-generation Accord, the 1994 model is available in three trim levels. Antilock brakes are standard on the EX and are finally available on the LX and DX. New engines across the board improve horsepower figures for all Accords.

Options	Price
Air Conditioning [Opt on DX]	+124
Antilock Brakes [Std on EX]	+187
Automatic 4-Speed Transmission	+198

Options	Price
Compact Disc Changer	+111
Leather Seats	+229
Rear Spoiler	+87

Honda

CR-V

2003

Body Styles	TMV Pricing		
	Trade	Private	Dealer
4 Dr EX 4WD SUV	17124	18217	20038
4 Dr LX 4WD SUV	15580	16574	18231
4 Dr LX SUV	15251	16224	17846

Options	Price
Automatic 4-Speed Transmission [Std on 2WD]	+624
Front Side Airbag Restraints [Std on EX]	+195

Mileage Category: L

Fully revamped last year, the CR-V receives no significant changes for 2003.

2002

Body Styles	TMV Pricing		
	Trade	Private	Dealer
4 Dr EX AWD SUV	15274	16317	18054
4 Dr LX AWD SUV	13889	14837	16418
4 Dr LX SUV	13578	14505	16050

Options	Price
Automatic 4-Speed Transmission [Opt on AWD]	+537
Front Side Airbag Restraints [Std on EX]	+168

Mileage Category: L

Redesigned for 2002, Honda's CR-V boasts a number of improvements and refinements. Major changes include more power, more interior room and increased passenger protection.

Honda
CR-V/Civic

2001
Mileage Category: L

A darker shade of silver debuts, and child seat-tether anchors are standard. EX and SE models have standard floor mats.

Body Styles	TMV Pricing			Body Styles	TMV Pricing		
	Trade	Private	Dealer		Trade	Private	Dealer
4 Dr EX AWD SUV	13187	14589	15884	4 Dr LX SUV	11807	13062	14221
4 Dr LX AWD SUV	11933	13202	14373	4 Dr SE AWD SUV	13776	15241	16594

Options	Price
Automatic 4-Speed Transmission [Opt on EX,LX AWD]	+480

2000
Mileage Category: L

The 2000 Honda CR-V gets a new SE (Special Edition) package that features a leather-lined cabin.

Body Styles	TMV Pricing			Body Styles	TMV Pricing		
	Trade	Private	Dealer		Trade	Private	Dealer
4 Dr EX AWD SUV	11496	12911	14297	4 Dr LX SUV	10259	11522	12759
4 Dr LX AWD SUV	10414	11695	12951	4 Dr SE AWD SUV	12069	13554	15010

Options	Price
AM/FM/CD Audio System [Std on EX]	+152
Automatic 4-Speed Transmission [Opt on EX,LX AWD]	+442

1999
Mileage Category: L

The CR-V gains 20 horsepower, bringing the total output to 146. Automatic transmission models have a revised column shifter with an overdrive switch. The power window buttons are illuminated, the spare tire cover has been upgraded and the front passenger seat is equipped with an armrest.

Body Styles	TMV Pricing		
	Trade	Private	Dealer
4 Dr EX AWD SUV	9291	10693	12153
4 Dr LX AWD SUV	8812	10141	11525
4 Dr LX SUV	8348	9609	10921

Options	Price
AM/FM/CD Audio System	+122
Automatic 4-Speed Transmission [Std on 2WD]	+353

1998
Mileage Category: L

A manual transmission debuts. Also available is a front-wheel-drive LX model, and the EX trim level now includes a CD player, antilock brakes and remote keyless entry.

Body Styles	TMV Pricing		
	Trade	Private	Dealer
4 Dr EX AWD SUV	7549	8862	10343
4 Dr LX AWD SUV	7152	8396	9800
4 Dr LX SUV	6776	7954	9283

Options	Price
Automatic 4-Speed Transmission [Std on 2WD]	+302

1997
Mileage Category: L

Priced competitively with mini-utes, the new CR-V offers more passenger room and cargo capacity than its peers. The CR-V is available with antilock brakes.

Body Styles	TMV Pricing		
	Trade	Private	Dealer
4 Dr STD AWD SUV	6608	7749	9143

Options	Price
Antilock Brakes	+254

Honda
Civic

2003

Body Styles	TMV Pricing			Body Styles	TMV Pricing		
	Trade	Private	Dealer		Trade	Private	Dealer
2 Dr DX Cpe	9060	9866	11209	4 Dr DX Sdn	9096	9905	11254
2 Dr EX Cpe	11587	12617	14335	4 Dr EX Sdn	11919	12979	14746
2 Dr HX Cpe	9535	10383	11797	4 Dr GX Sdn	14990	16323	18545

2003 (cont'd)

Body Styles	TMV Pricing		
	Trade	Private	Dealer
2 Dr LX Cpe	10487	11420	12975
2 Dr Si Hbk	12624	13743	15607

Body Styles	TMV Pricing		
	Trade	Private	Dealer
4 Dr Hybrid Sdn	13559	14765	16775
4 Dr LX Sdn	10650	11597	13176

Options	Price
Automatic 4-Speed Transmission	+624
Front Side Airbag Restraints [Std on Hybrid]	+195
Continuously Variable Transmission [Opt on Hybrid]	+780

Mileage Category: B

A host of minor changes bring the Civic into 2003. On the inside, all models gain improved seat fabrics, rear adjustable outboard headrests and new four-spoke steering wheels. On HX, LX and EX Civics, you'll find improved gauge illumination. There's a new center console for LX and EX, and a CD player is standard for HX and LX. On the outside, the Civic has freshened taillamps and new wheel designs. Also, there is a Hybrid Civic available for the 2003 model year.

2002

Body Styles	TMV Pricing		
	Trade	Private	Dealer
2 Dr DX Cpe	7570	8329	9594
2 Dr EX Cpe	9934	10930	12590
2 Dr HX Cpe	7992	8793	10129
2 Dr LX Cpe	8912	9806	11295
2 Dr Si Hbk	11271	12403	14289

Body Styles	TMV Pricing		
	Trade	Private	Dealer
4 Dr DX Sdn	7580	8340	9607
4 Dr EX Sdn	10288	11320	13039
4 Dr GX Sdn	13059	14344	16485
4 Dr LX Sdn	9030	9936	11445

Options	Price
Antilock Brakes [Opt on GX]	+671
Automatic 4-Speed Transmission	+537

Options	Price
Continuously Variable Transmission	+671
Front Side Airbag Restraints	+168

Mileage Category: B

The big news this year is the return of the Civic Si. Featuring an exclusive two-door hatchback body style, the new Si has a 160-horsepower engine. All Civic sedans and coupes feature a revised steering box for improved driving feel, added sound insulation and slightly tweaked suspension tuning. There are also some smattering of interior storage and comfort upgrades this year.

2001

Body Styles	TMV Pricing		
	Trade	Private	Dealer
2 Dr DX Cpe	6703	7798	8810
2 Dr EX Cpe	8868	10317	11655
2 Dr HX Cpe	7002	8146	9202
2 Dr LX Cpe	7865	9150	10336

Body Styles	TMV Pricing		
	Trade	Private	Dealer
4 Dr DX Sdn	6845	7964	8996
4 Dr EX Sdn	9174	10673	12057
4 Dr LX Sdn	7958	9259	10459

Options	Price
Automatic 4-Speed Transmission [Std on VP]	+480
Continuously Variable Transmission [Opt on HX]	+600
Front Side Airbag Restraints	+150

Mileage Category: B

Honda redesigns its cars and trucks every four to five years, whether they need it or not. For 2001, it's the Civic's turn. Larger inside and out, with more powerful engines but a less sophisticated suspension, coupes and sedans return in familiar DX, LX and EX trims, while HX models come with two doors only. The GX Sedan is powered by natural gas. Unfortunately, the hatchback dies just when Americans are once again figuring out how useful they can be, and the sporty Si goes on hiatus for a year or two.

2000

Body Styles	TMV Pricing		
	Trade	Private	Dealer
2 Dr CX Hbk	5708	6693	7659
2 Dr DX Cpe	5901	6920	7918
2 Dr DX Hbk	5780	6777	7755
2 Dr EX Cpe	7530	8829	10103
2 Dr HX Cpe	6397	7501	8583

Body Styles	TMV Pricing		
	Trade	Private	Dealer
2 Dr Si Cpe	10913	12829	14706
4 Dr DX Sdn	6157	7220	8261
4 Dr EX Sdn	8217	9635	11025
4 Dr LX Sdn	7221	8468	9689
4 Dr VP Sdn	7094	8318	9518

Options	Price
Air Conditioning [Opt on CX,DX,HX]	+469
AM/FM/Cassette/CD Audio System	+160
AM/FM/CD Audio System [Opt on DX,LX]	+138
Antilock Brakes [Std on Sdn]	+375
Automatic 4-Speed Transmission [Std on VP]	+442

Options	Price
Compact Disc Changer	+273
Continuously Variable Transmission [Opt on HX]	+553
Power Steering [Opt on CX]	+138
Rear Spoiler [Std on CX,Hbk]	+152

Mileage Category: B

No styling, content or trim changes for this year. The performance-oriented Si continues for 2000, and there have been paint comings and goings: Taffeta White has been added to the CX and DX Hatchback, and Dark Amethyst has been dropped; Titanium Metallic comes to the DX, LX and EX Sedan, and Vogue Silver is gone. Vintage Plum is now available to the LX and EX Sedan, and Inza Red has been eliminated.

1999

Mileage Category: B

The Civic gets new front and rear styling as well as an improved instrument panel. The DX trim gets a rear wiper and washer, a cargo cover and a low-fuel warning light. A hot-rod Si model is introduced midyear with a 160-hp VTEC engine.

Body Styles	TMV Pricing		
	Trade	Private	Dealer
2 Dr CX Hbk	4598	5541	6523
2 Dr DX Cpe	4918	5927	6977
2 Dr DX Hbk	4820	5809	6839
2 Dr EX Cpe	6044	7284	8574
2 Dr HX Cpe	5077	6119	7203

Options	Price
Air Conditioning [Opt on CX,DX,HX]	+375
AM/FM/Cassette/CD Audio System [Opt on DX,LX]	+128
Antilock Brakes [Std on SI,Sdn]	+333
Automatic 4-Speed Transmission [Std on VP]	+353

Body Styles	TMV Pricing		
	Trade	Private	Dealer
2 Dr Si Cpe	8848	10648	12522
4 Dr DX Sdn	4995	6020	7087
4 Dr EX Sdn	6438	7759	9134
4 Dr LX Sdn	5795	6984	8221
4 Dr VP Sdn	5778	6964	8198

Options	Price
Continuously Variable Transmission [Opt on HX]	+451
Leather Seats	+221
Rear Spoiler [Std on CX,Hbk]	+122

1998

Mileage Category: B

Select models get new wheel covers, a rear hatch handle and map lights.

Body Styles	TMV Pricing		
	Trade	Private	Dealer
2 Dr CX Hbk	3893	4810	5844
2 Dr DX Cpe	4195	5183	6297
2 Dr DX Hbk	4166	5147	6254
2 Dr EX Cpe	5172	6390	7764

Options	Price
Air Conditioning [Std on EX,LX]	+321
Antilock Brakes [Opt on Cpe]	+285
Automatic 4-Speed Transmission	+302

Body Styles	TMV Pricing		
	Trade	Private	Dealer
2 Dr HX Cpe	4316	5332	6478
4 Dr DX Sdn	4255	5257	6386
4 Dr EX Sdn	5362	6624	8048
4 Dr LX Sdn	4759	5880	7144

Options	Price
Compact Disc Changer	+225
Continuously Variable Transmission [Opt on HX]	+378

1997

Mileage Category: B

Honda deletes the Civic EX Coupe five-speed with ABS model. DX models receive new wheel covers, all Civics get 14-inch wheels, and the LX Sedan gets air conditioning.

Body Styles	TMV Pricing		
	Trade	Private	Dealer
2 Dr CX Hbk	3312	4108	5081
2 Dr DX Cpe	3765	4670	5776
2 Dr DX Hbk	3602	4467	5525
2 Dr EX Cpe	4735	5873	7264

Options	Price
Air Conditioning [Std on EX,LX]	+285
Antilock Brakes [Opt on Cpe]	+254
Automatic 4-Speed Transmission	+269

Body Styles	TMV Pricing		
	Trade	Private	Dealer
2 Dr HX Cpe	3793	4704	5818
4 Dr DX Sdn	3774	4681	5790
4 Dr EX Sdn	4911	6091	7534
4 Dr LX Sdn	4236	5255	6499

Options	Price
Compact Disc Changer	+200
Continuously Variable Transmission [Opt on HX]	+336
Leather Seats	+168

1996

Mileage Category: B

Honda engineers have created a more powerful and more contemporary Civic for 1996.

Body Styles	TMV Pricing		
	Trade	Private	Dealer
2 Dr CX Hbk	2705	3406	4375
2 Dr DX Cpe	3136	3949	5072
2 Dr DX Hbk	2931	3691	4740
2 Dr EX Cpe	3886	4893	6284

Options	Price
Air Conditioning [Std on EX]	+257
Antilock Brakes [Opt on LX,Cpe]	+229
Automatic 4-Speed Transmission	+243

Body Styles	TMV Pricing		
	Trade	Private	Dealer
2 Dr HX Cpe	3253	4096	5260
4 Dr DX Sdn	3237	4076	5235
4 Dr EX Sdn	4248	5349	6871
4 Dr LX Sdn	3470	4370	5613

Options	Price
Compact Disc Changer	+181
Continuously Variable Transmission [Opt on HX]	+303

1995

Body Styles	TMV Pricing			Body Styles	TMV Pricing		
	Trade	Private	Dealer		Trade	Private	Dealer
2 Dr CX Hbk	2155	2732	3693	2 Dr VX Hbk	2603	3299	4460
2 Dr DX Cpe	2237	2835	3831	4 Dr DX Sdn	2626	3329	4499
2 Dr DX Hbk	2223	2818	3810	4 Dr EX Sdn	3085	3911	5287
2 Dr EX Cpe	2881	3651	4936	4 Dr LX Sdn	2776	3518	4755
2 Dr Si Hbk	2836	3595	4859				

Options	Price	Options	Price
Leather Seats	+134	Antilock Brakes [Opt on LX,Cpe]	+203
Air Conditioning [Std on EX Sdn]	+228	Automatic 4-Speed Transmission	+215

Mileage Category: B

No changes for the last year of the current Civic.

1994

Body Styles	TMV Pricing			Body Styles	TMV Pricing		
	Trade	Private	Dealer		Trade	Private	Dealer
2 Dr CX Hbk	1714	2227	3083	2 Dr VX Hbk	2044	2656	3676
2 Dr DX Cpe	1745	2268	3139	4 Dr DX Sdn	2060	2677	3706
2 Dr DX Hbk	1735	2255	3121	4 Dr EX Sdn	2506	3257	4508
2 Dr EX Cpe	2366	3074	4255	4 Dr LX Sdn	2219	2884	3993
2 Dr Si Hbk	2316	3009	4165				

Options	Price
Air Conditioning [Std on EX Sdn]	+211
Antilock Brakes [Opt on LX,Si,Cpe]	+187
Automatic 4-Speed Transmission	+198
Leather Seats	+124

Mileage Category: B

The passenger airbag is now standard on all Civics. Antilock brakes are optional on the LX Sedan, EX Coupe and Si Hatchback.

1997

Body Styles	TMV Pricing		
	Trade	Private	Dealer
2 Dr S Cpe	5069	6071	7295
2 Dr Si Cpe	5857	7015	8430
2 Dr VTEC Cpe	6226	7457	8961

Options	Price
Air Conditioning	+285
Automatic 4-Speed Transmission	+336

Mileage Category: E

No changes to Honda's two-seater.

1996

Body Styles	TMV Pricing		
	Trade	Private	Dealer
2 Dr S Cpe	4408	5317	6572
2 Dr Si Cpe	5021	6056	7486
2 Dr VTEC Cpe	5478	6608	8168

Options	Price
Air Conditioning	+257
Automatic 4-Speed Transmission	+303

Mileage Category: E

The base S model gets more power by swapping its 1.5-liter four for a 1.6-liter unit, gaining four horsepower. The front fascia is freshened and the Si gets the suspension upgrades of the VTEC.

Honda
Civic del Sol/Element/Insight

1995
Mileage Category: E

Antilock brakes are now standard on VTEC models. Power door locks are also new to the standard equipment lists of Si and VTEC models. All del Sols get a remote trunk release.

Body Styles	TMV Pricing		
	Trade	Private	Dealer
2 Dr S Cpe	3944	4754	6105
2 Dr Si Cpe	4159	5013	6437
2 Dr VTEC Cpe	4729	5701	7320

Options	Price
Air Conditioning	+228
AM/FM/Cassette/CD Audio System	+94
Automatic 4-Speed Transmission	+268

1994
Mileage Category: E

VTEC technology makes its way to the del Sol, giving buyers a choice of three models. VTEC del Sols offer 35 more horsepower than the Si. A passenger airbag joins the standard equipment list for all models. VTEC del Sols gain performance-oriented upgrades that include a beefier suspension, larger tires and bigger brakes.

Body Styles	TMV Pricing		
	Trade	Private	Dealer
2 Dr S Cpe	3137	3868	5087
2 Dr Si Cpe	3508	4326	5689
2 Dr VTEC Cpe	3808	4696	6175

Options	Price	Options	Price
Leather Seats	+149	Automatic 4-Speed Transmission	+248
Air Conditioning	+211	Compact Disc Changer	+124

Honda
Element

2003

Body Styles	TMV Pricing			Body Styles	TMV Pricing		
	Trade	Private	Dealer		Trade	Private	Dealer
4 Dr DX 4WD SUV	13238	14227	15876	4 Dr EX 4WD SUV	15119	16249	18131
4 Dr DX SUV	12207	13119	14639	4 Dr EX SUV	14087	15140	16894

Options	Price
Automatic 4-Speed Transmission	+624
Front Side Airbag Restraints [Opt on EX]	+195

Mileage Category: L

The Element is a completely new vehicle for Honda. It's also the most adventurous Honda vehicle in quite a long time. Its blend of features, such as barn-style doors and waterproof seats, make it a good choice for those with active lifestyles.

Honda
Insight

2003

Body Styles	TMV Pricing		
	Trade	Private	Dealer
2 Dr STD Hbk	12628	13713	15521

Options	Price
Air Conditioning	+780
Compact Disc Changer	+394
Continuously Variable Transmission	+780

Mileage Category: B

No changes are in store for Honda's clever gas/electric hybrid vehicle.

2002
Mileage Category: B

No changes are in store for Honda's clever gas-electric hybrid vehicle.

Body Styles	TMV Pricing		
	Trade	Private	Dealer
2 Dr STD Hbk	9726	10770	12509

For the latest vehicle information, visit www.edmunds.com

Options	Price
Air Conditioning	+671
Compact Disc Changer	+339
Continuously Variable Transmission [Opt on HX]	+671

2001

Body Styles	TMV Pricing		
	Trade	Private	Dealer
2 Dr STD Hbk	8196	9676	11043

Options	Price
Air Conditioning	+600
Compact Disc Changer	+303
Continuously Variable Transmission	+600

Mileage Category: B

A continuously variable transmission (CVT) is available for 2001, and Monte Carlo Blue Pearl replaces Citrus Yellow on the color chart.

2000

Body Styles	TMV Pricing		
	Trade	Private	Dealer
2 Dr STD Hbk	7113	8509	9878

Options	Price
Air Conditioning	+552
Compact Disc Changer	+279

Mileage Category: B

Honda brings North America the first gasoline-electric hybrid for 2000.

Honda

Odyssey

2003

Body Styles	TMV Pricing		
	Trade	Private	Dealer
4 Dr EX Pass Van	21627	23085	25515
4 Dr LX Pass Van	19284	20583	22749

Options	Price
Leather Seats [Opt on EX]	+1170
Navigation System [Opt on EX]	+1560
DVD Entertainment System	+1170

Mileage Category: P

The Odyssey gains an intermittent rear window wiper this year, as well as an auto up-and-down driver-side window.

2002

Body Styles	TMV Pricing		
	Trade	Private	Dealer
4 Dr EX Pass Van	18763	20231	22678
4 Dr LX Pass Van	16981	18309	20523

Options	Price
DVD Entertainment System [Opt on EX]	+1006
Leather Seats	+1006
Navigation System	+1342

Mileage Category: P

The Odyssey gains a number of improvements this year. Included with the Odyssey 2.1 upgrade is more power, a new five-speed transmission, standard rear disc brakes and side airbags, optional leather seating and DVD entertainment, two new exterior colors and minor interior storage refinements.

2001

Body Styles	TMV Pricing				Body Styles	TMV Pricing		
	Trade	Private	Dealer			Trade	Private	Dealer
4 Dr LX Pass Van	15199	17053	18764		4 Dr EX Pass Van	16793	18842	20732

Options	Price
Navigation System	+1199

Mileage Category: P

Second- and third-row seats get new child seat-tether anchors, stereo speakers are upgraded, an intermittent feature for the rear window wiper is added and floor mats are made standard. LX models get a driver seat height adjuster and traction control, while EX models benefit from a new alarm feature for the remote control. A brighter Starlight Silver paint color replaces Canyon Stone Silver.

Honda
Odyssey

2000
Mileage Category: P

The only new feature is an optional navigation system on the EX.

Body Styles	TMV Pricing		
	Trade	Private	Dealer
4 Dr EX Pass Van	14609	16604	18559
4 Dr LX Pass Van	13524	15371	17181

Options	Price	Options	Price
Aluminum/Alloy Wheels [Std on EX]	+152	Leather Seats	+442
AM/FM/Cassette/CD Audio System	+193	Navigation System	+1104
Compact Disc Changer	+304		

1999
Mileage Category: P

Honda's latest minivan, the totally redesigned Odyssey, features the most powerful V6 in the minivan segment.

Body Styles	TMV Pricing		
	Trade	Private	Dealer
4 Dr EX Pass Van	13167	15140	17193
4 Dr LX Pass Van	11336	13034	14802

Options	Price
Leather Seats	+353

1998
Mileage Category: P

The engine is upgraded to a more sophisticated 2.3-liter, good for an extra 10 horsepower and seven pound-feet of torque. New looks up front come from a revised bumper and grille, and the interior gets dressed in new fabric.

Body Styles	TMV Pricing		
	Trade	Private	Dealer
4 Dr EX Pass Van	8729	10326	12127
4 Dr LX Pass Van	8345	9872	11594

Options	Price
6 Passenger Seating [Opt on LX]	+137
Compact Disc Changer	+226

1997

Body Styles	TMV Pricing		
	Trade	Private	Dealer
4 Dr EX Pass Van	6866	8383	10237
4 Dr LX Pass Van	6428	7848	9584

Mileage Category: P

No changes for the 1997 Honda Odyssey.

1996
Mileage Category: P

Minivan-wagon hybrid carries into 1996 sans changes.

Body Styles	TMV Pricing		
	Trade	Private	Dealer
4 Dr EX Pass Van	6140	7532	9454
4 Dr LX Pass Van	5499	6745	8466

1995
Mileage Category: P

Honda gets its minivan in the form of the Odyssey. Unique to the Odyssey is a five-door design that includes four passenger carlike swing-out doors. LX and EX models come standard with antilock brakes and dual airbags.

Body Styles	TMV Pricing		
	Trade	Private	Dealer
4 Dr EX Pass Van	5613	6808	8801
4 Dr LX Pass Van	4999	6063	7837

2002

Body Styles	TMV Pricing		
	Trade	Private	Dealer
4 Dr EX 4WD SUV	15851	16975	18848
4 Dr EX SUV	14420	15443	17147

Body Styles	TMV Pricing		
	Trade	Private	Dealer
4 Dr LX 4WD SUV	14070	15068	16731
4 Dr LX SUV	12369	13246	14707

Options	Price
AM/FM/Cassette/CD Changer Audio System	+265
Automatic 4-Speed Transmission [Opt on LX]	+772

Options	Price
Leather Seats	+436
Power Driver Seat	+161

Mileage Category: M

There are no significant changes to the Passport this year.

2001

Body Styles	TMV Pricing		
	Trade	Private	Dealer
4 Dr EX 4WD SUV	13354	14822	16178
4 Dr EX SUV	12244	13591	14834

Body Styles	TMV Pricing		
	Trade	Private	Dealer
4 Dr LX 4WD SUV	11952	13267	14480
4 Dr LX SUV	10532	11690	12759

Options	Price
Automatic 4-Speed Transmission [Std on EX]	+690
Compact Disc Changer	+240
Leather Seats	+420

Mileage Category: M

Honda adds a LATCH child seat-tether anchor system to the Passport, and all models get a new eight-speaker audio system.

2000

Body Styles	TMV Pricing		
	Trade	Private	Dealer
4 Dr EX 4WD SUV	11384	12828	14244
4 Dr EX SUV	10437	11761	13059

Body Styles	TMV Pricing		
	Trade	Private	Dealer
4 Dr LX 4WD SUV	10187	11480	12747
4 Dr LX SUV	8979	10118	11235

Options	Price
AM/FM/Cassette/CD Audio System	+221
Automatic 4-Speed Transmission [Std on EX]	+635

Options	Price
Compact Disc Changer	+304
Leather Seats	+553

Mileage Category: M

The Passport receives new front and rear fascias, a modified grille, redesigned front combination lamps and a host of fresh features for a new top-of-the-line EX-L trim level.

1999

Body Styles	TMV Pricing		
	Trade	Private	Dealer
4 Dr EX 4WD SUV	10275	11731	13247
4 Dr EX SUV	9395	10726	12112

Body Styles	TMV Pricing		
	Trade	Private	Dealer
4 Dr LX 4WD SUV	9017	10295	11625
4 Dr LX SUV	7919	9042	10210

Options	Price
AM/FM/Cassette/CD Audio System	+177
Automatic 4-Speed Transmission [Std on VP]	+507
Leather Seats	+441

Mileage Category: M

Last year, the Passport and the identical Isuzu Rodeo were completely redesigned, so there are no new changes this year.

1998

Body Styles	TMV Pricing		
	Trade	Private	Dealer
4 Dr EX 4WD SUV	7892	9371	11039
4 Dr EX SUV	7234	8590	10119

Body Styles	TMV Pricing		
	Trade	Private	Dealer
4 Dr LX 4WD SUV	6952	8255	9724
4 Dr LX SUV	6268	7443	8768

Options	Price
Leather Seats	+377
AM/FM/Cassette/CD Audio System	+151
Automatic 4-Speed Transmission [Opt on LX]	+434

Mileage Category: M

Like its Isuzu Rodeo counterpart, the Passport has been completely revised from top to bottom. The Passport gets modernized styling, a user-friendly interior, more powerful V6 and added room for passengers and cargo.

Honda
Passport/Pilot

1997

Body Styles	TMV Pricing		
	Trade	Private	Dealer
4 Dr EX 4WD SUV	6044	7307	8851
4 Dr EX SUV	5985	7236	8765

Body Styles	TMV Pricing		
	Trade	Private	Dealer
4 Dr LX 4WD SUV	5201	6288	7616
4 Dr LX SUV	4691	5672	6870

Options	Price
Air Conditioning [Std on EX,4WD]	+201
AM/FM/Cassette/CD Audio System	+134
Automatic 4-Speed Transmission [Opt on LX,4WD]	+326

Options	Price
Compact Disc Changer	+185
Leather Seats	+336
Premium Audio System [Opt on EX]	+134

Mileage Category: M

Honda drops the slow-selling DX four-cylinder Passport.

1996

Mileage Category: M

New wheels, dual airbags, available ABS and a stronger V6 engine are the changes for the 1996.

Body Styles	TMV Pricing		
	Trade	Private	Dealer
4 Dr DX SUV	3522	4325	5434
4 Dr EX 4WD SUV	5189	6371	8004
4 Dr EX SUV	5063	6217	7810

Body Styles	TMV Pricing		
	Trade	Private	Dealer
4 Dr LX 4WD SUV	4493	5517	6932
4 Dr LX SUV	4119	5058	6354

Options	Price
Air Conditioning [Std on EX,4WD]	+182
Automatic 4-Speed Transmission [Opt on LX,4WD]	+243

1995

Mileage Category: M

Midyear change gives the Passport driver and passenger airbags in a redesigned dashboard.

Body Styles	TMV Pricing		
	Trade	Private	Dealer
4 Dr DX SUV	2883	3555	4675
4 Dr DX Wgn (1995.5)	3244	4000	5260
4 Dr EX 4WD SUV	4312	5316	6990
4 Dr EX 4WD Wgn (1995.5)	4856	5987	7873
4 Dr EX Wgn (1995.5)	4402	5428	7137

Body Styles	TMV Pricing		
	Trade	Private	Dealer
4 Dr LX 4WD SUV	3785	4667	6136
4 Dr LX 4WD Wgn (1995.5)	4294	5295	6962
4 Dr LX SUV	3476	4286	5635
4 Dr LX Wgn (1995.5)	3694	4555	5989

Options	Price
Air Conditioning [Opt on DX,LX]	+161
Automatic 4-Speed Transmission	+215
Leather Seats	+268

1994

Mileage Category: M

Based on the highly successful Isuzu Rodeo, the Honda Passport has very little to distinguish it from its less expensive twin. Two- and four-wheel-drive models are available in three trim levels ranging from the budget-minded DX to the top-end EX.

Body Styles	TMV Pricing		
	Trade	Private	Dealer
4 Dr DX SUV	2533	3156	4193
4 Dr EX 4WD SUV	3880	4833	6422

Body Styles	TMV Pricing		
	Trade	Private	Dealer
4 Dr LX 4WD SUV	3336	4156	5522
4 Dr LX SUV	3037	3783	5027

Options	Price
Air Conditioning [Opt on DX,LX]	+149
Automatic 4-Speed Transmission	+303

Honda
Pilot

2003

Mileage Category: M

The Pilot is an all-new crossover SUV from Honda. It features eight-passenger seating, standard four-wheel drive, a 240-horsepower V6 and optional DVD-based navigation and entertainment systems.

Body Styles	TMV Pricing		
	Trade	Private	Dealer
4 Dr EX 4WD SUV	23978	25333	27591
4 Dr LX 4WD SUV	22068	23315	25393

Honda

2003 (cont'd)

Options	Price
Leather Seats [Opt on EX]	+1170
Navigation System [Opt on EX]	+1560
DVD Entertainment System	+1170

Honda
Prelude

2001

Body Styles	TMV Pricing		
	Trade	Private	Dealer
2 Dr STD Cpe	13206	14616	15918
2 Dr Type SH Cpe	14610	16170	17610

Options	Price
Automatic 4-Speed Transmission	+690

Mileage Category: E

Floor mats, rear child seat-tether anchors and an emergency trunk opener are added to the '01 Prelude. Two new colors, Electron Blue and Satin Silver, are also available.

2000

Body Styles	TMV Pricing		
	Trade	Private	Dealer
2 Dr STD Cpe	11448	12844	14213
2 Dr Type SH Cpe	13029	14618	16176

Options	Price	Options	Price
AM/FM/Cassette Audio System	+124	Compact Disc Changer	+276
Automatic 4-Speed Transmission	+553	Rear Spoiler [Opt on STD]	+193

Mileage Category: E

The 2000 Prelude is a carryover from 1999 and remains unchanged.

1999

Body Styles	TMV Pricing		
	Trade	Private	Dealer
2 Dr STD Cpe	10483	11850	13273
2 Dr Type SH Cpe	11744	13276	14870

Options	Price
Automatic 4-Speed Transmission	+441
Compact Disc Changer	+221
Rear Spoiler [Opt on STD]	+154

Mileage Category: E

Prelude gets another five horsepower, bringing it up to 200 horsepower with the manual transmission and 195 horsepower with the automatic. A remote keyless entry system is added, as is an air filtration system, mesh-style grille and new interior color choices.

1998

Body Styles	TMV Pricing		
	Trade	Private	Dealer
2 Dr STD Cpe	8149	9511	11046
2 Dr Type SH Cpe	8904	10392	12069

Options	Price
Automatic 4-Speed Transmission	+377
Compact Disc Changer	+189
Rear Spoiler [Opt on STD]	+132

Mileage Category: E

The Prelude doesn't change for 1998.

Honda
Prelude/S2000

1997

Mileage Category: E

The Prelude is totally redesigned for 1997. A base model is available with a five-speed manual or four-speed automatic gearbox, but the top-of-the-line Type SH model, featuring Honda's new Active Torque Transfer System, can only be had as a manual. Both the base and Type SH Preludes feature last year's VTEC engine which produces 195 horsepower for 1997.

Body Styles	TMV Pricing		
	Trade	Private	Dealer
2 Dr STD Cpe	7162	8463	10054
2 Dr Type SH Cpe	7731	9136	10854

Options	Price
Automatic 4-Speed Transmission	+336
Compact Disc Changer	+168

Options	Price
Leather Seats	+218
Rear Spoiler	+117

1996

Body Styles	TMV Pricing		
	Trade	Private	Dealer
2 Dr S Cpe	5060	6103	7544
2 Dr Si Cpe	5730	6911	8543
2 Dr VTEC Cpe	6441	7769	9603

Options	Price
Automatic 4-Speed Transmission	+243

Mileage Category: E

This is the last year for the current-generation Prelude.

1995

Mileage Category: E

The Si 4WS is dropped from the Prelude lineup. The fourth-generation Prelude is nearing the end of its life. Few changes for 1995, except the addition of air conditioning to the standard equipment list of S models.

Body Styles	TMV Pricing		
	Trade	Private	Dealer
2 Dr S Cpe	4499	5423	6964
2 Dr SE Cpe	5221	6294	8081

Body Styles	TMV Pricing		
	Trade	Private	Dealer
2 Dr Si Cpe	5044	6081	7808
2 Dr VTEC Cpe	5649	6810	8744

Options	Price
Automatic 4-Speed Transmission	+215
Leather Seats	+174

1994

Mileage Category: E

Dual airbags are standard on all Preludes this year. Improved interior ergonomics, freshened front-end styling and environmentally conscious CFC-free air conditioning are also welcome changes to this car.

Body Styles	TMV Pricing		
	Trade	Private	Dealer
2 Dr S Cpe	3677	4535	5964
2 Dr Si 4WS Cpe	4802	5922	7788

Body Styles	TMV Pricing		
	Trade	Private	Dealer
2 Dr Si Cpe	4335	5346	7030
2 Dr VTEC Cpe	4833	5960	7838

Options	Price
Air Conditioning [Opt on S]	+136
AM/FM/Cassette/CD Audio System	+87

Options	Price
Automatic 4-Speed Transmission	+198
Rear Spoiler [Opt on S]	+87

Honda
S2000

2003

Body Styles	TMV Pricing		
	Trade	Private	Dealer
2 Dr STD Conv	24209	25591	27894

Mileage Category: F

There are no changes this year for Honda's high-performance roadster.

2002

Body Styles	TMV Pricing		
	Trade	Private	Dealer
2 Dr STD Conv	21418	22836	25198

Mileage Category: F

For 2002, Honda has added a glass rear window with a defroster, an improved transmission and a more powerful audio system. There are also a handful of minor changes that only '00-'01 S2000 owners would notice, such as chrome-bezel taillights, an upgraded center console, door panel net storage pockets, a new shifter knob, an aluminum-accented foot rest and silver trim interior accents. There's also a new color for 2002: Suzuka Blue.

2001

Body Styles	TMV Pricing		
	Trade	Private	Dealer
2 Dr STD Conv	18793	20673	22408

Mileage Category: F

Indy Yellow is a new color for 2001. Floor mats, a rear wind deflector, a clock and an emergency trunk release are also new standard items. Midyear, a removable aluminum hardtop became available and can be retrofitted to all S2000s.

2000

Body Styles	TMV Pricing		
	Trade	Private	Dealer
2 Dr STD Conv	16894	18647	20366

Mileage Category: F

Honda brings out the high-revving, high-horsepower S2000 for 2000. The S2000's naturally aspirated inline four makes an amazing 240 horsepower, sending it to the rear wheels through a six-speed manual gearbox.

Hyundai
Accent

2003

Body Styles	TMV Pricing		
	Trade	Private	Dealer
2 Dr GL Hbk	5059	5896	7290
2 Dr STD Hbk	4625	5390	6665
4 Dr GL Sdn	5502	6412	7929

Options	Price	Options	Price
Air Conditioning [Opt on STD]	+502	Power Windows [Opt on GL]	+134
AM/FM/CD Audio System [Opt on GL]	+134	Rear Spoiler [Opt on GL]	+117
Automatic 4-Speed Transmission [Opt on GL]	+435	Sport Suspension [Opt on GL]	+124

Mileage Category: A

For 2003, the base single overhead cam 1.5-liter engine is dropped from the L hatchback; all Accents now come with the dual-overhead cam 1.6-liter inline four-cylinder. The 1.6 is rated at 104 horsepower -- a drop of only one horsepower following Hyundai's September 2002 announcement that it had misstated engine outputs across the board. Note that the engine itself is unchanged. In other news, all Accents get a facelift this year. In front, you'll see a new bumper, grille, hood and headlight assemblies, and in the back, the bumper, rear quarter panels and taillight units are new.

2002

Mileage Category: A

Air conditioning becomes standard equipment on GS and GL models. Otherwise, Hyundai's bargain-basement car soldiers on to 2002 with no changes in store. In September 2002, Hyundai announced that it had misstated the horsepower ratings for all of the models in its lineup -- the Accent's 1.5-liter four-cylinder engine is now rated for 89 hp and the 1.6-liter is rated for 103. To compensate, the company is offering owners (of 2000 models and newer) three options: 10 years of roadside assistance, 6-year/72,000-mile basic warranty coverage or 12-year/120,000-mile powertrain coverage.

Body Styles	TMV Pricing		
	Trade	Private	Dealer
2 Dr GS Hbk	3766	4524	5787
2 Dr L Hbk	3400	4084	5225
4 Dr GL Sdn	4094	4919	6294

Options	Price	Options	Price
Air Conditioning [Opt on L]	+440	Power Windows	+117
AM/FM/CD Audio System	+117	Rear Spoiler	+232
Automatic 4-Speed Transmission	+352		

2001

Mileage Category: A

For 2001, Accent GL and GS get a more powerful and fuel-efficient 1.6-liter, DOHC inline four-cylinder engine.

Body Styles	TMV Pricing		
	Trade	Private	Dealer
2 Dr GS Hbk	3095	4093	5015
2 Dr L Hbk	2945	3895	4771
4 Dr GL Sdn	3379	4469	5476

Options	Price	Options	Price
Air Conditioning	+386	Power Windows	+126
AM/FM/CD Audio System	+181	Rear Spoiler	+203
Automatic 4-Speed Transmission	+309		

2000

Mileage Category: A

The Accent has been completely redesigned for the 2000 model year.

Body Styles	TMV Pricing		
	Trade	Private	Dealer
2 Dr GS Hbk	2570	3552	4514
2 Dr L Hbk	2387	3297	4188
4 Dr GL Sdn	2768	3825	4861

Options	Price	Options	Price
Air Conditioning	+424	Automatic 4-Speed Transmission	+341
AM/FM/CD Audio System	+150	Rear Spoiler	+168

1999

Mileage Category: A

The L model has power steering standard, the GS and GL models have standard alloy wheels and a couple of new paint options are available. Hyundai's new industry-leading buyer assurance program is also worth taking note of.

Body Styles	TMV Pricing		
	Trade	Private	Dealer
2 Dr GS Hbk	2129	3117	4146
2 Dr L Hbk	1841	2695	3584
4 Dr GL Sdn	2176	3185	4236

1999 (cont'd)

Options	Price
Air Conditioning	+340
AM/FM/CD Audio System	+119
Automatic 4-Speed Transmission	+273

Options	Price
Rear Spoiler	+135
Sunroof	+151

1998

Mileage Category: A

The Accent GSi replaces the Accent GT this year. New front and rear fascias, and new engine mounts, which reduce engine vibration and harshness, are the only other changes to Hyundai's smallest car.

Body Styles	TMV Pricing		
	Trade	Private	Dealer
2 Dr GS Hbk	1678	2587	3612
2 Dr GSi Hbk	1860	2869	4006

Body Styles	TMV Pricing		
	Trade	Private	Dealer
2 Dr L Hbk	1269	1958	2736
4 Dr GL Sdn	1749	2697	3765

Options	Price
Air Conditioning	+259
Antilock Brakes	+199

Options	Price
Automatic 4-Speed Transmission	+199
Sunroof	+117

1997

Mileage Category: A

In the absence of truly ground-breaking improvement, Hyundai revises trim levels, adding GS hatchback and GL sedan midrange models.

Body Styles	TMV Pricing		
	Trade	Private	Dealer
2 Dr GS Hbk	896	1472	2176
2 Dr GT Hbk	1012	1663	2458

Body Styles	TMV Pricing		
	Trade	Private	Dealer
2 Dr L Hbk	824	1354	2001
4 Dr GL Sdn	931	1530	2263

Options	Price
Air Conditioning	+204
Antilock Brakes	+156
Automatic 4-Speed Transmission	+156

1996

Mileage Category: A

Hyundai is painting the Accent in some new colors this year, and height-adjustable seatbelt anchors are standard. Front and rear center consoles with cupholders debut, and optional air conditioning is now CFC-free. A new 105-horsepower GT hatch debuted midyear.

Body Styles	TMV Pricing		
	Trade	Private	Dealer
2 Dr GT Hbk	667	1207	1953
2 Dr L Hbk	529	957	1549

Body Styles	TMV Pricing		
	Trade	Private	Dealer
2 Dr STD Hbk	559	1012	1638
4 Dr STD Sdn	590	1068	1728

Options	Price
Air Conditioning	+131

1995

Mileage Category: A

Dramatically improved Accent replaces Excel in lineup. Dual airbags are standard, and ABS is optional. Power comes from the 1.5-liter Alpha engine which debuted in 1993 Scoupe.

Body Styles	TMV Pricing		
	Trade	Private	Dealer
2 Dr L Hbk	355	696	1264
2 Dr STD Hbk	376	737	1339
4 Dr STD Sdn	397	777	1411

Options	Price
Air Conditioning	+109
Antilock Brakes	+91
Automatic 4-Speed Transmission	+90

Hyundai
Elantra

2003

Body Styles	TMV Pricing		
	Trade	Private	Dealer
4 Dr GLS Sdn	7355	8336	9971
4 Dr GT Hbk	7660	8682	10384
4 Dr GT Sdn	7650	8670	10370

Options	Price	Options	Price
AM/FM/CD Audio System [Opt on GLS]	+211	Power Moonroof	+469
Antilock Brakes	+455	Rear Spoiler [Opt on GLS]	+265
Automatic 4-Speed Transmission	+536	Traction Control System	+167
Cruise Control [Opt on GLS]	+124	AM/FM/CD/MP3 Audio System [Opt on GLS]	+295

Mileage Category: B

Hyundai has added a GT sedan to the lineup. It has the same price and equipment as the GT hatchback, save for a rear wiper, and it gets a body-color rear spoiler. The hatchback will wear a black rear lip spoiler, and both GTs will come with floor mats. Meanwhile, the value-packed GLS sedan remains unchanged, except ABS will be slightly more affordable, as it has been added to the Accessory Group 3 options package, which costs $925. Finally, Hyundai announced that it had misstated the horsepower ratings for all of the models in its lineup -- the Elantra is now rated at 135 hp, rather than 140, though the engine itself is unchanged.

2002

Mileage Category: B

Hyundai's Elantra sedan was redesigned last year, but the big news for 2002 is the release of the GT version, an all-new five-door hatchback that boasts such upscale standard equipment as a leather-trimmed interior, European suspension tuning, four-wheel disc brakes, 15-inch wheels, foglamps and a CD player. In September 2002, Hyundai announced that it had misstated the horsepower ratings for all of the models in its lineup -- the Elantra is now rated at 135 hp, rather than 140. To compensate, the company is offering owners (of 2000 models and newer) three options: 10 years of roadside assistance, 6-year/72,000-mile basic warranty coverage or 12-year/120,000-mile powertrain coverage.

Body Styles	TMV Pricing		
	Trade	Private	Dealer
4 Dr GLS Sdn	5286	6210	7749
4 Dr GT Hbk	5949	6989	8721

Options	Price	Options	Price
AM/FM/CD Audio System	+185	Power Moonroof	+381
Antilock Brakes	+399	Traction Control System	+117
Automatic 4-Speed Transmission	+352		

2001

Mileage Category: B

Bigger inside and out, the redesigned 2001 Elantra boasts stylish sheet metal, a refined 140-horsepower engine and improved noise, vibration and harshness characteristics. Poised to tackle the best in the class, the Elantra comes well equipped for less than $13,000. Though the useful station wagon model has been stricken from the lineup, a five-door hatchback is set to debut next year.

Body Styles	TMV Pricing		
	Trade	Private	Dealer
4 Dr GLS Sdn	4337	5595	6756
4 Dr GT Hbk	4731	6103	7370

Options	Price	Options	Price
AM/FM/CD Audio System	+167	Cruise Control	+129
Antilock Brakes	+443	Power Moonroof	+386
Automatic 4-Speed Transmission	+309		

2000

Body Styles	TMV Pricing		
	Trade	Private	Dealer
4 Dr GLS Sdn	3491	4769	6021
4 Dr GLS Wgn	3858	5269	6653

Options	Price	Options	Price
AM/FM/CD Audio System	+139	Power Moonroof	+320
Antilock Brakes	+367	Rear Spoiler	+168
Automatic 4-Speed Transmission	+341		

Mileage Category: B

In an effort to mold its image into that of a serious first-rate automobile manufacturer, Hyundai has recently added standard equipment and enhanced the performance of several of its cars. The redesigned Accent and new Sonata are proving that this South Korean automaker has finally learned how to build a good car. The current Elantra provides even more proof, and the company offers an industry-leading warranty program to back it up.

1999

Body Styles	TMV Pricing		
	Trade	Private	Dealer
4 Dr GL Sdn	2862	4155	5501
4 Dr GL Wgn	2902	4213	5577

Options	Price
Rear Spoiler	+135
Antilock Brakes	+294

Body Styles	TMV Pricing		
	Trade	Private	Dealer
4 Dr GLS Sdn	2946	4276	5661
4 Dr GLS Wgn	3037	4409	5837

Options	Price
Automatic 4-Speed Transmission [Std on GLS Wgn]	+273
Power Moonroof	+256

Mileage Category: B

The 1999 Elantra boasts a more powerful engine, styling changes and the best buyer assurance program of any car in this class.

1998

Body Styles	TMV Pricing		
	Trade	Private	Dealer
4 Dr GLS Sdn	2111	3279	4596
4 Dr GLS Wgn	2163	3360	4710

Options	Price
Air Conditioning	+262
Antilock Brakes	+227

Body Styles	TMV Pricing		
	Trade	Private	Dealer
4 Dr STD Sdn	1961	3047	4271
4 Dr STD Wgn	2015	3130	4387

Options	Price
Automatic 4-Speed Transmission [Std on GLS Wgn]	+210
Power Moonroof	+197

Mileage Category: B

No changes to the Elantra for 1998.

1997

Body Styles	TMV Pricing		
	Trade	Private	Dealer
4 Dr GLS Sdn	1599	2639	3911
4 Dr GLS Wgn	1697	2802	4152

Options	Price
Air Conditioning	+187
Antilock Brakes	+156

Body Styles	TMV Pricing		
	Trade	Private	Dealer
4 Dr STD Sdn	1355	2237	3315
4 Dr STD Wgn	1437	2373	3516

Options	Price
Automatic 4-Speed Transmission [Opt on STD]	+166
Power Moonroof	+155

Mileage Category: B

Elantra rolls into 1997 with zero changes, save for a slight price increase.

1996

Body Styles	TMV Pricing		
	Trade	Private	Dealer
4 Dr GLS Sdn	866	1560	2518
4 Dr GLS Wgn	877	1580	2550

Body Styles	TMV Pricing		
	Trade	Private	Dealer
4 Dr STD Sdn	768	1382	2231
4 Dr STD Wgn	829	1493	2409

Options	Price
Air Conditioning	+131
Automatic 4-Speed Transmission [Opt on STD,Sdn]	+116

Mileage Category: B

All-new Elantra is a slickly styled sedan or wagon featuring dual airbags, side-impact protection and a more powerful engine. Pricing is up as well, pushing this Hyundai squarely into Dodge Neon and Honda Civic territory.

1995

Body Styles	TMV Pricing		
	Trade	Private	Dealer
4 Dr GLS Sdn	490	984	1806
4 Dr SE Sdn	439	881	1618
4 Dr STD Sdn	432	868	1594

Options	Price
1.8L I4 DOHC 16V FI Engine [Opt on SE,STD]	+119
Air Conditioning	+109
Antilock Brakes	+91

Options	Price
Automatic 4-Speed Transmission	+97
Power Moonroof	+91

Mileage Category: B

No changes.

1994

Body Styles	TMV Pricing		
	Trade	Private	Dealer
4 Dr GLS Sdn	303	745	1482
4 Dr STD Sdn	270	665	1324

Mileage Category: B

Styling is updated, and a driver airbag is standard. ABS is optional on GLS models. CFC-free refrigerant replaces freon in Elantra's air conditioning system.

1994 (cont'd)

Options	Price
Antilock Brakes	+76
Automatic 4-Speed Transmission	+81

Options	Price
1.8L I4 DOHC 16V FI Engine [Opt on STD]	+99
Air Conditioning	+91

Hyundai
Excel

1994

Body Styles	TMV Pricing		
	Trade	Private	Dealer
2 Dr GS Hbk	265	611	1189
2 Dr STD Hbk	201	464	901
4 Dr GL Sdn	245	566	1101

Options	Price
Air Conditioning	+81

Mileage Category: A

Four-speed manual dropped from base car in favor of five-speed unit. Base sedan is discontinued. New interior fabrics and wheel covers spruce up the Excel. Air conditioners get CFC-free coolant.

Hyundai
Santa Fe

2003

Mileage Category: L

For 2003, side airbags become standard equipment for every Santa Fe. New this year is Homelink and a Monsoon sound system with a six-CD changer – these are standard items on the LX, and the audio upgrades are optional for the GLS. There is a newly available 3.5-liter V6 which will be offered in addition to the 2.4-liter inline four and the 2.7-liter V6.

Body Styles	TMV Pricing		
	Trade	Private	Dealer
4 Dr GLS AWD SUV	15700	16986	19131
4 Dr GLS SUV	15296	16549	18638
4 Dr LX AWD SUV	17369	18792	21163

Body Styles	TMV Pricing		
	Trade	Private	Dealer
4 Dr LX SUV	16251	17582	19801
4 Dr STD SUV	12834	13885	15637

Options	Price
Alarm System [Opt on STD]	+127
Antilock Brakes [Opt on GLS,STD]	+455
Automatic 4-Speed Transmission [Opt on STD]	+536
Cruise Control [Opt on STD]	+134
Monsoon Audio System [Opt on GLS]	+131

Options	Price
Power Moonroof [Opt on GLS,LX]	+399
Traction Control System [Opt on GLS]	+134
AM/FM/CD Changer Audio System [Opt on GLS]	+134
3.5L V6 DOHC 24V FI Engine [Opt on GLS,LX]	+389

2002

Mileage Category: L

Entering its second year of production, the Santa Fe gets four-wheel disc brakes as standard equipment as well as an optional upgraded stereo system. In May 2002, Hyundai responds to customer requests and makes a power sunroof optional for GLS and LX models. Besides that, all models benefit from midyear interior upgrades, among these larger air conditioning vents; a center stack-mounted clock; illumination for the power window buttons and glovebox; chrome accents; ISOFIX child-seat anchors for the outboard rear seating positions and an improved rear-seat recliner and folding mechanism. In September 2002, Hyundai announced that it had misstated the horsepower ratings for all of the models in its lineup -- the Santa Fe's 2.4-liter four-cylinder is now rated for 138 hp and its V6 is now at 173 hp. To compensate, the company is offering Hyundai owners (of 2000 models and newer) three options: 10 years of roadside assistance, 6-year/72,000-mile basic warranty coverage or 12-year/120,000-mile powertrain coverage.

Body Styles	TMV Pricing		
	Trade	Private	Dealer
4 Dr GLS AWD SUV	13555	14828	16950
4 Dr GLS SUV	12601	13784	15757
4 Dr LX AWD SUV	14974	16380	18724

Body Styles	TMV Pricing		
	Trade	Private	Dealer
4 Dr LX SUV	13999	15314	17504
4 Dr STD SUV	11075	12115	13849

Options	Price
Antilock Brakes [Opt on GLS,STD]	+399
Automatic 4-Speed Transmission [Opt on STD]	+469
Cruise Control [Opt on STD]	+117

Options	Price
Power Moonroof	+349
Traction Control System [Opt on GLS,STD]	+117

2001

Body Styles	TMV Pricing		
	Trade	Private	Dealer
4 Dr GL AWD SUV	10972	12453	13821
4 Dr GL SUV	9253	10502	11655
4 Dr GLS AWD SUV	11494	13046	14478

Options	Price
2.7L V6 DOHC 24V FI Engine [Opt on GL]	+618
Antilock Brakes	+350
Automatic 4-Speed Transmission [Opt on GL]	+309

Body Styles	TMV Pricing		
	Trade	Private	Dealer
4 Dr GLS SUV	10712	12159	13494
4 Dr LX AWD SUV	12117	13753	15264
4 Dr LX SUV	11335	12866	14279

Options	Price
Heated Front Seats	+134
Limited Slip Differential [Opt on GL,GLS]	+129

Mileage Category: L

For 2001, Hyundai brings to market its very own sport-utility. The Santa Fe is based on a modified Sonata midsize car platform and is available with either front-wheel drive or full-time four-wheel drive with either a four-cylinder or V6 engine.

Hyundai
Scoupe

1995

Body Styles	TMV Pricing		
	Trade	Private	Dealer
2 Dr LS Cpe	540	1033	1855
2 Dr STD Cpe	474	906	1627
2 Dr Turbo Cpe	596	1141	2048

Options	Price
Air Conditioning	+97
Automatic 4-Speed Transmission	+78

Mileage Category: E

No changes.

1994

Body Styles	TMV Pricing		
	Trade	Private	Dealer
2 Dr LS Cpe	321	717	1376
2 Dr STD Cpe	286	637	1223
2 Dr Turbo Cpe	364	811	1557

Options	Price
Air Conditioning	+81

Mileage Category: E

Base and LS models receive new interior fabrics, wheel covers and revised trim molding. CFC-free refrigerant is added to the air conditioner.

Hyundai
Sonata

2003

Body Styles	TMV Pricing		
	Trade	Private	Dealer
4 Dr GLS Sdn	10885	12012	13889
4 Dr LX Sdn	10982	12119	14013
4 Dr STD Sdn	9454	10432	12063

Options	Price
Antilock Brakes [Opt on STD]	+455
Automatic 4-Speed Transmission	+335
2.7L V6 DOHC 24V FI Engine [Opt on STD]	+569

Mileage Category: C

After receiving significant upgrades last year, the Sonata receives only minor changes this year. Among these are a battery-saver feature (in the event that any of lights are left on); illuminated window switches; a 12-volt power point in the trunk; and electronic, rather than cable-operated, releases for the trunk lid and fuel door. Additionally, Hyundai announced that it had misstated the horsepower ratings for all of the models in its lineup in previous years, so the Sonata's four-cylinder is now rated at 138 horsepower (down from 149) and its V6 is rated at 170 (down from 181), though the engines themselves are unchanged.

Hyundai
Sonata

2002

Mileage Category: C

The 2002 Sonata receives a new look, a refined suspension and an available automanual transmission. The standard features list is lengthened to include such niceties as remote keyless entry and, on GLS and new-for-2002 LX models, 16-inch wheels. In September 2002, Hyundai announced that it had misstated the horsepower ratings for all of the models in its lineup – the Sonata's 2.4-liter four-cylinder is now rated for 138 hp, while the V6 is now at 170, the previously advertised 2002 power upgrade (11 horsepower) apparently notwithstanding. To compensate, the company is offering owners (of 2000 models and newer) three options: 10 years of roadside assistance, 6-year/72,000-mile basic warranty coverage or 12-year/120,000-mile powertrain coverage.

Body Styles	TMV Pricing		
	Trade	Private	Dealer
4 Dr GLS Sdn	7993	9130	11024
4 Dr LX Sdn	8624	9850	11894

Options	Price
2.7L V6 DOHC 24V FI Engine [Opt on STD]	+293
Antilock Brakes	+399
Automatic 4-Speed Transmission	+293

Body Styles	TMV Pricing		
	Trade	Private	Dealer
4 Dr STD Sdn	7399	8451	10203

Options	Price
Power Moonroof	+323
Traction Control System	+147

2001

Mileage Category: C

The Sonata gets only minor trim changes for 2001, such as a new grille design and some tweaks to the rear deck lid. Additional features are ladled onto the standard equipment list.

Body Styles	TMV Pricing		
	Trade	Private	Dealer
4 Dr GLS Sdn	6380	7946	9391

Options	Price
AM/FM/CD Audio System [Opt on STD]	+155
Antilock Brakes [Opt on GLS]	+350
Automatic 4-Speed Transmission	+258
Leather Seats	+682

Body Styles	TMV Pricing		
	Trade	Private	Dealer
4 Dr STD Sdn	5577	6946	8210

Options	Price
Power Moonroof	+335
Rear Spoiler	+227
Traction Control System [Opt on GLS]	+129

2000

Mileage Category: C

With new standard 15-inch alloy wheels, standard side airbags and some option changes, Hyundai's 2000 Sonata maintains the same base MSRP as last year.

Body Styles		TMV Pricing		
		Trade	Private	Dealer
4 Dr GLS Sdn		5198	6711	8194
4 Dr STD Sdn		4422	5709	6971

Options	Price
AM/FM/Cassette/CD Audio System	+192
AM/FM/CD Audio System [Opt on STD]	+128
Antilock Brakes	+290
Automatic 4-Speed Transmission	+213

Options	Price
Leather Seats	+341
Power Moonroof	+277
Rear Spoiler	+177

1999

Mileage Category: C

Hyundai's Sonata is completely new and much improved for 1999.

Body Styles		TMV Pricing		
		Trade	Private	Dealer
4 Dr GLS Sdn		4113	5563	7073
4 Dr STD Sdn		3553	4806	6111

Options	Price
AM/FM/Cassette/CD Audio System	+153
Antilock Brakes	+258
Automatic 4-Speed Transmission	+303

Options	Price
Leather Seats [Opt on GLS]	+273
Power Moonroof	+222
Rear Spoiler	+142

1998

Mileage Category: C

No changes to the Sonata for 1998.

Body Styles	TMV Pricing		
	Trade	Private	Dealer
4 Dr GL Sdn	2124	3144	4294
4 Dr GL V6 Sdn	2250	3331	4549

Options	Price
AM/FM/Cassette/CD Audio System	+118
Antilock Brakes	+199
Automatic 4-Speed Transmission [Opt on STD]	+234

Body Styles	TMV Pricing		
	Trade	Private	Dealer
4 Dr GLS Sdn	2601	3851	5260
4 Dr STD Sdn	2079	3079	4206

Options	Price
Leather Seats	+210
Power Moonroof	+175

Hyundai
Sonata/Tiburon

1997

Body Styles	TMV Pricing		
	Trade	Private	Dealer
4 Dr GL Sdn	1441	2345	3449
4 Dr GLS Sdn	1732	2819	4147
4 Dr STD Sdn	1385	2253	3314

Options	Price
Leather Seats	+166
Power Moonroof	+145
3.0L V6 SOHC 12V FI Engine [Opt on GL]	+230

Options	Price
Antilock Brakes	+156
Automatic 4-Speed Transmission [Opt on STD]	+184

Mileage Category: C

Sheet metal is all new, and gives Sonata a more substantial look despite somewhat controversial retro-style front fascia and grille. Flush-fitting doors and restyled exterior mirrors help quiet the ride, while horn activation switches from spoke button to center steering wheel pad.

1996

Body Styles	TMV Pricing		
	Trade	Private	Dealer
4 Dr GL Sdn	922	1621	2586
4 Dr GL V6 Sdn	981	1724	2749

Body Styles	TMV Pricing		
	Trade	Private	Dealer
4 Dr GLS Sdn	1077	1892	3017
4 Dr STD Sdn	916	1610	2569

Options	Price
Automatic 4-Speed Transmission [Opt on STD]	+121
Leather Seats	+116

Mileage Category: C

Noise, vibration and harshness are quelled with the addition of insulation to the floor and cowl, and liquid-filled V6 engine mounts. ABS is available as a stand-alone option on the GLS, and Steel Gray joins the color chart. Upgraded seat fabric comes in the base and GL models, while all Sonatas get CFC-free A/C.

1995

Body Styles	TMV Pricing		
	Trade	Private	Dealer
4 Dr GL Sdn	703	1267	2206
4 Dr GL V6 Sdn	748	1348	2349

Body Styles	TMV Pricing		
	Trade	Private	Dealer
4 Dr GLS Sdn	816	1471	2562
4 Dr STD Sdn	633	1140	1986

Options	Price
Antilock Brakes	+91
Automatic 4-Speed Transmission [Opt on STD]	+101

Options	Price
Leather Seats	+97
Power Moonroof	+78

Mileage Category: C

Brand-new Sonata debuted in mid-1994. Dual airbags are standard. A 137-horsepower engine powers base and GL models while a 142-horsepower V6 is optional on midlevel GL and standard on GLS. Both engines are Mitsubishi-based designs. New car meets 1997 side-impact standards. Air conditioning and cassette stereo are standard on all models.

1994

Body Styles	TMV Pricing		
	Trade	Private	Dealer
4 Dr GLS Sdn	484	962	1759
4 Dr GLS V6 Sdn	537	1066	1948

Body Styles	TMV Pricing		
	Trade	Private	Dealer
4 Dr STD Sdn	441	874	1595
4 Dr V6 Sdn	490	974	1781

Options	Price
Antilock Brakes	+76
Automatic 4-Speed Transmission	+84
Leather Seats	+81

Mileage Category: C

No changes.

Hyundai
Tiburon

2003

Mileage Category: E

Completely redesigned for 2003, the Tiburon has progressed from a sporty economy hatchback to a legitimate sport coupe. And it's the sleekest Hyundai we've ever laid eyes on -- more than a few journalists have compared it to the Ferrari 456GT. The previous generation's 134-horsepower inline four will still power the base coupe, but Hyundai predicts that the volume leader will be the 170-hp Tiburon GT V6. Of course, this Tiburon will cost more than its predecessor, but you can still get into a GT V6 for less than 20 grand. Available features include a six-speed manual transmission, 17-inch wheels and a seven-speaker Infinity sound system. Note that the engines were originally rated for 140 hp and 181 hp, respectively; Hyundai downgraded the output for both in September 2002 (along with all of the other models in its lineup). To compensate, the company is offering owners (of 2000 models and newer) three options: 10 years of roadside assistance, 6-year/72,000-mile basic warranty coverage or 12-year/120,000-mile powertrain coverage.

Hyundai
Tiburon

2003 (cont'd)

Body Styles		TMV Pricing		
		Trade	Private	Dealer
2 Dr GT V6 Hbk		10220	11418	13415
2 Dr STD Hbk		8965	10016	11768

Options	Price	Options	Price
AM/FM/Cassette/CD Audio System [Opt on STD]	+134	Leather Seats [Opt on STD]	+335
Antilock Brakes	+455	Power Moonroof	+435
Automatic 4-Speed Transmission	+603	Rear Spoiler [Opt on STD]	+131
Infinity Audio System [Opt on STD]	+251		

2001

Body Styles		TMV Pricing		
		Trade	Private	Dealer
2 Dr STD Hbk		5308	6672	7931

Options	Price	Options	Price
AM/FM/Cassette/CD Audio System	+207	Leather Seats	+386
Antilock Brakes	+386	Power Sunroof	+361
Automatic 4-Speed Transmission	+412		

Mileage Category: E

Following last year's freshening, the Tiburon sees only minor trim changes for 2001, such as redesigned wheels and the addition of a rear spoiler as standard equipment.

2000
Mileage Category: E

Hyundai's Tiburon is now offered in just one trim level. It receives new interior and exterior styling as well as alloy wheels, a power package and four-wheel disc brakes standard.

Body Styles		TMV Pricing		
		Trade	Private	Dealer
2 Dr STD Hbk		4437	5760	7057

Options	Price	Options	Price
Alarm System	+122	Leather Seats	+320
AM/FM/Cassette/CD Audio System	+171	Power Moonroof	+299
Antilock Brakes	+320	Rear Spoiler	+213
Automatic 4-Speed Transmission	+341		

1999
Mileage Category: E

Nothing changes on the Tiburon for 1999.

Body Styles		TMV Pricing		
		Trade	Private	Dealer
2 Dr FX Hbk		4008	5487	7026
2 Dr STD Hbk		3651	4999	6402

Options	Price	Options	Price
Air Conditioning	+307	Automatic 4-Speed Transmission	+273
Aluminum/Alloy Wheels [Opt on STD]	+171	Leather Seats	+256
AM/FM/Cassette/CD Audio System	+136	Power Sunroof	+239
AM/FM/CD Audio System	+119	Rear Spoiler [Opt on STD]	+171
Antilock Brakes	+258		

1998
Mileage Category: E

Base Tiburons get the 2.0-liter 140-horsepower engine as standard equipment.

Body Styles		TMV Pricing		
		Trade	Private	Dealer
2 Dr FX Hbk		2876	4292	5888
2 Dr STD Hbk		2557	3815	5234

Options	Price	Options	Price
Air Conditioning	+237	Leather Seats	+197
Aluminum/Alloy Wheels [Opt on STD]	+131	Power Sunroof	+185
Antilock Brakes	+199	Rear Spoiler [Opt on STD]	+118
Automatic 4-Speed Transmission	+210		

1997

Body Styles	TMV Pricing		
	Trade	Private	Dealer
2 Dr FX Hbk	1865	3166	4755
2 Dr STD Hbk	1681	2854	4287

Options	Price	Options	Price
Antilock Brakes	+156	Power Sunroof	+145
Automatic 4-Speed Transmission	+166	Air Conditioning	+182
Leather Seats	+155		

Mileage Category: E

Loosely based on the 1993 HCD-II concept car, the Tiburon (Spanish for shark) debuts as a budget sport coupe that promises to gobble competitors such as the Toyota Paseo like so much chum.

Hyundai
XG350

2003

Body Styles	TMV Pricing		
	Trade	Private	Dealer
4 Dr L Sdn	13552	14870	17066
4 Dr STD Sdn	13300	14593	16748

Options	Price
Compact Disc Changer	+335

Mileage Category: D

For 2003, Hyundai's flagship sedan gets a new instrument panel and trip computer. Otherwise, the XG350 is unchanged.

2002

Body Styles	TMV Pricing		
	Trade	Private	Dealer
4 Dr L Sdn	11053	12314	14416
4 Dr STD Sdn	10360	11542	13512

Options	Price
Compact Disc Changer	+293

Mileage Category: D

The XG300 becomes the XG350, as engine displacement is bumped up 0.5 liters to 3.5. Although horsepower is only increased by 2 to 194, 39 more pound-feet of torque is on tap for a grand total of 217, which should provide quicker acceleration.

Hyundai
XG300

2001

Body Styles	TMV Pricing		
	Trade	Private	Dealer
4 Dr L Sdn	8702	10199	11581
4 Dr STD Sdn	8189	9598	10898

Options	Price
Compact Disc Changer	+258
Power Moonroof [Opt on STD]	+386

Mileage Category: D

Hyundai goes after the Honda Accord V6 and Toyota Camry V6 by offering more for less. Fully loaded with equipment, the new XG300 undercuts both competitors on price. But, as we all know, there's more to the value equation than an attractive MSRP, especially in the meat of the sedan marketplace.

FX35/FX45/G20

Infiniti
FX35

2003

Mileage Category: H

The FX35 is an all-new crossover SUV from Infiniti. It is performance-oriented, and boasts a powerful V6, sharp handling and available all-wheel drive. It's also a less expensive alternative to the V8-powered FX45.

Body Styles	TMV Pricing		
	Trade	Private	Dealer
4 Dr STD AWD SUV	29665	31261	33921
4 Dr STD SUV	28394	29922	32468

Options	Price
Bose Audio System	+382
Heated Front Seats	+267
Leather Seats	+649
Navigation System	+1375
Power Moonroof	+687
Sport Suspension	+191
Adaptive Cruise Control	+611

Options	Price
Satellite Radio System	+305
20 Inch Wheels	+573
DVD Entertainment System	+993
Keyless Ignition System	+531
Rear View Camera	+382
Power Driver Seat w/Memory	+191

Infiniti
FX45

2003

Mileage Category: H

The FX45 is an all-new crossover SUV from Infiniti. It is performance-oriented, and therefore boasts V8 power, sharp handling and standard all-wheel drive.

Body Styles	TMV Pricing		
	Trade	Private	Dealer
4 Dr STD AWD SUV	37292	38925	41646

Options	Price
Bose Audio System	+382
Navigation System	+1375
Power Moonroof	+687
Sport Suspension	+191
Adaptive Cruise Control	+611

Options	Price
Satellite Radio System	+305
DVD Entertainment System	+993
Keyless Ignition System	+531
Rear View Camera	+382

Infiniti
G20

2002

Body Styles	TMV Pricing		
	Trade	Private	Dealer
4 Dr STD Sdn	11674	12701	14413

Options	Price
16 Inch Wheels	+213
Automatic 4-Speed Transmission	+487
Heated Front Seats	+173

Options	Price
Leather Seats	+426
Power Driver Seat	+143
Power Moonroof	+456

Mileage Category: H

A Sport package featuring a body-color grille, dark tint headlight trim and 16-inch aluminum-alloy wheels debuts this year, as do two new exterior colors -- Silver Crystal and Maui Blue. The G20t, as Infiniti dubs the Touring package-equipped model, disappears this year.

2001
Mileage Category: H

G20t comes with standard leather and a power sunroof this year. Luxury models can be equipped with leather and a manual transmission simultaneously. And hold on to your hat -- the side marker lights switch from amber lenses to clear.

Body Styles	TMV Pricing		
	Trade	Private	Dealer
4 Dr STD Sdn	9796	11118	12338
4 Dr Touring Sdn	11463	13009	14437

2001 (cont'd)

Options	Price
Automatic 4-Speed Transmission	+409
Compact Disc Changer	+235
Heated Front Seats	+128
Infiniti Communicator	+817

Options	Price
Leather Seats	+434
Power Heated Mirrors	+115
Power Moonroof	+485

2000

Mileage Category: H

The G20 entry-level compact receives numerous mechanical improvements, exterior and interior enhancements and safety additions for 2000, including more horsepower, revised transmissions and a new muffler.

Body Styles	TMV Pricing		
	Trade	Private	Dealer
4 Dr STD Sdn	8858	10211	11538

Body Styles	TMV Pricing		
	Trade	Private	Dealer
4 Dr Touring Sdn	9431	10872	12285

Options	Price
Automatic 4-Speed Transmission	+359
Compact Disc Changer	+322

Options	Price
Power Moonroof	+426

1999

Mileage Category: H

The G20 returns to the Infiniti lineup after a two-year hiatus. This entry-level compact is based on the European- and Japanese- market Primera, which has garnered a great deal of acclaim from the foreign automotive press.

Body Styles	TMV Pricing		
	Trade	Private	Dealer
4 Dr STD Sdn	7270	8507	9794

Body Styles	TMV Pricing		
	Trade	Private	Dealer
4 Dr Touring Sdn	8063	9435	10862

Options	Price
Automatic 4-Speed Transmission	+273
Leather Seats	+291

Options	Price
Power Moonroof	+325

1996

Mileage Category: H

Emergency locking front and rear seatbelts have been installed, and fake wood is applied on models equipped with the Leather Appointment Package. This is the last year for the entry-level Infiniti.

Body Styles	TMV Pricing		
	Trade	Private	Dealer
4 Dr STD Sdn	3281	4159	5372

Body Styles	TMV Pricing		
	Trade	Private	Dealer
4 Dr Touring Sdn	3559	4511	5826

Options	Price
Automatic 4-Speed Transmission	+186
Leather Seats [Opt on STD]	+158

Options	Price
Power Moonroof [Opt on STD]	+186

1995

Mileage Category: H

All-season tires are added to the G20. No other changes are made to the entry-level Infiniti.

Body Styles	TMV Pricing		
	Trade	Private	Dealer
4 Dr STD Sdn	2685	3454	4736

Body Styles	TMV Pricing		
	Trade	Private	Dealer
4 Dr Touring Sdn	2881	3706	5081

Options	Price
Automatic 4-Speed Transmission	+117
Leather Seats [Opt on STD]	+125

Options	Price
Power Moonroof [Opt on STD]	+139

1994

Body Styles	TMV Pricing		
	Trade	Private	Dealer
4 Dr STD Sdn	2073	2739	3849

Options	Price
Automatic 4-Speed Transmission	+105
Leather Seats	+111

Options	Price
Power Moonroof	+124

Mileage Category: H

No changes to the G20.

Infiniti
G35/I35/I30

Infiniti
G35
2003

Body Styles	TMV Pricing		
	Trade	Private	Dealer
2 Dr STD Cpe	25216	26608	28927

Options	Price
Bose Audio System	+420
Heated Front Seats [Opt on Sdn]	+267
Navigation System	+1527
Power Moonroof	+687

Body Styles	TMV Pricing		
	Trade	Private	Dealer
2 Dr STD Cpe	25216	26608	28927

Options	Price
Power Passenger Seat	+210
Satellite Radio System	+305
Automatic Climate Control (2 Zone) - Driver and Passenger	+210
Power Driver Seat w/Memory	+191

Mileage Category: H

The G35 is Infiniti's new entry-level luxury sport sedan and coupe. Aimed at buyers who would otherwise choose an Audi A4, BMW 3 Series or Lexus IS 300, the G35 offers impressive performance and comfort for a price that's less than most of the competition's.

Infiniti
I35
2003

Body Styles		TMV Pricing		
		Trade	Private	Dealer
4 Dr STD Sdn		20273	21446	23400

Options	Price
Automatic Stability Control	+267
Compact Disc Changer	+225
Power Heated Mirrors	+130
Heated Front and Rear Seats	+229
Navigation System	+1527

Options	Price
Power Moonroof	+706
Sport Suspension	+218
17 Inch Wheels - Chrome	+573
Power Rear Window Sunshade	+286
Satellite Radio System	+305

Mileage Category: H

There aren't that many changes for the I35 this year. It gains the option of having an integrated satellite radio, and on the inside the use of wood-tone trim is expanded on the center console

2002
Mileage Category: H

The I35 is an evolution of the second-generation I30 entry-level luxury sedan. It features a more powerful engine, updated exterior styling, standard 17-inch wheels, an upgraded braking system, stability control and more luxurious interior appointments.

Body Styles		TMV Pricing		
		Trade	Private	Dealer
4 Dr STD Sdn		17002	18145	20051

Options	Price
17 Inch Wheels	+347
Automatic Stability Control	+213
Chrome Wheels	+974
Compact Disc Changer	+335
Heated Front and Rear Seats	+183

Options	Price
Navigation System	+1096
Power Moonroof	+548
Power Rear Window Sunshade	+213
Rear Spoiler	+304
Sport Suspension	+173

Infiniti
I30
2001

Body Styles	TMV Pricing		
	Trade	Private	Dealer
4 Dr STD Sdn	14553	16110	17548

Options	Price
Compact Disc Changer	+307
Heated Front Seats	+192
Infiniti Communicator	+817

Body Styles	TMV Pricing		
	Trade	Private	Dealer
4 Dr Touring Sdn	14574	16133	17573

Options	Price
Navigation System	+1022
Rear Spoiler	+128
Traction Control System	+153

Mileage Category: H

This year, two new colors are added along with steering wheel-mounted controls, an antiglare rearview mirror with integrated compass and an emergency inside trunk release. The brilliant blue xenon headlights previously available only on Touring models can now be ordered on base trim cars, as well.

2000

Body Styles	TMV Pricing		
	Trade	Private	Dealer
4 Dr STD Sdn	12832	14388	15913

Options	Price
Compact Disc Changer	+269
Heated Front Seats	+168

Body Styles	TMV Pricing		
	Trade	Private	Dealer
4 Dr Touring Sdn	13006	14583	16129

Options	Price
Infiniti Communicator	+363

Mileage Category: H

The year 2000 marks the introduction of an all-new Infiniti I30.

1999

Body Styles	TMV Pricing		
	Trade	Private	Dealer
4 Dr STD Sdn	9892	11322	12810

Options	Price
Automatic 4-Speed Transmission [Opt on Touring]	+341
Compact Disc Changer	+228
Heated Front Seats	+142

Body Styles	TMV Pricing		
	Trade	Private	Dealer
4 Dr Touring Sdn	10275	11760	13306

Options	Price
Infiniti Communicator	+307
Leather Seats [Opt on STD]	+342
Power Moonroof [Opt on STD]	+325

Mileage Category: H

Traction control is available as an option, the audio faceplate has been updated and an ignition immobilizer is offered on the I30.

1998

Body Styles	TMV Pricing		
	Trade	Private	Dealer
4 Dr STD Sdn	7807	9160	10686

Options	Price
Automatic 4-Speed Transmission [Opt on Touring]	+281
Compact Disc Changer	+187
Heated Front Seats [Opt on STD]	+117

Body Styles	TMV Pricing		
	Trade	Private	Dealer
4 Dr Touring Sdn	8173	9590	11187

Options	Price
Infiniti Communicator	+253
Leather Seats [Opt on STD]	+281
Power Moonroof [Opt on STD]	+267

Mileage Category: H

Side-impact airbags make their way into the Infiniti I30, as do new headlamps, taillamps, center console and wheels.

1997

Body Styles	TMV Pricing		
	Trade	Private	Dealer
4 Dr STD Sdn	6090	7389	8977

Options	Price
Automatic 4-Speed Transmission	+231
Leather Seats [Opt on STD]	+231

Body Styles	TMV Pricing		
	Trade	Private	Dealer
4 Dr Touring Sdn	6380	7741	9405

Options	Price
Power Moonroof [Opt on STD]	+220

Mileage Category: H

A few new paint colors are the only changes to the 1997 I30.

1996

Body Styles	TMV Pricing		
	Trade	Private	Dealer
4 Dr STD Sdn	5074	6253	7880

Options	Price
Automatic 4-Speed Transmission	+186
Leather Seats [Opt on STD]	+185
Power Moonroof [Opt on STD]	+176

Body Styles	TMV Pricing		
	Trade	Private	Dealer
4 Dr Touring Sdn	5317	6552	8258

Mileage Category: H

New luxo-sport sedan based on the Nissan Maxima arrived during 1995. Slotted between the G20 and the J30, the I30 competes with the Lexus ES 300, BMW 3 Series and the new Acura TL-Series. If you like big chrome grilles, this is the car to buy.

Infiniti
J30

1997

Body Styles	TMV Pricing		
	Trade	Private	Dealer
4 Dr STD Sdn	6529	7931	9644
4 Dr STD Sdn (1997.5)	6529	7931	9644

Body Styles	TMV Pricing		
	Trade	Private	Dealer
4 Dr Touring Sdn	6144	7463	9076
4 Dr Touring Sdn (1997.5)	6144	7463	9076

Mileage Category: H

Last year for the J30.

Infiniti
J30/M45/Q45

1996

Mileage Category: H

Three new colors join the paint palette.

Body Styles	TMV Pricing		
	Trade	Private	Dealer
4 Dr STD Sdn	5340	6581	8294
4 Dr Touring Sdn	5480	6754	8513

1995

Mileage Category: H

Redesigned taillights, power lumbar support for the driver seat and an antiglare mirror mark the changes for the 1995 J30.

Body Styles	TMV Pricing		
	Trade	Private	Dealer
4 Dr STD Sdn	3925	4998	6787

Options	Price
Forged Alloy Wheels	+82
Touring Suspension	+114

1994

Mileage Category: H

Heated front seats and the addition of two speakers further pamper passengers in the J30.

Body Styles	TMV Pricing		
	Trade	Private	Dealer
4 Dr STD Sdn	3385	4449	6221

Options	Price
4 Wheel Steering	+240
Touring Suspension	+102

Infiniti
M45

2003

Body Styles	TMV Pricing		
	Trade	Private	Dealer
4 Dr STD Sdn	31334	32900	35510

Options	Price	Options	Price
Navigation System	+1375	18 Inch Wheels - Chrome	+764
Power Moonroof	+916	Satellite Radio System	+305
Rear Spoiler	+412	Automatic Dimming Sideview Mirror(s)	+134
Ventilated Seats (Front)	+573	Voice Recoginition System	+496
Adaptive Cruise Control	+535		

Mileage Category: I

The M45 performance sport sedan comes standard with class-leading V8 performance and a long list of world-class amenities.

Infiniti
Q45

2003

Body Styles	TMV Pricing		
	Trade	Private	Dealer
4 Dr STD Sdn	37876	39734	42831

Options	Price	Options	Price
Electronic Damping Suspension Control	+649	Power Rear Window Sunshade	+382
Heated Front and Rear Seats	+382	Adaptive Cruise Control	+611
Navigation System	+1527	Satellite Radio System	+305
Runflat Tire System	+191	18 Inch Wheels	+496
Ventilated Seats (Front)	+496	Air Conditioning - Front and Rear	+191

Mileage Category: I

The Q45 enters into 2003 with a few changes. Refinements include a higher numerical final drive ratio for better acceleration, slightly revised front and rear styling, new exterior colors, the addition of standard heated seats and a full-size spare tire. An optional satellite radio is now being offered along with some new optional equipment packages.

2002

Mileage Category: I

Body Styles	TMV Pricing		
	Trade	Private	Dealer
4 Dr STD Sdn	30239	32254	35611

Options	Price	Options	Price
18 Inch Wheels	+396	Navigation System	+1217
Adaptive Cruise Control	+487	Power Rear Seat	+487
Electronic Damping Suspension Control	+517	Power Rear Window Sunshade	+304
Heated Front Seats	+274		

Infiniti takes aim at the BMW 5 Series, Lexus GS and the Mercedes-Benz E-Class with the all-new Q45 sedan. Unlike the forgettable previous version, the new Q has power and panache, just what it takes to woo the mid-luxury crowd.

2001

Mileage Category: I

Body Styles	TMV Pricing		
	Trade	Private	Dealer
4 Dr STD Sdn	21623	24043	26277
4 Dr Touring Sdn	22017	24481	26756

Options	Price	Options	Price
Compact Disc Changer	+307	Navigation System	+1022
Heated Front Seats	+215	Rear Spoiler	+271
Infiniti Communicator	+817	Two-Tone Paint	+256

Few changes accompany the current Q45 as it gasps a few final breaths before a welcome, and long overdue, redesign debuts in spring of 2001. A new Luxury model replaces last year's Anniversary Edition. All Qs get body-colored door handles and license plate surrounds, revised taillights, real bird's eye maple wood interior trim and a leather-wrapped steering wheel rim trimmed in ersatz timber. The Touring model has standard bright-finish 17-inch wheels.

2000

Mileage Category: I

Body Styles	TMV Pricing		
	Trade	Private	Dealer
4 Dr Anniv Sdn	19009	21350	23645
4 Dr STD Sdn	18065	20291	22473
4 Dr Touring Sdn	18501	20780	23014

Options	Price	Options	Price
Compact Disc Changer	+269	Infiniti Communicator	+363
Heated Front Seats	+157	Rear Spoiler	+157

For 2000 the Q45 celebrates a decade of production with a special 10th Anniversary model. All Qs receive a new 100,000-mile tune-up interval and special child seat tethers.

1999

Mileage Category: I

Body Styles	TMV Pricing		
	Trade	Private	Dealer
4 Dr STD Sdn	13730	15660	17668
4 Dr Touring Sdn	14208	16205	18284

Options	Price	Options	Price
Compact Disc Changer	+228	Infiniti Communicator	+307
Heated Front Seats	+133	Rear Spoiler	+133

Several small exterior and interior enhancements have been added to the Q for 1999, including a new sunroof, revised front styling and the return of the analog clock.

1998

Mileage Category: I

Body Styles	TMV Pricing		
	Trade	Private	Dealer
4 Dr STD Sdn	11551	13399	15483
4 Dr Touring Sdn	11881	13783	15927

Options	Price
Compact Disc Changer [Opt on STD]	+187
Infiniti Communicator	+253

The Q45 gets front seatbelt pre-tensioners. No other changes for Infiniti's flagship.

1997

Mileage Category: I

Body Styles	TMV Pricing			Body Styles	TMV Pricing		
	Trade	Private	Dealer		Trade	Private	Dealer
4 Dr STD Sdn	9372	10965	12913	4 Dr Touring Sdn	9713	11365	13384
4 Dr STD Sdn (1997.5)	9659	11302	13309	4 Dr Touring Sdn (1997.5)	9897	11580	13636

This totally redesigned car has almost nothing in common with its predecessor. Power now comes via a 4.1-liter V8 engine and is still delivered through the rear wheels. The Q45 no longer has aspirations to be a sport sedan, its prime duties now are interstate cruising.

Infiniti
Q45/QX4

1996
Mileage Category: I

Active suspension model is canceled, but two new exterior colors are available.

Body Styles	TMV Pricing		
	Trade	Private	Dealer
4 Dr STD Sdn	7273	8696	10662
4 Dr Touring Sdn	7384	8828	10822

Options	Price
Traction Control System	+124

1995

Body Styles	TMV Pricing		
	Trade	Private	Dealer
4 Dr A Sdn	6250	7510	9609
4 Dr STD Sdn	6040	7258	9288

Options	Price
Compact Disc Changer [Std on A]	+115
Touring Package	+273
Traction Control System [Std on A]	+115

Mileage Category: I

Alloy wheels for the base model are about the only changes for the Q45.

1994
Mileage Category: I

A passenger airbag appears on the restyled 1994 Infiniti. The addition of a grille, along with new bumpers and foglights distinguish this car from previous models.

Body Styles	TMV Pricing		
	Trade	Private	Dealer
4 Dr A Sdn	5026	6248	8285
4 Dr STD Sdn	4743	5896	7818

Options	Price
4 Wheel Steering	+240
Traction Control System [Opt on STD]	+87

Infiniti
QX4

2003

Body Styles	TMV Pricing		
	Trade	Private	Dealer
4 Dr STD 4WD SUV	23162	24528	26805
4 Dr STD SUV	22858	24207	26454

Options	Price		Options	Price
Camper/Towing Package	+321		Two-Tone Paint	+382
Chrome Wheels	+1222		VCR Entertainment System	+993
Heated Front and Rear Seats	+382		Adaptive Cruise Control	+611
Navigation System	+1527		DVD Entertainment System	+1222
Power Moonroof	+764			

Mileage Category: O

For 2003, QX4 receives packaging enhancements, including the addition of previously optional Premium Package as standard equipment. This includes 17-inch wheels and tires, a leather and genuine wood steering wheel, driver seat memory and steering wheel-mounted audio control switches.

2002
Mileage Category: O

For 2002, the QX4 receives a few interior enhancements including a refined audio system, a faster functioning in-dash CD changer and a newly optional wood-trim steering wheel with audio controls. It also gets an available Intelligent Cruise Control system, the same system found on the Q45. Rounding out the updates are optional chrome-plated 17-inch wheels and seven new exterior colors.

Body Styles	TMV Pricing		
	Trade	Private	Dealer
4 Dr STD 4WD SUV	20388	21835	24247
4 Dr STD SUV	19563	20952	23266

2002 (cont'd)

Options	Price	Options	Price
17 Inch Wheels	+274	Limited Slip Differential	+183
Adaptive Cruise Control	+487	Navigation System	+1217
Camper/Towing Package	+256	Power Driver Seat w/Memory	+134
Chrome Wheels	+974	Power Sunroof	+609
DVD Entertainment System	+974	Two-Tone Paint	+304
Heated Front and Rear Seats	+304	VCR Entertainment System	+791

2001

Body Styles	TMV Pricing		
	Trade	Private	Dealer
4 Dr STD 4WD SUV	18068	20019	21820
4 Dr STD SUV	17337	19209	20937

Options	Price	Options	Price
Camper/Towing Package	+166	Navigation System	+1022
DVD Entertainment System	+818	Power Moonroof	+486
Heated Front and Rear Seats	+230	Two-Tone Paint	+256
Limited Slip Differential	+153	VCR Entertainment System	+664

Mileage Category: O

For 2001, the QX4 gets a substantial power boost from a brand-new V6 engine. Cosmetic updates include the addition of standard xenon high-intensity headlights, revised exterior styling, new alloy wheels and a more upscale interior. A navigation system is available, as is an on-board entertainment system. A less costly 2WD model is offered for the first time, and Infiniti's signature analog clock has been added to the dash, along with electrofluorescent gauge illumination.

2000

Body Styles	TMV Pricing		
	Trade	Private	Dealer
4 Dr STD 4WD SUV	15823	17603	19347

Options	Price	Options	Price
Camper/Towing Package	+146	Infiniti Communicator	+363
Compact Disc Changer	+269	Limited Slip Differential	+135
Heated Front Seats	+157	Power Moonroof	+426

Mileage Category: O

Infiniti's luxury SUV gets minor improvements to its emissions system but is otherwise a carryover from the 1999 model year. A more powerful QX4 will be available soon as a 2001 model.

1999

Body Styles	TMV Pricing		
	Trade	Private	Dealer
4 Dr STD 4WD SUV	12553	14280	16077

Options	Price	Options	Price
Camper/Towing Package	+123	Infiniti Communicator	+307
Compact Disc Changer	+228	Power Moonroof	+325
Heated Front Seats	+133	Running Boards	+123

Mileage Category: O

Infiniti's luxury sport-ute enters its third year with no major changes.

1998

Body Styles	TMV Pricing		
	Trade	Private	Dealer
4 Dr STD 4WD SUV	10402	12011	13826

Options	Price
Compact Disc Changer	+187
Power Moonroof	+267

Mileage Category: O

No changes to the QX4.

1997

Body Styles	TMV Pricing		
	Trade	Private	Dealer
4 Dr STD 4WD SUV	8663	10093	11841

Options	Price
Power Moonroof	+220

Mileage Category: O

A version of Nissan's wonderful four-wheeler is introduced by Infiniti, aiming to compete with the Mercury Mountaineer, Acura SLX and Land Rover Discovery. Differences between the QX4 and the Pathfinder include the Q's full-time four-wheel-drive system, a more luxurious interior and some different sheet metal.

Isuzu
Amigo

2000

Mileage Category: L

Redesigned front styling and several new colors are available for the new year. The Ironman package offers the Rodeo's Intelligent Suspension Control system.

Body Styles	TMV Pricing			Body Styles	TMV Pricing		
	Trade	Private	Dealer		Trade	Private	Dealer
2 Dr S Conv	4644	5656	6648	2 Dr S V6 4WD SUV	6083	7409	8708
2 Dr S SUV	4961	6043	7103	2 Dr S V6 Conv	5520	6723	7902
2 Dr S V6 4WD Conv	5844	7118	8366	2 Dr S V6 SUV	5390	6565	7716

Options	Price	Options	Price
Air Conditioning	+372	Compact Disc Changer	+196
Aluminum/Alloy Wheels	+157	Ironman Package	+377
AM/FM/CD Audio System	+137	Side Steps	+139
Automatic 4-Speed Transmission [Opt on V6 4WD Conv]	+313		

1999

Mileage Category: L

Two body styles are available, hardtop or soft top, and an automatic transmission is now offered with the V6 engine.

Body Styles	TMV Pricing			Body Styles	TMV Pricing		
	Trade	Private	Dealer		Trade	Private	Dealer
2 Dr S 4WD Conv	4476	5680	6933	2 Dr S V6 4WD SUV	4530	5749	7017
2 Dr S Conv	3990	5063	6179	2 Dr S V6 Conv	4388	5568	6796
2 Dr S SUV	4062	5154	6291	2 Dr S V6 SUV	4546	5769	7041
2 Dr S V6 4WD Conv	4504	5715	6975				

Options	Price	Options	Price
Air Conditioning	+288	Automatic 4-Speed Transmission	+237
Aluminum/Alloy Wheels	+182	Compact Disc Changer	+197
AM/FM/CD Audio System	+152		

1998

Mileage Category: L

Isuzu reintroduces its convertible sport-utility after a three-year hiatus. This model comes with a modest four-cylinder engine, but the powerful V6 from the Rodeo is available and turns this 4WD droptop into a screamer.

Body Styles	TMV Pricing		
	Trade	Private	Dealer
2 Dr S 4WD Conv	3591	4651	5847
2 Dr S Conv	2975	3852	4842
2 Dr S V6 4WD Conv	3934	5095	6404

Options	Price	Options	Price
Air Conditioning	+253	AM/FM/CD Audio System	+133
Aluminum/Alloy Wheels	+133	Compact Disc Changer	+173

1994

Mileage Category: L

Automatic transmission disappears from options list, and base 2.3-liter, four-cylinder engine is no longer available. Power steering, power outside mirrors, a center floor console and 16-inch tires are all newly standard.

Body Styles	TMV Pricing			Body Styles	TMV Pricing		
	Trade	Private	Dealer		Trade	Private	Dealer
2 Dr S 4WD Conv	2022	2667	3741	2 Dr XS 4WD Conv	2068	2727	3826
2 Dr S Conv	1793	2364	3316	2 Dr XS Conv	1867	2463	3455

Options	Price
Air Conditioning	+156

Isuzu
Ascender

2003

Body Styles	TMV Pricing			Body Styles	TMV Pricing		
	Trade	Private	Dealer		Trade	Private	Dealer
4 Dr LS 4WD SUV	23078	24583	27090	4 Dr Limited SUV	23760	25309	27890
4 Dr LS SUV	21424	22821	25148	4 Dr S 4WD SUV	20743	22095	24349
4 Dr Limited 4WD SUV	25414	27071	29832	4 Dr S SUV	18991	20229	22292

Ascender/Axiom/Hombre

Options	Price
Power Heated Mirrors [Opt on S]	+126
Power Driver Seat [Opt on S]	+196
5.3L V8 OHV 16V FI Engine [Opt on LS]	+960

Mileage Category: M

With its product lineup getting stale, Isuzu has called up the Ascender from the bull pen. Essentially a rebadged GMC Envoy XL, the Ascender offers seating for seven and V8 power.

Isuzu
Axiom
2003

Body Styles	TMV Pricing			Body Styles	TMV Pricing		
	Trade	Private	Dealer		Trade	Private	Dealer
4 Dr S 4WD SUV	16954	18249	20408	4 Dr XS 4WD SUV	18167	19555	21868
4 Dr S SUV	15277	16444	18390	4 Dr XS SUV	17286	18606	20807

Options	Price
Chrome Wheels [Opt on XS]	+254
Power Moonroof [Opt on S]	+644
AM/FM/Cassette/CD Changer Audio System [Opt on S]	+190

Mileage Category: M

There are no major changes for the Axiom this year.

2002

Body Styles	TMV Pricing			Body Styles	TMV Pricing		
	Trade	Private	Dealer		Trade	Private	Dealer
4 Dr STD 4WD SUV	14075	15437	17707	4 Dr XS 4WD SUV	15164	16632	19078
4 Dr STD SUV	12846	14089	16161	4 Dr XS SUV	13954	15304	17555

Options	Price
Leather Seats [Std on XS]	+426
Power Moonroof [Std on XS]	+428

Mileage Category: M

Debuting this year as Isuzu's fifth sport-ute model, the Axiom attempts to blend the rugged nature of a sport-utility with the style and driving dynamics of a sedan. It features a retuned version of the Trooper's 3.5-liter V6, Isuzu's Torque On Demand (TOD) four-wheel-drive system, an Integrated Monitor System (IMS) that controls both the climate control and audio systems and a trick trip computer synchronized with the U.S. Atomic clock.

Isuzu
Hombre
2000

Body Styles	TMV Pricing			Body Styles	TMV Pricing		
	Trade	Private	Dealer		Trade	Private	Dealer
2 Dr S 4WD Std Cab SB	6469	7877	9257	2 Dr XS 4WD Ext Cab SB	7722	9403	11050
2 Dr S Ext Cab SB	4959	6038	7096	2 Dr XS Ext Cab SB	5948	7242	8511
2 Dr S Std Cab SB	4571	5566	6541	2 Dr XS Std Cab SB	4832	5883	6914
2 Dr S V6 4WD Ext Cab SB	6770	8244	9688	2 Dr XS V6 Ext Cab SB	6426	7825	9196
2 Dr S V6 Ext Cab SB	6067	7388	8682				

Options	Price	Options	Price
Air Conditioning [Opt on S,S V6]	+373	AM/FM/CD Audio System	+215
Aluminum/Alloy Wheels [Opt on 2WD,XS V6]	+196	Automatic 4-Speed Transmission [Opt on S,XS]	+419
AM/FM/Cassette Audio System [Opt on S,S V6,Std Cab]	+149	Hinged Third Door	+147

Mileage Category: J

Hombres receive an upgraded standard suspension package and V6 engines get a horsepower boost. The three-door Spacecab gets a bare-bones S trim model.

Isuzu
Hombre/Oasis

1999
Mileage Category: J

Hombres receive additional exterior colors and a new bumper fascia. A three-door spacecab model is now available.

Body Styles	TMV Pricing		
	Trade	Private	Dealer
2 Dr S 4WD Std Cab SB	4918	6080	7289
2 Dr S Std Cab SB	3581	4427	5307
2 Dr XS 4WD Ext Cab SB	6356	7857	9420

Body Styles	TMV Pricing		
	Trade	Private	Dealer
2 Dr XS Ext Cab SB	4910	6070	7277
2 Dr XS Std Cab SB	3924	4851	5816
2 Dr XS V6 Ext Cab SB	5537	6845	8206

Options	Price
Air Conditioning	+288
Aluminum/Alloy Wheels [Std on 4WD]	+152
AM/FM/Cassette Audio System	+115

Options	Price
AM/FM/CD Audio System	+167
Automatic 4-Speed Transmission [Std on XS V6]	+324

1998
Mileage Category: J

Four-wheel drive arrives, finally. Also new are a theft-deterrent system and dual airbags housed in a revised instrument panel, with a passenger-side airbag cutoff switch so the kiddies can ride up front.

Body Styles	TMV Pricing		
	Trade	Private	Dealer
2 Dr S 4WD Std Cab SB	4297	5373	6586
2 Dr S Std Cab SB	3150	3938	4827
2 Dr XS 4WD Ext Cab SB	5518	6899	8457

Body Styles	TMV Pricing		
	Trade	Private	Dealer
2 Dr XS Ext Cab SB	4130	5164	6329
2 Dr XS Std Cab SB	3239	4050	4964
2 Dr XS V6 Ext Cab SB	4562	5704	6992

Options	Price
Air Conditioning	+222
Automatic 4-Speed Transmission [Std on XS V6]	+285

1997
Mileage Category: J

A Spacecab model debuts, with seating for five passengers and your choice of four-cylinder or V6 power. Other news includes two fresh paint colors and revised graphics.

Body Styles	TMV Pricing		
	Trade	Private	Dealer
2 Dr S Std Cab SB	2715	3444	4334
2 Dr XS Ext Cab SB	3465	4395	5531

Body Styles	TMV Pricing		
	Trade	Private	Dealer
2 Dr XS Std Cab SB	2768	3511	4418
2 Dr XS V6 Ext Cab SB	3763	4773	6007

Options	Price
Air Conditioning	+187
Automatic 4-Speed Transmission [Opt on S,XS]	+219

1996
Mileage Category: J

Isuzu clones a Chevy S-10 and dumps its Japanese-built compact truck. Sheet metal is unique to Isuzu, but everything else is pure General Motors.

Body Styles	TMV Pricing		
	Trade	Private	Dealer
2 Dr S Std Cab SB	2245	2902	3809
2 Dr XS Std Cab SB	2439	3153	4139

Options	Price
Air Conditioning	+159

Isuzu
Oasis
1999

Body Styles	TMV Pricing		
	Trade	Private	Dealer
4 Dr S Pass Van	6293	7649	9060

Options	Price
6 Passenger Seating	+582
AM/FM/CD Audio System	+142
Compact Disc Changer	+171
Power Sunroof	+288

Mileage Category: P

Only one trim level is available for 1999. Oasis has a new seating arrangement, interior and exterior refinements and a couple of new colors.

1998

Body Styles	TMV Pricing		
	Trade	Private	Dealer
4 Dr LS Pass Van	5341	6599	8018
4 Dr S Pass Van	5074	6269	7616

Options	Price
AM/FM/CD Audio System	+125
Compact Disc Changer	+150

Mileage Category: P

The engine is upgraded to a more sophisticated 2.3-liter, good for an extra 10 horsepower and 7 pound-feet of torque, and the transmission is revised. A tachometer is now standard, so you can better measure all that extra power.

1997

Body Styles	TMV Pricing		
	Trade	Private	Dealer
4 Dr LS Pass Van	4808	6024	7510
4 Dr S Pass Van	4421	5539	6905

Mileage Category: P

Cruise control is added to the S model's standard equipment list, and four new colors are available.

1996

Body Styles	TMV Pricing		
	Trade	Private	Dealer
4 Dr LS Pass Van	4342	5401	6863
4 Dr S Pass Van	3835	4770	6060

Mileage Category: P

New Isuzu minivan is a clone of the Honda Odyssey, except for the grille, badging and wheels. The Isuzu offers a better warranty, too.

Isuzu
Pickup

1995

Body Styles	TMV Pricing		
	Trade	Private	Dealer
2 Dr S 4WD Std Cab SB	2349	3063	4253
2 Dr S Std Cab LB	1689	2202	3057
2 Dr S Std Cab SB	1556	2029	2817

Options	Price
Air Conditioning	+139

Mileage Category: J

Spacecab, V6 power and automatic transmission are canceled for 1995. All that's left are four-cylinder regular-cab trucks in 2WD or 4WD. California didn't get any 1995 pickups, thanks to strict emissions regulations.

1994

Body Styles	TMV Pricing			Body Styles	TMV Pricing		
	Trade	Private	Dealer		Trade	Private	Dealer
2 Dr S 2.6 Ext Cab SB	1496	2057	2992	2 Dr S Ext Cab SB	1496	2057	2992
2 Dr S 2.6 Std Cab SB	1249	1717	2498	2 Dr S Std Cab LB	1279	1759	2558
2 Dr S 4WD Std Cab SB	1690	2324	3381	2 Dr STD Std Cab SB	1117	1536	2234

Options	Price
3.1L V6 OHV 12V FI Engine	+141
Air Conditioning	+131

Mileage Category: J

Vent windows are dropped. Models with 2.6-liter engine get standard power steering. Outside mirrors are revised.

Isuzu
Rodeo

2003

Body Styles	TMV Pricing		
	Trade	Private	Dealer
4 Dr S SUV	8245	9023	10319
4 Dr S V6 4WD SUV	11526	12613	14425
4 Dr S V6 SUV	10706	11716	13399

2003 (cont'd)

Options	Price
Air Conditioning	+531
Aluminum/Alloy Wheels [Opt on V6]	+258
Automatic 4-Speed Transmission [Opt on S,V6 4WD]	+644
Leather Seats [Opt on V6]	+512
Power Door Locks [Opt on V6]	+138
Power Driver Seat [Opt on V6]	+196

Options	Price
Power Moonroof [Opt on V6]	+451
Power Windows [Opt on V6]	+177
Running Boards	+213
Side Steps	+206
AM/FM/Cassette/CD Changer Audio System [Opt on V6]	+271
AM/FM/CD Changer Audio System [Opt on V6]	+225

Mileage Category: M

Rodeo receives no major changes for the 2003 model year.

2002
Mileage Category: M

For 2002, Isuzu has fiddled with the Rodeo's option packages and improved the available Intelligent Suspension Control (ISC) system.

Body Styles	TMV Pricing		
	Trade	Private	Dealer
4 Dr LS 4WD SUV	11877	13026	14942
4 Dr LS SUV	10662	11694	13414
4 Dr LSE 4WD SUV	12106	13278	15230
4 Dr LSE SUV	11938	13093	15019

Body Styles	TMV Pricing		
	Trade	Private	Dealer
4 Dr S SUV	6788	7445	8540
4 Dr S V6 4WD SUV	9611	10541	12092
4 Dr S V6 SUV	9530	10453	11990

Options	Price
18 Inch Wheels - Chrome [Opt on LS 4WD]	+392
Air Conditioning [Opt on S,S V6]	+452
Aluminum/Alloy Wheels [Opt on LS]	+190
Automatic 4-Speed Transmission [Opt on S,S V6]	+475
Electronic Suspension Control [Opt on LS 4WD]	+357

Options	Price
Power Moonroof [Opt on LS]	+333
Power Windows [Opt on S V6]	+131
Running Boards	+157
Side Steps	+119

2001
Mileage Category: M

An Anniversary Edition trim package that includes two-tone paint, leather seating and special chrome wheels is the only addition to 2001 Rodeos.

Body Styles	TMV Pricing		
	Trade	Private	Dealer
4 Dr LS 4WD SUV	8741	10074	11304
4 Dr LS SUV	7863	9062	10168
4 Dr LSE 4WD SUV	10548	12156	13640
4 Dr LSE SUV	8946	10310	11569

Body Styles	TMV Pricing		
	Trade	Private	Dealer
4 Dr S SUV	5896	6795	7624
4 Dr S V6 4WD SUV	8019	9242	10370
4 Dr S V6 SUV	7657	8824	9902

Options	Price
Air Conditioning [Std on LS,LSE]	+382
Aluminum/Alloy Wheels [Std on LS,LSE]	+161
AM/FM/Cassette/CD Changer Audio System [Opt on LS]	+142
Automatic 4-Speed Transmission [Std on LSE]	+402
Leather Seats [Opt on LS]	+402

Options	Price
Nakamichi Audio System [Opt on LS]	+362
Power Moonroof [Opt on LS]	+281
Power Windows [Opt on S]	+121
Running Boards	+145
Two-Tone Paint [Opt on LS]	+121

2000
Mileage Category: M

The Rodeo marches into the 2000 model year with an aggressive exterior restyle, a collection of ergonomic and quality improvements and interior upgrades.

Body Styles	TMV Pricing		
	Trade	Private	Dealer
4 Dr LS 4WD SUV	7647	9040	10406
4 Dr LS SUV	6876	8128	9356
4 Dr LSE 4WD SUV	9126	10788	12418
4 Dr LSE SUV	7789	9208	10599

Body Styles	TMV Pricing		
	Trade	Private	Dealer
4 Dr S SUV	5174	6117	7041
4 Dr S V6 4WD SUV	6926	8188	9425
4 Dr S V6 SUV	6008	7102	8175

Options	Price
Side Steps	+139
Air Conditioning [Std on LS,LSE]	+373
AM/FM/Cassette/CD Audio System	+167
AM/FM/CD Audio System	+145
Automatic 4-Speed Transmission [Std on LSE]	+392

Options	Price
Compact Disc Changer [Std on LSE]	+254
Ironman Package	+412
Power Moonroof [Opt on LS]	+274
Running Boards	+141

1999

Body Styles	TMV Pricing		
	Trade	Private	Dealer
4 Dr LS 4WD SUV	6197	7542	8942
4 Dr LS SUV	5519	6717	7964
4 Dr LSE 4WD SUV	7152	8704	10320
4 Dr LSE SUV	6485	7892	9357

Body Styles	TMV Pricing		
	Trade	Private	Dealer
4 Dr S SUV	4193	5103	6051
4 Dr S V6 4WD SUV	5634	6857	8129
4 Dr S V6 SUV	4875	5933	7034

Options	Price
Air Conditioning [Std on LS,LSE]	+288
AM/FM/Cassette/CD Audio System	+129
Automatic 4-Speed Transmission [Std on LSE 4WD]	+303

Options	Price
Compact Disc Changer	+197
Power Moonroof [Opt on LS]	+212

Mileage Category: M

Isuzu juggles minor standard and optional equipment for 1999, making items from last year's S V6 preferred equipment package standard on the LS, and last year's LS equipment standard on a new trim level called LSE.

1998

Body Styles	TMV Pricing		
	Trade	Private	Dealer
4 Dr LS 4WD SUV	5363	6681	8168
4 Dr LS SUV	4705	5861	7165
4 Dr S SUV	3192	3976	4861

Body Styles	TMV Pricing		
	Trade	Private	Dealer
4 Dr S V6 4WD SUV	4111	5122	6261
4 Dr S V6 SUV	3709	4620	5648

Options	Price
Air Conditioning [Std on LS]	+253
Automatic 4-Speed Transmission [Std on LS]	+266
Compact Disc Changer	+173

Options	Price
Leather Seats	+265
Power Moonroof	+186

Mileage Category: M

Though it may not look like it, Isuzu has completely revised the Rodeo from top to bottom, giving it more modern styling, a user-friendly interior, more V6 power and added room for passengers and cargo.

1997

Body Styles	TMV Pricing		
	Trade	Private	Dealer
4 Dr LS 4WD SUV	3834	4818	6020
4 Dr LS SUV	3642	4576	5717
4 Dr S SUV	2504	3147	3932

Body Styles	TMV Pricing		
	Trade	Private	Dealer
4 Dr S V6 4WD SUV	3267	4105	5129
4 Dr S V6 SUV	2975	3738	4671

Options	Price
Air Conditioning [Std on LS]	+213
Antilock Brakes	+179
Automatic 4-Speed Transmission [Opt on 4WD,S V6]	+217

Options	Price
Compact Disc Changer	+145
Leather Seats	+267

Mileage Category: M

All 4WD models get a standard shift-on-the-fly transfer case, and improvements have been made to reduce noise, vibration and harshness.

1996

Body Styles	TMV Pricing		
	Trade	Private	Dealer
4 Dr LS 4WD SUV	3343	4218	5427
4 Dr LS SUV	3248	4099	5273
4 Dr S SUV	2242	2829	3639

Body Styles	TMV Pricing		
	Trade	Private	Dealer
4 Dr S V6 4WD SUV	2898	3657	4704
4 Dr S V6 SUV	2643	3334	4289

Options	Price
Air Conditioning [Std on LS]	+180
Aluminum/Alloy Wheels [Std on LS]	+152
Antilock Brakes	+152

Options	Price
Automatic 4-Speed Transmission [Opt on 4WD,S V6]	+184
Compact Disc Changer	+124
Leather Seats	+227

Mileage Category: M

Finally, Isuzu's Rodeo can be equipped with four-wheel antilock brakes, and 4WD models get a standard shift-on-the-fly system. New style wheels debut, and the engine now makes 190 horsepower. Increased wheel track improves ride quality, and spare tire covers are redesigned.

1995

Body Styles	TMV Pricing		
	Trade	Private	Dealer
4 Dr LS 4WD SUV	2718	3475	4736
4 Dr LS SUV	2528	3232	4405
4 Dr S 4WD SUV	2291	2929	3992

Body Styles	TMV Pricing		
	Trade	Private	Dealer
4 Dr S SUV	1792	2292	3124
4 Dr S V6 SUV	2151	2750	3748

Mileage Category: M

Midyear change gives the Rodeo driver and passenger airbags in a redesigned dashboard. S V6 models can be equipped with a Bright Package that includes lots of chrome trim and aluminum wheels.

Isuzu
Rodeo/Rodeo Sport

1995 (cont'd)

Options	Price
Air Conditioning [Std on LS]	+165
Antilock Brakes	+139

Options	Price
Automatic 4-Speed Transmission [Opt on 4WD,S,S V6]	+168
Compact Disc Changer	+113

1994
Mileage Category: M

S model gets standard power steering. LS models are equipped with standard air conditioning. Front vent windows are dropped. All V6 models come with standard rear wiper/washer and tailgate spare tire carrier.

Body Styles	TMV Pricing		
	Trade	Private	Dealer
4 Dr LS 4WD SUV	2287	3046	4311
4 Dr LS SUV	2129	2836	4013
4 Dr S 4WD SUV	1845	2458	3479

Body Styles	TMV Pricing		
	Trade	Private	Dealer
4 Dr S SUV	1426	1900	2689
4 Dr S V6 SUV	1639	2184	3091

Options	Price
Air Conditioning [Std on LS]	+156
Automatic 4-Speed Transmission [Opt on 4WD,S,S V6]	+159

Isuzu
Rodeo Sport

2003

Mileage Category: L

Isuzu's two-door Rodeo Sport SUV is unchanged for 2003.

Body Styles	TMV Pricing		
	Trade	Private	Dealer
2 Dr S Conv	8440	9350	10866
2 Dr S SUV	8926	9888	11491

Body Styles	TMV Pricing		
	Trade	Private	Dealer
2 Dr S V6 4WD SUV	10375	11493	13356
2 Dr S V6 SUV	9529	10556	12267

Options	Price
AM/FM/CD Changer Audio System [Opt on S V6]	+217
AM/FM/Tape/CD Changer Audio System [Opt on S V6]	+217
Air Conditioning	+461
Alarm System [Opt on S V6]	+116
Aluminum/Alloy Wheels	+261

Options	Price
Automatic 4-Speed Transmission [Opt on S Utility]	+580
Power Door Locks [Opt on S V6]	+119
Power Windows [Opt on S V6]	+136
Side Steps	+186
Trailer Hitch	+130

2002
Mileage Category: L

Other than new 16-inch wheels, Isuzu's two-door Rodeo Sport SUV is unchanged for 2002.

Body Styles	TMV Pricing		
	Trade	Private	Dealer
2 Dr S Conv	7049	7909	9341
2 Dr S SUV	6962	7811	9227
2 Dr S V6 4WD Conv	10055	11281	13325

Body Styles	TMV Pricing		
	Trade	Private	Dealer
2 Dr S V6 4WD SUV	8588	9636	11382
2 Dr S V6 Conv	7950	8920	10536
2 Dr S V6 SUV	7896	8859	10464

Options	Price
Air Conditioning	+378
Aluminum/Alloy Wheels	+214
AM/FM/Cassette/CD Changer Audio System [Opt on S V6]	+178

Options	Price
AM/FM/CD Changer Audio System [Opt on S V6]	+178
Automatic 4-Speed Transmission [Opt on S 2 Dr]	+475
Side Steps	+152

2001
Mileage Category: L

Formerly the Amigo, Isuzu's two-door sport-ute gets a name change and two new colors. A wheezing four-cylinder automatic with either a hard- or soft top is also new for 2001.

Body Styles	TMV Pricing		
	Trade	Private	Dealer
2 Dr STD Conv	5664	6809	7866
2 Dr STD SUV	5453	6555	7573
2 Dr V6 4WD Conv	7135	8577	9909

Body Styles	TMV Pricing		
	Trade	Private	Dealer
2 Dr V6 4WD SUV	7137	8579	9911
2 Dr V6 Conv	6470	7778	8986
2 Dr V6 SUV	6379	7669	8859

Options	Price
Air Conditioning	+382
Aluminum/Alloy Wheels	+161
AM/FM/Cassette/CD Changer Audio System [Opt on V6]	+142

Options	Price
Automatic 4-Speed Transmission [Std on V6]	+402
Power Windows	+121
Running Boards	+143

2002

Body Styles	TMV Pricing		
	Trade	Private	Dealer
4 Dr LS 4WD SUV	13071	14336	16444
4 Dr LS SUV	12680	13907	15953
4 Dr Limited 4WD SUV	15506	17007	19508

Body Styles	TMV Pricing		
	Trade	Private	Dealer
4 Dr Limited SUV	15039	16494	18920
4 Dr S 4WD SUV	11310	12405	14229
4 Dr S SUV	10267	11261	12917

Options	Price
Automatic 4-Speed Transmission [Opt on S 4WD]	+404
Rear Spoiler [Opt on Limited]	+159
Running Boards [Opt on LS,S]	+152

Options	Price
Side Steps [Opt on LS,S]	+152
Special Factory Paint [Opt on Limited]	+250

Mileage Category: M

The flagship of the Isuzu line, the Trooper, receives minor changes for 2002. Privacy glass and solar green UV-cut glass are now standard for S models, and Trooper's famous extra-large power moonroof is now standard for the LS. Manual climate control and map lamps are now standard on S models, while LS models feature a new standard digital clock with outside temperature read-out, stop watch, average speed and service reminder. The Limited model now offers a Nakamichi premium audio system.

2001

Body Styles	TMV Pricing		
	Trade	Private	Dealer
4 Dr LS 4WD SUV	10493	12093	13569
4 Dr LS SUV	9966	11485	12888
4 Dr Limited 4WD SUV	11771	13565	15221

Body Styles	TMV Pricing		
	Trade	Private	Dealer
4 Dr Limited SUV	11053	12738	14293
4 Dr S 4WD SUV	9339	10763	12077
4 Dr S SUV	9098	10485	11765

Options	Price
Automatic 4-Speed Transmission [Opt on S]	+623
Leather Seats [Opt on LS]	+493
Nakamichi Audio System [Opt on LS]	+362

Options	Price
Pearlescent Metallic Paint	+181
Power Moonroof [Opt on LS]	+442
Running Boards	+136

Mileage Category: M

An Anniversary package commemorating Isuzu's 85th year is the only new option for 2001 Troopers.

2000

Body Styles	TMV Pricing		
	Trade	Private	Dealer
4 Dr LS 4WD SUV	8827	10435	12011
4 Dr LS SUV	8181	9671	11132
4 Dr Limited 4WD SUV	9859	11655	13416

Body Styles	TMV Pricing		
	Trade	Private	Dealer
4 Dr Limited SUV	9565	11307	13015
4 Dr S 4WD SUV	7803	9225	10618
4 Dr S SUV	7711	9115	10492

Options	Price
AM/FM/Cassette/CD Audio System	+245
AM/FM/CD Audio System	+215
Automatic 4-Speed Transmission [Opt on S]	+588
Compact Disc Changer [Opt on S]	+254

Options	Price
Power Moonroof [Opt on LS]	+431
Running Boards	+133
Side Steps	+133

Mileage Category: M

A two-wheel-drive model is available in the S trim, as well as the new midlevel LS and top-level Limited guises; all receive slight exterior restyling. The 10-year/120,000-mile powertrain warranty, the longest in America, ensures longevity.

1999

Body Styles		TMV Pricing		
		Trade	Private	Dealer
4 Dr S 4WD SUV		6064	7380	8750

Options	Price
AM/FM/Cassette/CD Audio System	+190
AM/FM/CD Audio System	+167
Automatic 4-Speed Transmission	+424

Options	Price
Compact Disc Changer	+197
Leather Seats	+379
Power Moonroof	+333

Mileage Category: M

A gold trim package is added to the Trooper's option list and Torque on Demand is now standard with the automatic transmission.

1998

Body Styles		TMV Pricing		
		Trade	Private	Dealer
4 Dr Luxury 4WD SUV		6345	7905	9664
4 Dr S 4WD SUV		5305	6609	8079

Mileage Category: M

A bigger and lighter engine provides huge improvements in horsepower and torque (up 13 and 22 percent, respectively). And the new Torque On Demand (TOD) drive system replaces conventional four-high mode for better performance on paved or slippery roads.

Trooper

1998 (cont'd)

Options	Price
AM/FM/Cassette/CD Audio System	+166
AM/FM/CD Audio System	+147
Automatic 4-Speed Transmission [Opt on S]	+370
Compact Disc Changer [Opt on S]	+173

Options	Price
Leather Seats [Opt on S]	+318
Performance/Handling Package	+296
Power Moonroof [Opt on S]	+325

1997
Mileage Category: M

Antilock brakes are now standard on all models, and dealers get a wider profit margin to help increase sales. Despite delirious requests by a certain consumer group, Isuzu will not equip the Trooper with training wheels for 1997.

Body Styles	TMV Pricing		
	Trade	Private	Dealer
4 Dr LS 4WD SUV	5086	6391	7986
4 Dr Limited 4WD SUV	5456	6856	8567
4 Dr S 4WD SUV	4668	5865	7329

Options	Price
Air Conditioning [Opt on S]	+179
AM/FM/CD Audio System	+123
Automatic 4-Speed Transmission [Opt on S]	+280

Options	Price
Compact Disc Changer [Opt on S]	+145
Leather Seats [Opt on LS]	+280
Power Moonroof [Opt on LS]	+246

1996
Mileage Category: M

More standard equipment, a horsepower boost for the SOHC V6 engine, and standard shift-on-the-fly debut for 1996.

Body Styles	TMV Pricing		
	Trade	Private	Dealer
4 Dr LS 4WD SUV	4125	5205	6696
4 Dr Limited 4WD SUV	4955	6252	8043

Body Styles	TMV Pricing		
	Trade	Private	Dealer
4 Dr S 4WD SUV	3686	4651	5984
4 Dr SE 4WD SUV	5135	6479	8335

Options	Price
Power Moonroof [Opt on LS]	+209
Air Conditioning [Opt on S]	+152
Antilock Brakes [Opt on LS,S]	+228

Options	Price
Automatic 4-Speed Transmission [Opt on S]	+237
Compact Disc Changer [Opt on LS,S]	+124
Leather Seats [Opt on LS]	+237

1995
Mileage Category: M

Dual airbags are standard. Styling is revised. A new top-of-the-line trim level debuts. The Limited has a power sunroof, leather upholstery, heated seats and wood grain trim. Suspensions have been reworked to provide a better ride.

Body Styles	TMV Pricing		
	Trade	Private	Dealer
2 Dr RS 4WD SUV	3311	4234	5771
4 Dr LS 4WD SUV	3330	4257	5803
4 Dr Limited 4WD SUV	3978	5086	6933

Body Styles	TMV Pricing		
	Trade	Private	Dealer
4 Dr S 4WD SUV	3059	3911	5331
4 Dr SE 4WD SUV	3938	5035	6864

Options	Price
Air Conditioning [Opt on S]	+139
Aluminum/Alloy Wheels [Opt on S]	+80
AM/FM/CD Audio System	+95
Antilock Brakes [Opt on S]	+208

Options	Price
Automatic 4-Speed Transmission [Opt on LS,S,RS]	+217
Compact Disc Changer [Opt on S,SE]	+113
Premium Audio System [Opt on S]	+78

1994
Mileage Category: M

Four-wheel ABS filters down to the Trooper S options sheet. Gray leather upholstery is a new option for the LS model, and it includes heated front seats with power adjustments. RS gets new alloys.

Body Styles	TMV Pricing		
	Trade	Private	Dealer
2 Dr RS 4WD SUV	2449	3262	4617
4 Dr LS 4WD SUV	2672	3559	5038

Body Styles	TMV Pricing		
	Trade	Private	Dealer
4 Dr S 4WD SUV	2054	2736	3873
4 Dr SE 4WD SUV	3238	4313	6104

Options	Price
Power Sunroof [Opt on LS]	+94
Air Conditioning [Opt on S]	+131
Aluminum/Alloy Wheels	+75
AM/FM/Cassette/CD Audio System	+102

Options	Price
AM/FM/CD Audio System	+90
Antilock Brakes [Opt on S]	+197
Automatic 4-Speed Transmission [Std on SE]	+205
Leather Seats [Opt on LS]	+205

2001

Body Styles	TMV Pricing		
	Trade	Private	Dealer
2 Dr STD 4WD SUV	12073	13913	15612

Mileage Category: M

Rear child seat-tether anchors are the only new additions for 2001.

2000

Body Styles	TMV Pricing		
	Trade	Private	Dealer
2 Dr STD 4WD SUV	9624	11377	13096

Options	Price
Ironman Package	+390

Mileage Category: M

Fat 18-inch wheels replace the previous 16-inchers. The new year also brings standard A/C, new exterior colors and a 10-year/120,000-mile powertrain warranty, the longest in America.

1999

Body Styles	TMV Pricing		
	Trade	Private	Dealer
2 Dr STD 4WD SUV	7771	9458	11213

Options	Price
Ironman Package	+302

Mileage Category: M

Isuzu imports its unique-looking SUV to the U.S. in 1999.

Jaguar
S-Type

2003

Body Styles		TMV Pricing	
	Trade	Private	Dealer
4 Dr 3.0 Sdn	27689	29189	31688
4 Dr 4.2 Sdn	32879	34660	37627

Options	Price	Options	Price
Alpine Audio System	+1202	Power Adjustable Foot Pedals [Opt on 3.0]	+167
Automatic Dimming Rearview Mirror [Opt on 3.0]	+120	Automatic 6-Speed Transmission [Opt on 3.0]	+922
Heated Front and Rear Seats	+334	Automatic Dimming Sideview Mirror(s) [Opt on 3.0]	+134
Navigation System	+1469	Voice Recognition System	+1503
Power Moonroof [Opt on 3.0]	+735	Power Driver Seat w/Memory [Opt on 3.0]	+167
Sport Package	+1336		

Mileage Category: I

For the 2003 S-Type, Jaguar has redesigned the interior, upgraded its hardware and added models to the range. The model lineup includes the S-Type 3.0 SE and 3.0 Sport, 4.2 V8 and the supercharged R. A new five-speed manual transmission is attached to the 3.0-liter V6 this year, while a new six-speed automatic transmission puts V8 power to the rear wheels. The suspension is also new in front and heavily revised in the rear. New standard safety features include stability control, panic assist brakes, anti-whiplash front seats, dual-stage front airbags, side curtain airbags for front and rear occupants and power adjustable pedals with a memory feature. Jaguar has also stiffened the body structure, made slight revisions to the exterior styling and added xenon headlights as an option (standard on the R). Audiophiles can opt for the 320-watt Alpine sound system, and technology buffs will appreciate the new touchscreen telematics system with improved voice recognition.

2002

Mileage Category: I

Jaguar's standard S-Type model comes tinted in three new hues for 2002: Aspen Green, Quartz and Zircon. The car also features a nifty new enhancement with regard to its cupholders: rear cupholders now deploy from the rear-seat cushion, putting them in a more easily accessed position for passengers. The manufacturer tosses performance hounds a tasty new bone with the addition of an S-Type Sport trim level, which comes with a choice of either a 3.0-liter V6 or 4.0-liter V8 engine. Its suspension reflects its performance aspirations; Computer Active Technology Suspension (CATS) ramps up handling with shock-absorber settings that automatically adjust to reflect road conditions. Additionally, a brand-new shade -- Pacific Blue -- is available only in Sport.

Body Styles		TMV Pricing	
	Trade	Private	Dealer
4 Dr 3.0 Sdn	23195	24799	27471
4 Dr 4.0 Sdn	25621	27393	30345

Options	Price	Options	Price
17 Inch Wheels	+444	Power Driver Seat w/Memory [Opt on 3.0]	+130
Automatic Stability Control	+296	Power Moonroof [Opt on 3.0]	+562
Electronic Suspension Control	+266	Premium Audio System [Opt on 3.0]	+888
Heated Front Seats	+169	Telematic System	+414
Navigation System	+1125		

2001

Mileage Category: I

The S-Type gets new 10-spoke alloy wheels for 2001, along with exterior color options Onyx White and Roman Bronze. The folks at Jaguar have decided to move the six-disc CD changer from the glovebox to the trunk. ISOFIX is added to the rear for securing child seats and Reverse Park Control now comes standard. An electronically controlled, speed-proportional power steering system is new this year and the software for the Voice Activation Control system has been upgraded. A Deluxe Communications Package featuring a Motorola Timeport digital phone system is a new option.

Body Styles		TMV Pricing	
	Trade	Private	Dealer
4 Dr 3.0 Sdn	20338	22471	24440
4 Dr 4.0 Sdn	21857	24149	26265

Options	Price	Options	Price
17 Inch Wheels	+256	Navigation System	+972
Automatic Stability Control [Opt on 3.0]	+256	Power Moonroof [Opt on 3.0]	+486
Compact Disc Changer	+409	Premium Audio System [Opt on 3.0]	+767
Electronic Suspension Control	+230	Sport Package	+563
Heated Front Seats	+146		

2000

Mileage Category: I

From the ground up, this is a completely new sport sedan based on the new Ford midsize platform. Lincoln worked with Jaguar to develop this platform, which is also used for Lincoln's LS sedan.

Body Styles		TMV Pricing	
	Trade	Private	Dealer
4 Dr 3.0 Sdn	17492	19573	21612
4 Dr 4.0 Sdn	17873	19999	22083

Options	Price	Options	Price
Automatic Stability Control	+213	Power Driver Seat w/Memory [Opt on 3.0]	+128
Compact Disc Changer	+341	Power Moonroof [Opt on 3.0]	+405
Heated Front Seats	+121	Power Passenger Seat w/Memory [Opt on 3.0]	+128
Navigation System	+809	Premium Audio System	+298
Park Distance Control (Rear)	+170	Sport Package	+445

Jaguar
S-Type R
2003

Body Styles	TMV Pricing		
	Trade	Private	Dealer
4 Dr S/C Sdn	43872	46248	50208

Options	Price	Options	Price
Navigation System	+1469	Voice Recognition System	+1503

Mileage Category: I

The muscle-bound S-Type R debuts. The S-Type R is the most powerful Jaguar sedan ever created, making about 400 horsepower and moving from rest to 60 mph in 5.3 seconds. A new six-speed automatic transmission puts the considerable power to the rear wheels. This super cat also benefits from the upgrades that all S-Types received this year, namely a revamped cabin, revised suspension and more safety features. Technology buffs will appreciate the new touchscreen telematics system with improved voice recognition.

Jaguar
X-Type
2003

Body Styles	TMV Pricing		
	Trade	Private	Dealer
4 Dr 2.5 AWD Sdn	18986	20349	22621

Options	Price
Alpine Audio System	+367
AM/FM/CD Audio System [Opt on 2.5]	+134
Automatic Stability Control	+267
Compact Disc Changer	+401
Heated Front Seats	+200
Navigation System	+1469
Power Moonroof	+601
Power Passenger Seat	+217
Rear Spoiler	+150

Body Styles	TMV Pricing		
	Trade	Private	Dealer
4 Dr 3.0 AWD Sdn	22337	23941	26613

Options	Price
Special Factory Paint	+384
Split Folding Rear Seat	+184
Sport Seats	+177
Sport Suspension	+184
Telematic System	+1102
17 Inch Wheels [Opt on 2.5]	+301
18 Inch Wheels	+2004
Park Distance Control (Rear)	+200

Mileage Category: H

Jaguar introduced its youth-oriented X-Type last year, so 2003 holds little changes for the baby Jag. There's a slight reduction in the price of the base model, and electrochromic mirrors are standard on all trim levels. Cars equipped with the 3.0-liter mill now get 17-inch wheels and a CD player as standard equipment.

2002

Body Styles	TMV Pricing		
	Trade	Private	Dealer
4 Dr 2.5 AWD Sdn	16965	18314	20563

Options	Price
17 Inch Wheels	+266
Alpine Audio System	+326
AM/FM/CD Audio System	+118
Automatic 5-Speed Transmission [Opt on 2.5]	+755
Automatic Stability Control	+237
Compact Disc Changer	+355
Heated Front Seats	+192
Metallic Paint	+326
Navigation System	+1302

Body Styles	TMV Pricing		
	Trade	Private	Dealer
4 Dr 3.0 AWD Sdn	19430	20975	23550

Options	Price
Park Distance Control (Rear)	+237
Power Moonroof	+533
Power Passenger Seat	+192
Rear Spoiler	+133
Split Folding Rear Seat	+163
Sport Seats	+157
Sport Suspension	+163
Telematic System	+888

Mileage Category: H

Jaguar beefs up its presence in the luxury category with the X-Type, a brand-new model that brings the company's range to four. The X-Type is a fresh breed of cat for the manufacturer: it's Jaguar's first-ever all-wheel-drive vehicle, and it's priced to tap the entry-luxury segment.

Jaguar
XJ-Series
2003

Body Styles	TMV Pricing		
	Trade	Private	Dealer
4 Dr Super V8 S/C Sdn	54479	57244	61851
4 Dr Vanden Plas Sdn	43572	45776	49448

Body Styles	TMV Pricing		
	Trade	Private	Dealer
4 Dr XJ Sport Sdn	35386	37176	40159
4 Dr XJ8 Sdn	33469	35161	37982

Jaguar
XJ-Series

2003 (cont'd)

Options	Price
Alpine Audio System [Opt on XJ,XJ8]	+217
Heated Front and Rear Seats [Opt on XJ,XJ8]	+334
Navigation System [Opt on Vanden Plas]	+1135

Mileage Category: I

In its final year of production, the current-generation XJ receives two new packages. XJ8s have the option of the Sovereign Package, offered with an Alpine premium sound system and six-disc changer, heated front and rear seats, wood and leather steering wheel and gearshift knob, boxwood-inlaid walnut trim, chrome grille and splitter, chrome mirror caps and door handles and special wheels. Meanwhile the XJR can be optioned with the R1 Performance Package, which includes Brembo brakes and 18-inch modular wheels.

2002

Mileage Category: I

A new XJ Sport trim debuts, which melds elements of the XJ8 and XJR. Additionally, the Vanden Plas Supercharged model -- previously available only on special order -- is now a regular-production sedan, called Super V8. The long-wheelbase XJ8L is discontinued.

Body Styles	TMV Pricing			Body Styles	TMV Pricing		
	Trade	Private	Dealer		Trade	Private	Dealer
4 Dr Super V8 S/C Sdn	49513	52090	56384	4 Dr XJ Sport Sdn	32249	33908	36673
4 Dr Vanden Plas Sdn	37081	39013	42232	4 Dr XJ8 Sdn	29086	30582	33076

Options	Price
Heated Front and Rear Seats [Opt on XJ8,XJ Sport]	+296
Navigation System	+1006
Premium Audio System [Opt on XJ8,XJ Sport]	+592

2001

Mileage Category: I

Jaguar's premium sedan receives only minor content changes for 2001. The XJ8 and XJ8 L both receive a six-disc CD changer as standard equipment. The Vanden Plas gets a premium sound system with the CD changer as standard, as well as heated front and rear seats. The navigation system is standard on the Vanden Plas Supercharged. For all models, Jaguar has added a new reverse parking control system and strengthened the chassis with new crush tubes, doors, hinges and steering columns. There are also new exterior colors, a new style of wheel for Vanden Plas models and an optional dealer-installed Motorola Timeport digital phone. Topping things off is a new no-cost scheduled maintenance program that covers four regular service visits under the four-year/50,000-mile limited warranty.

Body Styles	TMV Pricing			Body Styles	TMV Pricing		
	Trade	Private	Dealer		Trade	Private	Dealer
4 Dr Vanden Plas S/C Sdn	40509	43962	47149	4 Dr XJ8 Sdn	25060	27210	29195
4 Dr Vanden Plas Sdn	30610	33237	35661	4 Dr XJ8L Sdn	25462	27647	29663

Options	Price
Alpine Audio System [Opt on XJ8,XJ8L]	+512
Navigation System	+870

2000

Mileage Category: I

A fifth model -- the supercharged Vanden Plas -- has been added. All XJ8 Sedans gain all-speed traction control, improved ABS, rain-sensing windshield wipers, and child seat-anchor brackets as standard equipment. A new navigation system is being offered as optional equipment, as is an upgraded 320-watt Alpine system. The anti-theft system now has an encrypted key transponder. There are two new exterior colors and one new interior color.

The XJR gains all-speed traction control, improved ABS, rain-sensing windshield wipers, child seat-anchor brackets and an upgraded 320-watt Alpine system as standard equipment. A new navigation system is being offered as optional equipment. The anti-theft system now has an encrypted key transponder. The XJR also gets new 18-inch wheels and a different new style for the seats.

Body Styles	TMV Pricing			Body Styles	TMV Pricing		
	Trade	Private	Dealer		Trade	Private	Dealer
4 Dr Vanden Plas S/C Sdn	29129	31971	34757	4 Dr XJ8 Sdn	19994	21948	23864
4 Dr Vanden Plas Sdn	21607	23719	25790	4 Dr XJ8L Sdn	20227	22205	24143

Options	Price	Options	Price
Compact Disc Changer [Opt on Vanden Plas,XJ8,XJ8L]	+213	Heated Front and Rear Seats [Opt on Vanden Plas,XJ8,XJ8L]	+172
Harman Kardon Audio System [Opt on Vanden Plas,XJ8,XJ8L]	+490	Navigation System	+607

1999

Mileage Category: I

Jaguar's venerable XJ sedans enter '99 largely unchanged after a major workover in '98.

Body Styles	TMV Pricing			Body Styles	TMV Pricing		
	Trade	Private	Dealer		Trade	Private	Dealer
4 Dr Vanden Plas Sdn	18546	20796	23138	4 Dr XJ8L Sdn	17692	19839	22073
4 Dr XJ8 Sdn	16968	19027	21170				

1999 (cont'd)

Options	Price	Options	Price
Chrome Wheels	+302	Heated Front and Rear Seats [Opt on Vanden Plas,XJ8,XJ8L]	+133
Compact Disc Changer [Opt on Vanden Plas,XJ8,XJ8L]	+184	Traction Control System [Opt on Vanden Plas,XJ8,XJ8L]	+184
Harman Kardon Audio System [Opt on Vanden Plas,XJ8,XJ8L]	+422		

1998

Body Styles	TMV Pricing		
	Trade	Private	Dealer
4 Dr Vanden Plas Sdn	15044	17229	19693
4 Dr XJ8 Sdn	14254	16324	18659
4 Dr XJ8L Sdn	14784	16932	19354

Options	Price	Options	Price
Chrome Wheels	+259	Harman Kardon Audio System	+362
Compact Disc Changer	+158	Traction Control System	+158

Mileage Category: I

A new V8 engine, taken from the XK8 Coupe and Convertible, makes its way into the engine bay. A revised instrument panel greatly improves interior ergonomics. Cruise and satellite stereo controls are located on the steering wheel.

1997

Body Styles	TMV Pricing		
	Trade	Private	Dealer
4 Dr Vanden Plas Sdn	11055	12885	15121
4 Dr XJ6 Sdn	10379	12096	14195
4 Dr XJ6L Sdn	10805	12593	14779

Options	Price	Options	Price
Chrome Wheels	+203	Special Factory Paint	+127
Compact Disc Changer	+178	Traction Control System	+127
Harman Kardon Audio System	+279		

Mileage Category: I

The 1997 XJ-Series loses the V12 model that has been a mainstay of the Jaguar lineup for so many years. A long-wheelbase model becomes available this year, filling a niche between the XJ6 and the Vanden Plas. All models receive a contoured bench seat and three-point seatbelts for rear occupants. The XJ6 replaces last year's chrome-vane grille with a black-vane grille, and the convenience group becomes optional on this model.

1996

Body Styles	TMV Pricing			Body Styles	TMV Pricing		
	Trade	Private	Dealer		Trade	Private	Dealer
2 Dr XJS Conv	11636	13736	16637	4 Dr XJ12 Sdn	8510	10061	12203
4 Dr Vanden Plas Sdn	8888	10508	12745	4 Dr XJ6 Sdn	8516	10068	12212

Options	Price
Chrome Wheels	+155
Harman Kardon Audio System [Opt on Vanden Plas,XJ6]	+213

Mileage Category: I

On the XJ6, thicker side window glass insulates passengers from annoying wind noise and outside distractions. After a 20-year reign, the XJS coupe is put out to pasture. The only model offered for 1996 is the six-cylinder convertible; the most popular XJS in its unremarkable history. The changes for 1996 include new wheels, new bucket seats, additional chrome exterior trim and an adjustable wood-trimmed steering wheel.

1995

Body Styles	TMV Pricing			Body Styles	TMV Pricing		
	Trade	Private	Dealer		Trade	Private	Dealer
2 Dr XJS Conv	9217	10971	13895	4 Dr XJ12 Sdn	7464	8891	11268
2 Dr XJS Cpe	7240	8618	10915	4 Dr XJ6 Sdn	6980	8315	10539
2 Dr XJS V12 Conv	9863	11740	14869	4 Dr XJ6 Vanden Plas Sdn	7555	8999	11406
2 Dr XJS V12 Cpe	8566	10196	12913				

Options	Price	Options	Price
Chrome Wheels	+138	Power Sunroof	+156
Compact Disc Changer	+138	Special Factory Paint	+86
Harman Kardon Audio System [Opt on Vanden Plas,XJ6]	+173	Traction Control System	+86

Mileage Category: F

Horsepower is upped for naturally aspirated 4.0-liter engine, and inline-six and V12 engines. New sheet metal showcases a more traditional Jaguar; ironic considering the amount of input Ford had into the creation of this car. XJS V12 models get new wheels and a plethora of standard equipment such as heated seats and a multidisc CD changer.

Jaguar
XJ-Series/XJR

1994

Mileage Category: F

A passenger airbag joins the safety equipment roster. CFC-free air conditioning is added to the standard equipment list. For the XJS, a five-speed manual transmission is available as a new option for the 4.0-liter inline-six engine. An XJR-S derived XJ-S 6.0-liter V12 is available, they are differentiated by a rear spoiler, mirrors, grille and alloy wheels. The XJ-12 is available with a 301-horsepower engine and a four-speed automatic transmission.

Body Styles	TMV Pricing		
	Trade	Private	Dealer
2 Dr XJS Conv	7506	9177	11962
2 Dr XJS Cpe	5211	6371	8305
2 Dr XJS V12 Conv	7846	9593	12504
2 Dr XJS V12 Cpe	6543	8000	10427

Body Styles	TMV Pricing		
	Trade	Private	Dealer
4 Dr XJ12 Sdn	4787	5846	7611
4 Dr XJ6 Sdn	4548	5554	7231
4 Dr XJ6 Vanden Plas Sdn	5223	6378	8304

Options	Price
Dual Front Airbag Restraints	+194
Power Sunroof	+120
Sport Package	+108

Jaguar
XJR

2003

Body Styles	TMV Pricing		
	Trade	Private	Dealer
4 Dr S/C Sdn	45200	47494	51316

Options	Price
Performance/Handling Package	+1002

Mileage Category: F

In its final year of this generation, the XJR nonetheless gets a new option, the R1 Performance Package, which includes Brembo brakes and 18-inch modular wheels.

2002

Mileage Category: F

The XJR sees no changes as it nears the end of this generation's lifecycle.

Body Styles	TMV Pricing		
	Trade	Private	Dealer
4 Dr 100 S/C Sdn	51849	54547	59043
4 Dr S/C Sdn	41936	44074	47638

2001

Mileage Category: F

Jaguar's high-performance sedan receives only minor changes for 2001. Jaguar has added a new reverse parking control system and strengthened the chassis with new crush tubes, doors, hinges and steering columns. A heated rear seat and a premium audio system are now standard equipment, and there's a new optional dealer-installed Motorola Timeport digital phone. Topping things off is a no-cost scheduled maintenance program that covers four regular service visits under the four-year/50,000-mile limited warranty.

Body Styles	TMV Pricing		
	Trade	Private	Dealer
4 Dr S/C Sdn	37602	40808	43767

Options	Price
Navigation System	+870

2000

Mileage Category: F

The XJR gains all-speed traction control, improved ABS, rain-sensing windshield wipers, child seat-anchor brackets and an upgraded 320-watt Alpine system as standard equipment. A new navigation system is being offered as optional equipment. The anti-theft system now has an encrypted key transponder. The XJR also gets new 18-inch wheels and newly styled seats.

Body Styles	TMV Pricing		
	Trade	Private	Dealer
4 Dr S/C Sdn	28685	31484	34227

Options	Price
Navigation System	+660

1999

Mileage Category: F

Jaguar's potent XJR sedan enters '99 largely unchanged after a major workover in '98.

Body Styles	TMV Pricing		
	Trade	Private	Dealer
4 Dr S/C Sdn	23379	26178	29091

Options	Price
Chrome Wheels	+294

1998

Body Styles	TMV Pricing		
	Trade	Private	Dealer
4 Dr S/C Sdn	18650	21322	24335

Options	Price
Chrome Wheels	+252

Mileage Category: F

A new supercharged V8 engine makes its way into the engine bay. A revised instrument panel greatly improves interior ergonomics. Cruise and satellite stereo controls are located on the steering wheel.

1997

Body Styles	TMV Pricing		
	Trade	Private	Dealer
4 Dr S/C Sdn	13148	15295	17920

Options	Price
Special Factory Paint	+127

Mileage Category: F

Apart from gaining a contoured bench seat and three-point seatbelts for rear occupants (as with the rest of the XJ sedans) and losing the heater ducts for the same, the XJR cruises into this year unchanged.

1996

Body Styles	TMV Pricing		
	Trade	Private	Dealer
4 Dr S/C Sdn	11443	13509	16362

Mileage Category: F

After last year's rebirth, changes to the XJ sedans, including the XJR are limited to thicker side window glass that better insulates passengers from annoying wind noise and outside distractions.

1995

Body Styles	TMV Pricing		
	Trade	Private	Dealer
4 Dr S/C Sdn	10123	12050	15261

Mileage Category: F

Along with a new body that is more evocative of the classic XJ series comes this new model, the performance-oriented, supercharged XJR that boasts 322 horsepower under its bonnet.

Jaguar
XK-Series

2003

Body Styles	TMV Pricing		
	Trade	Private	Dealer
2 Dr XK8 Conv	51070	53404	57294
2 Dr XK8 Cpe	46032	48136	51642

Options	Price
Navigation System [Opt on XK8]	+1603
19 Inch Wheels [Opt on XK8]	+668

Mileage Category: F

Trying hard to keep up with blossoming competition, Jaguar makes significant modifications to its sports car. Changes to the exterior are limited to different wheels, slightly different badging, available (standard on the R) xenon headlamps and some new colors, including a lovely Jaguar Racing Green. The most important alterations lie under the hood, with two new engines managed by a six-speed automatic transmission. Standard safety equipment now includes a stability control system and BrakeAssist. In all, there are 900 changes to Jaguar's beautiful XK.

2002

Mileage Category: F

No major changes.

Body Styles	TMV Pricing		
	Trade	Private	Dealer
2 Dr XK8 Conv	43183	45205	48576
2 Dr XK8 Cpe	38060	39843	42814

Options	Price
18 Inch Wheels	+355
Navigation System	+1421

2001

Mileage Category: F

For 2001, there are standard child seat-anchor points for the rear seats and a reverse parking-control system. The premium audio system with a six-disc CD changer and the GPS navigation system are now standard equipment on XK8s. Topping things off are minor exterior styling changes and a new no-cost scheduled maintenance program that covers four regular service visits under the four-year/50,000-mile limited warranty.

Body Styles	TMV Pricing		
	Trade	Private	Dealer
2 Dr XK8 Conv	38895	41808	44496
2 Dr XK8 Cpe	34275	36842	39212

Options	Price
18 Inch Wheels	+256
Navigation System	+1228

2000

Mileage Category: F

No major changes.

Body Styles	TMV Pricing		
	Trade	Private	Dealer
2 Dr XK8 Conv	31510	34374	37182
2 Dr XK8 Cpe	29609	32301	34940

Options	Price
Compact Disc Changer	+256
Harman Kardon Audio System	+532
Heated Front Seats	+164
Navigation System	+607

1999

Mileage Category: F

The stunning XK returns for '99 with no significant changes.

Body Styles	TMV Pricing		
	Trade	Private	Dealer
2 Dr XK8 Conv	26531	29593	32779
2 Dr XK8 Cpe	25105	28002	31018

Options	Price	Options	Price
Chrome Wheels	+314	Heated Front Seats	+141
Compact Disc Changer	+220	Traction Control System	+220
Harman Kardon Audio System	+459		

1998

Mileage Category: F

The 1998 XK8 gets automatic on/off headlamps, an engine immobilizer feature as part of the security system and a cellular phone keypad integrated into the stereo controls. Other changes include the addition of two new exterior colors.

Body Styles	TMV Pricing		
	Trade	Private	Dealer
2 Dr XK8 Conv	22345	25405	28856
2 Dr XK8 Cpe	18711	21273	24163

Options	Price	Options	Price
Traction Control System	+189	Compact Disc Changer	+189
Heated Front Seats	+121	Harman Kardon Audio System	+394
Chrome Wheels	+269		

1997

Mileage Category: F

An all-new Jaguar debuts this year, replacing the stodgy XJ-S. This new sports car boasts the first V8 engine ever found in a Jag, as well as an all-new five-speed manual transmission that features normal and sport modes. The XK-Series is available in coupe and convertible forms, but Jaguar insiders expect a full 70 percent of sales to be of the convertible.

Body Styles	TMV Pricing		
	Trade	Private	Dealer
2 Dr XK8 Conv	19166	22126	25744
2 Dr XK8 Cpe	15850	18298	21289

Options	Price	Options	Price
Chrome Wheels	+217	Special Factory Paint	+127
Compact Disc Changer	+152	Traction Control System	+152
Harman Kardon Audio System	+305		

2003

Body Styles	TMV Pricing		
	Trade	Private	Dealer
2 Dr S/C Conv	61156	63951	68609
2 Dr S/C Cpe	57459	60085	64462

Options	Price	Options	Price
20 Inch Wheels	+4007	Performance/Handling Package	+6011
Adaptive Cruise Control	+1202	Recaro Seats	+1336

Mileage Category: F

Trying hard to keep up with blossoming competition, Jaguar makes significant modifications to its top-shelf sports car. Changes to the exterior are limited to different wheels, slightly different badging, standard xenon headlamps and some new colors, including a lovely Jaguar Racing Green. The most important alterations lie under the hood, with a new engine managed by a six-speed automatic transmission. In all, there are 900 changes to Jaguar's beautiful XKR.

2002

Body Styles	TMV Pricing		
	Trade	Private	Dealer
2 Dr 100 S/C Conv	64407	67424	72451
2 Dr 100 S/C Cpe	63461	66433	71386

Body Styles	TMV Pricing		
	Trade	Private	Dealer
2 Dr S/C Conv	52985	55466	59602
2 Dr S/C Cpe	48970	51264	55087

Mileage Category: F

XKR models get a burst of new color for 2002, with Aspen Green, Quartz and Zircon added to the palette. This year also ushers in a new trim level for the XKR; the limited-edition XKR 100 (created to honor the centenary of Jaguar's founder) offers unique features like special Anthracite paint and top-of-the-line Connolly leather seats.

2001

Body Styles	TMV Pricing		
	Trade	Private	Dealer
2 Dr S/C Conv	46005	49450	52630
2 Dr S/C Cpe	42424	45601	48534

Body Styles	TMV Pricing		
	Trade	Private	Dealer
2 Dr Silverstone S/C Conv	57444	61745	65716
2 Dr Silverstone S/C Cpe	55901	60087	63951

Mileage Category: F

For 2001, a limited-edition XKR "Silverstone" model will be offered, equipped with 20-inch BBS wheels, Brembo brakes and unique interior treatments. The Silverstone, as well as the regular XKR Coupe and Convertible, have additional safety equipment in the form of seat-mounted side airbags and an Adaptive Restraint Technology System (ARTS) that ultrasonically detects occupants. There are also standard child seat-anchor points for the rear seats and a reverse parking control system. Topping things off are minor exterior styling changes and a new no-cost scheduled maintenance program that covers four regular service visits under the four-year/50,000-mile limited warranty.

2000

Body Styles	TMV Pricing		
	Trade	Private	Dealer
2 Dr S/C Conv	38218	41692	45098
2 Dr S/C Cpe	34651	37801	40889

Options	Price
Navigation System	+607

Mileage Category: F

The performance-minded, supercharged, V8-powered XKR joins the lineup this year. It benefits from upgrades made to the rest of the XK8 family that include all-speed traction control, improved ABS and rain-sensing windshield wipers, while a new navigation system is being offered as optional equipment.

2001

Mileage Category: M

The 4.0-liter PowerTech inline-six engine, which now meets LEV requirements in all 50 states, is standard equipment in all 2001 Cherokees. The 2.5-liter inline four, along with the SE trim, is dropped midyear. The previous Limited trim is also dropped, with the former Classic trim now labeled Limited. All 2001 Cherokees offer child seat-tether anchors as standard equipment, and Steel Blue replaces Desert Sand as an exterior color choice. This is the last year for the Cherokee.

Body Styles	TMV Pricing		
	Trade	Private	Dealer
2 Dr SE 4WD SUV	8102	9306	10418
2 Dr SE SUV	7492	8605	9633
2 Dr Sport 4WD SUV	8612	9892	11073
2 Dr Sport SUV	8057	9255	10360
4 Dr Classic 4WD SUV	9567	10989	12302
4 Dr Classic SUV	8978	10312	11544

Body Styles	TMV Pricing		
	Trade	Private	Dealer
4 Dr Limited 4WD SUV	9720	11164	12497
4 Dr Limited SUV	9281	10661	11935
4 Dr SE 4WD SUV	8537	9806	10978
4 Dr SE SUV	7914	9091	10177
4 Dr Sport 4WD SUV	9499	10911	12215
4 Dr Sport SUV	8417	9668	10822

Options	Price
Air Conditioning [Std on Limited]	+415
Aluminum/Alloy Wheels [Opt on SE,Sport]	+120
AM/FM/Cassette/CD Audio System	+200
Antilock Brakes	+332
Automatic 4-Speed Transmission [Opt on SE,Sport]	+461
Camper/Towing Package	+120
Cruise Control	+122

Options	Price
Heated Front Seats	+269
Infinity Audio System	+171
Leather Seats [Opt on Limited]	+342
Locking Differential	+139
Off-Road Suspension Package	+354
Power Driver Seat [Opt on Classic,Limited]	+146
Power Passenger Seat [Opt on Limited]	+146

2000

Mileage Category: M

The 2000 Cherokee scores the '99 Grand Cherokee's redesigned 4.0-liter PowerTech inline six in addition to a new five-speed manual transmission. The Limited model sports bright chrome accents, including the front grille, the headlamp surrounds, the side graphics, the rear license-plate brow and the 16-inch wheels.

Body Styles	TMV Pricing		
	Trade	Private	Dealer
2 Dr SE 4WD SUV	6229	7256	8262
2 Dr SE SUV	5810	6767	7706
2 Dr Sport 4WD SUV	7058	8222	9362
2 Dr Sport SUV	6624	7715	8785
4 Dr Classic 4WD SUV	7966	9278	10565
4 Dr Classic SUV	7480	8713	9921

Body Styles	TMV Pricing		
	Trade	Private	Dealer
4 Dr Limited 4WD SUV	8376	9757	11110
4 Dr Limited SUV	8012	9332	10626
4 Dr SE 4WD SUV	6678	7778	8857
4 Dr SE SUV	6150	7164	8157
4 Dr Sport 4WD SUV	7507	8744	9956
4 Dr Sport SUV	6895	8032	9146

Options	Price
Antilock Brakes	+293
Automatic 3-Speed Transmission	+269
Automatic 4-Speed Transmission [Opt on SE,Sport]	+407
AM/FM/Cassette/CD Audio System	+205
Heated Front Seats	+237

Options	Price
Infinity Audio System	+151
Limited Slip Differential	+123
Power Driver Seat [Opt on Classic 4 Dr]	+129
4.0L I6 OHV 12V FI Engine [Opt on SE]	+428
Air Conditioning [Std on Limited]	+366

1999

Mileage Category: M

The Cherokee Sport gets a revised front fascia including body-colored grille and bumpers. New exterior colors include Forest Green and Desert Sand, to match the most common Cherokee surroundings.

Body Styles	TMV Pricing		
	Trade	Private	Dealer
2 Dr SE 4WD SUV	5286	6236	7224
2 Dr SE SUV	4778	5636	6529
2 Dr Sport 4WD SUV	5997	7074	8195
2 Dr Sport SUV	5552	6550	7589
4 Dr Classic 4WD SUV	6455	7615	8822
4 Dr Classic SUV	6200	7314	8474

Body Styles	TMV Pricing		
	Trade	Private	Dealer
4 Dr Limited 4WD SUV	6852	8083	9364
4 Dr Limited SUV	6550	7726	8951
4 Dr SE 4WD SUV	5528	6521	7555
4 Dr SE SUV	4981	5876	6808
4 Dr Sport 4WD SUV	6252	7375	8544
4 Dr Sport SUV	5742	6774	7848

Options	Price
4.0L I6 OHV 12V FI Engine [Opt on SE]	+343
Air Conditioning [Std on Limited]	+293
AM/FM/Cassette/CD Audio System	+164
Antilock Brakes	+260
Automatic 3-Speed Transmission	+214

Options	Price
Automatic 4-Speed Transmission [Opt on SE,Sport]	+324
Automatic Locking Hubs (4WD) [Opt on Utility]	+136
Heated Front Seats	+190
Infinity Audio System	+121

1998

Body Styles	TMV Pricing		
	Trade	Private	Dealer
2 Dr SE 4WD SUV	4406	5257	6217
2 Dr SE SUV	3937	4697	5555
2 Dr Sport 4WD SUV	4857	5796	6854
2 Dr Sport SUV	4597	5486	6488
4 Dr Classic 4WD SUV	5484	6544	7739
4 Dr Classic SUV	5109	6096	7209

Body Styles	TMV Pricing		
	Trade	Private	Dealer
4 Dr Limited 4WD SUV	6048	7216	8534
4 Dr Limited SUV	5627	6714	7940
4 Dr SE 4WD SUV	4590	5477	6477
4 Dr SE SUV	4124	4921	5820
4 Dr Sport 4WD SUV	5250	6264	7408
4 Dr Sport SUV	4799	5726	6772

Options	Price
4.0L I6 OHV 12V FI Engine [Opt on SE]	+294
Air Conditioning [Std on Limited]	+250
AM/FM/Cassette/CD Audio System	+140
Antilock Brakes	+223

Options	Price
Automatic 3-Speed Transmission	+196
Automatic 4-Speed Transmission [Opt on SE,Sport]	+278
Automatic Locking Hubs (4WD) [Opt on Utility]	+116

Mileage Category: M

Cherokee Classic and Limited replace the Cherokee Country. A new 2.5-liter four-cylinder engine is now the base engine for the SE, available with an optional three-speed automatic. New colors include Chili Pepper Red, Emerald Green and Deep Amethyst.

1997

Body Styles	TMV Pricing		
	Trade	Private	Dealer
2 Dr SE 4WD SUV	3664	4441	5391
2 Dr SE SUV	3071	3722	4517
2 Dr Sport 4WD SUV	4031	4886	5931
2 Dr Sport SUV	3848	4664	5662
4 Dr Country 4WD SUV	4846	5873	7129

Body Styles	TMV Pricing		
	Trade	Private	Dealer
4 Dr Country SUV	4572	5542	6727
4 Dr SE 4WD SUV	3803	4609	5594
4 Dr SE SUV	3528	4275	5189
4 Dr Sport 4WD SUV	4214	5108	6200
4 Dr Sport SUV	3983	4827	5859

Options	Price
4.0L I6 OHV 12V FI Engine [Opt on SE]	+263
Air Conditioning	+225
AM/FM/Cassette/CD Audio System	+126

Options	Price
Antilock Brakes	+200
Automatic 4-Speed Transmission [Std on Country]	+250
Leather Seats	+221

Mileage Category: M

A new interior sporting modern instrumentation debuts. Front and rear styling is refined, and the rear liftgate is now stamped from steel. Multiplex wiring is designed to improve reliability of the electrical system, while a new paint process aims to polish the finish of all Cherokees.

1996

Body Styles	TMV Pricing		
	Trade	Private	Dealer
2 Dr SE 4WD SUV	2445	2996	3756
2 Dr SE SUV	2263	2772	3476
2 Dr Sport 4WD SUV	2894	3546	4447
2 Dr Sport SUV	2663	3262	4090
4 Dr Country 4WD SUV	3895	4772	5984

Body Styles	TMV Pricing		
	Trade	Private	Dealer
4 Dr Country SUV	3286	4026	5047
4 Dr SE 4WD SUV	2677	3280	4112
4 Dr SE SUV	2397	2937	3683
4 Dr Sport 4WD SUV	3031	3714	4656
4 Dr Sport SUV	2850	3492	4378

Options	Price
4.0L I6 OHV 12V FI Engine [Opt on SE]	+159
Air Conditioning	+163
Antilock Brakes	+147

Options	Price
Automatic 4-Speed Transmission	+175
Leather Seats	+162
Off-Road Suspension Package	+204

Mileage Category: M

Cherokee rolls into 1996 with improved engines, new colors, upgraded Selec-Trac four-wheel-drive system, more standard equipment and the same sheet metal that it wore on introduction day in 1983.

1995

Body Styles	TMV Pricing		
	Trade	Private	Dealer
2 Dr SE 4WD SUV	2071	2553	3356
2 Dr SE SUV	1828	2253	2961
2 Dr Sport 4WD SUV	2313	2851	3748
2 Dr Sport SUV	2148	2648	3480
4 Dr Country 4WD SUV	2759	3401	4471

Body Styles	TMV Pricing		
	Trade	Private	Dealer
4 Dr Country SUV	2582	3183	4184
4 Dr SE 4WD SUV	2072	2554	3357
4 Dr SE SUV	1923	2370	3116
4 Dr Sport 4WD SUV	2430	2995	3937
4 Dr Sport SUV	2287	2819	3706

Options	Price
4.0L I6 OHV 12V FI Engine [Opt on SE]	+168
Air Conditioning	+173
Antilock Brakes	+156

Options	Price
Automatic 4-Speed Transmission	+186
Leather Seats	+172
Off-Road Suspension Package	+217

Mileage Category: M

Driver airbag is added on all models. SE model gets reclining bucket seats.

Jeep
Cherokee/Grand Cherokee

1994

Mileage Category: M

Side-door guard beams have been added, and center high-mounted brake light is new. Base model gets SE nomenclature.

Body Styles	TMV Pricing		
	Trade	Private	Dealer
2 Dr Country 4WD SUV	2119	2680	3616
2 Dr Country SUV	1908	2413	3255
2 Dr SE 4WD SUV	1720	2175	2934
2 Dr SE SUV	1426	1804	2434
2 Dr Sport 4WD SUV	1817	2298	3100
2 Dr Sport SUV	1752	2216	2990

Body Styles	TMV Pricing		
	Trade	Private	Dealer
4 Dr Country 4WD SUV	2361	2987	4029
4 Dr Country SUV	2055	2600	3507
4 Dr SE 4WD SUV	1771	2240	3022
4 Dr SE SUV	1636	2069	2791
4 Dr Sport 4WD SUV	2078	2628	3545
4 Dr Sport SUV	1791	2266	3057

Options	Price
4.0L I6 OHV 12V FI Engine [Opt on SE]	+154
Air Conditioning	+158
Antilock Brakes	+143

Options	Price
Automatic 4-Speed Transmission	+170
Leather Seats	+158

Jeep
Grand Cherokee
2003

Mileage Category: M

For 2003, the Jeep Grand Cherokee has received refinements that improve its ride and handling. The suspension features reduced pressure shocks and the brake master cylinder output has been increased to improve brake pedal feel. There are also new brake calipers and a revised steering gear. Available trims have been narrowed from five to three; the Sport and Special Edition trims have been discontinued. Standard on 2003 Laredo models is a new high-back cloth seat. Finally, in all Jeep Grand Cherokee interiors, a new cubby bin for holding sunglasses or cellular phones has been added to the instrument panel, replacing the ashtray.

Body Styles	TMV Pricing		
	Trade	Private	Dealer
4 Dr Laredo 4WD SUV	16822	18084	20186
4 Dr Laredo SUV	15777	16960	18932
4 Dr Limited 4WD SUV	19679	21155	23614

Body Styles	TMV Pricing		
	Trade	Private	Dealer
4 Dr Limited SUV	18295	19667	21953
4 Dr Overland 4WD SUV	23148	24884	27776

Options	Price
Compact Disc Changer [Opt on Laredo,Limited]	+256
Heated Front Seats [Opt on Laredo,Limited]	+171
Infinity Audio System [Opt on Laredo]	+153
Leather Seats [Opt on Laredo]	+580
Off-Road Suspension Package [Opt on Laredo,Limited]	+198
Power Moonroof [Opt on Laredo,Limited]	+546
Power Passenger Seat [Opt on Laredo]	+191

Options	Price
Quadra-Drive Transfer Case [Opt on Limited]	+375
Special Factory Paint	+136
17 Inch Wheels - Chrome [Opt on Limited]	+593
Quadra-Trac Transfer Case [Opt on Laredo]	+303
Front and Rear Head Airbag Restraints [Opt on Laredo,Limited]	+334
4.7L V8 SOHC 16V FI Engine [Opt on Laredo,Limited]	+303
4.7L V8 SOHC 16V FI HO Engine [Opt on Limited]	+1364

2002

Mileage Category: M

More power for the 4.7-liter V8 and three new trim levels (SE, Sport and Overland) are on tap for this year. Also, several important safety and convenience options such as side curtain airbags, power-adjustable pedals, a tire-pressure monitoring system and automatic windshield wipers debut this year.

Body Styles	TMV Pricing		
	Trade	Private	Dealer
4 Dr Laredo 4WD SUV	14221	15518	17679
4 Dr Laredo SUV	13197	14401	16407
4 Dr Limited 4WD SUV	16581	18093	20613
4 Dr Limited SUV	15361	16762	19097
4 Dr Overland 4WD SUV	19879	21692	24713

Body Styles	TMV Pricing		
	Trade	Private	Dealer
4 Dr Special Edition 4WD SUV	15720	17154	19543
4 Dr Special Edition SUV	14484	15805	18006
4 Dr Sport 4WD SUV	14163	15455	17608
4 Dr Sport SUV	13160	14360	16360

Options	Price
17 Inch Wheels - Chrome [Opt on Limited,Overland]	+523
4.7L V8 SOHC 16V FI Engine	+267
4.7L V8 SOHC 16V FI HO Engine [Opt on Limited]	+1202
AM/FM/Cassette/CD Changer Audio System [Opt on Limited]	+180
Compact Disc Changer [Std on Overland,Special Edition]	+225
Front and Rear Head Airbag Restraints [Std on Overland]	+295
Heated Front Seats [Std on Overland]	+150
Infinity Audio System [Opt on Laredo]	+135

Options	Price
Leather Seats [Opt on Laredo,Special Edition]	+394
Off-Road Suspension Package [Opt on 4WD - Laredo,Limited]	+174
Power Moonroof [Std on Overland]	+481
Power Passenger Seat [Opt on Laredo]	+147
Quadra-Drive Transfer Case [Opt on Limited 4WD]	+331
Quadra-Trac Transfer Case [Opt on Laredo 4WD]	+267
Special Factory Paint	+120

For the latest vehicle information, visit www.edmunds.com

2001

Body Styles	TMV Pricing		
	Trade	Private	Dealer
4 Dr Laredo 4WD SUV	12045	13835	15488
4 Dr Laredo SUV	11450	13152	14723

Options	Price
4.7L V8 SOHC 16V FI Engine	+522
AM/FM/Cassette/CD Audio System [Opt on Laredo]	+171
AM/FM/Cassette/CD Changer Audio System	+146
Automatic 5-Speed Transmission	+293
Camper/Towing Package	+120
Compact Disc Changer	+146
Heated Front Seats	+122

Body Styles	TMV Pricing		
	Trade	Private	Dealer
4 Dr Limited 4WD SUV	14737	16928	18950
4 Dr Limited SUV	13583	15602	17465

Options	Price
Leather Seats [Opt on Laredo]	+283
Locking Differential [Opt on 2WD]	+139
Off-Road Suspension Package	+281
Power Driver Seat [Opt on Laredo]	+146
Power Passenger Seat [Opt on Laredo]	+146
Power Sunroof	+391
Quadra-Trac Transfer Case [Opt on Laredo 4WD]	+217

Mileage Category: M

A new five-speed automatic tranny provides a second overdrive ratio, resulting in greater fuel economy and reduced noise, vibration and harshness in models equipped with the 4.7-liter V8. Chrome front tow hooks are now included if you get the skid plate group on the Limited model, while the Laredo model offers a Special Appearance Group package with 17-inch five-spoke aluminum wheels, colored metallic front fascia and body cladding, body-color license brow and liftgate handle, foglamps, body side stripe and leather seats. A hydraulically driven engine-cooling fan improves fuel economy on the 4.7-liter V8 and a quarter-turn fuel cap improves efficiency at the gas station. Limiteds get an AM/FM stereo with cassette and CD player as standard equipment, along with optional new "Euro-style" gathered leather seats. The Trailer Tow Group now includes an underdash connector to make plugging in aftermarket trailer wiring harnesses a snap. Finally, child seat-tether anchors improve the Grand Cherokee's family-friendly nature while a LEV-compliant 4.7-liter V8 makes this Jeep more earth-friendly.

2000

Body Styles	TMV Pricing		
	Trade	Private	Dealer
4 Dr Laredo 4WD SUV	10179	11857	13501
4 Dr Laredo SUV	9553	11128	12671

Options	Price
4.7L V8 SOHC 16V FI Engine	+461
AM/FM/Cassette/CD Audio System [Opt on Laredo]	+151
Compact Disc Changer	+129
Infinity Audio System [Opt on Laredo]	+219
Leather Seats [Opt on Laredo]	+250
Limited Slip Differential	+123

Body Styles	TMV Pricing		
	Trade	Private	Dealer
4 Dr Limited 4WD SUV	12621	14701	16740
4 Dr Limited SUV	11654	13575	15458

Options	Price
Power Driver Seat [Opt on Laredo]	+129
Power Passenger Seat [Opt on Laredo]	+129
Power Sunroof	+345
Quadra-Drive Transfer Case [Opt on Laredo]	+237
Quadra-Trac Transfer Case [Opt on Laredo]	+192

Mileage Category: M

New exterior cladding has been slapped onto the Laredo, and both models have received interior touch-ups. Two-wheel drive is available with the 4.7-liter V8. Shale Green and Silverstone are the new skin tones.

1999

Body Styles	TMV Pricing		
	Trade	Private	Dealer
4 Dr Laredo 4WD SUV	8693	10255	11881
4 Dr Laredo SUV	8080	9532	11043

Options	Price
AM/FM/Cassette/CD Audio System [Opt on Laredo]	+121
Infinity Audio System [Opt on Laredo]	+176
Leather Seats [Opt on Laredo]	+199
Power Driver Seat [Opt on Laredo]	+115
Power Passenger Seat [Opt on Laredo]	+115

Body Styles	TMV Pricing		
	Trade	Private	Dealer
4 Dr Limited 4WD SUV	10687	12607	14606
4 Dr Limited SUV	9291	10960	12698

Options	Price
Power Sunroof	+275
Quadra-Drive Transfer Case [Opt on 4WD]	+210
Quadra-Trac Transfer Case [Opt on Laredo 4WD]	+170
4.7L V8 SOHC 16V FI Engine	+330

Mileage Category: M

The new-for-'99 Grand Cherokee contains only 127 carryover parts from the previous model, and gets a new powertrain, rear suspension, braking and steering systems, 4WD system, interior and exterior styling.

1998

Body Styles	TMV Pricing		
	Trade	Private	Dealer
4 Dr 5.9 Limited 4WD SUV	9171	10942	12940
4 Dr Laredo 4WD SUV	6323	7545	8922
4 Dr Laredo SUV	5961	7113	8412
4 Dr Limited 4WD SUV	8126	9696	11466

Options	Price
Quadra-Trac Transfer Case [Opt on 4WD - Laredo,TSi]	+146
Power Sunroof [Std on Limited 5.9]	+224
5.2L V8 OHV 16V FI Engine	+259

Body Styles	TMV Pricing		
	Trade	Private	Dealer
4 Dr Limited SUV	7094	8465	10010
4 Dr TSi 4WD SUV	6871	8199	9696
4 Dr TSi SUV	6410	7648	9044

Options	Price
Infinity Audio System	+150
Leather Seats [Opt on Laredo]	+171

Mileage Category: M

A 5.9-liter V8 making 245 horsepower and 345 pound-feet torque powers the Grand Cherokee 5.9 Limited, making it the mightiest of all Jeeps. With the addition of the 5.9, the putrid Orvis model dies. Two new colors and "next-generation" airbags round out the changes.

Grand Cherokee/Liberty

1997

Mileage Category: M

Last year's integrated child safety seat has mysteriously disappeared from press kit and dealer order sheet radar. Other big news is the availability of the optional 5.2-liter V8 engine in 2WD models, and a six-cylinder that qualifies the JGC as a Transitional Low Emissions Vehicle (TLEV) in California. Refinements have been made to the ABS system, entry-level cassette stereo and floor carpet fit. In January, a sporty TSi model debuted with monotone paint, special aluminum wheels, and other goodies.

Body Styles	TMV Pricing		
	Trade	Private	Dealer
4 Dr Laredo 4WD SUV	5545	6720	8157
4 Dr Laredo SUV	4853	5882	7140
4 Dr Limited 4WD SUV	6961	8437	10241

Options	Price
5.2L V8 OHV 16V FI Engine	+221
Infinity Audio System [Std on Limited]	+135
Leather Seats [Std on Limited]	+153

Body Styles	TMV Pricing		
	Trade	Private	Dealer
4 Dr Limited SUV	6325	7666	9305
4 Dr TSi 4WD SUV	6149	7453	9047
4 Dr TSi SUV	5643	6840	8302

Options	Price
Power Sunroof	+201
Quadra-Trac Transfer Case [Opt on Limited,TSi]	+131

1996

Mileage Category: M

Jeep turns its flagship into an Explorer killer with dual airbags, revised styling, a better V6 engine, improved front suspension and an upgraded Selec-Trac four-wheel-drive system. Interiors have been restyled, featuring new luxury doodads and an optional integrated child safety seat. Trim levels are two: Laredo and Limited.

Body Styles	TMV Pricing		
	Trade	Private	Dealer
4 Dr Laredo 4WD SUV	4528	5548	6956
4 Dr Laredo SUV	4094	5016	6289

Body Styles	TMV Pricing		
	Trade	Private	Dealer
4 Dr Limited 4WD SUV	5822	7133	8944
4 Dr Limited SUV	4860	5955	7466

Options	Price
Power Sunroof	+148
5.2L V8 OHV 16V FI Engine	+169

1995

Mileage Category: M

Rear disc brakes are added to all models. An Orvis trim package is added to the Limited 4WD. New options are an integrated child safety seat and a flip-up liftgate window. Optional V8 engine gets a torque increase. A 2WD Limited model is newly available. A power sunroof is added to the options list.

Body Styles	TMV Pricing		
	Trade	Private	Dealer
4 Dr Laredo 4WD SUV	3875	4776	6278
4 Dr Laredo SUV	3431	4229	5559
4 Dr Limited 4WD SUV	4770	5879	7728

Options	Price
5.2L V8 OHV 16V FI Engine	+179
Infinity Audio System [Std on Limited]	+106
Leather Seats [Std on Limited]	+119

Body Styles	TMV Pricing		
	Trade	Private	Dealer
4 Dr Limited SUV	4054	4997	6568
4 Dr SE 4WD SUV	3544	4369	5743
4 Dr SE SUV	3030	3734	4908

Options	Price
Off-Road Suspension Package [Opt on SE 4WD]	+155
Power Sunroof	+157
Quadra-Trac Transfer Case [Opt on 4WD - Laredo,SE]	+102

1994

Mileage Category: M

Side-door guard beams are added for 1994. Grand Wagoneer trim level is dropped. Base model is now called SE. Limited gets rear disc brakes.

Body Styles	TMV Pricing		
	Trade	Private	Dealer
4 Dr Laredo 4WD SUV	3061	3872	5223
4 Dr Laredo SUV	3008	3805	5132
4 Dr Limited 4WD SUV	4026	5093	6870

Options	Price
Automatic 4-Speed Transmission [Std on 2WD,Limited]	+167
Infinity Audio System	+97
Leather Seats [Std on Limited]	+109

Body Styles	TMV Pricing		
	Trade	Private	Dealer
4 Dr SE 4WD SUV	2949	3730	5032
4 Dr SE SUV	2569	3250	4384

Options	Price
Premium Audio System [Opt on SE]	+97
Quadra-Trac Transfer Case [Opt on 4WD - Laredo,SE]	+94
5.2L V8 OHV 16V FI Engine	+164

Jeep

Liberty

2003

Body Styles	TMV Pricing		
	Trade	Private	Dealer
4 Dr Freedom Edition 4WD SUV	16016	17308	19462
4 Dr Freedom Edition SUV	15397	16639	18709
4 Dr Limited 4WD SUV	15927	17212	19353
4 Dr Limited SUV	14612	15791	17755

Body Styles	TMV Pricing		
	Trade	Private	Dealer
4 Dr Renegade 4WD SUV	16028	17321	19476
4 Dr Renegade SUV	15287	16520	18575
4 Dr Sport 4WD SUV	12567	13581	15271
4 Dr Sport SUV	11501	12429	13975

For the latest vehicle information, visit www.edmunds.com

2003 (cont'd)

Options	Price
Air Conditioning [Opt on Sport]	+477
Alarm System	+119
Aluminum/Alloy Wheels [Opt on Sport]	+211
Antilock Brakes [Opt on Freedom,Limited,Renegade]	+464
Automatic 4-Speed Transmission [Std on Limited]	+563
Camper/Towing Package [Opt on Freedom,Limited,Renegade]	+167
Cruise Control [Opt on Sport]	+205
Heated Front Seats [Opt on Limited]	+171
Keyless Entry System	+116
Leather Seats [Opt on Limited]	+512

Options	Price
Limited Slip Differential	+194
Power Door Locks [Opt on Sport]	+123
Power Driver Seat [Opt on Limited,Renegade]	+160
Power Moonroof	+477
Power Passenger Seat [Opt on Limited,Renegade]	+160
Power Windows [Opt on Sport]	+167
17 Inch Wheels - Chrome [Opt on Limited]	+610
Front and Rear Head Airbag Restraints	+334
3.7L V6 SOHC 12V FI Engine [Opt on Sport]	+580

Mileage Category: M

For 2003, a new overhead console, based on that of the Grand Cherokee, includes a unique interface that allows passengers to program the operation of nine convenience and safety items to their own preference. Liberty owners can now personalize several features, including which doors unlock with the first press of the remote keyless entry unlock button, the miles driven between service intervals and the amount of time the headlamps remain on when exiting the vehicle. Finally, an available six-disc in-dash CD player replaces the cargo area mounted unit. Standard four-wheel disc brakes endow the Jeep with improved brake feel, decreased stopping distances and reduced brake fade. Available electrochromic interior and driver-side rearview mirrors help reduce headlight glare from traffic at night, and standard sliding sun visors have been added, which serve to keep the sun out of your eyes by providing added windshield and side glass coverage.

2002

Body Styles	TMV Pricing		
	Trade	Private	Dealer
4 Dr Limited 4WD SUV	13707	14957	17040
4 Dr Limited SUV	12644	13797	15718
4 Dr Renegade 4WD SUV	13899	15167	17279

Body Styles	TMV Pricing		
	Trade	Private	Dealer
4 Dr Renegade SUV	13412	14635	16673
4 Dr Sport 4WD SUV	10748	11728	13362
4 Dr Sport SUV	9740	10628	12108

Mileage Category: M

Finally replacing the boxy Cherokee that has been in production since 1984, the handsome all-new 2002 Liberty serves as the affordable SUV in Jeep's lineup. Borrowing styling cues from the 1997 Jeep Dakar and 1998 Jeepster concept vehicles, the Liberty is available in three trim levels with your choice of two- or four-wheel drive, a four- or six-cylinder engine and a manual or automatic transmission.

Options	Price
16 Inch Wheels [Opt on Sport]	+165
3.7L V6 SOHC 12V FI Engine [Opt on Sport]	+511
Air Conditioning [Std on Limited]	+511
Aluminum/Alloy Wheels [Opt on Sport]	+186
Antilock Brakes	+409
Automatic 4-Speed Transmission [Std on Limited]	+496
Camper/Towing Package [Opt on Limited]	+147
Compact Disc Changer	+249
Cruise Control [Opt on Sport]	+180

Options	Price
Front and Rear Head Airbag Restraints	+295
Heated Front Seats [Opt on Limited]	+150
Leather Seats [Opt on Limited]	+451
Limited Slip Differential	+171
Power Driver Seat	+141
Power Passenger Seat	+141
Power Sunroof	+421
Power Windows [Opt on Sport]	+147

Jeep
Wrangler
2003

Body Styles	TMV Pricing		
	Trade	Private	Dealer
2 Dr Rubicon 4WD Conv	16604	17950	20193
2 Dr SE 4WD Conv	10677	11542	12984
2 Dr Sahara 4WD Conv	16505	17843	20073

Body Styles	TMV Pricing		
	Trade	Private	Dealer
2 Dr Sport 4WD Conv	13889	15015	16891
2 Dr X 4WD Conv	12851	13893	15629
2 Dr X Freedom Edition 4WD Conv	14241	15395	17318

Options	Price
Air Conditioning [Opt on Rubicon,SE,Sport,X]	+477
Aluminum/Alloy Wheels [Opt on SE,Sport,X]	+290
Antilock Brakes [Opt on Sahara,Sport,X,X Freedom]	+464
Automatic 4-Speed Transmission	+358
Automatic Dimming Rearview Mirror [Opt on Rubicon,Sport]	+150
Color Match Dual Roofs [Opt on Rubicon,Sahara,Sport]	+979

Options	Price
Cruise Control [Std on Sahara]	+171
Hardtop Roof	+542
Limited Slip Differential [Opt on Sahara,Sport,X,X Freedom]	+194
Split Folding Rear Seat [Opt on SE]	+307
Premium Audio System [Opt on Rubicon,Sport,X Freedom]	+201

2003 (cont'd)

Mileage Category: L

For 2003, the Wrangler gets a new trim level: the Rubicon. All trims have been bestowed with an all-new 42RLE four-speed automatic transmission which is supposed to provide smoother-shifting, better highway fuel efficiency and quieter engine operation at highway speeds compared to the previous three-speed automatic transmission. The SE trim gets a new NV1500 five-speed heavy-duty tranny, which promises to improve shift quality in cold weather, along with a new, more potent 2.4-liter Power Tech inline-four. Available four-wheel disc brakes debut this year, along with a new fold-and-tumble rear seat that can be more easily removed. Finally, the Wrangler's interior has been refurbished for 2003; it gets new front and rear seats, a new electrochromatic rearview mirror with map lights, temperature and compass display (standard on Sahara, optional on Sport and Rubicon trims), and a new four-spoke steering wheel.

2002

Mileage Category: L

A new "X" model is introduced, combining the potent 4.0-liter inline six with affordability. Sahara and Sport models receive upgrades, including hard doors with roll-up windows. New optional wheels, increased output from the climate control system and an improved premium sound system round out the changes to the tough and ready Wrangler.

Body Styles	TMV Pricing		
	Trade	Private	Dealer
2 Dr SE 4WD Conv	8713	9555	10957
2 Dr Sahara 4WD Conv	13739	15065	17276

Options	Price
Air Conditioning	+421
AM/FM/Cassette Audio System [Opt on SE]	+192
Antilock Brakes [Opt on Sport,X]	+409
Automatic 3-Speed Transmission	+189
Chrome Wheels [Opt on X]	+331
Cruise Control [Std on Sahara]	+150

Body Styles	TMV Pricing		
	Trade	Private	Dealer
2 Dr Sport 4WD Conv	11661	12787	14663
2 Dr X 4WD Conv	10696	11729	13450

Options	Price
Hardtop Roof	+478
Limited Slip Differential	+171
Off-Road Suspension Package [Opt on Sport,X]	+478
Premium Audio System [Opt on Sport]	+177
Split Folding Rear Seat [Opt on SE]	+270

2001

Mileage Category: L

The Wrangler gets a number of improvements for 2001. All models benefit from a new four-ply soft top that reduces wind and road noise at speed. Deep tint windows are now standard on the Sahara hardtop and optional on Sport and SE models with the solid-shell roof. Two new center console designs are available on all models, as is a premium subwoofer. The add-a-trunk feature and removable side steps have been redesigned to improve functionality, and a new instrument cluster, low-pivot steering column, rearview mirror, airbag cutoff switch, child seat-tether anchors and multifunction headlight/wiper stalk are standard across the entire model line. The ABS system is upgraded; intermittent windshield wipers are now standard, and the 4.0-liter inline six now meets LEV requirements in all 50 states. Sienna Pearl Coat, Amber Fire and Steel Blue exterior colors have been added, while Medium Fern Green and Desert Sand have been dropped.

Body Styles	TMV Pricing		
	Trade	Private	Dealer
2 Dr SE 4WD Conv	7595	8759	9833
2 Dr Sahara 4WD Conv	11536	13304	14936

Options	Price
Air Conditioning	+437
Aluminum/Alloy Wheels [Std on Sahara]	+242
AM/FM/Cassette Audio System [Opt on SE]	+156
Antilock Brakes	+332

Body Styles	TMV Pricing		
	Trade	Private	Dealer
2 Dr Sport 4WD Conv	9993	11524	12937

Options	Price
Automatic 3-Speed Transmission	+305
Cruise Control	+122
Hardtop Roof	+369
Locking Differential	+139

2000

Mileage Category: L

A reengineered 4.0-liter PowerTech inline six-cylinder that is more refined and quiet, with reduced emissions, is standard for Sport and Sahara for 2000. Shift quality kicks up a notch, thanks to an all-new five-speed manual transmission. A radio/cassette combo with four speakers is now standard for the Sport, and the Sahara gains a radio/CD. Solar Yellow, Patriot Blue and Silverstone are additional exterior colors.

Body Styles	TMV Pricing		
	Trade	Private	Dealer
2 Dr SE 4WD Conv	6842	7992	9120
2 Dr Sahara 4WD Conv	10194	11907	13587

Options	Price
Air Conditioning	+386
Aluminum/Alloy Wheels [Std on Sahara]	+214
AM/FM/Cassette Audio System [Opt on SE]	+138
AM/FM/CD Audio System [Std on Sahara]	+362
Antilock Brakes	+293

Body Styles	TMV Pricing		
	Trade	Private	Dealer
2 Dr Sport 4WD Conv	9017	10533	12019

Options	Price
Automatic 3-Speed Transmission	+269
Color Match Dual Roofs	+601
Hardtop Roof	+326
Limited Slip Differential	+123
Locking Differential	+123

1999

Body Styles	TMV Pricing		
	Trade	Private	Dealer
2 Dr SE 4WD Conv	6255	7362	8514
2 Dr Sahara 4WD Conv	8816	10376	11999
2 Dr Sport 4WD Conv	8090	9522	11012

1999 (cont'd)

Options	Price
Air Conditioning	+308
Antilock Brakes	+260
Automatic 3-Speed Transmission	+214

Options	Price
Color Match Dual Roofs	+480
Hardtop Roof	+260

Mileage Category: L

The Wrangler's interior finally enters the '90s with rotary HVAC controls, replacing the old slider control system. The hard- or soft top is available in Dark Tan, and new colors decorate both the exterior and the interior.

1998

Body Styles	TMV Pricing		
	Trade	Private	Dealer
2 Dr SE 4WD Conv	5546	6666	7928
2 Dr Sahara 4WD Conv	7752	9317	11082
2 Dr Sport 4WD Conv	7071	8498	10108

Options	Price
Antilock Brakes	+223
Automatic 3-Speed Transmission	+184
Color Match Dual Roofs	+411

Options	Price
Hardtop Roof	+223
Air Conditioning	+264

Mileage Category: L

Jeep has improved off-road capability by increasing the axle ratio offered with the 4.0-liter engine and revising the torsion bar for better steering. Optional this year are a tilting driver seat, automatic speed control, a combination CD/cassette stereo, a new Smart Key Immobilizer theft deterrent system and two new colors.

1997

Body Styles	TMV Pricing		
	Trade	Private	Dealer
2 Dr SE 4WD Conv	4607	5634	6890
2 Dr Sahara 4WD Conv	6657	8143	9959
2 Dr Sport 4WD Conv	5356	6551	8011

Options	Price
Air Conditioning	+237
Antilock Brakes	+200

Options	Price
Automatic 3-Speed Transmission	+165
Hardtop Roof	+200

Mileage Category: L

Jeep has totally redesigned this American icon. A Quadra-coil suspension improves on- and off-road manners; while dual airbags and optional antilock brakes increase the Wrangler's ability to keep occupants safe. Round, retro-style headlights add a nostalgic touch to this venerable ground-pounder. Fortunately, none of these refinements soften the Wrangler's tough exterior. A restyled interior includes integrated air vents, a glovebox and carlike stereo controls and accessory switches.

1995

Body Styles	TMV Pricing		
	Trade	Private	Dealer
2 Dr Rio Grande 4WD Conv	3701	4539	5935
2 Dr S 4WD Conv	3365	4126	5395

Body Styles	TMV Pricing		
	Trade	Private	Dealer
2 Dr SE 4WD Conv	3793	4651	6081
2 Dr Sahara 4WD Conv	4566	5599	7321

Options	Price
Air Conditioning	+186
Antilock Brakes	+156

Options	Price
Automatic 3-Speed Transmission	+129
Hardtop Roof	+156

Mileage Category: L

S model can be equipped with new Rio Grande package. Renegade is dropped from lineup. An optional dome light can be attached to the optional sound bar.

1994

Body Styles	TMV Pricing		
	Trade	Private	Dealer
2 Dr Renegade 4WD Conv	4033	5094	6861
2 Dr S 4WD Conv	2598	3282	4421
2 Dr SE 4WD Conv	3128	3951	5323

Body Styles	TMV Pricing		
	Trade	Private	Dealer
2 Dr Sahara 4WD Conv	3675	4641	6252
2 Dr Sport 4WD Conv	3364	4249	5724

Options	Price
Air Conditioning	+170
Antilock Brakes	+143

Options	Price
Automatic 3-Speed Transmission	+119
Hardtop Roof	+143

Mileage Category: L

The four-cylinder engine can be saddled with an automatic transmission this year. Base trim is now termed SE. Center high-mounted brake light is added.

Kia
Optima/Rio

2003

Body Styles	TMV Pricing		
	Trade	Private	Dealer
4 Dr LX Sdn	7899	8770	10221
4 Dr LX V6 Sdn	8404	9330	10874

Options	Price
AM/FM/Cassette/CD Audio System [Opt on LX,LX V6]	+354
Antilock Brakes [Opt on LX V6,SE V6]	+473
Automatic 4-Speed Transmission [Opt on LX]	+547

Body Styles	TMV Pricing		
	Trade	Private	Dealer
4 Dr SE Sdn	8539	9480	11048
4 Dr SE V6 Sdn	9063	10062	11727

Options	Price
Compact Disc Changer	+223
Leather Seats [Opt on SE,SE V6]	+446
Power Passenger Seat [Opt on SE,SE V6]	+149

Mileage Category: C

The Optima gets several revisions for its third year on the market. Most obvious is its new front-end styling, which replaces the Optima's reserved countenance with a more upscale European look -- double light clusters call to mind the Mercedes-Benz E-Class. Other changes include new wheel designs, and inside, a new center stack, new door panels and fresh seat fabric. A manual transmission will no longer be available on the four-cylinder SE model; all automatic four-cylinder models will offer Sportmatic manual-shift capability. The LX model now comes with cruise control and a CD player (at the expense of the cassette deck). The SE will include automatic climate control, an auto-dimming rearview mirror, Homelink and Infinity speakers; a wood- and leather-trimmed steering wheel is now part of the Leather Package. Lastly, engine horsepower ratings have been lowered following parent-company Hyundai's announcement that it had misstated outputs (the Optima is a corporate twin of the Sonata), but the engines themselves are unchanged.

2002

Mileage Category: C

Now in its second year, Kia's midsize sedan gets an upgraded V6 engine. Four-cylinder LX models trade their 14-inch wheels for standard 15s, while SE models get auto on/off headlights and two keyless remotes. The optional Leather Package for the SE now includes a four-way power passenger seat.

Body Styles	TMV Pricing		
	Trade	Private	Dealer
4 Dr LX Sdn	5613	6392	7691
4 Dr LX V6 Sdn	6427	7320	8807

Options	Price
AM/FM/Cassette/CD Audio System [Opt on LX,LX V6]	+289
Antilock Brakes [Opt on V6]	+386
Automatic 4-Speed Transmission [Opt on LX,SE]	+413

Body Styles	TMV Pricing		
	Trade	Private	Dealer
4 Dr SE Sdn	6160	7015	8441
4 Dr SE V6 Sdn	6948	7913	9521

Options	Price
Cruise Control [Opt on LX]	+121
Leather Seats [Opt on SE,SE V6]	+483

2001

Mileage Category: C

Kia joins the high-stakes poker game that is the midsize sedan market with the all-new Optima. Available in four- and six-cylinder models and two trim levels, the Optima offers a loaded deck of standard features, including air conditioning, side airbags, four-wheel independent suspension and power windows, locks and mirrors.

Body Styles	TMV Pricing		
	Trade	Private	Dealer
4 Dr LX Sdn	4776	5749	6647
4 Dr LX V6 Sdn	5651	6802	7864

Options	Price
AM/FM/Cassette/CD Audio System [Opt on LX,LX V6]	+241
Antilock Brakes [Opt on V6]	+322

Body Styles	TMV Pricing		
	Trade	Private	Dealer
4 Dr SE Sdn	5437	6544	7566
4 Dr SE V6 Sdn	6112	7357	8506

Options	Price
Automatic 4-Speed Transmission [Opt on LX,SE]	+345
Leather Seats [Opt on SE,SE V6]	+403

Kia
Rio

2003

Body Styles	TMV Pricing		
	Trade	Private	Dealer
4 Dr Cinco Wgn	5020	5850	7234
4 Dr STD Sdn	4710	5489	6787

Mileage Category: A

For 2003, Kia gives the Rio a number of upgrades. Among these are a new 104-horsepower 1.6-liter four-cylinder engine; various suspension tweaks to improve ride and handling; larger disc brakes; new engine mounts and exhaust tuning for a quieter cabin; and reinforcements to the steering wheel and column to minimize vibration. Inside, look for revisions to the instrument cluster, center console and door panels -- the latter will include storage bins and bottle holders -- as well as new seat fabric. New standard features include child-seat anchors, rear heater ducts, auto-off headlights, variable intermittent wipers and, on the wagon only, a CD player. In addition, Kia has added dual map lights and a sunglasses case to the sedan's Upgrade Package, and will offer the Power Package, which provides power windows and locks. Finally, both Rios get fresh front fascias and wheel covers; the sedan gets a sharper-looking tail and the wagon gets an optional body-color spoiler.

2003 (cont'd)

Options	Price
Air Conditioning	+446
Aluminum/Alloy Wheels	+164
AM/FM/CD Audio System [Opt on STD Sdn]	+253

Options	Price
Antilock Brakes	+405
Automatic 4-Speed Transmission	+399

2002

Body Styles	TMV Pricing		
	Trade	Private	Dealer
4 Dr Cinco Wgn	3722	4495	5783
4 Dr STD Sdn	3305	3992	5136

Options	Price
Air Conditioning	+364
Aluminum/Alloy Wheels	+134
AM/FM/Cassette Audio System [Opt on STD]	+155

Options	Price
Antilock Brakes	+330
Automatic 4-Speed Transmission	+425

Mileage Category: A

One of America's least expensive cars now comes in sedan or wagon flavor. Dubbed the Rio Cinco, the five-door Kia provides 44.3 cubic feet of storage space with the rear seat down.

2001

Body Styles	TMV Pricing		
	Trade	Private	Dealer
4 Dr STD Sdn	2790	3653	4449

Options	Price
Air Conditioning	+304
Aluminum/Alloy Wheels	+128
AM/FM/Cassette Audio System	+130

Options	Price
AM/FM/CD Audio System	+160
Antilock Brakes	+276
Automatic 4-Speed Transmission	+355

Mileage Category: A

With a base MSRP that makes it the least expensive car in America, the roomy little Rio is a peppy 96-horsepower entry-level sedan. While the design and materials used on this car are nothing to write home about, build quality is impressively tight. And Kia's new Long Haul Warranty Program offers the added security of a 10-year/100,000-mile limited powertrain warranty, along with impressive levels of bumper-to-bumper and roadside assistance coverage.

Kia
Sedona

2003

Body Styles	TMV Pricing		
	Trade	Private	Dealer
4 Dr EX Pass Van	12112	13356	15429
4 Dr LX Pass Van	10998	12128	14010

Options	Price
Antilock Brakes	+405
Leather Seats [Opt on EX]	+506
Power Moonroof [Opt on EX]	+342

Mileage Category: P

Minor upgrades are in store for the Sedona in its second year on the market. On the outside, buyers will find new taillights, and in the cabin, you'll note a new audio faceplate and a remote fuel-door release. The LX model gets a CD player, while the EX now comes with two keyless remotes, as well as additional leather on the armrests and lower portions of the seats. A trailer hitch is now available for all Sedonas.

2002

Body Styles	TMV Pricing		
	Trade	Private	Dealer
4 Dr EX Pass Van	10223	11401	13364
4 Dr LX Pass Van	9265	10332	12111

Options	Price
Antilock Brakes	+330
Leather Seats [Opt on EX]	+413
Power Moonroof [Opt on EX]	+279

Mileage Category: P

Kia joins the minivan rumble with the introduction of the Sedona, the lowest-priced minivan in America. Standard on the Sedona are such niceties as air conditioning, power windows, cruise control and auto on/off headlights. Upscale EX models get a CD player, interior wood trim and power front seats. All Sedonas benefit from Kia's impressive Long Haul Warranty with drivetrain protection for 10 years or 100,000 miles.

Kia
Sephia

2001

Body Styles	TMV Pricing		
	Trade	Private	Dealer
4 Dr LS Sdn	3092	4127	5082
4 Dr STD Sdn	2705	3610	4446

Options	Price	Options	Price
Air Conditioning	+365	Automatic 4-Speed Transmission	+395
Aluminum/Alloy Wheels	+138	Compact Disc Changer	+136
AM/FM/CD Audio System	+120		

Mileage Category: B

The 2001 Sephia features new safety items such as child seat anchors, front seatbelt pre-tensioners and an emergency internal trunk release. Changes for the 2001 model year also include dual visor vanity mirrors, a coin tray and a gas-cap tether.

2000
Mileage Category: B

The Sephia has improved seat fabric, a new audio system and two new colors for 2000.

Body Styles	TMV Pricing		
	Trade	Private	Dealer
4 Dr LS Sdn	2071	2892	3697
4 Dr STD Sdn	1882	2628	3360

Options	Price	Options	Price
Air Conditioning	+315	Antilock Brakes	+280
Aluminum/Alloy Wheels	+119	Automatic 4-Speed Transmission	+340
AM/FM/CD Audio System	+166	Power Windows	+122

1999
Mileage Category: B

The Sephia was entirely redesigned in '98 and enters '99 essentially unchanged.

Body Styles	TMV Pricing		
	Trade	Private	Dealer
4 Dr LS Sdn	1642	2439	3268
4 Dr STD Sdn	1464	2174	2913

Options	Price	Options	Price
Air Conditioning	+258	Automatic 4-Speed Transmission	+279
AM/FM/CD Audio System	+136	Leather Seats	+157
Antilock Brakes	+229		

1998
Mileage Category: B

The Sephia is totally redesigned for 1998.

Body Styles	TMV Pricing		
	Trade	Private	Dealer
4 Dr LS Sdn	1139	1875	2706
4 Dr STD Sdn	992	1632	2354

Options	Price
Air Conditioning	+216
Antilock Brakes	+192
Automatic 4-Speed Transmission	+234

1997

Body Styles	TMV Pricing		
	Trade	Private	Dealer
4 Dr GS Sdn	705	1290	2006
4 Dr LS Sdn	644	1178	1831
4 Dr RS Sdn	583	1066	1657

Options	Price
Air Conditioning	+171
Antilock Brakes	+175
Automatic 4-Speed Transmission	+172

Mileage Category: B

RS models get body-color bumpers this year, and a tan interior is newly available with black exterior paint.

Body Styles	TMV Pricing		
	Trade	Private	Dealer
4 Dr GS Sdn	538	1084	1838
4 Dr LS Sdn	469	946	1605
4 Dr RS Sdn	444	895	1518

Options	Price
Air Conditioning	+152
Antilock Brakes [Opt on GS]	+140
Automatic 4-Speed Transmission	+175

1996

Mileage Category: B

Styling and suspension tweaks, dual airbags and new twin-cam motors appeared with the introduction of the 1995.5 Sephia. These improvements, along with interior revisions and improved equipment levels, make the Kia more competitive in the compact sedan marketplace. Sephia now meets 1997 side-impact standards, and GS models can be equipped with antilock brakes. Sephia comes with five- year/60,000-mile powertrain coverage.

Body Styles	TMV Pricing			Body Styles	TMV Pricing		
	Trade	Private	Dealer		Trade	Private	Dealer
4 Dr GS Sdn	356	762	1439	4 Dr LS Sdn (1995.5)	332	712	1344
4 Dr GS Sdn (1995.5)	362	776	1465	4 Dr RS Sdn	293	627	1183
4 Dr LS Sdn	326	697	1316	4 Dr RS Sdn (1995.5)	306	656	1240

Options	Price
Automatic 4-Speed Transmission	+116
Air Conditioning	+115
Dual Front Airbag Restraints	+79

1995

Mileage Category: B

Oh no, another Korean manufacturer trying to break into the American market. But wait, this one is actually worth considering; a lot of help from Mazda and Ford mean that this little upstart is actually making fairly reliable little cars. The Sephia has plenty of Mazda parts and Kia has a long history of building durable, cheap cars.

Body Styles	TMV Pricing		
	Trade	Private	Dealer
4 Dr GS Sdn	293	657	1264
4 Dr LS Sdn	268	601	1156
4 Dr RS Sdn	247	553	1062

Options	Price
Air Conditioning	+84
Automatic 4-Speed Transmission	+85

1994

Mileage Category: B

New subcompact sedan from South Korea based on 1990-1994 Mazda Protege platform and powered by a 1.6-liter, 88-horsepower four-cylinder engine. Sold only in the Western and Southwestern regions of the U.S.

Kia
Sorento
2003

Body Styles	TMV Pricing			Body Styles	TMV Pricing		
	Trade	Private	Dealer		Trade	Private	Dealer
4 Dr EX 4WD SUV	15583	17048	19489	4 Dr LX 4WD SUV	13834	15134	17301
4 Dr EX SUV	14477	15838	18105	4 Dr LX SUV	12662	13852	15836

Options	Price	Options	Price
Aluminum/Alloy Wheels [Opt on LX]	+268	Heated Front Seats [Opt on EX]	+176
Antilock Brakes	+405	Leather Seats [Opt on EX]	+446
Automatic Load Leveling [Opt on EX]	+303	AM/FM/CD Changer Audio System [Opt on EX]	+193

Mileage Category: L

The Sorento is an all-new SUV from Kia. Larger and more powerful than the pint-size Sportage (which is expected to return for 2004 after a 2003 hiatus, by the way), the Sorento straddles the emerging middle ground between small SUVs and midsize SUVs. And it does so while offering interested buyers true off-road ability. Key competitors are the Ford Escape, the Honda CR-V, the Jeep Liberty, the Nissan Xterra and the Toyota Highlander.

Kia
Spectra

2003

Body Styles	TMV Pricing		
	Trade	Private	Dealer
4 Dr GS Hbk	5159	6012	7434
4 Dr GSX Hbk	6049	7050	8717

Body Styles	TMV Pricing		
	Trade	Private	Dealer
4 Dr LS Sdn	5648	6582	8139
4 Dr STD Sdn	4964	5785	7154

Options	Price
Air Conditioning [Opt on GS,STD]	+571
Aluminum/Alloy Wheels [Opt on LS]	+214
Antilock Brakes [Opt on GSX,LS]	+476
Automatic 4-Speed Transmission	+580

Options	Price
Compact Disc Changer	+199
Keyless Entry System [Opt on GSX,LS]	+125
Rear Spoiler [Opt on LS,STD]	+119

Mileage Category: L

For 2003, all Spectras will come with a CD player and body-color side moldings. Kia has attempted to make the cabin environment more hospitable via additional sound insulation in the roof and floor, an illuminated ignition and revised climate controls. Also, all hatchbacks get a standard rear wiper with an intermittent feature. Finally, note that engine specs have been revised this year -- the Spectra is now rated at 124 horsepower and 119 pound-feet of torque compared with 126 hp and 108 lb-ft for 2002. The four-cylinder engine itself is unchanged.

2002
Mileage Category: B

The Kia Sephia has officially been renamed the Spectra sedan. Got that? So now, there's the Spectra hatchback and the sedan; they've always shared mechanicals, so no big change there. The sedan will now sport some exterior styling cues borrowed from the five-door version.

Body Styles	TMV Pricing		
	Trade	Private	Dealer
4 Dr GS Hbk	3872	4631	5895
4 Dr GSX Hbk	4635	5543	7056

Body Styles	TMV Pricing		
	Trade	Private	Dealer
4 Dr LS Sdn	4322	5168	6579
4 Dr STD Sdn	3753	4488	5713

Options	Price
Air Conditioning [Opt on GS,STD]	+466
Aluminum/Alloy Wheels [Opt on LS]	+175
AM/FM/CD Audio System	+143

Options	Price
Antilock Brakes [Opt on GSX,LS]	+389
Automatic 4-Speed Transmission	+474
Compact Disc Changer [Opt on GSX,LS]	+163

2001
Mileage Category: B

2001 sees few changes to Kia's sporty five-door hatchback, which was introduced last year to attract younger customers to the brand. The top-rung GSX trim level gets a gas-cap tether, coin holder and dual visor vanity mirrors. Kia's Long Haul Warranty Program has also been introduced for this model year.

Body Styles	TMV Pricing		
	Trade	Private	Dealer
4 Dr GS Hbk	3031	4046	4983

Body Styles	TMV Pricing		
	Trade	Private	Dealer
4 Dr GSX Hbk	3627	4841	5962

Options	Price
Air Conditioning [Opt on GS]	+365
AM/FM/CD Audio System	+120
Antilock Brakes	+324

Options	Price
Automatic 4-Speed Transmission	+395
Compact Disc Changer	+136

2000
Mileage Category: B

The Spectra is new for 2000. Similar in size to the Sephia, Kia hopes the Spectra will attract younger buyers due to the versatile four-door hatchback design and sportier styling.

Body Styles	TMV Pricing		
	Trade	Private	Dealer
4 Dr GS Sdn	2272	3172	4055

Body Styles	TMV Pricing		
	Trade	Private	Dealer
4 Dr GSX Sdn	2519	3518	4497

Options	Price
Air Conditioning [Opt on GS]	+315
Antilock Brakes	+280

Options	Price
Automatic 4-Speed Transmission	+347
Compact Disc Changer	+138

Kia
Sportage

2002

Mileage Category: L

The Sportage is now in its eighth model year, so to help move its aged sport-ute along, Kia will offer the four-doors in just one trim level (eliminating the EX and Limited trim models) with more standard feature content than before, though you can no longer get leather upholstery. All Sportages are equipped with body-color door handles and an exterior latch on the rear hatch to ease loading cargo. A Two-Tone Package is available for hardtops; this option group contains two-tone cladding, bumpers and fenders and a cladding-color roof rack and hard-face spare tire cover. In addition, Kia has expanded the standard list of safety features to include seatbelt pre-tensioners and force limiters for the airbags. Finally, interested buyers should note that the Sportage will be going on hiatus for the 2003 model year (to make room for production of the new midsize '03 Sorento); a completely redesigned version (likely with unibody construction) is expected to return in the fall of 2003 as an '04 model.

2002 (cont'd)

Body Styles	TMV Pricing		
	Trade	Private	Dealer
2 Dr STD 4WD Conv	6839	7744	9251
2 Dr STD Conv	6602	7475	8930

Options	Price
Air Conditioning [Opt on Conv]	+449
Aluminum/Alloy Wheels [Opt on Conv]	+182
AM/FM/Cassette Audio System [Opt on Conv]	+170
Antilock Brakes [Opt on Wgn]	+330

Body Styles	TMV Pricing		
	Trade	Private	Dealer
4 Dr STD 4WD SUV	8072	9140	10919
4 Dr STD SUV	7713	8733	10434

Options	Price
Automatic 4-Speed Transmission [Opt on Wgn]	+486
Compact Disc Changer	+163
Cruise Control	+121

2001

Mileage Category: L

Kia's Long Haul warranty, introduced late in model-year 2000, provides powertrain coverage for 10 years or 100,000 miles, while a new Limited trim level includes lots of standard goodies over the already well-equipped Base and EX versions.

Body Styles	TMV Pricing		
	Trade	Private	Dealer
2 Dr STD 4WD Conv	5581	6853	8028
2 Dr STD Conv	5343	6561	7686
4 Dr EX 4WD SUV	6575	8074	9457

Options	Price
Air Conditioning [Opt on STD]	+365
Aluminum/Alloy Wheels [Opt on STD]	+138
AM/FM/Cassette Audio System	+130
AM/FM/CD Audio System [Opt on STD]	+193

Body Styles	TMV Pricing		
	Trade	Private	Dealer
4 Dr EX SUV	6177	7585	8884
4 Dr STD 4WD SUV	6028	7402	8670
4 Dr STD SUV	5669	6961	8154

Options	Price
Antilock Brakes	+276
Automatic 4-Speed Transmission [Opt on 4 Dr]	+405
Compact Disc Changer	+136
Leather Seats	+345

2000

Mileage Category: L

Kia ushers in the 2000 Sportage with a new sound system, dual airbags, new colors and some additional equipment, but keeps last year's MSRP.

Body Styles	TMV Pricing		
	Trade	Private	Dealer
2 Dr STD 4WD Conv	4397	5543	6666
2 Dr STD Conv	4167	5253	6317
4 Dr EX 4WD SUV	5041	6355	7642

Options	Price
Air Conditioning [Opt on STD]	+315
Aluminum/Alloy Wheels [Opt on STD]	+119
AM/FM/Cassette/CD Audio System	+166
AM/FM/CD Audio System [Opt on STD]	+166

Body Styles	TMV Pricing		
	Trade	Private	Dealer
4 Dr EX SUV	4697	5921	7120
4 Dr STD 4WD SUV	4659	5873	7063
4 Dr STD SUV	4488	5658	6804

Options	Price
Antilock Brakes	+238
Automatic 4-Speed Transmission [Opt on 4 Dr]	+349
Compact Disc Changer	+138
Leather Seats	+297

1999

Mileage Category: L

A new two-door convertible model joins the four-door Sportage in 1999. The convertible comes in either a 4x2 layout with automatic transmission or a 4x4 layout with five-speed manual transmission. It also boasts dual front airbags and a driver-side front knee bag.

Body Styles	TMV Pricing		
	Trade	Private	Dealer
2 Dr STD 4WD Conv	3781	4872	6008
2 Dr STD Conv	3526	4543	5602
4 Dr EX 4WD SUV	4200	5412	6673

Options	Price
Air Conditioning [Opt on STD]	+258
AM/FM/CD Audio System [Opt on STD]	+136
Antilock Brakes	+216

Body Styles	TMV Pricing		
	Trade	Private	Dealer
4 Dr EX SUV	3973	5120	6313
4 Dr STD 4WD SUV	3890	5013	6181
4 Dr STD SUV	3831	4936	6087

Options	Price
Automatic 4-Speed Transmission	+286
Leather Seats	+244

1998

Mileage Category: L

There are lots of improvements this year for the Sportage, including a new grille, new alloy wheels, tilt steering wheel, passenger-side airbag, better brakes, improved air conditioning and four-wheel ABS that replaces last year's rear-wheel ABS.

Body Styles	TMV Pricing		
	Trade	Private	Dealer
4 Dr EX 4WD SUV	3509	4620	5873
4 Dr EX SUV	3507	4618	5870

Body Styles	TMV Pricing		
	Trade	Private	Dealer
4 Dr STD 4WD SUV	3296	4340	5518
4 Dr STD SUV	3194	4205	5346

1998 (cont'd)

Options	Price
Air Conditioning	+216
Antilock Brakes	+181

Options	Price
Automatic 4-Speed Transmission	+240
Leather Seats	+216

1997

Mileage Category: L

An automatic transmission is offered on 2WD models, and the EX trim level is available in 2WD for the first time. Power door locks, a theft-deterrent system and a spare tire carrier are all standard on all Sportages for 1997. A new option is a CD player. Sportage gets a new grille. A tan interior can be combined with black paint for the first time. Base 2WD models lose their standard alloy wheels.

Body Styles	TMV Pricing		
	Trade	Private	Dealer
4 Dr EX 4WD SUV	2787	3782	4998
4 Dr EX SUV	2719	3689	4875
4 Dr STD 4WD SUV	2761	3746	4950
4 Dr STD SUV	2564	3479	4598

Options	Price
Air Conditioning	+177
Automatic 4-Speed Transmission	+196
Leather Seats	+196

1996

Mileage Category: L

The world's first knee airbag arrives in conjunction with a driver airbag, and a two-wheel-drive edition is available this year. A spirited twin-cam engine arrived late in 1995, and cured Sportage's power ills.

Body Styles	TMV Pricing		
	Trade	Private	Dealer
4 Dr EX 4WD SUV	2274	3200	4478
4 Dr EX SUV	2344	3298	4616
4 Dr STD 4WD SUV	2114	2975	4164
4 Dr STD SUV	1913	2692	3768

Options	Price
Automatic 4-Speed Transmission	+175
Leather Seats	+175
Air Conditioning	+158

1995

Mileage Category: L

Another mini-SUV is introduced, competing with everything from the Jeep Cherokee to the Geo Tracker. The Sportage offers comfortable seating for four, ample storage space and available four-wheel drive. Designed with Ford and Mazda, with suspension tuning by Lotus, the Sportage should provide a good deal of fun and durability.

Body Styles	TMV Pricing		
	Trade	Private	Dealer
4 Dr EX 4WD SUV	1815	2533	3729
4 Dr STD 4WD SUV	1582	2208	3252
4 Dr STD SUV	1432	1999	2944

Options	Price
2.0L I4 DOHC 16V FI Engine	+79
Air Conditioning	+119
Automatic 4-Speed Transmission	+132
Leather Seats	+112

1997

Body Styles	TMV Pricing		
	Trade	Private	Dealer
2 Dr 90 4WD Conv	22183	25234	28964
2 Dr 90 4WD SUV	23159	26345	30238

Options	Price
Air Conditioning	+409

Mileage Category: O

After a one-year hiatus, Defender 90 returns in convertible and hardtop body styles. A 4.0-liter V8 engine is standard, mated to a ZF four-speed automatic transmission. A redesigned center console includes cupholders, and hardtops have new interior trim. Convertibles get improved top sealing, while all Defender 90s are treated to fresh paint colors.

1995

Body Styles	TMV Pricing		
	Trade	Private	Dealer
2 Dr 90 4WD SUV	14324	16947	21318

Options	Price
Air Conditioning	+303
Aluminum/Alloy Wheels	+391
Special Factory Paint	+88

Mileage Category: O

Later in the model year, a new five-speed manual transmission (the only gearbox fitted to the Defender) debuts and features full syncromesh for reverse gear, decreasing the likelihood of embarrassing grinding noises when one attempts to back up. Land Rover claims the overall shift action is lighter and more precise, and that the new clutch requires less pressure to operate.

1994

Body Styles	TMV Pricing		
	Trade	Private	Dealer
2 Dr 90 4WD SUV	12710	15230	19430

Options	Price
Air Conditioning	+301
Aluminum/Alloy Wheels	+390
Hardtop Roof	+377

Mileage Category: O

After bringing the four-door Defender 110 to our shores last year, Land Rover decides to pull that model from the U.S. market and instead offer us the two-door version, called the Defender 90. As before, the number that is part of the Defender's name refers to the wheelbase length, rounded off in this case as it's actually 92.9 inches. A 3.9-liter, 182-horsepower V8, permanent 4WD and a five-speed manual gearbox are standard (no automatic is available). So are just two seats, though a small rear bench is optional. With its blocky body style, exposed door hinges and primitive cabin décor, the Defender 90 looks as if it could be a Land Rover from 30 years ago, but its simple and rugged design makes it an ideal means of transport for African Safari enthusiasts.

Land Rover
Discovery

2003

Body Styles	TMV Pricing		
	Trade	Private	Dealer
4 Dr HSE AWD SUV	28978	30537	33135
4 Dr S AWD SUV	24764	26096	28317
4 Dr SE AWD SUV	26423	27845	30214

Options	Price	Options	Price
Automatic Load Leveling [Opt on SE]	+535	Special Factory Paint	+214
Automatic Stability Control [Opt on HSE,SE]	+1213	Third Seat	+714
Dual Sunroofs [Opt on S]	+1070	Air Conditioning - Front and Rear	+464
Heated Front Seats	+214		

Mileage Category: O

Land Rover has made a number of updates to its 2003 Discovery. In terms of mechanical components, the company has installed a more powerful 4.6-liter V8 engine and has improved the steering, brakes and suspension. Styling is revised front and rear, including headlamps that mimic its bigger brother's, the Range Rover. New interior treatments grace the cabin, and a rear park distance control is now an option. Finally, Land Rover has dropped the "Series II" nomenclature, and it's now simply called "Discovery."

Land Rover
Discovery

1999

Mileage Category: O

The release of the 1999 Discovery Series II sees the first engineering redesign since the vehicle's European introduction 11 years ago. Traction Control, Active Cornering Enhancement and Hill Descent Control are new standard features.

Body Styles	TMV Pricing		
	Trade	Private	Dealer
4 Dr SD AWD SUV	12144	13736	15393
4 Dr Series II AWD SUV	12623	14277	15999

Options	Price	Options	Price
Air Conditioning - Front and Rear	+246	Jump Seat(s)	+212
Automatic Load Leveling [Opt on Series II]	+201	Leather Seats [Opt on Series II]	+320
Compact Disc Changer	+205	Performance/Handling Package	+904
Dual Power Moonroofs	+493	Power Driver Seat [Opt on Series II]	+119
Heated Front Seats	+164	Power Passenger Seat [Opt on Series II]	+119

1998

Mileage Category: O

Changes to the Discovery include interior trim nhancements for the LE and LSE. The rearview mirror also features map lights for the first time.

Body Styles	TMV Pricing		
	Trade	Private	Dealer
4 Dr 50th Anniv AWD SUV	10695	12219	13937
4 Dr LE AWD SUV	9792	11187	12761
4 Dr LSE AWD SUV	10178	11628	13263

Options	Price
Air Conditioning - Front and Rear	+207
Compact Disc Changer [Opt on LE]	+172
Jump Seat(s)	+345

1997

Mileage Category: O

A diversity antenna is added, and all interiors are trimmed with polished burled walnut. The sunroof has darker tinting, the airbag system benefits from simplified operation and engine management is improved. Three new exterior colors debut: Oxford Blue, Rioja Red and Charleston Green.

Body Styles	TMV Pricing		
	Trade	Private	Dealer
4 Dr LSE AWD SUV	8047	9370	10988
4 Dr SD AWD SUV	7484	8715	10219
4 Dr SE AWD SUV	7769	9047	10608

Body Styles	TMV Pricing		
	Trade	Private	Dealer
4 Dr SE7 AWD SUV	8527	9929	11643
4 Dr XD AWD SUV	7533	8772	10286

Options	Price
Compact Disc Changer	+213
Jump Seat(s) [Std on SE7]	+401
Leather Seats [Opt on SD]	+333

Options	Price
Power Driver Seat [Opt on SD]	+116
Power Passenger Seat [Opt on SD]	+116

1996

Mileage Category: O

Three new trim levels, a revised engine that gets better around-town fuel economy, new colors, increased seat travel and new power seats sum up the changes for 1996.

Body Styles	TMV Pricing		
	Trade	Private	Dealer
4 Dr SD AWD SUV	5947	7010	8479
4 Dr SE AWD SUV	6291	7416	8969
4 Dr SE7 AWD SUV	6403	7548	9130

Options	Price
Automatic 4-Speed Transmission [Std on SE]	+232
Compact Disc Changer	+126
Leather Seats [Opt on SD]	+197
Third Seat [Std on SE7]	+121

1995

Mileage Category: O

Introduced as a late-1994 model-year vehicle, the Discovery continues into its second year unchanged.

Body Styles	TMV Pricing		
	Trade	Private	Dealer
4 Dr STD AWD SUV	5083	6014	7566

1995 (cont'd)

Options	Price	Options	Price
Air Conditioning - Front and Rear	+189	Dual Power Moonroofs	+378
AM/FM/CD Audio System	+126	Leather Seats	+246
Automatic 4-Speed Transmission	+227	Special Factory Paint	+76

1994

Mileage Category: O

Body Styles	TMV Pricing		
	Trade	Private	Dealer
4 Dr STD AWD SUV	4562	5466	6972

Options	Price	Options	Price
Air Conditioning - Front and Rear	+188	Jump Seat(s)	+295
Automatic 4-Speed Transmission	+226	Leather Seats	+245
Dual Power Moonroofs	+377	Special Factory Paint	+75

Riding a short 100-inch wheelbase, the new Discovery is still able to seat up to seven if the optional rear jump seats are ordered. A raised roof over the rear compartment and a boxy, upright body with tall windows make the Discovery unmistakably Land Rover. The workhorse 3.9-liter V8 of 1960s GM origins sends its 182 horses to the permanent 4WD system through a choice of either a manual or automatic gearbox. Dual airbags and antilock brakes are standard on the Discovery.

Land Rover
Discovery Series II

2002

Body Styles	TMV Pricing		
	Trade	Private	Dealer
4 Dr SD AWD SUV	20192	21457	23564
4 Dr SE AWD SUV	22358	23758	26092

Options	Price	Options	Price
Air Conditioning - Front and Rear	+464	Heated Front Seats	+278
Automatic Load Leveling [Opt on SE]	+774	Special Factory Paint	+186
Dual Power Sunroofs [Opt on SD]	+928	Third Seat	+619

Mileage Category: O

Discovery gets new alloy wheels, along with a standard 300-watt Harman-Kardon sound system and an available factory-installed navigation system.

2001

Mileage Category: O

Body Styles	TMV Pricing		
	Trade	Private	Dealer
4 Dr LE AWD SUV	17843	19599	21219
4 Dr SD AWD SUV	17621	19355	20956
4 Dr SE AWD SUV	18918	20780	22498

Options	Price	Options	Price
Air Conditioning - Front and Rear	+386	Heated Front Seats	+257
Automatic Load Leveling	+386	Special Factory Paint	+154
Dual Power Moonroofs [Opt on LE,SD]	+772	Third Seat	+617

Land Rover introduces three new trim levels to the Discovery Series II lineup -- SD, LE and SE. New paint options are Oslo Blue and Bonatti Gray.

2000

Mileage Category: O

Body Styles	TMV Pricing		
	Trade	Private	Dealer
4 Dr STD AWD SUV	14529	16282	18001

Options	Price	Options	Price
Compact Disc Changer	+250	Power Driver Seat	+140
Dual Power Moonroofs	+600	Power Passenger Seat	+140
Heated Front Seats	+200	Special Factory Paint	+120
Jump Seat(s)	+232	Split Folding Rear Seat	+160
Leather Seats	+390	Air Conditioning - Front and Rear	+300
Automatic Stability Control	+260	Automatic Load Leveling	+220
Performance/Handling Package	+1101		

The Discovery was completely redesigned last year and sees only minor interior trim revisions for the 2000 model year.

Land Rover
Discovery Series II/Freelander/Range Rover

1999

Mileage Category: O

The release of the 1999 Discovery Series II sees the first engineering redesign since the vehicle's European introduction 11 years ago. Traction Control, Active Cornering Enhancement and Hill Descent Control are new standard features.

Body Styles	TMV Pricing		
	Trade	Private	Dealer
4 Dr SD AWD Wgn	14875	16496	18184
4 Dr Series II AWD Wgn	15460	17146	18900

Options	Price
Air Conditioning - Front and Rear	+287
Compact Disc Changer	+239
Dual Power Seats [Std on SD]	+259
Dual Sunroofs	+624
Heated Front Seats	+191

Options	Price
Jump Seat(s)	+247
Leather Seats [Std on SD]	+374
Performance/Handling Package	+1055
Special Factory Paint	+115

Land Rover
Freelander

2003

Body Styles	TMV Pricing		
	Trade	Private	Dealer
2 Dr SE3 AWD SUV	17421	18636	20661
4 Dr HSE AWD SUV	20774	22223	24638

Options	Price
Compact Disc Changer [Opt on S,SE,SE3]	+285
Harman Kardon Audio System [Opt on S,SE]	+535
Heated Front Seats	+214

Body Styles	TMV Pricing		
	Trade	Private	Dealer
4 Dr S AWD SUV	16521	17673	19594
4 Dr SE AWD SUV	18327	19605	21736

Options	Price
Power Moonroof [Opt on SE]	+624
Special Factory Paint	+143

Mileage Category: O

Engineering changes for Land Rover's mini-ute include a larger fuel tank and an improvement in the climate control system for quieter operation and more efficiency. Body side moldings have been added to protect the Freelander against scrapes. The 2003 model year sees the introduction of the three-door SE3 version, with removable top and rear panels for topless fun like a Jeep Wrangler.

2002

Mileage Category: O

The first new Land Rover to come to America since 1995, the compact Freelander is expected to boost U.S. sales by 50 percent by offering the go-anywhere cachet of the LR brand name and the daily drivability of a small SUV in a package priced under $30,000.

Body Styles	TMV Pricing		
	Trade	Private	Dealer
4 Dr HSE AWD SUV	18336	19724	22037
4 Dr S AWD SUV	14522	15621	17453
4 Dr SE AWD SUV	16166	17390	19429

Options	Price
Harman Kardon Audio System [Opt on S,SE]	+464
Heated Front Seats	+186
Power Moonroof [Opt on S,SE]	+541

Land Rover
Range Rover

2003

Body Styles	TMV Pricing		
	Trade	Private	Dealer
4 Dr HSE AWD SUV	56549	59305	63898

Options	Price
Heated Front and Rear Seats	+464
Special Leather Interior Trim	+1284

2003 (cont'd)

Mileage Category: O

As this is just the third new Range Rover in 31 years, one might hope that the 2003 Range Rover hosts some significant improvements. Indeed it does. Land Rover has focused on improving drivability and livability. As such, this updated flagship SUV features unit body construction, a four-wheel independent suspension and a BMW-engineered V8 mated to a five-speed automatic transmission. It also boasts more interior space, greater ground clearance and a beautifully revised interior.

Body Styles	TMV Pricing		
	Trade	Private	Dealer
4 Dr 4.6 HSE AWD SUV	40702	43251	47500

2002

Mileage Category: O

With an all-new Range Rover set to debut for 2003, the only change to the existing model for 2002 is the addition of a Westminster special edition.

2001

Mileage Category: O

Land Rover's venerable Range Rover will now come standard with a 4.6-liter V8 engine. A navigation system is now standard on the 4.6 HSE model and optional on the 4.6 SE, as is a new premium audio system. New exterior colors are Oslo Blue and Bonatti Grey.

Body Styles	TMV Pricing		
	Trade	Private	Dealer
4 Dr 4.6 HSE AWD SUV	31008	34057	36871
4 Dr 4.6 SE AWD SUV	25824	28363	30707

Options	Price
Navigation System	+1541
Special Factory Paint	+154

2000

Mileage Category: O

The 2000 Range Rover now qualifies as a low-emissions vehicle. Interior and exterior upgrades improve the vehicle's look and feel, and new trim levels allow buyers to further dress up their Range Rover's appearance

Body Styles	TMV Pricing			Body Styles	TMV Pricing		
	Trade	Private	Dealer		Trade	Private	Dealer
4 Dr 4.0 SE AWD SUV	20396	22718	24995	4 Dr 4.6 Vitesse AWD SUV	24182	26935	29634
4 Dr 4.6 HSE AWD SUV	24182	26935	29634	4 Dr County AWD SUV	20000	22277	24509

Options	Price
Navigation System	+1137
Special Factory Paint	+120

1999

Mileage Category: O

Engine upgrades, new color schemes, traction control and standard side-mounted airbags are some of the additions to the 1999 Range Rovers, which will be introduced later in the year. For now, interim Range Rover models called the 4.0 and 4.0S are available.

Body Styles	TMV Pricing			Body Styles	TMV Pricing		
	Trade	Private	Dealer		Trade	Private	Dealer
4 Dr 4.0 AWD SUV	17160	19409	21750	4 Dr 4.0 SE AWD SUV	17188	19441	21785
4 Dr 4.0 S AWD SUV	17378	19656	22027	4 Dr 4.6 HSE AWD SUV	20089	22722	25462

Options	Price
Navigation System	+747

1998

Mileage Category: O

Range Rover models get a new Harman Kardon audio system this year. Other changes include a new upholstery stitch pattern and a leather-wrapped gearshift knob.

Body Styles	TMV Pricing		
	Trade	Private	Dealer
4 Dr 4.0 SE AWD SUV	13409	15319	17473
4 Dr 4.6 HSE AWD SUV	17224	19678	22446
4 Dr 50th Anniv AWD SUV	15496	17704	20194

1997

Mileage Category: O

The 4.0 SE gets three new exterior colors (Oxford Blue, Rioja Red and White Gold, all matched to Saddle leather interior), a HomeLink transmitter and jeweled wheel center caps. The 4.6 HSE gets three new exterior colors (British Racing Green, Monza Red and AA Yellow), one new interior color (Lightstone with contrasting piping) and a leather shift handle.

Body Styles	TMV Pricing		
	Trade	Private	Dealer
4 Dr 4.0 SE AWD SUV	11578	13365	15550
4 Dr 4.6 HSE AWD SUV	13700	15815	18400

Options	Price
Vitesse Package	+239

1996

Mileage Category: O

Base 4.0 SE model is unchanged for 1996. A new, more powerful 4.6 HSE model debuts, giving buyers extra horsepower, fat wheels and tires, mud flaps and chrome exhaust for a $7,000 premium over the 4.0 SE.

Body Styles	TMV Pricing		
	Trade	Private	Dealer
4 Dr 4.0 SE AWD SUV	9281	10820	12946
4 Dr 4.6 HSE AWD SUV	10905	12714	15212

1995

Mileage Category: O

The new 4.0 SE is introduced as a late '95 model. Styling is an evolution of the classic Range Rover look. A new chassis sports an electronic air suspension and a 4.0-liter V8 that produces 190 horsepower. This top-of-the-line SUV also includes luxuries such as the obligatory leather and wood trimmed cabin and a premium stereo with a six-disc CD changer.

Body Styles	TMV Pricing		
	Trade	Private	Dealer
4 Dr 4.0 SE AWD SUV	7436	8798	11067
4 Dr County Classic AWD SUV	5767	6823	8584
4 Dr County LWB AWD SUV	6605	7814	9830

Options	Price
Special Factory Paint	+76

1994

Mileage Category: O

No changes this year for the official SUV of the rich and famous.

Body Styles	TMV Pricing		
	Trade	Private	Dealer
4 Dr County AWD SUV	4773	5719	7296
4 Dr County LWB AWD SUV	5603	6714	8566

2003

Body Styles	TMV Pricing		
	Trade	Private	Dealer
4 Dr STD Sdn	24395	25783	28096

Options	Price	Options	Price
Chrome Wheels	+1300	Traction Control System	+497
Compact Disc Changer	+421	Power Rear Window Sunshade	+161
Electronic Suspension Control	+474	Mark Levinson Audio System	+440
Heated Front Seats	+336	AM/FM/CD Changer Audio System	+421
Leather Seats	+765	Power Driver Seat w/Memory	+229
Navigation System	+1529		

Mileage Category: H

Completely redesigned last year, the 2003 ES 300's only change is the addition of power-adjustable pedals.

2002

Mileage Category: H

Body Styles	TMV Pricing		
	Trade	Private	Dealer
4 Dr STD Sdn	22571	23985	26342

Options	Price	Options	Price
AM/FM/Cassette/CD Changer Audio System	+268	Mark Levinson Audio System	+411
Automatic Stability Control	+286	Navigation System	+1431
Chrome Wheels	+1216	Power Driver Seat w/Memory	+215
Compact Disc Changer	+393	Power Moonroof	+644
Electronic Suspension Control	+443	Power Rear Window Sunshade	+150
Heated Front Seats	+315	Traction Control System	+179
Leather Seats	+715		

Lexus has introduced a completely redesigned ES 300 for 2002. The new car is roomier and quieter than the previous car, and in many ways has become more closely aligned with the LS 430 flagship model. Safety and feature quotients have been increased, and the car is wrapped in a svelte new body.

2001

Body Styles	TMV Pricing		
	Trade	Private	Dealer
4 Dr STD Sdn	18537	20405	22130

Options	Price	Options	Price
Automatic Stability Control	+349	Leather Seats	+635
Chrome Wheels	+1104	Nakamichi Audio System	+1034
Compact Disc Changer	+685	Power Driver Seat w/Memory	+190
Electronic Suspension Control	+393	Power Moonroof	+543
Heated Front Seats	+279		

Mileage Category: H

A glow-in-the-dark emergency trunk release handle is now located in the cargo compartment, while child seat-tether anchors have been added inside.

2000

Mileage Category: H

Body Styles	TMV Pricing		
	Trade	Private	Dealer
4 Dr STD Sdn	16501	18451	20362

Options	Price	Options	Price
AM/FM/Cassette/CD Audio System	+292	Leather Seats	+531
Automatic Stability Control	+292	Nakamichi Audio System	+637
Compact Disc Changer	+319	Power Driver Seat w/Memory	+159
Heated Front Seats	+186	Power Moonroof	+454

The Lexus ES 300 sports new front-end styling and taillights. The rearview and driver-side mirrors are now electrochromatic for improved nighttime performance. The interior gets new colors and additional wood trim on the audio/heater panel. The mirrors are added to the memory seat function. High-intensity discharge headlights are optional, as are 16-inch wheels. BrakeAssist is included in the Vehicle Skid Control option. A particle-and-odor air filter is a new option. The ES 300 also receives child seat-anchor brackets and three new colors.

1999

Body Styles	TMV Pricing		
	Trade	Private	Dealer
4 Dr STD Sdn	13845	15681	17592

Lexus
ES 300

1999 (cont'd)

Mileage Category: H

A new 3.0-liter V6 engine with VVT-i (Variable Valve Timing with intelligence) gives the 1999 ES 300 more horsepower, lower emissions and improved fuel economy. Optional Vehicle Skid Control (VSC) is available on the new ES as are one-touch open and close front windows and a one-touch operated moonroof.

Options	Price	Options	Price
AM/FM/Cassette/CD Audio System	+238	Leather Seats	+481
Chrome Wheels	+385	Nakamichi Audio System	+577
Compact Disc Changer	+289	Power Driver Seat w/Memory	+144
Heated Front Seats	+168	Power Moonroof	+411

1998

Mileage Category: H

Side-impact airbags debut on Lexus's entry-level car, as does an engine immobilizer anti-theft system and an optional Nakamichi audio system. Reduced force front airbags are also new on all 1998 Lexus models.

Body Styles		TMV Pricing		
		Trade	Private	Dealer
4 Dr STD Sdn		10885	12504	14329

Options	Price	Options	Price
AM/FM/Cassette/CD Audio System	+196	Leather Seats	+396
Chrome Wheels	+317	Nakamichi Audio System	+475
Compact Disc Changer	+238	Power Driver Seat w/Memory	+119
Heated Front Seats	+139	Power Moonroof	+339

1997

Mileage Category: H

The entry-level Lexus has been totally redesigned this year, growing in nearly every dimension. Lexus manages to eke out more power from the ES 300's 3.0-liter V6 engine. No longer just a dressed-up Camry, the ES 300 has finally come into its own.

Body Styles		TMV Pricing		
		Trade	Private	Dealer
4 Dr STD Sdn		9528	11096	13012

Options	Price	Options	Price
AM/FM/Cassette/CD Audio System	+160	Leather Seats	+324
Chrome Wheels	+259	Power Moonroof	+277
Compact Disc Changer	+194		

1996

Body Styles		TMV Pricing		
		Trade	Private	Dealer
4 Dr STD Sdn		7240	8539	10332

Options	Price	Options	Price
AM/FM/Cassette/CD Audio System	+130	Leather Seats	+263
Chrome Wheels	+211	Power Moonroof	+225
Compact Disc Changer	+158		

Mileage Category: H

Two new colors are available.

1995

Mileage Category: H

Styling is freshened, and chrome wheels are available. Trunk-mounted CD changer is a new option.

Body Styles		TMV Pricing		
		Trade	Private	Dealer
4 Dr STD Sdn		6288	7454	9397

Options	Price	Options	Price
Chrome Wheels	+189	Leather Seats	+236
Compact Disc Changer	+142	Power Moonroof	+202
Heated Front Seats	+83		

1994

Mileage Category: H

Passenger airbag added. New 3.0-liter engine has aluminum block and a few more horsepower. Several convenience features are now standard, including an outside temperature gauge.

Body Styles		TMV Pricing		
		Trade	Private	Dealer
4 Dr STD Sdn		4842	5894	7648

Options	Price	Options	Price
Compact Disc Changer	+126	Power Moonroof	+180
Leather Seats	+211		

2003

Body Styles	TMV Pricing		
	Trade	Private	Dealer
4 Dr STD Sdn	28559	30107	32688

Options	Price	Options	Price
Chrome Wheels	+1300	Rear Spoiler	+336
Compact Disc Changer	+497	Sport Suspension	+344
Heated Front Seats	+336	Mark Levinson Audio System	+459
Leather Seats	+956	Power Driver Seat w/Memory	+229
Navigation System	+1529		

Mileage Category: I

The only changes of note for the GS 300 this year are a now standard moonroof, an in-dash CD changer and wider tires (going from a 215mm tread to a 225mm tread).

2002

Body Styles	TMV Pricing		
	Trade	Private	Dealer
4 Dr STD Sdn	25374	26901	29447

Options	Price	Options	Price
Chrome Wheels	+1216	Navigation System	+1431
Compact Disc Changer	+536	Power Driver Seat w/Memory	+215
Heated Front Seats	+315	Power Moonroof	+715
Leather Seats	+894	Sport Suspension	+322
Mark Levinson Audio System	+429		

Mileage Category: I

After a number of upgrades last year, the GS 300 enters 2002 unchanged.

2001

Body Styles	TMV Pricing		
	Trade	Private	Dealer
4 Dr STD Sdn	22374	24677	26803

Options	Price	Options	Price
Automatic Dimming Sideview Mirror(s)	+127	Mark Levinson Audio System	+787
Chrome Wheels	+1079	Navigation System	+1269
Compact Disc Changer	+685	Power Driver Seat w/Memory	+190
Heated Front Seats	+279	Power Moonroof	+647
Leather Seats	+762		

Mileage Category: I

GS 430 gets a new ULEV-certified, 4.3-liter V8 good for 300 horsepower and 325 ft-lbs. of torque, resulting in sub-6-second acceleration times to 60 mph. GS 300 has new E-shift buttons on the steering wheel for manual control of the automatic transmission's shift points. On the safety front, standard side curtain airbags debut on both models, and a new sensor detects if the front passenger seat is unoccupied, deactivating the front passenger airbag if nobody is sitting in that seat. Additionally, a new child seat-tether restraint has been added, along with impact-detecting door locks and an emergency trunk release handle that glows in the dark inside the cargo area. Exterior changes include water-repellent front door glass, a new grille with a bigger "L" badge, revised taillights, larger exhaust pipes with stainless-steel tips and new six-spoke alloy wheels. HID headlights are optional on GS 300 but standard on GS 430. Inside, steering wheel controls for the audio system come standard, a compass has been added and a new DVD-based navigation system is optional. Bummer that it's bundled with trip computer, audio and climate control systems. Mark Levinson audio is newly optional, replacing Nakamichi as the premium sound supplier. GS 300 gets more wood trim inside the cabin, while GS 430 dashboards have new metallic-gray trim. A wood and leather steering wheel is optional on the 430. Four new colors round out this long list of updates for 2001.

2000

Body Styles	TMV Pricing		
	Trade	Private	Dealer
4 Dr STD Sdn	19701	21902	24059

Options	Price	Options	Price
Compact Disc Changer	+319	Chrome Wheels	+425
Heated Front Seats	+186	Platinum Series	+2411
Leather Seats	+637	Power Driver Seat w/Memory	+159
Nakamichi Audio System	+691	Power Moonroof	+505
Navigation System	+1062		

Mileage Category: I

The GS 300 gets a new BrakeAssist system and child seat-anchor brackets. The GS 300 is certified as a low-emission vehicle. Crystal White and Millennium Silver Metallic replace Diamond White Pearl and Alpine Silver Metallic.

GS 300

1999

Mileage Category: I

The GS 300 was totally redesigned last year with improvements in performance and a completely new look. As a result, the 1999 model goes unchanged except for the addition of daytime running lights and standard floor mats.

Body Styles	TMV Pricing		
	Trade	Private	Dealer
4 Dr STD Sdn	17178	19264	21435

Options	Price	Options	Price
Chrome Wheels	+385	Nakamichi Audio System	+626
Compact Disc Changer	+289	Navigation System	+770
Heated Front Seats	+168	Power Driver Seat w/Memory	+144
Leather Seats	+577	Power Moonroof	+457

1998

Mileage Category: I

A totally redesigned GS 300 appears for 1998. Featuring the familiar inline-six engine of the previous model, the new car lives up to the promise of providing serious fun in an elegant package.

Body Styles	TMV Pricing		
	Trade	Private	Dealer
4 Dr STD Sdn	14955	16908	19111

Options	Price	Options	Price
Chrome Wheels	+317	Nakamichi Audio System	+515
Compact Disc Changer	+238	Navigation System	+634
Heated Front Seats	+139	Power Driver Seat w/Memory	+119
Leather Seats	+475	Power Moonroof	+376

1997

Body Styles	TMV Pricing		
	Trade	Private	Dealer
4 Dr STD Sdn	12586	14429	16681

Options	Price	Options	Price
Chrome Wheels	+259	Nakamichi Audio System	+421
Compact Disc Changer	+194	Power Moonroof	+307
Leather Seats	+388	Traction Control System	+162

Mileage Category: I

No changes during final year before a redesign.

1996

Mileage Category: I

A five-speed automatic transmission makes the GS 300 feel more sporty, while rear styling revisions and five new exterior colors update the suave exterior. Side-impact standards for 1997 were met this year, and the power moonroof features one-touch operation.

Body Styles	TMV Pricing		
	Trade	Private	Dealer
4 Dr STD Sdn	10351	11994	14264

Options	Price	Options	Price
Chrome Wheels	+211	Nakamichi Audio System	+343
Compact Disc Changer	+158	Power Moonroof	+250
Leather Seats	+316	Traction Control System	+132

1995

Mileage Category: I

No changes.

Body Styles	TMV Pricing		
	Trade	Private	Dealer
4 Dr STD Sdn	8919	10362	12767

Options	Price	Options	Price
Power Moonroof	+212	Compact Disc Changer	+236
Traction Control System	+177	Heated Front Seats	+118
Nakamichi Audio System	+260	Leather Seats	+283

1994

Mileage Category: I

No changes.

Body Styles	TMV Pricing		
	Trade	Private	Dealer
4 Dr STD Sdn	7261	8553	10705

1994 (cont'd)

Options	Price	Options	Price
AM/FM/Cassette/CD Audio System	+126	Nakamichi Audio System	+274
Compact Disc Changer	+126	Power Moonroof	+200
Leather Seats	+253	Traction Control System	+105

Lexus
GS 400

2000

Body Styles		TMV Pricing	
	Trade	Private	Dealer
4 Dr STD Sdn	21440	23835	26183

Options	Price	Options	Price
Chrome Wheels	+425	Navigation System	+1062
Compact Disc Changer	+319	Platinum Series	+2544
Heated Front Seats	+186	Power Moonroof	+505
Nakamichi Audio System	+691	Rear Spoiler	+186

Mileage Category: I

The GS 400 gets a new BrakeAssist system and child seat-anchor brackets. Crystal White and Millennium Silver Metallic replace Diamond White Pearl and Alpine Silver Metallic.

1999

Mileage Category: I

The GS 400 was totally redesigned last year with improvements in performance and a completely new look. As a result, the 1999 model goes unchanged except for the addition of daytime running lights and standard floor mats.

Body Styles		TMV Pricing	
	Trade	Private	Dealer
4 Dr STD Sdn	18924	21222	23614

Options	Price	Options	Price
Chrome Wheels	+385	Navigation System	+770
Compact Disc Changer	+289	Power Moonroof	+457
Heated Front Seats	+168	Rear Spoiler	+168
Nakamichi Audio System	+626		

1998

Mileage Category: I

A totally redesigned GS 400 appears for 1998. Featuring a V8 with continuously variable valve timing, the new car lives up to the promise of providing serious fun in an elegant package.

Body Styles		TMV Pricing	
	Trade	Private	Dealer
4 Dr STD Sdn	15816	17882	20211

Options	Price	Options	Price
Chrome Wheels	+317	Navigation System	+634
Compact Disc Changer	+238	Power Moonroof	+376
Heated Front Seats	+139	Rear Spoiler	+139
Nakamichi Audio System	+515		

Lexus
GS 430

2003

Body Styles		TMV Pricing	
	Trade	Private	Dealer
4 Dr STD Sdn	36338	38122	41096

Options	Price	Options	Price
Chrome Wheels	+1300	AM/FM/Cassette/CD Changer Audio System	+497
Navigation System	+1529	Mark Levinson Audio System	+459
Rear Spoiler	+336		

Mileage Category: I

For the 2003 GS 430, Lexus has made the heated front seats, moonroof, CD changer and leather upholstery standard equipment.

Lexus
GS 430/GX 470/IS 300

2002

Mileage Category: I

After a number of upgrades last year, the GS 430 enters 2002 unchanged.

Body Styles	TMV Pricing		
	Trade	Private	Dealer
4 Dr STD Sdn	32693	34488	37479

Options	Price	Options	Price
17 Inch Wheels - Chrome	+536	Mark Levinson Audio System	+429
AM/FM/Cassette/CD Changer Audio System	+536	Navigation System	+1431
Chrome Wheels	+1216	Power Moonroof	+715
Heated Front Seats	+322	Rear Spoiler	+315

2001

Mileage Category: I

On the safety front, standard side curtain airbags debut, and a new sensor detects if the front passenger seat is unoccupied, deactivating the front passenger airbag if nobody is sitting in that seat. Additionally, a new child seat-tether restraint has been added, along with impact-detecting door locks and an emergency trunk release handle that glows in the dark inside the cargo area. Exterior changes include water-repellent front door glass, a new grille with a bigger "L" badge, revised taillights, larger exhaust pipes with stainless-steel tips and new six-spoke alloy wheels. HID headlights are standard. Inside, steering wheel controls for the audio system come standard, a compass has been added and a new DVD-based navigation system is optional. Bummer that it's bundled with trip computer, audio and climate control systems. Mark Levinson audio is newly optional, replacing Nakamichi as the premium sound supplier. Dashboards have new metallic-gray trim, and a wood and leather steering wheel is optional. Four new colors round out this long list of updates for 2001.

Body Styles	TMV Pricing		
	Trade	Private	Dealer
4 Dr STD Sdn	27204	29685	31976

Options	Price	Options	Price
AM/FM/Cassette/CD Changer Audio System	+476	Mark Levinson Audio System	+381
Chrome Wheels	+1079	Navigation System	+1269
Heated Front Seats	+279	Power Moonroof	+647
Leather Seats	+762	Rear Spoiler	+279

Lexus
GX 470

2003

Body Styles	TMV Pricing		
	Trade	Private	Dealer
4 Dr STD 4WD SUV	35751	37497	40407

Options	Price	Options	Price
Compact Disc Changer	+268	Telematic System	+929
Navigation System	+1376	Mark Levinson Audio System	+421
Rear Spoiler	+394	DVD Entertainment System	+1193
Third Seat	+1552		

Mileage Category: M

The Lexus GX 470 is a new midsize luxury SUV. It features standard V8 power, excellent off-road performance and the latest luxury and safety features.

Lexus
IS 300

2003

Body Styles	TMV Pricing		
	Trade	Private	Dealer
4 Dr STD Sdn	21623	22910	25055
4 Dr SportCross Wgn	21903	23207	25379

Options	Price	Options	Price
Automatic 5-Speed Transmission [Opt on STD]	+1048	Leather Seats	+765
Automatic Stability Control [Opt on SportCross]	+268	Limited Slip Differential	+298
Heated Front Seats	+336	Navigation System [Opt on STD]	+1529

2003

Options	Price
Power Driver Seat	+161
Power Moonroof	+382
Power Passenger Seat	+161

Options	Price
Rear Spoiler [Opt on STD]	+336
Sport Package [Opt on STD]	+1036

Mileage Category: H

Other than having some new wheel designs, the IS 300 is unchanged this year.

2002

Body Styles	TMV Pricing		
	Trade	Private	Dealer
4 Dr STD Sdn	19521	20819	22982
4 Dr SportCross Wgn	19698	21008	23190

Options	Price
17 Inch Wheels	+286
Automatic 5-Speed Transmission [Opt on Sdn]	+980
Automatic Stability Control	+250
Heated Front Seats	+315
Leather Seats	+715
Limited Slip Differential	+279

Options	Price
Navigation System	+1431
Power Driver Seat	+186
Power Moonroof	+358
Power Passenger Seat	+186
Rear Spoiler [Opt on Sdn]	+315

Mileage Category: H

Once a goal is set, Lexus is not a company to dillydally. Witness the 2002 IS 300. After just one year on the fiercely contested entry-level luxury sport sedan battlefield, Lexus has quickly moved to address the IS 300's short list of faults. A five-speed manual transmission is available, and it comes packaged with a sportier suspension than what is offered on the "regular" IS 300. The luxury side of the equation has also been upped. A navigation system and an all-leather interior are optional this year, and the rearview and driver-side mirrors are auto-dimming. Safety is also enhanced with the addition of head-protecting side curtain airbags (in addition to the regular side airbags), a BrakeAssist function and a stability control system. And for all of those golden retrievers out there tired of riding around in numbing RX 300s, take notice that Lexus has expanded the IS 300's lineup with a wagon version.

2001

Body Styles	TMV Pricing		
	Trade	Private	Dealer
4 Dr STD Sdn	17198	19036	20733

Options	Price
Heated Front Seats	+279
Leather Seats	+635
Limited Slip Differential	+247

Options	Price
Power Driver Seat	+133
Power Moonroof	+635
Power Passenger Seat	+133

Mileage Category: H

Lexus continues to change gears, moving away from single-minded relentless pursuits of perfection to chase performance. The new IS 300, complete with rear-wheel drive and a 215-horse inline six, chases the BMW 3 Series in the entry luxury sport marketplace, and will continue to do so until a proper manual transmission is available next year.

2000

Body Styles	TMV Pricing		
	Trade	Private	Dealer
4 Dr STD Sdn	24458	27190	29868

Options	Price
Automatic Load Leveling	+372
Chrome Wheels	+425
Compact Disc Changer	+319
Heated Front Seats	+186

Options	Price
Nakamichi Audio System	+637
Navigation System	+1062
Power Moonroof	+507

Mileage Category: I

Only minor changes are scheduled for 2000 LS 400s. BrakeAssist has been added to the Vehicle Skid Control system. A new onboard refueling vapor recovery system allows the LS 400 to meet transitional low emission vehicle status. Child seat anchor-brackets are standard.

1999

Body Styles	TMV Pricing		
	Trade	Private	Dealer
4 Dr STD Sdn	21270	23853	26541

Options	Price
Automatic Load Leveling	+337
Chrome Wheels	+385
Compact Disc Changer	+289
Heated Front Seats	+168

Options	Price
Nakamichi Audio System	+577
Navigation System	+770
Power Moonroof	+460

Mileage Category: I

After a number of improvements to the LS 400 last year, the 1999 model sees only minor upgrades to interior trim levels. Daytime running lights are now standard equipment and Mystic Gold Metallic replaces Cashmere Beige.

LS 400

1998

Mileage Category: I

Lexus further refines its flagship by introducing a new four-cam V8 engine that features continuously variable valve timing. Also new this year is a five-speed automatic transmission, Vehicle Skid Control (VSC) and a host of interior improvements.

Body Styles		TMV Pricing	
	Trade	Private	Dealer
4 Dr STD Sdn	17604	19903	22496

Options	Price	Options	Price
Automatic Load Leveling	+277	Nakamichi Audio System	+475
Chrome Wheels	+317	Navigation System	+634
Compact Disc Changer	+238	Power Moonroof	+378
Heated Front Seats	+139		

1997

Mileage Category: I

Side-impact airbags are standard.

Body Styles		TMV Pricing	
	Trade	Private	Dealer
4 Dr Coach Sdn	15415	17674	20435
4 Dr STD Sdn	12869	14755	17060

Options	Price	Options	Price
AM/FM/Cassette/CD Audio System	+194	Nakamichi Audio System	+388
Automatic Load Leveling	+226	Power Driver Seat w/Memory	+129
Chrome Wheels	+259	Power Moonroof	+306
Compact Disc Changer	+194	Traction Control System	+194

1996

Mileage Category: I

Deep Jewel Green Pearl is newly available on the paint palette.

Body Styles		TMV Pricing	
	Trade	Private	Dealer
4 Dr STD Sdn	10097	11700	13914

Options	Price	Options	Price
Automatic Load Leveling	+184	Nakamichi Audio System	+316
Chrome Wheels	+211	Power Moonroof	+252
Compact Disc Changer	+158	Traction Control System	+158

1995

Mileage Category: I

All-new car looks pretty much the same as it has for half a decade. The interior and trunk are larger, the engine more powerful, and the car is quicker than before. Six-disc CD changer is dash-mounted.

Body Styles		TMV Pricing	
	Trade	Private	Dealer
4 Dr STD Sdn	8745	10160	12517

Options	Price	Options	Price
Automatic Load Leveling	+236	Nakamichi Audio System	+260
Chrome Wheels	+260	Power Driver Seat w/Memory	+106
Compact Disc Changer	+236	Power Moonroof	+236
Heated Front Seats	+118	Traction Control System	+177

1994

Mileage Category: I

Minor trim revisions.

Body Styles		TMV Pricing	
	Trade	Private	Dealer
4 Dr STD Sdn	7306	8607	10774

Options	Price	Options	Price
AM/FM/Cassette/CD Audio System	+126	Power Driver Seat w/Memory	+95
Automatic Load Leveling	+169	Power Moonroof	+201
Compact Disc Changer	+126	Traction Control System	+126
Nakamichi Audio System	+253		

Lexus
LS 430/LX 450

2003

Body Styles	TMV Pricing		
	Trade	Private	Dealer
4 Dr STD Sdn	42427	44727	48561

Options	Price	Options	Price
Automatic Load Leveling	+535	Power Rear Seat	+574
Heated Front and Rear Seats	+593	Special Leather Seat Trim	+1606
Navigation System	+1529	17 Inch Wheels - Chrome	+1300
Power Moonroof	+841	Nappa Leather Seat Trim	+1116

Mileage Category: I

For 2003, 17-inch wheels are standard, replacing the 16-inchers. The climate control front seats and park-assist feature, formerly included only with the Ultra Luxury or Custom Luxury packages, are now available as stand-alone options. Finally, base cars ordered with the climate control front seats now feature perforated leather trim throughout.

2002

Body Styles	TMV Pricing		
	Trade	Private	Dealer
4 Dr STD Sdn	39862	42119	45879

Options	Price	Options	Price
17 Inch Wheels - Chrome	+572	Park Distance Control (Rear)	+429
Adaptive Cruise Control	+1252	Power Moonroof	+787
Air Conditioning - Front and Rear	+715	Power Rear Seat	+536
Automatic Load Leveling	+501	Power Rear Window Sunshade	+322
Heated Front and Rear Seats	+554	Telematic System	+869
Mark Levinson Audio System	+887	Ventilated Seats (Front)	+715
Navigation System	+1431		

Mileage Category: I

Lexus' flagship was completely redesigned last year. The only addition for 2002 is a new Platinum Blue Metallic exterior paint.

2001

Body Styles	TMV Pricing		
	Trade	Private	Dealer
4 Dr STD Sdn	35697	38953	41959

Options	Price	Options	Price
17 Inch Wheels - Chrome	+508	Park Distance Control (Rear)	+381
Adaptive Cruise Control	+1111	Power Moonroof	+711
Air Conditioning - Front and Rear	+635	Power Rear Seat	+888
Automatic Load Leveling	+444	Power Rear Window Sunshade	+286
Heated Front and Rear Seats	+558	Telematic System	+771
Mark Levinson Audio System	+787	Ventilated Seats (Front)	+635
Navigation System	+1269		

Mileage Category: I

The completely redesigned third-generation Lexus flagship features a larger 4.3-liter engine that meets ULEV standards, a freshened aerodynamic shape that allows for a more spacious interior and a new suspension that offers greater stability and a smoother ride. A richer, more stylish interior with advanced safety and luxury features also debuts.

Lexus
LX 450

1997

Body Styles	TMV Pricing		
	Trade	Private	Dealer
4 Dr STD 4WD SUV	15314	17389	19925

Options	Price
Compact Disc Changer	+194
Locking Differential	+262
Power Moonroof	+364

Mileage Category: O

There are no changes to the 1997 LX 450.

For the latest vehicle information, visit www.edmunds.com

Lexus
LX 450/LX 470

1996

Mileage Category: O

Lexus clones a Toyota Land Cruiser, puts some fancy wheels on it and slathers leather and wood all over the interior to capitalize on the booming sport-ute market.

Body Styles	TMV Pricing		
	Trade	Private	Dealer
4 Dr STD 4WD SUV	13057	14779	17158

Options	Price
Compact Disc Changer	+158
Locking Differential	+213
Power Moonroof	+296

Lexus
LX 470

2003

Body Styles	TMV Pricing		
	Trade	Private	Dealer
4 Dr STD 4WD SUV	48860	51139	54938

Options	Price	Options	Price
Rear Spoiler	+214	Telematic System	+929
Night Vision	+1682	Mark Levinson Audio System	+979

Mileage Category: O

In a move almost certainly meant to distance the LX 470 from the all-new GX 470, Lexus has made a number of enhancements for 2003. On the outside, the LX has received subtle changes to the headlights, taillights and front grille and bumper. Eighteen-inch wheels are now standard. Inside, there's a redesigned center stack, standard side and side-curtain airbags, additional audio controls for rear passengers, steering wheel-mounted audio controls and a new optional entertainment system (dealer-installed). Mechanically, Lexus has bumped horsepower output by five, added a new five-speed automatic transmission and improved the steering rack. There are also rain-sensing wipers and two new features -- a "Night View" night vision system and the Lexus Link emergency communications service.

2002

Mileage Category: O

The LX 470 was updated last year. As such, the only change for 2002 is that the navigation system is now standard equipment.

Body Styles	TMV Pricing		
	Trade	Private	Dealer
4 Dr STD AWD SUV	42684	44884	48550

Options	Price	Options	Price
Chrome Wheels	+930	Mark Levinson Audio System	+916

2001

Mileage Category: O

The LX 470 finally adds the all-important optional DVD-based navigation system (and if you turn down the nav, you get a compass on the rearview mirror). The optional Nakamichi audio system is gone in favor of an optional nine-speaker Mark Levinson system. The standard audio system is enhanced with an Automatic Sound Levelizer (ASL). Last year's optional wood and leather trim on the steering wheel and shift knob is now a standard feature. New security features include a key card immobilizer and a free-wheel key cylinder that prevents people from opening the door with anything other than the LX 470 key. Second-row passengers will benefit from child seat anchors and improved cupholders in the rear of the center console. The standard alloy wheels have a new surface treatment, and chrome wheels are optional. The fuel cap now has a tether to appease the absent-minded. Two new exterior colors will be offered -- Mystic Sea Opalescent and Blue Vapor Metallic.

Body Styles	TMV Pricing		
	Trade	Private	Dealer
4 Dr STD AWD SUV	36236	39508	42529

Options	Price	Options	Price
Chrome Wheels	+825	Mark Levinson Audio System	+812
Compact Disc Changer	+685	Navigation System	+1269

2000

Body Styles	TMV Pricing		
	Trade	Private	Dealer
4 Dr STD AWD SUV	29781	32922	36001

Options	Price
Nakamichi Audio System	+637

2000 (cont'd)

Mileage Category: 0

A Vehicle Stability Control system and a BrakeAssist system are now standard, as are last year's optional moonroof and illuminated running boards. The LX 470 also gets an optional wood and leather steering wheel and shift knob.

1999

Body Styles	TMV Pricing		
	Trade	Private	Dealer
4 Dr STD AWD SUV	25225	28053	30997

Options	Price	Options	Price
Nakamichi Audio System	+520	Power Moonroof	+550

Mileage Category: 0

For 1999 the LX 470 gets a redesigned roof rack, standard floor mats and an optional Nakamichi audio system featuring a dash-mounted, single-feed six-disc CD changer.

1998

Body Styles	TMV Pricing		
	Trade	Private	Dealer
4 Dr STD AWD SUV	21018	23649	26616

Options	Price
Power Moonroof	+453

Mileage Category: 0

Lexus' new LX 470 luxury SUV replaces the LX 450, offering a completely new body design, a more powerful engine, a roomier interior and more standard perks.

Lexus
RX 300

2003

Body Styles	TMV Pricing		
	Trade	Private	Dealer
4 Dr STD AWD SUV	27974	29464	31947

Options	Price
Automatic Dimming Rearview Mirror	+138
Camper/Towing Package	+122
Chrome Wheels	+1300
Compact Disc Changer	+826
Heated Front Seats	+336
Leather Seats	+765

Body Styles	TMV Pricing		
	Trade	Private•	Dealer
4 Dr STD SUV	26193	27588	29913

Options	Price
Navigation System	+1529
Rear Spoiler	+214
AM/FM/Cassette/CD Changer Audio System	+363
Automatic Dimming Sideview Mirror(s)	+153
Power Driver Seat w/Memory	+229

Mileage Category: 0

Nothing has changed for the RX 300 during its move from 2002 to 2003. Prospective buyers should note that it will get a complete redesign for 2004.

2002

Body Styles	TMV Pricing		
	Trade	Private	Dealer
4 Dr STD AWD SUV	25504	26991	29469

Options	Price
Automatic Dimming Rearview Mirror	+129
Automatic Dimming Sideview Mirror(s)	+143
Chrome Wheels	+1216
Compact Disc Changer	+536
Heated Front Seats	+315

Body Styles	TMV Pricing		
	Trade	Private	Dealer
4 Dr STD SUV	24349	25769	28137

Options	Price
Leather Seats	+715
Navigation System	+1431
Power Driver Seat w/Memory	+215
Power Moonroof	+644
Rear Spoiler	+200

Mileage Category: 0

Other than the Nakamichi audio system value package no longer being available, there are no changes for the RX 300 this year.

2001

Mileage Category: O

Vehicle Skid Control (VSC), traction control and BrakeAssist safety technologies are now standard, as is water-repellant front door and sideview mirror glass. Lights front and rear are revised, and the grille has been changed to a simpler design with chrome accents and a larger Lexus badge. HID headlights and chrome-plated wheels are optional for 2001, the full-size spare is newly mounted to a matching alloy wheel and a larger 19.8-gallon fuel tank increases driving range. Inside, new cloth upholstery debuts and an all-black leather option is available. Chrome door handles and scuff plates emblazoned with the Lexus logo class up the joint, while an additional cupholder is available to rear-seat occupants. Optional for 2001 is a wood-trimmed steering wheel and wood trimmed shift knob. Two-level seat heaters are also available. A DVD-based navigation system is optional, with the contiguous U.S. mapped onto a single disc. Child seat-tether anchors and ISO-FIX bars have been added this year. Models with 4WD get prewiring for towing and a standard rear bumper protector. Four new colors round out the list of changes for 2001.

Body Styles		TMV Pricing		
		Trade	Private	Dealer
4 Dr STD AWD SUV		22662	24816	26805
4 Dr STD SUV		21879	23959	25878

Options	Price	Options	Price
AM/FM/Cassette/CD Changer Audio System	+254	Leather Seats	+730
Automatic Dimming Sideview Mirror(s)	+127	Nakamichi Audio System	+1034
Camper/Towing Package	+197	Navigation System	+1269
Chrome Wheels	+1079	Power Driver Seat w/Memory	+190
Compact Disc Changer	+685	Power Moonroof	+635
Heated Front Seats	+279	Rear Spoiler	+178

2000

Mileage Category: O

The RX 300 remains mechanically unchanged. A Mineral Green Opalescent paint replaces Desert Bronze Metallic on the order sheet.

Body Styles		TMV Pricing		
		Trade	Private	Dealer
4 Dr STD AWD SUV		19973	22080	24145
4 Dr STD SUV		19091	21104	23078

Options	Price	Options	Price
Limited Slip Differential	+186	Rear Spoiler	+133
Nakamichi Audio System	+691	Traction Control System	+159
Power Driver Seat w/Memory	+159	AM/FM/Cassette/CD Audio System	+305
Leather Seats	+611	Compact Disc Changer	+319
Power Moonroof	+531	Heated Front Seats	+186

1999

Mileage Category: O

The RX 300 is an all-new car-based SUV from Lexus designed to compete in the luxury SUV segment.

Body Styles		TMV Pricing		
		Trade	Private	Dealer
4 Dr STD AWD SUV		17206	19136	21144
4 Dr STD SUV		16657	18525	20469

Options	Price	Options	Price
AM/FM/CD Audio System	+152	Nakamichi Audio System	+409
Compact Disc Changer	+289	Power Driver Seat w/Memory	+144
Heated Front Seats	+168	Power Moonroof	+481
Leather Seats	+553	Traction Control System	+144
Limited Slip Differential	+168		

2000

Mileage Category: I

The 2000 Lexus SC 300 is unchanged except for paint selection; Cinnabar Pearl replaces Baroque Red Metallic.

Body Styles		TMV Pricing		
		Trade	Private	Dealer
2 Dr STD Cpe		18750	20861	22930

Options	Price	Options	Price
Traction Control System	+319	Nakamichi Audio System	+637
Chrome Wheels	+425	Power Driver Seat w/Memory	+159
Heated Front Seats	+186	Power Moonroof	+531
Leather Seats	+637	Rear Spoiler	+186

1999

Body Styles	TMV Pricing		
	Trade	Private	Dealer
2 Dr STD Cpe	15980	17921	19941

Options	Price	Options	Price
Chrome Wheels	+385	Power Driver Seat w/Memory	+144
Heated Front Seats	+168	Power Moonroof	+481
Leather Seats	+577	Rear Spoiler	+168
Nakamichi Audio System	+520	Traction Control System	+289

Mileage Category: I

The SC 300 gets minor enhancements this year including new perforated leather inserts, larger brakes, daytime running lights and a new three-spoke steering wheel similar to the GS sport sedans.

1998

Body Styles	TMV Pricing		
	Trade	Private	Dealer
2 Dr STD Cpe	12996	14694	16608

Options	Price	Options	Price
Chrome Wheels	+317	Power Driver Seat w/Memory	+119
Compact Disc Changer	+238	Power Moonroof	+396
Heated Front Seats	+139	Rear Spoiler	+139
Leather Seats	+475	Traction Control System	+238
Nakamichi Audio System	+428		

Mileage Category: I

An engine immobilizer, depowered airbags and a sophisticated five-speed automatic transmission are standard this year as well. The SC 300 loses its five-speed manual transmission.

1997

Body Styles	TMV Pricing		
	Trade	Private	Dealer
2 Dr STD Cpe	10114	11596	13408

Options	Price	Options	Price
Automatic 4-Speed Transmission	+223	Nakamichi Audio System	+350
Chrome Wheels	+259	Power Moonroof	+324
Compact Disc Changer	+194	Traction Control System	+194
Leather Seats	+388		

Mileage Category: I

Minor interior and exterior enhancements update the look of the SC 300.

1996

Body Styles	TMV Pricing		
	Trade	Private	Dealer
2 Dr STD Cpe	8657	10031	11929

Options	Price	Options	Price
Automatic 4-Speed Transmission	+181	Nakamichi Audio System	+285
Chrome Wheels	+211	Power Moonroof	+263
Compact Disc Changer	+158	Traction Control System	+158
Leather Seats	+316		

Mileage Category: I

SC 300 boasts a larger options roster with the addition of a one-touch operation moonroof and electrochromatic rearview mirrors, and chrome wheels are available. Auto-dimming electrochromic inside and outside rearview mirrors are now standard, a new remote keyless entry system debuts and the optional moonroof now features one-touch operation.

1995

Body Styles	TMV Pricing		
	Trade	Private	Dealer
2 Dr STD Cpe	7194	8358	10299

Options	Price	Options	Price
Automatic 4-Speed Transmission	+212	Nakamichi Audio System	+255
Compact Disc Changer	+236	Power Driver Seat w/Memory	+106
Heated Front Seats	+94	Power Moonroof	+212
Leather Seats	+293	Traction Control System	+118

Mileage Category: I

Revised styling and new wheels spruce up the look of the SC 300. Side-impact standards for 1997 are met this year. A cupholder is added inside.

Lexus
SC 300/SC 400

1994

Mileage Category: I

Air conditioning is now CFC-free.

Body Styles	TMV Pricing		
	Trade	Private	Dealer
2 Dr STD Cpe	5819	6855	8582

Options	Price	Options	Price
Leather Seats	+253	Traction Control System	+126
Nakamichi Audio System	+228	Compact Disc Changer	+126
Power Driver Seat w/Memory	+95	Automatic 4-Speed Transmission	+145
Power Moonroof	+211		

Lexus
SC 400

2000

Body Styles	TMV Pricing		
	Trade	Private	Dealer
2 Dr STD Cpe	20990	23335	25633

Options	Price	Options	Price
Chrome Wheels	+425	Power Moonroof	+531
Heated Front Seats	+186	Rear Spoiler	+186
Nakamichi Audio System	+637	Traction Control System	+425

Mileage Category: I

The 2000 Lexus SC 400 is unchanged except for paint selection; Cinnabar Pearl replaces Baroque Red Metallic.

1999

Mileage Category: I

The SC 400 gets minor enhancements this year including new perforated leather inserts, daytime running lights and a new three-spoke steering wheel similar to the GS series sport sedans.

Body Styles	TMV Pricing		
	Trade	Private	Dealer
2 Dr STD Cpe	18017	20205	22482

Options	Price	Options	Price
Chrome Wheels	+385	Power Moonroof	+481
Heated Front Seats	+168	Rear Spoiler	+168
Nakamichi Audio System	+520	Traction Control System	+289

1998

Mileage Category: I

An engine immobilizer, depowered airbags and a sophisticated five-speed automatic transmission are standard this year as well.

Body Styles	TMV Pricing		
	Trade	Private	Dealer
2 Dr STD Cpe	15023	16985	19198

Options	Price	Options	Price
Chrome Wheels	+317	Power Moonroof	+396
Compact Disc Changer	+238	Rear Spoiler	+139
Heated Front Seats	+139	Traction Control System	+238
Nakamichi Audio System	+428		

1997

Mileage Category: I

Minor interior and exterior enhancements update the look of the SC 400.

Body Styles	TMV Pricing		
	Trade	Private	Dealer
2 Dr STD Cpe	11419	13092	15137

Options	Price	Options	Price
Chrome Wheels	+259	Power Moonroof	+324
Compact Disc Changer	+194	Traction Control System	+194
Nakamichi Audio System	+350		

1996

Mileage Category: I

Body Styles		TMV Pricing		
		Trade	Private	Dealer
2 Dr STD Cpe		9362	10848	12900

Options	Price	Options	Price
Chrome Wheels	+211	Power Moonroof	+263
Compact Disc Changer	+158	Traction Control System	+158
Nakamichi Audio System	+285		

The buttery V8 from the LS 400 is installed in the SC 400, and chrome wheels are available. Auto-dimming electrochromic inside and outside rearview mirrors are now standard, a new remote keyless entry system debuts and the optional moonroof now features one-touch operation.

1995

Mileage Category: I

Body Styles		TMV Pricing		
		Trade	Private	Dealer
2 Dr STD Cpe		7744	9059	11250

Options	Price	Options	Price
Compact Disc Changer	+236	Power Moonroof	+212
Heated Front Seats	+118	Rear Spoiler	+94
Nakamichi Audio System	+260	Traction Control System	+177

Revised styling and new wheels spruce up the look of the SC 400. Side-impact standards for 1997 are met this year. A cupholder is added inside.

1994

Mileage Category: I

Body Styles		TMV Pricing		
		Trade	Private	Dealer
2 Dr STD Cpe		7036	8284	10364

Options	Price	Options	Price
Compact Disc Changer	+126	Power Moonroof	+211
Nakamichi Audio System	+228	Traction Control System	+126

Air conditioning is now CFC-free.

Lexus
SC 430

2003

Body Styles		TMV Pricing		
		Trade	Private	Dealer
2 Dr STD Conv		48279	50066	53044

Options	Price
Rear Spoiler	+336
Runflat Tire System	+306
Telematic System	+929

Mileage Category: F

Other than the Lexus Link emergency and concierge service becoming available, there are no changes for the SC 430.

2002

Mileage Category: F

Body Styles		TMV Pricing		
		Trade	Private	Dealer
2 Dr STD Conv		42894	44620	47498

Options	Price
Rear Spoiler	+315
Runflat Tire System	+286

After nearly a decade out of the sport coupe spotlight, Lexus returns with a compelling entry. Since its debut of the SC coupe in 1992, Lexus has largely been overlooked by shoppers who wanted avant-garde styling, sports car performance and luxurious appointments. And it has never before offered a convertible roof. They need look no further. The new SC 430 delivers all that in spades.

Lincoln
Aviator
2003

Mileage Category: O

With the Aviator, Lincoln has thrown its hat into the midsize luxury sport-ute ring. It looks like a three-quarter scale Navigator, seats seven and is powered by a strong V8.

Body Styles		TMV Pricing	
	Trade	Private	Dealer
4 Dr STD AWD SUV	29778	31542	34483
4 Dr STD SUV	26752	28337	30979

Options	Price	Options	Price
Automatic Stability Control [Opt on AWD]	+314	Traction Control System [Opt on AWD]	+185
Camper/Towing Package	+185	17 Inch Wheels - Chrome	+436
Limited Slip Differential [Opt on 2WD]	+310	Climate Comfort Seats	+596
Navigation System	+1565	AM/FM/CD Changer Audio System	+561
Power Moonroof	+1000	DVD Entertainment System	+812
Special Factory Paint	+248		

Lincoln
Blackwood
2002

Body Styles		TMV Pricing	
	Trade	Private	Dealer
4 Dr STD Crew Cab SB	23411	24948	27510

Options	Price
Navigation System	+991

Mileage Category: O

For 2002, Lincoln introduces this cross between a luxury SUV and a pickup truck. Essentially a dolled-up Ford F-150 SuperCrew, the Blackwood offers a truckload of creature comforts and safety features but not a lot of utility.

Lincoln
Continental
2002

Body Styles		TMV Pricing	
	Trade	Private	Dealer
4 Dr STD Sdn	17108	18670	21274

Options	Price	Options	Price
Alpine Audio System	+286	Metallic Paint	+186
Chrome Wheels	+397	Power Moonroof	+745
Compact Disc Changer	+248	Premium Audio System	+137
Electronic Suspension Control	+201	Runflat Tire System	+489
Heated Front and Rear Seats	+199	Telematic System	+293

Mileage Category: I

The Continental remains relatively unchanged for 2002, its last year on the market. One new exterior color debuts, and an optional Vehicle Communication System (with portable analog-digital phone) is now offered. Available at no charge are a power moonroof, a six-disc changer and an Alpine audio system.

2001

Mileage Category: I

The Continental remains relatively unchanged for 2001. A universal garage door opener is standard, and the individual bucket seat option (five-passenger) now requires the Driver's Select System. Two new exterior colors have been added. Like all Lincoln products, the Continental now has complimentary maintenance at no additional charge for the first three years/36,000 miles in service.

Body Styles		TMV Pricing	
	Trade	Private	Dealer
4 Dr STD Sdn	13337	15361	17229

Options	Price	Options	Price
Alpine Audio System	+242	Heated Front Seats	+168
Chrome Wheels	+359	Power Moonroof	+641
Compact Disc Changer	+254	Runflat Tire System	+269

2000

Body Styles	TMV Pricing		
	Trade	Private	Dealer
4 Dr STD Sdn	9957	11661	13332

Options	Price	Options	Price
Alpine Audio System	+204	Power Moonroof	+548
Chrome Wheels	+305	Telematic System	+253
Compact Disc Changer	+216		

Mileage Category: I

The Continental receives additional safety features, including side airbags, an emergency trunk release, child seat-anchor brackets and Lincoln's Belt Minder system.

1999

Body Styles	TMV Pricing		
	Trade	Private	Dealer
4 Dr STD Sdn	8145	9671	11259

Options	Price	Options	Price
Alpine Audio System	+167	Power Moonroof	+447
Chrome Wheels	+250	Telematic System	+295
Compact Disc Changer	+176		

Mileage Category: I

Lincoln's luxury liner gets added safety in 1999 with the addition of standard side airbags for the driver and front passenger. There's also five new exterior colors, upgraded interior trim options, two new wheel designs and an improved audio system. Otherwise the Lincoln remains unchanged after its major rework in 1998.

1998

Body Styles	TMV Pricing		
	Trade	Private	Dealer
4 Dr STD Sdn	6768	8178	9768

Options	Price	Options	Price
Chrome Wheels	+219	Power Moonroof	+436
Compact Disc Changer	+171	Telematic System	+259
JBL Audio System	+163		

Mileage Category: I

Lincoln's front-wheel-drive luxo-barge gets a bigger grille (just what it needs) and rounded corners. It also gets an interior freshening that replaces the digital clock with an analog timepiece.

1997

Body Styles	TMV Pricing		
	Trade	Private	Dealer
4 Dr STD Sdn	5048	6242	7701

Options	Price	Options	Price
Chrome Wheels	+164	Power Moonroof	+294
JBL Audio System	+115	Telematic System	+194

Mileage Category: I

The changes to the 1997 Continental are minor this year. The first is the addition of a single-key locking system that locks the doors, glovebox and trunk with a turn of the wrist. The second is the addition of all-speed traction control.

1996

Body Styles	TMV Pricing		
	Trade	Private	Dealer
4 Dr STD Sdn	3708	4683	6030

Options	Price	Options	Price
Chrome Wheels	+125	Power Moonroof	+224

Mileage Category: I

The big news for Continental is an optional gee-whiz rescue unit that uses a Global Positioning Satellite to pinpoint your location for roadside assistance, medical and law enforcement personnel in the event of an emergency -- likely the greatest safety advance since airbags and antilock brakes. Also new are run-flat Michelin tires, a 75th Diamond Anniversary Edition and a standard anti-theft system. It's getting there.

1995

Body Styles	TMV Pricing		
	Trade	Private	Dealer
4 Dr STD Sdn	2825	3648	5020

Options	Price
Chrome Wheels	+108
Compact Disc Changer	+104
Power Moonroof	+194

Mileage Category: I

An all-new Continental is released with a DOHC V8. A new suspension system that adjusts the shock absorbers to the prevailing driving conditions debuts, as does a memory seat system that will retain the seating preferences for two people. The new Continental has swoopier styling which is geared toward attracting a more youthful audience.

Lincoln
Continental/LS

1994

Body Styles	TMV Pricing		
	Trade	Private	Dealer
4 Dr Executive Sdn	1625	2192	3138
4 Dr Signature Sdn	1729	2333	3339

Options	Price
Power Moonroof	+136

Mileage Category: I

Suspension changes improve the Continental's ride. A memory feature on the remote keyless entry automatically adjusts the driver seat to a preset position each time it's activated. Exterior changes include revised taillamps, grille and rocker moldings. A retractable trunk cord is standard on all Continentals; it is designed to keep the trunk from bouncing around when it has to be left open for large loads.

Lincoln
LS

2003

Body Styles	TMV Pricing		
	Trade	Private	Dealer
4 Dr V6 Sdn	19315	20593	22723

Body Styles	TMV Pricing		
	Trade	Private	Dealer
4 Dr V8 Sdn	22694	24196	26698

Options	Price
Aluminum/Alloy Wheels [Opt on V6]	+254
Automatic Dimming Rearview Mirror [Opt on V6]	+125
Automatic Stability Control	+367
Heated Front Seats [Opt on V6]	+219
Heated Front and Rear Seats [Opt on V8]	+251
Navigation System [Opt on V8]	+1878
Power Moonroof	+630
Special Factory Paint	+185

Options	Price
Spoke Wheels [Opt on V6]	+345
17 Inch Wheels - Chrome [Opt on V8]	+314
Premium Audio System [Opt on V6]	+361
AM/FM/CD Changer Audio System [Opt on V6]	+185
Automatic Dimming Sideview Mirror(s)	+157
Front Head Airbag Restraints	+248
Power Driver Seat w/Memory [Opt on V6]	+157
Park Distance Control (Rear)	+185

Mileage Category: H

Lincoln's sport sedan goes into 2003 with more than 500 changes. The V8 sports 28 more horsepower, while the V6 benefits from a 12-horsepower increase. Both engines are controlled by drive-by-wire throttle, and drink slightly less fuel than their 2002 counterparts. Unfortunately, Lincoln decided to kill the five-speed manual that was available with the V6. Meanwhile, the rack and pinion steering has been improved, and Lincoln says it has softened the ride without degrading the car's handling abilities. In terms of safety, Lincoln has added a BrakeAssist function, side curtain airbags (late availability) and power-adjustable pedals. As on the 2003 Jaguar S-Type, a new electronically activated parking brake improves the stowage capability of the center console. Also on the inside, you'll find vastly improved interior materials for the seat and dash, along with little touches like one-touch up and down front windows and a host of new options. Outside you'll find slightly altered fascias front and rear and a host of new wheel choices.

2002

Mileage Category: H

The LS' already handsome appearance can be further enhanced with the LSE appearance package that includes 17-inch two-tone Blade Grey wheels, a unique front fascia, round foglights, modified Blade Grey grille with color-keyed upper trim piece, side rocker panels and rear valance, low profile spoiler, dual stainless-steel exhaust tips and LSE floor mats. Lincoln makes an in-dash CD changer standard for 2002 (with Alpine Audiophile components on Sport models) and restyles the 16-inch alloy wheels on non-Sport V6 and V8 versions. A Vehicle Communication System, which provides a voice-activated Motorola Timeport mobile phone, is optional and includes safety and security services, route guidance and access to weather reports, stock quotes and sports scores. Three new colors replace three old ones.

Body Styles	TMV Pricing		
	Trade	Private	Dealer
4 Dr V6 Sdn	15111	16578	19022

Body Styles	TMV Pricing		
	Trade	Private	Dealer
4 Dr V8 Sdn	16439	18035	20694

Options	Price
17 Inch Wheels - Chrome	+248
Alpine Audio System	+286
Automatic Stability Control	+291
Heated Front Seats	+174

Options	Price
Metallic Paint	+147
Power Moonroof	+499
Rear Spoiler	+124
Telematic System	+293

2001

Body Styles	TMV Pricing		
	Trade	Private	Dealer
4 Dr V6 Sdn	12339	14264	16041
4 Dr V8 Sdn	12741	14728	16563

2001 (cont'd)

Options	Price
17 Inch Wheels - Chrome	+355
Alpine Audio System	+242
Automatic 5-Speed Transmission [Opt on V6]	+611
Automatic Stability Control	+309
Chrome Wheels	+355

Options	Price
Compact Disc Changer	+254
Heated Front Seats	+168
Power Moonroof	+422
Sport Suspension	+126

Mileage Category: H

V6 models now come with standard traction control and optional AdvanceTrac. All models receive a glow-in-the-dark manual trunk release and child safety-seat anchor points. The sport package has a new 17-inch chrome wheel design and a mini spare tire and wheel instead of the previous 16-inch nonmatching aluminum wheel (both late availability). Inside, there is an additional power point, a revised cupholder design, an optional in-dash six-disc CD changer and an optional mirror-mounted compass. The height-adjustable rear-seat head restraints have been deleted from V8 automatics. Four new exterior colors are offered. Lincoln now offers complimentary maintenance at no additional charge for the first three years/36,000 miles in service.

2000

Body Styles		TMV Pricing	
	Trade	Private	Dealer
4 Dr V6 Sdn	10823	12676	14492
4 Dr V8 Sdn	11547	13524	15462

Options	Price
5-Speed Transmission [Opt on V6]	+290
Alpine Audio System	+208
Automatic Stability Control	+266
Compact Disc Changer	+219
Heated Front Seats	+145

Options	Price
Power Moonroof	+364
Special Factory Paint	+136
Sport Package	+257
Telematic System [Opt on V8]	+394

Mileage Category: H

From the ground up, this is a completely new sport sedan based on an all-new midsize platform. Lincoln worked with Jaguar to develop this platform, which is also being used for Jaguar's S-Type sedan. It is the first Lincoln in over two decades not classified as a full-size vehicle, and should appeal to buyers looking for something sportier and smaller than the Town Car or Continental.

1998

Body Styles		TMV Pricing	
	Trade	Private	Dealer
2 Dr LSC Cpe	8502	10273	12270

Options	Price
Chrome Wheels [Opt on STD]	+219
Compact Disc Changer	+174

Body Styles		TMV Pricing	
	Trade	Private	Dealer
2 Dr STD Cpe	8221	9933	11864

Options	Price
Power Moonroof	+393

Mileage Category: I

No changes to Lincoln's muscle car for its last year.

1997

Body Styles		TMV Pricing	
	Trade	Private	Dealer
2 Dr LSC Cpe	6978	8628	10644

Options	Price
Chrome Wheels [Opt on STD]	+164
Compact Disc Changer	+130

Body Styles		TMV Pricing	
	Trade	Private	Dealer
2 Dr STD Cpe	6670	8247	10174

Options	Price
Power Moonroof	+294

Mileage Category: I

Lincoln thoroughly updates this personal coupe, lighting the darn thing up like a Christmas tree in the process. The Mark now has high-intensity discharge front headlamps, cornering lamps, a neon rear applique and puddle lamps. Wow, you'll see this thing from miles away. The hood, grille and interior have also been slightly redesigned.

1996

Body Styles		TMV Pricing	
	Trade	Private	Dealer
2 Dr LSC Cpe	5133	6483	8347

Options	Price
Compact Disc Changer	+121
Power Moonroof	+224

Body Styles		TMV Pricing	
	Trade	Private	Dealer
2 Dr STD Cpe	4927	6223	8012

Options	Price
Chrome Wheels [Opt on STD]	+125

Mileage Category: I

Last year's limited-edition LSC model goes full-time for 1996. Eight new colors are available, and borderless floor mats debut. A Touring Package and 75th Diamond Anniversary model are offered.

Lincoln
Mark VIII/Navigator

1995
Mileage Category: I

Lincoln's premium touring coupe receives significant changes across the board. A new instrument panel houses a new stereo with larger buttons. A feature called retained accessory power makes an appearance on the Mark VIII, allowing passengers 10 seconds to close the window after the car is turned off.

Body Styles	TMV Pricing		
	Trade	Private	Dealer
2 Dr LSC Cpe	3465	4473	6154

Options	Price
Chrome Wheels	+108
Compact Disc Changer	+104

Body Styles	TMV Pricing		
	Trade	Private	Dealer
2 Dr STD Cpe	3282	4238	5830

Options	Price
Power Moonroof	+194

1994
Mileage Category: I

Chrome wheels are now an available option on the Mark VIII. There is a memory feature for the seats and outside mirrors.

Body Styles		TMV Pricing		
		Trade	Private	Dealer
2 Dr STD Cpe		2834	3823	5472

Options	Price	Options	Price
Power Moonroof	+136	Chrome Wheels	+76

Lincoln
Navigator

2003

Body Styles	TMV Pricing		
	Trade	Private	Dealer
4 Dr STD 4WD SUV	32449	34287	37349

Options	Price
Automatic Stability Control	+314
Traction Control System	+185
Ventilated Seats (Front)	+373

Body Styles	TMV Pricing		
	Trade	Private	Dealer
4 Dr STD SUV	29478	31147	33929

Options	Price
Power Rear Liftgate	+282
DVD Entertainment System	+887
Power Third Seat	+408

Mileage Category: O

The 2003 Navigator may look like the previous year's, but significant changes underneath the sheet metal, such as a new suspension system and sophisticated new technologies, allow the Lincoln to continue to be a popular and respected choice in the luxury SUV market.

2002

Body Styles	TMV Pricing		
	Trade	Private	Dealer
4 Dr STD 4WD SUV	26174	27976	30980

Options	Price
17 Inch Wheels	+149
Alpine Audio System	+288
Chrome Wheels	+296
Navigation System	+991

Body Styles	TMV Pricing		
	Trade	Private	Dealer
4 Dr STD SUV	23849	25491	28228

Options	Price
Park Distance Control (Rear)	+127
Power Moonroof	+743
VCR Entertainment System	+636
Ventilated Seats (Front)	+296

Mileage Category: O

A new Limited Edition package is designed to drum up interest in the aging Navigator for 2002. It includes monochromatic black paint, special 17-inch machined aluminum wheels and a reverse sensing system.

2001
Mileage Category: O

Auxiliary climate control is standard on both two- and four-wheel-drive models. Both the second- and third-row seats get lower child safety-seat anchors. Lincoln now offers complimentary maintenance at no additional charge for the first three years/36,000 miles in service.

Body Styles	TMV Pricing		
	Trade	Private	Dealer
4 Dr STD 4WD SUV	21859	24178	26319

Options	Price
17 Inch Wheels - Chrome	+250
Alpine Audio System	+244
Compact Disc Changer	+250
Navigation System	+838

Body Styles	TMV Pricing		
	Trade	Private	Dealer
4 Dr STD SUV	20441	22610	24612

Options	Price
Power Moonroof	+628
VCR Entertainment System	+538
Ventilated Seats (Front)	+250

2000

Body Styles	TMV Pricing		
	Trade	Private	Dealer
4 Dr STD 4WD SUV	18604	20744	22841

Options	Price
Navigation System	+722
Power Moonroof	+599
Air Conditioning - Front and Rear	+259

Body Styles	TMV Pricing		
	Trade	Private	Dealer
4 Dr STD SUV	17806	19855	21863

Options	Price
Alpine Audio System	+206
Chrome Wheels	+127
Compact Disc Changer	+216

Mileage Category: O

The 2000 Navigator is now available with a fully integrated satellite navigation system, as well as a reverse-sensing system. Side airbags are standard, while new climate-controlled seats for the driver and front passenger are optional. The 2000 Navigator also features several exterior and interior styling changes.

1999

Body Styles	TMV Pricing		
	Trade	Private	Dealer
4 Dr STD 4WD SUV	16037	18007	20058

Options	Price
Air Conditioning - Front and Rear	+208
Alpine Audio System	+168

Body Styles	TMV Pricing		
	Trade	Private	Dealer
4 Dr STD SUV	15142	17003	18939

Options	Price
Compact Disc Changer	+176
Power Moonroof	+488

Mileage Category: O

Into its second year, Lincoln's Navigator enters 1999 with more power, adjustable pedals, speed-sensitive stereo volume and a hands-free cellular phone. Also, the optional third-row seat is mounted on rollers this year for easy installation and removal.

1998

Body Styles	TMV Pricing		
	Trade	Private	Dealer
4 Dr STD 4WD SUV	14022	15815	17837

Options	Price
Air Conditioning - Front and Rear	+183
Chrome Wheels	+206

Body Styles	TMV Pricing		
	Trade	Private	Dealer
4 Dr STD SUV	12686	14308	16137

Options	Price
Compact Disc Changer	+155
Power Moonroof	+389

Mileage Category: O

This all-new entrant into the luxury SUV market is the first truck ever sold by Lincoln. Based on the highly acclaimed Ford Expedition, the Navigator is powered by a 5.4-liter, SOHC V8 engine and has standard goodies that include illuminated running boards and a load-leveling air suspension. This truck also features one of the largest grilles this side of a Kenworth.

Lincoln
Town Car

2003

Body Styles	TMV Pricing		
	Trade	Private	Dealer
4 Dr Cartier L Sdn	30203	31839	34565
4 Dr Cartier Sdn	27019	28482	30921

Options	Price
Compact Disc Changer [Opt on Cartier,Signature]	+379
Navigation System [Opt on Cartier,Cartier L,Signature]	+1565
Power Moonroof [Opt on Cartier,Signature]	+956

Body Styles	TMV Pricing		
	Trade	Private	Dealer
4 Dr Executive Sdn	23962	25260	27422
4 Dr Signature Sdn	25518	26900	29203

Options	Price
Special Leather Seat Trim [Opt on Signature]	+314
Two-Tone Paint [Opt on Signature]	+185
Park Distance Control (Rear) [Opt on Executive]	+157

Mileage Category: I

Lincoln's full-size luxury car receives an extensive reengineering for 2003 designed to make it safer, quieter and more luxurious than before. Major hardware revisions include a redesigned frame and modifications to the suspension, steering and braking systems. The standard V8 engine is also more powerful. Visually, the Town Car is more formal in appearance, and the old-fashioned Lincoln "star" hood ornament is back by popular demand. Creature comforts are addressed by the addition of newly standard equipment, increased storage space, additional safety features and improved interior materials.

2002

Body Styles	TMV Pricing		
	Trade	Private	Dealer
4 Dr Cartier L Sdn	22398	23884	26360
4 Dr Cartier Sdn	20432	21787	24046

Options	Price
Alpine Audio System [Opt on Signature]	+174
Chrome Wheels [Opt on Signature]	+224
Compact Disc Changer	+300
Heated Front Seats [Opt on Signature]	+199

Body Styles	TMV Pricing		
	Trade	Private	Dealer
4 Dr Executive Sdn	17910	19098	21078
4 Dr Signature Sdn	19095	20362	22473

Options	Price
Power Moonroof [Opt on Signature]	+472
Telematic System	+293
Touring Suspension [Opt on Signature]	+286
Two-Tone Paint [Opt on Signature]	+129

Mileage Category: I

A new Vehicle Communication System (VCS) is optional. VCS includes a portable hands-free, voice-activated Motorola Timeport analog-digital phone; SOS safety and security services; access to news, stock quotes and weather; and route guidance assistance.

Lincoln
Town Car

2001

Mileage Category: I

Horsepower has been increased throughout the model lineup. Inside, the Town Car gains adjustable pedals, seat-belt pre-tensioners, upgraded map pockets and leather grab handles. Signature models have a wood-trimmed steering wheel as standard and the front seats in Executive models now have power lumbar adjustment. Lincoln now offers complimentary maintenance at no additional charge for the first three years/36,000 miles in service.

Body Styles	TMV Pricing		
	Trade	Private	Dealer
4 Dr Cartier L Sdn	18027	19918	21663
4 Dr Cartier Sdn	16902	18675	20312
4 Dr Executive L Sdn	16514	18246	19845

Options	Price
Chrome Wheels [Opt on Signature]	+292
Compact Disc Changer	+250

Body Styles	TMV Pricing		
	Trade	Private	Dealer
4 Dr Executive Sdn	14734	16279	17706
4 Dr Signature Sdn	15746	17398	18922

Options	Price
Heated Front Seats [Opt on Signature]	+168
Power Moonroof	+636

2000

Mileage Category: I

The Town Car receives additional safety features, including an emergency trunk release, child seat-anchor brackets and Lincoln's Belt Minder system. A new storage armrest has been placed on the front-passenger door-trim panel. One new exterior color has been added: Autumn Red Clearcoat Metallic.

Body Styles	TMV Pricing		
	Trade	Private	Dealer
4 Dr Cartier L Sdn	14053	15666	17247
4 Dr Cartier Sdn	13401	14939	16446
4 Dr Executive L Sdn	13094	14597	16070

Options	Price
Chrome Wheels [Opt on Signature]	+252
Compact Disc Changer	+208

Body Styles	TMV Pricing		
	Trade	Private	Dealer
4 Dr Executive Sdn	11333	12634	13909
4 Dr Signature Sdn	12239	13644	15021

Options	Price
Power Moonroof	+548
Two-Tone Paint	+136

1999

Mileage Category: I

Standard side airbags improve the Town Car's ability to protect occupants and a new JBL audio system makes getting there even more fun.

Body Styles	TMV Pricing		
	Trade	Private	Dealer
4 Dr Cartier Sdn	11391	12763	14190
4 Dr Executive Sdn	10016	11222	12477

Options	Price
Chrome Wheels [Opt on Signature]	+205
Compact Disc Changer	+176

Body Styles	TMV Pricing		
	Trade	Private	Dealer
4 Dr Signature Sdn	10705	11994	13336

Options	Price
Power Moonroof	+447

1998

Mileage Category: I

Lincoln redesigns its Town Car this year, making it lower, stiffer and faster. The interior is nicely improved as well, with softer seats and better positioned controls.

Body Styles	TMV Pricing		
	Trade	Private	Dealer
4 Dr Cartier Sdn	10050	11386	12892
4 Dr Executive Sdn	8579	9719	11005

Options	Price
Chrome Wheels	+181
Compact Disc Changer	+155
JBL Audio System [Opt on Signature]	+147

Body Styles	TMV Pricing		
	Trade	Private	Dealer
4 Dr Signature Sdn	9157	10374	11747

Options	Price
Leather Seats [Opt on Executive, Signature]	+148
Power Moonroof	+393

1997

Body Styles	TMV Pricing		
	Trade	Private	Dealer
4 Dr Cartier Sdn	7601	8760	10176
4 Dr Executive Sdn	6583	7586	8812

Options	Price
Power Moonroof	+294
JBL Audio System [Opt on Signature]	+158

Body Styles	TMV Pricing		
	Trade	Private	Dealer
4 Dr Signature Sdn	6923	7978	9268

Options	Price
Chrome Wheels	+134
Compact Disc Changer	+115

Mileage Category: I

The Town Car's power steering has been improved.

1996

Body Styles	TMV Pricing		
	Trade	Private	Dealer
4 Dr Cartier Sdn	5884	6821	8114
4 Dr Executive Sdn	5078	5886	7002

Body Styles	TMV Pricing		
	Trade	Private	Dealer
4 Dr Signature Sdn	5360	6213	7391

Options	Price
Power Moonroof	+224

Mileage Category: I

Engine upgrades, new automatic climate controls and real wood on the dashboard in Cartier models sum up the changes to the Town Car.

1995

Body Styles	TMV Pricing		
	Trade	Private	Dealer
4 Dr Cartier Sdn	4235	4977	6214
4 Dr Executive Sdn	3543	4164	5198

Body Styles	TMV Pricing		
	Trade	Private	Dealer
4 Dr Signature Sdn	3830	4501	5620

Options	Price
Compact Disc Changer	+104

Options	Price
Power Moonroof	+194

Mileage Category: I

Exterior changes on the Town Car include new headlights, grille, taillights, bumpers and bodyside molding. The outside mirrors have been moved forward slightly to increase visibility. An electronic steering switch selector allows the driver to select the type of steering effort he or she wants. The instrument panel includes a redesigned two-spoke steering wheel, illuminated switches and improved stereos with larger controls. Signature and Cartier models get steering wheel-mounted stereo and climate controls. A gate access unit integrated into the driver-side visor allows up to three frequencies to be programmed into its memory.

1994

Body Styles	TMV Pricing		
	Trade	Private	Dealer
4 Dr Cartier Sdn	2974	3667	4822
4 Dr Executive Sdn	2280	2811	3697

Body Styles	TMV Pricing		
	Trade	Private	Dealer
4 Dr Signature Sdn	2516	3102	4079

Options	Price
Power Moonroof	+136

Mileage Category: I

A dual exhaust system on the Town Car is made standard this year, upping horsepower to 210. All models receive solar-tinted glass. The Jack Nicklaus Special Edition has been dropped.

Mazda
323/6/626

1994

Body Styles	TMV Pricing		
	Trade	Private	Dealer
2 Dr STD Hbk	697	1047	1630

Options	Price
Air Conditioning	+131
Automatic 4-Speed Transmission	+123

Mileage Category: B

No changes. Final year for homely, slow-selling hatchback.

Mazda
6

2003

Mileage Category: D

Mazda introduces the successor to its 626 and Millenia midsize sedans, known as the 6. Touted for its sporty characteristics, the 6 hopes to make a splash in the congested family sedan marketplace.

Body Styles	TMV Pricing		
	Trade	Private	Dealer
4 Dr i Sdn	11611	12643	14364
4 Dr s V6 Sdn	14046	15295	17377

Options	Price
Aluminum/Alloy Wheels [Opt on i]	+267
AM/FM/Cassette Audio System	+133
Antilock Brakes [Opt on i]	+453
Automatic 4-Speed Transmission [Opt on i]	+567
Automatic 5-Speed Transmission [Opt on s]	+600
Bose Audio System	+167
Compact Disc Changer	+333
Heated Front Seats	+150
Leather Seats	+573

Options	Price
Power Driver Seat [Opt on i]	+167
Power Moonroof	+467
Rear Spoiler	+130
Front Side Airbag Restraints	+133
Traction Control System [Opt on i]	+167
AM/FM/CD Changer Audio System	+267
17 Inch Wheels	+250
Front and Rear Head Airbag Restraints	+167

Mazda
626

2002

Mileage Category: D

This year, to get any options on the LX four-cylinder or the ES-V6 model, you must order an automatic transmission. So much for that whole "zoom-zoom" philosophy. The former budget sport sedan, the LX-V6, can't be equipped with any options at all, save a slushbox. And the ES (in V6 format only for the new year) loses standard equipment; the moonroof, cassette player and Bose speakers are part of an optional ES Premium package.

Body Styles	TMV Pricing		
	Trade	Private	Dealer
4 Dr ES V6 Sdn	8426	9414	11061
4 Dr LX Sdn	7220	8067	9478
4 Dr LX V6 Sdn	7593	8483	9967

Options	Price
Alarm System [Std on ES V6]	+139
Aluminum/Alloy Wheels [Std on ES V6]	+250
AM/FM/Cassette/CD Audio System [Opt on ES V6]	+167
Antilock Brakes	+379
Automatic 4-Speed Transmission	+445
Compact Disc Changer	+125

Options	Price
Front Side Airbag Restraints	+195
Power Driver Seat [Std on ES V6]	+139
Power Moonroof	+445
Rear Spoiler	+220
Traction Control System [Opt on ES V6]	+153

2001

Mileage Category: D

The 626's interior gains a new modular audio system, a new rear deck with child safety-seat anchors and an internal emergency trunk release. Mazda has also made EZ-Kool glass standard on all models and side airbags a stand-alone option on models with a V6 and automatic transmissions. All 626s are now 50-state emission compliant.

Body Styles	TMV Pricing		
	Trade	Private	Dealer
4 Dr ES Sdn	7206	8510	9713
4 Dr ES V6 Sdn	7374	8709	9942

Body Styles	TMV Pricing		
	Trade	Private	Dealer
4 Dr LX Sdn	6280	7416	8465
4 Dr LX V6 Sdn	6422	7584	8656

2001 (cont'd)

Options	Price
Alarm System [Std on ES V6]	+122
Aluminum/Alloy Wheels [Std on ES,ES V6]	+219
AM/FM/Cassette/CD Audio System [Std on ES V6]	+170
Antilock Brakes	+331
Automatic 4-Speed Transmission [Std on ES]	+389
Bose Audio System [Std on ES V6]	+170

Options	Price
Front Side Airbag Restraints	+122
Power Driver Seat [Std on ES V6]	+122
Power Moonroof [Std on ES V6]	+438
Rear Spoiler	+192
Traction Control System	+122

2000

Body Styles	TMV Pricing		
	Trade	Private	Dealer
4 Dr ES Sdn	5887	7041	8173
4 Dr ES V6 Sdn	6447	7712	8951

Body Styles	TMV Pricing		
	Trade	Private	Dealer
4 Dr LX Sdn	5129	6135	7122
4 Dr LX V6 Sdn	5381	6436	7471

Mileage Category: D

Improvements in styling, handling, steering, interior content and options are the highlights of the 2000 626.

Options	Price
Rear Spoiler	+156
Aluminum/Alloy Wheels [Std on ES,ES V6]	+197
AM/FM/Cassette/CD Audio System [Std on ES V6]	+138
Antilock Brakes	+268

Options	Price
Automatic 4-Speed Transmission [Std on ES]	+315
Bose Audio System [Std on ES V6]	+138
Power Moonroof [Std on ES V6]	+355

1999

Body Styles	TMV Pricing		
	Trade	Private	Dealer
4 Dr ES Sdn	4938	5991	7086
4 Dr ES V6 Sdn	5259	6380	7547

Body Styles	TMV Pricing		
	Trade	Private	Dealer
4 Dr LX Sdn	4103	4978	5889
4 Dr LX V6 Sdn	4532	5498	6504

Mileage Category: D

After a major makeover in '98, the 626 slides into '99 with only one major change: a new height-adjustable seat for the driver.

Options	Price
Aluminum/Alloy Wheels [Std on ES V6]	+155
Antilock Brakes	+235

Options	Price
Automatic 4-Speed Transmission [Std on ES]	+249
Power Moonroof [Std on ES V6]	+280

1998

Body Styles	TMV Pricing		
	Trade	Private	Dealer
4 Dr DX Sdn	3406	4227	5152
4 Dr ES Sdn	4162	5165	6297

Body Styles	TMV Pricing		
	Trade	Private	Dealer
4 Dr LX Sdn	3627	4501	5486
4 Dr LX V6 Sdn	3963	4918	5995

Mileage Category: D

Mazda redesigns the 626, giving it more upscale styling, more powerful engines, a tighter body and increased cargo and people space while retaining the sedan's distinctive sporting nature.

Options	Price
Antilock Brakes [Opt on LX]	+200
Automatic 4-Speed Transmission	+211
Leather Seats [Opt on LX]	+184

Options	Price
Power Moonroof [Std on ES]	+238
Air Conditioning [Opt on DX]	+260
Aluminum/Alloy Wheels [Std on ES]	+132

1997

Body Styles	TMV Pricing		
	Trade	Private	Dealer
4 Dr DX Sdn	2869	3613	4522
4 Dr ES V6 Sdn	3715	4677	5853

Body Styles	TMV Pricing		
	Trade	Private	Dealer
4 Dr LX Sdn	3081	3879	4855
4 Dr LX V6 Sdn	3317	4177	5227

Mileage Category: D

LX V6 and ES models gain power and torque, while the four-cylinder LX gets a Lexus-like trim package that includes two-tone paint, chrome wheel covers, leather interior, and other creature comforts. Audio systems are revised and two new colors debut.

Options	Price
Air Conditioning [Opt on DX]	+232
Aluminum/Alloy Wheels [Opt on LX]	+118
Antilock Brakes [Std on ES]	+189

Options	Price
Automatic 4-Speed Transmission	+189
Leather Seats [Std on ES]	+164
Power Moonroof	+207

1996

Body Styles	TMV Pricing		
	Trade	Private	Dealer
4 Dr DX Sdn	2093	2701	3540
4 Dr ES V6 Sdn	2959	3819	5006

Body Styles	TMV Pricing		
	Trade	Private	Dealer
4 Dr LX Sdn	2304	2973	3897
4 Dr LX V6 Sdn	2573	3320	4352

Mileage Category: D

Chrome is tacked on front and rear, and the hood is raised a bit to give the 626 a more substantial look. ABS is available as a stand alone option on LX and LX-V6 models for the first time (formerly, you had to buy an option package), and side-impact protection meets 1997 standards.

Mazda
626/929

1996 (cont'd)

Options	Price
Air Conditioning [Opt on DX]	+202
Antilock Brakes [Std on ES]	+167
Automatic 4-Speed Transmission	+167

Options	Price
Leather Seats	+146
Power Moonroof [Std on ES]	+183

1995

Body Styles	TMV Pricing		
	Trade	Private	Dealer
4 Dr DX Sdn	1448	1906	2670
4 Dr ES V6 Sdn	2117	2786	3902

Body Styles	TMV Pricing		
	Trade	Private	Dealer
4 Dr LX Sdn	1698	2235	3130
4 Dr LX V6 Sdn	1890	2488	3484

Options	Price
Air Conditioning [Opt on DX]	+181
Aluminum/Alloy Wheels [Opt on LX]	+94
Antilock Brakes [Std on ES]	+142

Options	Price
Automatic 4-Speed Transmission	+151
Power Moonroof [Std on ES]	+165

Mileage Category: D

ES gets remote keyless entry, which is available on LX and LX-V6 models. New wheels and wheel covers are added across the board.

1994

Mileage Category: D

Passenger airbag added. LX-V6 debuts. Four-cylinder models get new Ford transmission for smoother shifting than previous Mazda unit. ABS becomes standard on ES trim level, as well as leather seats and power sunroof.

Body Styles	TMV Pricing		
	Trade	Private	Dealer
4 Dr DX Sdn	1157	1585	2299
4 Dr ES V6 Sdn	1635	2241	3251

Body Styles	TMV Pricing		
	Trade	Private	Dealer
4 Dr LX Sdn	1228	1683	2442
4 Dr LX V6 Sdn	1348	1848	2680

Options	Price
Air Conditioning [Opt on DX]	+168
Aluminum/Alloy Wheels	+87
Antilock Brakes	+132

Options	Price
Automatic 4-Speed Transmission	+140
Leather Seats	+121
Power Moonroof [Std on ES]	+153

Mazda
929

1995

Body Styles	TMV Pricing		
	Trade	Private	Dealer
4 Dr STD Sdn	2412	3133	4334

Mileage Category: H

Leather seats, wood trim and remote keyless entry are standard. Final year for sleek executive sedan.

1994

Mileage Category: H

Trimmed to one model. Console cupholder added, height-adjustable seatbelts debut and a limited-slip differential is included with the Cold Package. Premium Package adds remote keyless entry. New alloy wheels are standard.

Body Styles	TMV Pricing		
	Trade	Private	Dealer
4 Dr STD Sdn	1839	2461	3497

Options	Price
Compact Disc Changer	+126
Leather Seats	+214

2001

Body Styles	TMV Pricing		
	Trade	Private	Dealer
2 Dr B2300 SE Std Cab SB	6273	7421	8480
2 Dr B2300 SX Std Cab SB	5518	6527	7459
2 Dr B2500 SE Std Cab SB	5652	6686	7640
2 Dr B2500 SX Std Cab SB	4842	5728	6545
2 Dr B3000 DS Ext Cab SB	7203	8521	9737
2 Dr B3000 DS Std Cab SB	6386	7554	8633
2 Dr B3000 SE 4WD Ext Cab SB	8439	9983	11408

Body Styles	TMV Pricing		
	Trade	Private	Dealer
2 Dr B3000 SE 4WD Std Cab SB	7488	8858	10123
2 Dr B3000 SE Ext Cab SB	6966	8241	9417
2 Dr B3000 SE Std Cab SB	6362	7526	8601
4 Dr B3000 SE Ext Cab SB	7693	9101	10400
4 Dr B4000 DS Ext Cab SB	7771	9193	10505
4 Dr B4000 SE 4WD Ext Cab SB	8954	10592	12104

Options	Price
Air Conditioning [Opt on SX - B2500,B3000]	+391
Automatic 4-Speed Transmission	+486

Options	Price
Power Windows [Std on B4000 - SE,TL]	+117
Running Boards	+180

Mileage Category: J

More power is the big news for Mazda's '01 B-Series Pickups. The B4000 boasts a new 4.0-liter SOHC V6, while the B2300 has a new 2.3-liter, four-cylinder engine. The flexible-fuel feature on the 3.0-liter V6 has been dropped. Mazda has also made ABS standard on all models. A new 4x2 Dual Sport trim level gives a two-wheeler the raised-suspension look of a four-by. While they were at it, Mazda product planners also modified the exterior and interior styling. To the chagrin of Troy Lee but probably nobody else, the B-Series Troy Lee edition has been dropped.

2000

Body Styles	TMV Pricing		
	Trade	Private	Dealer
2 Dr B2500 SE Ext Cab SB	5191	6270	7328
2 Dr B2500 SE Std Cab SB	4193	5065	5919
2 Dr B2500 SX Std Cab SB	3444	4160	4862
2 Dr B3000 SE 4WD Std Cab SB	5688	6870	8029
2 Dr B3000 SE Ext Cab SB	5389	6509	7607
2 Dr B3000 SE Std Cab SB	4343	5245	6130
2 Dr B3000 SX Std Cab SB	3594	4341	5073

Body Styles	TMV Pricing		
	Trade	Private	Dealer
4 Dr B3000 SE 4WD Ext Cab SB	6587	7956	9298
4 Dr B3000 SE Ext Cab SB	5591	6753	7892
4 Dr B3000 TL Ext Cab SB	6089	7355	8595
4 Dr B4000 SE 4WD Ext Cab SB	7388	8923	10428
4 Dr B4000 SE Ext Cab SB	7087	8560	10004
4 Dr B4000 TL 4WD Ext Cab SB	7734	9341	10917

Options	Price
Air Conditioning [Opt on SX - B2500,B3000]	+317
Antilock Brakes	+268
Automatic 4-Speed Transmission	+431
Automatic 5-Speed Transmission [Opt on B4000 4WD]	+451

Mileage Category: J

Two B3000 regular-cab models are added: SX and SE. The B2500 Troy Lee edition has been discontinued. Foglights are standard on all 4x4 models. A CD-equipped audio system is standard on all B4000 models. P225/70R15 tires are standard on SX models, and air conditioning is standard on SE and Troy Lee edition models. A 6,000-pound trailer hitch is standard on B4000 4x4s and optional on B4000 4x2 models. Troy Lee editions get standard leather-wrapped steering wheels.

1999

Body Styles	TMV Pricing		
	Trade	Private	Dealer
2 Dr B2500 SE Ext Cab SB	4447	5424	6441
2 Dr B2500 SE Std Cab SB	3657	4460	5296
2 Dr B2500 SX Std Cab SB	2915	3555	4222
2 Dr B2500 TL Std Cab SB	3904	4762	5654
2 Dr B3000 SE 4WD Ext Cab SB	5546	6765	8033
2 Dr B3000 SE 4WD Std Cab SB	5011	6112	7257
2 Dr B3000 SE Ext Cab SB	4589	5597	6646
2 Dr B4000 SE 4WD Ext Cab SB	6325	7715	9161
2 Dr B4000 SE Ext Cab SB	5564	6786	8058

Body Styles	TMV Pricing		
	Trade	Private	Dealer
2 Dr B4000 SE Std Cab SB	4642	5662	6723
4 Dr B2500 SE Ext Cab SB	4600	5610	6662
4 Dr B3000 SE 4WD Ext Cab SB	5519	6731	7993
4 Dr B3000 SE Ext Cab SB	4843	5907	7014
4 Dr B3000 TL Ext Cab SB	5287	6448	7657
4 Dr B4000 SE 4WD Ext Cab SB	6398	7803	9266
4 Dr B4000 SE Ext Cab SB	5584	6810	8087
4 Dr B4000 TL 4WD Ext Cab SB	6817	8315	9874

Options	Price
Air Conditioning [Opt on B2500 SX]	+251
Antilock Brakes	+235

Options	Price
Automatic 4-Speed Transmission	+341
Automatic 5-Speed Transmission [Std on B4000 SE 2WD Ext Cab]	+341

Mileage Category: J

The B-Series Pickup now comes with a four-door option called the Cab Plus 4. Option packages have been consolidated and simplified this year to reduce buyer confusion. A class III frame-mounted hitch receiver is available with V6 applications.

1998

Body Styles	TMV Pricing		
	Trade	Private	Dealer
2 Dr B2500 SE Ext Cab SB	3767	4652	5649

Body Styles	TMV Pricing		
	Trade	Private	Dealer
2 Dr B3000 SE Ext Cab SB	3969	4901	5952

1998 (cont'd)

Mileage Category: J

Fresh styling, a revised front suspension, a larger regular cab, a more powerful 2.5-liter four-cylinder engine, a stiffer frame and a new 4WD system ensure that Mazda's compact truck will remain competitive through the end of the century.

Body Styles	TMV Pricing		
	Trade	Private	Dealer
2 Dr B2500 SE Std Cab SB	3114	3845	4670
2 Dr B2500 SX Std Cab SB	2614	3227	3919
2 Dr B3000 SE 4WD Ext Cab SB	4673	5770	7007
2 Dr B3000 SE 4WD Std Cab SB	4417	5454	6623

Options	Price
Air Conditioning	+213
Antilock Brakes	+200

Body Styles	TMV Pricing		
	Trade	Private	Dealer
2 Dr B3000 SX 4WD Std Cab SB	3861	4768	5790
2 Dr B4000 SE 4WD Ext Cab SB	5383	6647	8072
2 Dr B4000 SE Ext Cab SB	4371	5397	6555
4 Dr B2500 SE Ext Cab SB	3877	4787	5813

Options	Price
Automatic 4-Speed Transmission	+290
Automatic 5-Speed Transmission [Opt on B4000]	+299

1997

Mileage Category: J

The lineup is trimmed, leaving just B2300 and B4000 models available. SE-5 designation returns to bolster marketing efforts. B4000 pickups can be equipped with a new five-speed automatic transmission.

Body Styles	TMV Pricing		
	Trade	Private	Dealer
2 Dr B2300 SE Ext Cab SB	3125	3902	4852
2 Dr B2300 SE Std Cab SB	2570	3209	3991
2 Dr B2300 Std Cab SB	2167	2706	3364
2 Dr B4000 4WD Ext Cab SB	4363	5448	6775

Options	Price
Antilock Brakes	+178
Automatic 4-Speed Transmission	+252

Body Styles	TMV Pricing		
	Trade	Private	Dealer
2 Dr B4000 4WD Std Cab SB	3505	4376	5441
2 Dr B4000 SE 4WD Ext Cab SB	4782	5971	7425
2 Dr B4000 SE Ext Cab SB	3457	4317	5368

Options	Price
Automatic 5-Speed Transmission	+260
Air Conditioning	+189

1996

Mileage Category: J

A passenger-side airbag comes with SE Plus and LE trim levels, and it can be deactivated in the event that a rear facing child safety seat is installed. SE models also get new chrome bumpers.

Body Styles	TMV Pricing		
	Trade	Private	Dealer
2 Dr B2300 4WD Std Cab SB	2941	3684	4709
2 Dr B2300 Ext Cab SB	2528	3166	4047
2 Dr B2300 SE Ext Cab SB	2645	3313	4235
2 Dr B2300 SE Std Cab SB	2259	2829	3617
2 Dr B2300 Std Cab LB	2068	2590	3311
2 Dr B2300 Std Cab SB	1872	2345	2997

Body Styles	TMV Pricing		
	Trade	Private	Dealer
2 Dr B3000 4WD Ext Cab SB	3469	4344	5553
2 Dr B3000 SE Ext Cab SB	2895	3625	4634
2 Dr B4000 LE 4WD Ext Cab SB	5100	6387	8165
2 Dr B4000 LE Ext Cab SB	3351	4197	5366
2 Dr B4000 SE 4WD Ext Cab SB	4275	5354	6844
2 Dr B4000 SE 4WD Std Cab SB	3538	4431	5665

Options	Price
Air Conditioning [Std on B4000 LE]	+169
Antilock Brakes	+158
Automatic 4-Speed Transmission	+219

1995

Mileage Category: J

Redesigned dashboard with driver airbag debuts. Four-wheel ABS is standard on 4WD and 2WD B4000 models.

Body Styles	TMV Pricing		
	Trade	Private	Dealer
2 Dr B2300 4WD Std Cab SB	2544	3176	4228
2 Dr B2300 Ext Cab SB	2188	2731	3637
2 Dr B2300 SE Ext Cab SB	2325	2902	3864
2 Dr B2300 SE Std Cab SB	1977	2468	3285
2 Dr B2300 Std Cab LB	1798	2244	2988
2 Dr B2300 Std Cab SB	1637	2043	2720
2 Dr B3000 SE 4WD Ext Cab SB	2847	3554	4733

Body Styles	TMV Pricing		
	Trade	Private	Dealer
2 Dr B3000 SE Ext Cab SB	2367	2955	3934
2 Dr B3000 SE Std Cab SB	2155	2690	3581
2 Dr B4000 LE 4WD Ext Cab SB	4430	5530	7362
2 Dr B4000 LE Ext Cab SB	2807	3504	4665
2 Dr B4000 SE 4WD Ext Cab SB	3728	4653	6195
2 Dr B4000 SE 4WD Std Cab SB	3026	3777	5029
2 Dr B4000 SE Ext Cab SB	2412	3011	4008

Options	Price
Air Conditioning [Std on B4000 LE]	+152
Automatic 4-Speed Transmission	+197
Compact Disc Changer	+84

1994

Body Styles	TMV Pricing		
	Trade	Private	Dealer
2 Dr B2300 Ext Cab SB	1775	2296	3163
2 Dr B2300 SE Std Cab SB	1527	1975	2722
2 Dr B2300 Std Cab SB	1350	1746	2406
2 Dr B3000 4WD Ext Cab SB	2221	2873	3959
2 Dr B3000 4WD Std Cab SB	2212	2861	3942
2 Dr B3000 Ext Cab SB	1865	2412	3324
2 Dr B3000 SE Ext Cab SB	1906	2466	3398

Body Styles	TMV Pricing		
	Trade	Private	Dealer
2 Dr B3000 SE Std Cab LB	1819	2353	3243
2 Dr B3000 SE Std Cab SB	1739	2249	3100
2 Dr B4000 LE 4WD Ext Cab SB	3473	4493	6192
2 Dr B4000 LE Ext Cab SB	2372	3068	4228
2 Dr B4000 SE 4WD Ext Cab SB	3091	3998	5510
2 Dr B4000 SE 4WD Std Cab SB	2508	3244	4470
2 Dr B4000 SE Std Cab LB	1822	2357	3248

Options	Price
Air Conditioning	+141
Automatic 4-Speed Transmission [Std on B4000 LE]	+183

Mazda revises the styling of Ford's Ranger, slaps its name on the tailgate and has a new compact pickup to sell. Base, SE and LE trim levels are offered in two- or four-wheel drive and two body styles.

Mileage Category: J

2003

Body Styles	TMV Pricing		
	Trade	Private	Dealer
4 Dr ES Pass Van	15656	16940	19080
4 Dr LX Pass Van	13149	14228	16025
4 Dr LX-SV Pass Van	12634	13671	15398

Options	Price
Alarm System [Opt on ES]	+167
AM/FM/Cassette Audio System	+133
Automatic Dimming Rearview Mirror	+130
Compact Disc Changer [Opt on ES,LX]	+300
Power Dual Sliding Doors [Opt on ES,LX]	+533
Power Moonroof [Opt on ES,LX]	+467

Options	Price
Rear Spoiler	+127
Front Side Airbag Restraints [Opt on LX]	+183
AM/FM/CD Changer Audio System [Opt on LX]	+300
17 Inch Wheels [Opt on LX]	+150
Air Conditioning - Front and Rear [Opt on LX]	+397
DVD Entertainment System	+800

Mileage Category: P

For 2003, power sliding doors are an option for both the LX and ES trim levels. A towing package and a cargo organizer are two other new options. Also, an alarm and engine immobilizer are now part of a security package, and a cassette player is available on the ES trim level. The LX trim now rides on 16-inch wheels. Inside, floor and cargo mats are now standard on both trim levels, while outside, you'll see a new exhaust tip.

2002

Body Styles	TMV Pricing		
	Trade	Private	Dealer
4 Dr ES Pass Van	12857	14070	16092
4 Dr LX Pass Van	10591	11590	13256

Options	Price
16 Inch Wheels [Std on ES]	+209
Air Conditioning - Front and Rear [Std on ES]	+331
Automatic Dimming Rearview Mirror	+128
Compact Disc Changer	+250

Options	Price
Front Side Airbag Restraints [Std on ES]	+153
Power Driver Seat [Std on ES]	+148
Power Moonroof	+390
Traction Control System [Std on ES]	+142

Mileage Category: P

Mazda adds power to the MPV in the form of a 200-horsepower V6 engine governed by a five-speed automatic transmission, which is just what the doctor ordered for this previously underpowered minivan. The MPV also gains power-sliding doors, available 17-inch alloy wheels, traction control, an improved braking system and revised suspension tuning.

2001

Body Styles	TMV Pricing		
	Trade	Private	Dealer
4 Dr DX Pass Van	8435	9779	11020
4 Dr ES Pass Van	10301	11943	13458
4 Dr LX Pass Van	9137	10592	11936

Options	Price
Air Conditioning - Front and Rear [Std on ES]	+289
Aluminum/Alloy Wheels [Std on ES]	+122
Compact Disc Changer [Std on ES]	+219
Front Side Airbag Restraints [Std on ES]	+129

Options	Price
Power Moonroof	+340
Power Windows [Opt on DX]	+124
VCR Entertainment System	+776

Mileage Category: P

Not much changes on Mazda's minivan. Keyless entry is standard on MPV LX, and the AM/FM/CD/cassette audio system is standard on LX and ES models. Child safety-seat anchors have been added to all MPV models, as have new exterior color choices. The 2.5-liter V6 engine now complies with NLEV emissions standards.

Mazda
MPV

2000

Mileage Category: P

The MPV has been completely redesigned from top to bottom. Several unique features, like hinged rear doors and all-wheel drive, have disappeared. At the same time, items like roll-down windows in the sliding doors and tailgate seating in the third-row seats certify the MPV as a standout vehicle.

Body Styles	TMV Pricing		
	Trade	Private	Dealer
4 Dr DX Pass Van	7349	8691	10006
4 Dr ES Pass Van	9004	10648	12260
4 Dr LX Pass Van	7928	9375	10794

Options	Price
Power Moonroof	+276
Air Conditioning - Front and Rear [Std on ES]	+234
AM/FM/CD Changer Audio System [Opt on ES,LX]	+236

1998

Mileage Category: P

A CD player is now standard.

Body Styles	TMV Pricing		
	Trade	Private	Dealer
4 Dr ES 4WD Pass Van	6408	7810	9391
4 Dr ES Pass Van	5720	6971	8382

Options	Price
Air Conditioning	+159
Air Conditioning - Front and Rear	+318
Aluminum/Alloy Wheels [Std on ES 4WD]	+131
Automatic Load Leveling [Opt on LX]	+131

Body Styles	TMV Pricing		
	Trade	Private	Dealer
4 Dr LX 4WD Pass Van	5881	7167	8618
4 Dr LX Pass Van	4941	6022	7240

Options	Price
Captain Chairs (4) [Opt on LX 4WD]	+118
Leather Seats [Opt on LX]	+291
Power Moonroof	+318

1997

Mileage Category: P

Four-wheel ABS is standard across the board, and all but the LX 2WD model are dressed in goofy All-Sport exterior trim.

Body Styles	TMV Pricing		
	Trade	Private	Dealer
4 Dr ES 4WD Pass Van	5314	6588	8144
4 Dr ES Pass Van	4735	5871	7259

Options	Price
Air Conditioning	+141
Air Conditioning - Front and Rear	+259
Aluminum/Alloy Wheels [Std on ES,4WD]	+117

Body Styles	TMV Pricing		
	Trade	Private	Dealer
4 Dr LX 4WD Pass Van	4941	6125	7573
4 Dr LX Pass Van	4043	5013	6198

Options	Price
Automatic Load Leveling [Opt on LX]	+117
Power Moonroof	+283

1996

Mileage Category: P

New styling up front, a fourth door on the driver side, and a revised instrument panel with dual airbags sum up the changes to Mazda's attempt at a minivan.

Body Styles	TMV Pricing		
	Trade	Private	Dealer
4 Dr DX Pass Van	2846	3562	4550
4 Dr ES 4WD Pass Van	3899	4879	6233
4 Dr ES Pass Van	3338	4177	5336

Options	Price
Air Conditioning	+189
Air Conditioning - Front and Rear	+231
Power Moonroof	+251

Body Styles	TMV Pricing		
	Trade	Private	Dealer
4 Dr LX 4WD Pass Van	3549	4442	5674
4 Dr LX Pass Van	2990	3742	4781

1995

Mileage Category: P

New lineup includes L, LX and LXE trim levels. All come with seven-passenger seating. Four-cylinder engine has been dropped.

Body Styles	TMV Pricing		
	Trade	Private	Dealer
3 Dr L Pass Van	2432	3079	4156
3 Dr LX 4WD Pass Van	3054	3866	5219
3 Dr LX Pass Van	2516	3185	4300

Options	Price
Air Conditioning	+113
Air Conditioning - Front and Rear	+207
Aluminum/Alloy Wheels	+93

Body Styles	TMV Pricing		
	Trade	Private	Dealer
3 Dr LXE 4WD Pass Van	3324	4207	5679
3 Dr LXE Pass Van	2893	3662	4943

Options	Price
Automatic Load Leveling [Opt on LX]	+93
Power Moonroof	+226

Body Styles	TMV Pricing		
	Trade	Private	Dealer
3 Dr STD 4WD Pass Van	2232	2960	4173
3 Dr STD Pass Van	1808	2398	3381

Options	Price	Options	Price
3.0L V6 SOHC 18V FI Engine [Opt on STD]	+131	Automatic Load Leveling [Opt on STD]	+87
Air Conditioning	+105	Leather Seats	+192
Air Conditioning - Front and Rear	+192	Power Moonroof	+210
Aluminum/Alloy Wheels	+87		

Mileage Category: P

Side-door impact beams are added. Four-wheel disc brakes are new. Standard tire size increases.

Mazda

MX-3

1995

Body Styles	TMV Pricing		
	Trade	Private	Dealer
2 Dr STD Hbk	1829	2354	3228

Options	Price	Options	Price
Air Conditioning	+141	Automatic 4-Speed Transmission	+151
Antilock Brakes	+151	Power Sunroof	+132

Mileage Category: E

GS model, and its cool 1.8-liter V6, vanishes. ABS is available only with manual transmission.

1994

Body Styles	TMV Pricing		
	Trade	Private	Dealer
2 Dr GS Hbk	1759	2379	3413
2 Dr STD Hbk	1508	2040	2927

Options	Price	Options	Price
Air Conditioning	+131	Automatic 4-Speed Transmission	+140
Antilock Brakes	+140	Power Sunroof	+123

Mileage Category: E

Base model gets more power, and a passenger airbag is added. ABS can be ordered on base models for the first time. Can't get ABS on GS with automatic transmission. Base cars can be equipped with power sunroof. Both models get new wheels.

Mazda

MX-5 Miata

2003

Body Styles	TMV Pricing			Body Styles	TMV Pricing		
	Trade	Private	Dealer		Trade	Private	Dealer
2 Dr LS Conv	15847	17023	18984	2 Dr STD Conv	14126	15175	16922
2 Dr SE Conv	17512	18812	20979	2 Dr Shinsen Conv	15662	16825	18762

Options	Price	Options	Price
6-Speed Transmission [Opt on LS]	+433	Cruise Control [Opt on STD]	+130
Alarm System	+147	Keyless Entry System [Opt on STD]	+123
AM/FM/Cassette Audio System	+133	Limited Slip Differential [Opt on STD]	+263
Antilock Brakes [Opt on LS,SE]	+453	Power Door Locks [Opt on STD]	+137
Automatic 4-Speed Transmission	+533	Sport Suspension [Opt on LS,STD]	+263
Automatic Dimming Rearview Mirror	+153		

Mileage Category: E

Only minor changes are in store for the Miata this year. Base models receive standard 16-inch alloy wheels, a strut-tower brace, larger brakes and a child seat anchoring system. Cloth replaces vinyl on the top of the LS model, and tan leather gives way to a lighter parchment-colored hide. Also, the LS receives aluminum-colored interior trim and, for the first time, black leather is available as an option. New options include a cargo net, an auto-dimming mirror with an integrated compass and outside temperature display and special bezels for the headlights and taillights.

Mazda
MX-5 Miata

2002

Mileage Category: E

The addition of an optional in-dash six-CD changer, a perimeter theft alarm (on models with remote keyless entry) and a standard trunk light. LS versions get a revised stereo and speed-sensitive volume control. Later in the year, a new Special Edition trim debuts.

Body Styles	TMV Pricing		
	Trade	Private	Dealer
2 Dr LS Conv	12313	13533	15567
2 Dr SE Conv	12589	13836	15916
2 Dr STD Conv	11342	12466	14338

Options	Price	Options	Price
16 Inch Wheels [Opt on STD]	+306	Hardtop Roof	+835
6-Speed Transmission [Opt on LS]	+362	Limited Slip Differential [Opt on STD]	+139
Antilock Brakes	+379	Rear Spoiler	+164
Automatic 4-Speed Transmission	+445	Sport Suspension	+220
Compact Disc Changer [Std on SE]	+278		

2001

Mileage Category: E

For 2001, the Miata receives a host of minor changes. Horsepower has been increased, and a six-speed manual transmission is now optional on the Miata LS. Both the exterior and interior have been updated and there are four new exterior colors. Regular Miatas now have 15-inch wheels as standard equipment, while both the Miata LS and cars equipped with the optional suspension package get 16-inch wheels. Safety and security are improved via seatbelt pre-tensioners, improved ABS, an engine immobilizer, an internal trunk release and optional keyless remote (standard on Miata LS).

Body Styles	TMV Pricing		
	Trade	Private	Dealer
2 Dr LS Conv	10909	12600	14161
2 Dr STD Conv	9177	10600	11913
2 Dr Special Edition Conv	11163	12894	14491

Options	Price	Options	Price
6-Speed Transmission	+316	Hardtop Roof	+729
Antilock Brakes	+331	Limited Slip Differential [Opt on STD]	+122
Automatic 4-Speed Transmission	+438	Rear Spoiler	+143

2000

Mileage Category: E

The Miata's option packages have been simplified. There are now two models -- Miata and Miata LS -- and three option packages. A six-speed Miata Special Edition will also be available by spring 2000.

Body Styles	TMV Pricing		
	Trade	Private	Dealer
2 Dr LS Conv	8930	10411	11863
2 Dr STD Conv	7461	8698	9911
2 Dr Special Edition Conv	9849	11482	13083

Options	Price	Options	Price
Air Conditioning [Opt on LS,STD]	+355	Hardtop Roof	+473
Antilock Brakes	+268	Rear Spoiler	+118
Automatic 4-Speed Transmission	+335		

1999

Mileage Category: E

Mazda cautiously redesigns the MX-5 Miata, improving the car in every way without bumping up the price or diluting the car's personality.

Body Styles	TMV Pricing		
	Trade	Private	Dealer
2 Dr 10th Anniv Conv	7999	9566	11197
2 Dr STD Conv	5988	7161	8382

Options	Price	Options	Price
Air Conditioning	+280	Bose Audio System [Opt on STD]	+171
Antilock Brakes	+235	Hardtop Roof	+415
Automatic 4-Speed Transmission	+265	Leather Seats [Opt on STD]	+279

1997

Mileage Category: E

Mazda adds a Touring Package to the options list, consisting of alloy wheels, power steering, leather-wrapped steering wheel, power mirrors, power windows and door map pockets. Midyear a new M-Edition debuts, sporting Marina Green paint and chromed alloy wheels. Summertime brings the limited-production STO-Edition, of which 1,500 were produced.

Body Styles	TMV Pricing		
	Trade	Private	Dealer
2 Dr M-Edition Conv	6032	7351	8963
2 Dr STD Conv	4867	5931	7231
2 Dr STO Conv	5868	7151	8718

Options	Price	Options	Price
Air Conditioning [Opt on STD]	+212	Hardtop Roof	+314

1997 (cont'd)

Options	Price
Air Conditioning [Opt on STD]	+212
Antilock Brakes	+212
Automatic 4-Speed Transmission	+201

Options	Price
Hardtop Roof	+314
Leather Seats [Opt on STD]	+211

1996

Mileage Category: E

Side-impact standards for 1997 are met a year early, and to offset the added weight, Mazda boosts power and torque.

Body Styles	TMV Pricing		
	Trade	Private	Dealer
2 Dr M-Edition Conv	4802	6027	7718
2 Dr STD Conv	3646	4576	5861

Options	Price
Air Conditioning [Opt on STD]	+189
Antilock Brakes [Opt on STD]	+189
Automatic 4-Speed Transmission	+178

Options	Price
Hardtop Roof	+279
Leather Seats [Opt on STD]	+188
Sensory Audio System [Opt on STD]	+183

1995

Mileage Category: E

Option packages are revised, and a gorgeous M-Edition with Merlot Mica paint, tan top, tan leather interior and 15-inch BBS rims is available.

Body Styles	TMV Pricing		
	Trade	Private	Dealer
2 Dr M-Edition Conv	3667	4719	6472
2 Dr STD Conv	2806	3610	4951

Options	Price
Air Conditioning [Opt on STD]	+169
Antilock Brakes [Opt on STD]	+142
Automatic 4-Speed Transmission	+160

Options	Price
Hardtop Roof	+251
Leather Seats [Opt on STD]	+169
Sensory Audio System	+165

1994

Mileage Category: E

Dual airbags arrive, and a 1.8-liter four-cylinder making 128 horsepower replaces the original 1.6-liter engine. Sharp, new alloy wheels debut. Optional automatic gets electronic shift controls. Larger diameter disc brakes are standard. Bigger gas tank added. New R package debuts with sportier suspension. Superman Blue replaced by Montego Blue. M-Edition is painted Montego Blue with chromed alloys.

Body Styles	TMV Pricing		
	Trade	Private	Dealer
2 Dr M-Edition Conv	2530	3422	4909
2 Dr STD Conv	2151	2910	4174

Options	Price
Air Conditioning [Opt on STD]	+157
Antilock Brakes	+132
Automatic 4-Speed Transmission	+148

Options	Price
Hardtop Roof	+233
Leather Seats [Opt on STD]	+157

Mazda
MX-6

1997

Body Styles	TMV Pricing		
	Trade	Private	Dealer
2 Dr LS Cpe	4295	5235	6383
2 Dr STD Cpe	3601	4389	5351

Options	Price
Air Conditioning [Std on LS]	+212
Antilock Brakes	+189
Automatic 4-Speed Transmission	+189

Options	Price
Leather Seats	+164
Power Sunroof [Std on LS]	+177

Mileage Category: E

All LS models get a rear spoiler.

1996

Mileage Category: E

No changes for 1996.

Body Styles	TMV Pricing		
	Trade	Private	Dealer
2 Dr LS Cpe	3421	4205	5288
2 Dr M-Edition Cpe	4114	5057	6359

Body Styles	TMV Pricing		
	Trade	Private	Dealer
2 Dr STD Cpe	2883	3544	4457

Mazda
MX-6/Mazdaspeed Protege/Millenia

1996 (cont'd)

Options	Price
Air Conditioning [Std on STD]	+189
Antilock Brakes [Opt on LS,STD]	+167
Automatic 4-Speed Transmission	+167

Options	Price
Leather Seats [Opt on LS]	+146
Power Sunroof [Opt on STD]	+157

1995

Mileage Category: E

No changes for 1995.

Body Styles	TMV Pricing		
	Trade	Private	Dealer
2 Dr LS Cpe	2380	3063	4202
2 Dr STD Cpe	2024	2605	3573

Options	Price
Air Conditioning [Std on LS]	+169
Antilock Brakes	+151
Automatic 4-Speed Transmission	+151

Options	Price
Leather Seats	+131
Power Sunroof [Std on LS]	+141

1994

Mileage Category: E

Passenger airbag debuts. Air conditioning and power sunroof become standard on LS.

Body Styles	TMV Pricing		
	Trade	Private	Dealer
2 Dr LS Cpe	1986	2687	3854
2 Dr STD Cpe	1672	2262	3244

Options	Price
Air Conditioning [Std on LS]	+157
Antilock Brakes	+140
Automatic 4-Speed Transmission	+140

Options	Price
Leather Seats	+121
Power Sunroof [Std on LS]	+131

Mazda
Mazdaspeed Protege

2003

Body Styles	TMV Pricing		
	Trade	Private	Dealer
4 Dr Turbo Sdn	15451	16598	18509
4 Dr Turbo Sdn (2003.5)	15940	17124	19096

Mileage Category: E

Mazda introduces a new sport-tuned version of its Protege, dubbed Mazdaspeed.

Mazda
Millenia

2002

Body Styles	TMV Pricing		
	Trade	Private	Dealer
4 Dr Premium Sdn	13039	14192	16114
4 Dr Premium Special Edition Sdn	13546	14744	16740

Body Styles	TMV Pricing		
	Trade	Private	Dealer
4 Dr S S/C Sdn	14941	16262	18464
4 Dr S Special Edition S/C Sdn	16435	17888	20310

Options	Price
17 Inch Wheels - Chrome [Opt on S]	+334
Bose Audio System [Opt on Premium]	+445
Compact Disc Changer	+278
Heated Front Seats	+167

Options	Price
Special Factory Paint	+212
Traction Control System [Std on S]	+139
Two-Tone Paint	+212

Mileage Category: H

Now that the brilliant 6 sport sedan has been approved for production, the Millenia's days are numbered. Understandably, changes for 2002 barely register on the Richter scale. Are you ready for this? An auto-dimming mirror with compass is standard, and Snow White Pearl paint is changed to Snow Flake White Pearl paint. You can also get a Special Edition with a chrome-finished front grille, a black exterior and a black-and-ivory interior with titanium trim.

For the latest vehicle information, visit www.edmunds.com

2001

Mileage Category: H

Mazda has strengthened the Millenia's body structure to improve torsional rigidity by 30 percent. Combined with a new rear stabilizer bar and a larger front stabilizer bar, improved handling is the result. Visually, the car should be more appealing thanks to new front and rear styling. The interior has been updated significantly, as well. Hardware changes include larger disc brakes, a revised ABS system and standard side airbags for both models.

Body Styles	TMV Pricing		
	Trade	Private	Dealer
4 Dr Premium Sdn	10692	12300	13784
4 Dr S S/C Sdn	11055	12717	14252

Options	Price	Options	Price
17 Inch Wheels - Chrome	+292	Pearlescent Metallic Paint	+185
Bose Audio System [Opt on STD]	+389	Traction Control System [Opt on STD]	+146
Compact Disc Changer	+243	Two-Tone Paint	+185
Heated Front Seats	+146		

2000

Mileage Category: H

Millenia models receive considerable price reductions to make them more competitive in the market. Mazda is also offering a special 2000 Millenium edition of the Millenia. This version comes with 17-inch chrome wheels, an in-dash six-disc CD changer, suede seat and door trim and a choice of either Highlight Silver Mica or Millennium Red Mica paint.

Body Styles	TMV Pricing		
	Trade	Private	Dealer
4 Dr Millennium S/C Sdn	9438	10923	12378
4 Dr S S/C Sdn	9322	10789	12227
4 Dr STD Sdn	7939	9188	10412

Options	Price	Options	Price
Bose Audio System [Opt on STD]	+276	Power Moonroof [Opt on STD]	+364
Chrome Wheels [Opt on S]	+197	Power Passenger Seat [Opt on STD]	+138
Heated Front Seats	+118	Special Factory Paint	+150
Leather Seats [Opt on STD]	+433	Traction Control System [Opt on STD]	+118

1999

Mileage Category: H

Revised front- and rear-end styling, plus an optional two-tone color scheme, separate the '99 Millenia from past models.

Body Styles	TMV Pricing		
	Trade	Private	Dealer
4 Dr S S/C Sdn	7957	9295	10688
4 Dr STD Sdn	7067	8255	9492

Options	Price	Options	Price
Bose Audio System [Std on S]	+218	Power Moonroof [Std on S]	+288
Chrome Wheels	+155	Special Factory Paint	+118
Leather Seats [Std on S]	+342		

1998

Mileage Category: H

Millenia carries over into 1998 with no changes.

Body Styles	TMV Pricing		
	Trade	Private	Dealer
4 Dr S S/C Sdn	5994	7178	8513
4 Dr STD Sdn	5442	6517	7729

Options	Price	Options	Price
16 Inch Wheels [Opt on STD]	+147	Leather Seats [Opt on STD]	+291
Bose Audio System [Opt on STD]	+185	Power Moonroof [Opt on STD]	+265
Compact Disc Changer [Opt on STD]	+145		

1997

Mileage Category: H

Models equipped with leather are upgraded this year with an eight-way power passenger seat, 16-inch alloy wheels, and revised final drive ratio for better low-end response. S models also get the power passenger seat. All Millenias have a new rear-window-mounted diversity antenna, a new sound system with in-dash CD player, revised center console design and Michelin tires.

Body Styles	TMV Pricing		
	Trade	Private	Dealer
4 Dr L Sdn	4763	5825	7122
4 Dr S S/C Sdn	5211	6373	7793
4 Dr STD Sdn	4681	5725	7001

Options	Price
Bose Audio System	+165

Mazda
Millenia/Navajo/Protege

1996

Mileage Category: H

The Millenia S gets revised bright-finish alloy wheels.

Body Styles	TMV Pricing		
	Trade	Private	Dealer
4 Dr L Sdn	3529	4529	5910
4 Dr S S/C Sdn	3843	4932	6436
4 Dr STD Sdn	3352	4302	5613

Options	Price
Bose Audio System	+251
Compact Disc Changer	+115

1995

Mileage Category: H

Luxury-oriented model that was to be in Mazda's aborted upscale Amati luxury division. Positioned to do battle with entry-level Lexus, Infiniti and BMW models. S models have 2.3-liter V6 with Miller-cycle technology and 210 horsepower. Dual airbags and ABS are standard on all models. The Millenia S adds traction control.

Body Styles	TMV Pricing		
	Trade	Private	Dealer
4 Dr S S/C Sdn	2892	3756	5197
4 Dr STD Sdn	2498	3245	4489

Options	Price	Options	Price
Bose Audio System	+132	Leather Seats [Std on S]	+207
Compact Disc Changer	+103	Power Moonroof [Std on S]	+174

Mazda
Navajo

1994

Body Styles	TMV Pricing			Body Styles	TMV Pricing		
	Trade	Private	Dealer		Trade	Private	Dealer
2 Dr DX 4WD SUV	2225	2933	4112	2 Dr LX 4WD SUV	2468	3253	4561
2 Dr DX SUV	1739	2293	3215	2 Dr LX SUV	1900	2505	3513

Options	Price	Options	Price
Air Conditioning	+131	Leather Seats	+140
Automatic 4-Speed Transmission	+140	Moonroof	+148

Mileage Category: M

Restyled alloy wheels are new. Since Ford won't give Mazda a four-door version of the Explorer to sell, this is the final year for Navajo as Mazda picks up its toys and goes home to pout.

Mazda
Protege

2003

Mileage Category: B

Minor changes limited to feature content are in store for Mazda's economy sedan. The DX trim gets a CD player as standard equipment, while air conditioning is offered as a stand-alone option. The LX trim receives 15-inch wheels as standard. Last year's premium packages for the LX and ES have been discontinued, but you can still get the sunroof, side airbags and antilock brakes as options.

Body Styles	TMV Pricing		
	Trade	Private	Dealer
4 Dr DX Sdn	8183	9070	10547
4 Dr ES Sdn	9485	10512	12224
4 Dr LX Sdn	9083	10067	11706

Options	Price	Options	Price
Air Conditioning [Opt on DX]	+567	Compact Disc Changer	+333
Alarm System [Opt on ES,LX]	+147	Power Moonroof [Opt on ES,LX]	+333
AM/FM/Cassette Audio System	+133	Rear Spoiler [Opt on DX,LX]	+220
Antilock Brakes [Opt on ES,LX]	+453	Front Side Airbag Restraints [Opt on ES,LX]	+197
Automatic 4-Speed Transmission	+533	AM/FM/CD Changer Audio System [Opt on ES,LX]	+250
Automatic Dimming Rearview Mirror	+153		

Protege

2002

Mileage Category: B

Body Styles	TMV Pricing		
	Trade	Private	Dealer
4 Dr DX Sdn	6231	7067	8460
4 Dr ES Sdn	7433	8431	10093
4 Dr LX Sdn	6999	7938	9504

Options	Price
Air Conditioning [Opt on DX]	+445
Alarm System	+122
Antilock Brakes	+379
Automatic 4-Speed Transmission	+445
Automatic Dimming Rearview Mirror	+128

Options	Price
Compact Disc Changer	+278
Front Side Airbag Restraints [Opt on ES,LX]	+181
Power Moonroof	+167
Rear Spoiler [Std on ES]	+184

The enthusiast-oriented MP3 goes on hiatus as Mazda tries to extract more power from the engine. In other news, the base 1.6-liter engine is dropped, making the 130-horse 2.0-liter standard on all trim levels. Each model gets added equipment: larger tires and full wheel covers come on DX; air conditioning, body-colored mirrors and remote keyless entry are standard on LX; new carbon-fiber appearance decor and silver trim debut on the dash and doors of the ES. All models get a sporty three-spoke steering wheel and a 14.5-gallon fuel tank. Foglights and an auto-dimming mirror are available on any Protege for 2002.

2001

Mileage Category: B

Body Styles	TMV Pricing		
	Trade	Private	Dealer
4 Dr DX Sdn	4857	5872	6809
4 Dr ES Sdn	5922	7159	8301

Options	Price
2.0L I4 DOHC 16V FI Engine [Opt on LX]	+195
Air Conditioning [Std on ES]	+389
Antilock Brakes	+331
Automatic 4-Speed Transmission	+389

Body Styles	TMV Pricing		
	Trade	Private	Dealer
4 Dr LX Sdn	5135	6207	7197
4 Dr MP3 Sdn	7006	8469	9820

Options	Price
Compact Disc Changer	+243
Front Side Airbag Restraints	+122
Power Moonroof	+340
Rear Spoiler	+160

Already one of the best-looking economy sedans on the market, the Protege receives freshened exterior styling for 2001. ES models now have standard 16-inch wheels, and 15-inch wheels are optional on LX models. A larger 2.0-liter engine replaces the previous 1.8-liter engine. All Proteges get a revised interior and improvements to ride comfort, braking effort and steering feel. Front seatbelt pre-tensioners are standard.

2000

Mileage Category: B

Body Styles	TMV Pricing		
	Trade	Private	Dealer
4 Dr DX Sdn	3867	4815	5745
4 Dr ES Sdn	5102	6353	7580
4 Dr LX Sdn	4476	5574	6651

Options	Price
AM/FM/CD Audio System [Opt on DX]	+197
Antilock Brakes	+315
Automatic 4-Speed Transmission	+315

Options	Price
AM/FM/Cassette/CD Audio System	+138
Power Moonroof	+315
Air Conditioning [Std on ES]	+433

Front-seat side airbags and an improved ABS system are new to the LX premium and ES premium packages. The LX and ES also get illuminated power window switches. Chrome plating has been added to the inner door handles, and a Mazda symbol now appears on the steering wheel, the parking brake button and the automatic transmission shift-lever button. The Twilight Blue Mica exterior color has been discontinued and replaced with Midnight Blue Mica.

1999

Mileage Category: B

Body Styles	TMV Pricing		
	Trade	Private	Dealer
4 Dr DX Sdn	2909	3731	4587
4 Dr ES Sdn	4113	5275	6484
4 Dr LX Sdn	3331	4272	5252

Options	Price
Air Conditioning [Std on ES]	+342
Aluminum/Alloy Wheels	+125
AM/FM/CD Audio System [Opt on DX]	+155

Options	Price
Antilock Brakes	+249
Automatic 4-Speed Transmission	+249
Power Moonroof	+249

The Protege gets an extensive makeover for '99 that includes new exterior and interior styling, a more powerful engine lineup, additional luxury options and five new colors.

1998

Mileage Category: B

Body Styles	TMV Pricing		
	Trade	Private	Dealer
4 Dr DX Sdn	2229	2920	3700
4 Dr ES Sdn	2950	3866	4898

Options	Price
Air Conditioning [Std on ES]	+265
AM/FM/CD Audio System [Opt on DX]	+132
Antilock Brakes	+211

Body Styles	TMV Pricing		
	Trade	Private	Dealer
4 Dr LX Sdn	2507	3285	4162

Options	Price
Automatic 4-Speed Transmission	+211
Compact Disc Changer	+145
Power Moonroof	+185

A CD player is standard on ES and LX. It also comes on DX models equipped with an option package.

Mazda
Protege/Protege5

1997
Mileage Category: B

Styling revisions inside and out update this roomy compact sedan.

Body Styles	TMV Pricing		
	Trade	Private	Dealer
4 Dr DX Sdn	1957	2643	3481
4 Dr ES Sdn	2473	3339	4397
4 Dr LX Sdn	2120	2863	3770

Options	Price	Options	Price
Antilock Brakes	+189	Power Moonroof	+165
Automatic 4-Speed Transmission	+189	Air Conditioning [Std on ES]	+236

1996
Mileage Category: B

No changes for 1996.

Body Styles	TMV Pricing		
	Trade	Private	Dealer
4 Dr DX Sdn	1543	2157	3005
4 Dr ES Sdn	2023	2828	3940
4 Dr LX Sdn	1685	2355	3281

Options	Price	Options	Price
Air Conditioning [Std on ES]	+210	Automatic 4-Speed Transmission	+167
Antilock Brakes	+167	Power Moonroof	+147

1995
Mileage Category: B

Totally redesigned, the Protege grows substantially in interior volume and offers 10 more cubic feet inside than the Honda Civic. Dual airbags are finally added. ABS is standard on ES trim level; optional on LX.

Body Styles	TMV Pricing		
	Trade	Private	Dealer
4 Dr DX Sdn	1269	1819	2736
4 Dr ES Sdn	1534	2200	3309
4 Dr LX Sdn	1333	1912	2877

Options	Price	Options	Price
Air Conditioning [Std on ES]	+188	Automatic 4-Speed Transmission	+151
Aluminum/Alloy Wheels	+75	Power Moonroof	+132
Antilock Brakes [Opt on LX]	+151		

1994

Mileage Category: B

Minor styling revisions include new grille, headlamps, hood and front fascia.

Body Styles	TMV Pricing		
	Trade	Private	Dealer
4 Dr DX Sdn	931	1398	2176
4 Dr LX Sdn	1091	1639	2552
4 Dr Special Sdn	771	1158	1802

Options	Price
Air Conditioning	+175
Automatic 4-Speed Transmission	+140
Power Sunroof	+123

Mazda
Protege5

2003
Mileage Category: B

The Protege5 now has carpeted floor mats as standard equipment, and the moonroof can now only be had with an in-dash six-disc CD changer. There's also a new color this year: Laser Blue Mica.

Body Styles	TMV Pricing		
	Trade	Private	Dealer
4 Dr STD Wgn	10227	11268	13002

Options	Price		Options	Price
Alarm System	+147		Compact Disc Changer	+333
Aluminum/Alloy Wheels	+333		Leather Seats	+327
AM/FM/Cassette Audio System	+133		Power Moonroof	+333
Antilock Brakes	+453		Front Side Airbag Restraints	+197
Automatic 4-Speed Transmission	+600		AM/FM/CD Changer Audio System	+250
Automatic Dimming Rearview Mirror	+153			

Body Styles	TMV Pricing		
	Trade	Private	Dealer
4 Dr STD Wgn	8064	9086	10788

Mileage Category: B

The Protege is now available as a slick little sport wagon, adding another body style to the Protege lineup.

Options	Price		Options	Price
Alarm System	+122		Compact Disc Changer	+278
Antilock Brakes	+379		Front Side Airbag Restraints	+181
Automatic 4-Speed Transmission	+445		Leather Seats	+273
Automatic Dimming Rearview Mirror	+128		Power Moonroof	+390

Body Styles	TMV Pricing		
	Trade	Private	Dealer
2 Dr Turbo Hbk	11142	12311	14258

Options	Price		Options	Price
Automatic 4-Speed Transmission	+141		Power Sunroof	+132
Bose Audio System	+150		Sport Suspension	+141
Leather Seats	+151			

Mileage Category: F

CFC-free refrigerant is added to air conditioner. Touring package ousted. Red leather option dumped. Last year for RX-7.

Body Styles	TMV Pricing		
	Trade	Private	Dealer
2 Dr Turbo Hbk	8263	9338	11129

Mileage Category: F

Dual airbags appear, and softer suspension settings are available. Seat backs get map pockets, and power windows have a driver express-down feature.

Options	Price		Options	Price
Automatic 4-Speed Transmission	+131		Power Moonroof	+148
Bose Audio System	+140		Sport Suspension	+131
Leather Seats	+140			

Body Styles	TMV Pricing			Body Styles	TMV Pricing		
	Trade	Private	Dealer		Trade	Private	Dealer
4 Dr DX 4WD SUV	12975	14027	15779	4 Dr ES V6 SUV	14831	16033	18037
4 Dr DX SUV	11903	12868	14476	4 Dr LX V6 4WD SUV	14762	15959	17953
4 Dr ES V6 4WD SUV	15583	16846	18951	4 Dr LX V6 SUV	14485	15659	17616

2003

Options	Price	Options	Price
AM/FM/Cassette Audio System	+133	Power Moonroof [Opt on ES,LX]	+400
Antilock Brakes [Opt on LX]	+453	Rear Spoiler	+167
Automatic Dimming Rearview Mirror	+153	Front Side Airbag Restraints [Opt on LX]	+167
Camper/Towing Package [Opt on ES,LX]	+237	Side Steps	+233
Compact Disc Changer	+333	AM/FM/Cassette/CD Changer Audio System [Opt on ES,LX]	+337
Heated Front Seats [Opt on ES]	+150		
Power Driver Seat [Opt on LX]	+167	DVD Entertainment System	+800

Mileage Category: L

DX, LX and ES trims carryover, but the V6 is newly limited to LX and ES. If you want to see what's new on the 2003 Tribute, you'll need to look inside. This year, the dashboard is two-tone, and the insert trim is either brushed aluminum (DX and LX) or fake black wood (ES). ES models are equipped with upgraded leather and a cold package that includes heated seats and exterior mirrors. New options include an auto-dimming rearview mirror with compass and a DVD entertainment system. Four new colors round out the changes.

2002

Mileage Category: L

After an extremely successful introductory year, Mazda's Tribute SUV receives only minor modifications for 2002. DX models get additional standard equipment in the form of alloy wheels, dark-tinted glass and remote keyless entry. After a short production run, however, the DX-V6 model will be discontinued. Midgrade LX models can be ordered with ABS as a stand-alone option (last year it was bundled with side airbags) and with a six-way power driver seat. Both LX and ES models get a new driver lumbar support feature. Side step tubes are a new option on all Tribs, and four new colors debut for 2002.

Body Styles	TMV Pricing			Body Styles	TMV Pricing		
	Trade	Private	Dealer		Trade	Private	Dealer
4 Dr DX 4WD SUV	10918	11966	13713	4 Dr ES V6 4WD SUV	13201	14468	16580
4 Dr DX SUV	9960	10916	12510	4 Dr ES V6 SUV	12530	13733	15738
4 Dr DX V6 4WD SUV	12161	13328	15274	4 Dr LX V6 4WD SUV	12515	13717	15719
4 Dr DX V6 SUV	11351	12441	14257	4 Dr LX V6 SUV	11835	12971	14865

Options	Price	Options	Price
AM/FM/Cassette/CD Changer Audio System	+281	Front Side Airbag Restraints	+139
Antilock Brakes [Opt on LX V6]	+379	Power Driver Seat [Opt on LX V6]	+139
Automatic Dimming Rearview Mirror	+128	Power Moonroof	+334
Camper/Towing Package	+198	Rear Spoiler	+139
Compact Disc Changer	+278	Side Steps	+195

2001

Mileage Category: L

Mazda's first sport-utility vehicle since the departure of the Navajo half a decade ago, the Tribute combines carlike ride and handling with the ability to go in the snow and tote up to five passengers and a healthy amount of their luggage. With the most powerful V6 in its class, in addition to handsome looks and a spacious cabin, the Tribute should find huge success despite an increasingly crowded small-SUV marketplace.

Body Styles	TMV Pricing			Body Styles	TMV Pricing		
	Trade	Private	Dealer		Trade	Private	Dealer
4 Dr DX 4WD SUV	9564	10921	12173	4 Dr ES V6 4WD SUV	11705	13365	14898
4 Dr DX SUV	8506	9712	10826	4 Dr ES V6 SUV	11164	12747	14209
4 Dr DX V6 4WD SUV	10609	12114	13503	4 Dr LX V6 4WD SUV	11232	12825	14296
4 Dr DX V6 SUV	9882	11284	12578	4 Dr LX V6 SUV	10688	12204	13603

Options	Price	Options	Price
Aluminum/Alloy Wheels [Opt on DX]	+182	Front Side Airbag Restraints	+122
AM/FM/Cassette/CD Changer Audio System [Opt on ES,LX]	+246	Power Moonroof	+292
Antilock Brakes	+331	Premium Audio System	+246
Camper/Towing Package	+170		

Mazda
Truck

2003

Body Styles	TMV Pricing			Body Styles	TMV Pricing		
	Trade	Private	Dealer		Trade	Private	Dealer
2 Dr B2300 SE Ext Cab SB	10284	11281	12942	2 Dr B4000 SE 4WD Ext Cab SB	12133	13309	15270
2 Dr B2300 Std Cab SB	7540	8271	9489	4 Dr B3000 SE Ext Cab SB	10925	11984	13749
2 Dr B3000 Dual Sport Ext Cab SB	10413	11423	13106	4 Dr B4000 Dual Sport Ext Cab SB	11982	13143	15079
2 Dr B3000 Dual Sport Std Cab SB	9179	10069	11552	4 Dr B4000 SE 4WD Ext Cab SB	13093	14362	16477
2 Dr B4000 4WD Ext Cab SB	11480	12593	14447				

2003 (cont'd)

Options	Price
Air Conditioning [Opt on B2300]	+433
AM/FM/CD Audio System [Opt on B2300]	+183
Automatic 4-Speed Transmission	+667
Cruise Control	+123
Off-Road Suspension Package [Opt on B4000 SE]	+900
Power Windows	+133

Options	Price
Jump Seat(s)	+150
Side Steps	+247
Styled Steel Wheels [Opt on B2300]	+167
Tilt Steering Wheel	+117
Velour/Cloth Seats [Opt on B2300]	+267

Mileage Category: J

Two new extended cab models debut: a B2300 SE and a B3000 SE, and they include cosmetic changes like chrome bumpers and grille and alloy wheels. However, you can no longer order a four-wheel-drive B3000 Truck; 4WD is available on B4000 models only. Otherwise, only minor changes have been made to the rapidly aging Truck, such as the addition of A-pillar grab handles for the interior, thicker brake rotors for 4WD models, and the fact that the Power Package is no longer free when ordered with the Convenience Package.

2002

Body Styles	TMV Pricing		
	Trade	Private	Dealer
2 Dr B2300 Std Cab SB	6503	7251	8497
2 Dr B3000 4WD Ext Cab SB	10391	11585	13576
2 Dr B3000 Dual Sport Ext Cab SB	8649	9630	11266

Body Styles	TMV Pricing		
	Trade	Private	Dealer
2 Dr B3000 Dual Sport Std Cab SB	7925	8836	10354
4 Dr B4000 4WD Ext Cab SB	11235	12526	14678
4 Dr B4000 Dual Sport Ext Cab SB	10078	11236	13167

Options	Price
Air Conditioning [Opt on B2300]	+362
AM/FM/CD Audio System [Opt on B2300]	+153
Automatic 4-Speed Transmission	+557

Options	Price
Off-Road Suspension Package	+751
Running Boards	+206
Styled Steel Wheels [Opt on B2300]	+139

Mileage Category: J

The B-Series name gets dropped this year for the far more creative moniker "Truck." To celebrate, Mazda trims the lineup to just six models, all of which include a standard sliding rear window and none of which include SE or SX stickers on the beds because those trims have been killed. New packages include the SE-5 package for B2300s and an Off Road Package for B4000 four-bys. The Convenience package includes a bed liner this year. Color changes round out the updates for 2002.

Mercedes-Benz
C-Class

2003

Mileage Category: H

Changes are light this year. Mercedes'"4Matic" all-wheel-drive system is now available for sedan and wagon models (the C32 sport sedan being the lone exception) and the C230 Sport Coupe's supercharged engine has been revised for greater efficiency and lower emissions. A six-speed manual gearbox is available for the C320 models, and a supercharged C230 Sport Sedan is now available as well.

Body Styles	TMV Pricing		
	Trade	Private	Dealer
2 Dr C230 S/C Hbk	19362	20459	22286
2 Dr C320 Hbk	21214	22415	24417
4 Dr C230 S/C Sdn	21734	22965	25017
4 Dr C240 4MATIC AWD Sdn	25549	26995	29406
4 Dr C240 4MATIC AWD Wgn	26684	28195	30713
4 Dr C240 Sdn	23874	25226	27479

Body Styles	TMV Pricing		
	Trade	Private	Dealer
4 Dr C240 Wgn	24317	25694	27989
4 Dr C320 4MATIC AWD Sdn	29559	31233	34023
4 Dr C320 4MATIC AWD Wgn	30696	32434	35331
4 Dr C320 Sdn	27329	28877	31457
4 Dr C320 Wgn	27336	28884	31464

Options	Price
Automatic 5-Speed Transmission [Opt on C230,C240,C320]	+1037
Bose Audio System [Opt on C230,C240,C320]	+352
Compact Disc Changer	+313
Heated Front Seats	+509
Leather Seats [Opt on Hbk]	+705
Metallic Paint	+513
Power Moonroof [Opt on C230,C240,C320]	+705
Power Panorama Roof [Opt on Hbk]	+783
Special Leather Seat Trim [Opt on C230,C240,C320]	+1127
Split Folding Rear Seat [Opt on C230,C240,C320]	+196

Options	Price
Sport Suspension [Opt on C320]	+196
COMAND System	+1664
Power Rear Window Sunshade [Opt on C230,C240,C320]	+388
Telematic System [Opt on C230,C240,C320]	+607
17 Inch Wheels [Opt on C230,C320]	+411
Designo Charcoal Cinnamora Edition [Opt on Hbk]	+274
Power Driver Seat w/Memory [Opt on C230,C240,C320]	+254
Power Passenger Seat w/Memory [Opt on C230,C240,C320]	+254
Power Tilt and Telescopic Steering Wheel [Opt on C230,C240,C320]	+196

2002

Mileage Category: H

Two new models debut: the C230 Kompressor Sport Coupe and the C320 wagon.

Body Styles	TMV Pricing		
	Trade	Private	Dealer
2 Dr C230 S/C Hbk	17416	18602	20579
4 Dr C240 Sdn	21775	23258	25730

Body Styles	TMV Pricing		
	Trade	Private	Dealer
4 Dr C320 Sdn	24306	25944	28673
4 Dr C320 Wgn	24965	26647	29451

Options	Price
17 Inch Wheels [Opt on C230]	+523
Automatic 5-Speed Transmission [Opt on C230,C240]	+907
Bose Audio System [Opt on C230,C240]	+314
Compact Disc Changer	+398
Heated Front Seats	+314
Leather Seats [Opt on C230]	+984
Metallic Paint	+447
Navigation System	+1451
Power Driver Seat w/Memory [Opt on C240]	+227

Options	Price
Power Moonroof	+628
Power Panorama Roof [Opt on C230]	+1047
Power Passenger Seat w/Memory [Opt on C240]	+227
Power Rear Window Sunshade	+345
Power Tilt and Telescopic Steering Wheel [Opt on C240]	+174
Special Leather Seat Trim	+984
Split Folding Rear Seat [Opt on C240,C320 Sdn]	+174
Sport Package	+2100
Telematic System [Opt on C230]	+523

2001

Mileage Category: H

Ever expanding and improving its brood of stately vehicles, Mercedes gives the C-Class a complete overhaul for 2001. A choice of two new engines, increased safety features and sleeker sheet metal tempt those who seek to gain a foothold into the exalted realm of Mercedes ownership.

Body Styles	TMV Pricing		
	Trade	Private	Dealer
4 Dr C240 Sdn	17719	19511	21165

Body Styles	TMV Pricing		
	Trade	Private	Dealer
4 Dr C320 Sdn	21034	23161	25124

Options	Price
Automatic 5-Speed Transmission [Opt on C240]	+804
Bose Audio System [Opt on C240]	+368
Compact Disc Changer	+352
Heated Front Seats	+278
Metallic Paint	+386
Navigation System	+1258
Power Driver Seat w/Memory [Opt on C240]	+201

Options	Price
Power Moonroof	+587
Power Passenger Seat w/Memory [Opt on C240]	+201
Power Rear Window Sunshade	+306
Power Tilt and Telescopic Steering Wheel [Opt on C240]	+155
Split Folding Rear Seat	+155
Sport Package	+1824
Sport Seats	+247

For the latest vehicle information, visit www.edmunds.com

2000

Body Styles	TMV Pricing		
	Trade	Private	Dealer
4 Dr C230 S/C Sdn	16148	18096	20006

Options	Price
Bose Audio System [Opt on C230]	+301
Compact Disc Changer	+286
Heated Front Seats	+223
Leather Seats [Opt on C230]	+612
Metallic Paint	+317
Power Moonroof	+529

Body Styles	TMV Pricing		
	Trade	Private	Dealer
4 Dr C280 Sdn	16798	18825	20812

Options	Price
Power Passenger Seat [Opt on C230]	+239
Special Leather Seat Trim	+749
Split Folding Rear Seat	+132
Sport Seats	+370
Sport Suspension	+470

Mileage Category: H

TeleAid, which can assist in summoning help if you're ill or involved in a crash, is a brilliant new standard feature. A Touch Shift automanual transmission is added to all C-Class models, and stability control is standard this year. C-Class now comes with free scheduled service for the duration of the warranty period.

1999

Mileage Category: H

The SLK's 2.3-liter supercharged engine gets dropped into the C-Class, replacing the normally aspirated engine of the last C230. Performance has been turned up a notch. In addition, leather seating surfaces are now standard across the C-Class line.

Body Styles	TMV Pricing		
	Trade	Private	Dealer
4 Dr C230 S/C Sdn	13201	15026	16925

Options	Price
Automatic Stability Control [Opt on C280]	+272
Bose Audio System [Opt on C230]	+222
Compact Disc Changer	+233
Heated Front Seats	+182
Leather Seats [Opt on C230]	+500
Metallic Paint	+233

Body Styles	TMV Pricing		
	Trade	Private	Dealer
4 Dr C280 Sdn	13903	15825	17826

Options	Price
Power Moonroof	+431
Power Passenger Seat [Opt on C230]	+195
Special Leather Seat Trim	+611
Sport Seats	+272
Sport Suspension	+346
Traction Control System	+182

1998

Mileage Category: H

The C280 is the lucky recipient of Mercedes' new V-type engine technology, receiving a 2.8-liter unit for the engine bay. BabySmart car seats, BrakeAssist and side airbags also debut on the C-Class this year.

Body Styles	TMV Pricing		
	Trade	Private	Dealer
4 Dr C230 Sdn	10076	11672	13472

Options	Price
Heated Front Seats	+151
Leather Seats	+412
Metallic Paint	+194
Power Moonroof	+358
Power Passenger Seat [Opt on C230]	+162

Body Styles	TMV Pricing		
	Trade	Private	Dealer
4 Dr C280 Sdn	12218	14153	16335

Options	Price
Compact Disc Changer	+194
Sport Seats	+226
Sport Suspension	+287
Traction Control System	+226
Bose Audio System [Opt on C230]	+184

1997

Mileage Category: H

The C220 is replaced by a more powerful C230. All C-Class models have redesigned headlamps.

Body Styles	TMV Pricing		
	Trade	Private	Dealer
4 Dr C230 Sdn	8362	9796	11549

Options	Price
Bose Audio System [Opt on C230]	+158
Compact Disc Changer	+157
Heated Front Seats	+123
Leather Seats	+313
Metallic Paint	+158

Body Styles	TMV Pricing		
	Trade	Private	Dealer
4 Dr C280 Sdn	9470	11095	13082

Options	Price
Power Moonroof	+291
Power Passenger Seat [Opt on C230]	+132
Sport Suspension	+233
Traction Control System	+184

1996

Mileage Category: H

An infrared remote security system, dual cupholders in the console, a delayed headlamp dousing system and reconfigured option packages mark the changes to the baby Benz.

Body Styles	TMV Pricing		
	Trade	Private	Dealer
4 Dr C220 Sdn	6916	8166	9893

Body Styles	TMV Pricing		
	Trade	Private	Dealer
4 Dr C280 Sdn	7549	8914	10798

Mercedes-Benz
C-Class/C32 AMG

1996 (cont'd)

Options	Price
Bose Audio System [Opt on C220]	+130
Compact Disc Changer	+134
Leather Seats	+282
Metallic Paint	+140

Options	Price
Power Moonroof	+249
Sport Suspension	+210
Traction Control System	+157

1995

Mileage Category: H

No major changes.

Body Styles	TMV Pricing		
	Trade	Private	Dealer
4 Dr C220 Sdn	5966	7054	8868

Body Styles	TMV Pricing		
	Trade	Private	Dealer
4 Dr C280 Sdn	6698	7920	9956

Options	Price
Alarm System	+82
Bose Audio System [Opt on C220]	+116
Chrome Wheels [Opt on C280]	+84
Compact Disc Changer [Opt on C220]	+120
Heated Front and Rear Seats	+93
Heated Front Seats	+93

Options	Price
Leather Seats	+251
Metallic Paint	+125
Power Moonroof	+222
Power Passenger Seat [Opt on C220]	+92
Traction Control System	+140

1994

Mileage Category: H

This peppy replacement for the 190 is long-awaited. Longer and wider than the 190, the C-Class gives rear-seat passengers more room. Standard on the C-Class are dual airbags, a wood-trimmed interior, four-wheel antilock brakes and a power sunroof. The C-Class cars are available in four- or six-cylinder flavors with a standard automatic transmission.

Body Styles	TMV Pricing		
	Trade	Private	Dealer
4 Dr C220 Sdn	4805	5833	7547

Body Styles	TMV Pricing		
	Trade	Private	Dealer
4 Dr C280 Sdn	5862	7117	9209

Options	Price
Metallic Paint	+107
Power Moonroof	+190
Power Passenger Seat [Opt on C220]	+79
Traction Control System	+120

Options	Price
Bose Audio System	+99
Heated Front Seats	+80
Leather Seats	+215

Mercedes-Benz
C32 AMG

2003

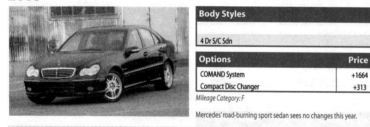

Body Styles			TMV Pricing		
			Trade	Private	Dealer
4 Dr S/C Sdn			38054	40226	43846

Options	Price
COMAND System	+1664
Compact Disc Changer	+313

Options	Price
Metallic Paint	+513
Power Rear Window Sunshade	+352

Mileage Category: F

Mercedes' road-burning sport sedan sees no changes this year.

2002

Mileage Category: F

Mercedes' in-house tuners, AMG, lay their hands on the little C-Class and the result is the stunning, 349-horsepower C32.

Body Styles			TMV Pricing		
			Trade	Private	Dealer
4 Dr S/C Sdn			34410	36141	39027

Options	Price
Compact Disc Changer	+398
Metallic Paint	+447

Options	Price
Navigation System	+1451
Power Rear Window Sunshade	+345

C36 AMG/C43 AMG

1997

Body Styles	TMV Pricing		
	Trade	Private	Dealer
4 Dr STD Sdn	15590	17390	19591

Options	Price	Options	Price
Compact Disc Changer	+157	Metallic Paint	+158
Heated Front Seats	+123	Traction Control System	+184

Mileage Category: F

For its last year in production, the C36 receives a slight boost in horsepower, which now stands at 276 ponies.

1996

Mileage Category: F

No changes to the hot-rod baby Benz for this year.

Body Styles	TMV Pricing		
	Trade	Private	Dealer
4 Dr STD Sdn	14126	15743	17977

Options	Price	Options	Price
Compact Disc Changer	+134	Metallic Paint	+140

1995

Mileage Category: F

After years of watching the tuning firm known as AMG modify its cars, Mercedes decides to bring it in-house. If the first effort of this union, the 268-horsepower C36, is any indication, it looks like this should be a happy marriage.

Body Styles	TMV Pricing		
	Trade	Private	Dealer
4 Dr STD Sdn	11866	13221	15478

Options	Price	Options	Price
Alarm System	+82	Metallic Paint	+125
Heated Front Seats	+93	Power Moonroof	+222

Mercedes-Benz

C43 AMG

2000

Body Styles	TMV Pricing		
	Trade	Private	Dealer
4 Dr STD Sdn	30446	33282	36062

Options	Price	Options	Price
Compact Disc Changer	+317	Metallic Paint	+317

Mileage Category: F

TeleAid, which can assist in summoning help if you're ill or involved in a crash, is a new standard feature. A Touch Shift automanual transmission is added to simulate the thrill of shifting gears manually. Free scheduled service for the duration of the warranty period has been added to the lengthy standard equipment list.

1999

Mileage Category: F

No major changes for this sizzling sedan.

Body Styles	TMV Pricing		
	Trade	Private	Dealer
4 Dr STD Sdn	20642	22845	25137

Options	Price	Options	Price
Compact Disc Changer	+233	Metallic Paint	+233

1998

Mileage Category: F

The C43 AMG bows as a successor to the late C36. Featuring an AMG-modified 4.3-liter V8 with 302 hp, the new C43 promises a high-performance thrill ride.

Body Styles	TMV Pricing		
	Trade	Private	Dealer
4 Dr STD Sdn	17856	19877	22155

Options	Price	Options	Price
Compact Disc Changer	+194	Metallic Paint	+194

CL-Class

2003

Body Styles	TMV Pricing		
	Trade	Private	Dealer
2 Dr CL500 Cpe	75763	78717	83640

Options	Price
Sport Package [Opt on CL500,CL600]	+3993
Ventilated Seats (Front) [Opt on CL500]	+920
Adaptive Cruise Control	+2309
Designo Espresso Edition	+8377
Designo Silver Edition [Opt on CL500,CL600]	+8377

Body Styles	TMV Pricing		
	Trade	Private	Dealer
2 Dr CL600 Turbo Cpe	97434	101233	107565

Options	Price
Power Trunk Closer	+368
Designo Cashmere Edition	+9003
Keyless Ignition System	+795
Park Distance Control (Front and Rear)	+810

Mileage Category: I

There is more power for the CL55 and CL600 models, both of which now put out nearly 500 horsepower. All CLs see a number of other subtle changes, such as new head- and taillight lenses, a Pre-Safe safety feature, revised switchgear and a larger COMAND screen.

2002

Mileage Category: I

The TeleAid system is enhanced. Now reservations for travel as well as tickets for sporting and theater events can all be acquired from the considerable comfort of the CL's cabin.

Body Styles	TMV Pricing		
	Trade	Private	Dealer
2 Dr CL500 Cpe	65185	68314	73528

Options	Price
Designo Espresso Edition	+6490
Designo Silver Edition	+6490
Dual Multi-Contour Seats [Opt on CL500]	+1047
Keyless Ignition System	+694

Body Styles	TMV Pricing		
	Trade	Private	Dealer
2 Dr CL600 Cpe	84745	88812	95591

Options	Price
Park Distance Control (Front and Rear)	+708
Power Trunk Closer	+321
Sport Package [Opt on CL500,CL600]	+3482
Ventilated Seats (Front) [Opt on CL500]	+820

2001

Mileage Category: I

The CL600 makes its debut with a 362-horsepower V12. Distronic cruise control, a high-tech system using radar, braking and acceleration to maintain a specified distance from other vehicles, is standard on the CL600 and optional on other CL models. Web-based services, such as e-mail and stock quotes, will also be on board for the 2001 model year.

Body Styles	TMV Pricing		
	Trade	Private	Dealer
2 Dr CL500 Cpe	57367	61798	65888

Options	Price
Designo Espresso Edition	+5132
Designo Silver Edition	+5132
Keyless Ignition System	+615

Body Styles	TMV Pricing		
	Trade	Private	Dealer
2 Dr CL600 Cpe	76735	82662	88133

Options	Price
Park Distance Control (Front and Rear)	+615
Sport Package	+3030
Ventilated Seats (Front) [Opt on CL500]	+727

2000

Mileage Category: I

2000 marks the introduction of an all-new CL500 that is lighter, less expensive, and more advanced than the previous version.

Body Styles	TMV Pricing		
	Trade	Private	Dealer
2 Dr CL500 Cpe	49209	53610	57923

Options	Price	Options	Price
Climate Comfort Seats	+668	Park Distance Control (Front and Rear)	+543
Dual Multi-Contour Seats	+585	Power Rear Window Sunshade	+276

1999

Body Styles	TMV Pricing		
	Trade	Private	Dealer
2 Dr CL500 Cpe	33663	37394	41278

Options	Price
Automatic Stability Control [Opt on CL500]	+272
Electronic Damping Suspension Control [Opt on CL500]	+590
Metallic Paint	+233

Body Styles	TMV Pricing		
	Trade	Private	Dealer
2 Dr CL600 Cpe	34583	38416	42406

Options	Price
Power Rear Window Sunshade [Opt on CL500]	+225
Traction Control System [Opt on CL500]	+182

Mileage Category: I

The CL coupes are carryover models for 1999 with no changes.

1998

Body Styles	TMV Pricing		
	Trade	Private	Dealer
2 Dr CL500 Cpe	26658	30122	34028
2 Dr CL600 Cpe	28441	32136	36303

Options	Price
Electronic Damping Suspension Control [Opt on CL500]	+491
Metallic Paint	+194
Power Rear Window Sunshade [Opt on CL500]	+187
Traction Control System [Opt on CL500]	+226

Mileage Category: I

In keeping with Mercedes' somewhat odd habit of changing its cars' names just as people are getting the hang of them, the former S-Class coupes are now dubbed the CL-Class. Other than that confusing switch, the only changes to these big coupes are the addition of BabySmart airbag technology and BrakeAssist to the standard equipment lists.

Mercedes-Benz
CL55 AMG

2003

Body Styles	TMV Pricing		
	Trade	Private	Dealer
2 Dr S/C Cpe	94896	98597	104764

Options	Price	Options	Price
Adaptive Cruise Control	+2309	Keyless Ignition System	+795
Designo Cashmere Edition	+8377	Park Distance Control (Front and Rear)	+810
Designo Espresso Edition	+7750	Power Trunk Closer	+368

Mileage Category: I

There is more power for the CL55 this year, thanks to the installation of a supercharger. Output is staggering at nearly 500 horsepower. Other changes include new head- and taillight lenses, a Pre-Safe safety feature, revised switchgear and a larger COMAND screen.

2002

Body Styles	TMV Pricing		
	Trade	Private	Dealer
2 Dr STD Cpe	78356	82117	88385

Options	Price	Options	Price
Designo Espresso Edition	+6978	Park Distance Control (Front and Rear)	+708
Designo Silver Edition	+6978	Power Trunk Closer	+321

Mileage Category: I

The CL55 AMG receives no major changes for this year.

2001

Body Styles	TMV Pricing		
	Trade	Private	Dealer
2 Dr STD Cpe	66168	71279	75997

Options	Price
Park Distance Control (Front and Rear)	+615

Mileage Category: I

AMG works its magic and creates the CL55 AMG with a 354-horsepower V8.

Mercedes-Benz
CLK-Class

2003

Body Styles	TMV Pricing			Body Styles	TMV Pricing		
	Trade	Private	Dealer		Trade	Private	Dealer
2 Dr CLK320 Conv	39489	41239	44156	2 Dr CLK430 Conv	47179	49270	52754
2 Dr CLK320 Cpe	36043	37640	40302	2 Dr CLK500 Cpe	41761	43612	46696

Options	Price	Options	Price
Appearance Package [Opt on CLK320]	+822	Power Moonroof [Opt on CLK320,CLK500]	+783
Compact Disc Changer	+313	Sport Package [Opt on CLK320]	+3679
Heated Front Seats [Opt on CLK320,CLK430,CLK500]	+485	COMAND System	+1664
Metallic Paint	+513		

2003 (cont'd)

Mileage Category: F

The CLK coupe is revamped this year and its sleeker body sports a grille that echoes the bigger (and much more expensive) CL coupe's. Other news include the CLK430 becoming the CLK500 via a larger, more powerful V8 engine. The convertible ("Cabriolet") models are unchanged.

Options	Price
Power Rear Window Sunshade [Opt on CLK320,CLK500]	+294
Adaptive Cruise Control [Opt on CLK320,CLK500]	+2309
Designo Espresso Edition [Opt on CLK430]	+4952

Options	Price
Designo Cashmere Edition [Opt on CLK430]	+5637
Keyless Ignition System [Opt on CLK320,CLK500]	+795
Park Distance Control (Front and Rear) [Opt on CLK320,CLK500]	+810

2002

Mileage Category: F

No changes this year.

Body Styles	TMV Pricing		
	Trade	Private	Dealer
2 Dr CLK320 Conv	36234	38074	41140
2 Dr CLK320 Cpe	31217	32832	35523
2 Dr CLK430 Conv	43601	45815	49506
2 Dr CLK430 Cpe	35476	37311	40369

Options	Price
Compact Disc Changer	+398
Designo Cashmere Edition	+4885
Designo Espresso Edition	+4327
Dual Multi-Contour Seats	+516
Heated Front Seats	+433

Options	Price
Metallic Paint	+447
Navigation System	+1451
Power Moonroof	+750
Power Rear Window Sunshade	+345
Sport Package [Opt on CLK320]	+3210

2001

Mileage Category: F

TeleAid comes standard on every CLK model this year, and the front windows lower slightly when you open the doors and seal (foop!) tight when you close them.

Body Styles	TMV Pricing		
	Trade	Private	Dealer
2 Dr CLK320 Conv	33272	36130	38769
2 Dr CLK320 Cpe	26949	29264	31401

Body Styles	TMV Pricing		
	Trade	Private	Dealer
2 Dr CLK430 Conv	38810	42143	45220
2 Dr CLK430 Cpe	32334	35112	37676

Options	Price
Compact Disc Changer	+352
Designo Espresso Edition	+3741
Designo Slate Blue Edition	+4236
Dual Multi-Contour Seats	+448
Heated Front Seats	+383

Options	Price
Metallic Paint	+386
Navigation System	+1258
Power Moonroof	+652
Power Rear Window Sunshade [Opt on Cpe]	+306

2000

Mileage Category: F

The CLK430 Convertible debuts, reminding us, for a premium price, what a drop-top muscle car from the '70s was like. Turn-signal indicators have been added to exterior mirrors, stability control is standard on all models, automatics get TouchShift manual gear selection and TeleAid emergency cellular service is standard. A new instrument cluster and multifunction steering wheel are added, and buyers can opt for the confusing COMAND navigation/phone/trip computer/sound system. CLK320s benefit from exterior cosmetic changes including new wheels, while 430s are enhanced inside with new black bird's eye maple wood trim. Free maintenance for the duration of the warranty is now included.

Body Styles	TMV Pricing		
	Trade	Private	Dealer
2 Dr CLK320 Conv	30082	32884	35631
2 Dr CLK320 Cpe	24189	26442	28651

Body Styles	TMV Pricing		
	Trade	Private	Dealer
2 Dr CLK430 Conv	34855	38102	41285
2 Dr CLK430 Cpe	28968	31667	34313

Options	Price
AM/FM/CD Audio System	+145
Compact Disc Changer	+317
Heated Front Seats	+139
Metallic Paint	+317

Options	Price
Navigation System	+1055
Power Moonroof	+587
Power Rear Window Sunshade [Opt on Cpe]	+276

1999

Mileage Category: F

These guys are still on a roll. Last year, Mercedes introduced an all-new sport coupe that is an amalgamation of C- and SLK-Class technologies, available this year with a larger engine in the CLK 430 model, and now they're rolling out the CLK 320 Cabriolet, a convertible version of the fabulous little car.

Body Styles	TMV Pricing		
	Trade	Private	Dealer
2 Dr CLK320 Conv	26371	29185	32114
2 Dr CLK320 Cpe	21538	23836	26228

Body Styles	TMV Pricing		
	Trade	Private	Dealer
2 Dr CLK430 Cpe	24945	27606	30377

Options	Price
Automatic Stability Control [Opt on CLK320]	+272
Compact Disc Changer	+233
Metallic Paint	+233

Options	Price
Power Moonroof	+431
Traction Control System [Opt on CLK320]	+182

1998

Body Styles	TMV Pricing		
	Trade	Private	Dealer
2 Dr CLK320 Cpe	18792	20918	23315

Options	Price	Options	Price
Compact Disc Changer	+194	Metallic Paint	+194
Heated Front Seats	+192	Power Moonroof	+358

Mileage Category: F

Mercedes rolls out an all-new sport coupe that is an amalgamation of C- and SLK-Class technologies, with E-Class style up front. The CLK-Class is infused with the same 3.2-liter V6 that has made its way into the ML320 and E320.

Mercedes-Benz
CLK55 AMG

2003

Body Styles	TMV Pricing		
	Trade	Private	Dealer
2 Dr STD Cpe	57137	59669	63889

Options	Price	Options	Price
Adaptive Cruise Control	+2309	Metallic Paint	+513
COMAND System	+1664	Park Distance Control (Front and Rear)	+810
Compact Disc Changer	+313	Power Rear Window Sunshade	+344
Keyless Ignition System	+795		

Mileage Category: F

A redesigned CLK55 coupe belatedly joins the rest of the revamped CLK family; the ragtop version takes a year off. The sleeker body sports a grille that echoes the bigger (and much more costly) Mercedes' CL coupe's and chassis improvements result in even better driving dynamics.

2002

Body Styles	TMV Pricing			Body Styles	TMV Pricing		
	Trade	Private	Dealer		Trade	Private	Dealer
2 Dr STD Conv	60761	63817	68911	2 Dr STD Cpe	51639	54236	58565

Options	Price	Options	Price
Compact Disc Changer	+398	Designo Espresso Edition	+3768
Designo Cashmere Edition	+4327	Navigation System	+1451

Mileage Category: F

A convertible version of this hot coupe debuts, adding the joy of open-air motoring to its scintillating performance.

2001

Body Styles	TMV Pricing		
	Trade	Private	Dealer
2 Dr STD Cpe	42180	45620	48795

Options	Price	Options	Price
Compact Disc Changer	+352	Designo Slate Blue Edition	+4236
Designo Espresso Edition	+3741	Navigation System	+1258

Mileage Category: F

The high-performance CLK55 AMG debuts this year. With 342 horsepower at its disposal, this muscle-bound CLK can sprint to 60 mph in just five seconds.

Mercedes-Benz
E-Class

2003

Body Styles	TMV Pricing			Body Styles	TMV Pricing		
	Trade	Private	Dealer		Trade	Private	Dealer
4 Dr E320 4MATIC AWD Wgn	40495	42074	44706	4 Dr E320 Wgn	38457	39956	42455
4 Dr E320 Sdn	37585	39051	41493	4 Dr E500 Sdn	46343	48150	51161

Mileage Category: I

The E-Class sedan is completely redesigned this year. A more elegant body, along with more power for the V8 model and more luxury (including four-zone climate control and an optional massaging driver seat), bring the latest midsize Benz up to date. Last year's E-Class station wagon, however, carries over into 2003 virtually unchanged.

For the latest vehicle information, visit www.edmunds.com

E-Class

2003 (cont'd)

Options	Price
Compact Disc Changer	+313
Harman Kardon Audio System [Opt on E320,E500]	+431
Heated Front Seats [Opt on E320,E500]	+497
Navigation System [Opt on E320]	+1664
Power Moonroof [Opt on E320,E500]	+826
Power Panorama Roof [Opt on E320,E500]	+1174
Special Factory Paint [Opt on E320,E500]	+513
Sport Package [Opt on E320,E500]	+1076

Options	Price
Dual Multi-Contour Seats [Opt on E320,E500]	+591
Ventilated Seats (Front)	+939
Power Rear Window Sunshade [Opt on E320,E500]	+344
Adaptive Cruise Control [Opt on E320,E500]	+2309
Automatic Climate Control (4 Zone) [Opt on E320]	+431
Keyless Ignition System [Opt on E320,E500]	+795
Drive Dynamic Seats [Opt on E320,E500]	+900
Park Distance Control (Front and Rear)	+810

2002

Mileage Category: I

The 2002 E-Class soldiers on unchanged, awaiting a redesign that will take place next year.

Body Styles	TMV Pricing		
	Trade	Private	Dealer
4 Dr E320 4MATIC AWD Sdn	34103	35740	38468
4 Dr E320 4MATIC AWD Wgn	34673	36337	39111
4 Dr E320 Sdn	32675	34243	36857

Body Styles	TMV Pricing		
	Trade	Private	Dealer
4 Dr E320 Wgn	33177	34769	37423
4 Dr E430 4MATIC AWD Sdn	35585	37293	40140
4 Dr E430 Sdn	35435	37136	39970

Options	Price
Bose Audio System [Opt on E320]	+283
Compact Disc Changer	+398
Designo Espresso Edition	+4327
Designo Silver Edition	+4327
Heated Front Seats	+443
Metallic Paint [Opt on E320]	+447

Options	Price
Navigation System	+1451
Power Moonroof	+736
Power Rear Window Sunshade	+345
Sport Package [Opt on Sdn - E320,E430]	+2913
Ventilated Seats (Front)	+820

2001

Mileage Category: I

Though it might not look different, the E55 AMG receives the same substantial freshening for 2000 that other E-Class models get, which includes an entirely new front end and a revised interior. A multifunction steering wheel debuts, and TeleAid, a cellular emergency service, comes with the package for 2000.

Body Styles	TMV Pricing		
	Trade	Private	Dealer
4 Dr E320 4MATIC AWD Sdn	29338	31862	34191
4 Dr E320 4MATIC AWD Wgn	29833	32399	34768
4 Dr E320 Sdn	27673	30053	32250

Body Styles	TMV Pricing		
	Trade	Private	Dealer
4 Dr E320 Wgn	28079	30494	32724
4 Dr E430 4MATIC AWD Sdn	31484	34192	36691
4 Dr E430 Sdn	30505	33129	35551

Options	Price
Bose Audio System [Std on E430]	+265
Compact Disc Changer	+352
Designo Espresso Edition	+3741
Designo Silver Edition	+3741
Dual Multi-Contour Seats	+448
Heated Front Seats	+383

Options	Price
Leather Seats [Opt on E320 Wgn]	+850
Navigation System	+1258
Power Moonroof	+652
Power Rear Window Sunshade [Opt on E320,E430]	+306
Sport Package [Opt on Sdn]	+2529
Ventilated Seats (Front)	+711

2000

Mileage Category: I

Though it might not look different, the E-Class receives a substantial freshening for 2000, with an entirely new front end and a revised interior. Stability control, a Touch Shift automanual transmission, and side airbags for all outboard seating positions are now standard. A multifunction steering wheel debuts, and E430 models can be equipped with 4matic all-wheel drive. TeleAid, a cellular emergency service, is standard and the confounding COMAND system is optional. For 2000, free maintenance is provided for the duration of the warranty period. The E300 turbodiesel model has been dropped. Other changes are limited to minor cosmetic and functional upgrades.

Body Styles	TMV Pricing		
	Trade	Private	Dealer
4 Dr E320 4MATIC AWD Sdn	26679	29293	31855
4 Dr E320 4MATIC AWD Wgn	26958	29599	32187
4 Dr E320 Sdn	24247	26623	28951

Body Styles	TMV Pricing		
	Trade	Private	Dealer
4 Dr E320 Wgn	24617	27028	29392
4 Dr E430 4MATIC AWD Sdn	27296	29970	32591
4 Dr E430 Sdn	27136	29794	32399

Options	Price
Bose Audio System [Std on E430]	+238
Compact Disc Changer	+317
Heated Front Seats	+223
Metallic Paint	+317
Nappa Leather Seat Trim	+899
Navigation System	+1055
Park Distance Control (Front and Rear) [Opt on E320,E430]	+543

Options	Price
Power Moonroof	+587
Power Rear Window Sunshade [Opt on Sdn]	+276
Rear Spoiler	+212
Special Leather Seat Trim	+605
Spoke Wheels	+238
Sport Package	+2199

E-Class

1999

Body Styles	TMV Pricing		
	Trade	Private	Dealer
4 Dr E300DT Turbodsl Sdn	21309	23601	25987
4 Dr E320 4MATIC AWD Sdn	22614	25047	27579
4 Dr E320 4MATIC AWD Wgn	23114	25601	28189

Options	Price
Automatic Stability Control	+272
Bose Audio System [Std on E430]	+175
Compact Disc Changer	+233
Heated Front Seats	+182
Leather Seats [Opt on E300DT,Wgn]	+515
Metallic Paint	+233

Body Styles	TMV Pricing		
	Trade	Private	Dealer
4 Dr E320 Sdn	21519	23834	26243
4 Dr E320 Wgn	21944	24305	26762
4 Dr E430 Sdn	23270	25773	28379

Options	Price
Power Moonroof	+431
Power Rear Window Sunshade [Opt on Sdn]	+225
Rear Spoiler	+155
Spoke Wheels	+175
Sport Package	+1794
Traction Control System [Opt on E300DT,Wgn]	+182

Mileage Category: I

More airbags find room in the E-Class, which now features a full curtain side airbag protection system. The E300 Turbodiesel and E320 wagon are enhanced with leather seat inserts, and all E-Class cars get fiber-optic technology in their sound system/optional telephone unit.

1998

Body Styles	TMV Pricing		
	Trade	Private	Dealer
4 Dr E300DT Turbodsl Sdn	18023	20239	22738
4 Dr E320 4MATIC AWD Sdn	19205	21566	24229
4 Dr E320 4MATIC AWD Wgn	19769	22200	24942

Options	Price
Automatic Stability Control [Opt on Sdn]	+302
Bose Audio System [Std on E430]	+184
Compact Disc Changer	+194
Heated Front Seats	+151
Leather Seats [Opt on E300DT,Wgn]	+427
Park Distance Control (Front and Rear)	+368

Body Styles	TMV Pricing		
	Trade	Private	Dealer
4 Dr E320 Sdn	17065	19164	21530
4 Dr E320 Wgn	17218	19335	21722
4 Dr E430 Sdn	19834	22273	25023

Options	Price
Power Moonroof	+358
Power Rear Window Sunshade [Opt on Sdn]	+187
Rear Spoiler	+129
Spoke Wheels	+145
Sport Package	+1490
Traction Control System	+323

Mileage Category: I

All-wheel drive comes to the Mercedes' E-Class lineup via the E320 sedan and all-new E320 wagon. Like the rest of Mercedes' model lineup, E-Class cars formerly powered by an inline-six engine now receive a more fuel-efficient V6 unit that is also supposed to improve the cars' low-end response. The 1998 E-Class cars receive the benefit of BabySmart airbags which are able to detect the presence of a Mercedes' car seat in the front passenger seat and disable the front passenger airbag. BrakeAssist is also a new feature, which aids drivers' stopping distance in a panic-stop situation.

1997

Body Styles	TMV Pricing		
	Trade	Private	Dealer
4 Dr E300D Dsl Sdn	14871	16812	19184
4 Dr E320 Sdn	14749	16674	19026

Options	Price
Heated Front Seats	+123
Leather Seats [Opt on E300D]	+347
Limited Slip Differential [Opt on E320]	+131
Power Moonroof	+286
Power Rear Window Sunshade	+152
Sport Package	+568

Body Styles	TMV Pricing		
	Trade	Private	Dealer
4 Dr E420 Sdn	16415	18557	21175

Options	Price
Dual Multi-Contour Seats [Std on S600]	+233
AM/FM/Cassette/CD Audio System	+230
Bose Audio System [Std on E420]	+147
Chrome Wheels	+144
Compact Disc Changer	+157

Mileage Category: I

The Mercedes-Benz E300D and E320 receive the driver-adaptable five-speed automatic transmission. The E-Class also has a smart sensor to determine if anyone is sitting in the passenger seat and to determine whether or not to deploy the airbag. The E420 can be had with a Sport Package.

1996

Body Styles	TMV Pricing		
	Trade	Private	Dealer
4 Dr E300D Dsl Sdn	12390	14013	16254

Options	Price
Bose Audio System	+130
Compact Disc Changer	+134
Leather Seats [Std on E320]	+312

Body Styles	TMV Pricing		
	Trade	Private	Dealer
4 Dr E320 Sdn	12695	14358	16655

Options	Price
Limited Slip Differential	+118
Metallic Paint	+162
Power Moonroof	+252

Mileage Category: I

All new and sporting a face anybody's mother could love, the E-Class comes in three flavors: E300 Diesel, E320 and E420. A new front suspension and larger wheels and tires provide better handling, while optional gas-discharge headlamps mark new technology. Side-impact airbags are included in the doors of all E-Class models. E420's can be had with ESP, which is a new safety system that makes sure the E420 is under control at all times. The E420 also gets a new five-speed transmission.

1995

Body Styles	TMV Pricing		
	Trade	Private	Dealer
2 Dr E320 Conv	17868	19973	23482

Body Styles	TMV Pricing		
	Trade	Private	Dealer
2 Dr E320 Cpe	10963	12255	14407

Mileage Category: I

No changes for the last year of this rendition of the E-Class.

1995 (cont'd)

Body Styles	TMV Pricing		
	Trade	Private	Dealer
4 Dr E300D Dsl Sdn	10034	11216	13187
4 Dr E320 Sdn	10202	11404	13407

Options	Price
AM/FM/CD Audio System	+128
Compact Disc Changer	+120
Heated Front Seats [Std on E420,Conv]	+93
Leather Seats [Opt on E300D,Wgn]	+279
Limited Slip Differential	+105

Body Styles	TMV Pricing		
	Trade	Private	Dealer
4 Dr E320 Wgn	10491	11727	13788
4 Dr E420 Sdn	10716	11979	14083

Options	Price
Power Driver Seat w/Memory [Std on E420,Cpe,Conv]	+82
Power Rear Window Sunshade [Opt on Cpe,Sdn]	+96
Premium Audio System	+95
Sport Package	+255
Traction Control System [Opt on E320 Sdn]	+210

1994

Mileage Category: I

In an effort at simplification, Mercedes renames its 300-Class, now calling it the E-Class. Like the new C-Class, the numeral after the E indicates the engine's size. Coupe, convertible, sedan and wagon body styles are still offered.

Body Styles	TMV Pricing		
	Trade	Private	Dealer
2 Dr E320 Conv	15287	17258	20542
2 Dr E320 Cpe	9644	10887	12958
4 Dr E320 Sdn	7872	8887	10578

Options	Price
Heated Front Seats [Std on E500]	+80
Leather Seats [Opt on Wgn]	+238
Power Rear Window Sunshade [Opt on Sdn,Wgn]	+80

Body Styles	TMV Pricing		
	Trade	Private	Dealer
4 Dr E320 Wgn	8249	9313	11085
4 Dr E420 Sdn	8565	9669	11509
4 Dr E500 Sdn	15289	17302	20656

Options	Price
Sport Package	+162
Sport Suspension	+117
Traction Control System [Std on E500]	+180

Mercedes-Benz
E55 AMG

2003

Body Styles	TMV Pricing		
	Trade	Private	Dealer
4 Dr S/C Sdn	59483	61828	65736

Options	Price
Adaptive Cruise Control	+2309
Compact Disc Changer	+313
Keyless Ignition System	+795
Park Distance Control (Front and Rear)	+810

Mileage Category: F

Options	Price
Power Panorama Roof	+1174
Power Rear Window Sunshade	+344
Power Trunk Closer	+372
Ventilated Seats (Front)	+509

A redesigned E55 AMG, sporting nearly 500 horsepower, belatedly joins the rest of the revamped E-Class family.

2002

Body Styles	TMV Pricing		
	Trade	Private	Dealer
4 Dr STD Sdn	49025	51491	55601

Options	Price
Compact Disc Changer	+398
Designo Espresso Edition	+3768
Designo Silver Edition	+3768

Mileage Category: F

Options	Price
Navigation System	+1451
Ventilated Seats (Front)	+820

Patiently waiting for a redesign, the E55 AMG continues with no changes.

2001

Mileage Category: F

No major changes for this AMG-massaged rocket.

Body Styles	TMV Pricing		
	Trade	Private	Dealer
4 Dr STD Sdn	40922	44259	47339

2001 (cont'd)

Options	Price
Compact Disc Changer	+352
Designo Espresso Edition	+3277
Designo Silver Edition	+3277

Options	Price
Navigation System	+1258
Ventilated Seats (Front)	+711

2000

Body Styles	TMV Pricing		
	Trade	Private	Dealer
4 Dr STD Sdn	35634	38954	42208

Options	Price
AM/FM/Cassette/CD Audio System	+223
Compact Disc Changer	+317

Options	Price
Metallic Paint	+317
Navigation System	+1111

Mileage Category: F

Though it might not look different, the E55 AMG receives the same substantial freshening for 2000 that other E-Class models get, which includes an entirely new front end and a revised interior. A multifunction steering wheel debuts, and TeleAid, a cellular emergency service, comes with the package for 2000.

1999

Body Styles	TMV Pricing		
	Trade	Private	Dealer
4 Dr STD Sdn	29962	33160	36488

Options	Price
AM/FM/Cassette/CD Audio System	+425
Compact Disc Changer	+233

Options	Price
Metallic Paint	+233
Power Rear Window Sunshade	+225

Mileage Category: F

The performance-oriented E55 AMG debuts, featuring a fire-breathing V8 that can rocket this sedate sedan to 60 mph in well under six seconds.

2003

Body Styles	TMV Pricing		
	Trade	Private	Dealer
4 Dr G500 4WD SUV	56923	59555	63942

Options	Price
Harman Kardon Audio System	+626
Designo Espresso Edition	+4971

Options	Price
Designo Silver Edition	+4971
Park Distance Control (Rear)	+431

Mileage Category: O

No changes this year.

2002

Body Styles	TMV Pricing		
	Trade	Private	Dealer
4 Dr G500 4WD SUV	49205	51895	56377

Options	Price
Designo Espresso Edition	+4327

Options	Price
Designo Silver Edition	+4327

Mileage Category: O

This vehicle is officially new to the U.S. market, though its basic design dates back over 20 years.

2003

Body Styles	TMV Pricing		
	Trade	Private	Dealer
4 Dr STD 4WD SUV	66486	69560	74685

Options	Price
Designo Espresso Edition	+4971
Designo Silver Edition	+4971

Options	Price
Harman Kardon Audio System	+626
Park Distance Control (Rear)	+431

Mileage Category: O

In-house tuner AMG lays its magic hands on the G-Class this year, empowering the SUV with a 5.4-liter V8 that generates 349 horsepower and a 0-to-60-mph time of 7.2 seconds.

Mercedes-Benz
M-Class

2003

Mileage Category: O

The M-Class' navigation system enters the 21st century by ditching the old CD-ROM-based design for a much more efficient DVD-based setup. This is the lone change as the MLs received numerous updates last year.

Body Styles	TMV Pricing		
	Trade	Private	Dealer
4 Dr ML320 AWD SUV	27317	28717	31051
4 Dr ML350 AWD SUV	27720	29141	31508

Options	Price
Automatic Dimming Rearview Mirror	+133
Bose Audio System [Opt on ML320,ML350,ML500]	+431
Compact Disc Changer [Opt on ML320,ML350,ML500]	+489
Heated Front Seats [Opt on ML320,ML350]	+509
Leather Seats [Opt on ML320,ML350]	+920
Metallic Paint [Opt on ML320,ML350,ML500]	+395
Power Moonroof [Opt on ML320,ML350,ML500]	+1057
Sport Package [Opt on ML320,ML350,ML500]	+2623
Third Seat [Opt on ML320,ML350,ML500]	+587
Nappa Leather Seat Trim [Opt on ML320,ML350,ML500]	+1315

Body Styles	TMV Pricing		
	Trade	Private	Dealer
4 Dr ML500 AWD SUV	35538	37359	40394

Options	Price
Designo Cognac Edition	+3288
Designo Mystic Green Edition [Opt on ML320,ML350,ML500]	+3288
Designo Pearl Edition [Opt on ML320,ML350,ML500]	+2740
Designo Savanna Edition [Opt on ML320,ML350,ML500]	+3053
Designo Sable Edition [Opt on ML320,ML350,ML500]	+2740
Automatic Dimming Sideview Mirror(s) [Opt on ML350]	+137
Power Retractable Mirrors [Opt on ML350,ML500]	+196
Power Driver Seat w/Memory [Opt on ML320,ML350,ML500]	+196
Power Passenger Seat w/Memory [Opt on ML320,ML350,ML500]	+196
Park Distance Control (Front and Rear)	+795

2002

Mileage Category: O

The ML430 is replaced by the ML500, which has a 5.0-liter V8 packing 288 horsepower. Over 1,100 parts of the truck have been modified, but the ML's exterior remains largely the same. New bumpers, clear-lens headlights and revised side mirrors are the most noticeable exterior changes. Inside, the center console sports a new look, and wood grain trim becomes standard on all models. A new automatic climate control system is now standard, and rear-seat passengers get dual cupholders and separate ventilation controls.

Body Styles	TMV Pricing		
	Trade	Private	Dealer
4 Dr ML320 AWD SUV	25356	26876	29409

Options	Price
Automatic Dimming Rearview Mirror [Opt on ML320]	+119
Automatic Dimming Sideview Mirror(s) [Opt on ML320]	+122
Bose Audio System	+366
Compact Disc Changer	+419
Designo Cognac Edition	+2861
Designo Mystic Green Edition	+2861
Designo Pearl Edition	+2373
Designo Sable Edition	+2373
Designo Savanna Edition	+2652
Heated Front Seats	+443

Body Styles	TMV Pricing		
	Trade	Private	Dealer
4 Dr ML500 AWD SUV	32025	33914	37062

Options	Price
Leather Seats [Opt on ML320]	+820
Metallic Paint	+345
Park Distance Control (Front and Rear)	+708
Power Driver Seat w/Memory	+174
Power Moonroof	+904
Power Passenger Seat w/Memory	+174
Power Retractable Mirrors	+174
Sport Package	+2338
Third Seat	+680

2001

Mileage Category: O

The TeleAid emergency calling system is now standard on every M-Class model, and smart dual-stage front airbags know when to deploy with partial force or full force. All models also feature expanded off-road capabilities with new downhill traction control and a new crawling mode for very slow and steep off-roading. Finally, a new M-Class sport package debuts this year.

Body Styles	TMV Pricing		
	Trade	Private	Dealer
4 Dr ML320 AWD SUV	20505	22521	24383

Options	Price
Automatic Dimming Sideview Mirror(s) [Opt on ML320]	+124
Bose Audio System	+309
Compact Disc Changer	+356
Designo Cognac Edition	+2473
Designo Mystic Green Edition	+2473
Heated Front Seats [Opt on ML320]	+383
Leather Seats [Opt on ML320]	+911

Body Styles	TMV Pricing		
	Trade	Private	Dealer
4 Dr ML430 AWD SUV	27076	29738	32196

Options	Price
Metallic Paint	+300
Power Driver Seat w/Memory	+155
Power Panorama Roof	+1515
Power Passenger Seat w/Memory	+155
Power Sunroof	+677
Sport Package	+2041
Third Seat	+835

2000

Body Styles	TMV Pricing		
	Trade	Private	Dealer
4 Dr ML320 AWD SUV	17312	19381	21409

Body Styles	TMV Pricing		
	Trade	Private	Dealer
4 Dr ML430 AWD SUV	22899	25635	28318

2000 (cont'd)

Options	Price
Heated Front Seats [Opt on ML320]	+251
Leather Seats [Opt on ML320]	+554
Metallic Paint	+286
Power Driver Seat w/Memory	+153
Power Moonroof	+522
Power Panorama Roof	+946

Options	Price
Power Passenger Seat w/Memory	+153
Running Boards	+159
Third Seat	+752
Bose Audio System	+214
Compact Disc Changer	+286

Mileage Category: O

All M-Class models get an interior facelift available in one of three new colors, optional third-row seating and a Touch Shift automanual transmission. ML320 buyers get body-color bumpers and trim, real walnut inside, leather-wrapped steering wheel and gearshift knob, revised interior fabric, seatback map pockets and footwell lamps. In addition to these items, a standard navigation system, high-grade leather, and heated seats come on all ML430s.

1999

Body Styles	TMV Pricing		
	Trade	Private	Dealer
4 Dr ML320 AWD SUV	15604	17609	19695

Body Styles	TMV Pricing		
	Trade	Private	Dealer
4 Dr ML430 AWD SUV	19710	22242	24878

Options	Price
Bose Audio System	+175
Compact Disc Changer	+233
Heated Front Seats	+184
Leather Seats [Opt on ML320]	+602
Metallic Paint	+233
Power Driver Seat [Opt on ML320]	+195

Options	Price
Power Moonroof	+425
Power Panorama Roof	+772
Power Passenger Seat [Opt on ML320]	+195
Running Boards	+159
Third Seat	+118

Mileage Category: O

Mercedes expands its M-Class with the addition of the more powerful and luxurious ML430 and gives the 320 more standard equipment.

1998

Body Styles	TMV Pricing		
	Trade	Private	Dealer
4 Dr ML320 AWD SUV	13951	15740	17757

Options	Price
Bose Audio System	+339
Compact Disc Changer	+194
Heated Front Seats	+153
Leather Seats	+500
Metallic Paint	+153

Options	Price
Power Driver Seat	+162
Power Moonroof	+354
Power Passenger Seat	+162
Running Boards	+189

Mileage Category: O

Mercedes enters the sport-ute fray with the introduction of the ML320. Designed from a clean sheet of paper, the ML320 offers the best of the car and truck worlds.

Mercedes-Benz
ML55 AMG

2003

Body Styles	TMV Pricing		
	Trade	Private	Dealer
4 Dr STD AWD SUV	50024	52588	56860

Options	Price
Designo Cognac Edition	+3288

Options	Price
Park Distance Control (Front and Rear)	+795

Mileage Category: O

The hot-rod ML55 benefits from the upgrades made to every M-Class for this year. Over 1,100 parts of the truck have been modified, but the ML's exterior remains largely the same. New bumpers, clear-lens headlights and revised side mirrors are the most noticeable exterior changes. Inside, the center console sports a new look, and wood grain trim becomes standard on all models. A new automatic climate control system is now standard, and rear-seat passengers get dual cupholders and separate ventilation controls.

2002

Body Styles	TMV Pricing		
	Trade	Private	Dealer
4 Dr STD AWD SUV	44597	47240	51644

Options	Price
Designo Cognac Edition	+2861

Options	Price
Park Distance Control (Front and Rear)	+708

Mileage Category: O

Extensive interior and exterior refinements enhance this fast SUV, though most changes will go unnoticed by the casual observer.

Mercedes-Benz
ML55 AMG/S-Class

2001

Mileage Category: O

AMG merges high-performance with SUV practicality with the new ML55 AMG.

Body Styles	TMV Pricing		
	Trade	Private	Dealer
4 Dr STD AWD SUV	36678	40353	43746

Options	Price
Designo Cognac Edition	+2473

2000

Mileage Category: O

Mercedes goes overboard on power and performance with the new ML55 AMG. Correct us if we're wrong, but weren't SUVs originally designed for rugged off-road travel?

Body Styles	TMV Pricing		
	Trade	Private	Dealer
4 Dr STD AWD SUV	30133	33734	37264

Options	Price
Metallic Paint	+251

Mercedes-Benz
S-Class

2003

Mileage Category: I

For 2003, there is more power for the S55 and S600 models, both of which now put out nearly 500 horsepower. Also Pre-Safe, a system that detects an imminent impact and quickly adjusts seating positions as well as seatbelt tension to better safeguard the occupants, debuts. Mercedes' 4Matic all-wheel-drive system becomes available on the S430 and S500 and a minor freshening inside and out are meant to keep these big Benzes near the top of luxury car buyer's shopping lists.

Body Styles	TMV Pricing		
	Trade	Private	Dealer
4 Dr S430 4MATIC AWD Sdn	59236	61688	65776
4 Dr S430 Sdn	56824	59176	63097
4 Dr S500 4MATIC AWD Sdn	65765	68488	73025

Options	Price
Compact Disc Changer [Opt on S430,S500]	+313
Four Place Seating [Opt on S500,S600]	+4607
Heated Front Seats [Opt on S430]	+352
Heated Front and Rear Seats [Opt on S430,S500]	+509
Power Rear Seat [Opt on S430,S500]	+1460
Sport Package [Opt on S430,S500,S600]	+3993
Dual Multi-Contour Seats [Opt on S430,S500]	+744
Nappa Leather Seat Trim [Opt on S430]	+658
Ventilated Seats (Front) [Opt on S430,S500]	+509
Adaptive Cruise Control	+2309

Body Styles	TMV Pricing		
	Trade	Private	Dealer
4 Dr S500 Sdn	61459	64003	68244
4 Dr S600 Turbo Sdn	96827	100835	107516

Options	Price
Designo Espresso Edition [Opt on S430,S500]	+6967
Designo Silver Edition [Opt on S430,S500]	+6967
Power Trunk Closer	+368
Automatic Climate Control (4 Zone) [Opt on S430,S500]	+1503
Ventilated Seats (Front and Rear)	+744
Designo Graphite Edition [Opt on S430,S500]	+6967
Keyless Ignition System	+795
Drive Dynamic Seats [Opt on S430,S500,S600]	+712
Armor Rear Protection [Opt on S500]	+25652
Park Distance Control (Front and Rear) [Opt on S430,S500]	+810

2002

Mileage Category: I

The TeleAid system is enhanced. Now reservations for travel as well as tickets for sporting and theater events can all be acquired from the considerable comfort of the S-Class' cabin.

Body Styles	TMV Pricing		
	Trade	Private	Dealer
4 Dr S430 Sdn	49261	51625	55565
4 Dr S500 Sdn	54110	56707	61035

Options	Price
Adaptive Cruise Control	+2006
Automatic Climate Control (4 Zone) [Std on S600]	+698
Automatic Load Leveling [Opt on S430,S500]	+879
Compact Disc Changer [Opt on S430,S500]	+398
Designo Espresso Edition	+5338
Designo Silver Edition	+6106
Electronic Suspension Control [Opt on S430,S500]	+1186
Four Place Seating [Opt on S500,S600]	+2756

Body Styles	TMV Pricing		
	Trade	Private	Dealer
4 Dr S600 Sdn	78442	82207	88482

Options	Price
Heated Front and Rear Seats [Std on S600]	+443
Heated Front Seats [Opt on S430]	+314
Keyless Ignition System	+694
Park Distance Control (Front and Rear) [Std on S600]	+708
Power Rear Seat	+1274
Power Trunk Closer	+321
Sport Package	+3472
Ventilated Seats (Front and Rear)	+649

2001

Body Styles	TMV Pricing		
	Trade	Private	Dealer
4 Dr S430 Sdn	40959	44275	47337
4 Dr S500 Sdn	46126	49861	53309

Options	Price
Adaptive Cruise Control	+1731
Automatic Climate Control (4 Zone) [Std on S600]	+618
Compact Disc Changer	+352
Designo Espresso Edition	+4638
Designo Silver Edition	+5287
Four Place Seating	+2393
Heated Front and Rear Seats	+383

Body Styles	TMV Pricing		
	Trade	Private	Dealer
4 Dr S600 Sdn	66870	72284	77281

Options	Price
Keyless Ignition System	+615
Park Distance Control (Front and Rear) [Std on S600]	+615
Power Rear Seat	+1104
Sport Package	+3030
Ventilated Seats (Front and Rear)	+563
Ventilated Seats (Front) [Std on S600]	+711

Mileage Category: I

One new model debuts this year with the S600. The S600 gets a powerful 12-cylinder engine along with standard Active Body Control and Internet access to keep up with life in the techno-savvy 21st century.

2000

Body Styles	TMV Pricing		
	Trade	Private	Dealer
4 Dr S430 Sdn	36408	39975	43471

Options	Price
Automatic Load Leveling [Opt on S430]	+515
Climate Comfort Seats	+668
Compact Disc Changer	+308
Air Conditioning - Front and Rear	+1002
Dual Multi-Contour Seats	+529
Four Place Seating	+3084

Body Styles	TMV Pricing		
	Trade	Private	Dealer
4 Dr S500 Sdn	39657	43542	47350

Options	Price
Heated Front and Rear Seats	+305
Park Distance Control (Front and Rear)	+543
Power Rear Seat	+529
Power Rear Window Sunshade	+276
Special Factory Paint	+243
Adaptive Cruise Control	+1113

Mileage Category: I

An all-new S-Class debuts for the millennium with enhanced performance and a snazzy COMAND system.

1999

Body Styles	TMV Pricing		
	Trade	Private	Dealer
4 Dr S320 LWB Sdn	24346	27045	29854
4 Dr S320 SWB Sdn	24120	26793	29576
4 Dr S420 Sdn	25049	27826	30716

Options	Price
Air Conditioning - Front and Rear [Opt on S500]	+913
Automatic Load Leveling [Std on S500,S600]	+420
Automatic Stability Control [Std on S600]	+450
Compact Disc Changer [Std on S600]	+226
Electronic Damping Suspension Control [Std on S600]	+573

Body Styles	TMV Pricing		
	Trade	Private	Dealer
4 Dr S500 Sdn	29234	32474	35847
4 Dr S600 Sdn	35651	39603	43716

Options	Price
Four Place Seating	+2516
Heated Front Seats [Std on S500,S600]	+225
Park Distance Control (Front and Rear)	+443
Power Rear Seat	+431
Power Rear Window Sunshade [Std on S600]	+225

Mileage Category: I

A limited-production Grand Edition S500 debuts.

1998

Body Styles	TMV Pricing		
	Trade	Private	Dealer
4 Dr S320 LWB Sdn	19545	21925	24609
4 Dr S320 SWB Sdn	18708	20986	23554
4 Dr S420 Sdn	19807	22218	24937

Options	Price
Air Conditioning - Front and Rear [Std on S600]	+758
Automatic Load Leveling [Std on S500,S600]	+349
Automatic Stability Control [Std on S600]	+374
Compact Disc Changer [Std on S600]	+188
Electronic Damping Suspension Control [Std on S600]	+476

Body Styles	TMV Pricing		
	Trade	Private	Dealer
4 Dr S500 Sdn	24019	26943	30240
4 Dr S600 Sdn	28183	31614	35483

Options	Price
Four Place Seating	+2090
Heated Front Seats [Std on S500,S600]	+186
Park Distance Control (Front and Rear)	+368
Power Rear Seat [Opt on S500]	+358
Power Rear Window Sunshade [Std on S600]	+187

Mileage Category: I

The uber-Mercedes are not changed much in anticipation of the cars' imminent replacement. BrakeAssist and BabySmart appear in the lineup, but the S320s don't receive the V6 engine that now powers the E320, instead, continuing with the inline six.

Mercedes-Benz
S-Class

1997
Mileage Category: I

Side-impact airbags debut in all S-Class cars this year. S-Class coupes get new front bumpers. All cars get new alloy wheels. A Parktronic system is available for those who aren't comfortable parking their $100,000 car in a smaller space. Mercedes' outstanding Automatic Slip Reduction (ASR) traction control system is finally available on the S320s. Lastly, a rain sensor system is now standard on all models. (It adjusts the speed of the wipers to the intensity of the rain.)

Body Styles	TMV Pricing		
	Trade	Private	Dealer
2 Dr S500 Cpe	20563	23202	26428
2 Dr S600 Cpe	23451	26461	30139
4 Dr S320 LWB Sdn	16592	18721	21324
4 Dr S320 SWB Sdn	16462	18575	21157

Body Styles	TMV Pricing		
	Trade	Private	Dealer
4 Dr S420 Sdn	17047	19234	21908
4 Dr S500 Sdn	19448	21944	24995
4 Dr S600 Sdn	22406	25281	28795

Options	Price
Air Conditioning - Front and Rear [Std on S600]	+357
Automatic Load Leveling [Opt on S320,S420]	+284
Automatic Stability Control [Std on S600]	+396
Electronic Damping Suspension Control	+685
Four Place Seating	+1675

Options	Price
Heated Front Seats [Opt on S320,S420]	+152
Park Distance Control (Front and Rear)	+299
Power Rear Seat	+529
Power Rear Window Shunshade [Std on S600]	+152
Traction Control System [Opt on S420,S500]	+179

1996
Mileage Category: I

No cosmetic improvements to the S-Class this year; everything new is under the skin. ESP is standard on the S600 and optional on V8 models. ESP is a stability control system designed to help the driver keep the S-Class under control at all times. V8 and V12 versions get a new five-speed automatic, and all models get a standard power glass sunroof and smog-sensing climate control system. The S350 Turbodiesel is history.

Body Styles	TMV Pricing		
	Trade	Private	Dealer
2 Dr S500 Cpe	17523	19818	22988
2 Dr S600 Cpe	19317	21848	25342
4 Dr S320 LWB Sdn	14371	16254	18854
4 Dr S320 SWB Sdn	13935	15760	18280

Body Styles	TMV Pricing		
	Trade	Private	Dealer
4 Dr S420 Sdn	14571	16479	19115
4 Dr S500 Sdn	15975	18068	20958
4 Dr S600 Sdn	18043	20407	23670

Options	Price
Air Conditioning - Front and Rear [Std on S600]	+305
Automatic Load Leveling [Std on S500,S600]	+232
Automatic Stability Control [Opt on S420]	+157
Compact Disc Changer	+137
Electronic Damping Suspension Control	+330

Options	Price
Four Place Seating	+1430
Heated Front Seats [Opt on S320,S420]	+136
Power Rear Seat [Opt on S500]	+445
Power Rear Window Sunshade [Std on S600]	+130

1995
Mileage Category: I

Minuscule exterior changes and a drop in price are about the only changes to the S-Class.

Body Styles	TMV Pricing		
	Trade	Private	Dealer
2 Dr S500 Cpe	15465	17464	20796
2 Dr S600 Cpe	16847	19025	22654
4 Dr S320 LWB Sdn	12708	14351	17089
4 Dr S320 SWB Sdn	11898	13436	15999

Body Styles	TMV Pricing		
	Trade	Private	Dealer
4 Dr S350D Turbodsl Sdn	12712	14355	17093
4 Dr S420 Sdn	12826	14484	17248
4 Dr S500 Sdn	14039	15854	18878
4 Dr S600 Sdn	16195	18289	21779

Options	Price
Compact Disc Changer	+122
Electronic Damping Suspension Control	+295
Four Place Seating	+958
Heated Front Seats [Std on S500,S600]	+121

Options	Price
Power Moonroof	+245
Power Rear Window Sunshade [Std on S600]	+116
Automatic Load Leveling [Std on S500,S600]	+207
Air Conditioning - Front and Rear [Std on S600]	+443

1994
Mileage Category: I

The big Benz gains Mercedes' new alphanumeric nomenclature that makes it easier to identify the vehicle family and engine size. Fuel economy is improved for the S-Class, and all but the S600 switch to H-rated tires for increased traction in inclement weather.

Body Styles	TMV Pricing		
	Trade	Private	Dealer
2 Dr S500 Cpe	14180	16264	19736
2 Dr S600 Cpe	15458	17730	21516
4 Dr S320 Sdn	10764	12346	14982
4 Dr S350D Turbodsl Sdn	11411	13088	15882

Body Styles	TMV Pricing		
	Trade	Private	Dealer
4 Dr S420 Sdn	11660	13373	16229
4 Dr S500 Sdn	12712	14580	17692
4 Dr S600 Sdn	14821	16999	20629

Options	Price
Air Conditioning - Front and Rear [Std on S600]	+368
Automatic Load Leveling [Std on S500,S600]	+177
Electronic Damping Suspension Control	+252
Four Place Seating	+660
Heated Front Seats [Std on S500,S600]	+104

Options	Price
Limited Slip Differential	+87
Power Moonroof	+210
Power Rear Seat [Std on S500,S600]	+240
Power Rear Window Sunshade [Std on S600]	+80
Traction Control System [Opt on S320,S420]	+116

2003

Body Styles	TMV Pricing		
	Trade	Private	Dealer
4 Dr S/C Sdn	81918	85309	90962

Options	Price	Options	Price
Adaptive Cruise Control	+2309	Keyless Ignition System	+795
Automatic Climate Control (4 Zone)	+1503	Park Distance Control (Front and Rear)	+810
Designo Espresso Edition	+8377	Power Rear Seat	+1460
Designo Graphite Edition	+8377	Power Trunk Closer	+368
Heated Front and Rear Seats	+509	Ventilated Seats (Front and Rear)	+1253

Mileage Category: I

There is more power for the S55 this year, thanks to the installation of a supercharger. Output is staggering at nearly 500 horsepower. Also Pre-Safe, a system that detects an imminent impact and quickly adjusts seating positions as well as seatbelt tension to better safeguard the occupants, debuts. As with other S-Class Benzes, the S55 receives a minor freshening inside and out.

2002

Body Styles	TMV Pricing		
	Trade	Private	Dealer
4 Dr STD Sdn	72975	76248	81704

Options	Price	Options	Price
Adaptive Cruise Control	+2006	Heated Front and Rear Seats	+443
Automatic Climate Control (4 Zone)	+698	Park Distance Control (Front and Rear)	+708
Designo Espresso Edition	+6211	Power Rear Seat	+1274
Designo Silver Edition	+6943	Ventilated Seats (Front and Rear)	+1092

Mileage Category: I

No changes for this thrilling luxury sedan.

2001

Body Styles	TMV Pricing		
	Trade	Private	Dealer
4 Dr STD Sdn	61246	65977	70344

Options	Price	Options	Price
Adaptive Cruise Control	+1731	Heated Front and Rear Seats	+383
Automatic Climate Control (4 Zone)	+618	Park Distance Control (Front and Rear)	+615
Designo Espresso Edition	+5380	Power Rear Seat	+1104
Designo Silver Edition	+6029	Ventilated Seats (Front and Rear)	+946

Mileage Category: I

The S55 AMG debuts this year, boasting a powerful V8, 18-inch wheels and suspension upgrades for improved handling.

2003

Body Styles	TMV Pricing		
	Trade	Private	Dealer
2 Dr SL500 Conv	70426	73202	77829

Options	Price	Options	Price
Panorama Removable Hardtop	+1409	Designo Espresso Edition	+5871
Sport Package [Opt on SL500]	+3993	Designo Graphite Edition	+5871
Dual Multi-Contour Seats [Opt on SL500]	+579	Keyless Ignition System	+795
Ventilated Seats (Front) [Opt on SL500]	+391	Park Distance Control (Front and Rear)	+810
Adaptive Cruise Control	+2309		

Mileage Category: F

What's new? Everything. A new SL debuts to replace the previous version, which dated back to 1990.

2002

Body Styles	TMV Pricing			Body Styles	TMV Pricing		
	Trade	Private	Dealer		Trade	Private	Dealer
2 Dr SL500 Conv	48713	51386	55842	2 Dr SL600 Conv	74776	78880	85721

2002 (cont'd)

Options	Price
Compact Disc Changer [Opt on SL500]	+471
Dual Multi-Contour Seats	+516
Electronic Damping Suspension Control [Opt on SL500]	+2826

Options	Price
Heated Front Seats [Opt on SL500]	+415
Panorama Removable Hardtop	+2812

Mileage Category: F

To make the last year of this generation SL special, Mercedes creates the Silver Arrow edition, a -- you guessed it -- silver-colored SL (available with either the V8 or the V12 engine) garnished both inside and out with polished aluminum trim.

2001

Mileage Category: F

The SL line gets some minor aerodynamic enhancements for 2001.

Body Styles	TMV Pricing		
	Trade	Private	Dealer
2 Dr SL500 Conv	42000	45771	49251

Body Styles	TMV Pricing		
	Trade	Private	Dealer
2 Dr SL600 Conv	59624	64977	69918

Options	Price
Compact Disc Changer [Opt on SL500]	+402
Designo Black Diamond Edition	+3092
Designo Slate Blue Edition	+3617

Options	Price
Dual Multi-Contour Seats	+448
Heated Front Seats [Opt on SL500]	+383
Panorama Removable Hardtop	+2442

2000

Mileage Category: F

Designo editions debut in Slate Blue and Black Diamond with special color-coordinated interior trim. Non-designo versions can be painted in Desert Silver. TeleAid is standard, as is a StarTAC digital phone with voice-recognition technology on the SL600. Free maintenance now covers you during the warranty period.

Body Styles	TMV Pricing		
	Trade	Private	Dealer
2 Dr SL500 Conv	37355	41206	44980

Body Styles	TMV Pricing		
	Trade	Private	Dealer
2 Dr SL600 Conv	49499	54602	59603

Options	Price
Compact Disc Changer [Opt on SL500]	+362
Electronic Damping Suspension Control [Opt on SL500]	+946
Heated Front Seats [Opt on SL500]	+315

Options	Price
Panorama Removable Hardtop	+1582
Sport Package	+1827

1999

Mileage Category: F

The SL500 gets a brand-spankin'-new 5.0-liter V8 that delivers better performance than ever before. Both SL models get sideview mirrors from the SLK, body-colored door handles and new side molding, new taillights, new exterior colors, a new instrument panel, new shifter and shift gate and a new four-spoke steering wheel.

Body Styles	TMV Pricing		
	Trade	Private	Dealer
2 Dr SL500 Conv	31507	34935	38503

Body Styles	TMV Pricing		
	Trade	Private	Dealer
2 Dr SL600 Conv	38081	42224	46536

Options	Price
Compact Disc Changer [Opt on SL500]	+295
Panorama Removable Hardtop	+1291
Sport Package	+1490

Options	Price
Compact Disc Changer [Opt on SL500]	+295
Panorama Removable Hardtop	+1291
Sport Package	+1490

1998

Mileage Category: F

The bargain basement SL320 was discontinued this year.

Body Styles	TMV Pricing		
	Trade	Private	Dealer
2 Dr SL500 Conv	28537	31738	35348
2 Dr SL500 SL1 Sport Conv	30289	33688	37520

Body Styles	TMV Pricing		
	Trade	Private	Dealer
2 Dr SL600 Conv	32428	36066	40169
2 Dr SL600 SL1 Sport Conv	33250	36981	41188

Options	Price
Electronic Damping Suspension Control [Opt on SL500]	+641
Heated Front Seats [Opt on SL500]	+192
Panorama Removable Hardtop	+1072
Traction Control System	+226

Options	Price
Compact Disc Changer	+245
AM/FM/CD Audio System [Opt on SL500]	+162
Automatic Load Leveling [Opt on SL500]	+283
Automatic Stability Control [Opt on SL500]	+374

1997

Body Styles	TMV Pricing		
	Trade	Private	Dealer
2 Dr SL320 Conv	24262	27064	30488
2 Dr SL500 Conv	26404	29453	33180

Options	Price
Automatic Load Leveling [Opt on SL320,SL500]	+230
Automatic Stability Control [Opt on SL320,SL500]	+304
Compact Disc Changer	+199
Electronic Damping Suspension Control	+521

Body Styles	TMV Pricing		
	Trade	Private	Dealer
2 Dr SL500 SL1 Sport Conv	28073	31316	35279
2 Dr SL600 Conv	29457	32859	37017

Options	Price
Heated Front Seats [Opt on SL320,SL500]	+156
Panorama Removable Hardtop	+872
Rear Spoiler	+131
Sport Package	+1007

Mileage Category: F

A Panorama hardtop is now available, and it helps improve top-up visibility. ASR traction control is now standard on the SL320. A rain sensor is now standard on all models as well.

1996

Body Styles	TMV Pricing		
	Trade	Private	Dealer
2 Dr SL320 Conv	20567	22923	26177
2 Dr SL500 Conv	23338	26012	29705

Options	Price
Automatic Load Leveling [Opt on SL320,SL500]	+196
Automatic Stability Control [Opt on SL320,SL500]	+490
Electronic Damping Suspension Control	+445

Body Styles	TMV Pricing		
	Trade	Private	Dealer
2 Dr SL600 Conv	25100	27976	31947

Options	Price
Hardtop Roof	+727
Heated Front Seats	+140

Mileage Category: F

Tweaked styling and new alloys freshen the exterior of the SL roadster. Underneath, ESP keeps drivers on track in lousy driving conditions. It comes standard on the SL600, and can be ordered for the SL320 and SL500. Side airbags are standard across the board. A five-speed automatic is included with SL500 and SL600. Cool gas-discharge headlamps are not available on the SL320.

1995

Body Styles	TMV Pricing		
	Trade	Private	Dealer
2 Dr SL320 Conv	18879	21034	24626
2 Dr SL500 Conv	20930	23320	27303

Options	Price
Automatic Load Leveling [Opt on SL320,SL500]	+175
Automatic Stability Control [Opt on SL320]	+231
Electronic Damping Suspension Control [Opt on SL320,SL500]	+397

Body Styles	TMV Pricing		
	Trade	Private	Dealer
2 Dr SL600 Conv	22276	24819	29057

Options	Price
Hardtop Roof	+649
Heated Front Seats [Opt on SL320,SL500]	+125

Mileage Category: F

Traction control is now standard on the SL320. Price cuts are the only other change for the Mercedes roadster.

1994

Body Styles	TMV Pricing		
	Trade	Private	Dealer
2 Dr SL320 Conv	16043	18179	21740
2 Dr SL500 Conv	18074	20480	24490

Options	Price
Automatic Load Leveling [Opt on SL320,SL500]	+150
Electronic Damping Suspension Control [Opt on SL320,SL500]	+340

Body Styles	TMV Pricing		
	Trade	Private	Dealer
2 Dr SL600 Conv	19496	22092	26418

Options	Price
Heated Front Seats [Opt on SL320,SL500]	+107
Traction Control System [Opt on SL320]	+126

Mileage Category: F

The 300SL becomes the SL320 as a new power plant slips into the engine bay. Offering the same horsepower as the previous engine, the SL320 throws out considerably more torque than last year's model. A Bose stereo is added to the standard equipment lists of the entire SL-Class.

Mercedes-Benz
SL55 AMG

2003

Body Styles	TMV Pricing		
	Trade	Private	Dealer
2 Dr S/C Conv	96783	100597	106955

Options	Price
Adaptive Cruise Control	+2309
Designo Espresso Edition	+5245
Designo Graphite Edition	+5245

Options	Price
Keyless Ignition System	+795
Panorama Removable Hardtop	+1409
Park Distance Control (Front and Rear)	+810

SL55 AMG/SLK-Class

2003 (cont'd)

Mileage Category: F

An all-new SL debuts this year, and along with it comes this near-500-horsepower AMG version that promises exotic car performance along with grand touring car comfort.

Mercedes-Benz
SLK-Class

2003

Mileage Category: F

There are no changes for this year.

Body Styles	TMV Pricing			Body Styles	TMV Pricing		
	Trade	Private	Dealer		Trade	Private	Dealer
2 Dr SLK230 S/C Conv	29953	31310	33572	2 Dr SLK320 Conv	33004	34499	36991

Options	Price	Options	Price
Automatic 5-Speed Transmission [Opt on SLK230,SLK320]	+1037	Power Passenger Seat [Opt on SLK230]	+235
Compact Disc Changer	+313	Sport Package [Opt on SLK230,SLK320]	+3362
Heated Front Seats [Opt on SLK230,SLK320]	+431	Telescopic Steering Wheel [Opt on SLK230]	+157
Metallic Paint	+513	Designo Silver Edition	+3836
Power Driver Seat [Opt on SLK230]	+235	Designo Terra Cotta Edition	+3836

2002

Mileage Category: F

No major changes.

Body Styles	TMV Pricing			Body Styles	TMV Pricing		
	Trade	Private	Dealer		Trade	Private	Dealer
2 Dr SLK230 S/C Conv	24627	26139	28658	2 Dr SLK320 Conv	27476	29163	31974

Options	Price	Options	Price
Automatic 5-Speed Transmission [Opt on SLK230]	+907	Metallic Paint	+447
Compact Disc Changer	+398	Power Driver Seat [Opt on SLK230]	+209
Designo Silver Edition	+3350	Power Passenger Seat [Opt on SLK230]	+209
Designo Terra Cotta Edition	+3350	Sport Package	+2945
Heated Front Seats	+384	Telescopic Steering Wheel [Opt on SLK230]	+140

2001

Mileage Category: F

A new V6-powered SLK320 joins the lineup while the SLK230 gets more power and a $2,100 price reduction. Both versions get a new six-speed manual tranny in addition to the five-speed automatic that's been available since the car's introduction, and all models benefit from a revised interior and exterior.

Body Styles	TMV Pricing			Body Styles	TMV Pricing		
	Trade	Private	Dealer		Trade	Private	Dealer
2 Dr SLK230 S/C Conv	22346	24352	26204	2 Dr SLK320 Conv	25086	27338	29417

Options	Price	Options	Price
Automatic 5-Speed Transmission	+587	Metallic Paint	+386
Compact Disc Changer	+352	Power Driver Seat [Opt on SLK230]	+192
Designo Copper Edition	+2968	Power Passenger Seat [Opt on SLK230]	+192
Designo Goldenrod Edition	+2690	Sport Package	+2557
Heated Front Seats	+383	Telescopic Steering Wheel [Opt on SLK230]	+186

2000

Mileage Category: F

Designo editions debut and include special paint and trim in either Copper or Electric Green hues.

Body Styles	TMV Pricing		
	Trade	Private	Dealer
2 Dr SLK230 S/C Conv	20164	22162	24121

Options	Price	Options	Price
Automatic 5-Speed Transmission	+501	Electric Green Edition	+2135
Compact Disc Changer	+334	Heated Front Seats	+337
Designo Copper Edition	+2361	Metallic Paint	+340

1999

Body Styles	TMV Pricing			Body Styles	TMV Pricing		
	Trade	Private	Dealer		Trade	Private	Dealer
2 Dr SLK230 S/C Conv	17087	18910	20808	2 Dr SLK230 Sport S/C Conv	19476	21554	23717

1999 (cont'd)

Options	Price
Automatic 5-Speed Transmission	+349
Compact Disc Changer	+272
Heated Front Seats	+232

Options	Price
Metallic Paint	+233
AM/FM/CD Audio System	+159

Mileage Category: F

This year, Mercedes gives the SLK-Class a standard five-speed manual transmission, optional Sport Package, a new-generation stereo with cassette that uses fiber-optic technology and integrated controls for a cellular phone.

1998

Body Styles	TMV Pricing		
	Trade	Private	Dealer
2 Dr SLK230 S/C Conv	15555	17315	19300

Options	Price
Compact Disc Changer	+226
Heated Front Seats	+192

Options	Price
Metallic Paint	+194

Mileage Category: F

Mercedes-Benz releases an all-new retractable-hardtop roadster. Powered by a supercharged 2.3-liter engine, which is hooked to a five-speed automatic transmission, the SLK-Class races to 60 mph in just over seven seconds.

Mercedes-Benz
SLK32 AMG

2003

Body Styles	TMV Pricing		
	Trade	Private	Dealer
2 Dr S/C Conv	44212	46215	49554

Options	Price
Compact Disc Changer	+313
Designo Silver Edition	+3836

Options	Price
Designo Terra Cotta Edition	+3836
Metallic Paint	+513

Mileage Category: F

The SLK32 rolls into 2003 with no changes.

2002

Body Styles	TMV Pricing		
	Trade	Private	Dealer
2 Dr S/C Conv	39845	41849	45189

Options	Price
Compact Disc Changer	+398
Designo Silver Edition	+3350

Options	Price
Designo Terra Cotta Edition	+3350
Metallic Paint	+447

Mileage Category: F

Mercedes-Benz gives BMW and Porsche something to think about by introducing an AMG version of its small, retractable-hardtop roadster. The SLK32 AMG brings a ripping 349 horsepower to the party by way of a supercharged 3.2-liter V6.

Mercury
Capri/Cougar

1994

Body Styles	TMV Pricing		
	Trade	Private	Dealer
2 Dr STD Conv	1174	1760	2737
2 Dr XR2 Turbo Conv	1362	2041	3173

Options	Price
Air Conditioning	+105
Automatic 4-Speed Transmission	+92
Hardtop Roof [Opt on STD]	+164

Mileage Category: E

A passenger airbag is added. A new suspension on the XR2 improves handling. Both trim levels get a freshened exterior. Slow sales make this the final year for this car.

Mercury
Cougar

2002

Body Styles	TMV Pricing		
	Trade	Private	Dealer
2 Dr I4 Hbk	7224	8173	9754
2 Dr V6 Hbk	7547	8539	10191

Options	Price	Options	Price
17 Inch Wheels [Opt on V6]	+148	Leather Seats [Opt on V6]	+433
Antilock Brakes	+329	Power Driver Seat	+116
Automatic 4-Speed Transmission	+481	Power Moonroof	+363
Front Side Airbag Restraints [Opt on V6]	+157		

Mileage Category: E

New colors spruce up the outside, and all Cougars get the formerly optional Convenience Group (cruise, remote keyless illuminated entry and rear wiper/washer) as standard equipment. Evidently, the Zn (Zinc Yellow) feature car from 2001 failed to get buyers' pulses up, so Mercury tries again for 2002 with the XR package, which includes special red or black paint, a rear spoiler, a fake hood scoop and special logos. The Cougar C2 feature vehicle makes a return engagement for 2002. Sadly, the shelved Cougar S never materialized.

2001

Mileage Category: E

Exterior and interior changes are extensive for the Cougar. At first glance outside, you'll notice new front and rear fascias, new headlights with a projector and reflector system, a new grille, a new spoiler, new foglights and 16-inch painted or 17-inch machined aluminum wheels. New clearcoat metallic colors include Dark Shadow Grey, Tropic Green, French Blue and Sunburst Gold. Later in the year, two special editions -- the Cougar Zn and C2-- will be offered.

Body Styles	TMV Pricing		
	Trade	Private	Dealer
2 Dr I4 Hbk	6224	7465	8611
2 Dr V6 Hbk	6415	7695	8876

Options	Price	Options	Price
Antilock Brakes	+280	Front Side Airbag Restraints	+161
Automatic 4-Speed Transmission [Opt on V6]	+336	Leather Seats	+247
Compact Disc Changer	+144	Power Sunroof	+254

2000

Mileage Category: E

Exterior and interior changes are extensive for the Cougar. At first glance outside, you'll notice new front and rear fascias, new headlights with a projector and reflector system, a new grille, a new spoiler, new foglights and 16-inch painted or 17-inch machined aluminum wheels. New clearcoat metallic colors include Dark Shadow Grey, Tropic Green, French Blue and Sunburst Gold. Later in the year, two special editions -- the Cougar Zn and C2-- will be offered.

Body Styles	TMV Pricing		
	Trade	Private	Dealer
2 Dr I4 Hbk	5493	6668	7819
2 Dr V6 Hbk	5659	6869	8056

Options	Price	Options	Price
Power Sunroof	+221	Compact Disc Changer	+126
Antilock Brakes	+244	Front Side Airbag Restraints	+135
Automatic 4-Speed Transmission	+292	Leather Seats	+321

1999

Body Styles	TMV Pricing		
	Trade	Private	Dealer
2 Dr I4 Hbk	4378	5445	6555
2 Dr V6 Hbk	4785	5951	7164

Options	Price	Options	Price
Antilock Brakes	+211	Power Sunroof	+172
Automatic 4-Speed Transmission	+227	Premium Audio System [Opt on V6]	+146
Leather Seats	+250		

Mileage Category: E

Mercury reintroduces the Cougar this year after a one-year hiatus that saw the departure of most of Ford Motor Co.'s personal coupes. The new model is built on the Mondeo global platform that is also the basis for the Ford Contour and Mercury Mystique. This new coupe is powered by the same engine choices as the Contour/Mystique, which means that buyers can choose between a zippy Zetec four-cylinder and a high-revving Duratec V6.

1997

Body Styles	TMV Pricing		
	Trade	Private	Dealer
2 Dr XR7 Cpe	2700	3603	4706

Options	Price
4.6L V8 SOHC 16V FI Engine	+233
Antilock Brakes	+155
Power Moonroof	+152

Mileage Category: D

Mercury gives you the chance to buy a special anniversary edition replete with plenty of badges, a special interior and a few luxury doo-dads.

1996

Body Styles	TMV Pricing		
	Trade	Private	Dealer
2 Dr XR7 Cpe	2030	2811	3890

Options	Price
Power Moonroof	+129
4.6L V8 SOHC 16V FI Engine	+196
Antilock Brakes	+131

Mileage Category: D

New styling and powertrain improvements highlight the 1996 Cougar. Some formerly standard equipment is now optional. New options include a revamped cruise control system and a Total Anti-Theft System. Four new colors debut.

1995

Body Styles	TMV Pricing		
	Trade	Private	Dealer
2 Dr XR7 Cpe	1364	1998	3055

Options	Price	Options	Price
4.6L V8 SOHC 16V FI Engine	+165	Leather Seats	+80
Antilock Brakes	+110	Power Moonroof	+108

Mileage Category: D

A Sport Appearance Package is offered to spruce up the Cougar with BBS wheels and a luggage rack. Unfortunately, the trunk-mounted CD changer is deleted from the option list. Antilock brakes and a traction-lock axle are available as separate options for the first time this year.

1994

Body Styles	TMV Pricing		
	Trade	Private	Dealer
2 Dr XR7 Cpe	978	1604	2647

Options	Price	Options	Price
4.6L V8 SOHC 16V FI Engine	+149	JBL Audio System	+76
Antilock Brakes	+99	Power Moonroof	+97

Mileage Category: D

Dual airbags are finally available on the Cougar. The standard four-speed automatic transmission gains electronic shift controls and an overdrive lockout switch. Optional traction control joins the lineup of safety features. Updated front and rear fascias, taillamps and headlights round out the changes.

Mercury
Grand Marquis

2003

Body Styles	TMV Pricing		
	Trade	Private	Dealer
4 Dr GS Sdn	12846	13779	15334
4 Dr LS Sdn	14524	15579	17337

Options	Price	Options	Price
AM/FM/Cassette/CD Audio System [Opt on GS]	+176	Front Side Airbag Restraints [Opt on LS]	+213
Automatic Load Leveling [Opt on LS]	+162	Special Leather Seat Trim [Opt on LS]	+430
Compact Disc Changer [Opt on LS]	+213	Sport Suspension [Opt on LS]	+170
Heated Front Seats [Opt on LS]	+159	Power Adjustable Foot Pedals [Opt on GS]	+146
Leather Seats [Opt on LS]	+267		

Mileage Category: G

The 2003 Grand Mark receives a number of updates. The most important ones are hidden. A new full-perimeter frame uses strong, lightweight hydroformed steel sections for the front rails to improve frontal and offset crash performance. Redesigned frame crossmembers and new optional side impact airbags improve side impact crash performance. Additionally, the new frame -- combined with a redesigned independent front suspension and new monotube shock absorbers at all four wheels -- contributes to a smoother, more controlled ride and improved handling. Other changes include a new variable ratio rack-and-pinion steering system with variable power assist and a new dual-rate brake booster that automatically supplies full braking power in a panic stop. On the inside, the seats have been changed to improve comfort and appearance, the cupholders are new, a three-point seatbelt has been added for the center rear passenger and the door trim has been redesigned for a cleaner appearance and better ergonomics. To spot a 2003 Marquis, look for the brighter headlights and subtle new styling applied to the front and rear of the vehicle.

2002

Mileage Category: G

Antilock brakes and traction control now come standard on all Grand Marks, while revised cupholders and a new front seat storage pouch improve the cabin. No-charge leather is available on LS Ultimate models. LS Ultimate and LSE models get standard steering wheel controls for the stereo and climate system, and a new trunk organizer is optional across the board. Three new colors are added this year.

Body Styles	TMV Pricing		
	Trade	Private	Dealer
4 Dr GS Sdn	10384	11297	12819
4 Dr LS Sdn	11817	12857	14589

Options	Price	Options	Price
Automatic Load Leveling	+218	Leather Seats	+481
Compact Disc Changer	+169	Sport Suspension	+363

2001

Mileage Category: G

Power from the V8 engine is improved. The interior gets minor improvements and an optional adjustable pedal assembly. Safety has been improved via a crash severity sensor, safety belt pre-tensioners, dual-stage airbags and seat position sensors.

Body Styles	TMV Pricing		
	Trade	Private	Dealer
4 Dr GS Sdn	8383	9627	10776
4 Dr LS Sdn	9280	10658	11930

Options	Price	Options	Price
Aluminum/Alloy Wheels	+132	Compact Disc Changer	+144
AM/FM/Cassette Audio System [Opt on LS]	+148	Digital Instrument Panel [Opt on LS]	+175
Antilock Brakes	+280	Leather Seats	+303
Automatic Load Leveling	+165	Power Passenger Seat [Opt on LS]	+144

2000

Mileage Category: G

The Marquis receives additional safety features, including an emergency trunk release, child seat-anchor brackets and Mercury's Belt Minder system. The interior gets a new trim color, Dark Charcoal. One new exterior color will be offered, Tropic Green. The handling package's rear-axle ratio changes from 3.27 to 3.55. The Grand Marquis Limited will be offered later in the 2000 model year.

Body Styles	TMV Pricing		
	Trade	Private	Dealer
4 Dr GS Sdn	6968	8139	9287
4 Dr LS Sdn	7618	8898	10152

Options	Price	Options	Price
Aluminum/Alloy Wheels	+115	Digital Instrument Panel [Opt on LS]	+152
Antilock Brakes	+244	Leather Seats	+264
Compact Disc Changer	+126	Power Passenger Seat [Opt on LS]	+129

Grand Marquis

1999

Body Styles	TMV Pricing		
	Trade	Private	Dealer
4 Dr GS Sdn	5806	6894	8026
4 Dr LS Sdn	6330	7516	8750

Options	Price
Antilock Brakes	+211
Digital Instrument Panel [Opt on LS]	+118
Leather Seats [Opt on LS]	+205

Mileage Category: G

This traditional American sedan got a revised rear suspension and exterior styling last year. This year all it gets are some new color options.

1998

Body Styles	TMV Pricing		
	Trade	Private	Dealer
4 Dr GS Sdn	4925	5930	7064
4 Dr LS Sdn	5343	6434	7664

Options	Price
Antilock Brakes	+184
Leather Seats	+174

Mileage Category: G

The last of the American rear-drive sedans gets substantial improvements this year, including a new instrument panel, new steering gear and an improved ride, thanks to a Watt's linkage suspension. All-speed traction control debuts this year as well.

1997

Body Styles	TMV Pricing		
	Trade	Private	Dealer
4 Dr GS Sdn	3827	4772	5926
4 Dr LS Sdn	4240	5287	6566

Options	Price
Leather Seats	+151
Antilock Brakes	+155

Mileage Category: G

After a mild facelift last year, the Grand Marquis soldiers on with a few color changes, improved power steering and the addition of rear air suspension to the handling package.

1996

Body Styles	TMV Pricing		
	Trade	Private	Dealer
4 Dr GS Sdn	2906	3751	4917
4 Dr LS Sdn	3275	4227	5542

Options	Price
Antilock Brakes	+131
Camper/Towing Package	+156

Mileage Category: G

This distant descendant of the Turnpike Cruiser gets engine and transmission upgrades, a new steering wheel and a new gas cap design. Passenger power lumbar support has been deleted.

1995

Body Styles	TMV Pricing		
	Trade	Private	Dealer
4 Dr GS Sdn	2103	2762	3860
4 Dr LS Sdn	2419	3177	4440

Options	Price	Options	Price
Antilock Brakes	+110	Leather Seats	+94
Camper/Towing Package	+131	Power Sunroof	+102

Mileage Category: G

Updated styling and an increased number of convenience features improve upon last year's model. A battery saver shuts off power to accessories or lights 10 minutes after the ignition is switched off. The mast antenna has been replaced by an integrated rear window antenna. Interior updates include a 12-volt outlet in a redesigned dashboard. Enlarged stereo controls improve ease of operation and bigger gauges improve the instrument panel.

1994

Body Styles	TMV Pricing		
	Trade	Private	Dealer
4 Dr GS Sdn	1599	2215	3241
4 Dr LS Sdn	1893	2622	3837

Mileage Category: G

The Grand Marquis passes the stringent 1997 side-impact standards this year. Wire-spoke wheel covers are now part of the standard equipment package.

1994 (cont'd)

Options	Price
Antilock Brakes	+99
Camper/Towing Package	+118
Leather Seats	+85

Mercury
Marauder

2003

Body Styles	TMV Pricing		
	Trade	Private	Dealer
4 Dr STD Sdn	18526	19766	21832

Options	Price
Compact Disc Changer	+213
Heated Front Seats	+159

Mileage Category: M

In an effort to generate interest in what seems to be a dying brand, Mercury takes a page out of a decade-old Chevrolet playbook and paints a Grand Marquis Amish-black, bolts on 18-inch wheels and stuffs a 300-horse V8 under the hood. The result is surprisingly appealing.

Mercury
Mountaineer

2003

Body Styles	TMV Pricing		
	Trade	Private	Dealer
4 Dr STD AWD SUV	18860	20141	22277
4 Dr STD SUV	17732	18937	20944

Options	Price	Options	Price
Camper/Towing Package	+216	AM/FM/CD Changer Audio System	+216
Heated Front Seats	+135	17 Inch Wheels	+311
Leather Seats	+376	Air Conditioning - Front and Rear	+330
Power Moonroof	+432	Automatic Climate Control (2 Zone) - Driver and Passenger	+189
Power Passenger Seat	+130		
Rollover Protection System	+135	Front and Rear Head Airbag Restraints	+135
Running Boards	+213	4.6L V8 SOHC 16V FI Engine	+449
Premium Audio System	+157	Park Distance Control (Rear)	+138

Mileage Category: M

The Mountaineer comes in three different versions for 2003: Convenience, Luxury and Premier. Mercury has added standard equipment this year, including security approach lamps, automatic headlamps, dual illuminated visor vanity mirrors, heated exterior mirrors and power-adjustable pedals. Luxury models receive color-keyed running boards and an Audiophile sound system as standard, and Premier adds to that a power sunroof and a Security Group that includes a Safety Canopy system of head airbags and rollover protection sensors bundled with a reverse-sensing system. Inside, Mountaineers get new trim for the doors and dash, a three-point seatbelt for the center of the second-row bench and an easy entry/exit system for the third-row seat. Luxury and Premier models can be outfitted with a new DVD entertainment system for the rear seats and a tire pressure monitoring system. A leather-upholstered center console cover is added and leather is a no-charge option for Luxury and Premier models.

2002

Mileage Category: M

Mercury has overhauled its Mountaineer for model-year 2002 in an attempt to make it more carlike than ever before. Among the changes are a 2.5-inch wider stance for better handling and roominess, a new independent rear suspension that improves ride and handling, while at the same time accommodating a standard third row of seats, larger door openings with a lower step-in height, standard six-way power-adjustable driver seat and optional power-adjustable pedals. With this year's redesign, Mercury is trying to further differentiate the Mountaineer from its lookalike cousin the Ford Explorer.

Body Styles	TMV Pricing		
	Trade	Private	Dealer
4 Dr STD AWD SUV	16021	17312	19464
4 Dr STD SUV	14950	16155	18163

Options	Price	Options	Price
17 Inch Wheels	+278	Leather Seats	+317
4.6L V8 SOHC 16V FI Engine	+336	Park Distance Control (Rear)	+123
Air Conditioning - Front and Rear	+295	Power Moonroof	+387
AM/FM/CD Changer Audio System	+193	Power Passenger Seat	+116

2002 (cont'd)

Options	Price
Automatic Climate Control (2 Zone) - Driver and Passenger	+169
Camper/Towing Package	+191
Front and Rear Head Airbag Restraints	+121
Heated Front Seats	+121

Options	Price
Premium Audio System	+140
Rollover Protection System	+121
Running Boards	+191

2001

Mileage Category: M

Not much changes for 2001, as Mercury's Explorer clone has a new child safety-seat tether anchor system. The rest of the vehicle is all carryover.

Body Styles	TMV Pricing		
	Trade	Private	Dealer
4 Dr STD 4WD SUV	12006	13567	15008
4 Dr STD AWD SUV	12176	13759	15220
4 Dr STD SUV	11259	12723	14074

Options	Price
5.0L V8 OHV 16V FI Engine [Opt on 2WD]	+192
AM/FM/Cassette/CD Audio System	+181
AM/FM/Cassette/CD Changer Audio System	+163
Automatic Load Leveling	+163
Chrome Wheels	+204
Front Side Airbag Restraints	+163

Options	Price
Leather Seats	+330
Limited Slip Differential [Std on AWD]	+146
Power Driver Seat	+126
Power Moonroof	+330
Power Passenger Seat	+126
Premium Audio System	+181

2000

Mileage Category: M

Mountaineer is uprated with new Premier and Monterey trim packages, which include tan leather upholstery, special paint, upgraded alloy wheels and wood-grain dash trim.

Body Styles	TMV Pricing		
	Trade	Private	Dealer
4 Dr STD 4WD SUV	9379	10890	12372
4 Dr STD AWD SUV	9576	11119	12632
4 Dr STD SUV	8594	9979	11336

Options	Price
5.0L V8 OHV 16V FI Engine [Opt on 2WD]	+166
AM/FM/Cassette/CD Audio System	+158
Automatic Load Leveling	+142
Chrome Wheels	+177
Compact Disc Changer	+133

Options	Price
Front Side Airbag Restraints	+140
Leather Seats	+341
Limited Slip Differential [Std on AWD]	+127
Power Moonroof	+287
Sport Seats	+215

1999

Mileage Category: M

For '99 the Mountaineer gets optional rear load leveling and a reverse parking aid. It also receives a new seat design.

Body Styles	TMV Pricing		
	Trade	Private	Dealer
4 Dr STD 4WD SUV	7104	8404	9758
4 Dr STD AWD SUV	7556	8939	10379
4 Dr STD SUV	6716	7946	9226

Options	Price
5.0L V8 OHV 16V FI Engine [Opt on 2WD]	+129
AM/FM/Cassette/CD Audio System	+123
Chrome Wheels	+138

Options	Price
Leather Seats	+265
Power Moonroof	+223
Sport Seats	+167

1998

Mileage Category: M

The Mountaineer gets minor front and rear styling tweaks as it enters its second year of production. In addition, a new model, with full-time four-wheel drive, receives the SOHC V6 and five-speed automatic transmission that became available on the Explorer last year.

Body Styles	TMV Pricing		
	Trade	Private	Dealer
4 Dr STD 4WD SUV	6147	7348	8702
4 Dr STD AWD SUV	6277	7503	8885
4 Dr STD SUV	5762	6887	8156

Options	Price
Power Moonroof	+190
Bucket Seats	+131

Options	Price
Chrome Wheels	+118
Leather Seats	+156

Mountaineer/Mystique

1997

Mileage Category: M

The all-new Mercury Mountaineer is yet another entrant into the booming luxury sport-utility market. Based on the wildly successful Ford Explorer, the Mountaineer is intended to appeal to outdoor sophisticates rather than true roughnecks. Distinguishing characteristics of the Mountaineer include four-wheel antilock brakes, a pushrod V8 engine and optional all-wheel drive.

Body Styles	TMV Pricing		
	Trade	Private	Dealer
4 Dr STD AWD SUV	5570	6657	7986
4 Dr STD SUV	5182	6194	7430

Options	Price
JBL Audio System	+171
Leather Seats	+135
Power Moonroof	+164

Mercury
Mystique

2000

Body Styles	TMV Pricing		
	Trade	Private	Dealer
4 Dr GS Sdn	4364	5468	6550
4 Dr LS Sdn	4848	6075	7277

Options	Price	Options	Price
Aluminum/Alloy Wheels [Opt on GS]	+152	Power Driver Seat [Opt on GS]	+126
Antilock Brakes	+244	Power Moonroof	+213
Automatic 4-Speed Transmission	+292		

Mileage Category: C

The Mystique comes standard with an emergency glow-in-the-dark trunk release, designed to allow a child or adult trapped in the trunk to open it from the inside. Two new exterior colors debut.

1999

Mileage Category: C

The Mystique gets a revised instrument panel and redesigned front seats this year. A six-way power-adjustable seat is now standard on the LS model and all Mystiques benefit from a revised suspension and larger fuel tank. Medium Steel Blue replaces Light Denim Blue as an exterior color. A final note to family-oriented shoppers: the optional integrated child safety seat is no longer available.

Body Styles	TMV Pricing		
	Trade	Private	Dealer
4 Dr GS Sdn	3541	4622	5748
4 Dr LS Sdn	3905	5098	6339

Options	Price	Options	Price
Aluminum/Alloy Wheels [Opt on GS]	+118	Automatic 4-Speed Transmission	+227
Antilock Brakes	+211	Power Moonroof	+166

1998

Mileage Category: C

The 1998 Mystique receives a freshened interior and exterior that includes new wheels and a new front end. Mechanical enhancements include 100,000-mile maintenance intervals for the 2.0-liter Zetec engine, improved manual transmission shifter feel, improved NVH and improved air conditioning performance. New interior pieces are intended to distinguish the Mystique from its otherwise-identical twin, the Ford Contour.

Body Styles	TMV Pricing		
	Trade	Private	Dealer
4 Dr GS Sdn	2637	3640	4772
4 Dr LS Sdn	2959	4085	5354

Options	Price	Options	Price
Antilock Brakes	+179	Leather Seats	+213
Automatic 4-Speed Transmission	+194	Power Moonroof	+141

1997

Mileage Category: C

The addition of a Spree Package for the GS model and the inclusion of a tilt steering wheel and standard trunk light are the only changes for the 1997 Mystique.

Body Styles	TMV Pricing		
	Trade	Private	Dealer
4 Dr GS Sdn	1835	2744	3855
4 Dr LS Sdn	2058	3077	4323
4 Dr STD Sdn	1825	2729	3834

Options	Price	Options	Price
Power Moonroof	+122	Antilock Brakes	+155
2.5L V6 DOHC 24V FI Engine	+204	Automatic 4-Speed Transmission	+168
Air Conditioning	+163	Leather Seats	+184

1996

Body Styles	TMV Pricing		
	Trade	Private	Dealer
4 Dr GS Sdn	1247	2009	3061
4 Dr LS Sdn	1367	2203	3357

Options	Price	Options	Price
2.5L V6 DOHC 24V FI Engine	+172	Antilock Brakes	+131
Air Conditioning	+135	Automatic 4-Speed Transmission	+142

Mileage Category: C

More rear seat room is the big story for Mystique in 1996. Gearshift effort has been improved on manual transmissions, a new Sport Appearance Package is available and five new colors are on the palette. Alloy wheels have been restyled on LS models.

1995

Body Styles	TMV Pricing		
	Trade	Private	Dealer
4 Dr GS Sdn	970	1572	2576
4 Dr LS Sdn	1062	1722	2821

Options	Price	Options	Price
2.5L V6 DOHC 24V FI Engine	+144	Automatic 4-Speed Transmission	+119
Air Conditioning	+114	Leather Seats	+87
Antilock Brakes	+110	Power Moonroof	+87

Mileage Category: C

Introduced to replace the aging Topaz, the Mystique is a virtual twin to the Ford Contour. Euro-styling combined with German engineering results in a $20,000 American car that can compete with import sedans that cost nearly twice as much. You may choose between two trim levels, the base GS or the more luxurious LS. A 170-horsepower V6 engine is optional.

Mercury
Sable

2003

Body Styles	TMV Pricing		
	Trade	Private	Dealer
4 Dr GS Sdn	8995	9926	11478
4 Dr GS Wgn	9666	10667	12334

Body Styles	TMV Pricing		
	Trade	Private	Dealer
4 Dr LS Sdn	10066	11108	12844
4 Dr LS Wgn	10522	11611	13426

Options	Price	Options	Price
AM/FM/CD Audio System [Opt on GS]	+143	Power Passenger Seat [Opt on LS]	+213
Antilock Brakes	+367	Front Side Airbag Restraints	+135
Chrome Wheels [Opt on LS]	+213	Special Leather Seat Trim [Opt on LS]	+213
Compact Disc Changer [Opt on LS]	+216	Spoke Wheels [Opt on GS]	+267
Leather Seats [Opt on LS]	+276	Traction Control System	+138
Power Driver Seat [Opt on GS]	+135	Power Adjustable Foot Pedals [Opt on GS]	+189
Power Moonroof [Opt on LS]	+538	MACH Audio System [Opt on LS]	+159

Mileage Category: D

Not much has changed for Mercury's 2003 Sable. All cars feature a new cupholder design, and the LS Premium trim level offers a no-charge leather trim. Mercury claims that "customers who appreciate understated sophistication will want to know more about the Platinum Edition," which includes aluminum wheels with a center cap ornament and interior trim pieces, perforated leather and a fender badge. Power windows, locks, tilt steering and floor mats are standard across the board, and two new colors brighten up the Sable.

2002

Body Styles	TMV Pricing		
	Trade	Private	Dealer
4 Dr GS Sdn	7069	7944	9403
4 Dr GS Wgn	7502	8431	9979

Body Styles	TMV Pricing		
	Trade	Private	Dealer
4 Dr LS Premium Sdn	7812	8780	10393
4 Dr LS Premium Wgn	8184	9197	10886

Options	Price	Options	Price
AM/FM/Cassette/CD Changer Audio System	+169	MACH Audio System	+131
AM/FM/CD Audio System [Opt on GS]	+128	Power Driver Seat [Opt on GS]	+121
Antilock Brakes	+329	Power Moonroof	+431
Chrome Wheels	+143	Power Passenger Seat	+169
Front Side Airbag Restraints	+133	Spoke Wheels [Opt on GS]	+191
Leather Seats	+247		

Mileage Category: D

Four new colors are added to the paint chart, while approach lighting and an auto-dimming rearview mirror with compass become standard equipment.

Mercury
Sable

2001

Mileage Category: D

A new child safety-seat restraint system is in place as well as a larger 18-gallon fuel tank. There's also a clearcoat metallic paint swap, trading Tropic Green for Spruce Green. Otherwise, no changes for the recently freshened Sable.

Body Styles	TMV Pricing		
	Trade	Private	Dealer
4 Dr GS Sdn	6004	7169	8245
4 Dr GS Wgn	6356	7589	8728
4 Dr LS Premium Sdn	6637	7926	9116

Body Styles	TMV Pricing		
	Trade	Private	Dealer
4 Dr LS Premium Wgn	6937	8284	9527
4 Dr LS Sdn	6119	7307	8404

Options	Price
3.0L V6 DOHC 24V FI Engine [Opt on LS]	+287
Aluminum/Alloy Wheels [Opt on GS Sdn]	+163
Antilock Brakes	+280
Chrome Wheels	+122
Compact Disc Changer	+144

Options	Price
Front Side Airbag Restraints	+161
Power Driver Seat [Opt on GS]	+163
Power Moonroof	+367
Power Passenger Seat [Opt on LS Premium]	+144
Premium Audio System	+276

2000

Mileage Category: D

The 2000 Mercury Sable gains new sheet metal and additional refinements. The freshened styling includes a raised hood and deck lid, a larger grille, improved headlamps and taillights and new mirrors. The instrument panel has been updated, and the new integrated control panel provides better functionality. The Sable also gains significant improvements to its safety and powertrain components.

Body Styles	TMV Pricing		
	Trade	Private	Dealer
4 Dr GS Sdn	4863	5904	6925
4 Dr GS Wgn	5301	6436	7548
4 Dr LS Premium Sdn	5538	6723	7884

Body Styles	TMV Pricing		
	Trade	Private	Dealer
4 Dr LS Premium Wgn	5758	6990	8198
4 Dr LS Sdn	5237	6358	7457

Options	Price
3.0L V6 DOHC 24V FI Engine [Opt on LS,Wgn]	+249
Aluminum/Alloy Wheels [Opt on GS Sdn]	+142
Antilock Brakes	+244
Chrome Wheels	+208
Compact Disc Changer	+126

Options	Price
Front Side Airbag Restraints	+140
Power Driver Seat [Opt on GS]	+142
Power Moonroof	+265
Power Passenger Seat [Opt on LS Premium]	+126

1999

Mileage Category: D

Still smarting from that 1996 "redesign" that had many longtime Sable fans running to the competition, Mercury performed some minor cosmetic surgery in '98 to help soften the Sable's front end. This year's changes are limited to new wheel designs, a revised gauge cluster and interior console, as well as suspension alterations designed to improve overall ride quality. The particulate filtration system has been deleted from this year's models.

Body Styles			TMV Pricing		
			Trade	Private	Dealer
4 Dr GS Sdn			3677	4565	5490
4 Dr LS Sdn			3889	4829	5807
4 Dr LS Wgn			4141	5141	6182

Options	Price
3.0L V6 DOHC 24V FI Engine	+155
Antilock Brakes	+211
Chrome Wheels	+161

Options	Price
Leather Seats	+250
Power Moonroof	+207

1998

Mileage Category: D

A mild facelift and fewer options are the only change to Mercury's midsize sedan.

Body Styles			TMV Pricing		
			Trade	Private	Dealer
4 Dr GS Sdn			3092	3977	4976
4 Dr LS Sdn			3255	4187	5239
4 Dr LS Wgn			3551	4569	5716

Options	Price
3.0L V6 DOHC 24V FI Engine	+118
Antilock Brakes	+179
Chrome Wheels	+138

Options	Price
Leather Seats	+213
Power Moonroof	+176

1997

Mileage Category: D

The 1997 Sable LS can now be had with Ford's outstanding Mach audio system. Other changes, occurring at the end of the 1996 model year, include the addition of a mass airflow sensor to the Vulcan V6, and improvements to the Duratec V6 to improve responsiveness.

Body Styles	TMV Pricing		
	Trade	Private	Dealer
4 Dr GS Sdn	2522	3366	4397
4 Dr GS Wgn	2583	3448	4505

Body Styles	TMV Pricing		
	Trade	Private	Dealer
4 Dr LS Sdn	2806	3745	4892
4 Dr LS Wgn	2806	3745	4892

1997 (cont'd)

Options	Price
Antilock Brakes	+155
Chrome Wheels	+120
Compact Disc Changer	+122

Options	Price
Leather Seats [Opt on GS]	+204
Power Moonroof	+152

1996

Body Styles	TMV Pricing		
	Trade	Private	Dealer
4 Dr G Sdn	1913	2649	3666
4 Dr GS Sdn	1989	2753	3809
4 Dr GS Wgn	2146	2972	4112

Body Styles	TMV Pricing		
	Trade	Private	Dealer
4 Dr LS Sdn	2209	3059	4232
4 Dr LS Wgn	2397	3319	4592

Options	Price
Antilock Brakes	+131
Leather Seats	+172
Power Moonroof	+129

Mileage Category: D

Fresh off the drawing boards for 1996, and it seems the drawing boards were poorly lit. Styling is heavy-handed and homely, but definitely not dull. Otherwise, the new Sable is an excellent car, powered by new engines, suspended by new components and innovative in nearly every way. Longer and wider sedan and wagon body styles are offered in GS and LS trim.

1995

Body Styles	TMV Pricing		
	Trade	Private	Dealer
4 Dr GS Sdn	1309	1917	2931
4 Dr GS Wgn	1391	2038	3115

Body Styles	TMV Pricing		
	Trade	Private	Dealer
4 Dr LS Sdn	1444	2115	3234
4 Dr LS Wgn	1578	2311	3532

Options	Price
3.8L V6 OHV 12V FI Engine	+77
Antilock Brakes [Opt on GS]	+110
Chrome Wheels	+85

Options	Price
Leather Seats	+131
Power Moonroof	+108

Mileage Category: D

Last year for the Sable in its current form. New cylinder heads and crankshafts are intended to decrease engine noise by reducing vibration. Solar control window glass makes a brief appearance on the sedan and wagon.

1994

Body Styles	TMV Pricing		
	Trade	Private	Dealer
4 Dr GS Sdn	921	1510	2492
4 Dr GS Wgn	935	1533	2530

Body Styles	TMV Pricing		
	Trade	Private	Dealer
4 Dr LS Sdn	982	1609	2655
4 Dr LS Wgn	1051	1722	2840

Options	Price
Antilock Brakes	+99
Leather Seats	+118
Power Moonroof	+97

Mileage Category: D

Rear window defroster becomes standard equipment on the sedan and wagon. The wagon gets a standard rear window wiper as well. CFC-free air conditioning is introduced to the Sable.

Mercury
Topaz

1994

Body Styles	TMV Pricing		
	Trade	Private	Dealer
2 Dr GS Cpe	594	967	1588
4 Dr GS Sdn	619	1008	1655

Options	Price
3.0L V6 OHV 12V FI Engine	+90
Air Conditioning	+105

Mileage Category: B

The Topaz receives CFC-free air conditioning. This will be the last year for the Topaz; Mercury is replacing it with an all-new compact called the Mystique.

Mercury
Tracer

1999

Body Styles	TMV Pricing		
	Trade	Private	Dealer
4 Dr GS Sdn	2616	3543	4508
4 Dr LS Sdn	2798	3789	4821
4 Dr LS Wgn	3052	4133	5258

Options	Price	Options	Price
Air Conditioning [Opt on GS]	+222	Automatic 4-Speed Transmission	+227
Antilock Brakes	+211	Leather Seats	+153

Mileage Category: B

The Tracer gets a new sport wagon model to help extend its appeal to young buyers. The LS Sport Wagon model comes standard with leather seating surfaces and 15-inch wheels. Other changes include a standard interior trunk release on all sedans. A remote keyless entry and AM/FM cassette player is standard on LS models.

1998
Mileage Category: B

No changes to Mercury's recently redesigned entry-level car.

Body Styles	TMV Pricing		
	Trade	Private	Dealer
4 Dr GS Sdn	2109	2988	3979
4 Dr LS Sdn	2241	3174	4227
4 Dr LS Wgn	2372	3360	4475

Options	Price	Options	Price
Air Conditioning [Opt on GS]	+189	Automatic 4-Speed Transmission	+194
Antilock Brakes	+179	Compact Disc Changer	+122

1997
Mileage Category: B

The Mercury Tracer is totally redesigned this year with enhancements across the board. The most noticeable improvements are in the powertrain and in the ride quality. New sheet metal gives the Tracer a rounder, more aerodynamic appearance as well. The speedy LTS sedan is discontinued.

Body Styles	TMV Pricing		
	Trade	Private	Dealer
4 Dr GS Sdn	1625	2372	3286
4 Dr LS Sdn	1689	2466	3416
4 Dr LS Wgn	1752	2558	3544

Options	Price
Air Conditioning	+163
Antilock Brakes	+155
Automatic 4-Speed Transmission	+168

1996

Body Styles	TMV Pricing		
	Trade	Private	Dealer
4 Dr LTS Sdn	1399	2101	3071
4 Dr STD Sdn	1214	1824	2667
4 Dr STD Wgn	1276	1917	2801

Options	Price
Air Conditioning	+136
Antilock Brakes	+131
Automatic 4-Speed Transmission	+142

Mileage Category: B

Automatic transmission modifications make base Tracers more responsive, and the standard 1.9-liter engine now goes 100,000 miles between tune-ups. Last year's integrated child seat continues, and Trio models are now available in all colors, including a new one called Toreador Red.

1995

Mileage Category: B

A passenger airbag is finally available for the Tracer. Unfortunately, some engineering genius decided to retain the annoying motorized shoulder belts. An integrated child seat is introduced as an optional safety feature. The Trio package is introduced, designed to give budget shoppers the option of purchasing some of the more popular LTS features such as the spoiler, aluminum wheels and leather-wrapped steering wheel.

1995 (cont'd)

Body Styles	TMV Pricing		
	Trade	Private	Dealer
4 Dr LTS Sdn	1031	1577	2487
4 Dr STD Sdn	936	1432	2259
4 Dr STD Wgn	958	1465	2311

Options	Price	Options	Price
Automatic 4-Speed Transmission	+119	Antilock Brakes	+110
Power Moonroof	+76	Air Conditioning	+114

1994

Body Styles	TMV Pricing		
	Trade	Private	Dealer
4 Dr LTS Sdn	825	1343	2206
4 Dr STD Sdn	668	1087	1785
4 Dr STD Wgn	675	1099	1805

Options	Price
Air Conditioning	+103
Antilock Brakes	+99
Automatic 4-Speed Transmission	+107

Mileage Category: B

A driver-side airbag is introduced on all models. New alloy wheels and optional antilock brakes show up on the LTS.

Mercury
Villager

2002

Body Styles	TMV Pricing		
	Trade	Private	Dealer
4 Dr Estate Pass Van	12358	13593	15651
4 Dr STD Pass Van	9185	10103	11632
4 Dr Sport Pass Van	11589	12747	14677

Options	Price	Options	Price
Air Conditioning - Front and Rear [Opt on STD]	+387	Digital Instrument Panel	+143
AM/FM/Cassette/CD Changer Audio System	+418	Power Driver Seat [Opt on STD]	+121
Antilock Brakes [Opt on Sport,STD]	+329	Power Moonroof	+375
Automatic Climate Control	+119	VCR Entertainment System	+626
Compact Disc Changer	+179		

Mileage Category: P

After 2002, it's outta here. As such, it comes as no surprise that there are virtually no significant changes to the Villager this year.

2001

Mileage Category: P

Numerous exterior and interior revisions are on tap for 2001. Also new are optional 16-inch wheels and tires, drivetrain changes for better engine smoothness, new seatbelt pre-tensioners to improve safety and the addition of an anchorage point for attaching a child seat.

Body Styles	TMV Pricing		
	Trade	Private	Dealer
4 Dr Estate Pass Van	10298	11930	13436
4 Dr STD Pass Van	8139	9429	10619
4 Dr Sport Pass Van	9984	11566	13027

Options	Price	Options	Price
Air Conditioning - Front and Rear [Opt on Sport]	+144	Power Driver Seat [Opt on STD]	+126
AM/FM/Cassette/CD Audio System	+357	Power Moonroof	+320
AM/FM/Cassette/CD Changer Audio System	+153	Premium Audio System [Opt on STD]	+128
Antilock Brakes	+280	Two-Tone Paint	+122
Digital Instrument Panel [Opt on Estate]	+122	VCR Entertainment System	+534
Leather Seats [Opt on Sport]	+328		

2000

Mileage Category: P

The convenience, comfort and luxury option packages have been simplified. All 2000 Villagers meet federal low-emission vehicle status and come standard with a child seat-anchor system. A new rear-seat video entertainment system is now optional.

2000 (cont'd)

Body Styles	TMV Pricing		
	Trade	Private	Dealer
4 Dr Estate Pass Van	8710	10265	11789
4 Dr STD Pass Van	7050	8309	9543
4 Dr Sport Pass Van	8066	9506	10918

Options	Price	Options	Price
Air Conditioning - Front and Rear [Opt on STD]	+166	Leather Seats [Opt on Sport]	+224
AM/FM/Cassette/CD Audio System	+246	Power Moonroof	+278
Antilock Brakes	+244	Premium Audio System [Opt on STD]	+253
Compact Disc Changer	+133	VCR Entertainment System	+251

1999

Mileage Category: P

The Mercury Villager is completely redesigned for '99. Improvements range from a more powerful engine to a larger interior to a second sliding door on the driver side. New styling features include larger headlights and a distinctive front grille. Inside, ergonomics have been addressed with easier to reach controls and an innovative storage shelf located behind the third seat.

Body Styles	TMV Pricing		
	Trade	Private	Dealer
4 Dr Estate Pass Van	6415	7750	9140
4 Dr STD Pass Van	5531	6682	7880
4 Dr Sport Pass Van	6218	7512	8858

Options	Price	Options	Price
Air Conditioning - Front and Rear	+129	Leather Seats	+174
AM/FM/Cassette/CD Audio System	+191	Power Moonroof	+217
Antilock Brakes	+211	Premium Audio System [Opt on STD]	+196

1998

Mileage Category: P

No changes to the 1998 Villager as Mercury readies a replacement.

Body Styles	TMV Pricing		
	Trade	Private	Dealer
3 Dr GS Pass Van	4323	5344	6496
3 Dr LS Pass Van	5085	6286	7641
3 Dr Nautica Pass Van	5202	6431	7817

Options	Price	Options	Price
Air Conditioning [Opt on GS]	+203	Compact Disc Changer	+161
Air Conditioning - Front and Rear	+203	Leather Seats [Opt on LS]	+148
AM/FM/Cassette/CD Audio System	+163	Power Moonroof	+184
Antilock Brakes	+179	Premium Audio System [Opt on GS]	+167

1997

Mileage Category: P

For 1997, the Villager offers a few more luxury items to distinguish it from the Nissan Quest. Quad captain's chairs are a nice alternative to the middle-row bench, and the addition of rear radio controls and rear air conditioning should also make rear-seat passengers happy.

Body Styles	TMV Pricing		
	Trade	Private	Dealer
3 Dr GS Pass Van	3522	4467	5623
3 Dr LS Pass Van	4140	5251	6609
3 Dr Nautica Pass Van	4179	5301	6672

Options	Price	Options	Price
Air Conditioning - Front and Rear	+176	Leather Seats [Opt on LS]	+128
AM/FM/Cassette/CD Audio System	+141	Power Moonroof	+160
Antilock Brakes [Opt on GS]	+155	Premium Audio System [Opt on GS]	+145
Captain Chairs (4) [Opt on LS]	+128	Air Conditioning [Opt on GS]	+176

1996

Mileage Category: P

A passenger-side airbag is installed in a redesigned dashboard for 1996, and fresh front and rear styling updates this versatile van. Villager also gets an optional integrated child seat, automatic climate control system and remote keyless entry system. Substantial trim and functional changes make Villager competitive once again.

Body Styles	TMV Pricing		
	Trade	Private	Dealer
3 Dr GS Pass Van	2886	3753	4951
3 Dr LS Pass Van	3252	4229	5578
3 Dr Nautica Pass Van	3397	4418	5827

Options	Price
Air Conditioning [Opt on GS]	+148
Air Conditioning - Front and Rear	+148
AM/FM/Cassette/CD Audio System	+119

Options	Price
Power Moonroof	+134
Premium Audio System [Opt on GS]	+122

1995

Mileage Category: P

No changes for the Villager.

Body Styles	TMV Pricing		
	Trade	Private	Dealer
3 Dr GS Pass Van	2124	2809	3951
3 Dr LS Pass Van	2544	3364	4730
3 Dr Nautica Pass Van	2751	3638	5117

Options	Price
Air Conditioning	+125
AM/FM/Cassette/CD Audio System	+100
Captain Chairs (4) [Opt on LS]	+89

Options	Price
Leather Seats [Opt on LS]	+91
Power Moonroof	+113
Premium Audio System	+103

1994

Mileage Category: P

A driver airbag is installed in the Villager and a special-edition luxury model debuts. Borrowing the name of an upscale men's clothier, the Nautica edition of the Villager includes such niceties as two-tone paint, alloy wheels and leather upholstery; all tastefully done in blue and white befitting a nautical theme.

Body Styles	TMV Pricing		
	Trade	Private	Dealer
3 Dr GS Pass Van	1699	2355	3449
3 Dr LS Pass Van	2114	2931	4292
3 Dr Nautica Pass Van	2210	3064	4488

Options	Price
AM/FM/Cassette/CD Audio System	+90
Captain Chairs (4) [Opt on LS]	+80
Leather Seats [Opt on LS]	+82

Options	Price
Power Moonroof	+102
Premium Audio System [Opt on GS]	+93
Air Conditioning [Opt on GS]	+112

Cooper

2003

Mileage Category: E

For their second season in the U.S. market, the Cooper and the Cooper S will now come with a second remote key and pre-wiring for a dealer-installed alarm system. Anthracite (smoke gray, that is) interior trim is available as a no-cost option for both cars, and the Cooper S is eligible for the high-gloss silver interior treatment found in the base Cooper. Sound systems will be satellite radio-ready this year, and the rear cargo area now has a power point.

Body Styles	TMV Pricing		
	Trade	Private	Dealer
2 Dr S S/C Hbk	17994	19168	21124
2 Dr STD Hbk	15142	16130	17776

Options	Price	Options	Price
Automatic Stability Control	+450	Power Panorama Roof	+758
Automatic Climate Control	+284	Sport Seats	+213
Harman Kardon Audio System	+521	Sport Suspension [Opt on STD]	+474
Heated Front Seats	+256	Traction Control System [Opt on STD]	+260
Power Heated Mirrors	+142	Runflat Tire System [Opt on STD]	+284
Heated Front and Rear Seats	+256	Continuously Variable Transmission [Opt on STD]	+1184
Leather Seats	+1184	16 Inch Wheels [Opt on STD]	+474
Metallic Paint	+379	17 Inch Wheels [Opt on S]	+497
Navigation System	+1515	Park Distance Control (Rear)	+284

2002

Mileage Category: E

BMW subsidiary, Mini, resurrects an unforgettable old favorite with the release of the Cooper. Available with either a 115-horsepower four-cylinder or a supercharged version of that engine worthy of 163 hp, the pint-sized but glamorous three-door hatchback features BMW-engineered suspension and steering and a base MSRP under 17 grand. Whether you're a 40-something hoping to relive earlier days, an autocross enthusiast or just the mild-mannered next-door neighbor, we expect that you'll run to the nearest BMW dealership in search of this coveted bundle of joy.

Body Styles	TMV Pricing		
	Trade	Private	Dealer
2 Dr S S/C Hbk	16386	17467	19267
2 Dr STD Hbk	13708	14612	16119

Options	Price	Options	Price
16 Inch Wheels [Opt on STD]	+343	Metallic Paint	+347
17 Inch Wheels	+455	Navigation System	+2038
Automatic Climate Control	+260	Park Distance Control (Rear)	+260
Automatic Dimming Rearview Mirror	+117	Power Heated Mirrors	+130
Automatic Stability Control	+412	Power Panorama Roof	+694
Continuously Variable Transmission	+1084	Runflat Tire System [Std on S]	+260
Harman Kardon Audio System	+477	Sport Seats	+195
Heated Front Seats	+234	Sport Suspension [Std on S]	+434
Leather Seats	+1084	Traction Control System [Std on S]	+238

1999

Body Styles	TMV Pricing		
	Trade	Private	Dealer
2 Dr SL Hbk	13013	14785	16629
2 Dr STD Hbk	9386	10664	11994
2 Dr VR-4 Turbo AWD Hbk	17031	19350	21764

Options	Price	Options	Price
AM/FM/Cassette/CD Audio System [Opt on STD]	+223	Compact Disc Changer	+184
AM/FM/CD Audio System	+122	Leather Seats [Opt on STD]	+253
Automatic 4-Speed Transmission [Opt on SL,STD]	+273		

Mileage Category: F

The 1999 3000GT sees some styling changes and a few choice pieces of standard equipment, including antilock brakes and a power sunroof for the SL. Last year for this once proud supercar.

1998

Mileage Category: F

SL and VR-4 models get a standard power sunroof this year.

Body Styles	TMV Pricing		
	Trade	Private	Dealer
2 Dr SL Hbk	10901	12468	14236
2 Dr STD Hbk	7947	9090	10378
2 Dr VR-4 Turbo AWD Hbk	14896	17038	19453

Options	Price	Options	Price
AM/FM/Cassette/CD Audio System [Opt on STD]	+192	Compact Disc Changer	+159
Antilock Brakes [Opt on SL]	+226	Leather Seats [Opt on STD]	+218
Automatic 4-Speed Transmission [Opt on SL,STD]	+236		

1997

Mileage Category: F

A value-leader base model is introduced. It has less than stellar performance and we think that it's embarrassing that this car is in the same lineup as the earth-scorching VR-4.

Body Styles	TMV Pricing		
	Trade	Private	Dealer
2 Dr SL Hbk	8665	10002	11635
2 Dr STD Hbk	7318	8447	9826
2 Dr VR-4 Turbo AWD Hbk	12620	14567	16946

Options	Price	Options	Price
Leather Seats [Opt on STD]	+199	Antilock Brakes [Opt on SL]	+205
Power Sunroof	+211	Automatic 4-Speed Transmission [Opt on SL,STD]	+210
AM/FM/Cassette/CD Audio System [Opt on STD]	+174	Compact Disc Changer	+144

1996

Mileage Category: F

Base model gets new cloth interior, while upper trim levels receive a choice of black or tan leather. Remote keyless entry gets panic feature, and several new colors are available.

Body Styles	TMV Pricing			Body Styles	TMV Pricing		
	Trade	Private	Dealer		Trade	Private	Dealer
2 Dr SL Hbk	7165	8231	9702	2 Dr Spyder VR-4 Turbo AWD Conv	13321	15302	18038
2 Dr STD Hbk	5735	6588	7765	2 Dr VR-4 Turbo AWD Hbk	9260	10637	12539
2 Dr Spyder SL Conv	12491	14349	16914				

Options	Price	Options	Price
Automatic 4-Speed Transmission [Opt on SL,STD]	+191	Compact Disc Changer	+123
Chrome Wheels [Opt on SL]	+120	Power Sunroof	+180

1995

Mileage Category: F

The VR-4 gains chrome-plated alloy wheels as standard equipment. A hardtop drop top joins the 3000GT family this year.

Body Styles	TMV Pricing			Body Styles	TMV Pricing		
	Trade	Private	Dealer		Trade	Private	Dealer
2 Dr SL Hbk	5491	6399	7911	2 Dr Spyder VR-4 Turbo AWD Conv	11276	13140	16247
2 Dr STD Hbk	4647	5415	6695	2 Dr VR-4 Turbo AWD Hbk	6912	8055	9959
2 Dr Spyder SL Conv	10376	12091	14950				

Mitsubishi
3000GT/Diamante

1995 (cont'd)

Options	Price
AM/FM/Cassette/CD Audio System	+120
Automatic 4-Speed Transmission [Opt on SL,STD]	+144
Chrome Wheels [Opt on SL]	+110

Options	Price
Compact Disc Changer	+99
Power Sunroof	+145

1994

Mileage Category: F

The 3000GT gets a passenger airbag. The 3000GT VR-4 gets a totally unnecessary 20 extra horsepower. But, hey, you won't find us complaining. To harness the extra power, the VR-4 switches to a six-speed manual gearbox. Freshened styling and CFC-free air conditioning round out the changes for all models.

Body Styles	TMV Pricing		
	Trade	Private	Dealer
2 Dr SL Hbk	4489	5485	7146
2 Dr STD Hbk	3856	4712	6138
2 Dr VR-4 Turbo AWD Hbk	5720	6990	9106

Options	Price
Automatic 4-Speed Transmission [Opt on SL,STD]	+129
Chrome Wheels	+87
Compact Disc Changer	+89

Options	Price
Leather Seats [Opt on SL]	+122
Sunroof	+131

Mitsubishi
Diamante

2003

Mileage Category: H

After introducing the sporty VR-X trim level halfway through 2002, the Diamante continues into 2003 with no changes.

Body Styles	TMV Pricing		
	Trade	Private	Dealer
4 Dr ES Sdn	13303	14411	16258
4 Dr LS Sdn	14543	15754	17773
4 Dr VR-X Sdn	13967	15130	17069

Options	Price
Heated Front Seats [Opt on LS]	+150
Infinity Audio System [Opt on VR-X]	+209
Leather Seats [Opt on VR-X]	+503

Options	Price
Rear Spoiler [Opt on VR-X]	+147
Traction Control System [Opt on LS]	+165

2002

Mileage Category: H

A sporty new trim level, the VR-X, debuts in an attempt to put some life into the Diamante's sales charts. Otherwise, only minor changes are in store for the Diamante this year. Slight styling tweaks have been applied to the front and rear, and the interior features redesigned audio controls and an emergency inside-trunk release. One mechanical change has been made this year -- Electronic Brakeforce Distribution (EBD) has been added to all trim levels.

Body Styles	TMV Pricing		
	Trade	Private	Dealer
4 Dr ES Sdn	9726	10689	12295
4 Dr LS Sdn	10815	11886	13672
4 Dr VR-X Sdn	10232	11246	12935

Options	Price
Heated Front Seats	+120
Infinity Audio System [Opt on VR-X]	+168

Options	Price
Power Moonroof [Opt on VR-X]	+409
Traction Control System [Opt on LS]	+132

2001

Mileage Category: H

This Mitsubishi model doesn't change much from last year, but product planners add tether anchors for child seats, foglights on the LS and new seat fabric and wheel cover for the ES. Greenies can rest easy knowing that it meets LEV standards for all states.

Body Styles	TMV Pricing		
	Trade	Private	Dealer
4 Dr ES Sdn	8304	9652	10896
4 Dr LS Sdn	9290	10797	12189

Options	Price
Traction Control System	+116

Diamante

Body Styles	TMV Pricing		
	Trade	Private	Dealer
4 Dr ES Sdn	7118	8435	9726
4 Dr LS Sdn	7924	9390	10827

Options	Price
Aluminum/Alloy Wheels [Opt on ES]	+301
AM/FM/Cassette/CD Audio System	+143
Compact Disc Changer	+215

Mileage Category: H

Other than bringing back the ES and LS trim levels, this Mitsubishi model doesn't change much from last year. Product planners add a couple of standard features, replace four colors and offer a new all-weather package for the LS buyer.

Body Styles	TMV Pricing		
	Trade	Private	Dealer
4 Dr STD Sdn	6207	7474	8792

Options	Price	Options	Price
Aluminum/Alloy Wheels	+258	Compact Disc Changer	+184
AM/FM/Cassette/CD Audio System	+122	Leather Seats	+276
AM/FM/CD Audio System	+122	Power Moonroof	+295
Chrome Wheels	+258		

Mileage Category: H

Only one Diamante model is available, replacing the ES and LS models. Mitsubishi also adds some new standard features, options and exterior colors to this top-level model.

Body Styles	TMV Pricing		
	Trade	Private	Dealer
4 Dr ES Sdn	4802	5883	7103
4 Dr LS Sdn	6028	7386	8917

Options	Price	Options	Price
Aluminum/Alloy Wheels [Opt on ES]	+222	Leather Seats [Opt on ES]	+238
Chrome Wheels	+222	Power Moonroof [Opt on ES]	+255
Compact Disc Changer	+159	Power Passenger Seat [Opt on LS]	+139

Mileage Category: H

All Diamantes get standard ABS and remote keyless entry for 1998.

Body Styles	TMV Pricing		
	Trade	Private	Dealer
4 Dr ES Sdn	3999	5018	6263
4 Dr LS Sdn	4835	6067	7573

Options	Price	Options	Price
Antilock Brakes	+182	Power Moonroof	+232
Compact Disc Changer	+144	Aluminum/Alloy Wheels [Opt on ES]	+202
Leather Seats [Opt on ES]	+217		

Mileage Category: H

After a one-year hiatus, the Diamante returns to the Mitsubishi lineup sporting clean and crisp styling, a full-load of luxury features and a lower price. The old car barely registered on near-luxury car buyers' radar; this new one deserves consideration and a close inspection.

Body Styles	TMV Pricing		
	Trade	Private	Dealer
4 Dr ES Sdn	3523	4499	5847

Mileage Category: H

The only Diamantes sold this year were for fleet sales. So unless you see one at a rental car auction, chances are not good that you'll find a used 1996 model.

Mitsubishi
Diamante/Eclipse

1995

Mileage Category: H

The base Diamante sedan is sent out to pasture, available only to fleet purchasers such as rental car agencies. No other changes for the Mitsubishi flagship.

Body Styles		TMV Pricing	
	Trade	Private	Dealer
4 Dr ES Sdn	2421	3208	4520
4 Dr LS Sdn	3102	4112	5794
4 Dr STD Wgn	2484	3293	4640

Options	Price
Antilock Brakes [Opt on STD]	+171
Compact Disc Changer	+136
Leather Seats [Opt on STD]	+181

Options	Price
Power Moonroof	+175
Power Passenger Seat w/Memory [Opt on LS]	+90
Traction Control System	+132

1994

Mileage Category: H

A passenger airbag and CFC-free air conditioning make the Diamante much friendlier to its passengers and the environment. A five-door wagon model introduced late last year comes with the 175-horsepower engine that is standard in the ES sedan. New wood trim and an upgraded Infinity stereo debut on the 1994 Diamante.

Body Styles		TMV Pricing	
	Trade	Private	Dealer
4 Dr ES Sdn	1790	2561	3845
4 Dr LS Sdn	2237	3200	4805
4 Dr STD Wgn	1854	2652	3983

Options	Price
Antilock Brakes [Std on LS]	+112
Compact Disc Changer	+115
Leather Seats [Std on LS]	+173

Options	Price
Power Moonroof	+142
Traction Control System [Opt on ES,LS]	+112

Mitsubishi
Eclipse

2003

Body Styles	TMV Pricing		
	Trade	Private	Dealer
2 Dr GS Hbk	10695	11598	13102
2 Dr GT Hbk	12304	13342	15073

Options	Price
Automatic 4-Speed Transmission	+479
Infinity Audio System [Opt on GS,GT]	+162

Body Styles	TMV Pricing		
	Trade	Private	Dealer
2 Dr GTS Cpe	13854	15023	16971
2 Dr RS Hbk	10385	11261	12722

Options	Price
Leather Seats [Opt on GT]	+365
Power Moonroof [Opt on GS,GT]	+479

Mileage Category: E

A new higher-performance Eclipse joins the lineup. Dubbed the GTS, its 3.0-liter V6 has 10 more horses than the same engine found under the hood of the GT, and a number of luxury features justify its standing as the top Eclipse. A new front fascia along with revised front and rear light clusters round out the changes.

2002

Mileage Category: E

Only trivial changes are in store for Mitsubishi's Eclipse this year. Two new exterior colors (Titanium and Flash Blue) are added, as well as a Mitsubishi triple-diamond chrome badge. GS and GT models get illuminated vanity mirrors and a glovebox lamp as standard equipment.

Body Styles		TMV Pricing	
	Trade	Private	Dealer
2 Dr GS Hbk	8961	9911	11494
2 Dr GT Hbk	10008	11069	12836
2 Dr RS Hbk	8537	9442	10950

Options	Price
17 Inch Wheels	+192
AM/FM/Cassette/CD Changer Audio System	+168
Antilock Brakes	+327
Automatic 4-Speed Transmission	+385
Front Side Airbag Restraints	+120

Options	Price
Infinity Audio System	+130
Leather Seats	+277
Power Driver Seat	+120
Power Moonroof	+349

2001

Mileage Category: E

Body Styles	TMV Pricing		
	Trade	Private	Dealer
2 Dr GS Hbk	7816	9133	10349
2 Dr GT Hbk	8681	10144	11494
2 Dr RS Hbk	7456	8713	9873

Options	Price
AM/FM/Cassette/CD Changer Audio System [Opt on GT]	+148
Antilock Brakes	+303
Automatic 4-Speed Transmission	+339

Options	Price
Infinity Audio System	+127
Leather Seats	+193
Power Moonroof [Std on GS]	+310

The new year for the Eclipse sees a standard spoiler, tether anchors for child seats and engines that meet LEV emissions standards.

2000

Mileage Category: E

Body Styles	TMV Pricing		
	Trade	Private	Dealer
2 Dr GS Hbk	6997	8228	9435
2 Dr GT Hbk	7425	8732	10013
2 Dr RS Hbk	6470	7608	8724

Options	Price
Leather Seats	+164
Power Moonroof [Std on GS]	+262
Rear Spoiler [Std on GT]	+115
AM/FM/Cassette/CD Audio System	+143

Options	Price
Antilock Brakes	+257
Automatic 4-Speed Transmission	+287
Compact Disc Changer	+215

Mitsubishi's 2000 Eclipse is redesigned inside and out and based on the Galant sedan platform, embodying a youthful image and providing a sporty drive. V6 power is now available, but the spunky turbocharged engine is gone as is the all-wheel-drive model.

1999

Body Styles	TMV Pricing		
	Trade	Private	Dealer
2 Dr GS Hbk	5902	7064	8274
2 Dr GS-T Turbo Hbk	6712	8034	9409

Body Styles	TMV Pricing		
	Trade	Private	Dealer
2 Dr GSX Turbo AWD Hbk	8949	10712	12546
2 Dr RS Hbk	5236	6267	7341

Options	Price
Air Conditioning [Opt on GS,RS]	+264
AM/FM/Cassette/CD Audio System [Opt on GS]	+122
AM/FM/CD Audio System [Opt on GS,RS]	+122
Antilock Brakes [Std on GSX]	+232

Options	Price
Automatic 4-Speed Transmission	+224
Compact Disc Changer	+184
Leather Seats [Std on GSX]	+169
Power Moonroof [Opt on GS,RS]	+224

Mileage Category: E

For 1999, the Eclipse gets a host of new standard equipment, and there is a new Sports Value Option Package for buyers of the GS.

1998

Mileage Category: E

Body Styles	TMV Pricing		
	Trade	Private	Dealer
2 Dr GS Hbk	4823	5907	7130
2 Dr GS-T Turbo Hbk	5554	6803	8211

Body Styles	TMV Pricing		
	Trade	Private	Dealer
2 Dr GSX Turbo AWD Hbk	6814	8346	10073
2 Dr RS Hbk	4204	5149	6215

Options	Price
Air Conditioning [Opt on GS,RS]	+228
Antilock Brakes	+200
Automatic 4-Speed Transmission	+183

Options	Price
Compact Disc Changer	+159
Leather Seats [Std on GSX]	+146
Power Moonroof [Std on GSX]	+194

The GSX gets a standard sunroof, power driver seat and remote keyless entry.

1997

Mileage Category: E

Body Styles	TMV Pricing		
	Trade	Private	Dealer
2 Dr GS Hbk	4124	5172	6453
2 Dr GS-T Turbo Hbk	4798	6018	7509
2 Dr GSX Turbo AWD Hbk	5469	6860	8559

Body Styles	TMV Pricing		
	Trade	Private	Dealer
2 Dr RS Hbk	3575	4484	5594
2 Dr STD Hbk	3281	4115	5134

Revised styling makes the attractive Eclipse drop-dead gorgeous. New interior fabrics and paint colors debut as well. Antilock brakes are now available on the GS model, and a CD player joins its standard equipment list. Two new exterior colors, new seat fabrics and a new interior color combination round out the changes.

1997 (cont'd)

Options	Price
Air Conditioning [Opt on GS,RS,STD]	+207
Antilock Brakes	+182
Automatic 4-Speed Transmission	+166

Options	Price
Compact Disc Changer	+144
Leather Seats	+132
Power Moonroof	+176

1996

Mileage Category: E

Three new colors debut. Audio systems are revised, and RS models can be ordered with a rear spoiler. Remote keyless entry systems get a new panic feature.

Body Styles	TMV Pricing		
	Trade	Private	Dealer
2 Dr GS Hbk	3306	4225	5495
2 Dr GS-T Turbo Hbk	3855	4928	6409
2 Dr GSX Turbo AWD Hbk	4052	5179	6736

Body Styles	TMV Pricing		
	Trade	Private	Dealer
2 Dr RS Hbk	2607	3332	4333
2 Dr STD Hbk	2353	3007	3911

Options	Price
Air Conditioning [Opt on GS-T,GSX]	+177
Antilock Brakes	+155
Automatic 4-Speed Transmission	+144

Options	Price
Compact Disc Changer	+123
Power Sunroof	+150

1995

Mileage Category: E

Radically redesigned, the new Eclipse sports bulging shoulders and no-nonsense looks, particularly in GSX guise. Engine ratings are improved for all models, while the turbocharged GS-T and GSX produce a mighty 210 horsepower at 6,000 rpm. Antilock brakes are optional on all models. Dual airbags are finally standard on the Eclipse.

Body Styles	TMV Pricing		
	Trade	Private	Dealer
2 Dr GS Hbk	2134	2849	4041
2 Dr GS-T Turbo Hbk	2549	3404	4828

Body Styles	TMV Pricing		
	Trade	Private	Dealer
2 Dr GSX Turbo AWD Hbk	3136	4187	5939
2 Dr RS Hbk	1847	2467	3500

Options	Price
Power Sunroof	+121
Air Conditioning [Opt on GS,RS]	+142
Antilock Brakes	+125

Options	Price
Automatic 4-Speed Transmission	+114
Compact Disc Changer	+99
Leather Seats [Opt on GS,RS]	+91

1994

Mileage Category: E

Last year for the current edition of the Diamond Star sport coupe. Turbo engines gain a minimal boost in horsepower. Several of the models get more standard equipment in an attempt to increase sales in this edition's final year.

Body Styles	TMV Pricing		
	Trade	Private	Dealer
2 Dr GS 2.0 Hbk	1574	2269	3428
2 Dr GS Hbk	1369	1974	2982

Body Styles	TMV Pricing		
	Trade	Private	Dealer
2 Dr GS Turbo Hbk	1895	2732	4128
2 Dr GSX Turbo AWD Hbk	2097	3024	4569

Options	Price
Air Conditioning [Opt on GS 1.8]	+128
Antilock Brakes [Opt on GS]	+112

Options	Price
Automatic 4-Speed Transmission	+102
Leather Seats	+82

2003

Body Styles	TMV Pricing		
	Trade	Private	Dealer
2 Dr GS Conv	14415	15461	17203
2 Dr GT Conv	15614	16747	18634
2 Dr GTS Conv	16949	18178	20227

Options	Price
Automatic 4-Speed Transmission	+598
Leather Seats [Opt on GS,GT]	+359

Mileage Category: E

A new, higher-performance Eclipse joins the lineup. Dubbed the GTS, its 3.0-liter V6 boasts 210 horses and a number of luxury features justify its standing as the top Eclipse. Unlike the 200-horse GT coupe, the Spyder GT gets the more powerful GTS engine. A new front fascia along with revised front and rear light clusters round out the changes.

Eclipse Spyder

2002

Body Styles	TMV Pricing		
	Trade	Private	Dealer
2 Dr GS Conv	11712	12704	14356
2 Dr GT Conv	12761	13841	15642

Options	Price	Options	Price
AM/FM/Cassette/CD Changer Audio System	+168	Front Side Airbag Restraints	+120
Antilock Brakes	+327	Leather Seats	+289
Automatic 4-Speed Transmission	+476	Power Driver Seat	+120

Mileage Category: E

Only trivial changes are in store for the Eclipse drop-top this year. Two new exterior colors (Titanium and Flash Blue) are added, and as well as a Mitsubishi triple-diamond chrome badge. The interior is upgraded slightly with illuminated vanity mirrors and a glovebox lamp.

2001

Body Styles	TMV Pricing		
	Trade	Private	Dealer
2 Dr GS Conv	10269	11626	12878
2 Dr GT Conv	11189	12668	14034

Options	Price	Options	Price
AM/FM/Cassette/CD Changer Audio System [Opt on GT]	+148	Automatic 4-Speed Transmission	+423
Antilock Brakes	+303	Leather Seats	+254

Mileage Category: E

Mitsubishi's 2001 Eclipse Spyder is all new inside and out and based on the recently redesigned Eclipse Coupe, embodying a youthful image and providing a sporty drive. But the turbocharged engine is no longer on the menu.

1999

Body Styles	TMV Pricing		
	Trade	Private	Dealer
2 Dr GS Conv	6812	8053	9344
2 Dr GS-T Turbo Conv	7767	9182	10654

Options	Price	Options	Price
Antilock Brakes	+232	Infinity Audio System [Opt on GS]	+134
Automatic 4-Speed Transmission	+224	Leather Seats [Opt on GS]	+174
Compact Disc Changer	+184		

Mileage Category: E

Sundance Plum Pearl exterior paint replaces Magenta Gray Pearl, black leather interior replaces the gray, and the GS-T model gets white-faced instrumentation.

1998

Body Styles	TMV Pricing		
	Trade	Private	Dealer
2 Dr GS Conv	5413	6549	7830
2 Dr GS-T Turbo Conv	6266	7582	9065

Options	Price	Options	Price
Antilock Brakes	+200	Infinity Audio System [Opt on GS]	+116
Automatic 4-Speed Transmission	+212	Leather Seats [Opt on GS]	+150
Compact Disc Changer	+159		

Mileage Category: E

Eclipse Spyder GS gets air conditioning, AM/FM stereo with CD player and wheel locks. The Spyder GS-T is now flashier than ever before thanks to standard 16-inch chrome-plated alloy wheels. All models have a fresh black interior appearance with gray cloth.

1997

Body Styles	TMV Pricing		
	Trade	Private	Dealer
2 Dr GS Conv	4047	5076	6334
2 Dr GS-T Turbo Conv	4872	6111	7625

Options	Price	Options	Price
Air Conditioning [Opt on GS]	+215	Compact Disc Changer	+144
Antilock Brakes	+182	Leather Seats [Opt on GS]	+132
Automatic 4-Speed Transmission	+205		

Mileage Category: E

The 1997 Spyder gets revised front and rear styling. Antilock brakes are now available on the GS model. Two new exterior colors, new seat fabrics and a new interior color combination round out the changes.

Mitsubishi
Eclipse Spyder/Expo/Galant

1996
Mileage Category: E

Sleek and eye-catching, the Spyder makes its debut this year. This convertible is based on the popular Eclipse.

Body Styles	TMV Pricing		
	Trade	Private	Dealer
2 Dr GS Conv	3380	4320	5617
2 Dr GS-T Turbo Conv	4073	5205	6768

Options	Price
Air Conditioning [Opt on GS,RS,STD]	+177
Antilock Brakes	+155

Options	Price
Automatic 4-Speed Transmission	+144
Compact Disc Changer	+123

Mitsubishi
Expo

1995

Body Styles	TMV Pricing		
	Trade	Private	Dealer
4 Dr STD 4WD Hbk	1406	2107	3276
4 Dr STD Hbk	1298	1946	3025

Options	Price
Air Conditioning	+116
Antilock Brakes	+125

Mileage Category: B

This is the last year for the Expo.

1994
Mileage Category: B

The Expo and LRV receive a driver airbag this year. Unfortunately, the Expo loses its uplevel SP model, but base models do receive better standard equipment as a result. LRVs are available only as two-wheel-drive models in 1994; the AWD has been axed. This is the last year for the Expo LRV, although it will live on as the Eagle Summit wagon.

Body Styles	TMV Pricing		
	Trade	Private	Dealer
2 Dr LRV 1.8 Hbk	850	1357	2201
2 Dr LRV 2.4 Hbk	877	1399	2270
2 Dr LRV Sport Hbk	1100	1757	2851

Body Styles	TMV Pricing		
	Trade	Private	Dealer
4 Dr STD 4WD Hbk	1125	1796	2915
4 Dr STD Hbk	1024	1635	2654

Options	Price
Power Sunroof	+97
Air Conditioning	+104

Options	Price
Antilock Brakes	+112
Automatic 4-Speed Transmission	+139

Mitsubishi
Galant

2003

Body Styles	TMV Pricing		
	Trade	Private	Dealer
4 Dr DE Sdn	8763	9613	11029
4 Dr ES Sdn	9044	9921	11384
4 Dr ES V6 Sdn	9865	10822	12416

Body Styles	TMV Pricing		
	Trade	Private	Dealer
4 Dr GTZ Sdn	11494	12609	14466
4 Dr LS Sdn	10695	11733	13462
4 Dr LS V6 Sdn	11183	12268	14076

Options	Price
Antilock Brakes [Opt on ES,ES V6]	+407
Infinity Audio System [Opt on ES,ES V6]	+162
Leather Seats [Opt on LS,LS V6]	+479

Options	Price
Power Driver Seat [Opt on LS,LS V6]	+168
Power Moonroof [Opt on ES,ES V6]	+509
Traction Control System [Opt on ES]	+132

Mileage Category: D

The ES Galant now offers a "Sun and Sound" option that provides a 210-watt Infinity audio system along with a power sunroof and 16-inch alloy wheels. LS models come equipped with traction control.

2002

Body Styles	TMV Pricing		
	Trade	Private	Dealer
4 Dr DE Sdn	6607	7425	8788
4 Dr ES Sdn	7058	7932	9389
4 Dr ES V6 Sdn	7749	8709	10308

Body Styles	TMV Pricing		
	Trade	Private	Dealer
4 Dr GTZ Sdn	9007	10122	11981
4 Dr LS Sdn	8463	9511	11257
4 Dr LS V6 Sdn	8798	9888	11704

Options	Price
Antilock Brakes [Opt on ES]	+327
Leather Seats [Opt on LS,LS V6]	+385

Options	Price
Power Driver Seat [Opt on LS,LS V6]	+135
Power Moonroof [Opt on ES,ES V6]	+409

Mileage Category: D

The 2002 Galant features new exterior and interior design changes and other improvements to enhance safety and functionality. A new LS model with the four-cylinder engine offers a standard sunroof and upgraded sound system plus the option of leather trim. Mechanically, changes include larger front ventilated disc brakes (four-cylinder models), an additional remote keyless-entry trunk-opening function, an emergency inside-trunk lid release and available ABS on ES models. The exterior features updated front and rear styling, new 16-inch wheels (GTZ and LS V6) and two new colors. Inside, Mitsubishi has spruced things up with a new audio system faceplate, a rear dome light with the optional sunroof and a redesigned gauge cluster. New titanium- and bronze-finish (ES and LS) or carbon fiber-finish (GTZ) trim panels have also been added.

2001

Body Styles	TMV Pricing		
	Trade	Private	Dealer
4 Dr DE Sdn	5451	6481	7431
4 Dr ES Sdn	5707	6785	7780
4 Dr ES V6 Sdn	6508	7737	8871

Body Styles	TMV Pricing		
	Trade	Private	Dealer
4 Dr GTZ Sdn	7760	9226	10579
4 Dr LS V6 Sdn	7434	8838	10135

Options	Price
Antilock Brakes [Opt on ES]	+408
Front Side Airbag Restraints [Opt on ES,ES V6]	+127
Power Moonroof [Opt on ES,ES V6]	+360

Mileage Category: D

Mitsubishi's fourth-generation Galant features some new standard and optional equipment, like a LATCH system for child seats and traction control and heated mirrors for cold-weather dwellers who purchase the all-weather package. It now meets LEV standards.

2000

Body Styles	TMV Pricing		
	Trade	Private	Dealer
4 Dr DE Sdn	4602	5531	6441
4 Dr ES Sdn	4773	5737	6681
4 Dr ES V6 Sdn	5592	6721	7828

Body Styles	TMV Pricing		
	Trade	Private	Dealer
4 Dr GTZ Sdn	6898	8291	9656
4 Dr LS V6 Sdn	6181	7428	8651

Options	Price
Antilock Brakes [Opt on ES]	+346
Compact Disc Changer	+242

Options	Price
Leather Seats [Opt on ES,ES V6]	+305
Power Moonroof [Opt on ES,ES V6]	+305

Mileage Category: D

After a '99 redesign, Mitsubishi's fourth-generation Galant features some new standard and optional equipment, like cruise-control memory function, an in-dash CD player, larger tires and four new colors.

1999

Body Styles	TMV Pricing		
	Trade	Private	Dealer
4 Dr DE Sdn	3680	4519	5392
4 Dr ES Sdn	4132	5074	6054
4 Dr ES V6 Sdn	4704	5776	6892

Body Styles	TMV Pricing		
	Trade	Private	Dealer
4 Dr GTZ Sdn	5930	7282	8688
4 Dr LS V6 Sdn	5423	6659	7945

Options	Price
AM/FM/CD Audio System	+122
Antilock Brakes [Opt on ES]	+296
Compact Disc Changer	+207

Options	Price
Leather Seats [Opt on ES,ES V6]	+261
Power Moonroof [Opt on ES,ES V6]	+261

Mileage Category: D

The all-new '99 Galant lineup features BMW-like styling, a new V6 engine option, more standard equipment and a GTZ model with a sport-tuned suspension.

1998

Body Styles	TMV Pricing		
	Trade	Private	Dealer
4 Dr DE Sdn	2869	3666	4565
4 Dr ES Sdn	3345	4275	5323
4 Dr LS Sdn	4014	5130	6388

1998 (cont'd)
Mileage Category: D

Solar-tinted glass makes it harder to tan in the new Galant. The ES gets a standard manual transmission, and the ES and LS have a new black grille with chrome accents. The LS also benefits from standard antilock brakes. All models have a new heavy-duty starter and battery.

Options	Price
Air Conditioning [Opt on DE]	+239
Antilock Brakes [Opt on ES]	+255
Automatic 4-Speed Transmission [Std on LS]	+207

Options	Price
Compact Disc Changer	+179
Leather Seats [Opt on ES]	+226
Power Moonroof [Opt on ES]	+226

1997
Mileage Category: D

Mitsubishi shuffles the Galant lineup, replacing the S sedan with a base model called the DE. Front and rear fascias have been redesigned, and the interiors of all models have been upgraded by the addition of more ergonomically correct center armrests, upgraded upholstery, additional sound deadening material and a new steering wheel.

Body Styles	TMV Pricing		
	Trade	Private	Dealer
4 Dr DE Sdn	2105	2797	3642
4 Dr ES Sdn	2600	3454	4498
4 Dr LS Sdn	3152	4187	5452

Options	Price
Leather Seats [Opt on ES]	+205
Power Moonroof [Opt on ES]	+192
Compact Disc Changer	+159

Options	Price
Air Conditioning [Opt on DE]	+217
Antilock Brakes	+232
Automatic 4-Speed Transmission [Opt on DE]	+210

1996
Mileage Category: D

A Homelink transmitter is available, and a panic feature debuts on keyless entry systems. New two-tone interiors debut, and four fresh exterior colors join the palette. Other changes include new wheel covers, expanded availability of alloy wheels, and a heavy-duty defroster with timer. LS models have standard leather seating and antilock brakes are available across the line.

Body Styles	TMV Pricing		
	Trade	Private	Dealer
4 Dr ES Sdn	2253	3074	4207
4 Dr LS Sdn	2558	3490	4778
4 Dr S Sdn	1735	2368	3241

Options	Price
Air Conditioning [Opt on S]	+185
Antilock Brakes	+198
Automatic 4-Speed Transmission [Opt on S]	+183

Options	Price
Compact Disc Changer	+136
Power Moonroof [Opt on ES]	+164

1995
Mileage Category: D

The much anticipated V6 engine never transpired in the 1995 Galant due to the increased costs and complexity involved in making the model. The 1995 Galants are available in three trim levels, all with the 141-horsepower four-cylinder.

Body Styles	TMV Pricing		
	Trade	Private	Dealer
4 Dr ES Sdn	1544	2210	3321
4 Dr LS Sdn	1572	2250	3381
4 Dr S Sdn	1170	1676	2518

Options	Price
Air Conditioning [Opt on S]	+149
Antilock Brakes	+159

Options	Price
Automatic 4-Speed Transmission [Opt on S]	+120
Leather Seats	+141

1994
Mileage Category: D

Dual airbags debut on this totally redesigned sedan. Four trim levels are offered, ranging from the low-level S to the luxury ES and sporty GS models. An automatic transmission is standard on the ES and LS models. GS Galants come with a twin-cam engine rated at 160 horsepower.

Body Styles	TMV Pricing		
	Trade	Private	Dealer
4 Dr ES Sdn	1097	1702	2711
4 Dr GS Sdn	1311	2034	3239

Body Styles	TMV Pricing		
	Trade	Private	Dealer
4 Dr LS Sdn	1192	1849	2945
4 Dr S Sdn	858	1331	2119

Options	Price
Air Conditioning [Opt on S]	+134
Antilock Brakes	+143

Options	Price
Automatic 4-Speed Transmission [Opt on GS,S]	+133
Leather Seats [Opt on LS]	+126

Lancer/Lancer Evolution/Mighty Max Pickup

Mitsubishi
Lancer
2003

Body Styles	TMV Pricing		
	Trade	Private	Dealer
4 Dr ES Sdn	7527	8519	10173
4 Dr LS Sdn	8427	9538	11389
4 Dr O-Z Rally Sdn	8159	9235	11027

Options	Price	Options	Price
Antilock Brakes [Opt on LS]	+407	Rear Spoiler [Opt on O-Z]	+215
Automatic 4-Speed Transmission [Opt on ES,O-Z]	+479	Front Side Airbag Restraints [Opt on LS]	+150
Power Moonroof [Opt on LS,O-Z]	+449	Split Folding Rear Seat [Opt on ES]	+150

Mileage Category: B

Midway through the year, Mitsubishi will unleash its Lancer Evolution, a rally racing-inspired road burner that sends 271 horsepower through all four of its 17-inch wheels.

2002

Mileage Category: B

Body Styles	TMV Pricing		
	Trade	Private	Dealer
4 Dr ES Sdn	5879	6783	8289
4 Dr LS Sdn	6782	7824	9561
4 Dr O-Z Rally Sdn	6591	7604	9292

Options	Price	Options	Price
Antilock Brakes [Opt on LS]	+327	Rear Spoiler	+173
Automatic 4-Speed Transmission [Opt on ES,O-Z]	+385	Split Folding Rear Seat [Opt on ES]	+120
Front Side Airbag Restraints [Opt on LS]	+120		

The '02 Lancer is Mitsubishi's replacement for its Mirage economy car, though the Mirage continues this year in coupe format only. The chief reason for the new name (for the U.S., as the car has always been called the Lancer elsewhere) is Mitsubishi's desire to emphasize that the Lancer is more upscale, larger and better-engineered than the old Mirage.

Mitsubishi
Lancer Evolution
2003

Body Styles	TMV Pricing		
	Trade	Private	Dealer
4 Dr Turbo AWD Sdn	22984	24456	26909

Options	Price
Power Moonroof	+449
AM/FM/CD Changer Audio System	+269

Mileage Category: E

The Lancer Evolution is not necessarily a new car; it's been around in Japan and Europe since 1989. However, this year marks the first time Mitsubishi is offering the Evo to American customers.

Mitsubishi
Mighty Max Pickup
1996

Body Styles	TMV Pricing		
	Trade	Private	Dealer
2 Dr STD Std Cab SB	1864	2497	3370

Options	Price
Air Conditioning	+156
AM/FM/CD Audio System	+118
Automatic 4-Speed Transmission	+265

Mileage Category: J

No changes this year, the Mighty Max's last.

Mitsubishi
Mighty Max Pickup/Mirage

1995
Mileage Category: J

The Mighty Max line is drastically reduced. Remaining is a four-cylinder two-wheel-drive regular-cab model.

Body Styles	TMV Pricing		
	Trade	Private	Dealer
2 Dr STD Std Cab SB	1542	2075	2963

Options	Price	Options	Price
Air Conditioning	+125	AM/FM/CD Audio System	+95
AM/FM/Cassette Audio System	+81	Automatic 4-Speed Transmission	+213

1994
Mileage Category: J

The Mighty Max gains a few safety features such as a high-mounted rear stoplight and side-impact door guard beams. The vehicle is otherwise unchanged.

Body Styles	TMV Pricing		
	Trade	Private	Dealer
2 Dr STD 4WD Std Cab SB	1790	2513	3719
2 Dr STD Ext Cab SB	1392	1955	2893
2 Dr STD Std Cab SB	1160	1629	2411

Options	Price
Air Conditioning	+112
Automatic 4-Speed Transmission	+192

Mitsubishi
Mirage

2002

Body Styles	TMV Pricing		
	Trade	Private	Dealer
2 Dr DE Cpe	4457	5227	6510
2 Dr LS Cpe	5484	6432	8011

Options	Price	Options	Price
Air Conditioning [Opt on DE]	+382	Automatic 4-Speed Transmission	+385
Aluminum/Alloy Wheels [Opt on LS]	+168	Power Moonroof [Opt on LS]	+385
AM/FM/CD Audio System [Opt on DE]	+132	Power Windows [Opt on DE]	+125

Mileage Category: B

Though the Mirage sedan has been discontinued to make room for the all-new Lancer sedan, Mitsubishi will continue to offer the Mirage coupe. Only a few minor changes -- a new audio faceplate, an emergency inside-trunk release and a new chrome badge -- are in store this year.

2001
Mileage Category: B

All 2001 Mirages now have tether anchors for child seats and meet LEV standards. A power sunroof is now available with the coupe's sport package. Sedan buyers can choose from the LS or the new base ES trim model that replaces the DE model. Nothing else has changed but the designation -- John Mellencamp? John Cougar? John Cougar Mellencamp?

Body Styles	TMV Pricing		
	Trade	Private	Dealer
2 Dr DE Cpe	3577	4670	5679
2 Dr LS Cpe	4080	5326	6476

Body Styles	TMV Pricing		
	Trade	Private	Dealer
4 Dr ES Sdn	3980	5195	6317
4 Dr LS Sdn	4033	5265	6403

Options	Price
Air Conditioning [Opt on DE]	+373
Aluminum/Alloy Wheels [Opt on LS]	+170
AM/FM/CD Audio System [Opt on DE]	+169

Options	Price
Automatic 4-Speed Transmission	+339
Power Moonroof [Opt on LS]	+339

2000
Mileage Category: B

The DE Sedan now comes with the more powerful 1.8-liter engine in place of last year's base 1.5-liter power plant. All DE models (sedans and coupes) get a host of luxury items and larger brakes as standard equipment. The LS Sedan also gets a few more standard goodies for 2000.

Body Styles	TMV Pricing		
	Trade	Private	Dealer
2 Dr DE Cpe	2641	3557	4455
2 Dr LS Cpe	3079	4147	5194

Body Styles	TMV Pricing		
	Trade	Private	Dealer
4 Dr DE Sdn	2951	3975	4978
4 Dr LS Sdn	3552	4784	5991

Options	Price
Air Conditioning [Opt on DE Cpe]	+316
Aluminum/Alloy Wheels [Opt on DE Sdn,LS]	+144
AM/FM/Cassette Audio System	+126

Options	Price
AM/FM/CD Audio System [Opt on DE Cpe]	+143
Automatic 4-Speed Transmission [Opt on DE,LS]	+273

For the latest vehicle information, visit www.edmunds.com

Mirage

1999

Body Styles	TMV Pricing		
	Trade	Private	Dealer
2 Dr DE Cpe	1971	2724	3507
2 Dr LS Cpe	2567	3547	4568

Options	Price
Air Conditioning [Std on LS Cpe]	+270
Aluminum/Alloy Wheels [Std on Cpe]	+123
AM/FM/CD Audio System [Std on LS Cpe]	+122

Body Styles	TMV Pricing		
	Trade	Private	Dealer
4 Dr DE Sdn	2180	3013	3879
4 Dr LS Sdn	2389	3302	4252

Options	Price
Antilock Brakes	+232
Automatic 4-Speed Transmission	+233
Power Moonroof	+243

Mileage Category: B

A new rear deck lid and taillamps, new seat fabric and some different exterior colors premier on the Mirage. The LS trim level also gets a few interior enhancements.

1998

Body Styles	TMV Pricing		
	Trade	Private	Dealer
2 Dr DE Cpe	1520	2176	2915
2 Dr LS Cpe	2001	2864	3837

Options	Price
Air Conditioning [Opt on DE,Sdn]	+233
Antilock Brakes	+200

Body Styles	TMV Pricing		
	Trade	Private	Dealer
4 Dr DE Sdn	1734	2481	3324
4 Dr LS Sdn	1920	2748	3682

Options	Price
Automatic 4-Speed Transmission	+180
Power Moonroof	+210

Mileage Category: B

Some new colors to choose from and a new heavy-duty starter and battery make the Mirage more reliable.

1997

Body Styles	TMV Pricing		
	Trade	Private	Dealer
2 Dr DE Cpe	1208	1796	2514
2 Dr LS Cpe	1571	2335	3268

Options	Price
Air Conditioning	+212
Antilock Brakes	+182

Body Styles	TMV Pricing		
	Trade	Private	Dealer
4 Dr DE Sdn	1414	2102	2943
4 Dr LS Sdn	1547	2300	3220

Options	Price
Automatic 4-Speed Transmission	+171
Power Moonroof	+176

Mileage Category: B

The Mirage is totally redesigned for 1997, sharing little with the model it replaces. Mitsubishi claims that interior size has been increased and that NVH have been reduced.

1996

Body Styles	TMV Pricing		
	Trade	Private	Dealer
2 Dr LS Cpe	1391	2071	3011
2 Dr S Cpe	1048	1561	2269
4 Dr S Sdn	1208	1799	2615

Options	Price
Automatic 4-Speed Transmission	+136
Air Conditioning	+181

Mileage Category: B

Four colors debut, and the Preferred Equipment Packages are revised a bit.

1995

Body Styles	TMV Pricing		
	Trade	Private	Dealer
2 Dr ES Cpe	967	1449	2253
2 Dr LS Cpe	991	1486	2310
2 Dr S Cpe	818	1226	1905

Body Styles	TMV Pricing		
	Trade	Private	Dealer
4 Dr ES Sdn	1065	1597	2483
4 Dr S Sdn	989	1483	2306

Options	Price
Air Conditioning	+145
Automatic 3-Speed Transmission [Opt on Cpe]	+89
Automatic 4-Speed Transmission	+109

Mileage Category: B

The often changing Mitsubishi Mirage is once again revised, this time with dual airbags. LS versions get bigger alloy wheels.

Mitsubishi
Mirage/Montero

1994

Mileage Category: B

The Mirage finally gains a standard driver airbag, but the LS loses its optional antilock brakes. The LS Coupe gets the 1.8-liter engine that was formerly available only on the LS and ES sedans. S and ES coupes get power steering added to their standard equipment lists, and LS sedans get alloy wheels.

Body Styles	TMV Pricing		
	Trade	Private	Dealer
2 Dr ES Cpe	739	1180	1914
2 Dr LS Cpe	742	1185	1922
2 Dr S Cpe	646	1030	1671

Body Styles	TMV Pricing		
	Trade	Private	Dealer
4 Dr ES Sdn	841	1342	2177
4 Dr LS Sdn	1051	1677	2721
4 Dr S Sdn	811	1295	2101

Options	Price
Air Conditioning	+131
Automatic 3-Speed Transmission	+80

Options	Price
Automatic 4-Speed Transmission [Opt on ES,Cpe]	+98
Compact Disc Changer	+89

Mitsubishi
Montero

2003

Body Styles	TMV Pricing		
	Trade	Private	Dealer
4 Dr Limited 4WD SUV	20899	22284	24593
4 Dr XLS 4WD SUV	18219	19427	21439

Options	Price
Automatic Climate Control [Opt on Limited]	+138
Infinity Audio System [Opt on XLS]	+150
Leather Seats [Opt on XLS]	+479

Options	Price
Power Moonroof [Opt on XLS]	+476
Power Passenger Seat [Opt on Limited]	+162
Air Conditioning - Front and Rear	+344

Mileage Category: M

A new grille, front fascia and headlights, designed to provide a "greater sense of luxury," as well as smoother body cladding and dechromed taillights update the Montero. A bigger (3.8 liter) V6 adds some much-needed power to this 4,700-pound SUV.

2002

Mileage Category: M

For 2002, Montero has several new features and refinements to greater enhance its market position. Montero Limited has new color-keyed exterior features, and both Limited and XLS now have a spare tire cover that matches the body color (except with Munich Silver).

Body Styles	TMV Pricing		
	Trade	Private	Dealer
4 Dr Limited 4WD SUV	17093	18461	20742

Body Styles	TMV Pricing		
	Trade	Private	Dealer
4 Dr XLS 4WD SUV	15028	16231	18236

Options	Price
Air Conditioning - Front and Rear	+361
Infinity Audio System [Opt on XLS]	+120
Leather Seats [Opt on XLS]	+385

Options	Price
Limited Slip Differential [Opt on XLS]	+120
Power Moonroof [Opt on XLS]	+382
Power Passenger Seat [Opt on Limited]	+130

2001

Mileage Category: M

The Montero is redesigned for 2001 and features a sculpted body, stiffer frame, improved suspension and more interior room.

Body Styles	TMV Pricing		
	Trade	Private	Dealer
4 Dr Limited 4WD SUV	14948	16873	18650

Body Styles	TMV Pricing		
	Trade	Private	Dealer
4 Dr XLS 4WD SUV	13153	14847	16411

Options	Price
Air Conditioning - Front and Rear	+275

Options	Price
Power Moonroof	+402

2000

Mileage Category: M

The Montero's list of standard features has been lengthened, and a new Endeavor package adds even more luxury items to Mitsubishi's largest SUV.

Body Styles	TMV Pricing		
	Trade	Private	Dealer
4 Dr STD 4WD SUV	10997	12676	14321

Options	Price
Compact Disc Changer	+242
Leather Seats	+431

Options	Price
Power Moonroof	+341

1999

Body Styles	TMV Pricing		
	Trade	Private	Dealer
4 Dr STD 4WD SUV	8953	10472	12053

1999 (cont'd)

Options	Price
AM/FM/CD Audio System	+122
Chrome Wheels	+284
Compact Disc Changer	+207

Options	Price
Leather Seats	+368
Power Moonroof	+291

Mileage Category: M

Nothing changes on the Montero this year, but one less paint color is available.

1998

Mileage Category: M

A revised front bumper and grille, new fenders and new rear quarter panels mark the exterior changes. Inside is a new steering wheel, while the standard equipment list now includes ABS, air conditioning, third-row seats and alloy wheels.

Body Styles	TMV Pricing		
	Trade	Private	Dealer
4 Dr STD 4WD SUV	7897	9381	11054

Options	Price
Chrome Wheels	+162
Compact Disc Changer	+179

Options	Price
Leather Seats	+318
Power Moonroof	+252

1997

Mileage Category: M

The Montero is unchanged for this year.

Body Styles	TMV Pricing		
	Trade	Private	Dealer
4 Dr LS 4WD SUV	5606	6793	8243

Body Styles	TMV Pricing		
	Trade	Private	Dealer
4 Dr SR 4WD SUV	7277	8818	10701

Options	Price
Air Conditioning [Opt on LS]	+217
Antilock Brakes	+182
Chrome Wheels	+223

Options	Price
Compact Disc Changer	+163
Leather Seats [Opt on LS]	+289
Power Moonroof [Opt on LS]	+229

1996

Mileage Category: M

Refinements result in a better SUV this year. A passenger airbag has been installed, optional side steps make it easier to clamber aboard and split-fold second-row seats increase versatility. New colors, new seat fabrics and better audio systems round out the package.

Body Styles	TMV Pricing		
	Trade	Private	Dealer
4 Dr LS 4WD SUV	4198	5185	6547

Body Styles	TMV Pricing		
	Trade	Private	Dealer
4 Dr SR 4WD SUV	5970	7373	9311

Options	Price
Leather Seats	+308
Power Moonroof [Opt on LS]	+180
Power Sunroof	+180
Air Conditioning [Opt on LS]	+185

Options	Price
Antilock Brakes [Opt on LS]	+238
Automatic 4-Speed Transmission [Opt on LS]	+183
Chrome Wheels	+191
Compact Disc Changer	+178

1995

Mileage Category: M

The Montero LS gets a more powerful V6 that offers a 26-horsepower boost over last year's marginal 151-horsepower rating. Towing capacity increases to 5,000 pounds for all models. Tricky electronic shock absorbers return to the Montero SR's standard equipment list, letting drivers choose between soft, medium or hard setting depending on their preferences.

Body Styles	TMV Pricing		
	Trade	Private	Dealer
4 Dr LS 4WD SUV	3296	4183	5661

Body Styles	TMV Pricing		
	Trade	Private	Dealer
4 Dr SR 4WD SUV	4136	5249	7104

Options	Price
AM/FM/Cassette/CD Audio System	+91
Antilock Brakes [Opt on LS]	+125
Automatic 4-Speed Transmission [Opt on LS]	+147
Chrome Wheels	+153

Options	Price
Compact Disc Changer	+111
Leather Seats	+248
Power Sunroof [Opt on LS]	+145

1994

Body Styles	TMV Pricing		
	Trade	Private	Dealer
4 Dr LS 4WD SUV	2465	3232	4511
4 Dr SR 4WD SUV	3246	4257	5941

Mitsubishi
Montero/Montero Sport

1994 (cont'd)
Mileage Category: M

Deciding to go the luxury sport-ute route, Mitsubishi drops its entry-level Monteros. The remaining models are the luxury-oriented LS and sporty SR. A driver airbag is standard on the 1994 Montero. Antilock brakes move from the standard equipment list to the option list of both trucks. CFC-free air conditioning, a third-row bench seat, heated outside mirrors and a leather-wrapped steering wheel become standard equipment. SR models finally receive a gutsier engine to move this scale-tipping SUV around; a 215-horsepower V6 engine is now standard on that model.

Options	Price
Air Conditioning [Opt on LS]	+133
AM/FM/Cassette/CD Audio System	+82
Antilock Brakes [Opt on LS]	+112
Automatic 4-Speed Transmission [Opt on LS]	+132

Options	Price
Chrome Wheels	+138
Compact Disc Changer	+101
Leather Seats	+178
Power Sunroof	+131

Mitsubishi
Montero Sport

2003

Mileage Category: M

Mitsubishi raises the Montero Sport's roof to provide more headroom and ups the wattage (from 100 to 140 watts) on the audio system.

Body Styles	TMV Pricing		
	Trade	Private	Dealer
4 Dr ES 4WD SUV	13721	14691	16308
4 Dr ES SUV	12521	13407	14883
4 Dr LS 4WD SUV	14972	16031	17796
4 Dr LS SUV	13826	14804	16433

Body Styles	TMV Pricing		
	Trade	Private	Dealer
4 Dr Limited 4WD SUV	17778	19035	21131
4 Dr Limited SUV	16954	18153	20151
4 Dr XLS 4WD SUV	16001	17133	19019
4 Dr XLS SUV	14879	15931	17685

Options	Price
Aluminum/Alloy Wheels [Opt on ES]	+162
Infinity Audio System [Opt on XLS]	+165
Keyless Entry System [Opt on ES]	+120
Leather Seats [Opt on XLS]	+553

Options	Price
Limited Slip Differential [Opt on XLS]	+150
Power Moonroof [Opt on XLS]	+509
Side Steps [Opt on ES]	+165

2002
Mileage Category: M

The 2002 Montero Sport receives a few changes and upgrades this year. Four-wheel-drive Montero Sports have a new mode called ALL4 four-wheel drive. This full-time all-wheel-drive mode automatically provides the appropriate traction for most on-road and light off-road situations -- without the driver having to activate anything. Engine choices remain the same, though the 197-horsepower, 3.5-liter V6 is now standard on XLS. In terms of features, there's a new appearance package for Montero Sport ES, and packages for XLS have been revised. Mitsubishi has also changed the seat fabrics and included metallic-faced gauges on LS, XLS and Limited. In case you are wondering, last year's XS "special edition" apparently wasn't special enough and has been discontinued.

Body Styles	TMV Pricing		
	Trade	Private	Dealer
4 Dr ES 4WD SUV	11197	12160	13766
4 Dr ES SUV	9934	10789	12213
4 Dr LS 4WD SUV	12189	13238	14985
4 Dr LS SUV	11256	12224	13837

Body Styles	TMV Pricing		
	Trade	Private	Dealer
4 Dr Limited 4WD SUV	14501	15748	17827
4 Dr Limited SUV	13832	15022	17005
4 Dr XLS 4WD SUV	13042	14164	16033
4 Dr XLS SUV	12116	13158	14895

Options	Price
Aluminum/Alloy Wheels [Opt on ES]	+130
Infinity Audio System [Opt on XLS]	+132
Leather Seats [Opt on XLS]	+445

Options	Price
Limited Slip Differential [Opt on XLS]	+120
Power Moonroof [Opt on XLS]	+409
Side Steps [Opt on ES]	+132

2001
Mileage Category: M

Because the Montero Sport underwent an update last year, this midsize SUV pretty much remains static for 2001. You can now get the base level ES trim in a 4WD configuration, and the XS trim level debuts with the 3.5-liter V6 from the pricey Limited model. A Lower Anchor Tether Child (LATCH) restraint system comes standard, and the light trucks meet LEV standards.

Body Styles	TMV Pricing		
	Trade	Private	Dealer
4 Dr 3.5XS 4WD SUV	11306	12871	14316
4 Dr 3.5XS SUV	10361	11795	13119
4 Dr ES 4WD SUV	9690	11032	12270
4 Dr ES SUV	8604	9795	10895
4 Dr LS 4WD SUV	10502	11956	13298

Body Styles	TMV Pricing		
	Trade	Private	Dealer
4 Dr LS SUV	9766	11119	12367
4 Dr Limited 4WD SUV	12490	14219	15815
4 Dr Limited SUV	11990	13649	15181
4 Dr XLS 4WD SUV	11372	12947	14400
4 Dr XLS SUV	10411	11852	13183

Options	Price
Infinity Audio System [Opt on XLS]	+149
Leather Seats	+423

Options	Price
Power Moonroof [Opt on XLS]	+360

2000
Mileage Category: M

The 2000 Montero Sport receives significant interior and exterior styling updates like a new grille, revised headlights, body-colored bumpers and new center console design, as well as several technical improvements, including a limited-slip differential on XLS and Limited models, and 16-inch alloy wheels.

Body Styles	TMV Pricing		
	Trade	Private	Dealer
4 Dr ES SUV	7049	8162	9253
4 Dr LS 4WD SUV	8438	9771	11077
4 Dr LS SUV	7842	9081	10295
4 Dr Limited 4WD SUV	10922	12647	14338

Body Styles	TMV Pricing		
	Trade	Private	Dealer
4 Dr Limited SUV	9529	11034	12510
4 Dr XLS 4WD SUV	9278	10744	12181
4 Dr XLS SUV	8637	10001	11338

Options	Price
Infinity Audio System [Opt on XLS]	+126
Leather Seats	+359

Options	Price
Power Moonroof [Opt on XLS]	+305
Compact Disc Changer	+215

1999

Body Styles	TMV Pricing		
	Trade	Private	Dealer
4 Dr ES SUV	5418	6319	7256
4 Dr LS 4WD SUV	7235	8437	9689
4 Dr LS SUV	6895	8041	9233
4 Dr Limited 4WD SUV	9645	11248	12916

Body Styles	TMV Pricing		
	Trade	Private	Dealer
4 Dr Limited SUV	8562	9985	11466
4 Dr XLS 4WD SUV	8508	9922	11394
4 Dr XLS SUV	7802	9099	10449

Mileage Category: M

A new Limited model joins the Montero Sport lineup and with it comes a powerful new V6 engine.

Options	Price
Air Conditioning [Opt on ES]	+281
AM/FM/CD Audio System [Opt on LS,XLS]	+122
Automatic 4-Speed Transmission [Opt on LS]	+264

Options	Price
Compact Disc Changer	+184
Power Moonroof [Std on Limited]	+261

1998

Body Styles	TMV Pricing		
	Trade	Private	Dealer
4 Dr ES SUV	4638	5555	6590
4 Dr LS 4WD SUV	6111	7320	8683
4 Dr LS SUV	5610	6719	7970

Body Styles	TMV Pricing		
	Trade	Private	Dealer
4 Dr XLS 4WD SUV	7541	9032	10713
4 Dr XLS SUV	6736	8068	9571

Mileage Category: M

Montero Sports get lots of features added to their option packages, and 4WD models now come with standard ABS.

Options	Price
Air Conditioning [Std on XLS]	+243
Appearance Package [Opt on LS]	+200
Automatic 4-Speed Transmission [Opt on LS 4WD]	+228

Options	Price
Compact Disc Changer	+179
Power Moonroof [Opt on LS]	+226

1997

Body Styles	TMV Pricing		
	Trade	Private	Dealer
4 Dr ES SUV	3725	4536	5527
4 Dr LS 4WD SUV	5201	6334	7718

Body Styles	TMV Pricing		
	Trade	Private	Dealer
4 Dr LS SUV	4828	5879	7164
4 Dr XLS 4WD SUV	6752	8222	10019

Mileage Category: M

This all-new entry from Mitsubishi is poised to steal sales in the ever-growing midsize sport-utility segment. Based on the same floorpan as the full-size Montero, the Montero Sport is shorter in length, lighter in weight and generally more nimble than its big brother.

Options	Price
Compact Disc Changer	+163
Leather Seats [Opt on LS]	+265
Power Moonroof [Opt on LS]	+191

Options	Price
Automatic 4-Speed Transmission [Std on 2WD,XLS]	+193
Air Conditioning [Std on XLS]	+220
Antilock Brakes	+182

Mitsubishi
Outlander
2003

Body Styles	TMV Pricing		
	Trade	Private	Dealer
4 Dr LS AWD SUV	12285	13301	14994
4 Dr LS SUV	11482	12432	14014

Body Styles	TMV Pricing		
	Trade	Private	Dealer
4 Dr XLS AWD SUV	13208	14300	16121
4 Dr XLS SUV	12403	13429	15139

Options	Price
Aluminum/Alloy Wheels [Opt on LS]	+165
Antilock Brakes [Opt on XLS]	+407
Heated Front Seats [Opt on XLS]	+165
Infinity Audio System [Opt on XLS]	+209

Options	Price
Leather Seats [Opt on XLS]	+464
Power Moonroof [Opt on XLS]	+479
Front Side Airbag Restraints [Opt on XLS]	+177

Mileage Category: L

Mitsubishi jumps into the mini-SUV battle with the Outlander, which offers different styling but little else to separate it from the likes of the Subaru Forester or Honda CR-V.

Nissan
200SX/240SX

1998

Body Styles	TMV Pricing		
	Trade	Private	Dealer
2 Dr SE Cpe	4007	4811	5717
2 Dr SE-R Cpe	4612	5536	6579

Options	Price
Air Conditioning [Opt on STD]	+297
AM/FM/CD Audio System	+139
Antilock Brakes	+224

Mileage Category: E

Body Styles	TMV Pricing		
	Trade	Private	Dealer
2 Dr STD Cpe	3305	3968	4715

Options	Price
Automatic 4-Speed Transmission	+238
Power Moonroof [Std on LE]	+148

Exterior enhancements include new headlights, taillights, front and rear bumpers and revised grille. Three new colors are available for 1998.

1997

Mileage Category: E

A spoiler is now standard on all models. An additional exterior color is the only other change for 1997.

Body Styles	TMV Pricing		
	Trade	Private	Dealer
2 Dr SE Cpe	3018	3698	4530
2 Dr SE-R Cpe	3771	4622	5661

Options	Price
Antilock Brakes	+198
Automatic 4-Speed Transmission	+210
Compact Disc Changer	+175
Power Moonroof	+118

Body Styles	TMV Pricing		
	Trade	Private	Dealer
2 Dr STD Cpe	2915	3572	4376

Options	Price
Air Conditioning [Opt on STD]	+262
AM/FM/Cassette Audio System [Opt on STD]	+118
AM/FM/CD Audio System	+123

1996

Mileage Category: E

Body-color door handles and outside mirrors are newly standard on SE and SE-R models.

Body Styles	TMV Pricing		
	Trade	Private	Dealer
2 Dr SE Cpe	2285	2886	3715
2 Dr SE-R Cpe	2925	3694	4757

Options	Price
Air Conditioning [Opt on STD]	+233
Antilock Brakes	+232
Automatic 4-Speed Transmission	+186

Body Styles	TMV Pricing		
	Trade	Private	Dealer
2 Dr STD Cpe	2173	2745	3534

Options	Price
Air Conditioning [Opt on STD]	+233
Antilock Brakes	+232
Automatic 4-Speed Transmission	+186

1995

Mileage Category: E

A Sentra-derived 200SX is introduced to the sporting public. Basically a two-door version of the redesigned Sentra, the 200SX comes equipped with dual airbags. The 200SX has two available power plants, a 1.6-liter four-cylinder that produces 115 horsepower or a 2.0-liter four that is good for 140 ponies.

Body Styles	TMV Pricing		
	Trade	Private	Dealer
2 Dr SE Cpe	1807	2323	3183
2 Dr SE-R Cpe	2159	2776	3804

Options	Price
AM/FM/Cassette Audio System [Opt on STD]	+94
Antilock Brakes	+159
Automatic 4-Speed Transmission	+168

Body Styles	TMV Pricing		
	Trade	Private	Dealer
2 Dr STD Cpe	1758	2260	3097

Options	Price
Power Moonroof	+94
Air Conditioning [Opt on STD]	+210

Nissan
240SX

1998

Body Styles	TMV Pricing		
	Trade	Private	Dealer
2 Dr LE Cpe	5987	7187	8541
2 Dr SE Cpe	5455	6549	7782

Options	Price
Aluminum/Alloy Wheels [Opt on STD]	+116
AM/FM/CD Audio System	+139
Antilock Brakes	+231
Automatic 4-Speed Transmission	+264

Body Styles	TMV Pricing		
	Trade	Private	Dealer
2 Dr STD Cpe	4568	5484	6517

Options	Price
Compact Disc Changer	+166
Power Moonroof [Std on LE]	+267
Air Conditioning [Opt on STD]	+297

Mileage Category: E

No changes to Nissan's sporty coupe.

1997

Mileage Category: E

Extensive exterior changes update the look of the 240SX. A luxury model is introduced midyear.

Body Styles	TMV Pricing		
	Trade	Private	Dealer
2 Dr LE Cpe	4530	5552	6800
2 Dr SE Cpe	4134	5066	6206

Options	Price
Air Conditioning [Opt on STD]	+262
AM/FM/CD Audio System	+123
Antilock Brakes	+203
Automatic 4-Speed Transmission	+233

Body Styles	TMV Pricing		
	Trade	Private	Dealer
2 Dr STD Cpe	3634	4453	5455

Options	Price
Compact Disc Changer	+175
Leather Seats [Opt on SE]	+196
Power Moonroof [Std on LE]	+235

1996

Mileage Category: E

Sporty new fabrics and a new grille are the only changes to the attractive 240SX.

Body Styles	TMV Pricing		
	Trade	Private	Dealer
2 Dr SE Cpe	3133	3957	5096

Options	Price
Air Conditioning [Std on SE]	+232
Antilock Brakes	+258
Automatic 4-Speed Transmission	+207

Body Styles	TMV Pricing		
	Trade	Private	Dealer
2 Dr STD Cpe	3055	3859	4969

Options	Price
Leather Seats	+175
Power Sunroof	+209

1995

Mileage Category: E

Totally redesigned, the 240SX loses its hatchback and convertible body styles. Available as a base or SE model, the 240 uses the same engine as the previous-generation model. Dual airbags are standard on the new 240SX as are side door beams that help the car meet federal side-impact standards.

Body Styles	TMV Pricing		
	Trade	Private	Dealer
2 Dr SE Cpe	2593	3334	4570

Options	Price
Air Conditioning [Std on SE]	+210
Aluminum/Alloy Wheels [Std on SE]	+82
AM/FM/CD Audio System	+99
Antilock Brakes	+233
Automatic 4-Speed Transmission	+187

Body Styles	TMV Pricing		
	Trade	Private	Dealer
2 Dr STD Cpe	2443	3142	4306

Options	Price
Leather Seats	+158
Power Moonroof	+189
Power Sunroof	+189
Special Factory Paint	+84

1994

Mileage Category: E

A convertible body style is the sole offering this year as the coupe is set for a complete redesign.

Body Styles		TMV Pricing		
		Trade	Private	Dealer
2 Dr SE Conv		2061	2722	3824

Options	Price
Air Conditioning	+187

Nissan
300ZX

1996

Body Styles	TMV Pricing		
	Trade	Private	Dealer
2 Dr 2+2 Hbk	9370	10903	13019
2 Dr STD Conv	11152	12976	15494

Options	Price
Automatic 4-Speed Transmission	+209
Leather Seats [Std on Conv]	+256
T-Tops - Glass [Std on 2+2,Turbo]	+335

Body Styles	TMV Pricing		
	Trade	Private	Dealer
2 Dr STD Hbk	9054	10535	12580
2 Dr Turbo Hbk	10423	12128	14482

Mileage Category: F

It's the end of the world as we know it. The final Z-car is produced for 1996.

Nissan
300ZX/350Z/Altima

1995
Mileage Category: F

No changes for the 300ZX.

Body Styles	TMV Pricing		
	Trade	Private	Dealer
2 Dr 2+2 Hbk	7676	8978	11147
2 Dr STD Conv	8996	10522	13065

Options	Price
Automatic 4-Speed Transmission	+189
Leather Seats [Std on Conv]	+231

Body Styles	TMV Pricing		
	Trade	Private	Dealer
2 Dr STD Hbk	7403	8659	10751
2 Dr Turbo Hbk	8470	9907	12301

Options	Price
Special Factory Paint	+84
T-Tops - Glass [Std on 2+2,Turbo]	+303

1994
Mileage Category: F

A passenger airbag is a new safety feature on the 300ZX, which allows the use of manual seatbelts. Remote keyless entry is another new feature for the 300ZX.

Body Styles	TMV Pricing		
	Trade	Private	Dealer
2 Dr 2+2 Hbk	6509	7790	9925
2 Dr STD Conv	7635	9138	11642

Options	Price
AM/FM/Cassette/CD Audio System	+94
Automatic 4-Speed Transmission	+169
Leather Seats [Std on Conv]	+207

Body Styles	TMV Pricing		
	Trade	Private	Dealer
2 Dr STD Hbk	6262	7495	9549
2 Dr Turbo Hbk	7007	8386	10685

Options	Price
Special Factory Paint	+75
T-Tops - Glass [Opt on STD]	+270

Nissan
350Z
2003

Mileage Category: F

Nissan's premier sports car has been resurrected after a six-year absence. Possessing excellent handling and power, the 350Z comes with a price tag that is thousands less than the competition's.

Body Styles	TMV Pricing		
	Trade	Private	Dealer
2 Dr Enthusiast Hbk	21793	23037	25110
2 Dr Performance Hbk	23437	24775	27004
2 Dr STD Hbk	20299	21457	23388

Options	Price
Automatic 5-Speed Transmission [Opt on Enthusiast,Touring]	+670
Navigation System [Opt on Performance,Touring, Track]	+1380
Front Side Airbag Restraints	+152

Body Styles	TMV Pricing		
	Trade	Private	Dealer
2 Dr Touring Hbk	25511	26967	29394
2 Dr Track Hbk	26191	27686	30177

Options	Price
18 Inch Wheels - Chrome	+1145
Front Head Airbag Restraints	+242

Nissan
Altima
2003

Mileage Category: D

After last year's debut to critical acclaim, Nissan's midsize sedan receives minor changes for 2003. Two new exterior colors, Sonoma Sunset and Crystal Blue add pizzazz to the wardrobe. There's a new charcoal seat fabric, padded cloth front center armrest cover (genuine leather on leather-equipped vehicles) and bright titanium interior accent colors for all models to spruce up the interior. The 2.5 SL receives a standard automatic transmission, heated front seats, heated outside mirrors and simulated wood trim. For the 3.5 SE, there is a Sport Package, which includes a sunroof and spoiler, and a Sport Package Plus, which includes sunroof, spoiler, Bose audio system and HID headlights. The 3.5 SE Leather Package now includes a Bose audio system, sunroof and heated seats, while the Leather Sport Package adds a spoiler and xenon headlights. Finally, a new 3.5 SE Premium Leather Package sports all of the above plus throws in fake wood to boot. How can you go wrong?

Body Styles	TMV Pricing		
	Trade	Private	Dealer
4 Dr 2.5 S Sdn	12649	13587	15150
4 Dr 2.5 SL Sdn	16072	17264	19250

Options	Price
Alarm System [Opt on S]	+117
Aluminum/Alloy Wheels [Opt on S]	+242
Antilock Brakes [Opt on S,SL,SE]	+469
Automatic 4-Speed Transmission [Opt on S,SE,STD]	+345
Bose Audio System [Opt on S,SE]	+207
Automatic Climate Control [Opt on 3.5 SE]	+173
Heated Front Seats [Opt on SE]	+190

Body Styles	TMV Pricing		
	Trade	Private	Dealer
4 Dr 2.5 Sdn	12165	13067	14570
4 Dr 3.5 SE Sdn	15831	17005	18961

Options	Price
Leather Seats [Opt on SE]	+587
Power Driver Seat [Opt on S]	+176
Power Moonroof [Opt on S,SL,SE]	+586
Rear Spoiler [Opt on SE]	+275
Front Side Airbag Restraints [Opt on S,SL,SE]	+173
AM/FM/CD Changer Audio System [Opt on S,SE]	+380
Front and Rear Head Airbag Restraints [Opt on S,SL,SE]	+173

2002

Body Styles	TMV Pricing		
	Trade	Private	Dealer
4 Dr 2.5 S Sdn	10680	11595	13120
4 Dr 2.5 SL Sdn	12798	13894	15721

Options	Price
16 Inch Wheels [Opt on 2.5 S]	+210
AM/FM/CD Changer Audio System	+330
Antilock Brakes [Opt on 2.5]	+408
Automatic 4-Speed Transmission	+480
Automatic Climate Control	+150
Bose Audio System	+180
Front and Rear Head Airbag Restraints [Opt on 3.5 SE,S,SL]	+150

Body Styles	TMV Pricing		
	Trade	Private	Dealer
4 Dr 2.5 Sdn	10283	11164	12632
4 Dr 3.5 SE Sdn	13814	14998	16970

Options	Price
Front Side Airbag Restraints	+150
Heated Front Seats	+165
Leather Seats	+510
Power Driver Seat [Opt on 2.5 S]	+153
Power Moonroof	+510
Rear Spoiler	+240

Mileage Category: D

The all-new third-generation 2002 Altima represents a total revision and rethinking of Nissan's midsize sedan -- it brings a level of design and performance that currently does not exist in its class. With a choice of a 240-horsepower, 3.5-liter V6 or 175-horsepower, 2.5-liter four-cylinder and an all-new four-wheel independent suspension, the Altima offers spirit with state-of-the-art technology. An aggressive new exterior design with increases in all major dimensions and a driver-oriented interior with myriad convenience and luxury features set the Altima apart in the highly competitive sedan marketplace.

2001

Body Styles	TMV Pricing		
	Trade	Private	Dealer
4 Dr GLE Sdn	8986	10392	11690
4 Dr GXE Sdn	7369	8522	9587

Options	Price
Air Conditioning [Opt on GXE,XE]	+266
AM/FM/Cassette/CD Audio System [Opt on GXE]	+212
AM/FM/Cassette/CD Changer Audio System [Opt on GLE]	+212
AM/FM/CD Audio System	+141
Antilock Brakes	+362
Automatic 4-Speed Transmission [Std on GLE]	+425
Compact Disc Changer	+233

Body Styles	TMV Pricing		
	Trade	Private	Dealer
4 Dr SE Sdn	8266	9560	10754
4 Dr XE Sdn	6850	7922	8911

Options	Price
Cruise Control [Std on GLE,SE]	+132
Front Side Airbag Restraints [Std on GLE]	+132
Leather Seats [Opt on SE]	+691
Power Driver Seat [Opt on SE]	+141
Power Moonroof	+452
Rear Spoiler [Std on SE]	+180

Mileage Category: C

GXE is available with a new Limited Edition package, which includes goodies like an eight-way power driver seat, remote keyless entry, floor mats, special badging and a security system.

2000

Body Styles	TMV Pricing		
	Trade	Private	Dealer
4 Dr GLE Sdn	7281	8564	9822
4 Dr GXE Sdn	6007	7066	8104

Options	Price
Air Conditioning [Std on GLE,SE]	+238
Aluminum/Alloy Wheels [Opt on GXE]	+284
AM/FM/Cassette/CD Audio System [Opt on GXE]	+131
AM/FM/CD Audio System	+126
Antilock Brakes	+323
Automatic 4-Speed Transmission [Std on GLE]	+380

Body Styles	TMV Pricing		
	Trade	Private	Dealer
4 Dr SE Sdn	6720	7905	9066
4 Dr XE Sdn	5449	6410	7351

Options	Price
Cruise Control [Std on GLE,SE]	+118
Front Side Airbag Restraints [Std on GLE]	+119
Leather Seats [Opt on SE]	+473
Power Driver Seat [Opt on SE]	+126
Power Moonroof	+404
Rear Spoiler [Std on SE]	+195

Mileage Category: C

For 2000 Altimas receive fresh ront and rear styling tweaks, comfort and convenience enhancements, engine refinements and a revised suspension.

1999

Body Styles	TMV Pricing		
	Trade	Private	Dealer
4 Dr GLE Sdn	5893	7119	8395
4 Dr GXE Sdn	4935	5962	7031
4 Dr SE Limited Sdn	5819	7029	8289

Options	Price
Air Conditioning [Opt on GXE]	+179
Aluminum/Alloy Wheels [Opt on GXE]	+215
Antilock Brakes	+271
Automatic 4-Speed Transmission [Std on GLE]	+287

Body Styles	TMV Pricing		
	Trade	Private	Dealer
4 Dr SE Sdn	5480	6620	7806
4 Dr XE Sdn	4357	5264	6207

Options	Price
Leather Seats [Std on GLE]	+358
Power Moonroof	+305
Rear Spoiler	+146

Mileage Category: C

All 1999 models get two new exterior colors, improved speakers and a new head unit for the three-in-one stereo combo. The GLE trim level gets alloy wheels added to its standard equipment list, and all alloy wheels now have a bright finish instead of a painted finish. All SE trim levels are now called SE Limited (SE-L) models and come with additional equipment.

Nissan
Altima

1998

Mileage Category: C

Altima is totally, and unnecessarily, redesigned for 1998. The Altima's new look is more wedge-shaped, with a trunk that looks like it has met the business end of a band saw. Standard equipment is up, including a CD player on every model except the XE.

Body Styles	TMV Pricing		
	Trade	Private	Dealer
4 Dr GLE Sdn	5141	6333	7678
4 Dr GXE Sdn	4079	5025	6092

Options	Price
Air Conditioning [Opt on XE]	+149
Antilock Brakes	+224
Automatic 4-Speed Transmission [Std on GLE]	+238

Body Styles	TMV Pricing		
	Trade	Private	Dealer
4 Dr SE Sdn	4490	5532	6706
4 Dr XE Sdn	3822	4708	5708

Options	Price
Leather Seats [Opt on SE]	+296
Power Moonroof	+252
Rear Spoiler [Std on SE]	+121

1997

Mileage Category: C

The 1997 models are virtually identical to 1996 models, except for the addition of new emissions equipment.

Body Styles	TMV Pricing		
	Trade	Private	Dealer
4 Dr GLE Sdn	4281	5488	6964
4 Dr GLE Sdn (1997.5)	4131	5297	6721

Options	Price
Air Conditioning [Opt on GXE,XE]	+131
AM/FM/CD Audio System	+123
Antilock Brakes	+198
Automatic 4-Speed Transmission [Std on GLE]	+210

Body Styles	TMV Pricing		
	Trade	Private	Dealer
4 Dr XE Sdn	2977	3816	4842
4 Dr XE Sdn (1997.5)	3089	3960	5025

Options	Price
Compact Disc Changer	+175
Leather Seats [Std on GLE]	+261
Power Moonroof [Std on GLE]	+222

1996

Mileage Category: C

New wheel covers, power lock logic and fresh GXE upholstery update this hot-selling sedan.

Body Styles	TMV Pricing		
	Trade	Private	Dealer
4 Dr GLE Sdn	2762	3705	5008
4 Dr GXE Sdn	2291	3073	4154
4 Dr SE Sdn	2574	3453	4667
4 Dr XE Sdn	2134	2863	3869

Options	Price
Air Conditioning [Opt on GXE,XE]	+116
Antilock Brakes	+176
Automatic 4-Speed Transmission [Std on GLE]	+193

Body Styles	TMV Pricing		
	Trade	Private	Dealer
4 Dr GLE Sdn	2762	3705	5008
4 Dr GXE Sdn	2291	3073	4154
4 Dr SE Sdn	2574	3453	4667
4 Dr XE Sdn	2134	2863	3869

Options	Price
Leather Seats	+232
Power Moonroof	+198
Power Sunroof [Std on SE]	+198

1995

Mileage Category: C

Minor exterior tweaks to the grille, taillights and wheels are the only changes for this attractive compact from Tennessee.

Body Styles	TMV Pricing		
	Trade	Private	Dealer
4 Dr GLE Sdn	2207	3043	4435
4 Dr GXE Sdn	1806	2490	3629

Options	Price
Air Conditioning [Opt on GXE,XE]	+105
AM/FM/CD Audio System	+99
Antilock Brakes	+159
Automatic 4-Speed Transmission [Std on GLE]	+168

Body Styles	TMV Pricing		
	Trade	Private	Dealer
4 Dr SE Sdn	2094	2886	4207
4 Dr XE Sdn	1577	2174	3169

Options	Price
Compact Disc Changer	+141
Leather Seats	+210
Power Moonroof [Opt on GXE]	+179

1994

Mileage Category: C

A passenger-side airbag is added to this hot-selling Tennessee-built compact. SE models gain a standard sunroof and GLEs have it as an available option.

Body Styles	TMV Pricing		
	Trade	Private	Dealer
4 Dr GLE Sdn	1727	2545	3907
4 Dr GXE Sdn	1271	1872	2874

Options	Price
Leather Seats	+187
Power Moonroof [Opt on GXE]	+165
Premium Audio System [Opt on GLE]	+94
Air Conditioning [Std on GLE,SE]	+94

Body Styles	TMV Pricing		
	Trade	Private	Dealer
4 Dr SE Sdn	1600	2358	3620
4 Dr XE Sdn	1221	1799	2761

Options	Price
AM/FM/CD Audio System [Opt on GXE]	+88
Antilock Brakes	+142
Automatic 4-Speed Transmission [Std on GLE]	+150
Compact Disc Changer	+126

For the latest vehicle information, visit www.edmunds.com

2003

Body Styles	TMV Pricing		
	Trade	Private	Dealer
2 Dr SC S/C 4WD Ext Cab SB	15219	16485	18594
2 Dr SC S/C Ext Cab SB	12772	13834	15605
2 Dr SE 4WD Ext Cab SB	14300	15490	17472
2 Dr SE Desert Runner Ext Cab SB	12593	13640	15386
2 Dr STD Ext Cab SB	8171	8851	9983
2 Dr SVE S/C 4WD Ext Cab SB	13751	14895	16801
2 Dr XE 4WD Ext Cab SB	12068	13072	14745
2 Dr XE Desert Runner Ext Cab SB	10414	11280	12724
2 Dr XE Ext Cab SB	9842	10661	12025
4 Dr SC S/C 4WD Crew Cab LB	16636	18020	20326
4 Dr SC S/C 4WD Crew Cab SB	16568	17946	20243
4 Dr SC S/C Crew Cab LB	15103	16359	18453

Body Styles	TMV Pricing		
	Trade	Private	Dealer
4 Dr SC S/C Crew Cab SB	14756	15983	18029
4 Dr SE 4WD Crew Cab LB	15731	17039	19220
4 Dr SE 4WD Crew Cab SB	15624	16923	19089
4 Dr SE Crew Cab LB	14142	15318	17279
4 Dr SE Crew Cab SB	13905	15062	16989
4 Dr SVE S/C 4WD Crew Cab LB	15550	16843	18999
4 Dr SVE S/C 4WD Crew Cab SB	15169	16431	18533
4 Dr XE 4WD Crew Cab LB	13809	14958	16872
4 Dr XE 4WD Crew Cab SB	13254	14356	16193
4 Dr XE Crew Cab LB	12152	13163	14847
4 Dr XE Crew Cab SB	11974	12970	14630

Options	Price
Air Conditioning [Opt on STD,XE]	+449
Aluminum/Alloy Wheels [Opt on XE]	+173
AM/FM/CD Audio System [Opt on STD,XE]	+169
Automatic 4-Speed Transmission [Opt on SC,SVE,XE]	+725
Automatic Stability Control [Opt on SE]	+293
Leather Seats [Opt on SC,SE]	+552

Options	Price
Power Door Locks [Opt on XE]	+131
Power Windows [Opt on XE]	+173
Side Steps [Opt on XE]	+179
Tilt Steering Wheel [Opt on XE]	+128
AM/FM/CD Changer Audio System [Opt on XE]	+207
Rockford Fosgate Audio System [Opt on SC]	+345

Mileage Category: J

Nissan's compact pickup rolls into 2003 with many new enhancements. Most interesting is a power-operated retractable top. The "Open Sky" top -- essentially a giant sunroof -- is optional on Crew Cab models. For safety, Nissan has added standard dual-stage front airbags for Crew Cabs, standard LATCH child seat anchors on King Cabs and Crew cabs, an optional stability control system and an optional tire pressure monitoring system. Other changes for 2003 include 10 more horsepower for normally aspirated V6 models, a driver seat-height adjuster and standard Electronic Brakeforce Distribution (EBD). King Cabs now have standard ABS, a new storage bin and a new first aid kit (V6 only).

2002

Body Styles	TMV Pricing		
	Trade	Private	Dealer
2 Dr SC S/C 4WD Ext Cab SB	12514	13709	15701
2 Dr SC S/C Ext Cab SB	11164	12230	14007
2 Dr SE 4WD Ext Cab SB	11940	13080	14981
2 Dr SE Desert Runner Ext Cab SB	10999	12049	13800
2 Dr STD Ext Cab SB	7236	7927	9079
2 Dr SVE S/C 4WD Ext Cab SB	12099	13254	15180
2 Dr XE 4WD Ext Cab SB	10656	11674	13370
2 Dr XE Desert Runner Ext Cab SB	9219	10100	11567
2 Dr XE Ext Cab SB	7914	8670	9929
4 Dr SC S/C 4WD Crew Cab LB	14494	15878	18185
4 Dr SC S/C 4WD Crew Cab SB	14478	15861	18165
4 Dr SC S/C Crew Cab LB	13169	14427	16523

Body Styles	TMV Pricing		
	Trade	Private	Dealer
4 Dr SC S/C Crew Cab SB	12872	14101	16150
4 Dr SE 4WD Crew Cab LB	13644	14947	17119
4 Dr SE 4WD Crew Cab SB	13324	14596	16717
4 Dr SE Crew Cab LB	12343	13522	15486
4 Dr SE Crew Cab SB	12036	13185	15101
4 Dr SVE S/C 4WD Crew Cab LB	13560	14855	17013
4 Dr SVE S/C 4WD Crew Cab SB	13227	14490	16595
4 Dr XE 4WD Crew Cab LB	11809	12937	14816
4 Dr XE 4WD Crew Cab SB	11632	12743	14594
4 Dr XE Crew Cab LB	10698	11720	13422
4 Dr XE Crew Cab SB	10573	11583	13266

Options	Price
Air Conditioning [Opt on Ext - STD,XE]	+390
Aluminum/Alloy Wheels [Opt on XE Ext]	+150
AM/FM/CD Audio System [Opt on Ext - STD,XE]	+147
AM/FM/CD Changer Audio System [Opt on Crew Cab,Ext Cab]	+210
Automatic 4-Speed Transmission [Opt on SC Ext Cab,STD,XE]	+630
Compact Disc Changer [Opt on Crew Cab]	+300

Options	Price
Leather Seats	+420
Limited Slip Differential [Opt on XE - Crew Cab,Ext Cab]	+120
Moonroof [Opt on SC,SE Ext Cab]	+168
Power Windows [Opt on SE Ext Cab,XE]	+150
Rockford Fosgate Audio System [Opt on Crew Cab]	+150

Mileage Category: J

Nissan continues to enhance its compact pickup line with the introduction of the 2002 Frontier Crew Cab Long Bed, the first compact crew cab pickup to offer a full-size bed. Other improvements for the Frontier lineup include a redesigned instrument panel and console and an available Rockford Fosgate-powered audio system.

2001

Body Styles	TMV Pricing		
	Trade	Private	Dealer
2 Dr SC S/C 4WD Ext Cab SB	10250	11825	13278
2 Dr SC S/C Ext Cab SB	9161	10568	11867
2 Dr SE 4WD Ext Cab SB	10065	11611	13038
2 Dr SE Desert Runner Ext Cab SB	8880	10244	11504
2 Dr XE 4WD Ext Cab SB	9043	10432	11714
2 Dr XE Desert Runner Ext Cab SB	7848	9053	10166
2 Dr XE Ext Cab SB	6722	7755	8708

Body Styles	TMV Pricing		
	Trade	Private	Dealer
2 Dr XE Std Cab SB	5855	6755	7585
4 Dr SC S/C 4WD Crew Cab SB	11162	12877	14460
4 Dr SC S/C Crew Cab SB	10192	11758	13203
4 Dr SE 4WD Crew Cab SB	11073	12774	14345
4 Dr SE Crew Cab SB	9862	11377	12775
4 Dr XE 4WD Crew Cab SB	10050	11594	13019
4 Dr XE Crew Cab SB	8855	10215	11471

2001 (cont'd)

Mileage Category: J

Fresh new styling with a decidedly industrial theme injects some much needed personality into the Frontier for 2001. A supercharged V6, making 210 horsepower and 246 pound-feet of torque (231 lb-ft with a manual tranny), is available on special Desert Runner, King Cab and Crew Cab models, which get black-chrome headlight surrounds. Supercharged Frontiers come standard with 17-inch wheels and a limited-slip differential and can be equipped with leather upholstery, bundled in a package that includes a premium audio system with in-dash CD changer and steering wheel controls, plus a security system. Interiors get new fabrics, gauges and dash trimmings, as well as a new steering wheel. Tailgate locks are standard across the board, and a number of new colors, with names straight out of a J.Crew catalog, are available, like Khaki, Salsa and Denim.

Options	Price
Air Conditioning [Std on Desert Runner SE,SE,Crew Cab]	+455
Aluminum/Alloy Wheels [Std on Desert Runner SE,SE]	+132
AM/FM/Cassette/CD Audio System	+160
AM/FM/CD Audio System	+249
Automatic 4-Speed Transmission	+558

Options	Price
Compact Disc Changer	+297
Leather Seats	+532
Moonroof	+160
Power Windows	+133
Running Boards [Std on SE]	+175

2000

Mileage Category: J

Nissan's pickup line expands to 11 models, including the new Desert Runner and a four-door Frontier Crew Cab.

Body Styles	TMV Pricing		
	Trade	Private	Dealer
2 Dr SE 4WD Ext Cab SB	8555	10054	11524
2 Dr SE Desert Runner Ext Cab SB	7412	8711	9985
2 Dr XE 4WD Ext Cab SB	7176	8434	9667
2 Dr XE Desert Runner Ext Cab SB	6554	7703	8829
2 Dr XE Ext Cab SB	5633	6620	7588
2 Dr XE Std Cab SB	4913	5774	6618
2 Dr XE Std Cab SB	5855	6755	7585

Body Styles	TMV Pricing		
	Trade	Private	Dealer
4 Dr SC S/C 4WD Crew Cab SB	11162	12877	14460
4 Dr SC S/C Crew Cab SB	10192	11758	13203
4 Dr SE 4WD Crew Cab SB	11073	12774	14345
4 Dr SE Crew Cab SB	9862	11377	12775
4 Dr XE 4WD Crew Cab SB	10050	11594	13019
4 Dr XE Crew Cab SB	8855	10215	11471

Options	Price
Power Windows	+119
Running Boards [Std on SE]	+119
Sunroof	+119
Air Conditioning [Std on Desert Runner SE,SE,Crew Cab]	+407
Aluminum/Alloy Wheels [Std on Desert Runner SE,SE]	+118

Options	Price
AM/FM/Cassette/CD Audio System	+143
AM/FM/CD Audio System	+223
Automatic 4-Speed Transmission	+499
Camper/Towing Package	+119
Compact Disc Changer	+265

1999

Mileage Category: J

Two new King Cab models debut with a powerful V6 engine under the hood, and new standard and optional equipment is available.

Body Styles	TMV Pricing		
	Trade	Private	Dealer
2 Dr SE 4WD Ext Cab SB	7352	8763	10231
2 Dr SE Ext Cab SB	5526	6587	7691
2 Dr XE 4WD Ext Cab SB	6274	7478	8731
2 Dr XE 4WD Std Cab SB	5734	6835	7980

Body Styles	TMV Pricing		
	Trade	Private	Dealer
2 Dr XE Ext Cab SB	4753	5665	6615
2 Dr XE Std Cab SB	4270	5090	5943
2 Dr XE V6 4WD Ext Cab SB	6618	7888	9210

Options	Price
Compact Disc Changer	+201
Automatic 4-Speed Transmission	+377

Options	Price
Air Conditioning [Std on SE]	+341
AM/FM/CD Audio System	+168

1998

Mileage Category: J

Nissan introduces an all-new truck for 1998. This model, named the Frontier, is larger than the model it replaces, and has improved interior ergonomics.

Body Styles	TMV Pricing		
	Trade	Private	Dealer
2 Dr SE 4WD Ext Cab SB	6077	7347	8779
2 Dr SE Ext Cab SB	5137	6210	7419
2 Dr STD Std Cab SB	3540	4279	5113
2 Dr XE 4WD Ext Cab SB	5442	6579	7861

Body Styles	TMV Pricing		
	Trade	Private	Dealer
2 Dr XE 4WD Std Cab SB	5034	6086	7272
2 Dr XE Ext Cab SB	4355	5264	6290
2 Dr XE Std Cab SB	3726	4504	5382

Options	Price
AM/FM/CD Audio System [Opt on XE]	+139
Automatic 4-Speed Transmission [Opt on 2WD]	+277
Compact Disc Changer	+166

1997

Mileage Category: J

No changes for 1997.

Body Styles	TMV Pricing		
	Trade	Private	Dealer
2 Dr SE 4WD Ext Cab SB	5114	6271	7684
2 Dr SE Ext Cab SB	4335	5315	6513

Options	Price
AM/FM/CD Audio System	+123
Automatic 4-Speed Transmission [Opt on 2WD]	+262
Compact Disc Changer	+144

Body Styles	TMV Pricing		
	Trade	Private	Dealer
2 Dr XE 4WD Ext Cab SB	4552	5581	6839
2 Dr XE Ext Cab SB	3813	4675	5729

Options	Price
Air Conditioning [Opt on XE]	+262
Aluminum/Alloy Wheels [Opt on XE]	+131

1996

Mileage Category: J

Heading into the last year of the current body style, Nissan adds a driver-side airbag to improve safety. Four-wheel-drive models get a new five-spoke alloy wheel design.

Body Styles	TMV Pricing		
	Trade	Private	Dealer
2 Dr SE 4WD Ext Cab SB	4167	5154	6518
2 Dr SE Ext Cab SB	3627	4486	5673

Options	Price
Air Conditioning [Opt on XE]	+232
Aluminum/Alloy Wheels [Opt on XE]	+116

Body Styles	TMV Pricing		
	Trade	Private	Dealer
2 Dr XE 4WD Ext Cab SB	3875	4794	6062
2 Dr XE Ext Cab SB	3084	3815	4824

Options	Price
Automatic 4-Speed Transmission [Opt on 2WD]	+233

1995

Mileage Category: J

King Cab models received no major changes for the 1995 model year as Nissan is preparing to introduce a completely redesigned truck within the next few years.

Body Styles	TMV Pricing		
	Trade	Private	Dealer
2 Dr SE V6 4WD Ext Cab SB	3576	4448	5902
2 Dr XE 4WD Ext Cab SB	3062	3809	5055
2 Dr XE Ext Cab SB	2277	2833	3759

Options	Price
Air Conditioning [Opt on XE]	+210

Body Styles	TMV Pricing		
	Trade	Private	Dealer
2 Dr XE V6 4WD Ext Cab SB	3439	4278	5677
2 Dr XE V6 Ext Cab SB	2670	3322	4408

Options	Price
Automatic 4-Speed Transmission	+210

1994

Mileage Category: J

A new XE trim level now slots between the standard and XE-V6 models. Compared to the standard model, the XE adds dual outside mirrors, styled steel wheels with trim rings, a sliding rear window and cloth seating. A Value Truck package can be added to XEs that includes air conditioning, an AM/FM cassette stereo, chrome wheels and trim, exterior body graphics, power mirrors, a digital clock and full instrumentation. The XE also offers an optional four-speed automatic transmission. All King Cabs get a refreshed interior with a more carlike dashboard design and a four-spoke steering wheel.

Body Styles	TMV Pricing		
	Trade	Private	Dealer
2 Dr SE V6 4WD Ext Cab SB	2579	3296	4491
2 Dr SE V6 Ext Cab SB	2361	3018	4112
2 Dr XE 4WD Ext Cab SB	2469	3156	4301

Options	Price
Air Conditioning	+187
Aluminum/Alloy Wheels	+94

Body Styles	TMV Pricing		
	Trade	Private	Dealer
2 Dr XE Ext Cab SB	1883	2407	3280
2 Dr XE V6 4WD Ext Cab SB	2541	3248	4426

Options	Price
Automatic 4-Speed Transmission	+188
Sport Package [Opt on SE]	+141

Nissan
Maxima
2003

Body Styles	TMV Pricing		
	Trade	Private	Dealer
4 Dr GLE Sdn	16651	17886	19943
4 Dr GXE Sdn	15450	16595	18504
4 Dr SE Sdn	15961	17145	19117

Mileage Category: D

Since the Maxima was updated last year and is scheduled for a redesign in 2004, there are no major changes in store for the family sedan in 2003. There's a Titanium Edition package available for the SE and side airbags are now standard on GLEs.

Maxima

2003 (cont'd)

Options	Price		Options	Price
Bose Audio System [Opt on SE]	+242		Power Moonroof [Opt on GLE,SE]	+621
Automatic Climate Control [Opt on SE]	+121		Power Passenger Seat [Opt on SE]	+228
Heated Front Seats [Opt on GLE,SE]	+173		Rear Spoiler [Opt on GLE,GXE]	+344
Power Heated Mirrors [Opt on GLE,SE]	+142		Front Side Airbag Restraints [Opt on SE]	+172
Leather Seats [Opt on SE]	+621		Traction Control System [Opt on GLE]	+206
Limited Slip Differential [Opt on SE]	+275		Power Driver Seat w/Memory [Opt on SE]	+142
Navigation System [Opt on GLE,SE]	+1380			

2002

Mileage Category: D

The Maxima receives updates this year that make it less of a family sedan and more of an entry-level luxury sport sedan. Headlining this year's upgrades is a 3.5-liter V6 that produces a stunning 255 horsepower. For maximum performance, sport-tuned SE models now combine this engine with a standard six-speed manual transmission. Other changes include revised exterior styling, additional feature content and an optional GPS navigation system.

Body Styles	TMV Pricing			Body Styles	TMV Pricing		
	Trade	Private	Dealer		Trade	Private	Dealer
4 Dr GLE Sdn	13934	15128	17117	4 Dr SE Sdn	13039	14156	16017
4 Dr GXE Sdn	12979	14091	15944				

Options	Price		Options	Price
Bose Audio System [Std on GLE]	+210		Power Driver Seat w/Memory [Opt on SE]	+123
Compact Disc Changer [Std on GLE]	+300		Power Heated Mirrors	+123
Front Side Airbag Restraints	+150		Power Moonroof	+540
Heated Front Seats	+150		Power Passenger Seat [Std on GLE]	+198
Leather Seats [Std on GLE]	+540		Rear Spoiler	+294
Limited Slip Differential	+240		Traction Control System	+180
Navigation System	+1200			

2001

Mileage Category: D

A 20th Anniversary edition includes the 227-horsepower version of the standard 3.0-liter V6 from the Infiniti I30, as well as goodies like bronze-lensed headlight covers, a body kit, ersatz carbon-fiber interior trim, drilled metal pedals and a number of features normally optional on the SE. This special model also gets an exclusive color: Majestic Blue. A new Meridian package is optional on all Maximas, bundling side-impact airbags and a low washer fluid indicator with heated front seats and side mirrors, as well as special trunk lid trim. Adding optional traction control to the SE or GLE results in a Z Edition Maxima, for some zany reason.

Body Styles	TMV Pricing			Body Styles	TMV Pricing		
	Trade	Private	Dealer		Trade	Private	Dealer
4 Dr GLE Sdn	11959	13612	15137	4 Dr SE 20th Anniv Sdn	12458	14180	15769
4 Dr GXE Sdn	10679	12155	13517	4 Dr SE Sdn	11287	12846	14286

Options	Price		Options	Price
Aluminum/Alloy Wheels [Opt on GXE]	+133		Heated Front Seats	+127
AM/FM/Cassette/CD Audio System [Opt on GXE]	+133		Leather Seats [Std on GLE]	+599
Automatic 4-Speed Transmission [Std on GLE]	+266		Power Driver Seat	+133
Bose Audio System [Std on GLE]	+478		Power Moonroof	+478
Chrome Wheels	+659		Power Passenger Seat [Opt on SE]	+175
Compact Disc Changer	+244		Rear Spoiler [Std on SE]	+255
Front Side Airbag Restraints	+133		Traction Control System	+159

2000

Mileage Category: D

The Maxima has been (controversially) redesigned, providing more power, more room and more amenities to the luxury/performance sedan buyer. Key among the improvements is 222 horsepower from the standard V6, a boost in rear-seat legroom and an available 200-watt Bose audio system.

Body Styles	TMV Pricing			Body Styles	TMV Pricing		
	Trade	Private	Dealer		Trade	Private	Dealer
4 Dr GLE Sdn	10712	12405	14064	4 Dr SE Sdn	9975	11551	13096
4 Dr GXE Sdn	9159	10606	12025				

Options	Price		Options	Price
Aluminum/Alloy Wheels [Opt on GXE]	+297		Leather Seats [Std on GLE]	+536
AM/FM/Cassette/CD Audio System [Opt on GXE]	+190		Power Driver Seat	+119
Automatic 4-Speed Transmission [Std on GLE]	+475		Power Moonroof	+428
Bose Audio System [Std on GLE]	+428		Power Passenger Seat [Opt on SE]	+121
Compact Disc Changer	+284		Rear Spoiler [Std on SE]	+227
Front Side Airbag Restraints	+119		Traction Control System	+142
Heated Front Seats	+119			

1999

Mileage Category: D

Traction control is now available on models with automatic transmissions and, in addition to minor interior enhancements, four new colors debut. The SE trim level has been renamed SE-Limited (SE-L) and offers new standard features.

Body Styles	TMV Pricing			Body Styles	TMV Pricing		
	Trade	Private	Dealer		Trade	Private	Dealer
4 Dr GLE Sdn	8888	10466	12108	4 Dr SE Limited Sdn	8085	9520	11014
4 Dr GXE Sdn	7018	8264	9560	4 Dr SE Sdn	8041	9468	10954

1999 (cont'd)

Options	Price
Aluminum/Alloy Wheels [Opt on GXE]	+224
AM/FM/Cassette/CD Audio System [Opt on GXE]	+143
Antilock Brakes	+271
Automatic 4-Speed Transmission [Std on GLE]	+358
Bose Audio System [Std on GLE]	+323

Options	Price
Compact Disc Changer	+215
Leather Seats [Std on GLE]	+404
Power Moonroof	+323
Power Passenger Seat [Opt on SE]	+130
Rear Spoiler [Opt on GLE,GXE]	+172

1998

Body Styles	TMV Pricing		
	Trade	Private	Dealer
4 Dr GLE Sdn	7200	8636	10255
4 Dr GXE Sdn	5916	7096	8426

Body Styles	TMV Pricing		
	Trade	Private	Dealer
4 Dr SE Sdn	6630	7952	9443

Mileage Category: D

Side-impact airbags are added to the optional equipment lists of the SE and GLE models. Sterling Mist is a new color choice for this sporty sedan.

Options	Price
Automatic 4-Speed Transmission [Std on GLE]	+297
Bose Audio System	+267
Compact Disc Changer	+178
Leather Seats [Opt on SE]	+334
Power Moonroof	+267

Options	Price
Rear Spoiler [Std on SE]	+127
Antilock Brakes	+224
Aluminum/Alloy Wheels [Opt on GXE]	+185
AM/FM/Cassette/CD Audio System [Opt on GXE]	+118

1997

Body Styles	TMV Pricing		
	Trade	Private	Dealer
4 Dr GLE Sdn	5927	7309	8998
4 Dr GXE Sdn	4741	5847	7198

Body Styles	TMV Pricing		
	Trade	Private	Dealer
4 Dr SE Sdn	5136	6334	7798

Mileage Category: D

The Nissan Maxima gets a new grille, headlights, bumpers and taillights. New alloy wheels and foglights on the SE, new wheel covers on the GXE and new aluminum wheels on the GLE round out the changes.

Options	Price
Aluminum/Alloy Wheels [Opt on GXE]	+163
Antilock Brakes	+198
Automatic 4-Speed Transmission [Std on GLE]	+314
Bose Audio System	+235

Options	Price
Compact Disc Changer	+157
Leather Seats [Opt on SE]	+294
Power Moonroof	+235

1996

Body Styles	TMV Pricing		
	Trade	Private	Dealer
4 Dr GLE Sdn	5039	6231	7878
4 Dr GXE Sdn	3876	4793	6060

Body Styles	TMV Pricing		
	Trade	Private	Dealer
4 Dr SE Sdn	4264	5273	6667

Mileage Category: D

All new for 1995, the excellent Maxima receives few changes for 1996. A four-way power passenger seat is available, a new center console cupholder will hold a Big Gulp and two new colors grace the Maxima's decidedly dull flanks. Taillights are as ugly as ever.

Options	Price
Aluminum/Alloy Wheels [Opt on GXE]	+145
Antilock Brakes	+176
Automatic 4-Speed Transmission [Std on GLE]	+233
Bose Audio System	+186

Options	Price
Compact Disc Changer	+139
Leather Seats [Opt on SE]	+261
Power Moonroof	+209

1995

Body Styles	TMV Pricing		
	Trade	Private	Dealer
4 Dr GLE Sdn	4071	5007	6566
4 Dr GXE Sdn	3411	4195	5502

Body Styles	TMV Pricing		
	Trade	Private	Dealer
4 Dr SE Sdn	3683	4529	5939

Mileage Category: D

Wow, what a beauty. The redesigned Maxima bows with an aerodynamic shape and a lengthened wheelbase. The new Maxima is available as a budget-minded GXE, sporty SE or luxurious GLE. All Maximas get the 190-horsepower engine previously exclusive to the SE.

Options	Price
Power Moonroof	+189
Rear Spoiler [Std on SE]	+90
Aluminum/Alloy Wheels [Opt on GXE]	+131
AM/FM/Cassette/CD Audio System [Std on GLE]	+84

Options	Price
Antilock Brakes	+159
Automatic 4-Speed Transmission [Std on GLE]	+210
Bose Audio System [Std on GLE]	+168
Leather Seats [Std on GLE]	+236

Nissan
Maxima/Murano/Pathfinder

1994

Body Styles	TMV Pricing			Body Styles	TMV Pricing		
	Trade	Private	Dealer		Trade	Private	Dealer
4 Dr GXE Sdn	2768	3479	4664	4 Dr SE Sdn	2878	3617	4849

Options	Price	Options	Price
Antilock Brakes	+142	Leather Seats	+211
Automatic 4-Speed Transmission [Opt on SE]	+188	Power Sunroof	+122
Bose Audio System [Std on SE]	+150		

Mileage Category: D

No changes for the 1994 Maxima.

Nissan
Murano

2003

Body Styles	TMV Pricing			Body Styles	TMV Pricing		
	Trade	Private	Dealer		Trade	Private	Dealer
4 Dr SE AWD SUV	23741	25135	27458	4 Dr SL AWD SUV	23130	24488	26751
4 Dr SE SUV	22519	23842	26046	4 Dr SL SUV	21910	23197	25341

Options	Price	Options	Price
Automatic Stability Control	+293	Power Passenger Seat	+176
Bose Audio System	+242	Traction Control System	+173
Camper/Towing Package	+365	AM/FM/Cassette/CD Changer Audio System	+155
Heated Front Seats	+242	Power Adjustable Foot Pedals	+173
Leather Seats	+587	18 Inch Wheels - Chrome	+828
Navigation System	+1380	Power Driver Seat w/Memory	+142
Power Moonroof	+621		

Mileage Category: M

Not satisfied with the current crop of crossover SUVs? Nissan rolls out the newest car-based SUV, the Murano. It boasts a powerful V6 engine, distinct styling.

Nissan
Pathfinder

2003

Body Styles	TMV Pricing			Body Styles	TMV Pricing		
	Trade	Private	Dealer		Trade	Private	Dealer
4 Dr LE 4WD SUV	18995	20366	22651	4 Dr SE 4WD SUV	17366	18620	20709
4 Dr LE SUV	18316	19638	21842	4 Dr SE SUV	16613	17812	19811

Options	Price	Options	Price
Automatic Stability Control	+293	Power Passenger Seat [Opt on SE]	+179
Bose Audio System [Opt on SE]	+138	Front Side Airbag Restraints [Opt on SE]	+207
Compact Disc Changer [Opt on SE]	+311	Traction Control System	+173
Heated Front Seats [Opt on SE]	+138	VCR Entertainment System	+897
Leather Seats [Opt on SE]	+621	Satellite Radio System	+275
Power Driver Seat [Opt on SE]	+179	DVD Entertainment System	+1104
Power Moonroof [Opt on SE]	+621		

Mileage Category: M

All 2003 Pathfinders will offer optional satellite radio, with a choice of XM or Sirius services. The LE model receives a standard leather-appointed interior, while SE models feature restyled wheels. Both models also feature a new four-spoke steering wheel and electronic rear-hatch window release. For safety, there is a new Vehicle Dynamic Control Package that bundles Vehicle Dynamic Control (VDC), traction control and a tire-pressure monitoring system. Two items no longer offered are the manual transmission and the optional navigation system. Guess you have to buy a map.

2002

Body Styles	TMV Pricing			Body Styles	TMV Pricing		
	Trade	Private	Dealer		Trade	Private	Dealer
4 Dr LE 4WD SUV	17043	18452	20800	4 Dr SE 4WD SUV	14914	16147	18201
4 Dr LE SUV	15649	16942	19098	4 Dr SE SUV	14355	15542	17519

2002 (cont'd)

Mileage Category: M

The 2002 Nissan Pathfinder receives only minor refinements. These include a new front grille, steering wheel and a revised audio system with new faceplate and faster functioning in-dash six-disc CD changer. The SE trim, now the base Pathfinder since the XE has been dropped, features a new titanium-accented step rail and roof rack with integrated air dam, body-color bumpers and fender flares, new 16-inch aluminum-alloy wheels and new seat cloth. Not to be outdone, the luxurious LE has 17-inch aluminum-alloy wheels as standard equipment this year.

Options	Price	Options	Price
Automatic 4-Speed Transmission [Opt on SE 4WD]	+600	Limited Slip Differential [Opt on LE]	+150
Bose Audio System [Std on LE]	+120	Navigation System	+1200
Compact Disc Changer [Std on LE]	+270	Power Driver Seat	+156
DVD Entertainment System	+960	Power Driver Seat w/Memory [Opt on LE]	+132
Front Side Airbag Restraints	+180	Power Moonroof [Std on LE]	+540
Heated Front Seats [Std on LE]	+120	Power Passenger Seat	+156
Leather Seats	+540	VCR Entertainment System	+780

2001

Mileage Category: M

A long overdue 250-horsepower V6 engine debuts for 2001, making Pathfinder the most powerful SUV in its class. An interior freshening and more standard goodies, as well as snazzy options like an in-dash navigation system and an entertainment system for rear-seat occupants, are new for 2001. Also added to the LE's options list this fall is the handy All-mode automatic 4WD system from the Infiniti QX4.

Body Styles	TMV Pricing			Body Styles	TMV Pricing		
	Trade	Private	Dealer		Trade	Private	Dealer
4 Dr LE 4WD SUV	14930	16824	18573	4 Dr SE SUV	12858	14489	15995
4 Dr LE SUV	13761	15507	17119	4 Dr XE 4WD SUV	13919	15685	17315
4 Dr SE 4WD SUV	13794	15544	17160	4 Dr XE SUV	12877	14510	16018

Options	Price	Options	Price
Automatic 4-Speed Transmission [Opt on SE]	+532	Navigation System	+1063
Compact Disc Changer	+382	Power Driver Seat [Opt on SE]	+120
Front Side Airbag Restraints	+160	Power Moonroof	+478
Leather Seats	+478	Power Passenger Seat [Opt on LE,SE]	+120
Limited Slip Differential	+132		

2000

Mileage Category: M

After a substantial update in the middle of the 1999 model year, the Pathfinder soldiers into the new millennium without change. However, rumor has it that later in 2000 the Pathfinder will get a massive power upgrade.

Body Styles	TMV Pricing			Body Styles	TMV Pricing		
	Trade	Private	Dealer		Trade	Private	Dealer
4 Dr LE 4WD SUV	12497	14227	15923	4 Dr SE SUV	10934	12448	13932
4 Dr LE SUV	11715	13337	14926	4 Dr XE 4WD SUV	11299	12863	14397
4 Dr SE 4WD SUV	11774	13404	15001	4 Dr XE SUV	10414	11856	13269

Options	Price	Options	Price
Automatic 4-Speed Transmission [Opt on SE]	+475	Limited Slip Differential	+118
Compact Disc Changer	+333	Power Door Locks [Opt on XE]	+119
Front Side Airbag Restraints	+143	Power Driver Seat	+147
Heated Front Seats	+143	Power Moonroof	+428
Leather Seats	+428	Power Windows [Opt on XE]	+136

1999

Mileage Category: M

Only the LE trim level sees change in 1999, with new body-color fender flares and SE-style alloy wheels, tires and tubular step rails.

Body Styles	TMV Pricing			Body Styles	TMV Pricing		
	Trade	Private	Dealer		Trade	Private	Dealer
4 Dr LE 4WD SUV	10897	12611	14395	4 Dr SE Limited Wgn (1999.5)	9302	10765	12288
4 Dr LE 4WD Wgn (1999.5)	10350	11978	13673	4 Dr XE 4WD SUV	8823	10211	11656
4 Dr LE SUV	9873	11426	13042	4 Dr XE 4WD Wgn (1999.5)	9587	11095	12664
4 Dr LE Wgn (1999.5)	9607	11118	12691	4 Dr XE SUV	8108	9383	10711
4 Dr SE 4WD SUV	9700	11226	12814	4 Dr XE Wgn (1999.5)	8920	10323	11783
4 Dr SE Limited 4WD Wgn (1999.5)	9782	11321	12922				

Options	Price	Options	Price
AM/FM/Cassette/CD Audio System [Std on LE]	+126	Leather Seats [Opt on LE,SE]	+323
Automatic 4-Speed Transmission [Opt on SE,XE]	+358	Power Moonroof	+323
Bose Audio System [Std on LE]	+161		

1998

Mileage Category: M

The only changes to the 1998 Pathfinder include chrome bumpers for the XE model, the addition of air conditioning to XE and SE standard equipment lists and additions to the XE Sport Package equipment.

Body Styles	TMV Pricing			Body Styles	TMV Pricing		
	Trade	Private	Dealer		Trade	Private	Dealer
4 Dr LE 4WD SUV	8391	9899	11599	4 Dr XE 4WD SUV	6590	7774	9109
4 Dr LE SUV	7779	9176	10752	4 Dr XE SUV	6098	7194	8430
4 Dr SE 4WD SUV	7308	8621	10102				

1998 (cont'd)

Options	Price
Power Moonroof	+267
AM/FM/Cassette Audio System	+116
Automatic 4-Speed Transmission [Std on LE]	+297

Options	Price
Bose Audio System [Opt on SE]	+178
Leather Seats [Opt on SE]	+267

1997

Mileage Category: M

Changes to the 1997 Nissan Pathfinder include storage pockets added at all doors, a new exterior color and an available Bose sound system.

Body Styles	TMV Pricing		
	Trade	Private	Dealer
4 Dr LE 4WD SUV	7587	9055	10849
4 Dr LE SUV	6849	8174	9793
4 Dr SE 4WD SUV	6305	7525	9016

Body Styles	TMV Pricing		
	Trade	Private	Dealer
4 Dr XE 4WD SUV	5661	6756	8094
4 Dr XE SUV	5251	6267	7508

Options	Price
Air Conditioning [Std on LE]	+262
Automatic 4-Speed Transmission [Std on LE]	+262
Bose Audio System [Opt on SE]	+157

Options	Price
Leather Seats [Opt on SE]	+235
Power Moonroof	+235

1996

Mileage Category: M

Outstanding new Pathfinder debuts with dual airbags and great interior styling. Engine output is up, but the Pathfinder is still not going to win any drag races. The new interior is open, airy and much more comfortable than most of its competitors.

Body Styles	TMV Pricing		
	Trade	Private	Dealer
4 Dr LE 4WD SUV	6308	7570	9312
4 Dr LE SUV	5837	7004	8616
4 Dr SE 4WD SUV	5397	6476	7967

Body Styles	TMV Pricing		
	Trade	Private	Dealer
4 Dr XE 4WD SUV	4771	5725	7043
4 Dr XE SUV	4297	5157	6344

Options	Price
Automatic 4-Speed Transmission [Std on LE]	+233
Leather Seats [Opt on SE]	+209

Options	Price
Power Moonroof	+209
Air Conditioning [Std on LE]	+232

1995

Body Styles	TMV Pricing		
	Trade	Private	Dealer
4 Dr LE 4WD SUV	4670	5693	7398
4 Dr LE SUV	4238	5167	6714
4 Dr SE 4WD SUV	4024	4906	6375

Body Styles	TMV Pricing		
	Trade	Private	Dealer
4 Dr XE 4WD SUV	3413	4160	5406
4 Dr XE SUV	3233	3941	5122

Options	Price
Air Conditioning [Std on LE]	+210
Automatic 4-Speed Transmission [Std on LE]	+210

Options	Price
Leather Seats [Opt on SE]	+189

Mileage Category: M

A two-wheel-drive version of Nissan's ancient sport-utility is now available in LE flavor.

1994

Mileage Category: M

The LE model is introduced for the country club crowd. Standard equipment on the LE includes leather upholstery, heated seats, a CD player and a luggage rack. All 1994 Pathfinders sport a redesigned dashboard and instrument panel. SE models get new alloy wheels and a sunroof.

Body Styles	TMV Pricing		
	Trade	Private	Dealer
4 Dr LE 4WD SUV	3557	4461	5968
4 Dr SE 4WD SUV	2967	3721	4978

Body Styles	TMV Pricing		
	Trade	Private	Dealer
4 Dr XE 4WD SUV	2504	3140	4201
4 Dr XE SUV	2407	3019	4039

Options	Price
Air Conditioning [Std on LE]	+187
Automatic 4-Speed Transmission [Std on LE]	+188

Options	Price
Leather Seats [Opt on SE]	+169

Nissan
Pickup
1997

Body Styles	TMV Pricing		
	Trade	Private	Dealer
2 Dr STD Std Cab SB	2803	3437	4212
2 Dr XE 4WD Std Cab SB	3906	4789	5869

Options	Price
Compact Disc Changer	+144
Air Conditioning	+262
Aluminum/Alloy Wheels	+131

Body Styles	TMV Pricing		
	Trade	Private	Dealer
2 Dr XE Std Cab SB	3187	3907	4788

Options	Price
AM/FM/CD Audio System	+123
Automatic 4-Speed Transmission [Opt on XE Std Cab]	+262

Mileage Category: J

The Value Truck package on XE models is now a no-cost option. It includes air conditioning, aluminum-alloy wheels, a tachometer, trip meter and an AM/FM/cassette stereo. All two-wheel-drive models with the Value Truck also get upgraded all-season tires and intermittent wipers. Two new exterior colors -- Autumn Sunburst and Starfire Blue Pearl -- have been added to the color palette.

1996

Body Styles	TMV Pricing		
	Trade	Private	Dealer
2 Dr STD Std Cab SB	2273	2812	3556
2 Dr XE 4WD Std Cab SB	3160	3908	4942

Options	Price
Air Conditioning	+232
Aluminum/Alloy Wheels	+116

Body Styles	TMV Pricing		
	Trade	Private	Dealer
2 Dr XE Std Cab SB	2569	3178	4019

Options	Price
Automatic 4-Speed Transmission [Opt on XE Std Cab]	+233

Mileage Category: J

Nissan adds a driver-side airbag to improve safety. Four-wheel-drive models get a new five-spoke alloy wheel design.

1995

Body Styles	TMV Pricing		
	Trade	Private	Dealer
2 Dr STD Std Cab LB HD	2220	2762	3665
2 Dr STD Std Cab SB	1745	2171	2881

Options	Price
Air Conditioning	+210

Body Styles	TMV Pricing		
	Trade	Private	Dealer
2 Dr XE 4WD Std Cab SB	2697	3356	4453
2 Dr XE Std Cab SB	2086	2595	3444

Options	Price
Automatic 4-Speed Transmission [Opt on XE]	+210

Mileage Category: J

Nissan compact pickups received no major changes for the 1995 model year in anticipation of a completely redesigned truck for 1996.

1994

Body Styles	TMV Pricing		
	Trade	Private	Dealer
2 Dr STD Std Cab SB	1499	1916	2612
2 Dr V6 Std Cab LB	1845	2359	3215

Options	Price
Air Conditioning	+187

Body Styles	TMV Pricing		
	Trade	Private	Dealer
2 Dr XE 4WD Std Cab SB	2185	2793	3807
2 Dr XE Std Cab SB	1785	2282	3109

Options	Price
Automatic 4-Speed Transmission	+188

Mileage Category: J

A new XE trim level now slots between the standard and XE-V6 models. Compared to the standard model, the XE adds dual outside mirrors, styled steel wheels with trim rings, a sliding rear window and cloth seating. A Value Truck package can be added to XEs that includes air conditioning, an AM/FM cassette stereo, chrome wheels and trim, exterior body graphics, power mirrors, a digital clock and full instrumentation. The XE also offers an optional four-speed automatic transmission. All trim levels get a refreshed interior with a more carlike dashboard design and a four-spoke steering wheel.

Nissan
Quest
2002

Body Styles	TMV Pricing		
	Trade	Private	Dealer
4 Dr GLE Pass Van	14436	15692	17784
4 Dr GXE Pass Van	12164	13222	14985
4 Dr SE Pass Van	13034	14168	16057

Mileage Category: P

This is likely the last year for the Quest before it is discontinued. As such, changes for 2002 are minimal. These include revised 16-inch alloy wheel designs for the GXE and SE, new exterior colors and revised option packages.

2002 (cont'd)

Options	Price
Air Conditioning - Front and Rear [Opt on GXE]	+375
AM/FM/CD Audio System [Opt on GXE]	+129
Automatic Dimming Rearview Mirror	+125
Captain Chairs (4) [Opt on GXE]	+450
Child Seat (1) [Opt on GXE]	+138
Heated Front Seats [Std on GLE]	+119
Leather Seats [Std on GLE]	+630

Options	Price
Power Driver Seat [Std on GLE]	+180
Power Moonroof	+510
Power Passenger Seat [Std on GLE]	+180
Running Boards	+324
Two-Tone Paint	+180
VCR Entertainment System	+420

2001

Mileage Category: P

Despite the company's decision to kill the Quest after a short 2002 model run, Nissan imbues the 2001 Quest minivan with a raft of minor improvements. Styling front and rear is freshened, and redesigned alloy wheels debut on all models. The entry-level GXE gains a rear stabilizer bar, while the sporty SE receives acceleration-sensitive strut valving and a strut tower brace. New interior gauges and fabrics spice things up, and a 130-watt Super Sound system is standard on SE and GLE. Luxury GLE models also get an in-dash six-CD changer and a wood 'n' leather steering wheel. An optional overhead family entertainment system replaces the former floor-mounted model, though that rather archaic unit can still be specified for SE and GLE Quests equipped with a sunroof. Front seatbelts now have pre-tensioners for improved occupant protection, and crash test scores are up this year, as well.

Body Styles	TMV Pricing		
	Trade	Private	Dealer
4 Dr GLE Pass Van	12429	14178	15792
4 Dr GXE Pass Van	10382	11842	13190

Body Styles	TMV Pricing		
	Trade	Private	Dealer
4 Dr SE Pass Van	11278	12864	14329

Options	Price
Air Conditioning - Front and Rear [Opt on GXE]	+345
AM/FM/Cassette/CD Audio System [Opt on GXE]	+186
Captain Chairs (2) [Opt on GXE]	+398
Child Seat (1) [Opt on GXE]	+122
Leather Seats [Opt on SE]	+583
Power Driver Seat	+165

Options	Price
Power Moonroof	+452
Power Passenger Seat [Opt on SE]	+175
Running Boards	+281
Two-Tone Paint	+159
VCR Entertainment System	+372

2000

Mileage Category: P

A stabilizer bar is now standard on the GLE model while new titanium-colored accents have been added to the 16-inch SE and 15-inch GXE alloy wheels. The SE gets auto on/off headlights and all Quests now come with a video entertainment system at no extra cost.

Body Styles	TMV Pricing		
	Trade	Private	Dealer
4 Dr GLE Pass Van	10296	11955	13582
4 Dr GXE Pass Van	8705	10108	11483

Body Styles	TMV Pricing		
	Trade	Private	Dealer
4 Dr SE Pass Van	9607	11155	12672

Options	Price
Air Conditioning - Front and Rear [Opt on GXE]	+308
AM/FM/Cassette/CD Audio System [Opt on GXE]	+204
Compact Disc Changer	+284
Leather Seats [Opt on SE]	+521

Options	Price
Power Driver Seat	+145
Power Moonroof	+404
Power Passenger Seat [Opt on SE]	+145
Running Boards	+237

1999

Mileage Category: P

Nissan redesigns its minivan for 1999 and adds a new SE trim level, standard driver-side sliding rear door and a more powerful engine.

Body Styles	TMV Pricing		
	Trade	Private	Dealer
4 Dr GLE Pass Van	8550	10178	11871
4 Dr GXE Pass Van	7361	8762	10220

Body Styles	TMV Pricing		
	Trade	Private	Dealer
4 Dr SE Pass Van	7607	9055	10562

Options	Price
Air Conditioning - Front and Rear [Opt on GXE]	+233
AM/FM/Cassette/CD Audio System	+153
Compact Disc Changer [Std on GLE]	+215
Leather Seats [Std on GLE]	+393

Options	Price
Power Driver Seat	+130
Power Moonroof	+305
Power Passenger Seat [Opt on SE]	+130

1998

Mileage Category: P

No changes to the 1998 Quest.

Body Styles	TMV Pricing		
	Trade	Private	Dealer
3 Dr GXE Pass Van	6349	7783	9399
3 Dr XE Pass Van	5770	7073	8542

Options	Price
Air Conditioning - Front and Rear [Opt on XE]	+215
AM/FM/Cassette/CD Audio System [Opt on XE]	+127
Antilock Brakes [Opt on XE]	+224
Captain Chairs (4) [Opt on XE]	+178

Options	Price
Compact Disc Changer	+178
Leather Seats	+325
Power Moonroof	+252

1997

Body Styles	TMV Pricing		
	Trade	Private	Dealer
3 Dr GXE Pass Van	5198	6606	8327

Options	Price
Power Moonroof	+223
Air Conditioning - Front and Rear [Opt on XE]	+189
Antilock Brakes [Opt on XE]	+198

Body Styles	TMV Pricing		
	Trade	Private	Dealer
3 Dr XE Pass Van	4593	5838	7359

Options	Price
Captain Chairs (4) [Opt on XE]	+157
Compact Disc Changer	+157
Leather Seats	+287

Mileage Category: P

A few new colors are the only changes to the 1997 Quest.

1996

Body Styles	TMV Pricing		
	Trade	Private	Dealer
3 Dr GXE Pass Van	4556	5921	7806

Options	Price
Air Conditioning - Front and Rear [Opt on XE]	+168
Antilock Brakes [Opt on XE]	+176

Body Styles	TMV Pricing		
	Trade	Private	Dealer
3 Dr XE Pass Van	3673	4774	6294

Options	Price
Compact Disc Changer	+139
Leather Seats	+255

Mileage Category: P

Substantial upgrades include dual airbags, integrated child safety seats, side-impact protection meeting 1997 passenger car standards, revamped fabrics, new colors, freshened styling and a cool in-dash six-disc CD changer. The Quest is still in the hunt.

1995

Body Styles	TMV Pricing		
	Trade	Private	Dealer
3 Dr GXE Pass Van	3600	4764	6704

Options	Price
Air Conditioning - Front and Rear [Opt on XE]	+152
AM/FM/Cassette/CD Audio System [Opt on GXE]	+90
Antilock Brakes [Opt on XE]	+159

Body Styles	TMV Pricing		
	Trade	Private	Dealer
3 Dr XE Pass Van	3060	4050	5699

Options	Price
Leather Seats	+231
Power Moonroof	+179
Power Sunroof	+137

Mileage Category: P

GXE models get standard captain's chairs for second-row occupants. The Extra Performance Package is renamed the Handling Package. No other significant changes for the Quest.

1994

Body Styles	TMV Pricing		
	Trade	Private	Dealer
3 Dr GXE Pass Van	2871	4024	5946

Options	Price
Air Conditioning - Front and Rear [Opt on XE]	+136
AM/FM/Cassette/CD Audio System	+81
Antilock Brakes [Opt on XE]	+142

Body Styles	TMV Pricing		
	Trade	Private	Dealer
3 Dr XE Pass Van	2415	3385	5002

Options	Price
Leather Seats	+206
Power Moonroof	+160

Mileage Category: P

The Quest gets a driver airbag added to its standard equipment list for 1994. GXE models can now be had with a premium audio package that includes a CD player.

Nissan
Sentra
2003

Body Styles	TMV Pricing		
	Trade	Private	Dealer
4 Dr 2.5 Limited Edition Sdn	10388	11444	13203
4 Dr GXE Sdn	8660	9541	11009
4 Dr SE-R Sdn	10336	11386	13137

Options	Price
Air Conditioning [Opt on XE]	+552
Aluminum/Alloy Wheels [Opt on GXE]	+173
AM/FM/CD Audio System [Opt on XE]	+242
Antilock Brakes [Opt on GXE,SE-R, SE-R Spec V]	+469
Automatic 4-Speed Transmission [Opt on GXE,SE-R,XE]	+552

Body Styles	TMV Pricing		
	Trade	Private	Dealer
4 Dr SE-R Spec V Sdn	10998	12116	13978
4 Dr XE Sdn	7539	8306	9584

Options	Price
Power Moonroof [Opt on 2.5 Ltd Ed,SE-R Spec V]	+483
Rear Spoiler [Opt on 2.5 Ltd Ed,GXE,XE]	+248
Front Side Airbag Restraints [Opt on GXE,SE-R,SE-R Spec V]	+173
Premium Audio System [Opt on GXE]	+224
Rockford Fosgate Audio System [Opt on SE-R Spec V]	+275

Mileage Category: E

For 2003, there is a new 2.5 Limited Edition trim, which includes GXE front fascia styling, the 165-horsepower QR25 4-cylinder engine, standard automatic transmission, standard Antilock Braking System (ABS) and side-impact supplemental airbags. The Sentra CA model is no longer available as all 1.8-liter engine-equipped Sentra XE and GXE models sold with California emission specifications offer zero evaporative emissions and meet SULEV (Super Ultra Low Emission Vehicles) standards. Other changes this year include a new power steering ratio for XE and GXE, a revised six-speed manual transmission for SE-R Spec V model and a new bright yellow exterior paint color for the SE-R and SE-R Spec V.

Nissan
Sentra

2002
Mileage Category: B

Beloved by compact car enthusiasts, the Nissan Sentra SE-R returns after a seven-year hiatus. The Sentra SE is no longer available, though Nissan has created additional options packages for the GXE to make it similar to the SE.

Body Styles	TMV Pricing		
	Trade	Private	Dealer
4 Dr CA Sdn	7049	7930	9397
4 Dr GXE Sdn	6735	7577	8979
4 Dr SE-R Sdn	8214	9226	10912

Body Styles	TMV Pricing		
	Trade	Private	Dealer
4 Dr SE-R Spec V Sdn	8830	9918	11730
4 Dr XE Sdn	5739	6456	7650

Options	Price
Air Conditioning [Opt on XE]	+480
Aluminum/Alloy Wheels [Opt on GXE]	+150
AM/FM/CD Audio System [Opt on XE]	+210
Antilock Brakes	+408
Automatic 4-Speed Transmission	+480

Options	Price
Compact Disc Changer	+240
Front Side Airbag Restraints	+165
Power Moonroof	+420
Rear Spoiler [Opt on GXE]	+132
Rockford Fosgate Audio System	+270

2001
Mileage Category: B

After last year's redesign, the 2001 Sentra is carrying over unchanged in XE, GXE, SE and super-ultralow emission California trims.

Body Styles	TMV Pricing		
	Trade	Private	Dealer
4 Dr CA Sdn	6144	7387	8534
4 Dr GXE Sdn	5736	6896	7967

Body Styles	TMV Pricing		
	Trade	Private	Dealer
4 Dr SE SDN	6458	7764	8970
4 Dr XE Sdn	4973	5979	6908

Options	Price
Air Conditioning [Opt on XE]	+425
Aluminum/Alloy Wheels [Std on SE]	+318
AM/FM/Cassette Audio System [Opt on XE]	+160
Antilock Brakes	+362
Automatic 4-Speed Transmission	+425

Options	Price
Compact Disc Changer	+212
Front Side Airbag Restraints	+160
Power Moonroof	+319
Rear Spoiler	+180

2000
Mileage Category: B

The Sentra has been completely overhauled for the 2000 model year. A better ride, more powerful engines and a new enviro-friendly version top the bill, and we likes what we sees.

Body Styles	TMV Pricing		
	Trade	Private	Dealer
4 Dr GXE Sdn	5034	6135	7214
4 Dr SE Sdn	5776	7040	8278

Body Styles	TMV Pricing		
	Trade	Private	Dealer
4 Dr XE Sdn	4173	5086	5980

Options	Price
Air Conditioning [Opt on XE]	+380
Aluminum/Alloy Wheels [Std on SE]	+284
AM/FM/Cassette Audio System	+143
Antilock Brakes	+323
Automatic 4-Speed Transmission	+380

Options	Price
Compact Disc Changer	+190
Front Side Airbag Restraints	+119
Power Sunroof	+262
Rear Spoiler	+161

1999

Mileage Category: B

Fresh front-end styling, a Limited Edition Option Package for GXE models and some new paint colors constitute the changes for 1999.

Body Styles	TMV Pricing		
	Trade	Private	Dealer
4 Dr GXE Sdn	4217	5246	6316
4 Dr SE Limited Sdn	4563	5676	6834

Body Styles	TMV Pricing		
	Trade	Private	Dealer
4 Dr SE Sdn	4478	5570	6706
4 Dr XE Sdn	3564	4433	5338

Options	Price
Air Conditioning [Opt on XE]	+287
Aluminum/Alloy Wheels [Opt on GXE]	+215
AM/FM/Cassette/CD Audio System	+170
Antilock Brakes	+271

Options	Price
Automatic 4-Speed Transmission	+287
Power Moonroof	+197
Rear Spoiler [Opt on GXE,XE]	+121

For the latest vehicle information, visit www.edmunds.com

Sentra

1998

Body Styles	TMV Pricing		
	Trade	Private	Dealer
4 Dr GLE Sdn	3631	4610	5713
4 Dr GXE Sdn	3399	4315	5348
4 Dr SE Sdn	3709	4708	5835

Options	Price
Air Conditioning [Opt on STD]	+238
AM/FM/Cassette/CD Audio System [Std on GLE]	+141
Antilock Brakes	+224

Body Styles	TMV Pricing		
	Trade	Private	Dealer
4 Dr STD Sdn	2626	3334	4132
4 Dr XE Sdn	2974	3775	4679

Options	Price
Automatic 4-Speed Transmission	+238
Compact Disc Changer	+166
Power Moonroof	+163

Mileage Category: B

A new Sentra SE debuts, sporting the same 140-horsepower engine and styling cues found in the 200SX SE-R coupe. Other changes include an exterior freshening that features new front and rear fascias.

1997

Body Styles	TMV Pricing		
	Trade	Private	Dealer
4 Dr GLE Sdn	3123	4078	5245
4 Dr GXE Sdn	2890	3773	4853

Options	Price
Air Conditioning [Opt on STD]	+195
AM/FM/CD Audio System	+123
Antilock Brakes	+198

Body Styles	TMV Pricing		
	Trade	Private	Dealer
4 Dr STD Sdn	2273	2968	3818
4 Dr XE Sdn	2548	3327	4278

Options	Price
Automatic 4-Speed Transmission	+210
Compact Disc Changer	+146
Power Moonroof	+144

Mileage Category: B

The base model is now simply called "Base" instead of S. Nissan works to quiet the Sentra's interior by using a bigger muffler and reducing the number of suspension-mounting points.

1996

Body Styles	TMV Pricing		
	Trade	Private	Dealer
4 Dr GLE Sdn	2314	3107	4203
4 Dr GXE Sdn	2246	3016	4079

Options	Price
Air Conditioning [Opt on STD]	+173
Antilock Brakes	+176

Body Styles	TMV Pricing		
	Trade	Private	Dealer
4 Dr STD Sdn	1684	2261	3057
4 Dr XE Sdn	1919	2577	3485

Options	Price
Automatic 4-Speed Transmission	+186

Mileage Category: B

Prices have crept up, making the Sentra a hard sell against the Neon, Prizm and Cavalier. Still, you may be able to find a good deal on a former rental vehicle. We've seen tons of them at the Alamo rental lots.

1995

Body Styles	TMV Pricing		
	Trade	Private	Dealer
4 Dr GLE Sdn	1792	2485	3640
4 Dr GXE Sdn	1666	2311	3385

Options	Price
Aluminum/Alloy Wheels	+126
Antilock Brakes	+159

Body Styles	TMV Pricing		
	Trade	Private	Dealer
4 Dr STD Sdn	1308	1814	2657
4 Dr XE Sdn	1525	2115	3098

Options	Price
Automatic 4-Speed Transmission	+168

Mileage Category: B

An all-new Sentra is released featuring aero styling and a stubby trunk. The 1995 Sentra is available only as a four-door sedan, the two-door model now being called the 200SX. Increased interior space is the most noticeable feature of the redesign. The engines remain unchanged from previous models.

1994

Body Styles	TMV Pricing		
	Trade	Private	Dealer
2 Dr E Cpe	966	1391	2100
2 Dr Limited Cpe (1994.5)	1224	1764	2663
2 Dr SE Cpe	1201	1730	2612
2 Dr SE-R Cpe	1531	2205	3328
2 Dr XE Cpe	1142	1645	2484

Options	Price
Power Sunroof	+103
Air Conditioning [Opt on E,SE,SE-R]	+140
Aluminum/Alloy Wheels [Std on GXE,SE-R]	+112

Body Styles	TMV Pricing		
	Trade	Private	Dealer
4 Dr E Sdn	1077	1551	2342
4 Dr GXE Sdn	1460	2103	3175
4 Dr Limited Sdn (1994.5)	1235	1779	2685
4 Dr XE Sdn	1171	1687	2547

Options	Price
AM/FM/Cassette/CD Audio System [Opt on XE]	+89
Antilock Brakes	+142
Automatic 4-Speed Transmission	+150

Mileage Category: B

CFC-free coolant is now standard on vehicles equipped with air conditioning. XE models get more standard equipment that includes air conditioning, cruise control and a stereo with cassette player.

Nissan
Xterra

2003

Mileage Category: M

Though the Xterra was updated just last year, Nissan has made further changes for 2003. Mechanically, the V6 has received a slight increase in power, and a stability control system (Nissan's VDC) will be a new option. Also for 2003, Xterra XE V6 models come with standard 16-inch alloy wheels and tubular step rails, and four new exterior colors are available, including Atomic Orange and Camouflage (limited and late availability). Inside, a driver seat-height and lumbar adjuster has been added to V6 models and a new roof headliner net (on nonsunroof models) and luggage side net have also been added, along with new metal ceiling tie-down hooks. A "rugged" leather package is now offered for the SE trim. Other refinements include a 300-watt rating for the Rockford Fosgate-powered eight-speaker audio system, an available tire-pressure monitoring system and Electronic Brakeforce Distribution. A heavy-duty alternator and dual 12-volt power outlets located in the engine compartment are also standard on SE trim.

Body Styles	TMV Pricing		
	Trade	Private	Dealer
4 Dr SE 4WD SUV	17171	18410	20476
4 Dr SE S/C 4WD SUV	17650	18924	21048
4 Dr SE S/C SUV	16414	17599	19574
4 Dr SE SUV	15292	16396	18236

Options	Price
Alarm System [Opt on XE V6]	+138
Automatic 4-Speed Transmission [Opt on XE V6]	+690
Automatic Dimming Rearview Mirror [Opt on XE,XE V6]	+151
Automatic Stability Control [Opt on SE]	+293
Cruise Control [Opt on XE,XE V6]	+128
Keyless Entry System [Opt on XE,XE V6]	+117
Leather Seats [Opt on SE]	+690
Limited Slip Differential [Opt on XE V6]	+173
Moonroof [Opt on SE]	+241

Body Styles	TMV Pricing		
	Trade	Private	Dealer
4 Dr XE SUV	11919	12779	14213
4 Dr XE V6 4WD SUV	14149	15170	16872
4 Dr XE V6 SUV	12966	13902	15462

Options	Price
Power Door Locks [Opt on XE,XE V6]	+155
Power Mirrors [Opt on XE,XE V6]	+128
Power Windows [Opt on XE,XE V6]	+176
Side Steps [Opt on XE]	+207
Tilt Steering Wheel [Opt on XE]	+117
Traction Control System [Opt on SE]	+173
AM/FM/CD Changer Audio System [Opt on XE V6]	+259
Rockford Fosgate Audio System [Opt on XE V6]	+207
Front and Rear Head Airbag Restraints	+344

2002
Mileage Category: M

Nissan's popular Xterra SUV receives a variety of updates for the 2002 model year. Front-end styling is updated, and the bulged hood hides a newly optional supercharged V6. Inside, there are revised gauges, seat fabrics, climate controls, two additional power points and a bigger glovebox. Also standard are dual-stage front airbags, rear child-seat anchors, variable intermittent front windshield wipers, a rear window wiper and a foot-operated parking brake. In terms of options, a new in-dash six-disc CD changer is available on XE Xterras and standard on SE models. Nissan has also made the sunroof optional instead of standard. Finally, as a tribute to dedicated Xterra owners, an Enthusiast Package is available only on XE V6 four-wheel-drive models. It includes ceiling tie clamps, a first aid kit, a tilt steering wheel, foglights, front tow hooks, map lights, a limited-slip differential, manually locking hubs and rubber floor mats.

Body Styles	TMV Pricing		
	Trade	Private	Dealer
4 Dr SE 4WD SUV	14156	15326	17277
4 Dr SE S/C 4WD SUV	14909	16142	18196
4 Dr SE S/C SUV	13753	14890	16784
4 Dr SE SUV	13014	14090	15883
4 Dr XE S/C 4WD SUV	14038	15198	17132

Options	Price
Alarm System [Opt on XE V6]	+120
Aluminum/Alloy Wheels [Opt on XE V6]	+240
Automatic 4-Speed Transmission	+600
Automatic Dimming Rearview Mirror	+132
Limited Slip Differential [Opt on XE V6]	+150

Body Styles	TMV Pricing		
	Trade	Private	Dealer
4 Dr XE S/C SUV	12890	13955	15731
4 Dr XE SUV	10142	10981	12378
4 Dr XE V6 4WD SUV	12017	13010	14666
4 Dr XE V6 SUV	10967	11873	13383

Options	Price
Moonroof [Opt on SE]	+210
Power Door Locks [Opt on XE,XE V6]	+135
Power Windows [Opt on XE,XE V6]	+153
Side Steps [Opt on XE,XE V6]	+180

2001
Mileage Category: M

SE models come with titanium interior accents as well as a premium audio system boasting 100 watts of peak power and an in-dash six-disc CD changer. New steering wheel-mounted audio controls can be used to operate this system. New colors, including one called Gold Rush, and restyled 16-inch alloy wheels round out the changes.

Body Styles	TMV Pricing		
	Trade	Private	Dealer
4 Dr SE 4WD SUV	13065	14723	16253
4 Dr SE SUV	12028	13554	14962
4 Dr XE SUV	9218	10387	11467

Options	Price
Aluminum/Alloy Wheels [Std on SE]	+318
AM/FM/Cassette/CD Audio System	+160
Automatic 4-Speed Transmission	+532
Automatic Dimming Rearview Mirror	+116
Compact Disc Changer	+233

Body Styles	TMV Pricing		
	Trade	Private	Dealer
4 Dr XE V6 4WD SUV	11108	12518	13819
4 Dr XE V6 SUV	10028	11300	12475

Options	Price
Limited Slip Differential [Std on SE]	+133
Power Door Locks [Std on SE]	+120
Power Windows [Std on SE]	+136
Side Steps [Opt on XE,XE V6]	+160

Mileage Category: M

A truck-based mini-SUV, the athletic new Xterra competes with several smaller vehicles built on car platforms.

Body Styles	TMV Pricing		
	Trade	Private	Dealer
4 Dr SE 4WD SUV	11642	13252	14831
4 Dr SE SUV	10638	12110	13552
4 Dr XE SUV	8229	9367	10483

Body Styles	TMV Pricing		
	Trade	Private	Dealer
4 Dr XE V6 4WD SUV	10115	11514	12886
4 Dr XE V6 SUV	8987	10230	11449

Options	Price
Automatic 4-Speed Transmission	+475
Camper/Towing Package	+119
Compact Disc Changer	+309
Limited Slip Differential [Std on SE]	+119

Options	Price
Power Windows [Std on SE]	+121
AM/FM/CD Audio System [Opt on XE]	+119
Aluminum/Alloy Wheels [Std on SE]	+284

Oldsmobile
Achieva/Alero

1998

Body Styles	TMV Pricing		
	Trade	Private	Dealer
4 Dr SL Sdn	2427	3144	3952

Mileage Category: C

Oldsmobile limited sales of the Achieva to fleets for 1998, so if you're considering one, it's probably a former rental car.

1997

Mileage Category: C

Side-impact standards are met, and standard equipment lists are enhanced. Series II Coupe gets new alloy wheels, and the lineup has been simplified.

Body Styles	TMV Pricing		
	Trade	Private	Dealer
2 Dr SC Cpe	1877	2592	3466

Options	Price
Power Moonroof	+118

Body Styles	TMV Pricing		
	Trade	Private	Dealer
4 Dr SL Sdn	1792	2476	3311

1996

Mileage Category: C

Substantial upgrades make the Achieva palatable for 1996. A new interior with dual airbags, standard air conditioning, a new base engine, daytime running lights, a theft-deterrent system and optional traction control make this Oldsmobile an excellent value in the compact class.

Body Styles	TMV Pricing		
	Trade	Private	Dealer
2 Dr SC Cpe	1260	1847	2658

Options	Price
Automatic 4-Speed Transmission	+156

Body Styles	TMV Pricing		
	Trade	Private	Dealer
4 Dr SL Sdn	1317	1930	2777

1995

Mileage Category: C

Fewer options and powertrains are available; SOHC and high-output Quad 4 engines are gone. Standard engine makes 150 horsepower this year, up from 115 in 1994. A V6 is optional. Air conditioning is standard.

Body Styles	TMV Pricing		
	Trade	Private	Dealer
2 Dr S Cpe	854	1304	2053

Options	Price
Air Conditioning	+89
Automatic 4-Speed Transmission	+124

Body Styles	TMV Pricing		
	Trade	Private	Dealer
4 Dr S Sdn	814	1243	1958

Options	Price
Power Moonroof	+79

1994

Mileage Category: C

Driver airbag debuts. A 3.1-liter V6 replaces 3.3-liter V6 on options sheet. Hot-rod SCX gone from lineup.

Body Styles	TMV Pricing		
	Trade	Private	Dealer
2 Dr S Cpe	560	958	1620
2 Dr SC Cpe	679	1160	1962

Options	Price
Automatic 4-Speed Transmission	+100

Body Styles	TMV Pricing		
	Trade	Private	Dealer
4 Dr S Sdn	569	973	1645
4 Dr SL Sdn	700	1197	2025

Oldsmobile
Alero

2003

Body Styles	TMV Pricing		
	Trade	Private	Dealer
2 Dr GL Cpe	8492	9372	10839
2 Dr GLS Cpe	9943	10973	12690
2 Dr GX Cpe	8028	8860	10246

Body Styles	TMV Pricing		
	Trade	Private	Dealer
4 Dr GL Sdn	8409	9281	10734
4 Dr GLS Sdn	9812	10829	12523
4 Dr GX Sdn	7815	8625	9975

Mileage Category: C

Any music lovers out there? For 2003, the Alero expands its scope of available sounds by offering XM Satellite Radio as an option. It's the only Oldsmobile to do so.

2003 (cont'd)

Options	Price
Antilock Brakes [Std on GLS]	+354
Power Driver Seat [Opt on GL]	+159
Power Moonroof [Opt on GL,GLS]	+336

Options	Price
Satellite Radio System	+169
3.4L V6 OHV 12V FI Engine [Opt on GL]	+312

2002

Body Styles	TMV Pricing		
	Trade	Private	Dealer
2 Dr GL Cpe	6504	7317	8671
2 Dr GLS Cpe	7723	8688	10296
2 Dr GX Cpe	6156	6926	8208

Body Styles	TMV Pricing		
	Trade	Private	Dealer
4 Dr GL Sdn	6423	7226	8563
4 Dr GLS Sdn	7583	8530	10109
4 Dr GX Sdn	5954	6698	7937

Options	Price
3.4L V6 OHV 12V FI Engine [Opt on GL]	+317
Aluminum/Alloy Wheels [Opt on GX]	+144

Options	Price
Power Moonroof	+288

Mileage Category: C

The biggest news for the 2002 Alero is an all-new four-cylinder engine on GX and GL1 models. Redesigned 15-inch wheels, a revamped interior console and two new exterior colors round out this year's changes.

2001

Body Styles	TMV Pricing		
	Trade	Private	Dealer
2 Dr GL Cpe	5403	6478	7470
2 Dr GLS Cpe	6462	7747	8933
2 Dr GX Cpe	5135	6156	7099

Body Styles	TMV Pricing		
	Trade	Private	Dealer
4 Dr GL Sdn	5289	6341	7311
4 Dr GLS Sdn	6330	7589	8751
4 Dr GX Sdn	4938	5920	6826

Options	Price
3.4L V6 OHV 12V FI Engine [Opt on GL]	+241

Options	Price
Power Moonroof	+239

Mileage Category: C

A five-speed manual transmission is now available with the four-cylinder engine; an eight-speaker premium sound system is now standard on the GLS (optional on GL); and a refined ABS system and 16-inch wheels are now standard on the GLS.

2000

Body Styles	TMV Pricing		
	Trade	Private	Dealer
2 Dr GL Cpe	4318	5281	6224
2 Dr GLS Cpe	5249	6419	7566
2 Dr GX Cpe	3959	4842	5707

Body Styles	TMV Pricing		
	Trade	Private	Dealer
4 Dr GL Sdn	4172	5102	6013
4 Dr GLS Sdn	5341	6532	7699
4 Dr GX Sdn	3815	4666	5500

Options	Price
Power Moonroof	+203
3.4L V6 OHV 12V FI Engine [Opt on GL]	+238
Aluminum/Alloy Wheels [Opt on GL,GX]	+124

Options	Price
Automatic 4-Speed Transmission [Opt on GL,GX]	+140
Leather Seats [Opt on GL]	+281

Mileage Category: C

A performance suspension is newly optional on GL models. The four-cylinder gets a composite intake manifold, while all models benefit from the addition of three rear-shelf anchors for child safety-seat restraints. If glitz is your thing, you can now opt for a new gold package on GL and GLS versions.

1999

Body Styles	TMV Pricing		
	Trade	Private	Dealer
2 Dr GL Cpe	3772	4709	5684
2 Dr GLS Cpe	4288	5353	6461
2 Dr GX Cpe	3330	4157	5018

Body Styles	TMV Pricing		
	Trade	Private	Dealer
4 Dr GL Sdn	3513	4385	5293
4 Dr GLS Sdn	4587	5726	6910
4 Dr GX Sdn	3378	4216	5089

Options	Price
3.4L V6 OHV 12V FI Engine [Opt on GL]	+188
Leather Seats [Opt on GL]	+222

Options	Price
Power Moonroof	+160

Mileage Category: C

Oldsmobile has dropped the slow-selling Achieva in favor of this new clean-sheet design patterned after the successful Intrigue midsize sedan. Available in both two- and four-door configurations with three well-equipped trim levels, the Alero represents a quantum leap forward over previous small Olds models.

Oldsmobile
Aurora

2003

Body Styles	TMV Pricing		
	Trade	Private	Dealer
4 Dr 4.0 Sdn	19123	20493	22776

Aurora

2003 (cont'd)

Options	Price
Bose Audio System	+260
Compact Disc Changer	+239
Heated Front Seats	+179
Navigation System	+538
Power Moonroof	+622

Options	Price
Power Passenger Seat	+125
Special Factory Paint	+286
17 Inch Wheels - Chrome	+416
Automatic Climate Control (2 Zone) - Driver and Passenger	+195

Mileage Category: H

The V6 has been dropped in the final year of production making the Aurora one of the few V8-only sedans on the market. Two new exterior colors -- Bordeaux Red and Steel Blue -- have also been added for the Aurora's going-away party.

2002

Mileage Category: H

A navigation radio supplements the OnStar system for easy-to-follow driving directions. Three new exterior colors debut along with chrome exhaust tips.

Body Styles	TMV Pricing		
	Trade	Private	Dealer
4 Dr 3.5 Sdn	13998	15275	17402

Body Styles	TMV Pricing		
	Trade	Private	Dealer
4 Dr 4.0 Sdn	15548	16966	19329

Options	Price
17 Inch Wheels - Chrome [Opt on 4.0]	+355
Automatic Climate Control (2 Zone) - Driver and Passenger [Opt on 3.5]	+166
Automatic Stability Control [Opt on 3.5]	+155
Bose Audio System	+222
Chrome Wheels	+355

Options	Price
Compact Disc Changer	+204
Heated Front Seats	+153
Navigation System	+731
Power Moonroof	+485
Special Factory Paint	+175

2001

Mileage Category: H

Oldsmobile has redesigned the Aurora, plopping its flagship sedan onto a more rigid but still front-drive platform. Remaining stylish and contemporary, Aurora is more conventional in appearance but overall, remains an enticing package. Both 3.5 V6 and 4.0 V8 versions are available, each equipped with a full load of luxury accoutrements.

Body Styles	TMV Pricing		
	Trade	Private	Dealer
4 Dr 3.5 Sdn	10721	12390	13931

Body Styles	TMV Pricing		
	Trade	Private	Dealer
4 Dr 4.0 Sdn	12162	14056	15804

Options	Price
Automatic Stability Control [Opt on 3.5]	+145
Bose Audio System	+184
Chrome Wheels	+294
Compact Disc Changer	+169

Options	Price
Heated Front Seats	+127
Power Moonroof	+402
Special Factory Paint	+145

1999

Body Styles	TMV Pricing		
	Trade	Private	Dealer
4 Dr STD Sdn	7746	9264	10844

Options	Price
Chrome Wheels	+197
Delco/Bose Audio System	+205

Options	Price
OnStar Telematic System	+245
Power Moonroof	+270

Mileage Category: H

It's the status quo again in Auroraville, except this year Olds has added two more hydraulic engine mounts (for a total of three) to better isolate engine vibrations. Other than that, a few new colors have been added (Galaxy Silver, Copper Nightmist and Dark Bronzemist).

1998

Mileage Category: H

Status quo in Auroraville, but second-generation airbags have been added.

Body Styles	TMV Pricing		
	Trade	Private	Dealer
4 Dr STD Sdn	5835	7289	8928

Options	Price
Chrome Wheels	+171
Delco/Bose Audio System	+177

Options	Price
OnStar Telematic System	+212
Power Moonroof	+212

1997

Body Styles	TMV Pricing		
	Trade	Private	Dealer
4 Dr STD Sdn	4604	5896	7475

For the latest vehicle information, visit www.edmunds.com

1997 (cont'd)

Mileage Category: H

Options	Price	Options	Price
Chrome Wheels	+152	Power Moonroof	+189
Delco/Bose Audio System	+158		

Larger front brakes, an in-dash CD player for the Bose sound system, a tilt-down right-hand exterior mirror for backing assistance, an integrated rearview mirror compass and a three-channel garage door opener are added this year.

1996

Mileage Category: H

Body Styles	TMV Pricing		
	Trade	Private	Dealer
4 Dr STD Sdn	3529	4639	6172

Options	Price	Options	Price
Chrome Wheels	+128	Power Moonroof	+160
Delco/Bose Audio System	+133		

Daytime running lights are added, and looking through the backlight won't make your eyes water from distortions anymore. We knew it was only a matter of time before some goofball decided chrome wheels and a gold package would look great on the otherwise classy Aurora. The new Oldsmobile? What's that? When do we get the fake convertible roof, guys?

1995

Mileage Category: H

Body Styles	TMV Pricing		
	Trade	Private	Dealer
4 Dr STD Sdn	2556	3435	4900

Options	Price	Options	Price
Delco/Bose Audio System	+105	Power Moonroof	+127

World-class V8 front-drive luxury sedan features cutting-edge styling, dual airbags, ABS and traction control.

Oldsmobile
Bravada

2003

Body Styles	TMV Pricing		
	Trade	Private	Dealer
4 Dr STD AWD SUV	19683	21075	23395

Body Styles	TMV Pricing		
	Trade	Private	Dealer
4 Dr STD SUV	18911	20249	22478

Options	Price	Options	Price
Automatic Load Leveling [Opt on AWD]	+195	Polished Aluminum/Alloy Wheels	+258
Bose Audio System	+258	Power Moonroof	+416
Compact Disc Changer	+153	Front Side Airbag Restraints	+182
Heated Front Seats	+130	DVD Entertainment System	+520

Mileage Category: M

Oldsmobile quietly added a two-wheel-drive model to the Bravada lineup last year, making it a bit more attractive to those who don't need the foul weather capability of all-wheel drive. This year 2WD Bravadas get standard traction control while AWD versions now feature a coil spring rear suspension. The previously standard air-spring setup is still an available option on AWD models. Side airbags have also been moved from the standard equipment package to the options list while the standard 4.2-liter engine has been given a 5 horsepower bump.

2002

Body Styles	TMV Pricing		
	Trade	Private	Dealer
4 Dr STD AWD SUV	17065	18432	20709

Body Styles	TMV Pricing		
	Trade	Private	Dealer
4 Dr STD SUV	15977	17256	19388

Options	Price	Options	Price
17 Inch Wheels	+199	DVD Entertainment System	+441
Bose Audio System	+219	Power Sunroof	+355
Compact Disc Changer	+131	Traction Control System	+197

Mileage Category: M

Olds brings out a new Bravada that's dramatically improved over its predecessor. A roomier interior, refined suspension, unique style and an all-new inline six packing more power than most competitors' V8s highlight the changes made to Oldsmobile's luxury ute.

2001

Body Styles	TMV Pricing		
	Trade	Private	Dealer
4 Dr STD AWD SUV	11188	12721	14137

2001 (cont'd)

Options	Price
Bose Audio System	+182
Compact Disc Changer	+145

Options	Price
OnStar Telematic System	+255
Power Moonroof	+294

Mileage Category: M

In the last model year before the long-awaited redesign, Oldsmobile adds a few goodies to distract us. Once a dealer-installed option, the OnStar communications system is now a factory-installed option. The Bravada's already comfortable seating is enhanced by new standard equipment such as an eight-way power passenger seat and memory control for the driver seat. A new option group includes the towing package, OnStar and white-letter tires. Previously available only with a package, the Platinum Edition (two-tone paint treatment) is now a stand-alone option. Those longing for a more understated green can now select Sage Green as an exterior color.

2000

Mileage Category: M

GM's OnStar communications system is now available as a dealer-installed option, and a new cargo management system is expected sometime this year. Special color treatments include a new Jewelcoat Red option that features a deep red base color finished with a red-tinted final top coat in place of the usual clearcoat. There's also a Platinum Edition option that adds pewter-colored lower body cladding.

Body Styles	TMV Pricing		
	Trade	Private	Dealer
4 Dr STD AWD SUV	8494	9815	11110

Options	Price
Power Moonroof	+234
Bose Audio System	+154

Options	Price
Compact Disc Changer	+123
OnStar Telematic System	+279

1999

Mileage Category: M

In the wake of last year's restyle, Bravada sees feature refinements for '99. The driver-side airbag has been redesigned into a mini-module to permit a clearer view of the instruments, while the turn signal stalk now provides a flash-to-pass feature. A telltale warning lamp has been added to alert the driver when the tailgate lift glass is ajar. And an anti-theft alarm system is now standard. There's also an option package that combines a driver-side memory seat and a power passenger-side seat, as well as sound system upgrades across the board.

Body Styles	TMV Pricing		
	Trade	Private	Dealer
4 Dr STD AWD SUV	6825	8058	9342

Options	Price
Bose Audio System	+122
OnStar Telematic System	+190

Options	Price
Power Moonroof	+185

1998

Mileage Category: M

Front styling is revised, and new body-side cladding alters the Bravada's profile. Inside, dual second-generation airbags are housed in a new dashboard. A heated driver-side exterior mirror is newly standard, while heated front seats have been added to the options roster. Battery rundown protection and a theft-deterrent system are new standard features.

Body Styles	TMV Pricing		
	Trade	Private	Dealer
4 Dr STD AWD SUV	5819	6995	8321

Options	Price
Power Moonroof	+160

1997

Mileage Category: M

Bravada drops the split-tailgate arrangement at the rear in favor of a top-hinged liftgate with separately lifting glass. So, tailgate parties aren't as convenient, but loading cargo sure is easier. Also new to the options list is a power tilt and slide sunroof. Included with the hole in the roof are a mini-overhead console, a pop-up wind deflector and a sun shade. Rear disc brakes replace the former drums, combining with the front discs to provide better stopping ability.

Body Styles	TMV Pricing		
	Trade	Private	Dealer
4 Dr STD AWD SUV	4560	5628	6934

Options	Price
Power Moonroof	+143

1996

Mileage Category: M

Nice truck, but how many luxury SUVs do we really need? Only a few things about the Bravada differentiate it from the Chevy Blazer and GMC Jimmy: the seats, front styling, trim -- and the price tag.

Body Styles	TMV Pricing		
	Trade	Private	Dealer
4 Dr STD AWD SUV	3975	4999	6413

1994

Mileage Category: M

New Special Edition model has gold trim. Doors get guard beams. Shock absorbers are softened for a better ride.

Body Styles	TMV Pricing		
	Trade	Private	Dealer
4 Dr STD AWD SUV	2474	3277	4616
4 Dr Special Edition AWD SUV	2297	3043	4285

Oldsmobile
Cutlass

1999

Body Styles	TMV Pricing		
	Trade	Private	Dealer
4 Dr GL Sdn	4249	5304	6402

Body Styles	TMV Pricing		
	Trade	Private	Dealer
4 Dr GLS Sdn	4638	5790	6988

Options	Price
Power Moonroof	+160

Mileage Category: C

No changes to Oldsmobile's fresh-in-'97 bread-and-butter sedan, except for two new colors, Bronze Mist and Dark Cherry, and the addition of a Gold Package.

1998

Body Styles	TMV Pricing		
	Trade	Private	Dealer
4 Dr GL Sdn	3354	4345	5463

Body Styles	TMV Pricing		
	Trade	Private	Dealer
4 Dr GLS Sdn	3634	4707	5918

Options	Price
Power Moonroof	+127

Mileage Category: C

No changes to Oldsmobile's fresh bread-and butter sedan, except for the addition of second-generation airbags.

1997

Body Styles	TMV Pricing		
	Trade	Private	Dealer
4 Dr GLS Sdn	2831	3909	5226

Body Styles	TMV Pricing		
	Trade	Private	Dealer
4 Dr STD Sdn	2508	3463	4630

Mileage Category: C

Oldsmobile retires the Ciera and introduces the Cutlass, based on the same platform as Chevy's new Malibu. Cutlass is more upscale that its Chevrolet counterpart, offering a slightly more powerful V6 engine on all models, and a sunroof option, standard leather interior and larger wheels on the GLS.

Oldsmobile
Cutlass Ciera

1996

Body Styles	TMV Pricing		
	Trade	Private	Dealer
4 Dr SL Sdn	1633	2264	3135
4 Dr SL Wgn	1764	2446	3388

Mileage Category: D

Best-seller prepares for retirement at the end of the year, receiving badge revisions, some additional standard equipment and an improved optional V6 engine.

1995

Body Styles	TMV Pricing		
	Trade	Private	Dealer
4 Dr SL Sdn	1147	1651	2490

Body Styles	TMV Pricing		
	Trade	Private	Dealer
4 Dr SL Wgn	1321	1900	2865

Options	Price
3.1L V6 OHV 12V FI Engine [Opt on Sdn]	+103

Options	Price
Automatic 4-Speed Transmission [Opt on Sdn]	+114

Mileage Category: D

Offered in a single trim level this year. Rear defroster and cassette player are standard. Brake/transmission shift interlock is new.

1994

Body Styles	TMV Pricing		
	Trade	Private	Dealer
4 Dr S Sdn	761	1196	1922
4 Dr S Wgn	815	1280	2056

Body Styles	TMV Pricing		
	Trade	Private	Dealer
4 Dr Special Edition Sdn	678	1066	1712
4 Dr Special Edition Wgn	804	1264	2030

Options	Price
Automatic 4-Speed Transmission [Std on S Sdn]	+82

Mileage Category: D

Driver airbag and ABS standard for all models. Four-cylinder engine back in base models, producing 120 horsepower. A 3.1-liter V6 replaces last year's 3.3-liter V6. Variable-assist steering is a new option on sedans. SL replaced by Special Edition models.

Cutlass Supreme/Eighty-Eight Royale

Oldsmobile
Cutlass Supreme

1997

Body Styles	TMV Pricing		
	Trade	Private	Dealer
2 Dr SL Cpe	2478	3382	4487

Options	Price
Leather Seats	+151

Body Styles	TMV Pricing		
	Trade	Private	Dealer
4 Dr SL Sdn	2730	3726	4944

Options	Price
Power Moonroof	+132

Mileage Category: D

Alloy wheels and a power trunk release are added to the standard equipment list, while coupes gain side-impact protection that meets federal safety standards. The 3.4-liter, DOHC V6 engine is dropped from the options list.

1996

Mileage Category: D

The convertible has been retired. The sedan and coupe enjoy their last year in production, receiving engine upgrades for 1996.

Body Styles	TMV Pricing		
	Trade	Private	Dealer
2 Dr SL Cpe	2001	2774	3842

Options	Price
3.4L V6 DOHC 24V FI Engine	+116

Body Styles	TMV Pricing		
	Trade	Private	Dealer
4 Dr SL Sdn	2122	2942	4075

Options	Price
Leather Seats	+128

1995

Mileage Category: D

Redesigned dashboard equipped with dual airbags debuts. Single trim level offered this year. Front bench seat is no longer available. Front seatbelts are mounted to door pillars instead of doors. Air conditioning, power windows, power locks, tilt steering and cassette player are standard on all models.

Body Styles	TMV Pricing		
	Trade	Private	Dealer
2 Dr S Cpe	1309	1883	2839
2 Dr STD Conv	1977	2844	4288

Options	Price
3.4L V6 DOHC 24V FI Engine	+92
Leather Seats [Opt on S]	+101

Body Styles	TMV Pricing		
	Trade	Private	Dealer
4 Dr S Sdn	1309	1883	2839

Options	Price
Power Moonroof	+89

1994

Mileage Category: D

Driver airbag added and ABS is made standard on all models. International Series dropped. Special Editions are on sale, carrying one-price stickers and a healthy load of standard equipment. The 3.1-liter V6 makes 20 more horsepower. The 3.4-liter V6 makes 10 more horsepower. New standard features include tilt steering, intermittent wipers, Pass-Key theft-deterrent system and rear defogger.

Body Styles	TMV Pricing		
	Trade	Private	Dealer
2 Dr S Cpe	872	1371	2203
2 Dr STD Conv	1377	2165	3478
2 Dr Special Edition Cpe	826	1299	2088

Body Styles	TMV Pricing		
	Trade	Private	Dealer
4 Dr S Sdn	885	1392	2237
4 Dr Special Edition Sdn	851	1337	2148

Options	Price
Leather Seats [Opt on S,Special]	+82

Oldsmobile
Eighty-Eight Royale

1999

Body Styles	TMV Pricing		
	Trade	Private	Dealer
4 Dr 50th Anniv Sdn	5927	7130	8383
4 Dr LS Sdn	5461	6569	7723

Options	Price
Leather Seats [Opt on LS]	+203
OnStar Telematic System	+245

Body Styles	TMV Pricing		
	Trade	Private	Dealer
4 Dr STD Sdn	5032	6053	7116

Options	Price
Power Moonroof	+256

Mileage Category: G

The Eighty-Eight gets two new exterior colors, Champagne and Evergreen, and the LS model gets the option of white-stripe 16-inch tires. Oh, wait. Oldsmobile is celebrating the nameplate's golden anniversary with a special 50th Anniversary Edition Eighty-Eight. It has 16-inch aluminum wheels fitted with 215/65SR blackwalls, a highly contented leather interior package and special badging finished in, what else? Gold.

1998

Body Styles	TMV Pricing		
	Trade	Private	Dealer
4 Dr LS Sdn	4396	5387	6505

Body Styles	TMV Pricing		
	Trade	Private	Dealer
4 Dr STD Sdn	4031	4940	5966

Options	Price
Leather Seats	+212

Mileage Category: G

Virtually nothing, unless you find a new fuel cap, better access to rear seatbelts, new ABS wheel-speed sensors and a couple of new colors intriguing. Second-generation airbags are standard.

1997

Body Styles	TMV Pricing		
	Trade	Private	Dealer
4 Dr LS Sdn	3260	4237	5432

Body Styles	TMV Pricing		
	Trade	Private	Dealer
4 Dr STD Sdn	2994	3892	4989

Mileage Category: G

Side-impact protection is upgraded to federal safety standards, interiors are improved and new Oldsmobile logos adorn the body.

1996

Body Styles	TMV Pricing		
	Trade	Private	Dealer
4 Dr LS Sdn	2619	3380	4431
4 Dr LSS S/C Sdn	3193	4120	5401

Body Styles	TMV Pricing		
	Trade	Private	Dealer
4 Dr LSS Sdn	3086	3982	5220
4 Dr STD Sdn	2332	3009	3944

Options	Price
Power Moonroof	+166

Mileage Category: G

Royale designation dropped, and the Eighty-Eight gets fresh Aurora-inspired styling front and rear. Standard equipment levels go up, and daytime running lights are added.

1995

Body Styles	TMV Pricing		
	Trade	Private	Dealer
4 Dr LS Sdn	1901	2500	3498
4 Dr LSS S/C Sdn	2247	2955	4134

Body Styles	TMV Pricing		
	Trade	Private	Dealer
4 Dr LSS Sdn	2075	2729	3818
4 Dr STD Sdn	1693	2226	3115

Options	Price
Compact Disc Changer	+83

Options	Price
Leather Seats [Std on LSS]	+101

Mileage Category: G

Engine upgraded to 3800 Series II status, and supercharged 3.8-liter V6 is a new option on LSS models. New onboard navigation system called Guidestar was a $1,995 option, originally available only in California.

1994

Body Styles	TMV Pricing		
	Trade	Private	Dealer
4 Dr LS Sdn	1485	2069	3041
4 Dr LSS Sdn	1454	2025	2976

Body Styles	TMV Pricing		
	Trade	Private	Dealer
4 Dr STD Sdn	1292	1799	2644
4 Dr Special Edition Sdn	1173	1634	2401

Options	Price
Leather Seats [Std on LS Special Edition]	+82

Mileage Category: G

Passenger airbag is housed in a new dashboard featuring more compact layout and new four-spoke steering wheel. Grille is body-color. Headlamps and turn signals are restyled. Traction control system can now reduce engine power as well as apply brakes to slipping wheel. New Special Edition model is available.

Oldsmobile
Intrigue

2002

Body Styles	TMV Pricing		
	Trade	Private	Dealer
4 Dr GL Sdn	8929	10050	11919
4 Dr GLS Sdn	10165	11441	13568

Body Styles	TMV Pricing		
	Trade	Private	Dealer
4 Dr GX Sdn	8352	9401	11148

Options	Price
Automatic Stability Control	+264
Bose Audio System [Opt on GL]	+122
Chrome Wheels [Opt on GL,GLS]	+233

Options	Price
Heated Front Seats [Opt on GL]	+120
Leather Seats [Opt on GL]	+366
Power Moonroof [Opt on GL]	+332

Mileage Category: D

LATCH child-seat anchors and two new colors are added, along with a standard CD player. GLS models receive additional standard equipment that includes a two-tone leather interior, sunroof and a HomeLink system. This is the last year for the Oldsmobile Intrigue.

Oldsmobile
Intrigue/LSS

2001

Mileage Category: D

The Intrigue receives only minor changes for 2001, including two new exterior colors and a standard air filtration system. The OnStar driver assistance system is now standard on GLS models while Precision Control System equipped models receive exterior "PCS" badging.

Body Styles	TMV Pricing		
	Trade	Private	Dealer
4 Dr GL Sdn	7083	8588	9977
4 Dr GLS Sdn	7754	9401	10921

Body Styles	TMV Pricing		
	Trade	Private	Dealer
4 Dr GX Sdn	6497	7877	9150

Options	Price
AM/FM/Cassette/CD Audio System [Opt on GL,GX]	+165
Automatic Stability Control	+219
Bose Audio System	+184
Chrome Wheels	+220

Options	Price
Compact Disc Changer	+169
Leather Seats [Opt on GL]	+366
Power Moonroof	+275

2000

Mileage Category: D

All Intrigues get restyled six-spoke 16-inch alloy wheels in either silver argent paint or chrome, and the option of adding Oldsmobile's Precision Control System (PCS). The full-function traction-control unit that's standard on the GL and GLS is now available on the GX. Retained accessory power becomes standard, and GL buyers can opt for the revised heated seats on the GLS.

Body Styles	TMV Pricing		
	Trade	Private	Dealer
4 Dr GL Sdn	5789	7212	8607
4 Dr GLS Sdn	6145	7656	9137

Body Styles	TMV Pricing		
	Trade	Private	Dealer
4 Dr GX Sdn	5187	6463	7713

Options	Price
AM/FM/Cassette/CD Audio System [Opt on GL,GX]	+140
Automatic Stability Control	+186
Bose Audio System [Opt on GL,GLS]	+133
Chrome Wheels	+187

Options	Price
Compact Disc Changer	+143
Leather Seats [Opt on GL]	+310
Power Moonroof	+234

1999

Mileage Category: D

Last year, Oldsmobile dumped the stodgy Cutlass Supreme for the Intrigue; a suave, sophisticated sporty sedan designed to take on the best of the imports. For '99 Olds is dumping the 3800 Series II V6 that powers the Intrigue for an all-new, 24-valve 3.5-liter twin-cam V6. Until production of the 3.5-liter (a design based on the Aurora V8) can be ramped up to meet the Intrigue build schedule, the new 215-horsepower engine will come standard only in the new top-line GLS model, and optional in the base GX and mid-line GL series. Full function traction control is now available in models equipped with the new power plant. Minor feature revisions, one new color and new badging rounds out the changes this year.

Body Styles	TMV Pricing		
	Trade	Private	Dealer
4 Dr GL Sdn	4296	5452	6655
4 Dr GLS Sdn	4542	5765	7037

Body Styles	TMV Pricing		
	Trade	Private	Dealer
4 Dr GX Sdn	3990	5064	6182

Options	Price
Chrome Wheels	+148
Leather Seats [Opt on GL]	+246

Options	Price
Power Moonroof	+185

1998

Mileage Category: D

Oldsmobile dumps the stodgy Cutlass Supreme for the Intrigue: a suave, sophisticated, sporty sedan designed to take on the best of the imports. Too bad refinement issues exist. Second-generation airbags are standard equipment.

Body Styles	TMV Pricing		
	Trade	Private	Dealer
4 Dr GL Sdn	3483	4510	5668
4 Dr GLS Sdn	3883	5027	6318

Body Styles	TMV Pricing		
	Trade	Private	Dealer
4 Dr STD Sdn	2887	3738	4698

Options	Price
Chrome Wheels	+128
Leather Seats [Opt on GL]	+212

Options	Price
Power Moonroof	+148

Oldsmobile
LSS

1999

Body Styles	TMV Pricing		
	Trade	Private	Dealer
4 Dr S/C Sdn	6844	8233	9679

Body Styles	TMV Pricing		
	Trade	Private	Dealer
4 Dr STD Sdn	5599	6735	7918

Options	Price
Chrome Wheels	+148

Options	Price
Power Moonroof	+256

Mileage Category: G

The LSS gets two new exterior colors (Champagne and Evergreen) for '99. Olds has also upgraded the standard radio to an AM/FM stereo cassette with CD player and seek-scan, auto tone control, digital clock and power antenna.

For the latest vehicle information, visit www.edmunds.com

1998

Body Styles	TMV Pricing		
	Trade	Private	Dealer
4 Dr S/C Sdn	5413	6634	8010

Options	Price
Chrome Wheels	+128

Body Styles	TMV Pricing		
	Trade	Private	Dealer
4 Dr STD Sdn	4805	5888	7110

Options	Price
Power Moonroof	+212

Mileage Category: G

New colors, improved ABS, a revised electrochromic rearview mirror, second-generation airbags and a redesigned fuel cap are the major changes for 1998.

1997

Body Styles	TMV Pricing		
	Trade	Private	Dealer
4 Dr S/C Sdn	4103	5152	6433

Options	Price
Power Moonroof	+189

Body Styles	TMV Pricing		
	Trade	Private	Dealer
4 Dr STD Sdn	3907	4905	6125

Mileage Category: G

Minor changes accompany Oldsmobile's euro-flavored sedan into 1997. The center console and shifter are new, and other interior upgrades have been made. New, more prominent badging has been added to the exterior. Finally, the final-drive ratio has been changed to 2.93-to-1 from 2.97-to-1.

Oldsmobile
Ninety-Eight

1996

Body Styles	TMV Pricing		
	Trade	Private	Dealer
4 Dr Regency Elite Sdn	3431	4510	6001

Options	Price
Power Moonroof	+177

Mileage Category: H

Supercharged engine dropped from this model, and daytime running lamps have been added. Don't expect a 1997 Ninety-Eight.

1995

Body Styles	TMV Pricing		
	Trade	Private	Dealer
4 Dr Regency Elite S/C Sdn	2516	3380	4821

Options	Price
Power Moonroof	+140

Body Styles	TMV Pricing		
	Trade	Private	Dealer
4 Dr Regency Elite Sdn	2387	3208	4576

Mileage Category: H

Engine upgraded to 3800 Series II status. Alloy wheels are standard. Flash-to-pass is new standard feature.

1994

Body Styles	TMV Pricing		
	Trade	Private	Dealer
4 Dr Regency Elite S/C Sdn	1756	2512	3772
4 Dr Regency Elite Sdn	1668	2387	3584

Options	Price
Leather Seats [Opt on Elite,STD]	+82

Body Styles	TMV Pricing		
	Trade	Private	Dealer
4 Dr Regency Sdn	1466	2098	3152
4 Dr Regency Special Edition Sdn	1409	2017	3029

Options	Price
Power Moonroof	+113

Mileage Category: H

Passenger airbag is housed in a new dashboard featuring more compact layout. Touring Sedan is dropped, and a Special Edition is added. Supercharged engine is now available on the Elite, and it gains horsepower and torque. Traction control system can now reduce engine power as well as apply brakes to slipping wheel. There is an additional inch of seat travel. The grille and headlamps are restyled.

Oldsmobile
Regency

1998

Body Styles	TMV Pricing		
	Trade	Private	Dealer
4 Dr STD Sdn	5584	6975	8543

Options	Price
Power Moonroof	+212

Mileage Category: H

Minor changes this year. The ABS is upgraded, it's easier to get at the rear seatbelts, colors are revised and the "unleaded fuel only" label is removed from the inside of the fuel door.

Oldsmobile
Regency/Silhouette

1997

Mileage Category: H

New name for an old concept. Look closely...see the old Eighty-Eight before 1996's restyle? Regency takes over where the Ninety-Eight left off, satisfying traditional Oldsmobile buyers.

Body Styles	TMV Pricing		
	Trade	Private	Dealer
4 Dr STD Sdn	4494	5755	7297

Options	Price
Power Moonroof	+189

Oldsmobile
Silhouette

2003

Body Styles	TMV Pricing		
	Trade	Private	Dealer
4 Dr GL Pass Van Ext	13276	14292	15984
4 Dr GLS AWD Pass Van Ext	18376	19782	22125
4 Dr GLS Pass Van Ext	14666	15788	17658

Options	Price
Chrome Wheels	+362
Power Dual Sliding Doors [Opt on GLS]	+182

Mileage Category: P

Body Styles	TMV Pricing		
	Trade	Private	Dealer
4 Dr Premiere AWD Pass Van Ext	19502	20994	23481
4 Dr Premiere Pass Van Ext	16286	17532	19608

Options	Price
Power Sliding Door [Opt on GL]	+234
AM/FM/CD Changer Audio System	+153

For 2003, traction control and 16-inch wheels are now standard on two-wheel-drive models.

2002

Mileage Category: P

Despite the fact that the Silhouette is headed to the graveyard with the rest of Oldsmobile's lineup, there are still minor changes on tap for the 2002 model. The Versatrak AWD system will now be available on GLS and Premiere models coupled with special 16-inch aluminum wheels. The standard front airbags are now dual-stage units that deploy according to the severity of the crash, and Premiere models equipped with the onboard video system get a DVD player in place of a standard VCR.

Body Styles	TMV Pricing		
	Trade	Private	Dealer
4 Dr GL Pass Van Ext	10914	11886	13506
4 Dr GLS AWD Pass Van Ext	15565	16951	19262
4 Dr GLS Pass Van Ext	12594	13716	15586

Options	Price
Air Conditioning - Front and Rear [Opt on GL]	+244
Aluminum/Alloy Wheels [Opt on GL]	+131
Chrome Wheels	+308
Compact Disc Changer	+131

Body Styles	TMV Pricing		
	Trade	Private	Dealer
4 Dr Premiere AWD Pass Van Ext	16544	18018	20474
4 Dr Premiere Pass Van Ext	13522	14727	16734

Options	Price
Park Distance Control (Rear) [Opt on GL]	+122
Power Dual Sliding Doors [Std on Premiere]	+155
Power Sliding Door [Opt on GL]	+199

2001

Mileage Category: P

Oldsmobile is giving minivan buyers good reason to shop the Silhouette for 2001, even if General Motors issues a death sentence for the brand. All models get freshened styling, a touring suspension package with self-leveling suspension and an air inflation kit, fold-flat second-row captain's chairs, improved sound-deadening insulation and standard OnStar communications. Upscale GLS and Premiere models have two-tone leather seating, a rear parking aid, an integrated universal garage door opener, 16-inch wheels with an available chrome finish, power-sliding driver door, in-dash CD changer, third-row captain's chairs, stowable third-row seat, wood grain accents, eight-way power front seats and dual-zone A/C as either optional or standard. The Premiere also gets an updated onboard entertainment system with a larger video screen.

Body Styles	TMV Pricing		
	Trade	Private	Dealer
4 Dr GL Pass Van Ext	9037	10354	11570
4 Dr GLS Pass Van Ext	10203	11690	13063

Options	Price
Air Conditioning - Front and Rear [Opt on GL]	+165
Chrome Wheels	+255

Body Styles	TMV Pricing		
	Trade	Private	Dealer
4 Dr Premiere Pass Van Ext	11366	13022	14551

Options	Price
Power Sliding Door [Opt on GL]	+165

2000

Mileage Category: P

Olds has canned its 112-inch wheelbase GS, meaning all 2000 Silhouettes (GL, GLS and Premiere) are now extended-length (120-inch wheelbase) seven-passenger models. The traction-control system has been improved, and heated front seats are available in leather. There's also a redesigned instrument cluster with dual trip odometers, as well as upgraded radios, interior lighting and electrical system functions.

Body Styles	TMV Pricing		
	Trade	Private	Dealer
4 Dr GL Pass Van Ext	7018	8185	9329
4 Dr GLS Pass Van Ext	7896	9209	10496

Options	Price
Air Conditioning - Front and Rear [Opt on GL]	+140
OnStar Telematic System [Opt on Premiere]	+279

Body Styles	TMV Pricing		
	Trade	Private	Dealer
4 Dr Premiere Pass Van Ext	8991	10486	11952

Options	Price
Power Sliding Door [Opt on GL]	+140

For the latest vehicle information, visit www.edmunds.com

1999

Body Styles	TMV Pricing		
	Trade	Private	Dealer
4 Dr GL Pass Van Ext	5759	6906	8100
4 Dr GLS Pass Van Ext	6360	7626	8945

Options	Price
Leather Seats [Opt on GS]	+234

Body Styles	TMV Pricing		
	Trade	Private	Dealer
4 Dr GS Pass Van	6081	7292	8552
4 Dr Premiere Pass Van Ext	6923	8302	9737

Options	Price
OnStar Telematic System [Opt on Premiere]	+245

Mileage Category: P

Olds is headlining its Premiere Edition, a loaded-up model that debuted in mid-'98 with a standard integrated video entertainment system in back. But other news for 1999 includes a horsepower and torque increase for Silhouette's 3.4-liter V6, plus the addition of a theft-deterrent system and heated outside rearview mirrors as standard equipment. And if four new exterior colors (Sky, Ruby, Silvermist and Cypress) weren't enough, then consider the availability of a new Gold Package (but only if you must).

1998

Body Styles	TMV Pricing		
	Trade	Private	Dealer
4 Dr GL Pass Van Ext	4513	5567	6757
4 Dr GLS Pass Van Ext	5047	6226	7555

Options	Price
Leather Seats	+186

Body Styles	TMV Pricing		
	Trade	Private	Dealer
4 Dr GS Pass Van	4642	5727	6950
4 Dr Premiere Pass Van Ext	5756	7101	8618

Options	Price
OnStar Telematic System [Opt on Premiere]	+212

Mileage Category: P

Side-impact airbags are standard for front seat passengers, and Oldsmobile is building more short-wheelbase vans with dual sliding doors. Front airbags get second-generation technology, which results in slower deployment speeds. Midyear, a Premiere Edition debuted, loaded with standard features including a TV/VCR setup in back.

1997

Body Styles	TMV Pricing		
	Trade	Private	Dealer
3 Dr GL Pass Van Ext	3827	4840	6079
3 Dr GLS Pass Van Ext	4158	5259	6604

Options	Price
Leather Seats	+165

Body Styles	TMV Pricing		
	Trade	Private	Dealer
3 Dr STD Pass Van	3423	4329	5437
3 Dr STD Pass Van Ext	3683	4658	5850

Options	Price
Power Moonroof	+132

Mileage Category: P

Completely redesigned, the new Silhouette comes in several trim levels and two sizes, each with a healthy load of standard equipment.

1996

Body Styles	TMV Pricing		
	Trade	Private	Dealer
3 Dr STD Pass Van	2775	3581	4694

Options	Price
Leather Seats	+140

Mileage Category: P

New 180-horsepower, 3.4-liter V6 makes the Silhouette even better able to imitate Japan's bullet train.

1995

Body Styles	TMV Pricing		
	Trade	Private	Dealer
3 Dr STD Pass Van	1960	2616	3710

Options	Price
Leather Seats	+110

Mileage Category: P

The 3.1-liter V6 engine is dropped in favor of the more powerful 3.8-liter V6.

1994

Body Styles	TMV Pricing		
	Trade	Private	Dealer
3 Dr STD Pass Van	1398	1974	2934
3 Dr Special Edition Pass Van	1397	1973	2932

Options	Price
3.8L V6 OHV 12V FI Engine [Opt on STD]	+82
Automatic 4-Speed Transmission [Opt on STD]	+82
Leather Seats	+89

Mileage Category: P

Driver airbag added to standard equipment list. Traction control and integrated child seats are new options. Power-sliding side door debuts. New Special Edition model is available.

Plymouth
Acclaim/Breeze

1995

Body Styles	TMV Pricing		
	Trade	Private	Dealer
4 Dr STD Sdn	930	1419	2234

Options	Price
3.0L V6 SOHC 12V FI Engine	+95

Mileage Category: C

Last year for Acclaim.

1994

Mileage Category: C

The Acclaim gains a motorized passenger seatbelt. The flexible-fuel model is now available to retail customers.

Body Styles	TMV Pricing		
	Trade	Private	Dealer
4 Dr STD Sdn	523	891	1503

Options	Price	Options	Price
Air Conditioning	+87	Automatic 4-Speed Transmission	+99
Antilock Brakes	+94	3.0L V6 SOHC 12V FI Engine	+84

Plymouth
Breeze

2000

Body Styles	TMV Pricing		
	Trade	Private	Dealer
4 Dr STD Sdn	4122	5165	6188

Options	Price	Options	Price
2.4L I4 DOHC 16V FI Engine	+171	Automatic 4-Speed Transmission	+399
Aluminum/Alloy Wheels	+260	Compact Disc Changer	+143
AM/FM/CD Audio System	+133	Power Sunroof	+264
Antilock Brakes	+258		

Mileage Category: C

New colors and child-seat tether anchorages update the Breeze for 2000.

1999

Mileage Category: C

Power windows, locks and mirrors, along with floor mats and a driver seat height adjuster are now standard on the Breeze. In addition, the suspension has been revised for a more pleasant ride.

Body Styles	TMV Pricing			Body Styles	TMV Pricing		
	Trade	Private	Dealer		Trade	Private	Dealer
4 Dr Expresso Sdn	3238	4170	5140	4 Dr STD Sdn	3198	4119	5077

Options	Price	Options	Price
2.4L I4 DOHC 16V FI Engine	+130	Automatic 4-Speed Transmission	+302
Aluminum/Alloy Wheels	+197	Power Sunroof	+200
Antilock Brakes	+218		

1998

Mileage Category: C

Availability of a 2.4-liter engine brings 150 horsepower and 167 pound-feet of torque, and that's just what the Breeze needs to live up to its name. Both engines can meet California emissions regulations, and new engine mounts help make them quieter. An Expresso package adds some aesthetic changes, a power sunroof is now optional and there are six new colors to choose from.

Body Styles	TMV Pricing			Body Styles	TMV Pricing		
	Trade	Private	Dealer		Trade	Private	Dealer
4 Dr Expresso Sdn	2676	3553	4542	4 Dr STD Sdn	2624	3484	4453

Options	Price	Options	Price
Power Sunroof	+159	Antilock Brakes	+173
Aluminum/Alloy Wheels	+156	Automatic 4-Speed Transmission	+240

1997

Body Styles	TMV Pricing		
	Trade	Private	Dealer
4 Dr STD Sdn	2124	2912	3874

For the latest vehicle information, visit www.edmunds.com

Breeze/Colt/Grand Voyager

Options	Price
Aluminum/Alloy Wheels	+158
Antilock Brakes	+175
Automatic 4-Speed Transmission	+197

Mileage Category: C

Plymouth is inching the Breeze up-market in both price and content. This year sees a fairly sizable price hike and the addition of luxury options such as an in-dash CD changer. Changes to the standard equipment list bring a nicer center console, improved basic stereos and increased-flow rear-seat heater ducts.

1996

Mileage Category: C

Body Styles	TMV Pricing		
	Trade	Private	Dealer
4 Dr STD Sdn	1564	2252	3203

The Breeze is introduced this year as Chrysler Corporation's bargain-basement midsize sedan. Nicely equipped with air conditioning and a decent stereo, the Breeze has a surprising amount of interior room.

Options	Price	Options	Price
Antilock Brakes	+138	Power Sunroof	+127
Automatic 4-Speed Transmission	+155		

1994

Body Styles	TMV Pricing		
	Trade	Private	Dealer
2 Dr GL Cpe	511	940	1655
2 Dr STD Cpe	444	817	1438
4 Dr GL Sdn	554	1018	1792
4 Dr STD Sdn	534	983	1732

Body Styles	TMV Pricing		
	Trade	Private	Dealer
4 Dr Vista AWD Wgn	817	1504	2650
4 Dr Vista SE Wgn	800	1472	2591
4 Dr Vista Wgn	724	1331	2343

Options	Price	Options	Price
Air Conditioning	+87	Automatic 4-Speed Transmission	+99
Antilock Brakes	+94		

Mileage Category: B

A driver airbag is now standard on the Colt and CFC-free air conditioning is optional.

2000

Body Styles	TMV Pricing		
	Trade	Private	Dealer
4 Dr SE Pass Van Ext	6637	7923	9183
4 Dr STD Pass Van Ext	6223	7429	8611

Options	Price	Options	Price
3.3L V6 OHV 12V FI Engine	+369	Camper/Towing Package	+159
Air Conditioning - Front and Rear [Opt on SE]	+323	Captain Chairs (4) [Opt on SE]	+255
Aluminum/Alloy Wheels [Opt on SE]	+158	Infinity Audio System [Opt on SE]	+274
AM/FM/Cassette/CD Audio System [Opt on SE]	+238	Power Driver Seat [Opt on SE]	+116
Antilock Brakes [Opt on STD]	+258		

Mileage Category: P

The Expresso trim level is discontinued, and Plymouth changes some of the standard features and options on base and SE models. Notably, base models now come with a cassette player. This is the last year for the Grand Voyager, as Chrysler begins dismantling the Plymouth division. Fortunately, the van's demise shouldn't pose much of a problem for shoppers, as the Dodge Grand Caravan gives you the same product with slightly different styling.

1999

Mileage Category: P

Body Styles	TMV Pricing		
	Trade	Private	Dealer
4 Dr Expresso Pass Van Ext	5515	6790	8118
4 Dr SE Pass Van Ext	5137	6325	7562

Body Styles	TMV Pricing		
	Trade	Private	Dealer
4 Dr STD Pass Van Ext	4760	5861	7006

SE models get body-color door and liftgate handles, as well as a body-colored front grille. All models add a cargo net between the front seats, and you can now get built-in child seats with the second-row captain's chairs.

Grand Voyager

1999 (cont'd)

Options	Price
3.3L V6 OHV 12V FI Engine	+280
Air Conditioning [Opt on STD]	+121
Air Conditioning - Front and Rear [Opt on Expresso,SE]	+245
AM/FM/Cassette/CD Audio System [Opt on SE]	+180

Options	Price
Antilock Brakes [Opt on STD]	+218
Camper/Towing Package	+121
Captain Chairs (4) [Opt on Expresso,SE]	+194
Infinity Audio System [Opt on Expresso,SE]	+208

1998

Mileage Category: P

Plymouth adds an Expresso trim level; intended to offer both style and value, this van has body-color door handles and silver exterior accents, and comes with privacy glass, keyless entry and a CD player. In other news, all Grand Voyagers get depowered, next-generation front airbags, adjustable front head restraints and new seat fabric. The four-speed automatic transmission receives upgrades for durability, and it can now be paired with the 3.0-liter V6 (which is LEV-certified in California). Other minor changes include an easy-entry feature for the left-hand captain's chair (in the second row) on vans with the left-hand sliding door, revised built-in booster seats and grocery bag hooks on the rear seat backs.

Body Styles	TMV Pricing		
	Trade	Private	Dealer
4 Dr Expresso Pass Van Ext	4069	5131	6328
4 Dr SE Pass Van Ext	3879	4890	6031

Body Styles	TMV Pricing		
	Trade	Private	Dealer
4 Dr STD Pass Van Ext	3402	4289	5290

Options	Price
Air Conditioning - Front and Rear [Opt on Expresso,SE]	+195
AM/FM/Cassette/CD Audio System [Opt on Expresso,SE]	+143
Antilock Brakes [Opt on STD]	+173
Captain Chairs (4) [Opt on Expresso,SE]	+153

1997

Mileage Category: P

Changes for 1997 include updated transmission software, an upgraded antilock brake system and an enhanced accident response system that unlocks the doors and turns on the interior lights if the front airbags deploy. Additionally, Plymouth has made improvements to the cabin insulation (to reduce noise and vibration) and cassette stereo units. Standard lighting elements now include front map lights and liftgate flood lamps; a cargo bay power point is also part of the deal. New options include an eight-way power driver seat and an overhead console with a trip computer, compass and outside temperature display. A Rallye decor package is available on SE models -- it includes a roof rack, tinted glass, alloy wheels and various silver accents and decals. Rounding out the changes are new wheel covers for the base model.

Body Styles	TMV Pricing		
	Trade	Private	Dealer
3 Dr SE Pass Van Ext	3185	4098	5214

Body Styles	TMV Pricing		
	Trade	Private	Dealer
3 Dr STD Pass Van Ext	2788	3587	4563

Options	Price
3.3L V6 OHV 12V FI Engine	+292
Air Conditioning - Front and Rear [Opt on SE]	+197
AM/FM/Cassette/CD Audio System [Opt on SE]	+144
Antilock Brakes [Opt on STD]	+175

Options	Price
Captain Chairs (4) [Opt on SE]	+144
Premium Audio System [Opt on SE]	+167
Sliding Driver Side Door	+138

1996

Mileage Category: P

The Grand Voyager is completely redesigned for 1996, and Chrysler's minivan designers and engineers have substantially improved upon the original formula: Interior comfort is top-notch, engines are more powerful (though you can no longer get the torquey 3.8-liter V6), and the available left-hand sliding door is an industry first.

Body Styles	TMV Pricing		
	Trade	Private	Dealer
3 Dr SE Pass Van Ext	2623	3447	4585

Body Styles	TMV Pricing		
	Trade	Private	Dealer
3 Dr STD Pass Van Ext	2292	3012	4006

Options	Price
3.0L V6 SOHC 12V FI Engine	+140
3.3L V6 OHV 12V FI Engine [Opt on SE]	+163
Air Conditioning - Front and Rear [Opt on SE]	+155

Options	Price
Antilock Brakes	+138
Captain Chairs (4) [Opt on SE]	+136
Premium Audio System [Opt on SE]	+131

1995

Mileage Category: P

Changes this year are minimal. ABS is now standard on LE models. SE models can be equipped with a snazzy Rallye package designed for those trying to disguise the fact that they are driving a minivan -- it includes two-tone paint treatment, tinted glass and 15-inch alloy wheels. Lastly, the four-speed automatic transmission benefits from engineering refinements.

Body Styles	TMV Pricing		
	Trade	Private	Dealer
3 Dr LE AWD Pass Van Ext	2273	3056	4362
3 Dr LE Pass Van Ext	2065	2777	3964
3 Dr SE AWD Pass Van Ext	1972	2652	3786

Body Styles	TMV Pricing		
	Trade	Private	Dealer
3 Dr SE Pass Van Ext	1825	2455	3504
3 Dr STD Pass Van Ext	1717	2309	3295

Options	Price
Air Conditioning - Front and Rear	+119
AM/FM/Cassette/CD Audio System [Opt on SE]	+88
Antilock Brakes [Opt on SE]	+106

Options	Price
Captain Chairs (4) [Opt on LE,SE]	+88
Leather Seats [Opt on LE]	+112
Premium Audio System [Opt on SE]	+101

1994

Body Styles	TMV Pricing		
	Trade	Private	Dealer
3 Dr LE AWD Pass Van Ext	1790	2587	3915
3 Dr LE Pass Van Ext	1548	2237	3386
3 Dr SE AWD Pass Van Ext	1487	2149	3253

Body Styles	TMV Pricing		
	Trade	Private	Dealer
3 Dr SE Pass Van Ext	1396	2017	3053
3 Dr STD Pass Van Ext	1320	1908	2887

1994 (cont'd)

Options	Price
Antilock Brakes	+94
Captain Chairs (4) [Opt on LE,SE]	+78

Options	Price
Leather Seats [Opt on LE]	+99
Premium Audio System [Opt on LE]	+90

Mileage Category: P

The Grand Voyager sees a number of changes for 1994. On the outside, the vans have revised front and rear fascias, body-side molding and lower-body cladding. Inside, you'll find a new instrument panel, various revisions to the controls and a front-passenger seat that offers fore/aft adjustment. In addition, Plymouth has made improvements to sliding-door operation and the windshield wipers, and taken measures to reduce noise and vibration in the cabin. On the safety front, all vans get a standard passenger-side front airbag this year, along with side-impact beams that meet 1997 federal passenger car standards and asbestos-free brakes. Antilock brakes are now standard on all-wheel-drive models. In terms of performance, the 3.3-liter V6 benefits from additional horsepower (now up to 162) and torque (now up to 194). LE models can be optioned with a larger-displacement 3.8-liter V6, which offers just 162 hp but makes a healthy 213 pound-feet of torque. Remote keyless entry is now standard on the SE and LE and optional on the base model. The optional built-in child seats now have a recline feature to improve comfort when kids are sleeping.

Plymouth
Laser
1994

Body Styles	TMV Pricing		
	Trade	Private	Dealer
2 Dr RS Hbk	787	1276	2090
2 Dr RS Turbo AWD Hbk	1003	1626	2665

Body Styles	TMV Pricing		
	Trade	Private	Dealer
2 Dr RS Turbo Hbk	923	1496	2451
2 Dr STD Hbk	732	1187	1944

Options	Price
Air Conditioning	+87
Antilock Brakes	+94

Options	Price
Automatic 4-Speed Transmission	+93

Mileage Category: E

The final year for the Laser brings automatic-locking retractors for rear seats, making them more compatible for child seats.

Plymouth
Neon
2001

Body Styles	TMV Pricing		
	Trade	Private	Dealer
4 Dr Highline LX Sdn	4580	5808	6941

Body Styles	TMV Pricing		
	Trade	Private	Dealer
4 Dr Highline Sdn	4251	5391	6443

Options	Price
Air Conditioning	+513
Aluminum/Alloy Wheels	+182
Antilock Brakes	+349
Automatic 3-Speed Transmission	+308
Compact Disc Changer	+192

Options	Price
Cruise Control	+115
Front Side Airbag Restraints	+179
Leather Seats	+338
Power Moonroof	+305
Power Windows	+131

Mileage Category: B

Side-impact airbags and leather seats are now available in Plymouth's economy car. A center shoulder belt for the rear seat and an internal emergency trunk release further improve this Plymouth's safety consciousness. A Sun and Sound or a Value/Fun option group is available this year, each of which includes a sunroof. New interior and exterior options for the Neon pump some life into this fading brand.

2000

Body Styles	TMV Pricing		
	Trade	Private	Dealer
4 Dr Highline Sdn	3005	3994	4964

Body Styles	TMV Pricing		
	Trade	Private	Dealer
4 Dr LX Sdn	3379	4492	5583

Options	Price
Air Conditioning [Std on LX Sdn]	+380
Aluminum/Alloy Wheels	+155
AM/FM/CD Audio System	+150
Antilock Brakes	+319

Options	Price
Automatic 3-Speed Transmission	+228
Compact Disc Changer	+190
Power Moonroof	+226

Mileage Category: B

Everything's new inside and out, as the second-generation Neon grows up, not old. A totally redesigned suspension and steering system, low-speed traction control and a complete exterior redesign head up the notable changes.

Plymouth
Neon

1999

Mileage Category: B

Nothing changes for '99.

Body Styles	TMV Pricing		
	Trade	Private	Dealer
2 Dr Competition Cpe	2176	3011	3881
2 Dr Expresso Cpe	2573	3561	4589
2 Dr Highline Cpe	2306	3192	4114

Body Styles	TMV Pricing		
	Trade	Private	Dealer
4 Dr Competition Sdn	2196	3040	3919
4 Dr Expresso Sdn	2639	3652	4707
4 Dr Highline Sdn	2345	3246	4184

Options	Price
Air Conditioning [Std on Comp Cpe,Expresso]	+288
Aluminum/Alloy Wheels	+118
Antilock Brakes	+242
Automatic 3-Speed Transmission	+192

Options	Price
Compact Disc Changer	+144
Competition Package	+288
Power Moonroof	+172

1998

Mileage Category: B

California and other emission-regulating states get an LEV (Low Emission Vehicle) engine calibration. Also changed this year are ABS, a new ignition key lock and the addition of four new colors.

Body Styles	TMV Pricing		
	Trade	Private	Dealer
2 Dr Competition Cpe	1761	2550	3439
2 Dr Expresso Cpe	1980	2866	3865
2 Dr Highline Cpe	1851	2680	3615
4 Dr Competition Sdn	1834	2655	3581

Body Styles	TMV Pricing		
	Trade	Private	Dealer
4 Dr Expresso Sdn	1917	2775	3743
4 Dr Highline Sdn	1867	2703	3645
4 Dr Style Sdn	2194	3176	4284

Options	Price
Air Conditioning [Opt on Competition,Highline]	+229
Antilock Brakes	+173
Automatic 3-Speed Transmission	+152

Options	Price
Competition Package	+229
Power Moonroof	+136

1997

Mileage Category: B

The 1997 Neons are made quieter with the addition of a structural oil pan. Other changes include new optional radios, a new seat fabric, new wheels and wheel covers and a few new paint colors.

Body Styles	TMV Pricing		
	Trade	Private	Dealer
2 Dr Expresso Cpe	1538	2332	3302
2 Dr Highline Cpe	1420	2153	3049
2 Dr STD Cpe	1327	2012	2849

Body Styles	TMV Pricing		
	Trade	Private	Dealer
4 Dr Expresso Sdn	1592	2414	3418
4 Dr Highline Sdn	1533	2324	3291
4 Dr STD Sdn	1360	2062	2920

Options	Price
Air Conditioning [Opt on STD]	+231
Antilock Brakes	+175
Automatic 3-Speed Transmission	+154

Options	Price
Compact Disc Changer	+115
Competition Package	+131
Power Moonroof	+138

1996

Mileage Category: B

Antilock brakes are optional across the line, and base models get more standard equipment for 1996. A value-packed Expresso package is aimed at 20-something first-time buyers. A base coupe is newly available, and all Neons are supposedly quieter than last year. A power moonroof joins the options list, and a remote keyless entry system with panic alarm is available.

Body Styles	TMV Pricing		
	Trade	Private	Dealer
2 Dr Highline Cpe	1080	1718	2600
2 Dr STD Cpe	1025	1631	2467
2 Dr Sport Cpe	1213	1930	2921

Body Styles	TMV Pricing		
	Trade	Private	Dealer
4 Dr Highline Sdn	1168	1858	2811
4 Dr STD Sdn	1038	1652	2500
4 Dr Sport Sdn	1220	1940	2935

Options	Price
Air Conditioning	+182
Antilock Brakes	+138

Options	Price
Automatic 3-Speed Transmission	+122
Competition Package	+331

1995

Mileage Category: B

The all-new Neon is introduced as Plymouth's entry in the compact car class. Roomy, cute and quick are three of the best adjectives we can find for this car. The Neon is available in coupe and sedan body styles in three trim-levels. Safety equipment includes standard dual airbags, optional antilock brakes and an optional integrated child seat.

Body Styles	TMV Pricing		
	Trade	Private	Dealer
2 Dr Highline Cpe	751	1252	2086
2 Dr Sport Cpe	920	1533	2555
4 Dr Highline Sdn	847	1412	2353

Body Styles	TMV Pricing		
	Trade	Private	Dealer
4 Dr STD Sdn	678	1130	1883
4 Dr Sport Sdn	896	1493	2488

Options	Price
Air Conditioning	+141
Antilock Brakes [Std on Sport]	+106

Options	Price
Automatic 3-Speed Transmission	+94
Leather Seats	+77

Prowler/Sundance

2001

Body Styles	TMV Pricing		
	Trade	Private	Dealer
2 Dr STD Conv	29053	31879	34488

Mileage Category: F

Get your Plymouth Prowler while you can. After 2001 it becomes the Chrysler Prowler. Sure, it will be the identical car, but that powerful Plymouth Prowler alliteration will be gone forever! You can get these in Copper Metallic and a silver/black combination this year. New adjustable damper shocks are offered as standard equipment.

2000

Mileage Category: F

Prowler Purple is discontinued, replaced by Prowler Silver for 2000. Chrome wheels are standard, as is a new leather shift boot and speed-sensitive volume for the stereo.

Body Styles	TMV Pricing		
	Trade	Private	Dealer
2 Dr STD Conv	26418	29249	32024

Options	Price
Special Factory Paint	+570

1999

Mileage Category: F

A brand-new 3.5-liter engine under the hood creates performance more fitting a hot rod. Also new for '99 is one more color option: Prowler Yellow.

Body Styles	TMV Pricing		
	Trade	Private	Dealer
2 Dr STD Conv	23764	26619	29592

Options	Price
Chrome Wheels	+288
Special Factory Paint	+288

1997

Mileage Category: F

Plymouth brings a hot-rod-style show car to market. Although the Prowler's V6 kicks out a respectable 214 horsepower, it comes only with a four-speed automatic transmission. More show than go, some enthusiasts will lament the Prowler's lack of a V8 and manual gearbox.

Body Styles	TMV Pricing		
	Trade	Private	Dealer
2 Dr STD Conv	21780	24329	27445

Plymouth
Sundance

1994

Body Styles	TMV Pricing		
	Trade	Private	Dealer
2 Dr Duster Hbk	511	940	1655
2 Dr STD Hbk	469	862	1518
4 Dr Duster Hbk	597	1098	1933
4 Dr STD Hbk	490	901	1586

Options	Price
3.0L V6 SOHC 12V FI Engine	+84
Air Conditioning	+87
Antilock Brakes	+94
Automatic 4-Speed Transmission	+93

Mileage Category: B

The Sundance gets a motorized passenger shoulder belt and CFC-free air conditioning.

Plymouth
Voyager

2000

Mileage Category: P

The Expresso trim level is discontinued. A new option package that Plymouth calls "T-Plus" allows buyers to pick up the 3.0-liter V6, cruise control, a tilt steering wheel and power windows, mirrors and locks, all for about $20,000. Base models now come standard with a cassette player. Note that this is your last opportunity to get a Plymouth-badged Voyager, as Chrysler dismantles its value-oriented division -- all future Voyagers will be badged as Chryslers.

Body Styles	TMV Pricing		
	Trade	Private	Dealer
3 Dr STD Pass Van	5268	6290	7291
4 Dr SE Pass Van	6544	7813	9057

Options	Price
Aluminum/Alloy Wheels	+158
AM/FM/Cassette/CD Audio System	+238
Antilock Brakes [Std on SE]	+258
Camper/Towing Package	+159
Captain Chairs (4)	+255
Infinity Audio System	+274
Power Driver Seat	+116

Options	Price
Sliding Driver Side Door [Opt on STD]	+226
3.0L V6 SOHC 12V FI Engine [Opt on STD]	+304
3.3L V6 Flex Fuel OHV 12V FI Engine [Opt on STD]	+369
3.3L V6 OHV 12V FI Engine	+369
7 Passenger Seating [Opt on STD]	+143
Air Conditioning [Opt on STD]	+159

1999

Mileage Category: P

SE models get body-color door and liftgate handles, as well as a body-colored front grille. All models add a cargo net between the front seats, and you can now get built-in child seats with the second-row captain's chairs.

Body Styles	TMV Pricing		
	Trade	Private	Dealer
3 Dr STD Pass Van	3913	4818	5759
4 Dr Expresso Pass Van	5270	6488	7756

Body Styles	TMV Pricing		
	Trade	Private	Dealer
4 Dr SE Pass Van	5028	6190	7400

Options	Price
Air Conditioning [Opt on STD]	+121
AM/FM/Cassette/CD Audio System [Opt on SE]	+180
Antilock Brakes [Opt on STD]	+218
Camper/Towing Package	+121
Captain Chairs (4)	+194

Options	Price
Infinity Audio System	+208
Sliding Driver Side Door [Opt on STD]	+172
3.0L V6 SOHC 12V FI Engine [Opt on STD]	+231
3.3L V6 OHV 12V FI Engine	+280

1998

Mileage Category: P

Plymouth adds an Expresso trim level; intended to offer both style and value, this van has body-color door handles and silver exterior accents, and comes with privacy glass, keyless entry and a CD player. In other news, all Voyagers get depowered, next-generation front airbags, adjustable front head restraints and new seat fabric. The four-speed automatic transmission receives upgrades for durability, and it can now be paired with the 3.0-liter V6 (which is LEV-certified in California). Other minor changes include an easy-entry feature for the left-hand captain's chair (in the second row) on vans with the left-hand sliding door, revised built-in booster seats and grocery bag hooks on the rear seat backs.

Body Styles	TMV Pricing		
	Trade	Private	Dealer
3 Dr STD Pass Van	3036	3828	4722
4 Dr Expresso Pass Van	3845	4848	5980

Body Styles	TMV Pricing		
	Trade	Private	Dealer
4 Dr SE Pass Van	3621	4566	5632

Options	Price
Sliding Driver Side Door [Opt on STD]	+136
3.0L V6 SOHC 12V FI Engine [Opt on STD]	+176
AM/FM/Cassette/CD Audio System [Opt on SE]	+143

Options	Price
Antilock Brakes [Opt on STD]	+173
Captain Chairs (4)	+153

1997

Mileage Category: P

Changes for 1997 include updated transmission software, an upgraded antilock brake system and an enhanced accident response system that unlocks the doors and turns on the interior lights if the front airbags deploy. Additionally, Plymouth has made improvements to the cabin insulation (to reduce noise and vibration) and cassette stereo units. Standard lighting elements now include front map lights and liftgate flood lamps; a cargo bay power point is also part of the deal. New options include an eight-way power driver seat and an overhead console with a trip computer, compass and outside temperature display. Finally, base models get new wheel covers.

Body Styles	TMV Pricing		
	Trade	Private	Dealer
3 Dr SE Pass Van	3004	3865	4917
3 Dr STD Pass Van	2569	3305	4205

Options	Price
3.3L V6 OHV 12V FI Engine	+341
AM/FM/Cassette/CD Audio System	+144
Antilock Brakes [Std on SE]	+175
Automatic 3-Speed Transmission [Opt on SE]	+121

Options	Price
Captain Chairs (4)	+144
Premium Audio System [Opt on SE]	+167
Sliding Driver Side Door	+138

1996

Body Styles	TMV Pricing		
	Trade	Private	Dealer
3 Dr SE Pass Van	2474	3251	4325
3 Dr STD Pass Van	2095	2753	3662

Options	Price
3.0L V6 SOHC 12V FI Engine	+140
3.3L V6 OHV 12V FI Engine	+163
Antilock Brakes [Opt on STD]	+138

Options	Price
Captain Chairs (4)	+136
Premium Audio System [Opt on SE]	+131

Mileage Category: P

The Voyager is completely redesigned for 1996, and Chrysler's minivan designers and engineers have substantially improved upon the original formula: Interior comfort is top-notch, engines are more powerful and the available left-hand sliding door is an industry first.

1995

Body Styles	TMV Pricing		
	Trade	Private	Dealer
3 Dr LE Pass Van	2022	2719	3880
3 Dr SE Pass Van	1728	2324	3316
3 Dr STD Pass Van	1516	2038	2909

Options	Price
Antilock Brakes [Std on AWD,LE]	+106
Captain Chairs (4)	+88
Premium Audio System [Opt on STD]	+101

Mileage Category: P

Changes this year are minimal. ABS is now standard on LE models. SE models can be equipped with a snazzy Rallye package designed for those trying to disguise the fact that they are driving a minivan -- it includes two-tone paint treatment, tinted glass and 15-inch alloy wheels. The four-speed automatic transmission benefits from engineering refinements, while the base model is no longer available with a manual transmission. A natural gas version of the 3.3-liter V6 is available in limited numbers this year.

1994

Body Styles	TMV Pricing		
	Trade	Private	Dealer
3 Dr LE Pass Van	1457	2106	3187
3 Dr SE Pass Van	1243	1797	2720
3 Dr STD Pass Van	1060	1533	2321

Options	Price
Air Conditioning - Front and Rear	+105
Antilock Brakes [Std on AWD]	+94
Captain Chairs (4)	+78
Leather Seats	+99

Mileage Category: P

The Voyager sees a number of changes for 1994. On the outside, the vans have revised front and rear fascias, body-side molding and lower-body cladding. Inside, you'll find a new instrument panel, various revisions to the controls and a front-passenger seat that offers fore/aft adjustment. In addition, Plymouth has made improvements to sliding-door operation and the windshield wipers, and taken measures to reduce noise and vibration in the cabin. On the safety front, all vans get a standard passenger-side front airbag this year, along with side-impact beams that meet 1997 federal passenger car standards and asbestos-free brakes. The 3.0-liter V6 becomes standard on the SE model; base vans can still get it as an option. The 3.3-liter V6, optional on the LE, benefits from additional horsepower (now up to 162) and torque (now up to 194). Remote keyless entry is now standard on the LE and optional on the SE. The optional built-in child seats now have a recline feature to improve comfort when kids are sleeping. Finally, note that all-wheel drive will no longer be offered; those who want it will need to step up to the longer-wheelbase Grand Voyager.

Pontiac
Aztek/Bonneville

2003

Mileage Category: L

For 2003, the Aztek offers a few new high-tech options like a DVD-based entertainment system and XM Satellite Radio. You'll also find additional wheel styles, a tire pressure-monitoring system and a new "luxury appointment group" for top-of-the-line models.

Body Styles	TMV Pricing		
	Trade	Private	Dealer
4 Dr STD AWD SUV	12542	13655	15510

Options	Price
Antilock Brakes [Opt on 2WD]	+385
Camper/Towing Package	+207
Heads-Up Display	+241
Heated Front Seats	+156
Leather Seats	+368
Power Driver Seat	+136
Power Moonroof	+136
Power Passenger Seat	+136

Body Styles	TMV Pricing		
	Trade	Private	Dealer
4 Dr STD SUV	11319	12323	13997

Options	Price
Front Side Airbag Restraints [Opt on 2WD]	+170
Traction Control System	+170
OnStar Telematic System	+269
Tire Inflation System	+156
AM/FM/CD Changer Audio System	+167
Satellite Radio System	+184
17 Inch Wheels	+167
DVD Entertainment System	+567

2002

Mileage Category: L

After a chilling reception from consumers in its first year, Pontiac is attempting to salvage the Aztek with a slight makeover that includes a monotone exterior and a new rear spoiler. Inside, numerous amenities that were optional on last year's model are now standard equipment.

Body Styles	TMV Pricing		
	Trade	Private	Dealer
4 Dr STD AWD Wgn	10381	11428	13173

Options	Price
17 Inch Wheels	+243
AM/FM/Cassette/CD Audio System	+207
AM/FM/CD Changer Audio System	+144
Camper/Towing Package	+178
Heads-Up Display	+207
Leather Seats	+414

Body Styles	TMV Pricing		
	Trade	Private	Dealer
4 Dr STD Wgn	9556	10520	12126

Options	Price
OnStar Telematic System	+338
Power Driver Seat	+117
Power Moonroof	+316
Power Passenger Seat	+117
Temperature Controls - Driver and Passenger	+170

2001

Mileage Category: L

Pontiac brings forth a new so-called Sport Recreation Vehicle, blending attributes of a station wagon, minivan, SUV and Pumbaa the talking pig (from "The Lion King") into an "interesting" offering.

Body Styles	TMV Pricing		
	Trade	Private	Dealer
4 Dr GT AWD Wgn	9371	10751	12025
4 Dr GT Wgn	9110	10452	11690

Options	Price
AM/FM/Cassette/CD Audio System	+136
AM/FM/CD Changer Audio System	+124
Camper/Towing Package	+153

Body Styles	TMV Pricing		
	Trade	Private	Dealer
4 Dr STD AWD Wgn	8980	10302	11523
4 Dr STD Wgn	8341	9569	10703

Options	Price
Captain Chairs (4)	+126
Heads-Up Display [Opt on GT]	+116
Power Moonroof	+273

Pontiac
Bonneville

2003

Mileage Category: G

The Bonneville gets only minor changes for 2003. Base SE models now sport newly styled 16-inch steel wheels and a standard AM/FM/CD stereo, while all models can be upgraded with optional XM Satellite Radio. Previously standard side airbags are now optional on SE and SLE models.

Body Styles	TMV Pricing		
	Trade	Private	Dealer
4 Dr SE Sdn	13185	14142	15738
4 Dr SLE Sdn	15305	16417	18269

Options	Price
Aluminum/Alloy Wheels [Opt on SE]	+212
Compact Disc Changer	+337
Heads-Up Display [Opt on SSEi]	+184
Heated Front Seats	+167
Leather Seats [Opt on SE,SLE]	+450
Power Moonroof	+623

Body Styles	TMV Pricing		
	Trade	Private	Dealer
4 Dr SSEi S/C Sdn	18782	20146	22419

Options	Price
Power Passenger Seat [Opt on SE,SLE]	+136
Front Side Airbag Restraints [Opt on SE,SLE]	+198
17 Inch Wheels - Chrome [Opt on SLE,SSEi]	+337
OnStar Telematic System [Opt on SE]	+394
Satellite Radio System	+184
Automatic Climate Control (2 Zone) - Driver and Passenger [Opt on SE,SLE]	+207

2002

Body Styles	TMV Pricing		
	Trade	Private	Dealer
4 Dr SE Sdn	11245	12190	13766
4 Dr SLE Sdn	12633	13695	15466

Body Styles	TMV Pricing		
	Trade	Private	Dealer
4 Dr SSEi S/C Sdn	15771	17097	19308

Options	Price
17 Inch Wheels - Chrome [Opt on SLE,SSEi]	+290
Automatic Climate Control (2 Zone) - Driver and Passenger [Opt on SE]	+219
Compact Disc Changer	+290
Heated Front Seats [Opt on SSEi]	+144

Options	Price
Leather Seats [Std on SSEi]	+414
OnStar Telematic System [Opt on SE]	+207
Power Moonroof	+526
Power Passenger Seat [Std on SSEi]	+258

Mileage Category: G

Only subtle changes are on tap for the 2002 Bonneville. Most notable on the list are new front and rear fascias for the base SE model, while new exterior badging and dual exhaust tips debut on the SLE and SSEi models. Newly styled 17-inch wheels, three new exterior colors, LATCH child-seat anchors, an improved Monsoon sound system and redesigned cupholders round out the changes.

2001

Body Styles	TMV Pricing		
	Trade	Private	Dealer
4 Dr SE Sdn	9182	10453	11626
4 Dr SLE Sdn	9940	11315	12585

Body Styles	TMV Pricing		
	Trade	Private	Dealer
4 Dr SSEi S/C Sdn	13348	15196	16902

Options	Price
17 Inch Wheels - Chrome	+250
Automatic Climate Control (2 Zone) - Driver and Passenger [Opt on SE]	+157
Compact Disc Changer	+250
Heated Front Seats	+124

Options	Price
Leather Seats [Std on SSEi]	+357
OnStar Telematic System	+199
Power Moonroof	+453
Power Passenger Seat [Std on SSEi]	+138

Mileage Category: G

Heated seats are available on the SE and SLE, and Ivory White is a new color for the year. OnStar telematics with a one-year membership is optional on the SE but comes standard with the SLE and SSEi.

2000

Body Styles	TMV Pricing		
	Trade	Private	Dealer
4 Dr SE Sdn	7271	8485	9674
4 Dr SLE Sdn	7777	9075	10348

Body Styles	TMV Pricing		
	Trade	Private	Dealer
4 Dr SSEi S/C Sdn	10660	12440	14184

Options	Price
Aluminum/Alloy Wheels [Opt on SE]	+123
AM/FM/CD Audio System	+121
Chrome Wheels	+225
Compact Disc Changer	+225
Leather Seats [Std on SSEi]	+322

Options	Price
OnStar Telematic System	+339
Power Driver Seat [Opt on SE]	+116
Power Moonroof	+371
Power Passenger Seat [Std on SSEi]	+116

Mileage Category: G

Brand-new from the ground up, Pontiac's flagship sedan moves onto a stiffer platform with rakish styling and high-tech goodies such as an integrated chassis control system.

1999

Body Styles	TMV Pricing		
	Trade	Private	Dealer
4 Dr SE Sdn	5628	6737	7892
4 Dr SLE Sdn	5906	7069	8280

Body Styles	TMV Pricing		
	Trade	Private	Dealer
4 Dr SSE Sdn	7520	9002	10544
4 Dr SSEi S/C Sdn	7597	9094	10652

Options	Price
Chrome Wheels	+178
Leather Seats	+254

Options	Price
OnStar Telematic System	+297
Power Moonroof	+293

Mileage Category: G

GM's dealer-installed OnStar mobile communications system is available.

1998

Body Styles	TMV Pricing		
	Trade	Private	Dealer
4 Dr SE Sdn	4409	5418	6555
4 Dr SLE Sdn	5103	6270	7587

Body Styles	TMV Pricing		
	Trade	Private	Dealer
4 Dr SSE Sdn	6013	7388	8939
4 Dr SSEi S/C Sdn	6442	7915	9576

Options	Price
Chrome Wheels	+160
Leather Seats	+228

Options	Price
OnStar Telematic System	+267
Power Moonroof	+263

Mileage Category: G

Second-generation airbags are standard, the SE comes with a standard deck lid spoiler, and the SSE gets more standard equipment. New colors freshen the aging Bonneville.

Pontiac
Bonneville/Firebird

1997

Mileage Category: G

Changes for 1997 are few. Supercharged Bonnevilles get a new transmission, a new Delco/Bose premium sound system is optional on the SSE, and the EYE CUE heads-up display has a new motorized adjustment feature. Two new exterior colors, a new interior color and a new interior fabric visually liven up the aging Bonneville.

Body Styles	TMV Pricing		
	Trade	Private	Dealer
4 Dr SE S/C Sdn	4120	5250	6632
4 Dr SE Sdn	3352	4272	5396

Options	Price
Chrome Wheels	+147
Electronic Suspension Control [Opt on SE]	+117

Body Styles	TMV Pricing		
	Trade	Private	Dealer
4 Dr SSE Sdn	4566	5819	7350
4 Dr SSEi S/C Sdn	4656	5934	7495

Options	Price
Leather Seats	+192
Power Moonroof	+242

1996

Mileage Category: G

The Series II V6 has been supercharged for 1996, pumping out 240 horsepower. Styling front and rear has been tweaked, and daytime running lights debut.

Body Styles	TMV Pricing		
	Trade	Private	Dealer
4 Dr SE S/C Sdn	2739	3645	4895
4 Dr SE Sdn	2389	3179	4269
4 Dr SLE Sdn	3023	4022	5401

Options	Price
Chrome Wheels	+125
Leather Seats	+164

Body Styles	TMV Pricing		
	Trade	Private	Dealer
4 Dr SSE S/C Sdn	3453	4594	6169
4 Dr SSE Sdn	3309	4403	5913

Options	Price
Power Moonroof	+206

1995

Mileage Category: G

Base engine is upgraded to 3800 Series II status, gaining 35 horsepower in the process. SE models with the SLE package can be ordered with the supercharged 3.8-liter V6. Computer Command Ride is made available on SE models.

Body Styles	TMV Pricing		
	Trade	Private	Dealer
4 Dr SE S/C Sdn	2036	2806	4088
4 Dr SE Sdn	1810	2494	3634

Options	Price
Leather Seats	+139
Power Moonroof	+174

Body Styles	TMV Pricing		
	Trade	Private	Dealer
4 Dr SSE Sdn	2359	3251	4737
4 Dr SSEi S/C Sdn	2555	3520	5129

Options	Price
Special Seats [Opt on SSE]	+209

1994

Mileage Category: G

Dual airbags are standard. SE and SSE trim levels are available. Californians get SLE model. SSEi is an option package on SSE. Supercharged engine in SSEi package gets 20 more horsepower. Automatic transmission gains "Normal" and "Performance" shift modes when hooked to supercharged engine. Traction control gains ability to retard engine power as well as apply brakes to slow spinning wheel(s). Get traction control on the SSE, and you can opt for Computer Command Ride, a suspension package that automatically adjusts the suspension to meet the demands of the driver.

Body Styles	TMV Pricing		
	Trade	Private	Dealer
4 Dr SE Sdn	1403	2068	3175
4 Dr SSE Sdn	1841	2713	4167

Options	Price
Leather Seats	+126
Power Moonroof	+159

Body Styles	TMV Pricing		
	Trade	Private	Dealer
4 Dr SSEi S/C Sdn	1988	2930	4500

Options	Price
Power Sunroof	+112
Sport Suspension	+81

Pontiac
Firebird

2002

Mileage Category: E

Entering its last year of production, the Firebird gets few changes for 2002. Power mirrors and a power antenna are now standard on all models, and Bright Silver Metallic replaces Blue-Green Chameleon on the color palette.

Body Styles	TMV Pricing		
	Trade	Private	Dealer
2 Dr Formula Hbk	14449	15539	17355
2 Dr STD Conv	14747	15859	17712
2 Dr STD Hbk	10266	11040	12331

Options	Price
17 Inch Wheels [Opt on Trans Am]	+365
5.7L V8 OHV 16V FI w/Ram Air Engine [Opt on Trans Am]	+1193
Automatic 4-Speed Transmission [Opt on STD Hbk]	+316
Chrome Wheels	+290
Compact Disc Changer	+290

Body Styles	TMV Pricing		
	Trade	Private	Dealer
2 Dr Trans Am Conv	18765	20180	22538
2 Dr Trans Am Hbk	14854	15974	17841

Options	Price
Leather Seats [Std on Trans Am]	+280
Limited Slip Differential [Opt on STD]	+173
Power Driver Seat [Opt on STD Hbk]	+131
Traction Control System	+122
T-Tops - Glass [Std on Trans Am]	+484

2001

Body Styles	TMV Pricing		
	Trade	Private	Dealer
2 Dr Formula Hbk	12033	13514	14881
2 Dr STD Conv	12513	14053	15475
2 Dr STD Hbk	8724	9798	10789

Body Styles	TMV Pricing		
	Trade	Private	Dealer
2 Dr Trans Am Conv	16101	18083	19912
2 Dr Trans Am Hbk	12925	14516	15985

Options	Price
Automatic 4-Speed Transmission [Opt on STD]	+342
Chrome Wheels	+250
Compact Disc Changer	+250
Leather Seats [Std on Trans Am]	+241
Limited Slip Differential	+126

Options	Price
Monsoon Audio System [Opt on STD Hbk]	+138
Power Windows [Opt on STD Hbk]	+124
Ram Air Performance Package	+1321
T-Tops - Glass [Std on Trans Am]	+418
T-Tops - Solid	+417

Mileage Category: E

For 2001, V8-equipped Formula and Trans Am receive five more horsepower and five more pound-feet of torque, new exterior and interior colors join the palette and the Ram Air Formula is dropped from the lineup.

2000

Body Styles	TMV Pricing		
	Trade	Private	Dealer
2 Dr Formula Hbk	10551	12013	13447
2 Dr SLP Firehawk Hbk	14492	16501	18470
2 Dr STD Conv	10969	12490	13980
2 Dr Formula Hbk	10551	12013	13447
2 Dr SLP Firehawk Hbk	14492	16501	18470
2 Dr STD Conv	10969	12490	13980

Body Styles	TMV Pricing		
	Trade	Private	Dealer
2 Dr Formula Hbk	10551	12013	13447
2 Dr SLP Firehawk Hbk	14492	16501	18470
2 Dr STD Conv	10969	12490	13980
2 Dr Formula Hbk	10551	12013	13447
2 Dr SLP Firehawk Hbk	14492	16501	18470
2 Dr STD Conv	10969	12490	13980

Options	Price
T-Tops - Glass [Std on Trans Am]	+377
Ram Air Performance Package	+568
17 Inch Wheels - Chrome [Opt on Trans Am]	+303
5.7L V8 OHV 16V FI w/Ram Air Engine	+890
AM/FM/Cassette/CD Audio System	+125

Options	Price
Automatic 4-Speed Transmission [Opt on STD]	+309
Chrome Wheels	+225
Compact Disc Changer	+225
Leather Seats [Std on Trans Am]	+218
Monsoon Audio System [Opt on STD Hbk]	+125

Mileage Category: E

New wheels, exterior and interior colors and engine revisions for improved emissions and better throttle response on manual transmission-equipped cars top the list of Firebird changes for 2000.

1999

Body Styles	TMV Pricing		
	Trade	Private	Dealer
2 Dr Formula Hbk	9046	10511	12036
2 Dr STD Conv	9372	10890	12470
2 Dr STD Hbk	6424	7464	8547

Body Styles	TMV Pricing		
	Trade	Private	Dealer
2 Dr Trans Am Conv	11450	13304	15234
2 Dr Trans Am Hbk	9499	11038	12639

Options	Price
17 Inch Wheels [Opt on Formula, Trans Am]	+158
5.7L V8 OHV 16V FI w/Ram Air Engine	+581
Automatic 4-Speed Transmission [Opt on STD]	+244
Chrome Wheels	+178
Compact Disc Changer	+178

Options	Price
Leather Seats [Std on Trans Am]	+172
Ram Air Performance Package	+448
Special Leather Seat Trim [Opt on Trans Am]	+274
T-Tops - Glass [Std on Trans Am]	+297

Mileage Category: E

Electronic traction control is now available on all models, with a bigger gas tank and an oil life monitor standard. A Torsen limited-slip rear axle comes with V8 models (and V6 cars with the performance package), while an eight-speaker Delco/Monsoon sound system goes into the convertible. A power-steering cooler is now available for V8s, and a Hurst shifter is optional on the six-speed manual transmission. The Ram Air WS6 package now sports dual outlet exhaust, and two new exterior colors debut, Pewter and Medium Blue Metallic. The 30th anniversary Trans Am sports an extroverted paint scheme that features two blue stripes running over the hood and deck lid.

1998

Body Styles	TMV Pricing		
	Trade	Private	Dealer
2 Dr Formula Hbk	7394	8741	10259
2 Dr STD Conv	7614	9000	10563
2 Dr STD Hbk	5307	6273	7363

Body Styles	TMV Pricing		
	Trade	Private	Dealer
2 Dr Trans Am Conv	9681	11443	13430
2 Dr Trans Am Hbk	7806	9227	10830

Options	Price
Performance/Handling Package	+316
Premium Audio System [Opt on Trans Am Hbk]	+115
Traction Control System	+121
T-Tops - Glass [Std on Trans Am]	+267
17 Inch Wheels [Opt on Formula, Trans Am]	+223

Options	Price
5.7L V8 OHV 16V FI w/Ram Air Engine	+700
Automatic 4-Speed Transmission [Opt on STD]	+219
Chrome Wheels	+160
Compact Disc Changer	+160
Leather Seats [Std on Trans Am]	+174

Mileage Category: E

Firebirds get a minor restyle that is most evident from the front end. Also on tap for Formula and Trans Am models is a detuned Corvette engine making 305 horsepower without Ram Air induction. Base models can be equipped with a new Sport Appearance Package, and two new exterior colors debut. Second-generation airbags are standard.

Pontiac
Firebird

1997

Body Styles	TMV Pricing		
	Trade	Private	Dealer
2 Dr Formula Conv	7102	8544	10306
2 Dr Formula Hbk	6096	7334	8847
2 Dr STD Conv	6660	8013	9666

Body Styles	TMV Pricing		
	Trade	Private	Dealer
2 Dr STD Hbk	4329	5208	6282
2 Dr Trans Am Conv	7725	9294	11211
2 Dr Trans Am Hbk	6223	7487	9031

Options	Price
17 Inch Wheels [Opt on Formula, Trans Am]	+206
5.7L V8 OHV 16V FI w/Ram Air Engine	+590
Automatic 4-Speed Transmission [Opt on STD]	+195
Chrome Wheels	+147

Options	Price
Compact Disc Changer	+147
Leather Seats	+199
Performance/Handling Package	+290
T-Tops - Glass	+246

Mileage Category: E

Pontiac upgrades the Firebird in several ways for 1997. Performance freaks will appreciate the addition of Ram Air induction to the options list of the Formula and Trans Am convertibles. Audiophiles will be blown away by the newly optional 500-watt Monsoon sound system. Luxury intenders can get power seats swathed in leather this year. Safety-conscious buyers will find daytime running lights. Additional cosmetic and comfort items keep the fourth-generation Firebird fresh for its fifth year.

1996

Mileage Category: E

A new standard V6 makes 40 more horsepower than the old one. The LT1 V8 also makes more power, particularly when equipped with Ram Air induction. A new color livens up the exterior, as if it needed it.

Body Styles	TMV Pricing		
	Trade	Private	Dealer
2 Dr Formula Conv	5900	7251	9116
2 Dr Formula Hbk	4583	5632	7081
2 Dr STD Conv	5053	6210	7808

Body Styles	TMV Pricing		
	Trade	Private	Dealer
2 Dr STD Hbk	3484	4282	5384
2 Dr Trans Am Conv	6366	7824	9837
2 Dr Trans Am Hbk	4726	5808	7303

Options	Price
17 Inch Wheels [Opt on Formula, Trans Am]	+175
5.7L V8 OHV 16V FI w/Ram Air Engine	+502
Automatic 4-Speed Transmission [Opt on STD]	+166

Options	Price
Compact Disc Changer	+125
Leather Seats	+169
T-Tops - Glass	+204

1995

Mileage Category: E

Traction control is added as an option on Formula and Trans Am. Trans Am GT is dropped from lineup. Californians get a 3.8-liter V6 equipped with an automatic transmission on base models instead of the 3.4-liter V6. The new engine meets strict emissions standards in that state, and makes 40 additional horsepower.

Body Styles	TMV Pricing		
	Trade	Private	Dealer
2 Dr Formula Conv	4420	5494	7285
2 Dr Formula Hbk	3442	4279	5674
2 Dr STD Conv	4098	5094	6755

Body Styles	TMV Pricing		
	Trade	Private	Dealer
2 Dr STD Hbk	2535	3152	4179
2 Dr Trans Am Conv	5354	6656	8826
2 Dr Trans Am Hbk	3891	4837	6414

Options	Price
Leather Seats [Opt on Formula, STD]	+102
Premium Audio System	+77
T-Tops - Glass	+173

Options	Price
T-Tops - Solid	+116
Automatic 4-Speed Transmission	+141
Air Conditioning [Std on Trans Am, Conv]	+89

1994

Mileage Category: E

Trans Am GT debuts. Six-speed transmission is saddled with a first-to-fourth skip shift feature designed to improve fuel economy. Automatic is new electronically controlled unit with the V8 engine, and it features Normal and Performance modes. Remote keyless entry, cassette player and leather-wrapped steering wheel move from the Trans Am standard equipment list to the options sheet. T/A also loses Batwing rear spoiler to GT, taking Formula's more subdued rear treatment. Convertible debuts at midyear. A 25th anniversary Trans Am, done up in white with blue accents, celebrates a quarter-century of Pontiac's performance flagship.

Body Styles	TMV Pricing		
	Trade	Private	Dealer
2 Dr Formula Conv	3456	4548	6369
2 Dr Formula Hbk	2743	3609	5053
2 Dr STD Conv	3291	4331	6064
2 Dr STD Hbk	2010	2645	3704

Body Styles	TMV Pricing		
	Trade	Private	Dealer
2 Dr Trans Am 25th Anniv Hbk	3415	4494	6292
2 Dr Trans Am GT Conv	3736	4917	6884
2 Dr Trans Am GT Hbk	3134	4124	5775
2 Dr Trans Am Hbk	2973	3913	5479

Options	Price
Leather Seats [Std on Trans Am GT Conv]	+93
T-Tops - Glass	+157

Options	Price
Air Conditioning	+81
Automatic 4-Speed Transmission	+128

2003

Body Styles	TMV Pricing		
	Trade	Private	Dealer
2 Dr GT Cpe	10691	11729	13459
2 Dr GT1 Cpe	11286	12382	14209
4 Dr GT Sdn	10726	11768	13504
4 Dr GT1 Sdn	11322	12422	14254

Body Styles	TMV Pricing		
	Trade	Private	Dealer
4 Dr SE Sdn	9111	9996	11471
4 Dr SE1 Sdn	9564	10493	12040
4 Dr SE2 Sdn	10598	11627	13342

Options	Price
Aluminum/Alloy Wheels [Opt on SE]	+170
Antilock Brakes [Opt on SE,SE1]	+385
Automatic 4-Speed Transmission [Opt on SE,SE1]	+482
Cruise Control [Opt on SE]	+142
Leather Seats [Opt on GT,GT1,SE2]	+326
Power Moonroof [Opt on GT,SE1,SE2]	+397

Options	Price
Power Windows [Opt on SE]	+144
Rear Spoiler [Opt on SE,SE1,SE2]	+127
Satellite Radio System [Opt on GT,SE1,SE2]	+184
3.4L V6 OHV 12V FI Engine [Opt on SE1]	+405
16 Inch Wheels - Chrome	+368

Mileage Category: C

A new trim level has been added -- SE2 -- that offers buyers more standard equipment and additional options, while the SE coupe is no longer available. All SE sedans now feature cleaner styling thanks to less body cladding and smoother front and rear fascias. XM Satellite Radio is an available option on all models, while the OnStar communications system is now standard on all models except the base SE.

2002

Body Styles	TMV Pricing		
	Trade	Private	Dealer
2 Dr GT Cpe	8257	9289	11008
2 Dr GT1 Cpe	8735	9826	11645
2 Dr SE Cpe	6774	7620	9031
2 Dr SE1 Cpe	7347	8265	9794

Body Styles	TMV Pricing		
	Trade	Private	Dealer
4 Dr GT Sdn	8289	9325	11051
4 Dr GT1 Sdn	8770	9865	11691
4 Dr SE Sdn	6807	7658	9075
4 Dr SE1 Sdn	7380	8302	9838

Options	Price
3.4L V6 OHV 12V FI Engine [Opt on SE1]	+348
Aluminum/Alloy Wheels [Opt on SE]	+146
Automatic 4-Speed Transmission [Opt on SE,SE1]	+402
Chrome Wheels	+290

Options	Price
Cruise Control [Opt on SE]	+117
Leather Seats [Opt on GT,GT1]	+280
Monsoon Audio System [Opt on SE1]	+139
Power Moonroof [Std on GT1]	+316

Mileage Category: C

Base model SEs get a new 2.2-liter four-cylinder engine, while GTs get newly styled 16-inch wheels. All models receive a console upgrade and two new exterior colors.

2001

Body Styles	TMV Pricing		
	Trade	Private	Dealer
2 Dr GT Cpe	6937	8293	9545
2 Dr GT1 Cpe	7276	8698	10010
2 Dr SE Cpe	5305	6342	7299
2 Dr SE1 Cpe	5947	7109	8182

Body Styles	TMV Pricing		
	Trade	Private	Dealer
4 Dr GT Sdn	7075	8458	9735
4 Dr GT1 Sdn	7462	8920	10265
4 Dr SE Sdn	5433	6495	7475
4 Dr SE1 Sdn	6073	7261	8357

Options	Price
3.4L V6 OHV 12V FI Engine [Opt on]	+275
Aluminum/Alloy Wheels [Opt on SE,SE1 Cpe]	+206
Automatic 4-Speed Transmission [Opt on SE,SE1]	+346
Chrome Wheels	+271

Options	Price
Leather Seats	+199
Monsoon Audio System [Opt on SE1]	+143
Power Moonroof [Std on GT1]	+250

Mileage Category: C

For 2001, the Grand Am gets audio improvements, a wheel upgrade and revised paint choices.

2000

Body Styles	TMV Pricing		
	Trade	Private	Dealer
2 Dr GT Cpe	5564	6792	7996
2 Dr GT1 Cpe	5866	7160	8429
2 Dr SE Cpe	4328	5283	6220
2 Dr SE1 Cpe	4711	5751	6771
2 Dr SE2 Cpe	5109	6237	7342

Body Styles	TMV Pricing		
	Trade	Private	Dealer
4 Dr GT Sdn	5681	6934	8163
4 Dr GT1 Sdn	6059	7397	8708
4 Dr SE Sdn	4458	5442	6407
4 Dr SE1 Sdn	4893	5974	7033
4 Dr SE2 Sdn	5618	6858	8073

Options	Price
3.4L V6 OHV 12V FI Engine [Opt on]	+248
Automatic 4-Speed Transmission [Opt on SE,SE1]	+297
Chrome Wheels	+244

Options	Price
Leather Seats	+180
Power Moonroof [Std on GT1]	+225

Mileage Category: C

Grand Am gets engine improvements, interior upgrades (including a revamped center console), new exterior appearance packages and revised paint choices.

1999

Mileage Category: C

New for 1999, the Grand Am offers a host of standard and optional equipment as well as a completely redesigned exterior.

Body Styles	TMV Pricing		
	Trade	Private	Dealer
2 Dr GT Cpe	4625	5847	7118
2 Dr GT1 Cpe	4904	6199	7546
2 Dr SE Cpe	3647	4610	5612
2 Dr SE1 Cpe	4111	5197	6327
2 Dr SE2 Cpe	4223	5337	6497

Options	Price
3.4L V6 OHV 12V FI Engine [Opt on SE1]	+196
Leather Seats	+164

Body Styles	TMV Pricing		
	Trade	Private	Dealer
4 Dr GT Sdn	4714	5959	7254
4 Dr GT1 Sdn	5121	6473	7880
4 Dr SE Sdn	3798	4800	5843
4 Dr SE1 Sdn	4174	5276	6423
4 Dr SE2 Sdn	4704	5946	7238

Options	Price
Power Moonroof [Std on GT1]	+178

1998

Body Styles	TMV Pricing		
	Trade	Private	Dealer
2 Dr GT Cpe	3217	4202	5313
2 Dr SE Cpe	2990	3905	4936

Options	Price
Automatic 4-Speed Transmission	+217
Leather Seats	+147

Body Styles	TMV Pricing		
	Trade	Private	Dealer
4 Dr GT Sdn	3387	4424	5593
4 Dr SE Sdn	3022	3946	4988

Options	Price
Power Moonroof	+160

Mileage Category: C

Second-generation airbags are newly standard, and option groups are simplified.

1997

Mileage Category: C

Very minimal changes this year as Pontiac concentrates on Grand Prix and Trans Sport launches. Air conditioning is now standard. Also, three new colors are added.

Body Styles	TMV Pricing		
	Trade	Private	Dealer
2 Dr GT Cpe	2564	3448	4528
2 Dr SE Cpe	2410	3241	4256

Options	Price
Automatic 4-Speed Transmission	+200
Leather Seats	+172

Body Styles	TMV Pricing		
	Trade	Private	Dealer
4 Dr GT Sdn	2513	3379	4438
4 Dr SE Sdn	2354	3164	4155

Options	Price
Power Driver Seat	+147
Power Moonroof	+147

1996

Mileage Category: C

New styling, a new base engine, dual airbags and body-mounted seatbelts.

Body Styles	TMV Pricing		
	Trade	Private	Dealer
2 Dr GT Cpe	1817	2556	3577
2 Dr SE Cpe	1682	2367	3314

Options	Price
Leather Seats	+146
Power Moonroof	+125
Automatic 4-Speed Transmission	+168

Body Styles	TMV Pricing		
	Trade	Private	Dealer
4 Dr GT Sdn	1926	2711	3794
4 Dr SE Sdn	1676	2358	3300

Options	Price
Air Conditioning [Opt on SE]	+175
AM/FM/Cassette/CD Audio System	+126

1995

Mileage Category: C

Base engine upgraded to a 150-horsepower version of the Quad 4. High-output Quad 4 motor is dropped from the GT, which now uses the same standard and optional power plants as the SE. Variable-effort power steering is a new option on GT models, rear suspensions are redesigned and SE models get restyled wheel covers and alloy wheels.

Body Styles	TMV Pricing		
	Trade	Private	Dealer
2 Dr GT Cpe	1214	1796	2765
2 Dr SE Cpe	1080	1598	2461

Options	Price
Air Conditioning [Opt on SE]	+148
Automatic 3-Speed Transmission	+80
Automatic 4-Speed Transmission	+142

Body Styles	TMV Pricing		
	Trade	Private	Dealer
4 Dr GT Sdn	1249	1848	2846
4 Dr SE Sdn	1155	1709	2631

Options	Price
Leather Seats	+98
Power Moonroof	+106

1994

Body Styles	TMV Pricing		
	Trade	Private	Dealer
2 Dr GT Cpe	859	1403	2310
2 Dr SE Cpe	828	1352	2224

Options	Price
Air Conditioning [Opt on SE]	+134
Leather Seats	+89

Body Styles	TMV Pricing		
	Trade	Private	Dealer
4 Dr GT Sdn	931	1521	2505
4 Dr SE Sdn	845	1382	2276

Options	Price
Power Sunroof	+97

Mileage Category: C

Driver airbag added. A 3.1-liter V6 replaces last year's optional 3.3-liter V6. Four-speed automatic debuts; standard with V6 and optional on four-cylinder models.

Pontiac
Grand Prix

2003

Body Styles	TMV Pricing		
	Trade	Private	Dealer
4 Dr GT Sdn	11908	13063	14988
4 Dr GTP S/C Sdn	14627	16046	18410

Options	Price
Antilock Brakes [Opt on GT,SE]	+385
Bose Audio System [Opt on GT,GTP]	+195
Heads-Up Display [Opt on GT,GTP]	+184
Heated Front Seats [Opt on GT]	+156
Leather Seats [Opt on GT,GTP]	+368

Body Styles	TMV Pricing		
	Trade	Private	Dealer
4 Dr SE Sdn	10938	11999	13767

Options	Price
Power Moonroof [Opt on GT,GTP]	+368
OnStar Telematic System [Opt on GT,SE]	+394
16 Inch Wheels [Opt on SE]	+170
16 Inch Wheels - Chrome [Opt on GT,GTP]	+198

Mileage Category: D

The Grand Prix coupe has been dropped from the lineup, leaving the SE, GT and GTP sedans as the remaining models. SE versions now come standard with an AM/FM/CD stereo, rear reading lamps and a ski pass-through, while all Grand Prix models now offer a standard overhead console with vanity mirrors and assist handles. A new Limited Edition package for GT and GTP models is available; it includes a new rear spoiler, special wheels, embroidered floor mats, blue foglamps, a monotone lower fascia, unique badging and door sill plates, white-faced gauges and special seats with leather inserts and blue stitching. ABS brakes are now optional on SE and GT models.

2002

Body Styles	TMV Pricing		
	Trade	Private	Dealer
2 Dr GT Cpe	9664	10798	12689
2 Dr GTP S/C Cpe	11091	12393	14563
4 Dr GT Sdn	9756	10901	12810

Options	Price
16 Inch Wheels [Opt on SE]	+146
Bose Audio System [Opt on GT]	+192
Chrome Wheels [Opt on GT,GTP]	+314
Heads-Up Display [Opt on GT]	+158

Body Styles	TMV Pricing		
	Trade	Private	Dealer
4 Dr GTP S/C Sdn	11766	13147	15449
4 Dr SE Sdn	8641	9655	11346

Options	Price
Leather Seats [Opt on GT,GTP]	+253
OnStar Telematic System [Opt on GT]	+207
Power Driver Seat [Opt on SE]	+117
Power Moonroof [Opt on GT,GTP]	+316

Mileage Category: D

A 40th Anniversary option package can be added to GT and GTP coupes and sedans. SE and GT models also gain additional standard equipment.

2001

Body Styles	TMV Pricing		
	Trade	Private	Dealer
2 Dr GT Cpe	7677	9152	10513
2 Dr GTP S/C Cpe	9435	11247	12920
4 Dr GT Sdn	7820	9322	10709

Options	Price
Aluminum/Alloy Wheels [Opt on SE]	+124
Bose Audio System	+155
Chrome Wheels	+271
Heads-Up Display [Opt on GT]	+116

Body Styles	TMV Pricing		
	Trade	Private	Dealer
4 Dr GTP S/C Sdn	9961	11874	13640
4 Dr SE Sdn	7005	8351	9593

Options	Price
Leather Seats	+199
OnStar Telematic System	+199
Power Driver Seat [Std on GTP]	+128
Power Moonroof	+240

Mileage Category: D

The Grand Prix receives only minor changes for 2001 including a Special Edition appearance package on GT and GTP models and optional 16-inch three-spoke aluminum wheels. The OnStar system is now available on GTP models while SE models receive a slight front-end revision.

2000

Mileage Category: D

Improvements to the base 3.1-liter V6 net a gain of 15 horsepower, as well as improved durability, reduced noise and lower emissions. A limited run (2,000 coupes) of Daytona Pace Car replicas will be built, featuring unique exterior and interior details. Also new are a revised anti-theft system, five-spoke silver-painted wheels, three new exterior colors and Cyclone cloth upholstery.

Body Styles	TMV Pricing		
	Trade	Private	Dealer
2 Dr GT Cpe	6569	7975	9354
2 Dr GTP S/C Cpe	8267	10036	11770
4 Dr GT Sdn	6806	8263	9692

Body Styles	TMV Pricing		
	Trade	Private	Dealer
4 Dr GTP S/C Sdn	8179	9930	11646
4 Dr SE Sdn	5857	7111	8341

Options	Price
3.8L V6 OHV 12V FI Engine [Std on GT]	+157
Bose Audio System	+150
Compact Disc Changer	+174
Leather Seats	+180

Options	Price
OnStar Telematic System [Opt on GT,GTP]	+339
Power Driver Seat [Opt on GT,SE]	+116
Power Moonroof	+216

1999

Mileage Category: D

The Grand Prix gets more muscle for '99 with low-restriction air-induction components giving the naturally aspirated 3.8-liter V6 five more horsepower, to 200. This engine is standard on the GT (sedan and coupe) and optional on the SE sedan. A traction control indicator and on/off button are now standard on GTP models. Minor revisions are in order inside, with front-door courtesy lamps and a six-speaker sound system now standard, and an eight-speaker Bose audio unit and OnStar mobile communications system optional. Outside, a rear deck spoiler is standard on the GT model, and two colors have been added to the 1999 exterior paint chart.

Body Styles	TMV Pricing		
	Trade	Private	Dealer
2 Dr GT Cpe	5325	6550	7826
2 Dr GTP S/C Cpe	6281	7727	9231
4 Dr GT Sdn	5589	6875	8213

Body Styles	TMV Pricing		
	Trade	Private	Dealer
4 Dr GTP S/C Sdn	6649	8179	9772
4 Dr SE Sdn	4889	6015	7186

Options	Price
3.8L V6 OHV 12V FI Engine [Std on GT]	+124
Bose Audio System	+119
Compact Disc Changer	+138

Options	Price
Leather Seats	+164
OnStar Telematic System [Opt on GT,GTP]	+297
Power Moonroof	+170

1998

Mileage Category: D

Supercharged GTP models get traction control, and new colors are available inside and out. Second-generation airbags debut as standard equipment.

Body Styles	TMV Pricing		
	Trade	Private	Dealer
2 Dr GT Cpe	4488	5738	7147
2 Dr GTP S/C Cpe	4579	5854	7292
4 Dr GT Sdn	4569	5841	7275

Body Styles	TMV Pricing		
	Trade	Private	Dealer
4 Dr GTP S/C Sdn	5138	6568	8181
4 Dr SE Sdn	4084	5221	6503

Options	Price
Compact Disc Changer	+160
Leather Seats	+147

Options	Price
Power Moonroof	+153

1997

Mileage Category: D

Pontiac redesigns the Grand Prix for 1997, giving buyers slick new styling, a longer and wider wheelbase and supercharged V6 power on GTP models. Traction control, antilock brakes, dual airbags and side-impact protection are standard. Optional is a built-in child safety seat.

Body Styles	TMV Pricing		
	Trade	Private	Dealer
2 Dr GT Cpe	3362	4467	5818
2 Dr GTP S/C Cpe	3692	4907	6392
4 Dr GT Sdn	3636	4832	6294

Body Styles	TMV Pricing		
	Trade	Private	Dealer
4 Dr GTP S/C Sdn	4193	5572	7257
4 Dr SE Sdn	3017	4010	5223

Options	Price
Compact Disc Changer	+147
Leather Seats	+136
Power Moonroof	+159

Options	Price
Compact Disc Changer	+147
Leather Seats	+136
Power Moonroof	+159

1996

Body Styles	TMV Pricing		
	Trade	Private	Dealer
2 Dr GTP Cpe	2504	3485	4839
2 Dr SE Cpe	2292	3189	4428

Body Styles	TMV Pricing		
	Trade	Private	Dealer
4 Dr GT Sdn	2470	3437	4772
4 Dr SE Sdn	2116	2944	4087

Options	Price
Antilock Brakes [Opt on SE]	+159
Leather Seats	+146

Options	Price
Power Moonroof	+136

Mileage Category: D

Minor trim and powertrain improvements to the only car in GM's stable that still has those stupid door-mounted seatbelts. Do yourself a favor, wait for the 1997 GP.

1995

Body Styles	TMV Pricing		
	Trade	Private	Dealer
2 Dr GTP Cpe	1808	2587	3886
2 Dr SE Cpe	1658	2372	3562

Options	Price
Antilock Brakes [Opt on SE]	+134
Compact Disc Changer	+82

Body Styles	TMV Pricing		
	Trade	Private	Dealer
4 Dr GT Sdn	1747	2500	3756
4 Dr SE Sdn	1446	2069	3108

Options	Price
Leather Seats	+124
Power Moonroof	+101

Mileage Category: D

Brake/transmission shift interlock is added. GT coupe dropped in favor of GTP Package. GT sedan continues. Variable-effort steering is added to GTP and GT. New alloys debut on GT and GTP. Coupes can be equipped with a White Appearance Package, which includes color-keyed alloys and special pinstriping. Floor consoles are redesigned on models with bucket seats.

1994

Body Styles	TMV Pricing		
	Trade	Private	Dealer
2 Dr SE Cpe	1073	1676	2682

Options	Price
3.4L V6 DOHC 24V FI Engine	+161
Antilock Brakes	+122

Body Styles	TMV Pricing		
	Trade	Private	Dealer
4 Dr SE Sdn	1058	1653	2644

Options	Price
Leather Seats	+113
Power Sunroof	+112

Mileage Category: D

Interior is redesigned to accommodate dual airbags. LE and STE sedans are dropped; GT and GTP become option packages on SE coupe. A GT package is available on SE sedan, and includes 3.4-liter V6, alloys, low-profile tires, ABS and sport suspension. Front seatbelts are anchored to pillars instead of doors on sedan; coupe retains door-mounted belts. The 3.1-liter V6 is up 20 horsepower. Twin-cam 3.4-liter V6 is up 10 horsepower. Five-speed manual and three-speed automatic transmissions are dropped in favor of four-speed automatic. Coupes gain standard equipment, including 16-inch alloys, cruise and leather-wrapped steering wheel with integral radio controls.

Pontiac

Montana

2003

Body Styles	TMV Pricing		
	Trade	Private	Dealer
4 Dr Montanavision AWD Pass Van Ext	17583	19088	21596
4 Dr Montanavision Pass Van Ext	15065	16354	18503
4 Dr STD AWD Pass Van Ext	15872	17230	19494
4 Dr STD Pass Van	13132	14256	16129

Body Styles	TMV Pricing		
	Trade	Private	Dealer
4 Dr STD Pass Van Ext	13911	15101	17085
4 Dr Value Pass Van	12238	13285	15031
4 Dr Value Pass Van Ext	13293	14431	16327

Options	Price
Aluminum/Alloy Wheels [Opt on STD, Value]	+142
Antilock Brakes [Opt on Value]	+538
Compact Disc Changer [Opt on MontanaVision, STD]	+224
Leather Seats [Opt on MontanaVision, STD]	+467
Power Driver Seat [Opt on STD, Value]	+136
Power Dual Sliding Doors [Opt on MontanaVision, STD]	+198

Options	Price
Power Sliding Door [Opt on STD]	+198
Sport Package [Opt on MontanaVision, STD]	+1456
OnStar Telematic System [Opt on MontanaVision, STD]	+241
Air Conditioning - Front and Rear [Opt on STD, Value]	+255
Park Distance Control (Rear) [Opt on MontanaVision, STD]	+227

Mileage Category: P

The Montana gets only a few minor upgrades for 2003. The most notable change is the addition of an extended-length version of the Special Value van with a 60/40-split bench second-row seat as standard. More available free flow options also give the Value van a greater range of equipment.

2002

Mileage Category: P

Pontiac's big news for the Montana this year is the availability of the Versatrak all-wheel-drive system. Also debuting this year on the Montana is the Thunder Sport package and a very cool DVD entertainment system.

Body Styles	TMV Pricing		
	Trade	Private	Dealer
4 Dr Montanavision AWD Pass Van Ext	14704	16166	18603
4 Dr Montanavision Pass Van Ext	12487	13729	15798
4 Dr STD AWD Pass Van Ext	13233	14549	16742

Body Styles	TMV Pricing		
	Trade	Private	Dealer
4 Dr STD Pass Van Ext	10926	12012	13823
4 Dr Value Pass Van	10066	11067	12736

Options	Price
7 Passenger Seating [Opt on STD]	+477
Air Conditioning - Front and Rear [Opt on STD Ext]	+316
Aluminum/Alloy Wheels [Opt on STD]	+122
Chrome Wheels [Opt on Ext]	+268
Compact Disc Changer [Opt on Ext]	+144
Leather Seats [Opt on Ext]	+389
OnStar Telematic System [Std on Montanavision]	+207

Options	Price
Park Distance Control (Rear) [Opt on STD]	+195
Power Driver Seat [Opt on STD Ext]	+117
Power Dual Sliding Doors [Opt on Ext]	+170
Power Passenger Seat [Opt on Ext]	+117
Power Sliding Door [Opt on STD Ext]	+170
Rear Spoiler [Opt on Ext]	+134
Touring Suspension [Opt on Ext]	+146

2001

Mileage Category: P

Updated styling and more feature content top the list of changes to the Montana for 2001, but perhaps most importantly, GM has figured out how to provide buyers with a third-row seat that flips and folds to create a flat load floor in extended-length models. New standard features include OnStar communications, power windows, a CD player and remote keyless entry. A rear parking aid sensor, power driver-side sliding door and an in-dash six-disc CD changer are new options. When you buy the available TV/VCP setup, you get a larger screen for 2001.

Body Styles	TMV Pricing		
	Trade	Private	Dealer
4 Dr Convenience Pass Van Ext	9363	10894	12308
4 Dr STD Pass Van	8606	10014	11313
4 Dr STD Pass Van Ext	8824	10268	11600
4 Dr Sport Pass Van	8963	10429	11783

Options	Price
Air Conditioning - Front and Rear	+189
Aluminum/Alloy Wheels	+117
Compact Disc Changer	+124

Body Styles	TMV Pricing		
	Trade	Private	Dealer
4 Dr Sport Pass Van Ext	9529	11088	12527
4 Dr Value Pass Van	8078	9399	10619
4 Dr Vision Pass Van Ext	10081	11730	13252

Options	Price
Leather Seats	+493
Park Distance Control (Rear) [Opt on Convenience]	+168

2000

Mileage Category: P

The 2000 Montana boasts improvements to its V6 and antilock brakes, an upgraded electrical system, a revised instrument cluster and radios, a quieter climate-control blower motor, the option of heated leather seats, reading lamps and oil-life monitoring as well as new paint schemes.

Body Styles	TMV Pricing		
	Trade	Private	Dealer
4 Dr STD Pass Van	6348	7622	8870
4 Dr STD Pass Van Ext	7038	8450	9834

Options	Price
Air Conditioning - Front and Rear	+170
AM/FM/Cassette/CD Audio System	+139
Leather Seats	+377
OnStar Telematic System [Opt on STD]	+339

Body Styles	TMV Pricing		
	Trade	Private	Dealer
4 Dr Vision Pass Van Ext	7401	8886	10341

Options	Price
Power Sliding Door	+170
Power Windows	+123
Sport Suspension	+353

1999

Mileage Category: P

The entire line gets a name change this year, from Trans Sport to Montana (the name pulled from '98's sporty trim package). Regular-wheelbase models come with one or two sliding doors, while extended wheelbase vans get two only with a right-side power-sliding door option. Side-impact airbags are standard, as are 15-inch 215-70R white-letter puncture sealant tires. New two-tone paint jobs are available and four new exterior colors are offered, as are options for front-row leather seats and an overhead video system. Better still, a special sport performance package adds cast-aluminum wheels, traction control and a specially tuned sport suspension for soccer dads (and moms) who are sport sedan wanna-bes.

Body Styles	TMV Pricing		
	Trade	Private	Dealer
3 Dr STD Pass Van	4811	5945	7126
4 Dr STD Pass Van	5230	6463	7746

Options	Price
Air Conditioning - Front and Rear	+135
Leather Seats	+297
OnStar Telematic System	+297

Body Styles	TMV Pricing		
	Trade	Private	Dealer
4 Dr STD Pass Van Ext	5545	6852	8213

Options	Price
Power Sliding Door	+135
Sport Suspension [Opt on 4 Dr]	+278

Pontiac
Sunbird

1994

Body Styles	TMV Pricing		
	Trade	Private	Dealer
2 Dr LE Conv	936	1504	2450
2 Dr LE Cpe	677	1087	1771

Options	Price
3.1L V6 OHV 12V FI Engine [Opt on LE]	+97
Air Conditioning	+113

Mileage Category: B

Body Styles	TMV Pricing		
	Trade	Private	Dealer
2 Dr SE Cpe	783	1258	2049
4 Dr LE Sdn	680	1093	1781

Options	Price
Automatic 3-Speed Transmission	+89

GT coupe, SE convertible and SE sedan vanish. Surviving are LE models and an SE coupe that comes standard with the GT's old bodywork. Convertibles get alloys and rear spoiler standard. SE comes with a 3.1-liter V6 standard.

Pontiac
Sunfire

2003

Body Styles	TMV Pricing		
	Trade	Private	Dealer
2 Dr STD Cpe	6665	7544	9008

For the latest vehicle information, visit www.edmunds.com

2003 (cont'd)

Options	Price
Aluminum/Alloy Wheels	+184
AM/FM/CD Audio System	+142
Antilock Brakes	+385
Automatic 4-Speed Transmission	+459
Cruise Control	+142
Power Door Locks	+125

Options	Price
Power Moonroof	+280
Power Windows	+135
Front Side Airbag Restraints	+212
OnStar Telematic System	+241
Satellite Radio System	+184
16 Inch Wheels	+184

Mileage Category: B

The Sunfire gets a refresh this year that adds new front and rear fascias, a revised sport suspension and four new wheel styles. The 2.2-liter Ecotec four-cylinder is now the only engine offered, as the GT model has been dropped from the lineup. Base model Sunfires no longer come with standard ABS brakes, but it remains an available option. On the inside, there's a 60/40-split folding rear seat, an upgraded interior seat fabric and new options like side-impact airbags, XM Satellite Radio and the OnStar system.

2002

Body Styles	TMV Pricing		
	Trade	Private	Dealer
2 Dr GT Cpe	6233	7159	8703
2 Dr SE Cpe	5181	5951	7234

Body Styles	TMV Pricing		
	Trade	Private	Dealer
4 Dr SE Sdn	5551	6376	7751

Options	Price
2.2L I4 DOHC 16V FI Engine [Opt on SE]	+219
AM/FM/CD Audio System [Opt on SE]	+117
Automatic 4-Speed Transmission	+394

Options	Price
Power Moonroof [Opt on Cpe]	+270
Power Windows	+124

Mileage Category: B

All models get a tilt steering wheel and an electric trunk release as standard equipment. Three new exterior colors debut, while the three-speed automatic transmission gets dropped from the lineup.

2001

Body Styles	TMV Pricing		
	Trade	Private	Dealer
2 Dr GT Cpe	4901	6037	7085
2 Dr SE Cpe	4039	4974	5838

Body Styles	TMV Pricing		
	Trade	Private	Dealer
4 Dr SE Sdn	4158	5121	6010

Options	Price
2.4L I4 DOHC 16V FI Engine [Std on GT]	+189
Aluminum/Alloy Wheels [Opt on SE]	+124
AM/FM/CD Audio System	+134

Options	Price
Automatic 4-Speed Transmission	+340
Power Moonroof	+250
Power Windows	+121

Mileage Category: B

A standard rear spoiler and a new exterior color are the only new additions to the Sunfire for 2001. The GT convertible is no longer available, leaving the sedan and coupe versions as the only available body styles.

2000

Body Styles	TMV Pricing		
	Trade	Private	Dealer
2 Dr GT Conv	4995	6270	7520
2 Dr GT Cpe	4142	5199	6236

Body Styles	TMV Pricing		
	Trade	Private	Dealer
2 Dr SE Cpe	3322	4170	5002
4 Dr SE Sdn	3358	4215	5056

Options	Price
2.4L I4 DOHC 16V FI Engine [Std on GT]	+170
AM/FM/Cassette/CD Audio System	+121
AM/FM/CD Audio System	+121

Options	Price
Automatic 3-Speed Transmission	+201
Automatic 4-Speed Transmission [Std on Conv]	+307
Power Moonroof	+225

Mileage Category: B

Redesigned front and rear fascias for a sportier appearance, a new five-speed manual transmission and the availability of the premium Monsoon audio system lead Sunfire's upgrade list for 2000. There are also restyled rocker-panel moldings, new wheels and exterior colors, as well as a revised instrument panel cluster, floor console and upholstery.

1999

Body Styles	TMV Pricing		
	Trade	Private	Dealer
2 Dr GT Conv	4240	5474	6758
2 Dr GT Cpe	3323	4289	5295

Body Styles	TMV Pricing		
	Trade	Private	Dealer
2 Dr SE Cpe	2658	3431	4236
4 Dr SE Sdn	2694	3478	4293

Options	Price
Power Moonroof	+178
2.4L I4 DOHC 16V FI Engine [Std on GT]	+135
Air Conditioning [Std on GT]	+248

Options	Price
Automatic 3-Speed Transmission	+176
Automatic 4-Speed Transmission [Std on Conv]	+262

Mileage Category: B

After Sunfire coupes got a rear spoiler last year, this year it's the sedan's turn, only as an option. The top-line 2.4-liter twin-cam engine is revised to improve breathing, including new fuel injectors, injection rails, exhaust manifold and catalytic converter. Fern Green Metallic is added to the paint color chart.

1998

Mileage Category: B

All coupes have a rear spoiler, a new six-speaker sound system is available, the base four-cylinder gets some additional low-end punch and Topaz Gold Metallic is added to the paint color chart. Second-generation airbags are added as standard equipment.

Body Styles	TMV Pricing			Body Styles	TMV Pricing		
	Trade	Private	Dealer		Trade	Private	Dealer
2 Dr GT Cpe	2871	3774	4793	2 Dr SE Cpe	2160	2840	3607
2 Dr SE Conv	3446	4531	5754	4 Dr SE Sdn	2246	2953	3750

Options	Price	Options	Price
Power Moonroof	+160	Automatic 3-Speed Transmission	+158
2.4L I4 DOHC 16V FI Engine [Opt on SE]	+121	Automatic 4-Speed Transmission [Opt on GT,SE]	+226
Air Conditioning [Std on GT,Conv]	+223		

1997

Mileage Category: B

SE convertible gets a higher level of standard equipment, including an automatic transmission. Coupes get a new front seatbelt guide loop, and a new Sports Interior trim debuts called Patina/Redondo cloth.

Body Styles	TMV Pricing			Body Styles	TMV Pricing		
	Trade	Private	Dealer		Trade	Private	Dealer
2 Dr GT Cpe	2304	3081	4030	2 Dr SE Cpe	1878	2512	3286
2 Dr SE Conv	2945	3938	5151	4 Dr SE Sdn	1914	2559	3348

Options	Price	Options	Price
Air Conditioning [Std on Conv]	+205	Automatic 4-Speed Transmission [Std on Conv]	+205
Automatic 3-Speed Transmission	+136	Power Moonroof	+147

1996

Mileage Category: B

Traction control, remote keyless entry and steering wheel radio controls are newly available. Old Quad 4 engine dumped in favor of new 2.4-liter twin-cam engine. Two new paint choices spiff up the exterior.

Body Styles	TMV Pricing			Body Styles	TMV Pricing		
	Trade	Private	Dealer		Trade	Private	Dealer
2 Dr GT Cpe	1897	2616	3610	2 Dr SE Cpe	1510	2083	2874
2 Dr SE Conv	2349	3241	4472	4 Dr SE Sdn	1545	2131	2940

Options	Price	Options	Price
Air Conditioning [Std on Conv]	+168	Power Moonroof	+125
Automatic 3-Speed Transmission [Std on Conv]	+116		

1995

Mileage Category: B

All-new replacement for aged Sunbird comes in SE coupe or sedan, and GT coupe trim levels. An SE convertible debuted midyear. Dual airbags, ABS, tilt steering and tachometer are standard. Base engine is a 2.2-liter four-cylinder good for 120 horsepower. GT models get a 150-horsepower Quad 4 engine, which is optional on SE. Order the four-speed automatic transmission and you'll get traction control.

Body Styles	TMV Pricing			Body Styles	TMV Pricing		
	Trade	Private	Dealer		Trade	Private	Dealer
2 Dr GT Cpe	1402	2047	3121	2 Dr SE Cpe	1052	1536	2342
2 Dr SE Conv	1652	2411	3677	4 Dr SE Sdn	1083	1581	2411

Options	Price	Options	Price
2.3L I4 DOHC 16V FI Engine [Opt on SE]	+116	Automatic 3-Speed Transmission [Std on Conv]	+98
Air Conditioning	+142	Power Moonroof	+106

Pontiac
Trans Sport

1998

Body Styles	TMV Pricing			Body Styles	TMV Pricing		
	Trade	Private	Dealer		Trade	Private	Dealer
3 Dr STD Pass Van	4019	5068	6251	4 Dr Montana Pass Van Ext	4789	6040	7450
4 Dr Montana Pass Van	4558	5748	7090	4 Dr STD Pass Van Ext	4494	5668	6991

Options	Price	Options	Price
Air Conditioning - Front and Rear	+121	Premium Audio System	+148
Captain Chairs (4)	+141	Sliding Driver Side Door [Opt on 3 Dr]	+117
Leather Seats	+354		

Mileage Category: P

Short-wheelbase models get the dual sliding doors and power-sliding door options. Side-impact airbags are standard, and a white two-tone paint job is new. Second-generation airbags are standard for front-seat occupants.

1997

Body Styles	TMV Pricing		
	Trade	Private	Dealer
3 Dr SE Pass Van	3603	4729	6106

Options	Price
Captain Chairs (4)	+130
Leather Seats	+260

Body Styles	TMV Pricing		
	Trade	Private	Dealer
3 Dr SE Pass Van Ext	3713	4874	6293

Options	Price
Power Moonroof	+172

Mileage Category: P

Pontiac redesigns the Trans Sport.

1996

Body Styles			TMV Pricing		
			Trade	Private	Dealer
3 Dr SE Pass Van			2624	3569	4874

Options	Price	Options	Price
7 Passenger Seating	+148	Leather Seats	+183

Mileage Category: P

A 180-horsepower, 3.4-liter V6 replaces weak base engine as well as the optional 3.8-liter V6. Front air conditioning is standard equipment for 1996.

1995

Body Styles			TMV Pricing		
			Trade	Private	Dealer
3 Dr SE Pass Van			1926	2666	3898

Options	Price	Options	Price
3.8L V6 OHV 12V FI Engine	+142	Automatic 4-Speed Transmission	+124
Air Conditioning	+80	Leather Seats	+155
Air Conditioning - Front and Rear	+80		

Mileage Category: P

A brake/transmission shift interlock is added. New overhead console includes outside temperature gauge, compass and storage bin.

1994

Body Styles			TMV Pricing		
			Trade	Private	Dealer
3 Dr SE Pass Van			1543	2234	3386

Options	Price	Options	Price
Automatic 4-Speed Transmission	+113	3.8L V6 OHV 12V FI Engine	+129
Leather Seats	+141		

Mileage Category: P

Driver airbag debuts and new front styling improves doorstop looks. Dashboard gets styling tweak to shorten visual acreage on top. A power-sliding side door and integrated child seats are newly optional. Automatic power door locks are added, and rear seats gain a fold-and-stow feature. Traction control is made available at midyear; requires 3.8-liter engine.

Pontiac
Vibe

2003

Body Styles	TMV Pricing		
	Trade	Private	Dealer
4 Dr GT Wgn	11798	12845	14589
4 Dr STD AWD Wgn	12003	13068	14843

Options	Price
Alarm System	+184
Aluminum/Alloy Wheels [Opt on STD 2WD,STD AWD]	+249
Antilock Brakes [Opt on STD 2WD]	+385
Appearance Package	+184
Automatic 4-Speed Transmission [Opt on STD 2WD]	+462
Navigation System	+907

Body Styles	TMV Pricing		
	Trade	Private	Dealer
4 Dr STD Wgn	10057	10949	12436

Options	Price
Power Moonroof	+280
Power Windows	+127
Front Side Airbag Restraints	+198
AM/FM/CD Changer Audio System	+184
17 Inch Wheels [Opt on GT,STD 2WD]	+227

Mileage Category: L

The Vibe is an all-new model in Pontiac's lineup designed to combine the best attributes of an SUV, a station wagon and a small van. Thankfully, the result is rather attractive and hip, not to mention utilitarian.

Porsche
911

2003

Mileage Category: F

Porsche finally puts a standard CD player in the 911. Five horsepower are mysteriously lost in non-Turbo 911s, meaning output is "only" 315 horses now.

Body Styles	TMV Pricing		
	Trade	Private	Dealer
2 Dr Carrera 4 AWD Conv	70382	73088	77598
2 Dr Carrera 4S AWD Cpe	66788	69356	73636
2 Dr Carrera Conv	64602	67086	71226
2 Dr Carrera Cpe	56250	58413	62018

Options	Price
Automatic 5-Speed Transmission	+2803
Automatic Dimming Rearview Mirror	+201
Bose Audio System	+652
Color To Sample Paint	+2861
Compact Disc Changer	+586
Cruise Control [Opt on GT2 Turbo]	+467
Heated Front Seats	+336
Hi-Fi Audio System	+680
Metallic Paint	+676
Metallic Paint To Sample	+2861
Navigation System	+2156
Performance/Handling Package	+11467
Special Factory Paint	+676
Special Leather Interior Trim	+984
Special Leather Seat Trim	+324

Body Styles	TMV Pricing		
	Trade	Private	Dealer
2 Dr Carrera Targa Cpe	62450	64851	68853
2 Dr GT2 Turbo Cpe	165375	171511	181737
2 Dr Turbo AWD Cpe	104836	108726	115208

Options	Price
Sport Chassis [Opt on Carrera,Carrera 4,Carrera Targa]	+578
18 Inch Wheels - Sport Design [Opt on Carrera,Carrera 4,Carrera Targa]	+2410
Sport Seats [Opt on Carrera,Carrera 4,Carrera Targa]	+328
Traction Control System [Opt on Carrera,Carrera Targa]	+1012
18 Inch Wheels - Turbo Look [Opt on Carrera,Carrera 4,Carrera Targa]	+1176
18 Inch Wheels - Sport Classic [Opt on Carrera,Carrera 4,Carrera Targa]	+2410
18 Inch Wheels [Opt on Carrera,Carrera 4,Carrera Targa]	+1176
Automatic Dimming Sideview Mirror(s)	+246
18 Inch Wheels - Sport Techno [Opt on Carrera 4S,Turbo]	+1484
Power Driver Seat w/Memory	+410
Park Distance Control (Rear)	+434

2002

Mileage Category: F

For those zealots who feel that a 911 Turbo isn't quite enough, Porsche rolls out the new-for-'02 GT2. Standard 911s receive new front-end styling and a bump in engine size (from 3.4 liters to 3.6) and power (from 300 horsepower to 320). Other 911 updates include a real glovebox, the option of a Bose stereo, a single cupholder and a gaggle of new wheels. Open-air versions were not overlooked when they were making improvements; the Cabriolet finally gets a glass rear window and the Targa model returns after a four-year hiatus.

Body Styles	TMV Pricing		
	Trade	Private	Dealer
2 Dr Carrera 4 AWD Conv	62553	65070	69266
2 Dr Carrera 4S AWD Cpe	60251	62675	66715
2 Dr Carrera Conv	59462	61855	65844
2 Dr Carrera Cpe	50954	53005	56423

Options	Price
18 Inch Wheels	+1007
18 Inch Wheels - Sport Classic	+2121
18 Inch Wheels - Sport Design	+2121
18 Inch Wheels - Turbo Look	+1740
Advanced Design Package	+3333
Advanced Technic Package	+2463
AM/FM/CD Audio System	+266
Arctic Silver Interior Package	+654
Automatic 5-Speed Transmission	+2607
Automatic Dimming Rearview Mirror [Std on GT2]	+266
Automatic Dimming Sideview Mirror(s) [Std on GT2]	+209
Automatic Stability Control [Opt on 2WD]	+608
Color To Sample Paint	+2630

Body Styles	TMV Pricing		
	Trade	Private	Dealer
2 Dr Carrera Targa Cpe	57165	59466	63300
2 Dr GT2 Turbo Cpe	153851	159734	169540
2 Dr Turbo AWD Cpe	98889	102650	108919

Options	Price
Compact Disc Changer	+543
Cruise Control [Opt on GT2]	+319
Design Package	+1505
Heated Front Seats	+315
Metallic Paint	+1695
Navigation System	+2691
Park Distance Control (Rear)	+399
Power Driver Seat w/Memory [Std on Turbo]	+228
Special Factory Paint	+627
Special Leather Seat Trim	+3724
Sport Chassis	+524
Traction Control System [Opt on 2WD]	+327

2001

Mileage Category: F

After a one-year hiatus, the 911 Turbo model makes its much anticipated return and brings with it 415 tire-shredding horsepower. All 911s get electric engine cover and trunk releases, improved interior lighting and improved trunk carpet. A new optional audio system includes a bass box, there are optional "Turbo Look 1" wheels, a self dimming day/night rearview mirror and a new three-spoke steering wheel with colored Porsche crests.

Body Styles	TMV Pricing		
	Trade	Private	Dealer
2 Dr Carrera 4 AWD Conv	55365	59457	63234
2 Dr Carrera 4 AWD Cpe	49885	53572	56975
2 Dr Carrera Conv	53220	57154	60785

Options	Price
18 Inch Wheels - Sport Classic [Opt on Cpe]	+1856
18 Inch Wheels - Sport Design	+1856

Body Styles	TMV Pricing		
	Trade	Private	Dealer
2 Dr Carrera Cpe	45174	48513	51595
2 Dr Turbo AWD Cpe	85404	91360	96857

Options	Price
Heated Front Seats	+265
Hi-Fi Audio System [Opt on Carrera]	+419

For the latest vehicle information, visit www.edmunds.com

2001 (cont'd)

Options	Price
18 Inch Wheels - Turbo Look [Opt on Non-Turbo]	+830
AM/FM/CD Audio System	+209
Arctic Silver Interior Package	+2149
Automatic 5-Speed Transmission	+2386
Automatic Dimming Rearview Mirror	+481
Automatic Dimming Sideview Mirror(s)	+192
Automatic Stability Control [Opt on Carrera]	+558
Color To Sample Paint	+2390
Compact Disc Changer	+492
Design Package	+2362
Digital Audio System [Opt on Turbo]	+401

Options	Price
Leather Seats [Std on Turbo]	+2243
Metallic Paint	+1538
Metallic Paint To Sample	+2390
Navigation System	+2470
Park Distance Control (Rear)	+363
Power Driver Seat w/Memory [Opt on Carrera]	+530
Power Passenger Seat [Opt on Carrera]	+530
Special Factory Paint	+1538
Sport Chassis [Opt on Carrera Cpe]	+481
Sport Suspension	+481
Traction Control System [Opt on Carrera]	+290

2000

Body Styles	TMV Pricing		
	Trade	Private	Dealer
2 Dr Carrera 4 AWD Conv	49119	53368	57532
2 Dr Carrera 4 AWD Cpe	46115	50105	54015

Body Styles	TMV Pricing		
	Trade	Private	Dealer
2 Dr Carrera Conv	48716	52930	57060
2 Dr Carrera Cpe	41193	44756	48249

Mileage Category: F

A new exhaust system bumps horsepower from 296 to 300. Already featured on Carrera 4 models, two-wheel-drive Carreras now get an electronic drive-by-wire throttle and optional PSM stability control. All models receive an upgraded interior console and materials. The formerly optional charcoal odor filter is now standard. There are two new standard and one new optional exterior colors.

Options	Price
18 Inch Wheels - Sport Classic [Opt on Cpe]	+1706
18 Inch Wheels - Sport Design [Opt on Carrera Cpe]	+1538
18 Inch Wheels - Turbo Look	+763
AM/FM/CD Audio System	+192
Automatic 5-Speed Transmission	+1980
Automatic Dimming Rearview Mirror	+346
Automatic Dimming Sideview Mirror(s)	+170
Compact Disc Changer	+430
Digital Audio System [Opt on Carrera]	+716
Heated Front Seats	+244

Options	Price
Limited Slip Differential [Opt on Carrera]	+740
Metallic Paint	+490
Navigation System	+2049
Power Driver Seat w/Memory	+463
Power Passenger Seat	+463
Special Factory Paint	+945
Special Leather Seat Trim [Opt on Carrera Conv]	+908
Sport Seats	+454
Traction Control System [Opt on Carrera]	+530

1999

Body Styles	TMV Pricing		
	Trade	Private	Dealer
2 Dr Carrera 4 AWD Conv	44579	49045	53694
2 Dr Carrera 4 AWD Cpe	38920	42820	46880

Body Styles	TMV Pricing		
	Trade	Private	Dealer
2 Dr Carrera Conv	42569	46834	51274
2 Dr Carrera Cpe	36302	39940	43726

Mileage Category: F

Everything just got better with the totally redesigned 911, internally named the 996. The 911 Coupe, Cabriolet and Carrera 4 (available as either a coupe or cabrio) are all available for the 1999 model year.

Options	Price
18 Inch Wheels - Sport Classic [Opt on Cpe]	+1572
18 Inch Wheels - Sport Design [Opt on Cpe]	+1343
18 Inch Wheels - Turbo Look	+704
AM/FM/CD Audio System	+160
Automatic 5-Speed Transmission	+1644
Automatic Dimming Rearview Mirror	+287
Compact Disc Changer	+357
Digital Audio System	+340
Hardtop Roof	+6156
Heated Front Seats	+202

Options	Price
Hi-Fi Audio System	+355
Limited Slip Differential [Opt on Carrera]	+616
Metallic Paint	+407
Navigation System	+2095
Power Driver Seat w/Memory	+450
Power Passenger Seat	+450
Special Factory Paint	+785
Special Leather Seat Trim	+882
Traction Control System [Opt on Carrera]	+440

1998

Body Styles	TMV Pricing		
	Trade	Private	Dealer
2 Dr Carrera 4 AWD Conv	41166	45527	50444
2 Dr Carrera 4S AWD Cpe	38745	42849	47477
2 Dr Carrera Conv	38001	42027	46566

Body Styles	TMV Pricing		
	Trade	Private	Dealer
2 Dr Carrera S Cpe	33708	37278	41304
2 Dr Carrera Targa Cpe	35359	39104	43328

Options	Price
Automatic 4-Speed Transmission	+1834
Automatic Dimming Rearview Mirror	+252

Options	Price
Power Driver Seat w/Memory	+427
Power Passenger Seat	+247

1998 (cont'd)
Mileage Category: F

The current-generation 911 goes the way of the dodo at year's end, replaced by the next evolutionary step toward the perfect driving machine.

Options	Price
Compact Disc Changer	+457
Hardtop Roof [Opt on Cabriolet]	+5844
Heated Front Seats	+325
Hi-Fi Audio System [Opt on S Cpe]	+337
Leather Seats	+742
Limited Slip Differential [Std on Carrera 4S,AWD]	+602
Metallic Paint	+1894

Options	Price
Special Factory Paint	+746
Special Leather Seat Trim [Opt on S Cpe]	+1364
Sport Chassis [Opt on S Cpe]	+378
Traction Control System [Opt on 2WD]	+602
AM/FM/CD Audio System	+177
17 Inch Wheels - Targa	+523
18 Inch Wheels - Sport Classic	+1492

1997
Mileage Category: F

The only change to this year's Porsche 911 is the availability of a Porsche-engineered child seat that will deactivate the passenger airbag when it is in place.

Body Styles	TMV Pricing		
	Trade	Private	Dealer
2 Dr Carrera 4 AWD Conv	38056	41310	45287
2 Dr Carrera 4S AWD Cpe	35557	38598	42314
2 Dr Carrera Conv	35998	39076	42839
2 Dr Carrera Cpe	31067	33723	36970

Body Styles	TMV Pricing		
	Trade	Private	Dealer
2 Dr Carrera Targa Cpe	32946	35763	39205
2 Dr Turbo AWD Cpe	60924	65856	71885
2 Dr Turbo S AWD Cpe	91985	99432	108534

Options	Price
Automatic 4-Speed Transmission	+1432
Automatic Dimming Rearview Mirror [Std on Turbo S]	+242
Compact Disc Changer	+439
Digital Audio System [Opt on Turbo]	+619
Hardtop Roof	+5619
Heated Front Seats [Std on Turbo S]	+267
Hi-Fi Audio System [Opt on Cpe - Carrera,Carrera 4S]	+502
Limited Slip Differential [Opt on Targa,RWD]	+579
Metallic Paint [Std on Turbo,Turbo S]	+1821

Options	Price
Pearlescent Metallic Paint [Opt on Cpe - Carrera,Carrera 4S]	+4805
Power Driver Seat	+271
Power Passenger Seat	+271
Special Factory Paint	+717
Special Leather Interior Trim	+834
AM/FM/CD Audio System	+146
17 Inch Wheels - Cup Design [Opt on Carrera Cpe]	+667
17 Inch Wheels - Targa [Opt on Carrera Cpe]	+502

1996
Mileage Category: F

Trick Targa model joins the lineup, and power is up in midrange revs. New Carrera 4S model provides Turbo looks without Turbo price or performance. Bigger wheels are standard across the line, as well as Litronic headlights. New stereos and exterior colors compliment one new interior color this year. Remote keyless entry system gets an immobilizer feature.

Body Styles	TMV Pricing		
	Trade	Private	Dealer
2 Dr Carrera 4 AWD Conv	34835	38366	43241
2 Dr Carrera 4 AWD Cpe	32400	35684	40219
2 Dr Carrera 4S AWD Cpe	31376	34556	38947
2 Dr Carrera Conv	32742	36060	40643

Body Styles	TMV Pricing		
	Trade	Private	Dealer
2 Dr Carrera Cpe	27865	30689	34589
2 Dr Carrera Targa Cpe	29842	32867	37044
2 Dr Turbo AWD Cpe	54110	59287	66436

Options	Price
17 Inch Wheels - Spoke [Opt on Carrera,Targa]	+721
18 Inch Wheels - Technology Design	+891
AM/FM/Cassette/CD Audio System	+247
AM/FM/CD Audio System	+142
Automatic 4-Speed Transmission	+1772
Compact Disc Changer	+366
Digital Audio System [Opt on Turbo]	+933
Heated Front Seats	+260

Options	Price
Hi-Fi Audio System [Opt on Carrera 4S]	+418
Leather Seats [Std on Turbo]	+694
Limited Slip Differential [Opt on 2WD]	+563
Metallic Paint	+465
Pearlescent Metallic Paint	+4676
Power Driver Seat	+251
Power Passenger Seat	+251
Spoke Wheels	+649

1995
Mileage Category: F

This year the optional Tiptronic automanual transmission allows driver to change gears either with the console-mounted gear selector as before or via buttons mounted on the steering wheel.

Body Styles	TMV Pricing		
	Trade	Private	Dealer
2 Dr Carrera 4 AWD Conv	31867	35373	41215
2 Dr Carrera 4 AWD Cpe	27730	30781	35865

Body Styles	TMV Pricing		
	Trade	Private	Dealer
2 Dr Carrera Conv	29128	32332	37673
2 Dr Carrera Cpe	24650	27362	31881

Options	Price
Chrome Wheels [Opt on Carrera Conv]	+463
Compact Disc Changer	+272
Digital Audio System	+889
Heated Front Seats	+154
Hi-Fi Audio System [Opt on Conv]	+399

Options	Price
Automatic 4-Speed Transmission	+1350
Metallic Paint	+310
Pearlescent Metallic Paint	+3666
Power Driver Seat	+185
Power Passenger Seat	+185

Options	Price
Leather Seats	+632
Limited Slip Differential [Opt on 2WD]	+469

Options	Price
AM/FM/CD Audio System	+128

1994

Body Styles	TMV Pricing		
	Trade	Private	Dealer
2 Dr America Roadster Conv	32941	36686	42928
2 Dr Carrera 4 AWD Cpe	25975	28929	33852
2 Dr Carrera Conv	26299	29290	34274
2 Dr Carrera Cpe	21979	24478	28642
2 Dr Carrera S Turbo Cpe	43867	48558	56375
2 Dr Carrera Targa Cpe	21692	24158	28268

Body Styles	TMV Pricing		
	Trade	Private	Dealer
2 Dr Carrera Turbo Cpe	41856	46331	53790
2 Dr RS America Cpe	15102	16819	19681
2 Dr Speedster Conv	21999	24501	28670
2 Dr Wide Body AWD Cpe	27656	30801	36043
2 Dr Wide Body Cpe	22950	25560	29909

Mileage Category: F

Porsche modernizes the 911, updating and improving the car without killing its character. A more aerodynamic body and various tweaks to the engine and suspension make this old favorite even better.

Options	Price
17 Inch Wheels - Spoke	+389
Air Conditioning [Opt on America, Speedster]	+305
AM/FM/Cassette Audio System [Std on Cabriolet Conv, Carrera 4WD Cpe]	+186
AM/FM/CD Audio System	+107
Automatic 4-Speed Transmission	+1050
Automatic Climate Control [Opt on RS America]	+203
Compact Disc Changer	+237
Cruise Control [Opt on Speedster]	+203

Options	Price
Hardtop Roof	+4118
Heated Front Seats	+135
Limited Slip Differential	+412
Metallic Paint	+272
Power Driver Seat	+123
Power Passenger Seat	+152
Power Sunroof [Std on Carrera]	+406

Porsche
928

1995

Body Styles	TMV Pricing		
	Trade	Private	Dealer
2 Dr GTS Hbk	26379	29260	34061

Options	Price
Heated Front Seats	+248
Leather Seats	+846

Mileage Category: F

After this year and close to two decades in production, the 928 dies a quiet death.

1994

Mileage Category: F

Body Styles	TMV Pricing		
	Trade	Private	Dealer
2 Dr GTS Hbk	19716	22169	26258

After last year's tweaks that included a bigger engine, the 928 continues into this year essentially unchanged.

Options	Price
Automatic 4-Speed Transmission	+931
Heated Front Seats	+170
Leather Seat Package	+559

Options	Price
Metallic Paint	+254
Power Passenger Seat w/Memory	+390
Sport Suspension	+301

Porsche
968

1995

Mileage Category: F

After this year, and like its 928 sibling, the 968 dies a quiet death.

Body Styles	TMV Pricing		
	Trade	Private	Dealer
2 Dr STD Conv	15089	16749	19516
2 Dr STD Cpe	12292	13644	15897

Porsche
968/Boxster

1995 (cont'd)

Options	Price
17 Inch Wheels - Spoke [Opt on Conv]	+444
AM/FM/CD Audio System	+128
Automatic 4-Speed Transmission	+1061
Compact Disc Changer	+534
Heated Front Seats	+193
Hi-Fi Audio System	+240

Options	Price
Leather Seats	+597
Limited Slip Differential	+193
Metallic Paint	+289
Power Driver Seat	+174
Power Passenger Seat	+174
Special Factory Paint	+251

1994

Mileage Category: F

The entry-level yet still gratifying Porsche receives the option of a Torsen limited-slip differential for the year.

Body Styles	TMV Pricing		
	Trade	Private	Dealer
2 Dr STD Conv	12726	14309	16948
2 Dr STD Cpe	10488	11793	13967

Options	Price
17 Inch Wheels - Spoke	+389
AM/FM/CD Audio System	+170
Automatic 4-Speed Transmission	+931
Compact Disc Changer	+237
Heated Front Seats	+170
Leather Seats	+525
Limited Slip Differential	+170

Options	Price
Metallic Paint	+254
Power Driver Seat	+152
Power Passenger Seat	+152
Premium Audio System	+288
Rear Spoiler	+152
Sport Chassis	+626

Porsche
Boxster

2003

Mileage Category: F

Minor visual updates, including revised front and rear fascias and gray (versus the previous yellow) tint for the turn signal lenses, along with a boost in output keep the Boxster relevant in the face of faster, more refined rivals.

Body Styles	TMV Pricing		
	Trade	Private	Dealer
2 Dr S Conv	39364	41927	46200
2 Dr STD Conv	32095	34185	37668

Options	Price
Alarm System [Opt on STD]	+369
Automatic 5-Speed Transmission	+2631
Automatic Dimming Rearview Mirror	+184
Bose Audio System	+1332
Color To Sample Paint	+3537
Compact Disc Changer	+586
Cruise Control	+467
Hardtop Roof	+1922
Heated Front Seats	+336
Hi-Fi Audio System	+680
Metallic Paint	+676
Metallic Paint To Sample	+3537
Navigation System	+2156
Special Factory Paint	+676

Options	Price
Special Leather Interior Trim	+1648
Special Leather Seat Trim	+299
Sport Chassis	+578
18 Inch Wheels - Sport Design	+2410
Traction Control System	+1012
18 Inch Wheels - Turbo Look	+1176
18 Inch Wheels - Sport Classic	+2410
Sport Design Package	+1143
17 Inch Wheels [Opt on STD]	+1012
18 Inch Wheels	+1176
17 Inch Wheels - Sport Classic [Opt on S]	+1070
Automatic Dimming Sideview Mirror(s)	+225
Power Driver Seat w/Memory	+279
Park Distance Control (Rear)	+434

2002

Mileage Category: F

The Boxster stands pat for '02.

Body Styles	TMV Pricing		
	Trade	Private	Dealer
2 Dr S Conv	35159	37681	41884

Options	Price
17 Inch Wheels - Boxster Design	+935
17 Inch Wheels - Sport Classic	+980

Body Styles	TMV Pricing		
	Trade	Private	Dealer
2 Dr STD Conv	28288	30317	33698

Options	Price
Design Package	+1262
Hardtop Roof	+1744

Options	Price
18 Inch Wheels - Sport Classic	+2044
18 Inch Wheels - Sport Design	+2044
18 Inch Wheels - Turbo Look	+912
AM/FM/CD Audio System	+266
Arctic Silver Interior Package	+551
Automatic 5-Speed Transmission	+2440
Automatic Dimming Rearview Mirror	+171
Automatic Dimming Sideview Mirror(s)	+209
Automatic Stability Control	+935
Bose Audio System	+836
Color To Sample Paint	+3249
Compact Disc Changer	+543
Cruise Control	+437

Options	Price
Heated Front Seats	+315
Metallic Paint	+627
Metallic Paint To Sample	+3249
Navigation System	+2691
Park Distance Control (Rear)	+372
Power Driver Seat w/Memory	+228
Power Passenger Seat	+570
Special Factory Paint	+627
Special Leather Interior Trim	+1512
Special Leather Seat Trim	+1820
Sport Chassis	+524
Sport Design Package	+1049
Traction Control System	+935

2001

Body Styles	TMV Pricing		
	Trade	Private	Dealer
2 Dr S Conv	30988	34361	37475
2 Dr STD Conv	25312	28068	30612

Options	Price
18 Inch Wheels - Sport Classic	+1856
18 Inch Wheels - Sport Design	+1856
18 Inch Wheels - Turbo Look [Opt on S]	+1908
AM/FM/CD Audio System	+209
Arctic Silver Interior Package	+2149
Automatic 5-Speed Transmission	+2240
Automatic Dimming Rearview Mirror	+481
Automatic Dimming Sideview Mirror(s)	+192
Automatic Stability Control	+848
Compact Disc Changer	+551
Cruise Control	+372
Design Package	+1799
Digital Audio System	+820

Options	Price
Hardtop Roof	+1601
Heated Front Seats	+265
Leather Seat Package	+1654
Metallic Paint	+2100
Navigation System	+2470
Park Distance Control (Rear)	+363
Power Driver Seat w/Memory	+530
Power Passenger Seat	+530
Special Factory Paint	+562
Sport Design Package	+1130
Sport Suspension	+481
Traction Control System	+848

Mileage Category: F

Minor interior changes are in store for 2001. The Boxster S' thicker roof lining has migrated to the regular Boxster. Both cars now feature a hidden cell phone antenna, a gauge cluster design similar to the 911's, improved interior lighting and better dashboard material quality. Porsche has also added a new button to the ignition key to control the driver seat and outside memory function. In terms of optional equipment, the sophisticated Porsche Stability Management system is now available for the Boxster and Boxster S.

2000

Body Styles	TMV Pricing		
	Trade	Private	Dealer
2 Dr S Conv	28368	31601	34770
2 Dr STD Conv	22329	24874	27369

Options	Price
17 Inch Wheels - Boxster Design	+740
17 Inch Wheels - Sport Classic [Opt on STD]	+1601
18 Inch Wheels - Sport Classic	+1706
18 Inch Wheels - Sport Design	+1706
18 Inch Wheels - Turbo Look [Opt on S]	+1754
AM/FM/Cassette/CD Audio System	+367
AM/FM/CD Audio System	+192
Automatic 5-Speed Transmission	+1860
Automatic Dimming Rearview Mirror	+344
Automatic Dimming Sideview Mirror(s)	+170
Compact Disc Changer	+507

Options	Price
Cruise Control	+342
Digital Audio System [Opt on STD]	+716
Hardtop Roof	+1398
Heated Front Seats	+244
Metallic Paint	+490
Navigation System	+2049
Special Factory Paint	+490
Special Leather Interior Trim	+1213
Special Leather Seat Trim	+287
Sport Package	+1286
Traction Control System	+530

Mileage Category: F

The big news for 2000 is the Boxster S. This more powerful version of the Boxster features a bigger engine that generates 250 horsepower. The regular Boxster (if you can call it that) also gets a horsepower boost in 2000, going from 201 to 217. Both models feature upgraded interior materials and new exterior colors.

1999

Body Styles	TMV Pricing		
	Trade	Private	Dealer
2 Dr STD Conv	20814	23269	25825

1999 (cont'd)
Mileage Category: F

The Boxster is slowly adding features and options. This year, a Classic Package includes metallic paint and all-leather seats, and adds special highlights to the interior. The gas tank is increased from a 12.5- to a 14.1-gallon capacity, and gas-discharge Litronic headlights are optional. All the features in the Sport Package are individually optional this year, and 18-inch wheels are now available.

Options	Price	Options	Price
17 Inch Wheels - Boxster Design	+748	Hardtop Roof	+1162
18 Inch Wheels - Sport Classic	+2417	Heated Front Seats	+202
18 Inch Wheels - Sport Design	+748	Hi-Fi Audio System	+355
AM/FM/Cassette/CD Audio System	+304	Metallic Paint	+407
AM/FM/CD Audio System	+160	Power Driver Seat w/Memory	+450
Automatic 5-Speed Transmission	+1545	Special Factory Paint	+407
Automatic Dimming Rearview Mirror	+286	Special Leather Interior Trim	+1007
Compact Disc Changer	+421	Special Leather Seat Trim	+1199
Cruise Control	+284	Sport Package	+1584
Digital Audio System	+340	Traction Control System	+440

1998
Mileage Category: F

Side airbags are standard for 1998.

Body Styles		TMV Pricing		
		Trade	Private	Dealer
2 Dr STD Conv		19608	21918	24522

Options	Price	Options	Price
Traction Control System	+418	Compact Disc Changer	+399
17 Inch Wheels - Boxster Design	+710	Cruise Control	+270
17 Inch Wheels - Sport Classic	+1366	Hardtop Roof	+815
Alarm System	+294	Heated Front Seats	+192
AM/FM/Cassette/CD Audio System	+289	Metallic Paint	+387
AM/FM/CD Audio System	+152	Special Leather Interior Trim	+937
Automatic 5-Speed Transmission	+1465	Special Leather Seat Trim	+1116
Automatic Dimming Rearview Mirror	+271	Sport Package	+1504

1997
Mileage Category: F

This all-new roadster is introduced to compete in the revitalized midpriced sports car category. The Boxster features a 2.5-liter six-cylinder engine, a five-speed manual or five-speed Tiptronic transmission and a power top that closes in an impressive 12 seconds.

Body Styles		TMV Pricing		
		Trade	Private	Dealer
2 Dr STD Conv		17954	20037	22583

Options	Price	Options	Price
Automatic Dimming Rearview Mirror	+261	Sport Package	+1393
Compact Disc Changer	+384	Traction Control System	+381
Cruise Control	+259	Automatic 5-Speed Transmission	+1408
Hardtop Roof	+783	17 Inch Wheels - Boxster Design	+683
Heated Front Seats	+391	17 Inch Wheels - Sport Classic	+1314
Leather Seats	+887	Alarm System	+283
Metallic Paint	+371	AM/FM/Cassette/CD Audio System	+278
Special Factory Paint	+371	AM/FM/CD Audio System	+146
Special Leather Seat Trim	+1060		

Porsche
Cayenne

2003

Mileage Category: O

We would've never imagined it, but Porsche jumps onto the SUV gravy train. The Cayenne, with a choice of two potent V8s and an available active suspension, promises performance that's more like a 911 than an SUV.

Body Styles		TMV Pricing		
		Trade	Private	Dealer
4 Dr S 4WD SUV		45117	47110	50432
4 Dr Turbo 4WD SUV		72049	75231	80535

Options	Price	Options	Price
Automatic Dimming Rearview Mirror	+287	Special Leather Seat Trim	+324
Automatic Load Leveling [Opt on S]	+2623	Sport Seats [Opt on S]	+1057
Comfort Seats [Opt on S]	+1057	Power Rear Liftgate	+287
Compact Disc Changer	+586	19 Inch Wheels	+697
Heated Front Seats [Opt on S]	+393	20 Inch Wheels	+1607
Heated Front and Rear Seats [Opt on S]	+787	Automatic Climate Control (4 Zone)	+1385
Metallic Paint [Opt on S]	+406	Automatic Dimming Sideview Mirror(s)	+225
Navigation System [Opt on S]	+2238	Keyless Ignition System	+816
Off-Road Suspension Package	+2336	Power Driver Seat w/Memory	+295
Power Moonroof	+902	Park Distance Control (Front and Rear) [Opt on S]	+811

2003

Body Styles	TMV Pricing		
	Trade	Private	Dealer
2 Dr SE Turbo Conv	26378	28268	31417
4 Dr Arc Turbo Sdn	18870	20200	22416

Options	Price
Automatic 4-Speed Transmission [Opt on SE]	+830
Automatic 5-Speed Transmission [Opt on Arc,Linear,Vector]	+830
Heated Front Seats	+315
Metallic Paint	+332
Power Driver Seat [Opt on Linear]	+216
Power Moonroof [Opt on Arc,Linear,Vector]	+797
Rear Spoiler [Opt on SE]	+216

Body Styles	TMV Pricing		
	Trade	Private	Dealer
4 Dr Linear Turbo Sdn	16426	17603	19564
4 Dr Vector Turbo Sdn	22555	24144	26793

Options	Price
Sport Seats [Opt on SE]	+166
Sport Suspension [Opt on Arc,Linear]	+166
AM/FM/CD Changer Audio System [Opt on Arc,Linear,Vector]	+196
16 Inch Wheels [Opt on Linear]	+332
17 Inch Wheels [Opt on Arc,Linear,SE]	+498
Automatic Climate Control (2 Zone) - Driver and Passenger [Opt on Linear]	+130
Park Distance Control (Rear) [Opt on Arc,Vector]	+216

Mileage Category: F

The 2003 9-3 is an all-new design from top to bottom. It rides on a new platform, has new engines and an interior that's considerably more modern than the previous version.

2002

Body Styles	TMV Pricing		
	Trade	Private	Dealer
2 Dr SE Turbo Conv	20817	22459	25196
2 Dr Viggen Turbo Conv	23970	25835	28943
2 Dr Viggen Turbo Hbk	19669	21199	23750

Options	Price
17 Inch Wheels [Opt on SE Conv]	+440
Automatic 4-Speed Transmission [Opt on SE]	+640
Automatic Climate Control [Opt on SE Hbk]	+120
Heated Front Seats [Opt on SE]	+253
Metallic Paint	+253
Power Driver Seat w/Memory [Opt on SE Hbk]	+120

Body Styles	TMV Pricing		
	Trade	Private	Dealer
4 Dr SE Turbo Hbk	12946	13967	15668
4 Dr Viggen Turbo Hbk	19742	21278	23838

Options	Price
Power Passenger Seat [Opt on SE Hbk]	+141
Premium Audio System [Opt on SE Hbk]	+173
Rear Spoiler [Opt on SE Hbk]	+173
Special Leather Seat Trim [Opt on SE Hbk]	+472
Sport Suspension [Opt on SE Conv]	+157

Mileage Category: F

The base 9-3 three- and five-door models have been replaced by a value-priced SE five-door. High-performance Viggen models get a new interior color and a carbon-fiber instrument panel.

2001

Body Styles	TMV Pricing		
	Trade	Private	Dealer
2 Dr SE Turbo Conv	16945	19277	21429
2 Dr Turbo Hbk	9464	10766	11967
2 Dr Viggen Turbo Conv	20485	23229	25761
2 Dr Viggen Turbo Hbk	16496	18705	20744

Options	Price
Automatic 4-Speed Transmission	+540
Heated Front Seats	+202
Leather Seats [Std on SE,Viggen,Conv]	+607

Body Styles	TMV Pricing		
	Trade	Private	Dealer
4 Dr SE Turbo Hbk	11531	13118	14582
4 Dr Turbo Hbk	9855	11210	12461
4 Dr Viggen Turbo Hbk	16649	18879	20937

Options	Price
Metallic Paint	+202
Power Moonroof [Opt on STD]	+517
Power Passenger Seat [Opt on SE Conv]	+157

Mileage Category: H

The base convertible has been dropped for this year while all other models get two new colors. The OnStar telematics system and traction control are now standard.

2000

Body Styles	TMV Pricing		
	Trade	Private	Dealer
2 Dr SE HO Turbo Conv	13270	15426	17539
2 Dr Turbo Conv	13183	15325	17424
2 Dr Turbo Hbk	7344	8537	9707
2 Dr Viggen Turbo Conv	14966	17316	19619
2 Dr SE HO Turbo Conv	13270	15426	17539
2 Dr Turbo Conv	13183	15325	17424
2 Dr Turbo Hbk	7344	8537	9707
2 Dr Viggen Turbo Conv	14966	17316	19619

Body Styles	TMV Pricing		
	Trade	Private	Dealer
2 Dr SE HO Turbo Conv	13270	15426	17539
2 Dr Turbo Conv	13183	15325	17424
2 Dr Turbo Hbk	7344	8537	9707
2 Dr Viggen Turbo Conv	14966	17316	19619
2 Dr SE HO Turbo Conv	13270	15426	17539
2 Dr Turbo Conv	13183	15325	17424
2 Dr Turbo Hbk	7344	8537	9707
2 Dr Viggen Turbo Conv	14966	17316	19619

Mileage Category: H

The base model gets restyled 15-inch alloy wheels, while the SE version gains performance enhancements and increased horsepower. The sporty 9-3 Viggen offers even more power, and is available as a five-door or convertible in addition to the coupe. All engines are now LEV compliant and GM's OnStar "Telematics" System becomes optional across the model lineup.

2000 (cont'd)

Options	Price
OnStar Telematic System	+338
Power Moonroof [Opt on STD]	+434
Metallic Paint	+132
Automatic 4-Speed Transmission	+453

Options	Price
Compact Disc Changer	+170
Heated Front and Rear Seats	+196
Heated Front Seats	+140
Leather Seats [Std on SE HO,Viggen,Conv]	+416

1999

Mileage Category: H

Saab changed the car's name to the 9-3, giving it a mild exterior freshening to boot. Around midyear, a high-output version of its 2.0-liter turbo four-cylinder (making an amazing 200 horsepower) becomes the standard engine in the uplevel SE five-door and SE Convertible models equipped with a manual transmission. All SEs also get new five-spoke 16-inch alloy wheels. All five-speed manual 9-3s get revised gearbox ratios and a numerically higher (4.05-to-1) final drive ratio for better off-the-line feel. A revised 9-3 interior headliner provides more padding for increased protection in the event of a crash. And five-door SE variants add an integrated driver-seat armrest and a centrally located cupholder that swings out from the instrument panel.

Body Styles	TMV Pricing		
	Trade	Private	Dealer
2 Dr SE HO Turbo Conv	10594	12291	14058
2 Dr SE Turbo Conv	10491	12173	13924
2 Dr Turbo Conv	7919	9188	10509
2 Dr Turbo Hbk	6514	7558	8644

Body Styles	TMV Pricing		
	Trade	Private	Dealer
2 Dr Viggen Turbo Hbk	10425	12031	13702
4 Dr SE HO Turbo Hbk	6959	8074	9235
4 Dr SE Turbo Hbk	6910	8017	9170
4 Dr Turbo Hbk	6607	7665	8767

Options	Price
Automatic 4-Speed Transmission	+316
Compact Disc Changer	+137
Heated Front and Rear Seats	+143

Options	Price
Leather Seats [Std on SE,SE HO,Viggen,Conv]	+370
Power Moonroof [Opt on STD]	+316

Saab
9-5

2003

Mileage Category: I

After last year's extensive round of improvements, the 9-5 received only minor upgrades for 2003. All five-speed automatic-equipped models now have the Sentronic manual-shift feature with steering wheel-mounted controls. Ventilated sport seats are now optional on the Aero, while electronic stability control is now standard on all models.

Body Styles	TMV Pricing		
	Trade	Private	Dealer
4 Dr Aero Turbo Sdn	24248	25951	28789
4 Dr Aero Turbo Wgn	24676	26409	29297
4 Dr Arc 3.0t Turbo Sdn	24236	25938	28774

Body Styles	TMV Pricing		
	Trade	Private	Dealer
4 Dr Arc 3.0t Turbo Wgn	24695	26429	29320
4 Dr Linear 2.3t Turbo Sdn	21207	22697	25179
4 Dr Linear 2.3t Turbo Wgn	21692	23216	25755

Options	Price
Automatic 5-Speed Transmission [Opt on Aero,Linear]	+897
Automatic Dimming Rearview Mirror [Opt on Linear]	+123
Harmon Kardon Audio System [Opt on Linear]	+365
Metallic Paint	+332

Options	Price
Ventilated Seats (Front) [Opt on Aero]	+661
Automatic Dimming Sideview Mirror(s)	+199
Power Driver Seat w/Memory [Opt on Linear]	+149
Park Distance Control (Rear)	+163

2002

Mileage Category: I

Although it looks similar to last year's model, the 2002 9-5 has undergone extensive changes. There are now three distinct models, each with its own look and feature content. A new five-speed automatic transmission is available on all models, while the top-of-the-line Aero gets more power. Revisions to both the steering and suspension systems increase performance, while a new electronic stability control system and adaptive front airbags improve safety.

Body Styles	TMV Pricing		
	Trade	Private	Dealer
4 Dr Aero Turbo Sdn	18447	20133	22942
4 Dr Aero Turbo Wgn	18709	20418	23267
4 Dr Arc 3.0t Turbo Sdn	18391	20071	22872
4 Dr Aero Turbo Sdn	18447	20133	22942
4 Dr Aero Turbo Wgn	18709	20418	23267
4 Dr Arc 3.0t Turbo Sdn	18391	20071	22872

Body Styles	TMV Pricing		
	Trade	Private	Dealer
4 Dr Aero Turbo Sdn	18447	20133	22942
4 Dr Aero Turbo Wgn	18709	20418	23267
4 Dr Arc 3.0t Turbo Sdn	18391	20071	22872
4 Dr Aero Turbo Sdn	18447	20133	22942
4 Dr Aero Turbo Wgn	18709	20418	23267
4 Dr Arc 3.0t Turbo Sdn	18391	20071	22872

Options	Price
Automatic 4-Speed Transmission [Std on Arc]	+640
Automatic Stability Control [Opt on Linear]	+211
Harmon Kardon Audio System [Opt on Linear]	+173

Options	Price
Heated Front and Rear Seats [Opt on Linear]	+293
Metallic Paint	+253
Park Distance Control (Rear) [Opt on Aero,Arc]	+131

2001

Mileage Category: I

Entry-level models get more horsepower from the turbo four-cylinder while all models get the OnStar telematics system, turbo gauges and two new colors.

Body Styles	TMV Pricing		
	Trade	Private	Dealer
4 Dr 2.3t Turbo Sdn	13916	15838	17612
4 Dr 2.3t Turbo Wgn	14094	16040	17836
4 Dr Aero Turbo Sdn	15996	18204	20242

Body Styles	TMV Pricing		
	Trade	Private	Dealer
4 Dr Aero Turbo Wgn	16112	18337	20390
4 Dr SE V6t Turbo Sdn	15282	17392	19340
4 Dr SE V6t Turbo Wgn	15557	17705	19688

2001 (cont'd)

Options	Price
Automatic 4-Speed Transmission [Std on SE V6t]	+540
Harmon Kardon Audio System [Opt on 2.3t]	+292
Heated Front and Rear Seats	+268

Options	Price
Leather Seats [Opt on 2.3t]	+360
Metallic Paint	+202
Ventilated Seats (Front)	+448

2000

Body Styles	TMV Pricing		
	Trade	Private	Dealer
4 Dr 2.3t Turbo Sdn	10793	12433	14041
4 Dr 2.3t Turbo Wgn	10990	12661	14299
4 Dr Aero Turbo Sdn	13601	15668	17695
4 Dr Aero Turbo Wgn	14008	16137	18224

Body Styles	TMV Pricing		
	Trade	Private	Dealer
4 Dr Gary Fisher Edition Turbo Wgn	12820	14769	16680
4 Dr SE V6t Turbo Sdn	12942	14909	16838
4 Dr SE V6t Turbo Wgn	12942	14909	16838

Options	Price
Automatic 4-Speed Transmission [Std on SE V6t]	+453
BBS Wheels	+623
Harmon Kardon Audio System [Opt on 2.3t]	+246
Heated Front and Rear Seats	+196
Leather Seats [Opt on 2.3t]	+510

Options	Price
Metallic Paint	+132
OnStar Telematic System	+338
Power Driver Seat w/Memory [Opt on 2.3t]	+225
Ventilated Seats (Front)	+359

Mileage Category: I

Saab debuts the high-performance 9-5 Aero Sedan and Wagon with 230 horsepower. Entry-level sedans and wagons sport new 16-inch 10-spoke alloy wheels, and all SE versions offer a turbo V6 and auto-dimming rearview mirror. The 9-5 Wagon Gary Fisher Edition offers a sportier exterior design and a Saab Limited Edition Gary Fisher mountain bike. A sunroof and traction-control system (TCS) have been added to the standard equipment list.

1999

Body Styles	TMV Pricing		
	Trade	Private	Dealer
4 Dr 2.3t Turbo Sdn	8566	10114	11726
4 Dr 2.3t Turbo Wgn	8991	10616	12307
4 Dr SE 2.3t Turbo Sdn	9167	10824	12548

Body Styles	TMV Pricing		
	Trade	Private	Dealer
4 Dr SE V6t Turbo Sdn	10231	12080	14005
4 Dr V6t Turbo Wgn	10347	12217	14163

Options	Price
Automatic 4-Speed Transmission [Std on SE V6,V6 Turbo Wgn]	+316
Heated Front and Rear Seats	+143
Leather Seats [Opt on STD,STD Turbo Wgn]	+370

Options	Price
Power Moonroof [Opt on STD]	+316
Ventilated Seats (Front)	+282

Mileage Category: I

Saab's replacement for the 9000 line of cars is called the 9-5. Available as a sedan with a turbocharged four-cylinder or turbocharged V6 engine, the 9-5 is designed to compete against conventional cars like the BMW 5 Series and Infiniti I30.

1998

Body Styles	TMV Pricing		
	Trade	Private	Dealer
2 Dr S Conv	6478	7790	9269
2 Dr S Turbo Hbk	5346	6428	7649
2 Dr SE Turbo Conv	7494	9011	10722

Body Styles	TMV Pricing		
	Trade	Private	Dealer
2 Dr SE Turbo Hbk	5554	6678	7946
4 Dr S Hbk	5420	6517	7754
4 Dr SE Turbo Hbk	5860	7046	8384

Options	Price
Automatic 4-Speed Transmission	+213
Leather Seats [Std on SE,Conv]	+246

Options	Price
Power Moonroof [Opt on S]	+213

Mileage Category: H

The Saab 900 three-door hatchback gets the same turbocharged engine as the SE models this year. Other changes include the addition of body-color front and rear bumpers.

1997

Body Styles	TMV Pricing		
	Trade	Private	Dealer
2 Dr S Conv	5476	6670	8129
2 Dr S Hbk	4499	5480	6679
2 Dr SE Talladega Turbo Conv	6498	7915	9647
2 Dr SE Talladega Turbo Hbk	5143	6264	7634
2 Dr SE Turbo Conv	6289	7661	9337
2 Dr SE Turbo Hbk	4807	5855	7135

Body Styles	TMV Pricing		
	Trade	Private	Dealer
2 Dr SE V6 Conv	6513	7933	9669
4 Dr S Hbk	4618	5625	6855
4 Dr SE Talladega Turbo Hbk	5304	6461	7874
4 Dr SE Turbo Hbk	5233	6374	7769
4 Dr SE V6 Hbk	5425	6608	8054

Mileage Category: H

No changes this year.

Saab
900/9000

1997 (cont'd)

Options	Price
Automatic 4-Speed Transmission [Std on SE V6]	+182
Leather Seats [Opt on S Hbk]	+212

Options	Price
Power Moonroof [Opt on S]	+182

1996

Mileage Category: H

The popular Saab 900 SE five-door is available this year with the turbocharged four-cylinder engine. An automatic transmission is now optional on turbos. V6 models come only with an automatic. Adjustable driver's lumbar support is now standard on all 900 models.

Body Styles	TMV Pricing		
	Trade	Private	Dealer
2 Dr S Conv	4671	5752	7245
2 Dr S Hbk	3676	4527	5701
2 Dr SE Turbo Conv	5469	6734	8482
2 Dr SE Turbo Hbk	4338	5342	6728

Body Styles	TMV Pricing		
	Trade	Private	Dealer
2 Dr SE V6 Conv	5769	7104	8948
4 Dr S Hbk	3751	4619	5818
4 Dr SE Turbo Hbk	4470	5504	6933
4 Dr SE V6 Hbk	4582	5643	7108

Options	Price
Automatic 4-Speed Transmission [Opt on S,SE]	+164
Leather Seats [Std on SE,SEV6,Conv]	+193

Options	Price
Power Moonroof [Opt on S]	+164

1995

Mileage Category: H

Daytime running lights (DRLs) are now standard on the 900. A new convertible 900 appears, and all 900 models get a new three-spoke steering wheel and an anti-theft alarm.

Body Styles	TMV Pricing		
	Trade	Private	Dealer
2 Dr S Conv	3901	4796	6288
2 Dr S Hbk	2966	3646	4780
2 Dr SE Turbo Conv	4226	5196	6812
2 Dr SE Turbo Hbk	3705	4556	5973

Body Styles	TMV Pricing		
	Trade	Private	Dealer
2 Dr SE V6 Conv	4342	5338	6998
4 Dr S Hbk	2904	3570	4681
4 Dr SE V6 Hbk	3335	4100	5375

Options	Price
Automatic 4-Speed Transmission	+137
Leather Seats [Std on SE,SE,Conv]	+162

Options	Price
Power Moonroof [Opt on S]	+137

1994

Mileage Category: H

A totally new Saab is introduced with a little help from GM. The new 900 will be available only as a four-door hatchback initially, with a new two-door and convertible to follow. The 900SE four-door features a V6 engine that was developed by GM for use in its Opels. Saab gets a new optional automatic transmission as well that offers three types of driving modes: sport, winter and economy. Saab's black panel instrument cluster and dual airbags debut on this vehicle as well.

Body Styles	TMV Pricing		
	Trade	Private	Dealer
2 Dr Commemorative Turbo Conv	3716	4723	6401
2 Dr S Conv	2822	3587	4861
2 Dr S Hbk	1959	2490	3375
2 Dr SE Turbo Hbk	2785	3540	4798

Body Styles	TMV Pricing		
	Trade	Private	Dealer
2 Dr Turbo Conv	3280	4169	5651
4 Dr S Hbk	1935	2459	3333
4 Dr SE V6 Hbk	2782	3536	4793

Options	Price
2.5L V6 DOHC 24V FI Engine [Opt on S]	+208
Automatic 3-Speed Transmission	+84
Automatic 4-Speed Transmission	+106

Options	Price
Leather Seats [Opt on S]	+125
Power Moonroof [Opt on S]	+106
Power Sunroof	+102

Saab
9000

1998

Body Styles			TMV Pricing		
			Trade	Private	Dealer
4 Dr CSE Turbo Hbk			5524	6747	8126

Options	Price
Automatic 4-Speed Transmission	+197

Mileage Category: I

No changes to the aging 9000.

1997

Body Styles	TMV Pricing		
	Trade	Private	Dealer
4 Dr Aero Turbo Hbk	5352	6593	8110
4 Dr CS Turbo Hbk	4082	5029	6186
4 Dr CSE Anniv Turbo Hbk	5009	6170	7589

Body Styles	TMV Pricing		
	Trade	Private	Dealer
4 Dr CSE Turbo Hbk	4907	6045	7435
4 Dr CSE V6 Hbk	5224	6435	7915

Options	Price
Power Moonroof [Opt on CS]	+202
Automatic 4-Speed Transmission [Std on CSE V6]	+188
Leather Seats [Opt on CS]	+280

Mileage Category: I

No changes to this aging model.

1996

Body Styles	TMV Pricing		
	Trade	Private	Dealer
4 Dr Aero Turbo Hbk	4237	5245	6637
4 Dr CS Turbo Hbk	3503	4337	5488
4 Dr CSE Turbo Hbk	4196	5194	6572
4 Dr CSE V6 Hbk	4218	5222	6608

Options	Price
Automatic 4-Speed Transmission [Opt on CS,CSE]	+172
Leather Seats [Opt on CS]	+251
Power Moonroof [Opt on CS]	+204

Mileage Category: I

The 9000 sedans are dropped, leaving only the hatchback body style. Cupholders for rear-seat passengers, new upholstery for the CS and new three-spoke alloy wheels for the CS and CSE round out the major developments for this year's model.

1995

Body Styles	TMV Pricing		
	Trade	Private	Dealer
4 Dr Aero Turbo Hbk	3594	4472	5934
4 Dr CDE Sdn	3395	4224	5606
4 Dr CS Turbo Hbk	2930	3646	4838
4 Dr Aero Turbo Hbk	3594	4472	5934
4 Dr CDE Sdn	3395	4224	5606
4 Dr CS Turbo Hbk	2930	3646	4838

Body Styles	TMV Pricing		
	Trade	Private	Dealer
4 Dr Aero Turbo Hbk	3594	4472	5934
4 Dr CDE Sdn	3395	4224	5606
4 Dr CS Turbo Hbk	2930	3646	4838
4 Dr Aero Turbo Hbk	3594	4472	5934
4 Dr CDE Sdn	3395	4224	5606
4 Dr CS Turbo Hbk	2930	3646	4838

Options	Price
Automatic 4-Speed Transmission [Opt on S,SE]	+130
Leather Seats [Std on SE,SE V6,Conv]	+213
Power Moonroof [Opt on S]	+153

Mileage Category: I

Saab adds a light-pressure turbo and a V6 to its large-car engine roster. V6 cars come only with an automatic transmission. Daytime running lights (DRLs) become standard on all 9000s this year.

1994

Body Styles	TMV Pricing		
	Trade	Private	Dealer
4 Dr Aero Turbo Hbk	2520	3321	4657
4 Dr CD Turbo Sdn	1936	2552	3579
4 Dr CDE Sdn	1956	2578	3615
4 Dr CDE Turbo Sdn	2402	3166	4439

Body Styles	TMV Pricing		
	Trade	Private	Dealer
4 Dr CS Hbk	1575	2076	2912
4 Dr CS Turbo Hbk	1993	2627	3683
4 Dr CSE Hbk	1977	2606	3654
4 Dr CSE Turbo Hbk	2317	3054	4283

Options	Price
Automatic 4-Speed Transmission	+101
Leather Seats [Opt on CD,CS]	+166
Power Moonroof [Opt on CD]	+119

Mileage Category: I

Dual airbags debut this year. CS models get front and rear foglights. Traction control is dropped for all models.

Saturn
ION/L-Series

Saturn
ION
2003

Mileage Category: B

After 12 long years in production, Saturn is finally retiring its aging S-Series sedan and coupe in favor of the all-new Saturn Ion sedan and innovative quad coupe.

Body Styles	TMV Pricing		
	Trade	Private	Dealer
4 Dr 1 Sdn	5895	6672	7968
4 Dr 2 Cpe	7094	8029	9588
4 Dr 2 Sdn	6921	7833	9354

Body Styles	TMV Pricing		
	Trade	Private	Dealer
4 Dr 3 Cpe	8496	9616	11482
4 Dr 3 Sdn	7596	8597	10266

Options	Price
Air Conditioning [Opt on 1]	+579
Aluminum/Alloy Wheels [Opt on 2]	+226
AM/FM/CD Audio System [Opt on 1]	+238
AM/FM/Cassette/CD Audio System [Opt on 1,2]	+307
Antilock Brakes	+422
Automatic 5-Speed Transmission [Opt on Sedans]	+543
Automatic Dimming Rearview Mirror [Opt on 2,3]	+121
Cruise Control [Opt on 2]	+142
Leather Seats [Opt on 3]	+479

Options	Price
Power Moonroof [Opt on 2,3]	+437
Power Windows [Opt on 2]	+148
Traction Control System	+121
OnStar Telematic System [Opt on 2,3]	+419
Premium Audio System [Opt on 2,3]	+175
Continuously Variable Transmission [Opt on Coupes]	+739
AM/FM/CD Changer Audio System [Opt on 2,3]	+410
Front and Rear Head Airbag Restraints	+238

Saturn
L-Series
2003

Body Styles	TMV Pricing		
	Trade	Private	Dealer
4 Dr L200 Sdn	8635	9529	11018
4 Dr L300 Sdn	10331	11401	13183

Body Styles	TMV Pricing		
	Trade	Private	Dealer
4 Dr LW200 Wgn	9801	10815	12506
4 Dr LW300 Wgn	10838	11960	13829

Options	Price
Aluminum/Alloy Wheels [Opt on L200,LW200]	+241
AM/FM/Cassette/CD Audio System	+307
Automatic 4-Speed Transmission [Opt on L200]	+482
Automatic Climate Control	+121
Heated Front Seats	+151
Leather Seats	+479
Power Driver Seat	+196

Options	Price
Power Moonroof	+437
OnStar Telematic System	+419
Premium Audio System	+121
AM/FM/Cassette/CD Changer Audio System	+479
DVD Entertainment System	+934
16 Inch Wheels - Chrome	+151

Mileage Category: D

Saturn's L-Series sedan and wagon receive a significant exterior and interior freshening for 2003. Both front and rear fascias have been redesigned for a new look. Front-end restyling includes clear wraparound headlamps with chrome trim, optional foglamps with chrome bezels integrated into the new fascia, a larger grille with a new Saturn badge and a raised hood. The rear end sports new taillamps and a revised fascia with additional chrome trim. No more black rocker panels and lower fascias -- the whole car is now offered with body-color trim. The interior now features brushed nickel-finish trim plates, silver faceplates in the instrument cluster and European-style upholstery. Ride and handling has been improved by adjusting spring rates; optional 16-inch wheels and tires should help, too.

2002

Mileage Category: D

Safety enhancements are the big news for 2002. All Saturn L-Series models now feature standard head curtain airbags, antilock brakes and traction control. Other enhancements include four-wheel disc brakes (on all models except L100), automatic headlamps, LATCH child seat anchors and post airbag-deployment signals. A DVD entertainment system will be available later in the year along with the OnStar communications system. New options packages add even more value with features like an in-dash six-disc CD changer and automatic climate control. New 15-inch alloy and 16-inch chrome wheels round out the upgrades.

Body Styles	TMV Pricing		
	Trade	Private	Dealer
4 Dr L100 Sdn	6314	7125	8476
4 Dr L200 Sdn	6632	7483	8902
4 Dr L300 Sdn	7842	8849	10526

Body Styles	TMV Pricing		
	Trade	Private	Dealer
4 Dr LW200 Wgn	7562	8533	10151
4 Dr LW300 Wgn	8386	9463	11257

Options	Price
Aluminum/Alloy Wheels [Std on 300]	+175
AM/FM/Cassette/CD Audio System	+255
AM/FM/Cassette/CD Changer Audio System	+398
Automatic 4-Speed Transmission [Std on 300]	+406

Options	Price
Heated Front Seats	+125
Leather Seats	+398
Power Driver Seat	+163
Power Moonroof	+363

2001

Body Styles	TMV Pricing		
	Trade	Private	Dealer
4 Dr L100 Sdn	5012	6041	6991
4 Dr L200 Sdn	5550	6689	7741
4 Dr L300 Sdn	6341	7643	8845

Options	Price
Aluminum/Alloy Wheels [Opt on 200]	+148
AM/FM/Cassette/CD Audio System	+215
AM/FM/CD Audio System	+166
Antilock Brakes	+295
Automatic 4-Speed Transmission [Opt on L100,L200]	+362

Body Styles	TMV Pricing		
	Trade	Private	Dealer
4 Dr LW200 Wgn	6277	7566	8755
4 Dr LW300 Wgn	7011	8450	9779

Options	Price
Front and Rear Head Airbag Restraints	+166
Leather Seats	+335
Power Driver Seat	+137
Power Sunroof	+306

Mileage Category: D

Saturn has addressed safety concerns by making front and rear head curtain airbags optional on all trim levels. All sedans are now equipped with a three-point seatbelt in the rear center seat, but this feature is still not available in wagons. Sedans also will get an emergency trunk release handle. New colors include Cream White, Bright Silver, Silver Blue and Straight Shade Black. Bright White, Silver, Silver Plum and Blackberry have been discontinued.

2000

Body Styles	TMV Pricing		
	Trade	Private	Dealer
4 Dr LS Sdn	4451	5444	6417
4 Dr LS1 Sdn	4683	5727	6751
4 Dr LS2 Sdn	5422	6631	7817

Options	Price
Aluminum/Alloy Wheels [Opt on LS1,LW1]	+129
AM/FM/Cassette/CD Audio System	+188
AM/FM/CD Audio System	+146
Antilock Brakes	+258

Body Styles	TMV Pricing		
	Trade	Private	Dealer
4 Dr LW1 Wgn	5190	6347	7482
4 Dr LW2 Wgn	5862	7169	8451

Options	Price
Automatic 4-Speed Transmission [Opt on LS,LS1]	+317
Leather Seats	+293
Power Driver Seat	+120
Power Sunroof	+267

Mileage Category: D

The L-Series is a new midsize line of sedans and wagons that was developed for Saturn customers moving up from the smaller cars. Offered in three trim levels, with two engines and manual or automatic transmissions (depending on model), the L-Series is based on the European-market Opel Vectra platform, and consequently carries a distinct import feel.

Saturn

S-Series

2002

Body Styles	TMV Pricing		
	Trade	Private	Dealer
3 Dr SC1 Cpe	5326	6141	7499
3 Dr SC2 Cpe	6314	7279	8888
4 Dr SL Sdn	4231	4878	5956

Options	Price
Air Conditioning [Std on SC2,SL2]	+413
Aluminum/Alloy Wheels	+175
AM/FM/Cassette/CD Audio System	+255
AM/FM/CD Audio System [Std on SC]	+198
Antilock Brakes	+350
Automatic 4-Speed Transmission	+431

Body Styles	TMV Pricing		
	Trade	Private	Dealer
4 Dr SL1 Sdn	5020	5788	7067
4 Dr SL2 Sdn	5532	6378	7787

Options	Price
Cruise Control	+118
Front and Rear Head Airbag Restraints	+163
Leather Seats	+398
Power Sunroof	+363
Power Windows [Std on SC2]	+123

Mileage Category: B

New aluminum 15-inch wheels and four new exterior colors are the only notable changes for 2002.

2001

Body Styles	TMV Pricing		
	Trade	Private	Dealer
3 Dr SC1 Cpe	4445	5495	6465
3 Dr SC2 Cpe	5266	6510	7659
4 Dr SL Sdn	3564	4406	5183

Options	Price
Air Conditioning [Opt on SC1,SL,SL1]	+348
Aluminum/Alloy Wheels	+148
AM/FM/Cassette/CD Audio System	+215
AM/FM/CD Audio System	+166
Antilock Brakes	+295

Body Styles	TMV Pricing		
	Trade	Private	Dealer
4 Dr SL1 Sdn	4132	5109	6011
4 Dr SL2 Sdn	4608	5697	6703
4 Dr SW2 Wgn	4917	6079	7151

Options	Price
Automatic 4-Speed Transmission	+362
Front and Rear Head Airbag Restraints	+137
Leather Seats	+335
Power Sunroof	+306

Mileage Category: B

The S-Series sees no change from last year, save for optional head curtain airbags.

S-Series

2000

Mileage Category: B

Saturn has redesigned the body panels and cockpit of its S-Series SL Sedan and SW Wagon this year. GM's OnStar communications system will now be available as a dealer-installed option across the Saturn line.

Body Styles	TMV Pricing		
	Trade	Private	Dealer
3 Dr SC1 Cpe	3745	4701	5639
3 Dr SC2 Cpe	4273	5364	6433
4 Dr SL Sdn	3083	3870	4641

Options	Price
Leather Seats	+293
Power Sunroof	+267
Premium Audio System [Opt on Cpe]	+129
Automatic 4-Speed Transmission	+317
Air Conditioning [Opt on SC1,SL,SL1]	+304

Body Styles	TMV Pricing		
	Trade	Private	Dealer
4 Dr SL1 Sdn	3464	4348	5215
4 Dr SL2 Sdn	3799	4769	5719
4 Dr SW2 Wgn	4012	5036	6040

Options	Price
Aluminum/Alloy Wheels	+129
AM/FM/Cassette/CD Audio System	+188
AM/FM/CD Audio System	+146
Antilock Brakes	+258

1999

Mileage Category: B

Starting in the late fall of 1998, all coupes will be fitted with a rear-access door on the driver side designed to provide easier entry to the backseat. Drum brakes replace the rear discs previously available on SC2s and SL2s equipped with ABS. Engines benefit from engineering upgrades that improve fuel economy and reduce noise, vibration and emissions. Finally, the SC2 gets new plastic wheel covers and a new optional alloy wheel design.

Body Styles	TMV Pricing		
	Trade	Private	Dealer
2 Dr SC1 Cpe	3093	3993	4930
2 Dr SC2 Cpe	3441	4443	5485
3 Dr SC1 Cpe	3132	4043	4991
3 Dr SC2 Cpe	3498	4516	5576
4 Dr SL Sdn	2574	3323	4102

Options	Price
Air Conditioning [Std on SC2,SL2,SW2]	+295
AM/FM/CD Audio System	+135
Antilock Brakes	+239

Body Styles	TMV Pricing		
	Trade	Private	Dealer
4 Dr SL1 Sdn	2941	3797	4687
4 Dr SL2 Sdn	3148	4064	5018
4 Dr SW1 Wgn	3118	4025	4969
4 Dr SW2 Wgn	3320	4286	5292

Options	Price
Automatic 4-Speed Transmission	+264
Leather Seats	+272
Power Sunroof [Opt on SC,SL]	+248

1998

Mileage Category: B

All models get reduced-force front airbags, and sedans and wagons get new seat fabrics. The SC2, SL2 and SW2 are equipped with new headrests, and the optional alarm system now has a programmable passive arming feature. On the mechanical side, structural upgrades to the engine blocks and transmission case housing are said to reduce noise and increase durability. Additionally, the automatic transmission's programming has been tweaked to reduce hunting on hills and improve shift quality. And Saturn says that revised shock absorbers on all cars provide a smoother ride. Restyled alloy wheels and plastic wheel covers round out the changes.

Body Styles	TMV Pricing		
	Trade	Private	Dealer
2 Dr SC1 Cpe	2716	3620	4639
2 Dr SC2 Cpe	2930	3905	5005
4 Dr SL Sdn	2163	2884	3696
4 Dr SL1 Sdn	2554	3404	4363

Options	Price
Air Conditioning [Std on SC2,SL2,SW2]	+269
AM/FM/CD Audio System	+123
Antilock Brakes	+218

Body Styles	TMV Pricing		
	Trade	Private	Dealer
4 Dr SL2 Sdn	2770	3693	4734
4 Dr SW1 Wgn	2597	3461	4436
4 Dr SW2 Wgn	2825	3765	4825

Options	Price
Automatic 4-Speed Transmission	+241
Leather Seats	+248
Power Sunroof [Opt on SC,SL]	+226

1997

Mileage Category: B

Coupes get a new look inside and out for 1997. No longer stubby in appearance, all coupes adopt the longer wheelbase used by the sedans and wagons, as well as their softer, rounder styling cues. The SC1 and SC2 are now virtually identical in appearance (the SC2's body-color door handles being one of the few differences); both have exposed headlamps and standard daytime running lights. In other news, all models pick up a low-fuel indicator light and can be equipped with a single in-dash CD player. And Saturn has again taken measures to reduce engine noise and vibration.

Body Styles	TMV Pricing		
	Trade	Private	Dealer
2 Dr SC1 Cpe	2340	3227	4312
2 Dr SC2 Cpe	2367	3264	4360
4 Dr SL Sdn	1846	2546	3401
4 Dr SL1 Sdn	2200	3034	4053

Options	Price
Air Conditioning	+245
AM/FM/CD Audio System	+116
Antilock Brakes	+205

Body Styles	TMV Pricing		
	Trade	Private	Dealer
4 Dr SL2 Sdn	2313	3191	4263
4 Dr SW1 Wgn	2279	3143	4199
4 Dr SW2 Wgn	2357	3250	4341

Options	Price
Automatic 4-Speed Transmission	+221
Leather Seats [Opt on SC2,SL2,SW2]	+233
Power Sunroof [Opt on SC,SL]	+212

Body Styles	TMV Pricing		
	Trade	Private	Dealer
2 Dr SC1 Cpe	1784	2600	3726
2 Dr SC2 Cpe	1921	2800	4013
4 Dr SL Sdn	1464	2133	3058
4 Dr SL1 Sdn	1653	2409	3452

Body Styles	TMV Pricing		
	Trade	Private	Dealer
4 Dr SL2 Sdn	1810	2637	3780
4 Dr SW1 Wgn	1720	2507	3593
4 Dr SW2 Wgn	1818	2649	3797

Options	Price
Air Conditioning	+217
Antilock Brakes	+183
Automatic 4-Speed Transmission	+196

Options	Price
Compact Disc Changer [Opt on Cpe]	+147
Leather Seats [Opt on SC2,SL2,SW2]	+208
Power Sunroof [Opt on Cpe,Sdn]	+190

Mileage Category: B

Sedans and wagons get new exterior styling -- resulting in a softer, rounder appearance -- along with redesigned rear seats and standard daytime running lights. Traction control is now available on cars equipped with a manual transmission. Finally, both engines now use sequential-port fuel injection in place of multiport injection.

Body Styles	TMV Pricing		
	Trade	Private	Dealer
2 Dr SC1 Cpe	1318	1976	3073
2 Dr SC2 Cpe	1502	2251	3500
4 Dr SL Sdn	929	1393	2166
4 Dr SL1 Sdn	1173	1758	2733

Body Styles	TMV Pricing		
	Trade	Private	Dealer
4 Dr SL2 Sdn	1399	2097	3259
4 Dr SW1 Wgn	1240	1858	2888
4 Dr SW2 Wgn	1406	2107	3276

Options	Price
Air Conditioning	+183
Antilock Brakes	+155
Automatic 4-Speed Transmission	+165

Options	Price
Compact Disc Changer	+124
Leather Seats [Opt on SC2,SL2,SW2]	+175
Power Sunroof [Opt on Cpe,Sdn]	+160

Mileage Category: B

All models add a standard front-passenger airbag, along with non-motorized seatbelts and a redesigned dash and steering wheel. Improvements to the base engine result in 15 more horsepower (for a total of 100) and slightly more torque. An in-dash CD player is no longer available, but a trunk-mounted changer is now optional. SC1 coupes receive new high-back front seats, while all coupes get new front-end treatments and revised wheel covers.

Body Styles	TMV Pricing		
	Trade	Private	Dealer
2 Dr SC1 Cpe	992	1571	2535
2 Dr SC2 Cpe	1137	1800	2904
4 Dr SL Sdn	773	1224	1975
4 Dr SL1 Sdn	994	1573	2539

Body Styles	TMV Pricing		
	Trade	Private	Dealer
4 Dr SL2 Sdn	1037	1642	2650
4 Dr SW1 Wgn	1033	1635	2638
4 Dr SW2 Wgn	1058	1675	2702

Options	Price
Air Conditioning	+160
AM/FM/CD Audio System	+76
Antilock Brakes	+135

Options	Price
Automatic 4-Speed Transmission	+144
Leather Seats [Opt on SC2,SL2,SW2]	+153
Power Sunroof [Opt on Cpe,Sdn]	+140

Mileage Category: B

Saturn makes minimal changes for 1994. The air conditioning system now uses CFC-free refrigerant, and the automatic transmission has been recalibrated to provide smoother, quieter shifts. A new alloy wheel design is available on the SC1, SL2 and SW2.

Saturn
VUE
2003

Body Styles		TMV Pricing	
	Trade	Private	Dealer
4 Dr STD AWD SUV	12241	13254	14941
4 Dr STD SUV	10489	11357	12803
4 Dr V6 AWD SUV	13986	15143	17070
4 Dr V6 SUV	13509	14626	16488

Options	Price	Options	Price
Alarm System [Opt on STD]	+151	Power Moonroof	+437
Aluminum/Alloy Wheels [Opt on STD]	+241	Power Windows [Opt on STD]	+154
AM/FM/CD Audio System [Opt on STD]	+238	Traction Control System [Opt on STD]	+121
AM/FM/Cassette/CD Audio System	+307	OnStar Telematic System	+419
Antilock Brakes	+422	Premium Audio System	+178
Keyless Entry System [Opt on STD]	+115	AM/FM/Cassette/CD Changer Audio System	+479
Leather Seats	+479	Continuously Variable Transmission [Opt on STD]	+739
Power Door Locks [Opt on STD]	+130	Front and Rear Head Airbag Restraints	+238

Mileage Category: L

New last year, the Vue gets only minor changes for 2003. V6 models are now available with front-wheel drive, while a new options package bundles together heated leather seats and a leather-wrapped steering wheel. A new optional audio system includes a subwoofer, 180-watt amplifier and six door-mounted speakers.

2002

Mileage Category: L

The Vue is an all-new sport-utility vehicle in Saturn's lineup, designed to compete on the lower end of the scale with models like the Ford Escape and Honda CR-V.

Body Styles		TMV Pricing	
	Trade	Private	Dealer
4 Dr STD AWD SUV	10436	11373	12935
4 Dr STD SUV	8989	9797	11143
4 Dr V6 AWD SUV	12555	13683	15562

Options	Price	Options	Price
Alarm System [Std on V6]	+125	Continuously Variable Transmission [Std on STD 4WD]	+613
Aluminum/Alloy Wheels [Std on V6]	+200	Front and Rear Head Airbag Restraints	+198
AM/FM/Cassette/CD Audio System	+255	OnStar Telematic System	+348
AM/FM/Cassette/CD Changer Audio System	+398	Power Sunroof	+363
AM/FM/CD Audio System [Std on V6]	+198	Power Windows [Std on V6]	+128
Antilock Brakes	+350		

Body Styles	TMV Pricing		
	Trade	Private	Dealer
4 Dr STD AWD Crew Cab SB	16563	17730	19676

Options	Price
Alarm System	+131
Automatic 4-Speed Transmission	+553
Automatic Dimming Rearview Mirror	+127

Body Styles	TMV Pricing		
	Trade	Private	Dealer
4 Dr Sport AWD Crew Cab SB	15211	16283	18070

Options	Price
Compact Disc Changer	+311
Premium Audio System	+185

Mileage Category: J

The Baja is all new for 2003. It's similar to the Subaru Outback, but it has an open cargo bed. Certainly a niche vehicle, it should appeal to people with active lifestyles, especially those who ski or surf.

Body Styles	TMV Pricing		
	Trade	Private	Dealer
4 Dr 2.5 X AWD Wgn	13996	15072	16864

Options	Price
Alarm System	+138
Aluminum/Alloy Wheels [Opt on 2.5 X]	+449
Automatic 4-Speed Transmission	+553
Automatic Dimming Rearview Mirror	+127
Compact Disc Changer [Opt on 2.5 X]	+311

Body Styles	TMV Pricing		
	Trade	Private	Dealer
4 Dr 2.5 XS AWD Wgn	15268	16441	18397

Options	Price
Leather Seats [Opt on 2.5 XS]	+519
Power Moonroof [Opt on 2.5 XS]	+553
Rear Spoiler	+242
Premium Audio System	+138

Mileage Category: L

Subaru's well-regarded Forester crossover sport-ute has been completely redesigned to be an even more enjoyable addition to your family. Engineers have given the tall wagon more interior room, a stiffer body structure, a revised chassis and more standard feature content -- all while keeping exterior dimensions the same and reducing the curb weight by 90 pounds.

2002

Body Styles	TMV Pricing		
	Trade	Private	Dealer
4 Dr L AWD Wgn	11921	12947	14656

Options	Price
Aluminum/Alloy Wheels [Std on S]	+365
AM/FM/CD Audio System [Std on S]	+221
Automatic 4-Speed Transmission	+490
Compact Disc Changer [Std on S]	+319
Front Side Airbag Restraints [Opt on S]	+151

Body Styles	TMV Pricing		
	Trade	Private	Dealer
4 Dr S AWD Wgn	13452	14609	16538

Options	Price
Leather Seats	+429
Power Moonroof [Opt on S]	+398
Premium Audio System	+164
Rear Spoiler	+181

Mileage Category: L

Subaru's mini-SUV/tall wagon gains three new standard features: a cargo area cover, daytime running lights and an intermittent mode for the rear wiper. Other changes include a new color for the Forester S' lower body cladding (from Titanium Pearl to Graystone Metallic) and the option of leather seating for S models equipped with the Premium package and automatic transmission.

2001

Body Styles	TMV Pricing		
	Trade	Private	Dealer
4 Dr L AWD Wgn	10182	11566	12844

Options	Price
Aluminum/Alloy Wheels	+333
AM/FM/CD Audio System	+235
Automatic 4-Speed Transmission	+447
Compact Disc Changer	+385
Front Side Airbag Restraints [Opt on S]	+140

Body Styles	TMV Pricing		
	Trade	Private	Dealer
4 Dr S AWD Wgn	11481	13041	14481

Options	Price
Keyless Entry System	+125
Leather Seats	+724
Power Moonroof [Opt on S]	+364
Premium Audio System	+559
Rear Spoiler	+165

Mileage Category: L

The 2001 Forester receives slight alterations to the front and rear fascias, a new Premium Package and upgrades to the interior.

Subaru

Forester/Impreza

2000

Mileage Category: L

Forester L gets standard cruise control and Forester S receives a viscous limited-slip rear differential at base price increases of $100.

Body Styles	TMV Pricing		
	Trade	Private	Dealer
4 Dr L AWD Wgn	8805	10132	11432
4 Dr S AWD Wgn	9740	11208	12646

Options	Price
Aluminum/Alloy Wheels	+292
AM/FM/Cassette/CD Audio System	+206
AM/FM/CD Audio System	+206

Body Styles	TMV Pricing		
	Trade	Private	Dealer
4 Dr L AWD Wgn	8805	10132	11432
4 Dr S AWD Wgn	9740	11208	12646

Options	Price
Automatic 4-Speed Transmission	+393
Compact Disc Changer	+339
Leather Seats	+440

1999

Mileage Category: L

Forester's engine makes more torque and the automatic transmission has been improved. L and S models have longer lists of standard equipment and two new colors are available.

Body Styles	TMV Pricing		
	Trade	Private	Dealer
4 Dr L AWD Wgn	7595	8846	10148
4 Dr S AWD Wgn	8651	10075	11557

Options	Price
Aluminum/Alloy Wheels [Std on S]	+229
AM/FM/Cassette/CD Audio System	+162
AM/FM/CD Audio System	+162

Body Styles	TMV Pricing		
	Trade	Private	Dealer
4 Dr STD AWD Wgn	8161	9505	10904

Options	Price
Automatic 4-Speed Transmission	+308
Compact Disc Changer	+265
Leather Seats	+422

1998

Mileage Category: L

Subaru attacks the mini-SUV market head-on with the Forester, which actually constitutes an SUV body on an Impreza platform with a Legacy engine under the hood. The most carlike of the mini-utes, Forester is also the most powerful. Airbags remain the full power variety, despite new rules allowing lower deployment speeds.

Body Styles	TMV Pricing		
	Trade	Private	Dealer
4 Dr L AWD Wgn	6528	7601	8812
4 Dr S AWD Wgn	7420	8640	10016

Options	Price
Aluminum/Alloy Wheels [Std on S]	+195
AM/FM/CD Audio System	+138
Automatic 4-Speed Transmission	+262

Body Styles	TMV Pricing		
	Trade	Private	Dealer
4 Dr STD AWD Wgn	7105	8273	9590

Options	Price
Compact Disc Changer	+226
Leather Seats	+359

Subaru

Impreza

2003

Mileage Category: B

As the Impreza was redesigned just last year, not much changes for 2003. Convenience has been improved; keyless entry is now standard equipment on the 2.5 RS, TS Sport Wagon and Outback Sport. For the WRX, Subaru will offer a standard rear spoiler on the sedan (though you can still get the car without, if you want) and Sonic Yellow is available as an exclusive WRX color.

Body Styles	TMV Pricing		
	Trade	Private	Dealer
4 Dr Outback Sport AWD Wgn	13167	14314	16227
4 Dr RS AWD Sdn	13312	14472	16405
4 Dr TS AWD Wgn	11548	12554	14231

Options	Price
Alarm System	+138
Aluminum/Alloy Wheels [Opt on TS]	+373
Automatic 4-Speed Transmission	+553
Automatic Dimming Rearview Mirror [Opt on Outback,WRX]	+127
Compact Disc Changer [Opt on Outback,RS,TS]	+311

Body Styles	TMV Pricing		
	Trade	Private	Dealer
4 Dr WRX Turbo AWD Sdn	16912	18381	20829
4 Dr WRX Turbo AWD Wgn	16027	17418	19738

Options	Price
Keyless Entry System [Opt on TS]	+124
Performance/Handling Package [Opt on WRX]	+554
Rear Spoiler	+248
Premium Audio System	+185

2002

Mileage Category: B

Body Styles	TMV Pricing		
	Trade	Private	Dealer
4 Dr Outback Sport AWD Wgn	11420	12457	14185
4 Dr RS AWD Sdn	11809	12881	14669
4 Dr TS AWD Wgn	10059	10972	12494

Options	Price
Aluminum/Alloy Wheels [Opt on TS]	+322
Automatic 4-Speed Transmission	+490

Body Styles	TMV Pricing		
	Trade	Private	Dealer
4 Dr WRX Turbo AWD Sdn	15683	17058	19350
4 Dr WRX Turbo AWD Wgn	14245	15494	17575

Options	Price
Premium Audio System	+164
Rear Spoiler [Opt on Sdn]	+215

Subaru completely redesigns the Impreza and brings a high-performance turbocharged WRX variant into the fold to offer enthusiasts the opportunity to drive a powerful, all-wheel-drive sport sedan without breaking the bank. All Imprezas benefit from improvements in performance, refinement and safety. Along with the Impreza's trip upmarket come revised trim levels consisting of two sedans (WRX and 2.5 RS) and three wagons (WRX, Outback Sport and 2.5 TS Sport Wagon). The coupe body style has been dropped.

2001

Body Styles	TMV Pricing		
	Trade	Private	Dealer
2 Dr L AWD Cpe	8315	9765	11104
2 Dr RS AWD Cpe	10056	11810	13429
4 Dr L AWD Sdn	8520	10006	11378

Options	Price
Aluminum/Alloy Wheels [Opt on L]	+294
AM/FM/CD Audio System	+187
Automatic 4-Speed Transmission	+447

Body Styles	TMV Pricing		
	Trade	Private	Dealer
4 Dr L AWD Wgn	8750	10275	11683
4 Dr Outback Sport AWD Wgn	9480	11133	12659
4 Dr RS AWD Sdn	9804	11513	13091

Options	Price
Keyless Entry System	+125
Leather Seats	+724
Premium Audio System	+458

Mileage Category: B

RS models get carbon-fiber patterned interior trim, a CD player and embroidered floor mats.

2000

Mileage Category: B

Body Styles	TMV Pricing		
	Trade	Private	Dealer
2 Dr L AWD Cpe	6498	7781	9038
2 Dr RS AWD Cpe	7802	9342	10852
4 Dr L AWD Sdn	6481	7761	9015

Options	Price
Aluminum/Alloy Wheels [Opt on L, Outback]	+270
AM/FM/Cassette/CD Audio System	+206
AM/FM/CD Audio System	+206

Body Styles	TMV Pricing		
	Trade	Private	Dealer
4 Dr L AWD Wgn	6914	8279	9617
4 Dr Outback Sport AWD Wgn	7201	8623	10017
4 Dr RS AWD Sdn	8427	10091	11723

Options	Price
Automatic 4-Speed Transmission	+393
Rear Spoiler [Std on RS, Cpe]	+172

For 2000, Subaru introduces the new Impreza 2.5 RS Sedan, a cross between an aggressive driver's car and a sedan. More standard equipment comes on the 2.5 Coupe and Sedan while the L model remains unchanged. The Outback Sport receives some exterior design changes. All Impreza models now come with 24-hour roadside assistance.

1999

Mileage Category: B

Body Styles	TMV Pricing		
	Trade	Private	Dealer
2 Dr L AWD Cpe	5204	6365	7573
2 Dr RS AWD Cpe	6466	7908	9408
4 Dr L AWD Sdn	5640	6898	8207

Options	Price
Aluminum/Alloy Wheels [Std on RS]	+225
AM/FM/CD Audio System	+162

Body Styles	TMV Pricing		
	Trade	Private	Dealer
4 Dr L AWD Wgn	5952	7279	8660
4 Dr Outback Sport AWD Wgn	6032	7377	8778

Options	Price
Automatic 4-Speed Transmission	+308
Rear Spoiler [Opt on Sdn]	+135

More horsepower, more torque and a more efficient automatic transmission are the big news this year. Multireflector halogen headlights are new and Outback Sport gets a revised grille. The 2.5 RS gets silver alloy wheels, a new front bumper, white gauge faces and more torque, as well as an upgraded leather-wrapped steering wheel and shift knob. Two new colors are available for 1999.

1998

Mileage Category: B

Body Styles	TMV Pricing		
	Trade	Private	Dealer
2 Dr L AWD Cpe	4343	5516	6838
2 Dr RS AWD Cpe	5363	6811	8443
4 Dr L AWD Sdn	4523	5744	7120

Options	Price
Aluminum/Alloy Wheels [Std on RS]	+192
AM/FM/CD Audio System	+138
Automatic 4-Speed Transmission	+262

Body Styles	TMV Pricing		
	Trade	Private	Dealer
4 Dr L AWD Wgn	4594	5835	7234
4 Dr Outback Sport AWD Wgn	5285	6712	8321

Options	Price
Leather Seats	+377
Rear Spoiler [Opt on Sdn]	+115

Impreza gets a new dashboard and revised door panels. The entry-level Brighton coupe is dropped, and the high-end 2.5RS coupe is added. No depowered airbags here.

1997

Mileage Category: B

Imprezas receive a facelifted front end that includes a Hemi-size hood scoop. A new Outback Sport Wagon debuts, with over six inches of ground clearance, foglights and a slightly raised roof. LX model disappears, which means only the Outback is equipped with ABS. Power and torque for both Impreza engines are up for 1997, and some new colors are available. HVAC controls are revised.

Body Styles	TMV Pricing		
	Trade	Private	Dealer
2 Dr Brighton AWD Cpe	2587	3430	4460
2 Dr L AWD Cpe	3229	4281	5567
4 Dr L AWD Sdn	3351	4443	5777

Body Styles	TMV Pricing		
	Trade	Private	Dealer
4 Dr L AWD Wgn	3422	4537	5900
4 Dr Outback Sport AWD Wgn	3916	5192	6752

Options	Price
Aluminum/Alloy Wheels	+150
Automatic 4-Speed Transmission	+180

1996

Mileage Category: B

The formerly optional 2.2-liter engine is standard across the board, except in the new budget-minded Brighton AWD Coupe. A new grille accompanies the bigger engine, and a five-speed is available as well.

Body Styles	TMV Pricing		
	Trade	Private	Dealer
2 Dr Brighton AWD Cpe	1831	2553	3551
2 Dr L AWD Cpe	2270	3167	4405
2 Dr LX AWD Cpe	2765	3857	5364
4 Dr L AWD Sdn	2334	3256	4528

Body Styles	TMV Pricing		
	Trade	Private	Dealer
4 Dr L AWD Wgn	2353	3282	4565
4 Dr LX AWD Sdn	2798	3902	5427
4 Dr LX AWD Wgn	2927	4082	5677
4 Dr Outback AWD Wgn	2766	3858	5365

Options	Price
Aluminum/Alloy Wheels [Std on LX AWD Cpe]	+134
Antilock Brakes [Opt on L]	+173

Options	Price
Automatic 4-Speed Transmission [Opt on L ,Outback,Cpe]	+184
Compact Disc Changer	+126

1995

Mileage Category: B

An Impreza coupe and an Outback wagon are added to Subaru's subcompact line of cars in an attempt to broaden their appeal with sporting and outdoor enthusiasts. Top-of-the-line LX model is introduced, replacing the LS trim level, with a 2.2-liter engine taken from the Legacy. Unfortunately it is available only with an automatic transmission.

Body Styles	TMV Pricing		
	Trade	Private	Dealer
2 Dr L AWD Cpe	1847	2645	3974
2 Dr L Cpe	1589	2275	3419
2 Dr LX AWD Cpe	2170	3107	4668
2 Dr STD Cpe	1379	1975	2969
4 Dr L AWD Sdn	1847	2645	3974
4 Dr L AWD Wgn	1860	2664	4004
4 Dr L Sdn	1589	2275	3419
4 Dr L Special Edition AWD Sdn	1877	2687	4038

Body Styles	TMV Pricing		
	Trade	Private	Dealer
4 Dr L Special Edition Sdn	1659	2375	3569
4 Dr L Special Editition AWD Wgn	1901	2721	4089
4 Dr LX AWD Sdn	2155	3086	4637
4 Dr LX AWD Wgn	2281	3266	4908
4 Dr Outback AWD Wgn	2130	3050	4583
4 Dr Outback Special Edition AWD Wgn	1901	2721	4089
4 Dr STD Sdn	1379	1975	2969

Options	Price
Air Conditioning [Opt on L AWD Cpe,STD]	+151
Aluminum/Alloy Wheels [Std on LX AWD Sdn]	+111
AM/FM/CD Audio System	+79

Options	Price
Antilock Brakes [Opt on L]	+143
Automatic 4-Speed Transmission [Std on L Spec Edition,LX]	+168

1994

Mileage Category: B

A passenger airbag joins the driver airbag on all models. LS Imprezas have standard antilock brakes, automatic transmission and sunroof.

Body Styles	TMV Pricing		
	Trade	Private	Dealer
4 Dr L AWD Sdn	1380	2096	3289
4 Dr L AWD Wgn	1431	2173	3411
4 Dr L Sdn	1201	1824	2862
4 Dr L Wgn	1240	1883	2955

Body Styles	TMV Pricing		
	Trade	Private	Dealer
4 Dr LS AWD Sdn	1923	2922	4586
4 Dr LS AWD Wgn	1841	2796	4389
4 Dr STD Sdn	1125	1709	2682

Options	Price
Antilock Brakes [Std on LS]	+127
Automatic 4-Speed Transmission [Std on LS]	+117
Air Conditioning [Std on LS]	+135

Options	Price
Dual Front Airbag Restraints [Std on LS]	+101
Power Sunroof [Std on LS]	+117

Subaru
Justy
1994

Body Styles	TMV Pricing		
	Trade	Private	Dealer
2 Dr DL Hbk	568	862	1352

Body Styles	TMV Pricing		
	Trade	Private	Dealer
4 Dr GL 4WD Hbk	694	1054	1654

Options	Price
Air Conditioning	+117

Mileage Category: A

Continuously variable transmission is no longer available. Base models gain a standard rear-window defroster. Last year for the Justy runabout.

Subaru
Legacy
2003

Body Styles	TMV Pricing		
	Trade	Private	Dealer
4 Dr 2.5 GT AWD Sdn	14802	16053	18137
4 Dr 2.5 GT AWD Wgn	15402	16703	18872
4 Dr L AWD Sdn	12456	13508	15262

Body Styles	TMV Pricing		
	Trade	Private	Dealer
4 Dr L AWD Wgn	12856	13942	15752
4 Dr L Special Edition AWD Sdn	12690	13762	15549
4 Dr L Special Edition AWD Wgn	12964	14059	15885

Options	Price
Alarm System	+131
Aluminum/Alloy Wheels [Opt on L]	+363
Automatic 4-Speed Transmission	+553
Automatic Dimming Rearview Mirror	+127

Options	Price
Compact Disc Changer [Opt on L,L SE]	+311
Rear Spoiler	+204
Premium Audio System [Opt on L,L SE]	+185

Mileage Category: D

For 2003, Subaru has added standard equipment and slightly altered available trim levels. The previous Legacy GT and GT Limited models have been consolidated into one 2.5 GT series, with all GT Limited equipment now standard. The new 2.5 GT's optional four-speed automatic now comes with a Sportshift manual mode. To fill the void created by the GT consolidation, Subaru has created an L Special Edition Package that adds several features from the 2.5 GT. Base L models now come with a standard CD player and keyless entry. 2.5 GTs have an upgraded sound system with an in-dash six-disc CD changer. Finally, all Legacys receive slightly freshened front-end styling.

2002

Mileage Category: D

Body Styles	TMV Pricing		
	Trade	Private	Dealer
4 Dr GT AWD Sdn	12430	13562	15448
4 Dr GT AWD Wgn	12957	14137	16102
4 Dr GT Limited AWD Sdn	13467	14693	16736

Body Styles	TMV Pricing		
	Trade	Private	Dealer
4 Dr L AWD Sdn	10304	11242	12805
4 Dr L AWD Wgn	10696	11670	13293

Options	Price
Aluminum/Alloy Wheels [Opt on L]	+322
AM/FM/CD Audio System [Opt on GT,L]	+221
Automatic 4-Speed Transmission	+490

Options	Price
Compact Disc Changer [Opt on GT,GT Limited]	+306
Premium Audio System	+165
Rear Spoiler	+181

Only minor changes are in store for Subaru's midsize Legacy sedan and wagon. GT Limiteds receive a standard All-Weather Package that includes heated front seats, heated outside mirrors and a windshield wiper de-icer. GT models now have larger front brakes, a new ignition switch illumination ring, standard floor mats and wood grain-patterned door switch trim. Other upgrades for all Legacys include a dome light off-delay and an internal trunk release (sedans only).

2001

Mileage Category: D

Body Styles	TMV Pricing		
	Trade	Private	Dealer
4 Dr GT AWD Sdn	11066	12578	13973
4 Dr GT AWD Wgn	11527	13102	14556
4 Dr GT Limited AWD Sdn	11833	13449	14940

Body Styles	TMV Pricing		
	Trade	Private	Dealer
4 Dr L AWD Sdn	9195	10451	11610
4 Dr L AWD Wgn	9538	10840	12042

Options	Price
Aluminum/Alloy Wheels [Opt on Brighton,L]	+294
AM/FM/CD Audio System	+235
Automatic 4-Speed Transmission	+447

Options	Price
Compact Disc Changer	+278
Premium Audio System	+559
Rear Spoiler	+165

The Brighton model is stricken from the Legacy lineup. All 2001 Legacys comply with low-emission vehicle (LEV) standards and come with standard 24-hour roadside assistance. Legacy L models now include an ambient temperature gauge, a dual-mode digital trip odometer and a fixed intermittent rear wiper with washer on the wagons. GT models feature a power moonroof, six-way power driver seat, limited-slip rear differential and multireflector halogen foglights.

Subaru
Legacy

2000

Mileage Category: D

Subaru's Legacy is completely redesigned for the new millennium.

Body Styles	TMV Pricing		
	Trade	Private	Dealer
4 Dr Brighton AWD Wgn	7857	9126	10370
4 Dr GT AWD Sdn	9577	11124	12640
4 Dr GT AWD Wgn	9946	11553	13127

Body Styles	TMV Pricing		
	Trade	Private	Dealer
4 Dr GT Limited AWD Sdn	10236	11889	13509
4 Dr L AWD Sdn	8064	9367	10644
4 Dr L AWD Wgn	8242	9573	10879

Options	Price
Leather Seats [Std on GT Limited]	+455
Power Moonroof [Opt on L]	+443
Rear Spoiler [Opt on GT Sdn,L Sdn]	+145
Aluminum/Alloy Wheels [Opt on Brighton,L]	+292

Options	Price
AM/FM/Cassette/CD Audio System [Opt on L Wgn]	+206
AM/FM/CD Audio System	+206
Automatic 4-Speed Transmission	+393
Compact Disc Changer	+244

1999

Mileage Category: D

Subaru celebrates 30 years of selling cars in the United States by adding special editions to the Legacy lineup. The L sedan and wagon are available with a package of goodies that includes power moonroof, alloy wheels, rear spoiler or roof rack, body-color trim, power antenna and seat height adjuster. New colors include Sandstone Metallic and Winestone Pearl. The 2.5GT Limited is newly available with a manual transmission, while all 2.5GT, Limited and Outback models receive standard remote keyless entry.

Body Styles	TMV Pricing		
	Trade	Private	Dealer
4 Dr 30th Anniv AWD Sdn	7947	9427	10967
4 Dr Brighton AWD Wgn	5854	6943	8077
4 Dr GT AWD Sdn	7518	8918	10375
4 Dr GT AWD Wgn	8011	9502	11054
4 Dr GT Limited 30th Anniv AWD Sdn	8055	9554	11115

Body Styles	TMV Pricing		
	Trade	Private	Dealer
4 Dr L AWD Sdn	6398	7589	8828
4 Dr L AWD Wgn	6819	8089	9410
4 Dr Limited 30th Anniv AWD Sdn	8932	10595	12325
4 Dr Outback AWD Wgn	7353	8722	10147

Options	Price
Aluminum/Alloy Wheels [Opt on Brighton,L]	+229
AM/FM/Cassette/CD Audio System [Opt on Outback]	+162
AM/FM/CD Audio System [Std on GT Limited 30th,Outback Limited 30th,SUS]	+162
Automatic 4-Speed Transmission	+308

Options	Price
Compact Disc Changer	+191
Dual Power Moonroofs [Opt on Outback 30th]	+347
Leather Seats [Opt on 30th Anniversary,GT,Outback]	+433
Power Moonroof [Opt on L]	+347

1998

Mileage Category: D

Prices remain stable while equipment is shuffled and the LSi model is dropped. All Legacy sedans and wagons, except the Outback, sport the grille and multireflector halogen lights found on the 2.5GT. A new Limited model joins the 2.5GT lineup, and a dual power moonroof package is available for the Outback Limited wagon. Outbacks get new alloy wheels, an overhead console and longer splash guards, while midyear Outback Limiteds with revised trim and added content were dubbed 30th Anniversary models. The cold weather package has heated windshield wiper nozzles this year instead of an engine block heater. The Brighton wagon's stereo loses half its wattage, Limited models have a standard CD player and the base Outback comes with a weatherband radio. Full power airbags continue, despite new government rules allowing automakers to install reduced force bags to better protect small adults.

Body Styles	TMV Pricing		
	Trade	Private	Dealer
4 Dr Brighton AWD Wgn	4287	5226	6286
4 Dr GT AWD Sdn	5822	7098	8538
4 Dr GT AWD Wgn	5856	7140	8588
4 Dr GT Limited AWD Sdn	6632	8086	9725

Body Styles	TMV Pricing		
	Trade	Private	Dealer
4 Dr L AWD Sdn	5046	6152	7399
4 Dr L AWD Wgn	5088	6203	7461
4 Dr Outback AWD Wgn	5623	6855	8245
4 Dr Outback Limited AWD Wgn	6562	8001	9623

Options	Price
Aluminum/Alloy Wheels [Opt on Brighton,L]	+195
AM/FM/Cassette/CD Audio System	+138
AM/FM/CD Audio System [Std on Limited]	+138
Automatic 4-Speed Transmission [Std on GT Limited]	+262

Options	Price
Compact Disc Changer	+163
Dual Power Moonroofs [Opt on Outback 30th]	+295
Leather Seats [Opt on GT,Outback]	+369
Spoke Wheels	+209

1997

Mileage Category: D

Front-wheel-drive models are given the ax as Subaru returns to its all-wheel drive roots. Power and torque are up marginally with the base 2.2-liter engine. The 2.5-liter motor (also stronger this year and now available with a manual transmission) is now the only engine mated to the Outback. L models gain cruise control, antilock brakes and power door locks as standard equipment. GTs get a manual transmission, larger tires and revised styling. The Outback lineup is expanded with the introduction of a Limited model, which includes a leather interior, new alloy wheels, fresh exterior colors and wood grain interior trim.

Body Styles	TMV Pricing		
	Trade	Private	Dealer
4 Dr Brighton AWD Wgn	3167	3950	4907
4 Dr GT AWD Sdn	4960	6186	7685
4 Dr GT AWD Wgn	5090	6348	7885
4 Dr L AWD Sdn	3974	4956	6157
4 Dr L AWD Wgn	4240	5288	6568

Body Styles	TMV Pricing		
	Trade	Private	Dealer
4 Dr LSi AWD Sdn	5422	6762	8400
4 Dr LSi AWD Wgn	5738	7156	8889
4 Dr Outback AWD Sdn	5012	6250	7764
4 Dr Outback AWD Wgn	4890	6098	7574
4 Dr Outback Limited AWD Wgn	5346	6668	8283

Options	Price
Aluminum/Alloy Wheels [Opt on Brighton,L]	+153
Automatic 4-Speed Transmission [Std on LSi]	+206
Compact Disc Changer [Std on LSi]	+128

Options	Price
Leather Seats	+290
Spoke Wheels	+153

For the latest vehicle information, visit www.edmunds.com

1996

Mileage Category: D

Body Styles	TMV Pricing		
	Trade	Private	Dealer
4 Dr Brighton AWD Wgn	2488	3202	4189
4 Dr GT AWD Sdn	4192	5395	7057
4 Dr GT AWD Wgn	4363	5616	7346
4 Dr L AWD Sdn	3088	3974	5197
4 Dr L AWD Wgn	3459	4452	5824
4 Dr L Sdn	3025	3893	5092

Body Styles	TMV Pricing		
	Trade	Private	Dealer
4 Dr L Wgn	3069	3950	5167
4 Dr LS AWD Sdn	4135	5322	6962
4 Dr LS AWD Wgn	4337	5583	7303
4 Dr LSi AWD Sdn	4453	5731	7497
4 Dr LSi AWD Wgn	4868	6266	8197
4 Dr Outback AWD Wgn	4104	5282	6910

Options	Price
2.5L H4 DOHC 16V FI Engine [Std on GT,LSi]	+166
Aluminum/Alloy Wheels [Opt on L]	+134
AM/FM/Cassette/CD Audio System	+128

Options	Price
Antilock Brakes [Opt on L]	+173
Automatic 4-Speed Transmission [Std on GT,LS,LSi]	+115

A new sport model debuts, with a larger, more powerful engine. The 2.5GT is available in sedan or wagon format. The luxury-oriented LSi model also gets the new motor. A knobby-tired, raised-roof Outback wagon appears, offering 7.3 inches of ground clearance and an optional 2.5-liter engine. Designed specifically for American consumers, the Outback provides a carlike ride with light-duty off-road ability.

1995

Mileage Category: D

Body Styles	TMV Pricing		
	Trade	Private	Dealer
4 Dr Brighton AWD Wgn	1955	2606	3691
4 Dr L AWD Sdn	2194	2924	4142
4 Dr L AWD Wgn	2529	3371	4775
4 Dr L Sdn	2030	2706	3832
4 Dr L Wgn	2113	2816	3988
4 Dr LS AWD Sdn	2565	3419	4842

Body Styles	TMV Pricing		
	Trade	Private	Dealer
4 Dr LS AWD Wgn	2910	3879	5493
4 Dr LSi AWD Sdn	3102	4135	5857
4 Dr LSi AWD Wgn	3218	4289	6075
4 Dr Outback AWD Wgn	2556	3407	4824
4 Dr STD Sdn	1763	2350	3327

Options	Price
Air Conditioning [Opt on STD]	+151
Aluminum/Alloy Wheels [Opt on Brighton,L,LSi]	+111
AM/FM/Cassette/CD Audio System [Opt on L,LSi]	+79
AM/FM/CD Audio System	+79
Antilock Brakes [Opt on L]	+143

Options	Price
Automatic 4-Speed Transmission [Std on LS,LSi]	+151
Compact Disc Changer	+94
Leather Seats	+213
Power Moonroof [Opt on L]	+170

New sheet metal freshens the flanks of one of our favorite compact sedans and wagons. Unfortunately the turbocharged engine has been dropped, leaving the Legacy with a rather anemic 2.2-liter four-cylinder that produces a meager 135 horsepower. The value leader Brighton wagon is introduced for budding naturalists. It includes all-wheel drive, air conditioning and a stereo with cassette. The Outback Wagon is also introduced as an alternative to the burgeoning SUV market.

1994

Body Styles	TMV Pricing		
	Trade	Private	Dealer
4 Dr L AWD Sdn	1576	2273	3434
4 Dr L AWD Wgn	1974	2847	4302
4 Dr L Sdn	1421	2050	3098
4 Dr L Wgn	1520	2193	3314
4 Dr LS AWD Sdn	2055	2964	4478
4 Dr LS AWD Wgn	2209	3186	4815

Body Styles	TMV Pricing		
	Trade	Private	Dealer
4 Dr LS Sdn	1983	2860	4322
4 Dr LS Wgn	2050	2957	4468
4 Dr LSi AWD Sdn	2191	3160	4774
4 Dr LSi AWD Wgn	2376	3426	5177
4 Dr Sport Turbo AWD Sdn	2151	3102	4687
4 Dr Touring Turbo AWD Wgn	2437	3515	5311

Options	Price
Power Moonroof [Opt on L,LS AWD Sdn]	+151
Premium Audio System	+93
Air Conditioning [Opt on L]	+135

Options	Price
Aluminum/Alloy Wheels [Opt on L]	+98
Antilock Brakes [Opt on L]	+127
Automatic 4-Speed Transmission [Opt on L]	+135

Mileage Category: D

Antilock brakes become optional on the L sedan.

Subaru

Loyale

1994

Body Styles	TMV Pricing		
	Trade	Private	Dealer
4 Dr STD 4WD Wgn	1051	1620	2568

Options	Price
Automatic 3-Speed Transmission	+93

Mileage Category: C

The Loyale is available only in the wagon body style and is seeing its last year as the Impreza is set to take over the duties of all-wheel-drive subcompact in Subaru's lineup.

Subaru
Outback

2003

Body Styles	TMV Pricing		
	Trade	Private	Dealer
4 Dr H6-3.0 AWD Sdn	18181	19377	21371
4 Dr H6-3.0 AWD Wgn	17525	18678	20600
4 Dr LL Bean AWD Wgn	19607	20897	23047
4 Dr Limited AWD Sdn	17200	18332	20218

Body Styles	TMV Pricing		
	Trade	Private	Dealer
4 Dr Limited AWD Wgn	17390	18534	20442
4 Dr STD AWD Wgn	15085	16077	17731
4 Dr VDC AWD Sdn	19744	21043	23208

Options	Price
Alarm System [Opt on H6,Limited,STD]	+131
Automatic 4-Speed Transmission [Opt on Limited,STD]	+346
Automatic Dimming Rearview Mirror	+127

Options	Price
Compact Disc Changer [Opt on H6,STD]	+311
Rear Spoiler	+225
Premium Audio System [Opt on H6,STD]	+185

Mileage Category: D

Only minor changes have been made to the 2003 Subaru Outback. All models have freshened front-end styling and revised front struts. The struts feature internal rebound springs that are said to reduce body roll when cornering, as well as brake dive. In terms of features, the four-cylinder powered Outbacks gain the formerly optional All-Weather Package as standard equipment. The base Outback now has a standard CD player, and Outback Limiteds have an upgraded audio system with an in-dash six-disc CD changer. All six-cylinder Outbacks now have the OnStar communications system. Finally, the Outback H-6 3.0 VDC's premium McIntosh audio system has been fitted with an in-dash six-disc CD changer.

2002

Mileage Category: D

Subaru has expanded the availability of its new 3.0-liter six-cylinder engine to the Outback sedan. The result is two additional sedan trim levels: 3.0-H6 and 3.0-H6 VDC. Minor upgrades to all trim levels this year include a dome light off-delay, an ignition switch illumination ring and wood grain-patterned door switch trim. Cars with the Vehicle Dynamics Control system now have a button to turn the system off, and sedans receive an internal trunk release. The automatic climate control system is upgraded with an air filtration system.

Body Styles	TMV Pricing		
	Trade	Private	Dealer
4 Dr H6-3.0 AWD Sdn	15471	16546	18336
4 Dr L.L. Bean Edition AWD Wgn	16780	17945	19888
4 Dr Limited AWD Sdn	14665	15683	17380
4 Dr Limited AWD Wgn	14829	15859	17576

Body Styles	TMV Pricing		
	Trade	Private	Dealer
4 Dr STD AWD Wgn	12541	13412	14865
4 Dr VDC AWD Sdn	16864	18035	19987
4 Dr VDC AWD Wgn	17763	18997	21053

Options	Price
AM/FM/CD Audio System [Opt on STD]	+215
Automatic 4-Speed Transmission [Opt on STD,Limited Wgn]	+490
Compact Disc Changer	+306
Heated Front Seats [Opt on STD]	+184

Options	Price
Power Heated Mirrors [Opt on STD]	+123
Premium Audio System [Std on H6,LL Bean]	+169
Rear Spoiler	+199

2001

Mileage Category: D

Two new models, the H6-3.0 L.L. Bean Edition and the H6-3.0 VDC, both featuring a more powerful 3.0-liter engine, join the happy Outback family. Braking is upgraded this year via larger front rotors with twin piston calipers.

Body Styles	TMV Pricing		
	Trade	Private	Dealer
4 Dr L.L. Bean Edition AWD Wgn	14565	16222	17751
4 Dr Limited AWD Sdn	12896	14363	15717
4 Dr Limited AWD Wgn	13045	14528	15898

Body Styles	TMV Pricing		
	Trade	Private	Dealer
4 Dr STD AWD Wgn	10813	12042	13177
4 Dr VDC AWD Wgn	15364	17111	18723

Options	Price
AM/FM/CD Audio System [Opt on STD Wgn]	+202
Automatic 4-Speed Transmission [Opt on Wgn]	+447
Compact Disc Changer	+291

Options	Price
Heated Front Seats	+140
Premium Audio System	+559
Rear Spoiler	+165

2000

Mileage Category: D

As with the Legacy platform it's based on, Subaru's hot-selling Outback is completely redesigned for the millennium.

Body Styles	TMV Pricing		
	Trade	Private	Dealer
4 Dr Limited AWD Sdn	10583	12152	13689
4 Dr Limited AWD Wgn	10861	12471	14049
4 Dr STD AWD Wgn	9402	10795	12161

Options	Price
AM/FM/Cassette/CD Audio System	+206
AM/FM/CD Audio System [Opt on STD Wgn]	+206
Automatic 4-Speed Transmission [Opt on Wgn]	+393

Options	Price
Compact Disc Changer	+244
Heated Front Seats	+123

1997

Body Styles	TMV Pricing		
	Trade	Private	Dealer
2 Dr L AWD Cpe	4517	5635	7002
2 Dr LSi AWD Cpe	5276	6582	8178

Options	Price
AM/FM/CD Audio System	+167

Mileage Category: E

A body-color grille debuts, along with P215/55VR16 tires.

1996

Body Styles	TMV Pricing		
	Trade	Private	Dealer
2 Dr L AWD Cpe	3692	4730	6164
2 Dr LSi AWD Cpe	4238	5430	7075

Options	Price
AM/FM/CD Audio System	+149

Mileage Category: E

The L model gets standard solar-reduction glass this year.

1995

Body Styles	TMV Pricing		
	Trade	Private	Dealer
2 Dr L AWD Cpe	2737	3579	4982
2 Dr L Cpe	2282	2984	4154
2 Dr LS Cpe	2081	2721	3788
2 Dr LSi AWD Cpe	3421	4473	6227

Options	Price
AM/FM/CD Audio System	+123

Mileage Category: E

Dual airbags are extended to the base model.

1994

Body Styles	TMV Pricing		
	Trade	Private	Dealer
2 Dr L Cpe	1672	2327	3419
2 Dr LS Cpe	1709	2378	3493
2 Dr LSi AWD Cpe	2677	3725	5472

Options	Price
Dual Front Airbag Restraints [Opt on L]	+84
AM/FM/CD Audio System	+109

Mileage Category: E

Subaru introduces two-wheel-drive "value leaders" to the SVX lineup called the L and LS. These new SVXs offer the same 3.3-liter Flat-6 found in the LSi, and antilock brakes are standard on the LS. A passenger airbag becomes standard on the uplevel LS and LSi models.

2003

Body Styles	TMV Pricing				Body Styles	TMV Pricing		
	Trade	Private	Dealer			Trade	Private	Dealer
4 Dr GS AWD Sdn	7997	8936	10501		4 Dr SX AWD Wgn	8137	9092	10684
4 Dr GS Sdn	7084	7915	9301		4 Dr SX Wgn	7105	7939	9329
4 Dr S Sdn	6434	7189	8448					

Options	Price	Options	Price
Antilock Brakes [Opt on GS,SX]	+390	Automatic 4-Speed Transmission [Opt on S]	+573

Mileage Category: B

As the Aerio is a recent introduction to the market, there aren't that many changes for 2003. Suzuki has bumped the horsepower up by four to 145 and nudged the torque up one pound-foot to 135. Other additions include integrated cruise control buttons on the steering wheel, a three-point seatbelt and headrest for rear center seat and a new cloth design. The GS and SX models drop the rear-seat armrest, get a six-disc in-dash CD player and have the optional all-wheel-drive available.

2002

Mileage Category: B

The Aerio is Suzuki's new compact car. Available in both sedan and wagon format, the Aerio boasts a powerful engine, distinctive styling and an affordable price.

Body Styles	TMV Pricing		
	Trade	Private	Dealer
4 Dr GS Sdn	5628	6350	7552
4 Dr S Sdn	5224	5893	7009
4 Dr SX Wgn	5628	6350	7552

Options	Price
Antilock Brakes	+307
Automatic 4-Speed Transmission	+452

2002

Body Styles	TMV Pricing				Body Styles	TMV Pricing		
	Trade	Private	Dealer			Trade	Private	Dealer
4 Dr GL Sdn	4259	4876	5903		4 Dr GLX Sdn	4598	5263	6372
4 Dr GL Wgn	4429	5070	6139		4 Dr GLX Wgn	4763	5452	6601
4 Dr GLX Plus Wgn	5995	6862	8308					

Options	Price
Automatic 4-Speed Transmission [Std on GLX Plus Wgn]	+452

Mileage Category: B

Not much changes for the 2002 Esteem. The seat upholstery is new, and sedans now have an inside trunk release handle. Suzuki has changed with the trim levels, and last year's GLX+ and GLX Sport sedan trims are no longer available. Suzuki now offers a 24-hour roadside assistance program.

2001

Mileage Category: B

Suzuki has equipped every model with an in-dash CD player. Stereo head units also get larger controls. Elsewhere, you will find gentle cosmetic changes: The front grille has been restyled, the seats are wrapped in a new fabric and floor mats are standard. Sky Blue Metallic is no longer available as an exterior color.

Body Styles	TMV Pricing				Body Styles	TMV Pricing		
	Trade	Private	Dealer			Trade	Private	Dealer
4 Dr GL Sdn	3512	4342	5109		4 Dr GLX Sdn	3659	4524	5323
4 Dr GL Wgn	3541	4378	5150		4 Dr GLX Sport Sdn	4397	5436	6396
4 Dr GLX Plus Sdn	4707	5820	6847		4 Dr GLX Wgn	3762	4651	5472
4 Dr GLX Plus Wgn	4905	6065	7135					

Options	Price
Automatic 4-Speed Transmission	+393

Esteem

2000

Body Styles	TMV Pricing		
	Trade	Private	Dealer
4 Dr GL Sdn	2434	3125	3802
4 Dr GL Wgn	2642	3392	4128

Options	Price
1.8L I4 DOHC 16V FI Engine [Opt on GL]	+158
Antilock Brakes	+215

Body Styles	TMV Pricing		
	Trade	Private	Dealer
4 Dr GLX Sdn	2749	3529	4294
4 Dr GLX Wgn	2856	3667	4461

Options	Price
Automatic 4-Speed Transmission	+316
Power Moonroof	+206

Mileage Category: B

All Esteems get the 1.8-liter engine, starting with the September 1999 production run. GLX and GLX+ models receive 15-inch wheels and tires as standard equipment. Two new paint colors, Bluish Black Pearl and Cassis Red Pearl, replace Mars Red and Midnight Black.

1999

Body Styles	TMV Pricing		
	Trade	Private	Dealer
4 Dr GL Sdn	1944	2642	3369
4 Dr GL Wgn	2032	2761	3520

Options	Price
1.8L I4 DOHC 16V FI Engine	+122
Antilock Brakes	+184

Body Styles	TMV Pricing		
	Trade	Private	Dealer
4 Dr GLX Sdn	2137	2904	3703
4 Dr GLX Wgn	2223	3021	3852

Options	Price
Automatic 4-Speed Transmission	+244
Power Sunroof	+158

Mileage Category: B

A restyled front end with multireflector headlights and an overall smoother body distinguishes the 1999 Esteem line from its predecessors. Base GL models come with the 14-inch wheels that were standard on GLX models. Interior surfaces have been upgraded and a Clarion AM/FM cassette is available. An all-new 1.8-liter inline four that makes 122 horsepower.

1998

Body Styles	TMV Pricing		
	Trade	Private	Dealer
4 Dr GL SE Wgn	1720	2487	3352
4 Dr GL Sdn	1409	2037	2745
4 Dr GL Wgn	1474	2132	2873

Body Styles	TMV Pricing		
	Trade	Private	Dealer
4 Dr GLX SE Wgn	1867	2699	3638
4 Dr GLX Sdn	1554	2247	3028
4 Dr GLX Wgn	1620	2342	3157

Options	Price
Antilock Brakes	+161
Automatic 4-Speed Transmission [Opt on GL, GLX]	+214
Power Sunroof	+139

Mileage Category: B

A wagon adds diversity to the Esteem lineup.

1997

Body Styles	TMV Pricing		
	Trade	Private	Dealer
4 Dr GL Sdn	1051	1654	2392

Options	Price
Antilock Brakes	+147

Body Styles	TMV Pricing		
	Trade	Private	Dealer
4 Dr GLX Sdn	1200	1889	2732

Options	Price
Automatic 4-Speed Transmission	+195

Mileage Category: B

No changes to the economical Esteem.

1996

Body Styles	TMV Pricing		
	Trade	Private	Dealer
4 Dr GL Sdn	815	1314	2002

Options	Price
Automatic 4-Speed Transmission	+169

Body Styles	TMV Pricing		
	Trade	Private	Dealer
4 Dr GLX Sdn	1024	1650	2515

Options	Price
Antilock Brakes	+128

Mileage Category: B

New for 1996 are daytime running lights, standard air conditioning and body-color bumpers on the GL.

1995

Body Styles	TMV Pricing		
	Trade	Private	Dealer
4 Dr GL Sdn	647	1019	1640

Body Styles	TMV Pricing		
	Trade	Private	Dealer
4 Dr GLX Sdn	774	1220	1962

Options	Price
Air Conditioning	+105
Antilock Brakes	+119
Automatic 4-Speed Transmission	+158

Mileage Category: B

The 1995 Esteem is Suzuki's entry in the subcompact car market. The Esteem has standard dual airbags and is available with antilock brakes but is saddled with a 1.6-liter engine.

Grand Vitara

2003

Body Styles	TMV Pricing			Body Styles	TMV Pricing		
	Trade	Private	Dealer		Trade	Private	Dealer
4 Dr STD 4WD SUV	10115	11205	13022	4 Dr STD SUV	9930	11000	12783

Options	Price
Aluminum/Alloy Wheels	+287
Antilock Brakes	+390
Automatic 4-Speed Transmission	+573

Mileage Category: L

For 2003, Suzuki has updated the dashboard and console for a higher quality look. Other additions this year include aluminum wheels, a seven-speaker stereo system with a CD player, adjustable center armrest with CD storage, an overhead console with reading lamps and storage compartments and a smaller rear headrest design for better reward visibility. Also of note: the Limited model has been dropped this year and last year's JLS and JLX models have been merged, leaving only one trim level for 2003.

2002

Mileage Category: L

For 2002, the Grand Vitara's model matrix has been simplified. The JLS (rear-wheel drive) and JLX (four-wheel drive) share most equipment, and the Limited Edition is available with either drive system. Hoping to better match the competition, Suzuki upped the V6's power for 2002, improving acceleration and throttle response. In terms of equipment, all Vitaras get the LATCH child seat system, 4WD vehicles now have heated side mirrors and optional heated seats, and the Limited Edition trim gains a leather-wrapped steering wheel and shift knob. Wrapping things up, Suzuki is now offering 24-hour emergency roadside assistance and towing for the duration of the vehicle's warranty to increase customer satisfaction.

Body Styles	TMV Pricing			Body Styles	TMV Pricing		
	Trade	Private	Dealer		Trade	Private	Dealer
4 Dr JLS SUV	6641	7434	8756	4 Dr Limited 4WD SUV	9009	10085	11878
4 Dr JLX 4WD SUV	7943	8892	10473	4 Dr Limited SUV	8511	9527	11221

Options	Price	Options	Price
Aluminum/Alloy Wheels [Opt on JLS,JLX]	+226	Automatic 4-Speed Transmission [Opt on JLS,JLX]	+452
Antilock Brakes [Opt on JLS,JLX]	+307	Heated Front Seats [Opt on Limited 4WD]	+135

2001

Mileage Category: L

Standard Grand Vitaras get redesigned front and rear bumpers and a restyled grille. New interior features include a redesigned AM/FM stereo with an in-dash CD player, adjustable front-seat armrests, redesigned head restraints, child seat-tether hooks and a new seat fabric. Top-of-the-line Grand Vitara Limiteds also get the improved stereo along with a tilt-and-slide power sunroof and new aluminum wheels.

Body Styles	TMV Pricing			Body Styles	TMV Pricing		
	Trade	Private	Dealer		Trade	Private	Dealer
4 Dr JLS Plus SE 4WD SUV	7737	9100	10358	4 Dr JLX 4WD SUV	6770	7962	9063
4 Dr JLS Plus SE SUV	7400	8704	9907	4 Dr JLX Plus 4WD SUV	7156	8417	9581
4 Dr JLS Plus SUV	6743	7931	9028	4 Dr Limited 4WD SUV	7894	9284	10568
4 Dr JLS SUV	6012	7070	8047	4 Dr Limited SUV	7450	8762	9974

Options	Price
Automatic 4-Speed Transmission [Std on Limited]	+393

2000

Mileage Category: L

The 2000 Limited Edition Grand Vitara comes with leather seats, privacy glass, foglamps, a hard spare tire cover, an armrest, gold emblems and a special black-and-white paint scheme. The spare tire cover on regular Grand Vitaras features a new design. The '99 model's base trim levels JS and JS+ have been renamed JLS and JLS+. A CD changer is standard equipment on JLS+ and JLX+ models.

Body Styles	TMV Pricing			Body Styles	TMV Pricing		
	Trade	Private	Dealer		Trade	Private	Dealer
4 Dr JLS SUV	5108	6115	7102	4 Dr Limited 4WD SUV	6246	7477	8684
4 Dr JLX 4WD SUV	5466	6544	7600	4 Dr Limited SUV	5974	7152	8306

Options	Price
Antilock Brakes [Opt on JLS,JLX]	+253
Automatic 4-Speed Transmission [Opt on JLS,JLX]	+316
Compact Disc Changer [Opt on JLS,JLX]	+174

1999

Mileage Category: L

The Grand Vitara is a completely new design from Suzuki and offers a standard V6 engine.

Body Styles	TMV Pricing			Body Styles	TMV Pricing		
	Trade	Private	Dealer		Trade	Private	Dealer
4 Dr JLX 4WD SUV	4700	5732	6807	4 Dr JS SUV	4103	5005	5943

Options	Price	Options	Price
Antilock Brakes	+195	Automatic 4-Speed Transmission	+244

1995

Body Styles		TMV Pricing		
		Trade	Private	Dealer
2 Dr JL 4WD Conv		1019	1375	1969

Options	Price
Air Conditioning	+102

Mileage Category: L

The Samurai is retired this year with no changes.

1994

Body Styles		TMV Pricing		
		Trade	Private	Dealer
2 Dr JL 4WD Conv		870	1217	1796

Options	Price
Air Conditioning	+93

Mileage Category: L

The two-wheel-drive model is no longer available. Other changes are limited to the addition of a high-mounted rear brake light.

1998

Body Styles	TMV Pricing				Body Styles	TMV Pricing		
	Trade	Private	Dealer			Trade	Private	Dealer
2 Dr JS Conv	2031	2652	3352		4 Dr JX FLT 4WD SUV	3274	4274	5401
2 Dr JX 4WD Conv	2594	3386	4279		4 Dr Sport JLX 4WD SUV	3410	4451	5625
2 Dr JX SE 4WD Conv	2826	3689	4663		4 Dr Sport JS SUV	2836	3702	4679
4 Dr JS SUV	2546	3323	4200		4 Dr Sport JX 4WD SUV	2998	3914	4946
4 Dr JX 4WD SUV	2819	3680	4650		4 Dr Sport JX SE 4WD SUV	3325	4340	5485

Options	Price		Options	Price
Automatic 4-Speed Transmission	+226		Antilock Brakes [Std on Sport JLX]	+161
Air Conditioning [Opt on JS,JX]	+164		Automatic 3-Speed Transmission	+142

Mileage Category: L

A couple of new colors debut.

1997

Body Styles	TMV Pricing				Body Styles	TMV Pricing		
	Trade	Private	Dealer			Trade	Private	Dealer
2 Dr JS Conv	1736	2312	3016		4 Dr Sport JLX 4WD SUV	3070	4087	5331
2 Dr JX 4WD Conv	2233	2973	3877		4 Dr Sport JS SUV	2488	3312	4319
4 Dr JS SUV	2166	2883	3759		4 Dr Sport JX 4WD SUV	2633	3505	4571
4 Dr JX 4WD SUV	2460	3275	4271					

Options	Price		Options	Price
Air Conditioning [Opt on JS,JX]	+162		Automatic 3-Speed Transmission	+130
Antilock Brakes [Opt on Sport JLX]	+147		Automatic 4-Speed Transmission	+206

Mileage Category: L

A JS Sport 2WD model is added to the Sidekick lineup. It has a DOHC engine that makes 120 horsepower at 6,500 rpm. There are no changes to the rest of the Sidekick line.

1996

Body Styles	TMV Pricing				Body Styles	TMV Pricing		
	Trade	Private	Dealer			Trade	Private	Dealer
2 Dr JS Conv	1504	2027	2750		4 Dr JX 4WD SUV	2153	2902	3936
2 Dr JX 4WD Conv	1955	2635	3574		4 Dr Sport JLX 4WD SUV	2696	3633	4928
4 Dr JS SUV	1865	2513	3409		4 Dr Sport JX 4WD SUV	2282	3076	4172

Options	Price
Air Conditioning [Opt on JS,JX]	+129
Antilock Brakes [Opt on JS,JX]	+128
Automatic 4-Speed Transmission	+179

Mileage Category: L

Lots of changes to this mini SUV: the 16-valve, 95-horsepower engine is available across the board (except in the Sport), and dual airbags are housed in a revised instrument panel. New fabrics, colors and styling revisions update the Sidekick. All new for 1996 is a Sport variant, equipped with lots of exclusive standard equipment, a 120-horsepower twin-cam motor, a wider track, two-tone paint and a chrome grille.

Suzuki
Sidekick/Swift

1995
Mileage Category: L

The convertible model gets a new top.

Body Styles	TMV Pricing		
	Trade	Private	Dealer
2 Dr JS Conv	1323	1786	2558
2 Dr JX 4WD Conv	1557	2102	3009
4 Dr JLX 4WD SUV	1878	2535	3630

Body Styles	TMV Pricing		
	Trade	Private	Dealer
4 Dr JS SUV	1560	2106	3015
4 Dr JX 4WD SUV	1861	2512	3597

Options	Price
Air Conditioning	+120
Automatic 3-Speed Transmission	+105

Options	Price
Automatic 4-Speed Transmission	+166

1994
Mileage Category: L

All Sidekicks get an alarm and a tilt steering wheel as standard equipment this year. A high-mounted rear brake light is a new safety item found on all Sidekicks.

Body Styles	TMV Pricing		
	Trade	Private	Dealer
2 Dr JS Conv	1138	1593	2351
2 Dr JX 4WD Conv	1273	1782	2630
4 Dr JLX 4WD SUV	1445	2022	2984

Body Styles	TMV Pricing		
	Trade	Private	Dealer
4 Dr JS SUV	1299	1818	2683
4 Dr JX 4WD SUV	1616	2262	3338

Options	Price
Air Conditioning	+109
Automatic 3-Speed Transmission	+95

Options	Price
Automatic 4-Speed Transmission	+150

Suzuki
Swift

2001

Body Styles	TMV Pricing		
	Trade	Private	Dealer
2 Dr GA Hbk	1873	2634	3336

Body Styles	TMV Pricing		
	Trade	Private	Dealer
2 Dr GL Hbk	2102	2956	3744

Options	Price
Automatic 3-Speed Transmission	+255

Mileage Category: A

The 2001 Suzuki Swift remains mechanically unchanged. Suzuki has changed the exterior color options slightly: Bright White and Platinum Silver Metallic replace Polar White and Mercury Silver Metallic.

2000
Mileage Category: A

The 2000 Suzuki Swift remains mechanically unchanged. Two new exterior colors – Brilliant Blue Metallic and Catseye Blue Metallic – are offered.

Body Styles	TMV Pricing		
	Trade	Private	Dealer
2 Dr GA Hbk	1413	2136	2844

Body Styles	TMV Pricing		
	Trade	Private	Dealer
2 Dr GL Hbk	1493	2257	3006

Options	Price
Air Conditioning [Std on GL]	+253

Options	Price
Automatic 3-Speed Transmission	+206

1999
Mileage Category: A

With the exception of some color changes, the Suzuki Swift remains unchanged for '99.

Body Styles	TMV Pricing		
	Trade	Private	Dealer
2 Dr STD Hbk	1127	1819	2540

Options	Price
Air Conditioning	+195

Options	Price
Automatic 3-Speed Transmission	+158

1998
Mileage Category: A

Swift's engine makes nine more horsepower this year, and one more pound-foot of torque.

Body Styles	TMV Pricing		
	Trade	Private	Dealer
2 Dr STD Hbk	979	1635	2374

1998 (cont'd)

Options	Price
Automatic 3-Speed Transmission	+128
Antilock Brakes	+161

Options	Price
Air Conditioning	+171

1997

Body Styles	TMV Pricing		
	Trade	Private	Dealer
2 Dr STD Hbk	761	1340	2047

Options	Price
Air Conditioning	+156

Options	Price
Antilock Brakes	+147

Mileage Category: A

New paint colors (Victory Red and Bright Teal Metallic) and new seat coverings are the only changes to the 1996 Swift.

1996

Body Styles	TMV Pricing		
	Trade	Private	Dealer
2 Dr STD Hbk	633	1138	1836

Options	Price
Air Conditioning	+136

Options	Price
Antilock Brakes	+128

Mileage Category: A

Two new colors and new seat fabrics.

1995

Body Styles	TMV Pricing		
	Trade	Private	Dealer
2 Dr STD Hbk	495	873	1504

Options	Price
Air Conditioning	+126
Antilock Brakes	+119

Options	Price
Automatic 3-Speed Transmission	+86

Mileage Category: A

The sedan is dropped and dual airbags are added. Antilock brakes become a much appreciated option. The two-door GT hatchback has also been dropped.

1994

Body Styles	TMV Pricing		
	Trade	Private	Dealer
2 Dr GA Hbk	341	626	1102
2 Dr GT Hbk	492	905	1592

Body Styles	TMV Pricing		
	Trade	Private	Dealer
4 Dr GA Sdn	380	698	1228
4 Dr GS Sdn	442	812	1428

Options	Price
Air Conditioning	+114

Options	Price
Automatic 3-Speed Transmission	+78

Mileage Category: A

The GA hatchback gets a cargo cover and both GA models get a right sideview mirror.

Suzuki
Vitara

2003

Body Styles	TMV Pricing		
	Trade	Private	Dealer
2 Dr STD 4WD Conv	8022	8996	10618
2 Dr STD Conv	7836	8787	10372

Body Styles	TMV Pricing		
	Trade	Private	Dealer
4 Dr STD 4WD SUV	8454	9480	11189
4 Dr STD SUV	7897	8856	10453

Options	Price
Aluminum/Alloy Wheels	+287
Antilock Brakes	+390

Options	Price
Automatic 4-Speed Transmission	+573

Mileage Category: L

Besides the merging of the JLS and JLX trim levels, not much has changed for the Suzuki Vitara this year.

2002

Body Styles	TMV Pricing		
	Trade	Private	Dealer
2 Dr JLS Conv	6066	6879	8235

Body Styles	TMV Pricing		
	Trade	Private	Dealer
4 Dr JLS SUV	6387	7244	8672

Suzuki
Vitara/X-90

2002 (cont'd)
Mileage Category: L

The previous base-level Vitara JS and JX have been discontinued. The Vitara now comes only in fully equipped JLS (rear-wheel drive) and JLX (four-wheel drive) trim in either body style. Additionally, motivation for all Vitaras now comes from the 2.0-liter engine as the 1.6-liter has been dropped. Other changes for the new year include the addition of the LATCH child seat system, a new fender-mounted antenna, new donut-style headrests for better visibility and new exterior colors. Suzuki offers 24-hour emergency roadside assistance and towing for the duration of the vehicle's warranty to increase customer satisfaction.

Body Styles	TMV Pricing		
	Trade	Private	Dealer
2 Dr JLX 4WD Conv	6498	7370	8823

Options	Price
Aluminum/Alloy Wheels	+226

Body Styles	TMV Pricing		
	Trade	Private	Dealer
4 Dr JLX 4WD SUV	6863	7783	9317

Options	Price
Automatic 4-Speed Transmission	+452

2001
Mileage Category: L

All Vitara models get a restyled front grille, new seat fabric, a larger audio unit with an in-dash CD player and new exterior colors.

Body Styles	TMV Pricing		
	Trade	Private	Dealer
2 Dr JLS Conv	5122	6217	7227
2 Dr JLX 4WD Conv	5875	7130	8289
2 Dr JS Conv	4390	5328	6194
2 Dr JX 4WD Conv	5280	6408	7450

Options	Price
Aluminum/Alloy Wheels	+196

Body Styles	TMV Pricing		
	Trade	Private	Dealer
4 Dr JLS SUV	5688	6904	8026
4 Dr JLX 4WD SUV	6213	7541	8767
4 Dr JS SUV	5304	6438	7484
4 Dr JX 4WD SUV	5975	7252	8431

Options	Price
Automatic 4-Speed Transmission	+393

2000
Mileage Category: L

Four-door models receive a new luggage cover for 2000. The Vitara two-door JLS/JLX is equipped with air conditioning as standard equipment. There are three new paint colors, and four-wheel-drive models have a "4x4" sticker in the rear-quarter windows.

Body Styles	TMV Pricing		
	Trade	Private	Dealer
2 Dr JLS Conv	3952	4905	5839
2 Dr JLX 4WD Conv	4513	5601	6667
2 Dr JS Conv	3118	3869	4606
2 Dr JX 4WD Conv	4022	4992	5942

Body Styles	TMV Pricing		
	Trade	Private	Dealer
4 Dr JLS SUV	4325	5367	6389
4 Dr JLX 4WD SUV	5142	6381	7596
4 Dr JS SUV	4061	5040	5999
4 Dr JX 4WD SUV	4589	5695	6779

Options	Price
Automatic 4-Speed Transmission	+316

1999
Mileage Category: L

The Vitara is an all-new model that replaces the Sidekick as Suzuki's entry into the mini-SUV class.

Body Styles	TMV Pricing		
	Trade	Private	Dealer
2 Dr JS 1.6 Conv	2619	3328	4065
2 Dr JS 2.0 Conv	2906	3692	4511
2 Dr JX 1.6 4WD Conv	3228	4102	5011

Options	Price
Air Conditioning	+195

Body Styles	TMV Pricing		
	Trade	Private	Dealer
2 Dr JX 2.0 4WD Conv	3445	4377	5348
4 Dr JS SUV	3336	4239	5179
4 Dr JX 4WD SUV	3695	4695	5736

Options	Price
Automatic 4-Speed Transmission	+244

Suzuki
X-90

1998

No changes this year.

Body Styles	TMV Pricing		
	Trade	Private	Dealer
2 Dr SE 4WD SUV	3117	4007	5010
2 Dr STD 4WD SUV	2965	3811	4766

Options	Price
Air Conditioning [Opt on STD]	+171
Antilock Brakes [Opt on STD]	+166

Mileage Category: L

No changes this year.

Body Styles	TMV Pricing		
	Trade	Private	Dealer
2 Dr STD SUV	2576	3312	4141

Options	Price
Automatic 4-Speed Transmission	+203

1997

Body Styles	TMV Pricing		
	Trade	Private	Dealer
2 Dr STD 4WD SUV	2218	2946	3835

Options	Price
Air Conditioning	+156
Antilock Brakes	+147

Body Styles	TMV Pricing		
	Trade	Private	Dealer
2 Dr STD SUV	1906	2532	3296

Options	Price
Automatic 4-Speed Transmission	+185

Mileage Category: L

No changes to Suzuki's alternative to AWD vehicles.

1996

Body Styles	TMV Pricing		
	Trade	Private	Dealer
2 Dr STD 4WD SUV	1596	2107	2813

Options	Price
Air Conditioning	+136

Body Styles	TMV Pricing		
	Trade	Private	Dealer
2 Dr STD SUV	1333	1760	2350

Options	Price
Automatic 4-Speed Transmission	+161

Mileage Category: L

Based on Sidekick platform, this new concept features a two-seat cockpit, T-top roof, conventional trunk and available four-wheel drive.

Suzuki

XL-7

2003

Body Styles	TMV Pricing		
	Trade	Private	Dealer
4 Dr Limited 4WD SUV	13429	14494	16268
4 Dr Limited SUV	13038	14072	15795

Options	Price
Aluminum/Alloy Wheels [Opt on Touring]	+287
Antilock Brakes [Opt on Touring]	+390
Automatic 4-Speed Transmission [Opt on Touring]	+573

Body Styles	TMV Pricing		
	Trade	Private	Dealer
4 Dr Touring 4WD SUV	12721	13730	15411
4 Dr Touring SUV	12333	13311	14940

Options	Price
Heated Front Seats [Opt on Limited]	+172
Third Seat	+430

Mileage Category: M

For 2003, Suzuki has updated the Grand Vitara XL-7's dash and console with wood grain trim, chrome accents and a 12-volt accessory outlet. Other additions to the interior include a new seven-speaker system, integrated audio and cruise control buttons on the steering wheel, an adjustable center armrest with CD storage and smaller rear headsets for better rearward visibility.

Suzuki has also changed some of its trim names for 2003. The previous "Standard" trim has now simply become the XL-7, while the "Plus" has become the XL-7 with the option of third-row seating. The "Touring" model has been dropped all together. The Limited model is now being offered with a six-disc in-dash CD changer. Finally, a Limited model with the third-row option is also available with climate control and a rear air conditioning switch.

2002

Body Styles	TMV Pricing		
	Trade	Private	Dealer
4 Dr Limited 4WD SUV	11332	12273	13841
4 Dr Limited SUV	11065	11983	13514
4 Dr Plus 4WD SUV	10173	11018	12425
4 Dr Plus SUV	9809	10624	11981

Options	Price
Antilock Brakes [Std on Limited, Touring]	+307
Automatic 4-Speed Transmission [Std on Limited, Touring 2WD]	+452

Body Styles	TMV Pricing		
	Trade	Private	Dealer
4 Dr STD 4WD SUV	9655	10456	11792
4 Dr STD SUV	9084	9838	11095
4 Dr Touring 4WD SUV	10864	11766	13269
4 Dr Touring SUV	10770	11664	13155

Options	Price
Heated Front Seats [Opt on Limted 4WD]	+135

Mileage Category: M

For 2002, the XL-7's 2.7-liter V6 engine has been upgraded to produce more power. Inside, all XL-7 models have gained features such as the LATCH child seat system, improved cargo floor design and new upholstery. All Standard and Plus models now offer optional ABS brakes, while the line-topping Limited Edition's interior gains woodgrain trim and a leather-wrapped steering wheel and shift knob. Suzuki offers 24-hour emergency roadside assistance and towing for the duration of the vehicle's warranty to increase customer satisfaction.

2001

Body Styles	TMV Pricing		
	Trade	Private	Dealer
4 Dr Plus 4WD SUV	8463	9662	10769
4 Dr Plus SUV	8199	9360	10432
4 Dr STD 4WD SUV	8070	9213	10269

Body Styles	TMV Pricing		
	Trade	Private	Dealer
4 Dr STD SUV	7609	8687	9682
4 Dr Touring 4WD SUV	8840	10092	11248
4 Dr Touring SUV	8764	10005	11151

Options	Price
Automatic 4-Speed Transmission [Opt on Plus, Touring]	+393

Mileage Category: M

The Suzuki XL-7 is an all-new midsize SUV based on a stretched Grand Vitara. It is the first in this class to offer third-row seating and a starting price of under $20,000.

2003

Mileage Category: M

Toyota's popular midsize SUV has been completely redesigned this year. Though it stays true to its truck-based roots, it comes with many new upscale features, including an available V8 engine and an optional navigation system.

Body Styles	TMV Pricing		
	Trade	Private	Dealer
4 Dr Limited 4WD SUV	25501	27144	29884
4 Dr Limited SUV	22966	24446	26914
4 Dr SR5 4WD SUV	20502	21823	24025

Options	Price
Alarm System [Std on Limited]	+166
JBL Audio System	+321
Navigation System	+1434
Power Moonroof	+679
Rear Spoiler	+151

Body Styles	TMV Pricing		
	Trade	Private	Dealer
4 Dr SR5 SUV	18732	19939	21951
4 Dr Sport Edition 4WD SUV	21170	22534	24808
4 Dr Sport Edition SUV	19616	20880	22987

Options	Price
Front Side Airbag Restraints	+189
AM/FM/Cassette/CD Changer Audio System	+151
Front and Rear Head Airbag Restraints	+359
4.7L V8 SOHC 16V FI Engine	+717

2002

Body Styles	TMV Pricing		
	Trade	Private	Dealer
4 Dr Limited 4WD SUV	22289	23879	26530
4 Dr Limited SUV	20674	22149	24608

Options	Price
16 Inch Wheels [Opt on SR5]	+328
Leather Seats [Opt on SR5]	+579
Power Sunroof	+562

Body Styles	TMV Pricing		
	Trade	Private	Dealer
4 Dr SR5 4WD SUV	18443	19759	21951
4 Dr SR5 SUV	16744	17939	19931

Options	Price
Premium Audio System	+138
Sport Package [Opt on SR5]	+1093
Sport Seats [Opt on SR5]	+197

Mileage Category: M

Not much has changed this year for Toyota's truck-based 4Runner SUV. The SR5's optional Sport package has gained a front skid plate, floor mats and new tube step-up bars (optional). Handsome 15-inch alloy wheels are now standard, there's a new chrome package available, and Golden Pearl has been added to the Limited's selection of exterior colors.

2001

Mileage Category: M

Base models have been dropped, leaving Limited and SR5 trim levels equipped with a standard automatic transmission, Vehicle Skid Control (VSC), traction control and ABS with Electronic Brakeforce Distribution and BrakeAssist. All 4Runners have power door locks this year, as well as a prewired trailer hitch harness, a modified grille design and freshened taillights. New wheels for Limited and Sport debut, and a new premium 3-in-1 audio system with a CD changer is available. Revised sun visors with extensions and a HomeLink programmable transmitter come standard on Limited and can be ordered on SR5. Limited also gets a new color of wood trim, and standard front seat heaters. There's bad news for hard-core off-roaders -- the optional differential lock has been discontinued with the demise of the manual transmission. Three new colors replace two old ones on the color chart.

Body Styles	TMV Pricing		
	Trade	Private	Dealer
4 Dr Limited 4WD SUV	19559	21748	23769
4 Dr Limited SUV	18247	20289	22175

Options	Price
Aluminum/Alloy Wheels [Opt on SR5]	+261
AM/FM/Cassette/CD Changer Audio System [Opt on Limited]	+126
Leather Seats [Opt on SR5]	+529
Power Sunroof	+513

Body Styles	TMV Pricing		
	Trade	Private	Dealer
4 Dr SR5 4WD SUV	16675	18541	20264
4 Dr SR5 SUV	15187	16887	18456

Options	Price
Running Boards [Opt on SR5]	+217
Sport Package [Opt on SR5]	+997
Sport Seats [Opt on SR5]	+179

2000

Mileage Category: M

Optional color-coordinated fender flares are available on the SR5. An AM/FM/cassette/CD is now available on base models, and is standard on SR5 and Limited models. Daytime running lights are now included with the antilock brake package.

Body Styles	TMV Pricing		
	Trade	Private	Dealer
4 Dr Limited 4WD SUV	17117	19321	21481
4 Dr Limited SUV	16000	18060	20079
4 Dr SR5 4WD SUV	13979	15779	17543

Options	Price
Cruise Control [Opt on STD]	+138
Compact Disc Changer	+366
Keyless Entry System [Opt on SR5]	+124
Leather Seats [Opt on SR5]	+464
Limited Slip Differential	+188
Power Door Locks [Opt on STD,SR5 V6 2WD]	+135
Power Moonroof	+450

Body Styles	TMV Pricing		
	Trade	Private	Dealer
4 Dr SR5 SUV	13220	14922	16590
4 Dr STD 4WD SUV	12996	14669	16308
4 Dr STD SUV	11725	13235	14714

Options	Price
Power Windows [Std on Limited]	+146
Running Boards [Std on Limited]	+191
Sport Package	+770
Sport Seats	+157
Steel Wheels	+332
Tilt Steering Wheel [Opt on STD]	+135
Wide Tires And Wheels [Opt on SR5,STD]	+541

Options	Price
Air Conditioning [Std on Limited]	+544
Alarm System [Std on Limited]	+177
Aluminum/Alloy Wheels [Std on Limited]	+229
AM/FM/Cassette/CD Audio System [Opt on STD,SR5 V6 2WD]	+387

Options	Price
AM/FM/CD Audio System	+221
Antilock Brakes [Opt on STD]	+376
Automatic 4-Speed Transmission [Opt on STD,SR5 V6 4WD]	+497

1999

Body Styles	TMV Pricing		
	Trade	Private	Dealer
4 Dr Limited 4WD SUV	14790	16960	19219
4 Dr Limited SUV	13560	15550	17621
4 Dr SR5 4WD SUV	12255	14054	15925

Body Styles	TMV Pricing		
	Trade	Private	Dealer
4 Dr SR5 SUV	11029	12647	14332
4 Dr STD 4WD SUV	10696	12266	13899
4 Dr STD SUV	9325	10693	12117

Options	Price
Air Conditioning [Std on Limited]	+420
Alarm System [Std on Limited]	+137
Aluminum/Alloy Wheels [Std on Limited]	+177
AM/FM/Cassette/CD Audio System	+299
AM/FM/CD Audio System [Std on Limited]	+171
Antilock Brakes [Std on Limited,SR5]	+323
Automatic 4-Speed Transmission [Opt on STD,SR5 V6 4WD]	+385
Compact Disc Changer	+282
Leather Seats [Opt on SR5]	+534

Options	Price
Locking Differential	+145
Power Moonroof	+349
Power Windows [Std on Limited]	+203
Running Boards [Std on Limited]	+147
Sport Package	+596
Sport Seats	+177
Steel Wheels	+256
Wide Tires And Wheels [Opt on SR5,STD]	+419

Mileage Category: M

The 4Runner receives a number of upgrades this year, starting with a new and improved four-wheel-drive system equipped with a center differential and featuring a full-time 4WD mode in addition to the current two-high, four-high and four-low modes. New exterior features include a front bumper redesign, multireflector headlamps and an enhanced sport package with fender flares and a hood scoop on the SR5 model. Inside, a new center console/cupholder design will improve beverage-carrying capacity of the 4Runner and an automatic climate control system will be featured on the Limited models.

1998

Body Styles	TMV Pricing		
	Trade	Private	Dealer
4 Dr Limited 4WD SUV	12187	14148	16360
4 Dr Limited SUV	11463	13308	15388
4 Dr SR5 4WD SUV	10434	12113	14007

Body Styles	TMV Pricing		
	Trade	Private	Dealer
4 Dr SR5 SUV	9611	11158	12902
4 Dr STD 4WD SUV	8785	10199	11793
4 Dr STD SUV	7849	9112	10536

Options	Price
Air Conditioning [Opt on SR5,STD]	+370
Alarm System	+120
Aluminum/Alloy Wheels [Opt on SR5,STD]	+156
AM/FM/Cassette/CD Audio System	+263
AM/FM/CD Audio System [Opt on SR5,STD]	+150
Antilock Brakes [Opt on STD]	+284
Automatic 4-Speed Transmission [Opt on STD,SR5 4WD]	+338
Compact Disc Changer	+248

Options	Price
Leather Seats [Opt on SR5]	+470
Locking Differential	+122
Power Moonroof	+344
Power Windows [Opt on SR5,STD]	+174
Running Boards [Opt on SR5,STD]	+129
Sport Seats	+156
Steel Wheels	+226

Mileage Category: M

For 1998, the Toyota 4Runner gets rotary HVAC controls, a new four-spoke steering wheel and revised audio control head units.

1997

Body Styles	TMV Pricing		
	Trade	Private	Dealer
4 Dr Limited 4WD SUV	10697	12538	14788
4 Dr Limited SUV	9949	11662	13755
4 Dr SR5 4WD SUV	9380	10995	12968

Body Styles	TMV Pricing		
	Trade	Private	Dealer
4 Dr SR5 SUV	8641	10128	11946
4 Dr STD 4WD SUV	7499	8790	10367
4 Dr STD SUV	6834	8011	9449

Options	Price
Power Moonroof	+294
Power Windows [Opt on SR5,STD]	+141
Sport Seats	+219
Steel Wheels	+193
Air Conditioning [Opt on SR5,STD]	+316
Aluminum/Alloy Wheels [Opt on SR5,STD]	+133

Options	Price
AM/FM/Cassette/CD Audio System	+225
AM/FM/CD Audio System	+129
Antilock Brakes [Opt on STD]	+242
Automatic 4-Speed Transmission [Opt on STD,SR5 4WD]	+289
Compact Disc Changer	+209
Leather Seats [Opt on SR5,STD]	+401

Mileage Category: M

Toyota's SUV receives minor changes. The most noticeable is the addition of the 2WD Limited to the model lineup. SR5 models receive new interior fabrics.

Toyota
4Runner/Avalon

1996

Mileage Category: M

A new 4Runner with a potent V6, updated styling and more interior room debuts.

Body Styles	TMV Pricing		
	Trade	Private	Dealer
4 Dr Limited 4WD SUV	8965	10636	12943
4 Dr SR5 4WD SUV	7917	9392	11430
4 Dr SR5 SUV	7504	8902	10833

Options	Price
Sport Seats	+194
Steel Wheels	+162
Air Conditioning [Opt on SR5,STD]	+266
AM/FM/Cassette/CD Audio System	+189
Antilock Brakes [Opt on STD]	+204

Body Styles	TMV Pricing		
	Trade	Private	Dealer
4 Dr STD 4WD SUV	6051	7178	8735
4 Dr STD SUV	5443	6457	7858

Options	Price
Automatic 4-Speed Transmission [Opt on STD,SR5 4WD]	+244
Compact Disc Changer	+176
Leather Seats [Opt on SR5]	+338
Power Moonroof	+248

1995

Mileage Category: M

V6 models get new tape stripes.

Body Styles	TMV Pricing		
	Trade	Private	Dealer
4 Dr Limited 4WD SUV	6872	8155	10295
4 Dr SR5 4WD SUV	5177	6144	7756

Options	Price
Compact Disc Changer	+156
Leather Seats [Opt on SR5 V6]	+300
Power Moonroof	+196
Power Windows [Opt on 2WD,SR5 V6]	+76
Premium Audio System	+156
Running Boards	+79
Sport Seats	+99

Body Styles	TMV Pricing		
	Trade	Private	Dealer
4 Dr SR5 SUV	5578	6620	8357
4 Dr SR5 V6 4WD SUV	6210	7370	9303

Options	Price
Automatic 4-Speed Transmission [Std on 2WD]	+216
Air Conditioning [Std on Limited]	+236
Alarm System	+77
Aluminum/Alloy Wheels [Opt on SR5]	+99
AM/FM/Cassette/CD Audio System	+168
AM/FM/CD Audio System	+96
Antilock Brakes	+181

1994

Mileage Category: M

Four-wheel ABS available on models with V6 engine. Side-door guard beams added. Air conditioners get CFC-free refrigerant. Optional leather can be had in new Oak color.

Body Styles	TMV Pricing		
	Trade	Private	Dealer
4 Dr SR5 4WD SUV	4388	5310	6847
4 Dr SR5 V6 4WD SUV	5187	6277	8095

Options	Price
Air Conditioning	+209
Aluminum/Alloy Wheels	+88
AM/FM/Cassette/CD Audio System	+148
AM/FM/CD Audio System	+84
Antilock Brakes	+160
Automatic 4-Speed Transmission [Std on 2WD]	+190

Body Styles	TMV Pricing		
	Trade	Private	Dealer
4 Dr SR5 V6 SUV	4635	5609	7233

Options	Price
Compact Disc Changer	+137
Leather Seats	+265
Power Moonroof	+173
Power Windows	+81
Sport Seats	+88

Toyota
Avalon
2003

Body Styles	TMV Pricing		
	Trade	Private	Dealer
4 Dr XL Sdn	17977	19056	20853
4 Dr XLS Sdn	20324	21543	23575

Mileage Category: G

A few minor changes are in store for Toyota's large sedan. On the outside, you'll find freshened styling that consists of a new grille, new taillamps and redesigned bumpers. Inside, the 2003 Avalon has been upgraded with dual-stage airbags and ISO-FIX child safety seat anchor points. XLS models also have more features this year, including an autodimming driver-side mirror, rain-sensing wipers, a simulated wood-trimmed steering wheel and an optional navigation system.

Options	Price
Alarm System [Opt on XL]	+241
Aluminum/Alloy Wheels [Opt on XL]	+340
Heated Front Seats [Opt on XLS]	+238
JBL Audio System [Opt on XL]	+223
Keyless Entry System [Opt on XL]	+132
Leather Seats [Opt on XL]	+642
Navigation System [Opt on XLS]	+1510
Power Driver Seat [Opt on XLS]	+181

Options	Price
Power Moonroof	+679
Power Passenger Seat [Opt on XL]	+181
Special Factory Paint	+166
Split Front Bench Seat	+619
Traction Control System [Opt on XLS]	+491
AM/FM/Cassette/CD Changer Audio System [Opt on XLS]	+264
16 Inch Wheels	+291
Power Driver Seat w/Memory [Opt on XLS]	+155

2002

Body Styles	TMV Pricing		
	Trade	Private	Dealer
4 Dr XL Sdn	16278	17395	19257

Body Styles	TMV Pricing		
	Trade	Private	Dealer
4 Dr XLS Sdn	17903	19132	21179

Mileage Category: G

Toyota has tinkered with the options packages, but otherwise left the Avalon alone. A new luxury package for the XL includes power leather-trimmed seats, 15-inch alloy wheels, remote keyless entry and a JBL audio system. There's also a Sport Luxury package that adds 16-inch alloy wheels and a rear spoiler in addition to the items in the luxury package.

Options	Price
16 Inch Wheels	+266
Aluminum/Alloy Wheels [Opt on XL]	+155
AM/FM/Cassette/CD Changer Audio System [Opt on XLS]	+241
Automatic Stability Control [Opt on XLS]	+448
Heated Front Seats [Opt on XLS]	+217
JBL Audio System [Opt on XL]	+204
Keyless Entry System [Opt on XL]	+121
Leather Seats	+586

Options	Price
Pearlescent Metallic Paint	+152
Power Driver Seat [Opt on XL]	+166
Power Driver Seat w/Memory [Opt on XLS]	+145
Power Moonroof	+621
Power Passenger Seat	+166
Rear Spoiler [Opt on XL]	+172
Split Front Bench Seat	+566
Traction Control System [Opt on XLS]	+186

2001

Body Styles	TMV Pricing		
	Trade	Private	Dealer
4 Dr XL Sdn	13681	15145	16496

Body Styles	TMV Pricing		
	Trade	Private	Dealer
4 Dr XLS Sdn	15949	17656	19231

Mileage Category: G

Two colors, Cognac Brown and Constellation Blue Pearl, are dumped for 2001, and an emergency trunk release has been added.

Options	Price
Aluminum/Alloy Wheels [Opt on XL]	+242
AM/FM/Cassette/CD Changer Audio System [Opt on XLS]	+252
Automatic Stability Control [Opt on XLS]	+409
Heated Front Seats	+198
JBL Audio System [Opt on XL]	+227
Leather Seats	+535
Pearlescent Metallic Paint	+138

Options	Price
Power Driver Seat [Opt on XL]	+132
Power Driver Seat w/Memory [Opt on XLS]	+132
Power Moonroof	+573
Power Passenger Seat [Opt on XL]	+132
Split Front Bench Seat	+516
Traction Control System	+170

2000

Body Styles	TMV Pricing		
	Trade	Private	Dealer
4 Dr XL Sdn	12156	13662	15139

Body Styles	TMV Pricing		
	Trade	Private	Dealer
4 Dr XLS Sdn	13642	15333	16990

Mileage Category: G

Entering its second generation, the 2000 Avalon is roomier, more powerful and more technically advanced. The Kentucky-built Avalon features new styling inside and out, enhanced safety features, increased engine performance, and more comfort and convenience than its predecessor.

Options	Price
Alarm System [Opt on XL]	+220
Aluminum/Alloy Wheels [Opt on XL]	+213
Automatic Stability Control [Opt on XLS]	+359
Compact Disc Changer	+304
Heated Front Seats	+174
JBL Audio System [Opt on XL]	+199
Leather Seats	+470

Options	Price
Power Driver Seat [Opt on XL]	+133
Power Driver Seat w/Memory [Opt on XLS]	+134
Power Moonroof	+486
Power Passenger Seat [Opt on XL]	+133
Special Factory Paint	+122
Traction Control System	+149

1999

Body Styles	TMV Pricing		
	Trade	Private	Dealer
4 Dr XL Sdn	8573	9885	11251

Body Styles	TMV Pricing		
	Trade	Private	Dealer
4 Dr XLS Sdn	10131	11682	13296

Toyota
Avalon

1999 (cont'd)

Options	Price
Power Passenger Seat [Opt on XL]	+178
Traction Control System	+128
Alarm System [Opt on XL]	+170
Aluminum/Alloy Wheels [Opt on XL]	+164
AM/FM/CD Audio System	+143

Options	Price
Compact Disc Changer	+235
Heated Front Seats	+135
Leather Seats	+363
Power Driver Seat [Opt on XL]	+178
Power Moonroof	+385

Mileage Category: G

After a body makeover and safety improvements (side airbags) last year, the Avalon heads into '99 with only minor updates. Daytime running lights with auto-off color-keyed foglamp covers and dual heated color-keyed power mirrors are new this year. A new three-in-one ETR/cassette/CD sound system is optional on the XL model and Lunar Mist Metallic replaces Golden Sand Metallic.

1998

Mileage Category: G

The Avalon gets side-impact airbags, new headlights and taillamps, a new grille, a new trunk lid and pre-tensioner seatbelts with force limiters.

Body Styles	TMV Pricing		
	Trade	Private	Dealer
4 Dr XL Sdn	7002	8160	9465

Options	Price
Alarm System [Opt on XL]	+120
Aluminum/Alloy Wheels [Opt on XL]	+164
Compact Disc Changer	+206
Heated Front Seats	+119

Body Styles	TMV Pricing		
	Trade	Private	Dealer
4 Dr XLS Sdn	8640	10068	11679

Options	Price
Leather Seats	+492
Power Driver Seat [Opt on XL]	+157
Power Moonroof	+368
Power Passenger Seat [Opt on XL]	+157

1997

Mileage Category: G

More power, more torque and added standard features make the Avalon one of the most appealing full-size sedans

Body Styles	TMV Pricing		
	Trade	Private	Dealer
4 Dr XL Sdn	5482	6482	7704

Options	Price
AM/FM/Cassette/CD Audio System	+196
Compact Disc Changer	+239
Leather Seats	+322
Power Bench Seat [Opt on XL]	+273

Body Styles	TMV Pricing		
	Trade	Private	Dealer
4 Dr XLS Sdn	7012	8290	9853

Options	Price
Power Driver Seat [Opt on XL]	+134
Power Moonroof	+315
Power Passenger Seat [Opt on XL]	+134
Aluminum/Alloy Wheels [Opt on XL]	+139

1996

Mileage Category: G

No changes.

Body Styles	TMV Pricing		
	Trade	Private	Dealer
4 Dr XL Sdn	4373	5230	6414

Options	Price
Aluminum/Alloy Wheels [Opt on XL]	+118
AM/FM/Cassette/CD Audio System	+203
Antilock Brakes [Opt on XL]	+265
Compact Disc Changer	+148

Body Styles	TMV Pricing		
	Trade	Private	Dealer
4 Dr XLS Sdn	5742	6867	8421

Options	Price
Leather Seats	+272
Power Bench Seat	+230
Power Moonroof	+265
Premium Audio System [Opt on XL]	+397

1995

Mileage Category: G

Marginally larger than the Camry, the Avalon is a true six-passenger sedan set to conquer Buick LeSabre and Ford Crown Victoria. Dual airbags, power windows, power mirrors and power locks are standard. ABS is optional. Mechanicals are mostly Camry-based.

Body Styles	TMV Pricing		
	Trade	Private	Dealer
4 Dr XL Sdn	3735	4424	5573

Options	Price
Aluminum/Alloy Wheels [Opt on XL]	+92
Antilock Brakes [Opt on XL]	+235
Compact Disc Changer	+132
Leather Seats	+204
Power Bench Seat [Opt on XL]	+204

Body Styles	TMV Pricing		
	Trade	Private	Dealer
4 Dr XLS Sdn	4879	5779	7279

Options	Price
Power Driver Seat [Opt on XL]	+99
Power Moonroof	+211
Power Passenger Seat [Opt on XL]	+99
Premium Audio System [Opt on XL]	+353

Camry

Body Styles	TMV Pricing		
	Trade	Private	Dealer
4 Dr LE Sdn	13401	14379	16010
4 Dr LE V6 Sdn	15529	16663	18553
4 Dr SE Sdn	14224	15262	16993

Options	Price
Alarm System [Opt on LE,SE]	+271
Aluminum/Alloy Wheels [Opt on SE,XLE]	+309
Antilock Brakes [Opt on LE,SE]	+513
Automatic 4-Speed Transmission [Opt on LE,SE]	+626
Automatic Stability Control [Opt on LE V6,SE V6,XLE V6]	+321
Heated Front Seats [Opt on SE,SE V6,XLE,XLE V6]	+238

Body Styles	TMV Pricing		
	Trade	Private	Dealer
4 Dr SE V6 Sdn	16445	17646	19648
4 Dr XLE Sdn	15550	16685	18578
4 Dr XLE V6 Sdn	17534	18815	20949

Options	Price
JBL Audio System [Opt on LE,SE]	+155
Leather Seats [Opt on SE,XLE]	+566
Power Moonroof [Opt on LE,LE V6,XLE]	+600
Front Side Airbag Restraints	+189
AM/FM/Cassette/CD Changer Audio System [Opt on LE,SE]	+302
Front and Rear Head Airbag Restraints	+359

Mileage Category: D

Other than the added availability of power-adjustable pedals, the Camry is unchanged for 2003.

Body Styles	TMV Pricing		
	Trade	Private	Dealer
4 Dr LE Sdn	11476	12410	13965
4 Dr LE V6 Sdn	13420	14512	16331
4 Dr SE Sdn	12270	13268	14932

Options	Price
16 Inch Wheels [Opt on XLE,XLE V6]	+190
Aluminum/Alloy Wheels [Opt on SE]	+283
AM/FM/Cassette/CD Changer Audio System	+276
Antilock Brakes [Opt on LE,SE]	+469
Automatic 4-Speed Transmission [Opt on LE,SE]	+573
Automatic Stability Control [Opt on V6]	+293
Front and Rear Head Airbag Restraints	+207
Front Side Airbag Restraints	+172
Heated Front Seats [Opt on SE V6,XLE,XLE V6]	+217

Body Styles	TMV Pricing		
	Trade	Private	Dealer
4 Dr SE V6 Sdn	14269	15429	17363
4 Dr XLE Sdn	13443	14537	16359
4 Dr XLE V6 Sdn	15282	16525	18598

Options	Price
JBL Audio System [Std on XLE,XLE V6]	+141
Keyless Entry System [Std on XLE,XLE V6]	+128
Leather Seats [Opt on SE V6,XLE,XLE V6]	+517
Navigation System	+1345
Power Driver Seat [Std on XLE,XLE V6]	+193
Power Moonroof	+548
Spoke Wheels [Opt on SE,XLE]	+283
Traction Control System [Opt on V6]	+207

Mileage Category: D

One of America's favorite cars is all new for 2002. Toyota's design goals for the new Camry included larger interior packaging, reduced noise, more advanced safety features, better driving dynamics and, of course, a new standard of value.

Body Styles	TMV Pricing		
	Trade	Private	Dealer
4 Dr CE Sdn	8758	9864	10884
4 Dr LE Sdn	10324	11628	12832
4 Dr LE V6 Sdn	11297	12723	14039

Options	Price
Air Conditioning [Opt on CE]	+632
Aluminum/Alloy Wheels [Opt on LE,LE V6]	+242
AM/FM/Cassette/CD Changer Audio System [Opt on XLE,XLE V6]	+252
Antilock Brakes [Opt on CE,LE]	+428
Automatic 4-Speed Transmission [Opt on CE,LE V6]	+503
Cruise Control [Opt on CE]	+157
Front Side Airbag Restraints	+157
JBL Audio System [Opt on LE,LE V6]	+182

Body Styles	TMV Pricing		
	Trade	Private	Dealer
4 Dr XLE Sdn	11380	12816	14142
4 Dr XLE V6 Sdn	12753	14363	15849

Options	Price
Leather Seats	+581
Power Door Locks [Opt on CE]	+148
Power Driver Seat	+196
Power Moonroof	+629
Power Windows [Opt on CE]	+167
Traction Control System	+189
Two-Tone Paint	+126

Mileage Category: D

Want air conditioning, power windows/locks/mirrors and variable intermittent wipers on the CE? Buy the Value Package. To get remote keyless entry or a power driver seat on the LE, you must buy a Value Package. A power moonroof and an in-dash six-disc CD changer require the Leather Value Package on XLE models. LE V6 models get daytime running lights standard, while JBL audio is optional on all LEs. The anti-theft system with engine immobilizer is restricted to XLE V6 models.

Body Styles	TMV Pricing		
	Trade	Private	Dealer
4 Dr CE Sdn	7553	8703	9830
4 Dr LE Sdn	8934	10294	11628
4 Dr LE V6 Sdn	9622	11088	12524

Body Styles	TMV Pricing		
	Trade	Private	Dealer
4 Dr XLE Sdn	10106	11645	13153
4 Dr XLE V6 Sdn	10925	12589	14219

2000 (cont'd)

Mileage Category: D

The Camry sedan receives minor updates for the 2000 model year. The exterior benefits from new front and rear styling. Camry LE models get 15-inch tires with new wheel covers while the XLE gets standard 16-inch tires. Four-cylinder models make three more horsepower than last year. Interior upgrades include an available JBL premium audio system, automatic climate control, larger buttons on the audio faceplate, imitation wood trim on XLE models, optional leather seats with driver-side power on LE models and new LE model seat fabric. The hood is now supported with struts and dampers.

Options	Price
Traction Control System	+166
Air Conditioning [Opt on CE]	+555
Alarm System [Opt on CE]	+220
Aluminum/Alloy Wheels [Std on XLE,XLE V6]	+202
AM/FM/Cassette/CD Audio System [Opt on CE]	+387
Antilock Brakes [Opt on CE,LE]	+376
Automatic 4-Speed Transmission [Opt on CE,LE V6]	+442
Compact Disc Changer	+304
Front Side Airbag Restraints	+138

Options	Price
JBL Audio System [Opt on LE,LE V6]	+160
Leather Seats	+511
Power Door Locks [Opt on CE]	+130
Power Driver Seat	+172
Power Mirrors [Opt on CE]	+124
Power Moonroof	+552
Power Windows [Opt on CE]	+146
Rear Spoiler	+193

1999

Mileage Category: D

Two new audio systems are available and both include three-in-one ETR/cassette/CD features. Also available are daytime running lights with auto-off. Vintage Red Pearl, Sable Pearl and Woodland Pearl replace Sunfire Red Pearl, Ruby Red and Classic Green Pearl.

Body Styles	TMV Pricing		
	Trade	Private	Dealer
4 Dr CE Sdn	6062	7172	8328
4 Dr LE Sdn	7404	8760	10172
4 Dr LE V6 Sdn	8001	9467	10992

Body Styles	TMV Pricing		
	Trade	Private	Dealer
4 Dr XLE Sdn	8387	9923	11523
4 Dr XLE V6 Sdn	8955	10596	12304

Options	Price
Air Conditioning [Opt on CE]	+429
Alarm System [Std on XLE,XLE V6]	+170
Aluminum/Alloy Wheels [Std on XLE,XLE V6]	+155
AM/FM/Cassette/CD Audio System	+299
AM/FM/CD Audio System [Std on XLE,XLE V6]	+143
Antilock Brakes [Opt on CE,LE]	+323
Automatic 4-Speed Transmission [Opt on CE]	+342

Options	Price
Compact Disc Changer	+235
Leather Seats	+394
Power Driver Seat	+132
Power Moonroof	+427
Rear Spoiler	+150
Traction Control System	+128

1998

Mileage Category: D

Side-impact airbags debut. Depowered front airbags further enhance this car's ability to protect its occupants in a crash. An engine immobilizer feature is now part of the theft-deterrent package.

Body Styles	TMV Pricing		
	Trade	Private	Dealer
4 Dr CE Sdn	5082	6114	7277
4 Dr CE V6 Sdn	6004	7222	8596
4 Dr LE Sdn	6368	7660	9117

Body Styles	TMV Pricing		
	Trade	Private	Dealer
4 Dr LE V6 Sdn	6868	8262	9834
4 Dr XLE Sdn	7370	8866	10553
4 Dr XLE V6 Sdn	7798	9381	11167

Options	Price
Aluminum/Alloy Wheels [Std on XLE,XLE V6]	+156
AM/FM/Cassette/CD Audio System	+263
AM/FM/CD Audio System [Std on XLE,XLE V6]	+126
Antilock Brakes [Opt on CE]	+284
Automatic 4-Speed Transmission [Opt on CE,CE V6]	+301
Compact Disc Changer	+206

Options	Price
Leather Seats	+347
Power Driver Seat	+116
Power Moonroof	+376
Rear Spoiler	+132
Air Conditioning [Std on XLE,XLE V6]	+378
Alarm System [Std on XLE,XLE V6]	+149

1997

Mileage Category: D

Toyota plays the market conservatively with the all-new Camry, giving consumers exactly what they want; a roomy, attractive, feature-laden car with available V6 performance and the promise of excellent reliability as well as resale value. The Camry is the new standard for midsize sedans.

Body Styles	TMV Pricing		
	Trade	Private	Dealer
4 Dr CE Sdn	4414	5396	6597
4 Dr CE V6 Sdn	5184	6337	7747
4 Dr LE Sdn	5518	6746	8247

Body Styles	TMV Pricing		
	Trade	Private	Dealer
4 Dr LE V6 Sdn	5762	7044	8611
4 Dr XLE Sdn	6231	7618	9312
4 Dr XLE V6 Sdn	6563	8023	9808

Options	Price
Air Conditioning [Opt on CE,CE V6]	+322
Alarm System [Std on XLE,XLE V6]	+116
Aluminum/Alloy Wheels [Std on XLE,XLE V6]	+133
AM/FM/Cassette/CD Audio System	+225
Antilock Brakes [Opt on CE]	+242

Options	Price
Automatic 4-Speed Transmission [Opt on CE]	+257
Compact Disc Changer	+177
Leather Seats	+297
Power Moonroof	+321

1996

Body Styles	TMV Pricing		
	Trade	Private	Dealer
2 Dr DX Cpe	3470	4276	5389
2 Dr LE Cpe	3730	4596	5793
2 Dr LE V6 Cpe	4631	5707	7192
2 Dr SE V6 Cpe	5019	6184	7793
4 Dr Collector V6 Sdn	6027	7426	9358
4 Dr DX Sdn	3567	4395	5539
4 Dr LE Sdn	4001	4930	6213

Body Styles	TMV Pricing		
	Trade	Private	Dealer
4 Dr LE V6 Sdn	4793	5906	7443
4 Dr LE V6 Wgn	5094	6277	7911
4 Dr LE Wgn	4560	5619	7081
4 Dr SE V6 Sdn	5236	6452	8132
4 Dr XLE Sdn	4738	5839	7358
4 Dr XLE V6 Sdn	5394	6646	8376

Options	Price
Compact Disc Changer	+148
Leather Seats [Std on Collector V6]	+250
Power Moonroof	+270
Air Conditioning [Opt on DX]	+272

Options	Price
AM/FM/Cassette/CD Audio System [Std on Collector V6]	+189
AM/FM/CD Audio System	+124
Antilock Brakes [Std on XLE,XLE V6]	+204
Automatic 4-Speed Transmission [Opt on DX]	+216

Mileage Category: D

The 1996 Camry remains virtually unchanged from last year's model. Minor engine adjustments mean that the four-cylinder is fully compliant with all on-board diagnostic standards, and is now certified as a transitional low emission vehicle power plant. Additionally, the interior of the DX line gets a new seat fabric, the LE Sedan is available with a leather package, and the Wagon can now be ordered with a power-operated driver seat.

1995

Body Styles	TMV Pricing		
	Trade	Private	Dealer
2 Dr DX Cpe	2615	3223	4236
2 Dr LE Cpe	3281	4043	5314
2 Dr LE V6 Cpe	3650	4499	5912
2 Dr SE V6 Cpe	4064	5008	6582
4 Dr DX Sdn	2884	3555	4672
4 Dr LE Sdn	3444	4244	5578

Body Styles	TMV Pricing		
	Trade	Private	Dealer
4 Dr LE V6 Sdn	3800	4683	6155
4 Dr LE V6 Wgn	3896	4801	6310
4 Dr LE Wgn	3574	4404	5789
4 Dr SE V6 Sdn	4192	5166	6790
4 Dr XLE Sdn	3727	4593	6037

Options	Price
Power Moonroof	+240
Premium Audio System	+80
Leather Seats	+222
Rear Spoiler	+84
Third Seat	+82
Air Conditioning [Opt on DX]	+241

Options	Price
Aluminum/Alloy Wheels	+87
AM/FM/Cassette/CD Audio System	+168
AM/FM/CD Audio System	+80
Antilock Brakes [Std on XLE,XLE V6]	+181
Automatic 4-Speed Transmission [Opt on DX]	+192
Compact Disc Changer	+132

Mileage Category: D

Front and rear styling is updated, ABS is standard on XLE model, and Camry now meets 1997 side-impact protection standards. DX wagon dumped from lineup.

1994

Body Styles	TMV Pricing		
	Trade	Private	Dealer
2 Dr DX Cpe	2115	2668	3589
2 Dr LE Cpe	2692	3396	4569
2 Dr LE V6 Cpe	2651	3344	4499
2 Dr SE V6 Cpe	3342	4216	5672
4 Dr DX Sdn	2324	2932	3944
4 Dr DX Wgn	2694	3398	4572
4 Dr LE Sdn	2799	3531	4750

Body Styles	TMV Pricing		
	Trade	Private	Dealer
4 Dr LE V6 Sdn	3132	3951	5316
4 Dr LE V6 Wgn	3243	4091	5504
4 Dr LE Wgn	3006	3792	5103
4 Dr SE V6 Sdn	3300	4163	5602
4 Dr XLE Sdn	3090	3898	5244
4 Dr XLE V6 Sdn	3423	4318	5811

Options	Price
Air Conditioning [Opt on DX]	+213
Aluminum/Alloy Wheels [Std on XLE V6]	+77
AM/FM/Cassette/CD Audio System	+148
Antilock Brakes	+160
Automatic 4-Speed Transmission [Opt on DX - Sdn,Cpe]	+170

Options	Price
Compact Disc Changer	+117
Leather Seats	+196
Power Moonroof [Std on XLE,XLE V6]	+212
Power Sunroof	+170

Mileage Category: D

Coupe body style debuts in DX, LE and SE form. All Camrys get passenger airbag. V6 engine is tweaked for more power. New fuzzy logic controls govern automatic transmission. SE models get standard power windows, locks, mirrors and cruise control.

Toyota
Camry Solara

2003

Mileage Category: D

For 2003, the manual transmission is no longer available with the V6 engine.

Body Styles	TMV Pricing		
	Trade	Private	Dealer
2 Dr SE Conv	18846	20066	22099
2 Dr SE Cpe	13578	14457	15922
2 Dr SE V6 Conv	20329	21645	23838

Body Styles	TMV Pricing		
	Trade	Private	Dealer
2 Dr SE V6 Cpe	14980	15950	17567
2 Dr SLE V6 Conv	21863	23278	25637
2 Dr SLE V6 Cpe	17541	18676	20569

Options	Price
Alarm System [Opt on SE,SE V6]	+362
Aluminum/Alloy Wheels [Opt on SE]	+189
Antilock Brakes [Opt on SE]	+513
Automatic 4-Speed Transmission [Opt on SE]	+604
Automatic Climate Control [Std on SLE]	+166
Heated Front Seats [Opt on SE V6,SLE V6]	+238
JBL Audio System [Opt on SE,SE V6]	+155
Keyless Entry System [Opt on SE,SE V6]	+140
Leather Seats [Opt on SE V6]	+660

Options	Price
Power Driver Seat [Opt on SE,SE V6]	+211
Power Moonroof [Opt on SE,SE V6,SLE V6]	+679
Rear Spoiler [Opt on SE,SE V6]	+162
Front Side Airbag Restraints	+189
Special Factory Paint	+166
Traction Control System [Opt on SLE V6]	+226
AM/FM/Cassette/CD Changer Audio System [Opt on SLE V6]	+151
16 Inch Wheels [Opt on SE V6]	+223

2002
Mileage Category: D

More power is in store from a new 2.4-liter four-cylinder engine. On the outside, Toyota has added a redesigned front grille and bumper, new headlights and taillights and a bolder rear bumper. A new appearance package (only available on the SE Coupe) includes alloy center caps for the wheels, a three-spoke perforated leather-wrapped steering wheel and shift knob, black trim and Black Pearl emblems. Rounding out the changes are standard daytime running lights, optional seat heaters (coupes only) and a trunk-opener function for the keyless remote.

Body Styles	TMV Pricing		
	Trade	Private	Dealer
2 Dr SE Conv	16819	18028	20044
2 Dr SE Cpe	11452	12275	13647
2 Dr SE V6 Conv	18145	19449	21623

Body Styles	TMV Pricing		
	Trade	Private	Dealer
2 Dr SE V6 Cpe	12756	13673	15201
2 Dr SLE V6 Conv	19556	20962	23305
2 Dr SLE V6 Cpe	14001	15008	16686

Options	Price
16 Inch Wheels [Opt on SE V6]	+204
Aluminum/Alloy Wheels [Opt on SE]	+172
AM/FM/Cassette/CD Changer Audio System [Opt on SLE V6]	+138
Antilock Brakes [Opt on SE]	+469
Automatic 4-Speed Transmission [Std on SLE V6]	+552
Front Side Airbag Restraints	+172
Heated Front Seats [Opt on V6 Cpe]	+217
JBL Audio System [Std on SLE V6]	+141

Options	Price
Keyless Entry System [Std on SLE V6]	+128
Leather Seats [Std on SLE V6]	+604
Pearlescent Metallic Paint	+152
Power Driver Seat [Std on SLE V6]	+193
Power Moonroof [Opt on Cpe]	+621
Rear Spoiler [Std on SLE V6]	+148
Traction Control System [Opt on SLE V6]	+207

2001
Mileage Category: D

Top-level SLE models can be equipped with a new JBL audio system, so long as you order leather upholstery. Option package fiddling makes it easier to equip a Solara the way you like. The anti-theft and engine immobilizer system is restricted to SLEs, while SEs now come standard with a six-speaker cassette stereo. Twilight Blue Pearl is replaced by Indigo Ink as an exterior color.

Body Styles	TMV Pricing		
	Trade	Private	Dealer
2 Dr SE Conv	14828	16510	18062
2 Dr SE Cpe	10152	11303	12366
2 Dr SE V6 Conv	16468	18335	20059

Body Styles	TMV Pricing		
	Trade	Private	Dealer
2 Dr SE V6 Cpe	11498	12802	14006
2 Dr SLE V6 Conv	17817	19838	21703
2 Dr SLE V6 Cpe	12462	13875	15180

Options	Price
Aluminum/Alloy Wheels [Opt on SE,SE V6]	+274
AM/FM/Cassette/CD Changer Audio System [Opt on SLE V6]	+126
Antilock Brakes [Opt on SE]	+428
Automatic 4-Speed Transmission [Std on SLE V6,Conv]	+503
Front Side Airbag Restraints	+157
JBL Audio System [Opt on SE,SE V6]	+126

Options	Price
Leather Seats [Opt on SE V6]	+566
Pearlescent Metallic Paint	+138
Power Driver Seat [Opt on SE,SE V6]	+245
Power Moonroof	+566
Rear Spoiler [Opt on SE,SE V6]	+135
Traction Control System	+189

2000
Mileage Category: D

Solara four-cylinder models will achieve ultralow emission vehicle (ULEV) status. A convertible version is now offered for topless fun. SLE models get a JBL premium audio system as standard equipment, and an in-dash six-disc CD changer is optional. Two new exterior colors are offered.

Body Styles	TMV Pricing		
	Trade	Private	Dealer
2 Dr SE Conv	13012	14710	16375
2 Dr SE Cpe	8883	10042	11179
2 Dr SE V6 Conv	14002	15830	17622

Body Styles	TMV Pricing		
	Trade	Private	Dealer
2 Dr SE V6 Cpe	9155	10350	11522
2 Dr SLE V6 Conv	15734	17788	19800
2 Dr SLE V6 Cpe	10881	12302	13694

2000 (cont'd)

Options	Price
Alarm System [Opt on SE,SE V6]	+213
Aluminum/Alloy Wheels [Opt on SE,SE V6]	+240
Antilock Brakes [Opt on SE]	+376
Automatic 4-Speed Transmission [Std on SLE V6,Conv]	+442
Compact Disc Changer	+276
Front Side Airbag Restraints	+138
JBL Audio System [Opt on SE,SE V6]	+276

Options	Price
Leather Seats [Opt on SE,SE V6]	+497
Power Driver Seat [Opt on SE,SE V6]	+215
Power Moonroof	+497
Rear Spoiler [Std on SLE V6,Conv]	+119
Special Factory Paint	+122
Traction Control System	+166

1999

Body Styles	TMV Pricing		
	Trade	Private	Dealer
2 Dr SE Cpe	6766	7913	9106
2 Dr SE V6 Cpe	7326	8567	9859

Body Styles	TMV Pricing		
	Trade	Private	Dealer
2 Dr SLE V6 Cpe	8934	10448	12023

Mileage Category: D

This all-new coupe is based on the Camry platform. Designed jointly by the Toyota Motor Corporation in Japan and the Toyota Technical Center in Ann Arbor, Michigan, the Solara is targeted at consumers who want the style of a sports car but the room and comfort of a larger, more practical vehicle.

Options	Price
Alarm System [Std on SLE]	+183
Aluminum/Alloy Wheels [Std on SLE]	+186
AM/FM/Cassette/CD Audio System [Std on SLE]	+119
Antilock Brakes [Opt on SE]	+323
Automatic 4-Speed Transmission [Std on SLE]	+380
Front Side Airbag Restraints	+119

Options	Price
JBL Audio System [Std on SLE]	+237
Leather Seats [Std on SLE]	+427
Power Driver Seat [Std on SLE]	+185
Power Moonroof	+427
Traction Control System	+142

2003

Body Styles	TMV Pricing		
	Trade	Private	Dealer
2 Dr GT Hbk	12955	13912	15508

Body Styles	TMV Pricing		
	Trade	Private	Dealer
2 Dr GT-S Hbk	15427	16567	18466

Options	Price
Alarm System	+301
Aluminum/Alloy Wheels [Opt on GT]	+291
Antilock Brakes	+513
Appearance Package	+1117
Automatic 4-Speed Transmission	+604
Cruise Control [Opt on GT]	+151
JBL Audio System [Opt on GT]	+396

Options	Price
Keyless Entry System	+174
Leather Seats [Opt on GT-S]	+498
Power Door Locks [Opt on GT]	+170
Power Moonroof	+679
Power Windows [Opt on GT]	+185
Rear Spoiler	+328
Front Side Airbag Restraints	+189

Mileage Category: E

The Celica has been revised for 2003 with freshened front and rear styling. In front, the Celica gets a new bumper and fascia with a wider upper air intake. Newly available high-intensity discharge (HID) headlights complement the car's advanced styling, and redesigned rear lights echo the projector-style look. Inside, Toyota has redesigned the center dash cluster for improved legibility and added a standard JBL audio system to the GT-S model. A power antenna is now standard on JBL-equipped models. Finally, you can get two new colors: Solar Yellow and Zephyr Blue Metallic.

2002

Body Styles	TMV Pricing		
	Trade	Private	Dealer
2 Dr GT Hbk	11187	12110	13648

Body Styles	TMV Pricing		
	Trade	Private	Dealer
2 Dr GT-S Hbk	13304	14401	16231

Mileage Category: E

No changes this year.

Options	Price
Aluminum/Alloy Wheels [Std on GT-S]	+266
Antilock Brakes	+469
Appearance Package	+1097
Automatic 4-Speed Transmission	+552
Cruise Control [Std on GT-S]	+138
Front Side Airbag Restraints	+172

Options	Price
Leather Seats [Opt on GT-S]	+455
Power Door Locks [Std on GT-S]	+155
Power Moonroof	+621
Power Windows [Std on GT-S]	+169
Premium Audio System [Std on GT-S]	+228
Rear Spoiler	+300

2001

Mileage Category: E

No changes this year.

Body Styles	TMV Pricing		
	Trade	Private	Dealer
2 Dr GT Hbk	9698	10975	12153

Options	Price
Aluminum/Alloy Wheels [Opt on GT]	+242
Antilock Brakes	+428
Automatic 4-Speed Transmission	+440
Cruise Control [Opt on GT]	+126
Front Side Airbag Restraints	+157
Leather Seats	+683

Body Styles	TMV Pricing		
	Trade	Private	Dealer
2 Dr GT-S Hbk	11405	12906	14292

Options	Price
Power Door Locks [Opt on GT]	+142
Power Moonroof	+554
Power Windows [Opt on GT]	+154
Premium Audio System [Opt on GT]	+208
Rear Spoiler	+274

2000

Mileage Category: E

The all-new 2000 Celica is considerably more performance-oriented than the previous model. Highlights include a sleek exterior, a 180-horsepower engine and six-speed gearbox for the GT-S, and sharp handling.

Body Styles	TMV Pricing		
	Trade	Private	Dealer
2 Dr GT Hbk	8708	9963	11192

Options	Price
Alarm System	+235
Aluminum/Alloy Wheels [Opt on GT]	+240
Antilock Brakes	+376
Automatic 4-Speed Transmission	+387
Compact Disc Changer	+304
Front Side Airbag Restraints	+138

Body Styles	TMV Pricing		
	Trade	Private	Dealer
2 Dr GT-S Hbk	9805	11218	12603

Options	Price
Leather Seats	+599
Power Door Locks [Opt on GT]	+124
Power Moonroof	+486
Power Windows [Opt on GT]	+135
Rear Spoiler	+240

1999

Body Styles	TMV Pricing		
	Trade	Private	Dealer
2 Dr GT Conv	9330	10855	12443

Options	Price
Alarm System	+181
Aluminum/Alloy Wheels [Std on Conv]	+186
AM/FM/Cassette/CD Audio System [Std on Conv]	+235
Antilock Brakes	+323
Automatic 4-Speed Transmission	+342

Body Styles	TMV Pricing		
	Trade	Private	Dealer
2 Dr GT Hbk	7732	8996	10311

Options	Price
Compact Disc Changer	+235
Leather Seats	+463
Power Moonroof	+376
Sport Suspension	+224

Mileage Category: E

The Celica GT Sport Coupe has been discontinued along with the color Galaxy Blue Metallic.

1998

Mileage Category: E

Celica ST is eliminated. GT's get more standard features and one new color: Caribbean Green Metallic.

Body Styles	TMV Pricing		
	Trade	Private	Dealer
2 Dr GT Conv	7514	8897	10456
2 Dr GT Cpe	6384	7559	8885

Options	Price
Alarm System	+159
Aluminum/Alloy Wheels [Std on Conv]	+164
AM/FM/Cassette/CD Audio System [Opt on Hbk]	+206
AM/FM/CD Audio System	+162
Antilock Brakes	+284
Automatic 4-Speed Transmission	+338

Body Styles	TMV Pricing		
	Trade	Private	Dealer
2 Dr GT Hbk	6577	7788	9153

Options	Price
Compact Disc Changer	+206
Keyless Entry System	+149
Leather Seats	+407
Power Moonroof	+285
Rear Spoiler [Opt on Cpe]	+164
Sport Suspension	+197

1997

Mileage Category: E

GT Coupe is gone, and Fiesta Blue Metallic can be specified for cars equipped with black sport cloth interior.

Body Styles	TMV Pricing		
	Trade	Private	Dealer
2 Dr GT Conv	6387	7643	9178
2 Dr GT Hbk	5736	6864	8243
2 Dr GT Limited Edition Conv	6883	8236	9890

Body Styles	TMV Pricing		
	Trade	Private	Dealer
2 Dr ST Cpe	4670	5588	6711
2 Dr ST Hbk	4979	5958	7154
2 Dr ST Limited Edition Hbk	5444	6515	7823

Options	Price		Options	Price
Air Conditioning [Opt on GT,ST]	+322		Keyless Entry System	+127
Alarm System	+136		Leather Seats	+348
Aluminum/Alloy Wheels [Opt on GT,ST]	+139		Power Moonroof	+244
AM/FM/Cassette/CD Audio System [Opt on GT]	+241		Premium Audio System [Opt on GT]	+273
AM/FM/CD Audio System	+138		Rear Spoiler [Opt on GT,ST]	+133
Antilock Brakes	+242		Sport Seats	+311
Automatic 4-Speed Transmission	+257		Sport Suspension	+160
Compact Disc Changer	+177			

1996

Body Styles	TMV Pricing			Body Styles	TMV Pricing		
	Trade	Private	Dealer		Trade	Private	Dealer
2 Dr GT 25th Anniv Conv	6041	7322	9091	2 Dr ST 25th Anniv Hbk	4531	5491	6818
2 Dr GT Conv	5642	6838	8491	2 Dr ST Cpe	3654	4429	5498
2 Dr GT Cpe	4692	5687	7062	2 Dr ST Hbk	3856	4674	5803
2 Dr GT Hbk	4764	5774	7170				

Mileage Category: E

Front and rear styling tweaks, a new spoiler, new wheel covers, two new colors and revised fabrics debut this year.

Options	Price		Options	Price
Air Conditioning [Opt on GT,ST]	+272		Automatic 4-Speed Transmission	+216
Alarm System [Opt on GT,ST]	+115		Compact Disc Changer	+148
Aluminum/Alloy Wheels	+118		Leather Seats	+225
AM/FM/Cassette/CD Audio System [Opt on GT]	+203		Power Moonroof [Opt on GT,ST]	+206
AM/FM/CD Audio System [Opt on GT,ST]	+116		Premium Audio System [Opt on GT]	+230
Antilock Brakes	+204			

1995

Body Styles	TMV Pricing			Body Styles	TMV Pricing		
	Trade	Private	Dealer		Trade	Private	Dealer
2 Dr GT Conv	4627	5651	7359	2 Dr ST Cpe	2947	3599	4686
2 Dr GT Cpe	3646	4453	5798	2 Dr ST Hbk	3320	4055	5279
2 Dr GT Hbk	3760	4592	5980				

Mileage Category: E

GT Convertible returns to lineup, available in red, white, blue or black.

Options	Price		Options	Price
Compact Disc Changer	+132		Sport Suspension	+120
Automatic 4-Speed Transmission	+192		Air Conditioning	+241
Keyless Entry System [Opt on ST]	+95		Alarm System	+102
Leather Seats	+260		Aluminum/Alloy Wheels	+104
Power Moonroof	+183		AM/FM/Cassette/CD Audio System	+132
Premium Audio System [Opt on GT]	+204		AM/FM/CD Audio System	+103
Rear Spoiler	+99		Antilock Brakes	+181
Sport Seats	+232			

1994

Body Styles		TMV Pricing		
		Trade	Private	Dealer
2 Dr GT Cpe		3106	3876	5158
2 Dr GT Hbk		3074	3835	5105
2 Dr ST Cpe		2488	3104	4131
2 Dr ST Hbk		2768	3453	4595

Mileage Category: E

Redesigned coupe and liftback debut. Turbocharged All-Trac is gone. ST and GT are only trim levels. Dual airbags are standard; ABS is optional. Power mirrors and driver seat height adjuster are standard.

Options	Price		Options	Price
Air Conditioning	+213		Power Sunroof	+159
Aluminum/Alloy Wheels	+92		Premium Audio System [Opt on GT]	+180
AM/FM/Cassette/CD Audio System	+117		Rear Spoiler	+88
Antilock Brakes	+160		Sport Seats	+205
Automatic 4-Speed Transmission	+170		Sport Suspension	+106
Leather Seats	+229			

Toyota
Corolla

2003

Mileage Category: B

Toyota's Corolla is all-new for 2003. Far removed from the original Corolla, this one is the biggest yet. It's also more luxurious. The return is more interior room, a more substantial feel and changes aimed at fixing the previous model's shortcomings. Though pricing has increased, Toyota has made more equipment standard in the hopes of keeping the Corolla's reputation for value intact.

Body Styles	TMV Pricing		
	Trade	Private	Dealer
4 Dr CE Sdn	9062	9982	11515
4 Dr LE Sdn	9339	10287	11867

Options	Price
Alarm System [Opt on LE,S]	+241
Aluminum/Alloy Wheels [Opt on LE,S]	+294
Antilock Brakes	+513
Automatic 4-Speed Transmission	+604
Automatic Dimming Rearview Mirror [Opt on LE]	+170
Cruise Control	+189
Keyless Entry System [Opt on S]	+151

Body Styles	TMV Pricing		
	Trade	Private	Dealer
4 Dr S Sdn	9141	10069	11615

Options	Price
Leather Seats [Opt on LE]	+449
Power Door Locks [Opt on CE]	+223
Power Moonroof [Opt on LE,S]	+566
Power Windows [Opt on S]	+181
Rear Spoiler [Opt on S]	+208
Front Side Airbag Restraints	+189

2002

Mileage Category: B

Pricing for optional value packages has been lowered for all trim lines.

Body Styles	TMV Pricing		
	Trade	Private	Dealer
4 Dr CE Sdn	6983	7764	9066
4 Dr LE Sdn	7643	8498	9924

Options	Price
Air Conditioning	+414
Aluminum/Alloy Wheels [Opt on LE,S]	+252
Antilock Brakes [Opt on LE,S]	+469
Automatic 3-Speed Transmission [Opt on CE]	+286
Automatic 4-Speed Transmission [Opt on LE,S]	+562

Body Styles	TMV Pricing		
	Trade	Private	Dealer
4 Dr S Sdn	7432	8263	9649

Options	Price
Cruise Control [Opt on LE,S]	+172
Front Side Airbag Restraints	+172
Power Door Locks	+145
Power Moonroof [Opt on LE,S]	+493
Rear Window Defroster [Opt on CE,S]	+141

2001

Mileage Category: B

Midgrade CE trim replaces entry-level VE, top-line LE replaces midgrade CE and a sporty new CE-based S model debuts. Front and rear lighting is restyled, and the fascia up front is tweaked and now includes a chrome-ringed grille. An internal trunk release has been added, along with a push-button fresh/recirculate control for the ventilation system. Two new colors replace an equal number of shades that are fading away.

Body Styles	TMV Pricing		
	Trade	Private	Dealer
4 Dr CE Sdn	6004	7073	8059
4 Dr LE Sdn	6562	7729	8807

Options	Price
Air Conditioning	+597
Aluminum/Alloy Wheels	+230
AM/FM/Cassette Audio System [Opt on CE,S]	+132
Antilock Brakes	+428
Automatic 3-Speed Transmission	+261
Automatic 4-Speed Transmission	+513

Body Styles	TMV Pricing		
	Trade	Private	Dealer
4 Dr S Sdn	6324	7449	8488

Options	Price
Cruise Control	+157
Front Side Airbag Restraints	+157
Power Door Locks	+170
Power Moonroof [Opt on LE,S]	+450
Power Windows [Opt on LE,S]	+180
Rear Window Defroster [Opt on CE,S]	+129

2000

Mileage Category: B

The Corolla receives increased performance from VVT-i engine technology. Horsepower jumps from 120 to 125. The Corolla also achieves low emission vehicle status this year.

Body Styles	TMV Pricing		
	Trade	Private	Dealer
4 Dr CE Sdn	5447	6500	7533
4 Dr LE Sdn	5626	6714	7780

Options	Price
Automatic 3-Speed Transmission	+332
Automatic 4-Speed Transmission	+442
Compact Disc Changer	+304
Cruise Control	+119
Front Side Airbag Restraints	+138
Power Door Locks [Opt on CE]	+124
Power Moonroof	+406

Body Styles	TMV Pricing		
	Trade	Private	Dealer
4 Dr VE Sdn	5333	6365	7376

Options	Price
Power Windows [Opt on CE]	+158
Rear Spoiler	+163
Antilock Brakes	+376
Air Conditioning [Std on LE]	+524
Alarm System	+220
Aluminum/Alloy Wheels	+229
AM/FM/CD Audio System	+166

1999

Body Styles	TMV Pricing		
	Trade	Private	Dealer
4 Dr CE Sdn	4389	5354	6359
4 Dr LE Sdn	4831	5894	7000

Body Styles	TMV Pricing		
	Trade	Private	Dealer
4 Dr VE Sdn	4253	5189	6163

Options	Price
Alarm System	+170
Aluminum/Alloy Wheels	+177
AM/FM/Cassette/CD Audio System	+192
AM/FM/CD Audio System	+128
Air Conditioning [Std on LE]	+406
Antilock Brakes	+323

Options	Price
Automatic 3-Speed Transmission	+256
Automatic 4-Speed Transmission	+342
Compact Disc Changer	+235
Power Moonroof	+315
Power Windows [Std on LE]	+122
Rear Spoiler	+126

Mileage Category: B

The VE model features a deluxe AM/FM ETR four-speaker audio system as standard equipment. A Touring Package is standard equipment on the Corolla LE model. Five new exterior colors include Silver Stream Opal, Venetian Red Pearl, Dark Emerald Pearl, Aqua Blue Metallic and Twilight Blue Pearl.

1998

Body Styles	TMV Pricing		
	Trade	Private	Dealer
4 Dr CE Sdn	3776	4730	5805
4 Dr LE Sdn	4105	5142	6311

Body Styles	TMV Pricing		
	Trade	Private	Dealer
4 Dr VE Sdn	3511	4398	5398

Options	Price
Air Conditioning [Opt on VE]	+357
Alarm System	+150
Aluminum/Alloy Wheels	+156
AM/FM/Cassette/CD Audio System	+169
Antilock Brakes	+284

Options	Price
Automatic 3-Speed Transmission	+188
Automatic 4-Speed Transmission	+301
Compact Disc Changer	+206
Power Moonroof	+276

Mileage Category: B

The Toyota Corolla is completely redesigned this year with a new engine, new sheet metal and a new standard for safety in compact cars: optional front passenger side-impact airbags.

1997

Body Styles	TMV Pricing		
	Trade	Private	Dealer
4 Dr CE Sdn	3166	4041	5110
4 Dr DX Sdn	3118	3979	5032

Body Styles	TMV Pricing		
	Trade	Private	Dealer
4 Dr STD Sdn	2971	3792	4795

Options	Price
Compact Disc Changer	+177
Power Sunroof	+191
Air Conditioning [Std on CE]	+305
Aluminum/Alloy Wheels	+133

Options	Price
AM/FM/Cassette/CD Audio System	+144
Antilock Brakes	+242
Automatic 3-Speed Transmission	+160
Automatic 4-Speed Transmission	+257

Mileage Category: B

The Classic Edition (CE) debuts and the slow-selling DX Wagon gets the ax.

1996

Body Styles	TMV Pricing		
	Trade	Private	Dealer
4 Dr DX Sdn	2767	3541	4610
4 Dr DX Wgn	2946	3770	4909

Body Styles	TMV Pricing		
	Trade	Private	Dealer
4 Dr STD Sdn	2450	3135	4082

Options	Price
Air Conditioning	+257
Antilock Brakes	+204
Automatic 3-Speed Transmission	+135

Options	Price
Automatic 4-Speed Transmission	+216
Compact Disc Changer	+148
Power Sunroof	+161

Mileage Category: B

The Toyota Corolla heads into 1996 with redesigned front and rear fascias, three new colors, new wheel covers, an optional integrated child seat and a revised interior. Additionally, the five-speed manual transmission has been revised for a better feel and more positive gear engagement.

1995

Body Styles	TMV Pricing		
	Trade	Private	Dealer
4 Dr DX Sdn	2449	3116	4227
4 Dr DX Wgn	2491	3169	4298

Body Styles	TMV Pricing		
	Trade	Private	Dealer
4 Dr LE Sdn	2772	3526	4783
4 Dr STD Sdn	2098	2669	3620

Mileage Category: B

The 1.8-liter engine loses 10 horsepower to meet stricter emissions regulations but torque is up. DX models get new interior fabric.

Corolla/ECHO

1995 (cont'd)

Options	Price		Options	Price
Air Conditioning [Std on LE]	+228		Automatic 4-Speed Transmission	+192
Aluminum/Alloy Wheels	+99		Compact Disc Changer	+132
Antilock Brakes	+181		Power Sunroof	+143
Automatic 3-Speed Transmission	+120		Premium Audio System [Opt on DX Wgn]	+96

1994

Mileage Category: B

Passenger airbag added. Passenger seatbelts have automatic locking retractors. CFC-free refrigerant is added to air conditioning system.

Body Styles	TMV Pricing			Body Styles	TMV Pricing		
	Trade	Private	Dealer		Trade	Private	Dealer
4 Dr DX Sdn	1786	2384	3380	4 Dr LE Sdn	1866	2491	3532
4 Dr DX Wgn	1941	2591	3675	4 Dr STD Sdn	1496	1997	2833

Options	Price		Options	Price
Antilock Brakes	+160		Power Sunroof	+126
Automatic 3-Speed Transmission	+106		Air Conditioning [Opt on DX,STD]	+201
Automatic 4-Speed Transmission	+170		Aluminum/Alloy Wheels	+88
Compact Disc Changer	+117			

Toyota
ECHO

2003

Body Styles	TMV Pricing			Body Styles	TMV Pricing		
	Trade	Private	Dealer		Trade	Private	Dealer
2 Dr STD Cpe	6627	7485	8916	4 Dr STD Sdn	7298	8244	9820

Options	Price		Options	Price
Air Conditioning	+642		Power Steering	+189
Alarm System	+377		Power Windows [Opt on SDN]	+147
AM/FM/Cassette/CD Audio System	+181		Rear Spoiler	+226
Antilock Brakes	+513		Rear Window Defroster	+132
Automatic 4-Speed Transmission	+604		Front Side Airbag Restraints	+189
Keyless Entry System	+132		Split Folding Rear Seat	+125
Power Door Locks	+136			

Mileage Category: A

For 2003, the Echo receives a new look with redesigned front and rear fascias. The front bumper and fenders feature sharper and more prominent lines, a new chrome-slat grille and new headlamps with a distinctive bulb layout. Optional round foglamps accent the new front-end design. In the rear, a new trunk lid with chrome plate garnish, a new bumper and redesigned combination clear-lens taillights provide a more upscale look.

A new Appearance Package adds aerodynamic body enhancements, including overfenders that blend into the front and rear underbody. A rear trunk spoiler incorporates the LED high-mounted stop lamp.

The standard 14-inch wheels get a new wheel cover design, and, for the first time, the Echo can be had with optional 15-inch wheels. The new styling is topped off with five new colors.

2002

Mileage Category: A

Toyota has left the Echo untouched for 2002.

Body Styles	TMV Pricing			Body Styles	TMV Pricing		
	Trade	Private	Dealer		Trade	Private	Dealer
2 Dr STD Cpe	5512	6295	7600	4 Dr STD Sdn	5830	6658	8038

Options	Price		Options	Price
Air Conditioning	+586		Keyless Entry System	+121
AM/FM/Cassette/CD Audio System	+186		Power Door Locks	+124
Antilock Brakes	+469		Power Steering	+172
Automatic 4-Speed Transmission	+614		Power Windows	+183
Front Side Airbag Restraints	+172		Rear Window Defroster	+141

2001

Mileage Category: A

In an effort to better protect occupants of this lightweight economy car, Toyota makes side airbags optional for 2001. Brilliant Blue Pearl is a new color.

Body Styles	TMV Pricing		
	Trade	Private	Dealer
2 Dr STD Cpe	4704	5759	6733
4 Dr STD Sdn	5065	6200	7248

Options	Price		Options	Price
Air Conditioning	+581		Front Side Airbag Restraints	+157
AM/FM/Cassette/CD Audio System	+170		Power Door Locks	+142
Antilock Brakes	+428		Power Windows	+167
Automatic 4-Speed Transmission	+503		Rear Window Defroster	+129

Body Styles	TMV Pricing				Body Styles	TMV Pricing		
	Trade	Private	Dealer			Trade	Private	Dealer
2 Dr STD Cpe	4266	5277	6267		4 Dr STD Sdn	4515	5584	6631

Options	Price		Options	Price
Air Conditioning	+511		Automatic 4-Speed Transmission	+442
Aluminum/Alloy Wheels	+138		Compact Disc Changer	+318
AM/FM/Cassette/CD Audio System	+149		Power Door Locks	+124
AM/FM/CD Audio System	+124		Power Steering	+149
Antilock Brakes	+376			

Mileage Category: A

The 2000 Toyota Echo brings a new name and a fresh concept to the Toyota lineup. Designed to attract youthful buyers, the Echo features a roomy and comfortable interior, superb gas mileage and an affordable price.

Toyota

Highlander

Body Styles	TMV Pricing				Body Styles	TMV Pricing		
	Trade	Private	Dealer			Trade	Private	Dealer
4 Dr Limited AWD SUV	23753	25157	27498		4 Dr STD SUV	18650	19753	21590
4 Dr Limited SUV	22665	24005	26239		4 Dr V6 AWD SUV	21247	22503	24596
4 Dr STD AWD SUV	19740	20907	22852		4 Dr V6 SUV	19877	21052	23010

Options	Price		Options	Price
Alarm System [Std on Limited]	+271		Limited Slip Differential	+294
Aluminum/Alloy Wheels [Std on Limited]	+377		Power Driver Seat [Std on Limited]	+294
Camper/Towing Package	+121		Power Moonroof	+679
Heated Front Seats [Opt on Limited]	+332		Front Side Airbag Restraints	+189
Keyless Entry System [Std on Limited]	+166		Traction Control System	+491
Leather Seats [Opt on Limited]	+808		AM/FM/Cassette/CD Changer Audio System [Opt on Limited]	+151

Mileage Category: M

There are no changes for the Highlander this year.

Body Styles	TMV Pricing				Body Styles	TMV Pricing		
	Trade	Private	Dealer			Trade	Private	Dealer
4 Dr Limited AWD SUV	21960	23217	25313		4 Dr STD SUV	17146	18128	19765
4 Dr Limited SUV	20905	22103	24099		4 Dr V6 AWD SUV	19335	20430	22256
4 Dr STD AWD SUV	18197	19239	20977		4 Dr V6 SUV	18313	19362	21110

Options	Price		Options	Price
Aluminum/Alloy Wheels [Std on Limited]	+345		Leather Seats [Opt on Limited]	+738
AM/FM/Cassette/CD Changer Audio System [Opt on Limited]	+138		Limited Slip Differential [Opt on 4WD]	+269
Automatic Stability Control	+448		Power Driver Seat [Std on Limited]	+269
Front Side Airbag Restraints	+172		Power Moonroof	+621
Heated Front Seats [Opt on Limited]	+304		Traction Control System	+448
Keyless Entry System [Std on Limited]	+148			

Mileage Category: M

Toyota's car-based Highlander SUV receives no changes this year.

Body Styles		TMV Pricing		
		Trade	Private	Dealer
4 Dr STD AWD SUV		16417	17964	19392
4 Dr STD SUV		15299	16740	18071
4 Dr V6 AWD SUV		17427	19069	20585
4 Dr V6 SUV		16516	18072	19509

Mileage Category: M

Based on the same platform as the Lexus RX 300, Toyota's new Highlander SUV represents the best blend of a station wagon, a minivan and a sport utility available on the market today. Available only with a V6 and an automatic transmission driving power to the front or all the wheels, Highlander will be sold in one trim level with a Limited package listed on the option sheet.

Toyota
Highlander/Land Cruiser

2001 (cont'd)

Options	Price
Alarm System	+135
Aluminum/Alloy Wheels	+315
AM/FM/Cassette/CD Changer Audio System [Opt on V6]	+252
Automatic Climate Control	+157
Automatic Stability Control	+409
Camper/Towing Package	+182
Front Side Airbag Restraints	+157

Options	Price
Heated Front Seats	+277
Keyless Entry System	+138
Leather Seats	+639
Limited Slip Differential	+245
Power Driver Seat	+245
Power Sunroof	+513
Traction Control System	+535

Toyota
Land Cruiser

2003

Body Styles	TMV Pricing		
	Trade	Private	Dealer
4 Dr STD 4WD SUV	42213	44461	48207

Options	Price
Navigation System	+2264
Running Boards	+260

Options	Price
Front Side Airbag Restraints	+189
Front and Rear Head Airbag Restraints	+302

Mileage Category: O

Mechanically, the 2003 Land Cruiser delivers five more horsepower and has a new five-speed automatic transmission. On the outside, you'll find standard 17-inch wheels, optional 18-inch wheels, slightly freshened front-end styling and clear-lens rear turn signals. Inside, Land Cruiser features a new dashboard design, a power tilt and telescoping steering wheel, rear seat audio and steering wheel-mounted audio controls. There is also a new optional rear DVD entertainment system and available front- and second-row side curtain airbags.

2002
Mileage Category: O

Toyota's flagship SUV receives no changes this year.

Body Styles	TMV Pricing		
	Trade	Private	Dealer
4 Dr STD 4WD SUV	35534	37588	41012

Options	Price
Navigation System	+1932

Options	Price
Running Boards	+238

2001
Mileage Category: O

A navigation system is optional (and plays DVD movies when the vehicle is not in motion). Standard equipment includes an electrochromic rearview mirror with compass and JBL audio with an in-dash six-disc CD changer. Each of the power windows now features one-touch up and down control. Three new colors replace Desert Bronze on the color chart, and the alloy wheels have a new chromelike finish.

Body Styles	TMV Pricing		
	Trade	Private	Dealer
4 Dr STD 4WD SUV	30838	33658	36261

Options	Price
Navigation System	+1888

Options	Price
Third Seat	+1425

2000
Mileage Category: O

The Land Cruiser receives new standard equipment features, such as vehicle skid control and an Active TRAC electronic four-wheel-drive system with torque transfer capability. Additional standard equipment includes illuminated entry for the remote keyless-entry system, power tilt/slide moonroof and a leather interior. The optional third-row seat now includes rear air conditioning.

Body Styles	TMV Pricing		
	Trade	Private	Dealer
4 Dr STD 4WD SUV	26342	29036	31676

Options	Price
Automatic Climate Control (2 Zone) - Front and Rear	+315
Running Boards	+428

Options	Price
Third Seat	+627

1999
Mileage Category: O

No changes this year.

Body Styles	TMV Pricing		
	Trade	Private	Dealer
4 Dr STD 4WD SUV	21719	24315	27016

Options	Price
Air Conditioning - Front and Rear	+243
Leather Seats	+777
Locking Differential	+150

Options	Price
Power Moonroof	+451
Running Boards	+331
Third Seat	+539

1998

Body Styles	TMV Pricing		
	Trade	Private	Dealer
4 Dr STD 4WD SUV	18489	21136	24120

Options	Price	Options	Price
Leather Seats	+684	Running Boards	+291
Locking Differential	+132	Third Seat	+459
Power Moonroof	+445		

Mileage Category: O

For 1998, the all-new Land Cruiser gets a powerful V8 engine, standard ABS, an increase in structural rigidity, an improved suspension system, increased passenger and cargo room and several new colors.

1997

Body Styles	TMV Pricing			Body Styles	TMV Pricing		
	Trade	Private	Dealer		Trade	Private	Dealer
4 Dr 40th Anniv Limited 4WD SUV	15695	18172	21199	4 Dr STD 4WD SUV	14107	16333	19053

Options	Price	Options	Price
Compact Disc Changer	+257	Running Boards	+223
Keyless Entry System	+127	Third Seat	+540
Leather Seats [Opt on STD]	+392	Alarm System	+124
Power Driver Seat [Opt on STD]	+134	Aluminum/Alloy Wheels	+169
Power Moonroof	+304	AM/FM/Cassette/CD Audio System	+303
Power Passenger Seat [Opt on STD]	+134	AM/FM/CD Audio System	+144

Mileage Category: O

The Black Package is discontinued, but black becomes an available color choice. A 40th-anniversary package lets buyers outfit their Cruiser with leather and choose one of two unique paint schemes.

1996

Body Styles	TMV Pricing		
	Trade	Private	Dealer
4 Dr STD 4WD SUV	11310	13236	15895

Options	Price	Options	Price
Power Moonroof	+320	AM/FM/Cassette/CD Audio System	+255
Running Boards	+188	AM/FM/CD Audio System	+121
Third Seat	+455	Compact Disc Changer	+216
Aluminum/Alloy Wheels	+142	Leather Seats	+331

Mileage Category: O

The Black Package debuts, featuring black paint along with chrome mirrors and door handles.

1995

Body Styles	TMV Pricing		
	Trade	Private	Dealer
4 Dr STD 4WD SUV	9018	10598	13232

Options	Price	Options	Price
Aluminum/Alloy Wheels	+126	Power Driver Seat	+99
AM/FM/Cassette/CD Audio System	+244	Power Moonroof	+227
Compact Disc Changer	+192	Power Passenger Seat	+99
Leather Seats	+360	Running Boards	+167
Locking Differential	+84	Third Seat	+404

Mileage Category: O

Redesigned dashboard carries dual airbags, and ABS is now standard. Revised grille carries Toyota logo rather than nameplate.

1994

Body Styles	TMV Pricing		
	Trade	Private	Dealer
4 Dr STD 4WD SUV	6898	8253	10511

Options	Price	Options	Price
Aluminum/Alloy Wheels	+111	Limited Slip Differential	+106
AM/FM/Cassette/CD Audio System	+200	Power Moonroof	+201
Antilock Brakes	+160	Running Boards	+147
Leather Seats	+385	Third Seat	+190

Mileage Category: O

Standard sound system has nine speakers instead of five. Passenger seatbelts have automatic locking retractors.

Toyota
MR2/MR2 Spyder

Toyota
MR2

1995

Body Styles	TMV Pricing		
	Trade	Private	Dealer
2 Dr STD Cpe	3716	4538	5909
2 Dr Turbo Cpe	4971	6071	7905

Options	Price	Options	Price
Sunroof	+91	Antilock Brakes	+253
T-Tops - Glass [Opt on STD]	+402	Automatic 4-Speed Transmission	+192
Air Conditioning	+144	Compact Disc Changer	+156
AM/FM/Cassette/CD Audio System	+100	Leather Seats	+240
AM/FM/CD Audio System	+96	Limited Slip Differential	+96

Mileage Category: E

Final year for Mister Two. Several states lose Turbo model, which wouldn't pass emissions regulations. Base models with T-bar roof get power windows and locks standard.

1994
Mileage Category: E

Passenger airbag debuts. ABS made standard. Taillights are revised, and the suspension gets further fine-tuning. Base models get standard air conditioning (made standard last year on turbo), which is CFC-free on both models.

Body Styles	TMV Pricing		
	Trade	Private	Dealer
2 Dr STD Cpe	3178	3966	5278
2 Dr Turbo Cpe	3995	4985	6634

Options	Price	Options	Price
AM/FM/Cassette/CD Audio System	+127	Leather Seats	+212
AM/FM/CD Audio System	+84	Limited Slip Differential	+84
Antilock Brakes	+223	Premium Audio System	+127
Automatic 4-Speed Transmission	+170	Sunroof	+80
Compact Disc Changer	+137	T-Tops - Glass	+370

Toyota
MR2 Spyder

2003

Body Styles	TMV Pricing		
	Trade	Private	Dealer
2 Dr STD Conv	16304	17555	19641

Options	Price
Alarm System	+195
Leather Seats	+498
6-Speed Sequential Semi-Manual Transmission	+1415

Mileage Category: E

For 2003, Toyota gives the MR2 Spyder a bolder look in front with a new bumper and fascia, dual-bulb projector-style headlights and integrated standard foglamps. The side air intakes are revised and now color-keyed. In the rear, the MR2 is distinguished by new combination lamps with cylindrical turn signals and reverse lights that mimic the dual-bulb look of the headlights. Further, the rear grille garnishes combines body-color vertical ribs and mesh to emphasize the midengine design. A larger oval chrome tailpipe puts the emphasis on performance capability, and a new power antenna contributes to the roadster's clean lines. Inside, instrument panel graphics have been revised, and there are new chrome trim accents. Additionally, the leather seating packages -- black or tan -- now include matching color convertible tops. Mechanically, an all-new six-speed sequential manual transmission (SMT) is optional, replacing last year's five-speed SMT. Toyota has also upped the rear wheels to 16 inches in diameter.

2002
Mileage Category: E

The MR2 Spyder rolls into 2002 with a new Formula One-style five-speed manual transmission. The only other change is that the yellow cloth interior has been discontinued.

Body Styles	TMV Pricing		
	Trade	Private	Dealer
2 Dr STD Conv	14298	15477	17443

Options	Price
5-Speed Sequential Semi-Manual Transmission	+931
Leather Seats	+455

2001

Body Styles	TMV Pricing		
	Trade	Private	Dealer
2 Dr STD Conv	12830	14518	16077

Options	Price
Leather Seats	+390

Mileage Category: E

No changes this year.

2000

Body Styles	TMV Pricing		
	Trade	Private	Dealer
2 Dr STD Conv	11343	12976	14576

Mileage Category: E

Toyota revives the MR2 nameplate on a minimalist two-seat roadster, set to compete directly with the ever-popular Mazda Miata. Only 5,000 are being built and sold.

Toyota
Matrix

2003

Body Styles	TMV Pricing		
	Trade	Private	Dealer
4 Dr STD AWD Wgn	12162	13140	14769
4 Dr STD Wgn	10473	11315	12718
4 Dr XR AWD Wgn	13080	14132	15884

Body Styles	TMV Pricing		
	Trade	Private	Dealer
4 Dr XR Wgn	11515	12441	13984
4 Dr XRS Wgn	13292	14360	16141

Options	Price
Alarm System	+241
Aluminum/Alloy Wheels [Opt on STD,XR]	+309
Antilock Brakes [Opt on STD,XR]	+513
Automatic 4-Speed Transmission [Std on AWD]	+604
Compact Disc Changer [Opt on XR,XRS]	+264
Cruise Control [Opt on STD,XR]	+189

Options	Price
Keyless Entry System [Opt on STD]	+151
Navigation System [Opt on XR,XRS]	+1162
Power Door Locks [Opt on STD]	+200
Power Moonroof [Opt on XR,XRS]	+566
Power Windows [Opt on STD]	+181
Front Side Airbag Restraints	+189

Mileage Category: L

The Matrix is an all-new model from Toyota. It offers sporty looks, enhanced cargo-carrying abilities and useful features not commonly found in small cars.

Toyota
Paseo

1997

Body Styles	TMV Pricing		
	Trade	Private	Dealer
2 Dr STD Conv	4155	4972	5970
2 Dr STD Cpe	3425	4098	4921

Options	Price
Air Conditioning	+297
Aluminum/Alloy Wheels	+133
AM/FM/CD Audio System	+147
Antilock Brakes	+242

Options	Price
Automatic 4-Speed Transmission	+257
Compact Disc Changer	+224
Rear Spoiler	+133
Sunroof	+131

Mileage Category: E

A convertible debuts. Coupes get dual-visor vanity mirrors, fresh door trim and rotary-heater controls.

1996

Body Styles	TMV Pricing		
	Trade	Private	Dealer
2 Dr STD Cpe	2887	3499	4345

Options	Price
Air Conditioning	+250
AM/FM/CD Audio System	+124
Antilock Brakes	+204

Options	Price
Automatic 4-Speed Transmission	+216
Compact Disc Changer	+189
Power Sunroof	+176

Mileage Category: E

All-new Paseo looks like last year's car, but is much improved. It now meets 1997 passenger car safety standards, and has a split-fold rear seat.

Paseo/Pickup

1995

Body Styles		TMV Pricing	
	Trade	Private	Dealer
2 Dr STD Cpe	2259	2759	3592

Options	Price	Options	Price
Air Conditioning	+222	Automatic 4-Speed Transmission	+192
Aluminum/Alloy Wheels	+99	Compact Disc Changer	+168
AM/FM/CD Audio System	+110	Power Sunroof	+156
Antilock Brakes	+181	Rear Spoiler	+99

Mileage Category: E

Several states with strict emissions laws get detuned Paseo for 1995.

1994

Mileage Category: E

CFC-free A/C added. Passenger seatbelts get automatic locking retractors.

Body Styles		TMV Pricing	
	Trade	Private	Dealer
2 Dr STD Cpe	1835	2290	3048

Options	Price	Options	Price
Air Conditioning	+196	Automatic 4-Speed Transmission	+170
Aluminum/Alloy Wheels	+88	Moonroof	+80
Antilock Brakes	+160	Rear Spoiler	+88

Toyota
Pickup

1995

Mileage Category: J

All models get a color-keyed center-high-mount-stop-lamp and redesigned audio systems.

Body Styles		TMV Pricing		Body Styles		TMV Pricing	
	Trade	Private	Dealer		Trade	Private	Dealer
2 Dr DX 4WD Ext Cab SB	3924	4723	6054	2 Dr DX V6 4WD Std Cab SB	3875	4664	5980
2 Dr DX 4WD Std Cab SB	3549	4272	5477	2 Dr DX V6 Ext Cab SB	3316	3991	5116
2 Dr DX Ext Cab SB	3034	3652	4682	2 Dr SR5 4WD Ext Cab SB	4810	5790	7422
2 Dr DX Std Cab SB	2380	2865	3673	2 Dr SR5 Ext Cab SB	3781	4551	5835
2 Dr DX V6 4WD Ext Cab SB	4251	5117	6559	2 Dr STD Std Cab SB	2147	2584	3313

Options	Price	Options	Price
Sunroof	+86	Antilock Brakes	+181
Air Conditioning	+192	Automatic 4-Speed Transmission	+204
AM/FM/CD Audio System	+108	Compact Disc Changer	+132

1994

Mileage Category: J

No major changes this year.

Body Styles		TMV Pricing		Body Styles		TMV Pricing	
	Trade	Private	Dealer		Trade	Private	Dealer
2 Dr DX 4WD Ext Cab SB	3113	3853	5085	2 Dr DX V6 4WD Std Cab SB	3072	3801	5017
2 Dr DX 4WD Std Cab SB	2680	3317	4378	2 Dr DX V6 Ext Cab SB	2506	3102	4094
2 Dr DX Ext Cab SB	2248	2782	3672	2 Dr SR5 V6 4WD Ext Cab SB	4063	5029	6638
2 Dr DX Std Cab SB	2034	2517	3322	2 Dr SR5 V6 Ext Cab SB	2854	3532	4662
2 Dr DX V6 4WD Ext Cab SB	3415	4227	5579	2 Dr STD Std Cab SB	1643	2034	2685

Options	Price	Options	Price
Moonroof	+76	AM/FM/CD Audio System	+95
Sunroof	+76	Automatic 4-Speed Transmission	+180
Air Conditioning	+170	Compact Disc Changer	+117
AM/FM/Cassette/CD Audio System	+132		

1997

Body Styles	TMV Pricing		
	Trade	Private	Dealer
3 Dr DX All-Trac S/C AWD Pass Van	5522	6672	8077
3 Dr DX S/C Pass Van	4974	6010	7276

Options	Price
Antilock Brakes	+253
Captain Chairs (2) [Opt on LE]	+246
Captain Chairs (4) [Opt on LE]	+279
Compact Disc Changer	+224
Keyless Entry System	+127
AM/FM/CD Audio System	+147
Leather Seats	+385

Body Styles	TMV Pricing		
	Trade	Private	Dealer
3 Dr LE All-Trac S/C AWD Pass Van	6815	8233	9967
3 Dr LE S/C Pass Van	6238	7536	9123

Options	Price
Moonroof [Opt on LE]	+129
Power Moonroof [Opt on LE]	+353
Premium Audio System [Opt on LE]	+273
Air Conditioning - Front and Rear [Opt on DX]	+359
Aluminum/Alloy Wheels	+139
AM/FM/Cassette/CD Audio System	+241

Mileage Category: P

The 2.4-liter supercharged engine received numerous improvements to reduce noise, vibration and harshness. Non-ABS models get larger brakes while all models received revised wheel covers. Two new colors added: Glacier Green Metallic and Deep Violet Pearl.

1996

Mileage Category: P

All Previas now have supercharged power.

Body Styles	TMV Pricing		
	Trade	Private	Dealer
3 Dr DX All-Trac S/C AWD Pass Van	4801	5863	7330
3 Dr DX S/C Pass Van	4317	5272	6591

Options	Price
Air Conditioning - Front and Rear [Opt on DX]	+303
Aluminum/Alloy Wheels	+118
AM/FM/Cassette/CD Audio System	+203
AM/FM/CD Audio System	+124
Antilock Brakes	+213
Captain Chairs (2) [Opt on LE]	+207

Body Styles	TMV Pricing		
	Trade	Private	Dealer
3 Dr LE All-Trac S/C AWD Pass Van	5603	6843	8555
3 Dr LE S/C Pass Van	5186	6333	7918

Options	Price
Captain Chairs (4) [Opt on LE]	+235
Compact Disc Changer	+189
Dual Power Moonroofs [Opt on LE]	+399
Leather Seats	+514
Power Moonroof [Opt on LE]	+298
Premium Audio System [Opt on LE]	+230

1995

Mileage Category: P

Seat back map pockets and an illuminated driver's visor vanity mirror are standard on all models.

Body Styles	TMV Pricing		
	Trade	Private	Dealer
3 Dr DX All-Trac AWD Pass Van	3749	4567	5930
3 Dr DX All-Trac S/C AWD Pass Van	3943	4803	6237
3 Dr DX Pass Van	3555	4331	5623
3 Dr DX S/C Pass Van	3688	4493	5834

Options	Price
Air Conditioning - Front and Rear [Opt on DX]	+269
Aluminum/Alloy Wheels	+104
AM/FM/Cassette/CD Audio System	+180
AM/FM/CD Audio System	+110
Antilock Brakes	+189
Captain Chairs (2)	+125
Compact Disc Changer	+168

Body Styles	TMV Pricing		
	Trade	Private	Dealer
3 Dr LE All-Trac AWD Pass Van	4514	5498	7139
3 Dr LE All-Trac S/C AWD Pass Van	4891	5958	7735
3 Dr LE Pass Van	4048	4931	6403
3 Dr LE S/C Pass Van	4210	5128	6659

Options	Price
Dual Power Moonroofs [Opt on LE]	+354
Leather Seats	+288
Moonroof	+96
Power Moonroof	+264
Premium Audio System [Opt on LE]	+204
Running Boards	+80

1994

Mileage Category: P

Passenger airbag added. Supercharged engine included on S/C models. Manual transmission is dropped. CFC-free air conditioning is new. Leather is available on LE models. New front bucket seats are installed.

Body Styles	TMV Pricing		
	Trade	Private	Dealer
3 Dr DX All-Trac AWD Pass Van	3400	4239	5638
3 Dr DX Pass Van	3050	3803	5058
3 Dr LE All-Trac AWD Pass Van	3963	4942	6573

Options	Price
Air Conditioning - Front and Rear [Opt on DX]	+237
Aluminum/Alloy Wheels	+92
AM/FM/Cassette/CD Audio System	+159
AM/FM/CD Audio System	+97
Antilock Brakes	+167
Captain Chairs (2)	+110

Body Styles	TMV Pricing		
	Trade	Private	Dealer
3 Dr LE All-Trac S/C AWD Pass Van	4304	5366	7137
3 Dr LE Pass Van	3552	4429	5890
3 Dr LE S/C Pass Van	3628	4524	6017

Options	Price
Compact Disc Changer	+148
Dual Power Moonroofs [Opt on LE]	+312
Leather Seats	+254
Power Moonroof	+233
Premium Audio System	+180

Toyota
Prius/RAV4

Toyota
Prius

2003

Body Styles	TMV Pricing		
	Trade	Private	Dealer
4 Dr STD Sdn	15770	17270	19770

Options	Price	Options	Price
AM/FM/Cassette/CD Audio System	+204	Front Side Airbag Restraints	+287
Cruise Control	+189	Special Factory Paint	+140
Navigation System	+2421	AM/FM/Cassette/CD Changer Audio System	+362

Mileage Category: B

The Prius, a gas/electric hybrid vehicle, is unchanged for 2003.

2002
Mileage Category: B

Initially offered as a single specification with no factory options, Toyota's advanced gasoline/electric hybrid now offers a choice of several new options for 2002. These include a navigation system, cruise control, side airbags and daytime running lights. There are also two new colors: Brilliant Blue and Blue Moon Pearl.

Body Styles	TMV Pricing		
	Trade	Private	Dealer
4 Dr STD Sdn	13741	15279	17841

Options	Price	Options	Price
AM/FM/Cassette/CD Audio System	+186	Front Side Airbag Restraints	+262
AM/FM/Cassette/CD Changer Audio System	+331	Navigation System	+2213
Cruise Control	+172		

2001
Mileage Category: B

Toyota's Prius, a gas/electric hybrid that follows in the more expensive Honda Insight's footsteps, offers space for five adults coupled with class-leading fuel economy.

Body Styles	TMV Pricing		
	Trade	Private	Dealer
4 Dr STD Sdn	11668	13744	15660

Options	Price	Options	Price
AM/FM/Cassette/CD Audio System	+170	Front Side Airbag Restraints	+239
AM/FM/Cassette/CD Changer Audio System	+302	Navigation System	+2018
Cruise Control	+157		

Toyota
RAV4

2003

Mileage Category: L

Already sporty-looking, the RAV4 compact SUV gets even sportier thanks to a new optional sport package that adds a new grille, a hood scoop, color-keyed door handles, heated exterior mirrors, tubular roof rack and gray-painted bumpers and overfenders. Inside, the package adds special sport fabric seats.

Body Styles	TMV Pricing			Body Styles	TMV Pricing		
	Trade	Private	Dealer		Trade	Private	Dealer
4 Dr STD AWD SUV	13076	14165	15980	4 Dr STD SUV	12550	13595	15337

Options	Price	Options	Price
Air Conditioning	+743	Limited Slip Differential	+294
Aluminum/Alloy Wheels	+302	Power Door Locks	+177
AM/FM/Cassette/CD Audio System	+283	Power Moonroof	+679
Antilock Brakes	+513	Power Windows	+200
Automatic 4-Speed Transmission	+792	Rear Spoiler	+151
Cruise Control	+166	Special Factory Paint	+166
Keyless Entry System	+174	Sport Package	+415
Leather Seats	+566		

2002

Body Styles	TMV Pricing			Body Styles	TMV Pricing		
	Trade	Private	Dealer		Trade	Private	Dealer
4 Dr STD AWD SUV	11744	12839	14663	4 Dr STD SUV	10977	12000	13705

For the latest vehicle information, visit www.edmunds.com

2002 (cont'd)

Options	Price
Air Conditioning	+680
Aluminum/Alloy Wheels	+276
AM/FM/Cassette/CD Audio System	+345
Antilock Brakes	+469
Automatic 4-Speed Transmission	+724
Cruise Control	+152
Keyless Entry System	+159
Leather Seats	+517

Options	Price
Limited Slip Differential [Opt on 4WD]	+269
Power Door Locks	+166
Power Moonroof	+621
Power Windows	+190
Rear Spoiler	+138
Side Steps	+172
Special Factory Paint	+152

Mileage Category: L

Toyota's mini-SUV receives just a couple cosmetic changes this year. Models ordered with the Quick Order package now have gray-painted bumpers and overfenders, and Toyota has added color-keyed bumpers and overfenders to the "L" package. There are also three new L package colors: Rainforest Pearl, Spectra Blue Mica and Pearl White (Natural White and Vintage Gold have been discontinued).

2001

Body Styles	Trade	Private	Dealer
4 Dr STD AWD SUV	10651	12125	13487

Body Styles	Trade	Private	Dealer
4 Dr STD SUV	9851	11214	12472

Mileage Category: L

Completely redesigned, RAV4 grows in size and gets a more powerful engine, along with edgy new styling.

Options	Price
Air Conditioning	+620
Aluminum/Alloy Wheels	+252
AM/FM/Cassette/CD Audio System	+315
Antilock Brakes	+428
Automatic 4-Speed Transmission	+598
Cruise Control	+157
Keyless Entry System	+138

Options	Price
Leather Seats	+472
Limited Slip Differential	+245
Power Door Locks	+151
Power Sunroof	+513
Power Windows	+173
Rear Spoiler	+126

2000

Body Styles	Trade	Private	Dealer
4 Dr L Special Edition AWD SUV	10589	12072	13526
4 Dr L Special Edition SUV	10201	11629	13029

Body Styles	Trade	Private	Dealer
4 Dr STD AWD SUV	9266	10564	11836
4 Dr STD SUV	8400	9576	10730

Mileage Category: L

The RAV4 SUV remains largely unchanged for 2000. A new cupholder design and the extinction of the two-door RAV4 convertible are the big news for '00.

Options	Price
Air Conditioning [Opt on STD]	+544
Alarm System	+193
Aluminum/Alloy Wheels [Opt on STD]	+271
AM/FM/Cassette Audio System [Opt on STD]	+193
AM/FM/Cassette/CD Audio System	+276
AM/FM/CD Audio System [Opt on STD]	+249
Antilock Brakes	+376
Automatic 4-Speed Transmission	+580

Options	Price
Compact Disc Changer	+332
Cruise Control [Opt on STD]	+138
Leather Seats	+414
Limited Slip Differential	+215
Power Door Locks [Opt on STD]	+133
Power Moonroof	+450
Power Windows [Opt on STD]	+152
Side Steps	+130

1999

Body Styles	Trade	Private	Dealer
2 Dr STD AWD Conv	8044	9410	10833
2 Dr STD Conv	7270	8505	9791
4 Dr STD AWD SUV	8110	9487	10921

Body Styles	Trade	Private	Dealer
4 Dr STD SUV	7357	8607	9908
4 Dr Special Edition AWD SUV	8357	9777	11254

Mileage Category: L

Leather seats and color-keyed body cladding are now available as part of the "L Special Edition" package. Color-keyed mirrors and door handles can also be had this year and the spare tire is now a full-size steel wheel with a soft cover.

Options	Price
Air Conditioning [Opt on STD]	+420
Alarm System	+150
Aluminum/Alloy Wheels	+209
AM/FM/Cassette Audio System [Opt on STD]	+150
AM/FM/Cassette/CD Audio System	+214
AM/FM/CD Audio System	+192
Antilock Brakes	+323

Options	Price
Automatic 4-Speed Transmission	+448
Compact Disc Changer	+256
Leather Seats	+321
Limited Slip Differential	+167
Power Moonroof	+349
Power Windows [Opt on STD]	+117

Toyota
RAV4/Sequoia

1998
Mileage Category: L

Toyota's mini SUV enters its third year of production with minor changes to the grille, headlights, taillamps and interior. Four-door RAV4s get new seat fabric. A late-year introduction of the new RAV4 convertible makes this sport-ute more appealing for those who live in the sunbelt.

Body Styles	TMV Pricing		
	Trade	Private	Dealer
2 Dr STD AWD Conv	6484	7650	8964
2 Dr STD AWD SUV	6135	7238	8482
2 Dr STD Conv	5990	7067	8282
2 Dr STD SUV	5799	6842	8018

Options	Price
Compact Disc Changer	+226
Automatic 4-Speed Transmission	+413
Leather Seats	+282
Limited Slip Differential	+141
Power Moonroof	+344
Spoke Wheels	+257
Air Conditioning	+370

Body Styles	TMV Pricing		
	Trade	Private	Dealer
4 Dr L Special Edition SUV	6574	7756	9089
4 Dr STD AWD SUV	6306	7440	8719
4 Dr STD SUV	5805	6849	8026

Options	Price
Alarm System	+150
Aluminum/Alloy Wheels	+184
AM/FM/Cassette Audio System	+132
AM/FM/Cassette/CD Audio System	+188
AM/FM/CD Audio System	+169
Antilock Brakes	+284

1997
Mileage Category: L

New fabric debuts on the two-door RAV, and a sunroof is finally available on the four-door. Improvements have also been made by using sound-deadening material in the dash area, reducing engine noise in the passenger compartment.

Body Styles	TMV Pricing		
	Trade	Private	Dealer
2 Dr STD AWD SUV	5470	6520	7804
2 Dr STD SUV	4833	5761	6895

Options	Price
Leather Seats	+241
Limited Slip Differential	+121
Power Moonroof	+294
Spoke Wheels	+219
T-Tops - Solid	+144
Air Conditioning	+316
Alarm System	+124

Body Styles	TMV Pricing		
	Trade	Private	Dealer
4 Dr STD AWD SUV	5480	6532	7818
4 Dr STD SUV	5137	6123	7328

Options	Price
Aluminum/Alloy Wheels	+157
AM/FM/Cassette/CD Audio System	+160
AM/FM/CD Audio System	+133
Antilock Brakes	+242
Automatic 4-Speed Transmission	+337
Compact Disc Changer	+174

1996
Mileage Category: L

A new mini-ute based on passenger car mechanicals debuts this year. It's available as a two-door or four-door.

Body Styles	TMV Pricing		
	Trade	Private	Dealer
2 Dr STD AWD SUV	4773	5671	6910
2 Dr STD SUV	4269	5072	6180

Options	Price
Air Conditioning	+266
Aluminum/Alloy Wheels	+133
Antilock Brakes	+204
Automatic 4-Speed Transmission	+284

Body Styles	TMV Pricing		
	Trade	Private	Dealer
4 Dr STD AWD SUV	4930	5856	7136
4 Dr STD SUV	4591	5454	6646

Options	Price
Compact Disc Changer	+148
Spoke Wheels	+185
Sunroof	+162
T-Tops - Solid	+121

Toyota
Sequoia

2003

Body Styles	TMV Pricing		
	Trade	Private	Dealer
4 Dr Limited 4WD SUV	34370	36223	39310
4 Dr Limited SUV	32291	34032	36934
4 Dr SR5 4WD SUV	28509	30046	32607
4 Dr SR5 SUV	25714	27100	29410

Mileage Category: N

For 2003, the eight-passenger Sequoia SUV features new 17-inch alloy wheels and tires and an inside rearview auto-dimming mirror as standard equipment on the top-of-the-line Limited grade, and as options on the SR5 model. A rear DVD entertainment system with two cordless headphones, and a load leveling rear suspension are new features available on both Sequoia models.

Options	Price
Automatic Load Leveling	+272
JBL Audio System [Opt on SR5]	+389
Keyless Entry System [Opt on SR5]	+185
Leather Seats [Opt on SR5]	+868
Power Driver Seat [Opt on SR5]	+226
Power Moonroof	+755
Power Passenger Seat [Opt on SR5]	+226
Rear Spoiler [Opt on Limited]	+151

Options	Price
Running Boards [Opt on SR5]	+302
Front Side Airbag Restraints	+189
AM/FM/Cassette/CD Changer Audio System	+151
17 Inch Wheels [Opt on SR5]	+415
Automatic Climate Control (2 Zone) - Driver and Passenger [Opt on SR5]	+430
DVD Entertainment System	+1336
Front Head Airbag Restraints	+189

2002

Mileage Category: N

The Sequoia is virtually unchanged for 2002. SR5 models have two additional stand-alone options this year: keyless remote and front foglamps.

Body Styles	TMV Pricing		
	Trade	Private	Dealer
4 Dr Limited 4WD SUV	32471	34303	37357
4 Dr Limited SUV	29936	31645	34493

Body Styles	TMV Pricing		
	Trade	Private	Dealer
4 Dr SR5 4WD SUV	26514	28027	30550
4 Dr SR5 SUV	23845	25206	27475

Options	Price
16 Inch Wheels [Opt on SR5]	+328
AM/FM/Cassette/CD Changer Audio System	+138
Automatic Climate Control (2 Zone) - Front and Rear [Opt on SR5]	+393
Front Head Airbag Restraints	+172
Front Side Airbag Restraints	+172
JBL Audio System [Opt on SR5]	+207
Keyless Entry System [Opt on SR5]	+169

Options	Price
Leather Seats [Opt on SR5]	+793
Power Driver Seat [Opt on SR5]	+207
Power Moonroof	+690
Power Passenger Seat [Opt on SR5]	+207
Rear Spoiler [Opt on Limited]	+138
Running Boards [Opt on SR5]	+276
Styled Steel Wheels [Opt on SR5]	+228

2001

Mileage Category: N

Toyota releases the Tundra pickup-based Sequoia, a full-size SUV that represents the first serious challenge to the Chevrolet Tahoe/Suburban, Ford Expedition and GMC Yukon from across either ocean.

Body Styles	TMV Pricing		
	Trade	Private	Dealer
4 Dr Limited 4WD SUV	28617	31168	33524
4 Dr Limited SUV	26436	28793	30969

Body Styles	TMV Pricing		
	Trade	Private	Dealer
4 Dr SR5 4WD SUV	23408	25495	27421
4 Dr SR5 SUV	21099	22979	24715

Options	Price
Air Conditioning - Front and Rear [Opt on SR5]	+359
Aluminum/Alloy Wheels [Opt on SR5]	+315
AM/FM/Cassette/CD Changer Audio System	+126
Front Head Airbag Restraints	+157
Front Side Airbag Restraints	+157
Keyless Entry System [Opt on SR5]	+138
Leather Seats [Opt on SR5]	+786

Options	Price
Power Driver Seat [Opt on SR5]	+204
Power Passenger Seat [Opt on SR5]	+204
Power Sunroof	+632
Rear Spoiler	+126
Running Boards [Opt on SR5]	+252
Styled Steel Wheels [Opt on SR5]	+208

Body Styles	TMV Pricing		
	Trade	Private	Dealer
4 Dr CE Pass Van	16508	17666	19596
4 Dr LE Pass Van	18266	19548	21684

Body Styles	TMV Pricing		
	Trade	Private	Dealer
4 Dr XLE Pass Van	19402	20763	23032

Mileage Category: P

The Sienna carries into 2003 virtually unchanged. The right-hand power-sliding door is now available on CE models, as are captain's chairs. A complete redesign is due for 2004.

Options	Price
Alarm System [Opt on CE,LE]	+233
Aluminum/Alloy Wheels [Opt on LE]	+359
Camper/Towing Package	+121
Captain Chairs (4) [Opt on CE,LE]	+245
Cruise Control [Opt on CE]	+136
Heated Front Seats [Opt on XLE]	+332
JBL Audio System [Opt on LE]	+245
Keyless Entry System [Opt on CE,LE]	+166
Leather Seats [Opt on XLE]	+868

Options	Price
Power Door Locks [Opt on CE]	+181
Power Driver Seat [Opt on LE]	+245
Power Dual Sliding Doors [Opt on LE,XLE]	+600
Power Moonroof [Opt on XLE]	+679
Power Sliding Door	+298
Power Windows [Opt on CE]	+204
Front Side Airbag Restraints	+189
Traction Control System	+415
AM/FM/Cassette/CD Changer Audio System [Opt on XLE]	+302

Sienna

2002

Mileage Category: P

Nothing major is in store for Toyota's minivan this year. The most significant change is the availability of a new "Symphony" special edition for LE models. This special edition includes items like keyless entry, a roof rack, captain's chairs for the first two rows (six-way power driver seat), a premium JBL audio system, power swing privacy glass, color-keyed heated power side mirrors, an overhead console with HomeLink and painted bumpers and cladding. There's also a new color this year exclusive to the Symphony: Lunar Mist Metallic. The base CE model's Extra Value package now includes a roof rack and keyless entry for no extra cost.

Body Styles	TMV Pricing		
	Trade	Private	Dealer
4 Dr CE Pass Van	13818	14958	16858
4 Dr LE Pass Van	15161	16412	18496

Options	Price
Aluminum/Alloy Wheels [Opt on LE]	+328
AM/FM/Cassette/CD Changer Audio System [Opt on XLE]	+276
Automatic Stability Control	+379
Captain Chairs (4) [Opt on LE]	+448
Cruise Control [Opt on CE]	+124
Front Side Airbag Restraints	+172
Heated Front Seats [Opt on XLE]	+304
JBL Audio System [Opt on LE]	+204
Keyless Entry System [Opt on CE,LE]	+128

Body Styles	TMV Pricing		
	Trade	Private	Dealer
4 Dr XLE Pass Van	16491	17851	20117

Options	Price
Leather Seats [Opt on XLE]	+793
Power Door Locks [Opt on CE]	+166
Power Driver Seat [Opt on LE]	+224
Power Dual Sliding Doors [Opt on XLE]	+548
Power Moonroof [Opt on XLE]	+621
Power Sliding Door [Opt on LE,XLE]	+272
Power Windows [Opt on CE]	+186
Traction Control System	+379

2001

Mileage Category: P

Like other minivans on the market, the 2001 Sienna can be equipped with an on-board entertainment system. Dual power-sliding doors are optional, and the safety-conscious will like the fact that side airbags and a stability control system are available. Sienna's smooth V6 makes more power and torque this year. A rear defroster is standard on all Siennas, while JBL audio, heated front seats and an electrochromic rearview mirror with integrated compass are optional on XLE models. Styling has been tweaked front and rear, four new colors replace four old colors and all Siennas come with a driver-side sliding door.

Body Styles	TMV Pricing		
	Trade	Private	Dealer
4 Dr CE Pass Van	12236	13825	15292
4 Dr LE Pass Van	13650	15422	17057

Options	Price
Aluminum/Alloy Wheels [Opt on LE]	+299
AM/FM/Cassette/CD Changer Audio System [Opt on XLE]	+324
Automatic Stability Control	+346
Captain Chairs (4) [Opt on LE]	+472
Child Seat (1) [Opt on LE]	+157
Front Side Airbag Restraints	+157
Heated Front Seats [Opt on XLE]	+277
Keyless Entry System [Opt on CE,LE]	+138

Body Styles	TMV Pricing		
	Trade	Private	Dealer
4 Dr XLE Pass Van	14732	16645	18410

Options	Price
Leather Seats	+887
Power Door Locks [Opt on CE]	+151
Power Dual Sliding Doors	+566
Power Moonroof	+554
Power Sliding Door	+249
Power Windows [Opt on CE]	+167
Traction Control System	+346

2000

Mileage Category: P

New for Sienna are two exterior colors and various audio enhancements. All grades feature a standard AM/FM/cassette audio system. XLE models add a CD deck and offer an optional in-dash six-disc changer.

Body Styles	TMV Pricing		
	Trade	Private	Dealer
3 Dr CE Pass Van	9985	11418	12823
4 Dr LE Pass Van	11751	13437	15089

Options	Price
Air Conditioning - Front and Rear [Opt on CE]	+326
Alarm System [Opt on CE,LE]	+177
Aluminum/Alloy Wheels [Opt on CE,LE]	+262
Captain Chairs (2)	+138
Captain Chairs (4) [Opt on LE]	+492
Child Seat (1)	+138
Compact Disc Changer	+304
Keyless Entry System [Opt on CE,LE]	+122

Body Styles	TMV Pricing		
	Trade	Private	Dealer
4 Dr XLE Pass Van	12855	14700	16509

Options	Price
Leather Seats	+779
Power Door Locks [Opt on CE]	+133
Power Moonroof	+486
Power Sliding Door	+218
Power Windows [Opt on CE]	+146
Rear Spoiler	+157
Running Boards	+329
Sliding Driver Side Door [Opt on CE]	+218

1999

Mileage Category: P

Entering its second full model year of production at Toyota's Kentucky plant, the Sienna minivan gets a right-side power-sliding door. An engine immobilizer system has been added to the keyless-entry security system and all Siennas will be equipped with daytime running lights. Selected models have a full-size spare tire and Woodland Pearl replaces Classic Green Pearl as an exterior color option.

Body Styles	TMV Pricing		
	Trade	Private	Dealer
3 Dr CE Pass Van	8502	9842	11236
4 Dr LE Pass Van	10031	11612	13257
4 Dr XLE Pass Van	11093	12841	14660

Options	Price
Rear Spoiler	+122
Running Boards	+254
Sliding Driver Side Door [Opt on CE]	+169
Air Conditioning - Front and Rear [Opt on CE]	+252
Alarm System [Opt on CE,LE]	+137
Aluminum/Alloy Wheels [Opt on CE,LE]	+203

Options	Price
AM/FM/CD Audio System [Opt on CE,LE]	+137
Captain Chairs (4) [Opt on LE]	+380
Compact Disc Changer	+235
Leather Seats	+602
Power Moonroof	+376
Power Sliding Door	+169

1998

Mileage Category: P

A new minivan from Toyota brings some innovation to the family transport market. A powerful 194-horsepower V6 engine rests under the hood of all models. Safety equipment includes standard antilock brakes, low tire-pressure warning systems and five-mph front and rear bumpers. Sienna boasts outstanding crash test scores.

Body Styles	TMV Pricing		
	Trade	Private	Dealer
3 Dr CE Pass Van	7110	8412	9881
3 Dr LE Pass Van	7732	9148	10745

Body Styles	TMV Pricing		
	Trade	Private	Dealer
4 Dr XLE Pass Van	9001	10649	12508

Options	Price
Air Conditioning - Front and Rear [Opt on CE]	+169
Alarm System	+149
Aluminum/Alloy Wheels [Opt on LE]	+229
AM/FM/Cassette/CD Audio System [Opt on LE,XLE]	+146
AM/FM/CD Audio System [Opt on CE,LE]	+120

Options	Price
Compact Disc Changer	+206
Leather Seats	+530
Power Moonroof	+368
Running Boards	+224
Sliding Driver Side Door	+141

Toyota

Supra

1998

Body Styles	TMV Pricing		
	Trade	Private	Dealer
2 Dr STD Hbk	14008	16051	18354

Body Styles	TMV Pricing		
	Trade	Private	Dealer
2 Dr Turbo Hbk	18368	21047	24067

Options	Price
AM/FM/Cassette/CD Audio System	+424
Automatic 4-Speed Transmission	+376
Compact Disc Changer	+313

Options	Price
Leather Seats [Opt on STD]	+459
Power Driver Seat [Opt on STD]	+117
Targa Top - Solid [Opt on STD]	+1044

Mileage Category: F

Variable Valve Timing with intelligence appears on the new Supra.

1997

Mileage Category: F

Turbo models get the six-speed manual transmission back, but the bigger news details massive price cuts. Turbos with automatics are $12,000 less expensive than last year! All Supras commemorate the nameplate's 15th anniversary with a rear spoiler, premium sound and special badging. Despite price cuts, equipment levels are enhanced across the board.

Body Styles	TMV Pricing		
	Trade	Private	Dealer
2 Dr STD Hbk	11974	13882	16215

Body Styles	TMV Pricing		
	Trade	Private	Dealer
2 Dr Turbo Hbk	15667	18164	21216

Options	Price
AM/FM/Cassette/CD Audio System [Std on Turbo]	+362
AM/FM/CD Audio System	+160
Automatic 4-Speed Transmission [Std on Turbo]	+321

Options	Price
Compact Disc Changer	+267
Leather Seats [Std on Turbo]	+392
Targa Top - Solid	+891

1996

Mileage Category: F

Manual transmission Turbo models are history, thanks to stringent emission regulations.

Body Styles	TMV Pricing		
	Trade	Private	Dealer
2 Dr STD Hbk	10714	12494	14951

Body Styles	TMV Pricing		
	Trade	Private	Dealer
2 Dr Turbo Hbk	12872	15010	17962

Options	Price
AM/FM/Cassette/CD Audio System	+195
Automatic 4-Speed Transmission [Std on Turbo]	+270
Compact Disc Changer	+225
Leather Seats	+331

Options	Price
Limited Slip Differential [Std on Turbo]	+152
Premium Audio System	+150
Rear Spoiler	+138
Targa Top - Solid	+751

Toyota
Supra/T100

1995
Mileage Category: F

No changes.

Body Styles	TMV Pricing		
	Trade	Private	Dealer
2 Dr STD Hbk	8987	10443	12869

Options	Price
AM/FM/Cassette/CD Audio System	+263
AM/FM/CD Audio System	+173
Automatic 4-Speed Transmission	+240
Compact Disc Changer	+200

Body Styles	TMV Pricing		
	Trade	Private	Dealer
2 Dr Turbo Hbk	10753	12495	15398

Options	Price
Leather Seats	+293
Limited Slip Differential [Opt on STD]	+123
Rear Spoiler	+112
Targa Top - Solid	+293

1994
Mileage Category: F

Base model gets revised final-drive ratio for improved launch.

Body Styles	TMV Pricing		
	Trade	Private	Dealer
2 Dr STD Hbk	7680	9026	11269

Options	Price
AM/FM/Cassette/CD Audio System	+205
Automatic 4-Speed Transmission	+212
Leather Seats	+212

Body Styles	TMV Pricing		
	Trade	Private	Dealer
2 Dr Turbo Hbk	8923	10487	13093

Options	Price
Limited Slip Differential [Std on Turbo]	+108
Rear Spoiler	+99
Targa Top - Solid	+259

Toyota
T100

1998

Mileage Category: K

No changes to Toyota's full-size truck.

Body Styles	TMV Pricing		
	Trade	Private	Dealer
2 Dr DX 4WD Ext Cab SB	7824	9130	10602
2 Dr DX Ext Cab SB	6406	7475	8681
2 Dr SR5 4WD Ext Cab SB	8184	9549	11089

Options	Price
AM/FM/Cassette Audio System [Std on SR5]	+143
Antilock Brakes	+284
Automatic 4-Speed Transmission	+338
Bucket Seats	+124

Body Styles	TMV Pricing		
	Trade	Private	Dealer
2 Dr SR5 Ext Cab SB	6926	8082	9385
2 Dr STD Std Cab LB	4643	5418	6291

Options	Price
Running Boards	+174
Aluminum/Alloy Wheels	+201
Air Conditioning	+226

1997
Mileage Category: K

Two new colors debut and the optional wheel and tire packages are larger this year. Standard models get radio prewiring, midlevel models get fabric door trim panels and SR5 models get chrome wheel arches.

Body Styles	TMV Pricing		
	Trade	Private	Dealer
2 Dr DX 4WD Ext Cab SB	6541	7765	9260
2 Dr DX Ext Cab SB	5616	6667	7951
2 Dr SR5 4WD Ext Cab SB	6892	8181	9757

Options	Price
Air Conditioning	+193
Aluminum/Alloy Wheels	+172
AM/FM/Cassette Audio System	+122
AM/FM/Cassette/CD Audio System	+160
AM/FM/CD Audio System	+147

Body Styles	TMV Pricing		
	Trade	Private	Dealer
2 Dr SR5 Ext Cab SB	5765	6843	8161
2 Dr STD Std Cab LB	3952	4691	5595

Options	Price
Antilock Brakes	+242
Automatic 4-Speed Transmission	+289
Premium Audio System	+134
Running Boards	+149

1996
Mileage Category: K

Essentially a carryover, but DX models are scrapped. Regular cabs can't be equipped with cruise control anymore. A new shade of red is offered, and tan interiors are offered in a wider variety of trucks.

Body Styles	TMV Pricing		
	Trade	Private	Dealer
2 Dr DX 4WD Ext Cab SB	5741	6839	8356
2 Dr DX Ext Cab SB	4782	5697	6961
2 Dr SR5 4WD Ext Cab SB	6129	7302	8922

Body Styles	TMV Pricing		
	Trade	Private	Dealer
2 Dr SR5 Ext Cab SB	4962	5912	7223
2 Dr STD Std Cab LB	3595	4283	5233

1996 (cont'd)

Options	Price
Air Conditioning	+244
Aluminum/Alloy Wheels	+163
AM/FM/Cassette/CD Audio System	+135
AM/FM/CD Audio System	+124
Antilock Brakes	+204

Options	Price
Automatic 4-Speed Transmission	+244
Chrome Wheels	+167
Power Sunroof	+135
Running Boards	+126

1995

Body Styles	TMV Pricing		
	Trade	Private	Dealer
2 Dr DX 1 Ton Std Cab LB	3646	4392	5636
2 Dr DX 4WD Ext Cab SB	4682	5641	7238
2 Dr DX 4WD Std Cab LB	4490	5409	6940
2 Dr DX Ext Cab SB	3858	4648	5964
2 Dr DX Std Cab LB	3585	4319	5542

Body Styles	TMV Pricing		
	Trade	Private	Dealer
2 Dr SR5 4WD Ext Cab SB	4980	5999	7698
2 Dr SR5 Ext Cab SB	3904	4703	6035
2 Dr STD Std Cab LB	2848	3431	4403
2 Dr V6 Std Cab LB	3181	3832	4918

Mileage Category: K

The 1995 T100 adds an extended-cab body style to fill out this midsize truck's lineup. A much more powerful DOHC V6 engine is introduced this year as are four-wheel antilock brakes. The antilock brakes are available only on DX and Xtracab models equipped V6 engine.

Options	Price
Antilock Brakes	+181
Automatic 4-Speed Transmission	+216
Running Boards	+111
AM/FM/Cassette/CD Audio System	+120

Options	Price
Air Conditioning	+144
Aluminum/Alloy Wheels	+128
AM/FM/Cassette Audio System	+91

1994

Body Styles	TMV Pricing		
	Trade	Private	Dealer
2 Dr DX 1 Ton Std Cab LB	2651	3267	4294
2 Dr DX 4WD Std Cab LB	3120	3845	5054
2 Dr DX Std Cab LB	2583	3184	4185

Body Styles	TMV Pricing		
	Trade	Private	Dealer
2 Dr SR5 4WD Std Cab LB	3914	4825	6342
2 Dr SR5 Std Cab LB	2913	3591	4720
2 Dr STD Std Cab LB	1810	2231	2932

Mileage Category: K

Driver airbag is added, and base models get four-cylinder engine. Side-door guard beams are installed, and beds get cargo tie-down hooks. Formerly standard rear ABS is now optional on base and DX trucks.

Options	Price
Air Conditioning	+127
Aluminum/Alloy Wheels	+113
AM/FM/Cassette Audio System	+80

Options	Price
AM/FM/Cassette/CD Audio System	+106
Automatic 4-Speed Transmission	+190

Toyota

Tacoma

2003

Body Styles	TMV Pricing		
	Trade	Private	Dealer
2 Dr Prerunner Ext Cab SB	12256	13240	14881
2 Dr Prerunner Std Cab SB	10202	11021	12386
2 Dr Prerunner V6 Ext Cab SB	13477	14559	16363
2 Dr S-Runner V6 Ext Cab SB	14696	15876	17844
2 Dr STD 4WD Ext Cab SB	13585	14676	16494
4 Dr Prerunner Crew Cab SB	13538	14625	16436

Body Styles	TMV Pricing		
	Trade	Private	Dealer
4 Dr Prerunner V6 Crew Cab SB	13926	15044	16908
4 Dr V6 4WD Crew Cab SB	16285	17592	19771
2 Dr STD 4WD Std Cab SB	12075	13045	14661
2 Dr STD Ext Cab SB	10682	11540	12969
2 Dr STD Std Cab SB	8764	9468	10640
2 Dr V6 4WD Ext Cab SB	14541	15708	17654

Mileage Category: J

The Tacoma compact pickup is upgraded for 2003 with standard antilock brakes on all models. Additionally, child restraint system lower anchors have been added to the front passenger seat on Regular and Xtracab models, and to the rear outboard seats on Double Cab models.

Options	Price
Air Conditioning [Std on S-Runner]	+442
Alarm System	+188
Aluminum/Alloy Wheels [Std on S-Runner]	+574
Automatic 4-Speed Transmission [Opt on STD]	+543
Chrome Wheels	+438
Keyless Entry System [Std on S-Runner]	+132
Locking Differential [Opt on V6]	+257

Options	Price
Power Door Locks [Std on S-Runner]	+174
Power Windows [Std on S-Runner]	+200
Running Boards	+238
Sport Seats [Opt on V6]	+189
TRD Off-Road Suspension Package [Opt on Prerunner,V6]	+626
Stepside Bed	+234

Tacoma

2002

Mileage Category: J

A moonroof is available now on PreRunners and S-Runners have color-keyed side badging.

Body Styles	TMV Pricing		
	Trade	Private	Dealer
2 Dr Prerunner Ext Cab SB	11058	12059	13728
2 Dr Prerunner Std Cab SB	9367	10215	11629
2 Dr Prerunner V6 Ext Cab SB	12374	13495	15362
2 Dr S-Runner V6 Ext Cab SB	12081	13175	14998
2 Dr STD 4WD Ext Cab SB	12400	13523	15393
2 Dr STD 4WD Std Cab SB	11058	12059	13728

Options	Price
Air Conditioning [Std on S-Runner]	+404
Aluminum/Alloy Wheels [Std on S-Runner]	+524
AM/FM/Cassette/CD Audio System	+172
Antilock Brakes	+469
Automatic 4-Speed Transmission [Std on Prerunner,V6 Crew]	+497
Chrome Wheels	+400
Locking Differential	+235

Body Styles	TMV Pricing		
	Trade	Private	Dealer
2 Dr STD Ext Cab SB	9790	10676	12154
2 Dr STD Std Cab SB	8073	8804	10022
2 Dr V6 4WD Ext Cab SB	13271	14473	16475
4 Dr Prerunner Crew Cab SB	12112	13209	15037
4 Dr Prerunner V6 Crew Cab SB	12670	13817	15730
4 Dr V6 4WD Crew Cab SB	14799	16139	18373

Options	Price
Moonroof [Opt on Crew Cab,Ext Cab]	+276
Power Door Locks	+121
Power Windows	+138
Running Boards [Opt on Crew Cab]	+217
Sport Seats [Opt on V6]	+172
Stepside Bed	+214
TRD Off-Road Suspension Package [Opt on Prerunner,V6]	+573

2001

Mileage Category: J

Toyota releases the Double Cab. A new StepSide version is available, and the S-Runner sport truck debuts. Revised front styling and new alloy wheels give Tacoma a more rugged look. New exterior colors and option package content shuffling sum up the obvious changes for 2001.

Body Styles	TMV Pricing		
	Trade	Private	Dealer
2 Dr Prerunner Ext Cab SB	10195	11577	12852
2 Dr Prerunner Std Cab SB	8295	9419	10457
2 Dr Prerunner V6 Ext Cab SB	11401	12946	14373
2 Dr S-Runner V6 Ext Cab SB	11047	12545	13927
2 Dr STD 4WD Ext Cab SB	11512	13072	14513
2 Dr STD 4WD Std Cab SB	10183	11563	12837

Options	Price
Air Conditioning [Std on Limited]	+315
Aluminum/Alloy Wheels [Std on Limited]	+233
AM/FM/Cassette/CD Audio System [Std on Limited]	+157
Antilock Brakes	+428
Automatic 4-Speed Transmission [Opt on SR5 V6,STD]	+453
Chrome Wheels	+296
Locking Differential [Opt on Prerunner]	+214

Body Styles	TMV Pricing		
	Trade	Private	Dealer
2 Dr STD Ext Cab SB	8829	10025	11130
2 Dr STD Std Cab SB	7187	8161	9060
2 Dr V6 4WD Ext Cab SB	11886	13497	14984
4 Dr Prerunner Crew Cab SB	11096	12599	13987
4 Dr Prerunner V6 Crew Cab SB	11699	13284	14748
4 Dr V6 4WD Crew Cab SB	13626	15473	17177

Options	Price
Moonroof	+245
Power Door Locks [Std on Limited]	+145
Power Windows [Std on Limited]	+167
Running Boards	+198
Stepside Bed	+126
TRD Off-Road Suspension Package	+503

2000

Mileage Category: J

Tacomas with four-cylinder engines and four-wheel drive achieve improved performance from an enhanced gear ratio. Base-grade Tacomas feature new designs for the interior fabric and exterior mirrors. Daytime running lights are now included with the antilock brake package. There are also two new colors as well as a color-keyed package for those who like the monochrome look.

Body Styles	TMV Pricing		
	Trade	Private	Dealer
2 Dr Limited 4WD Ext Cab SB	12762	14644	16488
2 Dr Prerunner Ext Cab SB	8741	10030	11294
2 Dr Prerunner Std Cab SB	6709	7698	8668
2 Dr Prerunner V6 Ext Cab SB	8921	10237	11526
2 Dr SR5 4WD Ext Cab SB	9629	11049	12440
2 Dr SR5 Ext Cab SB	8409	9649	10865
2 Dr SR5 V6 4WD Ext Cab SB	10462	12005	13517

Options	Price
Power Windows [Std on Limited]	+146
Power Steering [Opt on STD Std Cab]	+166
Running Boards	+158
Styled Steel Wheels [Std on STD 4WD Std Cab]	+260
Sunroof	+215
Tilt Steering Wheel [Std on Limited]	+135
TRD Off-Road Suspension Package	+442
Air Conditioning [Opt on Limited V6,V6,Std Cab]	+544
Alarm System	+138
Aluminum/Alloy Wheels [Std on Limited]	+204

Body Styles	TMV Pricing		
	Trade	Private	Dealer
2 Dr SR5 V6 Ext Cab SB	8688	9969	11225
2 Dr STD 4WD Ext Cab SB	8811	10110	11383
2 Dr STD 4WD Std Cab SB	8430	9673	10892
2 Dr STD Ext Cab SB	7049	8088	9107
2 Dr STD Std Cab SB	5623	6452	7265
2 Dr V6 4WD Ext Cab SB	9197	10553	11883
2 Dr V6 Ext Cab SB	8344	9574	10781

Options	Price
AM/FM/Cassette/CD Audio System [Std on Limited]	+320
AM/FM/CD Audio System	+376
Antilock Brakes	+376
Automatic 4-Speed Transmission [Opt on SR5 V6,STD]	+401
Automatic Locking Hubs (4WD)	+133
Compact Disc Changer	+332
Cruise Control [Opt on SR5 V6]	+138
Limited Slip Differential	+188
Off-Road Suspension Package	+729
Power Door Locks [Std on Limited]	+127

1999

Body Styles	TMV Pricing		
	Trade	Private	Dealer
2 Dr Limited 4WD Ext Cab SB	10839	12543	14317
2 Dr Prerunner Ext Cab SB	7634	8835	10085
2 Dr Prerunner Std Cab SB	6152	7119	8126
2 Dr Prerunner V6 Ext Cab SB	7646	8848	10100
2 Dr SR5 4WD Ext Cab SB	7748	8966	10235
2 Dr SR5 Ext Cab SB	6993	8092	9236
2 Dr SR5 V6 4WD Ext Cab SB	8834	10223	11668

Body Styles	TMV Pricing		
	Trade	Private	Dealer
2 Dr SR5 V6 Ext Cab SB	7358	8515	9719
2 Dr STD 4WD Ext Cab SB	7683	8891	10148
2 Dr STD 4WD Std Cab SB	7441	8611	9828
2 Dr STD Ext Cab SB	6177	7149	8160
2 Dr STD Std Cab SB	4771	5521	6302
2 Dr V6 4WD Ext Cab SB	7871	9109	10397
2 Dr V6 Ext Cab SB	7298	8445	9639

Options	Price
Air Conditioning [Opt on Limited,STD,V6]	+420
Aluminum/Alloy Wheels [Std on Limited]	+158
AM/FM/Cassette/CD Audio System	+248
AM/FM/CD Audio System [Std on Limited]	+290
Antilock Brakes [Opt on STD]	+323
Automatic 4-Speed Transmission [Std on Limited,SR5 2WD]	+309
Compact Disc Changer	+256

Options	Price
Locking Differential	+145
Power Steering [Opt on STD 4 cyl]	+128
Running Boards	+122
Styled Steel Wheels	+201
Sunroof	+167
TRD Off-Road Suspension Package	+380
Wide Tires And Wheels	+201

Mileage Category: J

Toyota adds new front seat belt pre-tensioners and force limiters. Optional on Xtra Cab models is an AM/FM four-speaker CD audio system while 4x4s get 15-by-7-inch steel wheels. The PreRunner adds a regular cab option to its model mix. Natural White, Imperial Jade Mica and Horizon Blue Metallic replace White, Copper Canyon Mica, Evergreen Pearl and Cool Steel Metallic as color options.

1998

Body Styles	TMV Pricing		
	Trade	Private	Dealer
2 Dr Limited 4WD Ext Cab SB	9038	10587	12334
2 Dr Prerunner Ext Cab SB	6286	7363	8578
2 Dr Prerunner V6 Ext Cab SB	6401	7498	8735
2 Dr SR5 4WD Ext Cab SB	6907	8091	9425
2 Dr SR5 Ext Cab SB	5583	6540	7620
2 Dr SR5 V6 4WD Ext Cab SB	7658	8970	10450
2 Dr SR5 V6 Ext Cab SB	6186	7246	8441

Body Styles	TMV Pricing		
	Trade	Private	Dealer
2 Dr STD 4WD Ext Cab SB	6488	7600	8854
2 Dr STD 4WD Std Cab SB	6300	7380	8598
2 Dr STD Ext Cab SB	4757	5572	6491
2 Dr STD Std Cab SB	4024	4714	5492
2 Dr V6 4WD Ext Cab SB	7042	8249	9610
2 Dr V6 Ext Cab SB	5871	6878	8013

Options	Price
Wide Tires And Wheels	+177
TRD Off-Road Suspension Package	+334
Air Conditioning [Opt on Limited,STD,V6]	+370
Aluminum/Alloy Wheels [Std on Limited]	+139
AM/FM/Cassette Audio System [Opt on STD,V6]	+139
AM/FM/Cassette/CD Audio System	+218

Options	Price
AM/FM/CD Audio System	+256
Antilock Brakes	+284
Automatic 4-Speed Transmission [Std on Prerunner,Prerunner V6]	+282
Compact Disc Changer	+206
Locking Differential	+122
Sunroof	+147

Mileage Category: J

The 1998 four-wheel-drive Tacomas receive fresh front-end styling that makes them more closely resemble their two-wheel-drive brothers. A new option package appears for 1998 as well; the TRD Off-Road Package for extended cab models is offered. On the safety front, Toyota introduces a passenger-side airbag that can be deactivated with a cut-off switch, making the Tacoma somewhat safer for children and short adults. Toyota also offers a new Tacoma PreRunner for 1998, billing it as a two-wheel-drive truck with four-wheel-drive performance.

1997

Body Styles	TMV Pricing		
	Trade	Private	Dealer
2 Dr SR5 4WD Ext Cab SB	6174	7381	8856
2 Dr STD 4WD Ext Cab SB	5059	6048	7256
2 Dr STD 4WD Std Cab SB	4795	5733	6879
2 Dr STD Ext Cab SB	3626	4335	5202

Body Styles	TMV Pricing		
	Trade	Private	Dealer
2 Dr STD Std Cab SB	3025	3617	4340
2 Dr V6 4WD Ext Cab SB	5503	6579	7894
2 Dr V6 4WD Std Cab SB	4983	5957	7148
2 Dr V6 Ext Cab SB	4743	5670	6803

Options	Price
Wide Tires And Wheels	+146
Sunroof	+125
Air Conditioning	+316
AM/FM/Cassette/CD Audio System	+186
AM/FM/CD Audio System	+147

Options	Price
Antilock Brakes	+242
Automatic 4-Speed Transmission	+257
Compact Disc Changer	+224
Power Sunroof	+125

Mileage Category: J

The 1997 Tacoma receives several new value packages that make optioning the truck easier. A locking rear-wheel differential is now available on all 4WD models. Bucket seats can be had on all Xtracab Tacomas this year; not just the SR5. Two-wheel-drive models have new headlamps and a new grille that make the vehicle look more like the T100.

Toyota

Tacoma/Tercel

1996
Mileage Category: J

Regular Cab 4WD models can be equipped with a new Off-Road Package.

Body Styles	TMV Pricing		
	Trade	Private	Dealer
2 Dr SR5 4WD Ext Cab SB	5351	6472	8020
2 Dr STD 4WD Ext Cab SB	3706	4482	5554
2 Dr STD 4WD Std Cab SB	3451	4174	5173
2 Dr STD Ext Cab SB	2934	3549	4397

Body Styles	TMV Pricing		
	Trade	Private	Dealer
2 Dr STD Std Cab SB	2231	2698	3344
2 Dr V6 4WD Ext Cab SB	3867	4677	5796
2 Dr V6 4WD Std Cab SB	3665	4433	5492
2 Dr V6 Ext Cab SB	3374	4081	5057

Options	Price
Antilock Brakes	+204
Automatic 4-Speed Transmission	+244
Compact Disc Changer	+189
Off-Road Suspension Package	+520

Options	Price
AM/FM/CD Audio System	+124
Air Conditioning	+266
AM/FM/Cassette Audio System [Std on SR5]	+153

1995
Mileage Category: J

New compact pickup with a real name debuted in March, 1995. Optional four-wheel ABS, a driver airbag and potent new engines are highlights of the new design. Rack-and-pinion steering replaces the old recirculating ball-type on the old truck. Front seatbelts are height-adjustable.

Body Styles	TMV Pricing		
	Trade	Private	Dealer
2 Dr SR5 4WD Ext Cab SB	4869	5861	7513
2 Dr STD 4WD Ext Cab SB	3068	3693	4734
2 Dr STD 4WD Std Cab SB	3037	3656	4687
2 Dr STD Ext Cab SB	2397	2885	3699

Body Styles	TMV Pricing		
	Trade	Private	Dealer
2 Dr STD Std Cab SB	1927	2320	2974
2 Dr V6 4WD Ext Cab SB	3086	3714	4762
2 Dr V6 4WD Std Cab SB	3030	3647	4675
2 Dr V6 Ext Cab SB	2985	3593	4607

Options	Price
Air Conditioning	+236
Aluminum/Alloy Wheels	+84
AM/FM/Cassette Audio System	+89
AM/FM/CD Audio System	+110

Options	Price
Antilock Brakes	+181
Automatic 4-Speed Transmission	+174
Sunroof	+94

Toyota

Tercel

1998

Body Styles	TMV Pricing		
	Trade	Private	Dealer
2 Dr CE Cpe	3054	3911	4878

Options	Price
AM/FM/CD Audio System	+171
Antilock Brakes	+284

Options	Price
Automatic 3-Speed Transmission	+188
Compact Disc Changer	+226

Mileage Category: A

For 1998, the Tercel is available exclusively as a two-door CE model with additional standard features like color-keyed grille and bumpers, rear seat headrests, AM/FM stereo with cassette, air conditioning, digital clock and power steering.

1997
Mileage Category: A

Standard and DX trim levels are shelved in favor of CE trim for all Tercels. All models have upgraded cloth trim, new rotary heater controls, a trip odometer and a storage console. New wheel covers adorn standard 14-inch wheels.

Body Styles	TMV Pricing		
	Trade	Private	Dealer
2 Dr CE Cpe	2044	2699	3499
2 Dr Limited Edition Cpe	2548	3364	4362

Body Styles	TMV Pricing		
	Trade	Private	Dealer
4 Dr CE Sdn	2628	3470	4498

Options	Price
Compact Disc Changer	+193
Rear Spoiler	+160
Air Conditioning	+297
AM/FM/CD Audio System	+147

Options	Price
Antilock Brakes	+242
Automatic 3-Speed Transmission	+160
Automatic 4-Speed Transmission	+225

1996
Mileage Category: A

Base cars can be equipped with fabric seats, and a "Sports" package is available.

Body Styles	TMV Pricing		
	Trade	Private	Dealer
2 Dr DX Cpe	1909	2575	3494
2 Dr STD Cpe	1550	2091	2837

Body Styles	TMV Pricing		
	Trade	Private	Dealer
4 Dr DX Sdn	2087	2814	3819

Options	Price
Air Conditioning	+250
AM/FM/CD Audio System	+124
Antilock Brakes	+204
Automatic 3-Speed Transmission	+189

Options	Price
Automatic 4-Speed Transmission	+192
Compact Disc Changer	+189
Power Sunroof	+135
Rear Spoiler	+135

1995

Body Styles	TMV Pricing		
	Trade	Private	Dealer
2 Dr DX Cpe	1495	2016	2883
2 Dr STD Cpe	1327	1789	2560

Body Styles	TMV Pricing		
	Trade	Private	Dealer
4 Dr DX Sdn	1540	2077	2972

Options	Price
Air Conditioning	+222
AM/FM/Cassette Audio System	+84
AM/FM/CD Audio System	+110
Antilock Brakes	+181

Options	Price
Automatic 3-Speed Transmission	+120
Automatic 4-Speed Transmission	+168
Compact Disc Changer	+144

Mileage Category: A

Redesigned, but based on 1991-1994 generation. Coupe and sedan body styles. Coupe available in Standard and DX trim; sedan comes in DX flavor only. Dual airbags are standard. Height-adjustable seatbelts are new. Car now meets 1997 side-impact standards. Engine is more powerful than before.

1994

Body Styles	TMV Pricing		
	Trade	Private	Dealer
2 Dr DX Cpe	1146	1593	2338
2 Dr STD Cpe	1044	1451	2130

Body Styles	TMV Pricing		
	Trade	Private	Dealer
4 Dr DX Sdn	1244	1729	2537

Options	Price
Air Conditioning	+196
Antilock Brakes	+160

Options	Price
Automatic 3-Speed Transmission	+106

Mileage Category: A

CFC-free refrigerant added to optional A/C. Passenger seatbelts get automatic locking retractors. LE Sedan is dropped.

Body Styles	TMV Pricing		
	Trade	Private	Dealer
2 Dr SR5 V8 4WD Std Cab LB	16958	18088	19970
2 Dr STD Std Cab LB	11270	12021	13272
4 Dr Limited V8 4WD Ext Cab SB	21738	23186	25600
4 Dr Limited V8 4WD Ext Cab Step SB	22052	23521	25970
4 Dr Limited V8 Ext Cab SB	19284	20569	22710
4 Dr Limited V8 Ext Cab Step SB	19727	21041	23231

Body Styles	TMV Pricing		
	Trade	Private	Dealer
4 Dr SR5 Ext Cab Step SB	17200	18346	20256
4 Dr SR5 V6 4WD Ext Cab SB	17461	18624	20563
4 Dr SR5 V6 Ext Cab SB	15097	16103	17779
4 Dr SR5 V8 4WD Ext Cab SB	19057	20327	22443
4 Dr SR5 V8 4WD Ext Cab Step SB	19520	20820	22987
4 Dr SR5 V8 Ext Cab SB	16829	17950	19818

Options	Price
Air Conditioning [Opt on STD]	+743
Alarm System [Opt on SR5]	+188
Aluminum/Alloy Wheels [Opt on SR5]	+302
Automatic 4-Speed Transmission [Opt on V6]	+581
Camper/Towing Package [Opt on Limited,SR5]	+325
Chrome Wheels [Opt on SR5]	+166
Keyless Entry System [Opt on SR5]	+132
Leather Seats [Opt on Limited]	+642

Options	Price
Limited Slip Differential [Opt on Limited,SR5]	+208
Power Door Locks [Opt on SR5]	+162
Power Driver Seat [Opt on Limited]	+181
Power Mirrors [Opt on SR5]	+136
Power Windows [Opt on SR5]	+189
Tilt Steering Wheel [Opt on STD]	+185
AM/FM/Cassette/CD Changer Audio System [Opt on SR5]	+370
17 Inch Wheels [Opt on Limited,SR5]	+298

Mileage Category: K

Toyota has expanded the Tundra's body style variety by adding a new StepSide model. Its distinctive styling includes flared rear wheel arches and special tail lamps. If you want to make the StepSide even sportier, there is a new sport suspension package available. All Tundras this year have a restyled front fascia, standard antilock brakes and a center console similar to the one found in the Sequoia SUV. For the top-line Limited trim, Toyota has added a power sliding rear window.

2002

Body Styles	TMV Pricing		
	Trade	Private	Dealer
2 Dr SR5 V8 4WD Std Cab LB	15223	16337	18193
2 Dr STD Std Cab LB	10216	10963	12209
4 Dr Limited V8 4WD Ext Cab SB	19431	20853	23222
4 Dr Limited V8 Ext Cab SB	17265	18528	20633

Body Styles	TMV Pricing		
	Trade	Private	Dealer
4 Dr SR5 V6 4WD Ext Cab SB	15662	16808	18718
4 Dr SR5 V6 Ext Cab SB	13570	14563	16218
4 Dr SR5 V8 4WD Ext Cab SB	17062	18311	20392
4 Dr SR5 V8 Ext Cab SB	15126	16233	18078

Mileage Category: K

SR5 models have new 16-inch wheels, and a limited-slip differential is available on V8-powered trucks. No other changes are in store for Toyota's full-size pickup this year.

Tundra

2002 (cont'd)

Options	Price
16 Inch Wheels [Opt on SR5 V8 Ext Cab]	+224
Air Conditioning [Opt on STD]	+680
Aluminum/Alloy Wheels [Opt on SR5]	+276
AM/FM/Cassette/CD Changer Audio System [Opt on SR5]	+224
Antilock Brakes [Std on Limited]	+469
Automatic 4-Speed Transmission [Std on V8]	+531
Captain Chairs (2) [Opt on Limted,SR5]	+207
Chrome Wheels [Opt on SR5]	+304
JBL Audio System [Opt on SR5]	+152
Keyless Entry System [Opt on SR5]	+121

Options	Price
Leather Seats [Opt on Limited]	+586
Limited Slip Differential [Opt on V8]	+190
Power Door Locks [Opt on SR5]	+148
Power Driver Seat [Opt on Limited]	+176
Power Mirrors [Opt on SR5]	+124
Power Windows [Opt on SR5]	+172
Styled Steel Wheels [Opt on SR5]	+152
Tilt Steering Wheel [Opt on STD]	+169
Two-Tone Paint [Opt on Limited]	+252

2001

Mileage Category: K

Newly optional on Limited is a package that matches the bumpers and tailgate handle to the body color. The TRD Off-Road package is now available on Access Cabs with a V8 engine, while models equipped with a V6 receive an upgraded alternator. A notepad holder is now optional on SR5 and Limited, while Base regular cab trucks lose their standard cassette player. Two new colors are available, filling slots left vacant by three old colors that have been discontinued.

Body Styles	TMV Pricing		
	Trade	Private	Dealer
2 Dr SR5 V8 4WD Std Cab LB	13987	15674	17231
2 Dr STD Std Cab LB	9212	10323	11348
4 Dr Limited V8 4WD Ext Cab SB	17307	19394	21320
4 Dr Limited V8 Ext Cab SB	15847	17758	19522

Body Styles	TMV Pricing		
	Trade	Private	Dealer
4 Dr SR5 V6 4WD Ext Cab SB	14045	15739	17302
4 Dr SR5 V6 Ext Cab SB	12496	14003	15394
4 Dr SR5 V8 4WD Ext Cab SB	15172	17001	18689
4 Dr SR5 V8 Ext Cab SB	13888	15562	17108

Options	Price
Air Conditioning [Opt on STD]	+620
Aluminum/Alloy Wheels [Std on Limited]	+239
AM/FM/Cassette/CD Changer Audio System	+126
Antilock Brakes	+428
Automatic 4-Speed Transmission [Opt on SR5 V6,STD]	+484
Leather Seats	+566

Options	Price
Power Door Locks [Std on Limited]	+138
Power Driver Seat	+135
Power Windows [Std on Limited]	+157
Styled Steel Wheels [Std on SR5 V8,Ext Cab]	+138
Tilt Steering Wheel [Opt on STD]	+126
Two-Tone Paint	+230

2000

Mileage Category: K

This is an all-new, full-size pickup truck designed to compete with the Ford F-150, Chevrolet Silverado 1500, GMC Sierra 1500 and Dodge Ram 1500. It features an optional V8 engine and can be ordered in a two- or four-door, regular- or extended-cab configuration.

Body Styles	TMV Pricing		
	Trade	Private	Dealer
2 Dr SR5 V6 4WD Std Cab LB	11111	12664	14185
2 Dr SR5 V8 4WD Std Cab LB	12302	14020	15705
2 Dr STD Std Cab LB	7852	8949	10024
4 Dr Limited 4WD Ext Cab SB	15499	17664	19786
4 Dr Limited Ext Cab SB	12963	14774	16549

Body Styles	TMV Pricing		
	Trade	Private	Dealer
4 Dr SR5 V6 4WD Ext Cab SB	12541	14292	16009
4 Dr SR5 V6 Ext Cab SB	11322	12904	14455
4 Dr SR5 V8 4WD Ext Cab SB	13367	15234	17065
4 Dr SR5 V8 Ext Cab SB	12246	13957	15633

Options	Price
Aluminum/Alloy Wheels [Std on Limited]	+122
AM/FM/Cassette/CD Audio System [Std on Limited]	+138
Antilock Brakes	+376
Automatic 4-Speed Transmission [Opt on SR5 V6,STD]	+464
Compact Disc Changer	+138
Cruise Control [Opt on SR5 V6]	+124
Leather Seats	+497
Power Door Locks [Std on Limited]	+122

Options	Price
Power Driver Seat	+119
Power Windows [Std on Limited]	+138
Split Front Bench Seat [Opt on SR5 V6 Std Cab]	+127
Spoke Wheels	+210
Styled Steel Wheels [Std on SR5 V8,Ext Cab]	+193
Two-Tone Paint	+180
Air Conditioning [Opt on STD]	+544

2002

Body Styles	TMV Pricing		
	Trade	Private	Dealer
2 Dr GL Conv	11313	12274	13875
2 Dr GLS Conv	12291	13335	15075

Body Styles	TMV Pricing		
	Trade	Private	Dealer
2 Dr GLX Conv	13269	14396	16274

Options	Price
Automatic 4-Speed Transmission	+559

Mileage Category: E

Reflex Silver with a gray top and Flannel Gray interior will be added to the spectrum, and Marlin Blue will replace Batik Blue. An on/off switch will allow you to govern the electrochromic mirror. For the 2002 model year, all-new Volkswagen vehicles will come standard with an improved four-year/50,000-mile bumper-to-bumper warranty, up from two years/24,000 miles. In addition, Volkswagen offers a fully transferable limited powertrain warranty that covers five years or 60,000 miles.

2001

Body Styles	TMV Pricing		
	Trade	Private	Dealer
2 Dr GL Conv	9836	11102	12271
2 Dr GLS Conv	10541	11898	13151

Body Styles	TMV Pricing		
	Trade	Private	Dealer
2 Dr GLX Conv	11283	12736	14077

Options	Price
Automatic 4-Speed Transmission	+494

Options	Price
Compact Disc Changer	+279

Mileage Category: E

A top-of-the-line GLX trim level has been added to the existing lineup for 2001. All models get an anti "trunk entrapment" button to keep people from getting stuck in the cargo hold.

2000

Body Styles	TMV Pricing		
	Trade	Private	Dealer
2 Dr GL Conv	8963	10234	11479

Body Styles	TMV Pricing		
	Trade	Private	Dealer
2 Dr GLS Conv	9465	10807	12122

Options	Price
Aluminum/Alloy Wheels [Opt on GL]	+182
Automatic 4-Speed Transmission	+431
Compact Disc Changer	+244

Options	Price
Heated Front Seats [Opt on GL]	+123
Power Windows [Opt on GL]	+125

Mileage Category: E

Volkswagen's Cabrio gets minor equipment updates for the millennium.

1999

Body Styles	TMV Pricing		
	Trade	Private	Dealer
2 Dr GL Conv	7129	8358	9637
2 Dr GLS Conv	7878	9236	10650

Body Styles	TMV Pricing		
	Trade	Private	Dealer
2 Dr New GL Conv	7476	8765	10106
2 Dr New GLS Conv	8104	9501	10955

Options	Price
Air Conditioning [Opt on GL]	+345
Aluminum/Alloy Wheels [Opt on GL,New GL]	+149
Automatic 4-Speed Transmission	+352

Options	Price
Compact Disc Changer	+199
Front Side Airbag Restraints [Opt on GL,GLS]	+159

Mileage Category: E

Volkswagen imparts new Euro-styling on the '99 Cabrios, making them more aerodynamic and adding twin headlights that show their elements through the lens. Cabrio interiors also receive makeovers.

1998

Body Styles	TMV Pricing		
	Trade	Private	Dealer
2 Dr GL Conv	5935	7118	8452

Body Styles	TMV Pricing		
	Trade	Private	Dealer
2 Dr GLS Conv	6633	7955	9445

Options	Price
Air Conditioning [Opt on GL]	+304
Aluminum/Alloy Wheels [Opt on GL]	+131
Automatic 4-Speed Transmission	+309

Options	Price
Compact Disc Changer	+175
Front Side Airbag Restraints	+140

Mileage Category: E

The Highline trim designation is replaced by more sensible GLS nomenclature. New GLS model gets a power top, making the Cabrio easier to live with. Optional are side-impact airbags mounted inside the seats. Standard on both base and GLS are door pocket liners, a trunk cargo net and sport seats with height adjustment.

Volkswagen
Cabrio/Corrado/Eurovan

1997

Mileage Category: E

Cabrio comes in two trim levels for 1997: Base and Highline. Base models are decontented versions of last year's car, priced a couple thousand dollars lower to entice young drivers. Highline models have standard alloy wheels, foglights and leather seats. Engines have a redesigned cylinder head resulting in quieter operation.

Body Styles	TMV Pricing		
	Trade	Private	Dealer
2 Dr Highline Conv	5741	6911	8340
2 Dr STD Conv	5407	6509	7855

Options	Price	Options	Price
Air Conditioning [Opt on STD]	+251	Compact Disc Changer	+145
Automatic 4-Speed Transmission	+255		

1996

Mileage Category: E

Daytime running lights and new body-color side moldings alter the exterior appearance of the 1996 Cabrio. A new color scheme also livens things up. Central locking and unlocking switch is dash-mounted.

Body Styles	TMV Pricing		
	Trade	Private	Dealer
2 Dr STD Conv	4625	5684	7147

Options	Price	Options	Price
Air Conditioning	+220	Compact Disc Changer	+127
Aluminum/Alloy Wheels	+149	Leather Seats	+327
Automatic 4-Speed Transmission	+224		

1995

Mileage Category: E

Dual airbags, ABS and 115-horsepower engine are standard on this Golf derivative. Manual top only.

Body Styles	TMV Pricing		
	Trade	Private	Dealer
2 Dr STD Conv	3614	4446	5833

Options	Price	Options	Price
Air Conditioning	+180	Automatic 4-Speed Transmission	+184
Aluminum/Alloy Wheels	+78	Compact Disc Changer	+104
AM/FM/CD Audio System	+105	Leather Seats	+268

Volkswagen
Corrado

1994

Body Styles	TMV Pricing		
	Trade	Private	Dealer
2 Dr SLC Hbk	3093	3958	5399

Options	Price
Automatic 4-Speed Transmission	+141
Compact Disc Changer	+105
Power Sunroof	+132

Mileage Category: E

Adaptive dual-mode automatic transmission debuts. Meets 1997 side-impact standards. Speed-activated spoiler rises at 55 mph instead of 45 mph.

Volkswagen
Eurovan

2003

Body Styles	TMV Pricing			Body Styles	TMV Pricing		
	Trade	Private	Dealer		Trade	Private	Dealer
3 Dr GLS Pass Van	16995	18242	20320	3 Dr MV Pass Van	17575	18865	21014

Options	Price	Options	Price
Heated Front Seats	+281	Power Moonroof	+703
Pearlescent Metallic Paint	+243	Weekender Package [Opt on MV]	+2345

Mileage Category: P

Volkswagen makes no changes to the EuroVan for 2003. Keep in mind that if you want a VW-branded minivan to go with the family Passat, the all-new Microbus isn't too far away -- it's supposed to arrive by the 2005 model year.

2002

Body Styles	TMV Pricing		
	Trade	Private	Dealer
3 Dr GLS Pass Van	14466	15628	17564
3 Dr MV Pass Van	15321	16551	18602

Options	Price	Options	Price
Heated Front Seats	+255	Power Sunroof	+638
Pearlescent Metallic Paint	+220	Weekender Package [Opt on MV]	+2119

Mileage Category: P

The EuroVan saw many upgrades for 2001, including a more powerful 201-horsepower V6 engine. This year, VW equips its minivan with a stability control system (ESP) to improve handling in inclement weather and adds Emerald Green, Reflex Silver and Black Magic Pearl exterior color choices on the MV with the Weekender package.

2001

Body Styles	TMV Pricing			Body Styles	TMV Pricing		
	Trade	Private	Dealer		Trade	Private	Dealer
3 Dr GLS Pass Van	12713	14332	15826	3 Dr MV Pass Van	13413	15121	16698

Options	Price	Options	Price
Heated Front Seats	+226	Power Sunroof	+565
Pearlescent Metallic Paint	+155	Weekender Package	+1874

Mileage Category: P

The EuroVan sees many upgrades for the 2001 model year; chief among them is a more powerful 201-horsepower V6 engine. Refinements have also been made to the electronic stability control system. Other changes include a new premium stereo, single seats for second-row seating and standard integrated foglights.

2000

Body Styles	TMV Pricing			Body Styles	TMV Pricing		
	Trade	Private	Dealer		Trade	Private	Dealer
3 Dr GLS Pass Van	11081	12602	14092	3 Dr MV Pass Van	11802	13422	15009

Options	Price	Options	Price
Weekender Package	+1637	Metallic Paint	+135
Compact Disc Changer	+222	Power Moonroof	+493
Heated Front Seats	+198		

Mileage Category: P

During its second year back in the U.S., Volkswagen's EuroVan receives remote central locking, dark-tinted glass on the side and rear windows and a brake-wear indicator. The GLS model receives additional reading lights in the rear and captain's chairs instead of a bench seat in the second row.

1999

Body Styles	TMV Pricing			Body Styles	TMV Pricing		
	Trade	Private	Dealer		Trade	Private	Dealer
3 Dr GLS Pass Van	9838	11331	12884	3 Dr MV Pass Van	10447	12032	13682

Options	Price	Options	Price
Compact Disc Changer	+181	Power Moonroof	+402
Heated Front Seats	+161	Weekender Package	+1334

Mileage Category: P

After a five-year hiatus, the EuroVan passenger van returns to the U.S. with a six-cylinder engine, structural improvements and new safety features.

1997

Body Styles	TMV Pricing		
	Trade	Private	Dealer
3 Dr Campmobile Pass Van	7601	9016	10745

Options	Price
Compact Disc Changer	+145

Mileage Category: P

The Eurovan camper remains unchanged for the 1997 model year.

1995

Body Styles	TMV Pricing		
	Trade	Private	Dealer
3 Dr Campmobile Pass Van	5515	6770	8861

Options	Price
Automatic 4-Speed Transmission	+178

Mileage Category: P

This Eurovan camper is an all-new model based on the extended wheelbase Eurovan. It features a 2.5-liter, five-cylinder engine with a standard five-speed manual and a four-speed automatic as an option. Winnebago Industries complete the camper conversion by adding a "pop-top" roof, a cooking range, sink, refrigerator, fresh water tank, power outlets and storage cabinets. Standard features include air conditioning, central locking, power windows and mirrors and cruise control.

Volkswagen
GTI

2003

Body Styles	TMV Pricing		
	Trade	Private	Dealer
2 Dr 1.8T Turbo Hbk	12810	13761	15345
2 Dr 20th Anniv Edition Turbo Hbk	16411	17629	19659
2 Dr VR6 Hbk	15155	16280	18155

Options	Price
Automatic 5-Speed Transmission [Opt on 1.8T]	+756
Automatic Stability Control [Opt on 1.8T,20th]	+197
Automatic Climate Control [Opt on VR6]	+186
Leather Seats [Opt on 1.8T,VR6]	+563

Options	Price
Monsoon Audio System [Opt on 1.8T,VR6]	+229
Power Moonroof [Opt on 1.8T,VR6]	+643
17 Inch Wheels [Opt on 1.8T]	+281

Mileage Category: E

VW's stability control system (ESP), which includes BrakeAssist, is now optional on the 1.8T model and standard on the VR6. A leather-wrapped three-spoke steering wheel, shift knob and hand brake are standard on both. Minor changes include increased padding for the head curtain airbags, backlighting for the buttons on the standard-issue stereo head unit, pinch protection for the sunroof's tilt function and upgraded wipers. Silverstone Gray replaces Matchstick Red on the exterior color list. Finally, it turns out that last year's special-edition 337 model was indeed special -- it's history for 2003.

2002

Mileage Category: E

For the 2002 model year, the GLS and GLX trim levels are dropped. Instead, choose from the juiced-up 180-horsepower turbocharged inline four (that can be mated to a five-speed manual or a five-speed automatic transmission with Tiptronic) or the VR6 engine. The current 174-horsepower, 12-valve VR6 will be replaced with a 24-valve unit good for producing 200 horsepower in the spring of 2002. Later on, a special-edition model called the GTI 337 will arrive with a six-speed manual hooked up to the 180-horse 1.8T, as well as 18-inch wheels, 225/45VR18 performance rubber, a ground effects kit, genuine Recaro seats and red accents inside and out. All-new Volkswagen vehicles come standard with an improved four-year/50,000-mile bumper-to-bumper warranty, up from two years/24,000 miles. In addition, Volkswagen offers a fully transferable limited powertrain warranty that covers five years or 60,000 miles.

Body Styles	TMV Pricing		
	Trade	Private	Dealer
2 Dr 1.8T Turbo Hbk	11410	12379	13994
2 Dr 337 1.8T Turbo Hbk	14055	15249	17239
2 Dr VR6 Hbk	13189	14309	16176

Options	Price
17 Inch Wheels [Opt on 1.8T]	+255
6-Speed Transmission [Opt on VR6]	+945
Automatic 4-Speed Transmission [Opt on 1.8T]	+686
Automatic Climate Control [Opt on VR6]	+169

Options	Price
Leather Seats	+447
Monsoon Audio System	+223
Power Moonroof	+511

2001

Mileage Category: E

The GTI benefits from a new 16-inch wheel design (for the GLX), optional 17-inch wheels, multifunction steering wheel controls and a revised cupholder design. Later in the model year, all GTIs will get side curtain airbags to protect the heads of front and rear passengers (in addition to the regular side airbags for front occupants already offered).

Body Styles	TMV Pricing		
	Trade	Private	Dealer
2 Dr GLS 1.8T Turbo Hbk	9922	11316	12602

Options	Price
Automatic 4-Speed Transmission [Opt on GLS]	+494
Compact Disc Changer	+279

Body Styles	TMV Pricing		
	Trade	Private	Dealer
2 Dr GLX VR6 Hbk	11057	12610	14043

Options	Price
Leather Seats [Opt on GLS]	+508
Monsoon Audio System [Opt on GLS]	+183

2000

Mileage Category: E

Volkswagen introduces the GLS Turbo model powered by the company's superb 150-horsepower 1.8T power plant to bridge the gap between the weak 115-hp inline four in the regular GLS and the potent VR6 available only in the pricey GLX model.

Body Styles	TMV Pricing		
	Trade	Private	Dealer
2 Dr GLS 1.8T Turbo Hbk	8504	9827	11123
2 Dr GLS Hbk	7949	9186	10398

Options	Price
AM/FM/CD Audio System	+135
Automatic 4-Speed Transmission	+431
Compact Disc Changer	+244

Body Styles	TMV Pricing		
	Trade	Private	Dealer
2 Dr GLX VR6 Hbk	9527	11010	12463

Options	Price
Heated Front Seats [Opt on GLS]	+123
Leather Seats [Opt on GLS]	+271
Monsoon Audio System [Opt on GLS]	+145

1999

Mileage Category: E

Volkswagen offers two generations of the sporty Golf-based GTI for sale in 1999. The third-generation GTI has been around since 1995, and it is a carryover. VW drops the sluggish four-cylinder version and offers only the VR6. Later in the model year, the company introduces a completely redesigned GTI with a smoother body and improved versions of the base inline four and VR6.

Body Styles	TMV Pricing		
	Trade	Private	Dealer
2 Dr New GLS Hbk	6208	7352	8543
2 Dr New GLX VR6 Hbk	7935	9398	10920

Options	Price
Automatic 4-Speed Transmission	+352
Compact Disc Changer	+199

Body Styles	TMV Pricing		
	Trade	Private	Dealer
2 Dr VR6 Hbk	7846	9292	10798

Options	Price
Front Side Airbag Restraints	+159
Leather Seats [Std on New GLX]	+221

1998

Mileage Category: E

The GTI VR6 receives several cosmetic upgrades taken from the 1997 Driver's Edition. Among them are a chrome-tipped exhaust pipe, silver/white-faced instruments, embossed sill covers, leather-wrapped steering wheel, shift boot and hand brake lever, new Sport-Jacquard seat fabric and the aluminum ball shift knob. Exclusive to the VR6 for 1998 are the Speedline 15-inch alloys from the Driver's Edition and one-touch up power windows with pinch protection. All GTIs get standard remote keyless entry, and side-impact airbags are optional.

Body Styles	TMV Pricing		
	Trade	Private	Dealer
2 Dr STD Hbk	4664	5594	6642

Options	Price
Automatic 4-Speed Transmission	+309
Compact Disc Changer	+175

Body Styles	TMV Pricing		
	Trade	Private	Dealer
2 Dr VR6 Hbk	6406	7683	9122

Options	Price
Front Side Airbag Restraints	+140
Leather Seats	+194

1997

Mileage Category: E

For 1997, the GTI VR6 gets new alloy wheels and a revised suspension that has been lowered by 10mm and includes stiffer shock absorbers, springs and stabilizer bars. Meanwhile, the 115-horsepower inline four that powers the base GTI is fitted with a new cylinder head for smoother power delivery. A cargo area light is now standard in the base model, and both models get a new high-mounted center brake light and open-door warning reflectors for all doors. Late in the 1997 model year, Volkswagen offers a limited run of the GTI VR6 Driver's Edition, which comes with a special set of seven-spoke alloys; an even lower, stiffer suspension with progressive antiroll bars; red brake calipers; chrome-tipped exhaust pipes; special cloth upholstery and floor mats; silver-faced gauges; a round aluminum/rubber shift knob; red stitching on the leather-wraps for the steering wheel, hand brake and shift boot and deluxe door sill covers embossed with the "GTI" name.

Body Styles	TMV Pricing		
	Trade	Private	Dealer
2 Dr STD Hbk	3915	4712	5687
2 Dr VR6 Driver's Edition Hbk	5168	6222	7510

Options	Price
Automatic 4-Speed Transmission	+255
Compact Disc Changer	+145

Body Styles	TMV Pricing		
	Trade	Private	Dealer
2 Dr VR6 Hbk	5054	6083	7342

Options	Price
Leather Seats	+161

1996

Body Styles	TMV Pricing		
	Trade	Private	Dealer
2 Dr STD Hbk	3270	4019	5053

Options	Price
Automatic 4-Speed Transmission	+224
Compact Disc Changer	+127

Body Styles	TMV Pricing		
	Trade	Private	Dealer
2 Dr VR6 Hbk	4346	5342	6717

Options	Price
Leather Seats	+141

Mileage Category: E

Last year's two-door Golf Sport and GTI VR6 models become a separate nameplate called simply the GTI, with respective base and VR6 trim levels. Like the Golf Sport, the base GTI will continue on with VW's 115-hp inline four but will get some additional content, including alloy wheels, bolstered sport seats, whip antenna and smoke-tinted taillights. Meanwhile, the GTI VR6 gets a black leather seating option. Both models will benefit from new cloth upholstery, the addition of a glovebox, retractor locking seatbelts (for more secure child-seat installation), easier-to-use height adjustment for the front belts, a central locking switch on the dash and a warning tone to remind you that you've left the headlights on. New exterior colors include Catalina Blue for the base GTI and Windsor Blue, Bright Surf Green and Sequoia Green for the GTI VR6.

1995

Mileage Category: E

The GTI returns with a vengeance after taking two years off -- based on the current-generation Golf, this pocket rocket has Volkswagen's 2.8-liter VR6 stuffed under its hood. Output is rated at 172 horsepower and 173 pound-feet of torque; the company says the GTI VR6 can go from zero to 60 mph in seven seconds flat. As before, the GTI rides on a sport-tuned version of the regular Golf suspension; a standard traction control system prevents its low-profile 205/50R15 Goodyear tires from slipping too much off the line. Standard equipment includes height-adjustable sport seats, a sunroof, a premium eight-speaker sound system and daytime running lights. The GTI meets 1997 side-impact standards, and its front seatbelts are height-adjustable and equipped with pre-tensioners.

Body Styles			TMV Pricing		
			Trade	Private	Dealer
2 Dr VR6 Hbk			3462	4260	5589

Options	Price
Compact Disc Changer	+104

Volkswagen
Golf

2003

Body Styles	TMV Pricing		
	Trade	Private	Dealer
2 Dr GL Hbk	9812	10687	12145
2 Dr GL TDi Turbodsl Hbk	11008	11989	13625
4 Dr GL Hbk	10000	10891	12377

Body Styles	TMV Pricing		
	Trade	Private	Dealer
4 Dr GL TDi Turbodsl Hbk	11235	12237	13906
4 Dr GLS Hbk	11434	12454	14153
4 Dr GLS TDi Turbodsl Hbk	11598	12632	14355

2003 (cont'd)

Options	Price
Automatic 4-Speed Transmission	+615
Automatic Stability Control	+197

Options	Price
Monsoon Audio System	+229

Mileage Category: B

The most affordable Volkswagen gets a few equipment changes for 2003. Probably the biggest of these is the availability of stability control (VW's ESP) on all trim levels. In other news, base GL models now include a CD player, cruise control and power windows and mirrors. GLS models now come with a sunroof and alloy wheels, while seat heaters and the premium Monsoon sound system will be optional across the line. Finally, VW has increased the padding on the side curtain airbag system; the base 2.0-liter four-cylinder now meets ULEV standards; and the standard stereo head unit will get backlighting for the buttons.

2002

Mileage Category: B

The speedy 1.8T four-door has been eliminated from the Golf lineup. A CD player now comes standard on the GLS model, and the GL trim level is available both in two- and four-door configurations. Mojave Beige joins the color spectrum. Also new for the 2002 model year, all Volkswagen vehicles come with an improved four-year/50,000-mile bumper-to-bumper warranty, up from two years/24,000 miles. In addition, Volkswagen offers a fully transferable limited powertrain warranty that covers five years or 60,000 miles.

Body Styles	TMV Pricing		
	Trade	Private	Dealer
2 Dr GL Hbk	7962	8816	10238
2 Dr GL TDi Turbodsl Hbk	9006	9971	11578
4 Dr GL Hbk	8156	9030	10486

Body Styles	TMV Pricing		
	Trade	Private	Dealer
4 Dr GL TDi Turbodsl Hbk	9234	10223	11872
4 Dr GLS Hbk	9301	10297	11958
4 Dr GLS TDi Turbodsl Hbk	9370	10374	12048

Options	Price
Aluminum/Alloy Wheels [Opt on GLS,GLS TDi]	+182
Automatic 4-Speed Transmission	+559

Options	Price
Monsoon Audio System [Opt on GLS,GLS TDi]	+207
Power Moonroof [Opt on GLS,GLS TDi]	+479

2001

Mileage Category: B

All Golf models get head protection airbags, higher quality interior fabrics, clear side marker lights, a trunk entrapment release button and a revised cupholder design.

Body Styles	TMV Pricing		
	Trade	Private	Dealer
2 Dr GL Hbk	7077	8283	9396
2 Dr GL TDi Turbodsl Hbk	7541	8825	10011
4 Dr GLS 1.8T Turbo Hbk	8543	9999	11342

Body Styles	TMV Pricing		
	Trade	Private	Dealer
4 Dr GLS Hbk	7756	9077	10297
4 Dr GLS TDi Turbodsl Hbk	8421	9855	11179

Options	Price
Aluminum/Alloy Wheels [Opt on GLS]	+155
Automatic 4-Speed Transmission	+494
Compact Disc Changer	+279

Options	Price
Heated Front Seats	+141
Monsoon Audio System	+183
Power Moonroof	+333

2000

Mileage Category: B

For 2000, the big news is the availability of the 150-horsepower 1.8T engine on the Golf GLS. In addition, the Golf receives several equipment updates, including child-seat anchor points, sun visor extenders, a glare-reducing shade band on the windshield, a brake wear indicator light in the instrument cluster, a theft-repelling engine immobilizer and a tether for the fuel cap. All Golfs are now eligible for dealer-installed in-dash CD player; a dealer-installed CD changer is also available. Finally, GLS buyers can opt for a premium Monsoon sound system in lieu of the standard eight-speaker system.

Body Styles	TMV Pricing		
	Trade	Private	Dealer
2 Dr GL Hbk	5881	6993	8082
2 Dr GL TDi Turbodsl Hbk	6515	7746	8953
4 Dr GLS 1.8T Turbo Hbk	7495	8913	10302

Body Styles	TMV Pricing		
	Trade	Private	Dealer
4 Dr GLS Hbk	6565	7806	9022
4 Dr GLS TDi Turbodsl Hbk	7383	8779	10148

Options	Price
Aluminum/Alloy Wheels	+135
Automatic 4-Speed Transmission	+431
Compact Disc Changer	+244

Options	Price
Heated Front Seats	+123
Monsoon Audio System	+145
Power Moonroof	+291

1999

Mileage Category: B

Volkswagen offers two generations of the Golf for sale in 1999. The third-generation Golf has been around since 1993, and it is a carryover for 1999. VW deletes the K2 model from the lineup and adds content to the upscale Wolfsburg, including cruise control, power windows (with one-touch operation) and heated power mirrors. Later in the model year, the company introduces a completely redesigned Golf with an improved version of the base inline four and an available turbodiesel four, which delivers up to 49 mpg on the highway. If you can hold out for a 2000 model, VW will offer a 150-hp 1.8-liter turbo for four-door hatchbacks.

Body Styles	TMV Pricing		
	Trade	Private	Dealer
2 Dr New GL Hbk	4738	5787	6879
2 Dr New GL TDi Turbodsl Hbk	5443	6648	7903
4 Dr GL Hbk	4418	5397	6415

Body Styles	TMV Pricing		
	Trade	Private	Dealer
4 Dr New GLS Hbk	5811	7099	8439
4 Dr New GLS TDi Turbodsl Hbk	6281	7673	9121
4 Dr Wolfsburg Hbk	5199	6351	7549

Options	Price
Air Conditioning [Opt on GL]	+345
AM/FM/Cassette Audio System [Opt on GL]	+195
AM/FM/Cassette/CD Audio System [Opt on Wolfsburg]	+120
Antilock Brakes [Std on VR6]	+311

Options	Price
Automatic 4-Speed Transmission	+352
Compact Disc Changer	+199
Front Side Airbag Restraints	+159
Power Moonroof [Std on VR6]	+237

1998

Body Styles	TMV Pricing			Body Styles	TMV Pricing		
	Trade	Private	Dealer		Trade	Private	Dealer
4 Dr GL Hbk	3712	4627	5659	4 Dr Wolfsburg Hbk	4256	5306	6490
4 Dr K2 Hbk	3892	4852	5934				

Options	Price	Options	Price
Front Side Airbag Restraints	+140	Antilock Brakes	+274
Power Moonroof [Opt on GL,K2]	+208	Automatic 4-Speed Transmission	+309
Air Conditioning [Opt on GL,K2]	+304	Compact Disc Changer	+175
AM/FM/Cassette Audio System [Opt on GL]	+171		

Mileage Category: B

The Trek and Jazz models disappear for 1998, but the winter-enthusiast K2 model sticks around. Late in the model year, Volkswagen offers the upscale Wolfsburg Edition, which comes standard with sport seats; upgraded velour upholstery; silver/white-faced gauges; leather-wrapped steering wheel, hand brake and shift knob; the eight-speaker sound system with cassette player; air conditioning; a power moonroof; a cargo net; alloy wheels; a chrome exhaust tip and a roof-mounted antenna. And you can option the Wolfsburg with useful features like cruise control, power windows with one-touch operation and heated power mirrors. All Golfs get keyless entry, and side-impact airbags are now optional across the line. The four-speed automatic gets a new shift logic pattern, which should enhance shift timing.

1997

Body Styles	TMV Pricing			Body Styles	TMV Pricing		
	Trade	Private	Dealer		Trade	Private	Dealer
2 Dr GL Hbk	3062	3885	4891	4 Dr K2 Hbk	3329	4223	5316
4 Dr GL Hbk	3287	4170	5249	4 Dr Trek Hbk	3398	4311	5427
4 Dr Jazz Hbk	3323	4218	5312				

Options	Price	Options	Price
Air Conditioning [Opt on GL,K2,Trek]	+251	Automatic 4-Speed Transmission	+255
AM/FM/Cassette Audio System [Opt on GL,K2,Trek]	+142	Compact Disc Changer	+145
Antilock Brakes [Opt on GL]	+226	Power Moonroof [Opt on GL,K2,Trek]	+172

Mileage Category: B

The Golf's 2.0-liter inline four engine is fitted with a redesigned cylinder head, resulting in smoother power delivery. Other changes include the addition of a cargo area light, a new high-mounted brake light and open-door warning reflectors for all doors. Memory Red is a new exterior paint choice. Later in the model year, Volkswagen releases special-interest K2, Trek and Jazz versions of the Golf. The K2 targets winter enthusiasts, and as such comes with the buyer's choice of skis or a snowboard; a roof rack to carry said gear; heated front seats, windshield washer nozzles and exterior mirrors; special cloth upholstery; silver-faced gauges; and an eight-speaker cassette stereo. The Golf Trek targets mountain bikers, and it comes with a 21-speed mountain bike and a bike rack for the roof; alloy wheels; sport seats; special cloth and carpeting; a leather-wrapped steering wheel; silver-faced gauges; and foglights. Finally, the Jazz is solely for those who fancy a Golf with a sound system, six-CD changer, velour upholstery and alloy wheels baked right in. Curiously, none of these special models are eligible for the basic GL model's optional antilock brakes.

1996

Body Styles	TMV Pricing			Body Styles	TMV Pricing		
	Trade	Private	Dealer		Trade	Private	Dealer
4 Dr GL Hbk	2436	3197	4247	4 Dr TDi Turbodsl Hbk	3171	4161	5528

Options	Price	Options	Price
Air Conditioning	+220	Automatic 4-Speed Transmission	+224
AM/FM/Cassette Audio System	+124	Compact Disc Changer	+127
Antilock Brakes	+199	Power Moonroof	+151

Mileage Category: B

Last year's two-door Golf Sport and GTI VR6 models become a separate nameplate called simply the GTI. Meanwhile, Volkswagen trims down the remaining Golf lineup, leaving only the four-door GL hatchback for 1996. Upgrades include a smoother shifting automatic transmission, new cloth upholstery, the addition of a glovebox, retractor locking seatbelts (for more secure child-seat installation), easier-to-use height adjustment for the front belts, a central locking switch on the dash and a warning tone to remind you that you've left the headlights on. Additionally, VW removes the Roman numeral "III" designation from the Golf's exterior badging and adds Catalina Blue as an exterior color.

1995

Body Styles	TMV Pricing			Body Styles	TMV Pricing		
	Trade	Private	Dealer		Trade	Private	Dealer
2 Dr GL Hbk	1874	2477	3482	4 Dr City Hbk	1608	2125	2987
2 Dr Sport Hbk	2130	2812	3949	4 Dr GL Hbk	1998	2641	3713
4 Dr Celebration Hbk	1825	2413	3392	4 Dr STD Hbk	1813	2396	3368

Mileage Category: B

Volkswagen doubles the number of trim levels in the Golf line: During the year, four-door models are offered in entry-level base and City trim, as well as midlevel Celebration trim; the GL remains the best-equipped four-door Golf. In addition, a two-door Sport model joins the lineup; it has distinctive styling cues like seven-spoke alloy wheels and blacked-out taillights, along with standard sport seats and a power sunroof. All Golfs meet 1997 side-impact standards, and the front seatbelts are now height-adjustable and equipped with pre-tensioners. Daytime running lights are standard across the line.

Volkswagen
Golf/Jetta

1995 (cont'd)

Options	Price
Air Conditioning [Std on GTI VR6,GL,Sport]	+180
AM/FM/Cassette Audio System [Opt on City,STD]	+102
Antilock Brakes [Std on GTI VR6]	+163
Automatic 4-Speed Transmission	+184

Options	Price
Compact Disc Changer	+104
Power Moonroof [Std on GTI VR6,Sport]	+124
Premium Audio System [Opt on Celebration]	+79

1994

Mileage Category: B

Two-door GL debuts. ABS is optional. Dual airbags are phased in shortly after 1994 production begins.

Body Styles	TMV Pricing		
	Trade	Private	Dealer
2 Dr GL Hbk	1386	1979	2968
2 Dr Limited Hbk	1571	2243	3363

Body Styles	TMV Pricing		
	Trade	Private	Dealer
4 Dr GL Hbk	1397	1995	2992

Options	Price
Air Conditioning	+151
AM/FM/Cassette Audio System	+85
Antilock Brakes	+137

Options	Price
Automatic 4-Speed Transmission	+154
Power Moonroof	+104

Volkswagen
Jetta

2003

Mileage Category: C

Volkswagen eliminates the GLX trim level for wagons -- this means that those who prefer the VR6 engine to the 1.8T engine will have to stick with the sedan. As a consolation, GLS wagons equipped with the 1.8T are eligible for a premium package, which bundles traditional GLX content like power seats, automatic climate control, an auto-dimming rearview mirror, rain-sensing wipers, wood interior trim and a trip computer. Additionally, VW makes the 1.8T available on both the GL sedan and wagon. GLs now have power windows and mirrors, cruise control and a CD player, while the GLS gets a standard sunroof and alloy wheels. All Jettas are available with stability control (ESP), heated seats and the Monsoon sound system. Other changes include a ULEV rating for the 2.0-liter four-cylinder, redesigned cupholders and backlit buttons on the standard stereo head unit.

Body Styles	TMV Pricing		
	Trade	Private	Dealer
4 Dr GL 1.8T Turbo Sdn	12680	13676	15336
4 Dr GL 1.8T Turbo Wgn	12921	13936	15628
4 Dr GL Sdn	11383	12277	13768
4 Dr GL TDi Turbodsl Sdn	12574	13562	15208
4 Dr GL TDi Turbodsl Wgn	13239	14279	16013
4 Dr GL Wgn	11893	12828	14385
4 Dr GLI VR6 Sdn	15351	16557	18567
4 Dr GLS 1.8T Turbo Sdn	13283	14327	16066

Body Styles	TMV Pricing		
	Trade	Private	Dealer
4 Dr GLS 1.8T Turbo Wgn	13862	14951	16766
4 Dr GLS Sdn	12697	13694	15356
4 Dr GLS TDi Turbodsl Sdn	13396	14449	16203
4 Dr GLS TDi Turbodsl Wgn	13639	14711	16497
4 Dr GLS Wgn	13045	14070	15778
4 Dr GLX VR6 Sdn	16900	18228	20441
4 Dr Wolfsburg Turbo Sdn	12889	13902	15589

Options	Price
Automatic 4-Speed Transmission [Opt on GL,GLS,TDI]	+615
Automatic 5-Speed Transmission [Opt on 1.8T]	+756
Automatic Stability Control [Std on GLI]	+197
Automatic Climate Control [Opt on GLS 1.8T Wgn]	+176
Leather Seats [Opt on GLS,GLI]	+563
Monsoon Audio System	+229

Options	Price
Power Moonroof [Opt on GLI,Wolfsburg]	+643
Power Passenger Seat [Opt on GLS 1.8T Wgn]	+193
Sport Suspension [Opt on GLS 1.8T]	+193
17 Inch Wheels [Std on GLI]	+281
Power Driver Seat w/Memory [Opt on GLS 1.8T Wgn]	+193

2002

Mileage Category: C

For 2002, the turbocharged four-cylinder engine receives 30 extra horsepower for a total of 180, which you can couple to a five-speed automatic with Tiptronic -- the 1.8T is now available for both sedans and wagons. In the spring of 2002, the Jetta GLX sedan's optional 12-valve 174-hp VR6 is replaced by a new 24-valve unit providing 200 ponies. A six-speed manual gearbox and the aforementioned five-speed automanual become available with the new VR6. Later on, the GLI sedan will appear -- it includes the new VR6, the six-speed and stability control without all the expensive GLX trimmings and replaces the manual-shift GLX. Other changes include the availability of the 1.9-liter turbodiesel engine for GL and GLS wagons. The base GL trim level is new to the wagon in 2002 -- previously, you had to step right up to the GLS model. A CD player is now standard on all GLS and GLX models, and all-new Volkswagen vehicles come with an improved four-year/50,000-mile bumper-to-bumper warranty, up from two years/24,000 miles. Volkswagen also offers a fully transferable limited powertrain warranty that covers five years or 60,000 miles. An on/off switch for auto-dimming rearview mirrors, a cruise control indicator light, a trunk escape handle for sedans and a new exterior color (Reflex Silver replaces Silver Arrow) complete the changes.

Body Styles	TMV Pricing		
	Trade	Private	Dealer
4 Dr GL Sdn	10093	10927	12317
4 Dr GL TDi Turbodsl Sdn	11030	11942	13461
4 Dr GL TDi Turbodsl Wgn	11708	12676	14288
4 Dr GL Wgn	10416	11277	12712
4 Dr GLI VR6 Sdn	13896	15045	16959
4 Dr GLS 1.8T Turbo Sdn	11861	12841	14475
4 Dr GLS 1.8T Turbo Wgn	12276	13291	14982
4 Dr GLS Sdn	10529	11399	12849

Body Styles	TMV Pricing		
	Trade	Private	Dealer
4 Dr GLS TDi Turbodsl Sdn	11774	12747	14369
4 Dr GLS TDi Turbodsl Wgn	11936	12923	14567
4 Dr GLS VR6 Sdn	12161	13166	14841
4 Dr GLS VR6 Wgn	12823	13883	15649
4 Dr GLS Wgn	11546	12500	14091
4 Dr GLX VR6 Sdn	15121	16371	18454
4 Dr GLX VR6 Wgn	15295	16559	18666

Options	Price
16 Inch Wheels [Opt on GLS VR6]	+310
17 Inch Wheels	+255
2.8L V6 DOHC 24V FI Engine [Opt on GLX VR6 Sdn]	+798
Aluminum/Alloy Wheels [Opt on GLS,GLS 1.8T,GLS TDi]	+182
Automatic 4-Speed Transmission	+559

Options	Price
Automatic 5-Speed Transmission [Opt on GLX VR6 Sdn]	+559
Leather Seats [Std on GLX VR6]	+511
Monsoon Audio System [Std on GLX VR6]	+207
Power Moonroof [Std on GLX VR6]	+543
Sport Suspension	+128

2001

Body Styles	TMV Pricing		
	Trade	Private	Dealer
4 Dr GL Sdn	8790	9896	10916
4 Dr GL TDi Turbodsl Sdn	9942	11193	12347
4 Dr GLS 1.8T Turbo Sdn	10386	11692	12898
4 Dr GLS Sdn	9448	10636	11733
4 Dr GLS TDi Turbodsl Sdn	10292	11586	12781
4 Dr GLS VR6 Sdn	10978	12359	13633

Options	Price
Aluminum/Alloy Wheels [Std on GLX VR6]	+161
Automatic 4-Speed Transmission	+494
Compact Disc Changer	+279

Body Styles	TMV Pricing		
	Trade	Private	Dealer
4 Dr GLS VR6 Wgn	11521	12970	14308
4 Dr GLS Wgn	10170	11449	12630
4 Dr GLS Wolfsburg Edition 1.8T Turbo Sdn	10732	12082	13328
4 Dr GLX VR6 Sdn	13401	15086	16642
4 Dr GLX VR6 Wgn	13577	15285	16861

Options	Price
Leather Seats [Std on GLX VR6]	+310
Monsoon Audio System [Std on GLX VR6]	+183
Power Moonroof [Std on GLX VR6]	+333

Mileage Category: C

For 2001, improved cloth and velour interior materials come standard in the GL and GLS trim. Side curtain airbags that offer head protection for front and rear passengers are introduced this year, and steering wheel controls for the audio and cruise systems are available on GLS/GLX trim models. Optional 17-inch wheels and a sport suspension can be had on GLX models and GLS models with the 1.8T or VR6 engine. The Wolfsburg Edition returns as a limited-edition model in early 2001 -- standard features include sport suspension, bolstered sport seats and 16-inch BBS wheels. All models get redesigned cupholders and a trunk entrapment release button. A wagon arrives in the spring of 2001.

2000

Body Styles	TMV Pricing		
	Trade	Private	Dealer
4 Dr GL Sdn	7374	8452	9509
4 Dr GL TDi Turbodsl Sdn	8276	9485	10671
4 Dr GLS 1.8T Turbo Sdn	8505	9749	10968
4 Dr GLS Sdn	7960	9124	10264

Options	Price
Aluminum/Alloy Wheels [Std on GLX VR6]	+141
AM/FM/Cassette/CD Audio System	+123
AM/FM/CD Audio System	+123
Automatic 4-Speed Transmission	+431
Compact Disc Changer	+244

Body Styles	TMV Pricing		
	Trade	Private	Dealer
4 Dr GLS TDi Turbodsl Sdn	8556	9807	11033
4 Dr GLS VR6 Sdn	9181	10524	11840
4 Dr GLX VR6 Sdn	10155	11640	13095

Options	Price
Heated Front Seats [Std on GLX VR6]	+123
Leather Seats [Std on GLX VR6]	+394
Monsoon Audio System [Std on GLX VR6]	+145
Power Moonroof [Std on GLX VR6]	+291

Mileage Category: C

VW's 2000 Jetta arrives with an optional turbocharged 1.8T engine on the GLS as well as minor equipment updates.

1999

Body Styles	TMV Pricing		
	Trade	Private	Dealer
4 Dr GL Sdn	5592	6514	7473
4 Dr GLX VR6 Sdn	8331	9704	11133
4 Dr New GL Sdn	6247	7276	8348
4 Dr New GL TDi Turbodsl Sdn	7466	8696	9977
4 Dr New GLS Sdn	7235	8428	9669

Options	Price
Air Conditioning [Opt on GL, TDI]	+345
AM/FM/Cassette Audio System [Opt on GL, TDI]	+195
Antilock Brakes [Std on GLX]	+311
Automatic 4-Speed Transmission	+352

Body Styles	TMV Pricing		
	Trade	Private	Dealer
4 Dr New GLS TDi Turbodsl Sdn	7688	8955	10273
4 Dr New GLS VR6 Sdn	7902	9204	10560
4 Dr New GLX VR6 Sdn	8797	10246	11755
4 Dr TDi Turbodsl Sdn	7002	8156	9357
4 Dr Wolfsburg Sdn	6239	7267	8337

Options	Price
Compact Disc Changer [Std on Wolfsburg]	+199
Front Side Airbag Restraints	+159
Leather Seats	+321
Power Moonroof [Std on GLX]	+237

Mileage Category: C

Volkswagen offers two generations of the Jetta for sale in 1999. The third-generation Jetta has been around since 1993, and it is a carryover for 1999. VW deletes the GT, K2 and GLS models from the lineup, leaving only the GL, GLX, TDI and Wolfsburg models. Later in the model year, the company introduces a completely redesigned Jetta with a smooth new European body, improved versions of the base inline four and the VR6 and a simplified lineup of GL, GLS and GLX models. If you can hold out for a 2000 model, VW will offer a 150-hp 1.8-liter turbo for the GLS.

1998

Body Styles	TMV Pricing		
	Trade	Private	Dealer
4 Dr GL Sdn	4477	5429	6502
4 Dr GLS Sdn	5191	6294	7538
4 Dr GLX VR6 Sdn	6839	8293	9933
4 Dr GT Sdn	4978	6036	7230

Options	Price
Leather Seats	+283
Power Moonroof [Std on GLX, Wolfsburg]	+208
Air Conditioning [Opt on GL, GT, TDI]	+304
AM/FM/Cassette Audio System [Opt on GL, GT, TDI]	+171
Antilock Brakes [Std on GLX]	+274

Body Styles	TMV Pricing		
	Trade	Private	Dealer
4 Dr K2 Sdn	4696	5694	6820
4 Dr TDi Turbodsl Sdn	5795	7027	8417
4 Dr Wolfsburg Sdn	5103	6187	7410

Options	Price
Automatic 4-Speed Transmission	+309
Bose Audio System [Opt on GLS]	+133
Compact Disc Changer [Std on Wolfsburg]	+175
Front Side Airbag Restraints	+140

Mileage Category: C

The TDI has finally arrived. New wheel covers and colors are offered, while remote keyless entry makes it easier to lock and unlock the Jetta. GLX models have new one-touch up power windows with pinch protection.

1997

Mileage Category: C

Wolfsburg models are gone, and the Jetta GT arrives sporting the look of the GLX without the VR6 engine. Trek gets alloy wheels. GL, GLS, Trek and GT run more quietly, thanks to a new cylinder head design.

Body Styles	TMV Pricing		
	Trade	Private	Dealer
4 Dr GL Sdn	3145	3990	5022
4 Dr GLS Sdn	4082	5178	6517
4 Dr GLX VR6 Sdn	4605	5841	7351
4 Dr GT Sdn	3401	4314	5429

Body Styles	TMV Pricing		
	Trade	Private	Dealer
4 Dr Jazz Sdn	3412	4331	5454
4 Dr TDi Turbodsl Sdn	3841	4872	6131
4 Dr Trek Sdn	3479	4413	5554

Options	Price
Air Conditioning [Std on GLS,GLX]	+251
AM/FM/Cassette Audio System [Std on GLS]	+142
Antilock Brakes [Std on GLX]	+226
Automatic 4-Speed Transmission	+255

Options	Price
Compact Disc Changer	+145
Leather Seats	+233
Power Moonroof [Opt on GLX]	+172

1996

Mileage Category: C

A new three-bar grille is added up front. GLX models get a firmer front suspension and new "Bugatti" style wheels. New colors sum up the changes.

Body Styles	TMV Pricing		
	Trade	Private	Dealer
4 Dr City Sdn	2434	3193	4241
4 Dr GL Sdn	2529	3318	4407
4 Dr GLS Sdn	3146	4127	5481
4 Dr GLX VR6 Sdn	3836	5032	6684

Body Styles	TMV Pricing		
	Trade	Private	Dealer
4 Dr TDi Turbodsl Sdn	3095	4060	5392
4 Dr Trek Limited Edition Sdn	2760	3620	4808
4 Dr Wolfsburg Sdn	2690	3529	4687

Options	Price
Air Conditioning [Std on GLS,GLX]	+220
AM/FM/Cassette Audio System [Std on GLS]	+124
Antilock Brakes [Std on GLX]	+199
Automatic 4-Speed Transmission	+224

Options	Price
Compact Disc Changer	+127
Leather Seats	+205
Power Moonroof [Std on GLX,Wolfsburg]	+151

1995

Mileage Category: C

The GL gets air conditioning, cruise control, power mirrors and a split-folding rear seat.

Body Styles	TMV Pricing		
	Trade	Private	Dealer
4 Dr Celebration Sdn	2036	2750	3941
4 Dr City Sdn	1723	2328	3336
4 Dr GL Sdn	2058	2780	3984

Body Styles	TMV Pricing		
	Trade	Private	Dealer
4 Dr GLS Sdn	2420	3269	4685
4 Dr GLX VR6 Sdn	3090	4175	5983
4 Dr STD Sdn	1839	2484	3560

Options	Price
Air Conditioning [Std on GL,GLS,GLX,STD]	+180
AM/FM/Cassette Audio System [Std on GL,GLS,GLX]	+102
Antilock Brakes [Std on GLX]	+163
Automatic 4-Speed Transmission	+184

Options	Price
Compact Disc Changer	+104
Leather Seats	+168
Power Moonroof [Std on GLS,GLX]	+124

1994

Mileage Category: C

GLS and GLX models arrive this year. ABS is optional on GL and GLS; standard on GLX. Dual airbags are phased in shortly after 1994 production begins. GLX features 2.8-liter V6 and traction control.

Body Styles	TMV Pricing		
	Trade	Private	Dealer
4 Dr GL Sdn	1314	1902	2883
4 Dr GLS Sdn	1562	2262	3428
4 Dr GLX VR6 Sdn	1927	2790	4227
4 Dr Limited Edition Sdn	1393	2017	3057

Options	Price
Air Conditioning [Std on GLS,GLX]	+151
Antilock Brakes [Std on GLX]	+137
Automatic 4-Speed Transmission	+154

Options	Price
Compact Disc Changer	+87
Leather Seats	+141
Power Moonroof	+104

2003

Body Styles	TMV Pricing		
	Trade	Private	Dealer
2 Dr GL 1.8T Turbo Hbk	12557	13525	15139
2 Dr GL Conv	13877	14947	16731
2 Dr GL Hbk	10994	11842	13255
2 Dr GL TDi Turbodsl Hbk	11729	12634	14141
2 Dr GLS 1.8T Turbo Conv	16286	17542	19635
2 Dr GLS 1.8T Turbo Hbk	13233	14253	15954

Body Styles	TMV Pricing		
	Trade	Private	Dealer
2 Dr GLS Conv	14801	15943	17845
2 Dr GLS Hbk	11982	12906	14446
2 Dr GLS TDi Turbodsl Hbk	13224	14244	15943
2 Dr GLX 1.8T Turbo Conv	17243	18573	20789
2 Dr GLX 1.8T Turbo Hbk	14488	15605	17467
2 Dr Turbo S Hbk	16225	17476	19561

Options	Price
Automatic 4-Speed Transmission [Opt on Hbk]	+615
Automatic Stability Control	+197
Leather Seats [Opt on GLS]	+563

Options	Price
Monsoon Audio System [Opt on GL,GLS]	+229
Automatic 6-Speed Transmission [Opt on Conv]	+826
17 Inch Wheels [Opt on GLS 1.8T,GLX]	+281

Mileage Category: E

Volkswagen makes the TDI and 150-horsepower 1.8T engines available on the base GL trim level. All GLs now come with power windows and cruise control, and the GL 1.8T and all GLS models get alloy wheels. Stability control (ESP), heated seats, and the Monsoon sound system will be available across the line. All models except the GL get a standard sunroof and a larger center console container, and the GL and GLS have new cloth upholstery. Note that last year's Sport model has been discontinued. All models have a more comfortable rear seat, a clock/temperature display on the rearview mirror and turn signals mounted on the outside mirrors. Finally, if you've been holding out for a Beetle convertible since 1998, your wait is almost over -- the first drop tops should arrive at the dealers just in time for, well, winter. The first ones will be 2.0 GL and GLS models in February 2003, 1.8T-equipped GLS and GLX models later in the spring.

2002

Body Styles	TMV Pricing		
	Trade	Private	Dealer
2 Dr GL Hbk	9425	10338	11859
2 Dr GLS 1.8T Turbo Hbk	11115	12191	13984
2 Dr GLS Hbk	9885	10842	12438
2 Dr GLS TDi Turbodsl Hbk	11050	12120	13903

Body Styles	TMV Pricing		
	Trade	Private	Dealer
2 Dr GLX 1.8T Turbo Hbk	12258	13445	15422
2 Dr Sport 1.8T Turbo Hbk	11431	12537	14381
2 Dr Turbo S 1.8T Hbk	14247	15626	17925

Options	Price
16 Inch Wheels [Opt on GLS,GLS TDi]	+223
17 Inch Wheels [Opt on GLS 1.8T,GLX 1.8T]	+255
Automatic 4-Speed Transmission	+559
Heated Front Seats [Std on GLX,Turbo S]	+172

Options	Price
Leather Seats [Opt on GLS,GLS 1.8T,GLS TDi]	+543
Monsoon Audio System [Opt on GLS,GLS 1.8T, TDi]	+207
Power Moonroof [Opt on GLS,GLS 1.8T,GLS TDi]	+511
Special Factory Paint [Opt on GLS]	+606

Mileage Category: E

A Turbo S model debuts, motivated by a 180-horsepower version of VW's 1.8-liter turbo engine teamed with a six-speed manual gearbox. Other exclusives for the Turbo S include Electronic Stabilization Program (ESP), a slightly stiffer suspension, 17-inch "Delta X" alloy wheels, revised turn signals and foglights, a front spoiler, a redesigned rear bumper with Turbo S badging and brushed alloy interior accents. Additionally, a rear spoiler will deploy from the hatch when these special Bugs reach 45 mph. Exterior paint for the S is limited to Reflex Silver, Black, Red and Platinum Gray. Later in the year, a Sport model debuts -- it's essentially a GLS 1.8T with a five-speed manual, 17-inch wheels, leather interior and a Sport badge on the deck lid. Changes for the rest of the lineup are minor: New colors such as limited-edition Snap Orange and Riviera Blue further enhance the Beetle's eye-candy appeal, and 16-inch wheels with 205/55 tires are now standard across the board. For 2002, all-new Volkswagen vehicles come standard with an improved four-year/50,000-mile bumper-to-bumper warranty, up from two years/24,000 miles. In addition, Volkswagen offers a fully transferable limited powertrain warranty that covers five years or 60,000 miles.

2001

Body Styles	TMV Pricing		
	Trade	Private	Dealer
2 Dr GL Hbk	7669	8821	9885
2 Dr GLS 1.8T Turbo Hbk	8987	10338	11585
2 Dr GLS Hbk	8018	9223	10336

Body Styles	TMV Pricing		
	Trade	Private	Dealer
2 Dr GLS TDi Turbodsl Hbk	8771	10090	11307
2 Dr GLX 1.8T Turbo Hbk	9840	11318	12683

Options	Price
Aluminum/Alloy Wheels [Opt on GLS]	+226
Automatic 4-Speed Transmission	+494
Compact Disc Changer	+282
Heated Front Seats [Opt on GLS]	+152

Options	Price
Leather Seats [Opt on GLS]	+480
Monsoon Audio System [Opt on GLS]	+183
Power Moonroof [Opt on GLS]	+452
Special Factory Paint [Opt on GLS,GLS 1.8T]	+536

Mileage Category: E

You can order 17-inch alloy wheels a la carte for GLS 1.8T and GLX models, while high-intensity discharge headlights are optional on all GLS and GLX models. New standard features for the Beetle's GLS and GLX models include the Monsoon sound system (optional for GLS), rain-sensing wipers and a self-dimming rearview mirror. All-new Beetles benefit from larger exterior mirrors, redesigned cupholders and a trunk entrapment release button.

2000

Body Styles	TMV Pricing		
	Trade	Private	Dealer
2 Dr GL Hbk	6935	8053	9149
2 Dr GLS 1.8T Turbo Hbk	8193	9514	10809
2 Dr GLS Hbk	7278	8452	9602

Body Styles	TMV Pricing		
	Trade	Private	Dealer
2 Dr GLS TDi Turbodsl Hbk	7968	9253	10513
2 Dr GLX 1.8T Turbo Hbk	9001	10452	11875

Mileage Category: E

Several minor equipment upgrades, such as improved theft protection, debut on the 2000 New Beetle.

2000 (cont'd)

Options	Price
Compact Disc Changer	+246
Heated Front Seats [Opt on GLS]	+133
Leather Seats [Opt on GLS]	+420
Power Moonroof [Opt on GLS]	+394

Options	Price
Special Factory Paint [Opt on GLS,GLS 1.8T]	+468
Aluminum/Alloy Wheels [Opt on GL,GLS]	+153
Automatic 4-Speed Transmission	+431

1999

Mileage Category: E

A high-performance turbo model debuts this year. A small spoiler over the rear window is the only exterior telltale that the Bug next to you has the 150-horsepower 1.8-liter turbocharged inline four from the larger Passat sedan under the hood.

Body Styles	TMV Pricing		
	Trade	Private	Dealer
2 Dr GL Hbk	6220	7367	8560
2 Dr GLS 1.8T Turbo Hbk	7212	8541	9925
2 Dr GLS Hbk	6441	7628	8863

Body Styles	TMV Pricing		
	Trade	Private	Dealer
2 Dr GLS TDi Turbodsl Hbk	7193	8518	9898
2 Dr GLX 1.8T Turbo Hbk	7406	8771	10192

Options	Price
Aluminum/Alloy Wheels [Opt on GLS]	+124
Automatic 4-Speed Transmission	+390
Compact Disc Changer	+223

Options	Price
Heated Front Seats [Opt on GLS]	+120
Leather Seats [Opt on GLS]	+380
Power Moonroof [Opt on GLS]	+357

1998

Mileage Category: E

Volkswagen revives a legend using retro styling touches wrapped around Golf underpinnings.

Body Styles	TMV Pricing		
	Trade	Private	Dealer
2 Dr STD Hbk	5067	6077	7215

Body Styles	TMV Pricing		
	Trade	Private	Dealer
2 Dr TDi Turbodsl Hbk	5681	6813	8089

Options	Price
Antilock Brakes	+284
Automatic 4-Speed Transmission	+373
Compact Disc Changer	+196

Options	Price
Heated Front Seats	+126
Power Moonroof	+349

2003

Mileage Category: D

For 2003, a base GL sedan and wagon are available. Think of the GL as a GLS 1.8T for buyers who don't require any extras like alloy wheels, leather upholstery, seat heaters or a sunroof. Meanwhile, alloy wheels and sunroof are now standard on GLS models. The 4Motion all-wheel-drive system will not be offered on GLS V6 models, forcing interested buyers to cross the 30-grand line; however, VW has made stability control (ESP) optional on all Passats (except the W8, which has this standard). Also this year, you'll be able to get W8 sedans and wagons with a six-speed manual transmission and a sport package that includes a firmer suspension and the requisite 17-inch wheels. Lastly, the standard stereo head unit gets backlighting for the buttons.

Body Styles	TMV Pricing		
	Trade	Private	Dealer
4 Dr GL 1.8T Turbo Sdn	14893	15864	17481
4 Dr GL 1.8T Turbo Wgn	15427	16432	18107
4 Dr GLS 1.8T Turbo Sdn	15600	16617	18311
4 Dr GLS 1.8T Turbo Wgn	16229	17287	19049
4 Dr GLS V6 Sdn	16470	17543	19332
4 Dr GLS V6 Wgn	17664	18815	20734

Body Styles	TMV Pricing		
	Trade	Private	Dealer
4 Dr GLX V6 4Motion AWD Sdn	21860	23284	25658
4 Dr GLX V6 4Motion AWD Wgn	22557	24027	26477
4 Dr GLX V6 Sdn	19121	20367	22444
4 Dr GLX V6 Wgn	19583	20859	22986
4 Dr W8 4Motion AWD Sdn	24109	25653	28227
4 Dr W8 4Motion AWD Wgn	24613	26190	28817

Options	Price
6-Speed Transmission [Opt on W8]	+1055
Automatic 5-Speed Transmission [Std on 4Motion]	+756
Automatic Stability Control [Opt on GLS,GLX]	+197
Heated Front Seats [Opt on GL,GLS]	+229

Options	Price
Leather Seats [Opt on GLS]	+668
Monsoon Audio System [Opt on GL,GLS]	+229
Sport Suspension [Opt on W8]	+193
17 Inch Wheels [Opt on W8]	+527

2002

Body Styles	TMV Pricing		
	Trade	Private	Dealer
4 Dr GLS 1.8T Turbo Sdn	13428	14331	15836
4 Dr GLS 1.8T Turbo Wgn	14472	15445	17067
4 Dr GLS V6 4Motion AWD Sdn	16124	17209	19016
4 Dr GLS V6 4Motion AWD Wgn	17116	18267	20185
4 Dr GLS V6 Sdn	14647	15632	17274
4 Dr GLS V6 Wgn	15794	16856	18627

Body Styles	TMV Pricing		
	Trade	Private	Dealer
4 Dr GLX V6 4Motion AWD Sdn	20051	21400	23647
4 Dr GLX V6 4Motion AWD Wgn	20593	21978	24286
4 Dr GLX V6 Sdn	17297	18460	20399
4 Dr GLX V6 Wgn	17554	18735	20702
4 Dr W8 4Motion AWD Sdn	22162	23595	25984
4 Dr W8 4Motion AWD Wgn	22624	24087	26525

2002 (cont'd)

Options	Price	Options	Price
Aluminum/Alloy Wheels [Std on GLX V6,W8]	+223	Leather Seats [Std on GLX V6,W8]	+606
Automatic 5-Speed Transmission [Std on 4Motion]	+686	Monsoon Audio System [Std on GLX V6,W8]	+207
Heated Front Seats [Std on GLX V6,W8]	+207	Power Moonroof [Std on GLX V6,W8]	+638

Mileage Category: D

The arrival of the 270-horsepower, all-wheel-drive W8 sedan and wagon disturbs the tranquility of the Passat lineup. Standard features in the W8 cars build upon the already impressive GLX equipment list, adding Electronic Stabilization Program with BrakeAssist, vented disc brakes all around (as opposed to solid discs in rear) xenon headlights with washers, wider 215/55R16 tires, an upgraded trip computer and extra chrome throughout the cabin. The rest of the Passats receive only minor upgrades for 2002, including a trunk escape release for the sedan, a cruise control indicator light and an on/off switch for the electrochromic mirror. In addition, all-new Volkswagens come standard with an improved four-year/50,000-mile bumper-to-bumper warranty, up from two years/24,000 miles. In addition, Volkswagen will offer a fully transferable limited powertrain warranty that covers five years or 60,000 miles.

2001

Body Styles	TMV Pricing			Body Styles	TMV Pricing		
	Trade	Private	Dealer		Trade	Private	Dealer
4 Dr GLS 1.8T Turbo Sdn	11353	12598	13747	4 Dr New GLS 1.8T Turbo Wgn	12297	13645	14889
4 Dr GLS 1.8T Turbo Wgn	12065	13388	14609	4 Dr New GLS V6 4Motion AWD Sdn	14690	16300	17787
4 Dr GLS V6 4Motion AWD Sdn	14115	15662	17090	4 Dr New GLS V6 4Motion AWD Wgn	14861	16490	17994
4 Dr GLS V6 4Motion AWD Wgn	14826	16452	17952	4 Dr New GLS V6 Sdn	12911	14326	15633
4 Dr GLS V6 Sdn	12555	13931	15202	4 Dr New GLS V6 Wgn	13769	15279	16672
4 Dr GLS V6 Wgn	13539	15023	16393	4 Dr New GLX V6 4Motion AWD Sdn	16663	18490	20176
4 Dr GLX V6 4Motion AWD Sdn	16533	18346	20019	4 Dr New GLX V6 4Motion AWD Wgn	16812	18655	20356
4 Dr GLX V6 4Motion AWD Wgn	16735	18570	20264	4 Dr New GLX V6 Sdn	14548	16143	17616
4 Dr GLX V6 Sdn	14188	15743	17179	4 Dr New GLX V6 Wgn	15560	17266	18840
4 Dr GLX V6 Wgn	14805	16428	17926				
4 Dr New GLS 1.8T Turbo Sdn	11743	13031	14219				

Options	Price	Options	Price
Aluminum/Alloy Wheels [Std on GLX,AWD]	+198	Leather Seats [Opt on GLS]	+480
Automatic 5-Speed Transmission [Std on 4Motion]	+607	Monsoon Audio System [Opt on GLS]	+183
Compact Disc Changer	+279	Power Moonroof [Opt on GLS]	+565
Heated Front Seats [Opt on GLS,GLS V6]	+183		

Mileage Category: D

The 2001.5 Passat arrives with updated exterior styling, minor interior changes and a more powerful four-cylinder engine. New features for the 2001 model year -- standard front and rear side curtain airbags, optional steering wheel controls for audio and cruise control for GLS (standard on the GLX) and a standard trunk entrapment release button -- carry over into 2001.5 Passats.

2000

Body Styles	TMV Pricing			Body Styles	TMV Pricing		
	Trade	Private	Dealer		Trade	Private	Dealer
4 Dr GLS 1.8T Turbo Sdn	10117	11391	12639	4 Dr GLS V6 Wgn	11745	13224	14673
4 Dr GLS 1.8T Turbo Wgn	10285	11579	12848	4 Dr GLX V6 4Motion AWD Sdn	13134	14787	16408
4 Dr GLS V6 4Motion AWD Sdn	11927	13428	14900	4 Dr GLX V6 4Motion AWD Wgn	13468	15163	16825
4 Dr GLS V6 4Motion AWD Wgn	11989	13498	14977	4 Dr GLX V6 Sdn	12190	13725	15229
4 Dr GLS V6 Sdn	11163	12568	13946	4 Dr GLX V6 Wgn	13009	14647	16252

Options	Price	Options	Price
Aluminum/Alloy Wheels [Std on GLX,AWD]	+173	Leather Seats [Opt on GLS]	+468
Automatic 5-Speed Transmission	+531	Monsoon Audio System [Opt on GLS]	+145
Compact Disc Changer	+244	Power Moonroof [Opt on GLS]	+493
Heated Front Seats [Opt on GLS,GLS V6]	+160		

Mileage Category: D

The radio display and anti-theft system have been updated. A brake-wear indicator is now standard on all models.

1999

Body Styles	TMV Pricing		
	Trade	Private	Dealer
4 Dr GLS 1.8T Turbo Sdn	8499	9808	11171
4 Dr GLS 1.8T Turbo Wgn	9064	10461	11914
4 Dr GLS V6 Sdn	9571	11046	12581
4 Dr GLX V6 Sdn	9962	11497	13095

Options	Price	Options	Price
Aluminum/Alloy Wheels	+140	Heated Front Seats [Opt on GLS]	+130
Automatic 5-Speed Transmission	+432	Leather Seats [Opt on GLS]	+381
Compact Disc Changer	+199	Power Moonroof [Opt on GLS]	+402

Mileage Category: D

After promising the availability of all-wheel drive this year, Volkswagen, in a last-minute product change, has cancelled the Synchro all-wheel-drive option on all Passats for 1999 and will not be offering the GLS wagon with a V6 engine.

Volkswagen
Passat

1998

Mileage Category: D

An all-new Passat arrives wearing updated sheet metal over a stretched Audi A4 platform. Engine choices include a spunky turbocharged four or a silky V6.

Body Styles	TMV Pricing		
	Trade	Private	Dealer
4 Dr GLS 1.8T Turbo Sdn	6661	7898	9292
4 Dr GLS 1.8T Turbo Wgn	7200	8537	10045

Options	Price
Automatic 5-Speed Transmission	+380
Heated Front Seats [Opt on GLS]	+115

Body Styles	TMV Pricing		
	Trade	Private	Dealer
4 Dr GLS V6 Sdn	7243	8588	10104
4 Dr GLX V6 Sdn	7660	9083	10687

Options	Price
Leather Seats [Opt on GLS]	+309
Power Moonroof [Opt on GLS]	+302

1997

Body Styles	TMV Pricing		
	Trade	Private	Dealer
4 Dr GLX V6 Sdn	5171	6400	7902
4 Dr GLX V6 Wgn	5177	6407	7911

Options	Price
Antilock Brakes [Opt on TDI]	+226
Automatic 4-Speed Transmission	+259
Compact Disc Changer	+145

Body Styles	TMV Pricing		
	Trade	Private	Dealer
4 Dr TDi Turbodsl Sdn	4936	6109	7542
4 Dr TDi Turbodsl Wgn	4994	6181	7632

Options	Price
Leather Seats	+255
Power Moonroof	+250

Mileage Category: D

GLS model vanishes from radar as Volkswagen prepares for launch of all-new Passat in mid-1997.

1996

Mileage Category: D

Daytime running lights debut, two new colors are added to the palette, and a new price-leader GLS model powered by a 2.0-liter, 115-horsepower, four-cylinder engine is introduced. Midyear, a Turbo Direct Injection (TDI) diesel model appears in sedan and wagon form.

Body Styles	TMV Pricing		
	Trade	Private	Dealer
4 Dr GLS Sdn	2938	3752	4876
4 Dr GLX V6 Sdn	3792	4843	6295
4 Dr GLX V6 Wgn	3930	5020	6525

Options	Price
Antilock Brakes [Std on GLX]	+199
Automatic 4-Speed Transmission	+228
Compact Disc Changer	+127

Body Styles	TMV Pricing		
	Trade	Private	Dealer
4 Dr TDi Turbodsl Sdn	3676	4695	6101
4 Dr TDi Turbodsl Wgn	3762	4804	6244

Options	Price
Leather Seats	+224
Power Moonroof	+219

1995

Mileage Category: D

Reskinned for 1995, VW adds dual airbags, three-point seatbelts, and side-impact protection that meets 1997 safety standards. Climate control system gains dust and pollen filter. GLX is only trim level.

Body Styles	TMV Pricing		
	Trade	Private	Dealer
4 Dr GLS Sdn	2026	2656	3705
4 Dr GLX V6 Sdn	2795	3664	5112

Options	Price
Antilock Brakes [Opt on GLS]	+163
Automatic 4-Speed Transmission	+187
Compact Disc Changer	+104

Body Styles	TMV Pricing		
	Trade	Private	Dealer
4 Dr GLX V6 Wgn	2949	3866	5394

Options	Price
Leather Seats	+184
Power Moonroof	+179

1994

Mileage Category: D

GL dropped, leaving only the V6 GLX. ABS and traction control are standard. Adaptive dual-mode transmission debuts.

Body Styles	TMV Pricing		
	Trade	Private	Dealer
4 Dr GLX V6 Sdn	2190	3023	4412
4 Dr GLX V6 Wgn	2372	3275	4779

Options	Price
Automatic 4-Speed Transmission	+171
Compact Disc Changer	+87
Leather Seats	+154

1997

Body Styles	TMV Pricing		
	Trade	Private	Dealer
4 Dr GLT Turbo Sdn	6147	7275	8654
4 Dr GLT Turbo Wgn	6539	7740	9207
4 Dr R Turbo Sdn	7259	8592	10221
4 Dr R Turbo Wgn	7951	9411	11195

Options	Price
Automatic 4-Speed Transmission [Opt on STD]	+219
Automatic Load Leveling [Std on R]	+123
Leather Seats [Std on R]	+241
Power Driver Seat w/Memory [Opt on STD]	+123

Body Styles	TMV Pricing		
	Trade	Private	Dealer
4 Dr STD Sdn	5230	6190	7364
4 Dr STD Wgn	5581	6606	7859
4 Dr T5 Turbo Sdn	6548	7750	9219
4 Dr T5 Turbo Wgn	6928	8200	9754

Options	Price
Power Moonroof [Opt on STD]	+236
Power Passenger Seat w/Memory [Opt on GLT,STD]	+123
Third Seat [Opt on Wgn]	+125

Mileage Category: H

The Turbo is now known as the T-5. GLT models get a new engine that makes 22 more horsepower than last year, and peak torque at a low 1,800 rpm. Base and GLT models meet Transitional Low Emission Vehicle (TLEV) regulations this year.

1996

Mileage Category: H

This year all Volvo 850s are equipped with front seat side-impact airbags, optional traction control (TRACS) and a life insurance policy that pays $250,000 to the estate of any occupant who loses their life in the 850 as the result of an accident.

Body Styles	TMV Pricing		
	Trade	Private	Dealer
4 Dr GLT Sdn	5129	6169	7605
4 Dr GLT Wgn	5309	6385	7872
4 Dr Platinum Limited Edition Turbo Sdn	6226	7488	9231
4 Dr Platinum Limited Edition Turbo Wgn	6671	8023	9891
4 Dr R Turbo Sdn	6287	7561	9321

Body Styles	TMV Pricing		
	Trade	Private	Dealer
4 Dr R Turbo Wgn	6828	8212	10124
4 Dr STD Sdn	4619	5556	6849
4 Dr STD Wgn	4710	5664	6982
4 Dr Turbo Sdn	5428	6528	8048
4 Dr Turbo Wgn	5661	6808	8393

Options	Price
Automatic 4-Speed Transmission [Opt on GLT,STD]	+200
Leather Seats [Opt on GLT,STD]	+221

1995

Mileage Category: H

Side airbags are standard on all 850 Turbos this year; optional on other 850s. All models get Turbo's rounded front styling.

Body Styles	TMV Pricing		
	Trade	Private	Dealer
4 Dr GLT Sdn	3865	4705	6105
4 Dr GLT Wgn	4490	5465	7091
4 Dr STD Sdn	3496	4256	5522
4 Dr STD Wgn	3524	4290	5566

Options	Price
Automatic 4-Speed Transmission [Std on T5R,Turbo]	+191
Compact Disc Changer	+88
Front Side Airbag Restraints	+108
Leather Seats [Std on T5R,Turbo Sdn]	+210
Power Driver Seat w/Memory [Opt on STD]	+107

Body Styles	TMV Pricing		
	Trade	Private	Dealer
4 Dr T5R Turbo Sdn	5147	6266	8130
4 Dr T5R Turbo Wgn	5381	6550	8499
4 Dr Turbo Sdn	4612	5614	7285
4 Dr Turbo Wgn	4774	5811	7540

Options	Price
Power Passenger Seat w/Memory [Opt on GLT,Turbo]	+107
Rear Spoiler [Std on T5R]	+75
Third Seat [Opt on Wgn]	+108
Aluminum/Alloy Wheels [Std on GLT,T5R,Turbo]	+78

1994

Mileage Category: H

Turbo model debuts with 222-horsepower, 2.3-liter five-cylinder engine, and a wagon body style is introduced with standard integrated child seat. Warranty is upped to four years/50,000 miles.

Body Styles	TMV Pricing		
	Trade	Private	Dealer
4 Dr GLT Sdn	2946	3701	4959
4 Dr GLTS Sdn	3264	4100	5494
4 Dr GLTS Wgn	3397	4267	5718

Options	Price
Aluminum/Alloy Wheels [Std on GLTS,Wgn]	+76
Automatic 4-Speed Transmission [Opt on GLT,GLTS,Sdn]	+170
Automatic Load Leveling	+93
Heated Front and Rear Seats [Opt on Turbo Wgn]	+76
Leather Seats [Opt on GLT,GLTS]	+188

Body Styles	TMV Pricing		
	Trade	Private	Dealer
4 Dr Turbo Sdn	3701	4649	6230
4 Dr Turbo Wgn	3833	4815	6452

Options	Price
Power Driver Seat w/Memory [Opt on GLT]	+93
Power Passenger Seat w/Memory [Opt on GLTS,Turbo]	+93
Spoke Wheels	+76
Third Seat [Opt on Wgn]	+94

Volvo
940/960

Volvo
940

1995

Body Styles	TMV Pricing			Body Styles	TMV Pricing		
	Trade	Private	Dealer		Trade	Private	Dealer
4 Dr STD Sdn	4260	5113	6535	4 Dr Turbo Sdn	4537	5446	6960
4 Dr STD Wgn	4566	5480	7004	4 Dr Turbo Wgn	4871	5847	7473

Options	Price
Leather Seats	+107
Power Driver Seat	+88
Power Moonroof	+176

Mileage Category: I

Daytime running lights debut. Level I and Level II trims are dropped in favor of less confusing base and Turbo designations.

1994

Mileage Category: I

940 gets passenger airbag. Level I 940s have 114-horsepower, 2.3-liter engine; equip a 940 with Level II trim and you get a turbocharged version of this engine.

Body Styles	TMV Pricing			Body Styles	TMV Pricing		
	Trade	Private	Dealer		Trade	Private	Dealer
4 Dr STD Sdn	3437	4188	5440	4 Dr Turbo Sdn	3822	4657	6049
4 Dr STD Wgn	3599	4386	5697	4 Dr Turbo Wgn	4086	4979	6467

Options	Price	Options	Price
Power Driver Seat w/Memory [Opt on STD]	+115	Compact Disc Changer	+110
Power Passenger Seat	+75	Leather Seats	+93
Power Sunroof [Std on Turbo]	+136		

Volvo
960

1997

Body Styles	TMV Pricing		
	Trade	Private	Dealer
4 Dr STD Sdn	7159	8513	10167
4 Dr STD Wgn	7702	9158	10938

Mileage Category: I

Automatic load leveling joins the options list for the wagon, while tailored leather seating is no longer available on the wagon.

1996

Mileage Category: I

This year all Volvo 960s are equipped with front seat side-impact airbags, a multistep power door locking system that increases driver safety when entering the vehicle in parking lots and a life insurance policy that pays $250,000 to the estate of any occupant who loses their life in the 960 as a result of a car accident.

Body Styles	TMV Pricing		
	Trade	Private	Dealer
4 Dr STD Sdn	6233	7486	9216
4 Dr STD Wgn	6626	7958	9797

1995

Mileage Category: I

Substantially revised with new sheet metal and detuned powertrain. Horsepower is down to 181 from 201, thanks to emissions standards. Daytime running lights are added. The dashboard is softened with more curves and contours. Suspensions are revised, and larger tires are standard. Other new standard equipment includes remote locking, an alarm system, headlight wipers and washers and wood interior trim.

Body Styles	TMV Pricing		
	Trade	Private	Dealer
4 Dr STD Sdn	4496	5396	6897
4 Dr STD Wgn	4689	5628	7193

Options	Price
Compact Disc Changer	+127
Leather Seats	+107

1994

Body Styles	TMV Pricing		
	Trade	Private	Dealer
4 Dr Level I Sdn	3556	4334	5630
4 Dr Level II Sdn	4102	4999	6493
4 Dr Level II Wgn	4223	5147	6686

Options	Price	Options	Price
AM/FM/Cassette/CD Audio System	+83	Power Moonroof [Opt on Level II]	+94
AM/FM/CD Audio System [Opt on Level II Wgn]	+94	Power Sunroof [Opt on Level I]	+136
Compact Disc Changer	+110	Premium Audio System	+93
Leather Seats [Opt on Level I]	+93		

Mileage Category: I

Base 960 is heavily decontented, and is available only in sedan format. Level II 960 adds leather, moonroof and other nice stuff.

Volvo
C70

2003

Body Styles	TMV Pricing		
	Trade	Private	Dealer
2 Dr HT Turbo Conv	31470	32865	35189
2 Dr LT Turbo Conv	29778	31098	33297

Options	Price	Options	Price
Automatic 5-Speed Transmission [Opt on HT]	+723	Dolby Pro Logic Audio System [Opt on HT]	+434
Compact Disc Changer [Opt on LT]	+867	17 Inch Wheels	+361

Mileage Category: F

For 2003, the C70 is only available in convertible form. Slight power increases are in store for both powertrains, with the LT engine now making 196 horsepower, an enhancement of six, and the HT engine producing 245, a boost of nine ponies over last year's output. The headlamps and taillamps have a jeweled effect, and the front grille is darkened. A rainbow of new colors -- Maya Gold, Ruby Red and Titanium Grey -- burst onto the scene.

2002

Body Styles	TMV Pricing		
	Trade	Private	Dealer
2 Dr HT Turbo Conv	27681	29156	31614
2 Dr HT Turbo Cpe	22654	23862	25874
2 Dr LT Turbo Conv	26882	28289	30634

Options	Price	Options	Price
17 Inch Wheels	+242	Compact Disc Changer [Std on HT Conv]	+726
Automatic 5-Speed Transmission [Opt on HT]	+605	Dolby Pro Logic Audio System [Opt on HT Conv]	+363

Mileage Category: F

Volvo will offer the C70 Coupe in just one trim level, and the contents of last year's SE model will come with it, including the unique sport grille, 17-inch wheels and tires, power sunroof, leather upholstery, trip computer, auto-dimming rearview mirror and special dash inlays. New standard features for all C70s include Volvo's stability and traction control system (STC), heated front seats and an emergency trunk release. Convertibles also get 17-spoke alloy wheels and ride on Z-rated 205/55R16 Pirelli tires. Genuine wood dash trim replaces the "wood effect" trim in the optional Touring Package for the C70 LPT convertible. Ash Gold is now an exterior color choice, while Turquoise Metallic and Venetian Red Metallic have been discontinued.

2001

Body Styles	TMV Pricing		
	Trade	Private	Dealer
2 Dr HT Turbo Conv	21689	23721	25597
2 Dr HT Turbo Cpe	17351	18977	20477

Options	Price
Automatic 4-Speed Transmission [Opt on HT]	+534
Automatic Stability Control [Opt on Conv]	+294
Compact Disc Changer	+214
Dolby Pro Logic Audio System [Opt on LT]	+427

Body Styles	TMV Pricing		
	Trade	Private	Dealer
2 Dr LT Turbo Conv	20771	22717	24514
2 Dr SE HT Turbo Cpe	18499	20233	21833

Options	Price
Heated Front Seats	+125
Power Moonroof [Opt on LT Cpe]	+641
Traction Control System	+288

Mileage Category: F

Volvo has dropped the C70 Coupe light-pressure turbo (LPT), meaning only the high-pressure turbo coupe (HPT) is offered. A new five-speed automatic transmission is optional equipment. Exterior styling remains the same, but there are new 16-inch wheels for all models, with the 17-inch wheels still being optional. Simulated wood trim replaces the previous car's burled walnut wood trim. The coupe's previously standard equipment of the trip computer, auto-dimming rearview mirror, simulated wood trim, leather upholstery and sunroof are now part of the Grand Touring option package. The premium audio system is optional on the HPT coupe and standard on the HPT convertible.

Volvo
C70/S40

2000
Mileage Category: F

Volvo introduces a high-pressure turbo (HPT) convertible and makes minor equipment changes to all C70s for 2000.

Body Styles	TMV Pricing		
	Trade	Private	Dealer
2 Dr HT Turbo Conv	17813	19867	21881
2 Dr HT Turbo Cpe	15112	16855	18563

Options	Price
Automatic 4-Speed Transmission [Opt on HT]	+443
Automatic Stability Control	+250
Dolby Pro Logic Audio System [Opt on LT]	+273
Leather Seats [Opt on LT Cpe]	+489
Power Moonroof [Opt on LT Cpe]	+546

Body Styles	TMV Pricing		
	Trade	Private	Dealer
2 Dr LT Turbo Conv	17096	19068	21000
2 Dr LT Turbo Cpe	14380	16038	17664

Options	Price
17 Inch Wheels - Spoke	+182
Special Leather Seat Trim	+728
Spoke Wheels	+182
Traction Control System	+246

1999
Mileage Category: F

Volvo offers a light-pressure turbocharged engine in the coupe. Both coupes and convertibles get a bit of new standard and optional equipment.

Body Styles	TMV Pricing		
	Trade	Private	Dealer
2 Dr HT Turbo Cpe	12546	14282	16089
2 Dr LT Turbo Conv	14444	16443	18524
2 Dr LT Turbo Cpe	11940	13592	15312

Options	Price	Options	Price
Automatic 4-Speed Transmission [Std on LT]	+349	Dolby Pro Logic Audio System [Opt on LT]	+212
Automatic Stability Control	+218	Traction Control System	+193

1998
Mileage Category: F

Modeled on the S70 chassis, the C70 shares sheet metal with the S70 from the windshield forward, and is powered by the same set of turbocharged power plants.

Body Styles	TMV Pricing		
	Trade	Private	Dealer
2 Dr HT Turbo Cpe	10901	12442	14180
2 Dr LT Turbo Conv	13060	14906	16988

Options	Price	Options	Price
Automatic 4-Speed Transmission	+281	Special Leather Seat Trim [Opt on LT]	+382
Compact Disc Changer	+130	Spoke Wheels	+574
Dolby Pro Logic Audio System	+190	Traction Control System	+128

Volvo
S40

2003

Body Styles	TMV Pricing		
	Trade	Private	Dealer
4 Dr Turbo Sdn	14404	15555	17475

Options	Price	Options	Price
Automatic Stability Control	+307	Power Moonroof	+687
Child Seat (1)	+217	Rear Spoiler	+181
Heated Front Seats	+192	Traction Control System	+163
Leather Seats	+687	Premium Audio System	+397
Metallic Paint	+325	16 Inch Wheels	+361
Power Driver Seat	+235		

Mileage Category: D

Output from the 1.9-liter turbocharged mill is bumped up by 10 to 170 horsepower. A CD player makes its way onto the standard features list, and the front fascia gets a slight freshening thanks to a black egg-crate grille and body-colored side molding and bumpers. Inside you'll find a new three-spoke steering wheel and a four-dial instrument cluster. The sport package adds front and rear spoilers, blackout headlamp surrounds and 16-inch wheels, and the premium package now includes a leather-wrapped hand brake handle and gearshift lever.

2002

Body Styles			TMV Pricing		
			Trade	Private	Dealer
4 Dr Turbo Sdn			12261	13363	15200

Options	Price	Options	Price
AM/FM/Cassette/CD Audio System	+227	Power Driver Seat	+197
Automatic Stability Control	+272	Power Moonroof	+575
Child Seat (1)	+181	Premium Audio System	+333
Heated Front Seats	+151	Rear Spoiler	+151
Leather Seats	+575	Traction Control System	+151
Metallic Paint	+242		

Mileage Category: D

Minor equipment changes have been made to Volvo's S40 for 2002. A Premium package now makes it easier for base sedan buyers to purchase desirable options like a sunroof, CD player, power driver seat and faux wood trim. And a Premium Plus package adds leather upholstery and a leather-wrapped steering wheel to the mix. The Sport package now includes aluminum interior accents, sport seats and an exclusive instrument cluster -- you can also get these items a la carte. A new center console design incorporates two integrated cupholders. Rear passengers will also have two cupholders at their disposal when they fold down the center armrest. And the S40 now comes with the an emergency trunk release. New exterior colors include Bamboo Green and Dark Blue.

2001

Body Styles			TMV Pricing		
			Trade	Private	Dealer
4 Dr SE Turbo Sdn			12286	14001	15584
4 Dr Turbo Sdn			10538	12038	13423

Options	Price	Options	Price
AM/FM/Cassette/CD Audio System	+259	Power Driver Seat [Std on SE]	+240
Automatic Stability Control	+294	Power Moonroof [Std on SE]	+588
Child Seat (1)	+160	Premium Audio System [Std on SE]	+374
Heated Front Seats	+133	Rear Spoiler [Std on SE]	+133
Leather Seats	+481	Traction Control System	+133
Metallic Paint	+214		

Mileage Category: D

Only a year after debuting them on U.S. shores, Volvo has updated the S40 and V40 for 2001. Both the sedan and wagon gain additional crash protection in the form of standard head-protection airbags, dual-stage front airbags and a new child seat-safety system. Under the hood, engine improvements have been made to increase power and lower emissions. There's also a new five-speed automatic transmission that takes the place of the previous four-speed. Other changes are found in the cabin, with new material colors, a redesigned center stack for better functionality, more durable front-seat materials and improved switchgear. Rounding out the S40 and V40's 2001 changes are restyled headlights, bumpers and fenders.

2000

Body Styles			TMV Pricing		
			Trade	Private	Dealer
4 Dr Turbo Sdn			9269	10744	12189

Options	Price	Options	Price
Automatic Stability Control	+250	Leather Seats	+409
Compact Disc Changer	+225	Power Moonroof	+501

Mileage Category: D

The S40 is Volvo's completely new entry-level sedan. Along with its wagon variant, the V40, this car rounds out Volvo's vehicle lineup. Safety, styling and comfort are its main attributes.

2003

Body Styles	TMV Pricing			Body Styles	TMV Pricing		
	Trade	Private	Dealer		Trade	Private	Dealer
4 Dr 2.4 Sdn	17028	18082	19839	4 Dr 2.5T Turbo AWD Sdn	21917	23274	25536
4 Dr 2.4T Turbo Sdn	20457	21723	23834	4 Dr T5 Turbo Sdn	22312	23693	25995

Options	Price	Options	Price
Automatic 5-Speed Transmission [Opt on 2.4,T5]	+723	Power Passenger Seat [Std on T5]	+235
Automatic Stability Control [Std on T5]	+502	Sport Suspension [Opt on 2.5T,T5]	+181
Automatic Climate Control [Opt on 2.4]	+150	Telematic System	+603
Heated Front Seats	+192	AM/FM/CD Changer Audio System	+867
Leather Seats	+759	16 Inch Wheels [Opt on 2.4]	+325
Metallic Paint	+325	17 Inch Wheels	+361
Navigation System	+1370	Power Driver Seat w/Memory [Opt on 2.4]	+235
Power Moonroof	+650		

Mileage Category: H

Minor changes are in store for Volvo's sport sedan for 2003. A leather-wrapped steering wheel, along with a stereo with a CD and a cassette deck, now grace the interior of the 2.4 and the 2.4T. The latter also gets foglights and wood dash trim in its standard equipment list. For the all-wheel-drive version, the 2.4 turbocharged engine receives a small bump in displacement and horsepower. Rain-sensing wipers and OnCall Plus (the telematics system) are available, and two new colors, Titanium Grey and Ruby Red, brighten the exterior.

Volvo
S60/S70

2002
Mileage Category: H

The big news is the arrival of the S60 2.4T AWD and its slick electronically controlled all-wheel-drive system. Additionally, all S60 models get Emergency Brake Assistance (EBA), enhanced traction control performance and improved throttle management, resulting in quicker response in everyday driving situations. Volvo's Dynamic Stability Traction Control (DSTC) system is now standard in T5 models and optional for the 2.4T AWD (starting in December 2001). Other model-specific changes include satellite controls on the steering wheel and rear cupholders for the base 2.4 model and a memory function for the power seats and mirrors in 2.4T and T5 models. The entire lineup gets revised rear headrests, ISO-FIX child restraint attachment points and an emergency trunk release handle.

Body Styles	TMV Pricing		
	Trade	Private	Dealer
4 Dr 2.4 Sdn	16067	17025	18622
4 Dr 2.4T Turbo AWD Sdn	20532	21769	23830

Options	Price
AM/FM/Cassette/CD Audio System [Std on T5]	+227
AM/FM/CD Changer Audio System [Opt on T5]	+726
Automatic 5-Speed Transmission [Opt on 2.4,T5]	+605
Automatic Stability Control [Opt on 2.4T,2.4T AWD]	+454
Heated Front Seats	+197
Leather Seats	+635

Body Styles	TMV Pricing		
	Trade	Private	Dealer
4 Dr 2.4T Turbo Sdn	19027	20162	22052
4 Dr T5 Turbo Sdn	20771	22009	24073

Options	Price
Metallic Paint	+242
Navigation System [Opt on T5]	+1146
Power Driver Seat [Opt on 2.4]	+197
Power Moonroof [Opt on 2.4]	+575
Power Passenger Seat [Opt on 2.4T,2.4T AWD]	+197
Sport Suspension [Opt on T5]	+151

2001
Mileage Category: H

The S60 is Volvo's new sedan that takes the place of the discontinued S70 Sedan. Smaller than the S80 but bigger than the S40, Volvo has designed the S60 to be sporty as well as safe.

Body Styles	TMV Pricing		
	Trade	Private	Dealer
4 Dr 2.4 Sdn	14435	15983	17411
4 Dr 2.4T Turbo Sdn	16375	18130	19751
4 Dr T5 Turbo Sdn	16603	18383	20025

Options	Price
AM/FM/Cassette/CD Audio System [Opt on 2.4,2.4T]	+259
AM/FM/CD Changer Audio System [Opt on T5]	+641
Automatic 5-Speed Transmission	+534
Automatic Stability Control [Opt on 2.4,2.4T]	+294
Compact Disc Changer	+641
Heated Front Seats	+125
Leather Seats	+641
Metallic Paint	+214

Options	Price
Navigation System	+1335
Power Driver Seat [Opt on 2.4]	+264
Power Moonroof	+641
Power Passenger Seat [Opt on 2.4T]	+187
Sport Seats [Opt on T5]	+133
Sport Suspension [Opt on T5]	+133
Traction Control System	+294

Volvo
S70

2000

Mileage Category: H

Engine improvements, a new transmission and equipment upgrades constitute the changes for the 2000 S70.

Body Styles	TMV Pricing		
	Trade	Private	Dealer
4 Dr GLT SE Turbo Sdn	13284	14977	16636
4 Dr GLT Turbo Sdn	12959	14611	16230
4 Dr SE Sdn	12720	14341	15930

Options	Price
AM/FM/Cassette/CD Audio System [Opt on AWD,GLT,STD]	+221
Automatic 4-Speed Transmission [Opt on T5]	+443
Automatic 5-Speed Transmission [Opt on SE,STD]	+443
Automatic Stability Control	+250
Leather Seats	+489

Body Styles	TMV Pricing		
	Trade	Private	Dealer
4 Dr STD Sdn	11058	12467	13848
4 Dr T5 Turbo Sdn	13366	15069	16739
4 Dr Turbo AWD Sdn	13373	15077	16748

Options	Price
Power Driver Seat w/Memory [Opt on STD]	+225
Power Moonroof	+546
Power Passenger Seat [Opt on AWD,GLT]	+205
Rear Spoiler	+134
Traction Control System	+246

1999
Mileage Category: H

Volvo adds an all-wheel-drive model (S70 AWD) to the lineup and makes a number of performance, safety and styling upgrades. All cars benefit from a new engine management system and an improved brake system that includes four-channel ABS and Electronic Brakeforce Distribution (EBD). In terms of safety, S70s now include head-protecting side airbags and dual-stage deployment for the front airbags. Stability and traction control is now standard on the T5, and all other front-drive models are equipped with traction control. On the cosmetic side, all S70s receive a new grille emblem and body-color side moldings, mirrors, door handles and bumpers.

Body Styles	TMV Pricing		
	Trade	Private	Dealer
4 Dr GLT Turbo Sdn	11142	12708	14338
4 Dr STD Sdn	9752	11122	12548

Options	Price
AM/FM/Cassette/CD Audio System [Opt on AWD,GLT,STD]	+173
Automatic 4-Speed Transmission [Opt on STD,T5]	+349
Leather Seats	+385

Body Styles	TMV Pricing		
	Trade	Private	Dealer
4 Dr T5 Turbo Sdn	11764	13417	15138
4 Dr Turbo AWD Sdn	11775	13430	15152

Options	Price
Power Driver Seat w/Memory [Opt on STD]	+116
Power Moonroof	+429
Traction Control System [Opt on GLT,STD,T5]	+193

1998

Body Styles	TMV Pricing		
	Trade	Private	Dealer
4 Dr GLT Turbo Sdn	8085	9444	10977
4 Dr GT Sdn	7281	8505	9886

Options	Price
Aluminum/Alloy Wheels [Opt on STD]	+130
AM/FM/Cassette/CD Audio System [Std on T5]	+139
Automatic 4-Speed Transmission [Std on GLT]	+281

Body Styles	TMV Pricing		
	Trade	Private	Dealer
4 Dr STD Sdn	6816	7963	9256
4 Dr T5 Turbo Sdn	8921	10421	12113

Options	Price
Leather Seats	+312
Traction Control System	+225

Mileage Category: H

Volvo's 850 sedan gets a new name, new nose, body-color trim, stronger side-impact protection, more powerful turbo engines, redesigned interior and revised suspension.

Volvo
S80

2003

Body Styles	TMV Pricing		
	Trade	Private	Dealer
4 Dr 2.9 Sdn	24329	25895	28506
4 Dr T6 Elite Turbo Sdn	31376	33396	36762
4 Dr T6 Turbo Sdn	28540	30377	33438

Options	Price
Automatic Stability Control [Opt on 2.9]	+502
Compact Disc Changer	+723
Heated Front Seats [Opt on 2.9, T6]	+192
Leather Seats [Opt on 2.9]	+759
Navigation System	+1370

Options	Price
Pearlescent Metallic Paint	+434
Power Moonroof [Opt on 2.9]	+650
Telematic System [Opt on 2.9]	+603
17 Inch Wheels [Opt on 2.9]	+361

Mileage Category: I

Only minor changes are in store for Volvo's flagship sedan. Rain-sensing wipers and On-Call Plus telematics are newly available features, and two new colors, Titanium Grey and Ruby Red, dress up the exterior.

2002

Body Styles	TMV Pricing		
	Trade	Private	Dealer
4 Dr 2.9 Sdn	20624	22100	24560
4 Dr T6 75th Anniv Edition Turbo Sdn	25525	27352	30396

Options	Price
17 Inch Wheels [Std on T6 75th]	+151
Automatic Stability Control [Opt on 2.9]	+454
Compact Disc Changer	+302
Heated Front Seats [Opt on 2.9, T6]	+197

Body Styles	TMV Pricing		
	Trade	Private	Dealer
4 Dr T6 Executive Turbo Sdn	26654	28561	31740
4 Dr T6 Turbo Sdn	22702	24327	27034

Options	Price
Metallic Paint [Opt on 2.9, T6]	+242
Navigation System	+1146
Pearlescent Metallic Paint [Opt on T6]	+363
Power Rear Window Sunshade [Opt on T6]	+227

Mileage Category: I

As a follow-up to the S80 T6 Executive, Volvo has released the T6 Elite, which combines the increased rear legroom, wider rear door openings and interior luxuries of the Executive with the convenience of a rear bench seat, thus providing room for five. Additionally, all S80s will get Emergency Brake Assistance (EBA), enhanced traction control performance and improved throttle management, resulting in quicker response in everyday driving situations. Other improvements include color-coordinated exterior trim (rather than the usual black moldings), an emergency release trunk release handle and the availability of a DVD-based navigation system and xenon headlamps. New exterior color choices are Pearl White and Black Sapphire. To commemorate the 75th anniversary of its first car, Volvo heightens comfort levels for rear-seat passengers with a special trim level. The car's wheelbase is the same, but special door hinges allow for a wider door opening in order to access a roomier rear seat. Executive leather upholstery and a sunshade are standard. A rear-seat entertainment system with dual 7-inch screens can play DVD, television or a video game. Another option is a refrigerator in the rear center armrest. The Special Edition S80 can be distinguished by the body-colored bumpers and moldings.

2001

Body Styles	TMV Pricing		
	Trade	Private	Dealer
4 Dr 2.9 Sdn	17097	19237	21212
4 Dr T6 Executive Turbo Sdn	20770	23369	25769
4 Dr T6 Turbo Sdn	18169	20443	22542

Options	Price
Compact Disc Changer	+360
Heated Front Seats	+240
Metallic Paint	+214

Options	Price
Navigation System	+1335
Power Moonroof	+641
Power Rear Window Sunshade [Opt on T6]	+200

Mileage Category: I

Volvo has added a new trim level, the luxurious S80 T6 Executive. Additional standard content for all trim levels comes in the form of leather seating, a luggage holder, remote retractable rear head restraints, memory position mirrors and Homelink. The 2.9 gets new 16-inch wheels and an auto-dimming rearview mirror as standard. All S80s get dual-stage airbags. The available Security Package for the S80 2.9 and T6 will now include the Interior Air Quality System (IAQS) which keeps the passenger cabin free from odors and pollutants.

Volvo
S80/S90/V40

2000

Mileage Category: I

The 2.9 and T-6 models go unchanged, save a few new colors and options.

Body Styles	TMV Pricing		
	Trade	Private	Dealer
4 Dr 2.9 Sdn	13210	15109	16970
4 Dr T6 Turbo Sdn	15319	17521	19679

Options	Price	Options	Price
Automatic Stability Control	+501	Leather Seats	+544
Compact Disc Changer	+307	Navigation System	+1137
Heated Front Seats	+205	Power Moonroof	+546

1999

Mileage Category: I

This long overdue redesign of the S90 counts several firsts to its credit: first with a transverse inline six, first with fully integrated GSM phone, first to carry an environmental specification (Europe only at introduction) and the S80 boasts the world's smallest manual transmission.

Body Styles	TMV Pricing		
	Trade	Private	Dealer
4 Dr 2.9 Sdn	11556	13424	15369
4 Dr T6 Turbo Sdn	13169	15298	17514

Options	Price	Options	Price
Automatic Stability Control	+218	Leather Seats	+427
Compact Disc Changer	+268	Navigation System	+713
Heated Front Seats [Opt on 2.9]	+161	Power Moonroof	+429

Volvo
S90

1998

Body Styles	TMV Pricing		
	Trade	Private	Dealer
4 Dr STD Sdn	8318	9788	11446

Options	Price
AM/FM/Cassette/CD Audio System	+139

Mileage Category: I

No changes this year.

1997

Mileage Category: I

The 960 sedan is now known as S90.

Body Styles	TMV Pricing		
	Trade	Private	Dealer
4 Dr STD Sdn	7373	8767	10471

Volvo
V40

2003

Body Styles	TMV Pricing		
	Trade	Private	Dealer
4 Dr Turbo Wgn	15133	16343	18359

Options	Price	Options	Price
Automatic Stability Control	+307	Power Moonroof	+687
Child Seat (1)	+217	Rear Spoiler	+181
Heated Front Seats	+192	Traction Control System	+163
Leather Seats	+687	Premium Audio System	+397
Metallic Paint	+325	16 Inch Wheels	+361
Power Driver Seat	+235		

Mileage Category: D

Output from the 1.9-liter turbocharged mill is bumped up by 10 to 170 horsepower. A CD player makes its way onto the standard features list, and the front fascia gets a slight freshening thanks to a black egg-crate grille and body-colored side molding and bumpers. Inside you'll find a new three-spoke steering wheel and a four-dial instrument cluster. The sport package adds front and rear spoilers, blackout headlamp surrounds and 16-inch wheels, and the premium package now includes a leather-wrapped hand brake handle and gearshift lever.

Body Styles	TMV Pricing		
	Trade	Private	Dealer
4 Dr Turbo Wgn	12969	14151	16122

Options	Price	Options	Price
AM/FM/Cassette/CD Audio System	+484	Metallic Paint	+242
Automatic Stability Control	+181	Power Driver Seat	+197
Child Seat (1)	+181	Power Moonroof	+575
Heated Front Seats	+197	Rear Spoiler	+133
Leather Seats	+696	Traction Control System	+151

2002

Mileage Category: D

Minor equipment changes are in store for Volvo's V40 in 2002. A Premium package now makes it easier for base wagon buyers to purchase desirable options like a sunroof, CD player, power driver seat and faux wood trim. And a Premium Plus package adds leather upholstery and a leather-wrapped steering wheel to the mix. The Sport package now includes aluminum interior accents, sport seats and an exclusive instrument cluster -- you can also get these items a la carte. A new center console design incorporates two integrated cupholders. Rear passengers will also have two cupholders at their disposal when they fold down the center armrest. New exterior colors include Bamboo Green and Dark Blue.

2001

Body Styles	TMV Pricing		
	Trade	Private	Dealer
4 Dr SE Turbo Wagon	12424	14163	15768
4 Dr Turbo Wgn	11048	12594	14021

Options	Price	Options	Price
AM/FM/Cassette/CD Audio System	+259	Metallic Paint	+214
Automatic Stability Control	+294	Power Driver Seat [Std on SE]	+240
Child Seat (1)	+160	Power Moonroof [Std on SE]	+588
Heated Front Seats	+133	Traction Control System	+133
Leather Seats [Std on SE]	+481		

Mileage Category: D

Only a year after debuting them on U.S. shores, Volvo has updated the S40 and V40 for 2001. Both the sedan and wagon gain additional crash protection in the form of standard head-protection airbags, dual-stage front airbags and a new child seat-safety system. Under the hood, engine improvements have been made to increase power and lower emissions. There's also a new five-speed automatic transmission that takes the place of the previous four-speed. Other changes are found in the cabin, with new material colors, a redesigned center stack for better functionality, more durable front-seat materials and improved switchgear. Rounding out the S40 and V40's 2001 changes are restyled headlights, bumpers and fenders.

2000

Body Styles	TMV Pricing		
	Trade	Private	Dealer
4 Dr Turbo Wgn	9117	10568	11991

Options	Price
Compact Disc Changer	+225
Leather Seats	+409
Power Moonroof	+501

Mileage Category: D

The S40 is Volvo's completely new entry-level sedan. Along with its wagon variant, the V40, this car rounds out Volvo's vehicle lineup. Safety, styling, and comfort are its main attributes.

Volvo
V70
2003

Body Styles	TMV Pricing			Body Styles	TMV Pricing		
	Trade	Private	Dealer		Trade	Private	Dealer
4 Dr 2.4 Wgn	19101	20233	22119	4 Dr 2.5T Turbo AWD Wgn	23093	24461	26741
4 Dr 2.4T Turbo Wgn	22037	23343	25519	4 Dr T5 Turbo Wgn	23974	25395	27762

Options	Price	Options	Price
Automatic 5-Speed Transmission [Opt on 2.4,T5]	+723	Power Passenger Seat [Opt on 2.4T,2.5T]	+246
Automatic Stability Control [Std on T5]	+325	Sport Seats	+199
Child Seat (1)	+217	Third Seat	+361
Child Seats (2)	+199	Traction Control System [Std on T5]	+177
Heated Front Seats	+192	Telematic System	+603
Leather Seats	+759	AM/FM/CD Changer Audio System	+867
Metallic Paint	+325	17 Inch Wheels [Opt on 2.5T]	+343
Navigation System	+1370	Power Driver Seat w/Memory [Opt on 2.4]	+235
Power Moonroof	+683		

Mileage Category: H

A new high-performance model, the V70R, making 300 horsepower, will be available later in the year. A leather-wrapped steering wheel and an audio unit with a CD and cassette player grace the interior of the 2.4 and 2.4T. The latter also gets real wood trim. For the all-wheel-drive version, the 2.4 turbocharged engine receives a small bump in displacement and horsepower. Rain-sensing wipers and OnCall Plus (the telematics system) are available, and two new colors, Titanium Grey and Ruby Red, brighten the exterior.

Volvo
V70

2002

Mileage Category: H

Like the rest of its platform mates (S60 and S80), the V70 gets emergency BrakeAssist, enhanced traction control performance and improved throttle management, resulting in quicker response in everyday driving situations. In addition, a V70 AWD model will be offered -- minus the armor and raised suspension of Volvo's Cross Country. Standard content has been increased, as well: All models get a cargo security cover; the 2.4T gets six-spoke alloy wheels and a leather gearshift knob; and the T5 gets Dynamic Stability and Traction Control (DSTC), special vinyl/cloth upholstery, leather wrappings on the steering wheel, hand brake and shift knob and aluminum mesh accents. Other new features include a DVD-based navigation system, xenon headlamps and an upgraded premium audio system. Cosmos Blue is now an exterior color choice. Finally, Volvo has plans to offer a limited number of special-edition V70s to commemorate the Volvo Ocean Race that begins in Fall 2001; these cars will come with leather upholstery, Ocean Blue exterior paint, silver body moldings, identifying badges and unique floor mats.

Body Styles	TMV Pricing		
	Trade	Private	Dealer
4 Dr 2.4 Wgn	17576	18573	20233
4 Dr 2.4T Turbo Wgn	20760	21937	23898

Options	Price
AM/FM/Cassette/CD Audio System [Std on T5]	+227
Automatic 5-Speed Transmission [Opt on 2.4,T5]	+605
Automatic Stability Control [Opt on AWD]	+454
Child Seat (1)	+151
Child Seats (2)	+181
Compact Disc Changer [Opt on T5]	+726
Heated Front Seats	+160
Leather Seats	+635

Body Styles	TMV Pricing		
	Trade	Private	Dealer
4 Dr T5 Turbo Wgn	22748	24038	26187
4 Dr Turbo AWD Wgn	21721	22965	25038

Options	Price
Metallic Paint	+242
Navigation System	+1146
Power Driver Seat w/Memory [Opt on 2.4]	+209
Power Moonroof [Opt on 2.4]	+726
Power Passenger Seat [Opt on 2.4T,AWD]	+206
Sport Seats [Opt on T5]	+181
Third Seat	+514

2001

Mileage Category: H

The Volvo V70 has been redesigned for 2001. Major changes include a new body structure, fresh styling, a revised interior and upgraded feature content. Safety figures prominently with the new V70 (as usual), but it is also more sporting than before, especially in T5 trim.

Body Styles	TMV Pricing		
	Trade	Private	Dealer
4 Dr 2.4M Wgn	15915	17369	18712
4 Dr 2.4T Turbo Wgn	18429	20114	21669

Options	Price
AM/FM/Cassette/CD Audio System [Std on T5]	+259
Automatic 5-Speed Transmission [Opt on 2.4,T5]	+534
Automatic Stability Control [Opt on 2.4,2.4T]	+294
Child Seats (2)	+160
Compact Disc Changer	+534
Heated Front Seats	+125
Leather Seats	+641
Navigation System	+1335

Body Styles	TMV Pricing		
	Trade	Private	Dealer
4 Dr T5 Turbo Wgn	19891	21710	23389
4 Dr XC Turbo AWD Wgn	22578	24642	26548

Options	Price
Power Driver Seat w/Memory [Opt on 2.4]	+187
Power Moonroof	+641
Power Passenger Seat [Opt on 2.4T,XC]	+187
Premium Audio System [Std on T5]	+187
Sport Seats [Opt on T5]	+133
Third Seat	+534
Traction Control System [Opt on 2.4,2.4T]	+294

2000

Mileage Category: H

Engine improvements, a new transmission and equipment upgrades constitute the changes for these 2000 Volvos. The V70 AWD and V70 T-5 have been discontinued.

Body Styles	TMV Pricing		
	Trade	Private	Dealer
4 Dr GLT Turbo Wgn	13689	15357	16992
4 Dr R Turbo AWD Wgn	18039	20236	22390
4 Dr SE Wgn	13434	15071	16675

Options	Price
AM/FM/Cassette/CD Audio System [Opt on GLT,Turbo,XC]	+221
Automatic 5-Speed Transmission [Opt on SE,STD]	+443
Leather Seats [Opt on GLT,STD,XC]	+489
Power Driver Seat w/Memory [Opt on STD]	+225

Body Styles	TMV Pricing		
	Trade	Private	Dealer
4 Dr STD Wgn	11965	13422	14851
4 Dr XC SE Turbo AWD Wgn	17198	19293	21347
4 Dr XC Turbo AWD Wgn	16451	18455	20420

Options	Price
Power Moonroof [Std on R,XC SE]	+546
Power Passenger Seat [Opt on GLT,XC]	+205
Rear Spoiler [Opt on GLT,STD]	+134
Traction Control System [Opt on GLT,SE,STD]	+246

1999

Mileage Category: H

Volvo makes a number of performance, safety and styling upgrades to the V70 line. All cars benefit from a new engine management system and an improved brake system that includes four-channel ABS and Electronic Brakeforce Distribution (EBD). In terms of safety, V70s now include head-protecting side airbags and dual-stage deployment for the front airbags. Stability and traction control is now standard on the T5, and all other front-drive models are equipped with traction control. On the cosmetic side, all V70s receive a new grille emblem and body-color side moldings, mirrors, door handles and bumpers.

Body Styles	TMV Pricing		
	Trade	Private	Dealer
4 Dr GLT Turbo Wgn	11910	13532	15220
4 Dr R Turbo AWD Wgn	15372	17465	19643
4 Dr STD Wgn	10569	12008	13506

Options	Price
AM/FM/Cassette/CD Audio System [Std on T5]	+173
Automatic 4-Speed Transmission [Opt on STD,T5]	+349
Automatic Load Leveling	+197
Leather Seats	+385

Body Styles	TMV Pricing		
	Trade	Private	Dealer
4 Dr T5 Turbo Wgn	12223	13888	15621
4 Dr Turbo AWD Wgn	12390	14077	15833
4 Dr XC Turbo AWD Wgn	13547	15392	17312

Options	Price
Power Driver Seat w/Memory [Opt on STD]	+116
Power Moonroof	+429
Traction Control System [Opt on GLT,STD,T5]	+193

Body Styles	TMV Pricing		
	Trade	Private	Dealer
4 Dr GLT Turbo Wgn	8914	10413	12104
4 Dr GT Wgn	8196	9574	11129
4 Dr R Turbo AWD Wgn	11960	13971	16240
4 Dr STD Wgn	7191	8400	9763

Body Styles	TMV Pricing		
	Trade	Private	Dealer
4 Dr T5 Turbo Wgn	10080	11775	13687
4 Dr Turbo AWD Wgn	9482	11077	12875
4 Dr XC Turbo AWD Wgn	10838	12660	14716

Options	Price
Leather Seats [Std on R,XC]	+315
Power Moonroof [Opt on STD,XC]	+345
Traction Control System [Std on AWD,R,XC]	+225

Options	Price
Automatic Load Leveling [Std on AWD,R,XC]	+158
AM/FM/Cassette/CD Audio System [Std on T5]	+139
Automatic 4-Speed Transmission [Std on AWD,GLT,R,XC]	+281

Mileage Category: H

Volvo's 850 wagon gets a new name, new nose, body-color trim, stronger side-impact protection, more powerful turbo engines, redesigned interior and revised suspension. All-wheel-drive versions arrive to battle luxury SUVs.

Volvo

V90

1998

Body Styles			TMV Pricing
	Trade	Private	Dealer
4 Dr STD Wgn	8243	9700	11344

Options	Price
AM/FM/Cassette/CD Audio System	+139
Automatic Load Leveling	+142

Mileage Category: I

Nothing changes on the V90.

1997

Body Styles			TMV Pricing
	Trade	Private	Dealer
4 Dr STD Wgn	6944	8257	9861

Mileage Category: I

The 960 wagon is now the V90.

Volvo

XC

2002

Body Styles			TMV Pricing
	Trade	Private	Dealer
4 Dr Turbo AWD Wgn	25134	26748	29438

Options	Price
AM/FM/Cassette/CD Audio System	+197
Automatic Stability Control	+454
Child Seat (1)	+151
Child Seats (2)	+181
Compact Disc Changer	+726
Heated Front Seats	+197

Options	Price
Leather Seats	+696
Metallic Paint	+242
Navigation System	+1146
Power Passenger Seat	+169
Special Factory Paint	+454
Third Seat	+514

Mileage Category: H

Like the rest of its platform mates (S60, S80 and V70), the V70 XC (the Cross Country) will get Emergency Brake Assistance (EBA), enhanced traction control performance and improved throttle management, resulting in quicker response in everyday driving situations. Integrated child booster cushions, previously optional, have been added to the standard features list. Other new features include a DVD-based navigation system, an upgraded premium audio system, xenon headlamps and deep-tinted windows. Cypress Green Metallic is now an exterior color choice. A limited-edition model aimed at sailing enthusiasts, the Ocean Race Cross Country, will offer leather upholstery, exclusive Ocean Blue exterior paint, silver body molding, special exterior badging, an additional rear skid plate and unique floor mats.

Volvo
XC70/XC90

Volvo
XC70

2003

Mileage Category: H

The psuedo-SUV formerly known as Cross Country gets a new name this year, to align itself more seamlessly with Volvo's revised SUV nomenclature. Now called the XC70, this all-wheel-drive, luxury crossover vehicle can be equipped with dark tinted windows, rain-sensing wipers and a new telematics system named On-Call Plus. Crystal Green is the new color for 2003.

Body Styles	TMV Pricing		
	Trade	Private	Dealer
4 Dr Turbo AWD Wgn	26866	28601	31494

Options	Price	Options	Price
Automatic Stability Control	+325	Power Moonroof	+683
Child Seat (1)	+217	Power Passenger Seat	+246
Child Seats (2)	+199	Third Seat	+361
Leather Seats	+759	Traction Control System	+177
Metallic Paint	+325	Telematic System	+603
Navigation System	+1370	AM/FM/CD Changer Audio System	+867

Volvo
XC90

2003

Mileage Category: O

Volvo throws in its hat into the luxury SUV ring with the XC90, a vehicle that offers an impressive list of safety and comfort features.

Body Styles	TMV Pricing		
	Trade	Private	Dealer
4 Dr 2.5T Turbo AWD SUV	30174	31797	34503
4 Dr 2.5T Turbo SUV	28700	30244	32818
4 Dr T6 Turbo AWD SUV	34285	36129	39203

Options	Price	Options	Price
Automatic Dimming Rearview Mirror [Opt on 2.5T]	+145	Power Passenger Seat [Opt on 2.5T]	+246
Automatic Load Leveling	+253	Third Seat	+361
Dolby Pro Logic Audio System	+361	AM/FM/CD Changer Audio System [Opt on 2.5T]	+199
Heated Front Seats	+192	17 Inch Wheels [Opt on 2.5T]	+361
Leather Seats [Opt on 2.5T]	+759	18 Inch Wheels [Opt on T6]	+271
Metallic Paint	+325	Air Conditioning - Front and Rear	+488
Navigation System	+1370	Power Retractable Mirrors [Opt on T6]	+181
Power Moonroof [Opt on 2.5T]	+683	Park Distance Control (Rear)	+289

Instructions:

Each vehicle in this book has a Mileage Category listed in its information. To determine the effect of the vehicle's mileage on its price, look up the mileage category in the rows along the left side of this table. Then find the vehicle's year along the top. Where the row and column meet, the average mileage range for that category and year is shown at the top of the box.

If the vehicle's mileage is less than the lower number in the mileage range, multiply the difference between the mileage and the lower number by the amount shown at the bottom of the box, and add to the price.

If the vehicle's mileage is greater than the higher number, multiply the difference by the amount shown and then subtract from the price.

Important: The mileage adjustment is not to exceed 50 percent of the vehicle's adjusted trade-in value!

Mileage Category	2003	2002	2001	2000	1999	1998	1997	1996	1995	1994
A, B, G	11,600-14,400	24,500-28,100	37,400-42,100	49,800-55,800	61,800-69,100	73,100-81,400	83,600-92,700	93,200-103,100	102,000-112,500	110,000-121,300
	+/- 7 cents	+/- 7 cents	+/- 6 cents	+/- 6 cents	+/- 6 cents	+/- 5 cents	+/- 5 cents	+/- 4 cents	+/- 4 cents	+/- 3 cents
C, D, E	11,300-14,000	23,900-27,400	36,500-40,900	48,500-54,200	60,200-67,000	71,300-78,900	81,800-90,200	91,400-100,700	100,100-110,300	108,300-119,300
	+/- 7 cents	+/- 7 cents	+/- 7 cents	+/- 6 cents	+/- 6 cents	+/- 6 cents	+/- 5 cents	+/- 5 cents	+/- 4 cents	+/- 4 cents
F	8,100-9,900	17,500-19,700	26,500-29,600	35,600-39,500	44,700-49,400	53,400-59,300	61,800-68,900	70,200-77,900	78,200-86,100	85,600-94,200
	+/- 10 cents	+/- 9 cents	+/- 9 cents	+/- 8 cents	+/- 8 cents	+/- 7 cents	+/- 6 cents	+/- 6 cents	+/- 6 cents	+/- 5 cents
H	10,600-13,200	22,800-26,100	34,300-38,900	45,800-51,800	57,600-64,600	69,500-76,900	81,100-89,000	92,500-100,800	102,900-111,700	111,800-121,200
	+/- 8 cents	+/- 8 cents	+/- 8 cents	+/- 7 cents	+/- 7 cents	+/- 6 cents	+/- 6 cents	+/- 5 cents	+/- 4 cents	+/- 4 cents
I	9,900-12,600	21,900-25,500	33,500-38,000	44,900-50,200	56,000-62,200	66,700-73,800	77,300-85,000	88,000-95,900	98,700-106,400	108,800-116,400
	+/- 10 cents	+/- 9 cents	+/- 9 cents	+/- 9 cents	+/- 8 cents	+/- 8 cents	+/- 7 cents	+/- 7 cents	+/- 6 cents	+/- 6 cents
J, L, O, P	11,050-13,800	23,400-27,150	35,825-40,825	47,975-54,275	59,825-67,325	71,100-79,500	81,475-90,725	91,050-101,000	99,900-110,550	108,375-119,575
	+/- 8 cents	+/- 8 cents	+/- 7 cents	+/- 7 cents	+/- 7 cents	+/- 6 cents	+/- 6 cents	+/- 5 cents	+/- 5 cents	+/- 4 cents
K, M, N, Q	11,700-14,600	24,575-28,700	37,475-42,975	50,150-57,150	62,525-71,025	74,325-84,100	85,450-96,325	95,875-107,725	105,350-118,325	114,100-128,050
	+/- 7 cents	+/- 7 cents	+/- 7 cents	+/- 7 cents	+/- 6 cents	+/- 6 cents	+/- 5 cents	+/- 5 cents	+/- 4 cents	+/- 4 cents
R	4,200-5,400	8,800-10,000	13,500-14,800	18,500-20,100	23,500-25,500	28,600-30,900	33,600-36,300	38,600-41,500	43,300-46,700	48,000-51,800
	+/- 13 cents	+/- 12 cents	+/- 12 cents	+/- 11 cents	+/- 11 cents	+/- 10 cents	+/- 9 cents	+/- 9 cents	+/- 8 cents	+/- 8 cents

Certified Used Vehicle Programs

Introduction

According to a recent J.D. Power and Associates study, sales of certified used cars have increased 46 percent since 2000. For many people, certified used cars have become affordable alternatives to new cars. "Certified" refers to used cars that are offered for sale by the original manufacturer, often with extended warranties beyond the initial coverage. The extended warranty typically takes effect when the original warranty expires, and like the new car warranty offers coverage for a certain number of years or miles, whichever comes first. Used cars sold with aftermarket warranties are sometimes advertised as "certified" but are not truly certified because the vehicle's manufacturer is not supporting the warranty in any way.

In many cases, a customer who purchases a certified used car will become eligible for benefits that a new car customer enjoys. Perks such as service loan cars, shuttle pick-up and drop-off service, roadside assistance, free maintenance and low-rate "incentive" loans can be one of many reasons to choose a certified used car over a less expensive used car bought from a private party or generic used car lot. Even if a specific perk is not part of the official certified program, you can sometimes negotiate additional features with your local dealer. Many certified programs will even offer longer warranties at an additional cost, but the real value lies in the factory-provided coverage that would be included in the purchase price of the car you're considering. Because some cars have a longer initial warranty when the car is purchased new, they therefore represent a better candidate as a certified used car. The attraction to certified used vehicles is clear — new car benefits at a used car price.

Many programs offer perks not directly related to the vehicle itself. For example, some certified programs offer services such as trip routing, and trip interruption protection. Trip interruption protection is a feature that will reimburse the owner of a certified used car for incidental costs such as car rental, lodging, meals and out-of-town repair expenses should he or she become stranded due a warranted mechanical breakdown when traveling out of town — usually an owner must be at least 100 miles from home in order to use the service. The rules and dollar amounts vary from brand to brand, so check with your local dealer for the specific details.

Each manufacturer runs its own certification program, and has different criteria for what kinds of cars will be accepted. In some cases, buying a certified used car will net the customer a longer warranty than if he or she bought the car new. Here is a breakdown of what each brand offers when purchasing a certified used car or truck.

Acura

Acura's "Certified Pre-Owned" program will only sell cars that are less than seven years old and with less than 80,000 miles. Acura offers its Certified Pre-Owned customers many of the same benefits as those customers who buy a new Acura. All Certified Pre-Owned Acuras include:

- 150-point vehicle inspection and history report
- Balance of new vehicle warranty
- Limited warranty of 12 months or 12,000 miles and a seven-year/100,000-mile powertrain warranty**
- No deductible
- Special financing through Honda Finance
- Three-day guarantee/exchange
- 24-hour roadside assistance*
- Rental car reimbursement*
- Trip routing and map service*

*Available only during the 12-month/12,000-mile period

**Seven-year/100,000-mile powertrain warranty starts on the date the new car warranty was first implemented

Audi

Certified used Audis are covered under the Audi Assured program. Audi Assured includes:

- 300-point inspection with condition report
- Balance of new vehicle warranty
- Limited two-year warranty or total of 100,000 miles, whichever comes first

Certified Used Vehicle Programs

- $50 deductible
- The remaining portion of free scheduled maintenance (if any)
- 24-hour roadside assistance (provided by AAA)
- Trip interruption service which provides up to $500 per day if you become stranded due to warranty-covered breakdown
- Audi Assured warranty is transferable for $150 fee

Aston Martin

Aston Martin does not have a certified used vehicle program at this time.

Bentley

Bentley offers all its pre-owned customers the same benefits as its new car customers. These perks include a personal invitation to visit the Crewe factory where the cars are built as well as a complimentary Bentley magazine. Bentley pre-owned cars must be newer than 17 years but the age of a covered car varies depending on country. Certified Bentley cars include:

- 154-point inspection
- Factory-authenticated service history
- One-year/unlimited mileage warranty

BMW

BMW Certified used cars must be five years old or less with less than 60,000 miles. BMW Certified used vehicles include:

- Multipoint inspection
- Balance of new car warranty
- Limited two-year/50,000-mile warranty — but not to exceed 100,000 miles or six years
- $50 deductible
- 24-hour roadside assistance
- Special financing through BMW

Buick

Certified used Buick vehicles are covered under the GM Certified program. GM Certified used vehicles must be less than five years old, and have less than 60,000 miles. GM Certified used vehicles include:

- 108-point inspection, and restored to factory standards through reconditioning process
- Three-day or 150-mile return/exchange program

If a GM vehicle is still in the three-year/36,000-mile warranty period, the warranty is extended to 39 months or 39,000 miles; if it's out of its warranty, the warranty period is three months or 3,000 miles bumper to bumper and no deductible.

Cadillac

Cadillac cars and trucks are covered under a program that is similar to GM Certified, but it offers a few more features as Cadillac is a luxury brand. Certified Cadillacs must be four years old or newer and/or have less than 50,000 miles. Certified Cadillacs include:

- 110-point inspection
- Limited warranty that extends the new car warranty to six years or 100,000 miles from date first sold
- No deductible
- 24-hour roadside assistance for the full term of the warranty

Certified Used Vehicle Programs

- Trip interruption protection
- Special GM financing rates
- Six months free OnStar and personal calling for eligible vehicles model year 1999 and newer
- Transferable warranty

Chevrolet

Certified used Chevrolet vehicles are covered under the GM Certified program. GM Certified used vehicles must be less than five years old, and have less than 60,000 miles.

GM Certified used vehicles include:

- 108-point inspection, and restored to factory standards through reconditioning process
- Three-day or 150-mile return/exchange program

If a GM vehicle is still in the three-year/36,000-mile warranty period, the warranty is extended to 39 months or 39,000 miles; if it's out of its warranty, the warranty period is three months or 3,000 miles bumper to bumper and no deductible.

Chrysler

Chrysler vehicles must pass a history check before they can be certified, and only five-star dealers can sell certified Chrysler cars. Certified Chrysler cars include:

- 125-point inspection
- Limited powertrain warranty of eight years/80,000 miles from original date of purchase
- 24-hour roadside assistance
- Trip interruption protection
- Rental car reimbursement if car is out of service for more than a day

Dodge

Dodge vehicles must pass a history check before they can be certified, and only five-star dealers can sell certified Dodge cars and trucks. Certified Dodge vehicles include:

- 125-point inspection
- Limited powertrain warranty of eight years/80,000 miles from original date of purchase
- 24-hour roadside assistance provided by Cross Country Motor Club
- Trip interruption protection
- Rental car reimbursement if car is out of service for more than a day

Ferrari

Ferrari does not offer a certified used vehicle program at this time.

Ford

Ford calls its certified program "Quality Checked." Certified Ford cars and trucks must be five years old or newer and have less than 50,000 miles. All Quality Checked Fords include:

- 115-point inspection
- Six-year/75,000-mile limited powertrain warranty from original date of purchase

Certified Used Vehicle Programs

- 24-hour roadside assistance
- Travel expense reimbursement of up to $500 per day for up to three days related to vehicle breakdown
- Destination expense assistance of up to $75 to cover cost of taxi or rental car to reach your destination
- Rental car reimbursement of up to $28 per day for up to five days if vehicle requires overnight repairs
- Warranty ID card

GMC

Certified used GMC trucks are covered under the GM Certified program. GM Certified used vehicles must be less than five years old, and have less than 60,000 miles. GM Certified used vehicles include:

- 3 month/3,000-mile limited warranty
- 108-point inspection, and restored to factory standards through reconditioning process
- Three-day or 150-mile return/exchange program
- No deductible

Honda

Honda Certified Used cars include:

- 150-point inspection
- Vehicle history report
- Seven-year/100,000-mile powertrain warranty from date first sold*
- Additional 12-month/12,000-mile warranty
- No deductible

*Insight battery covered for eight years/80,000 miles.

Hummer

Due to the low number of used Hummer vehicles, Hummer does not offer a certified used program at this time.

Hyundai

Hyundai certified protection cars must be less than four years old or have less than 48,000 miles. Hyundai certified vehicles include:

- 120-point inspection
- Extended limited warranty to six years/75,000 miles or five years/60,000 miles depending on age
- No deductible
- 24-hour roadside assistance
- Warranty is transferable

Infiniti

Infiniti certified used vehicles must be newer than six model years with various mileage restrictions. Infiniti certified vehicles include:

- 128-point inspection
- Balance of new car warranty
- One-year/12,000-mile warranty
- No deductible

Certified Used Vehicle Programs

- 24-hour roadside assistance for one year
- Service loan car for 12 months or 12,000 miles
- Trip interruption reimbursement up to $500 for breakdowns more than 100 miles from home

Isuzu

Isuzu has no certified used vehicle program at this time.

Jaguar

Select Edition is what Jaguar calls its certified used cars and the vehicle must be four years old or newer with less than 50,000 miles. Each Select Edition Jaguar includes:

- 120-point inspection
- Carfax history report backed up with its $10,000 guarantee
- New car warranty extended to six years/100,000 miles
- Free scheduled maintenance for model year 2001 and newer for the remainder of new car warranty period
- No deductible
- 24-hour roadside assistance for two years or 50,000 miles
- Special financing available through Jaguar
- Complimentary subscription to Jaguar Magazine

Jeep

Jeep vehicles must pass a history check before they can be certified, and only five-star dealers can sell certified Jeep cars. Certified Jeep vehicles include:

- 125-point inspection
- Eight-year/80,000-mile limited powertrain warranty
- 24-hour roadside assistance
- Trip interruption protection
- Rental car reimbursement if car is out of service for more than a day

Kia

Kia does not offer a certified used vehicle program at this time.

Lamborghini

Lamborghini does not offer a certified used vehicle program at this time.

Land Rover

Land Rover vehicles must be six years old or newer and have less than 75,000 miles to be certified. Certified Land Rover vehicles include:

- 97-point inspection
- Balance of new car warranty plus one year or 12,000 miles
- $100 deductible
- 24-hour roadside assistance for one year or 12,000 miles

Certified Used Vehicle Programs

- $50 fee to transfer warranty
- Special financing available

Lexus

All benefits and services enjoyed by new Lexus customers are offered to Lexus Certified Pre-Owned customers. Lexus Certified Pre-Owned vehicles include:

- 128-point inspection
- Three-year/100,000-mile total vehicle limited warranty
- No deductible
- 24-hour roadside assistance
- New car finance terms
- Complimentary loaner car for qualified repairs
- Reimbursement for meals, lodging and rental car if a breakdown occurs
- Complimentary first oil and filter change

Lincoln

Lincoln certified cars are called Premier Certified and only Lincoln cars from the current model year or four prior model years are eligible for certification, so long as they have less than 50,000 miles. Premier Certified Lincoln vehicles include:

- 141-point inspection
- Six-year/75,000-mile limited powertrain from the date the car was first sold
- Service can be obtained in any Ford, Mercury or Lincoln dealership
- 24-hour roadside assistance
- Complimentary first Motorcraft oil and filter change
- Warranty ID card

Maserati

Maserati does not offer a certified used vehicle program at this time.

Mazda

Only Mazda vehicles that are less than five years old with less than 50,000 miles qualify for Mazda's Pre-owned program. Mazda Pre-owned benefits include:

- 100-point inspection
- Balance of new car warranty plus one-year/12,000-mile warranty
- Limited warranty honored by all Mazda dealers in the U.S. and Canada
- 24-hour roadside assistance
- Warranty is transferable

Mercedes-Benz

Mercedes-Benz certified cars are referred to as Starmark vehicles. Mercedes-Benz automobiles that are less than nine years old and/or have less than 90,000 miles are eligible for the Starmark program. Starmark vehicles include:

- 132-point inspection

Certified Used Vehicle Programs

- Seven-day/500-mile exchange
- Balance of new car warranty plus one year or total of 100,000 vehicle miles
- No deductible
- Roadside assistance with no limit on years or mileage
- Transferable warranty
- Special financing available

Mercury

Mercury vehicles must be newer than model year 1997 and have less than 50,000 miles in order to qualify for Mercury's certified used program. Certified used Mercury vehicles include:

- 115-point inspection
- Balance of new car warranty
- Six-year/75,000-mile powertrain warranty from date vehicle was first sold
- $100 deductible
- 24-hour roadside assistance

Mini

Due to the low number of available used Minis, there is no certified used program at this time.

Mitsubishi

Mitsubishi has no certified used vehicle program at this time.

Nissan

Nissan certified used vehicles must be between six months and five model-years old, or with a mileage of 6,000 to 72,000. Nissan certified vehicles include:

- 128-point inspection
- 72-month or 100,000-mile warranty from date car was first sold
- Balance of new car warranty
- 24-hour roadside assistance
- No deductible

Oldsmobile

Certified used Oldsmobiles are covered under the GM Certified program. GM Certified used vehicles must be less than five years old, and have less than 60,000 miles.

- three-month/3,000-mile warranty
- 108-point inspection, and restored to factory standards through reconditioning process
- Three-day or 150-mile return/exchange program
- No deductible

Certified Used Vehicle Programs

Pontiac

Certified used Pontiac vehicles are covered under the GM Certified program. GM Certified used vehicles must be less than five years old, and have less than 60,000 miles.

- three-month/3,000-mile warranty
- 108-point inspection, and restored to factory standards through reconditioning process
- Three-day or 150-mile return/exchange program
- No deductible

Porsche

Porsche vehicles must be eight years old or newer, or have less than 125,000 miles to qualify for certification. Certified Porsches include:

- 100-point inspection
- Balance of new car warranty
- No deductible
- Limited warranty
- Warranty transferable between individuals only
- Roadside assistance

Rolls-Royce

Rolls-Royce does not have a certified used program at this time.

Saab

Saab vehicles must have less than 60,000 miles or be newer than model year 1998 in order to qualify for Saab's certified pre-owned program. Also, any used car with frame, fire or flood damage is immediately disqualified from the Saab certified program. Certified Saab cars include:

- 110-point inspection
- Carfax vehicle history report
- Balance of new car warranty
- 72-month/100,000-mile limited warranty from date car was first sold
- 24-hour roadside assistance

Saturn

Saturn is the only carmaker to certify other brands as part of its certified used program. Therefore it is possible to buy a "Saturn Certified" used car that might not be a Saturn. What Saturn dealers are really selling here is service — all Saturn Certified vehicles, regardless of brand, are offered with Saturn's no-haggle, no-pressure sales experience. A "Premium Certified" vehicle is a used Saturn that is certified while a car with only the "Certified" designation is a vehicle of any make other than Saturn. A Premium Certified Saturn must be less than four model-years old or have less than 60,000 miles. A Certified vehicle (any brand) has no mileage or age restrictions. Here is what the respective programs include:

- 150-point inspection*
- 100-point inspection**
- Three-day money-back guarantee
- 30-day/1,500-mile trade-in allowance*
- 12-month/12,000-mile limited warranty*
- 90-day/3,000-mile powertrain warranty**

Certified Used Vehicle Programs

- No deductible
- 24-hour roadside assistance*

*"Premium Certified" only

**Saturn "Certified" only

Subaru

Subaru does not have a certified used vehicle program at this time.

Suzuki

Suzuki does not have a certified used vehicle program at this time.

Toyota

While Toyota doesn't spell out the exact terms required for a vehicle to qualify for its certified used program, it does say "…only the best of the best are chosen to be Toyota Certified Used Vehicles." Toyota Certified vehicles include:

- 128-point inspection with vehicle history report
- Vehicle reconditioned to Toyota standards
- Limited six-year/100,000-mile powertrain warranty from date car was first sold
- 24-hour roadside assistance during warranty period
- Special financing available through Toyota

Volkswagen

VW's certified pre-owned vehicles must be newer than five years old, or have less than 75,000 miles. Any certified pre-owned VW with an original new car warranty in place must be in service for at least 12 months. Certified pre-owned Volkswagens include:

- 112-point inspection
- Two-year/24,000-mile limited warranty
- No deductible
- 24-hour roadside assistance with no mileage limit (provided by AAA)

Volvo

Only Volvo vehicles newer than model year 1999 (with mileage limit) can qualify for the Volvo certified pre-owned program. Volvo certified cars include:

- 130-point inspection
- Balance of new car warranty
- Six-year/100,000-mile warranty from date vehicle was first sold
- 24-hour roadside assistance
- Trip routing service
- Trip interruption allowance for qualified breakdowns

Please cut out or copy this page to order subscriptions to Edmunds.com Buyer's Guides.

All prices are in United States dollars.

2004 New Cars & Trucks Buyer's Guide 1 issue per year	Pay Only (includes Shipping & Handling)	Quantity
United States	$11.70	
Canada	$12.70	
International	$14.70	

2004 Used Cars & Trucks Buyer's Guide 1 issue per year	Pay Only (includes Shipping & Handling)	Quantity
United States	$11.70	
Canada	$12.70	
International	$14.70	

Make check or money order payable to:

Edmunds.com, Inc.
PO Box 338
Shrub Oaks NY 10588
USA

For more information or to order by phone, call (914) 962-6297. Please pay through an American bank or with American currency.

Rates subject to change without notice.

Name _____

Company/Library _____

Address _____

City _____ State/Province _____

ZIP/Postal Code _____ Country _____

Telephone _____

Credit Card # _____ Exp. Date _____

Cardholder Name _____

Signature _____